LEADERSHIP & MANAGEMENT

THEORY & PRACTICE

8TH EDITION

LEADERSHIP & MANAGEMENT

THEORY & PRACTICE

8TH EDITION

KRIS COLE
TIM RULE
JILL NOBLE
KIM SLINGO
BILLY WORTH

Leadership & Management: Theory & Practice
8th Edition
Kris Cole
Tim Rule
Jill Noble
kim Slingo
Billy Worth

Portfolio lead/Product manager: Sophie Kaliniecki
Content developer: Stephanie Davis/Lynley Bidlake
Project editor: Sutha Surenddar
Editor: Jade Jakovcic
Proofreader: Anne Mulvaney
Permissions/Photo researcher: Catherine Kerstjens
Cover designer: Chris Starr
Text designer: Mariana Maccarini
Art direction: Mariana Maccarini
Cover: iStock.com/dem10
KnowledgeWorks Global Ltd.

National Library of Australia Cataloguing-in-Publication Data
A catalogue record for this work is available from the National Library of Australia
NLApp103418
9780170453653

Cengage Learning Australia
Level 5, 80 Dorcas Street
Southbank VIC 3006 Australia

Cengage Learning New Zealand
Unit 4B Rosedale Office Park
331 Rosedale Road, Albany, North Shore 0632, NZ

For learning solutions, visit cengage.com.au

Printed in Singapore by C.O.S. Printers Pte Ltd.
1 2 3 4 5 6 7 26 25 24 23 22

BRIEF CONTENTS

CONTENTS

Guide to the text

As you read this text you will find a number of features in every chapter to enhance your study of management and help you understand how the theory is applied in the real world.

PART OPENING FEATURES

PART OPENING PARAGRAPHS

Part openers introduce each of the chapters within the part and give an overview of how the chapters in the text relate to each other.

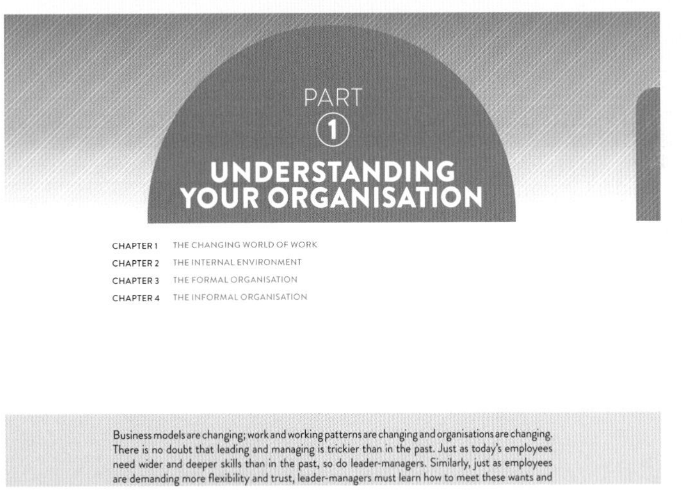
PART
1
UNDERSTANDING YOUR ORGANISATION

CHAPTER 1 THE CHANGING WORLD OF WORK
CHAPTER 2 THE INTERNAL ENVIRONMENT
CHAPTER 3 THE FORMAL ORGANISATION
CHAPTER 4 THE INFORMAL ORGANISATION

Business models are changing; work and working patterns are changing and organisations are changing. There is no doubt that leading and managing is trickier than in the past. Just as today's employees need wider and deeper skills than in the past, so do leader-managers. Similarly, just as employees are demanding more flexibility and trust, leader-managers must learn how to meet these wants and

CHAPTER OPENING FEATURES

KEY CONCEPTS

Identify the key concepts that the chapter will cover with the **Key Concepts** at the start of each chapter.

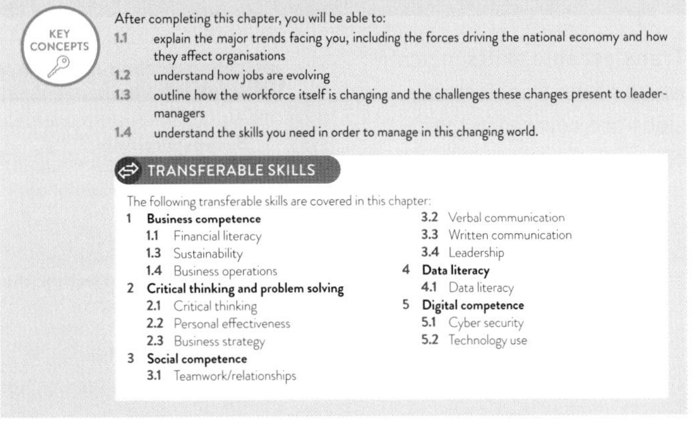
KEY CONCEPTS

After completing this chapter, you will be able to:

1.1 explain the major trends facing you, including the forces driving the national economy and how they affect organisations
1.2 understand how jobs are evolving
1.3 outline how the workforce itself is changing and the challenges these changes present to leader-managers
1.4 understand the skills you need in order to manage in this changing world.

TRANSFERABLE SKILLS

The following transferable skills are covered in this chapter:

1 **Business competence**
  1.1 Financial literacy
  1.3 Sustainability
  1.4 Business operations
2 **Critical thinking and problem solving**
  2.1 Critical thinking
  2.2 Personal effectiveness
  2.3 Business strategy
3 **Social competence**
  3.1 Teamwork/relationships
  3.2 Verbal communication
  3.3 Written communication
  3.4 Leadership
4 **Data literacy**
  4.1 Data literacy
5 **Digital competence**
  5.1 Cyber security
  5.2 Technology use

OVERVIEW

Chapter overviews provide a synopsis of the key concepts in each chapter and how these concepts connect to each other.

OVERVIEW

You can expect to spend a significant portion of your working hours communicating, and in many of these communication situations, you need to influence the opinions, actions or behaviours of others. To this end, all leader-managers need to be skilled influencers and persuaders (supported by your personal skills, discussed in Chapter 5, and your core communications skills, discussed in Chapter 6).

You may be called upon to represent your organisation officially or semi-officially; for example, in a sales or negotiation situation or at an industry conference. Or it may be in a one-on-one or a small group meeting or making a presentation to a client or a larger general audience. You might be required to convince a client that your business approach is appropriate to their needs. Or you may need to persuade in writing; for example, by preparing a formal proposal, letter of introduction, or a submission to a statutory agency. You may be called upon to mediate between employees in a conflict situation to redress any grievances and negotiate a way to prevent the conflict from escalating further, or you may find yourself at odds with another leader-manager, someone else in your organisation or even with a client or supplier. Even when you're chatting to employees informally, you may want to take the opportunity to help them understand a new or updated organisational strategy or a change in team or organisational direction.

In all of these situations, you have a number of things to consider, including the:

- other party's inclinations and background knowledge
- type of communication medium; for example, face-to-face, telephone or videoconference
- communication barriers that stand in your way
- pros and cons of your position for the other party and other stakeholders

SNAPSHOT

Gain an insight into how Management theories relate to the real world through the **Snapshot** at the beginning of each chapter.

SNAPSHOT

The strategic planning meeting

Charlotte is a paid, part-time leader-manager working on funding with a community arts organisation. She has just put the finishing touches on an updated induction outline for volunteers, a delegated responsibility she put her hand up for, thinking she'd like to give it a try. She found she didn't need to change much but updated the information on the source of the organisation's funding arrangements and how important bequests had become in the last few years. She also added information on the organisation's involvement in the local community and with similar organisations across the country and in Asia.

Now she's off to the strategic planning conference, which takes place every couple of years. Because it's a small organisation, with only one other part-time employee, one person seconded part-time from the local council and 12 volunteers, they have the luxury of being able to include everyone in the planning process. Apart from the good ideas everyone can contribute based on their different backgrounds and interests, the planning workshop is excellent for morale and for focusing everyone on the strategy and goals that they eventually agree on.

The external facilitator leading the planning workshop warms everyone up with a short creativity exercise. Next, they review their values, vision and mission and agree that there is no need to change or amend them, since they have been working well and they and all their stakeholders are familiar and comfortable with them.

Then they undertake a 'future search', exploring what changes or trends might affect them over the next few years regarding funding, the arts, and the closer and wider community. From there, they conduct a SWOT analysis and spend a fair bit of time discussing the constraints, direct and indirect, that influence the way they perform their roles and work towards their mission. The day ends by agreeing on some clear goals in the areas they highlighted as pivotal to their mission from their SWOT analysis, and assigning responsibilities for 'championing' them. The champions are to report at their next monthly meeting with suggested milestones and timelines.

NEW TRANSFERABLE SKILLS

Transferrable skills indicate which of the transferrable skills are covered in the chapter.

TRANSFERABLE SKILLS

The following transferable skills are covered in this chapter:

1 **Business competence**
- 1.1 Financial literacy
- 1.2 Entrepreneurship/small business skills
- 1.3 Sustainability
- 1.4 Business operations
- 1.5 Operations management

2 **Critical thinking and problem solving**
- 2.1 Critical thinking
- 2.2 Personal effectiveness
- 2.3 Business strategy

3 **Social competence**
- 3.1 Teamwork/relationships
- 3.2 Verbal communication
- 3.3 Written communication
- 3.4 Leadership

4 **Data literacy**
- 4.1 Data literacy

5 **Digital competence**
- 5.2 Technology use

FEATURES WITHIN CHAPTERS

NEW INDUSTRY INSIGHTS

Industry insights contextualise concepts from the chapter with workplace examples.

INDUSTRY INSIGHTS

Directors' independence: the pros and cons

Boards were once made up of people with useful contacts or a sound understanding of the organisation's industry. Then a series of catastrophic corporate governance failures around the world triggered regulatory strengthening, including new requirements for director independence.

In 2003, the Australian Securities Exchange (ASX) Corporate Governance Council recommended that a majority of board directors should be independent directors, that is, that they have no personal interests or stake in the organisation that could materially interfere with the impartial exercise of their judgement. Known as the 'Conflict Rule', in practice this means that directors should not hold more than 5 per cent of the company's stock and should not have worked in an executive capacity in the company or an associated company for at least three years.

But this is advice only and some believe it is occasionally best ignored in the case of individual directors. The important thing, they say, is the sum of the parts in terms of diversity, effectiveness, experience, independence and skills of the board as a whole. Directors with no prior experience with a company or its industry can't have the depth of knowledge they need to make sound decisions, however well-intentioned they may be.

However, a report by Macquarie Equities showed that companies whose directors are substantial shareholders outperformed the market. Many organisations prefer directors to hold substantial equity in the company because they believe directors with 'skin in the game' are more motivated to improve company performance. Suncorp directors, for example, must own at least $200 000 in company stock. In agreement with this sentiment, Australian Council of Superannuation Investors have stated their disappointment that a mere 89 per cent of S&P/ASX 100 and 82 per cent of ASX 200 directors own shares. They prefer all directors to be shareholders so that they identify more with the shareholders they represent. The Council believes that when directors have something to win or lose, they govern better.[7]

The question is whether shareholding might tempt directors into unethical behaviour. A large shareholding could lead to a material conflict of interest for a director who is, for example, responsible for signing off on financial statements or making strategic decisions. And it might incentivise them to make short-term decisions for personal gain at the expense of the long-term good of the company and all its shareholders. And would a small shareholding really make them govern better?

The jury, it seems, is still out but the consensus is that the right balance is needed between independence and impartiality on the one hand and vested interest on the other. What is your opinion?

NEW CASE STUDIES

Analyse in-depth **Case studies** that present issues in context, encouraging you to integrate the concepts discussed in the chapter and apply them to the workplace.

CASE STUDY 2

IBMERS REINVENT THEIR VALUES

In 1914, the start-up company International Business Machines Corporation (IBM) made cheese slicers, scales for weighing meat and tabulating machines. In 1962, then-president Thomas J Watson Jr announced what he called IBM's 'basic beliefs':

- respect for the individual
- superlative customer service
- pursuit of excellence.

These basic beliefs, or values, became the basis of IBM's culture and helped drive its success.[15]

In the 1990s, the company suffered the worst period in its history and was forced to cut its workforce of nearly 400 000 almost in half. IBM fought back under CEO Lou Gerstner, who took over in 1993, transforming it from a mainframe manufacturer into a provider of integrated hardware, networking and software solutions.

Sam Palmisano, who started with the company as a salesperson in 1973, took over as CEO in 2002. By then, IBM operated in 170 countries and had nearly 70 major product lines and countless supporting product lines, as well as more than a dozen customer segments. It employed more than 333 000 people, 40 per cent of whom didn't report daily to an IBM site but worked at clients' premises, from home or in mobile offices.

Despite its turnaround, something was still wrong. IBM's basic beliefs had become distorted. The company had stopped listening to its markets, its customers and its employees. 'Pursuit of excellence' had become arrogance. 'Respect for the individual' had become entitlement and a guaranteed job. So, statistically representative cross-section of the company – to participate in focus groups and surveys to inform the development of the new set of values. The resulting proposed values were:

- commitment to the customer
- excellence through innovation
- integrity that earns trust.

Despite this participative process, Palmisano knew that he couldn't simply announce these proposed corporate values:

> Traditional, top-down management processes … wouldn't work at IBM – or, I would argue, at an increasing number of twenty-first-century companies. You can't impose command-and-control mechanisms on a large, highly professional workforce. I'm not only talking about our scientists, engineers and consultants. More than 200 000 of our employees have college degrees. The CEO can't say to them, 'Get in line and follow me', or 'I've decided what your values are'. They're too smart for that. And, as you know, smarter people tend to be, well, a little more challenging; you might even say cynical.

In July 2003, Palmisano opened the values creation process to all employees. Using a specially tailored 'jamalyzer' software tool, a three-day debate on the company's values began. Known as ValuesJam, it took place on the company's intranet, opening unstructured employee discussions around four topics:

IN PRACTICE

Examine how theoretical concepts have been used in practice through the **In Practice** boxes.

IN PRACTICE

Spreading the costs – the advantages of sharing

An owner of a large café and a smaller delicatessen in different locations in the same street decides to merge operations on the advice of the accountant who reviewed the financial statement that follows.

	Delicatessen	Café	Total
Sales	$1100 000	$850 000	$1950 000
Cost of goods sold	$500 000	$350 000	$850 000
Gross profit	$600 000	$500 000	$1100 000
Wages	$200 000	$300 000	$500 000
Electricity	$50 000	$70 000	$120 000
Administration	$50 000	$50 000	$100 000
Rent	$50 000	$75 000	$125 000
Other expenses	$25 000	$25 000	$50 000
Profit/(loss)	**$225 000**	**($20 000)**	**$205 000**

The market value of the two businesses is $1000 000 for the delicatessen and $100 000 for the café. The owner had considered selling the café, but the accountant recommended relocating the deli to join the larger premises of the less profitable café. The accountant made the following projection of income and expenditure:

	Merged operation
Sales	$1950 000
Cost of goods sold	$750 000
Gross profit	$1200 000
Wages	$400 000
Electricity	$80 000
Administration	$65 000
Rent	$50 000
Other expenses	$40 000
Relocation and fit-out expenses	$75 000
Profit/loss	**$395 000**

Accepting the assumptions made by the accountant are correct, can you work out what has changed the financial situation for the owner?[2]

REFLECT

Gain a strategic overview of the concepts and theories from the chapter using the **Reflect** boxes.

REFLECT

In a culture where humour and 'getting a joke' is valued, people sometimes think they can get away with passive-aggressive humour, sarcasm and 'harmless' put-downs. They may be acceptable when aimed at yourself or others in your 'in group', but when someone in the 'in group' aims a 'joke' at someone in the 'out group', it is not acceptable. In workplaces where 'just joking' is the norm and 'get over yourself' is the response to someone not finding it funny, we have covert or even systemic discrimination at work.

Put-downs and 'humour' based on negative stereotypes have no place in the workplace. Call it out. And should you be called humourless for saying so, call it out again. And remember: 'The standard you walk past is the standard you accept.'[3]

If you're called out for an unfunny barb, your response should be something like: 'I'm sorry I offended you, thank you for telling me.' (Not 'I'm sorry *if* I offended you.')

Can you think of times when this has happened in your workplace, and the reactions from others?

FYI

Utilise the bonus information in the **FYI** boxes to develop your understanding of the chapter material.

Aligning goals and values

When employees' goals and values are not the same as their organisation's goals and values, they find it difficult to work well and even to remain within the organisation. So, how can organisations describe and communicate their vision, goals and strategies to employees in a way that builds loyalty and earns their support? How can they make employees feel part of and committed to a larger, worthwhile whole? What formal and informal communication channels can they establish to ensure that their key messages reach people?

One way is to keep employees informed about key events in their organisation so that they feel an important part of it. Corporate videos in a YouTube-style format; formal briefing meetings and papers; in-house magazines and newsletters; internal vacancy notices; intranet sites that are friendly, informative and interactive; noticeboards; senior managers' blogs and tweets; training programs and business conferences, and values and vision ambassadors, can all play an important role in aligning individual and organisational values.

Top-down communication alone isn't enough. Interactive communication is important, too, because to increase **employee engagement**, people need to feel that their voice is heard and that what they say matters. They want to know that their organisation considers them important enough not just to keep them informed about what is going on, but also to find out what they are thinking.

ICONS

The **transferrable skills icon** indicates where transferrable skills have been highlighted throughout the text.

END-OF-CHAPTER FEATURES

At the end of each chapter, you will find several tools to help you to review, practise and extend your knowledge of the key learning outcomes.

END-OF-CHAPTER ACTIVITIES

Test your knowledge and consolidate your learning through the **Extension activity**.

EXTENSION ACTIVITIES

Referring to the Snapshot at the beginning of this chapter, answer the following questions:

1 How would you rate Lee's performance at delivering the news to the HR team?
2 What does the constant use of the word 'we' create an assumption about regarding who was responsible for the failures identified – the entire company, just the decision-makers or just the members of the team?
3 How would you, as a leader-manager, have delivered this message and outcome to the team, and how do you think your method would have made it more effective?

CASE STUDY 31

CARMEN'S PROBLEM

'Come in, Carmen, and sit down. I want to talk to you about how you're getting on here. You seem a bit nervous and edgy lately and I'm worried that it seems to be affecting your work performance. Is anything wrong?'

'No, everything's fine ... (pause) ... It's just, well – oh, it's nothing, really. Not important.'

'I'd like to hear what it is, Carmen, although of course I'll understand if it's personal and you'd rather not tell me.'

'It's stupid – you'll think I'm just being silly ...'

'It seems to be bothering you, whatever it is. Why

'Well, they tease us a lot. It doesn't seem to bother the other girls much, but it makes me upset. I'm not used to that sort of thing. I don't know what to do about it.'

'What do you mean, they "tease" you?'

'For instance, when we have to climb up those ladders to get at the things stored up high, they make remarks. I don't always understand what they say, but they always laugh loudly and I get embarrassed. I sometimes drop things and they laugh even louder.'

'Is this only with you, or does this happen with the other women too?'

Guide to the online resources

FOR THE INSTRUCTOR

INSTRUCTOR RESOURCES PACK

Premium resources that provide additional instructor support are available for this text, including **instructor manual**, **mapping grid**, **PowerPoints**, **Testbank** and **cases**.

These resources save you time and are a convenient way to add more depth to your classes, covering additional content and with an exclusive selection of engaging features aligned with the text.

The Instructor Resource Pack is included for institutional adoptions of this text when certain conditions are met.

The pack is available to purchase for course-level adoptions of the text or as a standalone resource.

Contact your Cengage learning consultant for more information.

FOR THE STUDENT

MINDTAP

MindTap is the next-level online learning tool that helps you get better grades!

MindTap gives you the resources you need to study – all in one place and available when you need them. In the *MindTap Reader*, you can make notes, highlight text and even find a definition directly from the page.

If your instructor has chosen *MindTap* for your subject this semester, log in to *MindTap* to:

- Get better grades
- Save time and get organised
- Connect with your instructor and peers
- Study when and where you want, online and mobile
- Complete assessment tasks as set by your instructor

When your instructor creates a course using *MindTap*, they will let you know your course link so you can access the content. Please purchase *MindTap* only when directed by your instructor. Course length is set by your instructor.

PREFACE

In the industrial economy of the 20th century, organisations were shaped like pyramids, with deep layers of middle managers who passed information 'up the line' and orders 'down the line'. Workers did as they were told and were expected to work for the same organisation, doing much of the same work for most of their working lives. Management was mostly about forecasting and planning, organising people and resources, commanding, coordinating and controlling.

Leadership and management today in the 21st century is entirely different. The industrial economy is gone and the COVID-19 pandemic has had a profound effect on organisations across the globe and has potentially changed the way we work forever. Organisations and leaders have been forced to re-evaluate how they lead and manage their employees and teams. Organisations are more complex, business models are changing rapidly, and stand-alone functions are being replaced by capabilities-based processes. For many organisations, hybrid working is becoming the norm with a shift to staff working remotely either in full or in part. This has meant the leadership role played by managers in the past has changed. No longer can a manager wander over to a team member's desk and check on their progress. Staff performance is now results-focused more than ever before, and monitoring and support is provided more often via videoconferencing rather than a meeting in the office or boardroom.

The attitudes of employees to work have also changed. Most employees expect to change employers and their careers frequently, particularly now that working from home has become a realistic expectation for those who have seized the opportunity provided by the pandemic to create a better work–life balance. The 'Great Resignation', where workers are resigning from their positions in great numbers, has become a reality that organisations and their managers are now facing. Organisations must find different ways and offer new incentives to elevate themselves to the position of an employer of choice in an increasingly competitive and shrinking labour market.

How well equipped are you to lead and manage in the uncertainty of the 'new normal' in 21st-century Australia? Unlike past generations of managers, you may not see those reporting to you for days or weeks at a time. In fact, sometimes you may never meet them face-to-face because they work in another state or country. As a manager in this 'new world of work', the emphasis of your role will be on your ability to adapt and innovate amid the uncertainties and unpredictability of the global and hybrid working environment. Having effective communication skills that empower, energise and support teams across different mediums, and the ability to utilise innovative strategies to do so, is more important than ever. These skills are now the key ingredients to leading your team successfully and creating a work environment where it can prosper and thrive.

This revised and updated eighth edition of *Leadership & Management: Theory & Practice* re-examines the requirements of managing and leading in a post-pandemic world. Bridging the gap between theory and practice, it presents the current theory, research and practical application of management and leadership concepts into everyday language and an understandable context. You will learn models and frameworks you can use in leadership and management situations that will equip you with the vocabulary you need to communicate effectively. This text also considers the ongoing importance of sustainability in how we manage, and takes a more detailed look into the concepts of wellness and wellbeing.

Whether you are an aspiring manager, new to management or an old hand extending, refreshing or updating your skills, the goals of this edition are threefold:

1 to provide leading-edge information about the science and art of management that you can put into practice in your own unique way
2 to convey the information in a practical, everyday context so that it 'makes sense'
3 to provide you with a resource that you can refer to and apply the concepts contained within for many years to come.

As you lead and manage your team, it may be helpful to keep the following quote in mind: *Respect is earned, honesty is appreciated, trust is gained, loyalty is returned* (Oscar Auliq-Ice). In the new and somewhat-uncharted world of work we now face, approaching your role with a philosophy such as this will help you to lead and manage not only with fairness and equity, but also with the humanity that your employees not only expect but deserve.

Author team

ACKNOWLEDGEMENTS

Tim Rule would like to thank Robyn Rea, Kim Slingo, Billy Worth and Kate Dennett.

Kim Slingo would like to acknowledge Tim Rule, Billy Worth and Lara Collins for their professional guidance and friendship, and Eden Slingo and Mark Irvine for their ongoing support.

Billy Worth would like to acknowledge the guidance and input of the following people, not only in the development of this publication but in the shaping of his career: fellow authors Kim Slingo and Tim Rule; Johanna Worth, Mike Allingham (VET professional), Kate Dennett (VET professional), Brent McGregor (personal mentor and VET professional), Sandro Capocchi (training manager and VET professional), the late Gary Wicks (personal mentor and creative director), Stephanie Davis and the entire Cengage publishing staff.

Publisher's acknowledgements

Cengage would like to give a special thanks to Andrew Roadknight for his updates to Chapters 20, 21 and 27; Stephen Abrahams for his update to Chapter 22; and Shehan Rauff for his expertise in checking Chapter 17. Their efforts are very much appreciated.

The authors and Cengage Learning would like to thank the following people for their feedback during the development of this edition.

Michael Brown, South Regional TAFE
Glen Parker, Adapt Education
Roz Jani, Charles Darwin University
Kay Jones, Southern Institute of Technology
Mike Stoll, The Management Edge Pty Ltd
Anne Butler, Melbourne Polytechnic
Maree Hawkins, Bay of Plenty Polytechnic
Louise John, TAFE Digital
Barbara Barnes, Central Queensland University TAFE
Ray Noronha, Enable College
Heath Burton, SWSLHD CEWD – NSW Health RTO
Merran Renton, Bedford College
Louise Targett, Target Training
Julie Pisano, TAFE SA
Shirley Virtue, TAFE NSW
Peter Drapac, NBIA
Wendy Tagliabue, ABEX Training

ABOUT THE AUTHORS

Kris Cole has held significant management and human resources positions in the engineering, oil, food and education industries and holds a Bachelor of Science (Honours) in Organisational Psychology, a Post-Graduate Diploma in Manufacturing Technology and a Graduate Certificate in Adult Education. She has created and led management training programs and helped organisations in all sectors in Australia, New Zealand and South-East Asia to improve their workplace effectiveness, performance and productivity.

Tim Rule's career spans over 30 years and has seen him undertake leadership and management roles in the private, public, not-for-profit and education sectors. From his first management role as a frontline manager in the public service for the then named Department of Social Security, Tim moved into the education sector where he worked as a Business Management and Economics teacher and Head of Department before accepting a team leader and coordination role for a not-for-profit registered training organisation (RTO) in the vocational education and training (VET) sector. He went on to create his own resource development business, Training Solutions Australia, which operated successfully for the next decade, providing customised training resources to businesses and RTOs. During this period, he also co-authored *Training and Assessment: Theory and Practice* as well as developing the learning support materials for the sixth and seventh editions of *Leadership and Management: Theory and Practice* written by Kris Cole. In recent years, Tim's expertise and experience have seen him reprise his role as an instructional designer for Swinburne University of Technology and he now acts as a consultant providing professional guidance and learning materials to businesses operating in the VET sector.

Jill Noble is a business and human resources (HR) consultant. She delivers workshops focusing on behavioural change for leaders and individual contributors across 30 topics. Jill works extensively across Asia, North and South America, Europe and Australia. Jill hold a Master's Degree, Postgraduate Diplomas in Public Relations, Learning and Development and Career Counselling. She is a content creator for business and agriculture, also producing a podcast and a print magazine focused on her other passion, which is sheep!

Kim Slingo is described as an imaginative and adaptable leader, and has led teams successfully in office and retail environments before transitioning her leadership and management experience to the VET sector over 25 years ago. During this time, Kim applied her leadership experience and innovative mindset to create and deliver bespoke training solutions to assist individuals and organisations reach their full potential. Throughout Kim's most recent educational leadership positions her responsibilities have included analysing training needs and learning outcomes, identifying strategies to enhance the achievement of learning objectives at both a strategic and operational level, and creating engaging and innovative curriculum to enhance learning experiences for both the VET and higher education sectors. Kim's love of learning has seen her complete the Advanced Diploma in Business and the Bachelor of Adult Learning and Development, and she is currently completing a Graduate Certificate in Education Design.

Billy Worth has worked in business management and ownership across the globe in a number of industries, including entertainment, hospitality, filmmaking and tertiary education. He has created learning and assessment resources and end-to-end training solutions for the Australian tertiary and higher education industries for the past 15 years. Billy holds qualifications in hospitality management, retail management, leadership and management, training and assessment, and training design and development.

PART

1

UNDERSTANDING YOUR ORGANISATION

Business models are changing; work and working patterns are changing and organisations are changing. There is no doubt that leading and managing is trickier than in the past. Just as today's employees need wider and deeper skills than in the past, so do leader-managers. Similarly, just as employees are demanding more flexibility and trust, leader-managers must learn how to meet these wants and needs. To remain employable, you need to continually update your skills, your understanding of yourself and your employees, and your understanding of the world around you. The stronger your conceptual, personal, interpersonal and technical skills are, the more you can thrive and the more satisfaction you will glean from working in this brave new world of work.

In these first four chapters, you will discover the rapidly changing, shrinking-yet-expanding, turbulent and unpredictable environment that your organisation operates within and the challenges this presents to employees, leader-managers and organisations alike.

You will find out how organisations are responding by changing their structures and their operations to more 'hybrid' and flexible modes. You will find out how the nature and types of relationships inside organisations are changing and how the relationships that organisations have with their customers and suppliers are changing. An organisation's values, vision, mission and strategy are explained, and you will learn how to use them to manage your area of operations and lead your team.

You will also discover how to understand the 'formal organisation' (your organisation as it appears on paper) and the 'informal organisation' (some would say the organisation as it really operates). This can help you interpret and understand your organisation's culture and norms, the relationships between people and groups and how power and influence operate.

The basic and essential understanding of organisations discussed in Part 1 will equip you with the skills to quickly find your feet in the shifting sands of organisations.

CHAPTER

THE CHANGING WORLD OF WORK

KEY CONCEPTS

After completing this chapter, you will be able to:

1.1 explain the major trends facing you, including the forces driving the national economy and how they affect organisations

1.2 understand how jobs are evolving

1.3 outline how the workforce itself is changing and the challenges these changes present to leader-managers

1.4 understand the skills you need in order to manage in this changing world.

TRANSFERABLE SKILLS

The following transferable skills are covered in this chapter:

1 **Business competence**
- **1.1** Financial literacy
- **1.3** Sustainability
- **1.4** Business operations

2 **Critical thinking and problem solving**
- **2.1** Critical thinking
- **2.2** Personal effectiveness
- **2.3** Business strategy

3 **Social competence**
- **3.1** Teamwork/relationships
- **3.2** Verbal communication
- **3.3** Written communication
- **3.4** Leadership

4 **Data literacy**
- **4.1** Data literacy

5 **Digital competence**
- **5.1** Cyber security
- **5.2** Technology use

OVERVIEW

Transferable skills

1.4 Business operations

2.3 Business strategy

3.1 Teamwork/relationships

3.4 Leadership

You are leading and managing in an ever-changing reality. Business models, the economy, the marketplace, society and technology are transforming at unprecedented speeds and often in unpredictable ways. Among political, climatic, economic and societal healthcare volatility abound. Organisations and employees need to be adaptable and innovative to not only navigate, but to take advantage of swift and deep changes.

In an effort to respond effectively to such variables, organisations are changing the way they organise themselves, introducing new ways of working and changing their employee mix to be more diverse than ever before. The workforce is getting older and more skilled, and includes more women, minority groups, people with disabilities, people from other cultures, and those for whom English is not their first language. There are also more people being managed in name only, such as contract workers, temporary staff and those in outsourced roles. Casual workers, part-timers and full-timers are also part of the mix. Each of these groups has different needs, different motivations and different expectations of work and of their leader-managers. In turn, new ways of leading and managing are replacing traditional practices at an astonishing rate.

What does the future hold? The changing world of work (and living) and the challenges that leader-managers face as a result are described in this chapter.

SNAPSHOT

The connected world

An organisation is looking to globalise operations and expand its network. Its People and Culture department was instructed to advertise worldwide for the position of manager of the copywriting team. The outstanding candidate is Caroline, a Canadian living in Toronto, who is, on paper, the most qualified and experienced individual who has applied. She negotiates a deal with the organisation that her working hours (Melbourne time) will be 6 a.m. to 2 p.m., which works well for all parties because the business conducts most meetings and presentations over the internet. As the CEO told her: 'It's your expertise we need, not your physical presence in the office – especially as 80 per cent of the organisation is working remotely anyway. Let's go for it!'

Caroline's experience and determination shine through, and she quickly bonds with her team. She brings a fresh approach to the processes the team follow, and she imparts her considerable knowledge to the organisation. Despite some initial trepidation from the team regarding working hours, Caroline's worth soon becomes apparent, and they begin to function in a streamlined, efficient and effective way.

Transferable skills

1.4 Business operations

2.2 Personal effectiveness

3.1 Teamwork/relationships

3.2 Verbal communication

3.3 Written communication

3.4 Leadership

1.1 Get ready: the megatrends

> Politicians once had the power to set interest rates and the exchange rate, and to protect industries from overseas competition. There were mechanisms in place to set wages for the whole country. That all changed with the deregulation of the economy that began in the 1980s.
>
> Laura Tingle, 'Political amnesia: How we forgot to govern', *Quarterly Essay Issue 60*, 2015, Black Inc, Victoria, p. 3.

We're in a new age. Gone is the slowly evolving, reasonably predictable business environment. Gone are the managers sending orders 'down the line' and workers sending information back 'up the line'. Gone are the 'good old days' of certainty and protectionism and gone is an economy based on agriculture, mining and manufacturing. You are leading and managing in a world of open markets, fierce competition and new and complex business models and platforms. You are leading and managing in an Australian economy based on service, knowledge and information, where brains, not brawn, are an organisation's, and an individual's, chief value.

Australian society is changing as its people and the definition of the family unit continue to evolve. The physical and economic environments are less stable and more uncertain as **climate change**, globalisation and resource scarcity continue to drive the changes confronting organisations. Advancing technologies make the needed responses to these changes possible, enabling us to communicate, cooperate, innovate and work more efficiently.

The main changes making organisations more vulnerable and more difficult to guide than in the past are shown in Figure 1.1. These changes are deeper and occurring faster than ever before; the acronym VUCA says it all: Volatility, Uncertainty, Complexity and Ambiguity. Each of the trends discussed below affect both employers and employees, and each demands a different response from an organisation.

Transferable skills

1.4 Business operations

You can expect discomfort, friction and stress as the people you lead and manage, and who lead and manage you, struggle to come to terms with the changes around them and work out how they can navigate and make the most of these changes for themselves and for their organisation. Leader-managers need to find ways to turn people's uneasiness into flexibility and innovativeness in order to respond to, and make the most of, these changes and to flourish in a knowledge and service economy.

Let's explore the major trends that are causing organisations to fundamentally rethink their operating philosophies, strategies and tactics. The details of how these factors are transforming

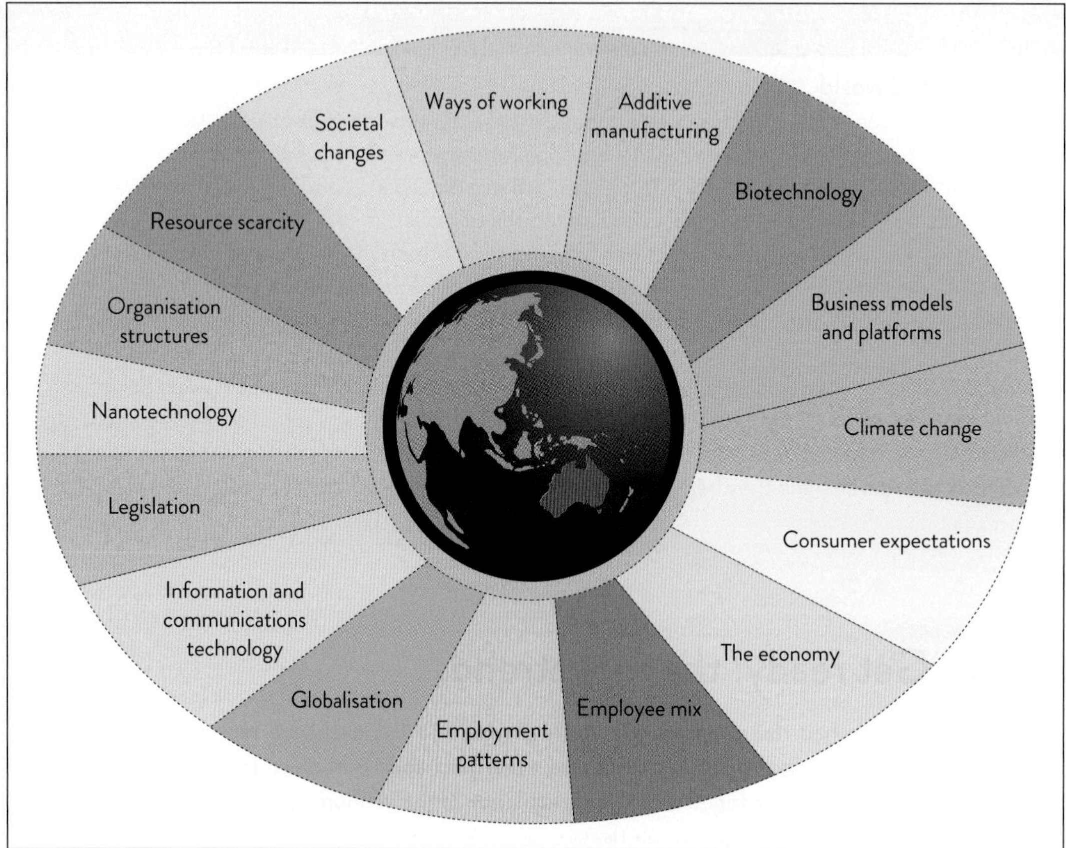

FIGURE 1.1 Change is all around us

workplaces are emerging as organisations test out different structures, ways of working and ways of organising people, jobs and operations to see what works best in this new age.

Climate change

Transferable skills

1.1 Financial literacy

1.4 Business operations

Scientists agree that the climate of the planet is changing, largely due to human activities. As a result, we can expect rising sea levels and increasingly severe and destructive weather events, such as droughts, floods and storms, to continue to threaten people's lives and livelihoods, corporate profits and global prosperity. These events have the potential to destroy infrastructure and ecosystems, disrupt agriculture, increase economic volatility and even render some regions of the country (or other parts of the world) uninhabitable. As Australia's population and population density increase, so does the potential impact of climatic events on the community.

Climate change has legal and business impacts. For example, the Australian Prudential Regulation Authority, which regulates financial institutions, expects them to monitor, disclose and discuss any risks resulting from their operations as part of their duty of care. Organisations need to predict and plan to manage disruptions to their operations and supply chains affected by climatic events. (Chapter 22 explains how to identify and manage risk and develop business continuity plans.) Organisations can also learn to adapt and benefit from climate change and share in the growing global market for environmental goods and services. 'Clean tech' is set to become a strategic priority for many companies. In Australia, potential winners from climate change include the alternative energy, engineering, recycling and sustainable property sectors, but there are also opportunities for innovative financial services, chemical agriculture and some healthcare companies.

The environmental performance of a company is increasingly affecting share prices and many companies are paying more attention to corporate social responsibility (CSR) and corporate responsibility (CR) and investing in improving their carbon footprint. (See 'A new way of assessing organisations' later in this chapter; see also Chapter 23.)

Pandemics and epidemics

Transferable skills

1.4 Business operations

2.3 Business strategy

As we have seen during the COVID-19 global pandemic, there are health-related events that, while seeming innocuous initially, can shut down large swathes of business across the planet. Despite the plethora of government assistance offered to many industries, the harsh reality is that some types of business have fared far better than others. For example, hospitality, travel and leisure industries have all suffered huge losses. Entire towns, cities and provinces overseas have been hit especially hard, with destinations that rely heavily on tourism dollars, such as Bali, experiencing not only business closures but also an impact on a large portion of the population, who have lost their means of income. Additionally, international border closures have had far wider-reaching effects than just delays or cancellations for travellers and tourists, with global transport and logistics industries heavily damaged, and the cost of import/export of goods increased exponentially. Additionally, international relations between trading partners soured, in some cases, almost beyond repair. The full cost of the pandemic – in financial and humanitarian terms – will no doubt take many years to be fully understood.

The only perceived upside of the COVID-19 pandemic is the necessity that employees and leader-managers, business owners and governments be better prepared to cope with these events in the future, without having to resort to economy-crippling lockdowns and the necessary removal of freedoms. Sensible organisations will now have plans in place to combat the effects of such disasters, and industries will be better placed to continue trading and reduce the loss of revenue and workforce that was so prevalent from the beginning of 2020.

Globalisation

Transferable skills

1.4 Business operations

2.3 Business strategy

It may sound trite, but it is true: It's a small world. Prior to COVID-19, globalisation saw transportation and communications technology drawing all areas of the world closer together. **Deregulation** was encouraging more trade between countries and was expanding the marketplace. Breaking up and selling off national monopolies in areas such as air transport, the finance and insurance industries and telecommunications had enabled trading systems, which linked the distribution and consumption of goods and services, finance and production, to span the globe. The result saw more and tougher competition, increasing pressure to customise products and services and improve efficiencies, productivity, quality and service. The world is recovering and is predicted to reach this level of industry behaviour again.

Companies are becoming more diverse in size and origin and economic power is shifting from West to East and from North to South as the world's economies realign themselves with Asia at the centre. Three of the four most populous countries in the world (China, India and Indonesia) and five of the 20 largest economies in the world (China, India, Japan, South Korea and Indonesia) are our neighbours. (The Australian economy is the sixth largest in the Asia-Pacific region despite our much smaller population.) Our region is the world's fastest-growing region; it represents nearly 40 per cent of the global economy and hosts more than half of the world's population.[1]

Transferable skills

1.4 Business operations

Some manufacturing and many professional services have moved overseas where labour costs less, and now more Australians are working overseas. While globalisation allows poorer countries to develop economically and raise their standard of living, and developed economies to purchase inexpensive goods and services, it also brings risks to individual organisations. For example:

- dependence on overseas suppliers and contractors makes it easier for climatic events and growing political destabilisation to wipe out part or all of an organisation's supply chain and a significant, possibly crippling, portion of its service providers
- epidemics and pandemics can more easily destroy or temporarily disable a significant part of an organisation's workforce
- organisations that exploit workers in developing countries or behave irresponsibly towards the local environment can face public relations disasters and consumer boycotts.

FYI

Not new, just faster and deeper

Globalisation used to be called 'international trade'. Even before industrialisation, there were periods of relative openness in cross-border trade. During the Middle Ages, for example, the Silk Road across Central Asia connected China and Europe. So international trade isn't new. However, the pace and extent of the current phase of globalisation is unprecedented. Pulitzer Prize-winning author, Thomas Friedman, described today's globalisation with the adjectives 'farther, faster, cheaper and deeper', compared to previous waves of international trade.[2] In fact, many observers believe that the pace of globalisation has ushered the world into a new phase of economic development.

Globalisation doesn't just affect the way we do business and manage organisations; it affects nearly every aspect of our lives, as summarised in Figure 1.2.

Transferable skills

1.3 Sustainability

1.4 Business operations

2.3 Business strategy

5.1 Cyber security

5.2 Technology use

Technology

Additive manufacturing (covered later in this chapter), augmented intelligence, **big data**, superfast broadband, Cloud computing, the digital economy, the internet of things (IoT) ... technology makes breathtaking leaps forward, with increasingly disruptive results, radically extending what we take for granted and changing – faster and faster – not just the rules, but the game itself. We need to innovate through the changes in order to adapt to them and use them well.

Computing power doubles every two years, as does the amount of data and funding for artificial intelligence (AI). The advances in communications technology and the IT-related revolution have been the main enablers of the massive changes that are taking place, affecting organisations of all sizes and in all industries and sectors of the economy.

Cyber security and data breaches notwithstanding, the internet, intranets, collaborative systems technology (or **groupware**) and powerful databases allow organisations to operate across time zones and borders, which in turn allows the growing flexible workforce to expand globally. As technology becomes more intelligent and intuitive, replicating aspects of human thought, it continues to reshape the workforce – the way we work and the skills we need, and access to information becomes even easier, allowing more efficient decision-making, in turn allowing for the implementation of better processes, policies and procedures.

Technology is changing the way we structure organisations and manage functions, projects and teams, and influencing how we use space, energy and materials. It is leading to new products and services and increasing competitive pressure as well as potential. It is enabling new business models

Cultural, influencing factors such as dress, food, language and entertainment as well as business ethics

Environmental and biological, as polluting industries move to developing countries and polluting transportation and distribution networks change natural habitats, they spread disease and affect the health and diets of living organisms (domestic and wild) in many ways

Financial, affecting currency rates and the financial markets and, as the Asian and global financial crises have shown, the economy of countries and regions

Political systems, putting pressure on authoritarian-style regimes to become more inclusive and democratic as the internet, the media and people working for transnational corporations expose those regimes' citizens to more open cultures

Social, increasing the movement of people between countries and bringing changes to societies; for example, in the nature of work, employment levels and prosperity

Spatial, as the changes in society and the environment influence the structure and layout of cities, the design of housing and the nature of working environments

FIGURE 1.2 The far reach of globalisation

and platforms that disrupt industries and change the way we work and live. To stay in the game, we – organisations and people – must innovate.

For some time, technology has been gradually changing how, when and where people work. It is taking over some jobs, fundamentally changing others, and eliminating others altogether. Rather than having to travel to work, technology brings work (as well as education and entertainment) to people. The managers who lead teams may seldom or never meet them face-to-face, and this calls for a new set of management skills. (Chapter 14 explains how to lead and manage virtual teams.)

Digital transformation

Transferable skills

1.4 Business operations

5.1 Cyber security

5.2 Technology use

This rapid technological advancement has been (and is being) led by the concept of **digital transformation**. Simply put, digital transformation is the integration of digital technology across many or all areas of an organisation. Such transformation, in terms of processes, people and, of course, technology, can fundamentally alter the way a company operates. Efficiency, value and innovation in delivering products and/or services are the key aims of digital transformation.

As the world of work changes and evolves apace, it becomes more and more apparent that digital transformation is an imperative target for all businesses, regardless of their size or their business offerings. Reasons for implementing digital transformations can include:

- changing market conditions
- economic fluctuations
- industry upheaval

- new and emerging customer requirements
- the after effects of a natural disaster, or a medical disaster such as the recent COVID-19 pandemic.

When considering digital transformation, it is important for leader-managers to know exactly what it will mean for the company. Often, the parameters of what the term signifies are too broad and can cause confusion, uncertainty and irritation among employees and managers alike. This is where executives and the organisation's decision-makers will determine the individual characteristics of the digital transformation they wish to implement. That is to say, just as every organisation has its own needs in terms of employees, facilities and resources; it will have its own individual requirements for meaningful digital transformation.

The company may wish to start with a Design Technology Mission Statement, tailored for its exact organisation. The statement should give an idea of what the aim is and why it is important to the business; for example: 'As a retail organisation, our aim is to digitalise all of our sales operations in order to streamline the service we provide to customers, allowing online transactions to be seamless and face-to-face shopping to be a smooth and easy experience for our customers – with the goal of our operations being considered industry **best practice**'. This will give a clear indication to employees of the purpose of the organisation's intended digital transformation plans. Indeed, if employees themselves are fully briefed and involved in the construction of a DT Mission Statement, they are far more likely to not only understand the purpose, but to actively and enthusiastically participate and promote the aims.

Transferable skills
5.1 Cyber security
5.2 Technology use

The digital economy

Airbnb, Alibaba, Amazon, Facebook, Google, Instagram, Netflix, Pinterest, Snapchat, Spotify, Tesla Motors, Twitter, Uber – just about everyone participates in, and to some extent depends on, the digital economy, the network of economic and social activities enabled by the internet and mobile and sensor networks.

The digital economy includes personal computers and computers embedded in everyday appliances; electronic banking and paying by credit card; game consoles; lecturers posting course outlines, study materials and videos online for students; mobile phones and other mobile devices; online maps and photo and video-sharing sites; and sensor networks that monitor traffic flows. High-speed broadband, analytics, augmented and AI are all part of the digital economy.

A successful digital economy can disrupt an industry. Airbnb, Netflix and Uber, for example, are digital disruptors to the hotel, entertainment and taxi industries. Additive manufacturing will change the way goods are made. The education and training, healthcare and social assistance, mining, professional, scientific and technical services, public administration, retail, outsourced home services and transport, postal and warehousing industries are all candidates for digital disruption.

Transferable skills
1.3 Sustainability
1.4 Business operations
5.2 Technology use

Additive manufacturing

No longer does material need to be bashed and bent, or removed and wasted or recycled. Additive manufacturing, or 3D printing, gradually builds up a product, layer upon layer, to make smaller and more complex and intricate products than conventional subtractive manufacturing. It uses a host of materials, from epoxy resin to ground glass, gold, nylon, stainless steel, wax and even stem cells and other living cells.

Because it uses far less material, additive or digital manufacturing is a sustainable and efficient way to produce goods. In fact, it looks as though digital manufacturing can lower the environmental impact of a range of goods by more than 40 per cent. It is seen as the way of the future – but in actual fact, it is already here. The hearing aid industry in the US converted to 100 per cent digital manufacturing in 500 days; not one company that stayed with traditional manufacturing methods survived. General Electric produces jet engines, medical devices and parts for home appliances; NASA has sped up and revolutionised its supply chain by putting a 3D printer on the space station that produces parts, saving delivering them by rocket; Aurora Flight Sciences makes drones, and Luxexcel makes lenses for light-emitting diodes, all with additive manufacturing.[3] Dentists can custom manufacture and fit bridges, crowns and dentures in their surgeries in under an hour. Soon, your shoes will be custom-printed for your feet right in the store, while you wait.

Additive manufacturing sometimes costs more per individual product, but it costs less overall; for example, it has cut the cost of manufacturing jet engine fuel nozzles by 75 per cent.[4] Additive manufacturing reduces costs in a number of ways:

- it eliminates assembly and inventories
- depending on what is being produced, it generally takes up less space than traditional manufacturing
- it needs less machinery and fewer people
- digital manufacturing machines, once going, can be left virtually unattended.

The patterns for digital manufacturing can be tweaked with a mouse, making customising, improving and updating products cheap and easy, and making it simple to meet customer needs and wants. No more expensive retooling and reconfiguring subtractive manufacturing machines.

4D printing takes 3D printing to the next level. Objects made by additive manufacturing can change shape depending on humidity, temperature, time or other factors, and so can self-repair and even self-build.

21st-century Industrial Revolution

The mechanisation of the textile industry in Britain in the late 1700s kicked off the first Industrial Revolution as machinery and steam power moved work from the home to the factory. The second began in the early 1900s when, aided by electricity, Henry Ford mastered the moving assembly line and mass production. The third was launched when the internet and early robots disrupted the second Industrial Revolution. The digital revolution, including additive manufacturing, AI, big data and the IoT (discussed later in this chapter), is now launching the fourth Industrial Revolution.

Just as farriers' jobs all but disappeared with the advent of motorised vehicles, additive manufacturing will displace most manufacturing jobs, replacing them with a few highly skilled manufacturing workers and creating other jobs for designers, IT whizzes, logistics experts, office staff, marketers and other professionals. Each Industrial Revolution disrupted the way work was previously carried out.

Automated intelligence

Through AI and intelligence augmentation (IA), computers can increasingly learn and perform human tasks and even have the sense of touch. As a result, many jobs are either set to disappear or change greatly, and others will be created.

Transferable skills

1.3 Sustainability

1.4 Business operations

2.3 Business strategy

5.2 Technology use

Work can be automated in three ways:

- *robotic process automation:* taking over tasks done by people (automation)
- *cognitive automation:* letting machines learn and do some of the thinking
- *social robotics:* humans and robots learning from working together.

The number of jobs at risk of being automated or altered by AI by 2030 is astounding – 40 per cent, or up to five million jobs in Australia alone, are at high risk and a further 18 per cent at medium risk. The most affected jobs are predicted to be in administration and in regional and rural Australia, where computers are set to swallow more than 60 per cent of jobs. For example, fruit trees have been grown in particular shapes since the 1970s so that robots can easily pick their fruit.[5]

And it isn't only the routine jobs and tasks at risk from automation. Many of the more predictable tasks of highly paid knowledge workers, such as doctors, executives, financial planners, market researchers, sales people and 'techies', can be done by adapting current technology. Automation and AI support jobholders in their analytic, creative and decision-making efforts, supply the raw data, options and conclusions, leaving jobholders to do what the computer cannot; that is, use good judgement to make the final decision.

Of course, this has already occurred to some extent. 'Off-peopling' has already relieved accountants, administrators, bank tellers, corporate planners, farmers, middle managers, product designers, salespeople and secretaries of many of their more mundane tasks and millions of routine jobs, such as clerical work and assembly-line work, have been automated. In fact, increasingly powerful and cheap computers have reshaped the labour market since the 1960s, resulting in an expansion of high-skill jobs and low-skill jobs (but not the in-between jobs).

As automation improves and becomes more common, it will reshape work more radically. For example, as driverless cars take over, jobs that involve driving, roughly 25 per cent of today's jobs, will change. The skill of driving will diminish while customer service aspects of those jobs are likely to become more important.

Transferable skills
1.4 Business operations
2.1 Critical thinking
2.2 Personal effectiveness

Other industries where AI can increase productivity and reduce jobs are in health (computers can analyse data for predictive diagnostics, assist in surgery, nursing and pharmaceutical dispensing), banking and legal advice (where analysing data is important and time-consuming).

However, these changes do not mean that there will be a raft of unemployed people scrabbling for a living, cursing the day that robots took over their jobs. We must move from *task performer* mode to *task monitor* mode. Machines can only go so far – the human factor will always play a part in the automation of tasks. As technology improves and automation becomes more prevalent, the overriding philosophy of engineers and designers is that automation should control complex systems, particularly those that can go beyond the normal human performance capabilities of individuals, while operators monitor the system performance. The key to success in implementing automation is to consider and define the role of the human operator within the automated system.

Transferable skills
5.2 Technology use

Really smart computers and algorithms

AI is increasingly intuitive, as in, for example, Google's algorithm AlphaGo, which beat South Korean Go Grandmaster Lee Se-dol by 4 to 1 in March 2016. Uber algorithms connect drivers and passengers. Alibaba uses algorithms to help others sell their products. A Hong Kong venture capital firm appointed an algorithm called VITAL to its board in 2014 to vote on whether to invest in companies. IBM's Chef Watson, the supercomputer, can create recipes based on what's in your refrigerator and pantry.

Transferable skills
4.1 Data literacy
5.2 Technology use

Big data

Big data, or analytics, gathers and uses statistical models and algorithms to analyse huge and disparate amounts of data at vast speeds to predict behaviour and trends with uncanny accuracy and find hidden patterns and relationships that you wouldn't otherwise be able to find or even guess. You can use these insights to analyse risks, make the most of opportunities, increase competitiveness, make decisions or decide on a course of action.

Airline bookings, credit and debit card transactions, digital images, Google searches, GPS signals, mobile phones, tweets and posts on social media, records of online purchases, sensors embedded in 'smart connected products' and videos posted online all provide data that goes into big data sets. (And once the data is in there, you can't remove it.)

For many organisations, big data has become a core asset that assists customer relations, innovation and productivity growth.

The Cloud

Transferable skills

1.4 Business operations

4.1 Data literacy

5.1 Cyber security

5.2 Technology use

The Cloud is a group of linked servers, some storing data, others running applications. Individuals and organisations can store and access data remotely on the Cloud, rather than on their own hard drive, so you can think of it as infrastructure outsourcing. Cloud computing is economical because you don't need to invest in your own infrastructure and you can share security costs with the Cloud hosting company. But there are concerns: security considerations aside, for example, who owns your stored data?

New business models

Transferable skills

5.2 Technology use

Platform business models aren't exactly new – shopping centres have brought customers and retailers together for years. But **digital platform business models** are new. With little infrastructure, Airbnb, Lyft and Uber bring the supplier or producer and the customer together digitally and are turning the accommodation, car hire and taxi industries upside down. Owning resources, such as shopping centres, hotels and cars, isn't what these new platforms do; they use technology and intellectual property (their algorithms) to spread resources around and make them useable. Revolutionary digital platform business models like these threaten organisations based on traditional business models by creating completely different ways of operating and bringing customers and suppliers together.

When you look at Table 1.1, which shows the differences between traditional business models and platform business models, you can see that digital platforms make competition more intricate

TABLE 1.1 Traditional vs platform business models

Traditional business models	Digital platform business models
Inputs go in; outputs come out in a linear process	Act as a network hub that brings users and providers together
Internal processes and procedures create value	Facilitate interactions between members and customers to create value
Depend on physical assets	Depend on digital assets
Own the needed physical assets	Their members own the needed physical assets
Rely on economies of scale and economies of scope	Rely on many members and users in order to create viable 'matches'
Rely on features	Rely on communities of members and users
Make profits from sales of products	Make money from commissions on interactions between members and users

and fluid. And it's hard for traditional businesses to predict the emergence of digital competition. Did Swatch and Timex, which can compete with each other, predict they'd have to compete with smart watches? Did map companies, which can compete with each other, realise they'd be competing with Google and Apple Maps?

What's more, digital platforms challenge traditional business models because they change or ignore the established ways of operating that encumber traditional business models and add costs. For example, taxis have fixed rates and must provide wheelchair accessibility at similar response times, but Uber and Lyft don't.

Traditional companies have few choices:

- take legal action to get the laws these platforms circumvent enforced
- join or replicate the new model for their own business
- do what they currently do but far better in order to keep their customers
- devise business procedures that give them a positive point of difference
- go out of business.

Table 1.1 summarises just how different the thinking behind platform, as opposed to traditional, business models is.

Two other well-known disruptive business models are peer-to-peer and the sharing economy. The gig economy (independent contracting) is also changing the way organisations manage their operations.

Transferable skills
5.2 Technology use

The internet of things

The internet of things (IoT) is devices (things) talking to other devices (other things) without human input. For example, an electronic sensor sends a message to the automatic watering system to switch on because it senses the ground is dry.

The 'things' in the IoT are traditional products combined with information communications technology (ICT). The resulting smart, connected 'things' contain physical components (e.g. mechanical parts), smart components (e.g. sensors, microprocessors, an operating system) and connectivity components (e.g. ports, protocols, a communication network to the product's Cloud, which contains the product's external operating system). Their connectivity means they can be customised and upgraded cheaply, easily and quickly. Smart dust, tiny microelectrical mechanical systems (MEMS), can detect factors such as temperature, light and movement to provide information to various devices, taking the IoT to the next level.

These smart, connected products can collect, analyse, store, send and receive data. For example, they can:

- let the marketing department know when, where and how they are being used – valuable information upon which to base decisions, customise products, segment customers and serve them better
- monitor and report on their environment and performance in real time, so that routine, preventative maintenance can be scheduled, reducing product down time
- diagnose whether they are performing as they should and adjust their performance accordingly
- exchange and integrate data with other 'things', such as related products and business systems, which allow organisations to collaborate and produce joint offerings
- be controlled through remote devices, which means their operation can be optimised easily
- predict what is likely to occur in the future
- run applications
- learn and adapt to their environment and user preferences, and some can even operate on their own.

These products have given rise to the continuous manufacturing model, where software upgrades and updates can continue long after a product is purchased. This means that a sale isn't just one transaction any more (I sell, you buy) but the beginning of an ongoing relationship where the product improves over time. This can be an important profit generator and can allow more sustainable manufacturing because such products can have longer life cycles.

The IoT increases value through new efficiencies for the customer and increases revenue for the seller. More than that, the IoT can disrupt business models and transform supply chains, turning the core functions of manufacturing, logistics, after-sales service, IT, product development, marketing and sales into internal value chains, rendering the traditional 'silos' (functions acting independently and treating each other as rivals) obsolete. This demands new skill sets in employees.

Social media

Transferable skills

1.4 Business operations

2.3 Business strategy

5.2 Technology use

Social media is no longer just a way for 'young people' to communicate with each other; over the last decade it has exploded as a business opportunity and is a crucial vehicle for communicating and engaging with stakeholders. Although the platforms change almost as quickly as what's trending on them, they all share the ability to build and to destroy the reputation of companies (as well as individuals). This alone puts social media on the radar of most organisations' marketing and risk management functions.

Social media also gives organisations a good insight into the worlds of their customers, investors and other stakeholders, helping them better relate to these groups. An organisation's own social media can be an important tool in customer relations, employee relations, shareholder relations and even crisis management.

Nanotechnology and biotechnology

Transferable skills

1.4 Business operations

2.3 Business strategy

Breakthroughs in nanotechnology, biotechnology and genetics point to a radically changed world of increased possibilities. Like the information and communications technologies discussed above, they, too, lead to new products and new work methods, making some skills obsolete, while creating a need for other skills and enabling organisations to evolve new ways of working.

Nanotechnology creates ultra-small devices, such as motors the size of a pinhead. Biotechnology uses living organisms (e.g. algae, bacteria, yeast), their products or their component cells (e.g. enzymes) to improve our health and environment. It is expected to lead to a sustainable 'bioeconomy', increasing food security, reducing the environmental impact of agriculture and fisheries and generating sustainable economic growth and jobs. New nanotechnology materials like graphene, a durable, flexible, lightweight, thin material with myriad uses, is said to be set to unleash a manufacturing and technological revolution akin to the changes enabled by electricity in the 19th century.

A transformed economy

Transferable skills

1.4 Business operations

2.3 Business strategy

The economy is becoming more collaborative and more 'sharing' or peer-to-peer; for example, non-competitive companies are forming strategic alliances (discussed further in Chapter 18). Airbnb, couch surfing and Uber are leading the trend to the direct sharing of resources. Crowdsourcing harnesses the power of many to innovate, make better decisions and solve problems.

Business disruption is commonplace as new, difficult-to-predict business models break all the rules. For example, Amazon has redefined bookshops, Google has redefined advertising and market research, and iTunes has redefined the music industry.

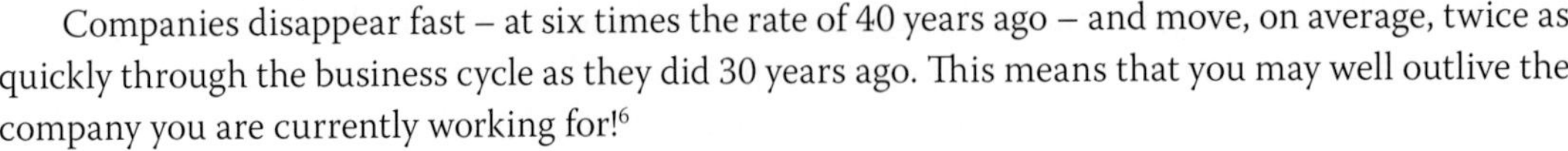

Companies disappear fast – at six times the rate of 40 years ago – and move, on average, twice as quickly through the business cycle as they did 30 years ago. This means that you may well outlive the company you are currently working for![6]

Transferable skills

1.3 Sustainability

1.4 Business operations

2.3 Business strategy

3.4 Leadership

5.2 Technology use

The knowledge and service economy

In order to remain competitive, scores of jobs that are dangerous or perceived as demeaning, dirty or dull in labour-intensive manufacturing and production processes have been automated or moved to developing markets with cheaper labour. In modern Australia, most of what we produce, whether it's a service or a product people can actually touch, is based on knowledge value rather than raw materials value (think of the fractions of a cent a microchip costs to make, for instance).

Although service industries don't actually produce any physical goods, they do create wealth – whatever consumers buy, either directly or indirectly, tangible or intangible, creates wealth. The income and profits of large manufacturing companies, such as General Electric, IBM and Xerox, increasingly come from their service divisions. Worldwide, trade in services is growing faster than trade in goods, and in most developed and developing countries, a growing proportion of the workforce works in the knowledge sector.

Biotechnology, business services, education, environmental services, health, hospitality, household services, nanotechnology, property services – all our service and knowledge industries are growing and four of the five most knowledge-intensive industries have grown faster than the Australian economy over recent years.[7] In the coming decades, more services and knowledge will be exported than anything else; overtaking minerals – just as minerals overtook manufacturing, which overtook agriculture.

Our knowledge and service economy demands a host of changes inside organisations, including business models, leadership styles, organisation strategies and organisation structure. It has changed how we earn our livings, how and where we work, and how we value companies and employees. In short, the new economy rewrites the rules of business and changes the skill sets employees and leader-managers need.

Transferable skills

2.3 Business strategy

Intangible, smart assets

Until the 1980s, tangible assets (e.g. money in the bank, plant and equipment, real estate and stock) made up about 80 per cent of a company's worth and the knowledge of its employees made up the remaining 20 per cent.[8] Today, it is intangible assets that count – including an organisation's:

- culture and capabilities (unique ways of doing things)
- goodwill and image in the marketplace
- intellectual capital (see the following section)
- organisation structure
- strategies.

These intangible assets are the building blocks of corporate prosperity. Because they are difficult for competitors to copy, they give a company its competitive edge. Their value has increased dramatically over the past 20 years, and they now make up as much as 80 per cent of a company's worth.[9] As a result, capabilities-based organisation structures, or organising around core capabilities, is becoming more common because it allows organisations to manage value-creating processes more effectively.

Intellectual capital

Transferable skills

1.4 Business operations

2.3 Business strategy

3.1 Teamwork/relationships

3.4 Leadership

Capital comes from the Latin word for head. It has come to stand for any strategic source of power. Three types of intellectual capital not yet included in the balance sheet are human, relationship and structural capital – an organisation's usable knowledge:

1. *Human capital* incorporates the competencies, health, motivation and productivity of an organisation's employees that can be lost when employees leave – unless a knowledge base captures their knowledge or it is incorporated into the organisation's procedures and structure. Measures include attrition rates among top performers, employee engagement and innovation.
2. *Relationship capital* is the value of an organisation's relationships with customers, suppliers and outsourcing and financing partners. It is built over time and reflected by loyalty to the company and its products, producing, for example, cross-selling, ideas sharing, referrals and repeat business. Measures include brand value, customer retention rate and customer satisfaction measures.
3. *Structural capital* could be described as the organisation's knowledge database. It is created by the organisation over time and includes competitive intelligence, copyrights, customer files, databases and the way it 'mines' big data, formulas, information systems, patents, policies, processes, software and trademarks. All of these remain with the organisation when employees go home. Measures include effectiveness of processes (are they helping or hindering?), estimated cost to replace databases, and time taken to develop new products and services and offer them to the marketplace ('time to market').

Resource scarcity

Non-renewable resources, for example, fossil fuels (e.g. coal, natural gas, petroleum) and some minerals (e.g. copper and gold), are becoming scarcer, more difficult to harvest and therefore more expensive. Companies that create products and services that eliminate wasted resources and keep them in use indefinitely will flourish.

You can find out more about reconciling consumption with ecosystem health and diminishing natural resources in Chapter 23.

Societal changes

Transferable skills

2.3 Business strategy

Migration continues to increase and we are becoming more diverse, getting older and living longer, marrying less and at older ages, and reproducing less. These and other societal shifts have a significant impact on people's work priorities and motivations, and on society as a whole.

Two factors in particular affect organisations:

1. the shrinking workforce, with the working age population likely to decline as Baby Boomers retire
2. changing consumer spending and customer expectations create additional pressures, as well as opportunities, for organisations in their product and service delivery.

The 'Great Resignation'

A new economic trend emerged in 2021, known as the 'Great Resignation'. This trend involves the large-scale resignation of swathes of employees across all industry sectors. There are a number of reasons for this uniquely 21st-century trend, including:

- COVID-19 causing a widespread rethink of employee goals, conditions and long-term career prospects

- workers becoming used to working from home and seeking alternatives with employers who continue to offer such flexible working conditions
- some employees in certain sectors, such as hospitality, realising that they would earn more money in furlough or government-funded schemes than actually working
- some employees who have contracted COVID-19 and/or suffered with post-viral syndrome ('long COVID') having their attitudes to work altered or completely diminished. This may also apply to those whose mental health was affected by loss of income, lockdowns and other restrictions.

Some may also see the Great Resignation as an unofficial strike, protesting the stagnation of wages despite the rising cost of living. When you add to this the large number of employees who were made redundant or 'let go' during the pandemic, particularly in hospitality, childcare and retail, unemployment numbers began to have an effect on most major economies.

At the time of writing, the Great Resignation has yet to reach a peak as far as we know; it may be an anomaly or simply a knee-jerk reaction to the COVID-19 pandemic. Regardless, as the world slowly returns to normal, we will know more and will surely find ways to understand and minimise the effects of this emerging economic trend.

Transferable skills

1.3 Sustainability

1.4 Business operations

2.2 Personal effectiveness

2.3 Business strategy

3.4 Leadership

1.2 New ways of working

> Our [Australian] manufacturing industry ... all told, has shed 205 000 jobs [since 1989]. But over the same time, we have created 3.9 million new jobs (almost 19 times more jobs than those lost from manufacturing) at a rate of 13 640 a month.
>
> Phil Ruthven (IBISWorld chair), 'Is it bye bye manufacturing?', *Company Director*, August 2013.

Tea ladies do the rounds. Smoking in the workplace is the norm. The standard working week is Monday to Friday, nine to five. No carer, paternity or personal leave. Men do 'men's jobs' and are the breadwinners, and women do 'ladies' jobs' or stay at home.

How the world has changed and continues to change. Where we work, when we work and how we work are changing. Dangerous, dirty, dull work (the mainstay of the manufacturing economy) has all but disappeared.

A job for life has become a life of jobs, and those jobs are becoming more collaborative. Career trajectories are lattices, not ladders. Work–life balance and work–life blending measures are important. People's working lives cover a wide range of hours and patterns, often related to their stage of life or family circumstances. They may have one or more jobs or they may be employees or self-employed. They may care for the elderly or children in addition to their paid and volunteering work.

Most large companies have trimmed down their permanent full-time workforce and now use casual, contract, part-time and temporary employees, allowing them to adjust their labour supply to meet the peaks and troughs of their business needs and access a range of specialist skills as required. Work that is not integral to the organisation's core business can be outsourced and 'offshored', saving yet more money. Organisations can further save money by making **teleworking** arrangements with those employees who can work from home or at a nearby office hub; teleworking can also increase productivity. These new ways of working affect the way organisations structure themselves and manage people. Welcome to the 'gig economy', which is worth almost US$350 billion, and is projected to reach US$455.2 billion within two years.[10]

Thanks to flattened organisation structures, many of the duties formerly carried out by middle managers now fall to leader-managers and, in turn, employees carry out many of their leader-manager's former duties. Goals and role descriptions are replacing job descriptions as job descriptions and organisation charts become less relevant and people and teams just 'get on with it'. The need to take personal responsibility and initiative is growing and employees are increasingly expected to use their judgement, learn from their mistakes and make sound decisions based on a careful consideration of alternatives and the potential effects of each.

Prior to the global COVID-19 pandemic, an estimated 9 per cent of Australians worked from 9 a.m. to 5 p.m. (compared to 70 per cent in the 1960s).[11] The effects of the pandemic on these statistics will not be known for some time. Some employees are 'time slaves', working long hours because of economic necessity or a toxic work culture; others are 'time lords', working long hours because they derive satisfaction, career and other benefits from doing so. Others are underemployed – they would like to and are able to work more hours than they currently work.

As discussed earlier in this chapter, technology has rendered traditional work–home demarcations obsolete because people can work anywhere, any time. Thanks to broadband, regional centres can blossom and we may see specialised centres with clusters of specialised producers or suppliers from multiple contributors in the way that Silicon Valley specialises in high technology.

What's a 'normal' job today? It's becoming harder to define. The following sections examine three other key features of changing work patterns in the new economy – the **casualisation** of the workforce, the outsourced and offshore workforce, and teleworking. These changes better suit a global, knowledge-driven economy, a hyper-competitive marketplace and consumer demand for inexpensive goods and services.

The casualised workforce

Transferable skills
3.4 Leadership

The casualised workforce refers to the loss of full-time jobs and the associated increase in casual, part-time and contracting jobs filled by agency workers, casual and temporary employees and independent contractors. The number of casual workers shot up by 70 per cent prior to 1998; since then, their numbers have held steady at about 20 per cent of the workforce.[12]

In fact, with the growth in professional, scientific and technical services, many of these temporary jobs are 'high end' jobs. Six-month 'gigs' are designed for CEOs, human resources and other managers, lawyers and similar highly skilled specialists. They can be genuinely independent contractors who operate their own businesses and are engaged under a commercial contract, or they can be temporary employees engaged for short-term or fixed-term work, contracting their skills to one, two or three organisations at a time. Their livelihoods depend on their ability to sell their skills and value proposition.

And the downsides? Is the security of a permanent job a fair trade for the freedom and flexibility of portfolio working? On the one hand, you can choose where you work, what you do and who you do it with or for, but how can you improve your earnings in order to buy or rent a house? Do the increased administrative obligations make temporary work satisfying and economically worthwhile? For example, you have to set up an ABN, manage your own tax, GST and superannuation, do your own secretarial work, provide your own indemnity insurance, sort out your own IT and so on – all the support that people in permanent employment, whether full-time, part-time or on permanent contracts, receive.

For organisations, the casualised workforce is a cheap workforce, without those associated employee costs – often equivalent to the actual wage – that contingent workers provide for themselves. Some say casualising jobs shifts risk and responsibility away from organisations to individuals who have no 'shock absorbers' against economic downturns and market fluctuations, yet are responsible for their own training and development, marketing and so on. Casualising jobs can also be a way for unscrupulous employers to circumvent laws and regulations, pay low wages and avoid their psychological contract responsibilities.

Yet, there is no doubt that these 'free agents' lower administrative overheads and reduce the legal obligations of employers. Employers call them in only when they're needed and pay them only for the hours they work, reducing wage costs. Many employers also save money by investing little or nothing in training and development activities for casual employees.

Transferable skills
1.4 Business operations
3.1 Teamwork/relationships
3.4 Leadership

Looking after the casualised workforce

Organisations need to guard against treating casual, contract and part-time workers as 'just a pair of hands'. When that happens, they can feel less committed, less engaged, and be less productive and less innovative – a poor return on the cost savings made from drawing skills from a large temporary pool of 'free agents'.

Dissatisfied and untrained casual, contract and part-time workers, especially when they're a large or strategically significant part of an organisation's workforce – for example, those who deal directly with customers – can damage an organisation's service levels and reputation. They need to be well led and managed so that they don't feel out of touch, ignored and unappreciated by their leader-managers and others they work with. You don't want disengaged employees who are not aligned with the values and vision of the organisation to become underperformers and a strain on the other team members.

Transferable skills
1.4 Business operations

The outsourced workforce

Many organisations contract out non-essential functions to independent businesses or individual contractors (called providers) who may be offshore or closer to home. This allows organisations to concentrate on their core functions and benefit from both the efficiencies of outsourcers' expertise and reduced direct labour and overhead costs. Another attraction is that should a provider be unsuited to a role, you can cancel the contract and find another provider. When the arrangement works well, contractors can be responsible for a large percentage of the value added to a product or service.

Commonly outsourced functions include administrative work such as invoicing, human resources (including training, payroll and recruitment and selection), IT, maintenance and other types of specialist work.

Transferable skills
1.4 Business operations
2.3 Business strategy

The offshore workforce

As the cost of living rises, Australian workers without the education, skills, temperament and training to do service and knowledge work are increasingly left behind. Employers can't afford to pay them cost-of-living wages and still produce a service or product at a price consumers are willing to pay, so their jobs go to technology (routine computer processing and robots) or to labour forces in less-developed countries where wages are lower. Organisations also routinely outsource knowledge work to rapidly developing economies with lower labour rates and advanced technological capabilities, such as India and eastern European countries.

The drawbacks of offshoring

You can call them 'external partners', but outsourcing still has its disadvantages, such as:

- concerns about protecting intellectual property
- ethical concerns (is it 'un-Australian' to send our jobs offshore?)

- greater ease of tweaking products with a supplier down the road than with a supplier thousands of kilometres away whose first language is unlikely to be English
- humanitarian concerns are increasing (e.g. Bangladesh's Rana Plaza factory collapse in 2013, killing 1129 people producing a range of clothing for Western companies; in India, children as young as 10 hand-stitching footballs for 12 cents a ball for up to 12 hours a day, seven days a week)[13]
- increasing transportation costs
- quality assurance concerns
- sustainability and risk concerns due to sourcing of raw materials, and supply chains that are economically and environmentally costly, long and risky-to-manage
- technology, particularly robotics and additive manufacturing, allowing cheaper production 'at home'.

As a result, many large corporations are considering 'reshoring' – bringing manufacturing and services 'back home'. Additive manufacturing, for example, allows goods to be easily customised and made at or close to where they're bought. For example, cars are now made in just a few hundred factories around the world but, thanks to additive manufacturing, they could be made in every metropolitan area in the not-too-distant future.[14]

Shamrock organisations

The shamrock symbolises the three main groups of employees found in most modern Australian organisations: core workers, contractors and flexible workers. The core workers perform the critical jobs of the organisation; those the organisation cannot afford to contract out. These may eventually make up less than one-quarter of an organisation's 'employees'. These indispensable managers, highly qualified professionals and technical specialists are likely to work long and hard hours and will be well remunerated in return.

Contractors, performing important administrative, marketing, training, accounting and other types of specialist work to support the core workers, may eventually be responsible for up to 80 per cent of the value that is added to a product or service. The temporary, part-time and casual workers the organisation needs to work on one-off projects and to fill in during busy times are the flexible workforce.[15]

Teleworking

Transferable skills

1.4 Business operations

2.3 Business strategy

3.1 Teamwork/relationships

3.4 Leadership

Before the COVID-19 pandemic, around 50 per cent of the workforce, substituted coming into the office for all or part of the day with teleworking – using the internet to work away from the office (mostly from home but also while travelling, including commuting and in workplace hubs) inside or outside of standard hours. Work is moving back into people's homes (ironically, where it was prior to the first Industrial Revolution).

Telecommuting lowers organisational, employee and environmental costs and reduces pressure on cities due to less traffic congestion and fewer car accidents. Employees see the benefits as flexibility, the ability to get more work done, access to home comforts and increased work–life balance or work–life blending. Despite doing 'more work', many teleworkers find working from home motivating, reporting reduced stress and increased job satisfaction. They can set up their workspaces to suit their own tastes and work habits. People who telework regularly may save money on lunch, clothes and commuting costs, and probably have less stress, too, from not commuting. Teleworking makes it easier to avoid office politics and it's great for people who are housebound; for example, people who have caring responsibilities or have a disability that makes leaving home difficult.

Employers consider teleworking essential for providing flexibility, increased productivity and the ability to retain skilled staff. With less office space to maintain, teleworking lowers real estate costs and overheads. Since about one-third of workers' compensation claims result from incidents travelling to or from work, those costs are reduced, too. Telecommuting can also provide continuity of operations, since operations are less affected by situations such as epidemics, extreme climatic events, personal (sick) leave, transport strikes and weather emergencies. During the COVID-19 pandemic, many employees in traditional office jobs were working from home for the first time – and the majority found it a positive experience.[16]

Happy employees and increased productivity sound good, although telecommuting requires work up-front, particularly if there is a health issue, such as a pandemic or epidemic, to take into consideration. There is also a new issue creeping in since the advancement of flexible working hours, known as 'proximity bias'. This occurs when leader-managers show bias towards employees who are in their immediate vicinity or prefer not to work off-site. This can be deliberate or unconscious; either way, it may result in remote workers having less opportunities for advancement, lower wages and less attractive or interesting tasks being assigned to them. As with any perceived or real unfair advantage in the workplace, proximity bias will not go unnoticed and could result in low morale, poor productivity, conflict and a high attrition rate. Bearing this in mind, leader-managers must regularly take stock of the way they allocate and measure the success of tasks, the way they offer opportunities for promotion and the way they ensure equity of treatment, in order to avoid proximity bias. (You can find more information on leading and managing off-site employees in Chapter 14. You can find out more about managing the health and safety risks for home workers in Chapter 30.)

Figure 1.3 shows the various ways to telecommute.

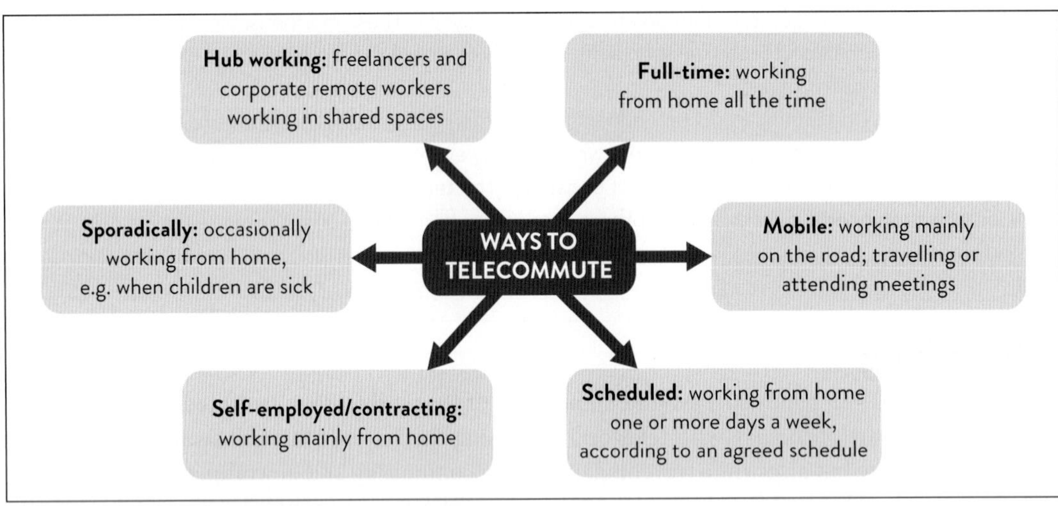

FIGURE 1.3 Ways to telecommute

Transferable skills

3.1 Teamwork/relationships

3.2 Verbal communication

3.3 Written communication

3.4 Leadership

The message for leader-managers

Each of these new ways of working has big implications for leader-managers:

- How do you know that employees you seldom see are pulling their weight?
- How do you manage people whose output is often intangible?
- How do you engage and motivate teams made up of vastly different groups of employees, each with different needs and expectations?

The quick (but not simple) answers are:

- building effective working relationships, based on open communication and trust
- making sure everyone understands their role and the part others play in achieving the team's goals
- providing the resources people need to do their jobs and removing obstacles that get in their way (difficulties that slow them down or frustrate them, or that make their work unnecessarily difficult or awkward)
- setting clear goals and managing by results and deliverables.

1.3 A new workforce

Transferable skills

1.4 Business operations

> Ever-smarter machines are performing ever-more human tasks – taking, replacing or eliminating the need for whole categories of employment.
>
> 'The New Work Order', a research report from the *Foundation for Young Australians*, Melbourne, 2015, p. 732.

As discussed earlier in this chapter, the workforce is becoming smaller and older and the employee mix is becoming more diverse. Blue-collar jobs have been decimated and those that are left have changed beyond recognition. White-collar jobs are being revolutionised by automation and computers.

Transferable skills

3.1 Teamwork/ relationships

3.4 Leadership

The skills that make people employable are largely mental rather than physical, and wider and deeper than ever before. Whether they are casuals, contractors, part-timers or permanent full-time employees or agency-based temporary fill-in staff (temps), and whether they work on-site or off-site, many of today's employees aren't 'workers' as much as individuals, professionals, specialists, executives or service providers, each with different expectations of leader-managers and organisations and with different levels of commitment to their employer. The 'flexible workforce' needs to be paid, led and organised differently from their permanent full-time colleagues and from each other, and they need to be encouraged to feel part of the organisation and engaged with its mission, values and vision.

As employees bring more of their knowledge and creativity to work, whether they work at home or their employer's premises, their work becomes a more important part of their lives, and not just what they do to pay the bills. Modern employees tend to have high expectations of their jobs, of the organisations they work for and of their leader-managers. Many expect their work to be meaningful and want to work for leader-managers they respect, in organisations that are 'green' and socially responsible, and to have a say in how their work is assigned, assessed and rewarded. You need the right sort of organisational policies and leadership that allow people to feel engaged and know that they're doing worthwhile work for a worthy organisation. Additionally, leading and managing employees who are skilled, educated, willing to speak up, make demands and challenge authority, requires skill.

Today's workforce has far-reaching effects on the way organisations operate.

A changing employee mix

Transferable skills

3.4 Leadership

A range of people make up today's employment pool. As discussed earlier in this chapter, you may be leading and managing full-time and part-time employees, casual and temporary employees, and people who may work on the road, at home, on the other side of Australia or in other countries. There are more distinct generations in the workforce than ever before; there are more employees from minority gender and ethnic groups, more employees with disabilities and more permanent and temporary migrants, many from other cultures and with English as a second language (see Chapter 32 for a more detailed discussion). Each of these distinct groups may have different:

- attitudes towards work
- expectations from work
- factors that motivate and engage them
- reasons for working
- reward and feedback expectations
- values and beliefs
- ways of working.

Leader-managers can help everyone integrate into the workplace, to assimilate into and feel part of their organisation's culture so that they can contribute fully. You can engage and incentivise the discrete groups of employees according to their requirements and offer them enough value from working with you that they don't move on with the next change in wind direction. You also can help everyone in your team develop the skills, knowledge and attributes that the organisation requires of them.

A more disgruntled workforce

The legacy of casualisation and downsizing of the workforce that began in the 1980s has left a bad taste in many mouths – not just of those affected but also the children who watched their parents and grandparents suffer the results. Severe downsizing brought with it a host of unfortunate repercussions:

- broken trust between management and the workforce due to breaking the psychological contract to provide long-term employment, career training and development in return for loyal and dependable service
- increased workloads, with some employees doing the jobs of two and even more employees, causing them to work long hours yet never feel on top of their jobs. The resulting stress, caused by overload, can, in some people, lead to bullying, illness and other unwanted outcomes
- less job security
- loss of experienced and knowledgeable employees to turn to for assistance, increasing the workload and pressures on those left behind, particularly when older, more experienced and more 'expensive' employees were let go and younger, less experienced but 'cheaper' employees were retained, as was often the case
- loss to the organisation of the strong networks, valuable relationships and knowledge of what works and what doesn't
- reduced levels of morale, motivation and job satisfaction
- underemployment of those who lost their jobs.

Employees who are dissatisfied with their employers and their jobs and uncommitted to the organisation are dangerous employees, particularly in knowledge and service organisations. They feel less loyalty and are more willing to leave. High attrition substantially increases an organisation's costs and prevents it from fully benefiting from word-of-mouth recommendations from past employees whose goodwill is lost.

A shrinking, greying workforce

We've already discussed the Great Resignation. Now we must consider the Great Retirement. By very simple calculations, seeing as there was a baby boom in the 1950s, there will be a 'baby bust' 70 years later – and we are there. Despite this, Boomers are going against the trend of previous generations – they're living longer, they're working for more years, commanding higher salaries, and being respected in a way that many of their ancestors were not in a workplace context. However, the economy cannot rely on the Baby Boomers for much longer. The global pandemic has made many older workers consider how they really want to spend their golden years, particularly as their generation is generally wealthier than those that went before them. Retirement is becoming more and more attractive to those who may, in the past, have continued in the workforce.

It has been forecast that 90 per cent of Australia's 5.3 million Baby Boomers will have retired by 2029, which could have cataclysmic consequences on the number of vacant positions available.[17] This makes recruitment difficult and retention imperative for many organisations.

Here are some tricky questions:

- How can we actively retain older workers and attract others to join to fill the employee shortfall?
- How can we make better use of females, people with disabilities and other untapped groups of employees who are underused in the workforce to fill the shortfall?
- How can we make the necessary adaptations as the new, smaller generations, each with different needs and expectations of their employer and work, replace the Baby Boomers?
- When we cannot find the people we need, what is Plan B?

The answers to these questions are different, depending on an organisation's customer expectations, market, strategy and vision. But whatever the answers are, they must be flexible enough to suit the range of people the organisation employs and must suit both the job and the jobholder, since not all options are feasible for all roles.

Transferable skills

1.4 Business operations

2.3 Business strategy

3.4 Leadership

Possible answers include career breaks and sabbaticals, job sharing, shortened working weeks or working years (e.g. nine-day fortnights, purchased leave), and phased retirement schemes. Developing an employer value proposition (EVP) and employer brand to attract and retain employees helps. Attracting, developing and retaining high-quality leader-managers, who can create an environment that employees want to remain in, is essential. It is also imperative to actively incentivise Baby Boomers to remain in the workplace long enough to train, coach, mentor and impart their knowledge to those taking on their roles.

A more skilled and educated workforce

Transferable skills

3.4 Leadership

In our service and knowledge economy, the trend is to design broad and flexible job roles rather than narrowly defined and prescriptive jobs. This means employees need to be adaptable, able to work without supervision and willing to take responsibility for the quality of their work. They need to understand the importance of continuous improvement and innovation and be able to work in teams, including project teams and multifunctional teams. There is less need to direct employees like this, to plan their work, organise them or 'keep an eye' on them – but they still need leading and managing.

Smart skills

In 10 years' time, more than half of today's jobs will require significant digital skills. How well can you find, evaluate, use, share and create information with information technology and the internet?

Here are the other skills to build: communication and interpersonal skills, critical thinking skills, learning skills, science and maths skills, and problem-solving skills.[18]

Transferable skills

3.1 Teamwork/relationships

3.2 Verbal communication

3.3 Written communication

3.4 Leadership

Knowledge workers

Brainpower, not muscle power, is the order of the day. Accountants, engineers, management consultants, software developers, and people who work in the advertising, media, pharmaceutical, public relations, and research and development industries are all part of the knowledge worker workforce. As a leader-manager, you are a knowledge worker yourself. In knowledge-intensive industries, these 'gold-collar workers', as they are sometimes called, often make up 70 to 90 per cent of all the employees, dominating their organisations numerically and culturally.[19]

Knowledge workers make today's world go round. They work with their brains, social skills and technology, creating and applying information, knowledge and ideas, and providing services and making contributions that, in many cases, don't have a tangible outcome. The 'three Is' of Ideas, Information and Intelligence describe the essence of knowledge-intensive organisations and knowledge and information workers.

Knowledge workers can operate anywhere – at home, in an office or a laboratory, in Apollo Bay, Beijing or Calcutta – because they carry their brainpower with them. But they're employable only as long as they keep their knowledge and learning up to date. (You can find out how to lead and manage knowledge workers earlier in this chapter and how to identify learning needs and develop learning and development plans in Chapter 29.)

Transferable skills

2.3 Business strategy

A new way of assessing organisations

Although emerging markets remain a growth engine of the global economy, critics of globalisation claim that Western multinational corporations benefit at the expense of local cultures, local enterprises and the environment. This, in part, gives rise to the notions of corporate social responsibility (CSR), corporate responsibility (CR), ethical investment funds and, more recently, conscious capitalism. These reflect the fact that organisations have fundamental responsibilities to stakeholders other than their shareholders and that those responsibilities go beyond mere compliance with local, state and federal government legislation and regulations.

Measured by the triple bottom line, **corporate citizenship** is now an important aspect of employer brand and EVP. The triple bottom line is:

- *People (human capital):* how the organisation's practices towards employees and the community benefit those constituencies rather than exploit or endanger them.
- *Planet (natural capital):* how sustainable the organisation's environmental practices are, how much they benefit (or at least do no harm to) the environment and whether the organisation is trying to reduce its carbon footprint through judicious consumption of energy and non-renewable resources, reducing waste and rendering waste less toxic before disposing of it.
- *Profit (the bottom line):* how much the organisation contributes to the economy.

CR is becoming more important because:

- many consumers prefer to purchase from socially responsible organisations
- many employees prefer to join socially responsible organisations
- many investors prefer to invest in socially responsible organisations.

When organisations contribute positively to, rather than undermine or have a zero impact on, society and the environment as they go about their business, they reap other benefits:

- enhanced corporate and brand image
- improved financial performance
- increased staff motivation
- reduced costs through environmental best practice
- reduced risk exposure.

Triple bottom line reporting is currently voluntary, although it is increasingly seen as mandatory for global companies and companies aspiring to become global. (Chapter 23 explains how to create sustainable workplaces.)

Who cares wins

Westpac is one of Australia's leaders in the field of CSR, ranking first on many local and global indices that measure companies' CSR and sustainability. These indices include Reputex, the Dow Jones Sustainability Index, the FTSE4Good Index and Australia's Corporate Responsibility Index. Other leaders in CSR are the broadcaster, ABC; professional services firms ARUP, GHD and PwC; miners Newmont Mining Corporation and Rio Tinto; the University of Queensland; Melbourne Water; National Australia Bank; and Main Roads Western Australia.[20]

Australian companies have adopted sustainability reporting more slowly than have companies overseas. For example, 80 per cent of Japanese companies and 75 per cent of British companies publish sustainability reports, while only 29 per cent of Australian companies publish a sustainability report and only six of them have their reports audited.[21]

Despite that, AMP Capital Investors found that strong financial performance is directly linked to CSR. Its research found that over four- and 10-year periods, companies with a higher CSR rating outperformed the Australian Securities Exchange Index by more than 3 per cent a year.[22]

1.4 Wanted: highly skilled leader-managers

Transferable skills
3.4 Leadership

Success in management requires learning as fast as the world is changing.

Warren Bennis, 'As online learning grows, the college campus lives on', *Bloomberg Businessweek*, 2012. Retrieved from: https://immagic.com/eLibrary/ARCHIVES/GENERAL//GENPRESS/B121224B.pdf

Management is becoming more demanding and challenging. You need different and broader skills than leader-managers of the past, particularly leadership and interpersonal skills. Flexibility, and the ability to cope with uncertainty and to think innovatively and strategically, can help you thrive in your changing environment. Continually developing, updating and refining your skills is essential.

More than ever, as a leader-manager you need strong 'right brain' skills for understanding yourself and working effectively with others. You also need strong 'left brain' skills for planning, solving problems, and identifying and managing risks. You need to be able to ask the right questions when confronted with a problem or decision, because what worked in the past may not work again.

The complex, fast-changing, unfamiliar competitive environment means that supervisors, team leaders and managers are now leader-managers who have stepped away from the 20th century and its traditions, as summarised in Table 1.2. The skills they need lie in three areas: conceptual, personal and interpersonal skills, and technical skills related to their job and to digital skills.

Conceptual skills

Transferable skills
3.4 Leadership

Increasing **business complexity**, capabilities-based competition, new business models, mushrooming risks and the quickening pace of change mean that the problems you face are increasingly new and unpredictable. This necessitates the ability to think holistically, to ask the right questions, to solve problems systematically and based on evidence, and to innovate unique and unexpected solutions and approaches to situations.

Solid conceptual skills help you anticipate future problems and implement preventative action; coordinate the many activities you and your team engage in; think through plans, ideas and decisions and recognise their possible implications and effects on others; and understand the processes and procedures that flow through your organisation and how a change in one section or system could affect other sections or systems.

TABLE 1.2 20th-century versus 21st-century leading and managing

20th-century management	21st-century management
Authoritarian management practices	Open, collaborative management practices
Chain of command	Flexible organisations, particularly multifunctional teams
Coercion	Cooperation
Control	Commitment
Cost control	Innovation
Decision by command	Decision by consensus
Hierarchy	Synergy
One-off learning	Continuous, lifelong learning
Periodic improvements	Continuous improvements
Scientific management: we can control people and find the 'one best way'	Empowered teams managing themselves and their work
'Us' and 'them'	Us together

Transferable skills
3.1 Teamwork/relationships
3.2 Verbal communication
3.3 Written communication
3.4 Leadership

Personal and interpersonal skills

Leading and managing begin with excellent interpersonal skills and personal skills. Personal skills deal with understanding yourself and managing your thoughts, emotions, actions and responses. Authenticity, confidence, ethics and integrity make open and transparent leadership possible. Emotional intelligence (EI or EQ) is a key workplace asset, as is thinking like a leader. Combined with a strong values system, personal skills help you set a good example and provide guidance and a sense of security and direction when 'the going gets tough'.

Your personal skills are the foundation of your interpersonal skills – critical for collaborative working and leading and managing a shrinking, more educated and demanding workforce. Your interpersonal skills allow you to build and maintain strong networks and effective working relationships across your organisation's value chain.

Strong personal and interpersonal skills help you build your cultural intelligence so that you can work effectively with people from other cultures and empathise with attitudes and viewpoints different from your own while speaking your mind clearly and respectfully.

Transferable skills
3.4 Leadership
5.2 Technology use

Technical skills

You don't have to be an expert in the work that your team members do, but you can develop an understanding of the nature of the jobs and the processes, methods, procedures and administration systems your team members use. Nor do you need to be the world's best computer programmer or data analyst. But you can keep your digital skills up to date so that you can organise data and research information, and use IT as a management tool to plan and monitor your own work and the work of your team. As managing and participating in virtual teams becomes more common, understanding and using collaboration and communications tools is important.

STUDY TOOLS

QUICK REVIEW

KEY CONCEPT 1.1 

a List and summarise the major trends affecting today's workplaces and organisations.

KEY CONCEPT 1.2 

a Discuss how the way we work is changing and the reasons for these changes.

b What are the pros and cons of a casualised workforce and of offshoring?

c What are the benefits of teleworking to employees, employers and society?

d What are the implications of our new ways of working for leader-managers? What skills can leader-managers develop to deal with them effectively?

e How has the global COVID-19 pandemic affected the way leader-managers treat their employees? What potentially negative outcomes could be caused by the pandemic?

KEY CONCEPT 1.3 

a What is meant by the term 'employee mix'? How is Australia's employee mix changing?

b What are the key characteristics of Australia's 'new' workforce?

KEY CONCEPT 1.4 

a What is meant by conceptual skills? Personal and interpersonal skills? Technical skills? Which do you excel in?

BUILD YOUR SKILLS

KEY CONCEPT 1.1 

a What skills, qualities and aptitudes do employees need in a service economy? A knowledge economy?

KEY CONCEPT 1.2 

a Do you know people who are casual or temporary employees? If so, interview them to find out what challenges and opportunities this way of working presents and whether or not, and why, they feel like a valued part of their organisation(s). Present your findings and conclusions to the class.

b Do you know people who work from home? If so, interview them to find out what challenges and opportunities working from home present, and how they perceive and manage their relationship with their leader-manager. Present your findings and conclusions to the class.

KEY CONCEPT 1.3 

a Referring to the information in this chapter concerning the current trends in organisations' external environments and any other information about trends you may be aware of, discuss what a typical organisation or workplace from your industry might look like in 2030. What might it be like to work in? Where might its employees be located? What might make the organisation valuable and what could reduce its value?

KEY CONCEPT 1.4 

a Describe the skills you believe are most important to lead and manage effectively in today's changing world of work.

b What new skills can you develop as Australia moves further into the knowledge economy? What are some strategies you can use to acquire and strengthen your skills? How can you know if you are succeeding and building these skills quickly enough?

WORKPLACE ACTIVITIES

KEY CONCEPT 1.1 

a Which of the trends discussed in this chapter have affected your workplace? Explain how they have affected your workplace and how you and your organisation have responded and plan to respond further.

b Referring to the information on globalisation's far-reaching effects (cultural, environmental, financial and so on), discuss whether each of these ramifications affects your workplace and if so, how.

KEY CONCEPT 1.2 

a What proportion of the employees at your workplace are casual? How can an organisation determine whether the ratio of flexible workers to full-time and part-time workers is appropriate?

b What proportion of the employees at your workplace telework? What teleworking arrangements does your organisation make? How can an organisation decide whether its teleworking arrangements are appropriate and effective?

KEY CONCEPT 1.3 

a Do you expect your work to be meaningful? What about the members of your work team? What does 'meaningful work' mean to you?

b According to the Corporate Responsibility Index, a meaningful code of ethics, cooperative employee relations, social and environmental audits and reporting, philanthropy, employee volunteering and community forums are all ways for organisations to nurture corporate social responsibility. Prepare a short report describing how your organisation employs or could usefully employ any of these, or other, strategies.

KEY CONCEPT 1.4 

a What skills do leader-managers in your workplace need? How do you measure up?

EXTENSION ACTIVITIES

Referring to the Snapshot at the beginning of this chapter, answer the following questions:

1. Consider the initial reactions of the copywriting team when they heard that they have a team manager who is based overseas. How do you think they would react, feel and behave when the news is delivered to them?
2. What obstacles do you think Caroline may face, and how can she overcome them?
3. What obstacles do you think team members may face, and how can they overcome them?
4. What potential issues may the organisation face, and how can it overcome them?

CASE STUDY 1

SITTING AND THINKING, OR JUST SITTING? MANAGING KNOWLEDGE WORKERS

Bethany is troubled. This is a new job with a specialist outsourcer and her first as a team leader – a double whammy, but a job she felt quite confident applying for. After completing her journalism course, working for two years with a regional newspaper as a general reporter, settling down with her partner and having a baby, she felt it was time for a change and was delighted to be offered the position.

She knows she is ultimately responsible for her team's results and is determined to do a good job. At the moment, she's struggling to find a way to relax and let the team get on with their work. They're smart people, very experienced, and yet, given the nature of their work, substantive results for their efforts sometimes aren't apparent for a week or two. To complicate matters, she doesn't see her team members for days at a time, since they can work where and when it suits them. As technical writers and translators for complicated equipment manuals, their work habits aren't really the point. She's comfortable with that, as it isn't so different from the newspaper, where people came and went all the time, too.

A few team members who live nearby make a point of coming into the office every week or so. Others have taken to phoning her every few days to let her know how they're getting on, and a couple send quick emails or text messages to let her know of any breakthroughs or setbacks. There are a few she's never met because they live in the bush and stay there, and a couple of others live overseas. Apparently, they moved when their partners relocated and the organisation didn't want to let them go, given their specialised skills and their experience, and so arranged for them to continue working remotely.

As a part-timer herself who often works from home, Bethany supposes they're working too, but it's hard to know. Even those who come into the office sometimes look like they're just 'sitting' there – hopefully sitting and thinking, not just sitting! These are honourable, professional people, she reminds

herself. Maybe their dedication isn't so much to the company or the clients as to their profession, but she wants to believe she can rely on them.

What she's really concerned about, as she thinks it through, is that some or all of the projects she is responsible for bringing to fruition on time might fall into a hole. She doesn't want to be left explaining to her boss any missed deadlines and her failure to keep on top of things.

Questions

1 What are Bethany's main concerns?
2 Which is the most important concern, which when solved will significantly reduce or remove the others?
3 What would be your objectives for resolving Bethany's major concern? How could you know whether your objectives were met?
4 What are some possible approaches for resolving Bethany's major concern?
5 What skills and work habits do you suggest Bethany develop to help her meet the demands of her new role?

CHAPTER ENDNOTES

1 Phil Ruthven, 'Growth barriers', Company Director, September 2002; Phil Ruthven, 'Our place in Asia', *Company Director*, June 2015, pp. 34–35.
2 Thomas L. Friedman, Michael Mandelbaum, *That used to be us*, Picador, 2012.
3 Richard D'Aveni, 'It's happening, and it will transform your operations and strategy', *Harvard Business Review*, May 2015, pp. 41–48.
4 Ibid.
5 'Australia's future workforce?', Committee for Economic Development of Australia, Melbourne, June 2015.
6 Martin Reeves, Simon Levin, Daichi Ueda, 'The biology of corporate survival', *Harvard Business Review*, Jan–Feb 2016, pp. 47–55.
7 Australian Bureau of Statistics (2015), Australian National Accounts: National Income, Expenditure and Product, Sep 2015, cat. no. 5206.0, table 6.
8 M. Blair, S. Wallman, *Unseen wealth*, Brookings Institution Press, 2000.
9 Ibid.
10 'Australia's future workforce?', CEDA, op. cit.
11 Larissa Ham, 'Working nine to five. Is this form of employment extinct?', *The New Daily*, 21 January 2014, http://thenewdaily.com.au/money/work/2014/01/21/nine-five-dead/, accessed 16 December 2021.
12 Mark Wooden, 'Fact check: Has the level of casual employment in Australia stayed steady for the past 18 years?', *The Conversation*, 23 March 2016, https://theconversation.com/factcheck-has-the-level-of-casual-employment-in-australia-stayed-steady-for-the-past-18-years-56212, accessed 16 December 2021.
13 *ABC News*, http://www.abc.net.au/news/2013-10-25/bangladesh-factory-collapse-victime-wiat, accessed 15 January 2014; *Sydney Morning Herald*, http://www.smh.com.au/national/ball-backdown-as, accessed 16 December 2021.
14 Richard A. D'Aveni, '3-D printing will change the world', *Harvard Business Review*, March 2013, p. 34.
15 Charles Handy, *The empty raincoat*, Random House, Sydney, 1994.
16 Australian Government Productivity Commission, 'Working from home research paper, 2021', https://www.pc.gov.au/research/completed/working-from-home/working-from-home.pdf
17 Robert Half Talent Solutions, '86% of Australian businesses concerned Baby Boomer departure will worsen skills shortage', https://www.roberthalf.com.au/press/86-australian-businesses-concerned-baby-boomer-departure-will-worsen-skills-shortage, July 2019, accessed 14 December 2021.
18 'The new work order', Foundation for Young Australians, op. cit.
19 The Work Foundation, 'Knowledge workers and knowledge work', http://www.theworkfoundation.com/assets/docs/publications/213_know_work_survey170309.pdf, accessed 16 December 2021.
20 'Australia's CSR top 10', Pro Bono Australia, https://probonoaustralia.com.au/news/2014/06/australias-csr-top-10, accessed 201416 December 2021.
21 'Corporate responsibility', *Management Today*, April 2006.
22 Matthew Rey, Thong Nguyen, 'Financial payback from environmental and social factors in Australia', research report, AMP Capital Investors, 2005.

CHAPTER

2

THE INTERNAL ENVIRONMENT

After completing this chapter, you will be able to:

2.1 understand which of the three sectors of the economy an organisation is part of

2.2 explain the roles and responsibilities of the four levels of management

2.3 outline the six stakeholder groups every organisation answers to

2.4 understand the importance of values, vision, mission and strategy in guiding an organisation and its employees.

TRANSFERABLE SKILLS

The following transferable skills are covered in this chapter:

1 **Business competence**
- **1.4** Business operations

2 **Critical thinking and problem solving**
- **2.1** Critical thinking
- **2.3** Business strategy

OVERVIEW

Amid the vast changes described in Chapter 1, some aspects of an organisation's environment haven't changed. Your leadership and management takes place in the same sectors as always – the private, the public and the not-for-profit sectors. You can manage from the top-, the middle- or the first-line level.

You still have stakeholders around you, each with expectations (sometimes conflicting) of how the organisation should perform. Overall, though, stakeholders expect organisations to be socially, culturally and environmentally responsible and well governed in order to avoid the numerous scandals we have recently seen.

At the core of every organisation is a set of values and behaviours that guide its operations: a vision, a mission and strategies that give purpose, meaning and direction to the organisation's operations. These guide its essential activities, such as attracting, engaging and retaining employees and providing them with worthwhile goals to move the organisation towards its vision.

This chapter helps you understand, support and work with these four aspects of your organisation's internal environment.

SNAPSHOT

The strategic planning meeting

Charlotte is a paid, part-time leader-manager working on funding with a community arts organisation. She has just put the finishing touches on an updated induction outline for volunteers, a delegated responsibility she put her hand up for, thinking she'd like to give it a try. She found she didn't need to change much but updated the information on the source of the organisation's funding arrangements and how important bequests had become in the last few years. She also added information on the organisation's involvement in the local community and with similar organisations across the country and in Asia.

Now she's off to the strategic planning conference, which takes place every couple of years. Because it's a small organisation, with only one other part-time employee, one person seconded part-time from the local council and 12 volunteers, they have the luxury of being able to include everyone in the planning process. Apart from the good ideas everyone can contribute based on their different backgrounds and interests, the planning workshop is excellent for morale and for focusing everyone on the strategy and goals that they eventually agree on.

The external facilitator leading the planning workshop warms everyone up with a short creativity exercise. Next, they review their values, vision and mission and agree that there is no need to change or amend them, since they have been working well and they and all their stakeholders are familiar and comfortable with them.

Then they undertake a 'future search', exploring what changes or trends might affect them over the next few years regarding funding, the arts, and the closer and wider community. From there, they conduct a SWOT analysis and spend a fair bit of time discussing the constraints, direct and indirect, that influence the way they perform their roles and work towards their mission. The day ends by agreeing on some clear goals in the areas they highlighted as pivotal to their mission from their SWOT analysis, and assigning responsibilities for 'championing' them. The champions are to report at their next monthly meeting with suggested milestones and timelines.

2.1 The three sectors

> My role, and the role of senior executives, is to make our people as successful as they possibly can be.
>
> Nev Power (CEO, Fortescue Metals), quoted in Andrew Burrell, *The deal*, August 2012.

Which are you more familiar working with: private enterprise, the government or not-for-profit organisations? Each of these sectors of the Australian economy needs top-quality leader-managers.

Each sector faces its own challenges. The **not-for-profit (NFP) sector** has to compete effectively for funding and skilled and motivated volunteers and paid employees. The **private sector** must learn to thrive in a global environment and a constantly changing marketplace. The **public sector** must learn to deal with budget cuts, deregulation and privatisation (i.e. transferring ownership of a statutory organisation to the public sector). We will discuss more about each in the following sections.

The not-for-profit sector

Non-commercial, non-government organisations make up the large and diverse NFP sector. The sector's activities and services cover animal welfare, arts and culture, business and professional associations and unions, education and research, environment, health, human rights, religion, social services and sport and recreation. Together, they account for about 600 000 organisations in Australia, mostly small and dependent on voluntary members.[1]

About 57 000 NFPs are incorporated or established as legal entities, and about the same number of them contribute significantly to the Australian economy.[2] Together, they employ around one million people – about 9 per cent of the workforce – many of whom are permanent full-time employees. Their 4.6 million volunteers contribute $15 billion in unpaid work, or 521 million hours of their time, equating to an equivalent of 265 600 full-time employed persons. Most NFP organisations are democratically controlled and have a controlling body, often called a **board of directors**, which is usually made up of volunteers.[3]

The NFP sector forms an important part of the Australian economy, contributing around $55 billion annually to Australia's GDP, making it similar in size to government administration and defence, transport and storage and the wholesale trade sectors, and larger than the agriculture industry. More important than its economic contributions, though, are the NFP sector's cultural, environmental and social contributions.[4]

Money isn't the goal for NFPs as it is in private enterprise; rather, their goal is to achieve social objectives. Their **measures of success** revolve around controlling costs through efficient operations and the quantity and quality of the services they provide. They can measure their success directly (e.g. the number or percentage of people receiving a service) or indirectly (e.g. the impact of a service, such as the reduced number of people going through the court system or the increased number of people completing tertiary education).

Nevertheless, NFPs are concerned with money – they have to be. Money is the means to the end. NFPs must continually raise funds in a competitive marketplace, often in competition with private providers and other NFPs; and to attract that money, they must perform. The days of big business, the government and even the wider community writing a cheque and turning their backs are over.

Corporate philanthropy is giving way to a partnership model. Business wants a return on its donations. Governments pit NFPs against each other in a race for outcomes and efficiency, and those at the bottom of the ladder are dropped from the next round of funding. In short, funders, whether governments, organisations or private individuals, want to know what NFPs do and how they do it, and they discontinue funding when professionalism and results don't eventuate.

Many NFPs have begun to partner with for-profit organisations to provide services, and the public–private partnership (PPP) **business model** has become more prevalent in this sector. As a result, today's NFPs are outcome driven as well as **mission** driven.

Many NFPs are taking the lead in **organisation design**, leadership and management style and **performance management**. Perhaps more than in any other sector, the leader-managers and key officers of NFP organisations must know how to attract, empower and retain workers, and they must be able to make the most of workers' skills and energies. After all, many of the workers are volunteers who can easily leave when they feel they are not appreciated or not contributing in a meaningful way.

The private sector

The majority of Australian employees and employers are in the private sector, businesses whose owners expect to earn a profit by providing goods or services. Many of their measures of success, or **key performance indicators (KPIs)**, therefore, revolve around financial indicators. Increasingly, they also include social and environmental measures (see Chapter 1 for information on new ways of assessing organisations). These businesses come in many sizes, from one-person businesses to organisations employing thousands of people.

Corporations

A **corporation**, or company, exists independently of its owners (the **shareholders**) and the people it employs. A corporation is an 'artificial person' (hence the expression 'the body corporate'). This means that the corporation continues even though its managers and employees come and go. Companies can behave as a natural person and hold property, issue shares, sue and be sued in the corporate name, and so on. About 4 per cent of Australia's corporations are owned by overseas investors.[5] The Australian Securities and Investments Commission (ASIC) regulates all corporations.

There are two kinds of corporations: **proprietary limited companies** and **public companies**. Unlike **sole traders** and **partnerships**, both can issue shares to raise capital for the operation and expansion of the business. Should a company fail, the shareholders' responsibility, or liability, for paying its debts is limited to the amount (if any) of their respective shares.

Proprietary limited companies

Proprietary limited companies (**private companies** in Queensland) are registered under the provisions of the various companies Acts. They can have no more than 50 owners (excluding employee shareholders). The right to transfer shares is restricted and a proprietary company cannot invite the general public to purchase its shares. These companies must have the words 'Proprietary Limited' or their abbreviation (Pty Ltd or P/L) after their business name.

Smaller proprietary limited companies tend not to have a board of directors, although many have an informal board, sometimes called a 'kitchen cabinet', made up of friends with business acumen and expertise who act as advisers and sounding boards.

Public companies

A public company, or listed company, must include the word 'Limited' or its abbreviation (Ltd) after its business name. These are the companies listed on the stock exchange and any individual or company can loan them money, or invest in them, by purchasing their shares. Public companies must have a minimum of three directors to represent the shareholders and one company secretary to organise board and shareholder meetings, induct new board members regarding company protocols and act as the conduit between the board and senior managers. There is no limit on the number of shareholders.

Sole traders

Transferable skills
1.4 Business operations

Sole traders are companies with a single owner who usually manages the business, although sometimes a paid manager is employed. Sole traders can trade under their own name or can register a business name with their state or territory fair trading department (or equivalent). Sole traderships are the simplest and most inexpensive businesses to set up and have the fewest reporting requirements. They tend to be small because of the difficulty in raising large amounts of capital for expansion.

The sole trader takes on all the responsibilities and financial risks of running the business. Although all the profits belong to the sole trader, when the business ceases trading, the owner is also responsible for paying any debts.

Partnerships

Transferable skills
1.4 Business operations

In a partnership, two or more people (or companies) own the business. Partnerships are useful when a sole trader cannot cope single-handedly with the amount of work available, when more money is required to expand the business or when the original sole trader lacks all the skills needed to manage a growing business successfully. When many partners are involved, the business is often referred to as a firm.

The partners usually share the day-to-day management of the business and all the profits of the business. Like sole traders, partners have unlimited liability. In the event of the firm failing or becoming insolvent, the partners are totally responsible for paying all the firm's liabilities (debts).

Unless a partnership agreement states otherwise, the law assumes that the partners split the profits and contribute to the payment of business debts equally.

The public sector

The public sector protects the country, administers justice, educates its residents and provides public and community services according to the policies and directives of the elected government.

The Commonwealth Government takes responsibility for matters of national concern, such as defence, health, foreign policy and social services. State and territory governments manage their own affairs and, within each, there are local and city councils as well as a range of statutory semi-autonomous bodies. Together, they own and run businesses across 22 per cent of the economy.[6]

The structure of the various forms of public sector organisations is determined, in the first instance, by the *Commonwealth of Australia Constitution Act 1900 (UK)*, the set of rules by which the country has been governed since Federation, when Australia became independent of the UK in 1901. The federal or relevant state parliament sets out the structure of statutory bodies in a charter, leaving the fine detail to the appointed senior managers.

Government departments

The activities of government are divided into functions, each with its own department. The head of each department is a public servant, employed by the government and responsible for structuring, leading and managing the department to achieve the government's objectives.

Most departments are run along the lines of the private sector business model, with, for example, a workplace bargaining system, corporate values, vision and mission statements and managing performance in ways similar to the private sector.

Statutory authorities

Sometimes referred to as a 'quango' (quasi-autonomous government organisation), a statutory **authority** is a government agency established by a statute, or Act of Parliament. Statutory authorities generally tend to have more independence than government departments. While most are subject to some form of ministerial control, the degree of control depends on the amount of freedom, or autonomy, the establishing government thought they would need to function effectively. The way statutory authorities are structured and operate normally falls somewhere between that of government departments and large private sector organisations.

Transferable skills

1.4 Business operations

2.2 The four levels of management

> Australia is now at the forefront of governance changes that are taking place worldwide. We have traditionally punched above our weight in terms of governance and financial reform, and now Australian boards are right up there with the world's best.
>
> David Crawford quoted in Tony Featherstone, 'Q and A with David Crawford', *Company Director*, 1 May 2014.

Although the traditional **organisation structure**, shaped like a pyramid, is giving way to other forms of organisation, and the organisational pyramid has become 'flatter', you can still find the four levels of management, shown in **Figure 2.1**, in most organisations. (Chapter 3 discusses the new ways organisations are restructuring their operations, and Chapter 1 explains why they are restructuring.)

Because of the ways the working environment and the capabilities that make organisations successful are changing, today's management and non-management employees alike need different

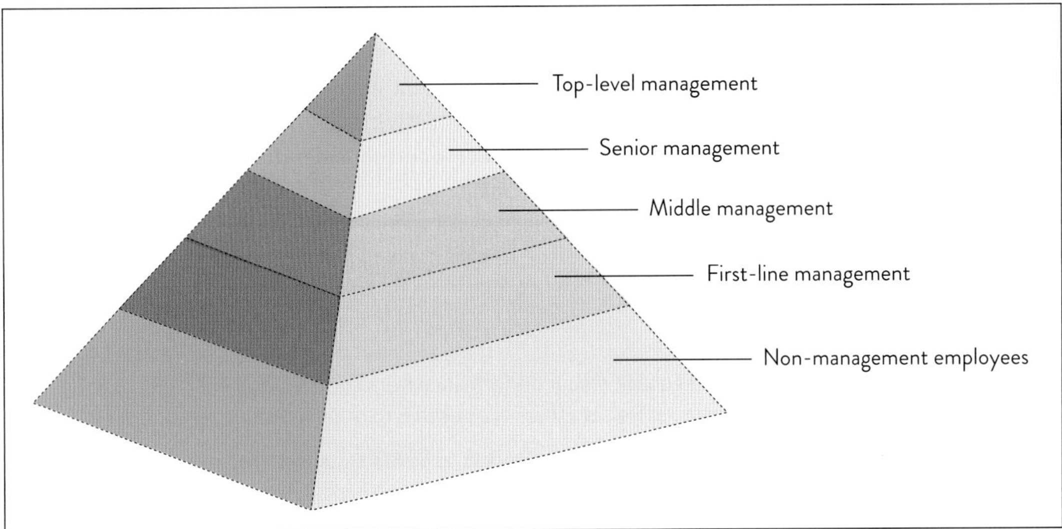

FIGURE 2.1 The traditional pyramid of employment levels

skill sets than they needed even 20 years ago. In particular, the ability to develop effective working relationships with a wide range of colleagues, customers and suppliers, and skills in communication, innovation, managing change, maths, **networking**, problem-solving, science, technology and team working are must-haves.

Different levels of leader-managers take care of different things. Top-level and senior leader-managers scan the external environment and set strategic direction. Middle leader-managers build and maintain efficient operations and enable performance so that targets are met. First-line leader-managers create the climate needed for innovation and performance. Whatever their level, leader-managers use a range of conceptual, people and technical skills, although the mix of those skills varies, as shown in Figure 2.2.

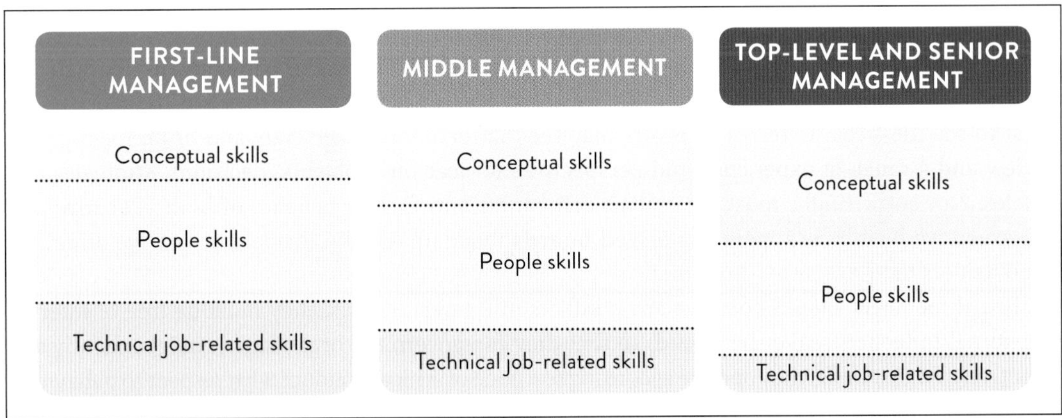

FIGURE 2.2 Skills needed at different levels of management

Top-level management

The chief executive officer or permanent head of a government department and the board of directors make up an organisation's **top-level management**. This highest management level is responsible for guiding the organisation's direction and setting its 'tone': its ethics and standards, values and culture.

In some organisations, it sets a range of policies, such as for hiring and retaining employees, **risk management** and **sustainability**; in other organisations senior management develops those policies for approval by top-level management. Top-level management also oversees the appointment and development of senior leader-managers and monitors their activities.

Many boards conduct a formal board evaluation process and consider the performance indicators shown in Table 2.1. How does your board measure up?

TABLE 2.1 How good is the board?

Diversity	Does our composition reflect our operating base, customers, local community and employees?
Feedback	Do we seek enough feedback on our performance from the management team, external advisers and regulators, as well as others in a position to observe the way we operate?
Fresh blood	Is there sufficient turnover of board members to provide fresh insights and ideas while retaining board stability?
Skills	Is there a range of skills among directors that reflects the needs of the organisation's operations?
Strategies	Have we provided a clear strategy and is it understood by all employees?

Small-to-medium enterprises generally have up to five board members and larger organisations usually have seven to nine board members. The board works with senior managers to determine the organisation's vision, mission, strategies and policies, enables the acquisition of the resources needed to carry them out, and monitors and guides the operations of the enterprise on behalf of the shareholders.

Board members can be **executive directors** or **non-executive directors**. Executive directors work full-time in the company, usually as senior managers, although some may be worker representatives, while non-executive directors are involved with the company only part-time, through the board. When all the directors work in the company, the board is known as an **inside board**, or executive board. A non-executive or **external board** is made up of directors who are not employed by the company full-time and hold no other roles in the company.

The advantages of an inside board are that its members know the company, its markets, its operations and its problems intimately. Yet this can sometimes mean that they are 'too close to the forest to see the trees'. External directors may see matters more objectively and bring fresh points of view and a range of experience and perspectives to bear on problems, decisions, strategies and policies. Not surprisingly, most Australian companies aim for the benefits of both executive and non-executive boards by appointing **mixed boards** made up of both insiders (executive directors) and outsiders (non-executive directors).

Board members should not have any conflicts of interest, that is, they must be free of internal or external influence (real or perceived) so that they can govern the organisation independently and objectively. For example, they operate according to a code of ethical conduct with respect to behaviour, communication and the use of official information and resources. Board members contribute best when they have a range of skills consistent with the organisation's strategic goals and direction. Directors should also be able to add 'competitive value' to the organisation.

'Nose in, fingers out' is a way that is often used to describe the way the best boards operate. They ask questions, formulate strategy and understand risks, trends and key business drivers, but they don't get involved in day-to-day operations. Boards have two main roles of advising and monitoring the overall performance of the organisation and the performance and behaviour of the senior management team. Their legal responsibilities and other best practice duties are shown in Figure 2.3.

LEGAL RESPONSIBILITIES	BEST PRACTICES
• Act in good faith in the organisation's best interests (e.g. not take decisions for their own personal advantage); breaches can lead to a civil penalty or criminal liability if the breach is reckless or intentionally dishonest. • Disclose material, or significant, personal interests (i.e. conflicts of interest) relating to the affairs of the organisation; a breach is a criminal penalty. (Directors can have a conflict of interest as long as they disclose it.) • Honour their duty of care and take due diligence, showing an interest in the organisation and taking their responsibilities seriously; breaches can result in a civil penalty. • Not allow the organisation to trade while insolvent; i.e. when it doesn't have enough money to pay its bills when they are due; breaches can result in a civil penalty and when dishonest, a criminal penalty. Directors should always know the organisation's financial position. • Not improperly use their position or information to gain benefit for themselves, or to cause harm to the organisation; breaches result in a civil penalty or criminal liability when the breach is reckless or intentionally dishonest.	• Appoint senior managers and auditors. • Approve, scrutinise and monitor budgets (including executive pay), key decisions, performance, plans, risk management and strategies. • Avoid overemphasising short-term goals. • Clearly define board and senior management responsibilities to avoid confusion. • Decide how to distribute the organisation's profits: some are returned to the shareholders; some are used to purchase plant and equipment or to acquire another organisation; some are invested in intangibles, such as training, research and development, and brand building. • Ensure compliance with policies, laws and regulations. • Ensure succession planning for senior managers and other key managers and employees. • Ensure the organisation meets its obligations to its stakeholders (see Section 2.3 in this chapter). • Keep abreast of trends, threats and opportunities, and ensure the organisation responds appropriately and proactively. • Manage communication with stakeholders. • Oversee external communications (e.g. with shareholders). • Set the strategic direction for key business drivers. • Take professional advice.

FIGURE 2.3 Board key responsibilities

 INDUSTRY INSIGHTS

Directors' independence: the pros and cons

Boards were once made up of people with useful contacts or a sound understanding of the organisation's industry. Then a series of catastrophic corporate governance failures around the world triggered regulatory strengthening, including new requirements for director independence.

In 2003, the Australian Securities Exchange (ASX) Corporate Governance Council recommended that a majority of board directors should be independent directors, that is, that they have no personal interests or stake in the organisation that could materially interfere with the impartial

exercise of their judgement. Known as the 'Conflict Rule', in practice this means that directors should not hold more than 5 per cent of the company's stock and should not have worked in an executive capacity in the company or an associated company for at least three years.

But this is advice only and some believe it is occasionally best ignored in the case of individual directors. The important thing, they say, is the sum of the parts in terms of diversity, effectiveness, experience, independence and skills of the board as a whole. Directors with no prior experience with a company or its industry can't have the depth of knowledge they need to make sound decisions, however well-intentioned they may be.

However, a report by Macquarie Equities showed that companies whose directors are substantial shareholders outperformed the market. Many organisations prefer directors to hold substantial equity in the company because they believe directors with 'skin in the game' are more motivated to improve company performance. Suncorp directors, for example, must own at least $200 000 in company stock. In agreement with this sentiment, Australian Council of Superannuation Investors have stated their disappointment that a mere 89 per cent of S&P/ASX 100 and 82 per cent of ASX 200 directors own shares. They prefer all directors to be shareholders so that they identify more with the shareholders they represent. The Council believes that when directors have something to win or lose, they govern better.[7]

The question is whether shareholding might tempt directors into unethical behaviour. A large shareholding could lead to a material conflict of interest for a director who is, for example, responsible for signing off on financial statements or making strategic decisions. And it might incentivise them to make short-term decisions for personal gain at the expense of the long-term good of the company and all its shareholders. And would a small shareholding really make them govern better?

The jury, it seems, is still out but the consensus is that the right balance is needed between independence and impartiality on the one hand and vested interest on the other. What is your opinion?

Transferable skills

1.4 Business operations

Governance

Governance refers to the way organisations are managed and controlled. Good governance means that a board uses due care and diligence to carry out its responsibilities independently and objectively, without domination by one individual or faction, to oversee and advise senior management and ensure they manage the organisation in a prudent way. Effective governance provides reasonable assurance to stakeholders that the organisation is achieving its goals in an acceptable and responsible way and ensures the enterprise is ready, willing and able to prosper in the long term.

INDUSTRY INSIGHTS

The price of negligence

The first documented death of an asbestos worker from lung failure was in 1906 in London; by 1908, insurance companies in the United States and Canada began decreasing insurance cover while increasing premiums for people who worked with asbestos. By the 1970s, many of those people had died of 'asbestosis'. Despite the consistent health warnings since that time, asbestos mining and use not only continued, but increased.

James Hardie was established in Melbourne in 1888 and listed on the Australian Stock Exchange in 1951. It mined and manufactured a wide range of asbestos products as well as other building and industrial products. In 2001, the board of James Hardie announced to the Australian Stock Exchange a compensation fund for asbestos victims, claiming it was sufficient to meet all legitimate claims. It was later found that the fund was short $1.5 billion and the Supreme Court of New South Wales found that the James Hardie statement to the stock exchange was false and misleading and that directors were in breach of their duties. They also found that the company engaged in deceptive and misleading conduct. As a result, many of the company's most senior executives received significant fines for their negligence in this matter.[8]

Corporate governance

The excesses of the 1980s, the business scandals in Australia and overseas in the late 1990s and early 2000s, and the global financial crisis that began in 2008 were all related to corporate governance, so you can understand why corporate governance is a hot issue. In corporations, the directors' *fiduciary duty* is their obligation to act solely in the interests of the owners, or shareholders. This includes avoiding conflicts of interest and other matters that may lead to corporate governance concerns being raised. Directors are expected to create wealth by contributing to shareholder value, raising the share price, being profitable, paying out large dividends and generally making the business attractive to investors. However, corporations should take more into account than short-term share prices in order to run their businesses properly.

Standing committees

Because standing committees enable deeper consideration of issues than could occur in a board meeting, the Australian Securities Exchange requires ASX 300 companies to have standing (i.e. permanent) audit and remuneration committees. Many boards have other standing committees for strategically important issues and they can add significant value (contrary to the popular jokes about committees). For example, banks often have standing technology committees and technology companies have standing innovation committees. Finance, risk management and sustainability committees are also common. Boards can also form temporary, ad hoc committees as needed, so there aren't too many committees to slow down decision-making.

Public sector boards

Transferable skills

1.4 Business operations

The key role of the boards of government enterprises is to help the organisation achieve its charter. Boards of government enterprises differ from boards of private sector companies in other ways, too; for example, they:

- don't have the same disclosure requirements
- have different stakeholders and can suffer from stakeholder interference (the government minister is a stakeholder)
- often don't have the power to hire and fire the CEO or appoint directors
- are usually paid less.

In addition, management prerogative is diminished by a range of public service policies and guidelines on matters such as entertainment, forced redundancies and relocations, as well as overseas travel, making it difficult to manage the enterprise commercially. And disgruntled special-interest groups can always pop through the ministerial back door to get their way.

Unlike the private sector, the overriding driver for the public sector isn't profit and, ultimately, the government calls the shots. For this reason, some suggest that the boards of government-owned enterprises be called 'advisory boards' or 'councils', so that it is clear that these boards are there to give input, while the government makes the decisions.[9]

Two board duties growing in importance

Two board duties growing in importance are risk management and developing environmentally sustainable operations. In particular, cyber-attack is becoming a 'when' question, not an 'if' question, making and having robust and well-communicated plans to respond to cyber-attacks and their effects on the organisation, its customers and other stakeholders critical.

Legal eagles believe that company directors who fail to consider climate change risks could be found liable for breaching their duty of care. Climate change is foreseeable and is associated with a plethora of economic, environmental and social risks that may affect the interests of their organisation. In fact, the Australian Prudential Regulation Authority (APRA), which oversees financial institutions such as banks, insurance companies and the superannuation industry, has warned members that it considers it their duty to take into account the financial risks associated with climate change.

Senior management

Senior management is the next-highest level of management. Senior managers, sometimes called executives, develop long-term 'roadmaps' of values, vision, mission, strategies, plans and policies to guide the organisation and add value for its stakeholders. It is their responsibility to see that the organisation achieves the goals established by the board and follows the agreed roadmap.

Middle management

Middle management comprises the level(s) between senior management and first-line management. They are the bridge connecting senior management's vision and strategies to the work priorities and aspirations of lower-level staff by developing the tactics and shorter-term plans to guide the organisation's day-to-day activities.

Large organisations can have several layers of middle managers while others have two or three. Generally, though, delayering, downsizing and restructuring are decreasing the number of middle management jobs and increasing the number of first-line leader-manager jobs. Communications and information technology can replace middle managers as transfer and control points for information and can undertake many of middle management's traditional duties, such as monitoring performance and providing feedback, and even creating reports. Other (formerly) middle-management responsibilities have moved to first-line leader-managers.

Transferable skills

1.4 Business operations

First-line management

First-line leader-managers used to be known as 'supervisors' but are now known by varied titles such as coordinators, first-line managers, front-line managers, section heads, team leaders or, simply, managers. They work in shorter timeframes than more senior managers, typically in weeks or months rather than quarters and years. They are the indispensable link between non-management employees and the rest of management. Because they are the only managers who have direct and daily contact with the workforce, their role is unique and one of the most important in any organisation.

First-line leader-managers are ideally positioned to influence the morale, motivation, productivity, service levels and cost-effectiveness of the employees they supervise. To many employees, they personify the organisation as a whole. They serve as a focal point for attitudes and values and are role models for how to behave towards customers, the organisation and the job itself.

First-line leader-managers translate the enterprise's vision and goals to employees and explain employees' feelings and views to more senior management. Unfortunately, this can sometimes lead to a 'pig-in-the-middle' feeling because first-line managers can easily see, and often identify with, both sides of an issue.

This closeness can also lead to loyalty problems. On the one hand, first-line leader-managers work very closely with non-management employees and, in many cases, were part of this group before their promotion to management. They may continue to identify with the workforce and more senior managers may mentally continue to place them there, too. Certainly, in some organisations first-line managers are 'glorified workers', expected to carry out the same tasks as the people they supervise with their management duties an added-on extra.

2.3 The six stakeholders

> While one should never underestimate the ability of risk-besotted financiers to wreak havoc, the real threat to capitalism isn't unfettered financial cunning. It is, instead, the unwillingness of executives to confront the changing expectations of their stakeholders.
>
> Gary Hamel (US management expert), 'Capitalism is dead. Long live capitalism', *The Wall Street Journal*, 21 December 2012.

Whichever sector and level managers work in, they need to understand not just their day-to-day duties and responsibilities but also their wider responsibilities. Who do you think managers are primarily accountable to? Is it to their own managers, the organisation's owners, the general public or those they lead? And what are managers' wider responsibilities? It might be to deliver profits to shareholders, reduce costs, nurture an organisation so it can survive in the long term, provide meaningful work, contribute to society or do no harm to the environment, to name a few.

Ethics, **corporate responsibility** (CR) and governance are increasingly important ingredients in an organisation's success. All managers need to understand and adhere to their organisation's policies concerning matters such as:

- bribery, corruption, facilitation payments and money laundering
- conflicts of interest
- entertainment and gifts
- harassment and discrimination, diversity
- privacy, security, and data and intellectual property protection
- supply-chain management
- whistle-blowing
- work–life balance/workplace flexibility.

Organisations and employees at all levels are increasingly seen as having responsibilities to the six groups of people shown in Figure 2.4.

The community and the wider society

Organisations have more than a responsibility to adhere to the laws and regulations of the governments of the countries in which they operate. They are increasingly expected to contribute to, or at least not harm, the environment and the economies in which they operate and to give something back to the communities in which their employees and customers live, and in which they make their money or provide their services. Organisations meet these expectations in a variety of ways, such as implementing sustainable operations, providing time off for employees to undertake community service work, sponsoring local sports teams and environmental projects, and partnering with or supporting charities.

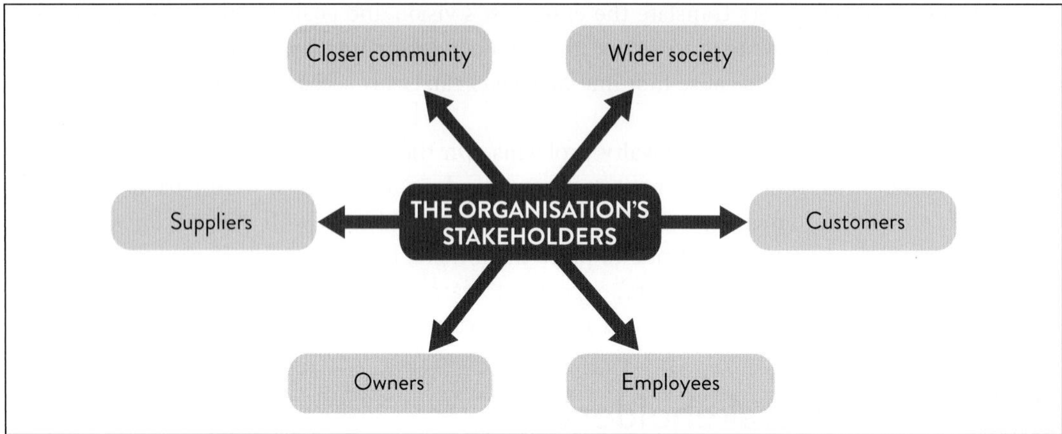

FIGURE 2.4 Stakeholders

Customers and/or clients

Senior managers determine the nature and level of services or product quality the organisation offers, while middle managers develop and monitor the necessary procedures and guidelines to provide it. First-line managers ensure that those products or services are produced or provided within the established guidelines. This includes continually striving to improve their products or services and the ways they are produced so that they represent better-and-better value for customers and, in turn, enhance the organisation's reputation.

Employees

As discussed in Chapter 1, people's expectations of work and the workplace itself have changed. Today's organisations have a variety of policies that help meet their diverse employees' needs and all managers need to understand, support and carry out those policies. Effectively, it is the responsibility of first-line leader-managers to treat employees fairly and to safeguard their health, safety and wellbeing, job satisfaction and morale. Leader-managers can also build good working environments by ensuring that employees have clear and specific goals to work towards.

Leader-managers can ensure employees are properly trained and fully use their skills and abilities. They can help employees feel appreciated and that they are receiving organisational support. Finally, they can help employees to carry out their duties efficiently.

Owners

An organisation's main duty is generally considered to be to its owners. In the private sector, these are the shareholders – private individuals as well as institutional investors – who invest in an organisation to make money. You can think of taxpayers as the 'owners' of the public sector because they fund the operations through their taxes. In an NFP organisation, you can think of those individuals and organisations that contribute funds to its operations as the 'owners'.

Owners want to know that the organisation is prudently managing their investments and they want a fair return for their investments. In the private sector, the return is profit. For public and NFP organisations, an effective service, or fulfilment of their mission, is considered a fair return.

Suppliers

Senior managers establish the desired outcomes and set the guidelines for working with suppliers that middle and first-line managers execute, in part by developing and maintaining cooperative relationships with people from supplier organisations. Believing that strength comes from mutually beneficial relationships, many organisations aim to forge genuine **trading partnerships** with their suppliers of goods and services. As more organisations outsource services, such as accounting, training, computing, maintenance and so on, many organisations also try to ensure their **contractors** 'buy into' their core values and principles so that they can actively help the organisation achieve its vision.

2.4 The roadmap

> The rule used to be that you'd reinvent yourself once every 7–10 years. Now it's every two to three years.
>
> Indra Nooyi, CEO, PepsiCo, quoted by Adi Ignatius, 'How Indra Nooyi turned design thinking into strategy', *Harvard Business Review*, September 2015.

It takes careful thought and planning to manage an organisation that achieves worthy goals in a worthy way. A vague ambition, such as 'Let's make great shirts' or 'Let's help people find jobs' may be a place to start, but it's only the first step.

Whatever the sector, the people employed in an organisation need a clear understanding of:

- what the organisation aims to achieve
- what needs to be done to achieve it, taking into account the changing external environment
- how to define and measure results
- how it intends to behave responsibly towards the environment and its stakeholders
- how employees should behave as they work towards achieving it.

The organisation also needs to know:

- what makes it distinct, to employees as well as to customers
- what its core competencies are and how those competencies contribute to results.

This is the foundation for an organisation's values, vision and mission. Together, they:

- enhance an organisation's reputation and help it attract like-minded employees
- position the organisation in the consumer and employee marketplace
- provide a framework for the organisation's strategy, business plans and day-to-day operations
- send a clear message to all stakeholders about what the organisation stands for, what it aims to achieve and, in broad terms, how it plans to attain its aims.

Based on the organisation's values, vision and mission, you can develop a strategy, or approach, to steer the organisation towards its destination. A strategy needs to be flexible but specific enough to help the organisation and its employees navigate the diversions, opportunities and problems they meet on the way.

Clear values, vision, mission and strategy ensure that each part of the organisation works in harmony with all other parts to achieve its aims by:

- acting as a reference point for decision-making
- guiding employees' day-to-day activities
- helping employees concentrate on what's important.

Figure 2.5 shows the range of board involvement in developing the organisation's roadmap of values, vision, mission and strategy. In small organisations and NFP organisations, the board is likely

Source: Adapted from research by Dr Peter Cebon, University of Melbourne, 2015. Used by permission.

FIGURE 2.5 Board involvement in the roadmap

to be fairly hands-on due to limited resources. In large organisations, the board reviews the values, vision, mission and strategy to ensure that the culture, incentives, organisation structure, people, **risk appetite**, succession plans, systems and so on can support the organisation's roadmap.

Who makes a strategy succeed?

Although senior managers are generally considered responsible for creating the values, vision, mission and strategy for board approval, many organisations involve employees at all levels in developing them. For example, the e-technology consulting company EDS involves thousands of employees in developing its strategy.

Whoever sets the strategy, it is the middle and first-line leader-managers who decide which ideas to push and which to let languish.[10] These leader-managers establish the 'rules' and set a daily example for how to adhere to the values and how to carry out the strategy in pursuit of the organisation's vision. Salespeople decide what to sell, to whom and how. Individual employees reveal whether and how much they support the values, vision and strategies in their day-to-day behaviours. As a result, some strategies are modified and others abandoned. Intel's middle managers, for example, pushed the company towards microprocessors when its senior executives were still concentrating on memory chips.

Once agreed, the roadmap is communicated throughout the organisation under the guidance of senior management. The board, usually through the chairperson, communicates the roadmap to large shareholders, such as superannuation funds, while senior management communicates the shorter-term strategy and results to these groups.

There are no hard-and-fast rules about how to write an organisation's roadmap. In fact, there are many contradictory definitions of the terms floating about. Some organisations combine their vision and mission, some have a six-word strategy and some have a six-page strategy. The point is not to get hung up on definitions but to ensure the organisation and its employees understand clearly:

- what the organisation stands for (values)
- what it wants to achieve (vision and mission)
- how it intends to achieve it (strategy).

Technology and the digital economy have become strategic issues for most enterprises. Both have the potential to destroy, create or reshape business models, industries and marketplaces with breathtaking speed. Threats and opportunities abound as technology redefines industry boundaries, creates new or unlikely competitors, and enables organisations to reinvent themselves in global markets.

Values: what we believe in

Transferable skills
1.4 Business operations

Iconic investor Warren Buffett told his employees: 'If you lose money for the company, I will be understanding. If you lose one shred of the company's reputation, I will be ruthless.'[11] An organisation's values point to the reputation the company wants. They describe what it believes is important and how it intends to operate. They form the basis of the organisation's culture, guide its operations and show its employees how they are expected to behave every day. All employees have a duty to abide by and promote their organisation's values.

Equally importantly, values are what people fall back on when they're unsure what to do. In fact, 60 per cent of first-line leader-managers, 62 per cent of middle managers, 85 per cent of senior managers, 84 per cent of CEOs and 78 per cent of executive directors refer to their organisation's values statement when making decisions.[12]

Many organisations in all sectors also use values to drive cultural change and improve the services they offer. One way to use values this way is to rate managers and employees in their formal **performance reviews** on how well their actions uphold the organisation's values.

Vision: where we are heading

You can think of an organisation's vision as its purpose, noble cause or *raison d'être*. It adds to the guidance values provide for an organisation's operations and its employees' actions. The best vision statements are short and snappy, easily remembered and inspiring to employees. Henry Ford's early vision was to 'democratise the automobile'. There's no point in being modest, but they should be believable, because when they're too divorced from reality, they invite cynicism. Clear, compelling and credible visions achieve the seven goals shown in Figure 2.6.

Corporate responsibility and conscious capitalism

The mantra of 'big business' has long been 'shareholder returns' (as in: 'We *must* give our shareholders a good return on their money' with 'or else they'll sell up' left unsaid). But there is no legal obligation for companies to aim exclusively to maximise shareholder value. In fact, they can choose any strategy

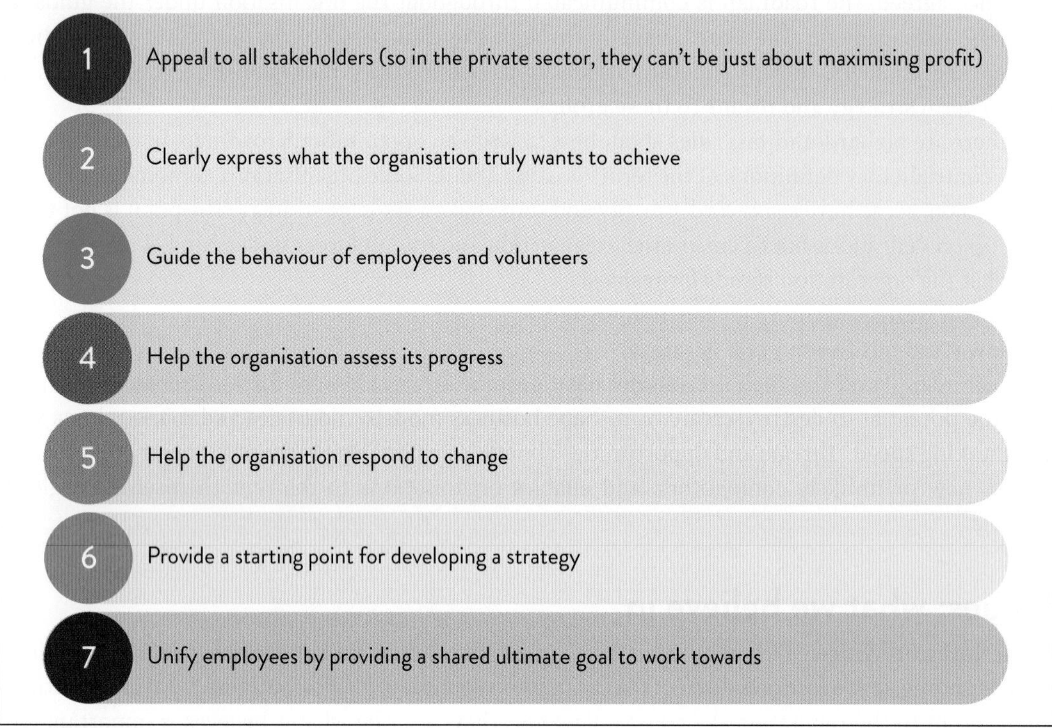

FIGURE 2.6 The seven goals of visions

they like, and some do. Some companies have realised that the short-term thinking of the stock market has restricted their ability to be vehicles for long-term employment, economic advancements, retirement security and, in general, to contribute to the wellbeing of the world and the communities they reside in and sell to. Their key question is not: 'How can we maximise profits?' but: 'How can the world be better off because we exist?'

Transferable skills

1.4 Business operations

Organisations are moving from the more prescriptive **corporate social responsibility** (CSR) to CR, which seeks to identify and meet the key environmental and social expectations and needs of all stakeholders. A consistent CR strategy often divides initiatives between three areas:

1 philanthropy (e.g. donations of money or products to community organisations and employee volunteering)
2 sustainable operations (e.g. reducing emissions, resource use and waste)
3 transforming the business model to address social and environmental challenges.

All three areas should enhance the company's reputation and employer brand, and the second and third areas should also increase revenue or decrease costs. Each initiative should be carefully aligned with the organisation's values and vision and have clear measures of success. A **cross-functional team** is often established to drive and coordinate all initiatives.

A global movement called **B corporations**, or B corps, has entered the CR arena. These companies have stated their commitment to environmental and social goals, as well as profit goals – to do good while doing business – and they are regularly audited against those achievements. There are now more than 2400 B corps in over 50 countries from 130 industries registered as Certified B Corps, including 224 companies in Australia and New Zealand with total revenues of over A$1 billion. All subscribe to the movement called **conscious capitalism**, founded by Raj Sisodia of Harvard University and John Mackey of Whole Foods.

Mission: our map

While the vision expresses an organisation's noble cause – and seldom changes, the mission sets out 'what we seek to achieve' – and changes and adapts as the world and the marketplaces change. The mission is more specific than the vision and reflects the organisation's standards in areas central to its vision (e.g. customer service, employee relations, product or service quality and reliability, as well as profitability).

Like visions, missions need to be clear, concise and memorable in order to motivate employees, guide their actions and inform their decisions. Everyone in your team should understand what the values, vision and mission mean for the organisation as a whole, for the team as a whole and for them personally. Don't confuse vision and mission with making money. Vision and mission is the purpose; making money is the result.

Whether or not an organisation has its vision and values written down, all organisations have them, if only by implication. You can infer them from employees' and managers' behaviour and actions and the way they organise their activities. In whatever format they are, they guide the organisation's decisions, directions and operations.

Aligning goals and values

When employees' goals and values are not the same as their organisation's goals and values, they find it difficult to work well and even to remain within the organisation. So, how can organisations describe and communicate their vision, goals and strategies to employees in a way that builds loyalty and earns their support? How can they make employees feel part of and committed to a larger, worthwhile whole? What formal and informal communication channels can they establish to ensure that their key messages reach people?

One way is to keep employees informed about key events in their organisation so that they feel an important part of it. Corporate videos in a YouTube-style format; formal briefing meetings and papers; in-house magazines and newsletters; internal vacancy notices; intranet sites that are friendly, informative and interactive; noticeboards; senior managers' blogs and tweets; training programs and business conferences, and values and vision ambassadors, can all play an important role in aligning individual and organisational values.

Top-down communication alone isn't enough. Interactive communication is important, too, because to increase **employee engagement**, people need to feel that their voice is heard and that what they say matters. They want to know that their organisation considers them important enough not just to keep them informed about what is going on, but also to find out what they are thinking.

Strategy: the road we'll take

Transferable skills
1.4 Business operations
2.1 Critical thinking
2.3 Business strategy

With the values, vision and mission in place, a strategy can be developed containing more detailed information about how to achieve the organisation's aims. The key to survival these days is organisational agility. How far strategies extend is different for every organisation, but because the world is changing so fast, the time period they cover is shrinking. Not all organisations are like Infosys, with a 200-year roadmap; most look three to five years ahead and review their strategies annually to check whether any risks or opportunities have emerged that make it necessary to adjust them. (Having said that, some say that these days, planning for more than a year ahead is optimistic, given the rate of change.) Meanwhile, strategies for start-ups and companies testing new business models are more of a rolling hypothesis until they find their feet.

Some organisations break their strategy down into *strategic imperatives*, giving each function or capability a strategic imperative to guide the development of its business plans and goals. Strategy is about what makes the organisation unique within the marketplace. Don't confuse strategy with aspirations, goals or vision. Nor is strategy an action, such as a merger or outsourcing. Strategy is not financial performance or operational effectiveness, either; these, like shareholder value, are results. Strategy is also different from tactics – strategy envisions and plans over time, while tactics react *now*.

An organisation's strategy should be based on its competitive edge, its strategically valuable capabilities that enable it to perform more competitively or better than its rivals. These might be **intangible assets**, **tangible assets** or a combination of both. Whatever strategically valuable capabilities the strategy is based on, it should be controlled by the organisation (not its employees, suppliers or customers). It should depreciate slowly and be difficult to copy and superior to any competitor's similar resource.

INDUSTRY INSIGHTS

The difference between strategy and tactics

Here is an example of strategy: Procter & Gamble (P&G) incorporated entering the bleach business into its *strategy*. It developed a colour-safe, low-temperature bleach – a differentiated and superior product to Clorox bleach, its main competitor. P&G's *business plan* was to test market its bleach in the East coast, in Portland, Maine, hoping to 'fly under the radar' since Clorox's headquarters were on the West coast of the US, in Oakland, California. P&G arranged full retail distribution, heavy product sampling and couponing (Americans love their coupons), and major TV advertising in order to create high consumer awareness that would entice them to try its new product.

Here's where it gets interesting. Clorox's *tactical response* was to deliver to the front door of every household in Portland a free gallon (nearly 4 litres) of Clorox bleach and a coupon for their next purchase of Clorox bleach. That sent a clear message to P&G: don't even think about entering the bleach market. P&G had already bought the advertising space and spent most of its launch budget on sampling and couponing. But no one in Portland, Maine, was going to need bleach for many months.

When Clorox decided to enter the laundry detergent market a few years later, P&G sent it a similarly clear and direct message and it, too, withdrew its product. The moral of the story: you need a good strategy, but tactics win you the game or lose it.[13]

Transferable skills

1.4 Business operations

2.1 Critical thinking

2.3 Business strategy

Two ways to develop a strategy

Organisations have two choices when deciding what to offer and how to offer it. One is to stick with your business model and leverage your key capabilities to find ways to execute your business model better and offer better value to your customers. This is the way most organisations have traditionally developed their strategies.

A completely different way to develop and execute a strategy, made possible by today's information technology combined with innovative brains, is to 'break the mould' and develop a completely new business model, or way of doing business. For example, dream up a way of travelling in a city from Point A to Point B that is completely different from the traditional taxi and chauffeur-driven hire car service business model; or dream up way to find and book accommodation when you're travelling that is completely different from the traditional hotel accommodation business model. Figure 2.7 shows the steps traditionally involved in developing a strategy.

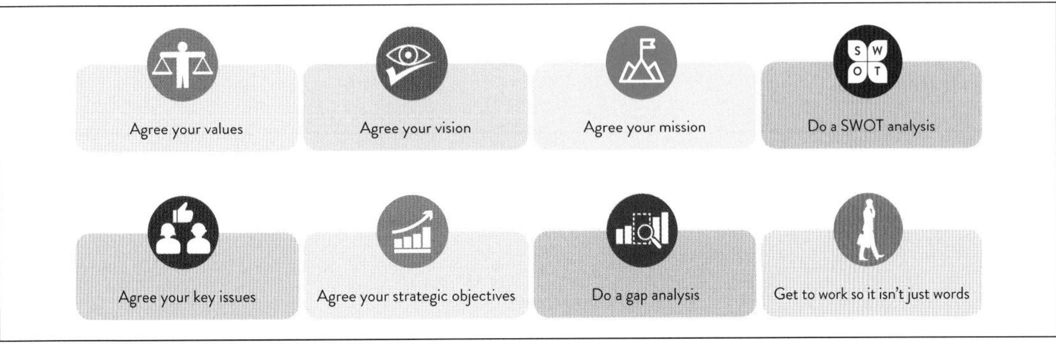

FIGURE 2.7 Developing a strategy

Five critical capabilities support an organisation's vision, mission and strategy, combining to create the value of an organisation. Figure 2.8 shows the five key capabilities.

Transferable skills

1.4 Business operations

2.1 Critical thinking

2.3 Business strategy

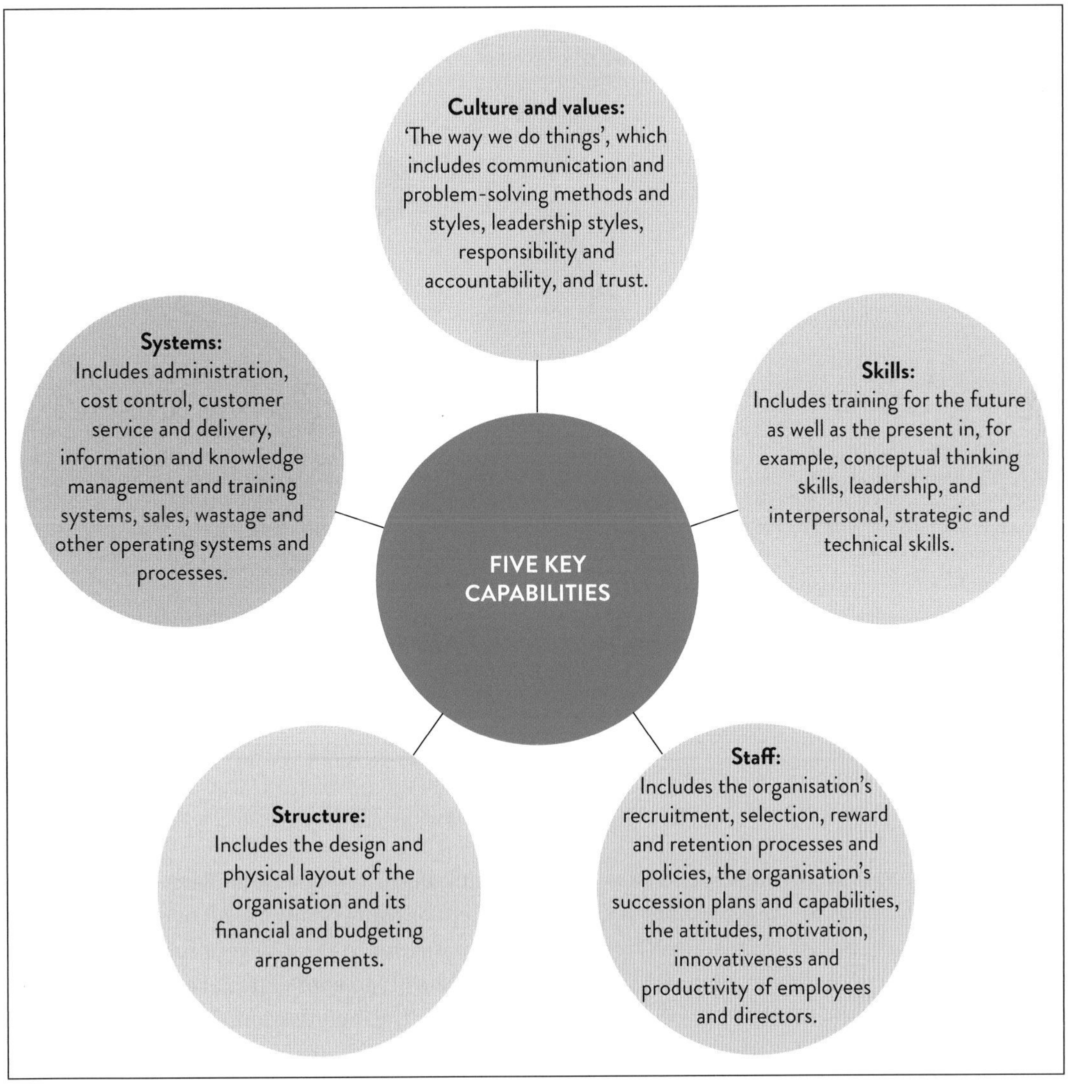

FIVE KEY CAPABILITIES

Culture and values:
'The way we do things', which includes communication and problem-solving methods and styles, leadership styles, responsibility and accountability, and trust.

Skills:
Includes training for the future as well as the present in, for example, conceptual thinking skills, leadership, and interpersonal, strategic and technical skills.

Staff:
Includes the organisation's recruitment, selection, reward and retention processes and policies, the organisation's succession plans and capabilities, the attitudes, motivation, innovativeness and productivity of employees and directors.

Structure:
Includes the design and physical layout of the organisation and its financial and budgeting arrangements.

Systems:
Includes administration, cost control, customer service and delivery, information and knowledge management and training systems, sales, wastage and other operating systems and processes.

FIGURE 2.8 Five key capabilities that support an organisation

Figure 2.9 shows how the strategic plan relates to the organisation's external and internal environments. From it, you can see the damage that would be caused if just one area resisted the selected strategy.

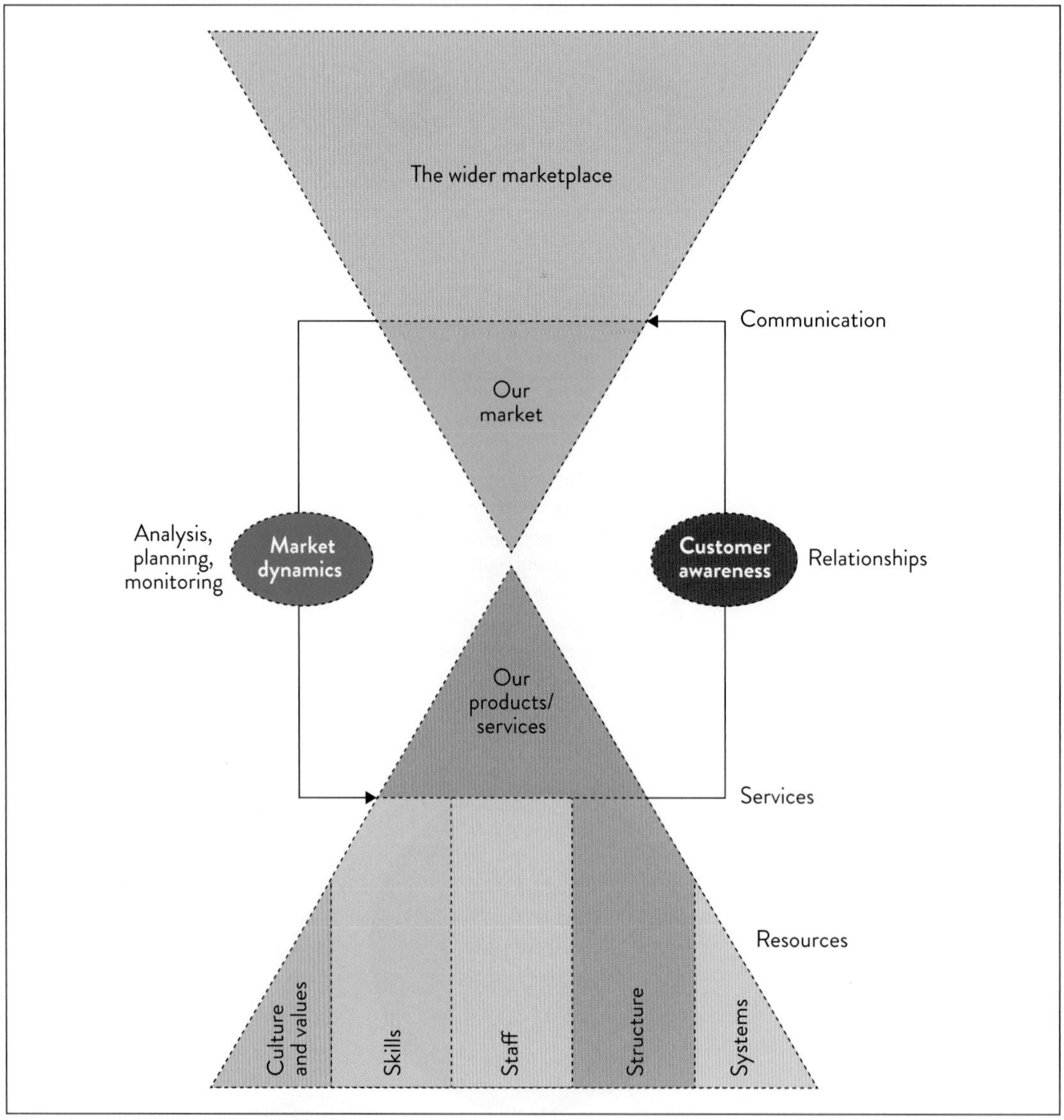

The wider marketplace
Communication
Our market
Analysis, planning, monitoring
Market dynamics
Customer awareness
Relationships
Our products/ services
Services
Resources
Culture and values
Skills
Staff
Structure
Systems

FIGURE 2.9 The strategic plan in context

SWOT analysis

Transferable skills

1.4 Business operations

2.1 Critical thinking

2.3 Business strategy

A **SWOT analysis** can provide a solid basis for developing both strategies and plans. You can use a SWOT analysis to look for ways to improve your department or team, or any aspect of your operations (e.g. sustainability and risk management) too. It is a systematic way to identify your internal strengths (S) and weaknesses (W) and the opportunities (O) and threats (T) in your external environment. You end up with a list of the many factors that could help or hinder the organisation, department, team or the plan you have devised. You can find out how to conduct a SWOT analysis in Chapter 22.

Key issues and strategic goals

Based on the SWOT analysis, the five to seven key issues (positive or negative) facing the organisation are identified. Beginning with the highest priority issue facing the organisation, ways to address that issue are discussed and agreed (bearing in mind the values, vision and mission, not just the strength, weakness, opportunity or threat under discussion).

Once the best ways to deal with the important issues facing the organisation are agreed, a series of challenging, clear, compelling and measurable strategic goals, or strategic imperatives, are developed. Some examples are shown in Table 2.2.

TABLE 2.2 Examples of strategic goals

Administration	Standardise the financial reporting and accounting systems across all sites by 30 April 2025
Employees	Achieve an employee retention rate of 90% by 30 June 2025
Innovation	Achieve 40% of sales from new products by 2025
Operations	Open six factories in three politically and economically stable neighbouring countries by 30 June 2026; develop and implement a self-financing equipment upgrade plan by 1 July 2025
Safety	Achieve an injury-free factory environment by 1 July 2024
Sales	Achieve $1 billion annual sales and a profit of $60 million by the end of the 2024 financial year

Notice that the goals shown in Table 2.2 begin with verbs such as 'standardise', 'achieve' and 'open', and end with the date by which the goal should be achieved. Notice also that they are written in positive, not negative, language. Finally, notice that these goals are measurable, or their attainment can be proved in some other way.

Strategic goals should also be ambitious, flexible and consistent with the rest of the organisation's values, vision and mission. They should be easy to understand and inviting to achieve. Clear strategic goals like these are the basis for developing detailed business and operational plans to move the organisation forward towards its vision and mission.

It's easy to end up with dozens of strategic goals, but it isn't necessary, or possible, to accomplish all of them. The top six or eight to concentrate on are generally selected so as not to dilute everyone's efforts.

Gap analysis

Transferable skills

1.4 Business operations

2.1 Critical thinking

2.3 Business strategy

A **gap analysis** helps you work out where you want to be and how to get there from where you are now. It asks the three questions shown in Figure 2.10 to help develop your strategy (see also Chapter 20 for more).

The following questions are important to ask during the third part of the gap analysis:

- Should we go for inorganic growth (through acquisitions or mergers) or organic growth (by expanding the core business to serve more markets or increase market share)?
- Should we move towards **horizontal** or **vertical integration**?
- Which would best help us achieve our goals – a virtual organisation, an actual organisation or a mixture of both?

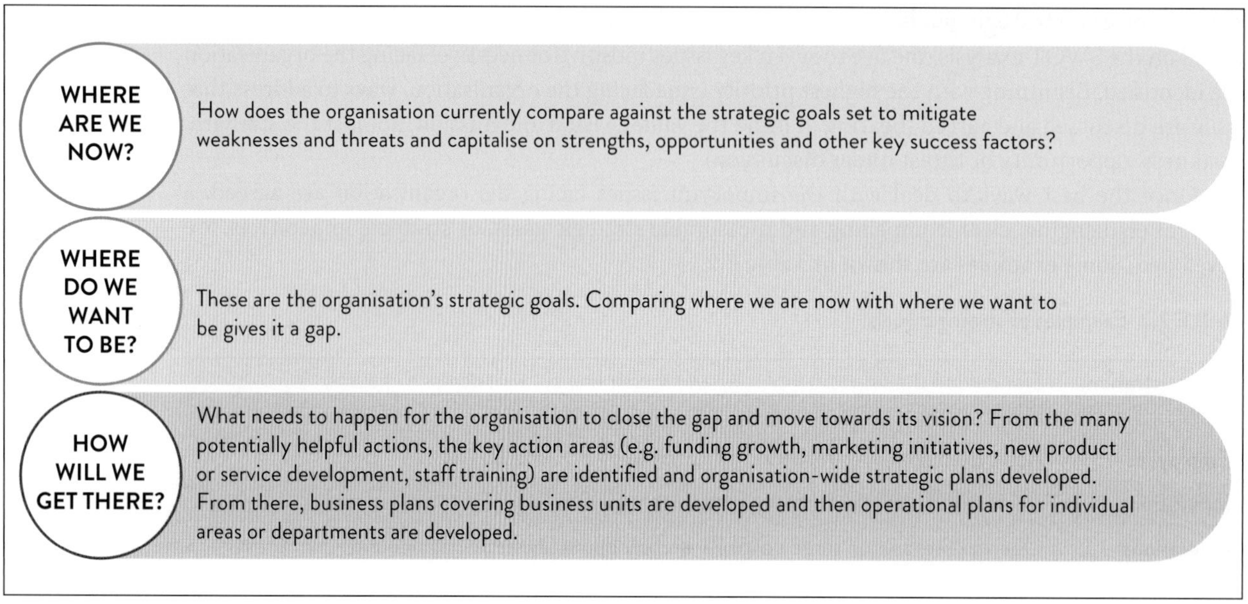

WHERE ARE WE NOW?	How does the organisation currently compare against the strategic goals set to mitigate weaknesses and threats and capitalise on strengths, opportunities and other key success factors?
WHERE DO WE WANT TO BE?	These are the organisation's strategic goals. Comparing where we are now with where we want to be gives it a gap.
HOW WILL WE GET THERE?	What needs to happen for the organisation to close the gap and move towards its vision? From the many potentially helpful actions, the key action areas (e.g. funding growth, marketing initiatives, new product or service development, staff training) are identified and organisation-wide strategic plans developed. From there, business plans covering business units are developed and then operational plans for individual areas or departments are developed.

FIGURE 2.10 Three questions to develop a strategy

Horizontal or vertical integration?

Horizontally integrated organisations seek complementary products or complementary uses for their products and facilities. For example:

- a bed linen manufacturer might begin designing and producing beds or nightwear
- a chain of optometrists might build on its market image of healthcare and find an additional complementary use for its retail outlets by including hearing care in its services
- a clothing designer might produce belts, spectacle frames, homewares (e.g. glasses, plates, towels), perfumes, scarves and shoes.

Vertically integrated organisations secure control of critical 'upstream' suppliers and 'downstream' buyers of their products and services. They own and often manage their upstream suppliers in order to create a consistent quality and secure supply of raw materials, as well as to set up subsidiaries downstream (or forward) to distribute and market their products or services, or they use those products or services themselves. For example:

- a movie studio might own a theatre chain
- a company producing breakfast cereals might decide to farm its own crops and/or produce its own packaging
- a retail pharmacy chain might invest in a research and development facility to create its own medicines and purchase a factory to manufacture them.

INDUSTRY INSIGHTS

A virtual harvest

The Harvest Company, a third-generation, Australian-owned family business, supplies supermarkets with fresh products gathered mainly from small family farmers. Most of these farmers had to learn new skills, hire managers and develop systems to meet quality and other **supply chain** demands as their businesses grew rapidly.

The growers themselves pick, pack, quality assess and deliver their products direct to the supermarket. The Harvest Company doesn't even see the produce before it arrives on the shelves. It arranges the contracts and manages the supply chain. Its business is totally intertwined with its suppliers, making them mutually reliant partners.

In virtual organisations, the real skill is in optimising a value chain of partners. Amazon, Apple, Dell and Nike outsource virtually everything (pun intended). Apple, for example, designs computers in California and manufactures them in Asia. Dell outsources everything except marketing. Nike outsources everything except design and marketing. A small team of hard-working, top-level senior managers and specialists oversees the various operations and links them all together.

Business plans: how we will navigate the road

Transferable skills

1.4 Business operations

2.1 Critical thinking

2.3 Business strategy

From the strategy, even more detailed *business plans* and *operational plans* are developed, which in turn feed down into team and individual **performance plans**. (Operational plans are explained in Chapter 20, team performance plans are explained in Chapter 13, and individual performance plans are discussed in Chapters 15 and 19.) Business plans show how the organisation's strategy is to be achieved. Depending on the organisation and how dynamic and volatile its operating environment is, business plans can look ahead six months, or two or three years, although the pace of change means that long-term planning, which assumes a certainty that no longer exists in many industries, is fast being replaced by continuous replanning, or *iterative planning*, making business planning a continuously evolving process.

Create more value for stakeholders

Transferable skills

1.4 Business operations

2.1 Critical thinking

2.3 Business strategy

Stakeholders are important. Some ways to create more value for them include:

- *Behaviour and culture*: ensure that the attitudes and behaviours of employees support the organisation's values and vision. For example, develop a learning culture or participative leadership, provide training and development, and build strong, productive teams.
- *Future scanning*: define factors critical to future success. For example, use **scenario planning** as a basis for strategy.
- *Operating methods*: design cheaper, more efficient, more reliable, safer or quicker ways of producing your products or services. For example, apply **benchmarking**, **continuous improvements**, **empowerment**, **business process management**, new technologies, time savings or total quality management.

STUDY TOOLS

QUICK REVIEW

KEY CONCEPT 2.1 

a Briefly review the three sectors of the economy and describe the main challenges each faces.

KEY CONCEPT 2.2 

a List the four levels of management and outline the main responsibilities of each.

KEY CONCEPT 2.3 

a List an organisation's six stakeholder groups and explain what each expects from the organisation in each of the three sectors. Are there any conflicting expectations within any of the sectors? If so, what are they and how can organisations manage them effectively?

KEY CONCEPT 2.4 

a Explain how clear organisational values, vision, mission and strategy flow down to the business plan and operational plans. What happens when employees don't understand, care about and/or support their organisation's values, vision, mission and strategy?

b What is meant by corporate responsibility, B corporations and conscious capitalism?

BUILD YOUR SKILLS

KEY CONCEPT 2.1 

a Select a not-for-profit organisation, private or public sector organisation to investigate. Describe how it is organised and how it manages its day-to-day operations to achieve its vision and mission. What particular challenges does it face and what are its strategies for responding to those challenges?

KEY CONCEPT 2.2 

a What do you believe are the three most important duties of a not-for-profit sector board? Of a private sector board? Of a public sector board?

KEY CONCEPT 2.3 

a List five organisations of which you are a stakeholder. What are your expectations of each organisation?

KEY CONCEPT 2.4 

a Look up the values of six or seven organisations (e.g. Alzheimer's Australia, ANZ, Amazon, the Australian Army, BHP Billiton, Bulla Dairy Foods, the Cancer Council, Garvan Research Foundation, the Girl Scouts, Google, Harley-Davidson, Kmart Australia, Telstra, WD-40, Wesfarmers). As you read through them, consider how living these values every day, as you go about your work, could guide your actions. Which are you most drawn to? Why? Which do you think would appeal most to investors and other stakeholders? Why?

b Explain how a set of lasting values can drive an organisation forward; if possible, give an example from your own experience.

c It has been said that everyone in the organisation needs to understand and support their organisation's strategy because, when they don't, they will put a different strategy in its place. Explain how that might happen and, if it does, what you think the likelihood is that the replacement strategy is well thought out and in the best interests of the organisation.

d Discuss how the five key groups of resources each help to create value for an organisation.

e Look up the visions of six well-known organisations. Which are you drawn to? Why? Which could best guide your actions? Which are concrete enough to provide a clear picture of where the organisation is heading?

f Look up the mission statements of some well-known organisations. Which do you find most compelling? Least compelling? Why?

WORKPLACE ACTIVITIES

KEY CONCEPT 2.1 

a To what sector does the organisation you work for belong? What are its key challenges and how are its vision, values and strategies aiming to overcome them?

KEY CONCEPT 2.2 

a List the titles of three senior leader-managers, three middle leader-managers and three first-line leader-managers in your organisation and outline the key responsibilities of each. What general conclusions can you draw about the responsibilities of leader-managers at various levels in your organisation?

b Write a short report on the composition of your organisation's board and the duties of its directors. You might source this information from your organisation's website, intranet or annual report.

c Many companies in European countries are moving to broaden board diversity by including consumers and employees as non-executive directors. What are the advantages and disadvantages of this? Would that work in your organisation? Why or why not?

KEY CONCEPT 2.3 

a Which stakeholders do you work with in your current role? Describe your relationship with them and your understanding of their expectations from you, your work team and your organisation as a whole. Check with them that your understanding of their expectations of you is correct.

b What do you think your stakeholders want most from your organisation? Consider, for example, environmental responsibility, social responsibility, ethical behaviour, a clear vision and strategy, treating employees well, honest dealings with customers and clients, being responsive and adaptable to changes in the operating environment, identifying and managing risks and opportunities well, being a positive change for good, having a diverse workforce and management, a safety culture, leadership excellence at all levels, profitability (in the private sector), cost management (in the public and not-for-profit sectors), or open and clear communications with stakeholders. When you have completed this analysis, consider:

   i How you can confirm your assessment regarding stakeholder needs and wants is correct.

   ii How well your organisation is meeting its stakeholder needs and wants.

KEY CONCEPT 2.4 

a Ask a random sample of employees at various levels and in various parts of your organisation whether they can state your organisation's values, vision and mission and, assuming they can, what they mean to them personally. Then write a short paper summarising your findings, conclusions and recommendations.

b Explore http://bcorporation.com.au and summarise your findings. Would the concept work in your organisation? Why or why not? How would you go about preparing a business case for becoming a Certified B Corp?

c How far ahead does your organisation's strategic plan stretch? What factors were considered when establishing this time period?

d Henry Mintzberg said: 'Strategic planning can neither provide creativity nor deal with it when it emerges by other means.'[14] Do you agree? Do you believe it is possible for an organisation to be trapped by its strategy?

EXTENSION ACTIVITIES

Referring to the Snapshot at the beginning of this chapter, answer the following questions:

1 What do you think some of the SWOT analysis findings conducted at the strategic planning conference would be? Consider the type of organisation it is, its size, etc.

2 After considering the constraints that you think might be part of their findings, what sort of goals would you recommend Charlotte and her team set to address these?

CASE STUDY 2

IBMERS REINVENT THEIR VALUES

In 1914, the start-up company International Business Machines Corporation (IBM) made cheese slicers, scales for weighing meat and tabulating machines. In 1962, then-president Thomas J Watson Jr announced what he called IBM's 'basic beliefs':

- respect for the individual
- superlative customer service
- pursuit of excellence.

These basic beliefs, or values, became the basis of IBM's culture and helped drive its success.[15]

In the 1990s, the company suffered the worst period in its history and was forced to cut its workforce of nearly 400 000 almost in half. IBM fought back under CEO Lou Gerstner, who took over in 1993, transforming it from a mainframe manufacturer into a provider of integrated hardware, networking and software solutions.

Sam Palmisano, who started with the company as a salesperson in 1973, took over as CEO in 2002. By then, IBM operated in 170 countries and had nearly 70 major product lines and countless supporting product lines, as well as more than a dozen customer segments. It employed more than 333 000 people, 40 per cent of whom didn't report daily to an IBM site but worked at clients' premises, from home or in mobile offices.

Despite its turnaround, something was still wrong. IBM's basic beliefs had become distorted. The company had stopped listening to its markets, its customers and its employees. 'Pursuit of excellence' had become arrogance. 'Respect for the individual' had become entitlement and a guaranteed job. So, a few months after taking on the top job, Palmisano met with IBM's top 300 managers and raised the idea of reinventing the company's values as a way to manage and reintegrate the diverse and growing global company. He believed the basic beliefs, however distorted they had become over the years, should be the starting point for the future. Palmisano put forth four concepts, three of them drawn from the basic beliefs, as possible bases for the new values:

- respect
- customers
- excellence
- innovation.

After getting input from the top 300 executives, Palmisano invited more than 1100 employees – a statistically representative cross-section of the company – to participate in focus groups and surveys to inform the development of the new set of values. The resulting proposed values were:

- commitment to the customer
- excellence through innovation
- integrity that earns trust.

Despite this participative process, Palmisano knew that he couldn't simply announce these proposed corporate values:

> Traditional, top-down management processes … wouldn't work at IBM – or, I would argue, at an increasing number of twenty-first-century companies. You can't impose command-and-control mechanisms on a large, highly professional workforce. I'm not only talking about our scientists, engineers and consultants. More than 200 000 of our employees have college degrees. The CEO can't say to them, 'Get in line and follow me', or 'I've decided what your values are'. They're too smart for that. And, as you know, smarter people tend to be, well, a little more challenging; you might even say cynical.

In July 2003, Palmisano opened the values creation process to all employees. Using a specially tailored 'jamalyzer' software tool, a three-day debate on the company's values began. Known as ValuesJam, it took place on the company's intranet, opening unstructured employee discussions around four topics:

1. *Company values*: Do company values exist? If so, what is involved in establishing them? … What would a company look like that truly lived its beliefs? Is it important for IBM to agree on a set of lasting values that drives everything it does?
2. *A first draft*: What values are essential to what IBM needs to become? Consider this list of the three proposed values. How might these values change the way we act or the decisions we make? Is there some important aspect or nuance that is missing?
3. *A company's impact*: If our company disappeared tonight, how different would the world be tomorrow? Is there something about our company that makes a unique contribution to the world?

4 *The gold standard*: When is IBM at its best? When have you been proudest to be an IBMer? ... What do we need to do – or change – to be the gold standard going forward?

Most of the comments on Day 1 were cynical and scathing:

- 'The only value in IBM is stock price.'
- 'Company values (yea right).'
- 'I feel we talk a lot about trust and taking risks. But at the same time, we have endless audits, mistakes are punished and not seen as a welcome part of learning and managers (and others) are constantly checked.'

The comments were so bad that at least one senior manager wanted to pull the plug on ValuesJam.

But on Day 2, the counter-critics weighed in. Positive comments became more frequent and criticism became more constructive. By the end of Day 3, more than 50 000 employees had logged on and posted nearly 10 000 comments. IBM analysts sifted through over one million words and isolated key themes, such as 'a silo mentality pits one business unit against another'.

The final set of values emerged and were published on IBM's intranet in November 2003:

1 dedication to every client's success
2 innovation that matters, for our company and for the world
3 trust and personal responsibility in all relationships.

In the next 10 days, Palmisano received more than a thousand emails and many more comments were posted on the intranet. The language was often sharp, saying just where IBM's operations fell short of, or clashed with, these ideals.[16]

Questions

1 What could lead to a company's strong values becoming distorted? How can leader-managers guard against this happening?
2 If announcing the values to the rest of the company was good enough for Tom Watson Jr, why wasn't it good enough for Sam Palmisano? Explain your thinking.
3 Do you think something similar to ValuesJam would work in your own company? Why or why not?
4 When the emails and postings pointed out the contrast between IBM's new values and its operations, did this indicate that the exercise had been a failure or that people cared about the company? Explain your thinking.

CHAPTER ENDNOTES

1 Bill Shorten, Assistant Treasurer, speech given at the Australian Council of Social Service National Conference, Melbourne Convention Centre, 30 March 2011; Mark Lyons, UTS Director of Research, 'The non-profit sector in Australia: A fact sheet', 4th ed, 2009, National Roundtable of Non-profit Organisations, https://www.mdsi.org.au/pub/MDSI_-_Nonprofit_Fact_Sheet.pdf, accessed 3 March 2014.

2 Angela Faherty, 'Spotlight on innovation', *Company Director*, March 2015, p. 56.

3 Australian Bureau of Statistics, 'Australian National Accounts: Non-Profit Institutions Satellite Account (2012–13)', http://www.ausstats.abs.gov.au/ausstats/subscriber. nsf/0/0260992FB20E701ECA257D0400129476/$File/52560_2012-13.pdf, accessed 8 December 2014; Angela Faherty, 'Spotlight on innovation', op cit.

4 PricewaterhouseCoopers, 'The PwC-CSI Index (13 June 2013)', http://www.pwc.com.au/media-centre/2013/pwc-csi-community-index-jun13.htm, accessed 22 October 2014.

5 Australian Bureau of Statistics, 'Selected characteristics of Australian business 2012–13', http://www.abs. gov.au/AUSSTATS/abs@.nsf/DetailsPage/8167.02012-13?Open Document, accessed 8 December 2014; (ABS catalogue 8167.0, 2014), http://dfat.gov.au/trade/topics/investment/Pages/frequently-asked-questions.aspx

6 Phil Ruthven, 'Exposing political and union rhetoric', *Company Director*, March 2015, pp. 36–37.

7 Domini Stuart, 'The importance of independence', *Company Director*, March 2014; 'Pros and cons of "skin in the game"', *Company Director*, December 2015 to January 2016, p. 13.

8 James Hardie, 'Company history', http://www.jameshardie.com.au/company-history, accessed 7 June 2015; 'History of asbestos', http://www.asbestos.com/asbestos/history, accessed 7June 2015; L. Gettler, 'See no evil, speak no evil, hear no evil', *HR Monthly*, July 2009, p. 19.

9 Domini Stuart, 'In public service', *Company Director*, August 2009.

10 Henry Mintzberg, *Managing*, Berrett-Koehler, 2011.

11 Warren Buffett, quoted in M. L. Litwin, *The public relations practitioner's playbook*, AuthorHouse (US), 2009.

12 'Added values: The importance of ethical leadership', Institute of Business Ethics.

13 Karen Dillon, 'I think of my failures as a gift', *Harvard Business Review*, April 2011.

14 Henry Mintzberg, *The rise and fall of strategic planning*, Simon and Schuster, 1994.

15 Thomas J. Watson Jr, *A business and its beliefs: The ideas that helped build IBM*, McGraw-Hill Leadership Classic, 1963.

16 Paul Hemp, Thomas A. Stewart, 'Leading change when business is good', *Harvard Business Review*, December 2004.

CHAPTER

THE FORMAL ORGANISATION

After completing this chapter, you will be able to:

3.1 explain the general principles by which organisations link employees and functions or processes, and the main ways organisations are altering these links

3.2 understand the traditional ways in which to structure organisations and how these are changing

3.3 understand the new types of organisations you are likely to find.

TRANSFERABLE SKILLS

The following transferable skills are covered in this chapter:

1 **Business competence**
- **1.1** Financial literacy
- **1.2** Entrepreneurship/small business skills
- **1.3** Sustainability
- **1.4** Business operations
- **1.5** Operations management

2 **Critical thinking and problem solving**
- **2.1** Critical thinking
- **2.2** Personal effectiveness
- **2.3** Business strategy

3 **Social competence**
- **3.1** Teamwork/relationships
- **3.2** Verbal communication
- **3.3** Written communication
- **3.4** Leadership

OVERVIEW

Since ancient Roman times, the usual way to organise people has been to put them into a pyramid-shaped organisation, with a few people at the top calling all the shots. However, the massive change 'without' (discussed in Chapter 1) requires massive change within. Organisations are changing the way they operate internally because the world around them and the nature of work is changing – so much so that organisation design is now a matter of high priority in many organisations. The traditional pyramid has been relentlessly eroded as, in an effort to keep pace, organisations are testing other ways to structure themselves.

In fact, organisations are undergoing more radical restructuring since 1985 than at any other time since the modern organisation evolved in the 1920s. Capabilities-based competition is the new source of competitive advantage, and it requires flat and fluid structures. Business complexity is increasing dramatically. The employee mix continues to change, globalisation marches on, and flexible working and labour-intensive manufacturing continues to give way to knowledge- and service-based organisations. Outsourcing has become an accepted part of getting work done. All these, too, call for different types of organisation structures, enabled by advances in communications and information technology.

What will replace the crumbling command-and-control hierarchy that suited the industrial era now that Australia is a service and knowledge economy? This chapter will help you find your way around organisations without getting lost.

SNAPSHOT

Finding their way around

Human resources (HR) officer Macayle Mataac sits at her desk working out how best to induct this year's work-experience students to the Electricity Corporation. She brainstorms a list of the information she could give them and then organises it into a logical sequence.

She thinks, when they report to me on their first day, I'll explain how an Act of Parliament set up the Corporation in 1926 and how we were privatised in 1997 as part of government policy. That was when we split our vertically integrated structure into four distinct businesses to generate, transmit, distribute and retail electricity.

I'll outline the corporation's charter and talk about our mission, strategy and goals. I'll explain our key policies – and challenges – regarding customer service, the environment, equal opportunity employment and health, safety and welfare. And I'll present a series of organisation charts to show them how much we've changed over recent years, even since I've been here.

After that, I'll walk them through the current organisation chart so they can see how the different business divisions of the Corporation relate to each other. I'll talk a bit about the variety of employment options we have, ranging from full-time core employees to part-time, casual and temporary employees, self-employed contractors and employed-by-others contractors. I'll explain how a lot of our employees work from home – some infrequently, some always. And I'll explain how in some parts of the organisation, the 'office' has become a drop-in centre so that people whose base of work is elsewhere can catch up with each other and exchange information. Then I'll throw the discussion open for questions. I'm sure they'll ask what we're doing about work–life balance, sustainability and other interesting topics.

I might close by taking them through a few examples of employees whose careers have taken some interesting paths within the corporation – it won't hurt to get these students thinking about the wealth of options open to them in their working lives. Then I'll ask them to think about what experience they particularly want to gain while they're with us. We're set for a couple of interesting inaugural hours.

3.1 Designing the (changing) organisation

Transferable skills

1.2 Entrepreneurship/ small business skills

1.4 Business operations

2.1 Critical thinking

2.2 Personal effectiveness

2.3 Business strategy

3.1 Teamwork/ relationships

3.2 Verbal communication

3.3 Written communication

3.4 Leadership

> There is nothing quite so useless as doing with great efficiency something that should not be done at all.
>
> Peter Ducker

Have you ever thought about how your organisation is arranged? Are activities grouped together into specialisms (e.g. administration, customer service, finance, production and sales)? Or is it more like a stream of activities, each building on the other to produce a product or service (e.g. welcoming hotel customers, checking them in and showing them to their rooms, or making a product from beginning to end)? The way people and functions or business processes are linked together is called organisation design.

Poorly designed organisations suffer from:

- lack of flexibility and responsiveness to change
- lack of innovation
- lack of trust and cooperation
- slow decision-making and poor-quality decisions
- time wasted on 'administrivia' – unnecessary and trivial administrative issues

- unclear reporting lines and relationships
- unclear roles, goals and responsibilities.

Organisation design doesn't just create or prevent problems. It also influences the type of employees and technologies an organisation needs. For example, hierarchical organisations with highly functionalised activities need specialist employees willing to carry out a narrow range of highly prescribed tasks, and they need sophisticated ways to monitor and control work and workflow; whereas, organisations with flat, open structures, a flexible approach and clusters of team-based employees with broad job responsibilities need multiskilled, self-directed employees, and systems that can store and retrieve information and knowledge easily. When the organisation is virtual or partially virtual, **collaborative systems technologies** is required that facilitate teamwork and open communication.

The way an organisation is designed also influences how it operates. For example tall, vertical organisation structures, or hierarchies with lots of levels, slow down communication and decision-making and encourage power-based relationships and organisational politics. But flat structures encourage accountability, participation, teamwork and more rapid and responsive communication and decision-making. So which is it to be? Tall or flat? Or maybe round?

The general principles of organisation design

Transferable skills

1.2 Entrepreneurship/ small business skills

1.4 Business operations

1.5 Operations management

Whatever the design selected, good organisation designs share a number of characteristics. They:

- are simple and flexible enough to accommodate change
- centralise overall policy and strategy development
- centre on core activities and support the organisation's strategy and main goals
- create feasible job roles in which employees are neither overworked nor underworked and that contain realistic groupings of skills and an interesting range of tasks
- eliminate or minimise duplication of effort so that activities are completed only once
- give leader-managers enough time to **coach** and **mentor** employees, offer **feedback** and guidance, etc.
- provide services and 'back office' functions to as wide a base as possible to achieve **economies of scale**
- suit the organisation's general environment and stakeholders.

Well-designed organisations are 'aligned' in the sense that the formal and informal structures support each other. Some key considerations are illustrated in Figure 3.1.

Four broad principles have traditionally guided the way organisations link their functions, which we will now discuss. These principles continue to apply, but as you see in the following four sections, three of them are changing.

Group size

People feel most comfortable and work best in worksites when there are fewer than 150 people. This size allows people to get to know each other, learn a bit about each other's families, chat about their daily lives and so on. When worksites get bigger than this, the number of people employees know suddenly shrinks to around 60 to 70 people, taking the worksite from friendly to a more formal atmosphere with far less personal interaction (which, it should be noted, some people prefer).

Interestingly, the Ringelmann effect – derived from a classic study of the effect of group size on how much effort people put into a 'tug of war' (pulling on a rope) – introduced the notion of 'social loafing' – the result being that when a group gets big enough, it's easy to 'hide' and not pull your weight.[1]

FORMAL CONSIDERATIONS	INFORMAL CONSIDERATIONS
Decisions • Decision-making processes • Governance • Policies • Values, vision and mission **Performance management** • Career pathing • Performance planning • Performance measurements • Reward systems • Talent management • Training and development **Knowledge management** • Systems for capturing knowledge • Systems for sharing knowledge • Systems for securing intellectual property **Structure** • Business process flows • Degree of centralisation • Degree of formalisation of roles • Degree of functionalism/departmentalisation • Division of responsibilities • Method of grouping functions (by customers, location, product, etc.) • Reporting structure/chain of command • Span of management • Reporting mechanisms • Degree of work specialisation	**Norms** • Day-to-day behaviours • Expectations and ethical standards • Leadership and management practices **Motivation and engagement** • Arrangements for flexible working • Employer brand • Psychological contract • Psychological rewards **Culture** • Focus on customers, innovation, quality, etc. • Shared assumptions, beliefs, biases **Networks** • Degree and type of collaboration and cooperation

FIGURE 3.1 Aligned organisations

Individual contributor and manager positions

An individual contributor is a professional without management responsibilities who contributes to an organisation independently to help support its goals and mission. Although they usually have to report to someone within the organisation, an individual contributor is not responsible for managing anyone except for themselves. Both individual contributors and managers have managing responsibilities, but individual contributors may be the manager of a process or project that they can complete as part of a team or individually, and they perform more self-management. Managers are in charge of a group of people, which may include individual contributors, and the projects and processes they are working on. Individual contributors manage more tactile tasks, such as sorting online files; whereas a manager takes on the more strategic tasks of developing project teams and focusing on growth goals.

Span of management

The span of management (or span of control) is the number of people a person supervises. It's important to get this right because supervising too many people can lead to *under*supervision and supervising too few people can lead to *over*supervision.

The number of people a leader-manager can effectively supervise depends on the:

- ability of the employees to work without supervision
- amount of 'own work' the leader-manager has to do in addition to leadership and management activities
- complexity of the jobs
- degree of independence or interdependence in the work
- location of those being supervised – scattered or all in one place
- number of different jobs done by those being supervised
- skills of the leader-manager
- strictness of quality standards.

Today's flatter organisation structures mean that the span of management is becoming wider, requiring different leadership and management skills.

Unity of command

Convention has it that an employee should report only to one person. This is called **unity of command** and is based on the thinking that having more than one boss can create a situation of potential conflict and confusion. As you may have guessed from the military-style language, this principle flourished in the days of hierarchy and bureaucracy. Today, however, organisations need to be flexible and responsive to their environments and this principle is losing its hold on organisation designers.

Project teams, for example, often form to deliver a specific result and then disband, contractors and part-time workers are often brought in to work in one or more areas and employees are often temporarily seconded to other areas. **Matrix organisations** are purposely designed with people reporting to two or more managers.

Organisation structure

Transferable skills

1.1 Financial literacy

1.2 Entrepreneurship/small business skills

1.3 Sustainability

1.4 Business operations

1.5 Operations management

The speed of change in the external environment has forced organisations to modify their structures as often as every two years. As Chapter 24 explains, merely designing a new organisation and announcing it invites resistance and mistrust – you need to bring people along with you.

The main goal of redesigning organisations is to make cost savings, increase efficiencies and provide a better product or service to customers. To do this, organisation designers work out which type of structure would best suit an organisation's size and activities and look for ways to best link internal relationships between people and functions. This allows the organisation to make the best use of its internal resources, particularly people, so they can work with minimum cost and fuss and maximum effectiveness and satisfaction.

You can think of the resulting organisation structure as the organisation's 'framework' that ties together its various activities. This is the *formal organisation*, drawn as an organisation chart.

Organisation charts

Organisation charts show the links between employees and functions in organisations, illustrating the officially recognised lines of authority, relationships and responsibility, and support. They are typically a series of boxes representing individual jobs or groups of jobs, grouped into functions or process flows. Boxes for positions on the same authority level are shown on the same horizontal level (space allowing). The boxes are linked by lines, showing reporting relationships. Then there are dotted lines that show sources of advice and service, or partial reporting relationships. Organisation charts also show the levels in the organisation's hierarchy, as well as the spans of control of the various managers.

Organisation charts can highlight problems of duplication of effort, span of management and unity of command in a function, process or team. This alerts you to the need to adjust the organisation design. Organisation charts also help employees understand the organisation as a whole. The charts show how employees fit into the rest of the organisation and into their department.

Organisations that keep up-to-date organisation charts tend to be well structured, possibly because the charts keep people aware of the structure and make it easier to make changes when they are needed.

3.2 Designing organisations the traditional way

I don't actually think that the stereotype of a businessperson treading all over people to get to the top, generally speaking, works. I think if you treat people well, people will come back and come back for more.

Richard Branson (founder, Virgin group), with Chris Anderson Q&A, 'Life at 30,000 feet', *TED*, March 2007.

Transferable skills

1.2 Entrepreneurship/small business skills

1.3 Sustainability

1.4 Business operations

1.5 Operations management

Bureaucracies, developed by the Romans more than 2000 years ago, compartmentalise work and break it down into simple, discrete steps to try to obtain the advantages of economies of scale. This makes them well suited to making and moving things. They work well with large groups of relatively uneducated people, as was the case in the early part of the Industrial Revolution.

Bureaucracies are suited to large organisations operating in predictable and stable external environments. These large, 'tall' **centralised organisations** encourage consistency, reliability and uniformity through controls, checks and balances. The different levels denote an individual's formal status, or rank, in the organisation. Bureaucracies were still popular towards the end of the 20th century in both the public and private sectors, when they continued to suit the external environment. Figure 3.2 shows an organisation chart for a bureaucracy.

Bureaucracies have five central features:

1 They are organised around functions, or specialist groups, such as accounting, engineering, human resource management and marketing, often critically referred to as 'silos'.
2 Everyone has a clear boss and bosses have a clearly defined group of subordinates. Reporting relationships are vertical, with managers closely directing people's work; your level in the organisation chart denotes your formal status and level of authority and responsibility.
3 Knowledge is concentrated at the top and authoritarian leadership dominates, because managers 'know more' and telling people what to do is viewed as the most efficient way to get results.
4 As much as possible, work is divided into small, discrete, independent tasks with clear procedures or one best way of carrying them out. Individuals, rather than teams, are accountable for their performance. Employees and managers concentrate on how well individual tasks are carried out rather than on how they fit together to create value.
5 There are lots of rules and regulations.

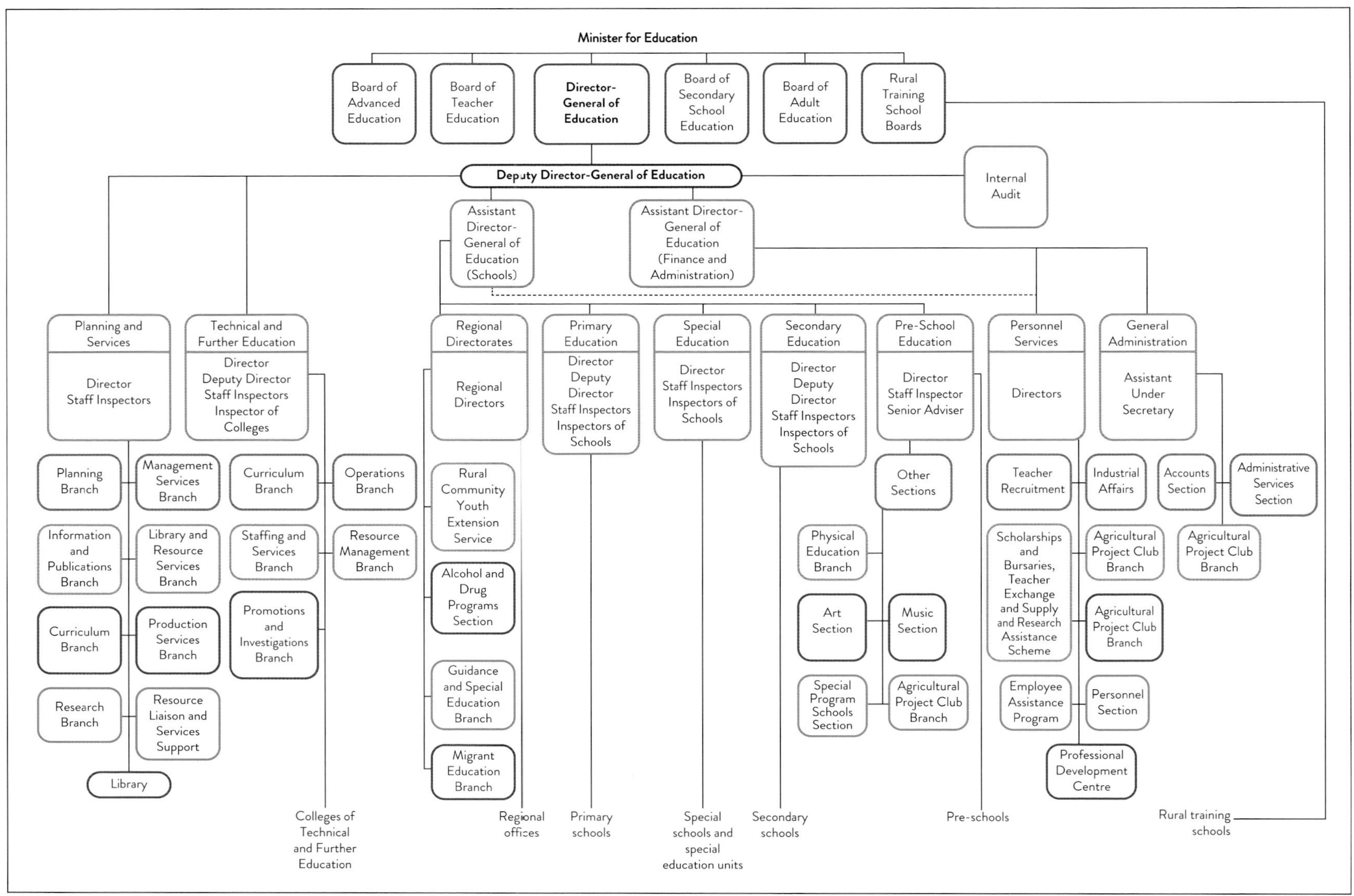

FIGURE 3.2 Organisation chart for the education department of a state government

By function

Mass production allows organisations to achieve economies of scale by centralising key functions. Centralised organisations also work well in companies seeking to create value from economies of scope. Figure 3.3 shows a typical functional organisation with one person responsible for each function. The organisation chart is drawn horizontally, with functional managers, each responsible for their particular function, reporting to a general manager. For example, the finance manager is responsible for all activities related to finance throughout the entire organisation.

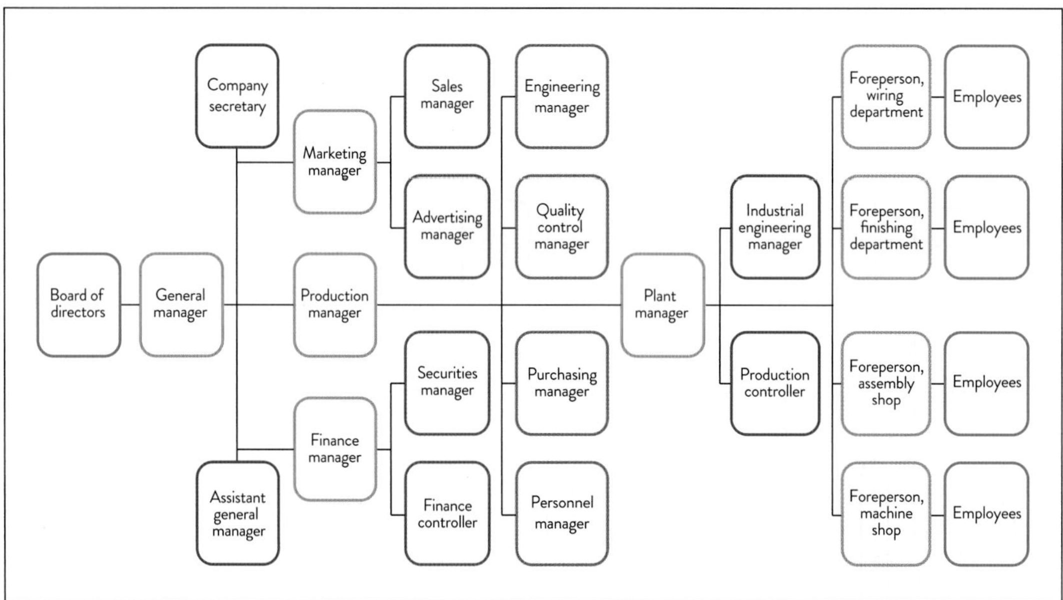

FIGURE 3.3 A sideways organisation chart for a manufacturing company with a functional structure

Functional structures can work reasonably well in smaller organisations, but as an organisation grows and becomes more complex, functional structures tend to become bureaucratic, creating problems of accountability and slowing decision-making. Because people are responsible for their tasks and to their function, no one is responsible for meeting customer needs, so the customer can fall into second place.

By customer or market type

As enterprises diversified their offerings and moved into new markets, new structures emerged that organised business units around customer type, geographic markets and products. These lost some economies of scale but their greater flexibility allowed them to adapt to local conditions.

In customer-type organisations, a separate division looks after each group of customers. Figure 3.4 illustrates a company with an upside-down organisation chart in which head office retains control of essential staff functions (distribution, finance and research and development).

Customer-type structures can work well in large organisations that offer a range of products or services to different groups of customers, especially where different manufacturing or processing techniques are used.

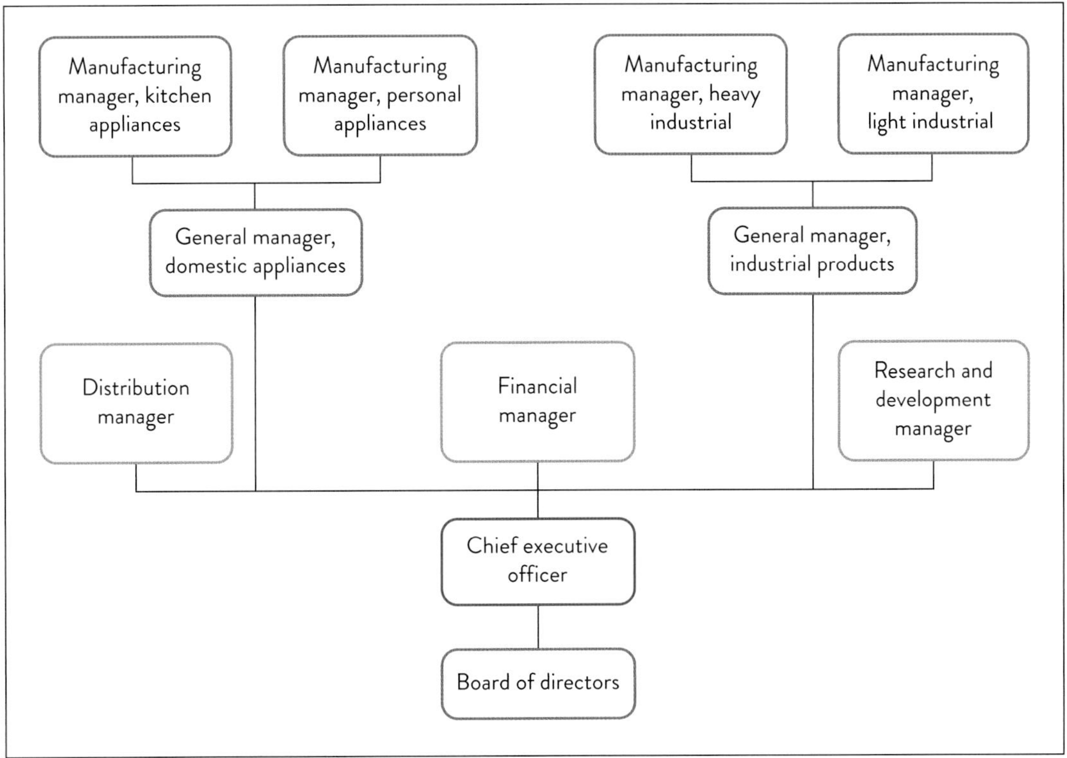

FIGURE 3.4 An upside-down organisation chart by customer type

By geographic location

When an organisation has manufacturing plants in one or more states or countries and sales branches in several major cities, organising by geographic location can make sense. This structure also allows organisations to customise their offerings to local preferences and regulations. Most organisations that are spread out geographically opt to organise along geographic lines. Figure 3.5 shows a larger company with the same product lines, as in the product organisation chart shown in Figure 3.6, but organised along geographic lines.

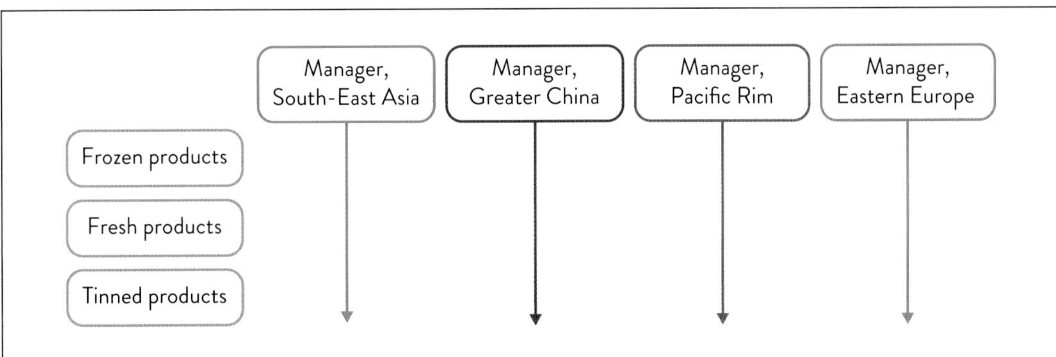

FIGURE 3.5 A geographic organisation chart

By product type

Organisations that arrange their operations by product have one division or department for each major product or service group. Figure 3.6 shows an organisation divided into three main product groups: frozen products, fresh products and tinned products. Organising by products can work well when the organisation is not big, not widely spread out geographically, and when the technology or brands are the organisation's key drivers of value. Organising by product type also encourages more entrepreneurial behaviour than organising by function, customer or market type or geographic location.

FIGURE 3.6 A product group organisation chart

Figure 3.7 shows another way to organise by product type. Here, each division has responsibility for its own finance, production, distribution and marketing.

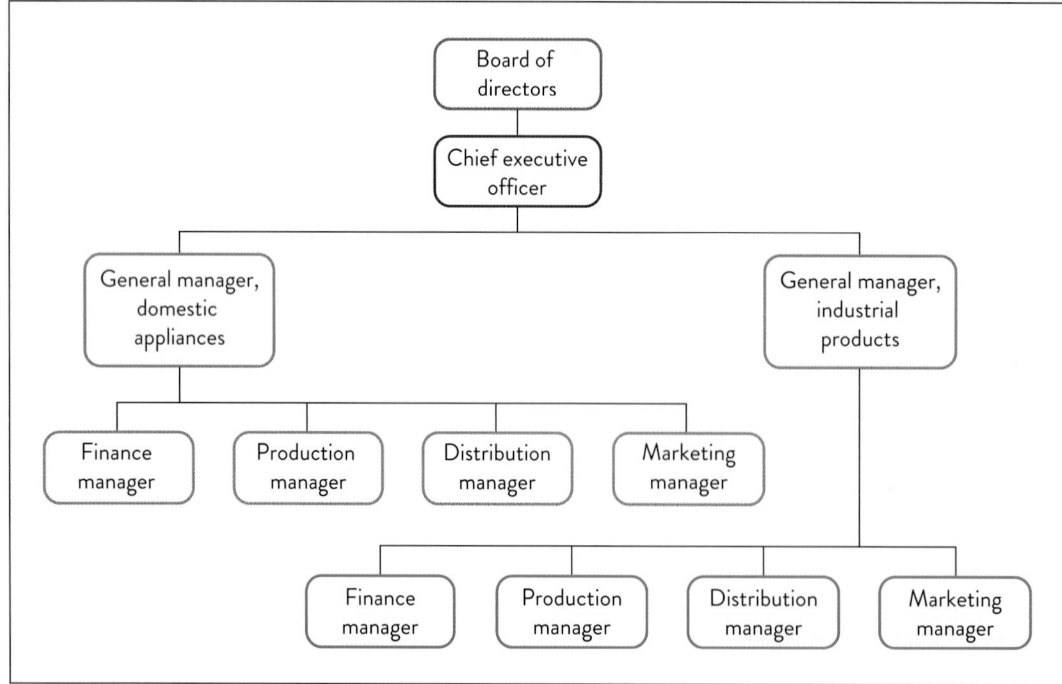

FIGURE 3.7 Structure by product, with each divisional general manager having control of each function

Organisations are ditching hierarchy with structures that are more effective in today's modern workplace. One example is **holacracy**, which is a 'comprehensive practice for structuring, governing and running an organisation that removes power from a management hierarchy and distributes it across clear roles, which can then be executed autonomously without a micromanaging boss' (see Figure 3.8).

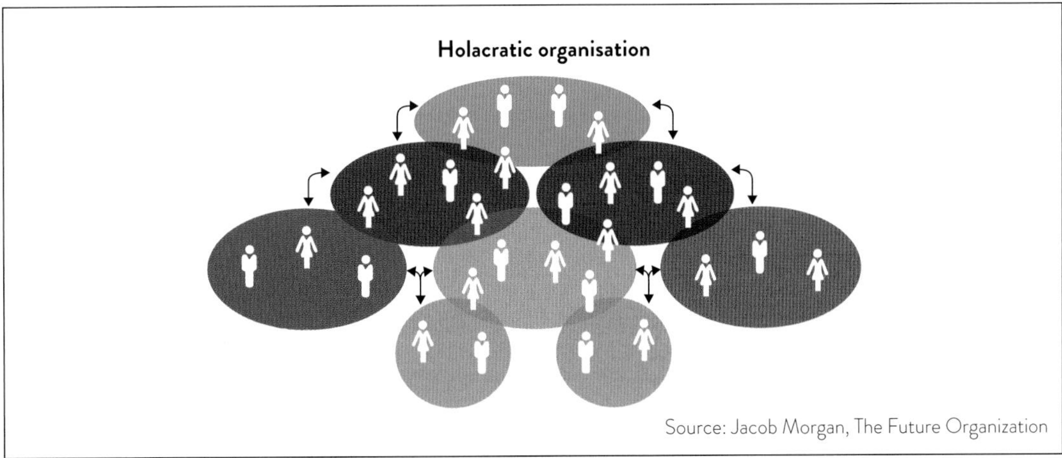

FIGURE 3.8 Example of a holacratic organisational structure

Companies like Zappos have adopted holacracy in order to create a more non-bureaucratic and flexible workplace. They have empowered their employees and catapulted their business productivity – merely by dropping hierarchy and becoming more collaborative. How is your organisation structured? Is it time to get rid of the hierarchies in your business?

Matrix structure

The organisation structures discussed above dominated organisations while the marketplace was relatively stable. As competition, customer demands and business complexity intensified at the end of the 20th century and, more recently, new ways of working these models became less effective. Organisations began experimenting with other ways to organise themselves. Two early models that are still around are the matrix structure and hybrid structures.

Many multinational companies adopted a matrix organisation structure in an attempt to retain the economies of scale and efficiencies of bureaucratic centralisation and the flexibility of customer, geographic location and product structures.

Matrix structures are popular in project-based organisations; for example, architecture, civil engineering and construction companies, where projects run for long periods. They make it possible to spread scarce professional skills around the organisation and tap into the skills and experience of people in other countries. Companies such as Procter & Gamble, Toyota and Unilever are organised in a complex form of the matrix. They coordinate their activities using products, functions and geographic areas. Figure 3.9 shows an organisation chart for a matrix organisation structured around project teams, with team members in each of the projects reporting to two people – their functional manager (vertically) and their project manager (horizontally).

However, matrix organisations are difficult to coordinate and can lead to confusion, conflict and delay due to the need to try to keep two or more bosses happy. They can also result in more bureaucracy, more meetings and slower decisions when people don't understand the reasoning behind how they are intended to work and when trust is absent.

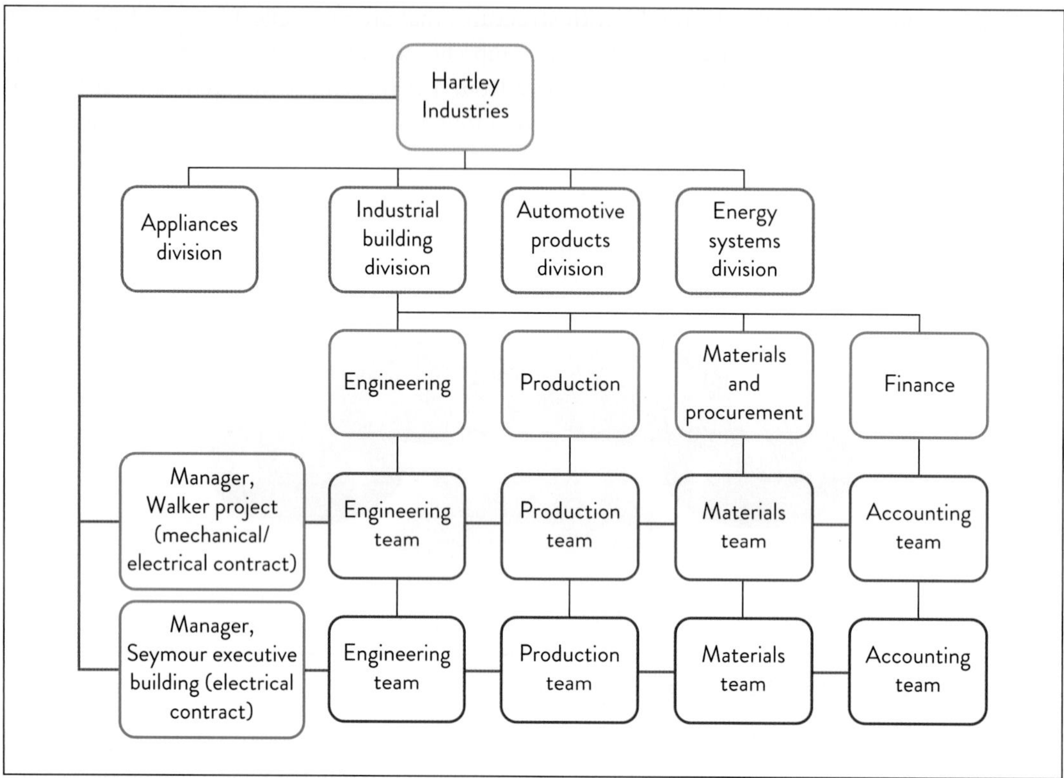

FIGURE 3.9 Matrix organisation chart

With changes to technology and increasingly flexible workplaces, power structures have begun to align more as a **wirearchy**, enabling the flow of power and authority to be based not on hierarchical levels, but on information, trust, credibility, and a focus on results. In general, over the past decade, it has become increasingly clear that through the forces of globalisation, competition and more demanding customers, the structure of many companies has become flatter, less hierarchical, more fluid and even virtual.

Hybrid structures

In the 1990s, business process management introduced another way to structure organisations: organising around core processes. This was a popular alternative to the confusing matrix structures. Few companies at that time adopted a pure core-process design, but rather overlaid a core process on a functional structure or a functional structure over a process structure.

For example, a company might organise its manufacturing operations around processes and arrange the rest of the organisation according to functions. Or it might organise around expert knowledge such as technical research and development, which feeds into the rest of the organisation, designed around product type.

Other organisations retain features such as formal lines of communication, responsibility and authority and formal rules for promotion, while eliminating some of the other features of the classic bureaucracy so that they can operate in a more 'open' way.

Another way to organise

There is one organisation that has thrived for more than 80 years, spans more than 170 countries and has more than two million members who join because they want to. It has virtually no hierarchy and its headquarters employs fewer than 100 people. Thousands of small, self-organising groups elect, not appoint, their leaders. The organisation does not operate according to budgets. It does have a mission but no detailed strategy or operational plans and yet it delivers a complex service to millions of people worldwide. The organisation? Alcoholics Anonymous.

Why traditional structures no longer work

Transferable skills

1.2 Entrepreneurship/small business skills

1.3 Sustainability

1.4 Business operations

1.5 Operations management

The centralised, functionally organised traditional organisation structure, with its vertical, command-and-control relationships, formal and specialised roles, sharp division of responsibilities and rigorous rules and regulations, is unsuited to today's vastly increased business complexity, **capabilities-based competition**, changing customer expectations, globalisation and the growth of knowledge workers, who direct their own performance. Each of these factors intensifies the need to link the relationships between people and functions horizontally rather than vertically.

The efficient execution of business processes (as opposed to discrete tasks) needs flexibility and local decision-making by knowledgeable employees who work together to optimise the process as a whole. It does not need centralised, slow decision-making. Employees need to be relatively autonomous and able to adjust complex processes to meet customer needs, not constrained by rules and hierarchy. They need information they have not traditionally had access to, as well as a strategic understanding of the organisation's strategy and goals. Employees like these don't respond well to the narrow roles and rules of bureaucracy.

Horizontal business processes, which emphasise the relationships between functions, break down 'silos' and allow products and services to be worked on in a continuous stream. The interdependence of tasks for which responsibilities are shared makes employees interdependent, too. To coordinate their efforts across functions, employees need strong horizontal relationships, teamwork and a large dollop of empowerment. Status, so important in hierarchies, is far less relevant than the value each employee can add to a process.

Today's customers often want a complete package of goods or services and effectively providing a product or service 'suite' calls for horizontal integration. The 'HQ' mentality of the centralised hierarchy doesn't work in a global economy, either. As organisations disperse their functions around the globe – design to one country, assembly to another and servicing their customers from call centres in yet another – organisations need flat, fluid structures to link their varied groups of employees and their internal and outsourced functions.

Australian enterprises today are increasingly knowledge- and service-based, and employees increasingly work from home some or all of the time, as well as in locations removed from their parent organisation and even their leader-manager (**virtual working**, **flexible working** and **hub working**).

3.3 Designing contemporary organisations

Organisations have become more complex, containing many diverse and interdependent parts. As you can see from Figure 3.10, it's difficult to predict what will happen when various parts of the business

FIGURE 3.10 Complex organisations

interact because of the interconnectedness of upstream and downstream effects. That means that seemingly simple changes can have unexpected consequences and those consequences can be more significant than expected.

You can also see that these organisations require the personal skills discussed in Part 2 of this text: **self-awareness** and emotional intelligence, the ability to communicate with influence, present information persuasively and negotiate effectively, developing effective working relationships based on trust and confidence, networking skills and taking responsibility for managing your personal productivity.

INDUSTRY INSIGHTS

Strategic capabilities

Changes to an organisation's strategy once occurred only periodically, in response to a major, often technology-based, innovation: think of horses and buggies to trains and then to vehicles; or wood to coal and then to oil. By the end of the 20th century, companies sought to gain a competitive edge by strategically focusing on market position, based on brand value, cost or economies of scale or scope. The recognition that capabilities create value and competitive advantage now makes business process management and capabilities-based organisation structures increasingly important to success.

For example:

- Airbus, Apple and Google excel at technology
- Amazon, Dell and Walmart excel at logistics
- BHP Billiton excels at mining
- Nestlé, Procter & Gamble and Ralph Lauren excel at brand marketing.

These are the strategic capabilities that they organise their business processes around.

Capabilities-based organisations

Autonomy, collaboration, continuous improvement, innovation, interdependence, job empowerment, self-management, shared accountability for performance, shared leadership and mutual trust characterise the multidisciplinary teams of **capabilities-based organisations**. These teams can't work well in authoritarian, hierarchical silo-type structures.

While more traditionally organised operations are likely to know their precise costs, value of sales and so on, they often don't know how frequently they fill orders correctly or how long it takes to get a new product to market profitably. Capabilities-based organisations do. They measure their success on process goals rather than on a function's efficiency. This encourages innovation and continuous improvement and improves productivity and profitability as well as customer and employee satisfaction.

Capabilities and processes

Capabilities are unique abilities, such as a reliable process, close relationships with customers and suppliers, or corporate culture. They are made up of sets of business processes and subprocesses that span functions and business units and that require cross-functional teamwork and strategic investment in support systems. For example, a store might combine a series of processes that effectively link shoppers with the store's website to make online shopping easy and efficient. They might also offer reliable and efficient delivery, based on the subprocesses of product picking and packing, route mapping and delivery, and customer after-service. Together, these processes and subprocesses create a core capability – a capability critical to success – of offering an excellent online shopping experience that is markedly better than that of the store's competitors and which is difficult for them to copy.

Process-based organisations concentrate on teamwork and customers. Because they are more flexible and responsive than traditional organisations, capabilities-based organisations handle change better. Figure 3.11 shows how a capabilities-based organisation might be structured.

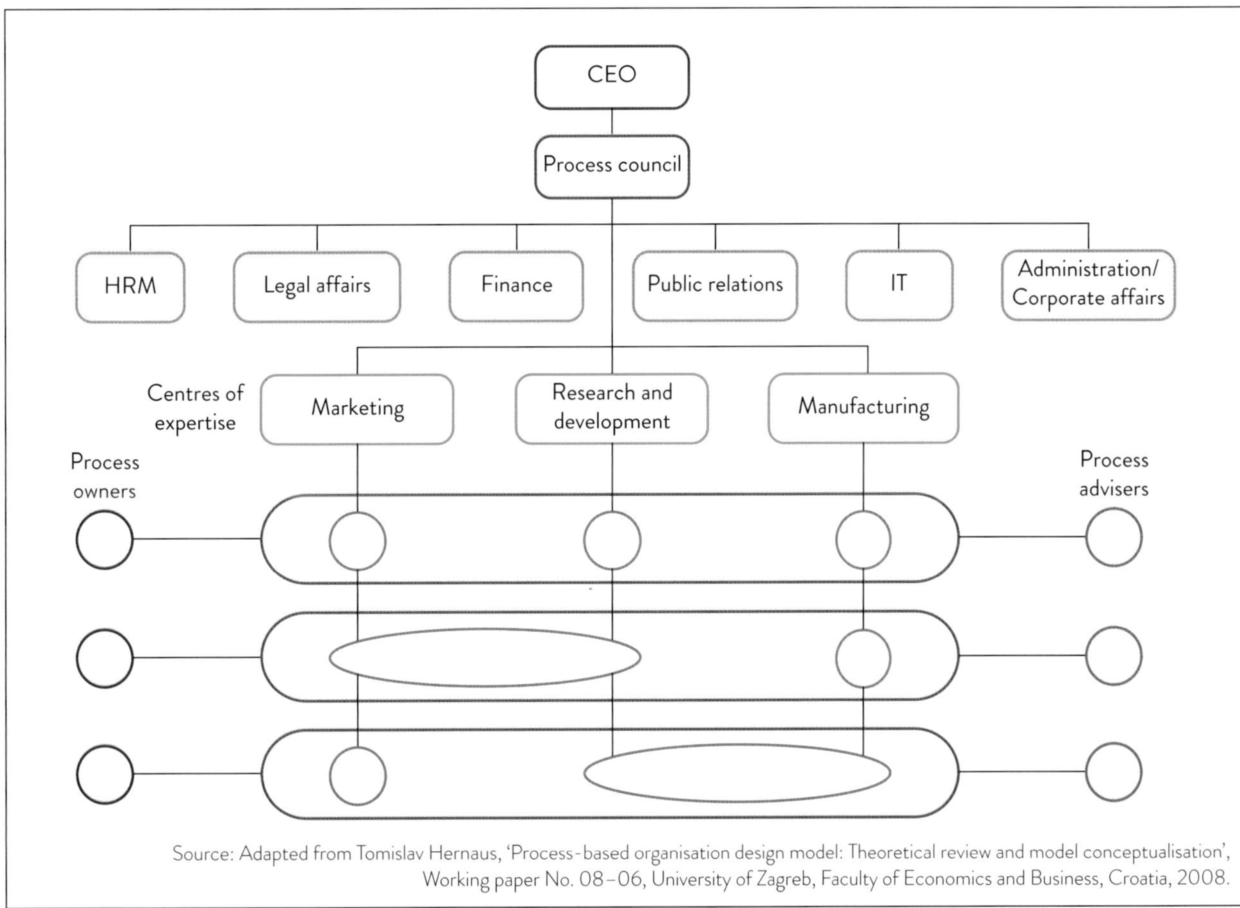

Source: Adapted from Tomislav Hernaus, 'Process-based organisation design model: Theoretical review and model conceptualisation', Working paper No. 08–06, University of Zagreb, Faculty of Economics and Business, Croatia, 2008.

FIGURE 3.11 A capabilities-based organisation structure

Each core process, from beginning to end, is the responsibility of a senior manager, or 'process owner', who has enough influence to obtain the resources needed to make the process flow smoothly. Process advisers support the process owners and centres of expertise, which create, gather and spread knowledge and provide specialist advice to each process. A process council coordinates the core processes and support units (human resource management, legal affairs, etc.), which provide staff support to the various processes.

Major trends in organisation design

Contemporary organisations are looking increasingly different to the traditional pyramidal structures described in Section 3.2. Silos are broken or at least permeable, reducing bureaucracy, increasing flexibility and eliminating non-value-adding work. The teamwork and strong horizontal relationships bring enhanced coordination, further enabling organisational flexibility and responsiveness and driving everyone's attention to the customer, thereby increasing customer satisfaction.

As the more traditional structures continue to give way to alternative structures, employees at all levels are likely to experience many psychological 'rubbing points'. Employees and leader-managers alike need different **mindsets** and skill sets. Employees need to have a more strategic understanding of the organisation's vision and goals, and solid interpersonal and teamworking skills. Leader-managers need to develop a range of interpersonal, conceptual, strategic and leadership skills, as discussed in Chapter 1.

In the following sections we will review the major trends in organisation design.

From actual to virtual

As organisations outsource their assets and non-core functions and activities, they are moving to a virtual structure. They may continue to be represented by a pyramid shape, or be shown in other forms, such as a doughnut, with a core of strategic decision-makers surrounded by contractors and outsourced workers; or perhaps as an atom, with a nucleus of essential core employees surrounded by electrons of contractors and protons of outsourced providers.

From big to small, and centralised to decentralised

Traditional organisation structures can eventually void economies of scale. Organisations have responded by 'deconglomerating' – slimming down divisions and departments through outsourcing non-essential work and saving many of the costs of employment (e.g. employee tax, insurance, office space and superannuation).

Many organisations have moved towards a flexible, **decentralised organisation** with simpler structures that emphasise autonomy and efficiency. Many of these flexible, decentralised organisations have become virtual, collaborative structures focused on capabilities and business processes, and they involve networks of outsourcers and suppliers that all add value.

From pyramids to pancakes

Thanks to extensive downsizing and de-layering, which has stripped out many middle management roles, the tall hierarchies of the past are largely gone; five levels is now more the norm. With fewer levels, leader-managers have wider spans of control, with as many as 10 or 12 people reporting to them.

Whether partially centralised or decentralised, today's flatter, leaner, meaner, nimble organisations push decision-making and responsibility down, opening up lines of communication and allowing information to circulate around the organisation more freely. Flatter organisations also tend to be less rigid and have fewer rules and regulations. This gives people at each level more autonomy and the broader responsibilities, greater creative latitude and decision-making authority that many want. This, in turn, encourages flexibility, innovation and empowerment, meaning, in theory, greater job satisfaction.

From mechanistic to organic, and from silos to clusters

Mechanistic organisations concentrate authority in a small management group at the top (making them centralised). They base their influence, power and prestige on a person's position in the hierarchy (making them bureaucracies). They have a simple, hierarchical structure, with formal channels of communication and chains of command, narrow spans of management, and formalised, specialised and standardised jobs. This suits highly specialised and standardised organisations, such as factories full of assembly lines and other stable, predictable environments. As we've seen, this traditional organisation structure is becoming increasingly redundant in modern Australia.

More organic ways of organising better suit today's dynamic and uncertain environment. There are wider spans of management, less standardisation of jobs and greater flexibility in organic organisations, where influence, power and prestige are based on people's skills and knowledge and the value they can add to the organisation. They may be more confusing, as you can see from Figure 3.12, but many of today's employees prefer the lack of hierarchy, more flexible roles, more open communication and participative decision-making that decentralised organic organisation structures offer.

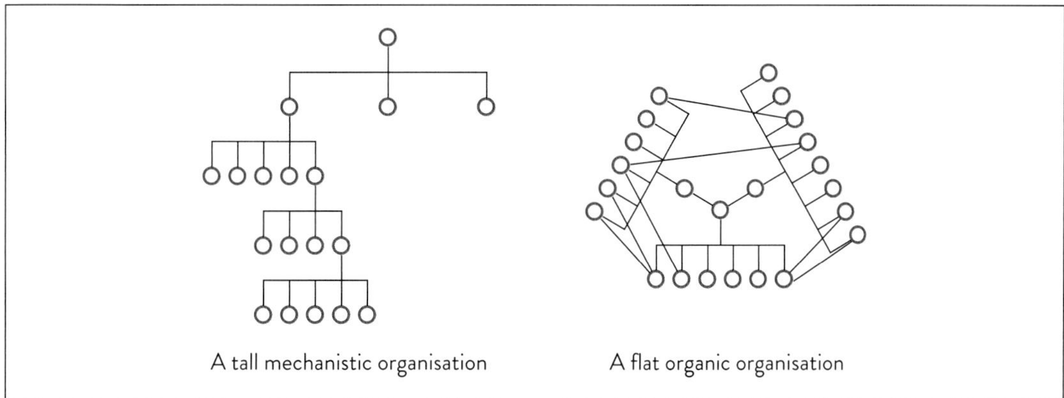

FIGURE 3.12 Mechanistic and organic organisations

As we've seen, silo-style, or functional organisation structures that group employees in terms of the roles they perform, are evolving to capabilities-based organisations made up of multifunctional clusters of people performing a range of roles that span many of the organisation's activities or functions. This increases job interest and provides more varied opportunities, which employees appreciate.

The new normal organisation

The exact future of what an organisation will look like is unclear, but we know that some things are here to stay. The line that separates work life and personal life has faded into true **work–life integration**. Ironically, technology has made this transition possible, but it has also led to a decidedly low-tech reality – this new corporate world has made us value collaboration, integration and togetherness more than ever before. Figure 3.13 lists a few of the 'new normal' elements in many organisations.

Corporate flexibility. Flexible working is here to stay and the productivity gains are clearly shown in our local economy	What the 'office' we once knew will become is not clear, but having a portion of the workforce working from home is proving to be profitable for organisations. This may mean that the office will become a place of interaction and collaboration rather than where we go to work, with conference rooms, meeting spaces and video studios taking up office space.
Work-ready homes. Our homes and internet connection will be relied upon more and more in the future	Home offices and even home video studios will become a priority. As new homes are built or existing ones are remodelled, working from home considerations will be the top priority for many. Technology will be developed to create an environment that more closely resembles hub working of the past than a suburban townhouse.
Embracing e-learning	We all know that learning is now front and centre, and many organisations realise that upskilling and right-skilling are essential for innovation and strategic advantage. Many corporate learning programs involved in-person workshops and seminars, and even though these won't disappear, they'll be utilised for targeted functions and certain employee populations. Face-to-face learning will likely be just a small element of a learning curriculum.
Video virtuosos	The developers behind Zoom, MS Teams, WebEx, Hangouts, Skype and other video communications tools made flexible working possible. Video became fully integrated into the work experience in an astonishing variety of ways, and this looks set to continue into the future.

FIGURE 3.13 The 'new normal' organisation

From purely profit driven to 'doing good'

Despite huge bottom-line pressures to perform financially, many organisations are taking environmental and social concerns, not just profit, into account. They also encourage employees to balance work responsibilities with responsibilities in other spheres of their lives.

Based on the principles of corporate responsibility and conscious capitalism, these organisations aim to offer fulfilling work, add meaning to employees' lives, and extend their focus from 'results only' to 'results plus employee and society's wellbeing'. These organisations expect higher productivity from their employees and increased shareholder value in return.

STUDY TOOLS

QUICK REVIEW

KEY CONCEPT 3.1 

a Review the four general principles of organisation design and explain the purpose of these principles.

KEY CONCEPT 3.2 

a What type of organisations and environments are best suited to structuring by function, customer or market type, geographic location and product type? What are the strengths and weaknesses of each of these types of organisation structure in today's operating environment?

b What is a matrix organisation structure? What are its strengths and weaknesses?

c List the reasons that traditional organisation structures are not as effective in today's operating environment.

KEY CONCEPT 3.3 

a What are the key characteristics of a capabilities-based organisation? What type of organisation and operating environment do they best suit?

b What has triggered the move towards virtual and partially virtual organisations?

c Why have organisations become flatter and more organic?

BUILD YOUR SKILLS

KEY CONCEPT 3.1 

a Explain how a suitable organisation structure can be a powerful competitive advantage.

b Interview someone who has experienced an organisational restructure firsthand. Find out all you can about the positives and negatives of their experience, for the employees as well as for the organisation as a whole, trying to understand what helped to make these experiences positive or negative. Draw some general conclusions about the best way to help your work team maintain its morale and productivity during and immediately after an organisational restructure.

KEY CONCEPT 3.3 

a Describe the organisation framework, either traditional or contemporary, that you believe is best suited to the present day for the industry you work in, or aspire to work in, and explain your reasoning.

b What would be the dangers in transforming the Australian Taxation Office into an organic, matrix-type organisation? Would these dangers be outweighed by the advantages? Why or why not?

WORKPLACE ACTIVITIES

KEY CONCEPT 3.2 

a Does a traditional organisation design suit your organisation? Why or why not? Which traditional organisation design would best suit your organisation?

KEY CONCEPT 3.3 

a Would a capabilities-based structure suit your organisation? Why or why not? If your organisation were to introduce a capabilities-based structure, which functions or departments would you recommend be linked first? What would be your objectives in linking them?

b What changes in organisation design can you predict for your organisation over the next few years? Why do you believe these changes will take place? Interview your HR manager if you need to.

c Obtain an organisation chart for your organisation and discuss how its structure affects internal relationships and your organisation's ways of working.

EXTENSION ACTIVITIES

Referring to the Snapshot at the beginning of this chapter, answer the following questions:

1 How could you disrupt this approach to an induction for these new recruits? What might make this formal induction more engaging or interactive for these participants?

2 Think about what you might need the inductees to know or understand as a result of their high-level introduction to the organisation as you look at ways to improve this approach.

CASE STUDY 3

LANCY'S LABORATORIES

Paul Lancy started his dental laboratory in 2004 as a sole trader, making dentures, dental implants and crowns. Due to the high quality of his work, his laboratory grew quickly and, in 2006, his brother Peter qualified and joined him as his partner. At Peter's urging, they began concentrating on customer service and the lab's business mushroomed to the point where they hired six additional technicians, a lab assistant and an office administrator. They also began doing facial reconstructive implants for the cranio-facial unit at City Hospital.

By 2011, Paul and Peter employed nine technicians, two full-time and one part-time lab assistants and two office administrators. On the advice of their accountant, Lancy's Laboratories became a proprietary limited company. They also began an apprenticeship scheme to ensure a continual flow of qualified technicians so that the business could continue to expand. As time went on, the brothers embraced the move towards partnering, developing strong and mutually beneficial links with their suppliers, which further strengthened the business.

In 2018, the company invested in 3D manufacturing technology, which initiated an organisational restructuring. Unfortunately, five technician jobs and the lab assistant's positions were made redundant by the new technology. Two technicians were retrained to program and operate the new 3D printers and the company ceased its apprenticeship scheme, replacing it with an ad hoc intake of people they could train to use the new technology.

With all the changes, the once-happy employees seemed a bit 'flat' and the brothers were wondering how to re-engage them so that productivity, quality and their trading partnerships don't suffer.

Questions

1 What are the key issues facing the company? Which is the most important to resolve and what would be your objectives for resolving it? How could you measure your success?
2 What are some possible approaches for resolving the major issues?
3 If you were advising Paul and Peter on organisation design, what general principles and organisation design concepts would you recommend, and why?
4 How would you expect a revised organisation structure to influence morale and efficiency in the lab? How might it affect relationships with partner labs, suppliers and customers, and among Lancy's employees?

CHAPTER ENDNOTE

1 Alan G. Ingham, George Levinger, James Graves, Vaughn Peckham, 'The Ringelmann effect: Studies of group size and group performance', *Journal of Experimental Social Psychology*, Vol. 10, No. 4, pp. 371–384.

CHAPTER

THE INFORMAL ORGANISATION

After completing this chapter, you will be able to:

4.1 understand the webs of human relationships in an organisation and how they influence each other

4.2 outline your organisation's culture, subculture and norms and why they are critical to your success, and the success of your organisation and your team

4.3 understand the effectiveness of the relationships inside your organisation and work team.

TRANSFERABLE SKILLS

The following transferable skills are covered in this chapter:

1 **Business competence**
- **1.4** Business operations
- **1.5** Operations management

2 **Critical thinking and problem solving**
- **2.1** Critical thinking
- **2.2** Personal effectiveness
- **2.3** Business strategy

3 **Social competence**
- **3.1** Teamwork/relationships
- **3.2** Verbal communication
- **3.3** Written communication
- **3.4** Leadership

OVERVIEW

When people come together, they develop specific ways of working and relating to each other; this is the organisation's culture. It is the mix of invisible, largely unconscious rules, values and rituals that regulate what people do and how they do it. An organisation's culture also includes what behaviours and practices are unwelcome. Then there's the power hierarchy that develops whenever people come together. Individuals jostle for their place in the pecking order – this is organisational politics and power. Organisational culture, politics and power affect everyone.

Understanding the culture – and subcultures – of your workplace, and aligning with them, helps you achieve your individual goals and your team's goals. And while understanding and working within the official hierarchy of your organisation is important (explained in Chapter 3), understanding and working within the unofficial hierarchies, the 'relational' networks and the 'political' structures of your organisation, is crucial. This chapter shows you how to weave your way through the complex and tricky maze of the informal organisation.

SNAPSHOT

Sussing out the team

Arana walks into his new department. He has been a line manager before but this is his first role at one of the company's subsidiaries. As per his plan, he asks everyone to grab a coffee and join him in his office. He begins by saying a few words about himself in order to establish his technical expertise as well as the fact that he has led successful teams at the company's head office. (He thinks it won't hurt his new team members to know that he knows important people at head office and has access to information and more than a few scarce resources.)

To get the team talking, he asks each person, in turn, for a quick rundown on their responsibilities and current projects. He also explains that he will meet with everyone individually over the next few days. Then he throws the meeting open for questions.

What Arana is really interested in is who pipes up first and what questions and comments they have. He watches the team members carefully to see how they interact with one another. In his experience, this is an important clue to how well a team works together and, therefore, how much work he has ahead of him to develop the team climate and culture he is looking for.

4.1 Uncovering the relationships

Organisation charts reflect the official organisation structure, or formal organisation. As important as the officially recognised lines of authority, communication, relationships and policies are to the way a workplace functions, they are only part of the picture. The other part of the picture is the network of people working together (or not) to achieve a shared purpose.

Transferable skills

2.2 Personal effectiveness

3.1 Teamwork/ relationships

3.2 Verbal communication

Human networks

The webs of human relationships and the unofficial power hierarchy inside organisations are known as the *informal organisation*. They determine how the organisation really works and are far more than the sum of the individual employees who are part of them. Each subgroup, or network, has its own beliefs, customs and energy.

When seen like this, organisations are complex, ever-evolving organic systems. The more that people trust each other, and the more attuned to sharing and learning the organisation **culture** is, the more people can talk freely, explore ideas and develop their own views. This is how tacit knowledge becomes fresh learning and innovation, and this is what a 'healthy' organisation is all about. (See Chapter 8 for more information on networking.)

What do people talk about in an organisation's networks? Conversation can be energising, enriching and positive, or it can be draining, manipulative and negative. Do the discussions in your organisation's networks and between your team members contribute to a healthy future for the organisation and your team?

Systematic chaos

When setting up responsibilities, procedures, measures of success and so on, management traditionally has worked on one part of an organisation at a time. Then came *systems theory*. A *system* is a collection of elements that together create a complex, meaningful whole. When you remove or change one part of a system, the rest of the system changes. A pile of sand is not a system – when you remove a grain of sand, you've still got a pile of sand. Bodies, cars, **ecosystems** and societies are systems – when you remove the kidneys, the body doesn't work; remove the battery, the car doesn't work; remove a species, the environment doesn't work. Each part, or *subsystem*, plays a special role, making the whole system far more than the sum of its parts.

Organisations are systems, too. When you change the way you provide a service, it affects the whole organisation. When you introduce a new way of working, like virtual working to a team (a subsystem), the people in that team change, as does their work together, which can affect the whole organisation.

Systems have inputs, processes, outputs and outcomes. Information and materials come in (inputs). Something is done with them (processes) to produce a product or service (outputs). The outcome is profit or some other measure of achievement for the organisation and satisfaction for the customer.

Systems can also share feedback to improve performance. Feedback can come from inside the system (e.g. the people working in it, and results attained) or from outside the system (e.g. from customers and the community).

Thinking about your organisation as a system made up of interwoven subsystems (functions, information, teams and processes) helps you see it from a broader perspective and find and interpret patterns and events. It helps you understand how the various parts of the organisation are interrelated and how each affects, and is affected by, all the others. This, in turn, helps you coordinate work so that the organisation as a whole runs smoothly and efficiently.

Chaos theory is an extension of systems theory. It considers unpredictable, complex systems and offers helpful information about organisational systems, including:

- Organisations are not machines that can be controlled by rules and procedures.
- Small, even seemingly insignificant, actions and events can have large and unpredictable consequences (or no consequences at all).
- Systems are always changing.
- Too much control kills creativity, innovation and productivity.
- You cannot predict the behaviour of a system from the behaviour of its parts because the whole is more than the sum of its parts.

This makes changing an organisation's culture difficult and time consuming. In fact, only two things can change an organisation's culture quickly: everyone needs to understand the need for the change (generally, so that the organisation can survive) and full support from the top.

4.2 Diagnosing organisation culture

Transferable skills

2.2 Personal effectiveness

2.3 Business strategy

3.1 Teamwork/relationships

3.2 Verbal communication

3.3 Written communication

3.4 Leadership

> Company culture is the promise you make to your candidates and employees about the environment they can expect to work in and the values upon which your business operates.
>
> Katie Burke, Chief People Office, Hubspot

Every organisation has a culture – it is impossible not to have one. No matter how awesome an organisation's vision and mission is, and how splendid its strategy, when it doesn't have a strong culture and operating system to pull it all together and make it happen, it is doomed to fail. Because it is difficult to reproduce, an organisation's culture is a core **capability** and can be a distinctive competitive advantage.

When employees feel 'at home' in a high-performance culture – when their values, mindsets and ways of operating are a good fit with the culture – the path to high performance is smooth. This makes culture one of an organisation's most powerful tools. In fact, the 'right' culture is increasingly essential to ensuring an organisation's long-term viability; it can make or break an organisation.

Technology is predictable, and work systems and people's behaviour are reasonably predictable – but only when you understand the culture. Organisation culture drives an organisation's performance. It can energise employees and drive engagement and productivity, or it can drain energy and drag down engagement and performance, which undermines long-term success. Culture is considered so important in driving behaviour that it and other qualitative information are now included, along with the usual quantitative data of hitting targets, when calculating remuneration and other non-financial benefits.

An organisation's culture is like a blueprint of how it operates internally and how it relates to its external environment. It determines the way people work together – the shared attitudes, behaviours, beliefs, understandings and values by which employees operate. Made up of employees' shared assumptions, expectations, mindsets and ways of working, culture is the glue that holds people, teams and functions together. It is also an essential part of an organisation's **employer value proposition** and its **employer brand**, which influences an organisation's ability to recruit, retain, engage and motivate employees. Figure 4.1 summarises the components of an organisation's culture.

It is easier to experience an organisation's culture and a team's **subculture** and **norms**, than to describe it. This is because the rules or codes of behaviour that influence employees to behave in certain ways are usually implicit, or not stated. Yet these unstated 'rules' affect how an organisation goes about its business, including:

- how carefully and quickly people make and execute decisions
- how much people collaborate with each other to produce a better product or service
- how seriously people view their accountabilities
- how thoroughly people do their work
- which emotions are expressed and which are concealed.

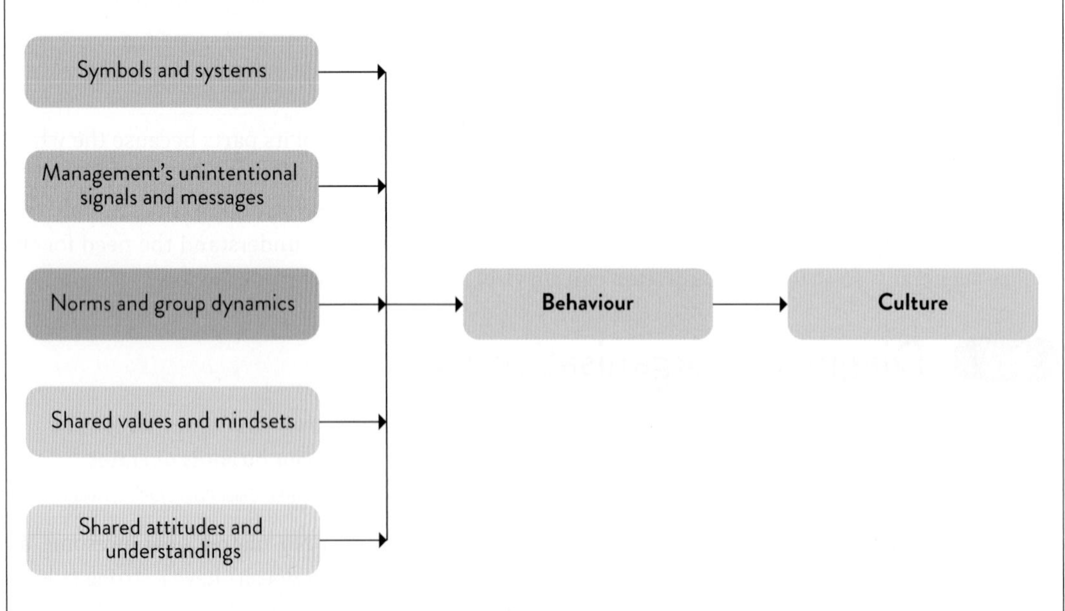

FIGURE 4.1 The components of culture

Four organisation cultures

The Organizational Culture Assessment Instrument (OCAI) was developed by University of Michigan business professors Robert E. Quinn and Kim S. Cameron. The framework focuses on four distinct types of company cultures: clan, adhocracy, hierarchy and market. These are shown in Figure 4.2. The framework is broken down in more detail in Table 4.1.

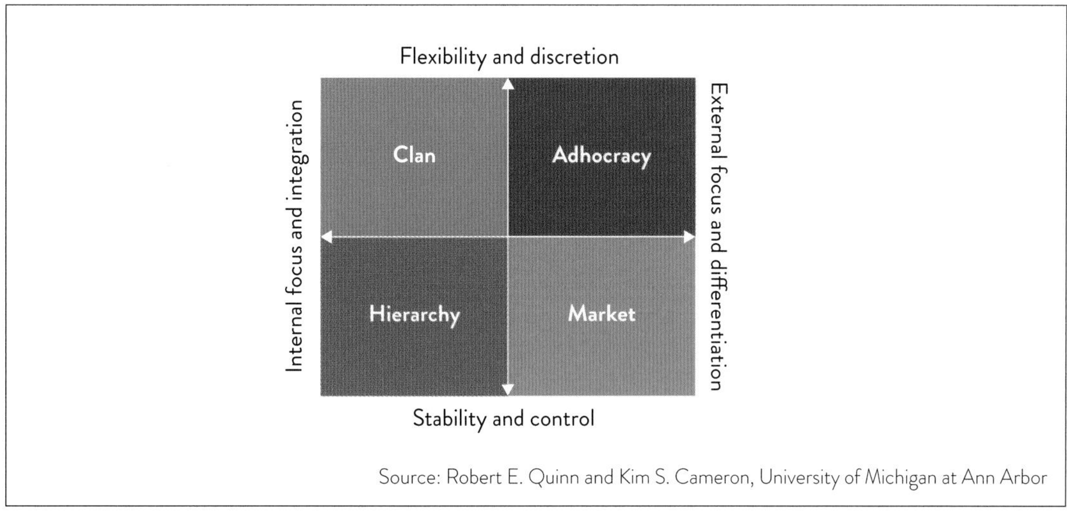

FIGURE 4.2 Competing values framework focuses on four types of company cultures: clan, adhocracy, hierarchy and market

TABLE 4.1 Four types of culture

Tribal culture	This culture is a safe tribe where everyone belongs and everyone has a lot in common with each other. This culture operates like a warm, comfortable and collaborative family. Examples are Google and Zappos.
Agile culture	This culture is fast paced, nimble and innovative. They disrupt, take risks and interrupt traditional models of business, assumptions and ways of thinking. Examples are Facebook, Uber, and Fintech companies.
Task focused culture	This culture is focused on delivering results, getting the job done and closing the deal. It is often competitive in nature both externally and internally. They are bottom line driven and aim to make as much profit and take as much market share as possible. Some Airlines, tech companies and hospitality businesses can have this type of culture.
Top down culture	This culture is about following the rules and having a procedure and process for everything. This keeps mistakes, risks and costs low. Managers focus on compliance and adherence rather than inspiration and innovation. Examples are Government, law enforcement and hospitals.

Source: Lin Grensing-Pophal, '4 distinct types of corporate culture – which is yours?' HR Daily Advisor, 12 April 2018. https://hrdailyadvisor.blr.com/2018/04/12/4-distinct-types-corporate-culture

Corporate culture is a somewhat vague term, but it can have a huge impact on the fortune of a company and the company's employees. What kind of culture does your organisation have? Is it the right culture to help you succeed in the market you're in and with the customers you wish to serve? While corporate culture is notoriously difficult to change, it's not something that should be left to chance or overlooked.

Transferable skills
3.1 Teamwork/relationships
3.2 Verbal communication
3.3 Written communication
3.4 Leadership

Toxic culture

A **toxic culture** is one where the workplace is plagued by fighting, drama and unhappy employees to the point that productivity and the wellbeing of the people in the office are affected. The following five signs might indicate a toxic culture:

1 little to no enthusiasm among employees
2 a pervasive fear of failure or fear of being blamed
3 constant dysfunction and confusion
4 never-ending gossip and drama
5 high employee turnover.

Subcultures

Inside every organisation there are subgroups made up of departments, work groups and networks. Each has its own subculture or operating code: its own common dress, 'hangouts', language, performance expectations and rituals.

Get to know the subgroups in your organisation, what functions they perform, which are the least and most influential, the least and most knowledgeable, and so on. Who are their **informal leaders**? Who is in the 'inner circle' and who is excluded from it? Knowing what makes one group different from another means that you can work with members of different subcultures more effectively. It means you can observe their unwritten rules and adjust your own behaviour and style to 'fit in'.

By and large, the CEO and senior managers, by their behaviours and actions, set the overall culture of an organisation. Employees interpret what they should and shouldn't do from what leader-managers do and don't do (not what they say). People take their cues from the team leader-manager.

Transferable skills
3.1 Teamwork/relationships
3.2 Verbal communication
3.3 Written communication
3.4 Leadership

Norms

Every team develops its own unique ways of how members work individually and together, solve problems and air disagreements, based on the wider organisation's culture, their leadership and the experiences group members have together. Gradually, a team's accepted behaviour patterns and ways of working together become clearer and more recognisable and, eventually, they become established habits. Known as norms, they are the unwritten traditions and codes of behaviour, the (usually) unspoken 'rules' of 'how we do things around here'.

Fit in or pay the price

A work group's norms and culture shape, and even dictate, its members' behaviour. Everyone wants to be accepted and liked. When people don't fit in by doing what is expected, the rest of the group snubs them. To avoid this, most new employees spend a lot of effort and energy trying to figure out the organisation's and team's culture and norms by analysing the organisation's corporate values and symbols, observing the people around them and working out their team's work habits and traditions.

When new team members struggle to understand the culture and norms that now surround them, they often unwittingly disrupt those norms and set the team back. It makes sense to save new team members any misunderstanding or embarrassment by taking the time to explain the team's culture and norms to them as soon as they start their new jobs. (Chapter 13 and Chapter 14 have more information on building your team's culture and norms and how to help new team members fit into your team quickly.)

Peter Drucker once said: 'Culture eats strategy for breakfast'; this indicates that it is important to ensure your team's culture and norms support your organisation's values, vision and strategy. You should also be sure that your team's culture and norms reward those who achieve goals and those who work well together. When you find your team's codes of behaviour holding the team back from achieving its task, meet the team members involved and discuss this openly to explore better ways of working together.

Here are some ways you can build a strong team culture and norms that support your organisation's values and goals:

- Be positive.
- Generate pride in the organisation and show how individual team members and the team as a whole contribute to it.
- Make it clear what you stand for.
- Make your team's purpose and goals clear to everyone.
- Pay attention to details.
- Walk your talk.

When you don't support your team and organisation in this way, be prepared to pay the price of a negative team culture and norms that deliver poor results.

The batik shirt

Paul Biddle works with a British Government body called the Stabilisation Unit, helping to establish peace and security in countries affected by conflict and instability. He needs to apply his management skills in extremely challenging, hostile and sometimes life-threatening situations. Thorough preparation and cultural insight, he believes, are keys to success in such difficult circumstances.

While researching Indonesian culture before deployment to Java, he discovered that all Indonesians, even those in uniform, traditionally abandon normal work attire every Friday and don a batik shirt showing the region they hail from. One of the first things he did when he arrived in Indonesia was purchase a bright batik shirt. A few days later, an important meeting with local officials fell on a Friday and he wore the shirt. The batik shirt broke down the barriers that normally take at least six months to crumble. 'Just a little thing like that ... opened all the doors.'[1]

Ethics

Transferable skills

3.1 Teamwork/relationships

An important part of culture is the ethics that employees live their working lives by. You've probably heard about the 'bad banks', and you may have heard about the 'good banks'. The Teachers Mutual Bank is the only Australian institution to make the Ethisphere Institute's 2020 list of the world's most ethical companies.[2]

Then there's PayPal, whose CEO Dan Shulman cancelled plans for PayPal's global operations centre in North Carolina, US, where people can be legally discriminated against for their sexuality, saying: 'Becoming an employer in North Carolina, where members of our teams will not have equal rights under the law, is simply untenable'. And while nearly two-thirds of Australia's 1500 largest companies pay tax, more than one-third do not, including Apple, ExxonMobil, Hoyts, Lendlease, McDonald's Asia Pacific, Qantas, the Ten Network, Virgin Australia and Vodaphone. (There are, of course, legitimate reasons not to pay tax, such as not making a profit.)[3]

An independent review exposed a dysfunctional culture of favouritism, unfairness and fear in the Australian Olympic Committee after months of bitter infighting.[4] Corporate culture is acknowledged to have been important in recent corporate scandals in Australia, such as underpaying 7-Eleven workers, manipulating financial data at Target, and ANZ's trading scandal. The Commonwealth Bank has been plagued by bad corporate behaviour, including its financial planning 'issue', CommInsure's unconscionable practices, and multiple money laundering breaches that resulted in an independent inquiry from the Australian Prudential Regulation Authority into accountability, culture and governance at the bank, an Australian Securities and Investments Commission investigation, a shareholder class action and the resignation of the CEO.

When an organisation's culture accepts shady practices, employees see their own behaviour through the organisation's cultural lens and their shady behaviour looks okay, even when it isn't. When an organisation's culture sets and upholds clear and ethical guidelines, employees know unmistakably what's expected of them and see their own behaviour through that cultural lens.

Denmark, Finland and New Zealand are the world's cleanest countries in terms of business ethics. 'Very clean' countries score over 80 (out of 100) in the Global Corruption Perception Index. Australia used to be up there with the best but slipped to 'clean' with a score of 79 in 2015 and declined further to 77 in 2020.[5]

With the public's increasing appetite for ethical investments, operating with integrity is a key component of success. The days of 'profit at any cost' are fast coming to an end (for more on this, see Chapter 2).

How do we get there?

For organisations, behaving in an ethical way means applying the highest ethical standards to decision-making. Managers should take the lead through their management actions. Some suggestions for fostering an ethical workplace and encouraging an ethical culture include:

- lead a discussion in your next team meeting about a problem within your workplace
- generate discussion about values and principles when a major decision needs to be made
- ensure you are familiar with your organisation's code of conduct and scrutinise your own behaviour
- challenge any misconduct within your workplace that you see
- in conjunction with the human resources department, plan steps on how you can become a values-based organisation
- display the values and employment principles in a prominent position within the workplace.[6]

Transferable skills

2.1 Critical thinking

2.2 Personal effectiveness

2.3 Business strategy

3.4 Leadership

What organisations do you think of when you think of an ethical organisation? What have they done that makes you believe they are an ethical organisation?

4.3 Working with group dynamics

Transferable skills

3.1 Teamwork/relationships

3.2 Verbal communication

3.3 Written communication

3.4 Leadership

Coming together is a beginning; keeping together is progress; working together is success.

Henry Ford (Ford Motor Company), in Erika Andersen, '21 quotes from Henry Ford on business, leadership and life', *Forbes*, 31 May 2013.

The way people develop and manage their relationships inside an organisation, within a team and with their external suppliers and customers is an important feature of culture and norms – and therefore another key element of an organisation's success. These relationships, based on the way people interact with each other, are known as **group dynamics**. A team's dynamics shape how its members go about doing the team's work, together and individually. Along with its culture, a team's dynamics is another key determinant of its productivity and results. Let's explore the main elements and influences on group dynamics.

Cohesion

The members of a cohesive team have a strong sense of 'us'. Its members want to belong to it and contribute to it. To build your team's cohesiveness, help members to develop a sense of team identity and pride along with a high-performance culture and norms. Provide opportunities for team members to get to know each other as diverse individuals, and respect what each member brings to the team.

A word of caution though! A highly cohesive team that is homogeneous (non-diverse), rather than heterogeneous (diverse), is prone to **groupthink**, particularly when it lacks robust group decision-making processes. This occurs when members of a team get along so well that they are loath to contradict what appears to be the wish or belief of the majority. This holds back the team's performance and even encourages the group to make dangerous decisions. When you think the team you lead may be suffering from groupthink, you need to act. (You can find out more about groupthink in Chapter 26, and what steps you can take to minimise it.)

Communication patterns

Transferable skills

1.4 Business operations

1.5 Operations management

2.1 Critical thinking

2.3 Business strategy

3.1 Teamwork/relationships

3.2 Verbal communication

3.3 Written communication

3.4 Leadership

Communication patterns influence your team's efficiency, productivity and morale. They can help you work out the informal status and power of its members, how effectively they use each other's skills to get the job done, and their working climate and cohesion. It is important to pay attention to whether members of your team speak to each other formally or informally, the tone of voice they use and their body language. Are their communications clear? What channels of communication do they use? Who talks to whom? When? Where? For how long? Who is left out? Do people really listen to each other? You should also note how you communicate with your team, and how they might view your communication style. Do you share information about yourself and your life outside work, and do you find out about theirs? You don't need to pry or become 'best friends' – just develop some bonds between yourself and team members to forge a strong team.

Decision-making

The more you need your team to participate in and support decisions that affect them and the team's operations, the more important it is to ensure that everyone in the team understands and follows effective decision-making procedures. Groups are constantly making decisions. What are these decisions about? How are they made? Does everyone have a say or do only a few people express opinions? Is silence taken for agreement? Are issues discussed so that consensus is reached or does one person or a subgroup make most of the important decisions?

Group roles

Everyone wants to have a role in the group, whether as a spokesperson, an expert or a clown. One person might generate enthusiasm and start the ball rolling on new initiatives. Someone else might be able to relieve tension with an appropriate joke. Another might be the one to bring people up to speed when they've been away on leave or travelling.

People take on roles that meet their own needs. Some of the roles people take it upon themselves to fill are helpful, or *functional*, while others are unhelpful, or *dysfunctional*, to the efficient functioning of a team. And some roles can be either functional or dysfunctional, depending on how they are 'played'. For instance, a *clown* can be disruptive or can relieve tension; a *gatekeeper* can shut people out or see that everyone has a say; a *devil's advocate* can pour water on good ideas or point out potential problems and how to fix them.

Observe your team to get a feeling for who performs which roles, and which roles help or hinder the way the team works together to achieve its tasks. Do you sense any friction over who holds certain roles? How noticeable is that friction? The roles that team members take up (and those they avoid) say a lot about the team's dynamics.

Team roles can be divided into task and process roles, although in practice, many serve both task and process functions, as shown in **Figure 4.3**. (For more on group roles and task and process matters in groups, see Chapter 13.)

FUNCTIONAL ROLES	DYSFUNCTIONAL ROLES
Task roles	**Task roles**
Analyser	Aggressor
Clarifier	Competer
Consensus builder	Complainer
Coordinator	Critic
Follower	Dissenter
Ideas builder	Dominator
Ideas person	Enthusiasm deflater
Information giver	Fault finder
Information seeker	Ideas squasher
Initiator	Manipulator
Mediator	Nit-picker
Opinion seeker	Saboteur
Standard setter	Show-off
Summariser	Special-interest speaker
Systems organiser	Stubborn donkey
Teacher, coach, trainer	Subject changer
	Sympathy seeker

FUNCTIONAL ROLES	DYSFUNCTIONAL ROLES
Process roles	**Process roles**
Compromiser	Approval seeker
Encourager	Conflict avoider/seeker
Friend	Disruptive clown
Gatekeeper	Recognition/status seeker
Harmoniser	Sarcastic remark maker
Tension reliever	Sniper/cynic
Withdrawer	
Yea sayer	

FIGURE 4.3 Functional and dysfunctional roles in teams

Informal leaders

Someone in your work team is probably an informal leader – the person others go to with ideas, questions or complaints, for advice, assistance or just a chat. Is it the person who gets the best results, who serves customers best, or who has the most expertise or technical knowledge? Or perhaps it's the most articulate and dissatisfied group member spearheading a group of discontented workers? Having an informal leader in your work team doesn't necessarily mean that you aren't leading properly. It may mean that the informal leader is meeting certain team and individual needs that you, the formal leader, cannot or should not meet.

Team members look to informal leaders, as much as they do to their official team leader, to see how they should and should not do things. The cues informal leaders send about how fast to work, how to dress, how much to cooperate with management, how courteous to be to customers and suppliers and so on, are stronger than official policy or procedures on these matters. This makes the role of informal leader important in establishing and maintaining group norms and team dynamics. These people 'set the pace' and this 'pace' can be in your favour or oppose what you're trying to accomplish. Rather than try to eliminate any informal leaders in your work group, ensure that they are working with you and not against you.

The standing of informal leaders is precarious, especially when the composition of the work group changes frequently or when the work location, product or task changes. As a group's needs change, so too does its choice of informal leader.

Participation

Transferable skills

3.1 Teamwork/relationships

3.4 Leadership

In your team, there will be individuals who are high participators and those who are low participators. How are the high and the low participators treated? Is anyone left out and, if so, why? Who generates enthusiasm and 'keeps the ball rolling'? Who contributes ideas and suggestions? Who is the first to notice something going wrong and bring it to the team's attention? Answering these questions will give you clues to the team's priorities and what it values.

Power and influence

Power and influence help you create productive relationships, engage and motivate employees, gain support, and inspire and persuade people. They can also often 'get you what you want' without resorting to coercion, manipulation or threats. Your position power comes from your official place in the organisation structure, and the resources you officially control. It gives you some authority over the behaviour of others. In the past, leader-managers relied heavily on this formal power, but this reliance has shrivelled in recent years to favour the 'servant leader' approach. This approach shares power and control in order to drive engagement.

People need autonomy – a feeling of choice – in order to be motivated. Position power generally removes that autonomy. People today are more likely to grant you respect because of your personal knowledge and qualities based on your personal authority, or personal power, than because of the position you hold. Attributes such as honesty, integrity, self-respect and respect for others, strength of personal vision and values and trustworthiness are particularly important in building personal power – the more important and reliable power base of today's leader-managers. (Part 2 of this text explains how to build your personal power.) As shown in **Figure 4.4**, three of the six sources of power are based on position power, or formal authority, and three are based on personal power, which you must earn.

LEGITIMATE POWER	Refers to your right to issue orders and instructions and someone else's duty to carry them out. When team members feel they 'should' do something because 'the boss says so', they are responding to legitimate power.
COERCIVE POWER	Based on fear. It rests on your ability to discipline. When employees do something in order to avoid an unpleasant outcome, for example to avoid criticism or to avoid you withholding overtime or cutting back their working hours (and therefore earnings), they are responding to coercive power.
REWARD POWER	Based on your ability to distribute something of value, such as overtime, interesting work assignments, pay increases, positive performance appraisals and promotion. When followers do as you ask in the hope of getting something in return, they are responding to reward power.
EXPERT POWER	Comes from your special skills and knowledge, usually gained through study and experience, and your 'track record'. When employees do as you ask because they assume you know best, your expert power is influencing them.
PROXIMITY POWER	Comes from the interesting information and knowledge you have and can share with others. When people do as you ask or suggest because you know or have access to someone important or assume you know something they don't know, your proximity power is influencing them.
REFERENT POWER	That special something that attracts followers, based on the goodwill, liking and respect that you have earned. When employees do as you ask because they want to support you or cooperate with you, your referent power is influencing them.

FIGURE 4.4 Six sources of power and influence

Power and influence rarely lie with just one person. More often they rest with a group of people, a coalition, who respect each other and share similar ideas, values and experiences. These people combine their power and influence to achieve a shared vision for their organisation or their work team.

Are you politically astute enough to know who has power and influence in your organisation and include them in your networks? To find out who actually has power and influence, you need to be able to read between the lines of your formal organisation chart and 'see' the invisible connections, like those shown in Figure 4.5.

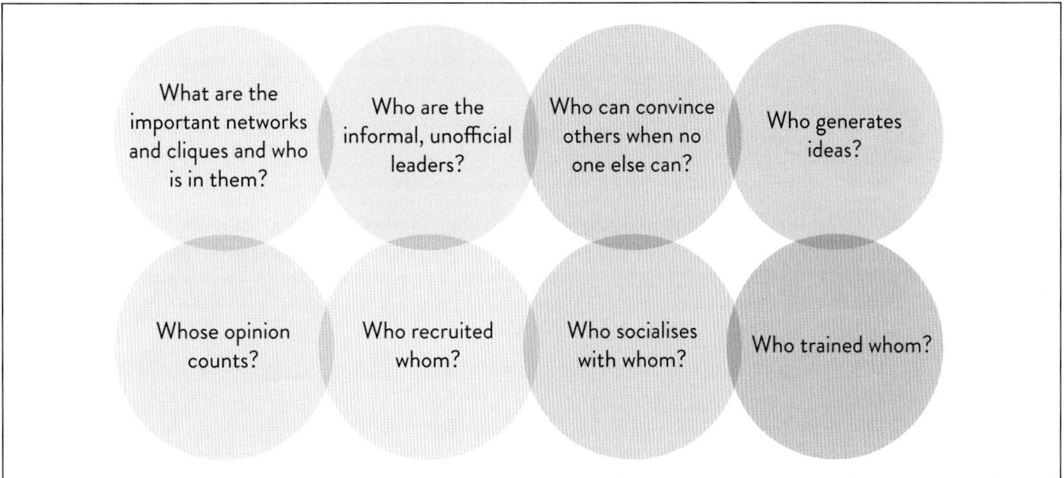

FIGURE 4.5 Invisible connections

Think about the influencers in your work group. Who influences whom and how? Who has the power to 'tell' others what to do? Who is listened to when they speak? Who do others copy? Who do others admire? When those wielding informal power and influence are doing so in ways inconsistent with the team's goals, trouble is brewing!

Your informal power

Expertise attracts both admiration and respect. You derive much of your authority as a leader-manager from your experience, job knowledge and training. You ideally have some expertise in the technology and work of your group. Knowledge of the organisation as a system and how it operates (its culture, subcultures and networks) is also part of job knowledge. Knowing what needs to be done, and where, when, why and how to do it, also earns you respect and influence. Consistency and dependability strengthen your expert power, as do your values and ethics.

Being 'in the know' brings you proximity power. This might include explaining the reasons behind a decision or passing on information about behind-the-scenes goings-on in the organisation. Proximity power lends itself to 'trade-offs' of favours, information or resources, and the scarcer those items are, the greater your proximity power.

Referent power is also known as 'charismatic power'. Your referent power comes in part from your ability to build cooperative and supportive working relationships; people skills play a part in building this aspect of referent power. Acting consistently to a clear set of personal guidelines and standards that complement and support the organisation's standards, and not deviating from them, is very powerful and attractive to others. Integrity is the other main contributor to referent power. Figure 4.6 lists four ways to build your influence.

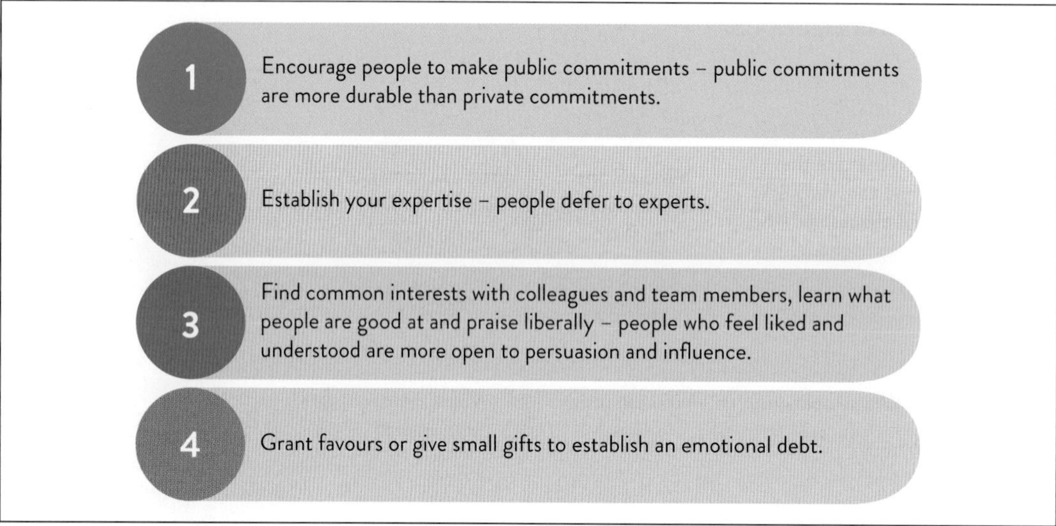

FIGURE 4.6 Four ways to build your influence

Work climate

Groups working in a supportive and relaxed atmosphere generally find it easy and enjoyable to complete their tasks and achieve their goals. Some signs of a positive working climate that is considerate, tolerant and trusting are when team members:

- feel free to express themselves and share their feelings
- support each other
- contribute to the group goals in the best way they can
- feel a sense of enjoyment as the team gets on with the job at hand.

Work climates can also be controlling, punishing and rigid, making task achievement difficult. Set a good example and set high standards to positively influence the climate of your work team.

Influences on group dynamics

Group dynamics are influenced by five groups of factors: what's happening in the surrounding environment, what's happening within the group itself, each group member's skills and personalities, the team's job or task and the leader-manager.

Together, these factors determine your team's internal relationships and how well it functions. Be particularly watchful for a change in any one of these five factors because it could lead to a shift in the dynamics of the group as a whole.

The environment

The environment determines what a team can and cannot do in a broad sense. It includes the organisation's culture, the closeness and type of other teams, the organisation's formal and informal rewards systems, the type of organisation structure, the power structure within the organisation, and the resources available (e.g. information, space, technology, time, tools). These aspects of the environment establish the boundaries within which teams operate, shaping the dynamics that are possible within teams.

The group as a whole

Team size is important. Groups including between five and 15 people work better together and enjoy the experience more than people in larger teams. Communication is less complicated, it's easier for members to get to know each other and members can help one another more easily. The turnover of membership (how rapidly people leave and enter the group) also matters because new team members often change the group's dynamics.

The extent to which team members have similar backgrounds, education, experiences and training is called the team's *homogeneity*. This also affects dynamics because a homogeneous team, while it can be cohesive and supportive, often has difficulty in adapting to change and innovating, and is more prone to groupthink.

While team members should be of like mind in their understanding of their purposes, goals, roles and procedures, strong teams are heterogeneous, or diverse, in their approaches and ways of thinking. With good group dynamics and a positive culture, this diversity leads to insight, continuous improvements, creativity and strength. With poor group dynamics and a poor culture, diversity leads to tension, conflict and mistrust. (Chapter 32 discusses the other benefits of diversity.)

Individual group members

Each team member's abilities, attitudes, **emotional intelligence (EI or EQ)**, experience, personality, role perceptions, skills and values – all the things that make people unique – determine what team members are able and willing to contribute. Add to that their level of motivation, the way they interact with other group members and the degree to which they accept group norms and the organisation's values and goals, and you can easily understand how much a team's dynamics depend on the skills of its individual members.

The job

Three groups of factors concerning the job affect a team's dynamics by encouraging or limiting the freedom of its members to make decisions concerning their work and the amount of interaction that is possible between them:

1 **job design** and the technology used
2 the working arrangements – virtual, flexible, activity-based working
3 the type of work involved.

The leader-manager

Every leader-manager needs to fit in with the type of leadership prevalent in the organisation and, to this extent, an organisation's leadership and management styles trickle down from the top. Effective leadership at every level is a vital ingredient of every organisation's success, just as it is for every team's success.

Employees take their cue from their leader-manager regarding such matters as work pace and what is, and isn't, important (customer service, quality, timekeeping, etc.). The leader-manager also establishes the working climate for the team.

Without a leader who 'paints the picture' and shows the way, a team is left floundering and looking to its informal leader for its cues. When that happens, it's the luck of the draw whether the team performs well. You can find out more about successful leadership throughout Part 2 of this text.

STUDY TOOLS

QUICK REVIEW

KEY CONCEPT 4.1 

a How does thinking about organisations as chaotic systems made up of ever-evolving networks of human relationships help you lead and manage operations and work teams and introduce change more effectively?

KEY CONCEPT 4.2 

a List and give some examples of the elements of culture.

b Define organisation culture and explain how an organisation's culture and subcultures relate to employee attraction and retention and to its overall success.

KEY CONCEPT 4.3 

a List and define the key elements of group dynamics.

b Make a list of words that describe a work group with poor group dynamics, and make another that describes one with good group dynamics. Describe what you think it would be like to work in each of the work groups and the degree to which each would be likely to reach its goals.

c Describe the six types and sources of organisational power and influence. Which of these are strongest in modern workplaces?

d Discuss six ways leader-managers can increase their personal power.

BUILD YOUR SKILLS

KEY CONCEPT 4.1 

a How can the way an organisation's internal networks operate help or hinder its achievement of a goal?

b What is systems theory and how does it differ from thinking about an organisation in terms of one function or process at a time? Can you give an example of how making a change in one part of an organisation can affect another part of the organisation in unexpected ways?

KEY CONCEPT 4.2 

a Explain how an organisation's culture can help or hinder its effectiveness and give an example from your own experience.

b Discuss how a work team's subculture and norms can help or hinder its effectiveness and give an example from your own experience.

KEY CONCEPT 4.3

a Who are the informal leaders in your study group and your work team? How do you know this? Considering both their personal qualities and the function they perform in the group, why do you believe they have become the informal leaders?

b Who wields power and influence in your study group and your work team? Which type of power and influence do they have and how do you believe they acquired it?

WORKPLACE ACTIVITIES

KEY CONCEPT 4.1 

a What human networks do you belong to at work? How effectively do they work for you? What actions can you take to make them more helpful to you?

KEY CONCEPT 4.2 

a What's your team culture like? Is it empowering? Is it work-focused? Is it service-oriented or safety-oriented? Or is it a toxic culture based on self-protection?

b From your experience, describe what it is like to enter a new organisation and join a new work team, particularly understanding the expected behaviours.

c Thinking about your own organisation, is the formal organisation or the informal organisation more important to the way employees do their jobs, achieve their goals and implement changes and new ideas? Provide examples to illustrate your reasoning.

d Describe your organisation culture and relate it to the types of culture described in **Table 4.1**. How effective is it in helping the organisation meet its stakeholders' needs?

e Analyse the culture and norms of your work group by thinking through the following questions:

- i Do people embrace flexible working as the norm and deliver outcomes regardless of having constant supervision?
- ii Do people socialise with each other?
- iii How do people treat each other, external customers and internal customers?
- iv How do employees speak about the organisation and its management, or about their customers?
- v How much attention to detail do people pay?
- vi How much fun do people have while they're working?
- vii How much do people focus on quality and customer satisfaction?
- viii How would you describe the management style of the organisation?
- ix Is the working atmosphere relaxed, formal or tense?
- x What are the attitudes and practices regarding health, safety and the environment?
- xi What are the systems and procedures like? For example, are they hierarchy driven, protocol driven, customer driven or production driven? Do they emphasise checks and controls, innovation or freedom to act?
- xii What behaviours are rewarded and respected? What behaviours are 'punished' or frowned upon?
- xiii What is the work ethic? For example, is it a 'She'll be right!' or a 'Get it right!' approach? How hard do employees work?
- xiv What priorities do people select?
- xv What style of language do people use (e.g. formal, informal, lots of jargon or technical terms)?
- xvi Where, how and by whom are decisions made?
- xvii On balance, do these attitudes and behaviours support or work against the team, the team leader, the organisation and its other stakeholders? What can you do to improve the balance?
- xviii Which is stronger in your workplace – power or influence? Give some examples to illustrate your answer.

f Describe the norms of your work team and discuss how effectively they support productivity and performance.

g Does your organisation have an ethics policy or a code of behaviour? Summarise it and share it with the class. What does it say people should do when they suspect unethical behaviour or behaviour that is not in accord with the code of conduct? Do people speak up when they see unethical behaviour or behaviour against the organisation's code of conduct? Who do they tell? How are they rewarded? What action is taken? Organisations that don't have a culture of open communication are in danger of learning about their own bad behaviour only when it hits the press.

KEY CONCEPT 4.3 

a How helpful or unhelpful is the behaviour of your team members to the way the team functions? Do they help or hinder other team members to do their best? Who plays which roles?

EXTENSION ACTIVITIES

Referring to the Snapshot at the beginning of this chapter, answer the following questions:

1 Why do you think that observing who speaks first and what questions or comments the team asks is an important clue as to how well the team works? Do you think this approach works better than one-on-one meetings with each team member? Why or why not?

2 What are some potential obstacles that Arana might face managing his new team? How would you suggest he address these obstacles?

CASE STUDY 4

TRANSFORMING A BANK'S CULTURE

When organisations get it right, their employees can be an important source of competitive advantage. Ah, but how to win back their trust and loyalty after years of automation and deep downsizing in an intensely competitive environment? Culture is the key. Here's how Money Bank, a solid performer in financial terms, attacked the gargantuan task of transforming its culture to make the most of its employees and reach the heights of superior performance.

Based on the philosophy that when people are happy and productive, they create more value for stakeholders, the bank's first task was to win the hearts and minds of the people inside the organisation. It began by surveying its employees and benchmarking a number of key measures with other high-performing organisations. It found that while some positive values, such as a results orientation, had become part of the culture, the bank needed to do more to engage its employees and reduce the bureaucracy and silo mentality.

So, Money Bank set about becoming 'the human bank' and established a three-fold strategy:

1 *Build our culture* to create the foundations for sustainable leadership and long-term success.

2 *Build on our success* by further strengthening our brand, leadership and revenue.

3 *Build our performance* to deliver improved financial performance and shareholder value.

Culture-building concentrated on creating a fundamentally different experience for the bank's key stakeholders: the broader community and the bank's customers, employees and shareholders. A dedicated culture team headed up three major initiatives:

1 personal and emotional development workshops in which participants examine the thoughts and values that drive their behaviour

2 process-improvement projects to streamline operations and support cultural transformation

3 cultural consulting providing diagnostic and consulting services to assist business units and teams to identify their current cultural climate, assess it against key principles, improve their culture and measure their progress.

It worked. Money Bank's financial results improved, and it was recognised as an employer of choice. Internal surveys of employee satisfaction rose from 50 per cent to 85 per cent over the next seven years and overall knowledge of Money Bank's values nearly doubled.[7]

Questions

1 It is generally accepted that the first step in maximising performance and gaining the people advantage is through an organisation's culture. Why is this the case?

2 Money Bank took a carefully thought-out approach to transform its culture. Discuss the key steps in its approach and the role each played.

3 Here are some important factors in successful cultural transformation. Read them through and discuss what each of them means to you in practical terms:

- a compelling vision and meaningful values
- aligning mindsets and behaviours with the organisation's business processes and systems
- being prepared to take risks and to learn from mistakes
- matching the organisation's people to its culture so there is a strong fit
- recognition that transformation is a journey, not a one-off program
- strong ownership of and commitment to change from the CEO and the executive management team.

CHAPTER ENDNOTES

1 Erika Lucas, 'View from the front line', *Professional Manager* (UK), © March–April 2011.

2 'A tale of two banks', *Leadership Matters*, May 2016, p. 23; https://bankaust.com.au/personal/, accessed 7 April 2017.

3 Dan Schulman, 'PayPal withdraws plan for Charlotte expansion', 5 April 2016, https://newsroom.paypal-corp.com/PayPal-Withdraws-Plan-for-Charlotte-Expansion

4 'Fit for purpose?', *Company Director,* October 2017, p. 15.

5 Transparency International, Corruption Perceptions Index 2020, https://www.transparency.org/en/cpi/2020/index/aus, accessed 1 March 2022.

6 Victorian Public Sector Commission, 'Ethics in the workplace', 2015, https://vpsc.vic.gov.au/ethics-behaviours-culture/public-sector-values/ethics-in-the-workplace

7 Based on Craig Donaldson, 'ANZ bank: Breaking out of the mould', *HC Online*, http://www.hcamag.com/profiles/anz-bank-breaking-out-of-the-mould-111735.aspx, accessed 16 January 2015.

PART 2
MANAGING YOURSELF

Are you a practising or aspiring leader-manager? Whether it's a rock band or a team of rocket scientists, an organisation employing thousands of people, a virtual team scattered around the world or a work team of five, when people come together to achieve their individual and shared goals, they need someone who can provide direction, guidance and a sense of purpose. They need someone who is willing and confident enough to take overall responsibility for their activities and achievements. They need someone who can inspire them, empower them and show them the way.

To be this person, you must first understand and manage yourself and communicate with panache. Only then can you successfully lead people and manage operations. Only then can you add real value to your organisation and to the team that looks to you for leadership.

People who possess the core competencies of self-understanding, communication and self-leadership seem to attract opportunities. They are noticed and given the chance to contribute. With those core competencies, you're well on your way to building a successful career, a successful organisation and, ultimately, a successful country.

In the next five chapters, you learn how to figure out what makes you 'tick' and what type of working environment you need in order to contribute optimally. You find out how to set meaningful and realistic life and career goals based on your values and interests and how to think your way into achieving them. The social and emotional intelligence you need to work effectively with others is explained so you can apply these skill sets to propel your career forward.

You examine how to communicate clearly, tactfully and thoughtfully, learn to develop and deliver polished presentations, and discover how to communicate in writing in a business-like way so that you don't let yourself or your organisation down.

You find out how to gain recognition for your contributions and skills, and how to build a well-earned reputation for getting things done, honouring your commitments and making a difference. You discover what it takes to work well with others, and you find out how to maximise your personal productivity and concentrate your efforts and attention on what matters most in order to achieve meaningful results.

CHAPTER

STRENGTHENING YOUR PERSONAL SKILLS

After completing this chapter, you will be able to:

5.1 recognise how well you understand yourself

5.2 recognise the values and motives that drive your behaviour and what you want from life

5.3 adopt the mindsets that empower you to act, make improvements and achieve the goals that are important to you

5.4 build the emotional intelligence and resilience you need to succeed

5.5 manage your career and prepare a professional development plan that identifies and develops the skills and abilities you need to succeed, and know when the time is right to make a move.

TRANSFERABLE SKILLS

The following transferable skills are covered in this chapter:

2 Critical thinking and problem solving
- **2.2** Personal effectiveness

3 Social competence
- **3.3** Written communication
- **3.4** Leadership

OVERVIEW

Do you know people who are great to be around because they're positive and make you feel good about yourself? Who are confident and assured, who are respected and who respect others? People who have a clear sense of who they are, what they stand for and what they believe in? Who know what they want from life and who can deal calmly with the ups and downs along the way?

These are personal skills that are vital to every leader-manager's success, from their first appointment to a leader-manager role, all the way to the top. They are critical because, before you can lead and manage anyone, you need to be able to manage yourself. And before you can do that, you need to understand yourself.

This chapter provides the principal resources you need to strengthen your personal skills and succeed in your personal and working life.

SNAPSHOT

David's dilemma

David is at a career crossroads because his position is being outsourced and made redundant. He has been offered a sideways move within the organisation, but in a different location less convenient to his home. It's a safe and easy option, although not particularly appealing. He considers his other options. One is that he could become a contractor, with all the attendant risks and expenses, as well as the benefits of being his own boss, setting his own hours and so on. This option is risky, and not particularly appealing.

Alternatively, he can brush up his résumé and launch a job search – check out the job sites and speak to people in his professional networks to let them know he's available. Something suitable is bound to turn up.

'What's my ideal job right now,' he muses? 'Do I even want another job? Maybe I should take a few months off and travel. Or go back to full-time study with a bit of casual work in between.' There are many options and a lot to think about, he realises. He 'slips, slops, slaps', picks up his journal and a pencil, and heads off to the surf for a bit of soul searching.

Transferable skills

2.2 Personal effectiveness

5.1 Understanding yourself

Who in the world am I? Ah, that's the great puzzle.

Lewis Carroll, *Alice's adventures in Wonderland*, Macmillan, UK, 1865.

Without self-awareness, you can't improve or become wiser; you are doomed to self-delusion. Without self-understanding, understanding others is next to impossible too. 'Know thyself' is even inscribed on the Temple of Apollo at Delphi, in Greece. 'Knowing thyself' is the basis of wisdom and the basis of leadership. People with self-knowledge understand how others see them. They are aware of their intentions, motivations, attitudes, biases and emotions. Self-understanding like this opens the door to understanding others, making it easier to develop effective working relationships (discussed in Chapter 8).

Transferable skills

2.2 Personal effectiveness

The Johari Window

Are you self-aware and open, or secretive, self-absorbed and blind to your effect on others? The **Johari Window** can help you increase your self-awareness in this area. It looks at two dimensions to understanding yourself:

1 Aspects of your behaviour and style that are known or not known to yourself.
2 Aspects of your behaviour and style that are known or not known to others.

Combining these two dimensions reveals four areas of self-awareness, shown in **Figure 5.1**. The top left square is your public self, or the 'open area', which contains information about yourself that you and others know, such as your name, your job and your experience in the organisation. The top right square is your 'blind area'. It contains information about yourself that others can see but of which you are unaware. For example, Kay is curious and keen to learn, yet is unaware that the way she asks questions often irritates people and makes them feel like she is cross-examining them. The 'closed area' in the bottom left square contains information you know about yourself but which others do not; it might be secret information or merely information you never thought or chose to reveal. For example, John's boss keeps him standing during informal meetings, which annoys John, but he says nothing; until John tells his boss that he would prefer to sit, this information remains in his closed area. Sometimes there is a good reason for privacy. Sometimes, opening up and telling others would improve communication, trust and teamwork. The final area is the 'unknown area' in the bottom right square, which contains information that is unknown to others and to yourself. This is the vast area of the unconscious.

The cubes in Figure 5.1 are shown equal in size, but for most people, this is not the case. The relative size of each cube is different for everyone. Imagine, for example, expanding the 'closed area' upwards, shrinking the 'open area'; people with a large 'closed area' are seen as puzzling, secretive and difficult to communicate and build relationships with. Now imagine expanding the 'open area' to the right (shrinking the 'blind area' to indicate a greater degree of self-knowledge) and down (shrinking the 'closed area' to indicate fewer 'secrets'). A large 'open area' helps you communicate openly, work well with others and develop honest and trusting relationships.

Transferable skills

2.2 Personal effectiveness

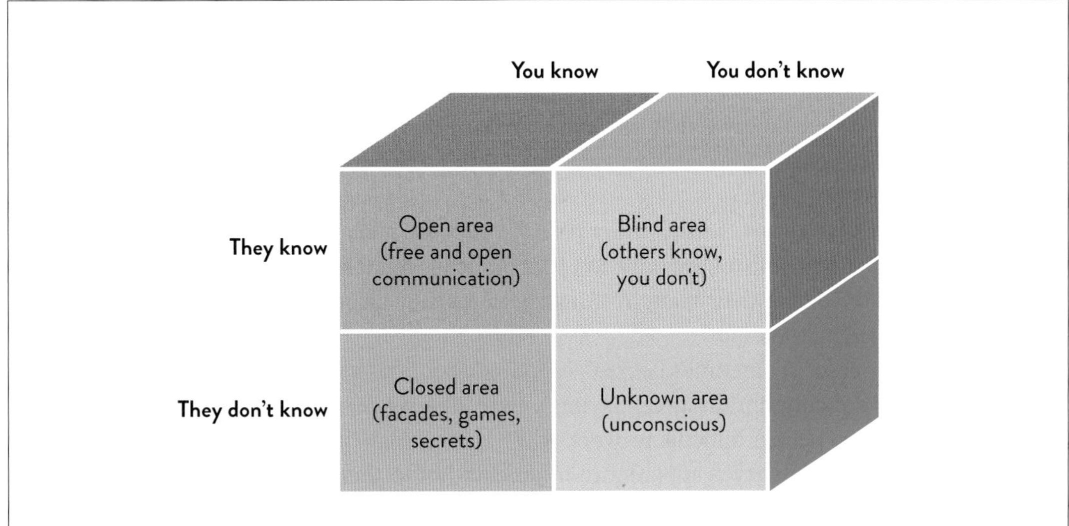

FIGURE 5.1 The Johari Window

Putting the Johari Window to work

You can increase the size of your 'open area' and shrink your 'blind area' through self-reflection and by asking for, listening to and acting on feedback from others (covered later in this chapter) and by being aware of the public aspects of yourself, such as your body language, facial expressions and tone of voice and their impact on others. Disclosing more of yourself to people you trust also increases your 'open area' by shrinking your 'closed area'.

When you work in your open areas, you can communicate and collaborate easily and be effective and productive. Large open areas between team members minimise conflict, mistrust and misunderstanding. You can encourage team members to be open, constructive and positive in their communication and offer feedback to team members on their 'blind areas'. (Chapter 13 has more ideas to help your team members.)

Espoused theories versus theories-in-use

Knowing your values, acting on them and making decisions based on them builds your integrity and self-respect, and earns you the respect of others. But does it always? News channels and websites and social media frequently carry stories about people who act on their values of self-interest and 'winning' at all costs. You may even know a manager who values self-preservation or self-promotion more than anything else. This is still value-directed behaviour, isn't it?

Then we have people who say one thing and do another. A leader-manager might say: 'I believe in participation and I really value the contributions of my work team'. This is known as espoused theory; that is, what people say. The way people behave is their theory-in-use. When that same leader-manager fails to listen to team members' ideas or suggestions, the theory-in-use might be something like this: 'People don't have any ideas worth listening to or valuable contributions to make'.[1]

Are these managers hypocrites? Possibly. More often, a theory-in-use that contradicts an espoused theory is due to one of three other reasons:

1 *The theory-in-use hasn't yet caught up with the person's espoused theory.* Take the leader-manager who consciously believes (i.e. in their head) that people are reliable and talks about how much they trust their team members (espoused theory) but who unconsciously believes the opposite, so they constantly check up on their employees' work (theory-in-use).
2 *A person feels pressured to conform to a set of values that is not their own.* A leader-manager values independence, however they work in an organisation that values teamwork. So they give 'lip-service' to teamwork (espoused theory) but continue to praise and reward individual results (theory-in-use).
3 *Another value, or theory-in-use, overrides the espoused theory.* A leader-manager values participation but works in an organisation that punishes mistakes. Therefore, to avoid mistakes they don't risk involving their team in things because they place higher value on staying out of trouble and keeping their job.

Whatever the reason, sometimes people's espoused theories (what they say) and their theories-in-use (what they actually do) disagree. Saying one thing and doing another indicates poor self-awareness and makes people difficult to work with. Incongruity like this often falls into people's blind spots (their inconsistency is apparent to others but not to them). People who have a large gap between their espoused theories and their theories-in-use lose credibility with their work teams and colleagues, harming their working relationships. To lead and manage effectively, you need congruence, or agreement, between your espoused theories and your theories-in-use. This is sometimes called 'walking your talk'.

Transferable skills
2.2 Personal effectiveness

5.2 Setting personal goals

Thought is the blossom; language is the bud; action is the fruit behind it.

Ralph Waldo Emerson

You've probably heard words to this effect: 'When you don't know where you're going, any road will do'. Put another way, you can either purposefully guide your life and your career, or you can accept whatever comes along. To guide your life well, you need to know what you value and what you want to achieve. Then you can decide how best to work towards your goals.

Your values and interests

Values are deeply and strongly held beliefs and principles. They express what you believe is right and wrong, good and bad, should and shouldn't be. They are so much a part of you that you may not even be conscious of what your values are.

Values give you deep roots. Do you have a strong sense of your own values and your organisation's values? People are happiest, do their best and achieve the most when they spend their time, at work and at home, on activities that are in line with their values.

Just as living according to your values leads to a satisfying life, choosing a career that supports your main values can give you genuine job satisfaction. (And as you will see in the final section of this chapter, a satisfying job must also link with your deep interests.)

What do you value most? Having fun? Money? Conserving resources? Justice? To find out, conduct an internet search for 'values test' and take one or two tests that are from reputable websites. Make a note of your results; it will be time well spent and you might be surprised!

Your life plan

Follow these four steps to set your personal goals and build an action plan to achieve them:

1 Think about your various life roles; for example, colleague, friend, leader-manager, parent, partner, sibling, student. Think about your major life areas; for example, your career, your family, your mental and physical health, your place in your community. What are you aiming at in each of these roles and areas? What sort of person do you wish to be in each of them? What contributions do you want to make?

2 Spend some time alone with a pen and notepad thinking about these questions. Some people like to imagine their 75th birthday party and what the 'significant others' in their life might say about them. Others like to sit quietly and write down the words and phrases that describe them, or that they would like to describe them. Other people make 'spidergrams', or mind maps. Do what feels right for you.

3 Look back over your thoughts. What are the common themes? Set some specific goals in the main areas of your life. Keep asking 'How can I know I've succeeded in this?' until you arrive at clear goals that you can 'see' yourself achieving.

4 Ask yourself: 'What needs to happen before I can achieve this goal?' Break your goals down into shorter-term milestones that you can realistically expect to achieve in, say, the next three to six months and write them down. Concentrate on these milestones and use them to assess your progress towards each goal.

5 List the first two or three steps you need to take towards achieving your first milestone in each of the main areas of your life.

Now you have a vision for your future. Invest time in it because your life plan gives overall direction and guidance to your life and power to your leadership. Setting goals is one of the best life skills you can master. Figure 5.2 has some tips for how you can start.

Work–life balance

Personal and work lives have merged; as workloads increase, we work longer hours and work from home offices. But we need to be sensible about this. All work and no play can lead to cynicism, interpersonal conflict, low productivity, substance abuse and tiredness – all symptoms of working too hard and feeling constantly under pressure. Balancing your various life roles (which you considered in the four-step life plan above) with your workplace roles is not only in your employer's interests (because people work better and more productively when they lead balanced lives), but also in your interest. **Work–life balance** increases your job satisfaction and improves your family life and your physical and psychological health.

A full, healthy and happy life – a well-balanced life – is a successful life. But it doesn't happen by itself. It takes planning and scheduling. You may not be able to find the time for everything, but you

FIGURE 5.2 How to set a great goal

can probably find the time for everything that is important to you. Go for 'quality time', not 'quantity time'. What matters isn't how long you spend in each life area, goal or role; it's how you use your time to make the most of them.

Remember to schedule some 'me time', in which you need not respond to the demands of your other life roles. This is time just for you and your mental and physical health; it might be bushwalking, gardening, jogging, learning a language, playing a sport or taking a painting class – whatever helps you unwind and relax. Activities like these keep your batteries charged, not just for your job but for your entire life.

Transferable skills

2.2 Personal effectiveness

3.4 Leadership

5.3 Thinking like a leader

> **We are all captives of the pictures in our head – our belief that the world we have experienced is the world that really exists.**
>
> Walter Lippmann, *Public opinion*, Harcourt Brace & Co., New York, 1922.

What do you believe, deep down, about yourself, other people and the world around you? Unquestioned and strongly held beliefs are known as mindsets or **paradigms**. They are your mental models of the world and how it operates, and they guide your thoughts and your behaviour. More than that, our beliefs are self-fulfilling prophecies because the brain filters out what doesn't support our mindsets, lets in what does support them and distorts the rest so that it appears to confirm our mindsets. Basically, the brain discards most information and uses what is left to create a 'parallel world' of its own. In this way, we each have our own reality, and everyone's reality is different.

Self-fulfilling beliefs

Leader-manager X believes, deep down inside, that employees are irresponsible, lazy and untrustworthy. X treats employees differently from leader-manager Y, who believes the opposite – that employees are hardworking, responsible and trustworthy. Driven by those mindsets, these two leader-managers develop different working relationships with their teams, and, in turn, those relationships confirm their deep-seated beliefs about employees. They each see what they expect to see.

Your mindsets form during childhood as your parents, siblings, friends and early experiences influence your development. As you continue to live your life, you expand your mindsets and adjust them according to your experiences and what your culture and society teach you. Your mindsets and values are key components of your personal skills. They direct your behaviour, usually without your awareness, colouring everything you say and do. It's worth taking the time to reflect on your mindsets to ensure they are up to date and based on facts.

There is a saying 'we are what our thoughts make us', and it's certainly true that successful leader-managers share remarkably similar mindsets. In the following sections we consider four important managerial mindsets – respect yourself, set high standards, see positives and possibilities, and pay attention.

 INDUSTRY INSIGHTS

How paradigms can work against you

Ford famously refused to add chrome and fancy bodywork to its cars, allowing Chrysler to steal Ford's number one spot with its 'Yank Tanks'. Eventually, the entire US car industry followed suit and then refused to believe consumers wanted smaller, simpler and more economical cars, leaving the door open for the Japanese car industry to usurp Ford's market dominance.

Kodak invented digital photography in 1975 but did nothing with it until it was too late and, even then, marketed it only half-heartedly, believing that people would never give up their hard copies of photographs and that digital imaging would compete directly with its lucrative film sales. Kodak filed for bankruptcy in 2012.

Respect yourself

Transferable skills

2.2 Personal effectiveness

How do you feel about yourself? Do you value yourself as a worthwhile individual? Are you self-confident and self-assured? Do you respect yourself? Your **self-esteem** describes your mindset about yourself. People with low self-esteem feel unworthy and uncomfortable within themselves. They lack self-confidence, which makes it difficult for them to reach decisions, state what's on their mind and tackle difficult issues. By contrast, high self-esteem gives you the confidence to deal with difficult issues and difficult people, to keep going when things get tough and to state your opinions and desires clearly. Whether it's high or low, your self-esteem is a self-fulfilling prophecy.

In case you're wondering whether holding yourself in high regard might make you seem arrogant, remember these four phrases:

1 I'm okay, you're okay.
2 I'm okay, you're not okay.
3 I'm not okay, you're okay.
4 I'm not okay, you're not okay.[2]

The first phrase describes people who hold themselves, as well as others, in high regard; these people are generally **assertive**. The second phrase describes people who are arrogant because, while they hold themselves in high regard, they do not hold others in high regard. These people are usually considered to be **aggressive**. The third phrase describes people who respect others, but not themselves and are generally **passive**. It is said, only half-jokingly, that the fourth phrase describes many people who populate our prisons – it is a 'going nowhere' position, characterised by a lack of respect for oneself as well as for others. This scenario plays out (often unconsciously) as: 'I don't respect others, so it's okay to steal from them or murder them. Sure, I may get caught and go to jail, but that's probably all I deserve anyway'. (See Chapters 6 and 7 to find out more about assertive, aggressive and passive behaviour.) The bottom line is that as long as you hold others, as well as yourself, in high regard, you are unlikely to behave in an arrogant or aggressive manner.

The imposter syndrome is something that many leader-managers may experience. If you ever feel you don't belong where you are, that you're winging it, that you are going to be found out to be a fraud and that you don't have the smarts or the talent to be in the position you're in, then you're experiencing imposter syndrome. And you wouldn't be alone – up to 70 per cent of professionals suffer from the imposter syndrome.[3] The higher they rise, the more like imposters they feel. It's something to do with 'the more you know, the more you know how much you don't know', so ironically, it's a natural symptom of learning and gaining expertise.

A realistically high sense of self-esteem helps you work through the impostor syndrome. So does:

- acknowledging that the skills you have are relevant
- acknowledging the skills you are missing or that are weak and asking for help
- faking it until you make it – not pretending you have skills you don't have, but pretending you're confident and getting on with the job at hand
- observing a role model and building their skills into your repertoire
- seeing the task you're not confident about as a chance to build your expertise and credibility
- thinking about similar challenges you've successfully faced and realising this one is similar, if not the same
- using confident body language – walk briskly, stand up straight, look people in the eye, speak clearly and so on.

Transferable skills
2.2 Personal effectiveness

Build your confidence with self-talk

A study found that 98 per cent of participants talked to themselves in their heads almost constantly in the course of a day.[4] So chances are, you are also talking to yourself constantly, whether you are aware of it or not. Maybe you even hold little conversations with yourself: 'Should I, or shouldn't I?' Your self-talk reflects your self-esteem and guides your behaviour, which boomerangs back to reinforce your beliefs about yourself. High self-esteem leads to positive, empowering self-talk, which strengthens your self-esteem; low self-esteem leads to negative, limiting self-talk, which crushes your self-esteem. Table 5.1 shows some examples of hurtful and helpful self-talk.

Whether it's empowering or limiting, and whether you're aware of it or not, your subconscious makes sure you follow the instructions of your self-talk, making true Henry Ford's observation, 'Whether you think you can or think you can't – you're right'. Some people are their own best friends, others their own biggest critics. Consider the examples of self-talk in Table 5.1 and think about how each could deflate or bolster a person's self-esteem. Do you recognise any of the examples as similar to your own self-talk?

TABLE 5.1 How to harm or help your self-esteem

Hurtful self-talk	Helpful self-talk
I always get things wrong	Next time I'll put more effort into it
I can never understand topics like this	I'm going to concentrate on making sure I understand this topic and stick with it until I master it
I'm always awkward around people I don't know	I will smile and be really friendly
I'm terrible at things like this	I'm not perfect, but I'm getting better
It's just like me to do something stupid	That isn't like me – I usually do things better than that
It's too complicated for me	I can work this through logically and carefully
I'm always so clumsy	I need to watch where I'm going

In our first example there are two leader-managers: the first believes she makes mistakes, doesn't communicate well with others and has few skills to offer. These self-limiting beliefs lead her to behave quite differently and get quite different results from the second leader-manager, who believes she is a skilled and effective leader-manager who communicates well and makes good decisions easily. Whether or not their beliefs accurately reflect reality, they do reflect their self-esteem and act as self-fulfilling prophecies, because each unconsciously finds ways to make their beliefs about themselves come true.

Imagine now that these leader-managers are asked to make a presentation at a meeting. The first, believing she is a poor communicator and makes many mistakes, is nervous. Imagine her self-talk: 'Oh no, I'll make a terrible presentation! I'll forget what I'm going to say. No one will pay any attention to me and I'll look like a fool'. This negative self-talk embeds itself in her subconscious and instructs her to fail. This manager unwittingly follows the very instructions she gives herself – to fail.

In contrast, the second leader-manager is more likely to give a good presentation because she believes in her own abilities. Her self-talk might be more like: 'Well, this is my first presentation. I'd better think it through carefully so that it makes sense and practise it thoroughly so that I deliver it well. People usually listen to me, and this is really no different from a conversation with several people and it's my chance to make a good impression in my new role'. Her subconscious acts on its instructions and she successfully delivers her presentation.

Elite athletes, sportspeople, businesspeople and many others repeatedly rehearse a first-class performance in their mind's eye before the actual event. This visualisation greatly increases their chances of achieving excellence.

Have you ever 'known' you were going to fail a test or miss kicking a goal? Even if you were mentally and physically able to succeed at the task, your own thoughts would probably have prevented you from doing so.

Think about an upcoming important event. Do you imagine yourself falling flat or sailing smoothly through? What does this tell you about your self-talk and your ability to visualise success?

Transferable skills

2.2 Personal effectiveness

Control yourself

People with low self-esteem generally have an **external locus of control** – other people and events control their behaviour, actions and reactions. People with an external locus of control tend to:

- allow others to make them angry
- be rude right back when someone is rude to them
- do tasks because they have to
- let someone else's bad mood bring their mood down
- react without thinking.

People with high self-esteem generally have an **internal locus of control**, making them masters of their own behaviour, communications and responses to others. They choose their behaviour, not other people or outside events. People with an internal locus of control tend to:

- act with integrity, according to their own values, and can ignore peer pressure
- choose whether, how and when to respond to rude or otherwise difficult people
- do tasks, even those they dislike, because they want to
- remain calm, cool and collected, even when people around them panic.

Develop an internal locus of control by learning to take a few deep breaths and thinking before responding. Ask yourself: 'What is my goal here?' Maintain your professionalism, regardless of how people around you are behaving. High self-esteem, positive self-talk and an internal locus of control are important personal skills not just for when you're leading and managing, but in all aspects of life. With high self-esteem and an internal locus of control, you appear more mature, self-contained and in charge. Others naturally trust you and look to you for guidance and leadership.

Build self-esteem in others

Think of the best boss or the best teacher you've worked with. Did they bring out the best in you? Did they help you achieve beyond what you thought you were capable of? Did they stretch you and extend your skills, talents and self-confidence? Help people feel good about themselves through **coaching**, encouragement and **positive feedback** and by placing them in jobs that stretch them and develop their skills. In this way, you can surround yourself with high-performing 'winners' and build a team that achieves results.

Transferable skills

2.2 Personal effectiveness

Set high standards

US essayist Logan Pearsall Smith observed: 'How can they say my life isn't a success? Have I not for more than 60 years got enough to eat and escaped being eaten?'[5] That's a pretty low standard for most Australians.

When you set high standards, your approach is more like 'Get it right', not 'It'll be right'. When your standards are high, you expect the best for yourself, from yourself and from the people around you. Whatever you attempt, you aim to do it to the best of your ability and expect others to do their best, too. High standards also encourage you to innovate and look for ways to continually do things better, easier, faster, more economically – critical in today's workplace.

Thanks to the self-fulfilling prophecy, this mindset brings out the best in everyone. Since most people enjoy stretching themselves, learning and working at their potential, most employees are glad of the opportunity to work with leader-managers who expect the best.

Establish priorities, set goals and act

What is the difference between a dream and a goal? A dream is a 'wish' while a goal is a plan to achieve followed by action. When you have high standards, you establish priorities, set realistic yet challenging goals and take responsibility for doing what is required to achieve them. The more concrete steps you take towards a goal, the more easily you achieve it. The higher your standards, the more you keep working towards making things happen, rather than complaining, daydreaming or seeing only problems and difficulties.

Is earning a diploma a high priority for you? Then you need to put in the work: attend class, pay attention, take notes, study them, read the textbook, take more notes and revise them several times, and complete your assessments on time. These are all actions that take you down the path to your qualification. Wanting to earn a diploma but not working at it practically guarantees failure.

Set goals and establish priorities for yourself as well as for your work team and individual team members. Establishing a clear vision and goals that employees can understand, share and feel good about contributing to is a critical part of your personal skill set, as is setting the pace for how action-oriented and goal-focused your work team is.

Concentrating on your goals, combined with taking responsibility and putting in the work, helps you to achieve them, especially when progress is slow or you run into difficulties. A mindset of consistently working towards your goals also ensures you look for ways around problems, rather than giving up and giving in to them.

You may have heard these phrases: 'The blame game' and 'If it's to be, it's up to me'. They illustrate two very different mindsets: blaming others and taking responsibility. The first leads you to do nothing while the second invites you to 'make things happen'. Table 5.2 gives some examples of self-talk that blames and self-talk that takes responsibility. Which of the following examples of self-talk do you use?

TABLE 5.2 The blame game versus taking responsibility

Blaming self-talk	Taking responsibility self-talk
Why doesn't my manager recognise how good I am?	How can I prove my value to my manager?
Why doesn't my manager spend more time with me?	What can I do to build a better relationship with my manager?
Why doesn't my team do as I tell them?	I'll explain what I want differently so they 'hear' it.
When are my team going to get motivated?	I need to take time to find out how they're feeling about their work and adjust everyone's roles so they're more in tune with their needs.
When will all this pressure let up?	I need to establish my priorities and learn to let go of what I can't control and what is low priority.

See positives and possibilities

Do you optimistically see the glass as 'half full' or pessimistically as 'half empty'? Or perhaps you see it realistically, as twice as big as it needs to be! Successful leader-managers have a mindset that says, 'Maybe the glass is a bit bigger than it needs to be, but it's nearly full – let's figure out how to fill it to the top!' A positive 'can do' approach makes your days and everyone else's that much brighter, thanks to the **boomerang principle**. When you smile at someone, they smile back. Give a compliment to someone and watch what happens. A positive outlook is refreshing and energising. It attracts people to you and it rubs off on others.

A large body of research shows that people with a positive approach are happier, healthier and live longer than gloomy people. For instance, an optimistic attitude can extend your life by up to 20 per cent (and for most Australians that's more than 10 years). By contrast, pessimists are two to eight times more at risk of cancer, depression and heart attack than optimists.[6]

During tough times, a leader's positive outlook helps rebuild dissolving confidence. It helps people concentrate on what they can do now and how they can do it, not on what they cannot do. For example, you can concentrate on what you want to happen, not on what you don't want to happen. Additionally, you can look for ways around, over and through obstacles, rather than give up.

Transferable skills

2.2 Personal effectiveness

See mistakes as learning opportunities

You may know someone who denies a problem exists, even when something has clearly gone wrong, or who blames other people or circumstances when a situation isn't working out perfectly. Or perhaps you know someone who is paralysed by guilt when they do something wrong and dare not take further action rather than risk making another mistake.

Mistakes are inevitable, natural and normal; learning from them, however, can take some effort. Successful people profit from their mistakes and try again in a different way. Acknowledging and learning from your mistakes helps you get better all the time and moves you out of the past and feeling bad, and into the future, where you find ways to improve and develop your skills. It makes you the sort of person others want to be around and take their lead from. (You can find out more about profiting from mistakes in Chapter 29.)

Pay attention

Avoid 'autopilot'. Pay attention to detail and to finding out the facts before making a decision or acting. Pay attention to everything you're doing as you do it. Psychologists call this **mindfulness**, and it helps you to:

- spot backtracking, bottlenecks, hiccups and wasted effort and resources so you can improve systems and procedures (see Chapter 19 for more information on making continuous improvements)
- spot ways to do tasks more easily, economically, reliably, safely or quickly
- keep energised
- stay involved, interested and out of 'ruts'
- improve your job satisfaction
- prevent mistakes.

You can find more information on mindfulness in Chapter 31.

5.4 Nurturing your emotional intelligence

Transferable skills
2.2 Personal effectiveness

> In the confrontation between the stream and the rock, the stream always wins – not through strength, but through persistence.
>
> Buddha, quoted in Finlay, *The vault of motivational quotes*, 2013.

Emotions are impulses to action in response to life situations. The degree to which you have mastered your emotions – not to snuff them out or keep them buried but to acknowledge them and choose how and when to act on them – describes your emotional intelligence (EI). (Teams have a collective EI; you can find out how to build it and how to help team members build their EI in Chapter 13.)

There are three components to EI:

1 *Perceiving:* the ability to recognise different feelings (e.g. angry, happy, nervous, surprise) in yourself and others.
2 *Understanding:* the ability to identify the causes and consequences of those different feelings.
3 *Regulating emotions:* how well you manage what you and others feel.

Social intelligence includes *interpersonal intelligence*, the ability to understand other people – what motivates them, how they work, how to work cooperatively with them and so on – and *intrapersonal intelligence*, the ability to understand oneself. Thus, EI includes skills that drive people's responses to both the external world and their internal world.

People with high EI can monitor their own and other people's emotions and use that information to guide their thinking and actions. Their *personal competence*, made up of self-awareness, self-regulation and motivation, enables them to manage themself while their *social competence*, made up of **empathy** and interpersonal skills, enables them to handle relationships and interactions with others.

Since part of EI is the ability to sense emotions in others, it can be useful to practise reading other people's emotions. When someone shows emotion, use **reflective listening** to test whether you're reading their emotions correctly; when you aren't, they can easily correct you. When someone talks about their emotions, listen reflectively and help them talk it through. Use your empathy to understand their feelings.

EI helps you to close the gap between *intent* (what you want to do) and *action* (what you actually do). For example, you may want to be a considerate leader-manager; high EI helps you overcome the frustrations and time scarcity of leading and managing so that you can pause and take the time to act considerately towards others, while low EI allows you to become caught up in the daily rush and pressures and speak curtly to people out of frustration.

By developing your EI, you can become more productive and successful, both personally and professionally, and you can help others become more productive and successful, too. Is it worth the effort? It depends on your job. EI helps job performance in high emotional labour jobs, such as those in customer service, counselling, leading-managing, sales and other roles that call for the job holder to work closely and cooperatively with others. But in jobs where people don't work closely with others, such as accountants, engineers, scientists and other jobs that deal mostly with data and ideas, EI actually detracts from job performance.[7] A meta-analysis of studies correlating job performance with EI and with general mental ability found that general mental ability can predict a person's work performance better than EI (26 per cent versus 8.4 per cent).[8] (You can find out how to nurture your team's EI in Chapter 13.)

Understand your own emotions

How well can you identify your own emotions? When you have EI, you can identify your own emotions and their impact on others. Can you name the emotions you feel? The most obvious label isn't necessarily the most accurate. Since we have a tendency to suppress strong emotions, you may need to look for what might lie beneath an emotion. Precisely labelling your emotions increases your sense of wellbeing and reduces the physical symptoms of stress. How intensely are you feeling an emotion on a scale of say, 1 to 10?

A good way to build your EI is, when you feel an emotion, name it accurately, identify its intensity and its trigger, and write about how effectively you managed it (handwriting is better than typing). Notice how the people around you are responding and note that down, too. No one needs to read it except you. Over time, this easy exercise builds your insights into your emotions. **Figure 5.3** shows some areas in which you can build your EI skills.

Self-awareness
Know your own drives, emotions, goals, strengths, values and weaknesses and understand the link between your emotions, thoughts and actions. This gives you self-confidence, a desire for constructive feedback and the ability to cope with stress, adversity and hardship.

Self-regulation
Control or redirect unwanted emotions and impulses. This makes you resilient, comfortable with ambiguity and change, and gives you integrity, resourcefulness and trustworthiness.

Motivation
Set out to do things well and delay gratification in order to succeed. This gives you energy and passion for your work and for new challenges.

Empathy
Understand your impact on others and attract, develop and retain a range of talented employees. This gives you cross-cultural sensitivity.

Social skills
Manage relationships and conflict productively and network well. This makes you persuasive and effective in building teams and leading change.

FIGURE 5.3 Building your EI

Think about the words you use to describe your emotions:

- Are you angry? Or are you perhaps annoyed, frustrated, irritated or offended?
- Are you sad? Or are you perhaps feeling disappointed or pessimistic?
- Are you anxious? Or are you perhaps feeling nervous or vulnerable?
- Are you hurt? Or are you perhaps feeling betrayed or shocked?
- Are you embarrassed? Or are you perhaps feeling isolated or self-conscious?
- Are you happy? Or are you perhaps feeling excited or relieved?

Manage your stress

As can be seen in Figure 5.4, performance goes up when stress goes up, but only to a point. For most of us, stress levels of 50 to 70 per cent of our ability to cope are tolerable; when stress levels rise to 90 per cent or more and remain there for some time, our performance falls off dramatically. So while some stress helps you concentrate better, use your time more productively and think clearly and creatively, too much stress at too high a level is debilitating and disables performance, and it is certainly unhealthy and can even be life-threatening.

The specific sources of stress are different for everyone. What one person deals with as invigorating **eustress**, another takes on as its flipside – debilitating distress. External events, people and situations (e.g. conflict, feeling rushed, organisational **restructuring**) can trigger stress. So can internal events; your own behaviour, feelings and thoughts about people, situations and events can exacerbate or calm these external events. 'Grrrr! Another traffic jam. It's going to make me late!' (stress) or 'Hmm, heavy traffic again today' (no stress). Stress can come also from having too much or too little to do, from working at tasks and carrying responsibilities far beyond your abilities, or at the interface of various facets of your life, as each competes for your time and attention.

Burnout is an early sign of poorly managed stress. Over time, stress accumulates and causes identifiable and increasingly severe physical, emotional and behavioural responses related to the **fight, flight or freeze response**. The body goes on 'full alert', which it can't do indefinitely without damaging itself.

Physical responses to stress include increased blood pressure, heart rate and muscle tension, and loss of appetite. When the physical responses aren't dealt with, *emotional symptoms* follow, for example, apathy, depression, mood swings, negativism, resignation and tension. People who fail to deal with stress at this point then display *behavioural responses*, for example, being short-tempered, easily upset over minor issues, procrastinating, and finding it difficult to concentrate, organise themself and make decisions.

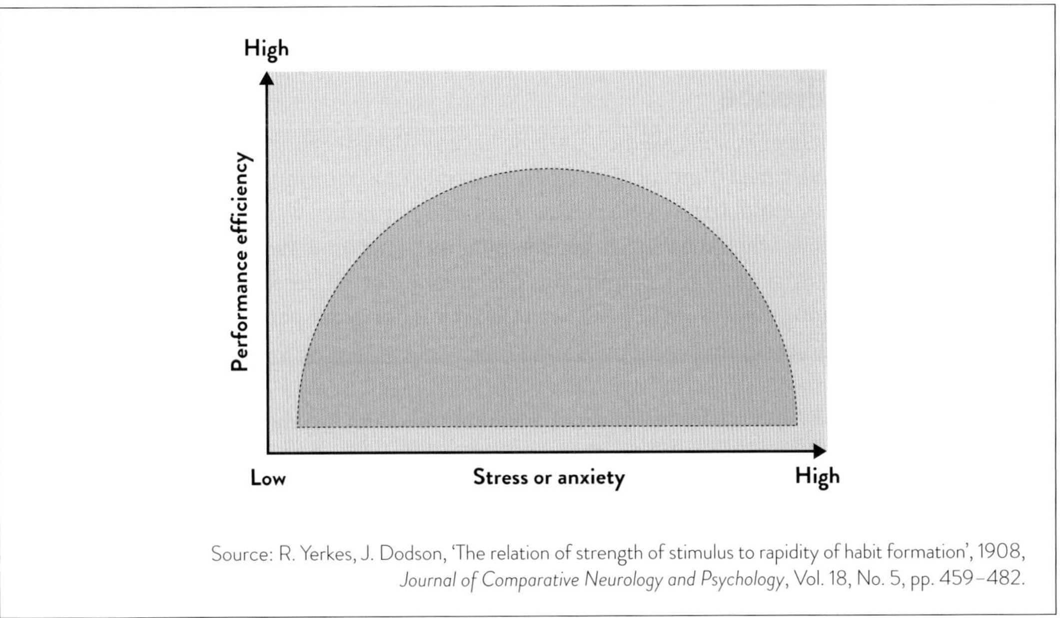

Source: R. Yerkes, J. Dodson, 'The relation of strength of stimulus to rapidity of habit formation', 1908, *Journal of Comparative Neurology and Psychology*, Vol. 18, No. 5, pp. 459–482.

FIGURE 5.4 The Yerkes–Dodson Curve

Here are some quick ways to avoid burnout:

- Avoid working unnecessarily long hours.
- Build your self-esteem so that you are more resilient.
- Develop and maintain interests outside work, including exercise, which lifts energy levels and produces feel-good endorphins that reduce stress.
- Keep your expectations about what you can achieve at work realistic.
- Say 'No' when you need to, so you don't take on more than you should.
- Slow down, take regular short (10-minute) breaks throughout the day, and take a full lunch break.[9]

Here are four steps to help you manage stress:

1. Learn to recognise your own physical, emotional and behavioural responses to stress. These alert you to the presence of a stressor so you can deal with it.
2. Identify the stressor, or source of stress. It (or they) may be at home (e.g. death of a loved one, going on holiday, illness or personal injury), in your job (e.g. demanding deadlines, major change in hours or conditions, actions or inaction of bosses, colleagues or customers, promotion or lack of promotion), in your finances (e.g. difficulty paying bills, making a major purchase), in your environment (e.g. noise, pollution, traffic) or within yourself (e.g. ageing, an outstanding personal achievement, a sense of inadequacy).
3. Reduce or eliminate the stressor or deal with it differently. When you can't prevent or reduce the stressor, perhaps by modifying the environment, change the way you perceive it and alter your self-talk.
4. If you continue to experience distress, act to reduce the stressor's negative effects. Alcohol, drugs, food, cigarettes or other short-term coping mechanisms might provide some temporary relief, but in the long run they are worse than doing nothing; they merely cover up the distress and fail to deal with its source or your responses to it. Experiment with various stress-management activities, such as exercise, meditation, relaxation training, self-talk and yoga, to help alleviate the symptoms of stress. Otherwise, you are at risk of serious health problems in the future.

Build your resilience

Winston Churchill lost every public election until he became British Prime Minister at age 62. Henry Ford went bankrupt five times. Vincent Van Gogh sold only one painting during his lifetime. Edith Cowan's mother died in childbirth when she was eight and her father was tried and hanged for the murder of his second wife when she was 15, but she went on to become the first woman elected to an Australian Parliament. Maude 'Lores' Bonney was deaf in one ear but became one of the world's best pilots. Evonne Goolagong Cawley, MBE, AO, was the first Aboriginal person to win a Grand Slam tennis title. They all had **resilience**. No doubt you know resilient people who are able to bounce back from adversity, too.

Closely related to EI and the leadership-management mindsets, psychological resilience is also a learnt set of skills. Resilience is mental toughness. It's the ability to adapt and find your way around, over or through adversity. It isn't about toughing it out and just plodding on, making lemonade out of lemons or brushing problems or difficulties aside; it's about keeping going in smart and imaginative ways and being resourceful and rolling with the punches *while* you adapt and keep going. Resilient people have the confidence and inner strength to deal with whatever life throws at them. Naturally, they become dismayed when the going gets tough, but can rein in their emotions in order to concentrate on working towards making the situation better or living through it. By contrast, people who lack resilience have a defeatist and pessimistic attitude. They fall apart under stress and don't bounce back quickly from difficult situations; they dwell on problems, feel victimised and are easily overwhelmed.

Increase your resilience

Increasing resilience is something that may require conscious effort at first but can become second nature to even the most die-hard pessimists over time. The following strategies can help you feel more able to bounce back from setbacks and increase resilience:

- ask for help when it is needed and offer help to others
- build strong networks of family, friends and colleagues who can listen to concerns and offer advice and support
- count your blessings, even when you have to hunt for them
- figure out what is needed to perform at your best and in which areas you have particular skills and abilities and concentrate on developing those skills (see information later in this chapter to learn about ways to identify how you work best and how to work to your strengths)
- get in the habit of interpreting negative events as temporary, thinking: 'This is one situation and it isn't going to last forever. I can get through it one step at a time'
- go with the flow, especially when it comes to change
- know what your priorities are and work towards accomplishing them every day (Chapter 9 explains how to establish and work towards your priorities)
- know which battles are worth fighting and are winnable and which are not
- learn from the past; even when you have dealt with similar situations poorly, they have information about what not to do again
- look after yourself, emotionally and physically, by participating in activities you enjoy, eating healthy food and taking time to rejuvenate
- know you can't change events but you can control the way you think about events beyond your control and set your sights on a positive outcome. Avoiding 'catastrophic thinking' – the tendency to assume the worst – helps to maintain performance in difficult circumstances. This is known as 'consistent competence under stress'
- monitor your self-talk and build self-confidence and self-esteem so you know you can get through setbacks
- stay flexible and keep working towards whatever it is you want to achieve. If you find that is no longer possible, adjust your goals and get to work on those
- take purposeful action. You cannot wish away or ignore problems and difficulties but you can see them in the broader context, decide what needs to be done and then do it, which may improve the situation, prevent it from happening again or help to reduce its impact if it does happen again
- use humour to help get through the difficult patches because laughter is a great healer.

Transferable skills

2.2 Personal effectiveness

5.5 Managing your career and professional development

> Know what success means for you, take responsibility for managing your career, know yourself – your strengths, weaknesses and passions – identify and excel at the tasks critical to success in your job, and demonstrate character and leadership.
>
> Robert Kaplan, 'Reaching your potential', *Harvard Business Review*, July–August 2008.

As working lives up to the age of 80 increasingly become the norm, you can expect to retrain, refocus and relearn at various points in your career. Working lives today already include five career changes and an average of 17 different jobs,[10] so you can expect to have several careers during your long working life and to work full-time, part-time, casually and for yourself. You can expect to have one job sometimes and two or more jobs at other times. You can expect to move up, down and across organisational hierarchies and to work in collaborative, **multifunctional teams**. You can expect to work when and where it suits you, sometimes at home, sometimes in a café. Never has it been more important to take charge of your career.

The questions to keep in the back of your mind are: 'What is the next role I am seeking either inside or outside my organisation?' and 'What transferable skills can I develop that I can bring to other jobs and careers?' With this in mind, you can strengthen the skills, experience and networks you need for your next move (see Chapter 8 for more on networking).

Your career vision: money, meaning or both?

You can earn your living in three ways – either through a vocation, or calling; through a career or line of work; or through 'just a job', working for whoever is employing you at that moment. Which way do you want to earn your living? Whether the career or vocation pathway, your work needs to align with your values, interests and what you're good at.

Part of your life plan is a career plan that helps you live and work according to your values. This is how your work can bring you both money and meaning.

Take the time to define what success means to you. Unless you know what you want, what you enjoy doing, what you're good at, what contribution you want to make and where you want to make it, and the skills and abilities you need to succeed, you can't manage your career. You're taking a chance that you can stumble into a job you love doing and that you're willing to do to the best of your ability. Think about your skills and aptitudes, the types of activities you enjoy, the roles you want to undertake and the impact you want to make, rather than the jobs you want to do. There are two reasons for this:

1 Organisations are changing their structures and the types of jobs they offer more frequently. Targeting specific jobs may leave you stranded. Targeting roles that can energise you, make good use of your skills and aptitudes, and satisfy you by allowing you to have the type of influence and achieve the types of results that are important to you, offers a variety of opportunities.
2 The life spans of organisations are shortening and the average life expectancy of companies is 10 years; only about 1 per cent of companies survive for 100 years.[11] This means you may well outlive your employer.

Know yourself

To begin planning and managing your career and professional development, you need to know yourself – your strengths and weaknesses, the ways in which you're smart, the skill gaps you need to fill, and the type of working environment and challenges that help you work best. You also need meaningful career goals regarding the role you want to play and the impact you want to make. This may sound like a lot of work, but it isn't when you think it through in the stages discussed in the following sections.

Work to your strengths

Transferable skills

2.2 Personal effectiveness

You probably know what you're *not* good at, but do you know what you *are* good at? What do you have a 'flair' for? What skills and knowledge have you picked up or worked hard to attain? What activities do you most enjoy? Everyone performs best when working from their strengths, not just avoiding their weaknesses. When you know your strengths, you can plan to develop them so you don't, at best, keep running in place and, at worst, get left behind by others who outperform you.

Ask 10 people who know you well – current and former work colleagues, family, friends, teachers and so on (the more diverse the better) – to describe your strengths. Ask in person or by email: 'What do you think I'm good at and can you give me one or two specific examples of how I have used this ability to help you or to make a contribution?' The answers may surprise you because a lot of what you do well is second nature, based on skills and abilities you use so automatically that you don't even realise you have them.

Here's what to do once you know your strengths:

- Identify areas where you have *no* strengths, talent or skill – these are areas to stay away from. Don't waste time developing them, either, as you have little chance of becoming even mediocre.
- Keep developing and improving your strengths.
- Look for gaps in your skills and knowledge, where you need to acquire new skills and knowledge or further strengthen existing skills and knowledge.
- Monitor your behaviour so that you avoid the trap of overusing your strengths. For example, if you're a good listener, make sure you don't listen when you should be talking. If being results-oriented is one of your strengths, think about whether you're oversupervising your team or being too task-oriented at the expense of considering people.
- Put yourself in roles where your strengths can help you produce results.
- Recognise, and take steps to remedy your bad habits. These may be actions or behaviours you do or fail to do that limit your effectiveness and performance.
- Redesign your job to include more of what you're good at, and delegate tasks that you find either too easy or too difficult. Make appropriate changes to the way you work, the composition of your team to cover your weaknesses and the way you spend your time.

You can't be great at everything, but you can:

- cover your weaknesses by building a well-balanced team
- keep out of situations in which your weaknesses are likely to be continually exposed and your self-confidence eroded
- pick the brains of a colleague or delegate the job to someone you can trust when you are given a task that requires a strength in which you are underdeveloped, and work with that colleague so you can learn from them as you complete the task.

Know the ways in which you're smart

People's minds work in different ways. Howard Gardner, professor of education at Harvard University, identifies nine types of intelligence,[12] shown in **Figure 5.5**. These nine 'smarts' are different ways of relating to the world and we all have them to some extent, in our unique combination. How does your smart-self operate?

The ways in which you're smart affect what you're interested in and the types of tasks you excel in. When you know the ways in which you are smart, you have more of a clue to your strengths. (When you know what types of intelligence the people you work with have, you know how to work well with them, too.)

Body smart
People with bodily kinaesthetic intelligence like to move and use their bodies in hands-on tasks.

Music smart
People with musical intelligence work well with melody, music and rhythms.

Nature smart
People with naturalist intelligence are keen observers of the natural order of things and are good at considering the broader principles in nature.

People smart
People with interpersonal intelligence enjoy participating and working cooperatively with others.

Philosophically smart
People with existential intelligence like to think matters through philosophically and form the big picture.

Picture and space smart
People with spatial intelligence are good at watching and observing and working with pictures and other images and representations, such as flow charts and maps.

Reasoning and number smart
People with logical-mathematical intelligence (the traditional 'IQ') are good at classifying information, using abstract thought, and finding basic principles and patterns.

Self-smart
People with intrapersonal intelligence enjoy thinking through ideas and working on their own.

Word smart
People with linguistic intelligence are good with words.

FIGURE 5.5 Nine types of intelligence

Transferable skills
2.2 Personal effectiveness

Know how you work best

Once you know what you're good at and smart about, you can work out how you work best, with others and with information. Then you can seek out career situations where you feel comfortable and can perform effectively. You can also work out how you prefer *not* to work because working in ways that don't suit you almost guarantees poor performance.

People work and perform differently. Think about your own preferred working styles while you read the list below and circle those that apply to you. Think about the working styles of those you work with, too, so you know how better to work with them.

- Are you a *decision-maker* or an *adviser*? Advisers don't excel under the burden and pressure of making decisions, while decision-makers, although decisive, often need advisers to help them think decisions through.
- Are you *practical, down-to-earth* and *present-oriented,* or *creative* and *future-oriented*?
- Do you pay attention to *facts* and *details,* or do you prefer the *big picture* and looking for *implications* and *possibilities*?
- Do you perform best in a *large* or a *small organisation*?
- Do you thrive on challenge and constant stimulation and tackling difficult problems or do you prefer routine?
- Are you more comfortable in *hierarchies* or in *informal, relaxed structures*?
- If you like working with people, in what relationship are you most comfortable – mutual interdependency in a *team* situation, as a *leader-manager,* as a *colleague* or as a *follower*? Or do you prefer to be near people but working *independently*?
- Do you work best with *things* or *ideas*?
- How do you best grasp information and learn – by *doing, listening, reading, talking* it through or by *writing* it down?
- What kind of work environment do you perform best in – a highly structured, orderly and *predictable* one, or a hectic and *unpredictable* one? And are you happier in an *action-oriented* environment or an *information-oriented* environment?
- What sort of job structures do you work best in; for instance, *formalised and prescribed* or *flexible and ever-changing*?
- What sorts of time frames (e.g. *tight, flexible* or *generous*) and results (e.g. *stretching* or *achievable, longer-term* or *shorter-term*) help you work best?
- How much autonomy do you like to have?
- Do you like to innovate, create and invent?

Work to improve yourself and the way you perform, but don't try to change yourself because you're unlikely to succeed. Try to avoid work and environments where you know you won't be able to perform well. (To find out more ways to understand yourself, see Section 5.1 of this chapter.) However you work, make sure you have a balance between work and the rest of your life, whether it's through work–life balance or **work–life blending**. When you don't, you risk burnout.

Your career plan

Transferable skills

2.2 Personal effectiveness

Once you know yourself and how you work best, you're in a good position to take charge of your career and professional development. Decide the direction you want your career to take and list the options open to you, remembering that you can accomplish a goal many ways. What types of tasks do you want more of and less of? What do you want to stay the same? What do you hope to be doing in three years' time? In five years? The answers help you target specific roles inside and outside your organisation. Set goals that stretch but don't strain, establish some career milestones and target dates to aim for, and make a commitment.

Think about your personal needs and situation as well your personality type and preferred ways of working. For instance:

- How much *flexibility, security and stability* do you need? Jobs with high security, such as accounting and medicine, have high barriers to entry because they rely on specialised technical knowledge or qualifications. When only a few people can do them, the jobs are not likely to be outsourced. Low-security jobs include customer service, marketing, human resources, IT and manufacturing.

- How much *personal contact* do you need? Do you enjoy interacting with others and forging strong relationships or are you more of a loner? If you enjoy interacting with others, do you prefer interaction based on, for instance, collaborating, helping and advising, mutual respect and cooperation or just passing the time pleasantly?
- What *type of boss* do you prefer? One who gives you the goal and leaves you alone to get on with it, or at the other end of the scale, a boss who does your thinking for you? Perhaps you're looking for a boss you can learn from, a boss who lavishes praise on your efforts and achievements, or a boss who respects your personal life and encourages work–life balance.
- Do you prefer to stay in one place or get out and about? Different jobs call for different levels of environmental *flexibility*.
- How much *potential for fulfilment* are you looking for? At the other end of the scale, do you just want to work for the money only?
- Do you want to be a generalist or build technical competence?
- Are you focused on your career or your whole pattern of living and lifestyle? Do you want to balance your work and life or integrate them?

The answers to these questions are likely to change at different points in your career and life stage.

Think of your career path as a lattice rather than a ladder. It may include a promotion or two (or even three). It may include one or more sideways moves in order to gain skills and experience in a range of jobs and tasks or to increase job interest. It may need a 'downward' move to learn something that is important to you or involve jobs with different working hours or responsibilities to give you more personal time. You may want to incorporate working on special **projects**, standing in for someone on leave, contributing to committees or moving into an entirely different field. You may decide to stay in your current role when it provides you with the level of interest and challenge you want, or you may develop your current job by adding to your duties and passing duties on to others that you've mastered and that no longer motivate you.

Let your networks know what types of roles you're interested in. Follow or join relevant social media sites like LinkedIn or Facebook, and develop networks in industries you're interested in moving into. You can find people through social media and invite them for a coffee, join the industry organisation or engage with them in some other way. You can also use a variety of online job boards like Seek. Then target a few organisations you're interested in and connect with people who work in them. Based on the 'six degrees of separation' principle, it won't take you long to arrange an introduction to people who recruit for roles you're interested in.

A career vision that plots the types of roles you want to undertake and the difference you want to make gives you a map to refer to as you journey through your career. It guides you to think about the additional skills, knowledge and experience you need to gain in order to achieve your career goals and decide how best to build your skills.

Plan your professional development

Transferable skills

2.2 Personal effectiveness

3.3 Written communication

Your initial learning and training cannot see you through the rest of your career; skills depreciate and need to be upgraded and replaced. Just as managing your career is up to you, so is keeping up to date in your field, industry and with personal development, management techniques and technology. Adding to, developing and sharpening your skills and knowledge, and gaining experience in a variety of areas keeps you employable and increases your earning potential.

As shown in Figure 5.6, leading and managing is about knowing, doing and being, or leading with your head, your hands and your heart. You can excel when you plan your professional development in all three of these areas.

To create a sustainable career, strengthen your current value as well as your future value in these areas. Your *current value* is what you create for the organisation in your current role. However, your *future value* is based on qualities and skills, such as your ability to adapt to change, to solve problems creatively and innovatively, to learn and to lead, your digital skills and digital literacy, and your willingness to tackle tough assignments, as well as the perceptions others have of you.

Seek to gain broad experience, technically and working in cross-cultural teams and in unfamiliar cultural contexts. Hone your ability to work with others in collaborative relationships. Include a variety of portable, adaptable skills in your professional development plan. Make sure your plan caters for adding to and building on your knowledge and strengths, filling skills, knowledge and experience gaps, and gradually rearranging or building up your job to make the best use of, and further develop, your skills and strengths. Notice how others manage their careers. Find ways to make the most of your passions and extend your experience through assignments, professional associations, project work, volunteer work and so on.

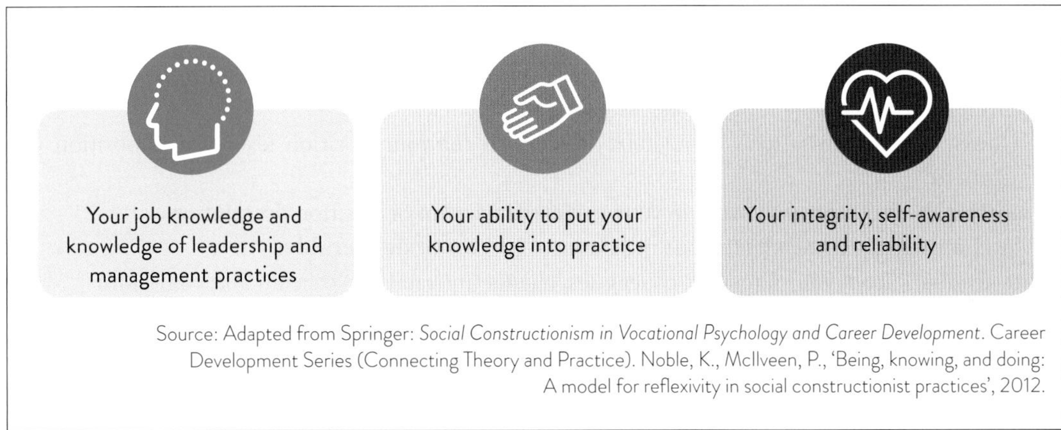

Source: Adapted from Springer: *Social Constructionism in Vocational Psychology and Career Development*. Career Development Series (Connecting Theory and Practice). Noble, K., McIlveen, P., 'Being, knowing, and doing: A model for reflexivity in social constructionist practices', 2012.

FIGURE 5.6 The knowing–doing–being model

'Digital' is the catch-all phrase for non-traditional skills and knowledge (See Chapter 1 for more on how technology affects jobs and organisations.) Digital literacy includes:

- basic software coding
- developing business processes
- knowing how digital systems and tools can deliver value to an organisation and its customers and extend its reach to potential customers
- understanding, interpreting and using analytics, online marketing platforms, social media and web processes to build an organisation's brand and offerings profile.

Here is a list of other new-economy knowing–being–doing skills you need in order to navigate the increasingly complex job market:[13]

- collaboration and team working
- cultural intelligence
- customer service
- effective follow-up
- goal setting

- initiative and enterprise
- innovating
- integrity-based self-promotion
- managing information
- sales and digital marketing
- self-management
- strategic planning and thinking
- strong interpersonal skills
- systems thinking.

Of course, you also need more traditional skills, such as:

- communication
- creativity and innovation
- critical thinking and analysis
- financial literacy
- project management.

Transferable skills

2.2 Personal effectiveness

3.3 Written communication

Assess your competencies

Competencies are the personal and technical knowledge, skills and attributes you need to carry out your day-to-day job tasks and duties effectively and efficiently and to move into future roles. To determine your development needs, assess your competencies:

- against your organisation's competency standards for your position level or the position you aspire to
- against the requirements listed in your performance plan or position description
- by comparing your results to your measures of success or **deliverables**
- by feedback from your manager, colleagues, clients (internal or external) and your team
- by observing others
- from performance reviews
- through personal reflection.

Below are the top 10 weaknesses that come up in online reference checks. Consider if you need to work on any of these:

1. self-confidence
2. communication
3. experience
4. industry-specific knowledge
5. time management and prioritising
6. delegation
7. taking on too much
8. further education/certification
9. handling stress
10. attention to detail/accuracy.[14]

Transferable skills

2.2 Personal effectiveness

By now, you may have quite a long list of development needs. Which are most important for you to develop over the next 12 months to achieve and maintain a competitive edge and protect your employability? Select two or three high-priority development areas on which you would like to concentrate.

Once you have identified and prioritised your development needs, set some short- to medium-term goals and look for opportunities to build your skills and maintain continuous learning. Accept roles that are a good fit for your values, interests, personality, working style, lifestyle and attributes, and that can extend your knowledge, skills and experience. There are many ways to build your knowledge and skills. You can build your knowledge and skills through:

- **action learning**, job exchange and job rotation, special and project assignments, temporary assignments and work experience
- asking questions
- asking other people for their thoughts on how you could improve your performance
- being coached and mentored
- **delegation** from your manager
- formal and informal learning programs: in-house, off-the-job or public
- internal and external training workshops, seminars and conferences
- general networking
- joining a professional association or industry group to extend your networks and support groups, and reading its journal to keep your thinking and knowledge up to date
- joining physical and virtual learning communities and knowledge exchanges
- learning from your manager, your peers, your reports and others you admire, especially those whose strengths are different from your own
- online tutorials
- part-time tertiary study, day-release courses or self-paced learning
- participation in committees and advisory groups
- personal study (e.g. reading, e-learning)
- shadowing and acting roles
- volunteer and committee work.

Looking over your shoulder for career competition from people or technology doesn't do you much good in today's globalised, technological world – your competition may be in another hemisphere, totally out of sight, or just a glimmer in an innovator's eye. Here are five essential ways to nurture your career:

1. Be innovative: technology can never replace innovative people.
2. Become a genuine leader: the ability to communicate a vision, set the pace and find willing followers practically guarantees lasting employment.
3. Keep learning.
4. Learn to be a skilful communicator.
5. Learn to work cooperatively and supportively with others: the adage 'no man is an island' couldn't be more appropriate.

Think about keeping a learning journal, because reflecting on what you've learnt, formally or informally, helps learning 'stick'. You can just keep general summary notes or follow the format of the **learning cycle** in Figure 5.7. Keep a good record of the professional development activities you undertake and your significant development experiences (e.g. participation in committees and on project teams, shadowing and acting roles, and so on). It's a good idea to file samples of your work too (avoiding strategic documents or trade secrets, of course). This could be useful when you're looking for your next job. Keep a 'smile file', too, with emails and thank you notes from bosses, customers and others complimenting your work, glowing performance appraisals and so on. (See Chapter 29 for more information on learning and how to learn from mistakes.)

Learn as you work

Life can be so hectic it can be hard to take time to reflect. Yet taking time to reflect helps your career as well as your job performance. Reflection keeps you conscious of what you learn, even from everyday mundane activities and routine procedures.

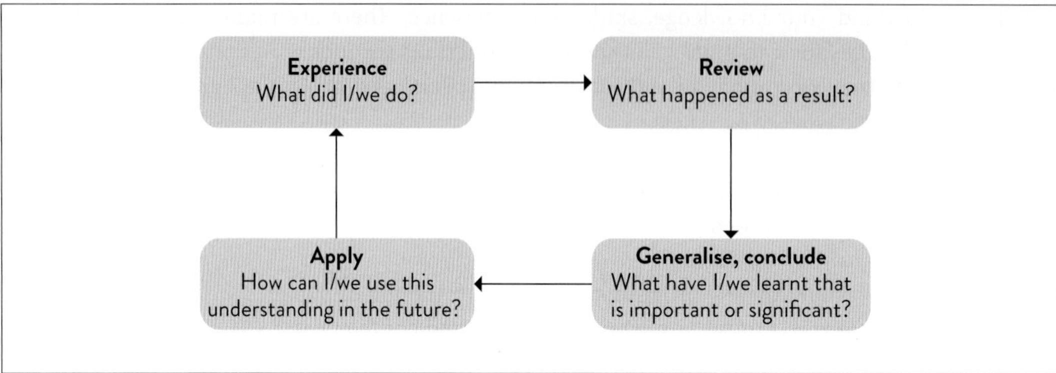

FIGURE 5.7 The learning cycle

Think of all the activities and tasks you have worked on in the past 24 hours. You may have calmed down a customer, developed or implemented a new procedure, problem-solved with a supplier, studied for an exam, trained an employee, worked on a project or written a report. You probably did some of these very well, some not as well as you could or should have, and others in an acceptable or average manner.

You are undertaking activities and tasks all the time. You could do just about all of them differently and often better, so it pays to take the time to think through what you have done to see what you can learn. This helps you complete the task better next time, continually improving your performance. Failing to update your opinions and knowledge condemns you to mediocrity.

Develop a habit of thinking through the learning cycle shown in Figure 5.7. This simple reflecting process helps individuals, groups and entire organisations continually improve their performance by learning from experience. To apply the learning cycle, first select an *experience* – something you've done. It doesn't matter whether you were successful or unsuccessful; you can still learn from it. Then *review* that experience: what did you say? What did you do? How did others react? What actually happened? What was your thinking at the time? Try to review it as if you were seeing it replayed on a cinema screen, or 'feel' yourself doing it in your mind's eye. Next, draw some *conclusions* about your performance. Be objective. What worked and what didn't work? What did you do well? What did you do poorly? What could you have done differently? Was your thinking correct? From these conclusions, plan to apply what you've learnt by thinking about what you can do the next time you're in a similar situation to improve your performance. Then practise what you've planned to build the skills and make them part of you. Look for learning opportunities in mistakes and setbacks, too.

Seek feedback

One of the most powerful ways to check your own performance is to ask others how they think you're doing and how you could improve. Colleagues, clients, your work team, your manager and people in your networks are all potential sources of valuable insights and information. Others can often see the details and effects of your actions and behaviour more clearly than you can and make valuable suggestions.

Make gathering information about how you're doing and how others see you an ongoing process because as new challenges and different demands present themselves, feedback helps you to improve.

You usually need to ask for feedback, and when you do, people see you as genuinely wanting to improve your performance and build your skills. Some ways to ask for feedback include:

- Can you see a better way to channel my efforts?
- Do you know of any other strategies I could use to achieve this goal?

- This is what I had intended; could I have reached that outcome more effectively?
- What could I do differently to be more effective in this area?
- What other ways of doing this do you think I could usefully explore?

Show that you are open and receptive to what you hear. Don't deny, defend or excuse yourself, or blame others, all of which could steal your chance to learn and improve and make the other person reluctant to give you feedback in the future.

Some feedback is bound to be accurate and useful, some of it less so. But all feedback is food for thought, and when similar information is given repeatedly, pay attention. When you're tempted to brush feedback away, remember the words of Socrates: 'Thank not those faithful who praise all thy words and actions, but those who kindly reprove thy faults'.

Sometimes, feedback is not delivered skilfully, and it may even sound more like criticism than help. But don't discount it just because of the poor skills of the person providing it because you don't like what you're hearing or because it doesn't immediately make sense. When you're doubtful, consider the possible motive of the person giving you the feedback. Consider all feedback carefully to see what you can learn. You're not obliged to take the advice when you don't want to.

Make sure you understand the feedback. When necessary, separate any emotional elements from the facts so you can respond to the useful information. Restate the feedback in your own words to check you understand it and ask questions when you need to. For example:

- 'If I understand correctly ...?'
- 'When you said X, could you give me an example of that so I can completely understand what you mean?'
- 'You said the report was incomplete. What could I add to it to make it more complete?'

Thank the person providing the improvement information. Say something like: 'I appreciate you telling me and ...', 'I agree and ...' or simply 'Thank you for your feedback', and commit to some change or at least to think through what they've said carefully. Figure 5.8 lists what you should do when receiving feedback.

If someone gives you negative feedback in public, move the discussion to somewhere private before continuing. Summarise your understanding of what they're saying and ask for improvement suggestions when you're still not clear. What does the person want you to do differently or suggest you do now or from now on? When feedback is worded aggressively or feels more like an attack, avoid a disagreement. Move the discussion forward by focusing on what you can do in the future.

Find a mentor

Wouldn't it be nice to have a knowledgeable and experienced person to 'show you the ropes', teach you, encourage you, help you learn from your mistakes, advise you on career options and fill you in on **organisational politics**? People who do this are called mentors. They are usually older, more experienced people who take an interest in you and your career. They are not necessarily your direct manager or even from your department; they may work in your organisation or be a member of one of your professional networks. Some mentors are experts in their field and help you grow mostly in that particular area. Others are more like 'wise counsellors' who share the wisdom and understanding that the experience of years brings. Whoever they are, they are people who can provide advice, help and support as you travel along your career path.

Although mentoring is formalised in some organisations, it is more often an informal, voluntary process. Mentors usually choose the people they help, so when you notice a more senior manager spending time with you and offering advice, listen carefully. (You can find out more about mentoring in Chapter 29.)

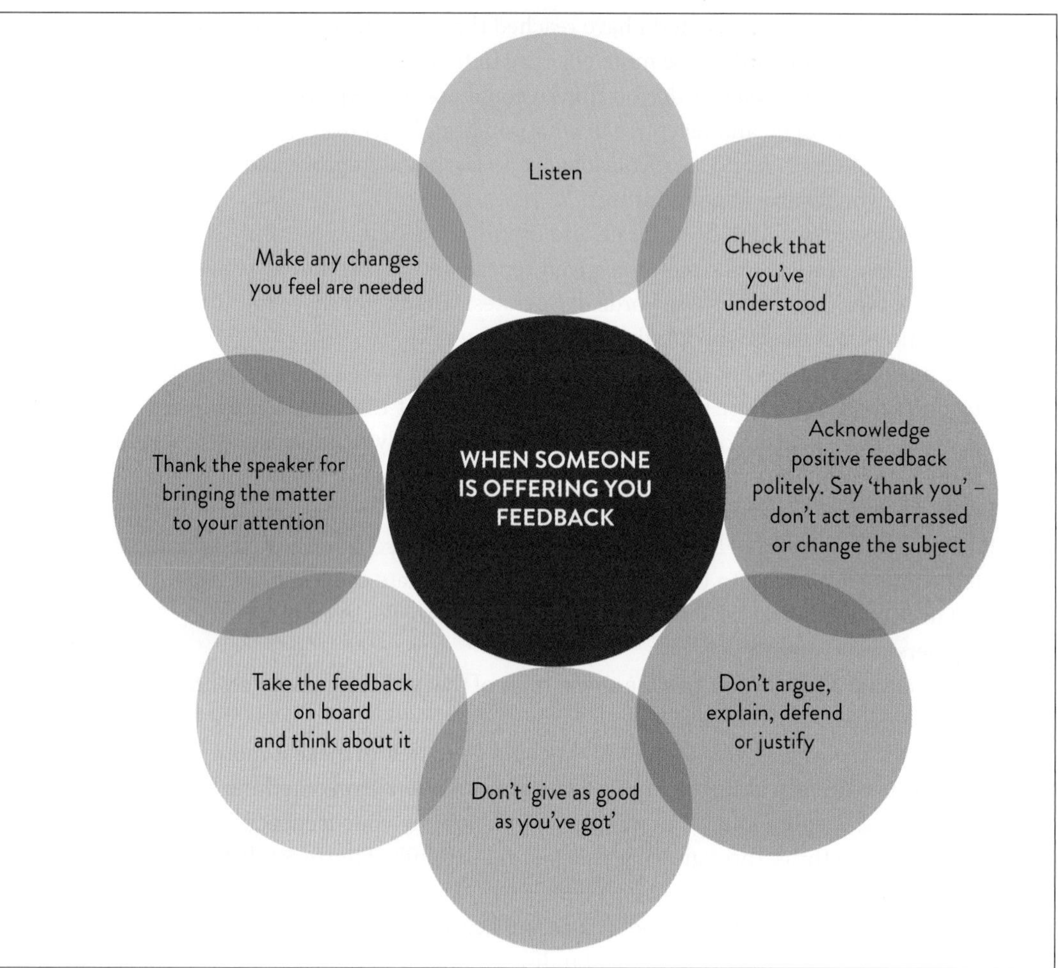

FIGURE 5.8 What you should do when receiving feedback

If you find you could benefit from a mentor, you can be proactive and make the first approach. Look for someone who:

- has the life and work experience and skills necessary to help you deal with issues that concern you
- is a good listener – you don't want them to solve problems for you but to help you uncover your own solutions
- is candid, so you get both the positive and the constructive feedback you need
- is well respected
- you can trust to keep your conversations confidential.

When you approach someone to be your mentor, make clear what help you think you need, and put limits on how much of the mentor's time you expect. Don't rush up and say, 'Will you be my mentor?'

Get a coach

Although people tend to use the two terms interchangeably, mentors tend to help you with your long-term career, often helping you achieve your personal goals as well as your professional goals, while coaches concentrate on helping you improve your current job performance. There are two types of coaches:

1. People who are particularly good at a skill and help others develop that skill.
2. People who are not necessarily experts in a particular area but follow a coaching process to help the people they coach uncover and develop their talents and skills.

Coaches can be from inside the organisation (internal coaches) or brought in from outside (external coaches). (You can read more about coaching in Chapter 29.)

Think through your roles

Everyone plays different roles in different situations – acting out the parts required at the time. Sometimes you're a leader, sometimes a learner, sometimes a caring friend, sometimes a fun friend. Playing a role doesn't mean that you are acting or in any way behaving falsely. Rather, it means you are behaving according to a set of concepts that defines, for you, how to behave in a particular situation. This personal set of concepts is called **role perception**.

In Section 5.2, you considered and set goals for some of your personal and professional roles: boss, colleague, supplier, community volunteer, parent and partner, to name just a few. You have a role perception of how you should act and behave, the sorts of attitudes you should hold, how you should dress and so on in each of those roles. You develop your role perceptions by watching and reading about others (role models) in similar situations. The family you grew up in, your friends and the organisation in which you work all contribute to your role perceptions.

Many of the ways you perform a role are *functional*. They help your group or the people you're with to function more effectively. Some of your role behaviours, however, may be *dysfunctional*. That is, they make it harder for people around you to work effectively. How do you know whether you're helping or hindering? Feedback from others and reflecting on your actions using the learning cycle are two excellent ways to determine how helpfully you play your roles and where you need to adjust your behaviour. (See Chapter 4 for information on the functional and dysfunctional roles you can find in your work team.)

You fine-tune your role perception to conform to the **role expectations** held by the people around you, to how they believe people should behave in a particular role. In some organisations, for example, managers dress very informally, while in others the expected dress is 'smart casual' or a business suit. Some organisations expect managers to be strictly task-oriented, while other organisations put people first. Your perception of acceptable behaviour might alter when you move to an organisation with a different culture and working climate, and you might change some of your behaviours as a result.

Earn a professional reputation

Just as an organisation's reputation is priceless, so is yours. When you've earned a professional reputation, people listen when you speak and seek out your opinions and advice. Your workplace reputation is built on how you walk, talk, dress and act, and on the results you consistently achieve. It's built on how you deal with difficult situations, write, present ideas and behave in meetings, and on the character and leadership you demonstrate. It's the ribbon that wraps around your competencies and the value you add to the organisation.

Most organisations have a characteristic 'type' of employee; for example, people share similar ways of dressing and behaving. Who is promoted in your organisation? Whose ideas are implemented? Who is offered the interesting assignments? What skills, traits and 'style' do these people have in common? Simply doing your job well isn't quite enough to forge a career, particularly in large organisations. Think about the image you want to project and make sure everything you do, say and write, including on social media, projects the image you want.

Show respect to people you come into contact with and be aware of your biases. Simple courtesies include knowing someone's name or being aware of their preferred pronoun. Professionalism helps people work together effectively and triggers cooperation and commitment. Ensure people can count on you for reliable and straightforward communications balanced with tact and consideration for others. (See Chapters 6 and 8 for more on this.)

Try to be in the right place at the right time and build actual and virtual relationships with people who can help you in your career and who you can also assist. Demonstrate, by word and deed, your loyalty and commitment to your job, your department, your organisation and your customers. (Chapter 8 discusses this in more detail.) Do more than you're asked for and deliver results and complete projects successfully. Have plans to streamline workflow and improve results and discuss them with others. Build a team of high performers by training your team and team members well and supporting their efforts. Generate enthusiasm, build their confidence and self-esteem, and set and achieve high performance standards (see Chapter 19 for more on this). Give credit where it is due and, without 'blowing your own trumpet', ensure that others know about your and your team's achievements, avoiding empty publicity that you cannot back up with solid achievement.

Look and act the part by maintaining a positive and professional attitude and dressing in the manner considered appropriate in your organisation for your job or the job to which you aspire. Blend your personal style with your organisation's culture so it is clear to others that you belong in your job.

You can find out more about how to earn a professional online reputation in Chapter 6 and how to build your personal brand by going to https://colemanagement.wordpress.com and searching for 'Building your personal brand'.

Let's leave the final word to Albert Einstein:

> 'Try not to become a man of success, but rather try to become a person of value.'[15]

Move on or fade out

In a working life that may last 60 years, you need to know how and when to change the work you do. The **S-curve of change** (shown in Figure 24.1 in Chapter 24) shows where, after a peak, an organism or an organisation either declines or makes a leap to a new level, and this also applies to careers. At some point, it's either time to move on or fade out.

When deciding whether to move on, think about the balance between what you've contributed to your role (e.g. the improvements you've initiated) and what you've gained from it (e.g. contacts, experience, skills). Think about whether you can continue to contribute to the role and whether you can still learn and develop in the role.

When you move too soon, you miss vital career experiences, learning, and personal and professional development that you need to succeed in your next role. In an ideal world, you move on once you have consolidated your contribution and your learning. When you leave making a change too late, you risk becoming complacent, working on autopilot and making mistakes. You risk curtailing your growth and experience and you could end up occupying a role to which someone with a fresh approach might be able to add more value.

When considering your options, look for an organisation, a department or a team that trains employees and for a boss with a reputation for coaching and developing staff. Make sure the organisation has values similar to your own so you can work effectively. When it's time to move on, tell your boss first and explain your handover plan for your successor. Do it in person or, when you work remotely, via a video meeting. Thank your boss and the organisation for the training, experience and opportunities you've received. (You can skip that bit when that's not true but, at all costs, stay professional – don't turn your resignation into a whinge fest.)

See out your notice period and complete your work as far as possible. Thank your colleagues personally, including mentors and any previous managers, and give them your new contact details. (They're now part of your network, so check in with them from time to time.) Enjoy your last few weeks, but don't use them as a chance to slack off. Leave on good terms.

Clarify your **job purpose, key result areas (KRAs)** and measures of success in your new role. Then aim to spend some time figuring out:

- what others expect from you
- your critical tasks and priorities and what you need to do to excel at them
- how best to divide and allocate your time to different activities
- mastering new skills and knowledge.

When you've done that, consolidate your learning and your performance before taking the role to a different level where you can make a unique contribution. That done, it may be time to move on again.

STUDY TOOLS

QUICK REVIEW

KEY CONCEPT 5.1 

a Using examples, explain why people need to understand themselves before they can understand others, and review some steps you could take to increase your self-understanding.

KEY CONCEPT 5.2 

a What are the benefits of knowing what you value and what you want from your career and your personal life?

KEY CONCEPT 5.3 

a Summarise the managerial mindsets explained in this chapter and discuss how you have observed them operating in yourself or by inference in other people's behaviour. What has been their effect?

b Discuss how the mindsets presented in this chapter help leader-managers succeed in their jobs and working relationships.

KEY CONCEPT 5.4 

a Explain the concepts of emotional intelligence and resilience and why they are important skills to develop, both professionally and personally.

KEY CONCEPT 5.5 

a What does knowing the ways you work best mean? What does knowing and working to your strengths and the ways you are smart, mean? Why are these important to know?

b Discuss the pros and cons of managing your career thoughtfully and purposely versus letting it evolve.

BUILD YOUR SKILLS

KEY CONCEPT 5.1 

a Based on **Figure 5.1**, draw your own Johari Window showing how large each square is in relation to the others. Ask five people you feel comfortable to ask whether they would draw the Johari Window for you with the same proportions. Can they offer you any feedback that would help increase your self-awareness?

b Explain the concept of espoused theories and theories-in-use to five people who know you well and ask them whether any of your espoused theories are contradicted by your behaviour (your theories-in-use); in short, do you 'walk your talk'?

c Ask 10 people who know you well to share a story about you when you were at your best. Then ask them to share a story about you when you were at your worst. Are there any themes of the 'best you' and the 'worst you'? What can these themes and stories teach you about yourself?

KEY CONCEPT 5.2 

a Search on the internet for ways organisations encourage work–life balance and for measures individuals can take to improve their own work–life balance, and summarise them.

b What do you hold dear? What is important to you?

c List your three primary roles, using one sentence for each. Describe your 'best self' in each of these roles. Then list three milestones for becoming your best self in each of these roles and the first three steps you can take to reach the first milestone for each.

KEY CONCEPT 5.3 

a What other mindsets, in addition to those discussed in this chapter, do you consider important to a leader-manager's success?

KEY CONCEPT 5.4 

a Who do you know that has high emotional intelligence? Observe their behaviour, particularly under difficult conditions, and note the particular skills you observe them using.

b Conduct an internet search for 'how to identify your emotions' and summarise your findings. How strong is your EI?

c What are your main stressors? How do you respond to them? Are your responses physical, emotional or behavioural? Develop a plan to remove or minimise the main stressors in your life so that you can savour life and prevent illness in the future.

KEY CONCEPT 5.5 

a You have decided you want to move to a different role within a year. List the steps you can take to make a satisfying and successful move.

b Find someone you know who either is a mentor or has been mentored. How do they describe the mentoring relationship? How did mentoring or being mentored come about for them? What do they see as the benefits of mentoring? Are there any disadvantages? Is a person at a huge disadvantage if they don't find a mentor?

c What role do you aspire to next? List the skills you need to develop in order to move into this role and prepare a plan to develop those skills over a time frame that suits you.

d Do you know the ways in which you're smart?

e What sort of career and job are you interested in and suited to?

WORKPLACE ACTIVITIES

KEY CONCEPT 5.1 

a What are your top 10 values? How do your values influence your decisions? How do you spend your leisure time and how do you approach your job and your career? How does your work support your values?

KEY CONCEPT 5.2 

a Investigate your organisation's policies and mechanisms for helping employees to achieve work–life balance and prepare a short report.

KEY CONCEPT 5.3 

a Select a person you believe to be an excellent leader-manager, sportsperson or athlete. Interview them to find out about their mindsets regarding their self-esteem, performance standards (self and others), optimistic or pessimistic attitudes, and mindfulness during their management, sporting or athletic activities. Summarise what you've learnt.

KEY CONCEPT 5.4 

a Ask your manager and/or a few colleagues and one or two people in your personal life for some feedback on how they view your emotional intelligence. Note any areas that you are strong in and any areas that you could strengthen. What are some specific measures you can take to strengthen your emotional intelligence?

b Begin a private 'emotions journal'. Every evening, note down the emotions you felt during the day. Label each emotion as accurately as you can and give it a number between one and 10 to indicate how strongly you felt that emotion. What triggered it? How did each emotion affect those around you?

How well did you control each emotion in order to respond effectively in the situation? Did your behaviour offer a positive role model to others?

c Draw a map of the stressors in the various facets of your life and circle the top three. (Remember that stress may come at the interface of various facets of your life as each competes for your time and attention.) Develop a plan for dealing with them more effectively so that you can savour life and prevent illness in the future.

KEY CONCEPT 5.5 

a How do you work best? How does understanding the way you work help you make more effective use of your strengths and compensate for your weaknesses? How does it affect the way you organise your job and progress your career?

b On one sheet of paper, summarise your strengths, the ways in which you're smart and the conditions and environment in which you work best. How can you bring your current working environment more into line?

c Given your current skill set and career trajectory, how likely do you think you are to lose your job to a computer during the next 12 years?

d Divide a sheet of paper in half. On one half, list 10 to 15 words that you believe others would use to describe you and your approach to work. On the other half, list 10 to 15 words that you would like to be used to describe you and your approach to work. How closely aligned are these descriptions? What actions can you take to align them even more closely?

EXTENSION ACTIVITIES

Referring to the Snapshot at the beginning of this chapter, answer the following questions:

1 Discuss David's approach to managing his career.
2 Who could David seek out to help him make an effective career decision?
3 What goals could David set for himself to help him move forward?
4 Does David know himself or his values?
5 Does he have a personal vision?

CASE STUDY 5

DES' MENTAL APPROACH

The sight of Des with his baggy brown trousers, crumpled shirt and tie that has seen better days is familiar around head office. He has been the oil company's technical trainer for decades, training the newly hired field representatives when they come to head office for their induction and touring the country running various training programs for franchisees' staff members.

In the staff kitchen, Des bumps into Lisa, the company's recruitment consultant, and takes the opportunity to tell her exactly what he thinks of the past few groups of newly hired field representatives. 'They just aren't up to scratch,' he says. 'They're not interested in the material they need to learn, they don't pay attention in meetings, they're totally irresponsible and are just plain thick. I hope the new group that starts next week will be better than your last couple of groups.'

'Irresponsible?' asks Lisa.

'Yes, for instance at lunchtimes, I always have to round them up to get started again, even though I warn them I won't. Even coffee breaks, for heaven's sakes – I need to herd them up after coffee, too. And thick. They don't pick up the material I teach them, they just don't seem bright enough or interested enough and they're too lazy to apply themselves. They just aren't up to standard, and you need to fix it or you'll find you'll be losing your contract with us.'

Lisa responded, 'Des, I'm really shocked to hear that because I've been totally happy with the people we've selected for you. I wonder – would it be possible for me to sit in on one of your training sessions with them?'

CASE STUDY 5

'Absolutely! I have them Wednesday to Friday next week and you're welcome to pop in any time,' Des replied.

'Thank you so much,' says Lisa. 'I appreciate that. I'd love to join you for your opening session on Wednesday – what time do you kick off?'

'Nine o'clock. See you then,' said Des as he returned to his office.

On Wednesday morning, Des tells everyone to take their seats and begins by laying down a few rules. 'Right,' he says, 'you people are going to have to work hard and apply yourselves because this technical material is difficult. In fact, a lot of new hires never come to grips with it, so some of you probably won't either. Just pay attention and do your best. Another thing – timekeeping. I'm sick of people waltzing in late from breaks and lunch and having to round people up. I want you here and ready to start at the appointed times. Now, switch off your mobiles and pass them to the front to me – I won't tolerate phones going off and texting in my class.'

'Ah,' thinks Lisa, 'I think I know what the problem may be …'

Questions

1 What frameworks discussed in this chapter can you apply to analyse this case study?
2 What specific conclusions can you make about Des' mindset regarding trainees from the case study? How might it affect his effectiveness as a trainer?
3 How would you describe the way Des went about informing Lisa of his dissatisfaction with the field representative recruits? What advice would you offer him?
4 What does Lisa's response to Des' feedback tell you about her emotional intelligence?

CHAPTER ENDNOTES

1 C. Argyris, D. Schön, *Theory in practice: Increasing professional effectiveness*, Jossey-Bass, San Francisco, 1974.

2 Thomas A. Harris MD, *I'm OK – You're OK*, Pan Books, London, 1973.

3 Caraniche at Work, 'How to overcome imposter syndrome', 2017, https://work.caraniche.com.au/how-to-overcome-imposter-syndrome; 'Brain food: Matters for the mind to chew on – are you suffering from Imposter syndrome?', *Management Today* (UK), May 2001.

4 Christopher L. Heavey, Russell T. Hurlburt, 'The phenomena of inner experience', *Consciousness and Cognition*, 17, 2008, pp. 798–810.

5 Logan Pearsall Smith, *Afterthoughts*, Constable & Co., London, 1931.

6 T. Maruta, R. Colligan et al., 'Optimists vs pessimists: Survival rate among medical patients over a 30-year period', *Mayo Clinic Proceedings*, February 2000, p. 140.

7 Dana Joseph, Daniel Newman, 'Emotional intelligence: An integrative meta-analysis and cascading model', *Journal of Applied Psychology*, Vol. 95, No. 1, January 2010, pp. 54–78.

8 Dana L. Joseph, Jing Jin, Daniel A. Newman, Ernest H. O'Boyle, 'Why does self-reported emotional intelligence predict job performance? A meta-analytic investigation of mixed EI', *Journal of Applied Psychology*, Vol. 100, No. 2, September 2014.

9 James Bradley, Employee Advisory Resource, a UK-based global Employee Assistance Programme provider, http://www.eap.co.uk, quoted in 'How to avoid burnout', *Human Resources Magazine*, 1 May 2007.

10 'The new work order', research report from the Foundation for Young Australians, Melbourne, 2017, http://www.fya.org.au/wp-content/uploads/2015/08/fya-future-of-work-report-final-lr.pdf, accessed 6 January 2018.

11 Paul Kerin, 'Business survival', *Company Director*, March 2016, p. 8.

12 Howard Gardner, *Multiple intelligences: New horizons*, Basic Books, New York, 2006; the theory originally proposed in H. Gardner, *Frames of mind*, Basic Books, New York, 1983.

13 'The new work order', Foundation for Young Australians, op. cit.

14 Adapted from an analysis of 12 800 online reference checks by SkillSurvey quoted in 'Talent: Room for improvement', *Harvard Business Review*, November 2016, p. 28.

15 Albert Einstein, quoted in 'Death of a genius', *Life*, 2 May 1955, p. 42.

CHAPTER

COMMUNICATING WITH INFLUENCE

KEY CONCEPTS

After completing this chapter, you will be able to:

6.1 recognise the main communication barriers that cause communications to fail and know how to avoid them

6.2 gather information effectively

6.3 give information effectively

6.4 understand and manage your body language and other non-verbal communications.

TRANSFERABLE SKILLS

The following transferable skills are covered in this chapter:

2 **Critical thinking and problem solving**
- **2.1** Critical thinking
- **2.2** Personal effectiveness
- **2.3** Business strategy

3 **Social competence**
- **3.1** Teamwork/relationships
- **3.2** Verbal communication
- **3.3** Written communication
- **3.4** Leadership

5 **Digital competence**
- **5.2** Technology use

OVERVIEW

Leader-managers play a pivotal communication role in organisations. As a leader-manager, you can expect to spend the bulk of your working hours communicating in one of four communication modes, whether face-to-face or virtually: listening, speaking, reading or writing. How well you communicate depends on your self-awareness, mindsets and emotional intelligence (discussed in Chapter 5) as well as on your communication skills. Together, they set the scene for productive work and effective working relationships (or make productive work and working relationships exceptionally difficult).

Poor communication is the most noted cause of frustration and poor performance in organisations and is at the root of most misunderstandings, mistakes and problems. It causes more havoc in work groups, teams and organisations than any other issue. Conversely, good communication can unite a group of employees and help them work as a team, and it can weld the various parts of an organisation together into an enterprising, efficient and effective whole.

There is no doubt that communication is a core employability skill. Communicating is about helping people understand and accept matters in the same way you do. The more important your message, the more often you need to communicate it, using as many channels as possible – formal and informal, written and spoken and even signals and sign language. This chapter gives you the solid foundation you need with which to apply your core communication skills as a leader-manager.

SNAPSHOT

Talk, talk, talk

Mila has been finding it hard to complete tasks lately, so she decided to keep a time log. She studies what she has recorded for the past week and is astonished to see that she spends about 80 per cent of each workday 'communicating'. She communicates with her staff, manager, other team leaders, people in other sections of the organisation, and people outside the organisation. She communicates on the telephone, in virtual and actual meetings, in individual discussions and in interviews. She communicates in writing through emails and texts, reports and proposals and through social media ... the list is endless.

Next, she turns her attention to the check sheets she has been keeping of complaints and rework from her section. It looks as though communication problems may well be at the bottom of many of those, too.

Faced with the difficulties caused by poor communications and the massive amount of time she spends each day simply getting messages across to people and understanding the messages of others, Mila decides she needs to become better at this business of communication.

6.1 Overcoming communication barriers

Communication is the conduit of leadership from the Prime Minister down to the leading hand of a small group of council workers fixing the roads.

General Sir Peter Cosgrove (appointed Australia's Governor-General, 2014), 'Boyer Lecture No. 3', ABC Radio National, 22 November 2009.

Transferable skills

2.1 Critical thinking

2.2 Personal effectiveness

3.1 Teamwork/relationships

3.2 Verbal communication

3.3 Written communication

To communicate effectively, someone – a *sender* – needs to communicate a message so that someone else – a *receiver* – grasps it in the same way. For that to happen, three factors are involved, and anything that hinders any of them impedes effective communication:

1 *noticing:* sender and receiver must each perceive the other's signals
2 *understanding:* occurs in the mind
3 *accepting:* occurs at an emotional level.

During this process of noticing, understanding and accepting, both sender and receiver need to navigate a multitude of communication barriers that can disrupt the flow of information and waste goodwill, money and time. Most barriers can't be removed, so you need to deal with them as best you can.

With every message you communicate, whether electronically or on paper, non-verbally or verbally, the following hurdles need to be overcome:

- environmental barriers
- barriers within receivers
- barriers within yourself.

How effectively you communicate depends on how successfully you and the receiver can overcome these three groups of barriers. Table 6.1 summarises the common communication barriers you can expect to face daily. Which of these barriers do you see in your work and personal life?

When you consider all the possible barriers to effective communication and all the varied ways people communicate, it is amazing that any communication is understood and accepted. But here's the good news: you can overcome many communication barriers with awareness and practice. For example, you can use reflective listening (also known as active listening) techniques and put your preconceptions, prejudices and personal interests to one side so that you can listen with an open mind. Ensure you avoid checking your messages and scanning your phone or documents when a team member comes in with some information or a question, so you don't send the message, 'I'm

TABLE 6.1 Common communication barriers

Barrier	Examples and effects
Environmental	• Distractions, interruptions, noise, etc. can make paying attention difficult • When not face-to-face, there are no expressions, gestures and other signals to help interpret a message or how it's being received • Technology interruptions can impact communication, whether it be communicating via phone or via a virtual platform • Distance can make it more difficult to ask questions, check meaning, convey confusion, establish rapport, etc.
Incongruity	• When words don't match voice or **body language**, most people believe the body language rather than the words • Poorly set-out documents, documents filled with typos, misspelled words and poor punctuation impede a positive reception of the written message
Individual factors	• The abilities, situations and even the mood and stress level of the sender and receiver affect communication • Age, cultural background and gender can affect a message or its reception • Differences in attitudes and values, ideas about time and space, etc. can interfere with communication
Language	• Complicated or unfamiliar words, jargon or slang, complex sentence structures, long sentences, etc. can hamper communication • Using emotive, critical, negative, pompous or vague words can detract from a message or alter its intended meaning • Poor word choice can obstruct communication, e.g. words with several meanings or connotations are open to different interpretations • Language differences and accents can make communication difficult
Listening	• Not giving a speaker your full attention blocks communication • Not actively listening
Message complexity and quantity	• Complicated messages can make understanding difficult • Too much information can cause 'information overload'
Perceptions, prejudice and stereotyping	• Senders' and receivers' backgrounds, beliefs, biases, expectations, experiences, mindsets, prejudices and stereotypes colour messages and their reception • When a message doesn't conform to the receiver's beliefs or expectations, their tendency may be to ignore it or twist it to fit in with their beliefs
Self-image	• How senders see themselves is reflected in their message • How receivers see themselves affects how they hear a message
Status	• A person's influence and power can prevent others from speaking freely
Time and timing	• Feeling rushed can result in a sender delivering an incomplete, unclear, curt or poorly planned message • Feeling rushed can cause receivers to listen with only 'half an ear' and 'hear' the message incorrectly

not listening properly because I don't consider you or your message worth my full attention'. You can create a climate of trust and openness and keep the channels of communication open by communicating regularly. When tasks don't require concentration, you can leave your office door open to signal you're ready and willing to communicate.

It is also important to take people's abilities and circumstances into account when communicating with them. Select an appropriate channel of communication and think through your messages in terms of timing, word choice and language style, and consider supporting your spoken or written communications with charts and diagrams. You can also take extra care when you're communicating with someone who has hearing difficulties, is in a wheelchair or whose second language is English. For example, you can face a person who is hard of hearing and speak up or speak more clearly; you can sit down to match the height level of someone seated in a wheelchair; you can speak clearly and a bit more slowly to someone with English as a second language and support your message with a diagram. Accommodations like these reduce barriers and smooth the passage of your message.

People from different age groups often have different values and world views from each other. 'Generation gaps' can make it difficult for people to empathise with and understand each other's point of view, which increases the chances of miscommunication. Similar gaps can exist when people from different cultures or backgrounds come together. You can develop your generational and **cultural intelligence** to smooth communications. (For more information on working with and leading people from different generations and cultures, see Chapter 32.)

When you're pushed for time, remember the consequences of a message not being received and acted on properly, and take the extra few moments to communicate fully. Think about timing, too; for example, you wouldn't explain a detailed new procedure to an employee who is just about to rush home and begin annual leave. You can ask for, or work out for yourself, specific times when your message would be most welcome or effective. Table 6.2 outlines six types of communication that occur in organisations.

We know that our beliefs, expectations and prejudices filter and alter the communications we receive so that we see what we expect to see, whether it's really there or not (as was discussed in Chapter 5). We also know that our beliefs, expectations and prejudices 'leak' out to others in subtle ways in the messages we send. For example, when you think employees are lazy and irresponsible, your mental filters let in information that supports that view; when you think employees are hard-working and do their best, that, too, is what you tend to see and hear. To further strengthen the prejudice and stereotyping barrier, people tend to rise or sink to meet your expectations.

Stereotyping and prejudice affect your ability to relate to and communicate with people in numerous ways:

- The **halo/horns effect**, which causes your positive or negative opinions of someone in one area to carry over to your opinion of them in other, unrelated, areas.

TABLE 6.2 Six types of communication

Term	Participants
Interorganisational	Communication between organisations (e.g. discussions with customers, outsourcers and suppliers)
Intraorganisational	Communication within an organisation (e.g. meetings or discussions between departments)
Intergroup	Communication between groups within an organisation
Intragroup	Communication within a work group or team
Interpersonal	Communication between individuals
Intrapersonal	Communication with yourself (e.g. to try to remember something or think something through)

- The **Pygmalion effect**, which causes people to 'live up to' or 'live down to' another's expectations.
- The **self-fulfilling prophecy**, or predictions that, directly or indirectly, cause them to become true.
- The **confirmation bias** trap that causes you to see what you expect to see.

The growing challenge of communication

Paradoxically, several trends are making organisational communication simultaneously more difficult and more important:

- the decrease in number of full-time employees as many organisations have downsized and increased their numbers of those who are contractors, **undertaking flexible work** and part-time or remote workers
- moves towards trading partnerships mean that relationships with customers and suppliers are more important, and community expectations are increasingly reflecting corporate responsibility and **triple bottom line** thinking
- communicating through virtual means, such as an online meeting platform.

Never has it been more important for organisations to improve the quality of their communications, both internally and externally.

6.2 Gathering good information

> Nature has given to men one tongue, but two ears, that we may hear from others twice as much as we speak.
>
> Epictetus (Greek stoic), Schweig (ed.), *Fragments*.

You can think of successful communication as a process of gathering and giving good information in order to achieve a goal. You need a goal (even when it's only to 'pass the time'). You need to know what's on people's minds and people need to know what's on your mind in order to work together effectively. You need to be able to express your thoughts clearly and considerately to build effective working relationships.

Effective communication generally begins with gathering good information. This is about asking smart questions, noticing, listening and understanding. It includes sorting through the information you're collecting: Is it an assumption? A fact? An inference? An opinion? It entails temporarily setting aside your own opinions, feelings and thoughts – which is not always easy, especially when you disagree or feel strongly about a topic.

Transferable skills
2.1 Critical thinking
2.2 Personal effectiveness
2.3 Business strategy
3.1 Teamwork/relationships
3.2 Verbal communication
3.3 Written communication

You use four senses to gather information efficiently:

1. your *ears*, as you listen carefully to the other person's words
2. your *eyes*, as you observe the other person's unspoken signals
3. your *head*, as you think about what the other person is saying (and not saying) and what might lie behind it
4. your *heart*, as you put yourself in the other person's place to understand how they might feel.

Gathering information before giving it puts you in a position of strength because once you find out what other people already know, think and believe, it's much easier to convey your information or ideas in a way that blends with and adds to their beliefs and knowledge. This makes your information more persuasive and helps people grasp and remember it more easily.

Ask good questions

Transferable skills

3.1 Teamwork/relationships

3.2 Verbal communication

3.3 Written communication

3.4 Leadership

When you're genuinely trying to understand what the other person is saying and meaning, asking the right questions tends to come naturally – with a bit of practice.

When you're asking questions to uncover information, facts and opinions, avoid making people feel like you're interrogating them. And don't leap straight into 'hard' questions that people might prefer to skirt around. Spend some time building rapport and trust first.

We also ask questions to facilitate thinking in others and help to diffuse strong emotions in others – enquiring questions show a level of emotional intelligence. Ask your questions in a neutral tone of voice, using neutral words, and show you're listening with attentive body language and occasional summaries to signal you're following. The following sections provide a rundown on the main types of questions.

General questions

General questions are good for introducing a topic or highlighting the one you want to pursue further. They're usually open questions: 'Please bring me up to date with the Cengage account?'

Open and closed questions

Open questions encourage elaboration and help you draw out the 'full story'. They also get the other party thinking deeper about the topic and can facilitate self-awareness. They encourage people to give more than a 'yes' or 'no' answer and leave the way open for a range of responses, helping you explore and understand the topic at hand:

- What did you learn from working on that project?
- What problems did you run into?
- What's that new client like?

Open questions can be statements, too:

- Tell me about your new client.
- Tell me about your meeting with Jim.

Closed questions can provide facts: 'Will you have that finished by the time you leave for the day?' and 'Did you say they'd send the report in this week or next week?' However, they don't provide much other than facts. When you want to uncover more information, ask an open question.

Both open and closed questions often begin with *who, what, where, when* or *how.* Avoid questions beginning with *why* because they can sound critical and make the other person feel defensive.

Questions to avoid

Questions can elicit valuable information. But they can also have pitfalls. Table 6.3. outlines some types of questions you should try to avoid.

TABLE 6.3 Questions to avoid

Transferable skills
2.1 Critical thinking
3.1 Teamwork/ relationships
3.2 Verbal communication
3.3 Written communication

Coercive questions	These narrow or limit the possible answers and can trap the responder into giving the answers you want: 'Don't you think …?' or '… right?' or 'Wouldn't you prefer …?'
'Gotcha' questions	These (seemingly innocently) show up the other person's weaknesses or mistakes: 'Didn't you say …?' (and look how wrong you were)
Imperative questions	These are really demands: 'Have you done anything about …?' or 'When are you planning to …?'
Leading questions	These imply the answer you're looking for: 'You won't have any problems with that, will you?' and 'Are you just about ready to leave for the meeting?'
Multiple questions	These ask several questions in succession, leaving the responder puzzled about which to answer: 'How did you get on with that assignment? Was everyone helpful? Did they give you the information you needed? Did you have any problems? Or did it go smoothly?' (A string of questions like this often ends up with a lame, closed question, which the confused responder answers, giving you little to no information)
Sarcastic questions	These mask what you really want to say, but the 'sting in the tail' gives it away: 'Did you have trouble with your car again?' (to someone late for work or a meeting, when what you really mean is 'Why are you late again?')
Screened questions	These ask for the other person's opinion in the hope that it is the same as yours: 'What do you think we should do first?' or 'What are your plans?'
Set-up questions	These set people up only for you to whack them down: 'Do you agree that time-keeping is important?' ('Yes, of course') 'Then can you please arrive on time in future?' (This example uses two leading questions)

Clarifying questions

Transferable skills
2.1 Critical thinking
2.2 Personal effectiveness
2.3 Business strategy
3.2 Verbal communication

When you are unsure about what someone is saying, ask a clarifying question: 'Les, when you said you're behind schedule, can I check how much behind schedule you are?' 'Carole, when you said you didn't think Mary was the right person for this assignment, can I ask in which particular way or ways you think she's unsuited?' Most people want to make themselves clear and appreciate your efforts to understand.

Clarifying questions can help you clear up cloudy information. For example:

- *Hazy generalisations:* 'Everyone knows …' (Who is 'everyone'?) or 'They all say …' (Who are 'they'?)
- *Meaningless comparisons:* 'That's the biggest botch-up I've ever seen!' ('Can you run through precisely what is wrong with it?')
- *Vague comments or ambiguous words:* 'I want a more interesting assignment.' ('What would a more interesting assignment involve?' or 'What would make an assignment more interesting for you?')

Probing questions

Probing questions help you delve deeper into a topic. They encourage the responder to flesh out the details: 'Sam, you mentioned you were having problems with finding that information. What avenues have you tried already?'

Unspoken questions

You're probably familiar with the raised eyebrow, the slight leaning forward, the 'Ummm?', which say 'Tell me more'. A short silence is another invitation to continue. So is repeating the last few words the other person has just said, or a key phrase they've used. Absorb and understand the information you're hearing by using the EARS technique in Figure 6.1.

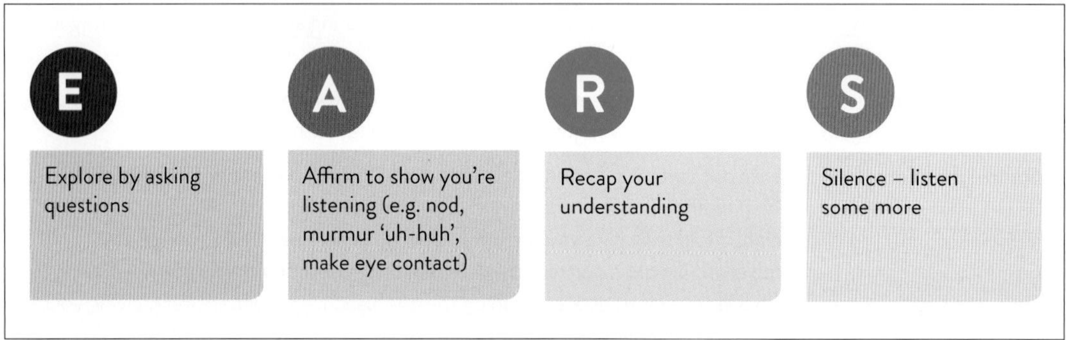

FIGURE 6.1 Use your EARS

Listen

Transferable skills

3.2 Verbal communication

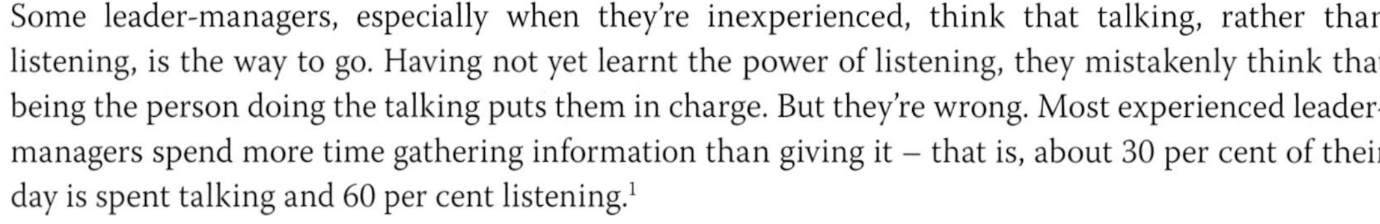

Some leader-managers, especially when they're inexperienced, think that talking, rather than listening, is the way to go. Having not yet learnt the power of listening, they mistakenly think that being the person doing the talking puts them in charge. But they're wrong. Most experienced leader-managers spend more time gathering information than giving it – that is, about 30 per cent of their day is spent talking and 60 per cent listening.[1]

Listen attentively

Transferable skills

3.2 Verbal communication

You can't build relationships without listening to people. Genuine listening is one of the finest compliments you can pay someone. According to the boomerang principle, when you listen to others, they are more likely to listen to you. Listening is about trying to understand how other people see situations and events, what the real meaning of their message is and what lies behind it.

Consider this: when you listen hard and concentrate, with your eyes, heart and mind as well as your ears, your blood pressure, body temperature and pulse rate all increase; these same physiological changes occur when you run a marathon. It doesn't just take energy to listen well. It also takes effort, patience, practice and a genuine desire to build empathy and understanding. Listening properly can be hard work, but the results are well worth it.

To interpret words and hear the meaning behind the words, think about:

- how those words are spoken
- the background to those words
- the person saying the words
- where you are now
- your relationship to the person speaking the words.

Show you're listening

Nobody likes talking to brick walls. When you are really listening, your body language shows the speaker that you're paying attention, which encourages them to give even more information. Looking at the speaker and repeating or rephrasing key words or phrases the speaker has used, and nodding your head in appropriate places, are ways to show you're following the speaker. Leaning slightly forward and making soft 'uh-huh' sounds also show you're listening. They help you listen better without disrupting the speaker's flow and encourage the speaker to continue.

Transferable skills

2.1 Critical thinking
2.2 Personal effectiveness
2.3 Business strategy
3.1 Teamwork/relationships
3.2 Verbal communication
3.3 Written communication
3.4 Leadership

Poor listening habits and skilful listening habits

Look at the characteristics of poor and effective listeners in Table 6.4 and circle two or three habits you intend to adopt and two or three habits you intend to stop to improve your listening skills.

TABLE 6.4 Characteristics of poor and effective listeners

Poor listeners' bad habits	Skilled listeners' good habits
• Being easily distracted • Not asking questions • Not checking whether you've understood before disagreeing • Not giving feedback • Fidgeting • Finishing people's sentences for them • Frequently (and often abruptly) changing the subject • Gazing passively at the speaker without giving non-verbal feedback that you are listening • Displaying inattentive body language (tapping a pencil, looking impatient) • Interrupting • Jumping to conclusions • Not responding to what others have said	• Asking questions • Checking your understanding by summarising the other's point of view • Giving speakers time to articulate their thoughts • Letting people finish what they are saying before giving an opinion • Looking alert and interested • Looking at the speaker in order to observe body language and pick up subtle nuances of speech • Remaining poised, calm and emotionally controlled • Responding with nods and 'uh-huhs' • Summarising frequently, repeating in your own words what the speaker has said (to check your understanding and give feedback that you are listening) • Using empathy like, 'I can see how concerned you are about this'

Concentrate on what you're hearing

Since we can think three to four times faster than people speak, it's tempting to let your thoughts wander. Instead, use that 'free mental time' to look at the speaker, observe their body language and concentrate on what you're hearing. Your thoughts also wander when you let your eyes wander, and you miss another opportunity to pick up more about the meanings behind the words.

When you're not sure you fully understand what someone is saying, ask some questions. Help people to be specific and encourage them to flesh out the details and other information you need by asking questions to clarify generalisations, jargon, meaningless comparisons and vague statements.

Jotting down key points can help you concentrate and understand more fully. This is because most people take in information best through their eyes (70–90 per cent of everything that gets into the brain enters through the eyes, while as little as 10 per cent goes in through the ears).[2] Mental or written notes in words, symbols or drawings keep your mind 'on track' and help you summarise what the speaker is saying and remember the main points of the message. (Don't write down all the details, though – this stops you from listening.)

Summarise often

To truly communicate, you need to 'send back' what you've heard – but count silently to three first, to make sure the other person has really finished speaking. *Recapping*, or summarising what the speaker has said, is a great way to confirm your understanding and keep gathering information smoothly. You can repeat a key word or phrase or put the gist of what the speaker has said in your own words, without agreeing or disagreeing with it, and without adding your own experiences, feelings, ideas or thoughts.

Summarising is perfect when you want to:

- disagree, but first show you have heard and understood the speaker's viewpoint
- find out what somebody really means but don't want to ask outright
- provide or gain feedback about whether, or how fully, you have understood.

When used appropriately, summarising your understanding of the discussion also:

- encourages the speaker to continue
- helps draw out the full story
- helps you concentrate on what the speaker is saying without letting your own thoughts get in the way
- prevents or minimises misunderstanding by giving the speaker a chance to correct or clarify any points you haven't fully understood.

Transferable skills
3.2 Verbal communication

Reflective or active listening

You can take summarising a stage further, to reflective listening (also known as *active listening*). You can briefly summarise (keeping the meaning the same) the speaker's meaning, feelings or both. Reflect this back to the speaker with a statement, rather than a question. Rather than summarise feelings or meanings in your own words, you can instead repeat a key word or phrase. Either way, when you haven't got it exactly right, the speaker can easily correct you. It also helps:

- defuse emotion by showing the other person that you have heard what they said
- people explore their feelings and thoughts
- you 'read between the lines'
- you understand and empathise, even when you don't agree with the speaker
- reassure the speaker that you are listening with an open mind
- show that you are listening and trying to understand, which provides an incentive to continue communicating with you, now and in the future.

When the speaker expresses several feelings, reflect the last one because that's usually the most accurate. **Table 6.5** gives some examples. Use objective words and a neutral tone of voice to avoid sounding judgemental or disapproving, and 'soften' your summary with phrases such as:

- 'I can hear that you might feel …'
- 'You think …'
- 'It seems to you …'
- 'You sound as though …'
- 'You look …'

When summarising or giving a reflective listening response, pause to let the speaker think about what you've said. Don't rush to fill their thoughtful silence with chatter. (Chapter 18 provides more information on effective listening and communicating.)

TABLE 6.5 Strong words need reflective listening

Speaker	Listener
'I'm so fed up I could scream! I'll never get through all this in time.'	'It sounds like you're feeling snowed under.' (feelings) or 'You've got a lot to do, and it seems like you'll never get it finished.' (meaning)
'Don't you have anything better to do than pick on me?'	'It sounds like you think I'm being unfair to you.' (feelings) or 'You'd prefer to do it the usual way.' (meaning)
'That way is no good – I'll do it my way!'	'You seem annoyed that I'm suggesting a different way to do that.' (feelings) or 'You feel a different approach won't work.' (meaning)
'Work, work, work and never a word of thanks. They treat us like cattle around here!'	'It's discouraging when no one seems to recognise all the hard work you put in.' (feelings and meaning)
'I'm loving my job; it's worked out better than I ever hoped it would.'	'You must be feeling really pleased with the way things have turned out.' (feelings) or 'It sounds like you're really glad you made the move.' (meaning)

Transferable skills

3.2 Verbal communication

Analyse information

Figure 6.2 shows how to listen effectively. Listen for the key ideas, then keep track of supporting information, listening for the five Fs:

- **F**act: Is this an indisputable fact that everyone would accept?
- **F**iction: Is this doubtful or questionable?
- **F**antasy: Is this someone's opinion?
- **F**eelings: Is this someone's intuition, ego or emotion?
- **F**olklore: Is this hearsay, gossip or rumour?

Transferable skills

2.1 Critical thinking

2.2 Personal effectiveness

3.2 Verbal communication

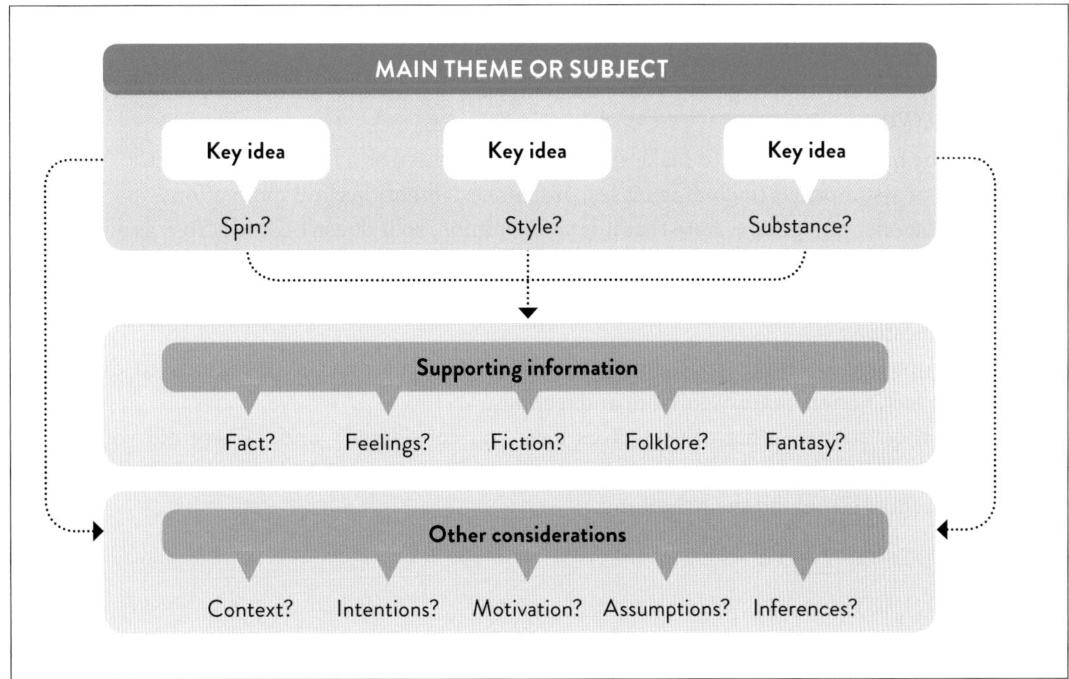

FIGURE 6.2 How to listen effectively

You probably deal with fewer *facts* than you might think. Many an expensive and embarrassing decision has been made by treating underlying assumptions, hearsay and opinions as facts and many a conflict has flared for the same reason. Often, what people present as a fact is actually *fiction* – inaccurate or incorrect information. Or sometimes they masquerade their opinion – their *fantasy* – as a fact. You may want to take these types of things into consideration, but don't treat them as facts.

Feelings have a place in organisations; after all, organisations are made up of people and people have feelings. Some feelings are useful, such as intuition – hunches and gut feelings – and with the world becoming more confusing and complex, this 'sixth sense' can be important. People's emotions, whether they are happy, sad, angry, motivated or uneasy, provide useful information, too. You also need to take feelings of the ego kind into account, although these are far less helpful than intuition or emotions. If you've ever seen someone backed into a corner and forced to save face or act macho, you've seen unhelpful ego feelings at work.

The last F, *folklore*, is based on hearsay, gossip or the rumour mill. As you probably know, most of it is fiction and should be treated as such. Although, it doesn't hurt to be tuned in because it can give you useful information about workplace dynamics and culture.

It is also important to consider the context or circumstances in which the communication is taking place. What intentions (i.e. desired outcomes) or motivations (i.e. reasons behind intentions or the strength of intentions) might be behind people's communications, and what assumptions (i.e. something people take for granted), including biases and prejudices, or inferences (i.e. conclusions drawn based on information available) they are making.

Transferable skills

3.2 Verbal communication

Be a detective when you listen. Don't be confused by style over substance, and listen for spin by making sure the speaker is answering your question or sticking to the point at hand, and not just delivering the message they want heard. Which of the three Ss shown in **Figure 6.3** do you hear? Listen 'between the lines' for what might lie beneath a speaker's words, too. This helps you analyse what you're hearing.

Use the five Fs along with the three Ss to help you think information through. When in doubt, ask the other person to make their thinking process clear: 'What leads you to conclude that?'

How to use the five Fs

When you give information or gather it, use the following tips to make sure what you're saying is true and to evaluate what others say:

- Get in the habit of checking to make sure what is presented as a fact really is a fact.
- Be alert to assumptions (including biases), inferences, intentions and motivations.
- When you offer an opinion, state that it is your opinion, so it doesn't come across as a fact.
- Don't spread folklore (but listen to it for the insights it can provide).
- Acknowledge and deal with feelings; listen to hunches and guard against ego-driven communications.
- When someone is telling you something, listen carefully and ask questions to distinguish between fact, fiction, fantasy, folklore and feelings.
- Ask good questions: 'What other factors have you considered?' and 'Where did you get that information?' Think about what their intentions and motives might be, and what assumptions and inferences lie behind their thinking.

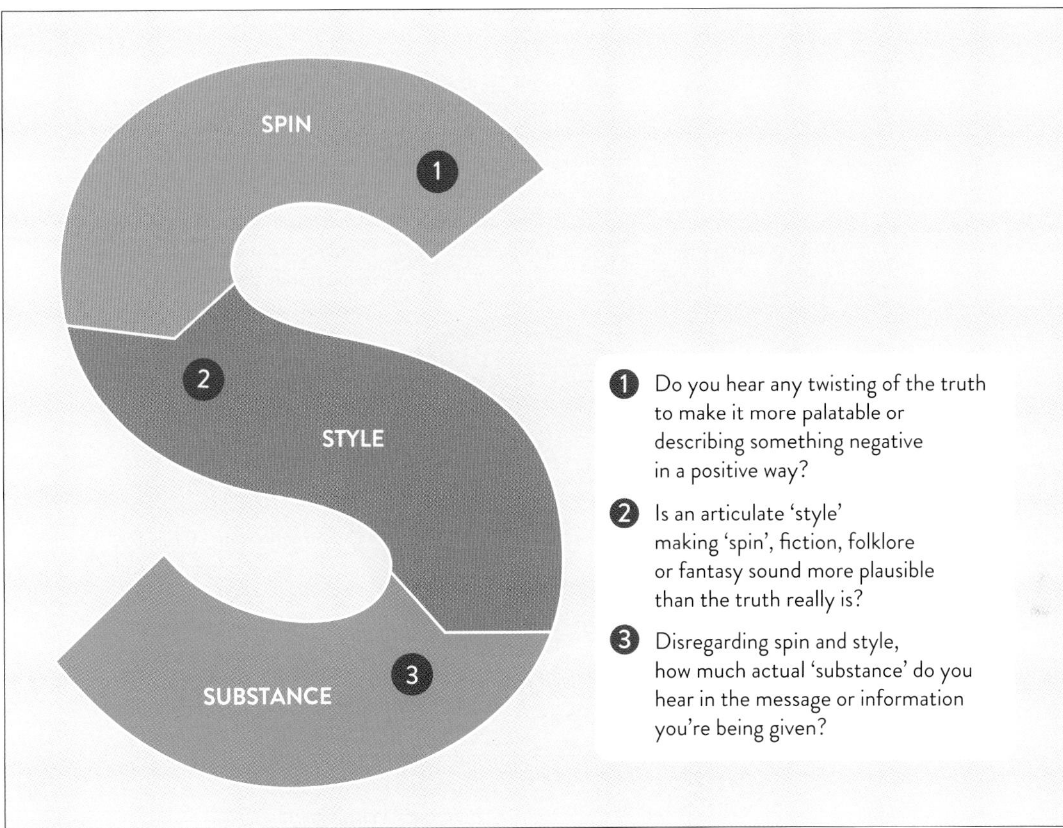

FIGURE 6.3 Spin, style or substance?

6.3 Giving good information

> To speak, and to speak well, are two things. A fool may talk, but a wise man speaks.
>
> Ben Jonson (dramatist), *Timber or discoveries made upon men and matter*, Ginn & Company, Boston, 1892, p. 101.

You are the link in the communication chain between your own and other departments in the organisation and between management and employees. This makes excellent communication skills indispensable. How well do you provide information? Do you just talk, or do you speak with intention? Do you notice and ask for feedback to make sure your messages are understood and accepted? Do you deliver bad news via email or text, or do you explain bad news in an assertive, courteous and empathic manner? Are your messages delivered in a tactful, positive way or a negative way that invites resistance? Do you take care to deliver information in small doses and often? Are you aware of your assumptions and perceptions and keep them in check to avoid distorting your communications? Do you think before you speak and try to put yourself in the other person's shoes, even when you disagree? Have you communicated the information shown in Figure 6.4 to your work team?

Transferable skills

3.1 Teamwork/relationships

3.2 Verbal communication

There's a lot to think about before you can communicate well. It's unlikely you've communicated by telling someone something – merely talking doesn't generally make for successful communication. The truth is that what you mean to say isn't what matters. What matters is the message others receive. When the two are the same, *intended* communication takes place. When the message received is not the same as the message you tried to send, *unintended* communication, or *miscommunication*, occurs.

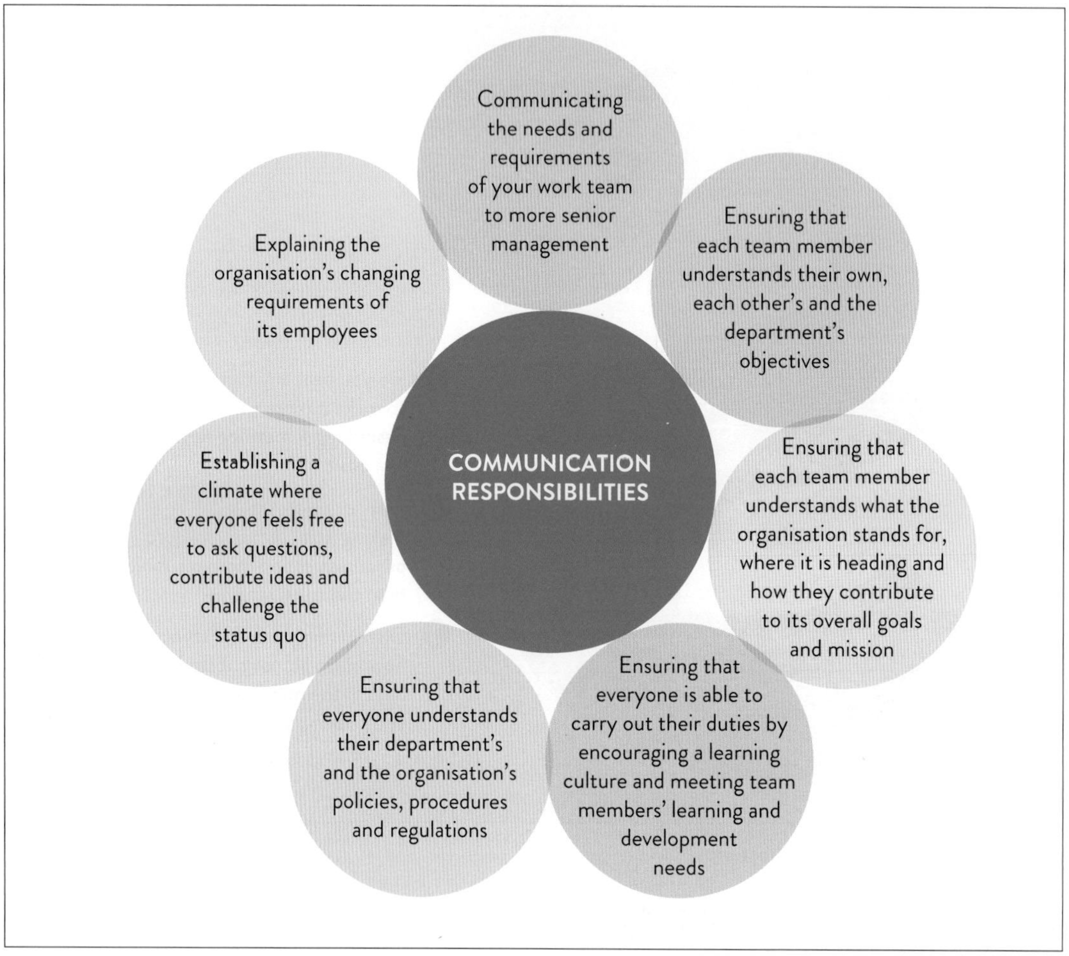

COMMUNICATION RESPONSIBILITIES

Communicating the needs and requirements of your work team to more senior management

Ensuring that each team member understands their own, each other's and the department's objectives

Ensuring that each team member understands what the organisation stands for, where it is heading and how they contribute to its overall goals and mission

Ensuring that everyone is able to carry out their duties by encouraging a learning culture and meeting team members' learning and development needs

Ensuring that everyone understands their department's and the organisation's policies, procedures and regulations

Establishing a climate where everyone feels free to ask questions, contribute ideas and challenge the status quo

Explaining the organisation's changing requirements of its employees

FIGURE 6.4 Your communication responsibilities to your work team

You need first to know your goal in communicating and then, having gathered information from the receiver, you can present your message clearly and persuasively, tailoring it to blend with what the receiver already knows, thinks and believes. This helps the receiver decode, or interpret, your message more easily and in the way you intended. This process is shown in **Figure 6.5**.

Transferable skills

3.1 Teamwork/ relationships

3.2 Verbal communication

However, this model is by no means the full story. You can enhance your message through drawings and other symbols. And as you probably know from your own experience, communication actually takes place quickly and simultaneously between people as each notices the other's body language signals, and consciously or unconsciously interprets them, while at the same time listening to the message and thinking it through.

Everything you do communicates. Your facial expressions, gestures, tone of voice – in fact, the whole package you present – are also part of your messages and these unspoken messages can be telltale signs of your motivations and intentions and even of your assumptions. This makes communication more like a complicated dance. It is a reciprocal process that happens between people, so the same message you give two people is received differently by each and probably given differently to each, too.

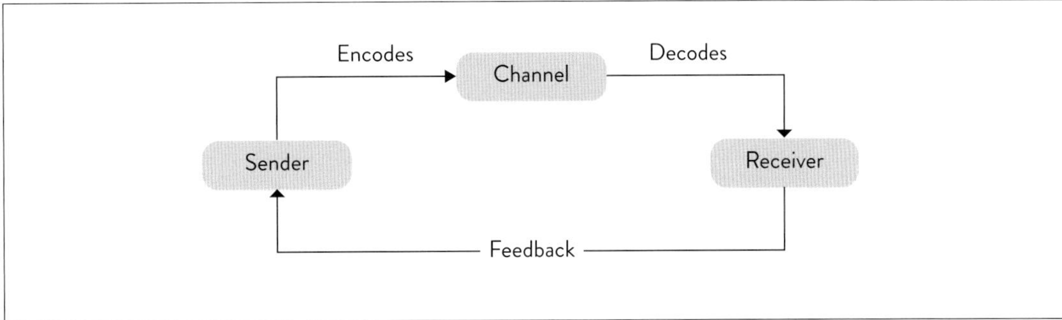

FIGURE 6.5 A two-way model of the communication process

Seven short tips for better communication

There's no such thing as a casual conversation when you're a leader-manager – employees repeat, dissect and interpret everything you say. This is just as true of the CEO's words spoken to the entire organisation as your words spoken to one or two employees at the water cooler.

Transferable skills

2.1 Critical thinking

2.2 Personal effectiveness

3.1 Teamwork/relationships

3.2 Verbal communication

Think it through first

Once you've said something badly – used a poor choice of words, given a bad example, delivered an order instead of making a request – you can't take it back. The more important or complex your message is, the more you benefit from thinking it through first. Even in ad hoc conversations, you don't have to blurt out a response. Pause and think first. Think about what you want to say and how to say it. Think about the words you want to use. Speak (and write) to be understood, not to impress. Use plain English to avoid the jargon barrier. Simple, clear language goes a long way towards achieving understanding. You can find out more about word choice in Chapter 7.

Select the location

When you can, reduce environmental barriers by talking somewhere that encourages open communication. Conversing in a quiet area, free from noise and distractions, is much easier than trying to hold a discussion in the hustle and bustle of a busy office or shop floor or 'on the run'. Try talking in the lunch area or going for a short walk to make communication flow more easily. You may not always be able to choose the best spot to talk but try to choose a suitable location whenever you can.

The six Cs of communication

The following six key words add up to clear communication. Try using them to test your messages. Is it:

1 clear?
2 complete?
3 concise?
4 concrete?
5 correct?
6 courteous?

Transferable skills

2.1 Critical thinking

2.2 Personal effectiveness

3.1 Teamwork/relationships

3.2 Verbal communication

Manage your expectations

Reduce the bias barrier by treating people in a way that shows you expect the best of them. Thanks to the self-fulfilling prophecy, when you expect the best, people generally give their best.

Use empathy

You may have heard the saying that to truly understand another, we must walk a mile in their shoes. Of course, before we can walk in another's shoes, we must first take off our own. Putting yourself in another's shoes means understanding how that person feels. This doesn't mean you have to agree; your goal is to see a situation as the other person sees it. Ask yourself: 'What must it be like for this person? What might be their feelings, opinions, desires, concerns and attitudes? How would I feel if I were in their position?'

Empathy helps you to understand others' communications and actions as well as the possible effects that your communication could have. Empathy helps you coach, offer feedback and provide other information, so it is well received, understood and accepted.

Be positive

Being positive can be the difference between successful and unsuccessful communication and can help ensure you achieve the goals of your communication. Which would you rather hear: the killer phrases on the left of Table 6.6, or the igniter phrases on the right?

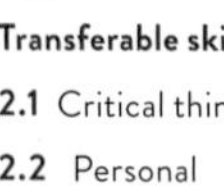

Transferable skills

2.1 Critical thinking

2.2 Personal effectiveness

3.1 Teamwork/relationships

3.2 Verbal communication

TABLE 6.6 Positive words make positive results

Killer phrases	Igniter phrases
'That won't work.'	'That might work if ...'
'That's wrong.'	'You're making great progress; try it like this – you'll find it easier.'
'Just put it over there for now.'	'You're finished? That's great! Thanks very much!'
'Where'd you get that idea?'	'That's an interesting idea – I wonder how we could make it work.'
'We haven't got the time.'	'Time might be a problem – let's see how we could get around it.'
'We've never done it like that.'	'Let's give it a go and see whether it makes the job easier or faster.'
'It isn't in the budget.'	'Let's test it out, and if it works well, we can find a way to get the funds.'

Transferable skills

2.1 Critical thinking

2.2 Personal effectiveness

3.1 Teamwork/relationships

3.2 Verbal communication

Chunk it and repeat it

Reduce the message complexity and quantity barrier by giving information in chunks of three or four, because that's all that people can keep in their working memory at a time.[3] This means that frequent communications on single topics are generally more effective than one big 'hit' of information.

Repetition helps your messages sink in. There are lots of subtle but effective ways to repeat a message so that you don't sound like you're stuck on replay. For example, you can use more than one channel of communication (e.g. confirming a telephone call with an email), or you can use different words, expressions or examples. Choose the number and type of repetitions to suit the other person's background and experience and the complexity and nature of the message.

Watch and ask for feedback

Transferable skills

2.1 Critical thinking

2.2 Personal effectiveness

3.1 Teamwork/ relationships

3.2 Verbal communication

3.4 Leadership

Because face-to-face communication permits immediate feedback, it's usually a more reliable way to transmit ideas and information. This is why so much business communication is spoken (and often followed up in writing for confirmation or future reference).

Talking directly with people allows you to ask questions and clear up any misunderstandings. The opportunity to observe body language can give you clues about how well someone has understood your message and can help you understand what the other person is saying. Look for non-verbal and signs of agreement, disagreement, confusion, hesitation, lack of understanding or surprise. Listen to people's tone of voice, which can indicate their degree of agreement, commitment and understanding and can reveal otherwise hidden thoughts. (Find out more about this in the next section.)

Encourage questions and comments. Questions can clear up confusion and help you assess whether you have communicated clearly. Establishing an atmosphere that encourages two-way communication helps people to add to, build on or disagree with your ideas, and present alternative ideas. Since unspoken opposition and concerns usually grow and cultivate resentment, it's better to discuss them early on and reach an understanding.

Encouraging questions and understanding

Transferable skills

3.2 Verbal communication

The way you ask questions is important. When you ask a closed question, such as 'Do you understand?', the response is likely to be 'Yes' to avoid looking stupid. It's better to use an open question to encourage a full response. Say something like 'What else can I tell you?' The response you receive will allow you to hear for yourself whether you have communicated successfully. When someone hasn't completely understood, take responsibility for not communicating fully or clearly. Rephrase your message; saying something in a different way often helps get your message across. Try giving an example, building on existing knowledge or giving a demonstration, or asking what in particular you need to clear up.

Make your messages stand out

You probably deal with many employees whose attention is permanently partial, which makes it difficult to capture their attention long enough for your message to get through. How can you make your information stand out and be remembered among the many streams of information most employees contend with – blogs, email, networking sites, RSS streams, smartphone apps, texts, tweets and voicemails? You can use multiple channels to 'spread the word' because the more communication channels you use, and the more often you communicate a message, the more your message stands out and the more likely it is that it gets across. Research shows that leader-managers who deliberately repeat their messages using different mediums get more buy-in than those who don't. Using multiple channels (e.g. combining emails, personal discussion and shared files) gives messages more weight and helps them sink in.[4] Table 6.7 gives some examples of the types of written, verbal and electronic communication you can use.

Assertiveness

Transferable skills

3.2 Teamwork/ relationships

Would others agree that you 'mean what you say and say what you mean without being mean'? Assertiveness is a style of communicating and relating to others that enhances mutual respect and leads to clear, open, direct and honest communication, both verbally and non-verbally. It is based on a strong set of personal skills and grounded in your beliefs about yourself and others. To be truly assertive, you need self-understanding and the mindsets discussed in Chapter 5. You also need:

- an internal locus of control
- clear and strong values that include openness and honesty

Transferable skills

3.2 Teamwork/relationships

3.2 Verbal communication

3.3 Written communication

3.4 Leadership

5.2 Technology use

TABLE 6.7 Communication channels

Written	Verbal	Electronic
• Articles and journals • Emails and letters • Organisation policies • Proposals • Reports • Signage • Social media	• Formal group meetings • Impromptu face-to-face meetings • Phone conversations • Recorded messages • Scheduled face-to-face meetings and interviews • Voicemails	• Collaboration technology • Emails, texts and tweets • Internet and intranet announcements and messages • VoIP (Voice over Internet Protocol), such as Skype • Virtual meetings

- high self-esteem
- mental models that include self-respect and respect for others
- positive self-talk.

Being assertive can be useful in many situations, for example:

- accepting and offering a compliment
- asking for a favour
- expressing annoyance
- initiating a conversation
- making a request
- responding to criticism
- saying positive things about yourself
- turning down requests.

Three styles of communicating

Transferable skills

2.2 Personal effectiveness

There are three broad styles of relating with others, as shown in **Figure 6.6**. They are aggressive, passive (also called submissive) and assertive.

Aggressive and passive styles are part of the fight, flight or freeze response that originates in a primitive part of the brain. All animals, including human beings, are born with the fight, flight or freeze response that instructs them to take one of three actions. They can stand their ground and fight, which leads to aggressive behaviour. They can flee (turn and run) or they can freeze (when there is no hope or when flight is impossible). Both fleeing and freezing lead to passive behaviour.

When the fight, flight or freeze response kicks in, blood moves from the brain into the muscles (preventing the ability to think clearly) and adrenalin courses through the body to provide the energy needed to fight or flee. When neither is possible, massive amounts of brain chemicals, hormones and painkillers are released into the bloodstream and we freeze, or stop moving.

Humans still have this ancient fight, flight or freeze response, although few face the life-threatening situations for which it was originally useful. Nevertheless, these passive and aggressive instincts can show up in the ways people communicate and in the types of relationships they develop.

People behaving aggressively are primarily concerned with achieving an outcome that satisfies them. This is called a win–lose position: *I win and you lose*. On the other hand, someone behaving passively is more concerned with making the other person happy. This is called a lose–win position: *I lose and you win*.

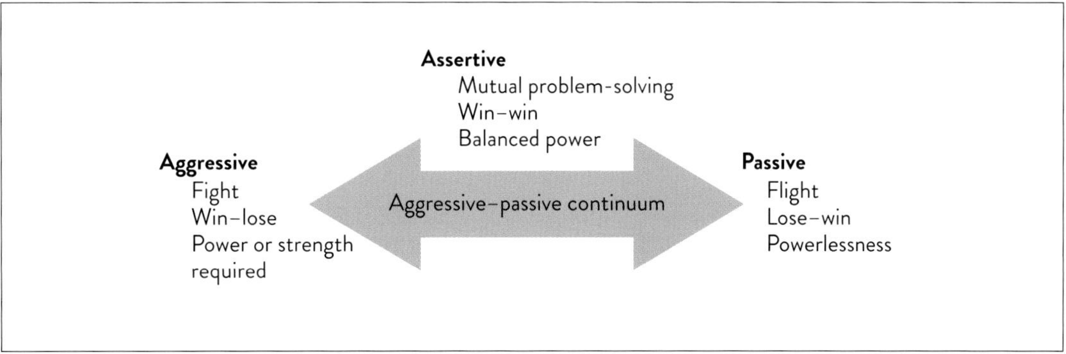

FIGURE 6.6 Three styles of communication

Assertiveness is a completely different style of behaviour and communication. Unlike aggression and submission, assertiveness is not instinctive and doesn't kick in automatically. Rather, it consists of a learnt set of skills. When you behave assertively, you work towards an outcome or solution that satisfies both or all parties. You honour your own rights as well as the other person's rights. This is called a win–win position: *I win and you win too.* Table 6.8 lists some characteristics of aggressive, passive and assertive behaviour, which are important to be able to recognise.

Transferable skills

2.2 Personal effectiveness

TABLE 6.8 Recognising aggressive, passive and assertive behaviour

Aggressive behaviour	Passive behaviour	Assertive behaviour
• Blaming, criticising, name-calling • Demanding or threatening (rather than requesting) • Expressing opinions as facts • Failing to respect other people • Focusing on own wants and needs • Generally behaving as if they are better than others • Making hostile remarks (e.g. derogatory, racist or sexist) • Speaking in a dominating or domineering manner • Using sarcasm to drive home a point • Invading other's personal space • Using 'standover tactics' • Displaying non-verbal cues, such as a jutting chin, set jaw, clenched or thumping fists, finger stabbing, glaring eyes	• Apologising ('Sorry, can I just say ...') • Dismissing own needs as unimportant ('What would you prefer?') • Lack of self-respect • Focusing on the other person's wants and needs • Frequent self-justifications • Seeking permission for thoughts or actions • Seldom expressing feelings, opinions and preferences, or expressing them in an indirect way (e.g. through hints) • Self-putdowns ('I'm hopeless', 'It's only my opinion, but ...') • Talking in a hesitant, rambling, singsong or whining manner, or in a dull, monotone or soft voice • Displaying non-verbal cues, such as downcast, evasive eyes, 'ghost' smiles when being criticised, and tense body posture accompanied by hand wringing, hunched shoulders, nervous movements, shrugs and shuffling feet	• Accepting and tolerant of others • Distinguishing between fact and opinion • Expressing feelings, needs and opinions in a way that doesn't punish or threaten others or ignore or discount others' feelings or wishes • Focusing on the issue or situation in order to reach agreement • Making statements that are clear and to the point, and that indicate self-respect as well as respect for others • Offering suggestions rather than giving 'advice' or orders, or making demands • Searching for ways to get around problems and differences of opinion • Appearing comfortable, relaxed, flexible and open • Appropriate eye contact that is neither too little (passive) nor a 'stare-down' (aggressive) • Facial expressions and other body language that accurately reflect feelings and messages • Open hand movements, emphasising key points

Your online professional 'Me Inc.'

Take care with how you present yourself online. Remember what you post is instant and permanent; even when you delete it, chances are someone saw it. What you write on social media needs to reflect your organisation's values and mission as well as your own. (If you can't do that honestly, you're in the wrong organisation.)

Keep up a professional profile on social media and use privacy settings to keep private matters private. Think about separate accounts for family and friends and another for colleagues and other professionals. Be aware that if you post too frequently, you may create an image that you're not working.

(You can find out more about earning a professional reputation in Chapter 5. To find out about building your personal brand, see Kris Cole's blog, 'Building your personal brand', at https://colemanagement.wordpress.com/2013/09/13/building-your-personal-brand.)

6.4 Managing your metacommunications or micro messages

> Eyes are vocal, tears have tongues. And there are words not made with lungs.
>
> Richard Crashaw (poet), *Upon the death of a gentleman in complete works of Richard Crashaw*, Robson & Sons, London, 1872.

Transferable skills

2.2 Critical thinking

2.2 Personal effectiveness

2.3 Business strategy

3.1 Teamwork/relationships

3.2 Verbal communication

3.3 Written communication

3.4 Leadership

Only a small portion of communication is achieved through the spoken or written word. Unspoken language says a lot, such as a downward glance, smile, sigh, silence, click of the tongue or tapping foot, and even the way you're dressed and the accessories you carry. Consciously or unconsciously, people notice this unspoken language, known as metacommunication, and make it part of the communication dance. What does your posture say about you? What does your clothing say? How open are your gestures? How convincingly do you show you're listening to someone? It all counts.

When your unspoken language doesn't match your spoken words, people believe the former. Every aspect of your communication adds to or detracts from your words. It all needs to 'add up' or you lose credibility.

A classic study by Albert Mehrabian showed that in a conversation between two people, only 7 per cent of the message is likely to come from the words that are spoken. The remaining 93 per cent of the message that is received and understood comes from body language (55 per cent) and tone of voice (38 per cent).[5] Of course, these figures can't hold true in every communication situation, but they make an important general point about the importance of body language and tone of voice.

This is not to say that words aren't important. Which would you rather hear: 'Your face makes time stand still' or 'Your face could stop a clock'? Or 'You look like the first day of spring' or 'You look like the last day of a long, hard winter'? Yes indeed, words count, too.

Body language

Transferable skills

2.2 Personal effectiveness

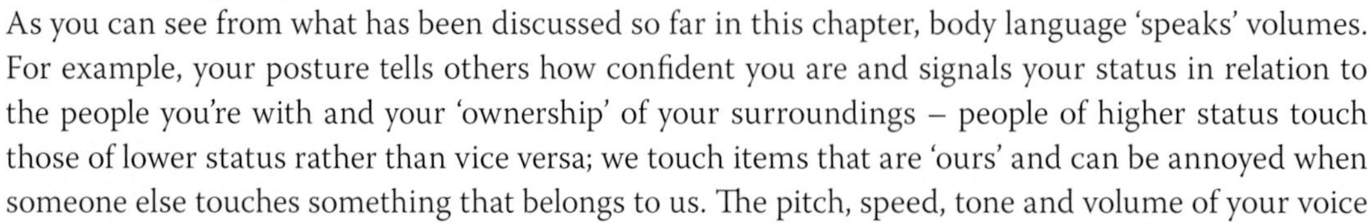

As you can see from what has been discussed so far in this chapter, body language 'speaks' volumes. For example, your posture tells others how confident you are and signals your status in relation to the people you're with and your 'ownership' of your surroundings – people of higher status touch those of lower status rather than vice versa; we touch items that are 'ours' and can be annoyed when someone else touches something that belongs to us. The pitch, speed, tone and volume of your voice subtly communicate the importance of your message, your degree of commitment to it and your emotional state; for example, whether you are feeling nervous or confident. Make sure your symbolic communication and body language 'match' your spoken message.

Monitor other people's body language, too, particularly any abrupt changes, as these could indicate agreement, disagreement or other emotions. Do people step back from you, indicating you are invading their personal space? Are they listening to you attentively? Or fidgeting so much that you would be better continuing the conversation another time?

Symbolic communication

Symbolic communication, such as the size of someone's office and the type of furnishings in it, are status symbols in some organisations. How tidy your desk is and the objects on it send messages about what's important to you. Clothing and personal grooming signal the way you expect others to treat you.

Personal space

Transferable skills

2.2 Personal effectiveness

Do you know that you have your own personal, invisible space bubble? When people enter it, you feel uncomfortable. With close friends and family, your personal space zone can shrink to as small as 15 to 45 centimetres; at work, most Anglo-Australians prefer others to keep to at least an arm's length – literally, while most Asians prefer more space. With people you don't know well, or dislike, your bubble expands even further.

You can observe differences in personal space zones between country and city dwellers; the personal space zone of people who live in high-density cities, for example, tends to be smaller than those of people who are used to wide open spaces in the bush. People from various cultures also have characteristic personal space zones.

Getting too close to people can make you seem pushy, while leaving too much distance can make you appear stand-offish. Keep your distance to the correct zone so that you don't invade anyone's personal space and make them feel uncomfortable around you. Figure 6.7 shows how to make sure your body language supports your communications, or be 'SO CLEAR'.

Build rapport with body language

Transferable skills

2.2 Personal effectiveness

3.1 Teamwork/relationships

Have you ever worked with someone who irritates you? Or someone you just couldn't seem to get on the same wavelength with? It's difficult to communicate with people you lack **rapport** with. When you have rapport with someone, you feel in sync or in harmony and have a sense of affinity and unity. You feel comfortable with them and communication flows. Rapport builds relationships, fosters cooperation and reduces conflict. It's essential to effective communication.

Rapport is based on similarity. We feel comfortable with people who are like us. You can see when two people have good rapport – they sit in a similar or even identical way, use the same type of words and style of language, make the same or similar gestures at the same speed, and speak in a similar tone of voice at the same or a similar speed. When one shifts position, so does the other; when one reaches for a drink, so does the other. They may even swing their leg or tap their foot to the same silent rhythm. Behaving in a similar way to the person you're with increases rapport, just as holding similar beliefs and values does.

S *Sit, stand and use space.* Sit or stand next to the person or at right angles and, as far as possible, on the same level so it is less confronting or domineering. When you're on the same level, it's easier to see things 'eye to eye'. Watch your use of space, too. In business situations, sit or stand about an arm's length away from others and avoid trespassing into their personal space with your belongings or using someone else's equipment

O *Open up.* Keep an open body posture and use open gestures. Most people interpret crossed arms and legs, hunched shoulders, or an averted face, eyes or body as closed and defensive, nervous and uncertain, or insincere

C *Concentrate your attention on the other person.* Centre your attention on the person and put any other thoughts to one side

L *Lean to show attention and apply or reduce pressure.* Lean slightly forward to show interest and attention. Lean a bit further forward to encourage people to provide more information. Lean slightly back to take the pressure off in a tense situation

E *Eye contact.* Remember too much is overpowering, and too little indicates lack of attention, lack of self-confidence or dishonesty

A *At ease.* Avoid fiddling, fidgeting and other nervous mannerisms that say, 'I'm not interested', 'I'm bored and want to get out of here', 'I'm nervous and uncomfortable' or 'I'm flustered'. Be relaxed and balanced, distributing your weight equally to both feet and sitting or standing straight (but not stiff)

R *Reflecting,* or mirroring, the other person's body posture, gestures, type of language (formal or informal, colloquial or proper) and voice tone. This smooths communication by increasing harmony and rapport and helps people feel more comfortable with you

FIGURE 6.7 The SO CLEAR acronym shows how body language should support communication

The more you like someone, the more 'like them' you are. People usually do this unconsciously, but you can do it consciously, too. It's called **mirroring**, or matching. Provided you're subtle about it, the other person subconsciously feels more comfortable with you – you're building rapport and establishing a bond that allows communication to flow more easily.

When you want to speed up the process of establishing rapport and put someone at ease, you can gently mirror them. But be discreet – subtlety is the key. Adjust your verbal and non-verbal communications to theirs but avoid copying them. You can also test whether someone feels in rapport with you by adjusting your body language or tone or speed of voice and observe whether they also adjust theirs. When you lead and they follow, you're in rapport.

STUDY TOOLS

QUICK REVIEW

KEY CONCEPT 6.1 

a Where do your communication barriers lie? Consider your own experience and the main barriers to effective communication you have faced and describe how you overcame them. For those you didn't overcome, discuss the signals that could have alerted you to the presence of those barriers; had you heeded them, what action could you have taken to remove those barriers or reduce their effects?

b Which of the barriers listed in **Table 6.1** do you see in your work and personal life? Give an example of each, explaining how you recognise the barrier and how you overcome it.

KEY CONCEPT 6.2 

a What does gathering good information entail? Give an example from your own experience.

b Describe the body language of someone who is listening closely. How does that aid communication?

c List and define the five Fs that help you think through what someone is saying. What else should you consider?

d What are the three Ss of listening?

KEY CONCEPT 6.3 

a Summarise the techniques for giving good information and, from your experience, give an example of each.

b What is empathy and how does it aid communication?

c Explain how a leader-manager can give clear directions without coming across as aggressive.

KEY CONCEPT 6.4 

a Explain how being aware of your own or someone else's metacommunications has helped you communicate more effectively, whether you were giving information or receiving it.

BUILD YOUR SKILLS

KEY CONCEPT 6.1 

a Think of an upcoming communication that is important to you. List the potential communication barriers and describe the actions you can take to overcome them or reduce their effect.

KEY CONCEPT 6.2 

a Think of an instance when you made an assumption without asking for clarification and the outcome of the communication was less than ideal. Write down at least five questions you could have asked during the communication that would have corrected your assumptions.

b Does effective communication mean you must agree with what the other person is saying or, conversely, that they must agree with what you are saying? Explain your reasoning and illustrate it with examples.

KEY CONCEPT 6.3 

a Review the differences between assertive, aggressive and passive behaviour and illustrate your explanation with examples from your experience – either your own behaviour or what you have observed in others. Do you think it's possible to lead and manage people effectively without the ability to be assertive? Why or why not?

b Explain why assertion can be mistaken for aggression if the asserting person isn't careful to respect the other person's rights, as well as protecting his or her own. Give an example to illustrate your explanation.

c Search on the internet for Mary T. Lathrap's poem 'Judge softly' and read it. What are its lessons concerning empathy?

KEY CONCEPT 6.4 

a Find a group of people talking together that you can observe quietly from a short distance away. Ignore what they are saying and, instead, observe their body language. Who seems to be the leader of the group? Who likes whom? Does anyone feel uncomfortable or left out? Is anyone impatient or bored? Is anyone angry? Are they good friends or just acquaintances? Give evidence for each answer.

b Observe two people in conversation. Are they in rapport? What is your evidence?

WORKPLACE ACTIVITIES

KEY CONCEPT 6.1 

a Keep a log of your communications at work for one day, noting any barriers that were present, what they were and the action you took to remove them or reduce their effect.

KEY CONCEPT 6.2 

a Describe a situation when you needed to ask a lot of questions and listen carefully to understand what someone was telling you. Discuss what, if anything, made it difficult for you to listen and how you overcame this and other barriers. Provide examples of the questions you asked.

KEY CONCEPT 6.3 

a Referring to a major communication process you have undertaken, explain how you took the context, environment and considerations regarding the receiver(s) of the communication into account when you developed your communication objectives, how you decided who to include in the communication and what communication channels or methods you considered. How successful was this communication in meeting its objectives? What factors were involved in its degree of success?

b Describe how you incorporate relevant business policies, procedures, regulations and legislation into your communications with your team.

KEY CONCEPT 6.4 

a Observe the people in positions one level above your own and describe their metacommunications.

b Observe people in a position you aspire to and describe their metacommunications.

EXTENSION ACTIVITIES

Referring to the Snapshot at the beginning of this chapter, answer the following questions:

1 What tips would you give Mila to manage her own communication strategies? What do you think she needs to do to become better at the business of communication?

2 How would you recommend Mila address her team's problems that have been caused by communication difficulties?

CASE STUDY 6

JIM IN JEOPARDY

The landline in the corner of Jim's office in Ceduna rang. That meant it was the State Manager. 'The Phone' was installed when the office opened over two years earlier, just so Wayne could communicate directly with Jim, even when Jim was on another phone call or in a meeting with his mobile switched off.

'Hello Wayne.'

'Jim, Canberra want to come out and review whether we should keep your office open. I want a brief report by the end of the week, and then I'll arrange for them to visit. Okay? Good. Thank you.' Click.

'Great, Wayne, nice to talk to you, too. Have a great weekend', Jim says into the air, hanging up the phone.

This was the third call on the landline in two years, when Jim was appointed to open a government-funded regional office of Aboriginal Business Development. It was quite different to Jim's former life in a city accounting office, though not much different to his time more recently living in an Aboriginal community as their accountant – except for all the written reports.

Still, people were people wherever you went. Spend time with them, sit down and do lots of listening, do your job and, above all, give them your respect and enjoy their company. That's the philosophy Jim carried with him to all his jobs.

Jim completed his report by the end of the week, following the tested and trusted 5WH principles:

CASE STUDY 6

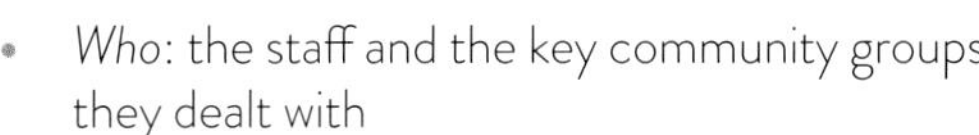

- *Who*: the staff and the key community groups they dealt with
- *What*: the work the office did, outstanding business and housing loans, financials
- *Why*: reasons the Ceduna office had been opened
- *When*: visits made to communities (once a week in one case)
- *Where*: the geographic area and key community groups
- *How*: improvements in operations since the office had opened.

Then came the field visit. Jim met the State Manager and the Canberra manager in Port Lincoln. Their first stop was the Mallee Park Football Club, one of the office's clients. Then Jim drove Wayne and Wayne's boss the 400 kilometres to Ceduna and Jim's office, where he'd arranged a meeting with some of the locals. The long drive gave Jim a lot of time to discuss how important the office's work is to the region and the local communities and the meeting in his office drove the message home further.

The next day, they drove two hours west to the Yalata Community to meet with the local Aboriginal Council and on the way back, they called into the community at Koonibba for a chat. Then back to the Ceduna office and more talking before shaking hands and saying their goodbyes.

After some time, the phone in the corner rang.

'Hello Wayne.'

'Well done, Jim. They've agreed with me that we should keep your office open. What got us over the line was the way the community people we met were clearly quite respectful and welcoming of you. You've developed good relationships. Your enthusiasm for the job and the people came through clearly – Canberra loved it. Well done.' Click.

Questions

1 What effective communication principles did Jim use to keep his office open?
2 What are some ways to communicate across diverse cultural groups?
3 What are the advantages and disadvantages of phone conversations, written reports and face-to-face discussions? What are some techniques you can use to overcome the disadvantages of each?
4 What are some guidelines for communicating in a professional, business-like yet friendly way on the telephone, in written reports, in emails and face-to-face?

CHAPTER ENDNOTES

1 A. C. 'Buddy' Krizan, Patricia Merrier et al., *Business communication*, 7th edn, Thomson, 2008, p. 408; Robert B. Denhardt, Janet V. Denhardt, Tara A. Blanc, *Public administration: An action orientation*, Cengage Learning US, 2013.

2 David Hyerle, *Visual tools for transforming information into knowledge*, Corwin Press, 2008, pp. 28, 52.

3 Jeffrey Rouder, Richard D. Morey, et al., 'An assessment of fixed-capacity models of visual working memory', *Proceedings of the National Academy of Sciences*, April 2008.

4 Tsedal Neeley, Paul Leonardi, 'Effective managers say the same thing twice (or more)', *Harvard Business Review*, May 2011.

5 A. Mehrabian, S. R. Ferris, 'Inference of attitudes from nonverbal communication in two channels', *Journal of Consulting Psychology*, Vol. 31, 1967, pp. 248–252.

CHAPTER

7

PRESENTING INFORMATION AND NEGOTIATING PERSUASIVELY

After completing this chapter, you will be able to:

7.1 present your ideas so they are understood and accepted
7.2 negotiate on behalf of your organisation or work team
7.3 turn conflicts into agreements
7.4 communicate clearly and persuasively in writing, following standard business protocols
7.5 deliver a successful group presentation.

TRANSFERABLE SKILLS

The following transferable skills are covered in this chapter:

2 **Critical thinking and problem solving**
  2.2 Personal effectiveness
3 **Social competence**
  3.1 Teamwork/relationships
  3.2 Verbal communication
  3.3 Written communication
  3.4 Leadership
5 **Digital competence**
  5.2 Technology use

OVERVIEW

You can expect to spend a significant portion of your working hours communicating, and in many of these communication situations, you need to influence the opinions, actions or behaviours of others. To this end, all leader-managers need to be skilled influencers and persuaders (supported by your personal skills, discussed in Chapter 5, and your core communications skills, discussed in Chapter 6).

You may be called upon to represent your organisation officially or semi-officially; for example, in a sales or negotiation situation or at an industry conference. Or it may be in a one-on-one or a small group meeting or making a presentation to a client or a larger general audience. You might be required to convince a client that your business approach is appropriate to their needs. Or you may need to persuade in writing; for example, by preparing a formal proposal, letter of introduction, or a submission to a statutory agency. You may be called upon to mediate between employees in a conflict situation to redress any grievances and negotiate a way to prevent the conflict from escalating further, or you may find yourself at odds with another leader-manager, someone else in your organisation or even with a client or supplier. Even when you're chatting to employees informally, you may want to take the opportunity to help them understand a new or updated organisational strategy or a change in team or organisational direction.

In all of these situations, you have a number of things to consider, including the:

- other party's inclinations and background knowledge
- type of communication medium; for example, face-to-face, telephone or videoconference
- communication barriers that stand in your way
- pros and cons of your position for the other party and other stakeholders

- best way to present your proposal, idea or position for maximum persuasiveness
- frequency of communication and the most suitable timing.

In this chapter, you find out how to think through and present your ideas, how to put key negotiating principles to use, and how to deal with conflict. You also learn a fail-safe way to think through and present written communications and develop and deliver presentations. (We discuss how to introduce and lead change in Chapter 24.) You will also consider how evolving forms of electronic and online communication can be used effectively in presenting and negotiating.

SNAPSHOT

What to do?

Trying to make it look like she's popping out for a coffee, Vailea storms out of the office, muttering to herself. 'Why isn't he ever ready on time? He knows I can't progress my work until I know the outcome of his, and then I need to work overtime to have my bit ready. He's a disorganised, arrogant ... I'm so over it. I've a good mind to complain to the boss!'

7.1 Promoting your ideas

> The tipping point is that magic moment when an idea, trend or social behaviour crosses a threshold, tips, and spreads like wildfire.
>
> Malcolm Gladwell, *The tipping point: How little things can make a big difference*, Little Brown, 2000.

You need more than a good idea or a sound negotiating position for it to be understood, accepted and acted on. Persuading people is a talent that begins with thorough preparation. You need to know 'who's who' in terms of power and influence in the organisation (see Chapter 4) and you need to think through how to link your idea and its benefits to their goals. You need to know what people want and why they want it, if and how you can provide it, and how to help overcome any objections they may have to your ideas. To succeed in this, you need to be up to date with your organisation's networks.

Think your idea through

Transferable skills

3.1 Teamwork/ relationships

First, give your ideas time to mature in your own mind – rather than rushing off with a proposal when you have a brainwave, step back for a moment. Think about the specific outcomes and benefits your ideas could achieve. Look at the objectives you are trying to meet from other departments' and key players' points of view. Who is likely to resist your ideas? How can your idea help them meet their goals? Think like the decision-maker(s). What do they want? What do they want to know? What sets your ideas apart from others?

Then float your ideas with a few people whose opinions you trust; find one or two colleagues you can use as sounding boards to assess the viability of your ideas and gather suggestions on how to improve them. If you're so positive about an idea that you can't see any potential resistance to it, ask what objections other people might have to it. It's not uncommon for people to be so blinded by the perceived perfection of their ideas that they can't possibly see any negatives, even if they're glaringly obvious.[1]

When developing your idea or considering your negotiating position, think about:

- how you can demonstrate a need for your idea, or build a business case for it

- how your idea fits in with or conflicts with other people's and team's main goals and how the success or failure of your idea would be advantageous or detrimental to these people and groups
- which people and groups might help or hinder the implementation of your idea – senior managers, other leader-managers at your own level, other departments or your work team, for example
- who might block your idea, why they might block it and what you can do to bring potential blockers onside
- who might support your idea, why they might support it and how you can bring these potential supporters onside
- who your idea will affect and how (e.g. your idea might lower a person's or a team's visibility, importance or influence, or it might make more work for a person or group)
- whose opinions you trust and whose support you need the most to have your idea accepted and implemented.

Gather supporting evidence so that you can build a sound business case. Facts are more valuable than opinions. Consider the following two statements and see which you find more powerful:

- We spent 54 hours last month alone just resolving incorrect invoices, at a cost of $1242. That's similar to our monthly average over the last year, which adds up to nearly $15 000 a year. I have a proposal to reduce that cost to the business dramatically.
- I think we're spending far too much money resolving incorrect invoices and I think we can reduce that cost dramatically.

When you believe your idea stacks up against the many other ways your organisation could spend time, effort and money on, it's worth moving forward with it. (How to prepare a business case is discussed in Chapter 29.)

Lay the groundwork

Once you've discussed your idea with trusted colleagues whose opinions you trust, thought about its ramifications across the organisation and for its stakeholders, and adjusted it to make it more palatable all round, you can gradually build a coalition of supporters. Who is most likely to support you and who should you get onside before formally putting forward your recommendations?

Think about the best way and order in which to approach them. There are important questions to ask yourself. Who should you speak to face-to-face and who would prefer an email or a short memo? How should you communicate with each of these people to be the most persuasive? For example, who should you enthuse with the 'big sky' overview and who should you entice with the finer details? Who should you stress results with and who should you stress the people aspects with? Who likes all the details and who prefers the overall picture? (Chapter 8 sheds light on this.)

Make your approach one of sharing your idea and involving others in shaping and strengthening the idea into its final form. Ask for people's views on your idea and listen to what they say, particularly when they have reservations. Pay attention to their body language, tone of voice and other clues to gauge how much they really support (or oppose) your idea.

With every proposal, some people and teams stand to lose and some stand to gain, so it would be naïve not to expect some opposition or scepticism. Don't take opposition personally and avoid becoming defensive – people naturally try to protect themselves and stay in their comfort zone, particularly if they have a fear of change. Work with resistance as if it's a file to help you smooth off your idea's rough edges. Ask questions and try to see concerns from the resistors' points of view. People are more likely to open up to your ideas when you acknowledge their opinions, and when you openly accept that you need their input in order to make the idea palatable for all. When 'my idea' becomes 'our idea', people respond more positively. Show people how you have incorporated their input to help them feel some ownership of the idea.

As you sound out the idea to a wider audience across the organisation, keep track of the responses, concerns and questions raised so you can prepare more thoroughly for your final presentation. Running your ideas by several people first also provides a 'comfort level' when you make your final presentation; that is, you will be more confident in your presentation and in the likelihood of its acceptance by decision-makers

Sell your idea to your team and colleagues

The decision-makers aren't the only ones you need to convince. Your colleagues, team and other stakeholders may not be the ones to give your idea the go-ahead, but you need to sell it to them just the same. Get their input and build in their ideas from the very beginning. Getting the buy-in of others could be the 'make or break' key to the success of your idea.

Transferable skills

3.1 Teamwork/relationships

Identify the most compelling suggestions of advantages and disadvantages that they raise. Then rework your proposal to minimise the drawbacks (or at least make them more manageable) and increase the benefits. Try to include a WIFM (what's in it for me) for everyone. Try saying 'What would you think of doing it this way?' rather than 'This is how we should do it'. The former seeks input and gives people a say. Make sure they understand that their doubts and misgivings are what you're looking for, and that their constructive input is invaluable. (Find out more about gaining support in Chapter 8.)

Present your idea

It goes without saying that your idea needs to be well thought out, practical and cost-effective. It's usually the best-packaged idea that wins approval, not necessarily the best idea. When your proposal is complicated, decision-makers may reject your idea rather than work hard to understand it, so make it easy for them by making your recommendation or proposed actions easily understood. Present your information assertively and in manageable chunks that can be easily 'digested'.

Transferable skills

3.2 Verbal communication

3.3 Written communication

When deciding how to best present your idea, think about the decision-makers' preferred modes of dealing with information (discussed in Chapter 8). When you present your idea in writing, explain it clearly and persuasively and set it out well; when you present your idea verbally, speak slowly enough that they can follow your argument (see Sections 7.4 and 7.5). This is also an opportunity to use visual aids and technology to assist you in getting your message across. A memorable presentation can have a huge impact on the audience, and could play a part in the eventual decision-making process. Take into account the decision-makers' evaluation criteria and who they might consult.

Frame your idea to show how it meets the organisation's main aims and strategy. For example, when cost containment is an important theme in the organisation, show how your idea limits or reduces costs. When building a cooperative, professional culture is the current priority, show how your idea helps build that culture. Clearly state the business benefits (e.g. the bottom line, effect on morale, public image). When people know you're motivated by the benefits to the organisation, they're more likely to support you than when they think you're just doing it for self-benefit.

Say 'because' after a statement. This greatly increases your chances of a 'Yes' because accurate facts and figures appeal to a person's sense of logic and reason – that's the *head*. Use the *heart* to strengthen your arguments further by aligning your ideas with the decision-makers' values and aspirations and link your idea into their priorities. Position your idea so that it is 'our idea' – the 'our' being influential key players, including experts and the decision-makers' peers, who have given you a positive response. The clearer it is that many people have been involved with and support your idea, the harder it is to reject it.

Show that you have considered the pros and cons of your idea and weighed them carefully; have your answers ready for probing questions about the pitfalls of your idea. Do the decision-makers have any positive or negative emotional attachments you may be asking them to accept or agree with? Have they had any previous positive or negative experiences with something similar? If it's positive, how can you link your idea to it? If negative, how can you show your idea is different from their past experience? When you can, link your idea with what the decision-makers have gone on record as saying they want or value, because people want to be consistent with what they have said or done in the past.

Think about how your idea can roll out when it is accepted – once that first step is completed, what comes next? When there are a number of steps, use a table to show who does what by when. Once your idea is up and running, how do you plan to make sure it doesn't collapse? (That's your 'keep it in place' strategy.)

Keep a list of the resources you will need at your disposal to implement your idea – physical, human and financial. Will you be able to convince others to consider using innovative or emerging technologies and ideas? The more information you have to hand regarding reasonable resource needs early on, the more likely it is that the idea will be considered viable to a business.

Know the risks of implementing your idea and how the risks can be addressed. Similarly, know the consequences of *not* implementing your ideas and be ready to present them. Should the mood of the decision-makers be 'Let's wait and see', you're armed with what the cost of waiting is.

Transferable skills

2.2 Personal effectiveness

7.2 Negotiating well

> Talking is like playing the harp; there is as much in laying the hand on the strings to stop their vibrations as in twanging them to bring out their music.
>
> Oliver Wendell Holmes, *The autocrat of the breakfast table*, Boston and New York Houghton, Mifflin and Company. The Riverside Press, Cambridge, MA, US. Copyright 1892, p. 11.

Not all negotiations are conducted by important people around a big conference table. We take part in negotiations every day – often without recognising them as such. Which film shall we see? What do you want for dinner? Can you stay late tonight to help me finish this project? Can I change my working hours tomorrow to fit in some personal appointments?

In most negotiating situations, you want to aim for an outcome that is beneficial, or at least acceptable, to all parties. In fact, the only time you might consider actively seeking to get the best deal at the expense of the other party is when you know you will never have to work with them again – but bear in mind the effect of that negotiating style on your own and your organisation's reputations. Such behaviour may also result in you questioning your own ethical standards and moral compass – are you really so ruthless as to be uncaring? Can you sleep soundly at night, comfortable with your actions? If you hesitate to answer these questions, it could also be possible that your actions may have a negative impact on your mental wellbeing.

As we see in Chapter 18, when organisations use their power to push supplier prices down, down, down, quality suffers and the suppliers eventually go out of business, forcing the organisation to begin the negotiations all over again with other potential suppliers – a lose–lose for everyone.

Frame the negotiation positively

You can think of negotiation as agreeing a path to move both parties forward for their mutual betterment. How can you best reach agreement on the issues? What goals do you share? If they differ, how can you move towards the same views and objectives? How can you reach a joint understanding and commitment?

The best long-term outcomes of negotiations come from agreements that satisfy both parties (at least to some extent, if not fully). They are built on mutual respect and trust, making establishing mutual respect and trust the first step in negotiating. (You can find out more about this in Chapter 8.)

Think of negotiating as a process of selling ideas (albeit sometimes to a less-than-receptive audience when the proceedings are adversarial). This may result in a simple process of give-and-take once each party has explained their position: 'If you agree to this, we can do that' or 'If I do this, I want that'. 'Horse-trading' like this works well when what is easy for one party to give is valuable to the other and vice versa, and not so well when the items under discussion are important to both parties – then you need to be more creative.

You can usually achieve the best outcomes by establishing an outcome that you both aim for, and look for ways to achieve the goals that meet the needs of both parties. For this to happen, each side needs to understand each other: where each is coming from; what each needs, wants and must have; what each is most concerned about losing. They each also need to understand the constraints of the other – what is and what is not possible to agree to. Aiming towards mutual goals takes more time but works well in high-stakes negotiations. The difference between these stances is summarised in Figure 7.1.

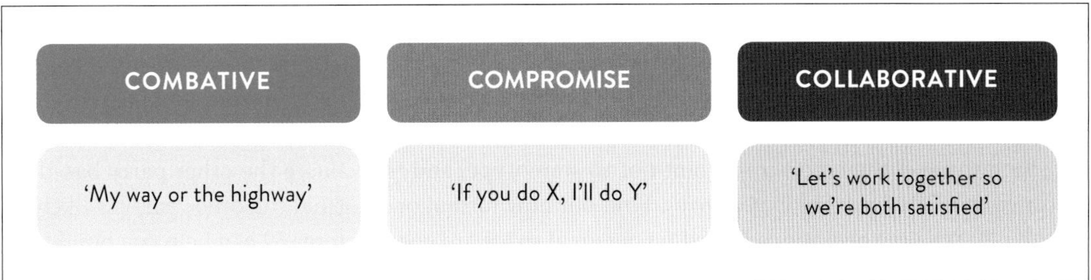

FIGURE 7.1 Three styles of negotiating

Do your homework

Transferable skills

2.2 Personal effectiveness

Do your research before sitting down at the negotiating table. Decide which issues matter most to the organisation and which are less important. Think through the organisation's strategic objectives and draft your negotiating stance and strategy by consulting others (as described in Section 7.1). For example, when you negotiate a workplace agreement, your strategy might be to provide a more flexible and forward-looking work environment that benefits everyone. Your strategic objectives might be to reach an agreement that helps the organisation attract and retain a quality workforce and to increase productivity and flexibility in ways that are cost-effective, time-effective and space-effective.

Work with your stakeholders to establish their musts, needs and wants and what they don't want to give away when the time comes to compromise. The better you understand your stakeholders' position(s), the more effectively you can negotiate. Ask them questions that help them suggest alternatives that meet your overall strategic objectives, too. In the workplace agreement example, they may be able to suggest a range of arrangements that could help meet your objectives.

Then work out your tactics – how can you guide the negotiation in a way that helps you achieve your objectives? Continuing with the workplace agreement example, think about the working arrangements that would best suit your business needs. What do you need, what do you want and what are you prepared to give up? Think about what the organisation needs to retain or gain, such as flexible rosters to meet peak demand or improved attendance, timekeeping or work practices. Think about any existing benefits the organisation needs to adjust, such as supplying tools of trade, guaranteed overtime or penalty rates for unsociable hours. Know where you can compromise and where you can't.

Then think about your goals, musts, wants and so on from the other party's perspective, using your 'audience analysis'. What are their major advantages and disadvantages to the other party? Then you can identify one or two of the most important benefits and one or two of the most important drawbacks from their perspective and rework your position to avoid, minimise or manage the drawbacks and highlight the benefits.

Use your audience analysis to think through what the other party's wants, needs, must-haves and must-not-lose items might be and what their opening position is likely to be. Decide how you can best establish mutual respect and trust, and then prepare your opening position so that it lines up with your strategic intentions. Some negotiators like to begin with an opening 'gambit', more like a wish than a realistic offer. The benefit of this is it anchors a 'high bar' in the other party's mind; the downside is that it's a well-known tactic. It's also worth noting that entering a negotiation with a high-level gambit can backfire; the other party may feel insulted by your opening, or even decide that you are so far apart in your needs that further negotiation is pointless and walk away completely. In contrast, you should be prepared for the other party to open with an unrealistic position, and be determined that it will not change your position.

When you're negotiating with people from other cultures, save yourself from looking naïve and unprepared by finding out what the other party's negotiation expectations are and fine-tune your approach to meet theirs. It's important not to stereotype, and to evaluate the other party based on historical negotiations and experiences. Find out how formal or informal the other party is likely to be and what their expectations regarding personal space are, too. Chapter 32 can help you build your cultural intelligence.

It's easy to try to achieve too much too soon. Make sure your requests and timeframes are realistic, so you can represent them with confidence. At the same time, you probably don't want to offer your 'bottom line' position. When you build some movement into your position, it allows the other party to look as though they've negotiated 'hard and well'. No negotiator wants to look like they gave in too easily.

Allowing for a small amount of movement also gives you flexibility to negotiate on other matters and manage the other party's expectations by setting a benchmark, or anchor, for the other party. (This is also why it's a good idea to make the first offer, at least on important issues.)

Remember that evidence convinces, so use facts, graphs and hard numbers to back up your points. You need to know what you're talking about and be thoroughly prepared so that you can persuade the other party of your case.

Depending on the negotiation, you can invite a colleague, stakeholders or your team to critique your opening position and the case you plan to present. When you haven't done much negotiating before, you may want to role-play a few discussions following different scenarios until you feel confident.

Transferable skills

3.1 Teamwork/ relationships

Gather your team

For lengthy or strategically important negotiations, gather a negotiating team who can support you with ideas and who have credibility with the other party. Even when you are the lead negotiator, split the negotiating among your team, perhaps assigning different areas to different people. This can work especially well if there are particularly technical or specialised aspects involved that require another person's expertise and ability to explain the issue in layperson's terms. When you do it all yourself, you're not only in danger of being caught out on areas you're not entirely confident in; you're also in danger of being seen to be the 'bad guy' all the time, which damages your working relationship with the other party.

Think about logistics

Manage the logistics when you can. For a potentially complex negotiation, you may wish to set a morning rather than an afternoon negotiation meeting in order to have more time to reach agreement. Investing more time in a negotiation also increases the odds of a happy outcome as you can build rapport, and neither party wants to lose their time investment due to a failed negotiation. Also consider the ongoing development of flexible working hours – will you be able to get all of the relevant stakeholders together at a time and date suitable for all, and using a medium they all have access to and are proficient in the use of?

You may also want to negotiate over several meetings. Even when you believe the negotiation will only last for one meeting, you can always plan a follow-up meeting to review your agreement and how it's working.

If you're meeting face-to-face, negotiate in your office or meeting room so that you can ensure the meeting place is comfortable, so you're both relaxed and ready to discuss cooperatively. Make coffee, tea, water and biscuits available. When you're meeting on neutral territory, make it a comfortable place that serves refreshments or bring some take-away coffee for both of you.[2] If you're meeting electronically, ensure that your environment is professionally laid out and that you are not going to be disturbed. This can be an unfortunately common occurrence, with the growing instances of flexible working hours and working from home arrangements meaning that disruptions, such as children, pets and doorbells, can often interrupt important work tasks.

During negotiations

Enter the negotiation with a win–win frame of mind. You're not negotiating against the other party; you're negotiating *with* them. Avoid standard negotiation terminology, which has been found to cause people to negotiate more aggressively. For example, avoid terms like 'accept', 'I'd be willing to ...', 'negotiate' and 'reject' and use cooperative words like 'collaborate', 'work together' and 'brainstorm'. Use 'our', 'us' and 'we' to emphasise your shared goals.

By the same token, avoid weak language and disclaimers: 'This might sound like we're asking for a lot, but ...'; 'I've been instructed to ask for ...'. You want to appear confident in your position but not arrogant.

Spend some time building rapport, mutual trust and respect. Disclosing some information about yourself unrelated to the negotiation – your interests, hobbies, family – whatever feels appropriate, smooths the wheels of negotiations. Matching the other party's non-verbal behaviour is a good way to build rapport (see Chapter 6 for more on building rapport with body language). Use the boomerang principle – treat the other party with respect, listen to and summarise their positions and so on to make it more likely they will return those cooperative behaviours. Your credibility is a precious asset during negotiations. Figure 7.2 shows four ways to build credibility.

Once you're past the 'getting to know you' stage, you can establish some ground rules. For lengthy negotiations, such as workplace agreements, this might include how often and where you will meet,

FIGURE 7.2 Four ways to gain credibility

how long meetings will last and who will take and distribute minutes. The more you agree up-front about how the process is to work, the more smoothly it will go.

Listen, listen, listen

It's vital to learn as much about the other party's needs and wants as possible. When you can, do this before expressing your organisation's position. As explained in Chapter 6, this helps you present your organisation's stance more effectively because you can explain it in a way that blends with their thinking. The more you understand each other's position, the reasoning behind it and background to it, the easier it can be to find ways to meet each other's needs.

Make eye contact and show you're listening. Nod, take short notes, summarise or recap your understanding of their position, using neutral language. When the other party stops talking, wait a few seconds before speaking yourself. This allows them to add any other information and shows you're considering what they've said; it also allows you to gather your thoughts.

Transferable skills

3.2 Verbal communication

Good questions help you draw out information, explore the other party's thinking and make sure you fully understand it. Questions like: 'To what end?' and 'Can you tell me a bit more about your thinking there?' can give you good insights into the other party's position. When you've asked a question, pause. Wait for the answer and pay attention to it. Try to keep your questions open; although closed questioning can play a part, information-gathering in negotiations is aided by offering the other party the opportunity to tell you as much as they can. Your goal here is to determine the other party's needs and wants and to try to get a feel for their importance in the eyes of the other party. Remember that the other party's real needs are not always the same as their stated needs, so listen carefully.

Remember that you need to be able to sell your stakeholders' demands to the other party as well as sell the other party's demands to your stakeholders. Keep asking questions until you fully understand the other party's position and the reasons behind it. (You can find out more about asking good questions in Chapter 6 and in **Figure 25.6**; see also **Figure 6.2** 'How to listen effectively' for ideas on what to listen for.)

Present your organisation's position clearly and reasonably

Avoid 'weak language', such as 'I hate to ask, but …' 'This may sound like a big ask but …' 'Could you possibly consider …' (discussed further in Section 7.4). Instead, be assertive, confident, firm and respectful in your requests and proposals.

Separate your offers rather than making several concessions as one; this makes them seem more valuable to the other party. However, when you make requests, or ask the other party to give something up, make that seem less difficult by bundling them up as much as you can. When you make a request, use the word 'because'; for example, 'I need to ask you to do this because …'

Manage your emotions (discussed in Chapter 5) and your body language (discussed in Chapter 6) and maintain a comfortable, assertive communication style (also discussed in Chapter 6) throughout the negotiation.

Keep your stakeholders informed throughout the negotiation. Work closely with the ultimate decision-maker and other key stakeholders as negotiations proceed so that they fully understand your negotiating strategy and reasoning and won't 'fold' at that critical time should negotiations become delicate and the organisation is put under pressure. You need their full backing to remain credible for this and future negotiations.

Work towards solutions

Test any assumptions you may have by bringing them out into the open to verify them. When you guess at what the other party does or doesn't know or want, you can end up going around in circles.

Rather than resolving elements of a negotiation one-by-one, it often pays to consider all the terms at once and resolve them together or in groups. This allows you more room to reach agreement. Each party might also list the various elements of the negotiation in order of importance. This is a good way to identify potential trade-offs; that is, items of high priority to one party that are low on the other party's priority list.

Many negotiators prefer to work on the 'big ticket items' first and when they're agreed, move on to items of lesser importance. These often fall into place easily, once the big items are sorted out. Beginning with the 'easy' items can leave you little room to manoeuvre when you finally begin to discuss the more important items.

Other negotiators prefer to reach agreement on a few issues quickly to build up some goodwill for when it comes time to make accommodations on tougher issues. Whichever way you go, remember to avoid standard negotiation terms.

Before putting an alternative point of view or proposal, outline your understanding of the other party's position. Then propose a solution rather than 'make an offer' and follow up with your reasoning. Avoid the word 'but', which builds barriers; instead, use the word 'and' to build bridges: 'I understand your point, and …'.

When you can't accept an item the other party puts forward, give a reason: 'I can't see us agreeing to that because …' and then come up with an alternative that you think could work. Think of differing viewpoints as issues to be agreed. Concentrate on a good outcome and work towards it. Think about how your actions and words will be perceived by the other party and what their response could be.

When you meet resistance, ask questions – who, how, what, when, where, why – so you can understand the nature of the resistance and deal with it more easily.

Before parting, double-check that the terms you think are agreed and included actually are. Last-minute add-ons or subtractions can mean you end up making compromises you did not factor in.

After the negotiation

Even informal negotiations benefit from a short email recapping what's been agreed. Thank the other party for meeting with you and for their time and then summarise your agreement in a document, or in your notes or minutes. Show that the benefits each party gains and what each party gives up are balanced. Even when you intend to draw up a formal agreement later, this can prevent the other party 'forgetting' an important part of what you've agreed on.

It never hurts to compliment the other party on their negotiation skills – everyone wants to do a good job and people are more satisfied when they believe they've done well. A compliment also makes it more likely they will sign off on the deal.[3]

7.3 Turning conflicts into agreements

People who fight fire with fire usually end up with ashes.

Abigail van Buren (US Agony Aunt), *It's the customer, stupid!*, Wiley, Hoboken, 2011, p. 207.

Transferable skills

3.1 Teamwork/ relationships

3.4 Leadership

Who do you know who has never had a conflict with anyone? No one? That's not surprising. Courteous and clear communication helps avoid some conflicts. Other conflicts, though, are inevitable because people are bound to have different opinions and want different outcomes. Some differences are merely minor irritations that people can quickly and easily forget, while others are more serious and can do lasting damage when not handled promptly and skilfully.

Think of conflict as verbally and/or non-verbally expressed disagreements between individuals or groups. It can occur between two individuals – between a leader-manager and an employee or between a customer and an employee, for example – or between team members. It can occur between an individual and a group, between groups in the same organisation or between organisations. Conflict can even exist within an individual; for example, when one part of you wants to stay in bed and sleep, while another part of you knows you should get up and go to work.

Direct or indirect aggression, such as backbiting, gossiping, malicious compliance, passive compliance and scapegoating are all consequences and signs of underlying, unresolved conflict that can poison the atmosphere of a workplace. You may be called upon to resolve conflict within your work team, between work teams within the organisation and, occasionally, between an employee and the organisation. As organisations strengthen relationships with contractors, customers, outsourcers and other suppliers, you may need to manage apparent conflicts with them, too. You may also have to resolve conflicts with other leader-managers in the organisation when the needs of your respective departments seem to be at odds. Clear thinking and the ability to communicate clearly and sensitively can help you reach solutions that are acceptable and beneficial to everyone in all of these situations.

Conflict can be useful

Conflict can lead to the formation of 'camps' (i.e. taking up strong stances), 'either/or' thinking, power struggles, quarrels, resentment and self-righteousness. It can be destructive, disagreeable, disruptive and stressful, lead to anxiety, anger and frustration, harm morale and productivity, strangle innovation and weaken teams and organisations. But that doesn't mean that the absence of conflict is good. Lack of conflict can indicate stagnant relationships or that people aren't sufficiently interested in an issue or each other to bother resolving their differences. At least when people argue, it shows that they care about the issue and each other. Figure 7.3 lists most common causes of conflict in workplaces.

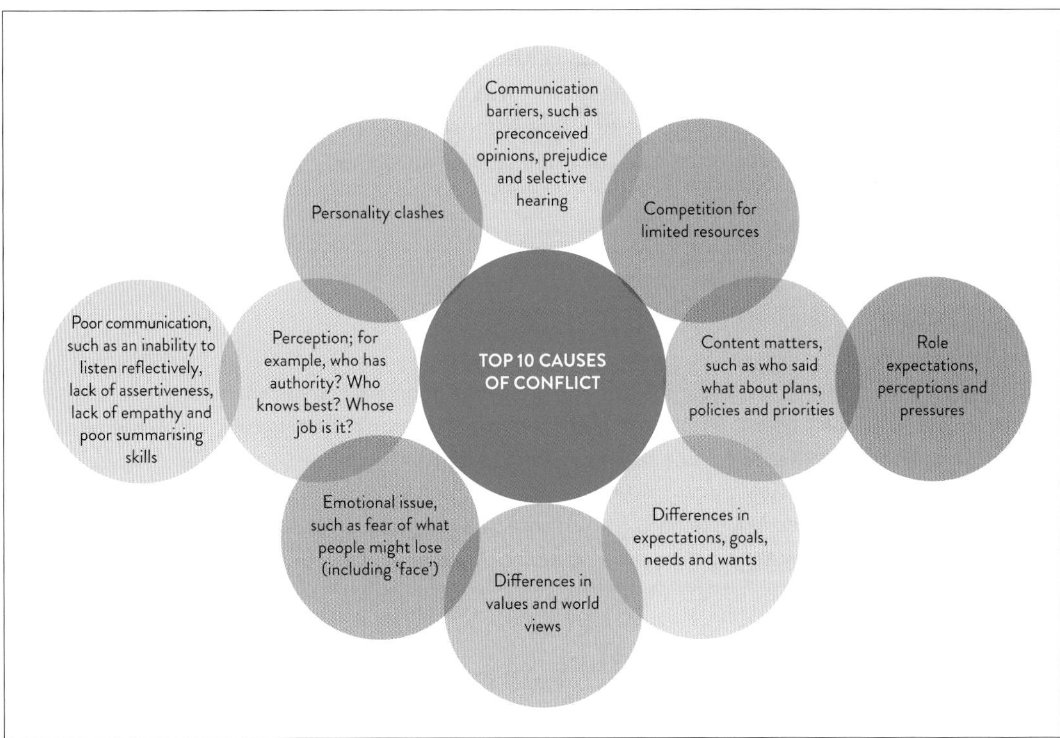

FIGURE 7.3 The most common causes of conflict

Some conflict is healthy, and it can be productive. When you point people's energies in the right direction – the **team purpose** or organisation's vision – conflict can produce the creative tension that results in discussion, innovation and increased understanding between people. It can also:

- allow people to discover the best way to resolve a situation
- bring hidden feelings into the open so people can deal with them constructively
- move a relationship out of a rut
- result in better ways of working.

So, conflict itself isn't the issue, it is how people resolve conflict that can be a problem.

Assertiveness and conflict

When what you want differs from what someone else wants, how do you approach it? Do you have to have your way no matter what? Would you do just about anything rather than have an open disagreement over it? Or do you want to figure out how you can both be satisfied?

Transferable skills

2.2 Personal effectiveness

The first way describes an aggressive, competitive, win–lose approach to conflict: 'I win–you lose', 'me versus you' or 'us versus them'. When you adopt an aggressive win–lose approach, you're sure to meet with grudging compliance or hostility, rather than cooperation and goodwill. You need to rely on threats and your formal authority to deal with the situation, and the outcome is never fully satisfactory.

The second stance is passive; it describes an avoiding, submissive or accommodating lose–win approach: 'I lose–you win.' When you take a passive approach – 'don't make waves', 'peace at any price', 'sweep it under the carpet' – you're likely to find that people take advantage of your good nature and difficult issues remain unresolved. Resentment can build up to such an extent that a passive-aggressive 'explosion' occurs.

The third approach describes an assertive, collaborative, win–win attitude: 'Let's see how we can both win.' The focus is 'us together' versus 'the problem'. When you confront and deal with conflict openly and constructively, seeking a win–win result that satisfies all or both parties, you keep exploring options until you find the one that is most acceptable to all parties. This style helps turn conflicts into agreements, or at least into satisfactory outcomes. (You can find out more about assertiveness in Chapter 6.)

Ego conflict

Have you ever had someone disagree with you repeatedly, even when (to you, at least) it was clear that you were both essentially saying the same thing? Some people automatically disagree out of habit. Ohers really think their position is different because they aren't listening to yours. Some might just be in an argumentative mood for a reason nothing to do with the discussion at hand. Depending on how important the debated point is to you, you can postpone the discussion to a 'more convenient' time or you can make it clear you're both on the same side, with both your body language and your words, and use reflective listening. (Chapter 6 explains how to manage your metacommunications.)

Common responses to conflict

The only internal responses to conflict available to a person lacking assertiveness skills are 'fight' (aggression), 'flight' or 'freeze' (submission), all of which are stressful. Stress responses to conflict include breathlessness, 'butterflies' in the stomach, clenched fists, a clenched jaw, grinding teeth, a thumping heart and tightening of the vocal cords (resulting in a higher than usual, or shrill, voice or the need for repeated throat clearing). When conflict is unresolved or unsatisfactorily resolved, long-term stress responses, such as problems associated with anxiety, tension, substance abuse, and domestic problems, can result. (See Chapter 5 for more information on the fight, flight or freeze response, and on stress and stress management.)

How you survive conflict depends on how negative or positive you can be. **Table 7.1** gives examples of responses to conflict that either inflame conflict or help reduce it. Harmful responses can create deadlocks, prevent mutual understanding, and leave losers resentful and even inclined to sabotage. Helpful responses can unlock creativity, build stronger relationships and achieve mutually satisfying outcomes. When you learn to deal with conflict successfully, either by watching others deal effectively with conflict or through formal or self-guided training, you can more easily respond to conflict assertively, avoiding much of the stress that conflict can cause.

How conflict grows

Each conflict is different. Having said this, most conflict passes through predictable phases, as shown in **Figure 7.4**. These stages are shown against a curved line. Think of this line as a hillside and think of the conflict as a ball. As a ball moves down a hill, it gains momentum and becomes increasingly difficult to stop. Like the ball, conflict gains momentum as it progresses through the stages and becomes increasingly difficult to deal with. This makes it important to stay alert to signs of potential or underlying conflict and address them early.

TABLE 7.1 Harmful and helpful responses to conflict

Harmful responses	Helpful responses
Apologising inappropriately	Clearly stating your position and goals
Being negative	Staying positive and showing mutual respect
Changing the subject	Isolating what you disagree about and what you agree about
'Either/or' thinking, unwillingness to explore options or compromise	Knowing what you want and your own limits and being willing to 'move' on some points
Getting angry	Keeping calm
Giving up and giving in – playing the martyr, pretending to agree	Agreeing shared goals and outcomes
Lack of empathy	Empathy
Personal attacks	Willingness to listen and respond objectively and non-judgementally, appointing a 'referee' if necessary
Refusing to see the other's point of view	Trying to understand the other's point of view
Trying to turn the conflict into a joke	A genuine desire to resolve the conflict, remaining respectful and polite while working towards a resolution
Win–lose or lose–win mindset	Win–win mindset

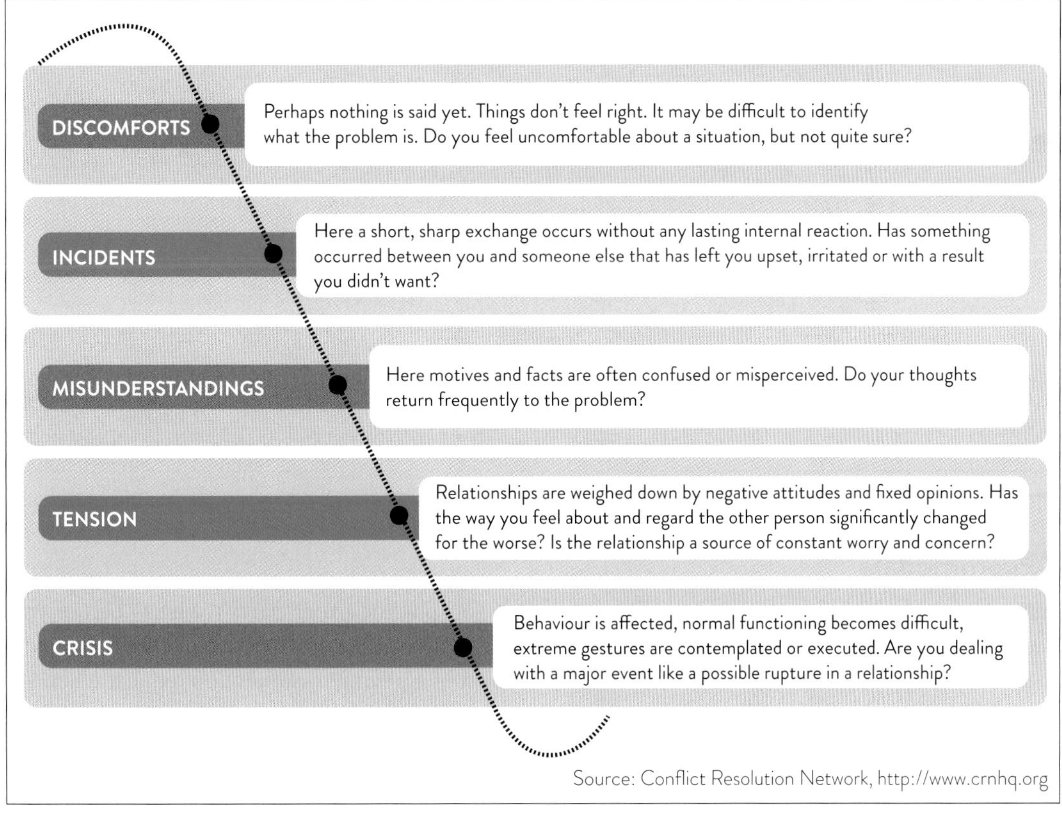

Source: Conflict Resolution Network, http://www.crnhq.org

FIGURE 7.4 Stages of conflict

When you ignore conflict, it can become increasingly serious until it reaches a crisis. When a mediation or confrontation is not possible, one or both of the parties may decide to take more drastic and harmful action, such as resigning. Or the people involved may become depressed, impatient, intolerant, irritable, moody or sulky – costly in terms of morale, performance and team harmony.

Is it wise to say something or not? When deciding, think about your goals, the issue and your relationship with the other person. How important to you is each? Say something when both your goals and the relationship are important to you. Say something when the issue itself is extremely important to you. Save your breath when neither is that important.

Five ways to manage conflict

Transferable skills
3.4 Leadership

The conflict modes shown in Figure 7.5 illustrate the five approaches people can take to conflict. The model is based on a person's or group's intentions along two dimensions: how much effort or energy they put into satisfying their *own concerns* and how much energy they devote to cooperation and satisfying the *concerns of the other party*. Each style is appropriate in some situations and inappropriate in others, so you need to be able to use each of them, as well as know when to use them.

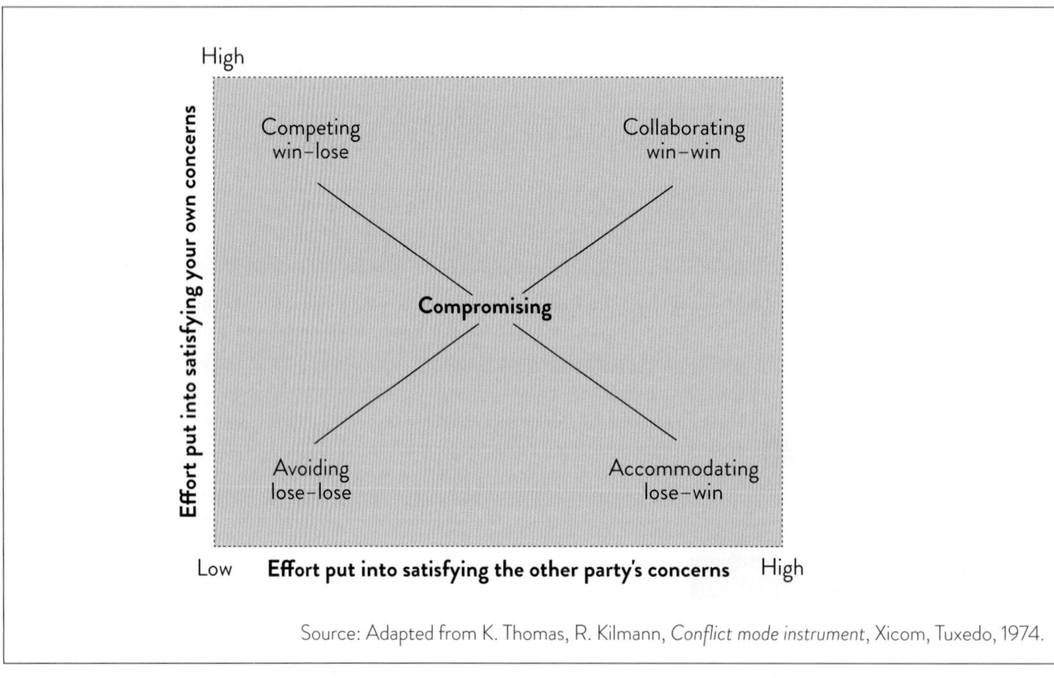

FIGURE 7.5 Conflict management styles

Accommodate

Accommodating takes cooperation to its extreme – you put the other party's wishes before your own. The message is 'I give up' or 'Go ahead – walk all over me' or 'I don't care – do what you want'. It is often passive or submissive and might take the form of agreeing to someone's request when you would rather not, or resentfully carrying out someone's request. Accommodating can also be selfless generosity or yielding to another's point of view against your better judgement.

Even when they are sure they are right, some people don't like taking a stand. Some leader-managers might be uncomfortable about using their power or afraid of losing the goodwill or cooperation of their staff and think it safer to 'give in'. The danger of too much accommodating or inappropriately accommodating is that others seldom take accommodators or their ideas seriously.

Accommodation can be a good choice when:

- the relationship or building the relationship is more important than the issue
- you have no hope of having your wishes met and accommodating minimises your losses and maintains a climate of cooperation with the other party
- your 'stake' in the conflict or issue isn't high.

Avoid

When you avoid conflict you 'let sleeping dogs lie', acting as if the conflict isn't there. Inappropriately avoiding issues leads to displacing your feelings, and general discontent and resentment, which can lead to griping and gossiping. Avoiding the conflict might be a good choice when neither the relationship nor the issue is important to you. Many potential conflict situations are just not worth the time and effort of taking a stand, or sometimes it isn't really your place to become involved. If you *do* decide to become involved, be prepared to follow through your involvement until the conflict is resolved. Avoiding can also have its uses, particularly when you want to:

- collect more information before taking action
- diplomatically sidestep an issue
- postpone discussion until a better time or to let people 'cool down'
- withdraw from a threatening situation.

Collaborate

Collaborating is cooperative and the opposite of avoiding. It involves establishing a constructive atmosphere and working with the other party (or facilitating such work between conflicting parties) to find an outcome that satisfies each side. It might take the form of exploring a disagreement to learn each other's concerns, needs, wants, perceptions and positions, and then working together to come up with a satisfactory resolution. This is not easy and it takes time, effort and skill in communication and problem-solving, and the willingness to remain objective and impersonal while searching for a solution.

This 'let's fix it together' approach is particularly useful in situations where both the issue and the relationship are important to you, and you want an outcome that satisfies both parties. Use it when you need all parties to be committed to the solution and when you need a creative solution.

Compete

Competing is when you automatically pursue your own concerns at the expense of the other person. This win–lose method of managing conflict relies on power (e.g. the ability to argue forcefully, pull rank or use financial incentives) to impose a solution on the other party. The usual response is hostility, lack of cooperation and resentment. 'Do it my way' is the message, so it isn't surprising that 'yes-men' and 'yes-women' often surround leader-managers who continually compete in conflict situations. People consider such leader-managers hard to get on with and, not surprisingly, habitual competitors find it difficult to form effective working relationships. The long-term effect of this is often negative; examples can include lack of productivity, further conflict and division, and, ultimately, a high level of employee turnover.

This is not to say, however, that competing is never an appropriate response. When decisiveness and speed are essential, as they are in emergencies, and when the issue is more important than the relationship, consciously taking a 'do it my way' approach might be the best option, at least in the short term; for example, when:

- nothing else has worked and 'no' isn't an option
- safety issues are at stake
- you need to make a difficult or unpopular decision
- you're in conflict with parties who refuse to cooperate and are trying to take advantage of you.

The point is to make the message assertive rather than aggressive. When you assertively choose a competitive stance, be aware that you may damage the relationship. Behaving assertively, not aggressively, and explaining your reasons, can help lessen the negative responses a competing style brings out.

Compromise

Compromising is the middle ground between accommodating and competing, where you give up more than in competing but less than in accommodating to arrive at a solution acceptable to both parties. 'Splitting the difference' or 'making a deal' is quicker and easier than collaborating. However, while it addresses issues more directly than avoiding them, it doesn't explore the issues in as much depth as collaborating.

Sometimes, settling for a workable compromise is the best you can do, so you might choose to collaborate. Some other occasions to consider looking for a compromise are when:

- collaboration or competition has failed
- time is running out
- you need a temporary, short-term solution to a conflict while collaborative discussions continue
- you want a quick solution and are willing to live with the fact that neither party is fully satisfied.

Your goal is to achieve a win–win outcome. The challenge is to work out how to achieve it. Table 7.2 shows you how.

TABLE 7.2 Win–lose, lose–win and win–win attitudes

Win–lose	Lose–win	Win–win
I'll 'attack' you personally if I have to	Let's not argue	Let's consider this objectively
I must win this battle	Have it your way	Let's solve our problem
I want a quick fix	I want a quick fix	We both need to be satisfied long term
I want total victory	You win	Let's see if we can both be satisfied
Me against you	You against me	We're in this together
My goals are most important	Your goals are more important than mine	Let's see if we can meet your goals, too. What are our common goals?
My way or the highway	Yours is the way to go	How can we resolve this?
This is a fight	Let's not fight	Let's deal with this amicably
This is how it is	We'll do it your way	Here's my point of view; what's yours?
We're on opposite sides	We're on opposite sides	We're on the same side

Four steps for reaching agreement

You can usually reach agreement, even in the most difficult workplace relationships. The four steps covered in the following sections can help get you there.

Step 1: Open a discussion

Make sure you have enough time to discuss the issue. Begin with a **framing statement** – a short, clear statement that 'sets the scene' and explains what you want to discuss. Make it clear that your aim is to reach an agreement that satisfies everyone as far as possible. (You can find out more about framing statements in Chapter 16.)

Transferable skills

3.2 Verbal communication

Step 2: Give good information

Helping the other party see the situation from your point of view can increase their willingness to collaborate. State it accurately, clearly and objectively, and stick to behaviour descriptions so the other person doesn't feel under attack. Explain the tangible, or real, effects the conflict or issue has on you, using neutral, non-emotive language, or **'I' language**. State your point of view assertively and congruently – look as though you mean what you say.

Table 7.3 contrasts the difference in expressing how a situation makes you feel, rather than directing the problem at the other person. Which would you rather hear?

TABLE 7.3 How 'I' language helps solve conflict

'I' language	'You' language
I can't think when you raise your voice	Don't shout
I feel I'm being pushed into a corner here. I need some time to think it through	You can't force me to ...
Let me show you a better way to do that	You did that the wrong way
I'm not following you	You're confusing me
I need you to be on time	You're late again
I see it differently	You're wrong
I'm annoyed because ...	You've annoyed me

Step 3: Gather good information

Listen to the other person's point of view. Use empathy and reflective listening to make sure you fully understand. Ask clarifying questions, paraphrase or summarise to check your understanding whenever you can, especially when the other person is using jargon or speaking indirectly or vaguely. Remember, you only want to understand the other person's viewpoint, not necessarily agree with it. Don't move on to Step 4 until you are sure you understand each other's points of view.

Discussing and listening to each other's views combined with *self-disclosure* (explaining how the conflict makes you feel) can help to bring your discussion into perspective and lead to greater understanding of the issues. Keeping calm can keep the discussion on track and prevent it from becoming heated.

Relationship statements (saying what you think or feel about the person with whom you have a conflict) also helps. For example, you might say, 'I'm really uncomfortable discussing this with you (self-disclosure using 'I' language) because I'm worried that it will damage the good working relationship we have and which I'd really like to see continue (relationship statement using 'I' language).'

Should a discussion become heated, stop – ask for some time out. For example, say, 'I'd like a minute or two to digest what you've said. How about a short break?' or 'I'd like to take a break now; can we meet again this afternoon?' Better still, suggest a break when you feel yourself tensing up or becoming angry – before tempers flare and one of you says or does something that will later be regretted or that could cause irreparable damage to the conflict resolution process.

Self-disclosure means letting people know what's going on for you. It sometimes requires courage, trust and a willingness to take a risk to build a better working relationship. Table 7.4 shows how expressing feelings can help resolve conflict. Choose one of these three categories and use the self-disclosures you feel comfortable with.

TABLE 7.4 Self-disclosure can assist in conflict resolution

Your situation	Your self-disclosure
How you are feeling	'I feel angry and disappointed to have to bring this up again. However, ...' 'I feel uncomfortable discussing this with you right now.'
How you are thinking	'As I see it, there are two options open to us right now ...' 'I'd like to take a break and continue our conversation this afternoon.' 'I think we've made excellent progress.' 'Our next step appears to be ...'
How you are reacting to something	'I really appreciate that. Thank you.' 'I'm not quite sure what you mean – would you go over that again, please?' 'I'm too upset to discuss this right now. Can we meet this afternoon?' 'It seems to me we're going round in circles.'

Step 4: Problem-solve

When both parties understand each other's views, you can turn to problem-solving. Chapter 26 explains how to solve problems and generate solutions, but the following is a short version:

1 *Summarise the problem:* what is the issue? What are the facts? What are the feelings and concerns of each party? Define the problem in terms of conflicting needs, not as a conflict between competing solutions. Make sure you agree on your differences.
2 *Search for mutually acceptable solutions:* think of as many ways to resolve the conflict as you can; the more solutions you have to choose from, the more likely you are to resolve your conflict successfully. It can be difficult to come up with a good solution right away, so be patient.
3 *Evaluate the possible solutions:* it generally becomes apparent when to move on to this step. Are there any reasons that a solution might not work? Might a solution be too hard to carry out or implement? Is each solution fair to each party? Remember, you are trying to reach a good, workable solution, not just any solution.

4 *Decide together:* shared commitment is essential. Choose the solution that is most acceptable to both parties and plan how to implement and evaluate its effectiveness together. Don't make the mistake of trying to persuade or push a solution onto the other party. When people don't freely choose a solution, they're unlikely to abide by the decision or implement it fully. If the chosen solution doesn't work, meet and begin the problem-solving process again at Step 1.

After you've resolved a conflict, review it and learn from it:

- What caused it? Have you removed the cause so it won't occur again?
- What helped you resolve it? What obstacles were in the way?
- What should you remember the next time a conflict occurs?
- What signs were there that the conflict was brewing? Would identifying and addressing them earlier have helped? What could you have done? What should you bear in mind for the future?

Tips to reach agreement

The following list includes some handy tips for turning conflicts into agreements:

- Act, don't react: pause and think, 'What outcome am I after and how can I best achieve that outcome?'
- Adopt a problem-solving approach by seeing the disagreement as a problem to solve rather than a battle to win.
- Agree on the content by stating your position and your understanding of the other party's position clearly to make sure you are both talking about the same issue.
- Agree on the process: right at the beginning, agree how to approach the discussions.
- Don't assume you have all the facts: find out what facts the other person has and what 'facts' you may have wrong.
- Emphasise the relationship because when you clearly state that you want a continuing good relationship, it's easier to work towards that end.
- Keep a long-term view in mind, which helps to keep what you say in perspective.
- Keep all verbal 'weapons' out of reach because hiding behind an outdated or irrelevant corporate 'policy', point scoring, pulling rank or threatening only adds fuel to the fire.
- Keep early discussions informal because it's easier to 'toughen up' than to 'soften down'.
- Limit each discussion to a few issues so that the 'mountain' doesn't appear insurmountable.
- Listen carefully and summarise frequently to ensure that the other person knows you have heard and understood their point of view; recap the other's point of view, especially before disagreeing.
- Look for and foster flexibility and creativity: how can you both get what you want? Don't limit yourself by grasping the first solution that comes to mind.
- Recognise that you're as likely to be biased as the other person by respecting each other's points of view, even when you don't agree.
- Test your assumptions by identifying them clearly and verifying them, to avoid going around in circles.
- Think of demands as opportunities to spot more ways of resolving the problem, which lessens possible resistance.
- Try tackling a few of the easier problems first, not to avoid the tough problems but because solving easier problems can encourage you to find solutions to the tougher problems.

Transferable skills

3.3 Written communication

7.4 Putting it in writing

The difficulty ... is not to write, but to write what you mean.

Robert Louis Stevenson (Scottish novelist and poet), *Virginibus puerisque and other papers*, C. Kegan Paul & Co, London, 1881, p. 70.

You can't always speak face-to-face, and electronic communications, letters, proposals, reports, submissions and tender documents are a daily part of most leader-managers' jobs. However, written communications can have the following shortcomings:

- they can be delayed or lost (even electronic communications)
- writing is not as personal as a face-to-face, or even a telephone, conversation
- the end result may be poorly written, difficult to read and open to misinterpretation
- there is no guarantee when they will be read or even that they will be read
- there is no guarantee that they will be understood and acted on as you expect.

Be clear about your aim

Before writing anything, decide precisely what you want to achieve. Is it to encourage someone to take action? To help someone make a decision? To inform? Persuade? When your purpose is unclear, your writing will be unclear, too. As part of your audience analysis, think about:

- What is the main point of this document?
- Who is receiving it?
- Why is it important to them?
- What do I want them to do after reading it?
- What do they need to know in order to do it?
- What do they already know and believe about the subject?
- How should I write it? With authority, as a subject matter expert, or am I communicating with peers? Am I cautioning someone or offering friendly advice? This helps you decide what 'tone' to adopt.

Jot down ideas

Spidergrams are a great way to think about what to include and put it in order. Write your topic or key idea in the centre of a sheet of paper or on a whiteboard and draw a circle around it. Then brainstorm what you could include and the supporting evidence you could use. Jot down your ideas as they occur to you. There's no need to write in full sentences; key words or phrases are enough.

Now look over your ideas. Cross out any that aren't necessary, keeping only the most relevant. To help decide what to cut out and what to keep in, consider:

- *Must know*: what must your readers (or the audience when the spidergram is for a presentation) know about your topic in order for you to achieve your objectives?
- *Should know*: ideally, what should the audience know about your topic?
- *Could know*: what is the non-essential but 'nice-to-know' information you could provide?

Put your information in a logical order. Keep it short and simple. Voila – you have an outline to start you off. Figure 7.6 shows a spidergram for this section of this chapter; it has been tidied up by removing the crossed-out possibilities.

With a clear aim, it's easy to think about what to write. Use the six 'trigger questions': What? Who? When? Where? Why? How? Jot down a few words under each heading. Next, think through what else to include. When you're having trouble, try imagining you're an expert on the subject and being interviewed: What would you be asked and how would you respond? Or draft a summary of

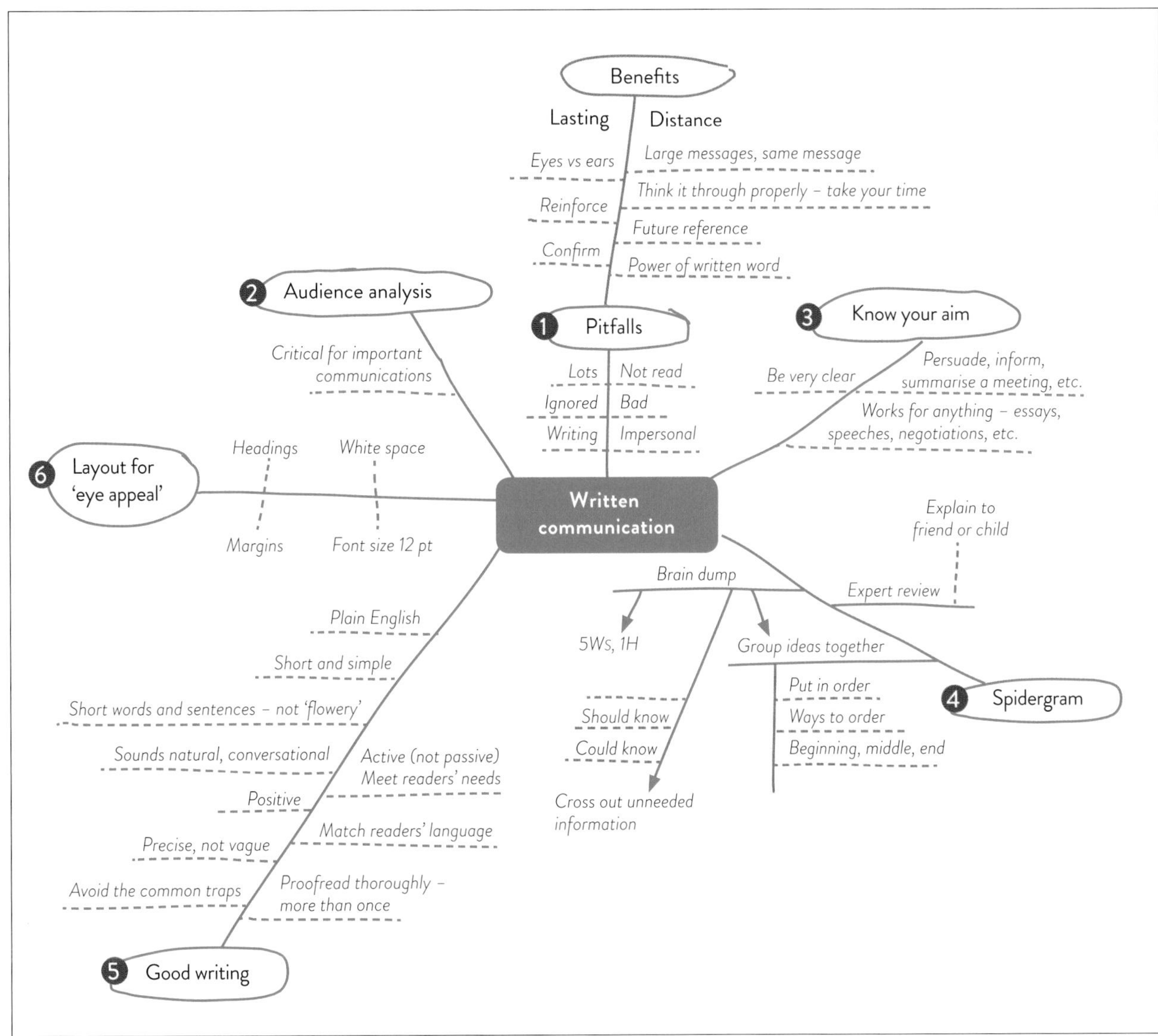

FIGURE 7.6 Spidergram

the highlights and 'call to action'. Or note how you would explain your subject over the phone to someone, or in person – a child, a friend or a colleague, for example.

Your spidergram doesn't have to be tidy or follow any order – that comes next. Think of it as a 'brain dump'.

Group your ideas

With your thoughts written down, cross out what you don't need and put the rest into a logical sequence. You can start from the beginning, for example, or begin with an overview or executive summary. Think about which approach would get your message across best. Here are some other ways to organise and structure your information:

- *Causal:* the facts and their results, or the problem and its causes.
- *Differing viewpoints:* outline one way of looking at the subject, then another way.

- *Principle:* from the theory to the practice.
- *Problem:* from the problem to the solution.
- *Process or sequence:* from the raw material to the finished product, from the beginning to the end.
- *Relative importance:* from the most to least important.
- *Space:* geographical, or from a central point outwards.
- *Time:* past to the present to the future.

Now it's time to start writing. Remember, every good communication has a beginning, a middle and an end. The beginning introduces the subject, the middle contains the information that you want to convey, and the end summarises what you have said and points towards the next steps. The middle will consist of the information you've collated. Put it in draft form, which you can polish later. You want each sentence to contain one idea and each paragraph to contain a group of related ideas.

It may be at this point where you come to a halt. It's common to have a feeling of not knowing where to start – writer's block happens to the most competent of written communicators. The best advice here is to simply walk away for a moment. Get some air, catch up on emails or messages. When you return to your written work you will probably find that you can continue with the communication with a clear head.

With the main section (the middle) of your writing organised and written in draft form, you need a beginning (the introduction) and an end (the conclusion). After that, all that is left is polishing your draft. Table 7.5 shows how to avoid common writing traps.

TABLE 7.5 Writing traps and how to avoid them

Writing trap	Antidote
Not making direct statements to avoid being held accountable	People will hold you accountable anyway; so use clear, precise, positive words and phrases
Being more concerned with proving yourself right and the reader wrong	Instead of assigning blame, look for a solution that is acceptable to yourself and your reader
Boring your readers to sleep	Write with a particular reader in mind and in a conversational tone
Brushing aside complaints, making demands rather than requests, and generally writing in a way that shows you think you are better than the reader	Courtesy is far more professional and business-like than arrogance and poor manners
Continually excusing and explaining	People generally don't care. Offer an apology and a solution to correct the situation; concentrate on what can be done to put matters right, not why a mistake was made
Insisting on so much precision that only a statistician can understand what you have written	Explain facts and figures to avoid misunderstandings, and only include the detail that is necessary
Mistaking brevity and terseness for conciseness	Warmth, friendliness and courtesy do not detract from professionalism

Writing trap	Antidote
Switching from one thought to another as you write, as they pop into your head	Jot down the points you want to make so you can number them to structure your information into a logical flow
Thinking bulk or length equals importance and displays intelligence	Pare down overly wordy writing by cutting out unnecessary words and phrases and write to express, not to impress
Using too much jargon, leaving the reader wondering what you're on about	Explain any technical terms or use terms you're sure your readers know
Writing in an unnatural, unnecessarily formal and flowery style	Think practical, not poetical, and write more as you would speak
Writing in clichés and platitudes	Concentrate on what you want to communicate, not flowery phrases

Use plain English, and keep it short and simple

Time is tight in most organisations. This makes it more important than ever that people write in clear, plain English. Write so that people can:

- read it easily
- understand it immediately
- act on it quickly.

Good writing follows the ABCs – *accurate, brief* and *clear*. People can easily read and understand accurate and clear writing, while brevity adds punch and force. Say what you want to say in as few words as possible. Then stop.

This is not to say that you should write only in short sentences or avoid details or explanations. Remember, it is difficult to accurately interpret tone when a message is not verbal. Be aware that an overly succinct message could be seen as aggressive or rude. The key is to use enough words to communicate your message while avoiding extra words and sentences that don't contribute any meaning or add information.

When you think you've finished, go back and search for and delete unnecessary words. Table 7.6 shows how to trim flowery, unnecessarily long and trite phrases that cloud your message. Table 7.7 shows how to avoid déjà vu by pruning unnecessary words.

TABLE 7.6 Wasting words when brief is better

Wordy	Better
a large number of	many
according to our records	we find
are of the opinion	believe
at the present time	now
consensus of opinion	consensus
despite the fact that	although
during the month of April	in April

Wordy	Better
during which time	while
for the reason that	because, since
give a description	describe
give consideration to	consider
has no confidence in	doubts
in addition to	also
in excess of	more than
in order that	so
in the absence of	without
in the event that	if
in the majority of instances	mostly
in the near future	soon
in view of the fact that	because
is sorry for	regrets
make application to	apply
on a regular basis	regularly
prior to	before
pursuant to your request	as you asked
reached an agreement	agreed
subsequent to	after
until such time	until
with reference to	about
with the exception of	except

TABLE 7.7 Why say it twice?

Redundant	Concise
absolutely necessary	necessary
advance warning	warning
as of now	now
at a price of $60	$60
basic fundamentals	fundamentals
during the course of	during
each and every one of us	each of us
enclosed herewith	enclosed
end result	result

Redundant	Concise
first and foremost	first
I am in the process of preparing	I am preparing
it is blue in colour	it is blue
made the statement that	said
my personal opinion	my opinion
one of the main factors is, of course, the question of quality	one of the main factors is quality
perform an analysis of	analyse
postponed until later	postponed
take into consideration	consider
reach a conclusion	conclude
we can supply them in the following colours: blue, red, green ...	we can supply them in blue, red, green ...
we seldom ever make this mistake	we seldom make this mistake

Use short words

When you need to use a long word, use it. Otherwise, go for familiar, precise, short words that have greater impact and readability. Only use a long word when it:

- adds richness or special meaning or is more exact than a short word (e.g. 'courier' is more precise than 'send')
- is economical, replacing a lot of small words (e.g. 'destination' is more economical than 'the place to which we are going')
- is more familiar to the reader than a short word (e.g. 'sponsorship' is more familiar to most people than 'aegis')
- is unique and can't be replaced by a short word (e.g. inventory, appreciation, communicate).

Table 7.8 demonstrates how to replace long words with shorter ones to keep your message clear and to the point.

TABLE 7.8 The long and the short of good writing

Long	Short	Long	Short
abbreviate	shorten	incorporate	include
abundance	a lot	indication	sign
accomplish	do	initiate	begin, start
administer	give	majority of	most
aggregate	total	manufacture	make
alternative	choice	participate	share, join
anticipate	expect	primarily	mostly

Long	Short	Long	Short
application	use	regulation	rule
apportion	assign, divide	reiterate	repeat
approximately	about	remunerate	pay
assistance	help	requirement	need
commencement	start	residence	home
consequence	result	similar	alike
demonstrate	show	subsequent	later
difficult	hard	terminate	end
endeavour	try	ultimate	final
frequently	often	utilise	use
fundamental	basic	visualise	see

Write naturally

It's easier and more effective to write the way you speak, using words that come naturally to you. Don't try to sound like someone you're not or be unnecessarily formal. If you would normally say, 'There's too much data that we don't need', don't write 'The level of information is superfluous to our requirements'. Elaborate, overblown words and phrases are off-putting and can cloud your meaning.

When you sit down to write, speak your thoughts mentally (or even aloud) as you put them on paper. (You can check the spelling and grammar later.) That way, you write more freely, and your writing is more alive, more interesting and easier to understand and act on.

Don't be glib

Business writing needs to be in full sentences and include vowels and correct punctuation. Writing as though you are texting – in phrases rather than sentences, shortening words by leaving out vowels and spelling them as they sound – is not acceptable in a business environment.

Overly casual writing lacks professionalism and sincerity and invites derision and mistrust. For business, write in Standard English, avoid written vernacular, slang words and expressions and avoid being overly familiar with your readers. Remember that the standard of your writing reflects the standard of the way you do business. **Figure 7.7** shows seven steps to writing success.

Be positive and precise

Most people don't like being told what is *not* the case or what they should *not* do. People want to know what *is* the case and what they *can* do. Avoiding negative statements and words improves your writing style and helps people remember your message more accurately. For example, instead of saying, 'We will not be able to fill your order this month because we are out of stock', leave out the negative and include specific information. Say, 'We will fill your order early next month, as soon as replacement stock arrives.'

FIGURE 7.7 The seven steps to good business writing

Write actively, not passively

'The moon was jumped over by the cow' is a passive sentence. It's boring. 'The cow jumped over the moon' is active and strong. Active writing is generally more interesting and easier to read. Placing the *actor* (in this example, the cow) in front of the *action* (jumped) makes the flow of the sentence active, clear and powerful.

Occasionally, for reasons of tact, you may decide to write in the passive voice. For example, it is more diplomatic to say: 'We believe there may have been an error in your last invoice', than 'You invoiced us incorrectly'.

Consider the way you put words together. The five most common words in the English language are *and, I, of, the* and *to*. Alone, they don't mean much, do they? It's the way you put them together that makes them count. The way you put words together is particularly important in written communications because you don't have the non-verbal cues to help people understand your meaning.

Write for your reader

Use words and terms your readers can readily understand, interpret and visualise, and avoid technical terms when writing to people with a non-technical background. To meet your readers' needs and word your message persuasively, think about what your readers are concerned about, what matters most to them, what opinions they may already hold on your topic and what background information they probably have.

Check spelling and grammar

It's easy to spell a word incorrectly. Use a dictionary or the spellcheck function on your word processing software to spot typos and check the spelling of unfamiliar words – but don't rely on it completely because spellcheck will not always know what you mean. Be careful of words that are often misspelled and words that are often misused. Some examples are given in Tables 7.9 and 7.10.

Watch your apostrophes, too. Use an *apostrophe s* (...'s) for one of two reasons:

1 *To indicate possession:* This is Deb's diary. That is Dave's desk.
2 *As a contraction, when the apostrophe takes the place of a letter:* Where is Deb's diary? (possession) It's (a contraction of It is) over there on Dave's desk. Where's (where is) my diary? Your diary's (diary is) there. You're (you are) right next to it. That's (that is) Dave's desk over there; why's (why is) Deb's diary on it?

When you want to pluralise a word, you don't need an apostrophe: *There are three computers on three different desks.*

TABLE 7.9 Frequently misspelled words

Correct	Incorrect
accidentally	accidently
calendar	calander or calender
committed	commited
license (verb)	licence
occasionally	occasionaly
occurrence	occurance or occurrance
publicly	publically
receive/receipt	recieve/reciept
separate	seperate

TABLE 7.10 Frequently misused words

Often misused	Correct use
accept, except	I will accept all ideas except bad ones
affect, effect	Their pleas did not affect my decision but my decision did effect a better solution
imply, infer	Did you imply that he is wrong or did I incorrectly infer it?
moral, morale	The moral of the story is to keep employee morale high
personal, personnel	It's improper to get too personal with the personnel
stationary, stationery	The wagon bringing the stationery supplies is stationary in the corridor
their, there, they're	Their files are over there where they're meeting
to, too, two	I, too, think that two is too many to have
your, you're	You're wearing your shirt inside out

A confusing exception to these rules is the possessive 'its': *The computer lost its memory when it crashed during the storm.* Here 'its' is not a contraction, so an apostrophe is not needed. 'Its' only needs an apostrophe when it is the contraction for 'it is': *The computer lost its memory and it's a major inconvenience.*

Grammar is sometimes more difficult to get correct, although most word-processing programs have a grammar checking function that can be useful. You can ask someone to look over your writing for errors, too. Basic errors of spelling and grammar seriously erode your professionalism and make your organisation look bad. Check, too, that there are no run-on sentences, no weasel words or waffle, and no clumsy comments.

Set out documents professionally

A document, letter or book filled with long paragraphs, tiny margins and small print invites the 'groan-response' and tempts people to shuffle it to the bottom of the pile. When your documents look reader-friendly and inviting to read, people are more likely to read them.

Most organisations have a variety of templates you can use. Use them or follow your organisation's protocol (or style guide, if they have one) for setting out business documents. If there is no common protocol or style guide, generally:

- break up the text with headings
- leave as much white space as possible
- leave margins of at least 5 cm
- use a font size of 12 point or larger.

Depending on your organisation's protocol, you may want to ask your manager to review your document before it reaches its final destination.

Award-winning emails

Like all of your communications, your emails represent you, as well as your organisation, so make sure they present you as a competent, consistent, reliable and thoughtful person. Here are some tips:

- Never write in anger – wait until you've calmed down or set up a meeting to discuss the situation.
- Don't use electronic communications when you could walk around the corner or to the next floor to speak to the person directly.

- Say 'please' and 'thank you'.
- Think carefully about who you copy in – do they really need it? Use CCs and Reply all only to keep people 'in the loop'.
- Follow your organisation's expectations regarding response times to other people's communications.
- Use a clear subject line and subheadings to help readers scan your message.
- Use 'you' rather than the third person.

Transferable skills

2.1 Personal effectiveness

3.2 Verbal communication

3.3 Written communication

7.5 Delivering successful presentations

Be sincere; be brief; be seated.

Franklin D. Roosevelt (32nd President of the United States), in Soper, *Basic public speaking*, Oxford University Press, NY, 1963, p. 12.

Since Aristotle wrote *The Art of Rhetoric* in the 4th century BCE, people have strived to make effective presentations. And without a doubt, preparing and delivering presentations is an important skill. Unfortunately, speaking in public rates high on most people's list of fears. Why? Nerves! Nerves can be caused by lack of knowledge, lack of preparation or lack of confidence. You can overcome any and all of these when you know your material thoroughly, prepare carefully and practise.

You are likely to find yourself making presentations to the following groups:

- customers and suppliers (e.g. to explain your organisation's or team's offerings or needs)
- industry groups and conferences (e.g. to represent your organisation and offer your experiences and insights)
- other managers (e.g. to present proposals or your team's results)
- your work team (e.g. to announce an important corporate decision, event or change, or to deliver training).

While presentations vary in their degree of formality and the size of the audience, preparing and delivering any presentation follows the same process, summarised in the 'Eight steps to proficient presentations':

1. Determine your purpose.
2. Analyse your audience.
3. Decide what to cover.
4. Develop an outline.
5. Write it up.
6. Practise, practise, practise.
7. Relax and enjoy delivering a proficient presentation.
8. Review your presentation and look for ways to improve the next one.

Step 1: Determine your purpose

Why are you making this presentation? Do you want to, for instance, offer your audience some insights, knowledge or skills, or do you want to persuade your audience to accept your ideas or provide information? Have a precise goal in mind and write it down: *After hearing my presentation, I want my audience to* ... Based on this, decide what your main message is: *My main message is* ... Write that down, too, in six or fewer words, and keep both clearly visible as you prepare your presentation.

Step 2: Analyse your audience

Successful communication in any form begins with understanding the person or people you are communicating with and tailoring your information accordingly. Who are you making the presentation to? Why are they listening to it? What is their background knowledge of, and previous experience with the subject? Are they likely to be sympathetic to your message, neutral or hostile to it? Tap into their needs and concerns – what do they want and need to hear in order to understand your message?

When you don't know your audience personally, get a feel for their demographics – their age, cultural and language backgrounds, literacy skills, numeracy skills and so on – and let this guide what you say, how you structure and explain your information, the examples you provide and your support material.

This is also the time to confirm logistics; for example, how much time you have to speak, the room set-up and the time of day.

Step 3: Decide what to cover

Bearing in mind your audience, your goal and your main message, take a piece of paper and use a spidergram (discussed earlier in this chapter) to brainstorm the points you could make. Include the 'must know' information and work your way through the 'should know' and then the 'could know' information, based on how much time you have available for your talk. Three to five main points with supporting information and examples are generally enough, as too much information can overwhelm an audience and may prevent them remembering it.

Step 4: Develop an outline

You now have several ideas or key words that you haven't crossed out. Number them into a logical sequence, bearing in mind the audience's attitude and current knowledge and understanding of your topic. Look for an order that flows well, with one point leading easily into the next. Remember, you are working on an outline in this step, just using key words and ideas.

Next, think about how you can help your audience to grasp your ideas. Maybe handouts, models or samples of what you are speaking about could help your points hit home. Here are some other ways to make your points memorable to your audience:

- analogies
- anecdotes or story-type examples
- case studies or stories
- charts, graphs, diagrams or flow charts
- computer simulations
- demonstrations
- facts and figures
- groups or pairs to practise a skill or discuss a topic
- lists
- metaphors
- rhetorical questions
- role-play or other simulations
- small group discussions.

Step 5: Write your talk

Some people prefer to write their presentation out in full, using complete sentences. Those who are more practised at making presentations often prefer to stick with a key-point outline using only words or phrases. This ensures a natural delivery style – no one wants to bore their audience by reading their presentation word for word.

As we have previously discussed, good communications have a beginning, a middle and an end. Once you've organised the main *body* of your presentation, develop a short *introduction* to make the audience sit up and listen. What will grab their attention? Is there a startling fact or piece of information you can begin with? Or a relevant anecdote that will lead nicely into your topic? You could state the dilemma or problem and how you recommend solving it.

Your introduction should also establish your objectives and indicate what you plan to cover. When appropriate, for example, in training presentations, you can give your audience an opportunity to add topics or remove unnecessary ones.

Finally, write a short *conclusion* summarising your main points and pointing to the next steps. Tie your closing comments back to your introduction when you can. Finally, thank people for their attention and, when appropriate, invite questions.

Work towards creating a user-friendly set of speaking notes to guide you through your talk. Use a large font or large handwriting so you can glance down and find key points easily. You could draw a line between key points when you use A4 sheets of paper, or use a separate index card for each key point. Number each card or page in case you drop them.

Develop some techniques to navigate through your speaking notes quickly and easily. For example, if you can draw, images are great memory joggers and different-coloured highlighter pens can signal important points or words.

Think about questions you could be asked so that you won't be caught by surprise and be at a loss for words. You should also be prepared to be asked questions that you are unable to answer immediately. In such situations, the audience will usually be satisfied with a promise to relay an answer to their question as soon as you are able to access the information required.

Transferable skills

5.2 Technology use

DON'T 'SLIDE' YOUR AUDIENCE TO SLEEP

Flip charts, PowerPoint or Prezi slides with video and audio recordings and whiteboards are other tools to help you drive your points home (but don't over-do the technical wizardry and don't over-use slides and cause 'death by PowerPoint'). You are the presentation, not your technology. Never stand there reading one slide after another. Your audience can read too, and more quickly than you can read slides out loud, so they'll be annoyed at you holding them up.

Your slides are not your speaking notes or even a memory crutch. They should highlight, and support your points and help your audience follow along, enhancing your presentation, not delivering it for you. Technology should add value to your presentation – not the other way around.

Here are some other tips to make sure technology enhances your presentation:

- Avoid fancy transitions and slide effects (building up slides word-by-word with text flying in, noises, meaningless cartoons and so on); they are distracting and detract from your message. Let what you say, and the way you say it, hold people's attention, not gimmicks.
- Bullet points are best – avoid sentences and paragraphs.
- Leave the lights on. Dimming the lights cues your audience to switch off and doze.
- Don't turn your back on your audience to read the slide to them or to check which slide is showing. (Use the computer screen in front of you.)

- Keep to one key idea per slide and limit the number of words per slide to about six.
- Use a big bold font, with high contrast to the background.
- Use clear headings.
- You don't want your audience reading through your slides and jumping ahead rather than listening to you, so avoid distributing copies of your slides to the audience before your presentation. An exception is a highly technical presentation when audience members can benefit from using copies of your slides to assist in note-taking.

Step 6: Practise your presentation

As they say, 'It's all in the delivery.' The more times you run through your presentation, the more confidence you gain and the better you can deliver it when the time comes. A common problem, generally caused by nerves, is speaking too quickly; avoid this by practising out loud – often – to get the right rhythm and speed embedded into your brain.

Rather than practising for hours the night before your presentation, practise often in the days or weeks leading up to it (just like studying for an exam, really). Practise in short sessions, running through the presentation fully each time. Stand up for your out-loud practice at least once, timing yourself to make sure you don't run over time.

Your practising has two goals:

1. Not to memorise your material but to know what you are going to say so thoroughly that an occasional glance at your notes is all you need to stay on track.
2. To become comfortable with a delivery style that includes facial expressions and gesturing that reinforce your message, eye contact with the audience, pauses to convey control, speaking clearly, and a varied speed and tone that conveys conviction.

Make sure your **self-talk** is positive and supportive as you think about and practise your presentation. (You can find out more about the importance of self-talk in Chapter 5.)

Tips for making presentations

Relax and send some oxygen to your brain by taking a few deep breaths before you begin. As you practise and during your presentation, remember:

- Before you begin, take a deep breath and smile at your audience. Thank the person who introduced you.
- Avoid filler words and non-words such as 'uhm', 'yeah' and 'ya know'.
- Be confident, natural and relaxed – be yourself.
- Gesture to emphasise key points. Don't distract the audience by being as stiff as a soldier at attention or a fidgeting bundle of nerves.
- Make eye contact with as many people as you can. Let your eyes meet the eyes of audience members for at least five seconds, or for a complete thought. This makes you look confident, establishes rapport, provides you with some feedback and personalises your information.
- Move around a bit to release tension, but avoid rocking, shuffling or pacing back and forth.
- Project your voice strongly and clearly so your audience can hear you, and speak clearly. People won't bother straining to hear or understand you for very long.
- Refer to your notes when you need them, but avoid reading out your presentation word for word.
- Speak in a conversational tone of voice that shows enthusiasm and commitment to your topic. A low-level, monotone or lifeless voice is guaranteed to put even the kindest audience to sleep.

Step 7: Deliver your presentation

Here is where all your hard work pays off. Don't worry about being nervous – that's normal. Channel your adrenalin from stage fright into enthusiasm so that you can deliver your talk with assurance and energy. Think of your presentation as an expanded conversation with a few friends and remember that the audience is on your side – no one wants to sit through a horrible presentation. Concentrate on communicating with your audience and making sure they understand your message.

Keep breathing and tune your brain into listening to what you're saying. This drains self-consciousness and nerves and helps you deliver a natural and powerful presentation. Have a glass of water nearby and take a sip when you feel you need to slow down.

Keep your eyes on your audience, not on your notes or other speaking aids, so you can watch for non-verbal signals that indicate you may need to explain further, slow down or speed up your delivery. Don't let audience members' distractions – jiggling legs, tapping feet, drumming fingers, etc. – put you off. Look elsewhere and block the disturbance from your mind; once you let it 'get to you', you're doomed.

When you're asked a question, paraphrase it in case some people didn't hear. Look around the audience as you answer because others may have the same question. If a question seems negative, hostile or designed to trap you, rephrase it more objectively. Treat all questions and questioners respectfully.

Believe it or not, once you've given several presentations, you'll begin to relax and enjoy them.

Step 8: Plan to keep improving

Afterwards, take a quiet moment to mentally replay your presentation. What worked well? Where did you run into problems? Ask audience members, your manager, the conference organiser and others involved in the presentation for their reactions and improvement suggestions. When the audience provides written feedback, read it through carefully. Then jot down a few useful notes to make your next presentation even better.

STUDY TOOLS

QUICK REVIEW

KEY CONCEPT 7.1 

a What aspects of an idea might cause people to block them? How can you bring potential blockers around to your way of thinking?

b Briefly review what to consider when presenting your ideas to decision-makers.

KEY CONCEPT 7.2 

a When, and why, is it particularly important to consider long-term relationships with the people you're negotiating with?

b Explain why it is important to understand the other party's position in a negotiation.

KEY CONCEPT 7.3 

a Look through the tips for turning conflicts into agreements. Which have you used successfully? Which can you incorporate into your agreement management repertoire?

b Discuss the types of workplace conflict that you are likely to meet and explain the most effective way to deal with each.

KEY CONCEPT 7.4 

a Describe the characteristics of a professional written business communication and analyse an example of a business letter, proposal or report you have written.

KEY CONCEPT 7.5 

a List the steps to making a successful presentation. How can following them help reduce your nerves?

BUILD YOUR SKILLS

KEY CONCEPT 7.1 

a Consider an improvement opportunity at your workplace; for example, a way to streamline a work process or a way to save money. Think it through as described in the first two parts of Section 7.1, jotting down notes as you go. Then develop a plan for presenting your idea to the decision-maker.

KEY CONCEPT 7.2 

a Of the three styles of negotiating illustrated in **Figure 7.1**, which is assertive? Which is aggressive? What are the long-term implications of each style?

b How does the way you frame a negotiation affect its outcome?

c Browse through https://www.karrass.com/en/glossary and select and summarise 10 negotiation tactics you think you could use in your next negotiation. You might, for example, start with 'Big pot approach', 'Bogey tactic', 'Foot-in-the-door technique', 'Hairy hand technique' and 'Pie expansion'.

KEY CONCEPT 7.3 

a Think of a conflict you have been involved in that did not have an ideal outcome. List any communication barriers that were present, such as preconceived opinions, prejudice and selective hearing. What was the cause of the conflict? Did it escalate in the way predicted in **Figure 7.4**? What conflict management style(s) were present (see **Figure 7.5**)? Develop a plan for managing a similar conflict in the future.

b In a situation where conflict may be looming, what skills would you need to use to identify the conflict?

KEY CONCEPT 7.4 

a Investigate the grammar options on the word-processing system you use, particularly the readability indices. Find out what each of them measures and what a 'readable' score is. Use the readability index to see how readable your last essay was.

b How well do you use words? Do you ever misuse words? You can find out by checking out http://www.businessinsider.com.au/harvard-steven-pinker-misused-words-2015-9.

KEY CONCEPT 7.5 

a Pay careful attention to the next few presentations you attend and note the techniques the speakers use to make them effective, as well as any distractions or other aspects of the presentations that could be amended to make them even more effective.

WORKPLACE ACTIVITIES

KEY CONCEPT 7.1 

a Describe how you went about promoting an improvement idea at your workplace and whether you were successful at having it adopted. On reflection, to what can you attribute your success (or lack of success)?

KEY CONCEPT 7.2 

a Consider an issue you have negotiated with someone recently, either formally or informally. What were your wants and needs? What were you keen to retain? What was your opening position and fallback position? Describe how you handled the negotiation effectively and what you plan to do to improve your negotiating skills the next time you're in a similar negotiation situation.

KEY CONCEPT 7.3 

a What are the most common causes of conflict at your workplace and in your work group?

b Describe a recent workplace conflict you have witnessed or been a party to and discuss its cause. Was the conflict useful or destructive? How cooperatively did the parties deal with the conflict and how satisfactorily was it resolved?

KEY CONCEPT 7.4 

a Describe a time when you planned and presented complex information successfully at work.

b Working with the last document of 500 words or more that you wrote, edit it to retain its meaning but make it clearer and easier to read by following the guidelines outlined in Section 7.4.

c Select one of your organisation's policies – for example, a human resource policy such as diversity, flexible working or sustainability – and write a series of two-paragraph summaries of the policy for the following groups of stakeholders: white-collar workers, blue-collar workers, employees who speak English as a second language, leader-managers, senior managers, local community residents and shareholders and potential investors. What factors are you taking into account as you write each of these summaries? When they're written, check them for accuracy, brevity, clarity, readability and layout.

KEY CONCEPT 7.5 

a What workplace presentations, either formal or informal, have you made in the past six months? Select two and describe how you developed those presentations, including your audience analysis. How well did you deliver those presentations? What are your improvement plans for your next presentation?

EXTENSION ACTIVITIES

Referring to the Snapshot at the beginning of this chapter, answer the following questions:

1 What are some possible sources of the difficulties between Vailea and her colleague? Would discussing the situation with her boss be preferable to discussing it directly with her colleague? Explain your reasoning. If Vailea decides to approach her colleague directly, how should she go about it? What should her main goal and her opening comments be? How could she use her influencing skills to progress the conversation from there?

2 Reflect on your own experiences with conflict. Can you identify with Vailea, and how? Think of three times you have been directly or indirectly involved in conflict, and how it was handled. Would you do anything differently?

CASE STUDY 7

THE CHRISTMAS PARTY

The annual Christmas party for the homeware company Interior Classics is, as usual, a family affair, with partners and children of employees invited. At the end of the party, Father Christmas appears with bags of goodies for the children and presents for the partners.

CEO Ben Goodman traditionally says a few words on the occasion.

'Fellow employees and friends: This has been a difficult year financially. The worldwide pandemic had a profound effect on sales, and profits have eroded because of this. As you know, we have to reduce labour costs, along with any other expenses we can control.

'I know that many of you are concerned. Some of your children are hard to manage at this hour and you want to be on your way, but I do want to take this opportunity to say a few words to you. Interior Classics is a huge part of our lives. We all have to nurture it, like we do our children, because we want to see it continue to innovate and grow.

'I know that there are rumours that we will be closing down, but I can assure you that is not the case at the moment.

'The 'new normal' world we find ourselves in forces us to look at our wage agreements, and I

hope that in the coming months we can generate new agreements in the true spirit of workplace collaboration.

'In summary, this has been a memorable year for both good and bad reasons – but I think the good has far outweighed the bad. So I am very happy to give each employee a bonus in the next pay cycle, to reflect the company's respect and esteem for you all.

'Finally, let me wish you all a Merry Christmas!'

When the party breaks up, some families head towards their cars. A good many, however, gather in small groups to talk, asking questions like: 'What did he mean?' 'Are they reducing head count again?'

Questions

1 Ben's intention is to reassure the employees that their jobs are safe and that the company can continue to develop in the new trading environment – provided some changes are made. What evidence is there for this in his speech?
2 Ben seems to be warning his employees about the hard times and redundancies to come. What evidence is there for this in his speech?
3 Why is it important that Ben gives a good presentation here?
4 From your reading of the Case study, conduct a short analysis of Ben's audience.
5 What do you think are Ben's objectives for his message? Write a short sentence describing them. Develop a key-point outline for Ben's speech that would help him to achieve these objectives.

CHAPTER ENDNOTES

1 Jennifer Whitman, Todd Woodward, 'Evidence affects hypothesis judgments more if accumulated gradually than if presented instantaneously', *Psychonomic Bulletin & Review*, Vol. 18, No. 6, 2011, pp. 1156–1165.

2 Lawrence E. Williams, John A. Bargh, 'Experiencing physical warmth promotes interpersonal warmth', *Science*, Vol. 322, No. 5901, 24 October 2008, pp. 606–607.

3 Jared R. Curhan, Hillary Anger Elfenbein, Gavin J. Kilduff, 'Getting off on the right foot: Subjective value versus economic value in predicting longitudinal job outcomes from job offer negotiations', *Journal of Applied Psychology*, Vol. 94, No. 2, 2009, pp. 524–534; Jared R. Curhan, Hillary Anger Elfenbein, Noah Eisenkraft, 'The objective value of subjective value: A multi-round negotiation study', *Journal of Applied Psychology*, Vol. 40, No. 3, pp. 690–709.

CHAPTER

8

BUILDING EFFECTIVE WORKING RELATIONSHIPS

After completing this chapter, you will be able to:

8.1 build and sustain people's confidence and trust

8.2 identify people's personality styles and adjust your approach in order to work effectively with them

8.3 establish, contribute to and benefit from professional networks

8.4 use organisational politics to achieve work priorities and goals.

TRANSFERABLE SKILLS

The following transferable skills are covered in this chapter:

2 Critical thinking and problem solving
2.2 Personal effectiveness

3 Social competence
3.1 Teamwork/relationships

OVERVIEW

Most people need to work with others to achieve results. The good working relationships you have with your work team, your own leader-manager and with people across and outside your organisation, your customers, suppliers and other stakeholders help you to achieve results effectively and enjoyably. Good relationships at work mean more than engaged and productive employees – people are naturally social creatures, and friendships and positive interactions with others are important for our psyches.

Good working relationships are critical to organisational success, too. Research has found that the single most important factor in extraordinary workplaces that are exemplars of productivity is the quality of working relationships – how people relate to each other as friends, colleagues and co-workers.

> The quality of working relationships represents the central pivot on which excellent workplaces are founded, underpinned by such key variables as good workplace leadership, clear values, having a say and being safe ... In excellent workplaces, the existence of mutual trust and respect is overwhelming. We became convinced that central to excellent workplaces is an understanding that to produce quality work in Australia, one must have quality relationships. ... The basic truth: Improved productivity in Australian workplaces is the outcome of the quality of working relationships on the job.[1]

Two sets of skills underpin quality working relationships: the self-awareness and personal skills discussed in Chapter 5, and the strong communication skills examined in Chapters 6 and 7. This chapter helps you build the relationships you need to work effectively as a leader-manager.

SNAPSHOT

Glenys designs her future

Everyone knows that Les plans to retire at some point during the next 18 months, and Glenys decides that she wants to be offered his leader-manager role. She has experienced no real problems on the many occasions she has acted in Les' position when he was away on leave, so she has no doubts about her ability to do the job from a technical point of view. But she suspects that she needs to develop more solid working relationships with her would-be staff and with the managers she hopes to make her peers.

She begins by reading up on the skills and techniques that forge effective working relationships. She finds several articles and blogs on these topics and learns that effective working relationships are based on understanding oneself and others, and on a collection of attitudes that underpin personal and interpersonal skills.

The information she learns and puts into practice really does seem to make it easier to get along with people – staff and management alike. Of course, it isn't easy, and she often feels uncomfortable, but according to what she has read, people can't improve their skills unless they take risks and try out new things.

Everyone seems impressed with the changes in Glenys and in her overall performance and it comes as no surprise when she is appointed to succeed Les. Although she realises that she still has a lot to learn, to her delight, she learns she is able to handle her new responsibilities. She is even able to get funds for extra staff and equipment – not an easy achievement! It seems to Glenys that all her hard work is paying off.

8.1 Building trust and confidence

> What you are thunders so loudly in my ears that I cannot hear what you say.
>
> Ralph Waldo Emerson, *Letters and social aims*, Belknap Press, 1875.

Without trust, good working relationships cannot develop. Customer loyalty, employee attraction, **retention** and morale, leadership effectiveness, profitability and gaining the benefits of diversity – all depend on trust. Without trust, teams and entire organisations grind to a halt.

Transferable skills

2.2 Personal effectiveness

3.1 Teamwork/relationships

As empowerment, multifunctional teams, **self-managed teams**, **virtual teams** and **teleworking** increase, not only must employees trust their leader-managers and their organisation to treat them fairly, but managers must also trust employees to do their jobs responsibly and correctly. Trust is truly a two-way street.

Because you depend on the goodwill of people above, below and at your level in the organisational hierarchy to achieve results, you need to build trust and confidence across, down and up the organisation.

Trust pays

Trust is important. But how important is it? Broken trust harms morale, loyalty and **productivity**, but does it show up on the bottom line? Research shows it does. For example, a survey of 6500 employees at 75 North American Holiday Inn hotels, using questionnaires in six languages and oral surveys for illiterate employees, asked for a response to statements such as 'My manager delivers on promises' and 'My manager practises what he preaches'. Researchers then correlated the responses with customer satisfaction surveys, personnel records and financial records.

The results were conclusive. Hotels with employees who strongly trusted their managers were substantially more profitable than hotels with employees who trusted their managers an 'average' amount or less. The link was so strong that a one-eighth point improvement in trust increased a hotel's profitability by 2.5 per cent of revenue, which translated to a profit increase of more than $250 000 per hotel per year.[2]

Trust is an absolute. You either trust someone, or you don't. It is also fragile – it takes time to develop but seconds to destroy and, once lost, it is difficult to earn back. An organisation's formal rules and policies can't build trust; only its culture, values and the integrity with which people work can breed and sustain trust.

Think of trust as 'relationship capital'. Like real capital, it takes time to amass and effort to preserve. When you keep drawing on it without replenishing it, your account quickly empties. Trust is deposited in your relationship accounts through genuineness, empathy, integrity and time; when you don't deposit enough, you can't draw on it.

Figure 8.1 shows six actions that can cost you trust, with suggestions for guarding against them.

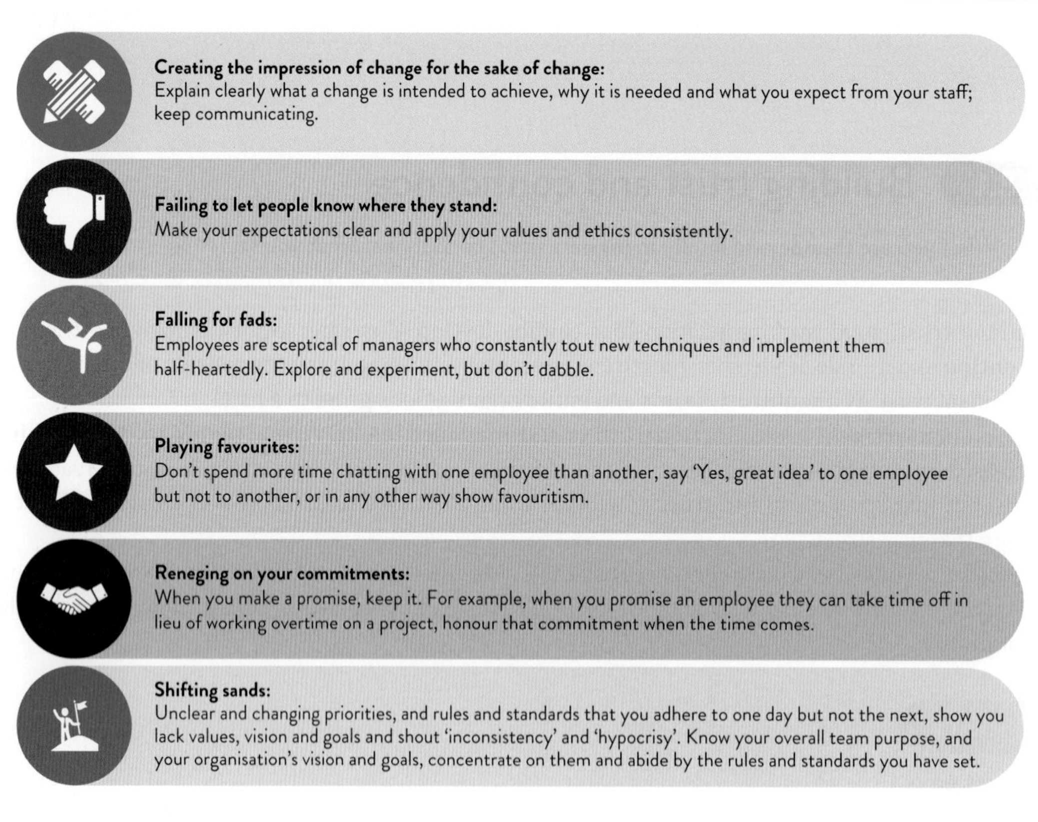

FIGURE 8.1 How to avoid breaking trust

Earn trust

How trustworthy are you? Do people confide in you and seek your advice? Do you admit when you've made a mistake and keep confidence? Or do you bend the truth or even tell lies when it benefits you to do so, gossip about others and take credit for things others have done? It takes only one untruth to be branded a 'liar', while you have to tell many truths to qualify as honest. 'Hypocrite' is a much stickier label than 'trustworthy'. Trust and credibility go hand in hand, and underpinning both is honesty.

People are only willing to follow leaders they believe uphold their rights and look after their best interests. When people believe this, they are willing to follow those leaders to the degree to which they rate their competence, honesty and ability to inspire.[3] You communicate these qualities every working hour, through everything you say and do (and don't say and don't do). Figure 8.2 shows the five components of trust.

Actively cultivating trust creates an expectation of trust so that people behave accordingly. When you trust your team, you can empower them and use consultative and participative leadership styles. Here are some actions that earn trust:

- Use power positively, to do the right thing, not to massage your ego.
- Stay true to your values and principles, which makes you consistent and reliable.
- Speak clearly and in a straightforward manner, without hidden agendas, so that people know where you stand.
- Pursue team or organisational goals rather than your personal goals.
- Keep confidences, so people can confide in you and tell you the truth.
- Give credit when tasks succeed and accept responsibility when they don't.

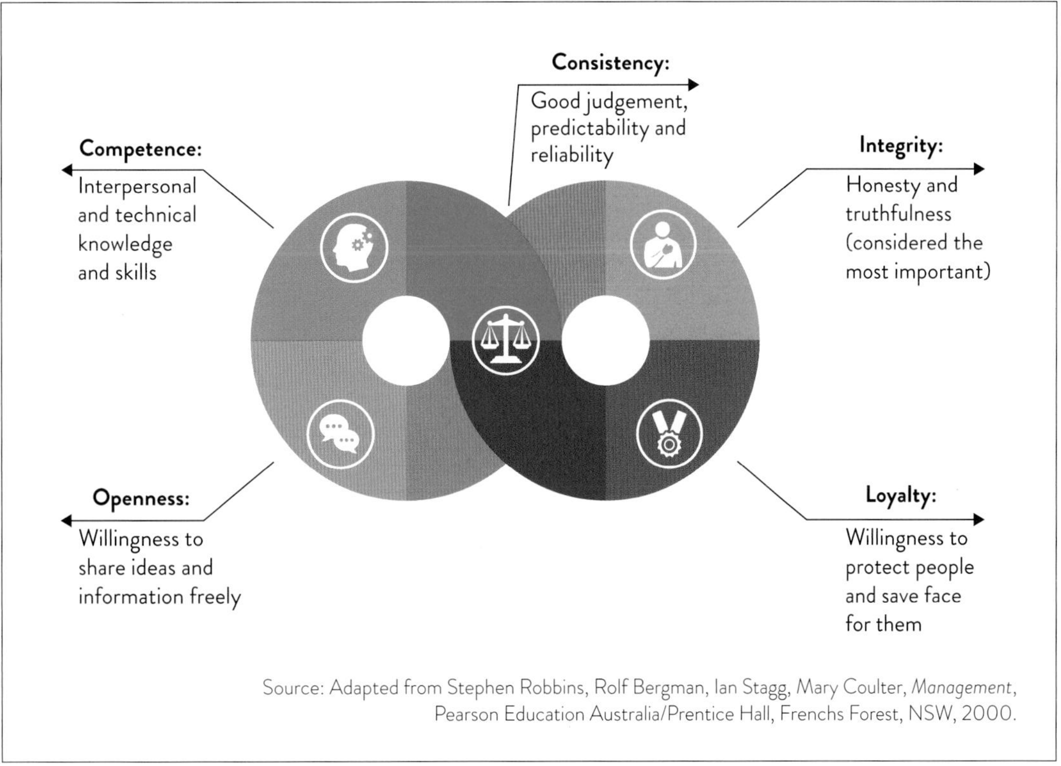

Source: Adapted from Stephen Robbins, Rolf Bergman, Ian Stagg, Mary Coulter, *Management*, Pearson Education Australia/Prentice Hall, Frenchs Forest, NSW, 2000.

FIGURE 8.2 Five components of trust

- Consider the impact of your actions or inactions on others.
- Confront people without being confrontational; for example, by tactfully tackling underperformance when necessary.
- Be enthusiastic about what is important to you, which motivates people and makes it easy to follow you.
- Admit when you get it wrong and learn from your mistakes, which enables others to do the same.

The late Maya Angelou summed it up nicely when she said, 'I've learned that people will forget what you said; people will forget what you did; but people will never forget how you made them feel'.[4]

Take responsibility

Transferable skills

2.2 Personal effectiveness

3.1 Teamwork/ relationships

Have you ever had a boss who blamed circumstances, the economy or other people when results were disappointing or a project didn't go according to plan? Or worked for someone who ranted and raved when people made mistakes rather than putting matters right or showing them how to avoid similar mistakes in the future? Not a good look. Here's a motto leader-managers like them could usefully adopt: 'Don't just see problems. Solve them.'

Taking responsibility for fixing mistakes, putting plans back on track and solving problems helps you to develop and maintain effective working relationships. Facing problems and mistakes head on and doing what you can to fix them makes you a pleasure to work with. Taking responsibility builds your **personal power** (Chapters 4 and 5 explain more about how to do this) and increases your overall effectiveness and people's confidence in you.

When you face problems and mistakes head on, take responsibility and do what you can to fix them. Don't:

- blame yourself, others or circumstances
- ignore them, hoping they'll go away or won't be noticed
- make excuses.

IN PRACTICE

Build trust first

Before people decide what they think of your message, they decide what they think of you. Two characteristics weigh heavily when people form an opinion of others: trustworthiness and competence. These characteristics answer two important questions:

1 What are this person's intentions towards me?
2 Is this person capable of acting on those intentions?

According to a growing body of research, projecting strength and competence before establishing trust risks a host of unwanted responses, including fear, which ultimately drags down productivity.

It's best to establish trust first; this is where the important qualities of employee engagement and **influence** begin. Even a few non-verbal signals, such as a nod, a smile and an open gesture, show you're pleased to see someone and are paying attention to them. A foundation of trust, supported by competence, leads to cooperation, flexibility, information sharing, innovation and openness, and makes planning, coordinating and executing easier.[5]

Show respect

Some people treat everyone with respect, regardless of their position or personal characteristics. Others grace just a select few with their high regard based on their seniority or on whether they 'like' them.

People who build and keep effective working relationships don't treat people differently based on what they do, where they're from or who they are. They treat **internal customers** and suppliers as valued colleagues, and contractors and **external customers** and suppliers as valued contacts – regardless of their size or the amount of business they do with them. (Chapter 18 explains how to develop effective relationships with customers and suppliers.)

Along with empathy and integrity, respect is another essential ingredient of effective working relationships. According to the principle of psychological reciprocity, which reminds us that mirror neurons in the brain are designed to encourage people to treat others the way others treat them, behaving respectfully and with empathy and integrity towards people encourages them to treat you the same way.

A mindset that accepts and respects people for what they are also helps you work effectively with people from different cultures and social backgrounds and people with special needs. (See Chapter 32 for information on working with a diverse range of people.)

Do the 'right thing'

When you're a leader-manager, people watch what you do, what you pay attention to, what you reward and what you discourage. They notice how you treat people every day and whether you say 'good morning' when you arrive at work and 'goodbye' before you leave the office. They notice when you return their emails promptly and whether you follow the rules and 'walk your talk'. And they make assumptions about the kind of person you are and what you value based on their observations.

Do you automatically want to do the 'right thing' because you owe it to yourself and to others? Even when the 'right thing' is awkward, inconvenient or uncomfortable, are your standards high enough to encourage you to make the 'right' decision and take the 'right' action? Doing the 'right thing' involves behaving ethically and with integrity and begins with self-awareness and knowledge of your core values (explained in Chapter 5).

How do you know what is the 'right thing' to do? Try the 'mirror test': ask 'What kind of person do I want to see when I look in the mirror?' Ask yourself whether a decision, idea, plan or strategy is morally defensible and whether reasonable people would agree with it. Ask yourself whether it would compromise your integrity, your reputation, your profession or your organisation's reputation. When the answers indicate doubt, the right answer is probably, 'No'. Here are some more questions to ask yourself:

- Is it legal?
- If someone did it to me, would I consider it fair?
- Would I be comfortable for it to appear on the front page of the newspaper?
- Would I like my mother to see me do it?

Think about the effects of your actions and decisions too. For example, consider how your decisions or actions affect those you work with internally and externally (e.g. your work team, your customers and your suppliers) and how they affect the wider community, the environment and other stakeholders. Straightforward? No. Easy? No. That's what management is all about – balancing the complex and the contrary.

Transferable skills

2.2 Personal effectiveness

3.1 Teamwork/ relationships

Being 'the boss' doesn't mean you can avoid having to explain yourself. The more you communicate your goals and intentions, the more you build understanding and trust and effective working relationships. Rather than assume people know or understand your motivations and aims, tell them. Especially when there is a chance that they could misinterpret your actions or decisions.

For example, when you have a difficult message to convey or have made a decision that can't please everyone, you can help people understand your intentions in three ways:

1 *Talk specifically about what's important to you:* the goals, purpose and values that guide your actions and decisions and the experiences that forged them. Explain both the business and personal reasons behind decisions.
2 *Through integrity:* keep your word and make sure what you do reflects what you say.
3 *Through consistency:* this comes naturally when you behave with integrity and follow your values and beliefs. When there are differences, explain them.

The psychological contract and mutual rewards

The package of unwritten and usually unspoken expectations between employers and employees, or the **psychological contract**, generally refers to intangible expectations regarding loyalty, salaries keeping pace with market rates, work performed in certain ways, and so on. When all parties honour the contract, it works well. Violating the contract erodes trust and relationships suffer as a result.

Make sure that your psychological contract with your team is a healthy one that respects individuals and their contributions, that it promotes relations that are cooperative and mutually rewarding, and that it includes all the stakeholders. You may also want it to include such expectations as employees turning up on time and sharing knowledge and information freely. You may want employees to treat customers and each other with respect, and have fun and enjoy each other's company while working towards achieving their goals. In return, you might allow, for example, flexibility in timekeeping to accommodate personal needs when required, provide formal and informal training and development, keep employees informed about matters that affect them and provide informal cakes and teas to celebrate team achievements. Unspoken agreements like this lead to cooperation and mutually rewarding behaviours.

Transferable skills

2.2 Personal effectiveness

3.1 Teamwork/relationships

Behave ethically and with integrity

Have you ever been placed in a situation where you were tempted to take the easiest course of action even though it was not the most ethical action, particularly when you took a longer-term perspective or the needs of other people or the organisation into account? Managers often face difficult choices. Choosing the ethical option or behaving according to your own or your organisation's set of values can sometimes be a difficult choice. What guides you in situations like this? Do you ask yourself, 'What do my organisation's and my own values and principles tell me to do?', or do you ask yourself, 'What do we usually do' or 'What does everyone else do?'

Acting with *integrity* means acting according to your own personal set of values and principles, which are different for everyone. Behaving *ethically* means behaving according to a set of standards that are the same for everyone, at least for everyone in the same culture. Acting with integrity and behaving ethically builds your credibility.

Most cultures share many ethical standards; for example, not killing people and not stealing from people. Other ethical standards are more culturally based; for example, in some societies it is expected that managers hire their relatives, even when the relatives are not particularly well suited to the job. Family responsibilities come first. Australians expect managers to hire the person best suited to the job and not show favouritism towards relatives or friends. 'Smoothing the way' with a tip, bribe or donation is considered normal and is even expected in some cultures but in others it is considered bribery. Caring for the environment might be mandatory in one culture and a luxury in another.

Having said that, you can think of management ethics as standards that are right or moral and that every manager should follow. Working ethically often involves managing competing tensions between an organisation's stakeholders. The ability to be **assertive** underpins your ability to behave ethically and with integrity. It helps you to state your needs, wants and opinions clearly and respectfully and to work with others to establish goals, agree responsibilities, identify and resolve problems and improve work performance. Stating your own point of view while respecting the rights of others earns you respect and a reputation for having the courage of your convictions.

Strong and professional relationships with your work colleagues can improve your position in their organisation and improve their positions as well. Figure 8.3 suggests eight ways you can nurture effective working relationships. (To find out more about building trust, confidence and effective working relationships, see Chapter 5.)

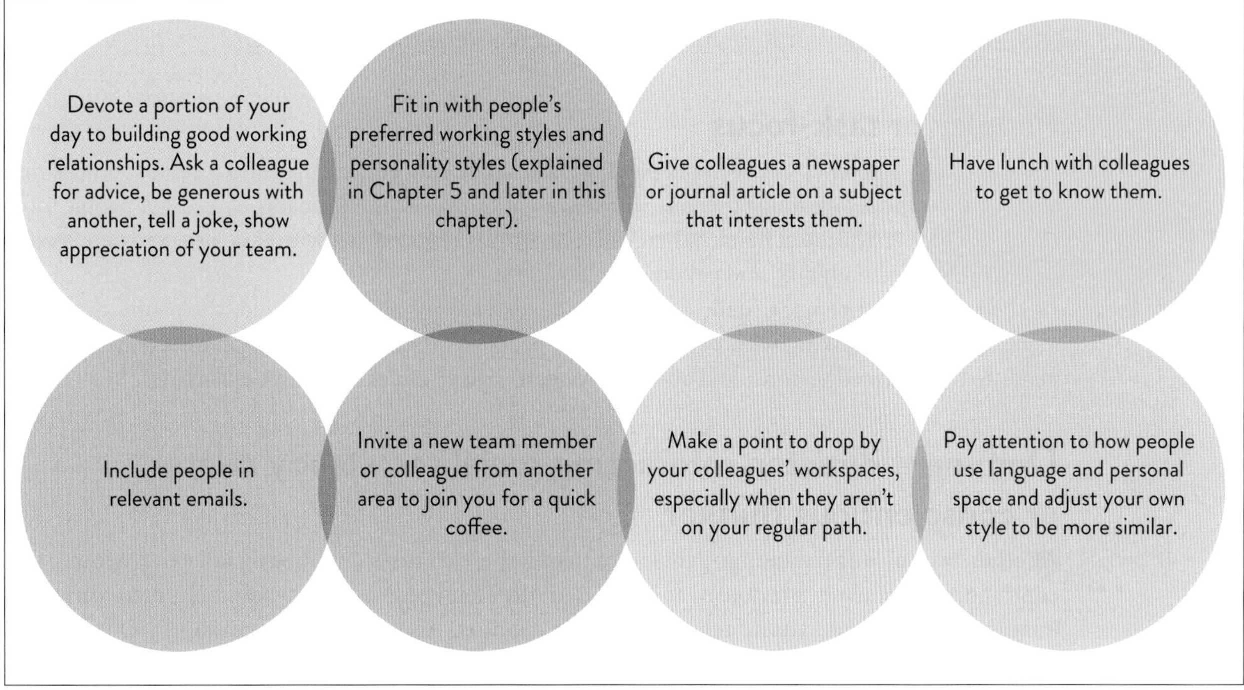

FIGURE 8.3 Eight ways to nurture effective working relationships

8.2 Understanding and working with personality styles

> To see ourselves as others see us is a most salutary gift. Hardly less important is the capacity to see others as they see themselves.
>
> Aldous Huxley, *The doors of perception*, Chatto & Windus (UK), 1954.

Part of what makes life interesting is individual differences, and it's these differences that help you and your team achieve results. Accepting that everyone has their own strengths and ways of working increases your flexibility and willingness to work differently with different people. Although people are extremely complex, you can learn to spot basic characteristics so that you can work more effectively with a range of people.

There are many ways to think about people's personalities, including your own. Each approach is valuable in its own way, with each offering different strengths, shortcomings, qualities and quirks. As you read through the following ways to think about people's personalities, consider which descriptions apply to you and which apply to the people you work with.

Transferable skills

2.2 Personal effectiveness

3.1 Teamwork/relationships

Extrovert or introvert

People face the world in two basic ways: as extroverts or introverts. Most people fall somewhere between the two types, leaning more towards the extrovert or more towards the introvert end of the spectrum.

Extroverts relate best to the external world of people and things and tend to be 'doers'. They love mixing with others and feel lost when by themselves. When persuading or explaining something to extroverts, show them how what you are saying fits in with other people's thinking and what others are doing, and how they can put it to immediate use.

Introverts are the thinkers, who prefer the inner world of concepts and ideas and are happiest when they are by themselves, doing their own thing. Although not necessarily shy, they do not seek out social or group activities. To communicate best with introverts, find out what ideas are important to them and try to fit your suggestions and instructions into that framework.

People- or task-focus

Another basic difference between people is whether they concentrate first and foremost on the *task* at hand or on the *people* doing the task. Those who put the task first probably care about people too – they just focus on the job at hand. When you're chatting to or meeting with task-oriented people, skip or minimise the 'small talk' and get down to business.

People-focused people usually care about the task too – they just consider the people aspects of a task first. When talking with people-oriented people, discuss how a decision affects people, who needs to be informed or consulted about a problem or decision and other people issues.

Dominant director, interacting socialiser, steady relater or conscientious thinker

Another way of understanding people combines the extroversion–introversion and people–task continuums discussed previously to give four different personality types: dominant directors, interacting socialisers, steady relaters and conscientious thinkers (DISC for short). One type or temperament is no better or worse than any other – they are just different.

Dominant directors

Dominant directors are extroverts who focus on the task. They provide energy, 'get the ball rolling' and make decisions. They are competitive, direct, outgoing and results-oriented. They are often ambitious, willing to speak up, make decisions easily, 'set the pace' and use their initiative. Strong-willed and practical, dominant directors often have a strong need for power, preferring to be in charge. They resist authority from others, often challenging the status quo. Dominant directors get to the point quickly – so quickly they can seem blunt, impatient and pushy. They are fast-paced, want things done *right now* and dislike sloppy results. But a team with too many dominant directors would be so busy fighting among themselves for control that they wouldn't get much work done.

To work effectively with dominant directors, communicate clearly and accurately and get to the point quickly. Turn in quality work that is practical and results-oriented. Don't try their patience with abstract theories and concepts or too much attention to people issues, which they view as 'fluffy'. Treat dominant directors with the respect they believe they deserve and let them think they're in charge (even when they aren't).

Interacting socialisers

Interacting socialisers are extroverts who focus on people – they like people and like to have people around them, and they enjoy working with and helping others and trying out new and better ways of doing things. They add enthusiasm, spirit and a sense of fun to the team and are impulsive, optimistic, persuasive, sociable and talkative. Interacting socialisers are good at influencing people and creating a motivating environment. They are creative, energetic and open with their feelings. They thrive on change, ideas and new trends and they need their achievements and contributions recognised. But interacting socialisers are often disorganised and inattentive to detail, excitable, manipulative, undisciplined and vain. A team might never get anything done with too many of these energetic, talkative people!

To develop good working relationships with interacting socialisers, keep details and detailed work well away from them. Focus on the big picture and vision and let them talk, participate, motivate and create an enjoyable atmosphere. Treat them as friends.

Steady relaters

Steady relaters are people-oriented introverts who pay attention to people and relationships in order to complete the task. Willing, reliable, cooperative, easygoing, consistent, helpful and relaxed, steady relaters may not be balls of fire, but they are valuable team players. Quiet and often unassertive, they are comfortable taking a back seat. They dislike conflict and need time to digest what a change might mean to them before they can embrace it. They prefer their known and stable routine to the untried and untested. Good thinkers and patient listeners, the stable, quiet manner of steady relaters makes them good at calming down upset people. Others sometimes see them as insecure conformists who are awkward, indecisive, possessive and unsure. Too many steady relaters could cause a team to stagnate and fail to improve.

To discover a steady relater's thoughts or opinions, ask a lot of open questions and listen carefully. Don't overlook them or take their contributions, hard work and loyalty for granted and don't spring changes on them without giving them time to think them through.

Conscientious thinkers

Conscientious thinkers are introverts who pay attention to the task and produce high-quality work. They look after the details, check things carefully, keep to timelines and produce accurate, comprehensive information. They have a strong need for achievement and 'getting things right'. They are deliberate, well-organised people who are good at analysing problems and thinking them through. They enjoy study and analysis, weighing up both sides of an issue and examining alternatives carefully. Their approach to work is accurate, diligent, exacting, objective, orderly, systematic and thorough. Conscientious thinkers are serious and well-organised perfectionists, but they can also be stuffy, fussy, judgemental, critical and slow at making decisions. A team with too many conscientious thinkers would suffer 'paralysis by analysis'.

Don't ask the conscientious thinkers to turn in a rushed, 'close enough is good enough' job and don't ever present sloppy work to them. When you need to criticise a conscientious thinker, do so gently and tactfully. Explain decisions, problems and situations fully and carefully and include the details they crave. When you need to make changes, for example to the departmental layout, a job assignment or a procedure, spell them out clearly, allow time for questions and give them time to adjust. Don't try to rush conscientious thinkers.

Stay flexible!

Treating everyone the same is a mistake. Adjust the way you assign and delegate work, ask for help or information and thank people for it, give information and present your ideas to suit each individual you work with.

8.3 Establishing and sustaining networks

Though most people recognise that networking is important to career advancement and success, few fully understand that a lack of access to influential networks can become a barrier to even the most talented employees.

Laura Sabattini (US talent management strategist), '6 unwritten rules to advancement in the workplace', *Encyclopaedia Britannica Blog*, 25 August 2008.

Transferable skills

2.2 Personal effectiveness

3.1 Teamwork/ relationships

Networks are relationships of people who share similar aspirations and interests. Networking helps you expand and share your information, knowledge, perspectives and skills and extend your sphere of influence. Networking is becoming more important as organisation structures become flatter and the power that was invested in the hierarchy moves to people with strong and cordial networks – these connected individuals are now an organisation's information brokers and persuaders.

Here's how the Australian Institute of Management defines networking: 'Connecting with others without the need for immediate gain. It is a proactive investment in the future aimed at building a relationship with another well before assistance is sought.'[6] Networking is not about seeing and being seen, or petty politicking. Think of networks as strategic alliances and the people in your networks as allies. The access to the advice, contacts, emotional support, resources and technical and task assistance they provide helps you contribute to your organisation and team. It also helps you to achieve your professional and personal goals more easily, effectively and quickly than you could on your own. Networking is a critical skill for managers and one of the key behaviours of effective leader-managers. Effective networks have some or all of these four characteristics – diversity, quality, size and strong bonds, as seen in Figure 8.4. How do your networks measure up?

When you make building networks part of your personal development plan, you benefit in three ways:

1 *Operational networks:* help you manage internal responsibilities. Networks, made up of people you report to, peers and more senior managers, as well as key customers, distributors and suppliers, help you do your job by ensuring coordination and cooperation. Your role and responsibilities largely determine the people you include in them.

1 The more varied your networks, in terms of people's backgrounds, interests and skills, the more powerful they can be in supplying a wide range of information and ideas. Don't just network with people who are similar to yourself or with whom you spend most time – mix it up

2 Network with the best. Network with skilled, smart and influential people who have strong networks themselves

3 Large networks have more potential for supporting you, so include lots of people from outside your organisation as well as from inside it

4 Mature networks that have been nurtured over time have strong rapport between members, which increases their willingness to support each other

Source: Peter Langford, 'Stay in touch', *HR Monthly*, October 2001.

FIGURE 8.4 Four characteristics of effective networks

2 *Personal networks:* are made up mostly of a range of people outside the organisation who assist your personal and professional development.

3 *Strategic networks:* build business acumen and help you figure out future priorities and challenges that the organisation (and therefore you) need to contend with.[7]

Your current and former bosses, colleagues and teachers can all be valuable to include in your professional circles. Friends, relatives, neighbours and acquaintances from professional and other groups can help you build knowledge, develop your ideas and broaden your perspectives. Include some customers, competitors, consultants and suppliers, too. Chapter 4 lists the types of informal networks you can link into in most organisations. Some organisations have introduced corporate social networking (CSN) to help employees connect and share information and ideas. CSNs can also include blogs, threaded discussion boards, Wikis and other web tools.

Add value to your networks without being asked, or you won't be in them for long. Find out what is important to people you network with, what they're thinking about and the challenges they face so you know how you can assist them. Mutual understanding helps you and the people in your networks achieve goals, develop and learn. Keep contact information up to date so that you can find each other when you need to do so. Build mutual respect and trust with everyone, concentrating your efforts on the people you plan to call on and support the most.

You can network anywhere (and even any time when you network on social media). All it takes is a smiling face, some business cards and some information that is useful to someone else who may pass on some of their information to you. Figure 8.5 suggests some ways to build useful networks. (See Chapter 6 for more information on presenting yourself professionally, online and in person.)

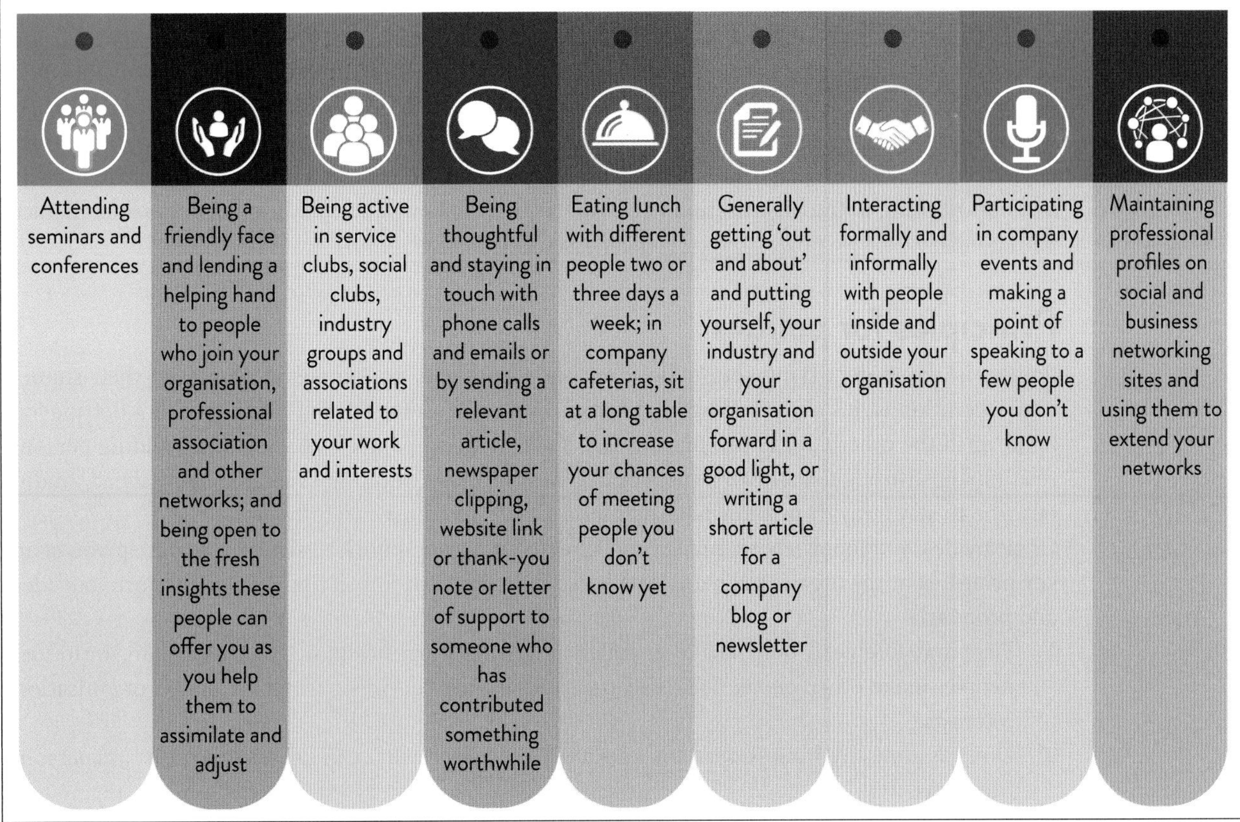

FIGURE 8.5 Some ways to network

8.4 Navigating organisational politics

The term office politics is often talked about in a negative sense, but it can be both beneficial and harmful. When you have people coming together, working towards a common goal and sharing resources and a workspace, there is going to be human interaction. This means differences of opinion and varied communication styles.

James Judge, CEO of Australian Human Resource Professionals, 'News: How to handle office politics in the public service', Australian Human Resource Professionals Pty Ltd, 27 February 2017, https://www.ahrp.com.au/handling-office-politics-public-service.

Transferable skills

2.2 Personal effectiveness

3.1 Teamwork/ relationships

Have you ever been amazed at someone's unexpected promotion, or watched someone float an idea at a meeting and it was immediately accepted? You were probably witnessing organisational politics at work. Politics has been called the 'shadow organisation', the unspoken alliances and coalitions of influence, and the often-hidden norms and networks of relationships discussed in Chapter 4. Politics is a reality in every organisation.

Awareness of, and sensitivity to, this shadow organisation – who is what to whom, what people want and need and why, and the patterns of loyalty criss-crossing the organisation – is known as *political intelligence*. It gives you the ability to read and understand the undercurrents of relationships and build good working relationships with the people around you, without being seen as 'self-serving' or labelled as 'political'. It can protect you against any unethical politicking and power plays too because you're 'in the loop'.

Certainly, some people could use the energy they expend on politicking much more productively. Fortunately, though, politicking without the underlying leadership and management competencies and values to support it can seldom sustain a career. When backed by sound leadership and management competencies and values, however, political intelligence increases your personal effectiveness.

Organisational politics is not about 'protecting your turf' or pursuing personal advantage (or it shouldn't be). It's about forming alliances with like-minded people across the organisation and with influential customers, suppliers and other stakeholders to help achieve team and organisational objectives. It's about managing your image in a positive way (discussed in Chapter 5), fitting in with and contributing to the organisation's culture, and recognising and building networks and alliances with people who have power and influence (discussed in Chapter 4).

Principles for politics

Politics is about identifying your supporters and opponents and knowing how deep their support and opposition is. It's about saying 'thank you' for people's support and helping others (letting 'one hand wash the other'). It's about sharing the credit, making people feel good and building personal relationships throughout the organisation. Politics is about thinking several 'moves' ahead, finding out who to stay away from and whose opinions to listen to most carefully.

Provided you follow these four 'prime directives', strong political alliances can help you shape key priorities in the organisation and line up supporters to promote change and support your ideas and proposals:

1 First and foremost, don't make enemies and don't burn bridges. Don't complain, intimidate people, make other people look bad or criticise anyone except in terms of the organisation's interests.

2 Don't assume anything you say stays secret. Think about what you say and don't discuss personal problems.

3 Be worth being around. Be assertive (but not tough or aggressive) when you need to and otherwise be pleasant, laugh and smile.
4 Play the political game in a professional, ethical way at all times.

Here are some other principles to help you succeed in organisational politics:

- Be visible and make sure that powerful people in your organisation hear about your and your team's achievements and contributions. Networking and progress reports are two ways to do this without coming across as a braggart. As a bonus, the more necessary to the organisation you seem to be, the more secure your employment is.
- Gain control of important and scarce organisational resources, knowledge and expertise. This expands your influence because you can bestow favours and offer information and help.
- Get a mentor and powerful allies who can guide you, keep you informed and speak up on your behalf.
- Remember that power is effective when it is in balance. As soon as you use it, especially against someone, it gets out of balance and people automatically seek to even things out.
- Speak and persuade in terms of benefits to the organisation and conceal any self-interest.
- Support your boss. When your boss is successful, you shine by association. When your boss is on the 'loser track', you suffer by association.

Work well with your boss

Transferable skills

2.2 Personal effectiveness

3.1 Teamwork/relationships

Your most important working relationship is probably the one you have with your manager. Although it can take time and energy, developing and nurturing it (yes, it's your responsibility, too), a good working relationship with your boss almost certainly increases your job effectiveness, avoids a host of problems and frustrations, and may open the door to interesting projects and career moves.

You need a good understanding of both yourself and your leader-manager, particularly regarding strengths, weaknesses, working and personality style and foremost concerns and goals. Find out what concerns and problems are uppermost in your boss' mind, what your boss' organisational and personal objectives are and what pressures are on your boss from their boss and colleagues. Use your empathy and pay attention to behavioural clues.

Find out how often your boss wants you to report progress, share general information and in what format. Establish what working style works best for your working relationship and serves both of your needs. When you understand each other's working style you can provide more effective (and appreciated) support.

Anticipate your manager's concerns and address them ahead of time, or as they surface, without being asked to do so, when possible. Or have clear communication lines between you and your manager so you can discuss any concerns you might have and work out how your manager might be able to best support you.

Four key questions to discuss with your boss include:

1 What are my key result areas and main goals?
2 How can we best measure my performance?
3 What operating guidelines do you want me to work within?
4 How can I support you to do your job better?

Maybe you already know the answers to these questions. If so, what does that tell you about your relationship with your boss and your organisation's culture?

Make it easy for your boss to give you feedback. Ask questions when you need to, listen to any tips your manager passes on about how you can do your job better and put those tips into practice. When your boss praises you, don't feign modesty – say 'Thank you' with confidence.

Feedback is a two-way street and your manager will not be perfect – no one is. Find ways to let your manager know what your own needs and expectations are. If you're unhappy with your boss' management style, suggest ways you could work better together, explaining what you would like (not what you don't like) in objective, uncritical terms. Focus on the future and what you'd like to happen.

Schedule regular meetings to update your manager on your work, what you've accomplished, what improvements you and your team have made, what problems you have resolved and are working on, and generally how your job and team are going. Be prepared, objective and factual. Anticipate problems and try to solve them before they grow. Report any problems you can't fix early on and have the facts with you.

See yourself as your manager's partner in achieving results. Just as you depend on your manager for help, guidance, resources and information, your manager depends on you for support and cooperation. Do what you're asked – in fact, 'go above and beyond'.

Lastly, don't take yourself too seriously. Your manager is an individual, not a job title. Show interest in your manager as a person and share a smile.

How to disagree with your boss

Transferable skills

2.2 Personal effectiveness

3.1 Teamwork/ relationships

When you and your boss don't see eye-to-eye, explain why and offer an alternative. Here's how to open a discussion:

1. Pick a good time and place to discuss the situation, a time when your boss is most likely to be receptive and when you're not angry, emotional or upset.
2. Find out what your boss thinks and any background information you may not know.
3. Offer your views; put them in positive terms and frame them as suggestions for your boss to consider and word your comments so you don't appear to be dogmatic or aggressive (e.g. 'I agree with ... On the other hand, I think we may get a better result by ...').

Here are some other pointers:

- Aim to see the situation from your boss' perspective as well as from your own.
- Consider the objective or goal of the conversation and what you would like to achieve from the discussion that will benefit yourself/the team/the organisation.
- Don't get personal – stay factual, objective, professional, respectful and thoughtful.
- Identify what you agree on.
- Show how your ideas benefit the boss and the team.
- Speak about common interests and needs.
- Unless you are speaking on behalf of others with their agreement, say 'I' rather than 'we'.

Your position is stronger when you have built a good working relationship, consistently made your boss look good, have shown you are committed to the overall success of your team and organisation and when you're straightforward and don't play games.

Reporting to more than one boss

Convention has it that an employee should report to only one person. Called unity of command, this is based on the thinking that having more than one boss can create conflict and confusion. This principle flourished in the days of hierarchy and **bureaucracy** but is eroding in today's organisations in which flexibility and responsiveness to the environment are critical. Temporary teams, for example, often form to undertake special projects and then disband; contractors and part-time workers are often brought in to work in one or more areas or in **matrix teams**. Employees are often temporarily seconded to other areas; and some organisations have opted for matrix organisation structures (see Chapter 3 for a discussion on matrix organisation structures).

Reporting to several managers, each making requests of you, and each with their own agenda and priorities, can be tricky. You're in danger of the following:

- *Competing demands on your time:* Which boss' work gets priority? This can be very tricky when each boss thinks their work deserves precedence.
- *Conflicting messages:* Different bosses have different expectations and communication styles, and they can unintentionally undermine each other's messages.
- Work overload: This occurs especially when each boss treats you as if you work only for them.

To protect yourself, work out who your primary boss is. This is the person you formally report to, who does your final performance review and who makes decisions about your pay. Make sure you have regular, at least monthly, meetings with this boss and ask for their help in mentoring or coaching to help you to work well with your other bosses.

Be open about your workload so all your bosses know your commitments. Share your electronic calendar with them and block off specific times for working on different projects and assignments so they know when not to interrupt you. Provide each with a document updating your progress on all of your projects and other work. However briefly, check in with each boss face-to-face or virtually once a week to maintain your good working relationships.

When you have several bosses, it's probably fair to ask each to adjust to your preferred working style so you don't have to keep chopping and changing, which is stressful in itself. Let them know whether you prefer to receive questions and requests via email, meetings or in some other way. Agree on mutual expectations regarding response time for queries, regularity of meetings and regularity and format of update briefings. Try to agree on one way that works for everyone.

As with working for one boss, be clear about your deadlines and deliverables, focus on results and keep communication flowing.

Reporting to a remote manager or working remotely

What if your manager is in Singapore and you're in Sydney? What if your role is based virtually? Because you can't see each other 'in the flesh', it's easy for each of you to miss the signals of energy, mood, personality and so on. When you report to a manager in a different location, it's critical that you communicate efficiently and build trust quickly.

As with any manager, agree on your job purpose, your key result areas (KRAs) and your **SMART targets** or deliverables and find out your manager's preferred working style so that you can fit in with it. What is the best time of day to contact them? What is the preferred method of contact? Does your boss prefer progress reports in virtual person, for example, by Skype, or in writing? How much detail should you include? Does your boss prefer to take queries or receive updates as they occur, or in regular batches?

Your other initial goal is getting to know your boss. When you can't meet face-to-face, make good use of virtual meetings and the telephone. Small talk is important, so avoid the temptation to move straight into task talk (unless that is your boss' clear preference).

Involve your manager in what they should be involved in (but avoid information overload). Schedule regular virtual meetings with an informal agenda and prepare the agenda to go to your boss in advance. This is your opportunity to summarise what you've achieved since your last virtual meeting. Ask any questions you have and finish with an outline of the next steps you are taking to achieve your mutual goals.

Confirm your commitments in a follow-up email, including date and time of your next scheduled virtual meeting. Design the email's content so that you can use it as a checklist or use it to list goals and create work schedules and plans to achieve them.

STUDY TOOLS

QUICK REVIEW

KEY CONCEPT 8.1 

a Explain how earning trust, taking responsibility, treating people with respect, doing the 'right thing' and behaving ethically and with integrity are linked and how they help develop effective working relationships.

KEY CONCEPT 8.2 

a What does working with people's personality styles and working styles mean?

KEY CONCEPT 8.3 

a The ability to network is becoming a key skill of employees at every level in the organisation. Discuss.

KEY CONCEPT 8.4 

a Why do managers need to be able to engage in organisational politics? At what point do you think politicking becomes counterproductive?

BUILD YOUR SKILLS

KEY CONCEPT 8.1 

a The novelist Aldous Huxley said: 'To see ourselves as others see us is a most salutary gift. Hardly less important is the capacity to see others as they see themselves.'[8] Discuss this advice in terms of establishing effective working relationships.

KEY CONCEPT 8.2 

a Explain how you can use an understanding of basic differences in personality styles and working styles to smooth the path to good working relationships without falling into the trap of 'pigeon-holing' people.

b This section considered a model of personality styles based on conscientious thinkers, dominant directors, interacting socialisers and steady relaters. Conduct an internet search for these two other ways to consider personality:

i 'analyst, empathist, legalist, realist'

ii 'feeler, intuitor, sensor, thinker'.

Summarise the characteristics of each personality style in these two models and explain how to lead and manage people from each of these personality styles most effectively. Which way of thinking about people are you more drawn to – the model described in this chapter or one of these two models?

c Who do you know that are dominant directors, interacting socialisers, conscientious thinkers and steady relaters? Which are you? Who do you know that are analysts, empathists, legalists and realists? Which are you? Who do you know that are feelers, intuitors, sensors and thinkers? Which are you? In what subtle ways might you need to adjust your behaviour towards people in each of these personality styles?

KEY CONCEPT 8.3 

a What are your personal and professional networks and how do these networks help you to do your job well? Provide two or three specific examples.

KEY CONCEPT 8.4 

a Do you think the ability to understand and employ organisational politics is more or less important today than it was 20 years ago? Why or why not?

WORKPLACE ACTIVITIES

KEY CONCEPT 8.1 

a Which manager in your organisation do you trust most? Brainstorm the characteristics and behaviours of this person that you believe earns this trust. Using this person as a role model, how can you adjust your behaviour?

b What are the elements of the psychological contract at your workplace? How does understanding and honouring it help people's working relationships? What is your role as a leader-manager in establishing and maintaining the psychological contract? What is your role as an employee in establishing and maintaining the psychological contract?

c Find out whether your organisation has a written code of conduct or ethics policy and an anonymous mechanism for reporting misconduct, fraudulent practices or dishonesty at work. If it does, review and summarise them.

KEY CONCEPT 8.2 

a List the people you work most closely with, including your direct reports, your manager, peers and internal customers and suppliers. Develop a matrix and, working through Section 8.2 and 'Build your skills' – Key concept 8.2, question (b), note each person's characteristics. Then analyse whether you need to adjust how you work with them and summarise your findings.

KEY CONCEPT 8.3 

a Explain why the ability to network may be more important for employees at all levels in the organisation today than it was 20 years ago. Is this true in your organisation? Why or why not?

KEY CONCEPT 8.4 

a Can you give an example of organisational politics used effectively for the benefit of a work team or the organisation and an example of politics 'gone too far'?

b Who in your organisation is able to 'make things happen' and obtain approval for their proposals? To what extent is this person's political intelligence helpful?

c Give two or three examples of how you have achieved outcomes you may not otherwise have achieved had it not been for political astuteness.

EXTENSION ACTIVITIES

Referring to the Snapshot at the beginning of this chapter, answer the following questions:

1 What are the top five skills and techniques you think would have assisted Glenys in her approach to improving workplace relationships?

2 What do you think are some of the potential problems Glenys might have faced, or situations that made her uncomfortable, and how would you address these?

CASE STUDY 8

DELUSIONS OF GRANDEUR?

David finally gets the break he has been hoping for. He is appointed team leader of the technical trainers of his company's learning and development unit. Now he really has a chance to show management what he is made of! His career is about to begin.

First, he intends to make some important changes in the way the team operates. He calls a team meeting and announces that, from now on, everyone is to adhere strictly to the standard working hours stated in their job contracts. Also, he intends to check everyone's expenses quite carefully when they return from their frequent interstate training trips. Under no circumstances does he intend to let his budget blow out.

The trainers point out that their frequent travel is often done outside working hours and a lot of their preparation for training is undertaken in their personal time. They see some of the 'relaxed' timekeeping when back at head office as *quid pro quo* – normal give and take. David replies that, on the contrary, this is a normal part of the job, and they'd better start getting used to it. Upon seeing David's rigid behaviour, the trainers keep the rest of their thoughts to themselves.

The next item on David's agenda is the training program he ran last week. The training manuals and training aids didn't turn up. 'Sheila was supposed to send them and, as usual, she messed up. I intend to find a replacement for her as soon as possible. I won't have my unit looking unprofessional in front of the trainees.'

Later, in the canteen, the trainers have quite a bit to say among themselves. 'Fancy him checking up on our expenses – he's the one who over-claims, not us!' They all agree on that point. 'David always says one thing and does another. And if he thinks I'm doing any travel or preparation in my own time, he's got another thing coming!' Once again, there is agreement all round.

'What really gets me,' says Margot, 'is that the only way David seems to feel good about himself is

CASE STUDY 8

by putting others down. He even does it in training sessions. I've seen him rip into trainees when they don't understand what he shows them first time around. All the trainees hate him – what in the world could management have been thinking when they made him team leader?'

'Perhaps they just wanted him out of the training room' suggests Andy, only half-jokingly. 'Great! So now he can take all his inadequacies out on us.'

'Poor Sheila. She never makes mistakes on our programs – only David's. That's because he leaves her such poor instructions about what he wants. I wonder how we can help her?'

'He won't listen to us. He always has to be the one with the answers and the good ideas. We might as well forget about suggesting anything or pointing anything out to him. I'm off to polish up my résumé and reach out to my networks!'

'Me too! He's such an aggressive person! I don't want to stay around here any longer than I have to.'

With that, the technical trainers amble back to their workstations.

Questions

1. Where is David going wrong in his working relationships with his team?
2. What advice can you give David to help him develop more effective working relationships with them?
3. Thinking about the Johari Window, what might some of David's blind spots be? If you were going to help David understand some of his blind spots, how would you go about it? Explain the general approach you would take and write down your opening comments.
4. Is David building trust with his team or is he draining his account? Explain your thinking.

CHAPTER ENDNOTES

1. Daryll Hull, Vivienne Read, *Simply the best*, Australian Centre for Industrial Relations Research and Training, University of Sydney, 2004.
2. Tony Simons, 'The high cost of lost trust', *Harvard Business Review*, September 2002.
3. Stephen Robbins, Rolf Bergman, Ian Stagg, Mary Coulter, *Management*, Pearson Education Australia/Prentice Hall, Frenchs Forest, NSW, 2000.
4. Quoted in B. Quirk, 'Women need to feel good about themselves', *The Capital Times*, 22 July 2003, p. 4.
5. Amy Cuddy, Matthew Kohut, John Neffinger, 'Connect, then lead', *Harvard Business Review*, July–August 2013, pp. 55–61.
6. Deborah Tarrant, 'Branching out', *Management Today* (Australia), August 2007.
7. Herminia Ibarra, Mark Hunter, 'How leaders create and use networks', *Harvard Business Review*, January 2007.
8. Aldous Huxley, *The doors of perception*, Chatto & Windus (UK), 1954.

CHAPTER

MANAGING YOUR PERSONAL PRODUCTIVITY

After completing this chapter, you will be able to:

9.1 see your role clearly enough to establish and work to priorities to carry out your role effectively

9.2 organise yourself and schedule your work to carry out your role efficiently.

TRANSFERABLE SKILLS

The following transferable skills are covered in this chapter:

2 **Critical thinking and problem solving**
 2.2 Personal effectiveness

3 **Social competence**
 3.3 Written communication

5 **Digital competence**
 5.2 Technology use

OVERVIEW

If you're a leader-manager, you already know that you often have only minutes between interruptions and seldom have 30 solid minutes to spend on a task. You know you work hard, and you probably switch attention from one task to another frequently. (If you aren't yet a leader-manager, you'll soon find out!) The trouble is that the human brain loses efficiency when it's forced to constantly switch mental gears and reorient itself to new and different tasks.

And there's more. The days of most leader-managers are hectic and difficult to plan precisely. It's incredibly easy to become caught up in the day-to-day and lose sight of the bigger picture. We call the ability to stay involved in the day-to-day, and at the same time to rise above it, as being 'in the dance and on the balcony'. All leader-managers need to be in the dance as well as on the balcony to be effective. But it's all too easy to work so hard on 'the dance' that you fail to take the time to stand 'on the balcony' to see your job as a whole, reflect on your performance and undertake activities that are vital to your longer-term success.

Managing your personal productivity is really about managing yourself. In this chapter, you will find out how to establish your priorities and plan your days accordingly, and how to maximise your productivity by working both effectively and efficiently.

SNAPSHOT

Seeds of doubt

As Jane takes her seat on the bus, her thoughts turn to what will no doubt be another frenetic workday. 'I know my job and I'm a good team leader, so why can't I ever finish my to-do list? I juggle so many tasks that I hardly know which are on time and on budget. It's a miracle that I manage to achieve anything at all! Yet I work like a dog.

'I wake up worrying about things I need to do, decisions I need to make, comments people have made. Sam seems to think that I'm more short-tempered than usual, and so do the kids. It's just that I worry a lot. And my boss doesn't seem to value my opinions. Sometimes I think I'm losing the support of the other leader-managers, but I can't think why. Really and truly, am I as good as I've always thought? Or am I kidding myself?

'What I need is a fairy godmother – someone who can explain how to make things happen and get results. All I want is to be a better team leader and for people to know I'm a good team leader, and I want to build a career that makes me feel good about myself, not like a loser.'

The bus jerks to a stop outside her workplace. 'Into the fray I go,' she sighs.

Transferable skills

2.2 Personal effectiveness

9.1 Standing on the balcony: establishing your priorities and goals

> **Things which matter most must never be left at the mercy of things which matter least.**
>
> Johann Wolfgang von Goethe (philosopher, scientist, author), 1749–1832.

The human brain craves structure and an overview, at home and at work. Standing on the balcony gives you that structure. From the balcony, you can see your job purpose, key result areas (KRAs) and measures of success (MoS). This doesn't just soothe your brain, it also highlights your important goals and priorities, guides your decisions and helps you decide how to use your time and organise your days. It prevents your job from seeming like an endless series of tasks.

A clear job purpose statement, KRAs and SMART targets provide **role clarity**. Together, they comprise the balcony overview that helps you manage your work priorities and increase your personal productivity. They tell you precisely what you expect to achieve, by when, and why achieving it is important. They also help you set priorities, establish a work schedule, focus your efforts and monitor your performance.

Your job purpose, KRAs and MoS (and those of your team members) should support the organisation's vision and mission. This produces an 'aligned' organisation – one in which everyone is working towards the same ends – and this provides a powerful competitive edge.

It helps you personally, too. When you're constantly 'on the dance floor', immersed in your daily tasks, you concentrate on what you need to do and try to do a good job. But understanding your work's overall purpose and how it fits into the organisation and links with its strategy, gives your performance an 'edge' (and can accelerate your career rapidly).

Job purpose

A clear job purpose is a one-sentence statement that answers the questions: 'What do I do?' and 'Why do I do it?' or 'To what end do I do it?' Your job purpose statement gives you an important overview of your job and, because it states why the job exists, it highlights what is important. This puts your role and responsibilities into context. A concise job purpose statement acts as your personal job vision or mission statement and provides overall guidance on how to do your job, showing you where to concentrate your efforts and mental energy. Really, you can't do a good job without a job purpose statement; Table 9.1 shows some examples.

TABLE 9.1 Examples of job purpose statements

Job	Purpose
Customer service team leader	Help my team follow company guidelines to delight our customers and feel proud of our work
Production team leader	Help my team take pride in producing quality products within time and cost budgets so that the organisation's reputation is enhanced in the marketplace both as a quality producer and a quality employer
Retail store manager	Achieve or exceed sales and other targets in a way that delights our customers, my team and myself

Key result areas

Key result areas (KRAs) describe your main areas of accountability and responsibility. They are not individual tasks and they are not goals. Rather, they are groups of tasks that, together, help achieve results in a specific area. Most jobs have five to nine KRAs; some examples are shown in Table 9.2.

Notice two important aspects of the KRAs in Table 9.2:

1. each is written using one to five words and without verbs – they single out areas of accountability
2. there is no 'pecking order' – each KRA is as important as every other. You might spend a lot more time on one KRA than another, but they're both important. When you fail to achieve results in any one key area, your entire job suffers.

To achieve results in each KRA, you complete tasks (e.g. assign work, coach team members, develop and implement improvements to procedures, lead meetings, monitor results, update your team). Carrying out a series of tasks well achieves results in a KRA. This is how KRAs put your tasks – even small, seemingly insignificant daily activities – into context and give them meaning. And here's the important rule to remember: every task you complete should in some way contribute to achieving results in a KRA. Otherwise, why are you doing it?

TABLE 9.2 Example key result areas for different types of leader-managers

Customer service team leader	Production team leader	Retail store manager
• Administration • Focus groups • Leadership • Problem resolution • Recruitment and selection • Service objectives and metrics • Staff induction, training and coaching • Staff rostering	• Equipment utilisation • Health and safety • Leadership • Output: quality, quantity, cost, timeliness • Staffing • Workplace relations	• Administration • Continuous improvement • Customer relations • Housekeeping • Leadership • Sales budgets • Stock

Measures of success

Transferable skills

2.2 Personal effectiveness

Once you know your job's overall purpose and key areas of responsibility, you can set measures of success (MoS; also called key performance indicators (KPIs) and measures of performance) for each KRA. MoS help you in two ways: they establish a performance standard, giving you something specific to aim for; and they help you track your progress and monitor your performance.

For each KRA, choose two or three targets that measure that KRA's most important aspects. Make each one 'SMART', as shown in the SMART acronym outlined in Figure 9.1.

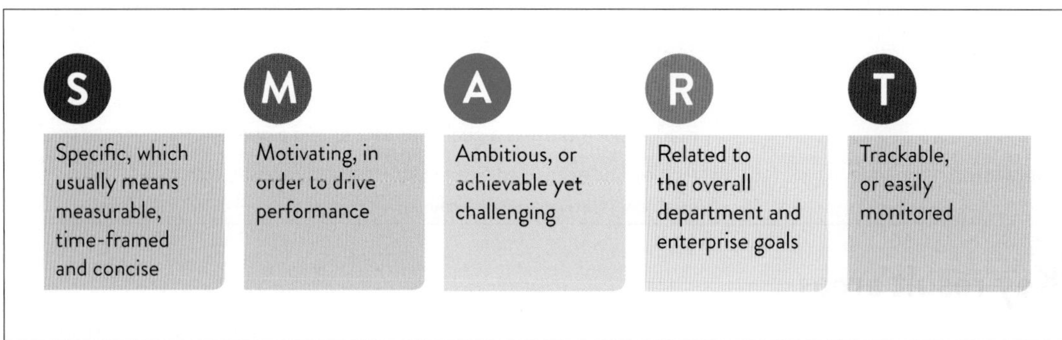

FIGURE 9.1 The SMART acronym

Ideally, establish your success measures jointly with your manager, for example, during a performance review and planning meeting. Together, identify, agree and write down what you are aiming to accomplish, by when and to what standards.

Beware, though. Goals should guide you, not constrain you. They should not become ends in themselves either, but rather encourage behaviours in harmony with your job purpose and your organisation's values and vision. And make sure they relate only to those parts of your job that are actually under your control.

Specific and concise

A target that is specific and concise is a clear target. It is usually measurable and time-framed, so no one needs to wonder whether or not the target has been met, or even what that means.

You probably don't want to wait for your manager to tell you whether you are doing a good job. You want to monitor your performance yourself. Specific targets that are measurable, time-framed and trackable allow you to do this. The more frequently you can measure your performance, the more your motivation and productivity are likely to increase, provided your targets are achievable (yet challenging).

Measurable MoS tend to fall into five main areas, which you can use to write your own MoS:

1 cost
2 quality (including expectations and behaviours)
3 quantity
4 safety
5 time.

Reject measures where a change in performance does not cause you (or your team) to act differently, that are difficult to interpret, that do not illustrate progress towards achieving an important objective, that replicate other measures or that are difficult or expensive to measure.

Difficult-to-measure targets

As the service and knowledge economies grow, organisations increasingly link MoS to their vision and values. It isn't always easy to set measurable, time-framed targets for adhering to corporate values and contributing to the vision, but that doesn't mean you shouldn't try.

For example, how do you specify and measure important responsibilities like 'leadership' or 'ethical behaviour'? For matters like these, use your imagination and knowledge of the job and its requirements to determine targets. For example, one of your KRAs might be leadership; you might choose to monitor your leadership achievements by whether you have developed a successor and by how thoroughly and how quickly you induct new employees into the department and train them; or you might work out a measure that indicates how well the employees reporting to you work as a team. You could attach timelines and ways to measure, or assess, your success for each of these factors.

Motivating

Targets that correspond to your interests and abilities are motivating and can power your performance and productivity. When the targets are also measurable and timeframed, you can track your success. You always know how well you're doing and where you need to make some adjustments to improve.

Ambitious yet achievable

Make your MoS ambitious. When you think about the accomplishments you are most proud of, they probably took effort and extended your skills. When a task is too easy you don't put much effort into it, yet when it's too hard and seems impossibly out of reach you probably don't put in much effort either. The lesson: set targets that stretch you, but don't break you.

Related to department and enterprise goals

Make sure your MoS contribute to overall organisational and departmental goals as well as to your own job purpose. Your goals should cascade down from your business', department's or unit's roadmap and goals. This also makes them meaningful. Success measures like these drive your performance and make rising to the challenge of meeting them motivating and satisfying.

Trackable

Trackable targets offer a measuring stick that allows you to judge for yourself how well you are doing. Try to select MoS that verify how you *are doing* (**lead indicators**), not how you *have done* (**lag indicators**).

Lag indicators are historical measures that tell you whether or not you succeeded. They are the scorecards of cost of production reports, financial reports, human resources monitoring systems, market-share reports, mystery shopper surveys, profit results and sales results. Lag indicators don't show you where you're going, only where you've been. By the time a below-target performance appears in a lag indicator, it has probably become a problem. All you can do is try to put the problem right and make sure something similar doesn't happen again. Retrospective corrective action is more difficult and less effective than the timely corrective action that lead indicators make possible. Lag indicators are the 'scoreboards', lead indicators the 'ball'.

Lead indicators measure what *is* happening. They are the best measures to track because they provide an early warning when plans are not going as expected. When results are below expectations, lead indicators help you take corrective action quickly before problems become more serious. Better still, they can point to the type of corrective action to take or the area in which to take it. Lead indicators also highlight when plans and activities are going particularly well so that you can work out how to retain or repeat those conditions. Keep your eye on the ball, not the scoreboard. Table 9.3 shows some terms for targets. Use positive terms so you can concentrate on what you want (not what you *don't* want).

TABLE 9.3 Terms for targets

Term	Examples
Absolute obligations	• All site personnel and visitors to wear hard hats and safety boots at all times • All staff and visitors to disinfect hands before entering the kitchen area • No smoking within 300 metres of the premises at any time
Averages	• Answer 90% of customer queries fully within three working days • Complete and enter into the system an average of 40 transactions per day per operator • Complete 500 documents each week/every day/each hour
Frequency of occurrence	• Check stock every three months • Contact 10% of key customers randomly every month to monitor satisfaction rates • Take product weight samples hourly
Percentages	• Achieve 95% of deliveries on time • Increase attendance rates by 3% over the next three months to 92% • Greet 90% of customers within 12 seconds
Time limits	• Investigate all minor accidents and near misses within two working days and serious accidents and incidents immediately • Answer all telephone calls within four rings • Take drinks orders within 10 minutes of patrons taking their seats

Decide what to do and when to do it

Transferable skills

2.2 Personal effectiveness

Your days are probably so busy that you find it impossible to do everything, and one of the worst ways to use your time is to do something well that you didn't need to do at all. Your goal is to concentrate your efforts on value-adding activities by referring to your overall job purpose and KRAs. Then you can develop a work schedule that concentrates on high-priority activities – those that contribute *directly* to your overall job goals, especially activities that:

- transform the product or service in some way
- your customer (whether internal or external) needs and appreciates.

Your personal productivity is as much a factor of what you *don't* do as what you do. How do you decide which of your important and support tasks to do straight away, which to defer, which to delegate and which to dump? The only way you can establish priorities, and know what to do and when, is by referring to your overall job purpose and KRAs. They help you to distinguish between what's important (and therefore should be attended to) and what's superfluous and unimportant (which can be delegated, worked on when time permits or ignored entirely).

Important or only urgent?

Importance is your first consideration when establishing priorities – *urgency* is your second. When a task must be done now, it's urgent. When it can wait, it isn't urgent. When a task contributes meaningfully to achieving results in a KRA, it's important; when it doesn't, it isn't important. As shown in Figure 9.2, these factors give you four ways to consider tasks and whether, and when, to do them.

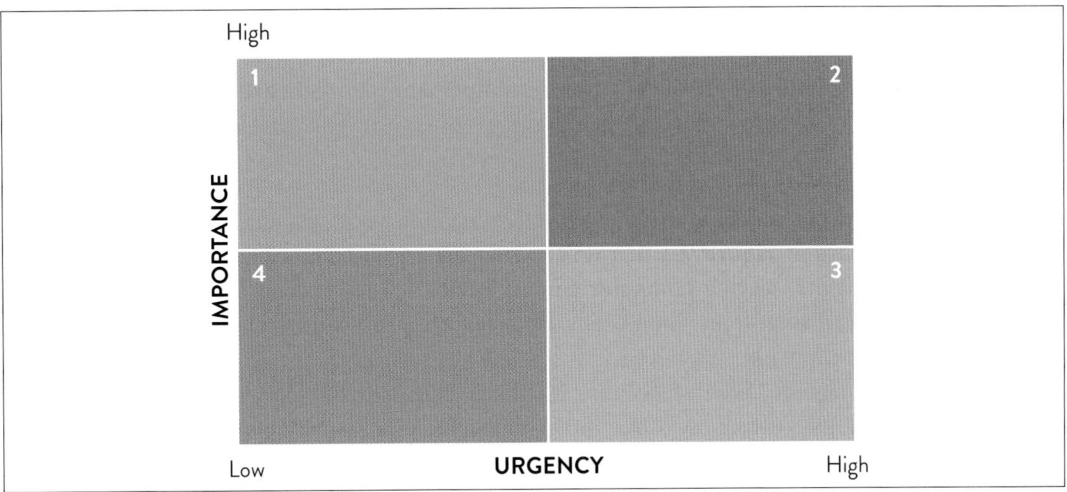

FIGURE 9.2 The establishing priorities model

Important but not urgent activities

Your view from the balcony shows you which tasks are important. Important but not urgent tasks are usually directed at longer-term contributions to goals in your KRAs; they are essential matters you must attend to. When you attend to them in a timely manner, you're dancing smartly and smoothly; when you don't, bad things happen.

Transferable skills

2.2 Personal effectiveness

Some of your important but not urgent tasks in the top left square in Figure 9.2 might include:

- building effective working relationships with your team, as well as with other leader-managers, customers and suppliers
- conducting **safety audits**
- finding ways to improve operations
- learning new skills
- planning routine maintenance
- solving problems
- training and coaching staff.

Important and urgent activities

Many activities that would appear in the top right square in Figure 9.2, such as customer queries or requests for important information needed quickly, begin their lives as both important and urgent activities and should be attended to straight away. Others become urgent through neglect: it's tempting to put important but not urgent tasks, like learning a new skill or conducting that safety audit, in the 'pending' file because there is no immediate consequence to not doing them. The truth is, most important but non-urgent activities that you do not attend to in a timely fashion eventually become urgent and you're forced to do them *immediately* – whether it's convenient to do so or not.

Convenience aside, whenever you tackle an important, urgent activity, you risk rushing and making mistakes. Whenever an important and urgent activity arises, take care to compose yourself first, so that there isn't an air of panic about you.

Unimportant but urgent activities

How often have you jumped to answer a ringing telephone only to find it was a wrong number, or a relatively unimportant matter that took you away from a more important task? Urgent and unimportant tasks in the bottom right square in Figure 9.2 might include dealing with routine 'administrivia', some interruptions, some meetings and some telephone calls. They often have a short-term nature and can be delegated or done later yourself (although why would you do them when they don't contribute to your KRAs?). Some unimportant yet urgent activities don't really need to be done at all.

Unimportant and non-urgent activities

Apart from the odd break, ask yourself why you're wasting your valuable time on activities in the bottom left square of Figure 9.2 that don't really need to be done. Excessively 'prettying up' unimportant documents, playing computer games, 'pouncing' on emails the second they arrive, some on-the-job socialising, some phone calls, unnecessary paperwork – these can be excuses for not getting on with 'real work'.

When you complete a task just because it's there, because you enjoy it, because it provides a convenient excuse for putting off other, more important or more difficult work, or because it's marginally worth doing, the result is the same – you're not attending to an important matter. When that happens a lot, you end up lurching from crisis to crisis while important tasks slide until they, too, become urgent crises. This makes for an uncoordinated, frenetic dance.

Evaluate your tasks: 'that can wait, this needs doing'

Get in the habit of using your balcony perspective to evaluate every task's degree of urgency and importance as it comes in so that you can deal with it appropriately, as shown in Figure 9.3. Tasks that seem urgent often aren't and can wait; other tasks might be 'nice but not necessary' – don't let them rule your life.

To find out whether a task really does have some time pressure or a deadline attached, or is necessary, ask yourself: 'What would happen (really) if I didn't do this right now?' When the answer is 'Something bad', ask yourself: 'Could or should someone else do it rather than me?' Answering those two questions helps you quickly assess how much value a task or an activity adds to your job. You can decide whether to delegate it or do it yourself now, later or not at all. That way, you can concentrate on work that directly contributes to your KRAs and goals, automatically channelling your efforts into high-priority matters. (Just make sure deferred tasks aren't holding anyone else up; delegate or attend to any that are.)

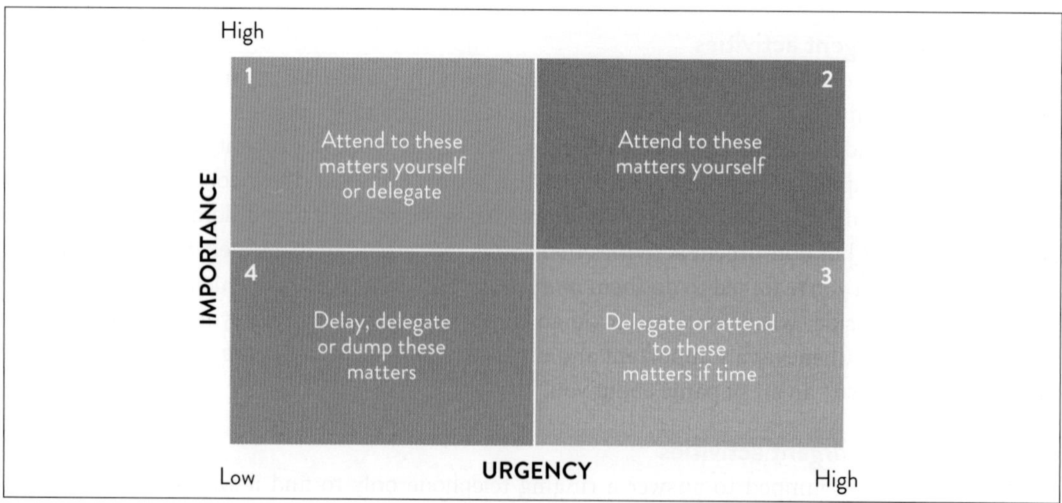

FIGURE 9.3 Putting the establishing priorities model to work

Types of tasks

No one can complete only important tasks and ignore all the unimportant tasks. Attending to the occasional unimportant, non-urgent task can offer a needed break. Sometimes, you need to deal with a question or problem that won't, strictly speaking, move you any closer to reaching your targets but may assist someone else to achieve their goals. There are also tasks you need to do, such as routine administration, to 'keep the system working'.

The trick to personal productivity is to find the balance between these three types of work:

1. *Manager-imposed work* is work that your manager asks you to do. Clearly, you can't ignore it. When your manager assigns you a lot of work, though, ask yourself why. Is it because you haven't shown that you can schedule your own work and determine priorities yourself? What kind of work is your manager assigning you? When it's unrelated to any of your KRAs, think about discussing this, especially when the work interferes with your ability to complete tasks that do contribute to your KRAs.
2. *System-imposed work* is required by the 'system' (e.g. routine administrative tasks such as filling out expense sheets and customer reports or taking a turn at tidying up the kitchen area). This work must be done, but when it takes up a large chunk of your time and stops you from completing your 'real work', think about how you could do these system-imposed tasks more efficiently.
3. *Imposed work* can be divided into two types: (a) discretionary and (b) other-imposed. *Discretionary work* is work you choose to do, whether it's work that achieves results in your KRAs or 'busy work' that doesn't. *Other-imposed work* includes tasks that your team members delegate 'upwards' to you, as well as other people's work; for example, work of other managers or your own manager, that lands on your desk.

When you find yourself doing a lot of other-imposed work, it could indicate that some of your team members or others you work with are unclear about your role and ask for your help with matters that relate to their KRAs rather than yours. Work like this can keep you from important work of your own and is usually better, and more properly, done by the people responsible for it. Spend some time on tasks to which you can uniquely add value. Otherwise, when people need help, show them how to do it. Don't do it for them. If your manager or the system continually imposes work on you that doesn't contribute to your job purpose and KRAs, discuss the situation with your manager with a view to achieving one of three things:

- adjusting your KRAs
- channelling the work to a more appropriate person
- fixing the system.

Use the balcony overview to improve your performance

Although your job purpose and KRAs are unlikely to change substantially, you may want to change a few success measures every six or 12 months or so to give your efforts a slightly different focus. This helps you steadily improve your performance. For example, you might be experiencing higher staff turnover than other comparable departments in your organisation and want to reduce it. You could set a success measure in your 'leadership' KRA of 'reaching a 90 per cent staff retention rate by the end of the third quarter'. When you achieve that and hold the improvement for another two quarters, you might decide to concentrate on developing a successor and replace the success measure relating to staff retention with 'develop a successor by the end of the calendar year'. When you've done that, you would select another success measure that would help you improve your results further. This is how to make continuous improvements to your job performance.

Chapters 13 and 19 explain how to use this balcony overview to build the productivity of your work team and team members.

REFLECT

Vilfredo Pareto, a late 19th-century Italian mathematical economist and sociologist, developed the 80:20 principle, or the 'law of the vital few', now often referred to as the **Pareto principle**. It states that a small proportion of effort, people or time (20 per cent) accounts for a large proportion of the results (80 per cent). For example, 20 per cent of salespeople in a sales team generate 80 per cent of the sales; 20 per cent of the customers yield 80 per cent of the profits; 20 per cent of the employees cause 80 per cent of the problems; fixing 20 per cent of software bugs avoids 80 per cent of the most common errors and crashes.

Are 20 per cent of your efforts giving you 80 per cent of your good results? Do 20 per cent of your interruptions account for 80 per cent of your wasted time? Are 80 per cent of your efforts not providing many benefits in terms of achieving meaningful results?

Monitor your performance

Transferable skills

2.2 Personal effectiveness

The balcony helps you keep an eye on your overall performance and how well you're in sync with the other dancers. That's important because, no matter how skilled you are, one of Murphy's best-known laws of management is going to kick in: in any field of endeavour, anything that can go wrong, will go wrong. Budgets change, resources are reallocated, work conditions vary. However, when you are working to and tracking clear and specific MoS for the KRAs of your job, monitoring is easy. You can identify variations in the quality of your work, spot tasks and processes going wrong and make the necessary adjustments.

Use the process shown in Figure 9.4 to monitor results. It involves three steps, although you use the third step only when your performance is below or well above expectations:

1 *Measure*: keep the information you need cheap and easy to collect. You can keep the information you gather about your actual performance to a minimum, but make sure that it's key information. What you are looking for are quick, clear, low-cost lead indicators that track how you are going.
2 *Compare*: how do your results compare with your success measures?
3 *Act*: decide what action you need to take. When your performance is short of expectations, take corrective action. When it has exceeded expectations, find out why and take steps to ensure your stellar performance continues.

As Figure 9.4 indicates, monitoring is a continual cycle. (See Chapter 20 for more information on how to monitor.)

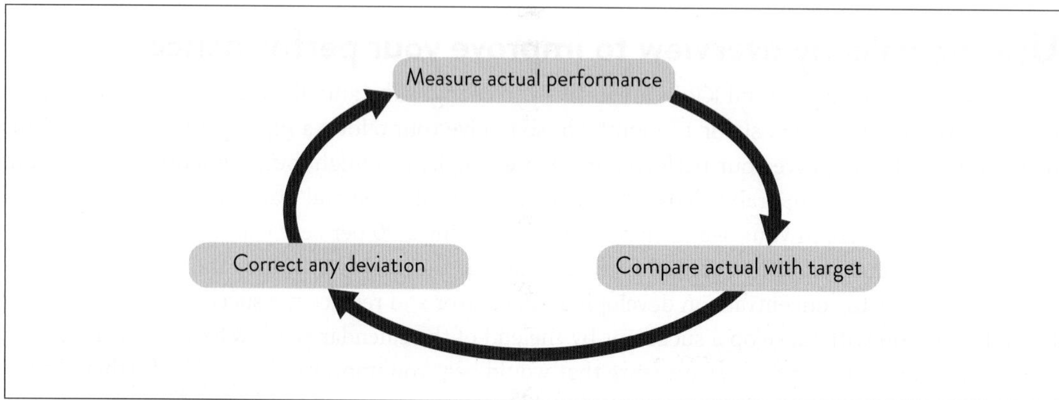

FIGURE 9.4 The monitoring cycle

Use a time log to check how well you manage your priorities

Transferable skills

2.2 Personal effectiveness

3.3 Written communication

Keeping a time log for two or three days gives you an objective balcony overview of how well you are managing your job. It helps you make sure you don't let urgent, unimportant matters get in the way of important tasks when you're on the dance floor. Time logs often show a lot of wasted time and frightening amounts of time spent on unnecessary and low-priority, unimportant activities that contribute little or nothing to people's KRAs. Equally sobering, a time log may well show that you aren't attending to some of the important tasks you should be doing.

You can ask yourself the following questions about the way you work when reviewing your time log:

- Which activities and tasks contribute to a KRA? In other words, which are *important* (squares 1 and 2 in Figure 9.2)? What percentage of my day do I spend on activities that directly contribute to achieving results in a KRA? (The more the better.)
- What *urgent* activities and tasks do I take on (squares 2 and 3 in Figure 9.2)? Why do I do them? Does something or someone else cause me to? Or do I set out to do them? (The answers tell you whether you or circumstances are in charge of your job.) What percentage of my day do I spend on urgent activities? (Unless your job is to manage crises, doing too many urgent tasks indicates a 'crisis management' style, which is stressful and undermines your performance.)
- Do I do a lot of *urgent, important* tasks (square 2 in Figure 9.2)? Have I left any important task to the last minute? Could I complete them more effectively by doing them before they become urgent? Does this indicate I work in crisis management mode? (Perhaps you need to learn to plan your work and stop procrastinating.)
- Do I do any tasks that are *urgent but not important* (square 3 in Figure 9.2)? Could I delegate any of them? How do they end up on my desk when they do not contribute to one of my KRAs? (Perhaps you need to learn to delegate and to say 'No' to easy work and to other people's work, and identify and work on high-priority matters.)
- Do I do any tasks that are *not important* and *not urgent* (square 4 in Figure 9.2)? If so, why do I bother with them? (Working on your own priorities rather than 'easy work' and other people's work is the way out of this trap.)
- Do I do many *non-urgent but important* tasks (square 1 in Figure 9.2)? (The more, the better, because this is a sign that you're in control of your job and concentrating on important, value-adding work.)
- What is the overall balance between *urgent* and *important* tasks? (While individual jobs vary, doing too many urgent tasks can be stressful and a sign of poor work scheduling, poor prioritising and poor productivity management.)

Which of the following personal productivity principles could you practise more of in order to work more effectively? The more of these you practise, the more easily you can maintain work–life balance, manage your stress and stay healthy.

- Set priorities based on important tasks – those that make maximum contribution to achieving results in your KRAs.
- Delay, delegate or dump anything that doesn't directly contribute to achieving goals in a KRA.
- Delegate work that you can safely leave to somebody else so you can concentrate on the most important aspects of your job that only you can do. (This **upskills** others as a bonus.)
- Don't let urgent, unimportant tasks override non-urgent but important matters.
- Set worthwhile (stretching yet realistic) SMART success measures and deadlines.

Work effectively and efficiently

Transferable skills

2.2 Personal effectiveness

The price you pay when you lack the balcony overview can spin your wheels – you work too hard, achieve little and pay the price in feelings of failure and stress. Clearly, working efficiently on the wrong or unnecessary tasks (unimportant tasks) is a waste of effort and time. Standing on the balcony – using your job purpose and KRAs – helps you set priorities and work on the *right tasks*. This means you work *effectively*.

Now it's time to dance. To dance smartly, you need to work *efficiently*: to do things right – in the easiest, fastest, least costly, safest, smoothest and most reliable and streamlined way possible. Working effectively and efficiently increases your personal productivity. You've just read about how to work effectively, so you probably have a good idea how smoothly (or feverishly) you're dancing. Section 9.2 explains how to work efficiently to dance smartly.

9.2 Dancing smartly: scheduling your work and organising yourself

> You can't overestimate the need to plan and prepare. In most of the mistakes I've made, there has been this common theme of inadequate planning beforehand. You really can't over-prepare in business.
>
> Chris Corrigan, former managing director of Patrick Corporation, http://www.australianinspiration.com.au/life/business-economics.html.

Dancing smartly needs planning and preparation as well as a bit of practice and commitment. Here are some quick questions to give you a feel for how smartly you dance:

- Are you often distracted from what you're working on by a crisis or an emergency?
- Do you often finish something just hours or even minutes before it's due?
- Do you lose important papers on your desk?
- Do you put things off until they become emergencies?
- Do people complain that you unload last-minute jobs on them?
- Do people write 'Since you haven't responded, I assume …'?
- Have you not looked at some of the papers or files on your desk for a week or more?

Answering 'Yes' to three or more of these questions suggests you need to find out how to dance smarter, not harder. Here are some ideas.

Keep a to-do list

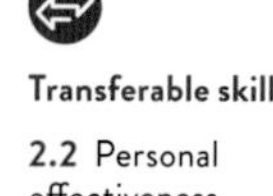

Transferable skills

2.2 Personal effectiveness

3.3 Written communication

You can easily spot leader-managers who fail to plan their work based on their priorities: they rush around, often trying to do several tasks at once, but actually achieve very little by the end of the day. They attend to whatever floats across their field of vision, whatever seems the most urgent at the time, or whatever 'makes the most noise'. Having fallen into the 'activity trap', they go home, and when asked what they did that day, they can't really say. They feel harassed and stressed and worry about all the tasks they have left undone. Their jobs control them, not the other way around. They may work hard, but they don't achieve results.

How you choose to spend your working days may not be obvious or even deliberate, but you do have choices. Tending to tasks as they crop up, or attending to tasks as the mood strikes you, is a choice – not a good choice but a choice nevertheless. You'll work hard but not achieve results. A better choice is to invest 15 minutes up front developing a daily or weekly to-do list. No matter how good your memory is, you're probably far too busy to remember everything you need to do, and the sense of order and peace of mind a to-do list provides more than compensates for the time it takes to write it. You also have a sense of accomplishment as you cross off or delete items on your list as you complete them.

A to-do list keeps what you need to do to achieve your goals 'front of mind', no matter how hectic your day becomes. This means you can work *proactively*, not *reactively*, which puts you in charge and lifts your self-esteem.

You can use your to-do list to:

- establish priorities
- group like tasks together, and do them together in blocks of time (which helps you work smoothly)
- note down promises and commitments you've made so you don't forget them
- plan your day or your week
- remind you to follow up on commitments others have made to you, tasks you've delegated or assigned to others and part-completed work
- remind you what you want to accomplish
- set aside time every day to think and reflect
- set aside time every week for personal and professional development.

Make your to-do list work for you

List the tasks you need to complete, grouping them into four or five categories that represent major task groups (e.g. follow-up, meetings, projects and ongoing, telephone, miscellaneous). Add new tasks as they arise and cross tasks off or delete tasks as you complete them. When you use a paper-based to-do list, turn the page and begin afresh when your list gets too messy. Transfer undone tasks to the new page and put the date at the top for future reference.

Grouping like tasks together gives you a clear overview of what you need to accomplish and helps you tackle tasks in blocks of time. For example, completing several phone calls in a block of time, writing emails and letters in another block of time and reading your incoming mail in a third block of time gives a flow to your work and means that you don't have to stop and mentally readjust as you do when you hop from one type of activity to another. Depending on your job, you probably need to review and update your to-do list at the end of each working day or week so that you can 'hit the road running' at the beginning of the next day or week.

Make sure that what you plan to achieve is realistic by keeping the anticipated timeframes, available resources and your overall targets in the back of your mind. Try to balance competing work demands and build in a cushion of time to allow for unforeseen events, such as impromptu meetings and technology problems.

When you are responsible for achieving results in a project environment – in other words, when it will be a lengthy period and many steps before your end results are accomplished – you may want to use scheduling software or a **Gantt chart** or **critical path analysis** (see Chapter 20 for more on this), which also provide a quick and easy way to visually monitor your progress.

When you find yourself transferring an item on your to-do list three or more times, or when it's been on your digital list for two or more weeks, it's a clear warning signal. Ask yourself why you haven't completed it. Are you procrastinating? Then there's no time like the present, as the saying goes – do it now and get it over with. Or perhaps it's a low-priority task that you can delegate or drop from your list. Perhaps it's a big job and dividing it into smaller parts can get you started.

Use the A-B-C method to work to priorities

Which items on your to-do list do you work on first? The easiest ones or those you can 'knock off' most quickly? Maybe that's a good choice when they're important; when they're unimportant, it's a poor choice. Working on the easiest and/or quickest items on your to-do list all day may provide the satisfaction of deleting several items, but when the tasks that are left behind are the ones that move you most towards achieving a meaningful goal in a KRA, you haven't really achieved much.

The A-B-C method prevents this by setting priorities so that you can work on tasks based on their importance. Here's how it works. Pop up to the balcony when you're fresh and thinking clearly. Consider each item's urgency and importance. Think about what you want to achieve by the end of the day and by the end of the week and, with this in mind, identify the most important tasks, those that most directly contribute to achieving results in your KRAs. Assign them an 'A' priority. Any items that are both urgent and important are 'A' priorities too. Which tasks contribute least to your KRAs and can wait until you have enough time to do them? Assign these unimportant, non-urgent tasks a 'C' priority. The rest are 'B' priorities.

Try to get through as much of your to-do list each day as you can, concentrating on your 'A' priorities. That way, when you don't complete every item, it's the less important items that are left. Don't ignore the 'Bs' and 'Cs', though, because many of them become urgent 'As' when you don't get on with them. When work comes in, even work that is seemingly 'urgent', ask yourself these questions:

- Does it contribute to achieving results in any of my KRAs? When the answer is yes, it's important, so schedule it in.
- Could someone else do it? When the answer is yes, delegate it.
- Must it be done now or can it be done later? When later is fine, delay it until it's convenient to attend to it.
- What would happen if it weren't done at all? You may not need to do it.

This gets you off the treadmill of attending to whatever crops up by letting you consciously choose to do the most important tasks.

INDUSTRY INSIGHTS

The price of nice

Trang manages the internal auditing section for a large firm. He is highly skilled at his work but he always seems to be rushing around trying to do several things at once. The result is that he completes few things on time or even well.

His boss, Denise, recently pointed this out to Trang and suggested that part of the problem was his exceptional computer skills and sound business acumen. People from all over the firm constantly ask him for advice and opinions. Denise explained that she understood that Trang was happy to help and that the business benefited overall, but she needed him to be aware that in spending so much time helping out other people, his own work was suffering. Denise suggested that this, combined with poor priority setting, was the source of Trang's apparently excessive workload and mediocre results.

Trang realised he'd better get on top of his job. He began using the A-B-C priority system to help him concentrate his efforts on his own priorities and to carefully think about requests for help in terms of his KRAs. He didn't want to let people down so, instead of doing things like complicated computer analyses for them, he began to show them how to do the analyses, providing written instructions, which he printed off from the program's help function, when necessary. He also began asking people questions aimed at helping them work out the answers themselves.

At first, people were taken aback, but then they appreciated the skills Trang was teaching them. For Trang's part, between the hours he saved by not doing other people's work for them and channelling his efforts and energies to his own work priorities, he was soon back on top of his job.

Clear your desk

Transferable skills

2.2 Personal effectiveness

Do you ever spend time looking for items that you know are 'right here, somewhere'? That's a sign you need to clear your desk and tidy your drawers. The less organised you are, the more you flail around trying to keep on top of your job. Too much clutter wastes your time, is emotionally draining and prevents you from concentrating. Your desk is not storage space. There should be only three or four things on your desk: your computer, the job you're currently working on, your telephone and, when it's paper not electronic, your to-do list. This means that no other items can compete for your attention and break your concentration.

To clear your work area, give everything its own 'home' and make a habit of putting items away so you know where to find them when you need them. Establish sensible electronic and paper filing systems and use them. Carefully name the files of information you decide to keep so that you can retrieve them easily later.

Clear your computer desktop, too. Get rid of old files and other distractions that slow your workflow. Select a wallpaper you like but keep the colours soft enough to avoid straining your eyes and the design simple enough that your icons show up. Delete or hide all but the icons you use daily or at least weekly and remove files from your desktop and put them in well-labelled folders.

Invest 10 minutes at the end of the week tidying and organising your desk. Evaluate any unfiled paperwork and electronic correspondence: can you discard or delete it? Delegate it? File it? This way, when you arrive on Monday morning, only what's most important is on your desk waiting for you.

It's as the philosopher Ralph Waldo Emerson said:

> Finish every day and be done with it ... You have done what you could; some blunders and absurdities no doubt crept in; forget them as soon as you can. Tomorrow is a new day; you shall begin it ... serenely, and with too high a spirit to be cumbered with your old nonsense.[1]

Have a system

Goals are good but you also need a system – a routine or habit. For example, your goal might be to build excellent workplace relationships and mutually beneficial networks; your system might be to join someone you don't know for lunch once a week and to invite two people you want to know better for coffee every week.

Build a habit for your most important goals, commit to following it and build in feedback to monitor your progress and alert you to adjust what you're doing for even greater success. For example, one great habit to build is, when a task is going to take two minutes or less to complete, do it straight away and get it out of the way.

Restrict interruptions

When you're interrupted every five minutes or so, it may seem like you get your real work done in the intermissions between interruptions. If only it were that simple. Once you've dealt with an interruption, it can take another 25 minutes to re-establish where you were and regain your concentration, unless your brilliant train of thought has been permanently derailed. Much of the time, you never return to the original activity. On top of that, all those interruptions leave you feeling tired and lethargic, reduce your creativity and keep you out of your 'flow zone', as we often say. Uninterrupted time is worth hours of interrupted time.

Research shows that 40 per cent of most people's interruptions are self-generated; in other words, you're nearly as likely to interrupt yourself as someone else is. The simple answer is – don't. When you're working on something and a stray thought reminds you that you need to phone someone or check up on some information, don't stop and do it immediately. Write it down on your to-do list and get back to what you were doing.

Limit human interruptions

You've probably tried the open-door policy and never had a moment's peace. You've probably tried 'quiet time', 'time out' or even 'power periods' to avoid interruptions and get on with some work that needs full concentration. That's fine, until someone needs you and they dare not disturb you because you're in 'quiet time', and their work suffers as a result.

Here's another way to limit human interruptions. Draw up a scale of interruptions with your team and ask them to use this with each other and with you. The scale might be like this:

- Interrupt for important matters that require the person's specific input.
- When you need a quick 'Yes' or 'No' answer and maybe a few words of discussion, save up about five, and see the person then.
- When someone else would do just as well, for example to talk something through or to provide some information that someone else or the files could provide, please go to that person or the files.

You can still use 'quiet times' – just keep them to an hour or less and, when appropriate, spread them across the entire department or work area. That way, everyone gets some time to concentrate when they know they won't be interrupted.

So that your team members don't feel deprived of your presence, schedule regular one-on-one 'catch-up' meetings with them. Ask them to create a running list of discussion points, a summary of what they've achieved since the last meeting, and any problems they're dealing with and how they're dealing with them. Keep a paper or electronic file or list for each of your team members to remind you of what you want to follow up with them in the 'catch-up' meeting.

As with any new ways of working, sticking to them takes steadfast determination. Especially early on, don't permit 'backsliding' to the old ways. Here are some other ways to discourage human interruptions:

- Sit at right angles, rather than facing the door or walkway. This makes it more difficult for people to catch your eye and 'drop in' for a chat. Because your back isn't to them, your computer screen isn't either, and no one can creep up on you unawares when you're deep in thought.
- Have a mental or written list of 'important' phone calls you need to make – 'Sorry, it's important that I phone this person now.'
- Steer the interrupter in another direction: 'The best person to help you with this is …' or 'Could you send me that in an email, please, so I can think it through when I have more time?'
- Try keeping your pen in hand, poised for action, or standing up, or looking at your watch, to discourage an interrupter from settling in.

When you need to deal with an interruption, note down what you need to do next on the task you are working on so you don't have to spend too much time reorienting yourself when you eventually return to it. Type it in a different colour on your word processor or write it in pencil or on a Post-it note placed in the document in the exact spot you left off. Then take a deep breath and give the interrupter your full attention.

Limit technological interruptions

Think about the mental clutter and the time you (and perhaps your team members) lose as you deal with information of limited or no real value. Tsunamis of emails, instant messages, push notifications, blogs, tweets, discussion forums on your areas of interest and the corporate intranet all demand your time and attention. Yet most people would agree that half of the information they receive is irrelevant and they never use most of what they keep.

Transferable skills
5.2 Technology use

Be bold. Technology is there to help you, not run your life. If you haven't already done so, switch off all your electronic alerts and push notifications for incoming mail, texts, tweets and so on. Automatically direct some incoming emails to folders and check them only when it's convenient to do so, such as when you want a break, have a few spare minutes or hit a pocket of down time or a period of low energy. Scan the rest for priority and subject titles, read only the most important and delete the unimportant and unwanted ones unopened.

Your mental traffic system

One of the brain's many automatic programs is called the '*control network*'. It helps you pay attention, block out distractions and impulses, and focus your efforts on your goals when you need to – even when you'd rather do something else. Amazingly, it does this by moving blood away from regions motivating your immediate desires to regions that help you achieve your longer-term objectives, in the same way you continually reallocate resources to meet the changing needs of the enterprise.

Directing your mental energy places quite a burden on your control network. You can lighten the load by removing distractions when you need to concentrate; for example, silencing the pings that alert you to incoming emails and texts, using earphones to dampen extraneous noise, avoiding multitasking, and keeping the goals you're working towards to a manageable few. Teach team members to do this too. Overworking ultimately reduces your productivity and the productivity of your employees.

Tame the telephone

Use voicemail in blocks of time to give you some uninterrupted working or thinking time. Leave a message saying when you are available to take calls and invite callers to leave their details. Resist the temptation to listen in each time the voicemail picks up. Return the calls so you don't get a reputation for being rude, unreliable or disorganised.

When someone calls you at a bad time, say so and arrange a time that is convenient for you both to talk, agreeing who phones whom. This is especially useful to discourage known 'talkers'. Explain that you're in the middle of something and offer to phone them back, and do so 15 minutes or so before the end of their day or when you know they'll soon need to leave for a meeting.

To prevent lengthy calls, stand up – your voice takes on a more 'urgent' tone, encouraging callers to be more 'to the point'. Standing also boosts your circulation and reduces fatigue. To politely end calls, say something like: 'I've just noticed it's 2.15 and I have to leave for a meeting in 10 minutes' or 'Just one more thing before we're finished ...' When the person you need to phone is a known 'talkaholic', begin by saying something like 'Hi, I've got three quick questions for you', or 'Hi, I'm in a bit of a rush but I want to give you the information you're looking for'.

Don't multitask while you're on the telephone. An alert caller can usually detect this, and your split attention is bound to make you miss something important. When a clicking keyboard or random 'uh-huhs' indicates someone is multitasking while they're talking to you, mention that it sounds like they're quite busy and ask whether they would prefer to speak later.

Make several outgoing calls together and respect people's time by asking whether they're free to talk. When someone isn't there, leave a message asking them to call back and saying when they can catch you at your desk. When you need some information, suggest what they do if you're not in when they call back: 'If I'm not in, please leave the figures with Zareena.' (And let Zareena know.)

Avoid telephone tag by scheduling a time to talk next. When the person you need to speak with isn't in, ask when the best time to reach them would be or see whether someone else can help you.

Rather than relying on your memory, use a software program or the reverse side of your paper to-do list to make notes about what you want to speak to people about and the telephone messages you have left for others. Cross people's names off when they return your call and follow up anyone who doesn't get back to you.

Transferable skills
2.2 Personal effectiveness

Don't procrastinate

For some people, procrastination is a way of life; for others it strikes only at certain times, such as when it comes time to attack a task they don't particularly enjoy. For others, it appears in a particular area of their life, such as studying or solving tricky longstanding problems. That's when 'better' tasks that need to be done can muscle in.

Putting it off won't make it go away or make it any easier. If procrastination is one of your problems, the following section discusses some ideas to help you stop putting tasks off and finish them off.

Break down 'big tasks'

When you think, 'I won't be able to finish this, so I'll do it later', you guarantee that it won't be done. Don't be discouraged by big tasks and projects that require a lot of time and effort – nothing is particularly hard when you divide it into smaller jobs. The salami, or layering, approach is to break big tasks down into smaller, manageable chunks, and do them 'one bite at a time' between interruptions. After a series of smaller 'attacks', all you usually need is one final 'assault' to pull everything together. Voila! Another big task completed.

Feel the fear and do it anyway

When fear of failure is stopping you from getting started, think of it as a 'chance to learn' instead. Embrace the opportunity – the only failure is not having a go. Or maybe it's fear of success that's making you dally and delay. If so, give yourself permission to succeed.

When it's a big task, is it fear of finishing? Some people drag their feet when they're coming to the end of a major task or project. They know they'll miss working on it and will have to get started on something else.

Find a reason

Examine your excuses and get realistic. 'I don't feel like it' isn't good enough. Motivate yourself with a good reason to do it. What's in it for you when you finish it? When you can't find a positive reason, try looking for a negative one: what will happen if you don't do it? When there's no good negative reason either, maybe it shouldn't be on your to-do list at all. Maybe you can pass it on to someone else or give it back to its proper owner.

Make a start

In physics, 'static friction' means that it's harder to move a stationary object than one that's already moving. The same applies to procrastination – once you make a start, the inertia of no movement disappears. Taking the first step makes taking the following steps easier. Since it's easier to revise than create, just begin; call it a 'pilot' or test run, if that makes you feel better.

When even taking the first step is too daunting, devote just five or 10 minutes to the task. Then decide whether to spend another five or 10 minutes. A journey starts with a small step, and once you've begun, you often find you're on a roll.

Adopt 'Do it now!' as your motto, at least regarding important tasks. And when you're feeling harassed and harried and everything seems to be getting on top of you, ask yourself the 'magic question', 'What's the most effective use of my time right now?' When several things are demanding your attention at the same time, this simple question can be a great help in establishing priorities and keeping you out of the activity trap. It helps you decide what to do, not leave it to chance to whatever is at the top of your in-tray or to the person calling you or standing at your door.

Make the most of your prime time

Everyone has their own energy cycle – periods when they are full of bounce and energy, periods when they are a bit flat, and periods in between. Use your peak energy periods for activities requiring careful thought and effort and try to avoid interruptions during this time.

When are you at your best? In the morning? Schedule work that takes the most thought, effort or energy then and avoid routine work, such as checking emails, until you've accomplished one or two important tasks. Perhaps you 'come good' later in the day. That's when to schedule in some uninterrupted 'quiet time' to tackle a few important jobs. When you need to attend an important meeting first thing in the morning, have clothes, paperwork and so on ready the night before.

Minimise multitasking

Splitting your attention between several tasks, particularly tasks that require concentration or tasks that are similar to each other, creates a mental traffic jam in the prefrontal cortex of your brain, reducing your productivity by up to 40 per cent.[2] The more work you have on the go at the same time, the more your brain struggles to keep tabs on all of it and the more you limit your available brainpower for each task. Too much multitasking also increases stress and can even reduce your memory and ability to concentrate for lengthy periods. Because so much is buzzing in your head, multitasking can also disrupt your sleep.

The truth is, you can concentrate on only one task at a time, and when you try to concentrate on more than one, you work more slowly and make more mistakes. That's inefficient, makes easy work hard and adds to your stress. Rather than mess up several tasks at once with multitasking, work on one activity at a time and pay attention to what you're doing so you don't have to go back and fix mistakes. Try to complete it before moving on to the next task. Never multitask when you need to absorb and retain information, because when you multitask the brain only pops the information into your short-term memory.

When you must multitask, work on tasks that are so simple you could practically do them in your sleep. That allows your subconscious brain to take over and do them for you, provided the tasks are dissimilar to each other. When they're too similar – for example, reading and listening to sing-along music are both word-oriented – forget multitasking.

STUDY TOOLS

QUICK REVIEW

KEY CONCEPT 9.1 

a Explain how standing on the 'balcony' helps you 'dance smoothly' in your job and how you can use the information the view from the balcony gives you.

b Explain how using the establishing priorities model shown in **Figures 9.2** and **9.3** helps you prioritise your work so that you complete the most important tasks and activities.

KEY CONCEPT 9.2 

a List the three main techniques you use to complete your work as a student or an employee efficiently.

BUILD YOUR SKILLS

KEY CONCEPT 9.2 

a Select three personal productivity techniques to work more efficiently that you haven't tried yet. Incorporate them into your routine for three weeks and at the end of that period, assess their effectiveness. Prepare a 50-word report for the class.

WORKPLACE ACTIVITIES

KEY CONCEPT 9.1 

a Discuss three strategies you currently use to establish and work to your priorities.

b Write your job purpose statement and list key result areas and measures of success. If you haven't discussed them with your boss, now is the time to do so.

c Think about how well you are currently using your time to achieve your work priorities and develop a plan for making better use of your time in order to improve your achievements in the key result areas of your job.

d Briefly explain the 80:20 rule, or Pareto principle, and use it to analyse how you have spent your time at work over the past week. Then develop a schedule to improve your use of work time.

KEY CONCEPT 9.2 

a Discuss five strategies you use to organise yourself at work in order to work efficiently.

EXTENSION ACTIVITIES

Referring to the Snapshot at the beginning of this chapter, answer the following questions:

1 What advice would you give to Jane to help her 'make things happen and get results'? What steps do you think she should take to achieve this?

2 Would you give Jane any other advice to feel better about her career and role as team leader?

CASE STUDY 9

HEEEELLLLP!

Eyes wide and hands to head, Maura mutters, 'Where did I put them? They're here, I know they are!'

The phone rings. 'Maura speaking ... Oh, yes, of course. I'm sorry, I'll get it to you this afternoon ... yes, sorry.'

'Hey Maura, have you got a minute? I've just about finished that outline and you wanted me to run it by you before carrying on.'

Maura's heart sinks, as she thinks, 'My first leader-manager role and it's out of control.'

Three months earlier, Maura was appointed to head up the workplace health and safety unit. Given her previous experience as a health and safety officer and a health and safety trainer, she was more than qualified and saw this appointment as her chance to join the ranks of management. 'I can manage myself all right, but I guess I can't manage a unit', she sighs. 'I miss deadlines, forget to do things, lose important papers ... I can't even think straight anymore.'

Her boss stops by. 'Ready Maura? Have you remembered we have a risk management committee meeting for health and safety?'

'Yes, Ron. I was just looking for my briefing papers and they seem to have disappeared. Just bear with me for a minute if you would.'

Questions

1 Maura needs help. What are her main problem areas?
2 What is Maura's most important problem (the one that will significantly improve her personal productivity if she solves it)?
3 What would be your objectives in assisting Maura and how could you measure your success?
4 What are some approaches you would suggest Maura try, and why?

CHAPTER ENDNOTES

1 Quoted in J. Elliot Cabot, *Memoir of Ralph Waldo Emerson*, Houghton, 1888, p. 485.

2 American Psychological Association, 'Multitasking: Switching costs', *Research in Action*, 20 March 2006, http://www.apa.org/research/action/multitask.aspx, accessed 25 October 2014.

PART

3

LEADING AND MANAGING OTHERS

'What's the biggest challenge in your job?' a senior manager asked a newly appointed leader-manager. 'Well, this job would be a hell of a lot easier if you took the people out of it!' Ah, the people. Every organisation can buy the same computer systems, the same furniture, the same everything. It's the way the people inside those organisations use those resources that makes the difference between success and failure.

High-calibre leader-managers harness people's energies, coach, guide and support them in their efforts and see that they have what they need to do their jobs to the best of their ability. They express goals clearly and in a way that encourages people to work willingly and cooperatively towards achieving them. More than this, they supply the vision – the overall sense of purpose – that inspires people and gives their work special significance.

Leaders with these skills don't grow on trees, which is why they are so valuable. In the long run, successful leadership is worth more to your organisation than modern technology, new buildings and a favourable quarterly result.

Part 3 explains the skills of leading and managing your team and its individual members. It helps you understand and build a work group that is innovative and energised, and creates competitive advantage for your organisation. Leading and managing is a big test and perhaps the most critical and most elusive skillset of all. You can expect challenges, surprises and self-development opportunities. So, here begins the never-ending journey of leading others.

CHAPTER

UNDERSTANDING LEADERSHIP

KEY CONCEPTS

After completing this chapter, you will be able to:

10.1 explain how Australian leadership is likely to develop as the 21st century progresses and which of your skills you can strengthen

10.2 apply the main approaches to leadership and extract useful information and tips from those approaches

10.3 recognise when you should lead and when you should manage.

TRANSFERABLE SKILLS

The following transferable skill is covered in this chapter:

3 Social competence

3.1 Teamwork/relationships

OVERVIEW

What is leadership? More importantly, what makes a good, or even great, leader? These are not questions with one-sentence answers. To lead well, you not only need a range of skills and personal characteristics but also the judgement and discretion to know when to use each. You need to have a vision, clearly articulate it to those you lead, and then inspire and support them to achieve it. Leaders also need to be good role models, exhibiting the types of positive behaviours they expect of their team members, such as caring for their customers, seeking continuous improvement and innovation, managing risk, working sustainably, being committed to learning and development and promoting safe work practices (discussed in Chapters 18, 19, 22, 23, 29, 30 and 31).

This chapter examines different approaches to leadership and how to apply them in a world of work where workplace environments are constantly changing. As you learn about the concepts and practices that make effective leaders, you will see that rather than being a stand-alone skill, leadership involves an array of knowing–doing–being skills. The interrelated and interconnected nature of leadership with management means there is considerable crossover between them. The references to other chapters throughout this chapter illustrate the intertwined relationship between the two.

SNAPSHOT

Leading a dysfunctional team

Malik knew this would be difficult. He had been brought in to take over management of the underperforming compliance team, bring them into the 21st century and transform them into a high-performance team. Nothing was off limits, but particular attention would need to be directed towards their inefficient processes, outdated technology and cumbersome workflows. But Malik's biggest challenge was going to be how to turn around the team's culture. Although not yet quite toxic, it was teetering on the brink with the team clearly divided into distinct cliques, leading to disagreements, communication breakdowns and almost non-existent cooperation.

The team was comprised of a diverse mix of people from different age groups, cultural backgrounds, levels of experience and genders. First, there were the 'old timers' who had been there for many years. They were set in their ways and believed they had the run of the place. 'We've been doing this for years; we know what we are doing' was their catchcry. In reality, most of them had very outdated skills and knew they were no longer really up to the job. Then there were the 'newbies' who had only joined the team in the past year and were made up of Gen Ys and Gen Zs and a couple of Millennials. They were full of new ideas and ways of improving how the work could be done but their initiatives were always quickly quashed by the 'old timers'. The rest of the team was an eclectic mix of people of varying ages and from different non-English speaking and gender diverse backgrounds, including Coen, hailing from a remote island in the Torres Straits; Jamala, a recent refugee from Sri Lanka; Mohammed, a highly skilled IT technician whose qualification was not recognised in Australia; and Justice, an astute legal compliance officer whose name was changed four years ago from Justine and who identified as gender neutral.

Malik thought to himself, 'This is going to be a real challenge, where do I start? There is some great talent in this group, but they are just not functioning as a team and seem to lack a clear view of what they are aiming for or need to achieve. Even if they did share a common goal, would this group know how to go about achieving it?'

After pondering some more, Malik emailed the team, calling them together for a whole-team meeting. First item on the meeting agenda was 'team protocols' with 'ground rules for communication and cooperation' in brackets beside it. Next item was 'decision-making processes'. 'That's a good start', Malik thought, 'now what else is needed to transform this team …'

10.1 The 21st-century Aussie leader-manager

Leadership is an elusive concept, hard to describe and impossible to prescribe. It is more evident in its absence, so that when leadership is needed, its lack is sorely felt.

Dodson, P. (1998). 'On leadership. Williamson Community Leadership Program Lecture', http://www.leadershipvictoria.org/speechesspeechdodson.html.

The ideal for the 21st-century leader is someone who guides rather than tells; who listens as much as they speak; who inspires, motivates and supports those that follow them; and who creates a sense of purpose through the articulation of clear goals and a meaningful vision. But the traits of an ideal leader also extend to their personal attributes. Their followers expect them to act ethically in their dealings as a representative of their organisation and with staff and customers. They must lead with integrity, act fairly, be sustainably responsible and manage the stress and the pressures of their position effectively. They need to be able to show empathy, use inclusive language and practices

Transferable skills

3.1 Teamwork/relationships

and understand how to motivate and manage a range of different workers, including Generation X, Generation Z, Millennials, the remaining Baby Boomers, those identifying as part of the LGBTIQ+ community, workers from non-English-speaking and diverse cultural backgrounds, First Australian and so on. Add in the skills required to lead the different types of teams – merged, mixed, project and virtual – as well as the increasing number of remote workers, often working from home, and the concept of the ideal modern leader seems to be one of fantasy rather than fact. But it does not end there. The 21st-century leader is also expected to maximise an organisation's most valuable resource, its people, by finding innovative ways to improve employee productivity, utilising workers' skills by empowering them to make the decisions they have the skills and training to make, and identifying, developing and drawing on their talents. This all seems like a tall order but for those leaders who can deliver on most or all of these fronts, loyalty, dedication and commitment from their followers, as well as the success of their team and organisation, is their likely reward.

Let's begin. As you go through your leadership journey, take time to reflect: what are you doing that's working? What do you need to correct?

INDUSTRY INSIGHTS

Jason Pellegrino, Managing Director, Google (2008–2018)

'Figuring out what you need to stop doing as you move from a manager to a leader is important. Often managers hope that what has made them successful in the past will make them successful in the future, and that's probably not the case. So, what do people look for in leaders that they don't look for in managers? They look for someone who paints a strong vision, they empower people to go after that vision and actively hold them accountable to the delivery against that vision.'[1]

AAP Image/Domain Holdings Australia Limited

How employees view leaders and leadership in Australia

Transferable skills

3.1 Teamwork/relationships

While it is dangerous to draw any firm conclusions on the basis of a few studies, the picture painted of Australian leaders by their employees does not appear promising. Recruitment agency Firebrand Talent conducted its Talent Ignition Report in 2018, which surveyed 1200 employees and found that the number one reason why employees left their employer was due to poor management and leadership.[2] The report asserted that leadership roles were still being assigned on the basis of industry experience or technical expertise rather than on a leader's 'human' or 'person' skills, the skills underpinning leaders' ability to produce high-performing teams. Studies such as this highlight the growing importance and need for leaders and their organisations to pay greater attention to developing and using their emotional intelligence skills so that they listen, empathise and provide the emotional, administrative and technical support that their teams need to perform at the highest level.

A leadership survey conducted by the Australian Institute of Management (AIM) in 2019 found that over 72 per cent of Australian workers left their jobs due to poor leadership, with communication skills and emotional intelligence seen as the critical skill gaps that Australian leaders are facing. Over 35 per cent of respondents in the survey highlighted communication as a skill their leaders needed to strengthen, while 48 per cent identified their leaders' ability to display emotional intelligence as being somewhat or not at all competent. The survey also found that 42.1 per cent of respondents identified authentic personal behaviour by their leaders as the most important personal behaviour that a leader needs to exhibit.[3] (The importance of authentic leadership will be explored later in this chapter.)

Transferable skills

3.1 Teamwork/relationships

Unfortunately, the skill level of Australian leaders being below their employees' expectations in areas such as communication, inclusiveness and other areas related to emotional intelligence is a common theme across different studies. This may indicate that leaders and leadership in Australia are still struggling to come to terms with how these skills are connected to, and determine, employee and team performance. Throughout this chapter, as well as many others in this text, the case for leaders and their organisations to sit up and take notice of these skills will become increasingly compelling. Those that fail to do so may find themselves with leaders who are not equipped to lead a modern workforce effectively and therefore will not deliver the results necessary to ensure their organisation's survival.

Team leaders

Leader-managers are increasingly leading and managing genuine teams rather than groups of individual performers. Team leaders need an additional skillset and a different style of leadership to leader-managers of individual performers. They need to be able and willing to:

- know when to be 'hands on' and when to be 'hands off'
- liaise with the supply chain
- share authority
- share information
- consult with team members
- troubleshoot problems and challenges
- trust their team.

Leader-managers of genuine teams, such as **project teams**, are more like team facilitators, empowering their teams and providing them with the support they require to achieve results. This approach is more synonymous with that of servant and Theory Y leaders, which are discussed in the next section.

The additional skills needed to lead virtual teams and mixed teams are outlined in Chapter 14 while a summary of the skills you need to lead the changing 21st-century workforce can be found in Chapter 1.

Four leadership skillsets to build

Today's leader-managers need to become adept in four interconnected areas: sensemaking, visioning, innovating and relating.[4] These four skillsets link well with the desirable qualities of Australian leaders and bosses and with team leaders.

Being skilled in all four of these areas might be a stretch; however, these skills can be developed. So, as you work on improving your skills in the areas where you are lacking, focus on utilising the skills you have while allowing others to utilise their skills to fill the gaps.

Sensemaking

Leaders need to make sense of the dynamic world of work, both inside and outside their workplace. The workplace landscape can be chaotic and unpredictable, making it important for leader-managers to understand how changes in society, new technologies and the changing labour force can offer both risks and opportunities. To make informed decisions, information needs to be gathered from a variety of sources, including competitors, customers, employees, funding bodies or investors, other functions and business processes and suppliers.

But don't keep this information to yourself. Discuss it with others, including people who have a different viewpoint from your own. You need to try to stay away from stereotypes and 'either/or' thinking and be open to new possibilities. When you think you understand what something means, you need to test your conclusions with trial runs or, at the very least, by sharing your conclusions with others and seeking their feedback. Focus on what's important to your operations and explain it to others so they can plan how best to deal with the important issues. In healthy organisations, sensemaking is continuous. (These matters are discussed in Chapters 6, 18, 26, 29 and 32.)

Visioning

Despite your workload and the daily pressures you face, you need to free up your mind to look into the future and create a vision of where you want your organisation or team to go, how you plan to get them there, and how you will deal with the problems and challenges that confront you along the way. Staying tuned into the ways the digital, globalised future is changing your industry, your organisation and your own work can open your mind to new information, ideas and opportunities.

Creating a compelling and reassuring picture of the future for employees to work towards is one of the most important responsibilities leader-managers have. While sensemaking helps you figure out what is going on, visioning helps you decide how to use this understanding to create and describe a desirable future. Explain your vision in a way that inspires others – what it can achieve and the benefits it will deliver. Use stories, metaphors, examples, images, anecdotes, affirmations and whatever else you can think of to impart your vision in a way that will inspire and motivate your team to join you on the journey. As you do so, ensure your actions reflect your words and embody the core values and ideas contained in your vision. (These skills are discussed in Chapters 8, 13, 14, 19 and 24.)

Innovating

Until we start making progress towards achieving a vision, it is nothing more than a dream. Innovating is about developing and implementing creative strategies to achieve a vision. Success is the reward for those leader-managers with the courage to find new ways to work together, organise, improve and refine.

Successful innovation requires you to encourage and support others to look for better, easier, faster, safer, better-value, more reliable and more sustainable ways to work towards the achievement of your organisation's and team's goals. This may require experimentation with different ways of organising work and linking people, but the potential rewards make it a more than worthwhile endeavour. (These skills are discussed in Chapters 2, 3, 19, 24, 26 and 32.)

Relating

Transferable skills

3.1 Teamwork/relationships

Successful leader-managers not only have to be able to establish and maintain effective working relationships, they need a broader and deeper understanding of their team members' motivations, values, contexts, communication styles and sensitivities. Diversity and inclusion are not just 'flavour of the month' business buzz words. Recognising diversity and inclusion is now expected and demanded and leader-managers need to embrace the concepts of tolerance, acceptance, inclusion, understanding and reconciliation, and embed them in daily operations and work practices.

No longer can leader-managers make decisions from their 'ivory tower', isolated from their team and **stakeholders**. They need to spend time with a variety of people, within and across the organisation, and with stakeholders outside it, encouraging them to speak up, listening with an open mind, and trying to understand their various perspectives, what they care about, what their concerns are and what they need to realise their potential.

Emotional intelligence is now an important skill or attribute for leader-managers to have. It allows them to analyse or predict how others will respond to information or news, and helps them to tailor the way they deliver information so it stands the greatest chance of being positively received. By using your emotional intelligence before you offer your own opinions and ideas, you can consider how others might react to them. This can help you to determine the best way to explain them.

There will be difficult issues and challenges along the way for which you may not have solutions. When those situations arise, it is important that you have built and maintained effective networks to whom you can turn to for help, who can support your initiatives and in other ways help you accomplish your goals. (These skills are discussed in Chapters 2, 4, 6, 8 and 32.)

Forces that are shaping leadership skills

As discussed in Chapters 1 and 3, the world and organisations are changing. A number of forces require a different style of leading and managing. Some examples of this are:

- A workforce of five generations working together, each working for different reasons and having different motivations and attitudes to work and the workplace, needs empathic and servant leader-managers.
- Flattened organisation structures need leader-managers who are creative, innovative and persuasive and who can make complex decisions based on sound ethics, judgement and analysis.
- Globalisation exposes every organisational weakness. Leader-managers need to be strong, dynamic and be able to see the big picture and think strategically.
- Organisational success increasingly depends on engaged, innovative people, because people, not equipment, make the difference and people need leader-managers who can bring out their best.
- Technology can simplify and even take over many of the planning, scheduling, monitoring and reporting functions that managers used to do.
- The greater number and magnitude of risks calls for leader-managers who can build a risk culture.
- The necessity to engage employees to attract and retain those you need calls for leader-managers who align people to a shared purpose and enable them to achieve it.
- The need to work successfully with suppliers, as even specialist expertise and technical and knowledge work is increasingly outsourced, calls for leader-managers with self-awareness and strong interpersonal skills who can successfully build relationships with diverse groups of people.
- Today's leader-managers have more responsibility and wider spans of management, requiring strong skills in self-organisation and managing personal productivity.

No one can be expected to know everything, stay on top of everything or be all things to all people. This means you need to continually examine and refine your leadership skills and understand yourself realistically – your strengths and limitations, preferences and blind spots (see Chapter 5 for more on this).

10.2 Understanding leadership

Absorb what is useful. Discard what is not. Add what is uniquely your own.

Bruce Lee, *Wisdom for the way*, Black Belt, 2009.

To begin your understanding of leadership, think of the best leader you've ever known or worked for. Write down about 10 words that describe this person. Now think of another good leader you've known and write down 10 words or so that describe this person. Take a look at the words you've written. Do they mostly describe this person's characteristics or personal qualities? That's the **trait approach to leadership**. Perhaps they describe what these leaders did that made them effective. That's the **behavioural approach to leadership**. Maybe your two lists were different because these people were leaders in very different situations. That's the **situational approach to leadership**. Or maybe the words you used to describe these effective leaders made clear they used rewards and punishments as incentives. That's the **transactional approach to leadership**.

Reviewing each of these approaches provides a sound foundation for understanding leadership. As you read each one, try to relate them to other leaders you know. Think about which approaches most reflect the way you lead and which aspects you feel would be valuable additions to your repertoire. (The more leadership styles you can draw on, the more effective your leadership is likely to be.)

How you lead – your leadership style – needs to reflect you and your unique skills, personality and values. Certainly, you should learn from others and from the different ideas about leadership outlined above and in the following sections, but you also need to be comfortable that the way you lead reflects who you really are. This is what makes you an authentic leader, and being an authentic leader is arguably the one thing, more than anything else, that will win over those that follow you.

Defining leadership

At a training program on leadership held at Uluru, more than 200 managers from across Australia developed the following list of things that leaders do:

- articulate and embody a vision and goals and enable others to share and achieve them
- attain results by establishing a vision and a strategy, and coaching, communicating, delegating and motivating people to achieve that vision
- communicate and achieve goals and plans effectively
- have the courage of their convictions and are fair and just in achieving their goals
- help others to achieve a shared goal without relying on position or power
- use an elusive quality that inspires others to perform, as well as a set of skills that help them persuade others to accept directions and goals willingly.[5]

Definitions of leadership abound and most agree that leaders are people who can influence and help others to achieve a shared goal. However, there is not one definition that covers all situations. We all have a view on what leadership is and a default leadership style. It might be telling people what to do or letting them work out what to do for themselves, for instance. Your default leadership style depends on:

- the culture you grew up in; some cultures are formal and hierarchical, and some are egalitarian and informal
- the organisational culture you work in
- the situation you're in; sometimes an emergency, sometimes not
- your role perceptions.

The important thing to remember is that the definition and style you adopt has to be 'right' for you.

The trait approach: what are leaders like?

What sort of people become leaders? The top three traits most commonly found in effective leaders are:

1 *Initiative:* independence and inventiveness, the capacity to see what needs to be done, and the willingness and ability to do it without being asked.
2 *Intelligence:* should be above average (but not at genius level) and include solid skills in solving abstract and complex problems.
3 *Self-assurance:* self-esteem and setting challenging personal goals.

Two other important leadership traits are the desire to lead and mental toughness. There aren't too many 'accidentally' great leaders who never wanted to lead in the first place. Similarly, the leaders who stick around long enough to become great almost always have weathered many storms and absorbed lots of knocks along the way. To use the term 'resilient leader' is somewhat of a tautology as resilience or mental toughness simply goes with the territory.

Being a resilient leader means:

- accepting that pressure comes with the territory and not being concerned by it
- compartmentalising and concentrating on the task at hand, despite personal or other distractions
- having the desire and determination to succeed
- having faith in your abilities
- raising your performance to keep going when the going gets tough, to get the result you need
- recovering from setbacks and using them as opportunities to learn and then come back stronger
- regaining psychological control following unexpected, uncontrollable events
- staying calm and keeping a lid on your nerves
- switching off as needed and being able to relax, recover and recharge your batteries.[6]

You don't have to be tough all the time; you just need to know when to be tough. (See Chapter 5 for more information on emotional intelligence and resilience.)

The trait approach is generally considered an oversimplification of a complex subject, for the following main reasons:

- The 'top three traits' of initiative, intelligence and self-assurance, while important, are not enough in themselves to make an effective leader.
- Many leadership traits are so ill defined as to be useless in practice.
- No one can have all the leadership traits identified by the research. In fact, researchers who analysed the results of more than 100 leadership studies found that, of the many traits identified for successful leaders, only 5 per cent of them were reported in four or more of the studies.[7]
- There are too many exceptions – many successful leaders do not display so-called 'necessary' leadership traits.

Despite the lack of hard data to support the trait approach to leadership, it has wide, popular appeal, perhaps because people intuitively know there is 'something to it'. The trait approach does make intuitive sense and it may make scientific sense, too. Evolutionary psychologists have long looked at how the brain is 'hardwired'. People have individual differences and are born with many character traits and predispositions that harden as we age into adulthood. Some personality traits, the evolutionary psychologists believe, are inborn in the form of deep-rooted inclinations – some people may be born to lead. Perhaps the trait approach just hasn't defined its terms well enough yet.

In the following section we consider five models of leadership associated with personal traits:

- charismatic leadership
- empathic leadership
- servant leadership

- narcissistic leadership
- transformational leadership.

Charismatic leadership

People with charisma can be charming and influential. Their enthusiasm acts like a magnet, drawing people to them, and they motivate people by tapping into their hopes and ideals. **Charismatic leaders** provide a sense of purpose and a clear vision that 'where we're going is better than where we are now', inspiring their followers to strive to achieve great results. They scan and read their environment, picking up people's concerns and moods. They hone their actions and words to suit different situations and are inspirational, often 'theatrical', communicators; using storytelling, symbolism and metaphor to reach people on an emotional level. They set challenging goals and hold high performance expectations of their followers.

Charismatic leaders have powerful personalities, and their charisma is made up of many traits, including self-confidence and self-awareness. They give their followers a unique identity by providing a distinct sense of belonging and building their team's image, particularly in the minds of the team members, as being superior to other teams. The downside is that the group success may depend on the leader, without whom the group may flounder and dissolve.

There have always been larger-than-life leaders, some of whom made the world a better place, and some who made it worse. For every Mahatma Gandhi, Nelson Mandela and Mother Teresa, there is an Adolf Hitler, Josef Stalin and Pol Pot. Each oozed charisma and created motivating, energetic environments. Each communicated a clear vision and was willing to pursue risky endeavours. It therefore follows that to be a good leader, you do not necessarily have to be a good person.

Some charismatic leaders appeal to reason and uplift their followers. Others appeal to emotions and manipulate ignorant followers for personal interests. When well intentioned, charismatic leaders can elevate and transform a team, a company and even a country. When self-driven and Machiavellian, they can bring people, companies or countries to the point of collapse.

While it can be argued that there is a place in organisations for charismatic leaders, particularly at senior levels to lead their charges through the dynamic and sometimes perilous waters of today's rapidly changing world, skilful charismatic leadership is possibly better suited to short-term projects, especially projects requiring energy and talent. Charismatic leaders are also useful in the early stages of an enterprise and when an enterprise needs to be transformed.

Charisma is a personality trait, though, and real leadership isn't about personality – it's about more than 'being' or 'appearing to be'. Charisma can help but it isn't essential to effective leadership. Certainly, relying on charisma alone, without the foundation of 'knowing' and 'doing' leadership skills, can lead to disastrous outcomes. Perhaps **transformational leadership** (discussed later in this chapter) is a better option if you want or need to turn around your team, organisation or country. However, if you want to develop your leadership charisma, you might consider the information in Figure 10.1.

Empathic leadership

Sir Edward 'Weary' Dunlop, an Australian surgeon who was captured during the Second World War, developed his approach to **empathic leadership** in Japanese prisoner-of-war (POW) camps.

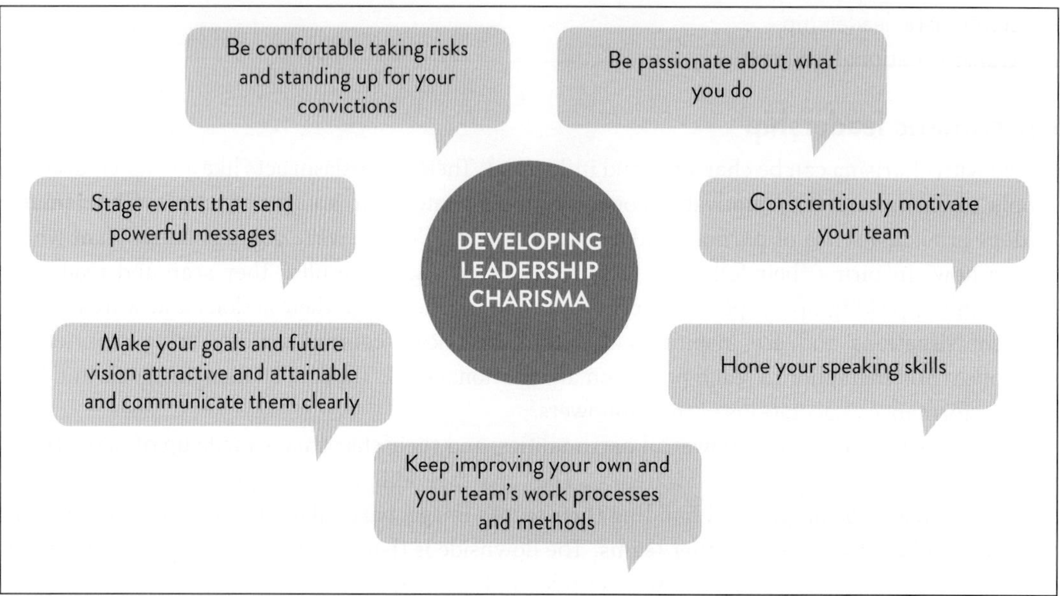

FIGURE 10.1 Being charismatic can help you to be an effective leader, but it isn't essential

The care and leadership he provided to debilitated men who were building the Thai–Burma railway restored morale and gave hope to the men forced to live and work in horrific conditions. On a number of occasions, he put his own life on the line by standing up to his captors to defend his fellow POWs against cruelty and brutality. In one instance, Dunlop saved the life of a blind amputee by physically positioning himself between the POW and the bayonets of the prison camp guards who had determined that his life was not worth maintaining. During his imprisonment, Dunlop identified 11 desirable aspects of leadership,[8] shown in **Figure 10.2**, which typify the concept of empathetic

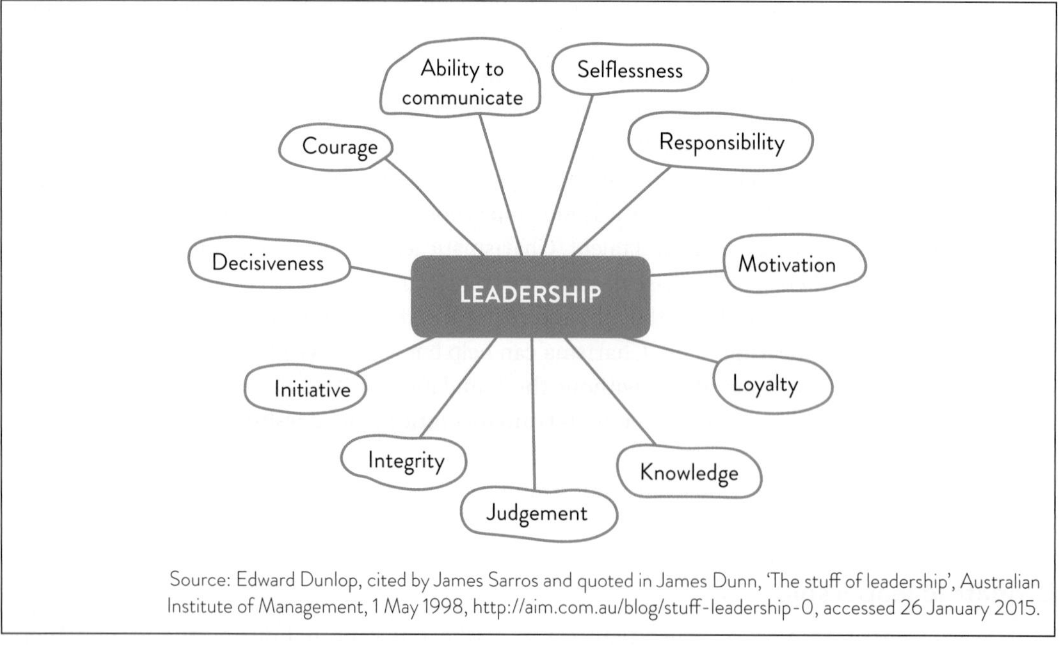

Source: Edward Dunlop, cited by James Sarros and quoted in James Dunn, 'The stuff of leadership', Australian Institute of Management, 1 May 1998, http://aim.com.au/blog/stuff-leadership-0, accessed 26 January 2015.

FIGURE 10.2 The 11 desirable aspects of leadership

leadership. In this style of leadership, a leader must be able to put themselves in the place of another so that they are able to experience a situation in the same way another person experiences it. By understanding how people may feel or react to difficult or stressful situations, empathetic leaders are able to develop strategies and solutions that consider people's feelings and emotions rather than just the needs of the task. Their decisions, therefore, are more likely to be met with acceptance and support.

Weary Dunlop was thinking of military leadership when creating his list of leadership qualities. Might these characteristics also help business leaders, not-for-profit leaders and public service leader-managers?

Servant leadership

Similar to empathic leadership (and forming a bridge to behavioural leadership because it combines personality traits with actions) is **servant leadership**. In essence, servant leaders help followers to grow and reach their potential in their jobs by allowing them the freedom to work to their strengths and so bring out their best. Servant leaders put aside self-interest and consider people's feelings to make balanced decisions. They incorporate the principles of stewardship: being responsible for the long-term welfare of others. The main attributes of servant leaders are shown in Figure 10.3. While desirable, demonstrating and 'living', these qualities may be easier in theory than in practice.

Transferable skills

3.1 Teamwork/relationships

You can find servant leaders in some public and not-for-profit organisations as well as in the private sector, particularly in companies practising conscious capitalism, where the leaders see themselves as serving not just their organisations and its employees, but also the wider society of which they are a part. The overlap between servant leadership and emotional intelligence make this leadership style increasingly relevant. In a changing and unpredictable world where workers face frequent challenges and difficulties they have not seen before, leaders need to be aware of the abilities of their employees' emotion control and play a role in managing this aspect within each person's psychological functioning.

Having empathy, understanding and the self-awareness to control one's own emotions so that you can tap into the emotional state of others is becoming more important for leaders managing a diverse cohort of workers (i.e. multi-generational, LGBTIQ+ community, workers from non-English-speaking and diverse cultural backgrounds, First Australians and so on) and navigating them through the challenging and uncertain times in the wake of the COVID-19 pandemic.

Narcissistic leadership

Narcissistic leaders are more concerned with themselves than with others. Indeed, they are the opposite of well-balanced, humble, empathic and servant leaders. Some narcissistic leaders are also charismatic, and some are transformational leaders (discussed next) who can inspire people and shape the future. They can be creative strategists who have the strength of will to push through massive transformations and the charm to convince others to help them do it. As unlikely as it may seem, there is a place for such leaders as they can 'rally the troops' and engage people's hearts and minds to achieve great things.

The downside is that these leaders can become emotionally isolated, distrustful of others and prone to feelings of grandiosity. They can become self-involved and unpredictable. Their self-belief is so high they can believe they're invincible, leading to flagrant risk-taking against all advice.

Brilliant or average, honest or corrupt, wise or foolish, narcissistic leaders share boldness and an unshakable conviction in their abilities and the value of their vision. But they hear only what they want to hear and prefer to indoctrinate rather than teach (this makes them terrible coaches

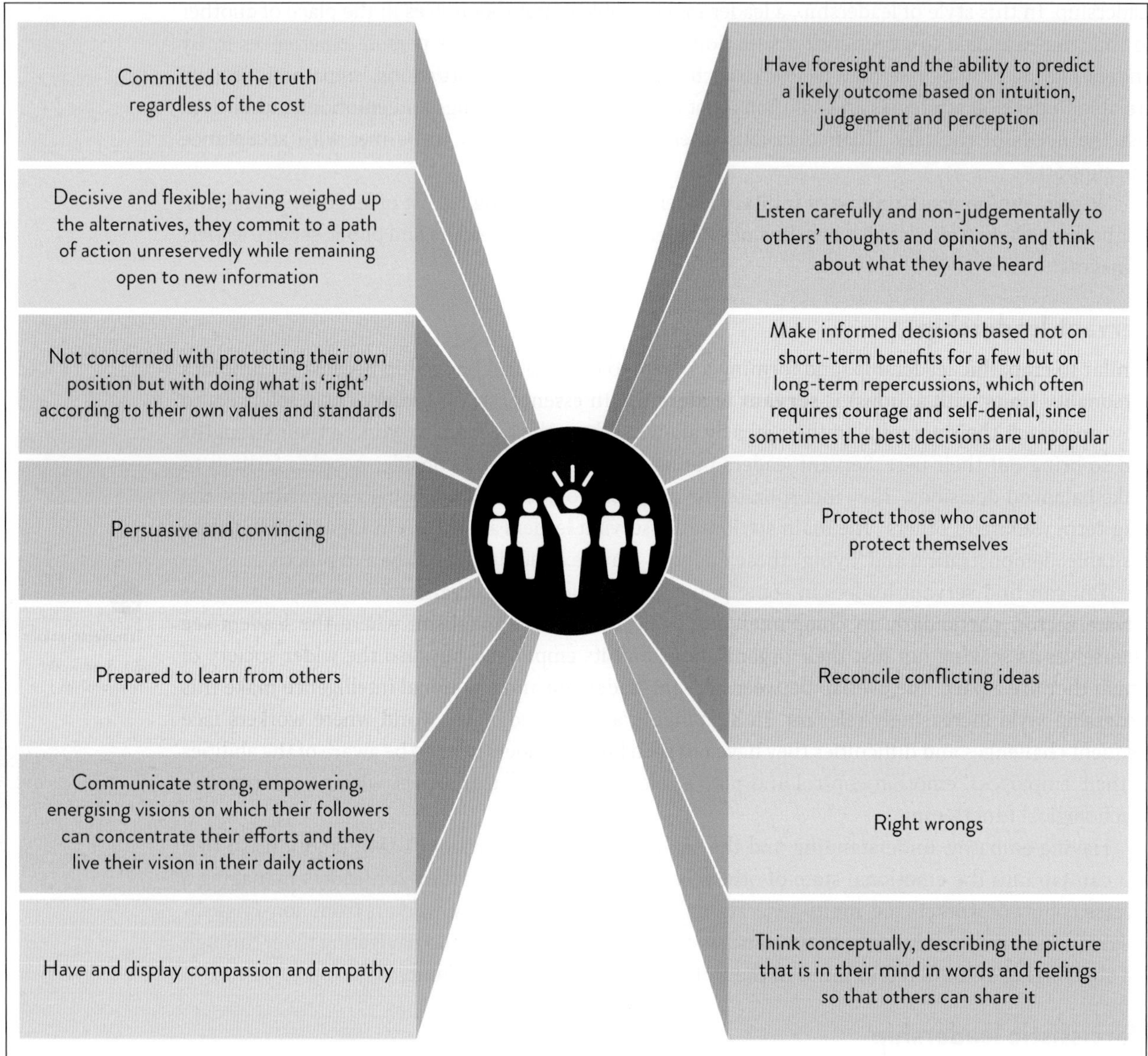

FIGURE 10.3 Attributes of servant leaders

and mentors). They dominate meetings and cannot tolerate criticism or dissent. They lack empathy, are hyper-competitive and are not restrained by conscience. Their self-absorption and need for admiration is obvious and unapologetic and they cut down anyone who challenges them, including those showing promise and those with new ideas or visions of their own.

Perhaps the real Achilles heel of narcissistic leaders is that their failures tend to become more pronounced the more successful they become. The dramatic collapse of Enron, an American energy, commodities and services company, is a good case in point. Headed by charismatic, determined, unscrupulous leaders, it was one of history's most spectacular business failures. Its former chief financial officer, Andrew Fastow, and chief executive, Jeff Skilling, were imprisoned and its chairperson, Kenneth Lay, died while on trial. All three displayed classic narcissistic behaviours: immune to consequences, unable to consider the needs of others, manipulating the environment for personal gain, and believing they can do no wrong. The company, with claimed revenues of nearly $101 billion during 2000, was bankrupt before the end of 2001.[9]

The good news is that narcissistic leaders can protect their Achilles heel in three ways: aligning those around them to their vision, finding a trusted confidant to keep them grounded in reality, and developing self-awareness.

Transformational leadership

Despite the limitations of charismatic leadership as a formula for success, the cult of the heroic leader remains strong. Transformational leaders often have charisma but there is a difference between the two types of leader: transformational leaders transform while charismatic leaders transfix.

Transformational leaders maintain high ideals, they seek to transform their organisations or society, cast their eyes and vision beyond present constraints and strike out in new directions, taking risks but influencing beliefs and values as they do so. The most significant functions of transformational leaders are:

- They develop a clear and compelling vision and mission that all employees understand and can commit to.
- They guide their organisation through revitalising change, redesigning it from top to bottom, with a goal of making it more effective, efficient and responsive, and better able to meet the changing requirements of the marketplace and society.
- They drum up enthusiasm for these changes throughout the organisation.

Transformational leaders seem to share a number of important core traits. They are strategic thinkers with a strong goal orientation and high levels of energy, personal integrity and trustworthiness. They act confidently and optimistically, and like charismatic leaders, they are excellent (and often theatrical) communicators and master motivators. They have the courage of their convictions, and their drive and enthusiasm set the pace for others to follow.

INDUSTRY INSIGHTS

Ann Sherry, transformational leader

Who would want to take over a cruise company whose reputation was still suffering from the tragic and highly publicised death of a young woman on one of its cruises five years previously? Ann Sherry was game. She began by setting a stretch goal – to have more than one million passengers a year travelling with the company. The staff thought she was mad.

Since Sherry took on the job of running the Carnival Australia cruising company, it has grown 20 per cent each year, and passenger numbers have increased ninefold, from 100 000 to 900 000 a year. A systematic analysis of the market helped Sherry establish two key elements of her strategy: building relationships with key stakeholders, including customers, the government, the media and suppliers; and improving the quality of the ships as well as destinations, entertainment, food and beverages.

Sherry is no stranger to creating transformational change. While running the office of childcare for the Victorian Government, she established after-school childcare programs and from the (federal) Office of the Status of Women, and was instrumental in extending mandatory superannuation to part-time and **casual employees**. She also obtained inaugural funding for the Breast Cancer Foundation at a time when that disease received virtually no funding, despite being the largest killer of women in Australia.

As a general manager of human resources, in the then very-blokey culture of one of Australia's major banks, Sherry demonstrated the bottom line benefits of introducing paid maternity leave, recruited several other women to senior roles in key functional areas, and provided training in sexual harassment for every executive – all part of the strategy to transform the bank into an employer of choice.[10] From early in her leadership career, Sherry demonstrated her ability to create transformational change.

At the time of writing, the company is now facing another monumental challenge with the fallout of the 'Ruby Princess' disaster. Owned by Carnival Australia, this cruise ship was linked to over 20 deaths as a result of the COVID-19 virus and is now facing a class action lawsuit. Sherry is no longer the company's CEO, or executive chairperson, but still acts as an adviser to the business. It remains to be seen whether the company has the sort of transformational leader needed to guide it through this still unfolding catastrophe.

Changing approaches to leadership

As authenticity and emotional intelligence overtake technical expertise and industry experience as the most important criteria for leaders in Australia, many leaders are sailing into uncharted waters. A massive transformation is required to move organisations and people towards effective leadership and future success. As we transform from the technical leadership style of the past, where leaders were often chosen for their smarts and ability to make the best decisions, today's leaders are faced with a complex environment of fast-paced change.

In a world where solutions to today's problems are largely undefined, leaders require new capabilities and skillsets to manage higher levels of uncertainty, complexity and change. As today's leaders are forced to be more adaptive to develop solutions for the future, they are faced with emotionally heightened situations involving higher levels of discomfort. This is where authenticity is essential.

The move towards authenticity and emotional intelligence is daunting for many, as we try to overcome the hangover of the past, where leaders were conditioned to leave their emotions at the door and get on with the job of recreating the traditional solutions – achieving targets and goals via a task-focused approach where employees were closely managed and directed with little regard given for their welfare or level of engagement.

We now expect our leaders to lead diverse teams, help us find meaning in our work and develop innovative solutions. So, it is essential for leaders to create an environment where people can be honest with their opinions and thoughts and take the risks necessary to get to previously unknown results.

What it means to be an authentic leader

To achieve innovative end-results, leaders must provide the freedom, permission and protection for their teams to develop new solutions. This means helping people show up to work with their competencies, as well as the vulnerability required to learn and grow. Authentic leadership is about capitalising on communication and interpersonal skills such as passion, motivation, transparency and integrity.

Creating an environment where a diverse group of people can be truthful enough to show their cards and reveal their deficiencies in order to move towards new insights, creates tension and discomfort. The ability to be an authentic leader means having the capacity to hold this discomfort in a room in a comfortable way.

This type of leadership change is not something organisations can arrive at overnight. Helping leaders grow and develop as human beings is a long-term undertaking that requires leaders to build enough personal agency to permanently develop these skills beyond short-term courses, to help carry the culture of an organisation forward in any environment in the future.

The behavioural approach: what do leaders do?

Effective leaders may be proactive, smart and self-assured, but how do you *do* smart? The behavioural approach sees leadership as a set of behaviours and looks at what effective leaders *do*.

Effective leaders take positive actions that poor leaders fail to. This means you can learn to be a better leader by adopting the behaviours of good leaders. Rather than copying them, take on board their behaviours and attitudes and incorporate them into your own leadership style in your own way, filtered through your own personality, experiences and knowledge.

Each of the behavioural approaches to leadership considered below offers useful insights and practical ways of thinking about leadership. (An additional behavioural approach to leadership, functional leadership, is discussed in Chapter 13.)

Leadership styles

One way to look at leaders is to divide them into three main styles of leadership:

1. autocratic
2. democratic
3. laissez-faire.

It was initially thought that the most effective leadership style was democratic because it brought out conscientiousness, friendliness and originality in followers, while **autocratic leadership** was supposed to lead to revolution, and laissez-faire, or 'do nothing', leadership wasn't motivating enough to bring out the best in followers.[11] However, it seems that each style has its uses, depending on the situation. This means you need to choose your leadership style to reflect the needs and objectives of the group, the prevailing circumstances, or the existing work environment and culture with which you're dealing.

Autocratic and dictatorial leaders

Autocratic leaders, also known as **authoritarian leaders**, use power and control to impose their will on their followers. They are task-centred leaders who avoid employee participation and retain information and the right to make all decisions themselves. They issue orders with no questions allowed and no explanations given. This tends to make followers dependent upon them for decisions and direction, and can result in the group feeling 'lost' or uncertain about which direction to take in the leader's absence.

Autocratic leaders may be thought of as 'harsh' and 'bossy', but they can also be polite and matter-of-fact while allocating duties. Leadership like this works with people doing highly routinised, prescribed jobs, such as assembly line work, although it isn't effective for bringing forth innovative ideas, motivating employees to give their best or establishing a friendly and relaxed work climate.

Dictatorial leadership, a more extreme version of authoritarian leadership, may be described as 'a loose grip around the throat'.[12] These leaders rule through force, holding threats of punishment over the heads of people to compel them to perform. This may get results in some work situations but, generally, the resulting quality and quantity of work does not remain high for very long. Instead, dictatorial leadership usually creates unrest and dissatisfaction. Employees eventually 'rebel' by doing the bare minimum of work or leaving for another job. This style of leadership has very limited application and is best avoided altogether.

Democratic leaders

While authoritarian leaders are task-centred, **democratic leaders** are people-centred. Sometimes called **participative leaders**, they encourage involvement, asking for employees' opinions and suggestions and involving them in solving work-related problems. Because employees are well informed and used to solving problems themselves, they can function effectively when their leader is absent. This makes democratic leaders effective when they need to call on the opinions and ideas of employees, establish cooperative working relationships and create a high-performing and innovative team culture.

Laissez-faire leaders

Laissez-faire leaders, also called *non-directive* and *free-rein leaders*, do not appear to lead at all. They provide the group with information and possibly some general direction and then let them get on with the job with little or no interference.

This delegative type of leadership can be effective when the work group is highly skilled and motivated and the work is complex or unstructured, as may be the case when managing professional employees and **knowledge workers**. However, when established standards and goals must be met regularly, this is probably not the most suitable style of leadership.

A team can, to a large extent, function in auto pilot mode when operations and people are working satisfactorily. But if the situation or work environment changes, then it's time for strong hands-on leadership. Table 10.1 shows when to be hands-off and when to be hands-on.

TABLE 10.1 Hands-on leadership can steer an organisation back on track

Laissez-faire 'hands-off' leadership when:	Strong 'hands-on' leadership when:
Everything is going well	There is a crisis
Followers understand the task clearly	The goal is unclear
Followers are committed to the task	Followers are unskilled or inexperienced
Followers are skilled and experienced	Followers are confused or uncertain
Followers are working well together	Followers are not working well as a team
Time is not an issue	Time is tight

The continuum of leadership styles

The continuum of leadership styles depicts leadership behaviour as ranging from leader-centred strategies to employee-centred strategies. Where do you sit on the leadership style continuum shown in Figure 10.4?[13] In this model, authoritarian leaders are at the left end of the continuum, laissez-faire leaders are at the right end, and democratic leaders are somewhere in the middle.

Choosing which leadership style to use depends on the circumstances. This is the contingency approach, which is covered later in this section. Can you use different leadership styles as the situation requires (see Table 10.2)?

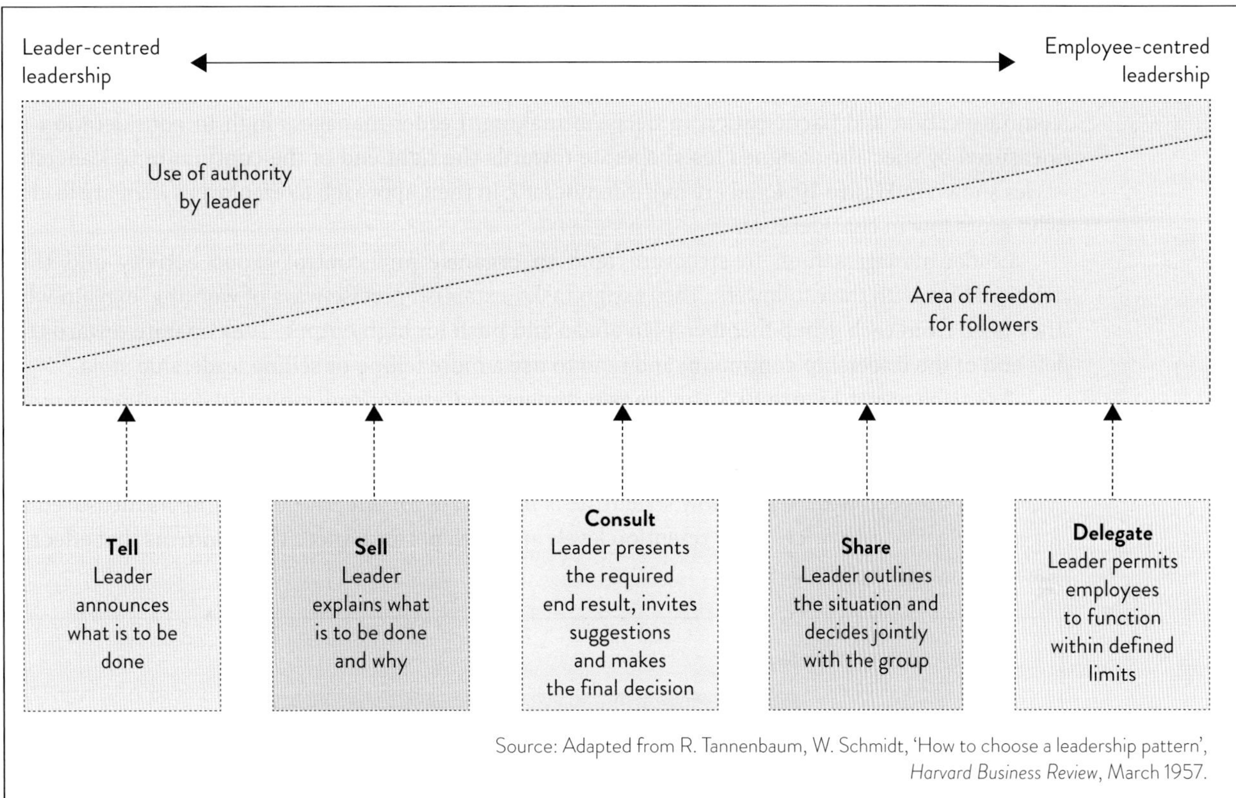

FIGURE 10.4 Continuum of leadership styles

TABLE 10.2 When to tell, when to delegate

Tell ____________ Sell ____________ Consult	____________ Share ____________ Delegate
when the task has a high degree of risk	when the task is low risk
with large numbers of followers	with smaller numbers of followers
with less skilled, experienced or motivated staff	with highly skilled, experienced or motivated staff
when employees have low involvement or are minimally affected	when employees are highly involved or very affected
when there is one best way	when there are many alternatives
when the task is critically important to the organisation	when the task is not critically important to the organisation
when time is short	when plenty of time is available

Consideration and structure

Thinking about two dimensions of leadership concern, called consideration (or concern for people) and structure (or concern for output or task), is also useful.[14] Consideration includes behaviour that indicates mutual trust, respect and rapport between the leader-manager and the work group.

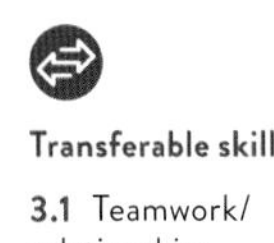

Transferable skills

3.1 Teamwork/relationships

Consideration does not mean a superficial pat on the back but, rather, a deeper concern for group members' needs and the empathy and emotional intelligence to demonstrate this concern in an authentic manner. Leader-managers high in consideration, for instance, encourage two-way communication and participation in decision-making. Leader-managers high in consideration (as measured by specially designed tests) operate towards the right end of the continuum of leadership styles shown in **Figure 10.4** and are more democratic in their approach to employees than are leaders who score low in consideration.

Leader-managers high in structure tend to organise and control group activity and their relationships with their followers. They assign tasks, establish precise ways of working, explain what they need from each group member, plan ahead and push for high output. They operate towards the left end of the leadership continuum and tend to use a more telling or selling leadership style.

As can be seen in **Figure 10.5**, this is a two-dimensional view of leadership that doesn't recommend one particular approach. It notes that some successful leaders are high in consideration and low in structure, while others are high in consideration and high in structure. But high consideration, whether combined with high or low structure, is important for effective leadership as measured by, for example, few grievances, high retention levels and high performance. This confirms that effective leaders need strong people skills.

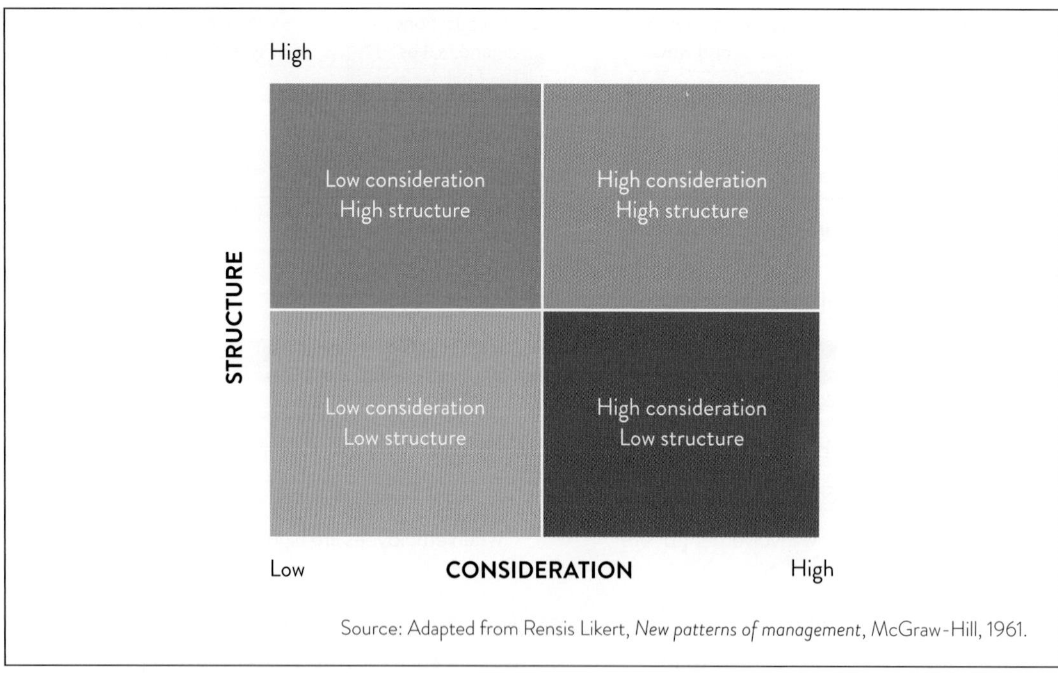

Source: Adapted from Rensis Likert, *New patterns of management*, McGraw-Hill, 1961.

FIGURE 10.5 The consideration and structure model

The managerial grid

The **managerial grid** is shown in **Figure 10.6**. This approach concludes that leaders can concentrate on one of two key factors – *people* or *output*. These two factors form the axes of the managerial grid, on which five possible leadership styles are positioned. A specially developed questionnaire ranks how much attention a leader pays to each of the two factors on a scale of one for low and nine for high. For example, the bottom left area of the grid in **Figure 10.6** reflects a low score of the two factors (people and output) – a low score of 1 for people and a low score of 1 for output.[15]

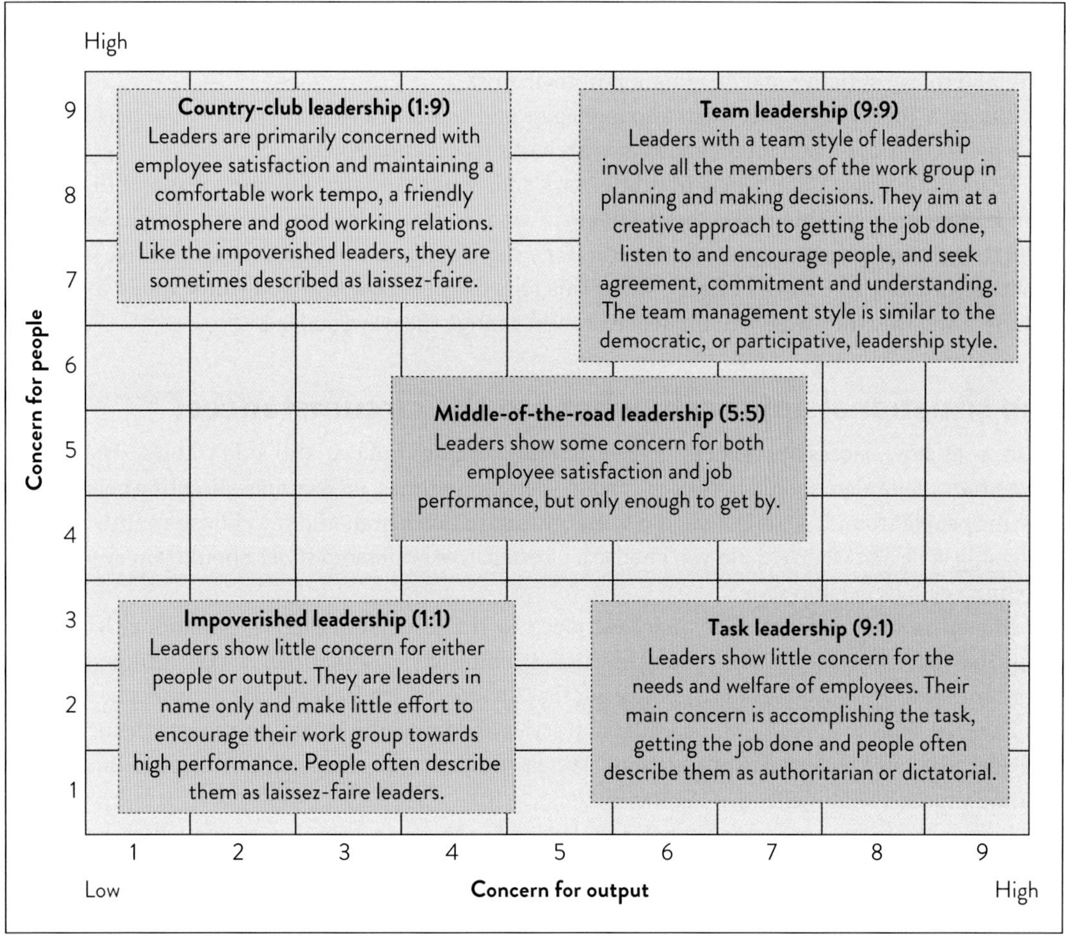

FIGURE 10.6 The managerial grid

In the past, it was believed that a team leadership style worked best in all situations, but we now know that this is not the case. Like authoritarian leadership, task leadership works better, for instance, when supervising repetitive work being done by inexperienced, unskilled or unmotivated employees. Similarly, country-club leadership, akin to delegating, often works well with highly experienced, skilled and motivated staff.

Theory X and Theory Y

What do you believe about the average employee? Do they work only for the money and try to get away with doing as little as possible? Or do they take pride in their work and try to do their best? This is another way to look at leadership; that is, from the leader's perspective. At one extreme is the **Theory X** mindset and at the other extreme is the **Theory Y** mindset. These mindsets describe two opposite beliefs that leader-managers can hold about how employees approach their jobs.[16]

Leaders with a Theory X mindset believe that employees are lazy, lack ambition and want to avoid responsibility. They believe employees work only because they have to and do as little as possible for their pay. When you believe that, it's natural to keep tight controls on employees, tell them what to do and threaten them with punishment to keep them in line.

Leaders with a Theory Y mindset believe that work is as natural as rest and play. With that mindset, you can believe that people want to do their jobs well and that they seek challenge and responsibility when they are committed to the overall objectives of their team or organisation. It is possible, and even probable, that employees want to be committed to goals and visions, to learn new skills, and to use initiative and imagination in their work.

Taking a Theory X approach can trap managers and teams in a vicious cycle of poor performance while a Theory Y approach forges ahead in search of success and growth.

Leaders advertise their beliefs in subtle ways and, sooner or later, followers respond in the way their leaders predict. This makes both Theory X and Theory Y leaders correct. People live up or down to their leader's expectations and predictions, depending on whether they are positive (the **halo effect**) or negative (the **horns effect**). What this tells us is that the way you think about your team members and why they work can influence or even change the way you lead.

The situational approach: what are the circumstances?

Looking at how successful leaders behave is enlightening, but we still don't know *when* or in *what situations* leaders should behave in certain ways. Sometimes, for example, directing behaviour – 'bossing people around' – is effective, and sometimes it isn't. When should you choose an authoritarian leadership style and when should you choose a participative leadership style? Should you ever choose a country-club leadership style?

The situational approach adds another piece to the leadership puzzle. Situational leadership shows us that effective leaders sometimes use a telling style, sometimes a consulting style and sometimes a delegating style. It is the situation that dictates which leadership style works best. When you have the skills to apply all of the leadership styles and know the right times to use them, you can lead effectively in a wide range of situations. When you can't, your leadership is likely to be effective in some situations but ineffective in others.

Let's look at three models of situational leadership that can help you decide which leadership style to choose. You may have heard the saying 'Horses for courses'. It means using an approach which suits the situation or circumstances. It applies to leadership as well as other spheres of life. Some situations call for leaders who wield authority while others need tactful, empathic leaders. For every situation there is a leadership approach suitable to handle it, but knowing which one and when to apply it is the skill and advantage that the most effective leaders have over the rest.

What unites successful leaders is not their particular sets of skills as much as the fact that their personality profiles meet the demands of the situation, that they *want* to lead, and that they have and use the leadership skills the situation calls for.

The contingency approach

The contingency approach says that the style of leadership that works best depends on the situation, or the environment in which you are leading. The following factors determine the appropriate leadership style in any given situation:

- *Leader–member relations:* how much the followers trust, respect and have confidence in their leader, which can be subjectively assessed as high (good) or low (poor).
- *Position power:* how much power and influence go with the leader's job – the power to hire, fire, reward and punish, which can be high (strong position power) or low (weak position power). (See Chapter 4 for more on this.)
- *Task structure:* whether established procedures must be followed (high structure) or whether employees have discretion in carrying out the task (low structure).[17]

An autocratic, telling style of leadership – one that emphasises a high concern with tasks – seems to work best in situations that are either favourable or unfavourable for the leader. For example, when there is high structure and little scope for followers to decide what to do, or low structure and the many options leave followers reeling, leaders should give clear instructions: what to do (and sometimes why), and when, where and how to do it. In moderate situations, a more democratic, people-centred approach is likely to be more successful.

The most favourable, or easiest, situation for a leader is one characterised by:

- good leader–member relations
- strong position power
- a highly structured task.

In contrast, the least favourable situation for a leader is characterised by:

- poor leader–member relations
- weak position power
- low task structure.

The elements of leadership approach

The elements of leadership approach incorporates the continuum of leadership styles and adds the several situational dimensions, discussed in the following sections, that need to be considered when deciding which leadership style to use.[18]

Consider the employees

What style of leadership is the work team used to and comfortable with? How much independence and responsibility do they want? How many followers are there? How competent and willing are they? Are they directly affected by a decision or involved in its execution? How experienced are they at working together? How confident are they? Do they understand and identify with the organisation's goals?

When people are used to, and expect participative leadership and are skilled and motivated, opt for participative leadership. Similarly, when a work team is used to highly directive leadership, a sudden change to democratic, consultative leadership would almost certainly fall flat, so it may be wiser to be more directive, at least initially.

Consider the task

Is there one best way to do the task or are there several ways? How routine or complex is it? How critically important to the organisation is the task or decision? Is a high degree of risk involved? Is time short?

A small, highly skilled team performing a flexible task in a changing environment generally responds best to democratic, people-centred leadership. On the other hand, when time is critical, or when a large work group is carrying out precisely specified, routine work, you can probably achieve better results by using more directive behaviour (remembering that directive behaviour can be polite and helpful). When the issue or task at hand is highly critical or sensitive and team members are skilled and willing, due diligence requires you to keep a reasonable amount of authority by consulting rather than sharing or delegating authority.

Consider the leader

Don't forget yourself in this. What style of leadership are you most comfortable with? What styles of leadership have you experienced yourself? Who are your role models? How confident are you about using each of the leadership styles? What is the expected leadership style in your organisation – its cultural norm of leadership? What are your organisation's values, traditions and policies? How dispersed are its work units? The answers to these questions may point you in a different direction altogether.

Whichever style of leadership you choose, you need to feel comfortable with it. Some people find it next to impossible to use an autocratic telling style convincingly, while others feel uncomfortable using a delegating or sharing style.

The task-readiness approach

The task-readiness approach to selecting a leadership style uses two dimensions of leadership behaviour:

1 *Directive behaviour:* how much task focus and supervision you provide; includes developing plans, programs and schedules related to employees' work, directing the way in which employees should carry out tasks, maintaining close and frequent supervision of the task, providing job training and setting objectives.
2 *Relationship behaviour:* how much support and encouragement you provide; looks at how much a leader includes employees in such tasks as developing plans, programming and scheduling employees' work and setting objectives. It also relates to how much the leader shares problem-solving and decision-making about how to carry out the task, and how much coaching, counselling and encouragement the leader provides.

Using this model, four styles of leadership are possible, as shown in Table 10.3. Notice that these four leadership styles are similar to the styles described in the continuum of leadership styles; both were developed around the same time.[19] Style 1 is referred to as S1, Style 2 is S2 and so on. Which leadership style do you mostly use?

TABLE 10.3 Leadership styles

Style	Style definition	Focus	Approach
S1	High directive/low relationship behaviour	The task at hand	Telling: 'I'll decide'
S2	High directive/high relationship behaviour	Both task and relationships with team members	Explaining: 'We'll talk; I'll decide'
S3	High relationship/low directive behaviour	Supporting and helping team members	Coaching, encouraging, participating: 'We'll talk. We'll decide'
S4	Low relationship/low directive behaviour	Monitoring tasks and relationships	Delegating: 'You decide. I'll be available'

Task-readiness level

How do you know which of the four leadership styles to use? The idea is to vary your leadership style according to each employee's 'readiness' to do a particular task, referred to as their task-readiness level.

The two factors that make up an employee's task-readiness level are:

1 *competence* or ability to do a particular task, which is a combination of skills, knowledge and experience in a particular task
2 *willingness* to take responsibility for doing the task, which is a combination of motivation and self-confidence.

The concept of task-readiness level relates to each task an employee does, not to an employee's overall competence for the job as a whole. This means that a person's readiness level might be high on some tasks and low on others. Therefore, you need to use different leadership styles with the employee depending on the task. Readiness levels are referred to as R1, R2 and so on.

Figure 10.7 shows ways of recognising employees at different levels of task readiness. (You'll notice there are two types of readiness; level 3: developing and regressing will be discussed shortly.)

Readiness level 1

I don't know how.
I can't do it.
I did my best, but ...
I've never done this before.

Readiness level 2

Show me.
I'll have a go!
I'm not sure.
I don't know how but I'll give it a try.

Readiness level 4

I've already done it.
Leave it to me.
No worries!
Here, let me help with that.

Readiness level 3 (developing)

How does this look?
Can I run this by you?
I'm not sure if I can.

Readiness level 3 (regressing)

I'll do it later.
It's someone else's turn.
What? Me again!
Been there, done that.

FIGURE 10.7 Assessing task-readiness level

When you know an employee's readiness level for a particular task, you know what leadership style to use with them:

R1 Low competence and low willingness to do a task unsupervised. This person needs direction, so an S1 or telling style of leadership is called for.

R2 Growing competence and willingness. This calls for an S2 or explaining style of leadership.

R3 Satisfactory competency but low willingness based on lack of confidence or lack of motivation. This person needs support, so an S3 or encouraging or participating style of leadership is needed.

R4 High levels of competence and willingness. This calls for an S4 or delegating, 'hands off' style of leadership.

This is illustrated in Figure 10.8. You can also apply the concept of task-readiness level to a work group to get a feel for the leadership styles you consider will be appropriate to use with them.

Using the task-readiness approach, you can see that you can change your behaviour towards employees as they develop skills, experience and confidence. That's why leaders need flexibility in the styles of leadership they apply.

Regression

This isn't the end of the story. As experienced leader-managers know, employees sometimes 'go off the boil'. An employee who was once skilled and motivated can, due to boredom, poor working relationships within the team or a poor working environment, become disgruntled, uncooperative and unwilling. Similarly, the productivity of a valued employee, distracted by problems at home, may drop away suddenly. Whatever the reason, people occasionally move backwards (regress) from being a skilled and willing employee (readiness level 4) to a competent but unwilling employee (readiness level 3). Figure 10.7 shows some ways to recognise a regressed employee.

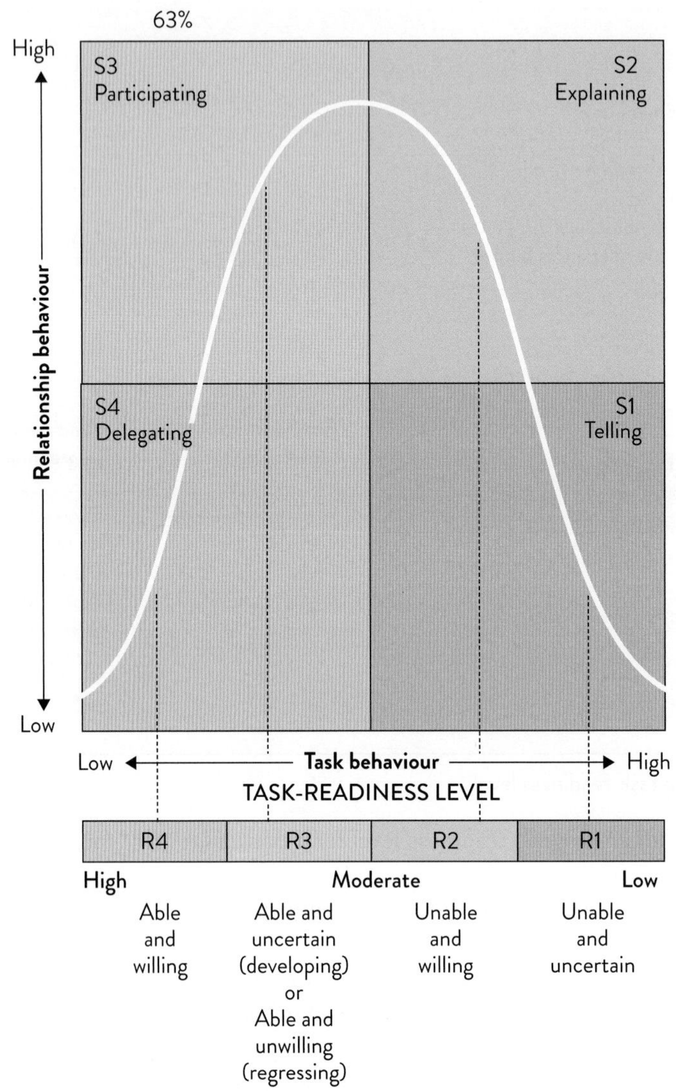

63%

High

S3
Participating

S2
Explaining

S4
Delegating

S1
Telling

Relationship behaviour

Low

Low Task behaviour High

TASK-READINESS LEVEL

R4	R3	R2	R1

High Moderate Low

Able and willing	Able and uncertain (developing) or Able and unwilling (regressing)	Unable and willing	Unable and uncertain

FIGURE 10.8 Selecting the right leadership style

Look at **Figure 10.8** and locate R3 on the task-readiness scale. Follow the line up to see what leadership style to use with R3 regressing employees. You can see that regressed employees need low-task, high-relationship behaviour. Telling them what to do or providing further training is a waste of time because they already *know* what to do. High-task behaviour is not the answer, although it is usually the first refuge of inexperienced or untrained leader-managers.

Transferable skills

3.1 Teamwork/relationships

An R3 regressing employee needs supportive, participative, relationship-building behaviour. Using your emotional intelligence skills , sit down and chat with the person, ask them questions and listen to their responses, showing them empathy as you do. You might find that boredom has set in and a new challenge is required, that the employee feels unappreciated and neglected, or that faulty tools or equipment or poor work systems are the source of the problem, and as a result the employee has given up trying. You can't act effectively until you find out what is causing the problem, so ask, listen, diagnose and then respond with the appropriate course of action. (Chapter 19 explains how to analyse the reasons that employees regress.)

The transactional approach: *quid pro quo*

If you like a nice, clear chain of command, think rewards and punishments motivate people, and want the people in your team to do what you say, you'll like the transactional approach to leadership. It's about *quid pro quo*; that is, rewards and punishments depend on performance.

Although bureaucracies have a poor name and are characterised as being hampered by red tape and a lack of innovation, many organisations continue to reward employees for good performance (e.g. a bonus or a commission) and punish them in some way for poor performance (even if only with a poor performance review or an undesirable job assignment). In fairness, this approach works well enough in situations where work is repetitive, problems are simple and judgement isn't required. However, it's generally considered a poor way to lead and manage today unless it's combined with other (more sophisticated) forms of leadership and motivation.

For transactional leadership to work, you need to make clear what you expect from the people who report to you (goals, measures of success) and the rewards they get when they achieve this. You need to provide the resources employees need to achieve their goals, monitor their performance (**management by exception** is generally fine), identify performance gaps and coach as necessary. When people perform above expectation, you need to provide positive feedback and other rewards; when people perform below expectation, you need to apply corrective action.

The transactional approach to leadership avails itself to a variety of leadership styles depending on the type of work employees are engaged in and the other factors shown in Table 10.2. Examples of leadership styles that can be applied include:

- *Achievement-oriented*: setting challenging work and personal development goals and setting high standards and expectations works best with complex tasks and knowledge workers.
- *Directive*: telling or explaining what needs to be done, providing coaching and guidance and so on works well with complex, unstructured tasks when followers are inexperienced.
- *Participative*: involving experienced and knowledgeable followers works well, provided you need and heed their advice.
- *Supportive, or high consideration leadership*: creating a friendly working environment, making jobs as interesting as possible, raising followers' self-esteem, showing concern for employees' welfare and so on works best as a reward when work is boring, hazardous or stressful.

Path-goal leadership

The path-goal approach to leadership is a type of transactional leadership where leaders specify the path (or the goal), remove any blocks or hindrances along the path, and provide followers with rewards as they move down the path towards the goal.[20]

You can set the path clearly or vaguely, remove only the biggest roadblocks or scour the path for pebbles, and give mild encouragement or be lavish with your praise. Your choice depends on the situation, the needs and expectations of followers, your own inclinations and the leadership culture of your organisation. Similarly, the choice is yours as to whether and how much to involve the followers in establishing the goals and identifying and removing the obstacles to achieving them, and whether to use lower-order or higher-order needs as rewards (described further in Chapter 11).

In conclusion

These approaches show that one style of leadership is no 'better' or 'worse' than any other. The art is to be able to use each of them when you need to, at the right time and in the right place. In the end, a leader may be 'best right now' but there is no 'best' for all situations.

10.3 Leading or managing?

Managers are people who do things right and leaders are people who do the right things.

Warren Bennis and Joan Goldsmith, *Learning to lead: A workbook on becoming a leader*, Basic Books, 2003.

The early concept of management was designed for the industrial era where job tasks were highly prescriptive, governed by strict rules and procedures and therefore suited a bureaucratic management approach. The goal of managers was to ensure that repetitive activities were performed efficiently and reliably so as to produce goods and services cheaply and in large quantities. Today's management landscape is very different. Global markets, complex supply chains, modern industrial agreements and work arrangements, value-added activities and so on have made the managerial role of the past virtually unrecognisable. The demand for employees who are engaged, flexible and innovative means a different sort of leadership and management is required.

This means that leadership based on authority, dominance and power is outdated and ineffectual. Leading and managing today is about creating a vision, setting goals, inspiring employees, leading by example, managing ethically and, most importantly, facilitating your team to achieve high performance. **Table 10.4** illustrates how the modern leader-manager's role and approach has changed. The right column represents the past, the left the column the present. It can be an interesting self-reflection to go through the list and see how many you tick in each column as being relevant to the way you manage. Maybe your approach to managing and leading is not as contemporary as you thought or perhaps you are the quintessential modern-day leader-manager. Take the test and see!

TABLE 10.4 Leaders and managers

Leaders	Managers
Align people	Organise people
Ask what and why	Ask how and when
Bring new perspectives and challenge the status quo	Protect the status quo
Coach and develop people	Control people
Create change	Work to established procedures
Create ideas and innovate	Control and administer, promote stability
Do the right things	Do things right
Encourage experimentation	Give direction
Empower and support	Use formal authority
Focus on people	Focus on results
Focus on the longer term	Focus on the short term
Give purpose and meaning	Plan and coordinate
Help people develop	Solve problems
Involve	Delegate
Lead by example, inspire	Give directions
Push out the boundaries	Work within the boundaries
Set direction and live values, vision and mission	Adhere to direction

Leaders	Managers
Tap into people's strengths	Monitor
Use empathy	Focus on the task
Use interpersonal skills	Use formal authority

From managing to leading to facilitating

Despite the shift in approach to management and leadership, managers are still an essential commodity. They are needed to allocate resources, increase efficiencies, deal with budgets and numbers, and optimise processes and structures. But organisations are now looking for managers who act more like leaders, who are role models that inspire their team, can adapt quickly to change and support others to do the same.

It's been said that the difference between leading and managing is the difference between '*path finding*' and '*path minding*'.[21] But it isn't the case of doing one or the other. Leader-managers need to do both. Managers need to be *good* leaders in order to be effective, and leaders need to be good managers in order to secure and coordinate resources, meet targets and so on. Managers who manage without leading are uninspiring, ineffectual and will quickly lose the confidence of their charges, while leaders who don't manage lose touch with what's going on and fail their team and organisation on an administrative and coordination front. So perhaps the best way to view leading and managing is as two distinct but complementary activities that are now part of the same whole.

You can't lead without managing or manage without leading. Regardless of your title, to achieve the results your organisation will demand of you in the 21st century, you need to exercise both leadership and management skills. When you have mastered the skills of both and successfully integrated them into the one role, then you are a leader-manager.

A final word

Leadership begins with your mindset (discussed in Chapter 5) so the most important step to becoming a leader is to think like a leader. As organisations become ever-leaner and more fluid, integrate their functions along process lines, work more closely with their suppliers and customers, and form strategic alliances with other organisations to offer shared services, leading and managing is becoming more demanding and the two roles have become inseparable.

Leadership is a journey of learning. Each aspiring leader needs to build their own leadership model and develop and refine it as they learn new skills and understand their natural style of leadership. Creating a vision, leading by example and inspiring others will make you a leader. But if you have the strength and conviction to lead in a way where your actions and behaviours are true to yourself and in harmony with your own personal style, you will then have become an authentic leader, one who others will willingly follow, and who will be keenly sought after by organisations.

STUDY TOOLS

QUICK REVIEW

KEY CONCEPT 10.1 

a List the main forces that require different attributes, skills and mindsets of those supervising the work of others in the industrial economy and in today's service and knowledge economy.

KEY CONCEPT 10.2 

a Which of the approaches to leadership discussed in this chapter can today's leaders apply to good effect? Does the industry and work environment you're thinking of affect the way you answer this question?

b Summarise the trait, behavioural, situational and transactional approaches to leadership and highlight the differences between them. Which of the three approaches are you more drawn to?

c Compare and contrast Theory X leadership with Theory Y leadership and explain how the two styles are self-fulfilling prophecies. Which do you believe is a more appropriate form of leadership in the 21st century and why?

KEY CONCEPT 10.3 

a What do you see as the main differences between leading and managing? Discuss the job of a leader-manager from a leadership point of view, and from a managing point of view.

BUILD YOUR SKILLS

KEY CONCEPT 10.1 

a 'Leaders can lead only when the followers are willing to follow.' Discuss the implications of this statement for leader-managers.

b Can you see any parallels between authentic leadership and authentic parenting or authentic friendship? What might they have in common?

c General Sir Peter Cosgrove said this in his third Boyer Lecture:

> **Overall, I think it is fair to say that while the sort of leadership on offer in Australia is pretty good, it can be 'patchy' – that is, spasmodic in practice. Sometimes leaders stop leading and sort of go on a leadership holiday and sometimes their leadership descends in quality so that the team wish they would go on holiday.**[22]

What actions can you as a leader take to avoid patchy leadership like this?

KEY CONCEPT 10.2 

a What is a leader? Illustrate your answer using each part of the following definition: 'A leader articulates and embodies a vision and goals and enables others to share and achieve them.'

b How do you define leadership? Explain why good leaders are vital to modern organisations.

c Which of the traits of charismatic, empathic, servant, narcissistic and transformational leaders do you possess?

d Referring to the situational approach to leadership, illustrate why different styles of leadership are appropriate in different situations using examples from your own experience.

e Give an example of each of the four approaches to leadership from your own experience.

KEY CONCEPT 10.3 

a 'Manage yourself. Lead others.' Discuss what this means to you.

b Are you a new leader? Check out the author's blogs 'Tips for new leaders Part I', at https://colemanagement.wordpress.com/2017/05/31/tips-for-new-leaders-part-i/ and 'Tips for new leaders Part II' at https://colemanagement.wordpress.com/2017/06/07/tips-for-new-leaders-part-ii/ and make some action point notes for yourself.

WORKPLACE ACTIVITIES

KEY CONCEPT 10.1 

a In what ways do the leader-managers in your workplace display the characteristics of 21st-century Australian leadership? Give at least three specific examples.

b General Sir Peter Cosgrove said:

> Part of our national wealth is not only the people but those people who lead them ... We want our leaders to be fair dinkum, as much among us as above us. If we think that they are hugely conscious of the temporary privilege they have in being in charge, then we are likely to grudgingly acknowledge that they are not a bad sort of man or woman: as under their stewardship we do marvellous things.[23]

What steps do you take to be 'fair dinkum' and not 'above' the people you work with?

KEY CONCEPT 10.2 

a Select one of the approaches to leadership discussed in this chapter and explain how you have used it to improve your own workplace leadership.

b Select and apply a situational approach leadership to four common situations in your workplace.

c Thinking about the people in your work team and your work situation, what leadership style does it indicate you should adopt?

d How do you rank your own task-readiness levels for the main tasks you perform at work? How do you rank your staff's task-readiness levels for the key tasks they perform? Are you using appropriate leadership styles according to the task-readiness approach to leadership?

KEY CONCEPT 10.3 

a Describe the nature of the jobs in your work group. Do they call for more leadership or more management? Explain your thinking.

EXTENSION ACTIVITIES

Referring to the Snapshot at the beginning of this chapter, answer the following questions:

1 Suggest two leadership approaches that would be appropriate for Malik to adopt to lead the compliance team into the 21st century. Outline your reasons for choosing each.

2 Suggest three more items that Malik could add to the meeting agenda in relation to strategies he could introduce to build a strong and unified team culture.

3 Outline how Malik could apply the task-readiness approach, to whom and what results he would seek to achieve by adopting such an approach.

4 Identify the key leadership skills that Malik needs to utilise to transform his team and how each can be used in relation to his team's situation.

CASE STUDY 10

MANAGEMENT BY FILING CABINET

How would you like to work for one of the most cited, distinguished and influential psychiatrists in the world? Daunting? Not when it's Professor of Psychiatry Gavin Andrews, AO, MD, FRCPsych, FRANZCP, the research director of the Clinical Research Unit for Anxiety and Depression of the University of New South Wales at St Vincent's Hospital in Sydney. His team includes two other MDs who rotate through the team as part of the hospital's psychiatry training unit; a chief psychologist and a team of clinical psychologists who work with patients combining face-to-face consultations with remote therapy over the internet; a trial manager, and a team of research fellows and research assistants, some of whom also have patient contact as well as research responsibilities. Non-medical staff – an administration assistant, an IT whiz and a project manager – complete the team of 18. A sprinkling of overseas team members and Australians who have worked overseas bring a variety of approaches and perspectives to the team.

Leading a team of knowledge workers is 'clean sailing' once you get the right people and the right culture, Professor Andrews says. 'The thing to do is hire stars and let them get on with it. It soon becomes self-perpetuating – the rumour gets around: "This is a great place to work". You become a magnet employer and the best people come to you.'

The team is set up so that members bounce ideas off each other, support each other and train each other, which builds a culture of collaboration, innovation and teamwork. The professor keeps that culture going, building camaraderie and gently monitoring performance and quality in several ways, as we describe next.

CASE STUDY 10

TUESDAY TEAM LUNCHES

The medical and non-medical staff, including the professor, take it in turn to bring in lunch for the rest of the team. 'Last week, it was make-your-own wraps with a variety of fillings, but the point is, these lunches encourage off-beat discussion and immersion in a stream of different ideas. After half an hour, I tap the table and kick off a more formal discussion. I take about five minutes talking about policy, plans going forward and what I've been up to; then we go around the table and everyone updates the rest of us on their week.'

THE QUALITY BOOK

At the end of the meeting the chief psychologist goes around with a book that lists people's KRAs, about four each, and people sign off on each one that there are no quality or safety issues in their areas of responsibility. When someone says 'Ah, well actually …' they have a chat and decide how to handle the situation based on our two prime directives:

1 Get people better.
2 No one comes to harm.

'That go-around only takes about five minutes at the end of our meeting, so we're pretty much done and dusted in an hour.'

The one-hour rule: 'Of course, if anyone is worried about something before Tuesday rolls around, the rule is – and they do this within one hour of becoming concerned about something – they come to me or another clinician and appropriate action is taken *instantly*. That might be, for instance, phoning the police to say someone is threatening self-harm.'

WEDNESDAY PRESENTATIONS

Each Wednesday, between 1 p.m. and 1.30 p.m. or 2 p.m., the professor's Anxiety and Depression team meets with the Schizophrenia team and someone gives a formal presentation about a paper recently published or about to be published. (Both teams are prolific writers of scientific papers for peer-reviewed journals.) This exposes everyone to different methodologies and ways of thinking. 'Cross-fertilisation of approaches and ideas is extremely important to our work', the professor explains.

WEDNESDAY IDEAS MEETINGS

Come 4 p.m., the professor's team meets to fly ideas, free associate, get feedback – whatever they want. People simply put their name on the board when they have something to discuss with the rest of the team. 'Last week I put my name up there. I am about to do a series of big talks around the country to teachers and educators and I wanted feedback on my presentation. As a result, I re-vamped quite a lot of it. These meetings are another way we build a culture of coming up with ideas.'

INDUCTION FOR ACCULTURATION AND COMFORT

When someone joins the team, I spend a lot of time sitting on the filing cabinet next to their desk; fortunately, we have low filing cabinets. We chat about what they're doing, how things are going, and so on. After two or three weeks, they usually let me know they're too busy with work to chat. Then I know they're comfortable with their roles and acculturated to our ways, and they know I'm there when they need me.'[24]

To find out about the unit, check out ABC TV's *Catalyst* program with Dr Norman Swan talking to the professor on the team's work, at https://www.youtube.com/watch?v=SP7_FYybMSY and link into the unit's website at https://thiswayup.org.au/clinic.

Questions

1 Based on the material in this case study, relate three of the approaches to leadership considered in Section 10.1 to Professor Andrews' leadership, giving examples to support your thinking.
2 Is the professor's leadership style more similar to the 'old fashioned' management styles or to the 21st-century Aussie leader-manager? Provide examples that illustrate your opinion.
3 How would you describe Professor Andrews' leadership approach? Explain your reasoning.

CHAPTER ENDNOTES

1 Six Degrees Executive, *The Future of Leadership Research Report*. Available at https://www.sixdegreesexecutive.com.au/your-career/news/future-leadership-research-report

2 Firebrand Recruitment, '2018 Talent Ignition Report'. Available at https://brand.aquent.com/2018-Talent-Ignition-Report

3 John Hilton, 'This is where Australia's leadership falls short', 5 March 2019. Available at https://www.hcamag.com/au/specialisation/leadership/this-is-where-australias-leadership-falls-short/160629

4 Deborah Ancona et al., 'In praise of the incomplete leader', *Harvard Business Review*, February 2007.

5 Kris Cole (author), a training program run by the author.

6 *Management Today* (UK), March 2003.

7 See, for example, J. Bono, T. Judge, 'Personality and transformational and transactional leadership: A meta-analysis', *Journal of Applied Psychology*, Vol. 89. No. 5, 2004, p. 901.

8 Edward Dunlop, cited by James Sarros and quoted in James Dunn, 'The stuff of leadership', Australian Institute of Management, 1 May 1998, http://aim.com.au/blog/stuff-leadership-0, accessed 26 January 2015.

9 M. Macoby, 'Learning the wrong lessons from Enron', *Research Technology Management*, Vol. 46, No. 6, 2002, pp. 57–58.

10 Ann Sherry, interview in Tom Skotnicki, 'Leaving all in her wake', *Management Today*, 8 June 2014.

11 K. Lewin, R. Lippitt, R. K. White, 'Patterns of aggressive behavior in experimentally created "social climates"', *The Journal of Social Psychology*, 1939, Vol. 10, No. 2, pp. 269–299.

12 Barry Hearn, quoted in J. Stokdyk, 'Better than a sporting chance', *Accountancy Age*, 3 March 1999.

13 R. Tannenbaum, W. Schmidt, 'How to choose a leadership pattern', *Harvard Business Review*, March 1958, pp. 95–101.

14 Rensis Likert, *New patterns of management*, Copyright © 1961 by McGraw-Hill Education. Used by permission. See also A.K. Korman, 'Consideration: Initiating structure and organizational criteria – a review', *Personnel Psychology: A Journal of Applied Research*, Vol. 19, No. 4, Winter 1966, pp. 349–361.

15 R. Blake, J. Mouton, *The managerial grid: The key to leadership excellence*, Gulf Publishing, 1964. See also R. Blake, J. Mouton, *The managerial grid III: The key to leadership excellence*, Gulf Publishing, 1985.

16 Douglas McGregor, 'The human side of enterprise', *Leadership and motivation: Essays of Douglas McGregor*, W. G. Bennis, E. H. Schein (eds), MIT Press, Cambridge, MA, 1966, pp. 3–20.

17 Fred Fiedler, *A theory of leadership effectiveness*, McGraw-Hill, 1967; also see Fred Fiedler, 'A contingency model of leadership effectiveness', *Advances in experimental social psychology*, 1964, pp. 149–190.

18 Robert Tannenbaum, Warren H. Schmidt, 'How to choose a leadership pattern', *Harvard Business Review*, March–April, 1957, pp. 95–101.

19 Paul Hersey, Kenneth Blanchard, *Management of organizational behavior: Utilizing human resources*, Prentice-Hall Inc.; see also William Reddin, 'The 3-D management style theory', *Training and Development Journal* (US), April 1967.

20 Robert House, Terence Mitchell, 'Path-goal theory of leadership', *Journal of Contemporary Business*, Vol. 3, 1974; see also Robert House, 'Path-goal theory of leadership: Lessons, legacy and a reformulated theory', *Leadership Quarterly*, Vol. 7, No. 3, pp. 323–352.

21 Harold J. Leavitt, *Corporate pathfinders: Building vision and values into organizations*, Dow Jones-Irwin, 1986.

22 Peter Cosgrove, 'Leading in Australia: Boyer Lecture No. 3', *ABC Radio National*, 22 November 2009.

23 ibid.

24 Kris Cole (author), case study based on telephone conversations with Professor Gavin Andrews and Jessica Smith, clinical trials manager, May 2014.

CHAPTER

11

UNDERSTANDING ENGAGEMENT, MOTIVATION AND RETENTION

After completing this chapter, you will be able to:

11.1 explain the difference between motivation and engagement and why they matter, and recognise the factors that engage employees

11.2 identify what motivates people

11.3 encourage people's motivation

11.4 help your organisation retain valuable employees.

TRANSFERABLE SKILLS

The following transferable skills are covered in this chapter:

3 Social competence

3.1 Teamwork/relationships

3.4 Leadership

OVERVIEW

Consider the following conundrum: we have two organisations of a similar size that offer a similar product, have an equal market share, are subject to the same market forces and have leader-managers and employees with similar skill sets. For all intents and purposes, they are identical. But while one is performing satisfactorily, the other's performance is exceptional. In fact, the second organisation's results are not only outstanding, but they are also still improving at an exponential rate, leaving the other organisation in its wake. How can this be for two organisations that are so similar? The answer lies not in the skills of its employees, but in their motivation and level of engagement. These are the two key ingredients that every leader-manager needs to unlock in their employees to create a high-performance team. Without them, a team may perform well, for a while, but gradually team members will move to other organisations and performance will decline accordingly. Motivating and engaging team members is therefore not only vital to achieve high-performance, but it is also an imperative for retaining talented employees as well as solid reliable performers who might otherwise go elsewhere.

Job contracts don't stipulate how hard an employee must work, how much cooperation and effort they must invest in their job, how much they must identify with and feel loyalty towards the organisation, or how long they must remain in the job. In short, a job contract provides no guarantees about an employee's motivation, engagement or retention. How hard an employee works, and the degree to which they commit to an organisation's values and strive to achieve its vision, are entirely up to them.

It is inevitable, therefore, that every leader-manager will at some stage have to ask the question: 'How do I motivate my staff?' But there is no single answer to this question – different staff are motivated by different things. This chapter explores the different aspects and theories of motivation as they apply to employees. It also examines the strategies that leader-managers can employ to keep their team members engaged, motivated and striving to perform at the highest level.

SNAPSHOT

The motivation to retain

It was late November and, once again, Josie's team members were waiting for their contract renewals to confirm their ongoing employment for the following calendar year. Being offered only one-year contracts was one thing, but for each of the six team members, not knowing until this late in the year whether they would even be offered a contract was extremely stressful and made planning their financial commitments for the following year next to impossible. On top of that, it had been a hard year, full of challenging projects and difficult clients.

Gil, one of the most experienced in the team, was feeling burnt out and in need of a break. At the other end of the spectrum was Rani, who had only joined the team 11 months ago. Initially starting full of enthusiasm, when she found out halfway through the year that she was being paid 30 per cent less than her more experienced colleagues, she had become disgruntled and agitated, and had even raised the matter with the HR manager, but to no avail. Her work output had steadily decreased over the five months following.

Sophia was the 'star performer' of the team. Her knowledge and skills were at the elite level, and she was at the top of her field, but because of this, whenever a really difficult project came along, it would always be assigned to her. For once, she would like to work on one of the easier projects that seemed to always be assigned to other members of the team. As this didn't seem likely to occur any time soon, she had taken matters into her own hands by consciously reducing her productivity in an attempt to make the allocation of work tasks fairer among the team.

Connor, Carly and Haley rounded out the team. Their skills were at a similar level, but they were all very different. Connor thrived on lively discussion and debate and working with other team members to come up with solutions. He was always animated and was forever coming up with new ideas and ways of doing things. Carly was the opposite; reserved, very task focused and preferred to simply come to work, achieve her daily goals and go home, not thinking about work again until the next day. Haley was the go-getter of the team. While she enjoyed her job, she was anxious to move up the organisational hierarchy as quickly as possible. She wanted more responsibility, more power and more money. She also wanted more job certainty, having just bought a house.

On 8 December, Josie finally announced that the contracts were ready. Once again, they were only for one year, ending on 31 December the following year. No one received a pay rise and for all intents and purposes, it would be business as usual going forward. Over the next two weeks, two of the team handed in their resignations and Gil applied for extended leave due to mental health issues. Ignoring the Christmas public holidays, it was less than a week before the new year would commence, and Josie had just lost half of her team. 'How did this happen', she thought, but, perhaps more importantly, how could it have been avoided?

11.1 Engaging employees

> You can buy a person's time. You can buy their physical presence at a given place. You can even buy a measured number of their skilled muscular motions per hour. But you cannot buy their enthusiasm or loyalty, the devotion of their hearts, their minds and souls. You must earn these.
>
> Clarence Francis (US businessman), in W. Bickham, *Liberating the human spirit in the workplace*, Irwin, 1996, p. 60.

Organisational success depends, to a significant degree, on the commitment, innovation and productivity of its employees. For employees to be committed, innovative and productive, and remain so, they need to be both engaged and motivated. Motivation is innate; it comes from within and provides an employee with the desire to do their job well, as well as a willingness to invest their effort and energy in their work. Engagement relates to the level of commitment an employee feels towards their organisation as a whole, not just to their job. Together, motivation and engagement inspire employees to put the extra effort into their work – extra time, energy and brain power to achieve that elite level of performance. The good news is, the more motivated and engaged an employee is, the more likely it is that their organisation will be able to retain them over the longer term.

INDUSTRY INSIGHTS

Loyalty lives

Apple's cult following means it has no shortage of job applicants and the retention rate in its Australian retail stores is 81 per cent – almost unheard of in the retail industry. The Apple culture engages employees and turns every job into a mission, allowing Apple to pay its employees a modest hourly wage and no commission. Yet they remain fiercely loyal.[1]

The bottom line benefits of engagement

There are many benefits to ensuring your employees are engaged. Engaged employees have 20 per cent higher performance and are at 87 per cent less risk of leaving the organisation.[2] They are also more loyal and enjoy better health and personal wellbeing than unengaged employees, and their enhanced feelings of self-worth reduce attrition and absenteeism. Organisations with engaged employees are significantly more profitable and have higher customer ratings and fewer safety incidents than those with actively disengaged employees, and they benefit from increased agility and improved efficiency in driving change initiatives.[3] The higher the ratio of engaged to disengaged employees, the better an organisation's performance.[4] But there is one caveat of which to be careful – highly engaged employees are at risk of burning out.[5]

Assessing the level of motivation and engagement of employees is not difficult. Measuring the factors shown in Table 11.1 for groups of employees, and comparing the measures with other similar organisations and organisations in the same area or industry, can provide motivation and engagement trends over time.

TABLE 11.1 Measuring motivation and engagement

Measuring motivation	Measuring engagement
Absenteeism/attendance	Attrition/retention
Attrition/retention	Costs per hire
Presenteeism	Revenue generated per employee compared with competitors
	Productivity improvement rates per employee
	Time to fill high revenue-generating positions

INDUSTRY INSIGHTS

Engagement pays

Brands like Baileys, Bundaberg Rum, Guinness, Johnnie Walker and Smirnoff have made Diageo the world's leading premium drinks producer. Four of the company's five values are closely linked to driving engagement:

1. Be the best.
2. Freedom to succeed.
3. Proud of what we do.
4. Value each other.

Diageo measures employee engagement through six questions in its annual employee survey. An employee that gives the most positive response to all six questions is super-engaged, the level the company is targeting. Quarterly surveys of three or four questions on topical issues around employee satisfaction measure progress by framing the questions in terms of whether they're doing better compared to a year ago.

The phrase 'Know me, focus on me and value me' guides leader-managers' conversations with employees when setting objectives and discussing career aspirations and development plans. The senior leadership team has a monthly agenda item on employee engagement and the team holds regular meetings with groups of 20 to 25 employees so they can ask questions and say what's on their minds.

Results have been impressive. The percentage of super-engaged employees doubled from 25 per cent to 50 per cent in three years and voluntary turnover dropped from 18.4 per cent to 13.5 per cent in 12 months, providing a measurable saving in recruitment costs.[6]

Three foundations of engagement

Transferable skills

3.1 Teamwork/relationships

3.4 Leadership

Organisations set the scene for engagement at a broad policy and strategic level, while individual leader-managers set the scene for motivation in their relationships with employees and the work they assign them. But fundamental to engaging employees is a leader-manager's ability to build, nurture and maintain positive relationships with their team members. They also need to be able to instil a team culture based on trust and integrity, ensure each employee is doing valuable work and is acknowledged for it, and keep team members connected with the organisation's vision and values. These aspects can be summarised as being the three Cs of engagement: connection, contribution and credibility.

Connection

Transferable skills

3.1 Teamwork/relationships

3.4 Leadership

Human beings are one of the most social species on the planet. Our need for connection brings us happiness, security, support and a sense of purpose. It forms an essential part in almost every aspect of our physical, social and psychological wellbeing. This need does not end when we step into the workplace. Understanding and relating to your organisation's goals and **vision**, and how the work you do contributes to achieving them, forms a significant part of your connection to your organisation. Combined with a sense of team unity, trust between team members and their leaders as well as with each other creates strong bonds between employees and their organisation. Keeping employees informed about what is happening in the organisation helps to maintain that trust. Additionally, seeking employees' ideas for improvement through effective upward feedback channels deepens the mutual sense of connection an employee feels with their organisation. Managing employees fairly and leading and acting with integrity demonstrates respect and provides employees with a feeling of security and safety. Taking the time to show interest in an employee by assisting them with planning their work goals and career aspirations, and making authentic enquires about their outside interests and relationships, increases the connection still further.

 INDUSTRY INSIGHTS

Engagement after death

Free gourmet food, fitness classes, haircuts, laundry services, company shares and car washes – what next? Regardless of how long you've worked there, Google pays the partner or spouse of a deceased employee half their salary for 10 years plus access to the deceased employee's shares, and pays the children US$1000 a month until they turn 19 (or 23 if the child is a full-time student). Although that must drive engagement and provide a powerful incentive to stay, Google says it's taking this approach because 'it's the right thing to do'.[7]

Contribution

For an employee to feel as though they have made a meaningful contribution they need to be placed in the right job; one that utilises their strengths and provides them with job satisfaction. The job must therefore be well designed and provide the employee with the opportunity to achieve results that contribute to both their team's and the organisation's goals. Knowing precisely what is expected of them, being supported with the resources they need to do their work and receiving an appropriate level of rewards and recognition for their contribution also forms part of this reciprocal relationship. Contribution can also include providing an employee with autonomy and flexibility in their roles, clear career paths, a chance to learn and grow in their job, and opportunities to develop skills and knowledge. This can help them to remain interested and feel 'fresh' in their role and steadily build engagement.

Credibility

Transferable skills
3.4 Leadership
3.1 Teamwork/relationships

An organisation's reputation for integrity, as evidenced by their commitment to corporate social responsibility, their employer brand and employer value proposition, are becoming increasingly important considerations for employees when choosing a new employer. Having a leader-manager who manages fairly, with integrity, and who acknowledges and appreciates their efforts will also be a significant factor in an employee's decision to remain with an organisation or go elsewhere. Building rapport and trust with their team members, showing them loyalty by backing and advocating for them, and communicating openly and honestly creates a positive team culture for which the reward is a committed and loyal team.

When countless **moments of truth**, or interactions, between employees, their leader-manager, other leader-managers and the organisation itself add up to an intrinsically rewarding work experience, employees feel appreciated, respected and valued. In this environment, employees form a bond with their team and organisation and strive to perform to the best of their ability.

Importance of job placement

Engagement levels may also vary according to seniority, occupation and length of service in an organisation, although not by sector. On the whole, more senior employees, hands-on employees and operational employees are all more likely to be engaged, while professionals and support staff are more likely to have the lowest levels of engagement, although this varies between organisations.[8]

Employees' perceptions of their workplace can also be influenced by where they live, their national culture, the stage of their country's economic development and their social environment.[9] Ultimately, engagement is a choice and depends upon what individual employees deem worthy of investing themselves in. This highlights the importance of correct **job placement**, not just between the employee and the job, but also between the employee and the organisation and its employer brand and employer value proposition.

The three levels of engagement

There are three levels of employee engagement, as shown in Figure 11.1: engaged, actively disengaged, and satisfied but not engaged. *Engaged employees* work with passion and pride. They identify with and are committed to their organisation's values and vision and voluntarily perform at levels that exceed their stated job requirements to help their organisation succeed. They see a direct connection between their efforts and the organisation's results and enjoy their jobs and the organisation they work for. They are even likely to act as advocates and recruiters for their organisation, encouraging those within their professional network to join them.

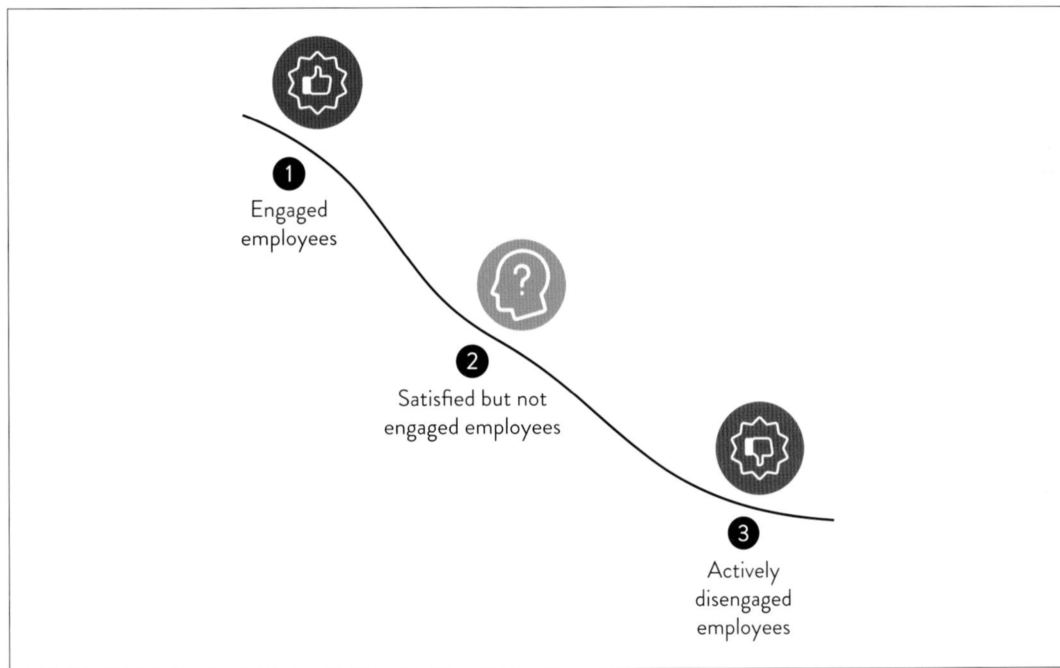

FIGURE 11.1 Levels of engagement

At the other end of the scale are *actively disengaged employees*. Their reason for coming to work is to get paid. They are likely to be actively looking for a job elsewhere. They are often so unhappy in their work that they undermine what their engaged colleagues accomplish and trash their organisation's reputation at every opportunity, draining their organisations of positivity and goodwill. Their active disengagement costs the Australian economy about $305 billion a year.[10]

In between engaged and disengaged employees are *satisfied but not engaged employees*. They might be quite content doing their jobs and put time – but not energy or passion – into their work. When something better comes along, it's easy for them to leave for greener pastures.

The engagement challenge

In Australia and New Zealand in 2013, 24 per cent of employees were engaged while 60 per cent were not engaged and 16 per cent were actively disengaged. The resulting ratio of engaged to actively disengaged employees – 1.5:1 – was one of the highest among all global regions and similar to results from the US and Canada (1.6:1). At this time, Australia was among the global leaders in the ratio of motivated and productive (engaged) employees versus the negative and disruptive (actively disengaged) employees in its workplaces.

Four years later, the news was not so good. The percentage of workers in Australia and New Zealand who were engaged had fallen sharply to 14 per cent. Of equal concern was the increased number of employees who were not engaged, jumping to 71 per cent with 15 per cent actively disengaged, ranking Australia 7th out of 11 global regions.[11] It was sobering reading. An even more recent study conducted by the ADP Research Institute in 2020 found the percentage of workers in Australia who were engaged had fallen even further to 13 per cent.[12]

Workplaces that are not psychologically safe, offer inadequate supervisory support, place unreasonable physical or psychological demands on employees, and afford workers little control over how they undertake their work roles are suggested to have contributed to this decline. Turning around this trend is imperative for Australian organisations and their leaders if they are to remain competitive in an already uncertain global market environment caused by the COVID-19 pandemic. This challenge will require leader-managers and organisations to:

- ensure they create and maintain psychologically safe work environments that are free from harassment, discrimination and bullying, and where employees feel comfortable and reassured in putting forward their views, ideas and concerns
- provide the supervisory and managerial support to their employees to enable them to perform their work role to the best of their ability
- ensure they clearly articulate the organisation's values and vision to their employees, align employees' work roles with the organisation's mission, and lead and manage in an authentic manner which reinforces their commitment to each.

How to be an engaging leader-manager

Engaging leader-managers may display many different characteristics. Some may be energetic extroverts, others shy and quiet; some are creative, others highly practical and still others intellectual. But the one thing they share is the impact on how they make their employees feel.

Transferable skills

3.1 Teamwork/relationships

3.4 Leadership

Engaging leader-managers are described as protectors, steadfast, able to keep calm in busy and confusing environments, and willing to stand by their beliefs and principles. They listen to employees, value them as people and involve them. They're approachable, honest and open, supportive and encouraging, and they develop people's skills and 'keep things interesting'. By developing quality relationships with their employees, they invite engagement and receive it in return. They are also good two-way communicators and give frequent positive, **constructive** and **corrective feedback**, using an encouraging, informal, coaching style. They respect and take an interest in people as individuals and develop and nurture their skills. At the same time, they have high standards, set clear goals and expectations, and address performance problems quickly, firmly and fairly. When they need to resort to dismissal in order to protect their team and their team's performance, they do so with empathy and follow the correct procedures.

Transferable skills

3.4 Leadership

Engaging leader-managers see the big picture and take immediate action when plans go wrong. They motivate employees and give them autonomy while making it clear they are there to support them when necessary. When employees need help, they guide them to solve problems, rather than hand them a solution on a plate.

Engaging leader-managers build strong teams where members work well together, 'share ups and downs' and help each other out. They are clear about the contribution of individual team members to the team as a whole and present their team in a positive light to the rest of the organisation and its supply chain. They encourage ideas and suggestions and are willing to make changes to improve workflow and work methods. They let team members work to their strengths and allow them be themselves. Feeling more comfortable being themselves, employees are likely to be more invested in their work and feel secure to engage more freely with their work team.

These traits can be learnt and honed over time and with experience, along with other behaviours, such as:

- articulating and agreeing upon clear goals
- allocating resources fairly
- encouraging and supporting their employees to achieve a better work–life balance
- including their team members in decision-making processes
- providing employees with development and learning opportunities
- leading in a manner that people respect
- providing worthwhile, meaningful work that fits into the organisation's and employees' value systems and matches their skills, strengths and interests.

11.2 Motivating employees

> In order that people may be happy in their work, these three things are needed: they must be fit for it; they must not do too much of it; and they must have a sense of success in it.
>
> John Ruskin (19th-century social reformer), *Pre-Raphaelitism*, Wiley, 1880, p. 7.

Skills, knowledge, self-belief and confidence – all key attributes to performing well and being successful. But without motivation, performance at an elite level will prove elusive. Motivation is the foundation upon which success is built. It is the key that unlocks a person's desire to go that extra step, put in that additional effort, continue to progress forward when faced with difficult times and strive for perfection.

But what is motivation? Motivation isn't about lighting a fire *under* a person – it's about lighting a fire *within*. Motivation is the internal engine that gets a person 'moving'. Knowing how to rev up the engine is perhaps the most powerful management tool a leader-manager can possess.

INDUSTRY INSIGHTS

Finding the gold within

Andrew Carnegie, the renowned steel magnate of the early 1900s, was at one time the wealthiest man in America. At one point, he had 43 millionaires working for him. These employees weren't millionaires when they began working for Carnegie; they became millionaires while working for him. When asked how he had developed them to become so valuable, he replied, 'Men are developed the same way gold is mined. When gold is mined, several tons of dirt must be moved to get one ounce of gold. But one doesn't go into the mine looking for dirt. One goes in looking for the gold.'[13]

Charles Schwab was the first person to earn more than US$1 million a year in Andrew Carnegie's steel mills. When asked what equipped him to earn US$3000 a day – was it his vast knowledge of steel – he replied, 'Nonsense! Lots of people work here who know lots more about steel than I do. I can inspire people. I consider my ability to arouse enthusiasm among employees, the greatest asset I possess.'[14]

What motivates?

The debate about what motivates people has raged for many years and continues to attract different theories and opinions. In the following sections we will discuss three of the most common explanations: fear, laziness and money.

Fear

Is fear a good motivator? Fear might motivate a person to drive at the speed limit to avoid a fine, turn up to work on time to avoid losing their job, or be careful with what they say to avoid embarrassing themselves or offending someone else. But this is only part of the story. These threats may light a fire under a person for a while, but generally the effect doesn't last long or work very well. Eventually, they drive faster than the allowable limit, turn up late for work and say something out of turn. The fear of the ramifications is simply not strong enough to motivate a person to maintain or change their behaviour.

The positive motivation of gaining something you want is more powerful than the negative motivation of fear and threats. But if you're tempted to motivate through fear, remember these consequences:

- Fear sets off an automatic adrenalin response in the body that triggers the fight, flight or freeze response. When managers manage through fear, employees instinctively want to either hit them, run from them or do nothing (or at least as little as possible) lest they do something else 'wrong'.
- Fear loses its power as people become accustomed to the threats.
- To motivate employees by fear, you must supervise them often and closely, which reduces your own productivity.

The conventional wisdom is to forget about using fear as your main motivational tool. Perhaps pull it out for particular employees in particular situations, but on the whole it will prove ineffective.

Laziness

There are no unmotivated people, only unmotivated employees. This popular saying is often true. Have you ever watched people rushing off home at the end of their shift? How many anglers do you know who leap out of bed at 3 a.m. to go on a fishing trip? Or perhaps you know skiers who are happy standing in freezing temperatures waiting for the chair lift, anticipating the run down the mountain? People are motivated to do things when they receive something they want in return.

Most people aren't inherently lazy. You probably don't like being lethargic and bored – neither do most employees. People welcome leader-managers who can help them enjoy their jobs and feel satisfied doing them. So, you don't have to worry about transforming lazy, unmotivated employees into industrious 'workaholics'. You just need to channel their existing energies into desirable work performance.

Money

Like fear, the theory that money motivates seduces many people. After all, it is undeniable that many employees calculate how much effort to put into a job based on how much money they receive in return for their efforts. Not only does this sound sensible, it also sounds fair and equitable. But how far will an employee go in relation to working to this 'formula'?

For repetitive or routine jobs, financial incentives, or pay for performance, can work. But that's mostly old economy, 20th-century jobs, where both white- and blue-collar jobs followed established steps. These jobs are now often automated or outsourced, which is not necessarily a bad thing – those jobs are, for the most part, dull and unsatisfying. That's why you have to coax people into doing them with external rewards and threaten them with external punishment – the old 'carrot and stick'. Even when money boosts productivity in those monotonous tasks, once the goal is achieved and the money is in your hand, productivity tends to fall.

Most jobs in Australia today are knowledge and service jobs that require creative and emotional work and brain power. Financial incentives can actually disincentivise, or reduce, performance. *Heuristic tasks*, where you have to work out what to do each time because each situation is different and calls for a novel solution, can't be automated or outsourced and, because they're generally more enjoyable and satisfying, they need intrinsic motivation.

Study after study shows that money does not motivate, at least not for long. People will forgo moving to a job that pays substantially more in order to remain working in a place where they enjoy the work and can use and develop their skills and talents and work with others in an atmosphere of mutual respect. Consider this: your manager walks up to you and says, 'My friend, in recognition of your excellent performance and because we think you're a terrific person, we have decided to double your pay.' Naturally you would be pleased and, perhaps in gratitude, work really hard for three, four or even five weeks. However, if you're like most people, you would quickly learn how to spend your increased earnings and come to take them for granted. They would then cease to motivate you, although the fear of losing them might motivate you for a little while longer!

Money is important, of course. Everybody needs it to pay for their bills, entertainment, holidays, clothes, food and so on. But as will be demonstrated, money for most people is what is known as a **hygiene factor** that helps satisfy their lower-order, or physiological and security needs. There are of course some people who do only go to work just for the money. Their reasons will vary; for example, they may be getting most of their psychological, higher-order needs met away from the workplace, or they may want to earn money to give their children a good life and educate them.

Money (in the form of a bonus, performance incentive or pay rise), when it is clearly paid to reward good performance, can motivate. In this case, though, it isn't so much the money itself that motivates but rather what it symbolises – the acknowledgement and recognition of good performance.

Climate, culture and content

Since laziness isn't a widespread problem and the carrot and stick don't motivate, what does? We've looked at the three Cs of engagement (connection, contribution and credibility). There are also three Cs of motivation: climate, culture and content. Research consistently identifies these intangible factors as much more effective ways to motivate people. They are the higher-order, psychological needs.

The importance of an organisation's climate and culture have been discussed earlier in the context of the 'informal organisation'. Job content is the third important piece of the motivation puzzle. Monotonous, boring jobs drain employees' interest and motivation and are a source of stress. Even when the surroundings and co-workers are congenial, dull jobs can still cause problems. Humans constantly seek stimulation, and when they don't receive it, or don't receive enough of it, they can fall into repetitive, harmful patterns of behaviour.

Environmental stimulation and job challenge fine-tune the brain, which is why job rotation and good job design increase job satisfaction and motivation as well as productivity. Job design refers to a job's content, or its specific duties, accountabilities and tasks. Well-designed jobs give employees autonomy, responsibility and the chance to work in teams. They provide variety, interest and challenge as well as opportunities to learn and grow, use skills and contribute ideas. Do you know the story of Sisyphus? The gods condemned him to endlessly rolling a rock up to the top of the mountain, from where it would fall back down, and he would push it up again. This tells us that even in ancient times, there was no more dreadful punishment than hopeless and futile labour. The founder of cybernetics,

Norbert Wiener, summed it up when he said, 'If the human being is condemned and restricted to perform the same functions over and over again, he will not even be a good ant, not to mention a good human being.'[15]

What do people need to be motivated?

To 'light the fire within', you need answers to the following three questions:

1 What does this person need to live a happy and satisfied life?
2 What does this person need from their work?
3 What happens when this person's needs are not met?

Values, beliefs and needs are powerful motivators for most people. Values express what a person holds dear and believes is right and wrong, good and bad, important and unimportant. Each person's values and belief systems – about themselves, others and the world around them – are unique to that person, based on their upbringing and life experiences.

Despite our apparent differences, human beings are also alike in many ways. Everyone shares the same basic needs, albeit in different strengths and combinations, and these needs combine with people's values and beliefs to motivate and guide their behaviour. Figure 11.2 gives some examples.

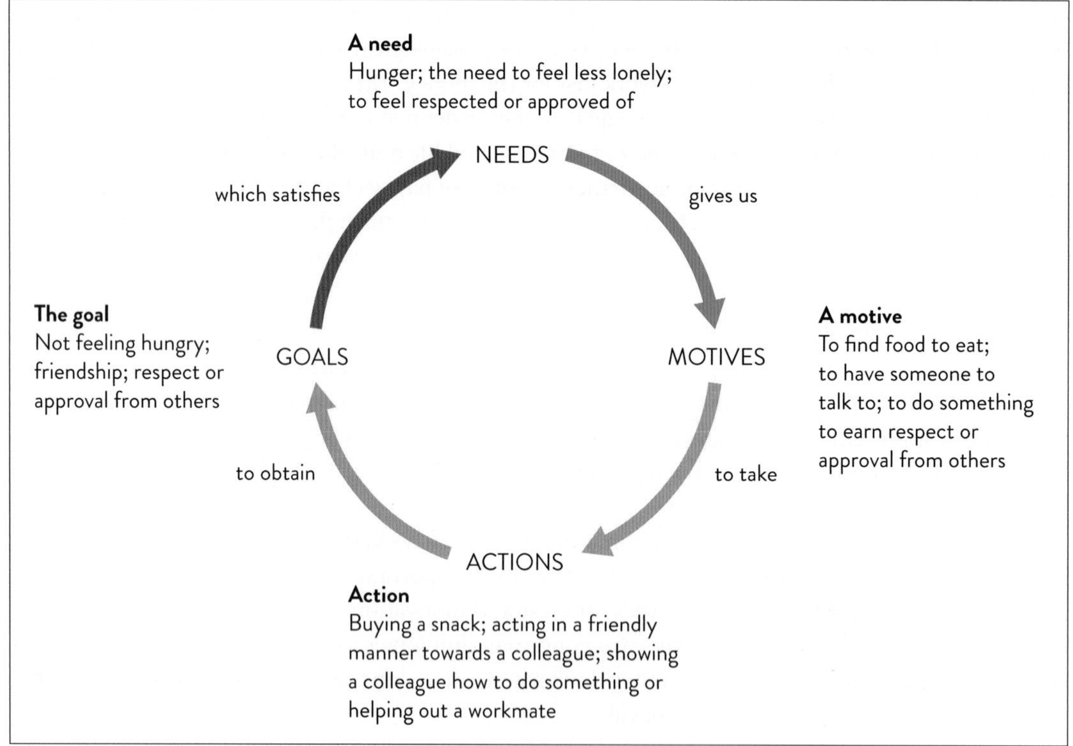

FIGURE 11.2 How needs drive goals

We consider four ways of thinking about motivation in the following sections: Maslow's hierarchy of needs, Herzberg's hygiene and motivation factors, and McClelland and Atkinson's trilogy of needs. They help to explain the basic needs that most people share. These needs motivate everyone to varying degrees, although for most people they are buried in the unconscious, so they have little or no awareness of them in their day-to-day lives.

Maslow's hierarchy of needs

Mahatma Gandhi spoke of people's basic needs when he said: ' ... those hungry millions who have no lustre in their eyes and whose only god is their bread.'[16] Human beings have physiological and psychological needs, which Abraham Maslow grouped into categories and arranged into a **hierarchy of needs**, as shown in Figure 11.3. The most basic, or lower order, physiological needs are displayed at the bottom, and once those needs are reasonably well satisfied, the person can focus on satisfying the next higher-level need – security needs. The level of need is also what primarily motivates the person.[17]

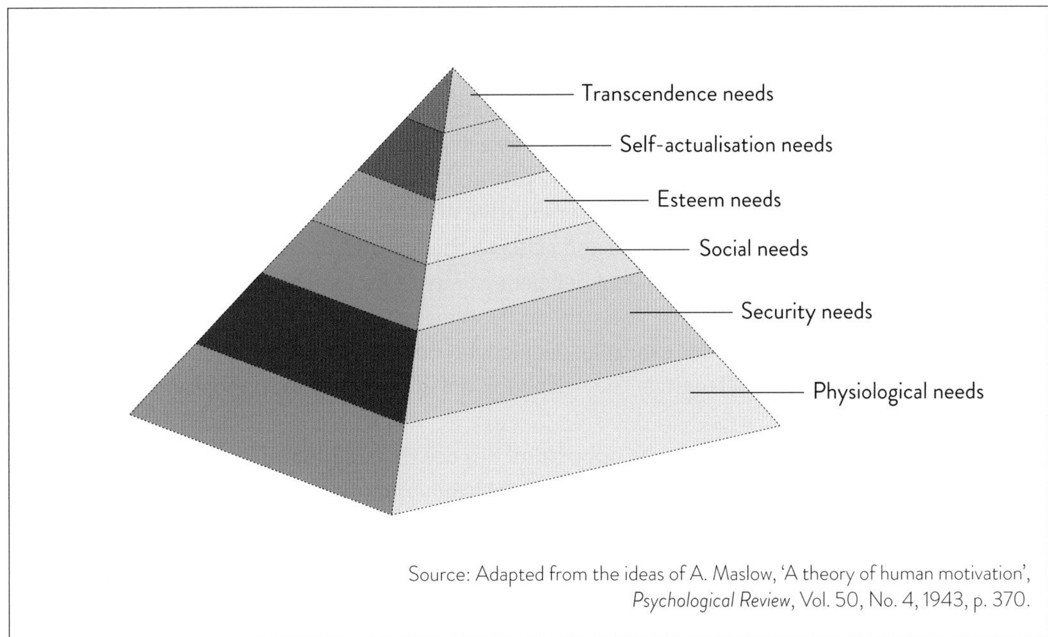

Source: Adapted from the ideas of A. Maslow, 'A theory of human motivation', *Psychological Review*, Vol. 50, No. 4, 1943, p. 370.

FIGURE 11.3 Maslow's hierarchy of needs

Consider each level, beginning at the bottom of the hierarchy, and what it might take to progress from each level to the next:

1 *Physiological needs*: this level of needs includes things people cannot live without, such as air, food, sleep, water, clothing and shelter. When any of these necessities are lacking, people spend most of their time and energy trying to obtain them.

   Organisations help to meet employees' physiological needs by providing basic working conditions, such as a safe and secure building, ergonomically designed workstations and chairs, labour-saving devices, rest periods, ventilated and temperature-controlled air, and paying a wage they can live on.

2 *Security needs*: people need to know they're safe – psychologically and physically. Once people's physiological needs are satisfied, they can turn their thoughts to satisfying their security needs. They can ensure continuity in their food and water supply, provide clothing and obtain a permanent, safe and secure shelter that protects them and their possessions from outside threats, such as the elements and other people.

   Organisations help to meet people's need for security by providing fair and just human resource policies and a safe and healthy working environment. Dependable leadership, job security, healthy working conditions and superannuation are other ways to help people feel secure in their work.

3 *Social needs*: once people have satisfied their physiological and security needs, they turn to social needs. They want to feel they 'belong' and begin to seek the company, acceptance, friendship and affection of others. Social needs are expressed, for example, in the need to be loved and to have someone to love, to be a friend and to have friends.

   Work can satisfy some social needs by providing an opportunity to be in the company of others and build friendly working relationships. Being informed, helping others out, organised employee activities, supportive management and trust can all help meet people's social needs.

4 *Esteem needs*: some esteem needs are satisfied internally, through autonomy, achievement, self-confidence and self-respect, for example. Other esteem needs are satisfied externally, through appreciation and respect from others and from status and recognition.

   Work is an important way for many people to satisfy both their internal and external esteem needs. Appreciation and recognition for work, delegated authority, opportunity for advancement, participation in decisions, status symbols, job title and responsibility can all meet esteem needs.

5 *Self-actualisation needs*: this is the need for creativity, learning, self-improvement and personal growth – the need to use your abilities and skills to the full and to reach your potential. At this level, you aren't spurred on by a sense of deficiency ('must find food', 'must make friends') but to explore and become more of what you can be. People at this level react against situations that prevent them from doing so. For example, people who find their job dull and boring often try to make it interesting and challenging. They also look outside of work for opportunities to develop and grow as a person.

   Assign work that gives people the opportunity to use their skills and learn new ones and that allows creativity, freedom to make work-related decisions and opportunities for personal growth. These can be important ways to satisfy self-actualisation needs and are under your control.

6 *Transcendence needs*: in later years, Maslow added this sixth level to his hierarchy. Transcendence includes feeling part of the greater whole as well as the need to serve and to help others achieve, find self-fulfilment and realise your potential.[18]

   At work, having 'grown' and self-actualised, people are ready to 'give back' through things like coaching, **mentoring** and passing on skills and knowledge to others in the workplace and their professional circles.

While Maslow's hierarchy can be thought of as a progression, as people move up the hierarchy, they can also move back down; for example:

- A young couple who have just taken on a large mortgage might have security as a primary motivator and step away from socialising with friends in their spare time in order to save money.
- As they near the age of retirement, many employees become concerned with security again.
- Someone with a satisfying job, a close group of friends and sufficient income, who then suddenly loses their job, might also revert to security as a key motivator.

Maslow's theory has been rigorously tested and proved correct time and again. Fulfilling the needs described in his hierarchy does indeed correlate with happiness. And, interestingly, you can also be happy if you have good social relationships and self-actualisation, even when your needs for food and safety aren't well fulfilled. To be specific, fulfilment of the lower-order needs (food and shelter) is closely linked to a positive evaluation of your life and satisfaction of the higher-order needs (respect, self-actualisation and self-transcendence), and is strongly related to enjoying your life.

Another finding is that people seem to feel more positive about their own lives when those around them also have their needs met and feel positive about their lives, and we enjoy our lives more when those around us are enjoying their lives.[19]

Herzberg's hygiene and motivation factors

Frederick Herzberg adapted Maslow's thoughts on motivation and applied them to a work setting. His model has also stood the test of time and is accepted as a credible theory in relation to motivation. While Maslow saw motivation operating across a single continuum of needs from physiological to self-transcendence, Herzberg divided people's needs into two groups of factors operating along two independent continuums. He called them hygiene factors and **motivation factors**.[20]

Hygiene factors don't motivate, but they can certainly dampen enthusiasm. They operate across a scale from dissatisfaction to no dissatisfaction, or 'neutral'. As Figure 11.4 shows, hygiene factors relate to the environment in which people do their jobs. When hygiene factors fail to meet employees' expectations, employees are dissatisfied. When an organisation meets its employees' hygiene needs, employees are in neutral and ready to be motivated by the second class of factors – *motivation factors*.

Motivation factors operate across a continuum from not motivated to highly motivated. In Figure 11.4 you can see that the work itself, not the environment in which it's done, provides job

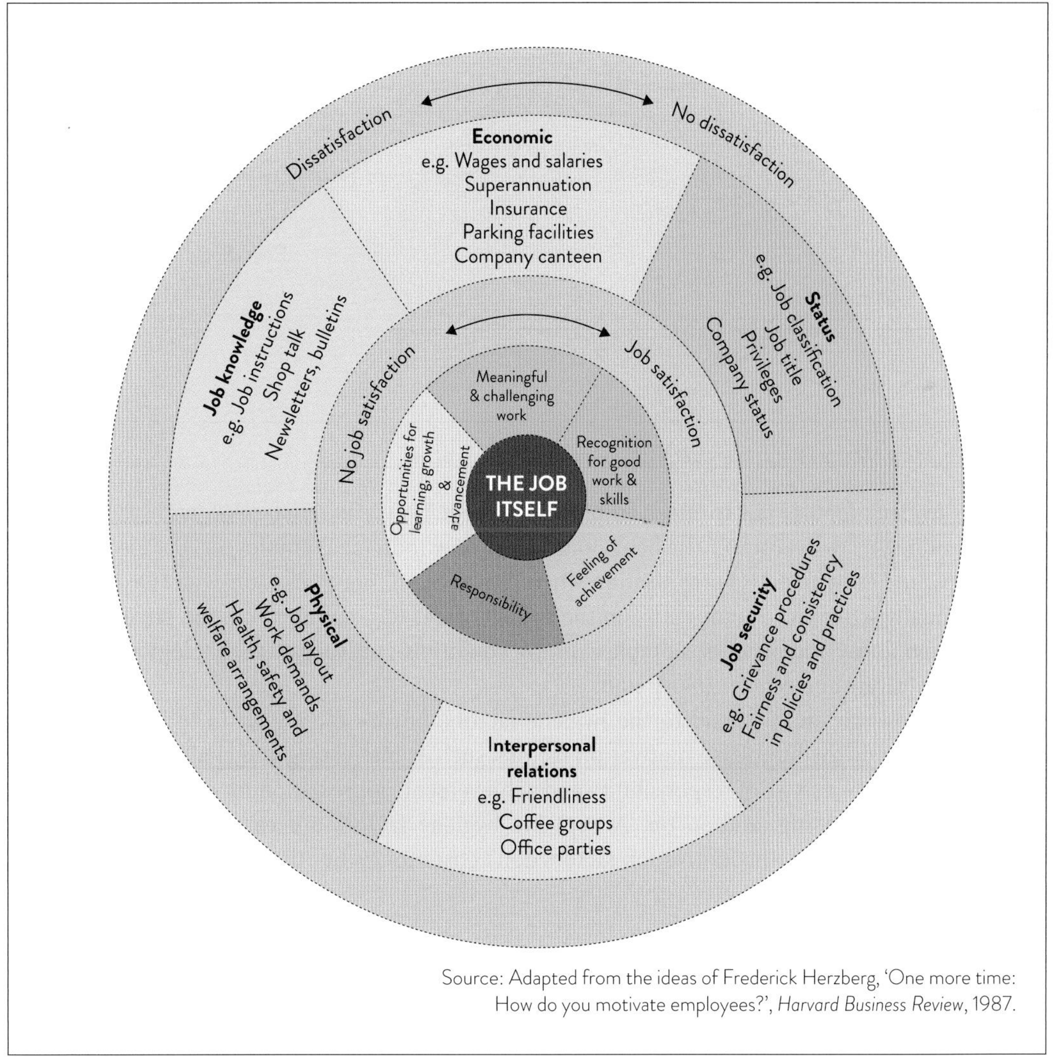

Source: Adapted from the ideas of Frederick Herzberg, 'One more time: How do you motivate employees?', *Harvard Business Review*, 1987.

FIGURE 11.4 Herzberg's hygiene and motivation factors

satisfaction and motivation. For example, employees need to be paid enough to ensure that money isn't a motivating factor. Once people consider their working terms and conditions (hygiene factors) to be adequate, they can find motivation when doing their jobs gives them satisfaction by providing meaningful and challenging work, a sense of accomplishment, recognition and responsibility, and opportunities to continue to learn and advance – or some combination of these factors. This illustrates the importance of climate, culture and content.

Figure 11.5 shows the relationship between Maslow's and Herzberg's ideas about motivation. Herzberg's hygiene factors relate roughly to the lower three levels of Maslow's hierarchy (physiological, security and social needs) and the motivators relate to the top levels (esteem, self-actualisation and self-transcendence needs).

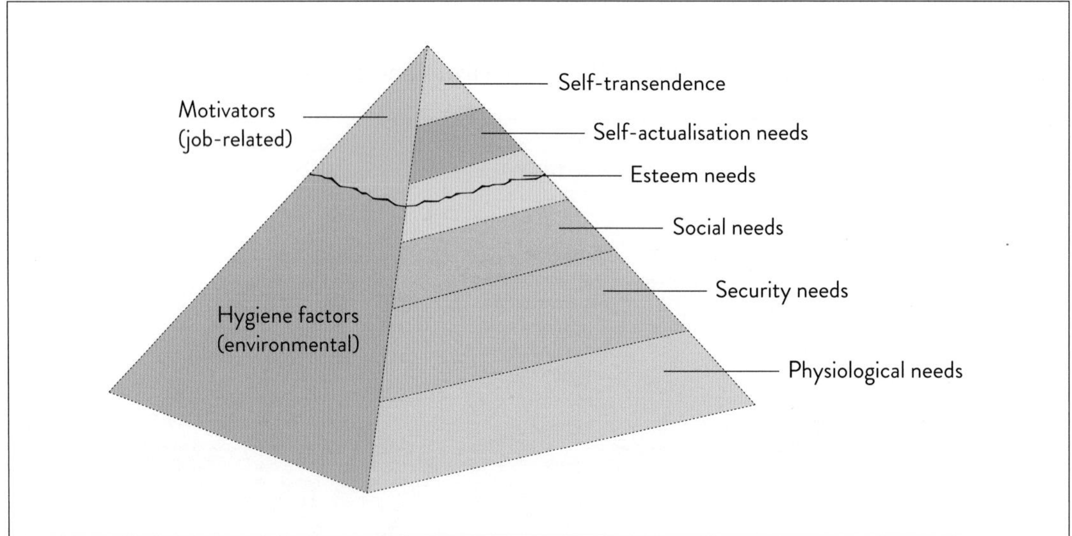

FIGURE 11.5 How Maslow's and Herzberg's ideas relate to each other

When hygiene factors fail to meet employees' expectations, dissatisfaction with the working environment begins to overpower the behaviour of not only individual employees, but also of whole work groups, and even an entire organisation when the problem is organisation-wide. Organisations must continually strive to be competitive in the hygiene areas (e.g. comfortable and attractive office furnishings, good pay and benefits, suitable working conditions, up-to-date technology, etc.) so they can attract, motivate and retain quality staff.

Organisations generally attend to the hygiene factors, but it's mostly up to individual leader-managers to provide the intangible motivation factors, such as interesting and challenging jobs with clear goals that allow a sense of responsibility and achievement, appreciation for one's contributions, opportunities for learning, and so on. Acceptable hygiene factors are easy enough to provide, although they cost money. The motivation factors don't cost money, but they do require high-calibre leader-managers.

McClelland and Atkinson's trilogy of needs

Maslow's hierarchy looks at innate, or inborn, needs. David McClelland and John Atkinson see these needs as being modified as people interact with their environment. Their model relates behaviour to three needs directly relevant to business drive and management:[21]

1 *Need for achievement:* (similar to Maslow's self-actualisation needs) the need to achieve, accomplish and make progress. People motivated by achievement are independent and gain

personal satisfaction from performing a task well; this means that in the right circumstances, they are high performers. They also need feedback on their achievement. Sportspeople, leader-managers and others with a strong achievement motive often excel in their fields.

2 *Need for affiliation:* (similar to Maslow's social and esteem needs) the need or desire to be with others or to belong to a group and be accepted, liked and held in popular regard. People motivated by affiliation often deal well with the public and make good customer service staff. Research has found that many Asian managers have high affiliation needs.

3 *Need for power:* the need for control, to be influential, to make an impact. Some individuals have an intense desire to be in charge and in a position of authority, for their ideas to prevail, and for personal status and prestige. Research has found that many managers in Western cultures have a high need for power.

Everyone has each of these three needs to some extent. The strength of each need relative to the others gives people their own unique 'needs profile', which affects their behaviour and working/management style. The task of leader-managers is therefore to identify the needs profile of each of their team members and meet it in ways that are within their control.

Proven ways to motivate employees

Here are some positive motivating strategies that you might consider implementing with your own team:

- Allow personal freedom with as few rules as possible; both being in charge and controlling one's own destiny motivate people who savour a high-risk, high-rewards environment.
- Build a culture of camaraderie and collaboration that values teamwork, openness and friendship. This will motivate people who enjoy working with others they trust and like and will help satisfy employees' social and esteem needs. Structure your team in a way that invites an exchange of ideas, interdependence and mutual support. Australia's basic mateship system encourages people to help one another, so ensure employees feel able to ask for and offer help and assistance.
- Build a sense of pride in the organisation's and your work team's mission, accomplishments and values; this motivates and engages most people.
- Build self-esteem and confidence because high self-esteem and confidence helps people perform at their best. This is one of the unrecognised keys to motivation.
- Consistently recognise employees' efforts.
- Make everyone a winner because nothing succeeds like success. Give every employee the opportunity to make a worthwhile contribution and be successful, or at least make a significant contribution to the team's success. Give credit to everyone involved in success.
- Match people with jobs and career paths that offer the greatest opportunity for satisfying their particular needs and that make the best use of their particular skills and abilities; then make sure that they understand precisely what is required of them.
- Match your thank-you strategy and its delivery to the person when recognising employees; for example, shy people may not feel comfortable being recognised in front of a large group, so do this in private.
- Offer well-designed jobs with clear measures of success and easy ways to track results. Worthwhile, interesting and challenging work motivates people who are into learning and developing their skills and abilities and who want to make a meaningful contribution and knowing what is expected, why it matters and how they are doing.

- Provide rewards employees value and connect them clearly to good job performance.
- Show appreciation and celebrate, because recognising and celebrating accomplishments motivates people who want a fun, supportive and interactive environment.
- Recognise people for the quality of their individual performance and the value they add to the work team as this motivates people who enjoy achieving goals and earning the respect of others.

Four basic emotional needs

Research from the fields of neuroscience, biology and evolutionary psychology combine with motivational research to identify four basic emotional needs that drive people. These four needs, or drives, are the product of our common evolutionary heritage. Because these four needs are hardwired into the human brain, the degree to which they are satisfied directly affects employees' emotions and, therefore, their behaviour in terms of how they work. They include:

- *The drive to acquire:* (similar to Maslow's esteem needs and McClelland and Atkinson's need for power) people are driven to acquire items that enhance their sense of wellbeing. This includes physical goods like clothing, housing and money, experiences like entertainment and travel, and indicators of status, such as a promotion and a private office.

  The organisation's reward system is perfect for satisfying this need, provided it discriminates between good and poor performers, ties rewards to performance and offers the best performers opportunities for advancement.
- *The drive to bond:* (similar to Maslow's social needs and McClelland and Atkinson's need for affiliation) human beings need to connect not only with their parents and kinship group, but also with larger collectives, such as organisations, associations and nations. Motivation receives an enormous boost when employees feel proud to belong to an organisation and it plummets when the organisation betrays them.

  An organisational culture that engenders a strong sense of 'us' and a team spirit, collaboration, friendship, openness and pride is the best way to satisfy the need to bond.
- *The drive to comprehend:* (similar to Maslow's self-actualisation needs and McClelland and Atkinson's need for achievement) people need to make sense of the world around them and contribute to it, which explains why learning and working out answers engages and energises employees.

  Job design is the key to satisfying this need – challenging, interesting, meaningful jobs that encourage employees to grow and learn motivate and retain employees, while dead-end, monotonous jobs demoralise and encourage attrition.
- *The drive to defend:* (similar to Maslow's security needs and somewhat to McClelland and Atkinson's need for power) as part of the fight, flight or freeze response, people naturally defend themselves, their family and friends, their property, and their accomplishments, beliefs and ideas against external threats. This extends to the desire for clear goals, **procedural fairness** and processes that allow people to express their ideas and opinions. Fulfilling this drive leads to feeling secure and confident while not fulfilling it leads to resentment and fear.

  Fair, transparent, trustworthy procedures for allocating resources, dealing with grievances, making decisions and managing performance, and policies and programs for enhancing work–life balance and employee welfare, satisfy this need.

An organisation's willingness and ability to meet the four needs explains employees' variance on the motivational indicators of engagement, satisfaction and commitment. It is necessary, therefore, that both organisations *and* individual leader-managers address all four of these drives to maintain employee motivation. In fact, individual leader-managers influence overall motivation as much as organisational policy. As with McClelland and Atkinson's ideas about motivation, the drives are independent, and people have each of them in different proportions (their needs profile). This makes it unwise, for example, to pay employees a lot (drive to acquire) and ignore their need to bond.

Employees may or may not be familiar with motivational theory, but they instinctively realise that many aspects linked to engagement and motivation are out of their boss' hands because they are a matter of organisational policy. However, employees also realise that many factors are squarely in their boss' hands.

11.3 Encouraging motivation

> If you want to build a ship, don't drum up people to collect wood and assign them tasks and work. Rather, teach them to long for the endless immensity of the sea.
>
> Attributed to Antoine de Saint-Exupéry (French author, aviator), quoted in M. Kruase, *Sell or sink: Strategies, tactics and tools every business leader must know to stay afloat!*, AuthorHouse, Bloomington, 2011, p. xii.

Motivation theory shows us that, although they're important for attracting and retaining employees, the lower-order needs, or hygiene factors, aren't good motivators. It's the higher-order, psychological needs that motivate. The interesting nature of work attracts people's best efforts, and this again highlights the importance of correct job placement.

With so many ways to appeal to people's higher-order needs, the question becomes: which ways are going to work best with which employees?

The secret to motivation: instilling belief and providing the reward

How highly people are motivated depends on how they answer three questions:[22]

1. *How hard will I have to work?* People need to know they have the necessary skills and the right resources (tools and equipment, time and information, etc. – see the section 'The Chance To Key' in Chapter 19) to succeed.
2. *What's in it for me if I do it?* People need to understand the relationship between performance and rewards and trust that they will receive those rewards.
3. *Is the reward worth my effort?* When someone wants better work–life balance, offering more money for overtime probably won't work.

When people believe they can succeed at the task and know they'll receive something they value in return, they'll be motivated. When they don't think they can succeed at the task or that it is too hard, or when they don't value the rewards on offer, they won't be motivated. Therein lies the secret to motivation – helping employees to believe that they can succeed and then letting them know they will receive something they want in return for succeeding. This will only work of course if you have taken the trouble to find out what each employee's needs are and how they can be satisfied in ways that are important to them for which, in return, they will deliver higher productivity and performance.

It is also worth remembering that as a need becomes satisfied, it tends to lose its importance as a motivator and another need replaces it, even if it's only 'more' of the same – a bigger bonus, a better office, more training or more responsibility. Don't forget also that while people may have similar needs, they have them in different combinations and express them differently, so their needs will need to be met in different ways.

The consequences of not meeting motivation needs

There are many employees who are not motivated because their motivation needs are not being met. It could be because they are in the wrong job, their employer or leader-manager has not made the effort to find out what motivates them or some other reason. The potential consequence is that you will end up having zombie employees who trudge in and out of work each day and simply go 'through the motions'. If you're lucky, they will just barely fulfil the requirements of their job role. If you're unlucky, you'll end up with workers who purposely go out of their way to do as little as possible and become the undercurrent of dissatisfaction and dissent.

When jobs don't satisfy enough of people's needs or satisfy them well enough, people still try to meet them in one of two ways:

1. They try to satisfy their needs off the job, perhaps by involving themselves in local clubs, undertaking volunteer work or taking up sports – whatever activity will provide them with a forum for having their needs satisfied. While the outlet they choose may help to meet their needs, the likely downside is that while they are motivated outside of work, the opposite becomes true when they are at work. They are likely to withdraw from their job and becoming unengaged 'nine-to-fivers', doing only the bare minimum – the zombie employee described earlier.
2. They become frustrated and express their frustration on the job, making life difficult for their leader-manager by arguing every little point, refusing to cooperate, stalling decision-making processes and even engaging in subtle acts of sabotage and malicious compliance. The dysfunction and division they cause eventually leaves their leader-manager with no option but to take action to terminate their employment. The damage done by this stage, however, may be substantial and take a long time to repair.

When employees keep asking for more

People seldom demand more responsibility, more respect or greater challenge, but commonly ask for more pay, better superannuation plans, better lighting and more comfortable desks and chairs. This is especially true when jobs fail to satisfy people's higher-order needs. Under these circumstances, when you 'give people what they ask for' and they still complain and lack motivation, it may be that what they asked for was not what they really wanted. Attempts to satisfy higher-order needs with better hygiene factors that target lower-order needs fail because satisfactory hygiene factors only put people in 'neutral', so that they can be motivated when their higher-order needs are satisfied. Therefore, don't forget the golden rule – hygiene factors don't motivate people, motivation factors do.

11.4 Retaining employees

> The brain is a wonderful organ. It starts working the moment you get up in the morning and it does not stop until you get into the office.
>
> Robert Frost (poet), quoted in S. Rathus, *Psychology: Concepts & connections*, Wadsworth, Belmont, 2013, p. 60.

The quote above is obviously a humorous take on how people may turn off their brains once at work but is, of course, completely untrue. Your brain never stops working, even when you're in a boring meeting or asleep. But what matters is what your brain is devoting its attention to – is it focused on the job at hand or on plans for the weekend?

No longer is it only **presenteeism** and poor productivity that managers need to worry about. Today's employees demand more from their employers and when employers don't deliver, they are happy to walk, or at the very least, rein in their efforts while they look for a new role.

Every time an employee leaves, you're faced with finding someone willing and able to fill the vacancy, bringing the replacement 'up to speed', and stabilising working relationships within your team and with customers and suppliers.

There are two types of voluntary employee turnover:

1 *Push turnover:* when the organisation is so bad it pushes people out.
2 *Pull turnover:* when the organisation is good but another organisation pulls the employee out.

The less engaged employees are, and the weaker the employer value proposition is, the more likely are both types of attrition. Conversely, organisations with a stronger employer brand and employer value proposition find it easy to retain the employees they want and to 'pull' the employees they want from other organisations.

Employee turnover

Recruitment and selection processes to fill job vacancies left by departing employees are time consuming and costly. But a certain level of employee turnover can actually be healthy. The generally accepted benchmark is in the 25th percentile for your industry in voluntary separations. This means that about 75 per cent of similar organisations have a turnover rate higher than yours, which puts your organisation in the preferred top 25 per cent of organisations to work for. Many organisations analyse the turnover figures separately for different areas of the business, which gives more meaningful measures.

To keep the staff you need, make sure you know what motivates and engages each of them and put in place strategies to achieve both. You should also know what they each need to be most productive, what team members like most and least about their work, how they prefer to be managed, how much and what type of recognition they need in return for a job well done, and what they want to learn to make their jobs more satisfying.

The main reason employees leave organisations is because of a poor relationship with their direct leader-manager so your ability to retain staff could well be a career maker – or a career breaker. Leader-managers with a high turnover of employees may soon be too costly for organisations to keep on, no matter how strong their skills are in other areas.

Exit interviews

Two factors increase the importance of monitoring how regularly and why people resign:

1 Employee turnover is expensive.
2 It is often difficult to find suitable replacements.

Moreover, especially in knowledge and service economies like Australia's, the right employees are valuable assets. Understanding why they leave (and why they stay) is therefore important. That's where **exit interviews** come in. When an employee resigns, an exit interview provides an opportunity to find out the source of dissatisfaction, if any, and perhaps take action to prevent others leaving for similar reasons in the future.

When an employee is terminated or **retrenched**, an exit interview provides an opportunity for the employee and the organisation to part formally and for the organisation to correct any misunderstandings that may have occurred. Any counselling or other form of support that might be needed can also be offered at this time.

Another benefit of exit interviews is that when employees leave on good terms, you have an advocate for the organisation, and when you remain in contact, you extend your networks.

Formal exit interviews

Employees leaving an organisation may hesitate to tell their leader-manager the real reasons they are leaving but may be willing to tell someone else. For that reason, someone from the human resources department or a neutral third party generally conducts exit interviews, which usually last from 15 to 30 minutes, and keeps records of them for future collation and analysis.

Alternatively, some organisations replace the traditional interview with an online exit survey, which can be less threatening for the departing employee and provides information that is easier to analyse. The aggregated findings are reported anonymously, further increasing the likelihood that departing employees will 'tell all'. The following are some typical interview questions that can be asked at an exit interview:

- Can you explain what led to your decision to leave us?
- Could your work environment have been improved in any way?
- What do you think of the work itself?
- How would you describe your work team and what it was like being part of it?
- Do you feel you had enough training and support?
- What are your ideas for improving the work, the work team and the leadership style of the team leader?
- If circumstances change, would you consider returning?
- We're not offering to do this, but if we were able to match (the new salary or other reason given for leaving), would you stay? If not, why not? If we could 'fix this' (whatever is mentioned), would you stay? (Keep asking until you get a 'yes' response – this tells you the genuine reason for leaving, not the 'polite' reason. You are not offering to match the salary or other things mentioned as an enticement for the employee to stay. You are asking hypothetical 'what if?' questions. This hypothetical series of questions helps you determine the real or most important reason/s the employee is leaving.)
- What are you intending to do?
- What are you most looking forward to in your new role?
- What did you enjoy most about working here? What did you enjoy least?
- What policies and practices do we follow that you feel are praiseworthy? Are there any you think we should scrap or change?
- Is there anything else you would like to mention at this time?

Informal exit interviews

Informal exit interviews can better suit small businesses with not many employees or even a larger business where there are no formal procedures for interviewing departing employees. The aims of conducting exit interviews are to part on good terms and to gather information that can help you improve your leadership and the way your team works. You also want to emphasise the potential ongoing nature of the relationship because in Australia's small employment market you may well find yourself working with former team members in a different capacity in another organisation.

When people leave your team, ask them these important questions:

- What outstanding promises or commitments have you made?
- What parts of your work are more in your head than written down?
- What does your replacement need to know to get off to a good start?
- What will you miss most about working here?
- What will you miss least about working here?

Keeping a database of former employees (including those outside your work team) and maintaining contacts via email and social media are good ways to expand your professional network. It also provides you with a list of people who potentially might be available to come back and perform short projects or undertake contract or casual work.

Key retention factors

Many types of employees, including casual, full-time, part-time and temporary employees, contractors and teleworkers, make up modern organisations; and within these groups are people born overseas, of varying abilities and from different generations. How is it possible to meet, at the same time and in the same workplace, the differing needs and expectations that these groups and types of employees have so that they remain engaged and motivated?

The following key factors in retaining Australian employees provide the answer:

- a culture of clear values
- effective leadership
- having a say
- mutual trust and respect
- the quality of working relationships – how people relate to each other as friends and colleagues.[23]

Although an organisation's policies and its reputation as a good place to work are important because they attract people in the first place, employees' relationships with their leader-managers largely determine how long they remain. That makes each employee's relationship with their direct leader-manager and colleagues the single most critical element in retaining people. When you're not the sort of leader-manager people want to work for, you will struggle to retain valuable, motivated, productive employees.

What you can do to retain employees

When employees don't like the culture, the organisation and what it stands for, or the people they work with, they leave. There are, however, many ways to retain employees without adding huge costs to your bottom line. Here are some of them:

- Build an organisation and a work team that people are proud to work for (e.g. by achieving results, being socially responsible and supporting your local community).
- Build social communities to develop bonds among employees, such as investment clubs, jogging clubs and other social activities, which can improve retention levels, even in notoriously mobile industries and occupations.
- Frame customers' letters that praise employees' work and hang them in a prominent place.
- Give employees a say in matters that affect them.
- Keep employees informed about the organisation's performance and other matters.
- Offer flexible working arrangements, help with childcare and elder care, and other modern, life-friendly practices.
- Organise an informal lunch (or breakfast) with the CEO, so the CEO and employees can brief each other about recent successes.
- Provide plenty of feedback and learning opportunities.
- Say 'happy birthday' and 'thank you' for jobs well done, ask how people's children are, and so on; in short, develop relationships that recognise people as individuals as well as employees.
- Send a letter to employees' homes on the anniversary of their joining the company to thank them for their support and saying that you appreciate their hard work.

It isn't rocket science, is it?

Look after high-flight-risk employees

Employees in the 20- to 30-year-old age group, who can change employer with less risk to their personal circumstances because they have few major commitments in their lives and can easily find another job, are almost twice as mobile (i.e. twice as likely to resign) as employees over the age of 30. Those with the skills, knowledge and attributes other organisations want are particularly at risk and it's difficult to find and train a replacement for them.

You can avoid 'push' turnover of new employees by providing them with support and adequate induction and onboarding. Showing younger employees how they are contributing to the organisation and growing professionally can help them understand the organisation's strategic priorities and provide them with a context for their work.

Other factors and things you can do include:

- maintaining a diverse and friendly work group
- providing coaching and development opportunities
- offering an effective and transparent career path
- having in place clear performance-management systems by which employees can see how they are performing
- making them feel valued
- offering generous health and wellbeing policies (including arrangements for flexible working)
- providing regular, constructive and specific feedback
- helping them to meet their career expectations by delegating tasks to them so that they can develop new skills or allowing them to take up secondments in other roles
- providing modern communications and information technology systems to support them in their work
- providing performance incentives (tangible as well as psychological)
- acting in a socially responsible manner.

All of the above are important aspects of an organisation's employer value proposition, particularly for younger employees, so find out what they want from work, try to provide it and honour the promises made at the recruitment stage.

An organisation's top performers are also high-flight risks, especially when your organisation is cutting back on staff and/or freezing pay to improve the bottom line. In addition to the above, make sure your top performers understand where the organisation is heading and how they fit in. Acknowledge their performance and value to the organisation and, where possible, and if appropriate, increase their remuneration accordingly.

STUDY TOOLS

QUICK REVIEW

KEY CONCEPT 11.1 

a What is the difference between employee motivation and engagement? Briefly describe the role of the leader-manager in each.

b List the three Cs of engagement and explain how each contributes to engaged employees.

c Discuss some ways that leader-managers can engage employees.

KEY CONCEPT 11.2 

a List the three Cs of motivation and explain how each contributes to motivated employees.
b What motivates you? Are these mostly motivators or hygiene factors? List the ways in which your role contributes to your motivation.
c Briefly explain, compare and contrast the four ways of thinking about employees' needs discussed under the heading 'What do people need to be motivated?' and explain how the three questions listed under the heading 'The secret to motivation: instilling belief and providing the reward' in Section 11.3 can help you use these four approaches to motivation.

KEY CONCEPT 11.3 

a What behaviour can you expect from employees whose motivation needs are not met?

KEY CONCEPT 11.4 

a Explain the leader-manager's role in retaining employees and outline two reasons why retention is important.

BUILD YOUR SKILLS

KEY CONCEPT 11.1 

a Explain the ways in which engaged employees benefit organisations.
b How can social media help engage employees?

KEY CONCEPT 11.2 

a What do you value? Search for a values test on the internet to find out more about your own values and belief systems.
b What do you think the quotation from Gandhi under the heading 'Maslow's hierarchy of needs' in Section 11.2 is referring to? Discuss it in relation to Maslow's hierarchy of needs. Contrast it with this statement: 'A person does not live by bread alone'. Can they both be correct?
c Based on Maslow's and Herzberg's ideas about motivation, and thinking about the higher-order needs and the lower-order needs, what do you think are the primary motivators of employees in Australia? Would the same things motivate employees in a country devastated by floods, earthquakes or a tsunami? What about workers in growing economies like India or China, where people might be very wealthy, middle class or so poor they can barely subsist?
d Atkinson and McClelland identified three areas of need that are at least partially learnt, and other researchers have identified four needs or drives they believe are instinctive. Briefly describe each of these seven needs and give an example of how you would recognise each need in an employee – what behavioural or other clues would you look for?
e Imagine three managers, one with a high need for achievement, another with a high need for affiliation and the third with a high need for power. How would each of them lead and manage their teams when they were at their best as managers? When they were at their worst as managers?

KEY CONCEPT 11.3 

a Give an example from your own experience that explains and illustrates how the three questions listed under the heading 'The secret to motivation: instilling belief and providing the reward' in Section 11.3 can help leader-managers motivate people.
b What are the necessary conditions for motivation to occur?
c Select three effective methods of motivating people that you have witnessed or experienced and explain them in terms of one or more of the approaches to motivation discussed in this chapter.

KEY CONCEPT 11.4 

a Explain how the specific ways in which an organisation manages its people affect how easily it can recruit and retain high-calibre staff.

WORKPLACE ACTIVITIES

KEY CONCEPT 11.1 

a Describe how your organisation triggers engagement in terms of the three Cs of engagement and the actions you take to support your organisation's efforts to invite engagement.

b Briefly define employee motivation and engagement and discuss how motivated and engaged the employees in your work group are, giving specific examples to support your case. List five additional actions you can take to further improve their engagement.

c What reference to your ability to engage employees is likely to be considered in your next performance review?

KEY CONCEPT 11.2 

a Watch Dan Pink's 18-minute TED talk, 'The puzzle of motivation', summarise the main points, and discuss how you can apply them to motivate the people in your work team and how the organisation as a whole can apply them to motivate employees. You can find the talk at https://www.ted.com/talks/dan_pink_on_motivation#t-1100463

b List the employees in your work group. What do you believe motivates each of them and why, in terms of Herzberg's hygiene and motivation factors? Then draw a bar chart to illustrate the needs profile of each employee using either McClelland and Atkinson's trilogy of needs or the four basic emotional needs discussed in this chapter.

c How well designed are the jobs in your work team? How can well-designed jobs motivate employees and encourage good performance? Explain how job placement factors into this equation.

d What reference to your ability to motivate employees is likely to be considered in your next performance review?

KEY CONCEPT 11.3 

a List three specific ways you can apply at your workplace the three questions listed under the heading 'The secret to motivation: instilling belief and providing the reward' in Section 11.3.

b People work well and hard for rewards that mean something to them. Discuss the rewards the people in your work team value and the actions you take to meet them.

KEY CONCEPT 11.4 

a How critical is each team member to the success of your team and your organisation? What is the impact if you lose team members? How ready are the key employees for promotion or a move to a new and challenging role? If they are ready now and no positions are available, what can you do to keep them? If you do lose them, who is ready to replace them in your team or who could you make ready? A staffing strategy like this is an important responsibility of all leader-managers.

b What is the rate of push attrition in your work team? How does it compare to similar teams in your organisation? What actions do you take to keep it low? List five other actions you could take.

c Based on the cost of recruitment given in this chapter (under the 'Employee turnover' heading in Section 11.4), how much has attrition cost in your work team over the last 12 months?

d What reference to your ability to retain employees is likely to be considered in your next performance review?

EXTENSION ACTIVITIES

Referring to the Snapshot at the beginning of this chapter, answer the following questions:

1 Which of Josie's team members appear not to have been engaged? Suggest why and what she could have done to address this issue.

2 Referring to one or more relevant theories of motivation, identify which staff members you think were the ones that resigned and why.

CASE STUDY 11

CRISIS IN THE KITCHEN

Gregory Kean was Manly Bistro's top apprentice six years ago and has always been a fast learner and an ambitious and willing worker. Because of his work ethic, his clear thinking and his organising abilities, the owner promoted Gregory to the position of head chef with a kitchen team of five. Upon his promotion, Gregory became more determined than ever to show his capabilities. His level of motivation was high, and he decided to make a clean sweep of the kitchen and really smarten the place up.

The previous chef had run the kitchen in a relaxed, informal manner and, for the most part, everyone did their work well. However, as far as Gregory could see, the previous head chef didn't really 'manage' at all – meals just 'happened'.

So in went Gregory, ensuring breaks weren't extended, handing out jobs at the beginning of each shift, tightening up systems and procedures, checking people followed them, continually monitoring everyone's work and generally ruling with the proverbial iron hand.

Now, four months later, the sous-chef has quit, the general kitchenhand is openly looking for another job and the team is no longer functioning as a unit. The four who are left seem to have withdrawn their cooperation, use no initiative and do only what Gregory tells them to do. The owner decides it is time to have a chat to get to the bottom of what can only be described as a crisis in the kitchen.

Questions

1 What, specifically, do you think led to this crisis?
2 Based on how the staff reacted to Gregory's new way of doing things, what do you think motivated them under the previous chef?
3 Which of the ways of thinking about motivation could Gregory use to help him correct the situation? Explain how your suggestion could help him turn the situation around.
4 Gregory concentrated on task matters rather than people matters. Many new leader-managers do this. Why can this be a mistake?

CHAPTER ENDNOTES

1 Chance Miller, 'Apple retail chief Ahrendts says she treats retail employees like executives, 81% retention in 2015', *9to5Mac*, 27 January 2016, https://9to5mac.com/2016/01/27/apple-retail-chief-ahrendts-says-she-treats-retail-employees-like-executives-81-retention-in-2015/

2 'Careerwise', *Human Resources Magazine*, 29 May 2008.

3 Gemma Robertson-Smith, Carl Marwick, 'Employee engagement: A review of current thinking', Report 469, Institute for Employment Studies, Brighton, UK, 2009; see also Tom Rath, Barry Conchie, *Strengths-based leadership*, Gallup Press, 2008; see also 'The state of the global workplace: Employee engagement insights for business leaders worldwide, 2011–2012', http://www.gallup.com/strategicconsulting/164735/state-global-workplace.aspx, accessed 27 December 2013.

4 The state of the global workplace, ibid.

5 Katie Truss, Emma Soane, 'Engaging the "pole vaulters" on your staff', *Harvard Business Review*, March 2010.

6 T. Russell, 'What makes a great place to work?', *HC Online*, 27 May 2009, http://www.hcamag.com/hr-resources/learning-and-development/what-makes-a-great-place-to-work-115299.aspx, accessed 26 November 2014; see also Diageo, 'About us', 'Our values', https://www.diageo.com, accessed 15 January 2015.

7 'Death benefits: Google workers get sweet perks for life and death', News.com.au, 10 August 2012, http://www.news.com.au/technology/death-benefits-google-workers-get-sweet-perks-for-life-and-death/story-e6frfro0-1226447351009, accessed 25 January 2015; see also Dylan Love, 'If a Google employee dies his spouse gets half his salary for the next 10 years', *Business Insider Australia*, http://www.businessinsider. com.au/google-spouse-death-benefits-2012-8, 10 August 2012, accessed 25 March 2014.

8 Robertson-Smith, Marwick, op. cit.

9 The state of the global workplace, op. cit.

10 Red Balloon, 'What to do about employee disengagement', https://www.redballoon.com.au/business/disengagement-is-costing-your-business-thousands-every-year-so-what-can-you-do-about-it/, accessed 2 October 2021.

11 Kochies Business Builders, 'Gallup report finds Australian employees stressed and disengaged', https://www.kochiesbusinessbuilders.com.au/gallup-report-finds-australian-employees-stressed-and-disengaged, viewed 2 October 2021.

12 Dr Mary Hayes, Dr Frances Chumney, Marcus Buckingham, *Global Workplace Study 2020*, ADP Research Institute, 2020, p. 13.

13 Andrew Carnegie, quoted in J. Maxwell, *Ultimate leadership: Maximise your potential and empower your team*, Thomas Nelson, 2007, p. 378.

14 Charles Schwab, quoted in Dale Carnegie, *How to win friends and influence people*, Vermillion, 2006, p. 24.

15 N. Wiener, *The human use of human beings: Cybernetics and society,* Da Capo, 1954, p. 52.

16 In N. K. Bose, *Selections from Gandhi*, Navajivan, 1948, p. 62.

17 Abraham Maslow, 'A theory of human motivation', *Psychological Review*, Vol. 50, No. 4, 1943, p. 370.

18 Mark Koltko-Rivera, 'Rediscovering the later version of Maslow's "hierarchy of needs": Self-transcendence and opportunities for theory, research and unification', *Review of General Psychology*, Vol. 10, No. 4, pp. 302–317, December 2006; see also Abraham Maslow, *The farther reaches of human nature,* Viking, New York, 1972.

19 Louis Tay, Ed Diener, 'Needs and subjective well-being around the world', *Journal of Personality and Social Psychology*, Vol. 101, No. 2, 2011, p. 354.

20 Frederick Herzberg, 'One more time: How do you motivate employees?', *Harvard Business Review*, January 2003, 1987.

21 David McClelland, *Power: The inner experience*, Irvington, 1975; see also David C. McClelland et al., *The achievement motive*, Appleton-Century Crafts Inc, 1953.

22 Victor H. Vroom, *Work and motivation*, Wiley, Oxford, 1964.

23 Daryll Hull, Vivienne Read, *Simply the best,* Australian Centre for Industrial Relations Research and Training, Sydney University, Sydney, 2004; see also DEEWR, 'Cultural imprints at work', op. cit.

CHAPTER

ASSIGNING WORK AND DELEGATING DUTIES

KEY CONCEPTS

After completing this chapter, you will be able to:

12.1 define the differences between the leadership style called delegating and delegating work, and between delegating work and assigning work

12.2 assign work in a way that achieves cooperation and commitment

12.3 delegate the right job in the right way and to the right person to ensure that it is done well

12.4 receive assignments and know what to do when you disagree with an instruction.

TRANSFERABLE SKILLS

The following transferable skills are covered in this chapter:

2 **Critical thinking and problem solving**
- **2.2** Personal effectiveness

3 **Social competence**
- **3.1** Teamwork/relationships
- **3.2** Verbal communication
- **3.4** Leadership

OVERVIEW

A key skill of successful managers who lead productive teams is the ability to allocate work and delegate duties effectively. This doesn't just involve choosing the team member with the right skills and knowledge to do the task and then handing it over to them. There are a number of factors to consider.

Transferable skills

2.2 Personal effectiveness

3.1 Teamwork/relationships

Ideally, you want the person being assigned the task to want to do it. A motivated team member is more likely to embrace the opportunity and produce the results you are looking for than one who is doing it because they have to. Seeking cooperation rather than compliance is therefore a preferable strategy where the circumstances, timeframe and degree of importance of the task allow it.

You also need to choose the person with the skills and knowledge required to complete the task to the requisite standard. While this may sound simple enough, there are also several things to consider. Not only do you need to know the capabilities of your team members, you need to think about what other skills might also be necessary that might not be immediately apparent. Possessing soft skills, such as listening, showing empathy or working cooperatively with others, may be critical, as may be the ability to work with employees from different generations, of different genders, from varying ethnic and cultural backgrounds, or who identify as part of the LGBTQI+ community. Having the emotional intelligence to defuse conflict, manage emotions and build strong relationships might also be as, or even more, important to the success of the assignment than analytical or technological skills.

How you assign the work can also affect how it is received. The words you use, your tone of voice and your body language reflect your respect for yourself and the person you are directing, which in turn affects the way employees hear and respond to your assignments. With portions of the workforce now working remotely, you also need to consider the most effective way of delegating duties via email, phone or even videoconferencing.

Conversely, receiving work instructions and accepting delegated duties aren't necessarily as straightforward as listening to what's wanted and then rushing off to do it. Many of the considerations just outlined again come into play.

This chapter examines what you need to think about and consider when you are on both the giving and receiving end of assignments.

SNAPSHOT

The end of the financial year

The end of the financial year is always a demanding period. Stocktaking is a major task requiring numerous reports to be prepared and with auditors milling around and checking on things, everyone feels under pressure and overworked.

Dilini Churuppu, the warehouse manager, is in charge of the stocktake. She understands the importance of an accurate count and takes the responsibility very seriously. Everyone is involved, from senior management to factory hands, and Dilini is the person from whom everyone takes the lead on stocktake day.

Dilini is finishing her email with instructions for carrying out the count. She wonders if she should use a different style when communicating the instructions for conducting the stocktake to the managing director, Isabelle Tollari, to how she tells the people who work for her in the warehouse. Isabelle is a strong and formidable leader who everyone fears because she demands perfection and doesn't accept excuses or 'fools'. Dilini is anxious that the direct tone of her email to the other staff might be misinterpreted by Isabelle as a challenge to her authority and put her off-side. This is the last thing Dilini wants at a time when she counts on Isabelle's support to help mobilise the staff so that the stocktake can be completed. But it is a new system this year and so Isabelle, like all of the other staff, needs to be properly briefed to avoid critical errors that could undermine the whole process.

12.1 Defining our terms

> **No person will make a great business who wants to do it all himself or get all the credit.**
>
> Andrew Carnegie (US industrialist), in Whitten, *Managing software development projects: Formula for success*, Wiley, 2nd ed., 1995, p. 63.

In the competitive, globalised, productivity-driven business environment of the 21st century, imprecise and unclear work instructions can lead to confusion and misunderstanding. While the autocratic order-giving managers of the 20th century are fast becoming extinct, modern organisations still require strong, decisive leaders. But with many organisations adopting a more participative style of leadership, how is this possible?

The laissez-faire style of leadership has long been criticised as being 'do-nothing' leadership. However, rather than being a 'do-nothing' leader, perhaps the leader-manager who provides little in the way of direction to their employees is an example of a modern, forward-thinking leader who empowers their employees and harnesses their collective skills and knowledge.

The dilemma of assigning work is not just a question of leadership style. Some leader-managers fear it is a way to lose the valued friendship, cooperation and support of their work team. With this conflict in the forefront of their mind, it's little wonder that some leader-managers choose to back away from assigning and delegating work. But assigning and delegating work are not the same thing:

- *Assigning work* means directing people to carry out duties and tasks that are part of their job.
- *Delegating work* means giving people the authority to carry out a task that is one of your duties.

Assigning work

Assigning work does not mean issuing orders in a dictatorial way. That sort of autocratic approach makes most 21st-century Australian leader-managers feel uncomfortable and it is out of touch with modern management practice. Giving orders without providing the opportunity for discussion and giving unnecessary orders are two ways to lose the goodwill and support of your team members.

In this chapter, the concept of assigning work is not being used in a harsh, commanding context, but rather in the sense of allocating duties to a team or team member. Does this detract from empowerment? In its strictest sense, full empowerment means that members of a work team have a great deal of autonomy and distribute duties among themselves. The members of synergistic, high-performing teams are competent and willing and generally need little direction or guidance.

Rather than telling people how to carry out tasks or complete an assignment, an alternative approach is to explain the desired outcomes, deadlines, constraints, resources available and so on, and work with the team or individual to decide how best to proceed. Guide people and use your emotional intelligence to ask questions which will help team members to work things out for themselves. When you need to explain how something should be done, instruct people following the steps explained in Chapter 29.

Transferable skills

2.2 Personal effectiveness

Delegating tasks

If you have completed Chapter 10, you probably remember a leadership style called delegating. You can use a delegating leadership style only with employees who are trained, competent, willing and confident. In this chapter, the term 'delegate' is not being used in the strict sense required by the leadership style of the same name. It is being used in the sense of a leader-manager of a work team assigning one of their own duties to someone who is already competent and willing to do the job; or it may be to someone who does not yet know how to do it and needs training.

12.2 Assigning work

> When I was first put in charge of a team 19 years ago, I had to come to terms with the fact that I was no longer a lone professional doing my own job. I had to manage in such a way that other people would be the ones making things happen, not me. With every year, the lesson has intensified.
>
> Olli-Pekka Kallasvuo (former chairman, Nokia), 'Humility', *Harvard Business Review*, January 2007.

When employees are uncertain of the reasons behind assignments or don't agree with them, they find it difficult to carry them out. Begin by establishing the task you want done and the specific outcome(s) you're after. Explain why the task is important and where it fits into the work of the team and the organisation. Being able to understand where tasks fit into a broader context gives people a better understanding of what is required and why, and increases commitment.

Explain what needs to be done in terms of:

- safety
- quality
- quantity
- time.

When an employee is unfamiliar with the task, and when you need to give direct and explicit work instructions, you may need to explain how to do the work. (Chapter 29 explains how to walk employees through a task, step-by-step.)

When an employee is clear about what needs to be done and why, establish measures of success (MoS) against which they can measure their progress and check that the employee understands all aspects of the assignment. Where necessary, revisit your expectations with the employee on multiple occasions and have them explain them back to you. Providing the employee with ample opportunity to ask questions will ensure they are able to clear up any areas of uncertainty or doubt.

As people perform best when utilising their strengths, select someone with both the ability and the desire to carry out the task. A good match between the person and the task is known as a good *job fit*. For example:

- When a task is repetitive, think about who is best suited to doing it.
- When a task requires a fine eye for detail, consider who in your team enjoys detailed work.
- When a task requires working with others cooperatively, select someone with a high level of emotional intelligence and strong interpersonal skills.
- When the unexpected might occur, pick someone who can 'roll with the punches' and who is an adept problem-solver.

(Chapters 8 and 28 explain more about matching people to tasks.)

Consideration should also be given to the timing of assigning work. It is unwise, for example, to assign work when you're angry. Other examples of poor timing include giving assignments when employees are about to go to lunch or finish for the day, or when the assignment comes on top of an incident that has lowered the morale of the group. Try to anticipate the employee's reactions and plan your explanations and timing so that there is a greater chance that the employee will willingly accept the assignment.

The main dos for assigning work include do:

- be consistent with what is to be done and the standards required
- ensure the employee has the skills or provide training/guidance
- where possible, distribute tasks evenly among employees
- double-check that the employee can do the job and knows what's expected
- select employees and plan your timing so that it is more likely the assignment will be willingly accepted
- ensure employees have completed the tasks within the expected timeframe and to the required standard
- know exactly what outcomes you want achieved before assigning tasks.

The main don'ts for assigning work include, don't:

- be careless or offhand when assigning work
- allocate the highly sought-after jobs to the same people all the time
- allocate the less desirable jobs to the same people all the time
- overload employees who accept tasks more willingly than others.

Assigning work is also not a case of 'set and forget'. You need to monitor the employee's progress so that, should things start to go wrong, you have time to rectify the situation. Thanking the employee and providing support, as well as timely and specific feedback on their efforts, will go a long way to securing their willingness to take on extra tasks in future. (Chapter 15 has information on how to provide feedback and Chapter 19 has information on establishing MoS.)

Transferable skills

2.2 Personal effectiveness

Assigning work systematically

In an ideal work environment, you assign tasks according to people's strengths, their likes and dislikes and the needs of the team or organisation. The reality, however, may be quite different. Many tasks are time-critical or become urgent, requiring you to pull a staff member off the task they have been assigned and onto something else. Not all staff have the same skills, meaning you may have to assign some tasks selectively. Then there is the potential 'elephant in the room', staff budgets, which ultimately may be the sole determining factor as to how and to whom you assign work.

Depending on the workplace and the nature of work, a systematic approach can be an effective way of assigning work. Based on organisational data, it can be used to ensure that all required tasks are assigned, completed, meet the quality standards expected and fall within staff budgeting parameters. A spreadsheet is an example of a systematic tool that can be used to implement such a strategy.

For instance, first you identify the level of quality and output required. Then review historical data in relation to how long a particular task may normally take and how long individual staff members may take to do particular tasks, and the level of quality they will produce (i.e. according to the task). By adding up the times and then dividing the total time required for each task by the number of staff, you can calculate the average time required for each task across your team and set this as your baseline. You may need to tweak these times slightly in order to get the desired level of quality. Alternatively, as you become familiar with the tasks, your staff and their level of quality, you can choose to take a more subjective approach and estimate this figure.

Referring back to your historical data, you can then allocate tasks according to 'best fit'. Some staff will complete their task above the baseline figure (i.e. they will take longer to do the task than the baseline indicates), others will come in below the baseline (i.e. they will complete the task quicker than the baseline indicates) and some will meet the baseline figure exactly. So long as the times of those above and below the baseline cancel each other out, all of the tasks should be completed on time.

The staff budget also needs to be considered. This may be predetermined higher up in your organisation, especially in the case of projects. While one approach is to simply divide the budget by the baseline figures previously calculated and allocate the staff accordingly, you may need to override this approach based on priority if one task is considered more important or urgent than another (i.e. you may allocate more staff to an area that is producing greater revenue for the business than another area not performing as well).

The key to a systematic approach is to align the right staff to the right tasks. While this is going to be easier where the work is homogenous and the staff are all at roughly or the same skill level, it can also be an effective tool for allocating work by modifying your baseline, as outlined above.

Different approaches to assigning work

The way you assign work depends on the situation and the employee. Emergencies and dangerous situations, for example, require prompt action. You need to be clear and decisive and may need to give a directive without explanation due to the urgency of the situation. At the other end of the scale are situations where there are many options and plenty of time to discuss and explain, so a more relaxed approach may be appropriate.

Team members may have different skill levels and expectations of their own jobs. Those who are highly motivated and self-directed generally respond best when you state the end result and let them decide the best way to achieve it. Those who are just learning a job need clear, step-by-step direction while those lacking motivation need clearly stated success measures and frequent 'check-ins'.

Direct and explicit assignments

When instructions must be followed without question, giving an explicit directive is the appropriate way in which to assign work – but avoid using the word 'order', which may illicit a response of resentment and even hostility. Clear directives are useful when time or outcomes are critical, such as in the case of workplace health and safety matters. For example, you might say: 'Close the machine guard *fully* and make sure you hear it *click* before proceeding' or 'Ensure you wash your hands before handling food'. When an employee is engaged in an unsafe work practice, immediate action is required, and this may mean giving an explicit directive to perform or refrain from a certain action. Some employees, due to past experiences or their attitude to the job, will respond only to explicit directives, so this may need to be the usual approach of communicating work assignments to these types of workers.

Explicit assignments state clearly the result required and describe precisely *who* is to do *what*, *when* it is to be done, *how* it is to be done and *where* it is to be done. Use explicit instructions with team members with limited experience or abilities, or those whose level of commitment is below that required to do the job.

Requests and implied assignments

Requests begin with, for example, 'Would you …' or 'Will you …' or 'Could you please …' . This approach can be used with nervous or sensitive workers as well as with skilled and motivated workers. Adopting a polite manner and using 'please' and 'thank-you' will help with this approach.

Implied assignments begin with, for example, 'We need to … '. This softens the instruction and encourages cooperation. This approach can be used with workers who readily accept responsibility or when you want to encourage innovation and continuous improvement.

Conditional assignments

For conditional assignments, explain the overall goal or desired outcome but allow initiative, judgement and latitude in *how*, *when* and *what* to do to achieve it. Since conditional assignments help maintain cooperation and commitment, use them whenever possible, particularly with experienced and responsible employees. This approach can also work well when training employees to upgrade their skills, although you should discuss with them how they plan to approach the task rather than simply letting them undertake it without any consultation, guidance or advice.

Undirected assignments

Occasionally you may need someone to do something 'above and beyond the call of duty'. Rather than selecting an employee and giving a direction, call your team together, explain the task and ask for a volunteer, explaining not only *what* is required but also *why*. The opportunity to volunteer can provide the motivation needed to do the job well, especially when the job allows the volunteer to satisfy one of their own motivational needs or goals. When your team is motivated, someone is likely to volunteer; otherwise, you may have to nominate a 'volunteer'.

Which way to choose and when

Generally, under normal working situations, assigning work with an explicit directive stifles ideas, initiative, innovation and suggestions. Too many explicit directives often reflect your uncertainty about the ability of your team, and seldom achieve more than grudging compliance where employees rarely do more than what you specifically tell them to do. You then face managing a team of reluctant staff. A wiser approach might be to assign work in a direct or explicit way only occasionally, so when you do, employees will know it's for a good reason and their response will more likely be positive.

The exception to this is team members who have low levels of task readiness. They are unlikely to be able to carry out requests and implied, conditional and undirected assignments successfully. This is because they lack either the skills or the willingness and so these approaches can be dangerous when used with inexperienced or unreliable staff. With these types of employees, it is better to avoid these approaches altogether.

Requests and implied, conditional and undirected assignments are particularly useful in complex situations, and also when employees are capable and willing, as they allow some discretion and initiative in carrying out the request. Many employees are capable of modifying or improving on assignments, too. Those with the skills and confidence to do so will generally put their own stamp on the way they complete tasks, and these methods of assigning work allow this latitude. Giving employees the opportunity to express their opinion and become creatively involved in the way they carry out a task also helps overcome resistance and encourages them to utilise the full range of their skills and experience.

Clear and respectful communication of your message will ensure it is received and understood in the manner intended. When allocating assignments, what communication strategies can you use to help ensure your instructions are understood?

Five levels of monitoring

Depending on an employee's task readiness level (i.e. skill level, experience and willingness to do the task) you may choose from five levels of monitoring:

1. *Over to you:* when employees are both skilled and motivated, you can safely assign them work and let them get on with it, provided you have a strategy in place to alert you to any potential problems.
2. *Keep me informed*: ask employees who are dependable, but slightly less skilled, experienced or willing to carry on with the task, to update you with certain key information or at milestones so you can satisfy yourself that the assigned work is progressing as planned.
3. *Check back first*: ask employees with even less experience or willingness to check back with you before proceeding at certain critical control points so that you can assure yourself that the work is being carried out correctly.
4. *Let's talk it through first*: ask employees who are trained but inexperienced in the task to decide what to do when a problem or something unexpected arises and then come and talk it through with you before acting. This is an expanded version of checking back and lets you review how the employee is thinking about approaching the task. It provides you with an opportunity to coach and develop the employee's skills.
5. *I'll walk you through it*: use the training approach discussed in Chapter 29 for employees new to a task.

Employees who seem reluctant to carry out directions

If an employee seems uncertain about taking on an assignment, before concluding that the reason is something related to them, consider whether the assignment is reasonable, whether you have clearly articulated its requirements and expectations, and whether you have offered the support and time necessary to complete it. Then consider whether the employee has the skills, ability and time to undertake it. It is also worth considering whether the work is something the employee enjoys doing, or at least doesn't dislike doing. Perhaps the task you assigned is unpleasant or interferes with something in the employee's work or private life. For example, it might be something as simple as requiring them to attend late afternoon meetings, which interferes with picking up their children from school.

Transferable skills

3.2 Verbal communication

When you are unable to determine why an employee isn't cooperating, ask them. They may have a valid reason or might have misunderstood or misinterpreted something you said. Asking open questions in a non-threatening and non-judgemental way can help you to understand the situation from the employee's point of view. There might be something in the 'Five Keys' (explained in Chapter 19) that is missing and is preventing the employee from starting. When you need to, review what you require, the importance of the task and why you're assigning the work to that employee. It may be better to assign the work to a less skilled but more willing team member than to someone who approaches it with a defeatist attitude from the start.

You could also try modifying the assignment, providing support and encouragement and constructively engaging with the employee to find out how they are going, what they need, what challenges they are facing and how you can help them overcome them. These strategies, plus maintaining a positive and cooperative attitude, may just be enough to turn the situation around.

Transferable skills

2.2 Personal effectiveness

3.1 Teamwork/relationships

Ultimately, your role and purpose as a leader-manager is to help the members of your team to accomplish their work. To achieve this you need to work with them rather than against them. Turning to your emotional intelligence is the key – listen, empathise, take the time to understand what someone is going through or what their concerns are, be aware of your own emotions and their impact on others, and pick up on social and emotional cues. Knowing your management tasks and functions is important, but knowing how to engage, motivate and inspire your team is critical to getting the job done.

The north-bound-bus approach

When your work assignments are reasonable, particularly regarding a change in policy or procedures, try the north-bound-bus approach. When you board a bus going north, you go north too. When you don't want to go north, the best thing to do is to get off that bus and find another one.

Organisations and work teams often alter course to head in a new direction. They might introduce a new customer service philosophy, establish new procedures and work methods based on a new technology, or reorganise and change established reporting structures. Symbolically, they are now heading 'north'.

Transferable skills

3.4 Leadership

Some employees may have trouble accepting the new direction. When an employee refuses to 'head north' with everyone else (even after you have followed the advice on introducing and leading change in Chapter 24), the north-bound-bus approach may be a last resort. Advising an employee of the consequences of them not following instructions or undertaking reasonable assignments given to them underpins this approach. Those consequences might be **demotion**, loss of pay or even termination of their employment. Similar to circumstances where you must invoke your organisation's formal discipline procedure, this is a method to adopt only when other approaches have failed.

When the task is done incorrectly

Transferable skills

3.4 Leadership

Everyone misunderstands sometimes. When an employee who has not carried out an assignment to your satisfaction says, 'I didn't know that was what you wanted', apologise for not making yourself clear and try to communicate your instructions better next time.

When you're sure you have communicated clearly, use Figure 12.1 to select the best course of action. Each quadrant suggests a possible cause of poor performance and a recommended approach to rectify it. In the first quadrant, the employee is willing but has insufficient job knowledge or skill, so training may be the answer. In the second, the employee is willing and has sufficient knowledge or skills, so you need to look to the environment or the 'Chance To Key' discussed in Chapter 19, for a clue. Perhaps the employee has insufficient resources (e.g. tools, equipment, time or information) or is constrained by cumbersome systems.

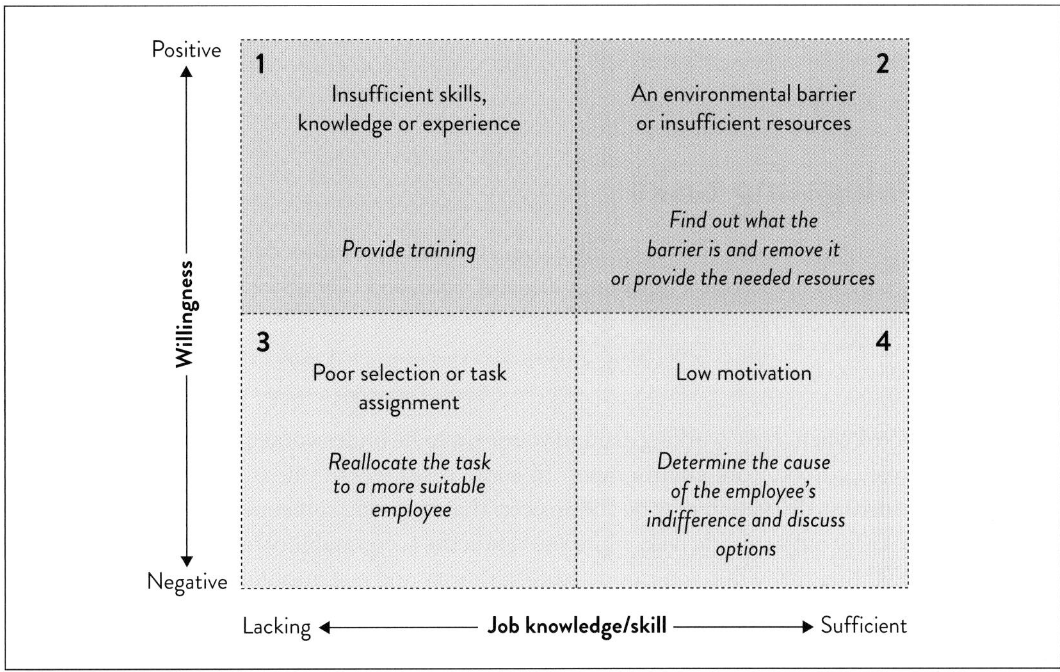

FIGURE 12.1 Poor performance?

In the third quadrant, the employee lacks the skills and knowledge and also the willingness to take on the assignment. This suggests that you should examine your selection procedures (to stop this happening in the future), select another employee to carry out the assignment and consider assigning the original employee other, more suitable work. In the fourth quadrant, the employee has sufficient job knowledge but lacks willingness, so the problem is a motivational one and you need to discuss options with the employee; perhaps the employee is looking for a new challenge, for example (as explained in Chapter 11).

Responsibility for assigning work

The principle of unity of command states that employees should receive their assignments from only one person. This avoids situations from occurring where employees feel conflicted and confused about whose directions should be given priority. As a general guideline, therefore, try to ensure that you are the only person who assigns work to your team members.

Organisations that have adopted a matrix organisational structure seem to go against this principle. Instead of the predictability of one boss, employees must deal with the ambiguity and potential of conflicting priorities that comes with reporting to two or more leader-managers. However, this need not necessarily go against the unity of command principle if each boss manages clearly defined, and different, aspects of a person's job.

When this is not the case, confusion and conflict are likely to arise. Some employees may be comfortable dealing with the uncertainty and conflict of having to report to more than one person. They may be willing and able to invest their personal energy, enthusiasm and creativity into dealing with multiple projects and overlapping challenges. The reality is that most employees find responding to more than one leader-manager a difficult task and problematic at best. Therefore, avoiding this situation is the wisest approach.

Transferable skills

2.2 Personal effectiveness

12.3 Delegating tasks

> **As all entrepreneurs know, you live and die by your ability to prioritise. You must focus on the most important, mission-critical tasks each day and night, and then share, delegate, delay, or skip the rest.**
>
> Jessica Jackley (American businesswoman and entrepreneur), *Forbes*, 2011, https://www.forbes.com/2011/04/21/pregnant-entrepreneur-ceo-and-the-venture-capitalist.html.

Feeling overworked when those working around you seem to be underworked can cause resentment, jealousy and create a toxic work environment. In some cases where this is occurring, or is being perceived as occurring, delegation may be the answer; that is, giving someone else the authority and responsibility to carry out a specific task, while you retain the accountability for its correct execution. It is worth highlighting that while you can delegate authority and responsibility, you cannot delegate accountability. Delegation is a tool for spreading the workload and responsibility but not for avoiding ultimate accountability for the results. An effective 'leader-delegator' transfers the responsibility for a task to another because it can enhance that person's skills, experience and job interest and at the same time allows the leader-manager to get on with adding value to their organisation by undertaking tasks which utilise the skills and experience that only they possess.

Think about occasions when you have successfully delegated tasks to members of your team. What aspects of the task or work you assigned contributed to this success and what factors in relation to the team member(s) to whom you assigned the work contributed to this success? Which do you consider were the most important?

What happens when you don't delegate?

When you find yourself using any of the excuses for not delegating shown in **Figure 12.2**, think again. These excuses just prevent you from increasing employee productivity and usefulness, developing and extending employees' skills and job interest, and freeing up some of your own time to do other things.

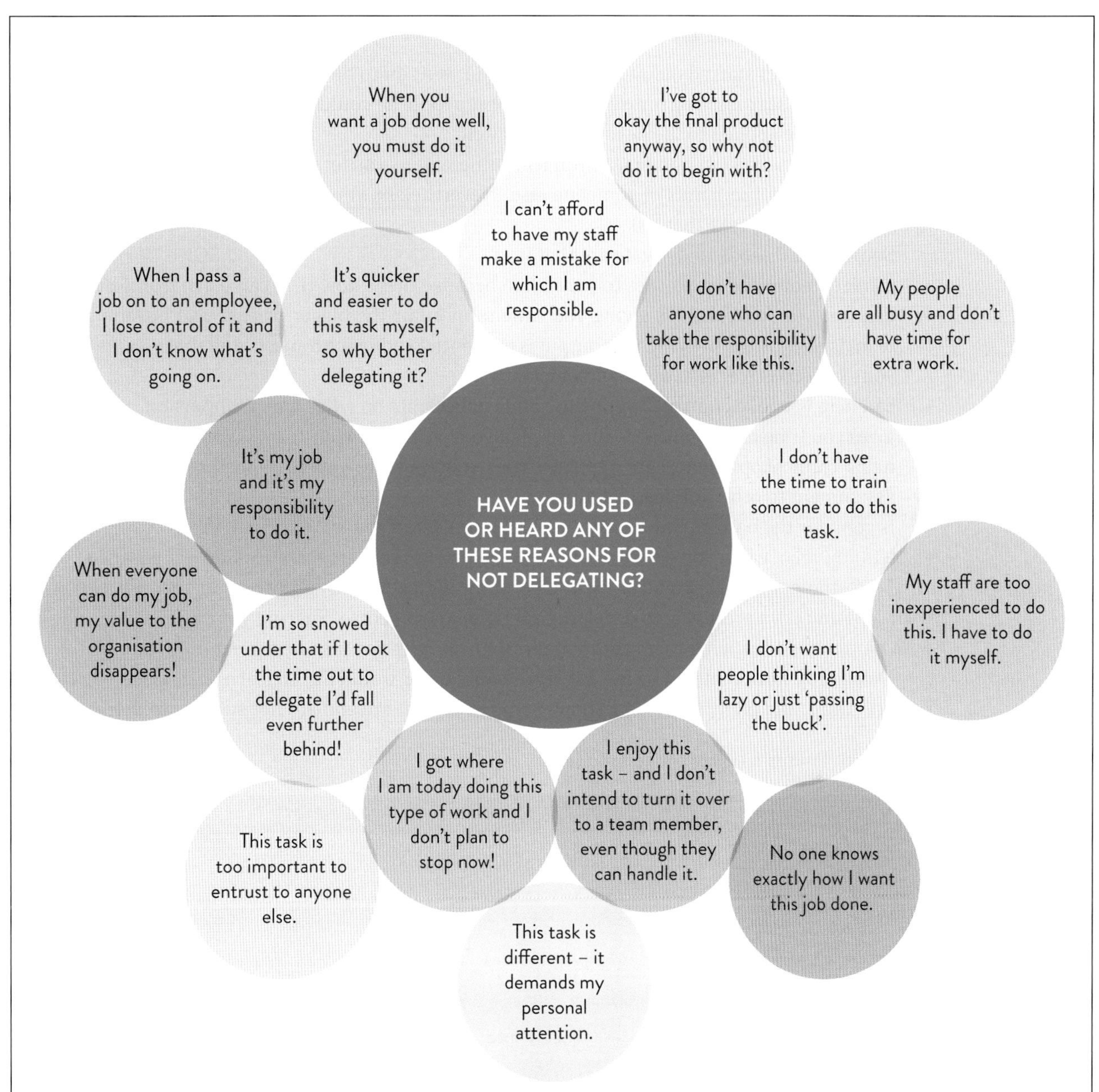

FIGURE 12.2 Common excuses for not delegating

When you don't delegate, you end up doing everything yourself. You become caught up in day-to-day tasks and don't have the time to devote to the *real* job of leading and managing – communicating, planning, thinking and so on. Your desk overflows, your team's work slows, and team members become confused because you've been too busy doing other jobs instead of those necessary to organise work and resources properly. Staying behind and working late is more likely to compound the problem than solve it.

The importance of delegation

John D. Rockefeller started out as an office boy and went on to become one of the richest men in the world. How? By surrounding himself with the best people he could find and delegating to them. This approach can be applied to life beyond work as well.

Delegating can be risky and make you feel vulnerable as you let go of a task that you're responsible for and place it in the hands of someone else. Nevertheless, you're unlikely to succeed as a leader-manager unless you take that risk.

Some good reasons to delegate are that it:

- attracts motivated employees to your team because they know they can learn from you
- can free you from details, giving you time to monitor the bigger picture and be sure that your team is operating smoothly, that output is integrated and synchronised, and that you are attaining your key objectives effectively and efficiently
- can help you take control of your time and concentrate on what's most important in your job
- gives you time to look ahead – time to plan your work and your team's work more effectively
- helps train people who can step into your role, putting you in a position for promotion or assignment to other interesting duties
- is good for the bottom line because jobs are completed at a less expensive level
- lets you relax when you go on holiday, knowing your team can carry on in your absence.

From the employees' point of view, delegating indicates faith and trust in them. It can enrich their jobs and it's a great way to develop, train and coach people. Sharing your knowledge and skills with employees and giving them additional responsibilities can also be a great motivator.

Delegating work that people in your team could do or would like to learn to do gives you time to sit back, think and plan. Table 12.1 shows some tasks that are and are not suitable to delegate.

TABLE 12.1 Tasks to delegate and tasks to keep

Tasks to delegate	Tasks to keep
Any tasks that you don't add value to by doing yourself	Boring jobs and unpleasant or otherwise disagreeable tasks that you don't like to do yourself
Recurring and routine duties	High-risk and high-cost tasks
Tasks that would train, develop and stretch employees	Matters dealing with organisational policy or security
Tasks that don't require your personal input	Planning and monitoring activities
Tasks that need to be done but you can't squeeze into your schedule, such as small projects, data collection, portions of larger projects and research	Sensitive or confidential matters such as pay or performance counselling
Tasks that require special skills or aptitudes that you may not have but team members have	Something that needs to be done quickly
Tasks that would make employees' jobs more interesting in some way	Tasks that are well beyond employees' training or experience – setting people up to fail is the worst possible kind of management

Five steps to effective delegation

Effective delegation takes planning and thought but it 'pays' for itself by saving you time in the long run. Like assigning work, delegating involves matching tasks to people, providing the right information and necessary training, and performing the necessary follow-up.

Step 1: Decide what to delegate

Use the work delegation plan shown in Figure 12.3 to help you decide which tasks you could or should be delegating. (Keep the delegation plan template handy and use it as required to make sure you're using recurring, routine, occasional and new tasks to develop team members' skills and to maintain their job interests.)

Recurring and routine tasks	Who can do it now?	Who could be trained to do it?
Tasks that would increase or develop an employee's skills or knowledge	Who can do it now?	Who could be trained to do it?
Occasional duties or tasks	Who can do it now?	Who could be trained to do it?
Tasks I do that are in someone's area of expertise or interest	Who can do it now?	Who could be trained to do it?

FIGURE 12.3 Work delegation plan

Think about your recurring and routine tasks that would increase or develop an employee's skills or knowledge, and your occasional duties or tasks and tasks that you do that are in one of your team members' areas of interest or expertise. When new work comes in, consider whether it might be appropriate and advantageous to delegate it.

Step 2: Select the delegate

Think about who in your team can already do these tasks, who could be trained to do them and who would enjoy or benefit from learning how to do them. Select suitable delegates based on whether or not they:

- are already able and willing to take on the responsibility for doing the task
- have a flair for the task (see, for example, Chapter 5)
- have shown interest in a particular type of work and delegating it can help them decide if they really enjoy it
- need to develop particular skills for future assignments or promotion
- want to learn the task in order to develop or extend their skills
- would appreciate learning the task because it adds interest or challenge to their job or because they enjoy that type of work.

Avoid the urge to delegate only to your most skilled or promising employees as everyone can benefit from the experience and knowledge that delegation provides.

Step 3: Delegate

When delegating, be clear as to the importance of the task, when or how often it needs to be done, the standard or end result you expect, what resources the employee can draw on and if there are any relevant constraints they need to take into consideration, such as time or money.

Delegate using these headings:

- Why the task is important
- Why you are delegating *this* task to *this* person
- Quality
- Quantity
- Safety
- Deadline.

Explaining why you are asking this particular person to do a task means you aren't just utilising their skills and knowledge but are also recognising them. One of the keys to effective delegation is reframing a task you can't realistically manage or don't have the time to handle so that delegates don't feel you've simply dumped it on them, but instead feel excited about taking it on.

Go through the task with the delegate, filling in knowledge or skills gaps with training or coaching. Discuss how the delegate intends to approach the task, any problems they might run into and how they could deal with them. Don't insist that it be done the way you would have done it – in other words, delegate according to the results desired, not according to the methods to use, unless these are very clear-cut and specific and really are the best way to approach the task.

Be clear that you are there to assist, give advice or help the delegate think through the task should any difficulties arise. 'I'm sure I can figure it out' or 'I think I understand' are code for 'I don't know what you want but I'm not about to say so' and a clear signal to explain more or ask what other information the employee needs. When delegated tasks are complicated or you're not sure the employee is completely clear about what you want, ask questions about how they could approach it or ask for a written summary to confirm their understanding.

Discuss how you will monitor the task to ensure that it is being completed correctly. Monitor only what is important, such as the critical success measures, and use **lead indicators** whenever you can to measure and track performance and progress.

Set up a systematic method of measuring progress against MoS or milestones to alert you and the delegate to deviations from the requirements. When the delegate is highly skilled and motivated, you can use management by exception where the delegate monitors progress and comes to you only when there is a deviation. Alternatively, you can arrange the system so that the actual results go directly to both you and the employee for comparison with the desired results. The results should never go only to you because this makes employees overly dependent on you for feedback on performance and can have the effect of reducing their motivation.

Don't be tempted to meddle unnecessarily. In other words, once you have delegated, don't hound the delegate by trying to keep on top of every detail. Release the task to the delegate and monitor only the critical control points upon which you have agreed. Also be careful to avoid the temptation to take the task back and do it for the delegate at the first sign of a problem.

Step 4: Inform others as necessary

When employees need to liaise with others to carry out a delegated task or duty, let those people know they can expect to be dealing with your delegate on this matter in the future. Reassure them that you have complete confidence in the delegate's ability to do the job well.

Step 5: Monitor results

Don't delegate a task and simply hope for the best. Whether or not your monitoring system is automated, keep on top of how the employee is progressing, whether they are carrying out the task safely and efficiently, and if they are on track to satisfactorily achieve the desired goal. When things are going wrong, you need to know in plenty of time so you can take corrective action yourself or guide the delegate in undertaking it.

From time-to-time discuss with the delegate how they are enjoying the task, what they are learning and how they can use the skills they are acquiring in other aspects of their job. Provide constructive feedback on how you see the delegate's performance, how it helps you and others, and express your appreciation for their help.

INDUSTRY INSIGHTS

Bill Gates

Alamy Stock Photo/Simon Serdar

Bill Gates, one of the richest people on earth, credits much of his success to skilful delegation. As he built his Microsoft empire, Gates was always careful to hire people who possessed slightly different skills to himself. He would then assign them tasks in relation to developing products and services and wait for them to come back to him with alternative suggestions and ideas. This resulted in the development of even better products and services than Gates himself could develop on his own.

But Gates went even further. He realised his strength was in software development rather than people management, so he brought in the energetic Steve Ballmer in 1980 who, as Gates put it, 'really liked people and management'. Ballmer became President of the company in 1998 and replaced Gates as CEO in 2000, filling that role for 14 years until 2014. By that stage, Microsoft was worth more than a trillion dollars and Gates was ready to step aside for good.

Not quite right?

Remember that reaching a goal is not the only important outcome of delegation. Facilitating team members' personal development by allowing them to learn is also important, even when on their first attempt they don't accomplish the task as quickly, efficiently or effectively as you could.

Part of the unwritten contract of delegating is that when you delegate you also offer the right to learn by mistakes. When a delegate makes a mistake or does something incorrectly, or when there is a better, easier or faster way to approach the delegated task, use it as an opportunity for training, coaching and guidance. Help the delegate fix any mistakes quickly and limit the fallout; then discuss what you will both do differently next time. (To find out more about coaching employees and offering constructive feedback, see Chapter 15 and Chapter 29.)

List five common mistakes that can be made when delegating that can undermine its effectiveness.

Delegate, don't abdicate

Leaving employees floundering and expecting them to 'get on with it' when they are clearly struggling is not delegation – it's the 'sink or swim' approach. Far from developing staff or 'testing' their skills, it's setting them up to fail. This kind of approach is likely to shatter their confidence and end up with the task having to be taken over or redone by someone else. The result is wasted time, an outcome that is unsatisfactory in terms of work quality, effort required to rebuild the staff member's confidence and possibly time and energy to also rebuild the relationship. Failing to ensure a delegate is approaching a task properly or failing to monitor progress is abdication, not delegation.

Dealing with unenthusiastic reactions to delegation

Not all employees receive a delegated task eagerly. Some employees who are delegated a task may respond with, 'I already have enough work to do' and this may well be true. On the other hand, the person might be poorly organised and so their response is an alert to you to provide coaching to help the employee improve their efficiency. Another employee might complain, 'I never know what I'm expected to do!' This may be a sign that you need to be more comprehensive or clear with the information you are communicating, or it could mean that the employee lacks confidence or is concerned about your reaction to mistakes. You may need to reflect on and improve your verbal communication and interpersonal skills if this is the basis for the employee's reaction.

When an employee indicates that they feel unappreciated for their efforts, you may need to review the information on motivation (see Chapter 11) and learn to give positive feedback (see Chapter 15). If an employee says, 'Tell me exactly what you want me to do', consider whether you have micro-managed them in the past and been too explicit in your work instructions. It might be time to provide them with greater scope in how they approach a task and allow them to be creative and problem solve. This will not only help their personal development, but also may lead to ideas and solutions that you might not have come up with.

Other negative reactions to delegation might include:

- 'I can't do it!': which may mean the employee lacks confidence and needs support.
- 'Why should I bother?' or 'Why should I be doing your job for you?': which may mean they are disenchanted with your lack of appreciation or recognition.
- 'Why should I help you out? You never do anything for me': which may indicate they feel unsupported and perhaps even unfairly overworked.

Transferable skills
3.4 Leadership

Whatever the reason for negative reactions like these, they should always be dealt with tactfully. Use your reflective listening skills and ask questions to fully understand the employee's objection to taking on the delegated task. The responses may be valid, or they may signal a deeper morale and motivation problem of which you were unaware and that requires your urgent attention.

12.4 Receiving assignments

Great ability develops and reveals itself increasingly with every new assignment.

Baltasar Gracián (17th-century Spanish Jesuit and philosopher), https://www.brainyquote.com/quotes/baltasar_gracian_100912.

When you are on the receiving end of work assignments or delegated duties, don't be embarrassed or reluctant to ask questions so that you thoroughly understand what your boss expects and are aware of any challenges and constraints that you need to consider. When you don't, you risk misunderstanding and underperforming.

Assumptions can be dangerous, so clarify any details you're unsure about, such as guidelines on timing, quality and quantity, and restrictions on money, time or other resources. You don't need to ask your boss to do the job for you or to explain it step-by-step, but specific operating parameters ensure that you are both on the same wavelength. When you need to enlist the cooperation of others or temporarily acquire any special authority, confirm your manager has made the necessary arrangements.

Find out what priority the task has to both your manager and the organisation. Be positive in your attitude and show through your words and actions that you are willing to complete the assignment with enthusiasm and professionalism. When your manager is inclined to 'shift the goalposts' or change priorities, it is a good idea to confirm your assignment in writing so if something goes wrong, you at least have a record of what you were basing your work efforts on and can defend your work performance and output up to that point.

STUDY TOOLS

QUICK REVIEW

KEY CONCEPT 12.1 

a What is the difference between assigning work, delegating work and the leadership style called delegation?

KEY CONCEPT 12.2 

a List and briefly explain the different ways to assign work, when to use each and what can happen when you assign work in the wrong way.

b List and give an example of each of the five levels of monitoring you can use after you have assigned or delegated work.

c Explain how you would handle an employee who is reluctant to carry out a directive.

KEY CONCEPT 12.3 

a What are some poor excuses for failing to delegate? What are the results of not delegating?

b What benefits can leader-managers expect to gain from effective delegation?

c How important is it for team leaders to know and understand the different strengths, working styles, work preferences, motivators and expectations of team members when assigning and delegating work?

KEY CONCEPT 12.4 

a List the information you need to know when receiving an assignment.

BUILD YOUR SKILLS

KEY CONCEPT 12.1 

a Discuss what leader-managers should consider before assigning or delegating work and how they can alter the leadership style they use to affect a good outcome.

KEY CONCEPT 12.2 

a How, in general terms, do you think knowledge workers should be assigned work? Would direct orders ever be suitable when assigning work to knowledge workers? Provide an example to illustrate your thinking.

b Discuss the reasons an employee might be reluctant to carry out an assignment and how leader-managers can deal with these situations.

KEY CONCEPT 12.3 

a Although delegation is a good time-management tool, you need to take care not to overuse it. Do you agree? Why or why not?

b What do you think are the dangers of delegating boring work?

c How should you handle the situation of an employee making a mistake or having trouble carrying out an assignment or a delegated duty? Discuss the four possible causes of an employee carrying out an assignment incorrectly and the remedies each cause suggests.

d Although it can be tempting to take work back that isn't done correctly, what could be the consequences?

e Explain how you would respond to an employee who says, 'I'm too busy to take on this task', and to an employee who asks for help with a problem.

KEY CONCEPT 12.4 

a What should you do when you disagree with an assignment or change in policy or procedure? Develop some action guidelines based on the information provided in this chapter.

WORKPLACE ACTIVITIES

KEY CONCEPT 12.1 

a Describe the last time you assigned work to someone in your work team.

b Describe the last task you delegated to someone in your work team.

KEY CONCEPT 12.2 

a Referring to the last time you assigned work to someone in your work team, described in question 12.1(a), how did you assign the work and why did you assign it in the way you did? How did you and the employee monitor the results? In retrospect, how effectively did you assign the work? What, if anything, would you do differently next time?

b What reference to your ability to assign work is likely to be commented on in your performance review?

KEY CONCEPT 12.3 

a Referring to the last time you delegated work to someone in your work team, described in question 12.1(b), describe the steps you took and how effectively the delegated task was carried out. What, if anything, would you do differently next time?

b What reference to your delegation skills is likely to be commented on in your performance review?

KEY CONCEPT 12.4 

a Thinking about the assignment or delegated duty you received, what was the effect on your level of motivation? What did you learn from it?

b How do you expect the way you receive and carry out delegated assignments to affect your performance review?

EXTENSION ACTIVITY

Referring to the Snapshot at the beginning of this chapter, answer the following question:

1 How would you advise Dilini about approaching the way she advises Isabelle about the new procedure in a way that won't get her 'off-side'?

CASE STUDY 12

WHAT HAPPENS WHEN YOU DO DELEGATE?

Seth Kehne, owner of Lawn Butler in East Tennessee in the United States, started his company in 1999 in his senior year of high school. It grew slowly over time and because the growth was gradual, he never took steps to implement the management system needed for a larger company. With everyone reporting to Kehne, his time was stretched thin as he worked too many hours – managing instead of delegating. But because managers didn't feel they had the freedom to do their jobs without input from him, the business' growth faltered.

'Deep down I knew what the problem was, but when I heard it spoken aloud from someone else it became real and my call to action was elevated,' Kehne says. 'By failing to delegate, I'd been holding back my managers. They didn't have the complete authority they needed to do what they needed to do.'

Part of the solution was to implement an organisation chart. It included managers' new duties and responsibilities. It also reduced the number of people reporting directly to Kehne from more than 20 down to four – three production managers and an asset manager.

'To be honest, I thought I had already delegated a lot of my responsibilities, but once we had this organisation chart in place, I realised that I really hadn't,' Kehne says. 'Suddenly my stress level was way down, and our efficiency was up. Jobs were able to be done correctly without everyone reporting to me. And I was no longer stretched too thin to take care of my own responsibilities.'

As managers and employees assumed their new roles, operations became increasingly smoother, allowing growth of the business to resume. Today, the company has expanded to 38 team members, up from 25 when the changes took place.

'Things just operate better now,' Kehne says, adding sales are up 50 per cent since he implemented the change two years ago. Other improvements include better work hours thanks to more efficient operations (at least five to 10 fewer hours per week), positive customer response and better employee job satisfaction.

'It's something we should have done a long time ago,' Kehne says. 'Personally, my stress level is at an all-time low despite the fact we're doing more work than we've ever done.'

Source: Casey Payton, 'Case study: Delegation dilemma', *Landscape Management Magazine*, 22 October 2014. Available at https://www.landscapemanagement.net/case-study-delegationdilemma

Questions

1 One of the most difficult aspects of delegation for leader-managers is to hand over the control for making decisions and taking responsibility. What can leader-managers do to ease their anxiety in relation to delegating and make it easier for them to 'hand over the reins' to others in the organisation?

2 Explore the benefits outlined in the case study that leader-managers and organisations can derive from effective delegation.

CHAPTER

BUILDING PRODUCTIVE WORK TEAMS

After completing this chapter, you will be able to:

13.1 recognise the 'upsides and 'downsides' of the various types of teams you are likely to participate in, and lead and manage

13.2 establish a performance plan for a team and for individual team members

13.3 help your team concentrate its efforts on its purpose and goals, and its members to work effectively together

13.4 build and sustain a high-performing team

13.5 support your team in its daily activities.

TRANSFERABLE SKILLS

The following transferable skills are covered in this chapter:

2 **Critical thinking and problem solving**
  2.2 Personal effectiveness

3 **Social competence**
  3.1 Teamwork/relationships
  3.4 Leadership

OVERVIEW

What does it feel like to be a member of your work team? For example, are your team members open or guarded, supportive or undermining, tolerant or judgemental, trusting or suspicious? Do they aim to fix problems or fix blame? Do they take responsibility or pass the buck? This depends on your organisation's culture, on how interpersonally skilled you and your team members are and how skilfully you build and support your team.

Managing in today's streamlined, informal team-based organisations is different from managing in the conformist hierarchical organisations of the past. If you aren't already, you will probably soon be leading a team whose members need to work together, rather than as independent performers, to achieve challenging goals. The ability to nurture high-performing teams and empower them to innovate and work productively is a prized skill in modern workplaces.

Understanding the interactions and dynamics that take place within teams and what it means to be a team helps you encourage and assist your work group to become a cohesive, highly productive team. Recognising the behaviours that effective team members display and how teams develop, set goals, make decisions, motivate their members, celebrate and reward success, and manage change, are all part of building effective work teams.

In this chapter, you will discover the real power of teams and how to build them and lead them to achieve meaningful, worthwhile results in an innovative, enjoyable way.

SNAPSHOT

Trouble in the team

Shenali is concerned about her team and not just its performance. Among the team there is constant complaining, negativity and a distinct lack of camaraderie or cooperation between team members. Each team member only concentrates on their particular tasks, and when Shenali asks for volunteers to do something, no one ever comes forward, which often means she has to do the task herself.

Shenali mentions her concerns to Jarrod, one of the other team leaders, 'Their attitudes are all wrong, they think that doing their job tasks is enough, but none of them have any sense of team or seem to understand or care about the team's goals – and this is starting to really affect the team's performance as a whole.'

'In what way?' asks Jarrod.

'Well, for instance, I can't get anyone to volunteer for things, so invariably I have to do them myself. This takes me away from important parts of my role, which affects the team, and when I do get them working together on joint tasks the disagreement and lack of cooperation means the tasks take much longer to complete and we miss our targets.

'They never help each other out either. When someone is overloaded, which happens often, no one lends them a hand without being told to. They've also got no sense of responsibility. The other day we had an important deadline, and we needed all hands-on-deck to meet it, but George and Caroline took their accumulated time-off-in-lieu and left early right on that day when we really needed them. And I know they are aware of the bottlenecks in the workflow and are smart enough to identify solutions for improvement, but do you think they bother to do so ...? Of course not.'

'You have certainly got some serious issues there,' Jarrod replies. 'What have you done so far to try to turn things around?'

'I'm a bit stumped, really. I don't know what I can do. Whatever I try I just get negativity and an unwillingness to help or go that extra yard. Gosh, maybe it's me, maybe it's my leadership. Maybe I'm not up to the job.'

'Whoa there Shenali, don't get ahead of yourself. Managing teams, and particularly unproductive ones, is a complex undertaking and there can be many different factors at play. Why don't we schedule a meeting where we can discuss this in greater detail together and see if we can come up with some ideas to address the challenges you're facing? I know of a few strategies that Caleb who manages the call centre team put into place with his team last year when they were in a similar place, and the results were quite remarkable.'

'Oh that would be great, Jarrod, I'll send you a Zoom invite when I get back to my desk for a catch up on Friday. Thanks so much.'

13.1 Understanding teams

> Most groups of people form into teams in order to strive for goals which are beyond the reach of an individual. The operative word of the previous sentence was strive.
>
> Governor-General Sir Peter Cosgrove, 'Leading in Australia', Boyer Lecture No. 3, ABC Radio National, 22 November 2009.

People join with others into teams because they can achieve more together than they can achieve alone and most people also enjoy being part of a team, particularly a successful team. For example, think of how much satisfaction people get from participating in and contributing to a winning sports team or a successful community project team, and how much time and effort they are willing to put into those teams as a result. Teams can be enjoyable, beneficial and motivating.

A group of individuals or a team?

People come together in differing ways. As Figure 13.1 shows, a collection of individuals with no sense of identity or team spirit can be at one end of the scale and at the other end is an interdependent team whose members share common goals, a sense of purpose and an identity.

A group of people working together in the same area or for the same leader-manager isn't necessarily a team. A work group becomes a work team when its members need to pool their efforts to achieve shared goals following a shared strategy. Teams share values and a vision that all members understand and are committed to. Members are collectively responsible for the end results and blend their complementary skills to achieve them.

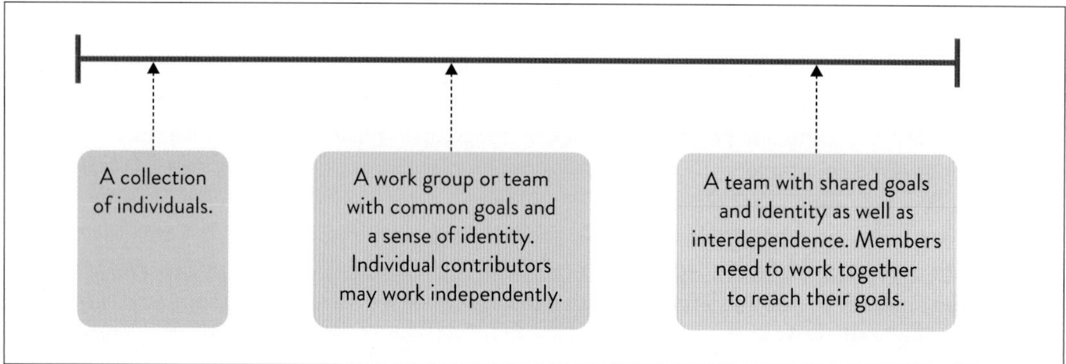

FIGURE 13.1 Me or we?

The good

Well-led teams can achieve cost savings, be innovative so as to solve problems and devise creative ideas and solutions, raise productivity, and respond quickly and decisively to customer needs. Increased creativity, innovation and problem-solving generated within a team environment can also reduce manufacturing and design flaws, leading to significant cost savings, increase efficiency in other ways, and reduce costs due to fewer layers of management.

Teams are an excellent way to benefit from people's skills and knowledge and the synergy created by the complementary mix of skills and expertise. They can increase morale and job satisfaction by providing people with more control over their jobs and the fulfilment of working collaboratively with others.

The bad and the ugly

There are downsides to teams, too. Not everyone has the skills or disposition to participate fully and effectively in a team. Maintaining high levels of cooperation and creativity takes skill and effort on everyone's part and not everyone is willing or capable to make the commitment necessary for a team to function effectively.

It isn't easy to introduce teams into the workplace or to find people with the skills to lead and support them. Failing to address poor performance or disruptive team members and allowing groupthink or dysfunctional conflict to develop are just four threats to effective teams brought about by poor leadership.

Many organisations have rushed into creating teams for the wrong kinds of jobs or have created the wrong kinds of teams. Not all jobs and activities are best handled by teams, and teams are often introduced when they aren't really needed or when another solution, such as automation, would be more effective. Some types of teams are better suited to certain activities than others; for example, when self-managed teams are called for, but the concept seems too 'radical' for the organisation and quality improvement teams are introduced instead, management is left wondering why the expected results have not materialised. Teams are also not needed when the leader is actually a better option in terms of having the knowledge and expertise to undertake the task or project. Similarly, sometimes assigning tasks to individuals to work on independently is a more efficient and effective option to achieve the desired goals.

When organisations introduce teams in isolation, as a quick fix or as a half-hearted experiment, team members may not be given sufficient training and support; they generally lack clear objectives, and the team can meet endlessly trying to figure out what it's supposed to do and how it's supposed to do it. Unsurprisingly, poorly introduced teams usually fail to achieve the expected results.

Ten types of teams

Teams vary in their leadership, longevity and purpose. Some teams carry out a range of tasks while others perform just a few; some are permanent while others, such as project teams, are temporary. Some teams have leader-managers to guide them, or a team facilitator who is also a member of the team, and some manage themselves. The number and types of different teams an organisation has depends on what the organisation does, its culture and size, and the expertise of its workforce.

Functional teams

Shannon is an accounting clerk in a large organisation. Her workstation is on the third floor, where all the finance people work. On the next floor is human resources, and on the next is sales and marketing. She only sees employees from these and other functions in the elevator and at the occasional training workshop. Her work group, and the other functional work groups in her organisation, are made up of individual contributors and so are teams only in a loose sense.

Functional teams like Shannon's carry out specific organisational functions and include members from several vertical levels of hierarchy.

Management teams

Juan is the marketing manager in the same company that Shannon works in. He leads the marketing team and is also part of the senior management team that meets monthly to review the company's performance, discuss corporate initiatives and proposals, coordinate work across the organisation, and update each other on their respective function's progress against targets. This is the only time the senior management team meets and works together as a team.

Matrix teams

Anika is an ergonomics engineer who works on three of the company's design teams, two based at head office and one a virtual team made up of employees from several offices. Each of these teams reports to a product manager and is responsible for either improving an existing product or developing a new product, depending on its brief. Because of her specialised knowledge, she contributes valuable advice on making the company's products safe and user-friendly. When she isn't meeting with a team, she is researching and developing designs, or consulting with other team members or outside experts.

In matrix organisations, employees are members of two or more teams, each made up of members from different functions. Members of matrix teams report to a different leader-manager for each aspect of their job.

Merged teams

Mingmei is the human resources manager of two recently merged banks. Her top two priorities currently are overseeing a temporary team responsible for combining the best of the two banks' policies (including the 'bring-your-own-device' policy, dress code and grooming policy, and leave policy) and working with the CEO and the other senior managers to firm up the organisation design and team composition.

Acquisitions, mergers and takeovers are common. Employees from once-competing organisations are asked to work together cooperatively for the good of the newly combined company. This presents special challenges as people mourn the loss of the old, struggle to come to terms with the new, and cope with new ways of working and a host of new people, cultures, procedures and systems. (For more information on leading merged teams, see Chapter 14.)

Organisations are also constantly looking for ways to reduce costs and become 'leaner' in the way they operate. To achieve this, organisations may sometimes merge teams to reduce duplication of tasks, enable cuts to staff and refine their operational processes to increase efficiency. Depending on the differences in the cultures of the teams being merged, their new leader may face some of the same challenges as those combining teams from different organisations. (For more on this refer to Chapter 14.)

Mixed teams

Youssef often works from a **workplace hub** alongside other remote workers from his organisation where they regularly congregate to share ideas and work on specific problems or client queries. He enjoys the freedom and flexibility of working with a range of specialists, some of whom are full-time and others part-time employees or contractors, with the odd casual freelancer brought in as necessary.

Full-time, part-time and casual employees, temporary employees and contractors, and off-site employees make up mixed teams like Youssef's. While most of Youssef's team members are off-site workers, most organisations have on-site mixed teams too where employees may come in on different days or during different periods of the day or may work in distinctly different locations on-site, meaning they rarely have contact with other team members. Leading these types of teams made up of various groups of workers presents special challenges and requires a range of different management strategies to ensure each type of worker remains motivated, engaged and supported. (For more on this refer to Chapter 14.)

Multifunctional or cross-functional teams

Anika, an ergonomics engineer who works in the matrix organisation discussed previously, belongs to three teams that are all cross-functional in that they are made up of specialists from across the organisation's functions who each perform their own specialised function.

Matrix teams are also multifunctional teams, as are project teams and other temporary teams, as well as teams in capabilities-based organisations. In teams like these, most of the members are from about the same hierarchical level. They may be responsible for delivering an entire product or service, from design to manufacturing, marketing, delivery and after-sales service, or they may be organised into customer account teams that handle every aspect of a customer's experience with the organisation.

Problem-solving and innovation teams

Junti has recently been seconded to a temporary, part-time innovation team along with six other leader-managers, each from functions whose workflows overlap. They have been tasked with devising streamlined workflows, or business processes, and opening communication channels between their functions. They have been asked to particularly consider the 'white space', or 'hands-off' work, as well as the 'dark space' or 'hands-on' work.

Problem-solving and innovation teams (sometimes called task forces) are generally temporary teams who meet to solve a specific problem, often through innovation, and then disband. Quality circles were an early form of this type of team; and they are still present today but usually are named differently, often with a 'corporate branding' flavour. They typically meet for a few hours a week to identify, analyse and rectify problems, particularly problems of workflows and systems.

Project teams and committees

Gillian has been asked to head up a project team to review her organisation's IT and communications requirements. Although the team won't begin its work for two months, giving Gillian time to second the members she needs and finalise the **project charter**, she has joined Junti's innovation team in order to get a feel for the sort of technology that may be helpful as the organisation moves towards becoming a capabilities-based organisation.

Project teams are generally temporary teams brought together to undertake a specific, usually large, assignment, such as introducing new technology throughout an organisation, launching a new product or managing the construction of a large building or residential development. Team members are generally chosen from across the organisation for their knowledge and experience in the project area, and may be assigned to the project full-time or work on it along with their normal duties. Once the project is completed, the team disbands. Increasingly, members of project teams come from all over the world and work together virtually using collaborative systems technology.

Other teams, often called committees, are permanent and undertake ongoing tasks. Their members often rotate in and out. Health and safety committees, internal communications committees and risk management committees are examples of this type of team.

Self-managed teams

Clayton's team manages its own budgets, plans and schedules its work, assigns tasks to team members and organises the resources it needs. It also improves work systems and workflows as needed and selects its own team members. Decisions are reached by **consensus** and team members evaluate each other's performance. Officially, leadership rotates among team members, although in practice, leadership moves between members informally, according to team needs, with the most knowledgeable or experienced team member 'stepping up'. (When the team first formed, an experienced leader-manager was appointed to help the team learn how to manage itself and coach them in the interpersonal and technical skills they needed.)

In self-managed, or self-directed teams like this, team members take on many of the responsibilities of their former leader-managers, and because of their broad responsibilities, they are usually kept informed about their company's financial affairs and how it is faring in the marketplace. Empowered teams like this can achieve impressive results in terms of cost savings, effective decision-making, employee commitment and motivation, improved customer satisfaction, and increased productivity and innovation. There is also, however, the potential for them to fall flat if the organisation doesn't provide them with the training and support they need.

Virtual teams

Anika – the ergonomics engineer we met earlier – is in a virtual team, which does everything her two other teams do. Sophisticated information technology makes it easy to communicate and work on documents together in real time. Although Anika's virtual team is temporary, there are other, permanent, virtual teams in her organisation, too. Some of those teams are made up entirely of employees from different locations while others have members from other organisations as well, usually suppliers and trading partners – some of them in different states and even different countries. Depending on team members' locations, they sometimes meet in person as well as via videoconferences, teleconferences and computer link-ups. (See Chapter 14 for more information on leading virtual teams.)

People make teams

To be an effective team leader or member of any type of team, you need sound communication and interpersonal skills, emotional intelligence (EI), self-awareness and training to work well together as a unit. The members of matrix, multifunctional, project, self-managed and virtual teams generally need extra training in these areas to develop the team-working skills they require, and members of virtual teams often need training in the technology of their team as well. This can be costly and time-consuming, but without targeted training, frustrations can mount and anticipated results can turn to smoke.

Members of merged and mixed teams often benefit from **team building**, while members of problem-solving and innovation teams need specialised training in problem identification and resolution, innovation, and statistical and systematic analytical tools and techniques, such as **check sheets**, **control charts** and **flow charts**.

13.2 Fixing the goalposts

> I think people are looking for inspiration. Work needs to have meaning, and they want to feel like they're part of something bigger. To do that well, you have to be thoughtful, and you have to communicate effectively.
>
> Adam Bryant quoting Amit Singh of Google, 'The corner office: A respectful clash of ideas', *The New York Times*, 22 January 2016.

What is needed to make a great or even just a good team? Is it team members with highly developed skills, experience and expertise? Or does it require an inspiring leader who can motivate and lift a team from mediocrity to greatness? For some teams, one or both of these requirements may be relevant. But for any team to be successful, there are a few must-haves.

The first is that every team needs a clear purpose, a reason for being if you like. Having a clear purpose enables team members to understand why the team exists and what it has been formed to do. The second thing is a clear understanding of the level at which it is required to perform. A sporting team, for example, may know it is there to win but unless its team members understand the level to which they must lift their skills and teamwork to defeat other teams, the team is likely to win some and lose some without ever establishing any real consistency in the results it achieves.

As well as understanding the team's performance requirements, each team member also needs to know what their individual role is and how it contributes to the success of the rest of the team. Even knowing this in addition to the team's purpose and required level of performance is still not quite enough.

The last thing each team member also needs to know is how their individual performance will be measured. This will provide them with a context as to how and in what aspects they can improve. All of these aspects can be incorporated into a team performance plan which provides a team with a road map of where it wants to get, how it is going to get there and how it will know when it does.

Team purpose and performance plan

To become a high performance team there needs to be a shared purpose, common goals and cooperation among team members to achieve them. High performance teams are able to overcome obstacles that block other teams and can find and fix the causes of poor performance.

The first step towards becoming a high-performance team starts with creating a short, clear statement of intent so that all team members understand what they are jointly working towards. A team purpose statement does this by defining why the team exists. It keeps everyone moving in the same direction and shows team members how their individual efforts contribute to the team's goals. The team purpose acts as a vision for the team and a touchstone for decision-making. It also acts as a guide for team members in relation to the expectations of their day-to-day behaviour. To serve both the team and the organisation, a team purpose should also relate to the wider context of the organisation's goals. Two examples of team purpose statements are shown in Figure 13.2.

Involving the whole team in crafting its purpose statement helps to strengthen buy-in from team members. Displaying it somewhere visible or making it available as a screensaver, for example, helps to keep it in the forefront of team members' minds.

Some other ways to keep your organisation's vision and team purpose alive include:

- Acknowledge and reward team members who support the vision and team purpose.
- Align your performance goals and measures with the vision and your team purpose.
- Refer to the vision and team purpose when reaching decisions.

Role clarification

Role clarification means making your expectations of the team and its members clear. To do this effectively, you need agreement regarding your team's purpose, individual team members' job purposes, key result areas (KRAs), measures of success (MoS), non-task goals and 'bottom-line rules' (see Chapter 19 for more on this).

It may be valuable to ask team members to write their own job purpose statements (they may want to refer to their role description or similar for this), read them to the rest of the team and then put it back to team members to help each other refine them. This ensures that everyone in the team understands and appreciates everyone else's role and contributions. People who do the same jobs may decide to combine their job purpose statements or to keep their own, slightly different statements to reflect their key concerns; either way is acceptable.

The **role clarity** this process provides ensures that everyone understands precisely what is expected of them in their job and as a team member, and how everyone else in the team contributes to the team purpose. On the process side, role clarity helps the team to openly discuss and agree the behaviours expected of all team members. You can do this through formal and informal individual and team discussions and in specially convened team-building workshops (explained in Section 13.4).

To enhance our company's reputation in the marketplace by working cooperatively together to produce a top-quality product that meets or exceeds our measures of success, continually refining our approach to increase our efficiencies and reduce waste and costs.

To organise and present our merchandise in an attractive and relaxing environment and serve our customers in a friendly, enjoyable, knowledgeable and helpful way, so that we win their repeat business and meet or exceed our key performance targets.

FIGURE 13.2 Two team purpose statements

Measures of success

SMART measures of success are explained in relation to individual jobs in Chapters 9 and 19. Teams also have SMART MoS; for example, a work team might be responsible for attaining the SMART target of 'designing, testing and implementing a streamlined workflow by the end of the next quarter'. To achieve this, it draws up a list of **milestones** or tasks that it needs to accomplish, each meeting the SMART criteria, and assigns these tasks, or deliverables, to individual team members. The team can measure its success by whether or not it meets its SMART targets and individual team members can measure their success by whether or not they're meeting their deliverables.

The advantage of outcome-based success measures is that team members can work anywhere, at any time, using whatever methods they want. Rather than needing to be watched, just check in with team members to find out whether they're on track or whether they have run into problems and need assistance. This makes outcome-based success measures ideal for teleworkers and other off-site employees, such as sales and service employees, and members of project and virtual teams. However, since the onset of the COVID-19 pandemic, this approach has been applied far more extensively to a range of different types of teams than might otherwise have been the case. So while there was an expectation that more teams would be working this way as more organisations became capabilities based, the fallout of the pandemic has meant that this method of managing teams has been fast-tracked to many teams regardless of their or their organisation's structure.

In addition to measuring whether team members meet their deliverables, you can also gauge the effectiveness of their contributions by looking at team members' abilities to 'add value' to a project or the team through their expertise, the ideas they help to generate, and the quality and timeliness of their contributions. Although subjective, these success criteria are at least clear and open.

As with individual performers, you can use MoS to continually improve a team's performance. For example, your team might have had a spate of near misses and you are concerned that an accident is waiting to happen. To concentrate everyone's attention on health and safety, you might introduce a team goal, such as 'to reduce incidents by 70 per cent next year'. When this is achieved, you could set a target of 'an incident-free quarter'. Once safety is back under control, you can shift the team's attention to a different improvement goal with another measure of success.

Now your team has a performance plan to build its performance. But there is a caveat to setting ambitious success measures: they should reflect what you believe is possible and what ought to happen given the conditions under which your team is working and their collective skills and abilities, rather than what you would like to happen in a perfect world where everything could be controlled and predicted. They should also help achieve the organisation's vision and objectives.

Monitoring performance

With both task and process expectations agreed and understood by all team members, it's easy to monitor performance and support team members in meeting these expectations. Monitoring performance also helps you to spot any training needs and manage performance by giving you a basis to discuss and uncover the reasons for performance not meeting expectations. (Chapter 19 explains how to uncover reasons for poor performance and productivity, Chapter 12 explains how to monitor performance, and Chapter 15 explains how to provide feedback on performance.)

13.3 Getting the team task and process right

> For all its technology, though, F1 is about people and finding the right staff and managing them well.
>
> Steve Nally, 'Pit-stop pressure', *Management Today*, June 2015, pp. 39–41.

To forge a group of diverse individuals into a team that works together to achieve a common goal isn't easy, but it is rewarding. To create an environment where team members participate in team activities, communicate openly and meaningfully with each other, work together to identify and resolve work problems and problems with the way they work together, and find ways to keep improving how they achieve their goals, you need to find the delicate balance between two aspects of team working: the team task and the team process.

The task

Task refers to the goal the team is working towards. It is 'what we do'. Make sure the team and job purpose statements, KRAs and MoS are crystal clear to each team member. You can increase task commitment by involving your team in planning, decision-making and other operational aspects of their work. To further boost teamwork, hold continuous improvement meetings, in which you identify and address issues and problems that prevent team members from working easily and smoothly to achieve their goals.

The process

The way the team approaches its task is referred to as its *process*. It is 'how we go about achieving our task'; how clearly and openly team members communicate and work, individually and together, to achieve results. Working together harmoniously and supportively, trusting each other and other elements of group dynamics set the stage for how fruitfully team members exchange ideas and information and how well they achieve their task. Remaining alert to team processes like these helps you recognise and diagnose problems early and deal with them effectively.

A team's process – how people work together – has a dramatic influence on its task achievement; it is the all-important lubricant that keeps the team's wheel turning. The specific communication patterns that characterise high-performing teams are observable, quantifiable and measurable.[1] Interestingly, they are better predictors of team success than the actual content of the communications and are as significant to a team's success as individual intelligence, personality, skill and the substance of discussions combined – particularly when the communications take place outside of formal meetings.

In successful teams, every team member talks to every other team member, not just to the team leader, and they talk and listen in roughly equal amounts. Exchanges among team members are numerous and the nature of these communications is more personal, such as face-to-face exchanges, phone calls or videoconferencing. When addressing the entire team, team members keep their contributions short, and when speaking one-to-one, they face each other and speak and gesture with energy. Social exchanges, as opposed to task discussions, account for at least half of all communications between individual team members, and new ideas and fresh perspectives obtained externally but shared with the team are also common.

Guide and shape your team's communication patterns; set an example by talking to team members face-to-face (or on the phone or via videoconference in virtual teams) as often as you can. Adjust the layout of the physical workplace so conversation between members is possible. Address the following issues with your team and revisit them periodically:

- How can we measure our team's success in working together to achieve results?
- How do we want to celebrate our successes?
- How do we want to communicate with each other?
- How do we want to share information with each other?
- How do we want to work, together and individually?
- How often do we want to meet?
- What can each team member contribute that will make it worthwhile for them to be a member of this team?
- What must we each do to achieve the team goals?

Write the answers down and give a copy to each team member to guide them in their daily activities. (For more information on what goes on inside a team, its culture, norms and group dynamics, see Chapter 14. For information on leading multicultural teams and team members from different generations, see Chapter 32.)

The delicate balance

Ironically, when you pay too much attention to the task and ignore the way the team works together, the task itself ends up suffering. And when you pay too much attention to process, the task ends up suffering, too. It's a delicate balance. Figure 13.3 shows that leaders and teams shift their efforts and attention between task and process, depending on the circumstances. Too much concentration on one or the other causes a team to flounder.

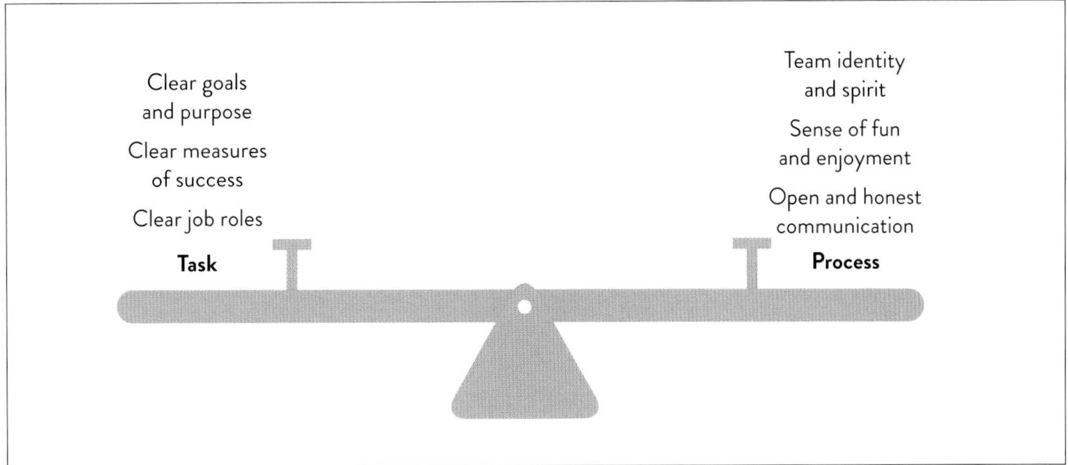

FIGURE 13.3 Task and process issues in a team

In times of crisis, for instance when there is a backlog of work to get through, when you're suddenly short-staffed and deadlines are looming, or the building is on fire, you almost certainly need to focus primarily on task issues as 'what needs to be done' is the highest priority. When the situation has calmed down, you can turn your attention to people and process issues to restore the balance. When the crisis is more emotional and affects team members, such as **downsizing** or a public relations disaster, you may need to be extra-supportive to team members to allay their concerns, and accept that a small, short-term loss of productivity is inevitable. When things are going really well, it's time to relax a bit, congratulate the team, celebrate and enjoy your success. The balance between task and process isn't constant or evenly split, which means you need to pay attention to your team's needs so that you can provide the time and effort required to support both, as your team's functioning dictates.

Here is a list of the things you need to do to address both your team's task and process needs:

- Address and redress task and process problems in the team quickly – don't avoid 'hard conversations'. (See Chapter 19 for more on this.)
- Build and maintain the team's sense of pride by making sure stakeholders understand the contribution the team makes to the organisation.
- Discuss matters affecting the team with team members, sharing as much information as you can.
- Make sure that nothing interferes with the members' ability to do their jobs. For example, equipment needs to work properly; members need to have the necessary information, time and other resources to do their jobs properly; any bottlenecks need to be removed; and cumbersome procedures need to be simplified. (Chapter 19 explains this in detail.)
- Make sure that team members know clearly what is expected of them, as individual contributors and as team members. This includes your bottom-line rules and the norms you expect them to follow. (See Chapters 4 and 19 for more on this.)
- Make sure that the best performers know how important they are to their team's success.
- Place team members in well-designed jobs that suit their personal skills and interests. (See Chapter 19 for more.)

- Protect your team – team members will return your loyalty.
- Reward the team when it reaches its goals, remembering that rewards come in many forms, not just money. (See Chapters 11 and 19 for more.)
- Take the time to get to know team members as individuals.
- Train team members and give them time to build their experience and confidence. (See Chapters 19 and 29 for a detailed explanation of how to train your team members.)
- Treat everyone not only as important individuals but also as valuable team members.

Task and process roles in teams

Team members characteristically behave and communicate in predictable ways, with predictable effects, called *roles*. Team members' roles can be functional (helpful) or dysfunctional (unhelpful). For example, the informal leader in your team can work with you or against you. The clown can be disruptive or can relieve tension. The gatekeeper can shut people out or make sure everyone has a say. The devil's advocate can pour water on good ideas or point out potential problems and how to fix them. (For more on task and process roles in teams, see Chapter 4.) Strengthen the way your team operates by helping people become aware of the roles they play and the effects these roles have on the team's task and process. Team members' skills improve when they become more sensitive to, and aware of, how they can help their team to function more effectively.

Three areas of team needs

To be an effective leader-manager, you need to satisfy three distinct areas of need:

1. *Individual needs:* the need for individuals to feel satisfied with their work – developing and motivating individuals.
2. *Task needs:* the need to succeed in reaching set goals – achieving the task.
3. *Team needs:* the need for the group to work as a team – building the team.[2]

This is called **functional leadership** or action-centred leadership. Ignoring any one area of need adversely affects the other areas.

Because these three areas of need overlap, as shown in **Figure 13.4**, it is sometimes possible to satisfy two or even all three areas of need with just one action. Training, for example, satisfies all

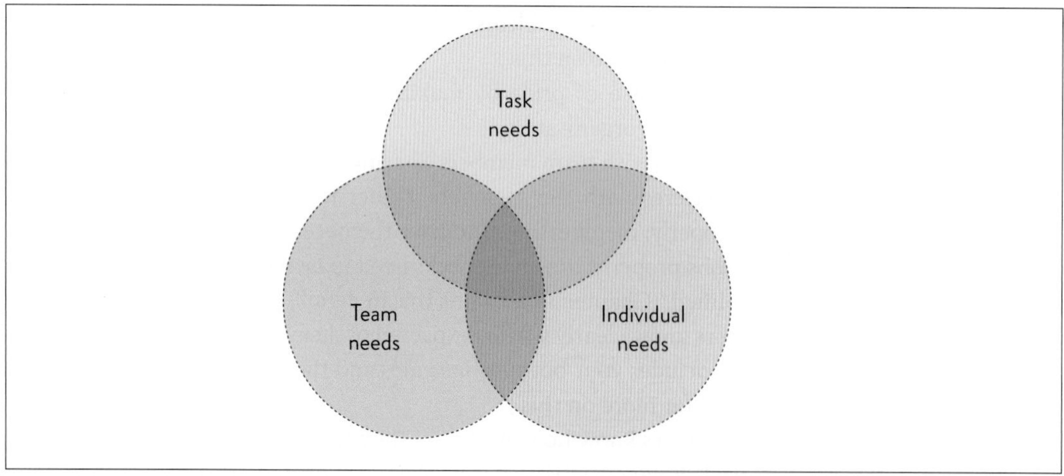

FIGURE 13.4 Overlapping needs

three areas: it helps to ensure that the task is performed well; it satisfies individuals' needs to increase their skills and knowledge; and it helps provide the team with a useful member.

13.4 Building and maintaining your team

> You are only as good as the people around you. You should hire people that think differently to you and have different skills. If you develop a crack team then you can do anything and once you have the team, you have to provide them with clear direction and let them get on with it.
>
> Ann Sherry (Executive Chairman, Carnival Australia), in T. Skotnicki, 'Leaving all in her wake', *Management Today*, 2014, pp. 12–15.

When your team members speak about their team, do they say 'they' and 'them', or 'we' and 'us'? The former indicates they don't feel part of things; the latter is what you want to hear. The more clearly people understand their own and each other's job purpose and KRAs – their roles and goals – the better they can work together and support each other's task achievement. When they understand each other's contributions and how their work is interdependent, they and the team as a whole have a sense of accountability for the team's actions, decisions and performance.

Teams, like people, have learning curves. The better team members come to know each other and how they each work; their individual experiences; approaches to problems, knowledge, skills, traits, strengths and work preferences; and how to put them to best use, the better they can perform.

INDUSTRY INSIGHTS

The power of food

It may sound simple, but it works – high-performing teams share meals. Research with firefighters found the special intimacy of sharing a meal makes a team feel like a family and increases performance. Cooperation is twice as high among firefighting teams that plan and prepare their shared meals and clean up afterwards, work out cooking schedules and share in the cost of the food than among those who don't.[3]

'Eating together is a more intimate act than looking over an Excel spreadsheet together. That intimacy spills back over into work', stated Kevin Kniffin, one of the authors of the research. While you don't have to take it that far with your team, sharing a meal in the cafeteria, a nearby park or a conference room occasionally can provide team members the opportunity to learn about each other as people, not just as co-workers, which is important in building a sense of 'us'.

Periodically, teams need to revisit both their team purpose and main goals on the task side, and the way they are going about achieving them with a view to making refinements and improvements (or getting the team back on track, as the case may be), on the process side. Prior to the COVID-19 pandemic, this could generally be achieved in a two- to three-day off-site team-building workshop led by an experienced facilitator who guided the team to examine and clarify its purpose and goals (task issues), and explored and strengthened the way team members worked together to achieve them (process issues). The same process can still be administered virtually by using videoconferencing software, and while this changes the dynamic somewhat to what might be experienced in a face-to-face environment, the same outcomes can still be achieved.

The shared experiences of a team-building session strengthen the ties between team members by helping them to see each other in a different light and appreciate each other's differences, similarities and contributions. The store of shared experiences helps to establish or strengthen the team's culture and translates into improved working relationships. It leads to a cohesive team – less 'they' and more 'us'.

Conducting a typical team-building meeting

When conducting a team-building meeting, you need to address both the task and process side. On the task side, have your team explore and define its purpose and goals, and get team members to explain their own job purpose, KRAs and MoS so that everyone understands everyone else's roles, responsibilities and contributions. This helps team members take responsibility for their own work and makes them more able to assist each other, increasing the likelihood that the team achieves the desired results.

Three important questions to discuss are:

1 What are our strong points as a team?
2 What holds us back or makes things harder for us?
3 How can we improve the way we work?

On the process side, specially designed and facilitated activities can be used to help the team explore the way members currently work together, identify areas for improvement and agree on specific actions to help them work together more effectively. For example, this may involve developing communication guidelines, learning how to give and receive feedback more effectively, and agreeing on ways to obtain and share information.

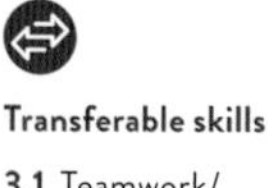

Transferable skills
3.1 Teamwork/relationships

While team building can be conducted once every 12 or 24 months, ongoing **team maintenance** is also essential for teams to work effectively. Every time you or a team member assists the team to clarify or work towards its agreed purpose, or to improve the way people work together, team maintenance occurs. Every time you make an announcement or the team celebrates achieving a goal, a major milestone or a member's birthday, team maintenance occurs. Every time team members spend some time enjoying each other's company and sharing a laugh, team maintenance occurs.

A team's daily interactions help it sustain the progress it makes during more formal team-building meetings, making team maintenance an essential ingredient for building and leading a successful team.

Team composition

Transferable skills
3.1 Teamwork/relationships
3.4 Leadership

People have different personalities and ways of working. That's good news because the most effective teams are made up of different types of people with different attributes, whose skills and working styles complement each other so that each contributes in their own special way. In fact, individual differences are essential for a team to perform effectively. The more diverse the team, the better they reach decisions, solve problems and innovate – provided they're led well and have an open and inclusive culture. Some teams might naturally have, or develop, an open and inclusive culture. However, don't assume that this will happen 'organically' as a matter of course. As the team's leader, you need to promote inclusivity and build and nurture diversity within your team, not only through emphasising a team culture that embraces these concepts, but also through your recruitment processes, training and organisational policies and procedures. (Strategies in relation to building diversity and inclusivity in your team are outlined in more detail in Chapter 32.)

Members of strong teams understand that everyone is different and that these differences strengthen their team. They don't personalise their disagreements but communicate honestly and deal openly with different viewpoints because they're all working towards the same outcomes. They may argue as they move towards their goals, but that's because they're intent on reaching the goal – together.

That's the good news. Here's the bad news: individual differences also have the potential to create conflict. Some people are simply unwilling to entertain opinions that differ to their own. As the leader, it is your job to ensure that team members make the most of their differences, and this means stamping out stereotypes, getting team members to understand their own personal biases and providing opportunities for each person's differences to be positively showcased so that others can see and understand the value that such differences bring to the team. (See Chapter 32 for information on how diversity strengthens a team and Chapter 8 for more information on different ways of working.)

Transferable skills

3.1 Teamwork/ relationships

3.4 Leadership

Stages of team growth

Just as people go through a life cycle from infancy through childhood, adolescence and adulthood to old age, teams also grow, develop and change. Just as an adult behaves differently from a child and has the capacity to cope with more complex tasks, members of mature teams behave differently from members of newly formed teams and are able to complete complex tasks more easily.

A team's maturity has nothing to do with how long it has been a team or the ages of its members; it relates to how effectively team members work together (process) and how well they fulfil their job purpose to achieve their team goals (task). Members of mature teams understand and contribute fully towards achieving the team's goals and work cooperatively together.

When you understand the stages of a team's growth, you can do a lot to help your team move through the growth stages to reach the mature 'performing' stage. According to the 'stages of group development' theory put forward by Bruce Tuckman in 1965, a team's life cycle has five predictable stages: forming, storming, norming, performing and adjourning.[4] These stages of team development are not always distinct but often merge into each other. Although the stages are described in a linear sequence below, teams move back and forth between the stages as new members join, new challenges emerge and changes are introduced. Growing teams is a complex process.

Very successful teams sit at one end of the continuum of team effectiveness, and unsuccessful teams are at the other end. Funnily enough, teams tend to be on one side or the other of the continuum – there are not many middle-ground teams. But it is just two factors that make the biggest difference between a successful team and an unsuccessful team: the leader, and how much the organisation provides the support that its teams need to be successful.

Forming

You may not set up a team from scratch (unless you're leading a project) but you can think of the forming stage as 'strangers' coming together to carry out a task or an activity. Teams whose members have little common understanding about the team's aims, and whose individual roles and responsibilities are unclear, exhibit characteristics of forming. Team members try to sort out exactly what their purpose is, what their relationships to each other are, where each fits into the team's 'pecking order' and what each can contribute.

Task issues take a back seat to personal feelings. People feel anxious and apprehensive and wonder what the group and its leader are really like and how to behave. This makes them careful, cautious and conscious of themselves and each other. They watch for clues about appropriate behaviour. Polite, impersonal discussions revolve around 'why are we here?' and getting acquainted. People's need for approval is strong and group identity is low or absent.

Teams like this depend on their leader-manager for guidance and direction, so it is important to take a strong leadership role. Inform people what you expect of them, how you want team members to work together, and how formally or informally you want them to behave. Give plenty of information about the team's purpose, its objectives, its customers and so on. Use the directing behaviour of the situational approach to leadership or the telling behaviour outlined in the **continuum of leadership styles** in Chapter 10.

Storming

The storming phase describes the conflict and in-fighting that surface as people begin to know each other and explore their differences in aims, values and working styles. Team members are tense as they vie to establish their 'turf' and group roles. Cliques may form, power struggles may develop and your leadership may be challenged.

Productivity remains low as the team deals with the difficulties of establishing common goals, work principles and procedures. Because of the many interactions between its members, a team learns through trial and error even more than individuals do, however well trained and professional the members are. Make it safe for them to experiment and try new ways so that they can recognise their mistakes and learn from them.

Storming teams often seem to be 'stuck' in some way. This may be due to internal conflicts about what the group should do or how it should be done or to a 'crisis of energy', where team members seem to lack their earlier spark and enthusiasm and seem reluctant to 'get stuck into it'. Disillusionment and frustration with the team and its capabilities may surface.

Teams at this stage need strong leadership that provides clear boundaries, direction and guidelines. No matter how bad the storming gets, help team members to concentrate on their goals rather than becoming distracted by relationship issues. Keep team members together and talking until they feel comfortable with each other and their goals and procedures.

Use the situational leadership coaching style or the continuum of leadership selling style and continue to show confidence in the team.

Norming

Some teams stay stuck in storming, but others emerge into the norming phase, where codes of behaviour and team customs are established both formally and informally as the team resolves how it functions day-to-day and how it makes decisions. This is the time to ensure that appropriate team norms develop. Norms, such as 'We insist on high quality', 'We put customers first', 'We listen to each other's views' and 'We turn up on time', are essential so that the team can reach the next stage, performing. (You can find out more about norms in Chapter 4.)

During the norming phase, team members settle into working rhythms, patterns and relationships. They begin making progress on the task and start to have fun with each other and enjoy being part of the team. Don't be alarmed if a short period of 'play' and celebration of their new-found working arrangements temporarily overrides task matters – they'll soon get down to work more seriously as the norming phase progresses.

As team members become more skilled in working with each other, they share accountability for results; they don't think 'That's not my problem' but 'That's our problem, how can we fix it?' Everyone's roles and responsibilities are now clear and accepted as members come to understand and appreciate each other's differences and talents and know where they stand in relation to the other members. Trust and openness between team members grows and commitment to the team strengthens. 'Me' gives way to 'we' and a team identity emerges towards the end of the norming phase.

Team members begin to depend less on the leader, although they continue to need your guidance and confirmation that work is progressing in the right direction. Become a facilitator and an enabler, applying both the situational leadership and continuum of leadership styles.

Performing

Performing teams are creative, harmonious and productive. They are clear about the task and why it is important, and members work independently or in any combination to achieve more together than they can individually, drawing on each other's unique strengths and knowing how to compensate for each other's weaknesses. Productivity is high on the task side, and satisfaction, loyalty and cohesion are high on the process side.

Performing teams achieve their goals and continually seek ways to improve and resolve any internal disputes openly and effectively. Members gain a sense of meaning from what they're doing and achieving. Open communication, close teamwork, flexibility, innovation, resourcefulness and trust are evident. You can practically feel the team spirit. Membership of a performing team brings out the best in all its members and members expect the best of each other.

High-performing teams are a team leader's dream-come-true because they need little direction. Their high autonomy means you can become a resource to help the team achieve its goals. Use the delegation 'hands-off' leadership style of situational leadership and the continuum of leadership styles and stand back to let the team itself set, monitor and achieve its goals.

Adjourning

Adjourning, or mourning, is the final stage of some teams. Temporary teams disband, worksites close down, a team or part of a team merges with another team, or the organisation makes a team redundant and contracts its work out. This leaves a hole or sense of emptiness in team members' lives, with feelings of loss and sadness, and promises to get together in the future.

Some sort of official closing celebration or 'ceremony' can help a team through this difficult phase – perhaps a shared meal or an informal get-together.

As teams grow and mature, predictable dynamics occur. These are summarised in Table 13.1.

TABLE 13.1 Key issues in the five stages of a team's development

	Stage 1: Forming
Key issues	Leader should show confidence
Key questions	What's 'the go' here? What can I offer this group? Who am I in this group? Who is in this group? Do I want to be in this group? What are our goals and objectives?
Process issues	The team depends on the leader to set ground rules
Task issues	The team depends on the leader to provide structure and guidance Team members become familiar with the team purpose, objectives and tasks
	Stage 2: Storming
Key issues	Conflict or crisis of energy may make the group seem 'stuck' The team can become disillusioned, so the leader should show confidence

Stage 2: Storming	
Key questions	How are decisions to be made? How much power and influence do I have? What are the coalitions, or cliques, in this team? Who has the formal/informal power? Who's really in charge?
Process issues	Conflict, hidden or out in the open, regarding leadership, power and authority roles may arise
Task issues	The team works out how best to work together and individually to achieve its goals
Stage 3: Norming	
Key issues	Leader should ensure appropriate norms develop The team may abandon the task and 'play' a while, enjoying their cohesiveness before getting down to work
Key questions	How should this team operate? What are our policies, rules and procedures? What are the ways to behave in this group?
Process issues	Cohesion and team identity emerge Openness and trust begin to develop Ideas, information and feelings start to be shared Team members strive for harmony
Task issues	Data and information begin to flow The team makes visible progress in achieving its goals and team purpose
Stage 4: Performing	
Key issues	How can we best achieve our goals and work together? Leader should take a back seat and act as coach and facilitator
Key questions	Are we getting the best results possible? How can I best contribute to the team's task? How can we improve our effectiveness and efficiency? What is the best way to do my job well?
Process issues	Interdependence is evident – team members can work singularly, in any combination of subgroups or in the whole team
Task issues	Team members continuously improve systems and the way they work, together and individually, and identify and solve problems Team members collaborate effectively and work 'in harmony' Task goals are clear to everyone Let's get on with the job and do it well! Strong commitment to the team and its tasks is evident

Stage 5: Adjourning	
Key issues	How do we achieve formal closure and goodbyes? The formal or informal leader should organise a 'closure' event
Key questions	How will I feel when I (or others) leave or when we disband? What are the consequences of leaving or disbanding?
Process issues	Team members feel both sadness and excitement about 'going it alone' Team members feel impending loss or anxiety about what comes next
Task issues	Final winding up ensures that achievements and learning aren't lost

The relationship between leadership styles and team growth

The stages of team growth model was developed around the same time as the continuum of leadership styles and situational leadership models. In each of these models, the principle is the same: as the team develops and becomes more skilled, the relationships between the members and between the members and the leader-manager change. The leader moves from a directing style through to coaching, then participating and finally to delegating. However, this progression does not happen by chance and teams don't become successful by chance. Most teams are either very successful or not at all. How they end up largely depends upon two factors: the leader, and how much the organisation provides the support that its teams need to be successful.[5] In the absence of these two factors, regardless of the talent a team contains, it will never succeed as a team and its success will be limited to the sum total of each team member's individual performance.

When your team is struggling to be effective, you need to take action to help lift them out of their slump. The following strategies are ways you can achieve this:

- Balance team membership with a range of backgrounds, experience, personalities and skills, and make the most of its diversity.
- Invite participation in decisions that affect the team; for example, involve your team in deciding what materials and equipment it needs and the best way to complete a job.
- Celebrate the team's successes and make sure the rest of the organisation hears about how well your team is doing.
- Communicate; for example, hold monthly update meetings about the organisation's activities and successes, customers and new initiatives to ensure a steady flow of information.
- Keep innovating and improving team procedures. People get bored when they're stuck in ruts and frustrated when the hassles, bottlenecks and extra, unnecessary steps that make their jobs harder aren't fixed.
- Provide training. Involve the team in deciding their own training needs and how best to train new team members.
- Revisit the team purpose and processes frequently. The team purpose may change in the light of changing organisational priorities; even when it doesn't change, the review serves as a useful reminder. Set new goals to challenge the team so that members don't become stale, and periodically review and update the team's process guidelines.
- Reward extra effort. When team members go 'beyond the call of duty' and put in extra time and effort or achieve something special, make sure they benefit in some special way.

- Rotate assignments. When there's a chance that people's tasks could become monotonous once mastered, cross-train team members and rotate tasks to keep interest and morale high.
- Support the team. Clearly define the team's goals and other expectations, and get them the resources they need. Make sure people have ways to evaluate the team's progress in both its task achievement and the way they're working together.

Transferable skills

2.2 Personal effectiveness

Changes in team membership

Team members leaving or new members joining can disrupt a team's productivity, which often falls as members adjust their relationships and roles. Now is the time to put extra effort into rebuilding your team. Use your understanding of the **team life cycle** and of group dynamics to help your team remain productive.

Departing members

Each time someone leaves, a kind of adjourning and a sense of impending loss occurs, and the team often takes a step backwards as it attempts to regain its sense of self and former efficiency levels. As soon as you know that a team member is leaving, bring the team together to discuss the departure and the reasons for it. Members may be proud of a teammate's promotion, sad about the loss or anxious about an increased workload. Be open and willing to listen and provide the support the team needs to rebuild itself.

Examine how the departure might affect each team member's productivity and the productivity of the team as a whole and how to lessen the negative effects of the departure. Discuss what projects or tasks might be at risk and how to keep the team's output on track. Talk about when and how the team member can be replaced and how to induct the new member into the team.

New team members

Each time a member joins a team, modified versions of forming, storming and norming begin all over again. A new member joining a team can dent the feelings of camaraderie and team spirit and alter the internal dynamics of the team, causing it to lose ground and revert to an earlier stage. Loyalties and alliances may shift as the new member settles in and learns the routines and rhythms of the team, which may be interrupted, at least temporarily. Group norms and morale may be threatened or changed, and dynamics often change permanently.

To get the team working well again, become more 'hands on' for a while. This restores the team's growth, carrying the new member along in the process. As the team moves forward into norming, allow it to explore its modified identity. Ensure the goals remain clear and that new team members have plenty of feedback on their performance and how they're fitting in. As the team moves into performing, step back into your former role of support.

Temporary members

Casual and temporary workers and contract workers often join teams to help out with the day-to-day work or to add their specialist expertise. They also need guidance.

They need to be engaged to make the most of their potential value and feel that they are part of the host organisation. This often means giving them a shortened version of the same induction and assimilation process that permanent employees receive. Your goal is to integrate them into the workplace and the team, so discuss the organisation's values, vision and mission, and the team's purpose. Make their role clear, too; discuss the value you expect them to add to the team – their own job purpose – and how they'll know they've succeeded – their KRAs and MoS.

Provide any supplies and tools temporary team members need to succeed, such as hardware, software, network access, equipment or background information. Make sure the permanent team members understand the contribution the temporary members are there to make and encourage them to welcome them and treat them as a valued part of the organisation. While they're with you, include temporary team members in corporate communications, newsletters, company events and so on so they feel part of the team.

13.5 Supporting your team

> Being a leader is not about you. It's about the people that are on your team and how you can help them be successful.
>
> Susan Vobejda, Global Head of Media Licensing and Distribution, Bloomberg, *I want her job*, 5 August 2013, http://www.iwantherjob.com/your-career/interview/susan-vobejda.

Even the most skilled, motivated and engaged team members can't keep up peak performance and productivity when their leader fails to support them, whether as individuals or the team as a whole. The following sections will discuss ways that you can support your team so they can continue to perform at optimum levels, maximise the benefits that team synergy offers and that this translates into results that would not be possible if they simply worked as a group of individuals.

Your managerial roles

You draw on a number of personas that utilise a wide range of skills, called *managerial roles*, as you carry out your duties. These are a good way of describing and understanding how you spend your time and support your team. The amount of emphasis you give to each role depends, of course, on your organisation and your job duties.

Managers play 10 roles that fall into three groups, as show in Table 13.2. Three *interpersonal roles* arise from your formal authority and involve communicating, building effective working relationships, leading, influencing and your official management duties. These interpersonal roles lead to three types of *informational roles* that serve to keep people informed on matters that affect them. These in turn lead to four *decisional roles* that call for you to exercise judgement in dealing with problems, allocating resources and working with others.[6]

TABLE 13.2 The 10 managerial roles divided into three groups

	Group 1: Interpersonal roles
Figurehead role	Acting in an official capacity (e.g. signing documents)
Leader role	Leading effectively
Liaison role	Communicating inside and outside the organisation
	Group 2: Informational roles
Monitor role	Collecting information in order to remain 'in the picture' and detect changes or problems
Disseminator role	Distributing information from both internal and external sources to more senior management, employees and colleagues
Spokesperson role	Representing the organisation to external people and groups, representing employees to management, and vice versa

Group 3: Decisional roles	
Entrepreneur role	Initiating changes and improvements, discovering problems, innovating solutions
Disturbance-handler role	Dealing with conflict, grievances and unexpected problems that arise, even with the most careful planning
Resource-allocator role	Deciding who does what, when and with which resources; scheduling time, tasks, materials and resources
Negotiator role	Making agreements with groups or individuals, inside and outside the organisation

Based on Henry Mintzberg, *The nature of managerial work*, Harper & Row, New York, 1973, pp. 392–393.

These roles were identified in the early 1970s, long before computers became commonplace and long before the explosion of information availability. Only a couple of decades ago, managers were disseminators of information; now, with the advent of the internet, managers' informational roles have changed to helping people make sense of all the information swirling around. You might do this by highlighting certain aspects or portions of information that are relevant to your team or directing them to sources that can provide updates, explanations or commentaries in relation to new legislation, processes, best practice, standards, quality and so on.

Transferable skills

3.1 Teamwork/relationships

Build your team's emotional intelligence

The ability to be aware of and take into account one's own emotions and the emotions of team members, the mood of the team itself, and the mood of other groups and individuals outside the team that the team interacts with, is not due simply to the sum of the team members' individual emotional intelligence (EI). It is due to their collective EI. (See Chapter 5 to find out how to strengthen your own EI.) There are three critical ingredients of a team's EI, each built on the one preceding it, as shown in Figure 13.5.

Transferable skills

3.1 Teamwork/relationships

Here are some specific actions you can take to develop your team's EI:

- Don't let factions develop.
- Don't let people push through a proposal where agreement has not yet been reached within the team – see that the team reaches genuine consensus.
- Encourage members to speak out when they disagree with something relating to team goals, decisions and ways of working.
- Ensure that members support a course of action once the team has agreed to it.
- Find quick and easy ways to express the team's emotions and fun ways to relieve stress.
- Make the team feel like winners. For example, acknowledge success and the importance of the team's purpose, note how the team members have successfully solved similar problems in the past and keep their attention on matters they can control.
- Provide a clear team purpose.
- Question any decisions that are made quickly.
- Respect everyone's contributions
- Build and facilitate trust based on empathy and shared values, known as identification-based trust.

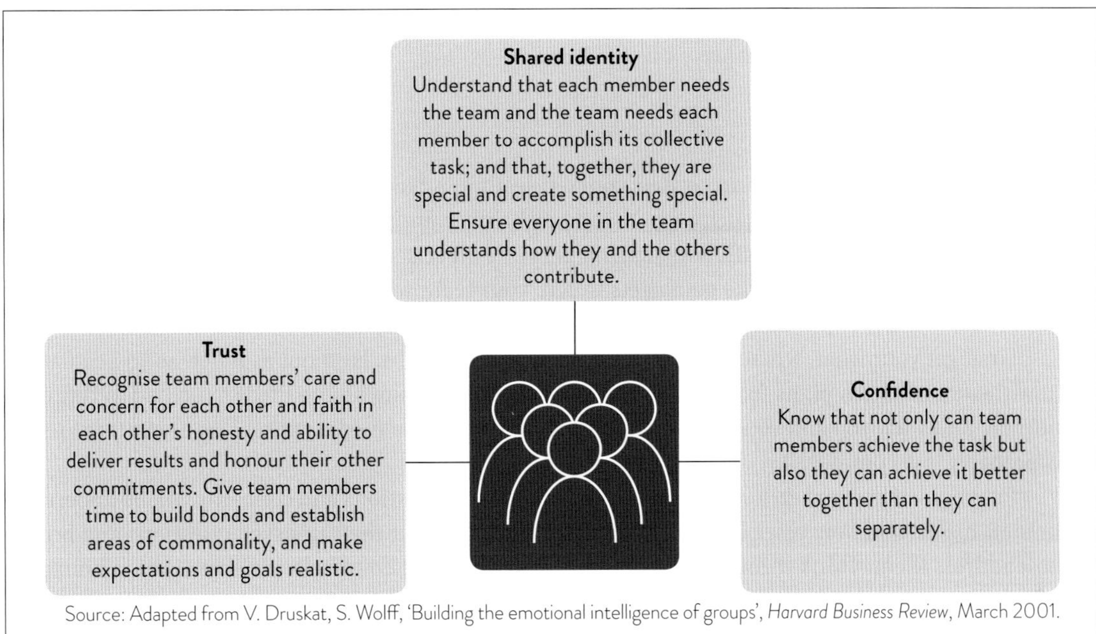

Source: Adapted from V. Druskat, S. Wolff, 'Building the emotional intelligence of groups', *Harvard Business Review*, March 2001.

FIGURE 13.5 Three critical ingredients of a team's emotional intelligence

Build individual team members' emotional intelligence

When a team member's emotions impinge on the team's morale and productivity, you can step in and help the employee strengthen their EI. Indeed, it is your job to do so. For people to change, they must first want to change. Here is where some honest feedback can help. You can use the Johari Window (described in Chapter 5) as a guide, combined with your coaching skills (see Chapter 29) and:

- ask what the team member's intention was regarding a particular interaction and what the outcome of the interaction was. When the two don't match up, you can open a discussion about EI
- conduct a gap analysis and encourage the employee to develop a plan for bridging the gap
- help the employee to find a personal vision for their future and discuss how managing their emotions is a key to realising that vision
- discuss how you managed an emotionally challenging situation yourself; this helps the employee learn from your good example and, as a bonus, enlarges the open area in your Johari Window
- use Socratic questioning (discussed in Chapter 29) to help them understand the effects of their emotions on others.

Think about how to open the discussion thoughtfully and considerately. Make sure the team member understands you have their best interests at heart and want to help them develop their skills and be successful. Sit next to the person, not opposite, to show you're 'on the same side', name the issue clearly (with tact and objectivity – think about how the employee would describe their behaviour) and be ready with concrete examples to help the employee understand the effect of their behaviour on others.

Provide constructive feedback privately and soon after the behaviour occurs. You might want to open the discussion towards the end of the workday so your team member can go home afterward, particularly if you suspect that the employee might become upset. Should the behaviour continue, affecting the team in a negative way, lowering the team's morale and productivity, you can begin counselling for underperformance.

Teams in crisis

Whatever the cause, you're sure to find yourself leading a team through stormy waters sooner or later – whether it be the security of customers being compromised, your organisation is going through a financial crisis, layoffs, lawsuits, mergers or a PR crisis, rumours about downsizing abound, or a global pandemic. When the going gets tough, your team will look to you more than ever, so it is not the time to be hands-off.

First, get your what, where, who, why and how facts straight. Find out as much as you can about how the organisation plans to deal with the difficulties, how long before life is expected to return to normal, and what you and your team members should say if the media approaches them (the answer is probably 'No comment').

Put yourself in your team's shoes and think about what questions and concerns will be uppermost in their minds and how you can best respond. Think also about their unasked questions and how to best address them. Think through what you and your team can do to help the organisation's image in relation to its stakeholders and what you and your team can do to stay productive.

When you can, alert your team about the storm in advance, preferably in person. But should you become aware of an imminent storm during holiday periods or late on a Friday night, gather your facts and send a group email or phone your team members individually. That would also be a good time to advise them how to respond to any media queries and, crucially, to warn everyone to say nothing on social media about the situation.

When you're leading a virtual or dispersed team (e.g. one with teleworkers and/or off-site workers) establish a time and place where you can all meet (somewhere private) even if only virtually. That personal touch can be ultra-important when the situation is dire. After that, you can hold teleconference or videoconference updates and meet again personally when there is sensitive or significant information to impart.

Perhaps the storm is distant and there is just conjecture so far. Your goal is to prevent the rumour mill magnifying the turbulence and draining productivity. Meet with your team and tell them the facts as you know them, and when you expect an official announcement or when you will update them again. Assure your team that you will keep them fully in the picture as best you can. Request they refrain from speculating among themselves (although they will anyway) and ask them to come to you with any questions or concerns.

Be a strong leader and tell the truth

While senior management is focused mostly on customers, the public and other stakeholders, your job is to make sure your team doesn't lose faith in the organisation – or themselves. A crisis is tough on your staff, too, and some may even want to abandon ship or turn against your organisation because they've lost faith in it. Be resilient and help your team be resilient. You can do a lot to allay their fears by being a strong leader, looking after task, team and individual needs (explained earlier in this chapter), and reinforcing that you have faith that the team will make it through the crisis and come out of it together. Calm, confident and consistent leadership is often what's required to steady the ship until it reaches calmer waters.

However, don't fall into the trap of being dishonest or covering up how bad things are if your team is going to find out. If you do, it is likely that your team will never trust you again. Don't withdraw either because saying nothing feeds the rumour mill and can have a worse effect on your team than if they knew the truth. Get out and about, communicate openly and honestly, and do as much as you can to reduce speculation and fear. Even when you can't share all the details, give as much information as you can, as quickly as you can and confirm you will provide information updates to your team as soon as they become available. But where information is sensitive, always confirm with your boss before sharing it.

Be aware of the silent messages you're sending out too – huddling with your manager or your peers, closing the door to your office for a phone call – as these can add to the tension and speculation and create feelings of insecurity, which can foster uneasy and negative team dynamics during a period where your aim is to create stability.

Depending on the severity of the crisis and how much team members are affected, you may need daily update meetings, perhaps a 'team huddle' each morning. When your team is dispersed or virtual, try a daily teleconference or videoconference update. Use this time to let your team members ask you questions, too. Keep your team aligned to the organisation's vision and values and your team purpose. Listen to their concerns, feelings and suggestions, and respond as honestly as you can.

Discuss with your team how and what to communicate with your external suppliers or customers because they too may need reassurance. Your organisation's senior managers or crisis manager will guide you, as will your organisation's values, vision and mission. This may add to everyone's work, so help your team stay organised and set priorities appropriately.

Stay productive

Don't forget the task. People still need clarity on roles and responsibilities, which may need to be adjusted during periods of crisis. Set a goal towards winning through the adversity, discuss how best to keep productivity on track and agree on a crisis management plan to get you through. Staying organised and productive also helps your team feel in control and assures them that together they can weather any future challenges they face.

Stay productive yourself. Dropping the ball signals to the team that it's okay for them to drop the ball, too. Make a 'To do' list of high-priority items and work through them. Budget for the extra time you're spending on communication with your team in your high-priority list. Look after yourself. Plan your exercise and go for a walk at lunchtime and get some fresh air and thinking time; this is often when good ideas and breakthrough insights hit, so make that a high priority. Look after yourself in other ways because your own stress levels are likely to rise. Remember, your team is looking to you for guidance and take their signals from you. When the difficult times have passed, look for what you can learn from the crisis and discuss it with your team.

If your team is the cause of the crisis, don't overreact and start casting blame. You need to focus on helping your team rise from the crisis by taking the following approach:

- Remain calm.
- Methodically collect the facts by asking the questions you need to and recording the answers.
- Identify the options available to you to address the crisis and evaluate which is/are the most suitable.
- Decide on a course of action to take and explain to your team why it has been chosen and how it will address the crisis.
- Support your team to implement the remedial actions decided upon and monitor their effectiveness, tweaking them as required along the way.

STUDY TOOLS

QUICK REVIEW

KEY CONCEPT 13.1 

a What characterises a true team?

KEY CONCEPT 13.2 

a List and define the elements of a performance plan. How can you use it to build a team's performance?

KEY CONCEPT 13.3 

a What is the difference between task and process? Is one more important than the other?
b What are the three areas of team needs? What happens when a leader pays insufficient attention to even one area?

KEY CONCEPT 13.4 

a What is the difference between team building and team maintenance? What are some ways you can maintain and support a team?
b What are the benefits and drawbacks of a diverse team? What actions can a leader-manager take to overcome the drawbacks?
c Explain the developmental stages of a team and the way team leadership needs to change as the team develops.

KEY CONCEPT 13.5 

a List your top three priorities for a leader-manager when their team is going through a crisis.

BUILD YOUR SKILLS

KEY CONCEPT 13.1 

a What was the most enjoyable team you have ever been a part of? Describe the team's characteristics. What goals did it set out to accomplish? Did they meet the SMART criteria and were they shared by the whole team? How well were the goals achieved? How did members work together? What were the task and process roles of each team member? What sort of task and process feedback was available?
b Discuss the types of teams you might find yourself leading and managing. Which type are you most drawn to and why? Would this type of team suit your current skill set?
c List and discuss the skills needed to build and lead a productive work team. In what ways do these skills differ depending on the type of team you're leading?
d Give an example of when you have worked collaboratively with others in a team situation and state at least six specific skills you used.

KEY CONCEPT 13.2 

a Discuss the elements of a team performance plan and how each element can lead to a productive team.
b Who should monitor a team's performance – the leader-manager, the team members or both? What factors would you base your decision on? Which style of monitoring suits which types of teams?

KEY CONCEPT 13.3 

a Explain why it is important to balance the attention you pay to task and process matters in a team.
b Describe how the three areas of team needs work together to build a productive team.
c Explain how having poor team dynamics could lead to an otherwise effective team failing to achieve its objectives.

KEY CONCEPT 13.4 

a What areas of the team's needs does team building work on?
b The stages of team growth model was developed in the 1960s. Do you think the model applies to today's diverse teams? Do you think a 21st-century team would come together to undertake a project and storm away until a pecking order and team 'rules' were normed? What about a team of knowledge workers?
c When a new team member is highly skilled at their job, would you expect any change to the way the team functions? Why or why not?

KEY CONCEPT 13.5 

a Which of the managerial roles described in this chapter have you observed a leader-manager use? What were the circumstances? Was the role effective in those circumstances?
b Why is a high level of emotional intelligence important to high-performing teams? What is the leader-manager's role in building their team's EI?
c List or flow chart what actions a leader-manager should take if an organisational crisis emerges.

WORKPLACE ACTIVITIES

KEY CONCEPT 13.1 

a Which of the 10 types of team is your team? Does it have a clear performance plan? Describe the team purpose and its process, or the way in which team members work together. What stage of development would you say the team has reached? What is your evidence for this?
b What do you believe are the key skills needed to build a productive work team and to be a member of one? Think about how you and your team measure up and develop a three-step plan to build your team-leadership skills and another to build your team's teaming skills.

KEY CONCEPT 13.2 

a What is your team's performance plan and how was it developed? Is every team member aware of the team purpose and the roles and goals of their teammates? How is the success of the performance plan monitored?

KEY CONCEPT 13.3 

a Observe your work team and list the task behaviours you notice. Then list the process and team maintenance behaviours. What behaviours most aid task achievement? In what ways did the task succeed or suffer because certain task or process behaviours were or were not used?
b What are your team's strengths and weaknesses in terms of task achievement and process?

KEY CONCEPT 13.4 

a In what ways is your work team diverse? Is the diversity used constructively; for instance, to innovate and solve problems, or does it cause tension? What steps can you take to build your team's strengths by recognising its diversity?
b Describe the last time a team member departed and another joined. Did it affect the way the team worked? In what way(s)?

KEY CONCEPT 13.5 

a Looking through the managerial roles in **Table 13.2**, describe the last time you used each. How could you carry out each of the roles better the next time?
b Describe your work group or team and your role and responsibilities as a leader-manager or member.
c List some of the ways in which you support your work team, including individual, task and team support.
d List the actions you took to support your team over the last three weeks.
e What reference to your ability to lead and manage a productive work team is likely to be considered in your next performance review?

EXTENSION ACTIVITIES

Referring to the Snapshot at the beginning of this chapter, answer the following questions:

1 How could establishing a team performance plan help to change the attitudes of Shenali's team?
2 Identify what Shenali needs to change in relation to her team on the 'process' side.
3 What stage of development do you consider Shenali's team to be in and why?
4 Outline three strategies that Shenali could implement to address her team's 'process' issues that you identified in question (3).
5 How can Shenali build trust, a sense of shared identity and confidence in her team? Suggest the likely benefits to the team if she is successful in building the team's collective emotional intelligence.

CASE STUDY 13

REBUILDING ITS CULTURE TO REBUILD ITS SUCCESS

SHAPE is a building contractor specialising in commercial interiors across several sectors. After instilling a new Board of Directors, the business embarked on an ambitious growth strategy and its staff numbers quickly swelled to 500. However, excessive layers of management, confusion over the direction the company should take, and competition for business between managers led to dysfunction and disagreement. In the midst of this internal crisis, the global financial crisis hit, causing the business to re-evaluate its position and direction.

It slashed its workforce by a third, losing many of its most talented employees in the process. This left it with an anxious workforce and with budgets also slashed, the pressure placed on managers and staff alike mounted.

To begin the rebuilding process, the business redefined its purpose as a premium provider and made the decision to reinvest in its 'people'. Its aim was to create a work environment and organisational culture that would attract the most talented employees in the industry.

After redefining its vision and purpose, the organisation created programs focused on building the leadership qualities, capabilities and behaviours that the organisation needed in order to attract the industry's high-end talent. Part of its overall strategy involved linking the organisation's culture to its performance. Its senior leaders began to understand that its strategies in relation to quality, safety, customer service and risk management would only be successful if supported by a positive, cooperative team-oriented culture. The senior leaders therefore became its most vocal advocates, redefining the organisation's culture to make it 'highly constructive', 'lived everyday' and 'the way we do things around here'.

Staff turnover declined, staff satisfaction increased, and profit and revenue rose significantly. The number of workplace injuries also declined and customer satisfaction soared. The general manager would address the problems brought to him by managers by asking them questions in return. At first, they were confused by this approach; however, this strategy served to empower them, forcing them to rely on their own expertise and use their own professional judgement to solve the problems they encountered.

By taking the decision to measure its culture, the organisation was able to see the link between this aspect and its overall business performance. By overlaying its cultural results (i.e. employee satisfaction) with its business performance data, the senior leaders were able to see the correlation between the two, realising that the culture had to be fixed if the organisation's performance was also going to be turned around.

As a result of this comparative analysis, it developed strategies to enhance communication and role clarity for its teams and provided team training for every team member. Finally, by adopting a balanced scorecard approach that aligned improvement in its culture to the organisation's key performance indicators (KPIs) and reward programs, cultural improvement became the key driver for the business' success.

Questions

1. Explain the relevance of both 'task' and 'process' playing an important role in turning SHAPE's fortunes around.
2. What was the importance of SHAPE's leaders comparing its cultural results with its business performance?
3. Why was it crucial for the business to find a way to measure its cultural results? What might have been the case if it had not found a suitable way to measure its cultural results or had chosen not to do so?
4. What do the phrases 'lived everyday' and 'the way we do things around here' indicate about the behaviour, attitudes and culture of the organisation's leaders and teams following its cultural reinvention?

CHAPTER ENDNOTES

1. Alex 'Sandy' Pentland, 'The new science of building great teams', *Harvard Business Review*, April 2012.
2. John Adair, *Action centred leadership*, McGraw-Hill, London, 1973.
3. Kevin M. Kniffin, Brian Wansink, Carol M. Devine, Jeffery Sobal, 'Eating together at the firehouse: How workplace commensality relates to the performance of firefighters', *Journal of Human Performance*, Vol. 28, No. 4, 2015, pp. 281–306.
4. Bruce Tuckman, 'Developmental sequence in small groups', *Psychological Bulletin*, Vol. 63, No. 6, June 1965, pp. 384–399.
5. 'Why some teams succeed (and so many don't)', *Harvard Management Update*, October 2006, https://hbr.org/2008/02/why-some-teams-succeed-and-so-1.html, accessed 29 November 2014.
6. Henry Mintzberg, *The nature of managerial work*, Harper & Row, New York, 1973.

CHAPTER

LEADING TODAY'S TEAMS

After completing this chapter, you will be able to:

14.1 support the productivity of merged teams and teams made up of a variety of team members, such as casual, contract, part-time, full-time and off-site employees, and knowledge workers

14.2 support the performance of project teams and virtual teams whose members you may seldom or never see face-to-face

14.3 identify technologies that can overcome distance between team members.

TRANSFERABLE SKILLS

The following transferable skills are covered in this chapter:

2 **Critical thinking and problem solving**
- **2.1** Critical thinking
- **2.2** Personal effectiveness

3 **Social competence**
- **3.1** Teamwork/relationships
- **3.2** Verbal communication
- **3.4** Leadership

5 **Digital competence**
- **5.2** Technology use

OVERVIEW

Advances in information and communications technology, combined with globalisation, increased business complexity, new business models and the COVID-19 global pandemic, mean that the types of teams discussed in this chapter are becoming more common and more widespread across many different types of businesses and industries. The new work patterns reviewed in Chapter 1 give rise to mixed teams of casual, contract, full-time, off-site, part-time and temporary employees. You can find business process teams and all sorts of project teams, from matrix to mixed to multifunctional to virtual, in many modern organisations.

Acquisitions, mergers and restructuring give rise to combined teams made up of people from different work cultures who are used to different work practices and who may even have once been competitors. Business complexity calls for capabilities-based organisations and project and multifunctional teams whose members are highly specialised and often scattered across the world. When teams are virtual or partly virtual and their members speak different languages and come from different cultures, managing these types of teams becomes all the more complicated.

Virtual and other non-traditional style teams present special challenges. They need different types of leadership and cultural and emotional intelligence in team leaders and members alike. They call for different types of organisational policies and procedures, and different ways and modes of communicating that meet their specific needs. Those tasked with leading such teams must utilise a variety of different strategies to build and maintain trust and working relationships, and to foster engagement and motivation. This can provide challenges for leader-managers and team members alike when they have been used to sharing a workspace and seeing each other every day.

This chapter explains how to develop and lead a non-traditional team so that it not only performs as well as a traditional team but actually thrives as a result of its distinct characteristics.

SNAPSHOT

Leading in the pandemic

'As of Friday, due to the new COVID-19 restrictions, no one will be permitted to work in the office. You will need to support each of your team members to set up their workspace at home, virtually of course, and put into place processes for communicating with and monitoring your teams. Oh, and don't forget that you will still need to maintain regular contact with clients to ensure that what was agreed to in the original high-level design meetings is actioned accordingly by your team and receives subsequent client approval as per the terms of each client's service contract. Any questions?'

Carmel left the meeting with her head spinning. Two weeks ago, the COVID-19 was just another flu virus that might keep a few staff home sick over the winter, but all of a sudden, the world seemed to be going into a tailspin.

Carmel's design and development team of eight consisted of four full-time staff, two contractors, one part-timer and a casual. The four full-time staff normally worked out of the office, while three of the others only came into the office for the extended Monday meeting every second week. Joshua, the e-learn specialist, employed as a casual, already worked from home because his role didn't require a physical presence in the office.

With only one day before the office lockdown was due to begin, Carmel immediately got to work. She started by sending out a group email to her team members advising them of the new 'work from home' arrangements commencing from Friday. In the email, she asked each of her team to confirm whether they had a suitable work area at home to undertake their role and whether there was anything they required, especially in relation to work health and safety. Attached to the email was a checklist for each team member to complete, including an ergonomic self-assessment so she could assess the suitability of their 'at home' office equipment and workspace.

She then sent another email to her team with a link to download Teams – videoconferencing software that would enable her and the team to have a virtual team briefing every Wednesday and Friday morning while maintaining their usual extended meeting, although now also to be held virtually, every Monday. It also provided the team with a virtual 'team room' where team members could instant message each other, share useful links and resources, and seek help and advice from each other. She then designed a 'weekly reporting' spreadsheet on which her team could self-report their progress on projects and tasks and email to her at the start of each week. She linked the calendars of all of the team so each team member could see when she and the rest of the team had meetings or other commitments and then emailed each of the team's clients, advising them of the new 'virtual meeting' arrangements.

Next, she asked herself what she could do, in addition to the meetings, briefings and reporting mechanism, to keep the team together, focused and engaged. She brainstormed some ideas: Friday lunch virtual trivia, personalised Teams backgrounds once a fortnight, one-on-one intermittent 'health checks' to make sure everyone was going okay. Carmel sat back and took a breath. Leading a virtual team seemed like it was going to be more effort than managing the team in the office. 'I wonder how long this will go on for.'

14.1 Developing productive merged and mixed teams

The technology and communications infrastructure is now robust and fast enough – no, really – for a wide range of employees to do their job effectively without going past their front door.

Rhymer Rigby, 'Homing in', *Management Today*, 1 March 2005, updated 31 August 2010, http://www.managementtoday.co.uk/homing/article/463771.

If you have been working as either an employee or leader-manager and haven't already been part of or led a merged or mixed team, you would now be in the minority. Although the trend towards these types of teams was already on the rise, the COVID-19 pandemic forced organisations all over the globe to change their structures to incorporate different types of teams. For many, it was a legal imperative as their countries legislated that employees had to work from home wherever possible in an attempt to stem the transmission of COVID-19. For others, it was a work health and safety issue due to the alarming spread of COVID-19 and the potential consequences of failing to provide a work environment where workers could safely 'social distance' from each other.

For most countries, once the virus was detected it was only a matter of months or even weeks before the workplace landscape was turned upside down. Arrangements for employees working remotely previously applied predominantly to contractors and volunteers. But as COVID-19 swept across the globe, employers had little choice but to offer similar arrangements to many other staff where it was feasible to do so. While **downsizing** or restructuring might have sent an organisation down this path based on an economic or financial imperative, by the middle of 2020, this trend had become firmly entrenched in organisations all around the world. Regardless of how long the pandemic continues, there seems little doubt that different types of non-traditional team arrangements are here to stay.

As Figure 14.1 shows, managing any team, traditional or non-traditional, requires similar actions. However, each type of non-traditional team also poses its own leadership challenges and requires additional skills, over and above the challenges and skills needed for leading and managing traditional teams.

Merged teams

Merged teams are becoming more common, whether it be due to a formal merging of organisations, internal organisational restructuring to increase efficiencies and reduce costs, or consolidating project resources. The merging process comes with its share of challenges, even when the teams being merged share commonalities. This may be due in part to the anxiety associated with such a change or because the members of the newly formed team have to establish and learn new work practices that meet the team's needs. But there is more to it than this.

Transferable skills
2.2 Personal effectiveness

Chapter 4 looked at the importance of organisational culture and the role it plays in establishing group norms, determining the roles, and even determining the relative power of group members. When teams are merged, the existing cultures of each team usually need to be replaced by a new team culture. Letting go can prove difficult for many, especially if the group has been together for a long time and has an entrenched team culture. What may appear as a conflict of personalities or ideas within the new team may often actually be an unwillingness or even refusal of team members to relinquish their previous team's culture. Left unaddressed, the feelings of tension and hostility associated with such a situation can lead to a toxic team environment and undermine the team's ability to cooperate, perform and achieve the results it is there to do. As this problem will rarely fix itself, this is where the leader-manager must step up, take control and lead the team towards its new 'state of being'. Let's look at how.

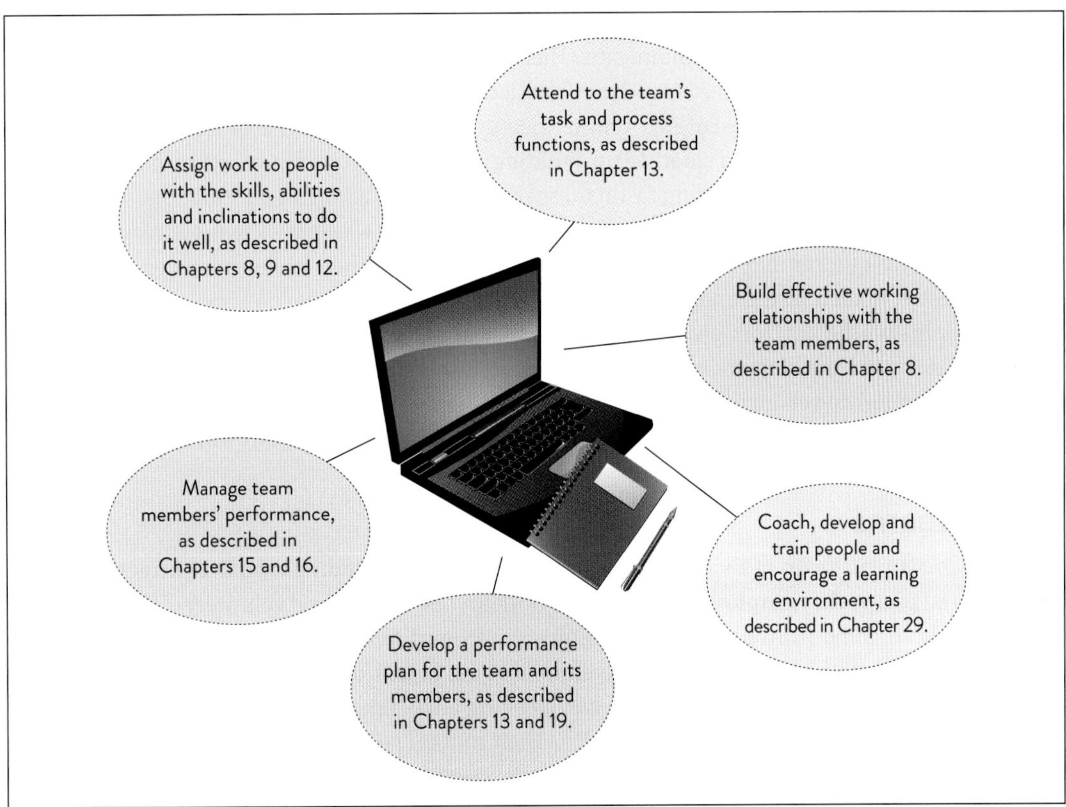

FIGURE 14.1 Leading and managing traditional and non-traditional teams

Whether a newly merged team is showing signs of disharmony or not, one of the first duties of its leader-manager is to align the members towards the new organisation's or new team's values and vision (see Chapter 2). Because the members of the merged team come from different cultures (as discussed in Chapter 4) and work in different ways, a considerable amount of effort may be required to gain agreement on team processes and to establish a team purpose and shared goals (see Chapter 13), and build a culture that works towards achieving them. Another priority is developing team norms quickly so that the new team can leave the 'storming' stage behind where conflict and power struggles drive down the team's productivity. The sooner the team is comfortable with and willing to embrace its identity and goals, the sooner it can progress to the 'performing' stage (see Chapter 13).

Leaders of merged teams have three options when a new team comes together:

1 Choose one culture to dominate the other and impose it on the team – this can be a risky strategy.
2 Take bits from each team's culture so as to merge the cultures.
3 Create an entirely new team culture.

Whichever option is chosen, it's important to establish the new culture as quickly as possible. Find ways to bring team members together, both physically and psychologically, whether it be in meetings, working together on short-term projects or participating in team-building activities. But make these interactions meaningful so that they produce outcomes that the new team can call their own. It might be that at meetings the team discusses and determines new work practices, that during team building exercises there is a takeaway in relation to ways in which the team can work better together or that the short-term projects produce immediate results that the team can hang their hat on as 'their achievement'.

Transferable skills
2.2 Personal effectiveness
3.1 Teamwork/relationships

Transferable skills

2.2 Personal effectiveness

3.1 Teamwork/ relationships

3.4 Leadership

5.2 Technology use

The highest priority during this period is to maintain communication. Set up multiple ways and modes by which the team can communicate. There are now many different options in addition to emails that provide a host of interconnectivity functions, such as sharing screens, instant messaging, videoconferencing, file sharing, calling, online meetings and so on. Some of these allow users to customise the background so a good team-building activity can be for meeting participants to upload a photo that means something to them, such as a favourite holiday destination, pet or social event and then share with the group why the photo is important to them. The more team members communicate, the quicker they will feel part of the new culture. As their leader-manager, answer their questions, listen to their issues and reassure them by keeping them in the loop about changes. When a change looms on the horizon, give them plenty of warning beforehand and provide support, such as training or by gradually introducing new processes. Where appropriate, utilise the strategies for introducing and leading change (which are outlined in Chapter 24). Above all, be honest, transparent and fair. If you fail to show these qualities as their leader, it is likely your team will follow your lead.

Mixed teams

Today's teams are made up of a variety of groups of employees, including casual, contract, full-time, part-time and **temporary employees**, knowledge workers, teleworkers and volunteers. Their members are also likely to come from diverse backgrounds, be from different age groups, and have varying abilities, education and expertise levels. Therefore, it is important to remember that collaboration is easier when team members perceive themselves as being alike. Emphasise similarities between your diverse team members, not differences, as well as their mutual goals and purpose.

Each of these groups of employees has different expectations of their leader and their work, and are motivated and engaged by different factors. Whatever their differing expectations, it is likely that all want to feel they are making a worthwhile contribution to the work of the team and the organisation. Your team purpose and a sound performance plan for the team and its members (job purpose, key result areas and measures of success, described in Chapter 13 and Chapter 19) are your best tools for ensuring that each team member feels wanted and needed and knows what to do. Ensure you clearly articulate and promote your organisation's values and vision as well as your employer brand so as to engage them and make them feel that they are part of that brand.

When many members of a mixed team don't see each other every day, it can be hard for them to feel like a team and develop the ties that create high performance and innovation. So, as is the case with building merged teams, create opportunities for get-togethers, either physically or virtually, and, where possible, mix in some social-related meetings among the work-related. Encourage members to communicate with each other and to share information, ideas and resources, and provide them with the communication tools to do so. Invite everyone to team meetings and include everyone in team celebrations, even if this is just an email to congratulate the team on receiving positive feedback or for completing a project ahead of schedule.

Transferable skills

3.1 Teamwork/ relationships

Use calendared social, cultural and community days, weeks and events to provide further opportunities for your team to mix with, learn about and bond with each other. There are a wide range to choose from, with some common examples being hosting events for Harmony Week, Cultural Diversity Week or LGBTIQ+ diversity days. Building relationships and creating bonds between team members strengthens their commitment to their team and their desire to perform both individually and as a part of their team.

Casuals, contractors and part-time team members

Casualisation of the workforce and increases in the number of people working on the basis of contract-to-contract means these types of workers are likely to make up an ever-growing part of your work team.

Don't make the mistake of thinking they aren't committed to the team or their jobs. With many of these types of workers, due to the often tenuous nature of their employment, they strive to outperform their full-time counterparts and look for ways to add value to their role. Encourage and support them as you would other employees and ensure you provide them with a safe workplace, including protection from psychological and physical hazards. Pay particular attention to female casual employees and contractors who, due to their work arrangements, may be more likely to experience higher levels of job stress and sexual harassment than those in full-time and permanent part-time jobs.

To bring out the best in casuals, contractors and part-time team members, keep them 'in the loop' on both task and process matters, and ensure that casuals and part-time employees have a chance to build working relationships across the rest of the organisation, as well as with their team. This ultimately increases the value they can add to your team. It may also seem obvious but because they spend less time in the workplace than full-time employees, be it physically or virtually, it is important to assess their performance results rather than time spent, so you are measuring their performance fairly and accurately.

Treating all types of employees as valued contributors involves not only including them in team meetings and social activities, but also seeking, listening to and incorporating their ideas and views into decisions. This demonstrates to the team that everyone's contributions are valued and can positively contribute to team outcomes while at the same time utilising valuable human resources.

Because casuals, contractors and part-time staff are not always present in the workplace, they may miss out on important information or not be ideally placed to pick up on the nuances that may develop within the team's culture. Therefore, as much as possible, make sure they are kept up to date with the goings-on in the team and the workplace and that there is a system in place where they can access the latest news, developments or minutes of meetings when you are not there to deliver the information personally. They also need to understand the team's workflows so they can prioritise their own tasks so as not to hold up others who may be relying on them.

Contractors (sometimes referred to as consultants and freelancers) generally operate their own business through an Australian Business Number (ABN) and contract out their service or skills without having the legal status of an employee. They may contract only to your organisation or to several. To be a successful contractor, they must be motivated, results driven and display a strong work ethic, so hold them in the high regard that they deserve. Think of them as specialist service providers, give them goals and success measures to work to, and establish a positive, respectful and professional working relationship with them. They can be a very useful resource during peak workload periods or where you need specific skills for a brief time or for a particular project that your own team doesn't possess.

As many contractors have a diverse range of experiences that include working with many different types of organisations, they can suggest different ideas and ways of approaching problems and work that your own team may not offer. Ask for their opinions and listen to what they have to say. When their contracted period or project is complete, find out what they enjoyed about working with your team and what changes, if any, they would make to improve the workflow and procedures. When they are particularly skilled and fit into your team well, you may want to find out their availability in the future.

Seasonal casual and contract workers

Due to seasonal working requirements and the peaks and troughs in demand in some businesses, such as those in hospitality, many teams have migrating membership with members joining and leaving according to the needs of the team.

When bringing casual and contract workers on board, review your team purpose and how their duties contribute to it, and explain what their measures of success are. Make them feel welcome and help them settle in. Towards the middle or end of their first week, catch up to find out how they're going and whether they have special skills or talents you're not using and should be. When some aspects of their work don't meet expectations, take the time to review what you expect. Treat them with the respect and fairness you would any other worker and offer them the same support and opportunities, where available. These workers are very important to some industries, so it is worth cultivating their allegiance as then when the peak seasonal period rolls around the next year, you have a skilled and mobile workforce ready to take up the slack.

Knowledge workers

Knowledge-intensive companies are the fastest growing and most successful in the world. Their workers, knowledge workers, are highly skilled professionals with specialised skills and often experience to match. They are destined to become the backbone of the Australian economy. In fact, by 2004 knowledge workers already comprised nearly 40 per cent of the Australian workforce.[1] (Chapter 1 explains why.) In New South Wales alone, around 80 per cent of the jobs created between 1997 and 2017 were knowledge-based and the overall share of knowledge-intensive jobs is expected to rise to 61 per cent by 2036.[2]

When you're leading knowledge workers, you're leading people who are intellectually gifted, have specialist knowledge at a deep level and who 'think for a living'. They're resourceful, have a large tacit knowledge base and generally work with complex tasks with high levels of uncertainty. They have good connections that extend beyond the team and even beyond the organisation. They can readily dissect a task, project or concept, so be ready for difficult questions and to be challenged when they're convinced they're right. Knowledge workers may tend to feel more 'entitled' due to their specialised niche in the market and may also be more demanding and dissenting than traditional workers. However, their upside balances this out by providing highly specialised skills and knowledge, and transferring that value to your organisation.

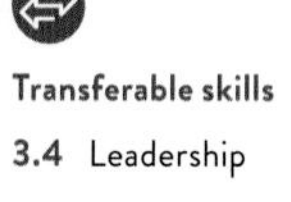

Transferable skills
3.4 Leadership

All of this can make knowledge workers tricky to manage, especially for managers who are into 'time spent' and 'overseeing' people while they work. Added to this, although you may manage them, you may not fully understand their work. How do you know whether or not they're just sitting, or sitting and thinking? How do you know whether or not they're producing, since their work is often intangible and invisible? The fact is, in most cases it doesn't matter. As long as you have clearly articulated the results and quality you require and the timeframe in which you require them, let them weave their magic while you revel in the time it affords you to do other things with one less employee to manage. Having said that, check in with them at agreed intervals to see how they are progressing and if there is anything they need.

Knowledge workers want competent and credible leader-managers who convey a vision, build a culture that supports its execution and provide the resources they need. Use your personal power, passion and vision to lead them and put your **position power** firmly on the backburner. Knowledge workers are secure in their knowledge, skills and market worth and will not respond to this type of leadership approach. Be confident in your abilities and say what you mean because knowledge workers are likely to be able to see through 'spin'. The more they respect you, the more likely it is that they will respond positively to your leadership.

INDUSTRY INSIGHTS

Managing knowledge workers in Silicon Valley

Rather than managing, monitoring and directing their workers, as has been the case with managers in the past, many of today's leaders are preferring a different approach. In Silicon Valley, organisational and management structures are flat and participative, promoting a culture where the expression and exploration of ideas is encouraged and supported and responsibility for decision-making shared. Step into a meeting room in most of Silicon Valley's companies and you will find a diverse mix of people, expertise, and ages. More importantly, the degree of openness and honesty that exists is a far cry from the 'do as I say' management approach of yesteryear.

As a fly on the wall in organisations such as Intel or Sun Microsystems, you are likely to witness an intense argument between a senior executive and an entry-level engineer. Status seniority and the value of opinions aren't based on age or position; they're based on what you know and can deliver.

In Silicon Valley, some corporations have implemented the 'five minute rule'. Anyone, at any level of the organisation, is able to suggest an idea, with the rule being that only positive comments are made about that idea for the first five minutes. This gives any idea the chance to become an impromptu brainstorm session, and has been the starting point for several truly great ideas.[3]

Stretch and inspire them

Knowledge workers have a low boredom threshold, so assign tasks that stretch and test their talents. Provide strategic direction to prevent them going off on a tangent that intrigues them but is unrelated to the team's or organisation's strategy.

Help them keep up to date in their fields by assigning work and projects that meet their needs for extending their skills and doing interesting work. Assist with their ongoing professional and personal development and cultivate a team **learning culture**. Let them network with their peers because knowledge workers work best when in contact with others in their field. For them, networking is a source of continual improvement, inspiration and new ideas.

Give them autonomy

Never micromanage a knowledge worker. Instead, set measurable goals, or deliverables, and explain the constraints and timelines. Organise the communications and information technology, equipment, information, time, funds and other resources they need, smooth out bottlenecks and provide a quiet space to think without distractions. Then give knowledge workers the freedom to get on with it. You will know you're leading them well when you hear them say you're not getting in the way too much!

Be accessible, meet for progress reports and be their chief coach and supporter rather than a traditional boss. In fact, think of your relationship to them as an inverted pyramid and yourself as a servant leader (see Chapter 10). Provide help and mentoring, not instructions. Shelter them from hierarchy and red tape and remove hassles and 'administrivia' that prevent them doing what they do best.

Measure the value knowledge workers add by what they achieve rather than by the tasks they do, how long they spend doing them or where they do them. It's quality, not quantity, that counts. Make sure you let them know they are contributing to a larger whole and doing meaningful work, but don't overdo it. Knowledge workers value recognition and respect from their peers and working for an organisation they also respect, so offering these things in a genuine and authentic way will help to engage and retain them. Where possible, recruit a diverse team of knowledge workers as the friction of different ideas that accompanies such a dynamic will help to mentally stimulate them and enhance their productivity.

Telecommuters and off-site team members

As outlined at the beginning of the chapter, the COVID-19 pandemic brought with it a pronounced shift in the way people have had to work, which has meant for many employees and the organisations that employ them, working remotely is the new normal. Just because this was forced on many organisations, it does not mean that the leader-managers of these employees have any fewer concerns about this type of work arrangement than they did previously. It may be difficult to know whether an employee working remotely is working at all, or whether they are doing something of value or struggling due to information technology issues, or even if they lack clarity about their role or task or some other issue. On the other side of the coin, many of these workers have been thrust into this work arrangement through no choice of their own and have their own concerns as to whether you know how hard they're working and are focusing on the correct priorities. The bottom line is that both employees and their leader-managers need to trust each other. More to the point, in this 'new normal', leader-managers need to trust that their employees are working and show appreciation for their work efforts, and employees need to be reassured that their leader-managers hold this view.

Even if this trust is absent, difficult to establish or will take time to develop, managing employees who work remotely still follows the same principles as managing employees in a physical work environment. You should set performance targets and goals and outline the timelines in which they are to be achieved. Then, regularly check in on the progress employees have made and see if additional support is required. Then, measure their performance against whether the goals are reached in the desired timeframe and the work produced is of the required standard. For leader-managers as well as off-site employees, the work equation remains the same, which is to get the work done. Where this occurs and how an employee achieves it is to a large extent immaterial, so there is little point in worrying about it. In fact, without the distractions of a busy, noisy, open-plan office, you may even see some employees raise their productivity and work output.

Of greater concern than whether telecommuters are working is how much they work. You may find that some have problems switching off and work longer hours than may be healthy in the context of work–life balance. Some may feel they can still work even when unwell because they don't have to actually attend a physical place of work, while parents may be reluctant to take leave when their children are sick for the same reason or because they are scared of how doing so might look. As their leader-manager, you need to make it clear to your team that leave entitlements still apply when working remotely and they should feel comfortable accessing them if they have a genuine need to do so. Some may take advantage of this for a 'day off' but would probably have called in 'sick' regardless of whether they were working from home or not. Monitor the health of your staff and if someone sounds obviously sick or they mention they have a sick child, reiterate their leave entitlements and the fact that you support them if they need to take time off. The more you show you trust them, the more likely it is that this trust will be reciprocated.

It is also important to keep in mind that not every worker makes a good telecommuter. For some, there are distinct advantages in having fewer directions, a more productive work environment, and avoiding time-consuming commutes to and from the workplace. For others, however, isolation from their work colleagues, the lack of social camaraderie and not having the opportunity to simply turn and ask someone a question can be demotivating and even depressing. So, where there is a choice in relation to people working remotely, choose those with excellent communication skills who are proactive in seeking out others for advice and support, are confident in making work-related decisions and solving basic technical problems and who you know are reliable and will meet deadlines. If they already have these qualities, it is likely that they will also be well-organised, independent and self-disciplined, which are other attributes to look for in workers who work remotely. For workers who need regular direction or validation that they are doing a good job, who do not have an ideal work environment at home due to space restrictions or distractions, or whose favourite part of their job is the social nature of their work environment, telecommuting is probably not for them.

Build the sense of 'us'

When people work autonomously, their sense of responsibility along with their sense of independence grows, which can lessen their sense of connection to their organisation. As their sense of connection to the organisation can be directly linked to their level of engagement, it is important to take particular care to keep that connection alive.

This can be done by taking the time and making the effort to 'catch up' with them regularly both virtually and when they are on-site. Keeping them informed and involved maintains their connection to the team and the organisation and can help to maintain their morale and team identity.

An alternative option for helping remote workers to cope better with the isolation of not working in a physical environment with their co-workers is to use workplace hubs. These are well-appointed bases for mobile workers set up by organisations for their own mobile employees or independent co-working spaces that cater for freelancers, can lessen the loneliness, and as a bonus allow the natural collaboration and innovation modern organisations depend on (there is even an online magazine devoted to hubs: https://www.deskmag.com/en).

For team members that are new to working remotely, provide them with guidelines and, if required, training in how to work remotely effectively. Plan how to help them adapt to the new style of work and new ways of communicating. For example, provide them with training and coaching in how to manage their time, communicate with far-flung and office-based colleagues and customers, set up a safe and ergonomically viable home office, separate work from private life, inject some social contact into their working day and so on. Provide them with the tools and training they need to not only meet their work commitments but to communicate with you and their team members as they need to and in a way that makes them feel part of the team.

Establish protocols in relation to accessibility by phone and instant messaging. For some teams or workers these communication lines may need to be open all of the time during work hours while for others it may be more productive to identify specified periods when people can be contacted. Remote workers should be left in no doubt as to what is the accepted practice of the team, so make sure all of them know at which times calling is fine, and when it can wait until later.

When you can, periodically bring everyone together for a meeting (and an informal coffee or meal) to help them maintain and strengthen relationships, provide adequate psychological interaction and facilitate information-sharing. Review the team's progress and successes together as a team to reinforce team bonds and discuss goals for the next period. Find out whether team members are experiencing any difficulties and bring everyone up to date on important organisational events, changes or news.

Transferable skills

3.2 Verbal communication

Where remote workers can't attend in person, link them to meetings by speakerphone or videoconferencing. When doing so, it is important to make sure they are included by inviting them to speak as well as respond. Reiterate the need for those physically present to speak clearly and perhaps more slowly so that those listening in remotely can hear and have time to process what has been said. Remembering the important role that body language plays in communication, try to verbally articulate the body language of those physically present where it helps to provide context. Some examples to illustrate this might include: 'Caleb just rolled his eyes because we all know how difficult this client can be', or 'Luala seems a bit confused, can you provide a bit more detail', or 'Marianna is smiling because she knows how much they love it when the designs contain the interactive graphical interfaces'.

Deal with any misunderstandings quickly. When you see each other in an office, it's easy and more automatic to discuss problems. This is harder for remote workers. Help team members share ideas and information, frustrations and triumphs. Even when your meetings are virtual because of distance, post the agenda before the meeting in your virtual team room (described later in this chapter), prepare for the meeting and follow it up as you would any other meeting. (See Chapter 25 for information on how to lead **virtual meetings**.)

Signal your understanding

Transferable skills

3.1 Teamwork/ relationships

Show an authentic and genuine understanding of the issues off-site workers may face, particularly those 'working on the road', such as lack of toilets, infrequent exercise, loneliness from spending a lot of time alone, the stress of driving and the temptation to eat quick, easy but unhealthy food. Provide them with resources and support, where you can, such as the website showing the location of public toilets in their areas at http://www.toiletmap.gov.au. Provide literature or website links in staff bulletins or newsletters explaining the benefits of healthy eating and exercise and showing them simple ways to stay fit and eat healthily on the road and at home. Listen to their issues when they raise them and follow up with solutions when you can provide them. Put into practice an empathetic style of leadership and utilise your emotional intelligence skills to show you understand what your off-site workers are dealing with. This will not only increase your credibility with these types of workers but will also build loyalty and trust.

Offset their loneliness with phone calls and videoconferencing. Texting doesn't provide the same psychological satisfaction that a real 'chat' does but can still be useful to fill the communication gaps in between. Keep your door open by responding quickly to queries and returning messages promptly as failing to do so communicates disrespect and disinterest.

Establish policies and procedures for issues that on-site employees normally take for granted; for example, how to obtain general office supplies and materials, what couriers to use and whether there are any specific times for meetings or brainstorming sessions.

When telecommuters work different hours or are in different time zones, agree in advance on the best times to contact each other as well on other matters, such as response times to answer emails, queries and telephone messages.

Other issues involving remote workers

There are other issues involving remote workers which can also pose tricky problems. Remuneration, a sensitive issue at the best of times, can become more so in the case of a virtual team whose members work at home or in co-working spaces in Hong Kong, India, Orange and Sydney. Each of these locations has different costs of living and people living there are on different salary scales, yet they're each doing the same job. 'Perks' can be problematic, too. When your main office offers a gym or subsidised canteen, how can you compensate home-based workers? Technology can also be tricky: computer software and hardware must be standardised, and people trained and provided with full technical support. Don't try to resolve all of these issues yourself. Technology and remuneration issues should be referred to IT support staff and help desks and issues relating to pay and conditions are the domain of the human resources (HR) manager or department.

Concentrate on results

When home workers do routine work, such as call centre operations or data entry, technology easily quantifies their productivity. Until you're comfortable that they're producing the results you need, you can use computer-monitoring programs to track whether people are working and provide summaries of, for example, what websites they're using and for how long. This way, you can keep an eye on their activities without being invasive. Remember that as part of building trust you should only track business-related activities and inform employees they're being monitored.

You can also monitor how your knowledge workers use their computers and use a shared calendar to track projects and scheduled meetings. Email, instant messaging and quick phone calls keep you in touch, and videoconferences give you virtual 'face time'. With videoconferencing, you can see whether your knowledge workers are walking in the park (where they may be thinking through a complex problem), and smartphone monitoring software can tell you where they are now and where they've been by tracking GPS locations. But if you really feel the need to resort to these methods of monitoring your staff, it seems likely that the relationship with them is already at ground zero and you might want to re-examine your management style or re-evaluate their employment arrangement/contract.

Of course, what really matters is their results. Whether it took them five inspirational minutes or 50 hard-slog hours to achieve the result is inconsequential. It is just important to know if they have produced the result you want in the time you need – period.

It's better to base clear individual goals on outcomes and not worry about time spent at a desk or on a telephone. Develop a solid performance management system to ensure that everyone knows exactly what is expected of them and how their contributions are measured. Agree how often and in what format you want progress reports. Make it easy for your team members to flag when they are struggling with something and need support and, when they do, provide the support they need. Remember that finding the right balance between autonomy and direction varies for each person and for each work context.

Maintain a safe and healthy work environment

As their leader-manager, you are responsible for ensuring that off-site team members work safely. Therefore, you need to satisfy yourself that their working environment is set up efficiently, ergonomically and safely. Train them to identify and manage risks and provide them with the same safety and emergency equipment found at their main workplace – fire extinguishers, first aid kits, personal protective equipment and other equipment they need to do their work in a healthy and safe way.

Consider visiting telecommuters' home workplaces to conduct your own safety audit. When it isn't feasible to complete a safety audit in person, obtain enough information about their home working environment to enable you to jointly assess risks and control hazards (as described in Chapter 30).

Discuss and put into place emergency plans too. While you hope they won't be needed if an emergency does occur, you need to be prepared by having them in place. Review these arrangements at least annually to make sure your agreed safety measures are up to date and working. (See Chapter 30 for more information about managing the health and safety risks for home workers.)

Provide different management solutions to different types of teams

In collaborative teams, people need to work together to manage their time well, and the way to effectively manage collective time needs to be based on the way the team works. When team members work across different time zones and feel pressured to be available around the clock to meet tight timelines or client expectations (or even just because they can be always available, thanks to technology), times and even a day should be agreed upon when everyone knows that they and the whole team are 'off' – not working and not available.

When teams are expected to work long hours, perhaps in periods of peak demand, provide extra time-off-in-lieu to recognise their efforts. When teams work in a hectic, interruption-filled environment with constant distractions (e.g. in open-plan offices or where meetings abound) provide a 'quiet time' when people can concentrate and complete their work so they don't have to take it home or leave it unfinished.

Whenever you are managing different teams with different circumstances, carefully analyse the similarities and differences between each and adopt a contingency style of managing that is relevant to deal with the issues and challenges particular to that person or team.

Transferable skills

2.1 Critical thinking

2.2 Personal effectiveness

14.2 Developing productive project and virtual teams

> Among the principal challenges in leveraging remote teams is finding managers with the right mix of skills, temperament and other attributes necessary to direct, monitor and motivate workers they may rarely, if ever, meet in person.
>
> Allan Schweyer, 'Managing the virtual global workforce', *HC Online*, 17 October 2006.

Does your organisation assign employees to temporary project teams, either full-time for the duration of a project or part-time while they continue to work on their other duties? Do you know anyone who works with people in different cities or countries some or all of the time? While project teams may or may not be virtual and virtual teams may or may not be temporary, these types of teams are becoming more common and so knowing how to manage them effectively is fast becoming a skill leader-managers are required to have in their management repertoire.

Yes, you still need to manage task and process matters of both of these teams. On the task side, you still need to clearly state the team purpose and shared goals and establish clear individual roles and responsibilities by implementing a performance plan centring on outcome-based success measures (as described in Chapters 13 and 19). You also still need to manage performance through coaching, training, and formal and informal feedback (as described in Chapters 15, 16 and 29).

On the process side, you still have a role in developing open communications and cooperation and building relationships and trust. As with any team, the culture, dynamics and norms (explained in Chapter 4) make or break the success of project and virtual teams. But getting the team norms and dynamics right and building a strong, high-performance culture is tricky at the best of times and even trickier with today's teams. Begin by establishing a team operating agreement (as explained in Chapter 21).

These and other customary team management activities are only part of what it takes to lead today's teams. Today's digital, dispersed, diverse, dynamic teams need two conditions to thrive:

1 a compelling vision that is challenging, worthwhile and shared by all
2 a strong and supportive structure, including the right mix of members, well-designed roles and procedures, suitable rewards and positive norms and group dynamics.

It takes time and a suite of strategies to lead today's teams effectively. Figure 14.2 outlines some of the strategies you can employ to achieve this. (See Chapter 19 for more on this.)

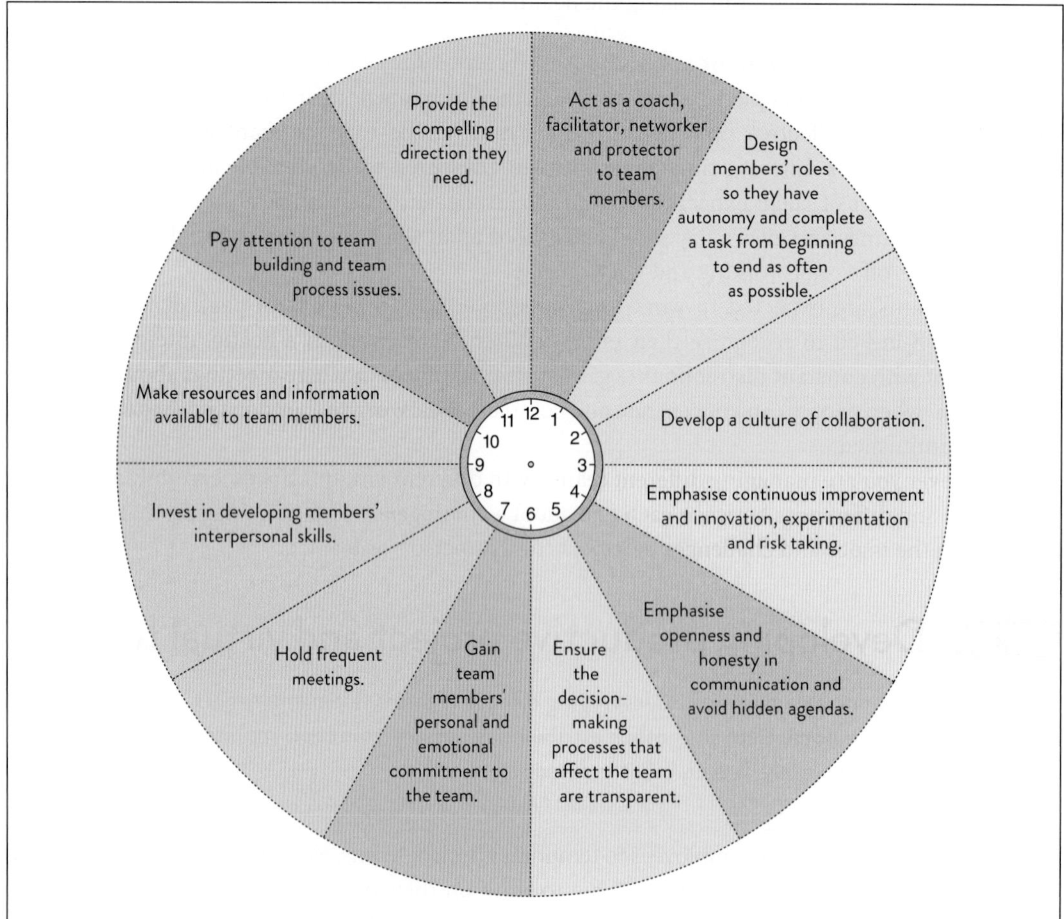

FIGURE 14.2 Leading today's teams takes time

Project and temporary teams

Project teams are formed to complete a specific, one-off assignment, such as:

- creating an innovative product, process or service (e.g. completing the protocols for a royal visit, designing a faster, more fuel-efficient passenger aircraft, developing a sensational customer-greeting experience that speeds up their hotel check-in)
- managing a large engineering project (e.g. building the Sydney Harbour Bridge, converting Adelaide Oval into a multi-sport facility, designing and building the Snowy Mountains Hydro-Electric Scheme)
- solving a problem (e.g. attracting more overseas visitors to the Flinders Ranges, making a city more pedestrian friendly, improving traffic flow in Sydney during rush hours).

Depending on the size of the assignment or project, the team leader-manager is generally full-time. Members are chosen for their different expertise or specialised skills (making the team multifunctional) and may be seconded either full-time or part-time in addition to their normal duties (the latter making the team a temporary matrix team). Some project teams have a mixture of full-time and part-time members; others have core team members supplemented with part-time and advisory members brought in to assist as needed. For large projects, the team is divided into subteams – sometimes many of them.

Project team members might be from the same organisation or from two or more organisations. Team members could include, for instance, customers and **service partners**, contractors and freelancers, permanent staff, volunteers, or any combination of these. When the work of the team is complex and the project large, team members may come from all over the world to form a virtual team.

When team members work part-time on a temporary or project team and belong to another team as well, try to ensure that split loyalties do not develop. For example:

- agree in advance how much time the members can commit to your team
- explain to your team members and their other managers how much they and the organisation stand to gain from their participation on your team
- keep the team members' other leaders informed about your temporary team's progress and the progress of their members 'on loan' to you so they aren't tempted to keep pulling them off their duties on your team for other work.

Most project teams disband once the assignment is completed, although some may be semi-permanent, with a few core members and other members who participate at certain times or for particular purposes; for example, to help out during busy seasons or other periods of high workload. In capabilities-based organisations, teams are often multifunctional and permanent, working together to design and bring to market ever-better products, produce specialised products or provide particular services, or service particular customers or customer groups. (See Chapter 3 to find out more about capabilities-based organisations and teams.)

Members of project teams not only have to learn new skills but also need to be able to dispense with the traditional roles and behaviours when they join non-traditional teams. This may require that they be provided with extra training, especially in organisations with a tradition of poor cooperation between **functions**. Rather than providing training for the team before it actually forms, if you feel its members need training in teamwork skills, spread it out over a period so that team members can absorb the information and put it into practice to see what works and what doesn't. As they do so, they can perfect certain skills and build on them as they complete each additional training module. (Chapter 21 explains how to manage the task side of project teams and support the team's process.)

Like knowledge workers, project teams thrive on the collaborative tension that comes from a diverse membership. That's easy to provide because project teams are made up of cross-functional specialists who are likely to think in different languages and follow different customs – the languages and working practices of their own specialisations. When the project team is also virtual and made up of people from other countries, they may think in different languages and follow different cultural customs too.

Add people to the mix from different backgrounds, experience, lifestyles and personality styles, and you've got the diversity you need to produce a stimulating and innovative work environment. But be on the lookout because while this diversity provides strength, it can also lead to misunderstanding and conflict. Have your conflict management and communication skills at the ready, just in case, and brush up on your knowledge of the relevant cultures and practices of your team members so that when you have to manage a misunderstanding between team members, you know what you're talking about!

Virtual teams

Thanks to advances in telecommunications technologies and access to high-speed internet, 34 per cent of Australians were already working from home prior to the commencement of the pandemic.[4] In some industries those numbers have risen rapidly in response to the pandemic, most notably finance and insurance (58 per cent), public administration and defence (51 per cent) and communication (47 per cent).[5] Almost 80 per cent of respondents to one survey believed that working from home would be more common after the pandemic.[6]

For those leader-managers out there who have a global mindset and cultural intelligence, and are good at relationship management, learning to lead virtual teams may prove to be a smart career move as the opportunities for these types of managers increase and become more widespread across the globe. But leading virtually is different from traditional team leadership and requires a different approach and different skills.

Virtual teams can be permanent or temporary, and the latter can work together either in the long-term or short-term. Their members may seldom or never meet face-to-face. They may be home-based or office-based employees at various locations, contractors or a mixture of all of these. They may be in different cities, time zones or hemispheres and have different ways of doing business. Your team may be their only team and they may work in it full-time or part-time, or they may also belong to other virtual or actual teams.

As with teleworkers and other off-site workers, you are the all-important link between the organisation and your virtual team members, so it is your role to build a sense of organisational identity and loyalty by passing on company news and information and making it accessible to team members. Provide opportunities for them to link into the organisation's formal and informal networks so they feel like effective members of the corporate team, as well as your team.

Build virtual trust

Building and maintaining trust with people you seldom (or never) see can be a tough task. Establishing trust is easier when 20 to 40 per cent of the team members already know each other and when team members have been trained to work effectively as part of a team and have worked in effective teams before. When this is not the case, provide training in areas like building effective working relationships, clear communication and resolving conflicts as these 'soft skills' are critical to your team's success.

It's easier to hide problems, sweep misunderstandings under the carpet and make wrong assumptions in virtual teams than in actual teams, which means that problems and conflicts can magnify and fester. Problems can escalate quickly over distance, and it isn't as easy to step in and mediate. So, while providing autonomy, stay on top of communications between team members by ensuring you are copied into emails and you know what communications and discussions are taking place within the team.

Transferable skills
3.1 Teamwork/ relationships

When team members are in different countries, virtual teams may also have cultural and language differences to overcome, and when they specialise in different areas, they may also need to overcome the different thinking and working habits of their various specialisations. To prevent a miscommunication disaster from occurring, make it clear from the outset to team members that they need to acknowledge the potential problems that will occur as a result of cultural and language differences. Set the scene for better working relationships from the first team meeting by establishing an understanding about how the team needs to work together. Then, discuss with them how they can prevent misunderstandings and conflicts from occurring by developing team norms that promote and value open communication, trust and acceptance of individual and cultural differences.

Unlike in traditional teams, where trust is built between team members over time, in virtual teams the level of trust is established right at the beginning and is usually what sticks. This makes the first few interactions of team members decisive in establishing which kind of trust becomes the norm for your virtual team.

With this in mind, avoid introductory messages that imply a lack of trust. This sets the scene for a virtual team plagued by low morale and poor performance, and you're stuck with deterrence-based trust. Instead try the following tips:

- Ask members to introduce themselves and provide some personal and professional background information before turning to the work at hand.
- Clarify each member's role and function in the team.
- Develop an action-oriented, enthusiastic team culture.

Support your team

Once your team is working well towards achieving a task, continue to support it as a whole while tailoring individual support to team members. Keep the team innovative and productive by reaffirming its cultural norms, setting the example, providing processes and opportunities where team members can generate ideas for innovation, and so on. Monitor team members' and the team's results as progress is made through the milestones. Help team members keep to their agreed timelines and deliverables, and address any problems of underperformance quickly before they mushroom and affect the entire project. Keep your feedback constructive and assist any team members with the support or direction they need to get back on track. Keep everyone up to date with corporate goings-on and the team's progress by posting regular progress reports in the team room and also use that space as a means of providing positive, enthusiastic feedback to the team as a whole, and to individual team members.

On the process side, monitor the team's dynamics and help it grow into a high-performing team (explained in Chapter 13). Remember that, as the team leader, one of your key result areas is relationship management – managing the relationships within the team and building your own relationship with each team member.

When you can't meet face-to-face often or at all, keep a record of team news, accomplishments, cultural events and celebrations relating to team members, birthdays and other personal milestone events so as to maintain team camaraderie and reinforce a sense of team pride and unity. You may even consider including some interesting information about the team's suppliers, customers and other stakeholders, and a photo of each team member with a paragraph about them (although check with them before making known information that they wish to keep private). Every so often, update the team with the record you have compiled and, where possible, make it interactive so team members can post comments and reactions which will further their sense of engagement with, and connection to, the team and organisation.

Communicate with care

We have explored the value of, and need for, ongoing communication when managing virtual teams. However, you should avoid contacting team members directly only when there's a problem – your communication needs to be balanced. You should provide both constructive positive feedback and constructive negative feedback. Also be careful not to stifle and shut down discussion even where there is disagreement. Team members need to feel comfortable airing alternative viewpoints and opinions and challenging those of others with whom they disagree. Build norms of open and honest communication so that team members aren't afraid to share bad news and instead look at it as a way of enlisting the support of the team to address a problem or make an improvement.

Be careful with emails. Once the 'send' button is pressed, there is no retracting what has been sent. The same is the case for instant messaging and other electronic means of communication. Before sending anything electronically, review why you are sending it (i.e. rather than saying it verbally), whether there is an alternative, and if you do decide electronic transmission is the right form, carefully review the content you have included by playing devil's advocate or putting yourself in the place of the recipient. Is there anything that could be misinterpreted or misunderstood? Have you made any assumptions or generalisations? Is there anything that could offend, even if it is unintentional? Does the content lack culturally and diversity-inclusive language and understanding? If the answer is 'yes' to any of these questions, consider removing or rewriting that part of the correspondence. You may even get a trusted colleague to review important electronic communiques before you hit the 'send' button.

From a security and efficiency perspective, your organisation's own collaboration tools are probably a better bet than email when team members need to communicate in writing or send each other documents. Email has poor documentation and filing features, making it hard to find information quickly, and emails sent through external servers are a security risk and a spam nuisance. A virus could not only compromise your team member's ability to work but also temporarily disable your organisation's communications system.

Virtual communication

In virtual teams, pay special attention to making regular contact since it doesn't occur automatically. In fact, the more dispersed team members are, the more you need to communicate, even when it's just to say hello and ask how everything is going or to listen to concerns, inspirations, setbacks and thoughts. Frequent contact builds bridges that can span vast distances and provides the essential contact that builds team members' loyalty and ties to the team.

When you communicate, resist the urge to get straight down to business, which could be interpreted as you only being concerned with work matters. Spend some time asking about your team members' partners and families, what they did on the weekend or how the holiday they just returned from was. Get to know your team member's personalities and parameters in relation to humour and communication so when you make a joke, use a sarcastic tone or be facetious, you can be confident that they won't be offended. If in any doubt, avoid these altogether. Remember that messages can easily be misinterpreted when communicating from a distance and in the absence of the usual body language clues that inform communications.

Working across different time zones means when you're at work, your team may not be and vice versa. Set clear guidelines around your availability during and outside of work hours. For instance, you may say, 'You can call me any time. When I'm not available, my phone will be switched off, so never worry that you're interrupting me. If my phone is switched off, just leave a message and I'll phone you back as soon as I can'.

14.3 Using technology to overcome distance

> A man is not idle because he is absorbed in thought. There is visible labour and there is invisible labour.
>
> Victor Hugo (French author), *Les misérables*, Penguin (UK), 2012.

Your virtual team can do just about everything an actual team can do. Thanks to collaborative systems technology, teleworkers and workers 'on the road' can keep in touch and work together remotely. Team members can drop short notes on each other's desks; have serendipitous interactions; share triumphs and successes via text and instant message; meet virtually as an entire team, in subgroups or in pairs with teleconferences and web meetings; and share data and documents online and work on them together in real time.

You can integrate all of your team's communications over an internet protocol (IP) network, making it possible to manage all your communications from a single web workspace. Collaborative systems technology – online workspaces, real-time application sharing, shared calendars and tasks lists, and so on – helps remote teammates work together creatively, flexibly and quickly. Chat messaging systems allow team members to see when their teammates are available.

Make sure every team member has precisely the same version of the same technology to allow full and easy collaboration. For example, sometimes when team members use different versions of even something seemingly simple, like instant messaging, they can't all contact each other, and cliques can form.

Sophisticated technology isn't enough – people need to know how and when to use it. Arrange training when you or any of your team members are not familiar with the advanced technologies you're using and when you upgrade. Figuring it out as you go and using the long route rather than efficient short cuts is frustrating and time wasting.

Establish ground rules for using your team technology. If your organisation does not already have a system in place, develop a set of core subject titles and a system to flag a message's importance, topic and urgency. Consider how to prioritise messages, how quickly to act on requests and respond to messages, when to copy in others or the entire team, how quickly to post responses to threaded discussions, when it's okay and not okay to contact team members using text and instant messaging, and so on. Agree how often people should check their messages and various sections of their actual or virtual team room and formulate guidelines for placing information on the bulletin board or organisation intranet. This also serves to overcome differences in individual communication styles and head off potential problems. Technology is there to aid people's work, not interrupt it. If it becomes apparent that it is causing more problems than it is solving, it might be time to review what technology is appropriate for your team and what should be discarded.

When some of the team is working while others sleep, team members should check the relevant sections of the team room when beginning their workday to make sure they're on the same page and decide whether to adjust the day's schedule and alter their priorities to fit in with other team members. This is particularly important when they are working closely together on a project or task.

Your virtual team room

A virtual team room is valuable for on-site project teams and essential for virtual teams. It should be informative, interactive and engaging, and only be accessible via password to relevant team members. It provides a virtual environment that team members can visit daily and see what's new, report their own progress, ask questions, share information and join threaded problem-solving and ideas-generating discussions. Because it's virtual, your team room is 'open' 24 hours a day, seven days a week. It should include everything the team needs to progress its work, together and individually, and be logically organised, easily navigated and up to date.

A good virtual team room builds a sense of team, trust and effective working relationships between team members. It gives team members a place to meet, discuss problems, share ideas and monitor progress. It can also act as a knowledge library where information, ideas, innovations, lessons learnt, and so on can be stored as a resource for later. In this way, it can contribute to innovation and continuous learning and help to build both a team learning culture and a learning organisation (i.e. one in which individual employees continually create, acquire and transfer knowledge through the organisation, enabling the organisation itself to learn and improve as its employees learn and share what they have learnt).

As team leader, you would normally manage the virtual team room, keep it up to date and moderate discussion threads. **Figure 14.3** shows some of the sections within the team room for each aspect of the team's work that you can create.

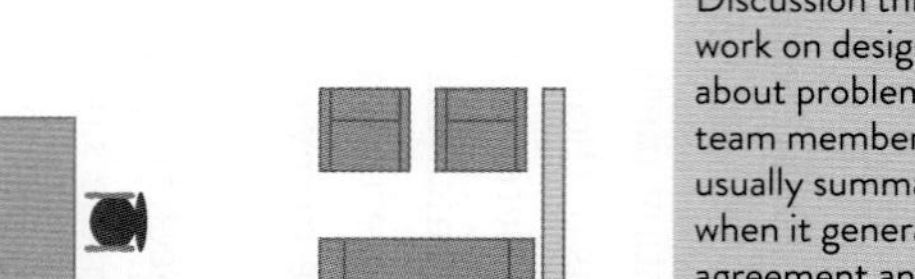

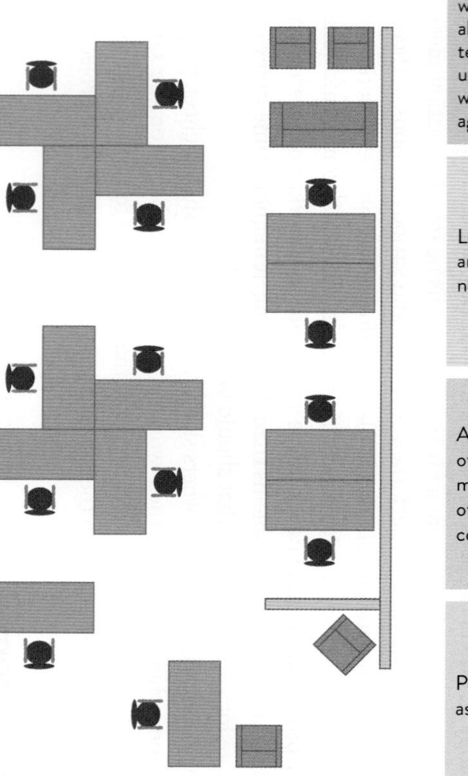

FIGURE 14.3 Your virtual team room

STUDY TOOLS

QUICK REVIEW

KEY CONCEPT 14.1 

a List and describe the types of teams and team members you are increasingly likely to lead and the special considerations you need to be aware of when leading each of them.

b Explain why you need to take particular care to develop a high-performance team culture and norms and to build trust in today's mixed and merged teams. List some of the ways you can do this.

c Explain why leading merged and mixed teams is even trickier than leading traditional teams.

KEY CONCEPT 14.2 

a Explain why you need to take particular care to develop a high-performance team culture and norms and to build trust in temporary project teams and virtual teams. Discuss some of the ways you can do this.

b Explain why communicating becomes even more important when leading project and virtual teams.

KEY CONCEPT 14.3 

a In what ways can technology help you run today's teams efficiently and effectively?

BUILD YOUR SKILLS

KEY CONCEPT 14.1 

a Interview two or three leaders of mixed teams and find out what techniques they use to overcome the problems inherent in such teams. For example, how do they measure and build their teams' performance and keep in touch with team members, and make everyone feel part of the team and part of the organisation?

b Have you ever worked from home? What are the benefits and drawbacks of regular telecommuting? In your opinion, what does it take to be an effective and contented home worker?

c Outline the qualities needed for leading knowledge workers.

KEY CONCEPT 14.2 

a Do you know anyone who leads or works in a virtual team? If so, ask them about the technologies they use and the advantages and disadvantages of virtual teams from their point of view. Ask whether they have any tips on leading or participating in a virtual team and prepare a short report to discuss with the class.

b Discuss the importance of frequent check-ins with remote team members.

KEY CONCEPT 14.3 

a Describe the purpose and content of a virtual team room in terms of both process and task.

b Investigate the collaboration technology currently available and predicted to become available in the near future and prepare a short report on how you could use it to lead a mixed, project or virtual team.

WORKPLACE ACTIVITIES

KEY CONCEPT 14.1 

a Do people in your organisation work from home for all or part of the time? Do salespeople, service people or tradespeople spend more time on the road and with customers than in the office? They still need to be part of a team, so how is your organisation managing this? If you lead a mixed team, how do you make everyone feel part of the same team?

b Does your organisation allow occasional or regular telecommuting? If so, what arrangements does it make for setting up home offices?

KEY CONCEPT 14.2 

a If you have participated in or led and managed any temporary knowledge, project or virtual teams, select one and describe how the team developed, using the stages of team growth. Discuss the leader's role and the team members' roles in the team's development and the factors that helped and hindered the team to achieve its goals. What lessons did you learn for the next time you work with or lead and manage a temporary or virtual team?

KEY CONCEPT 14.3 

a What technologies are you familiar with that can be useful to mixed and virtual teams? How could they be used to increase a team's efficiency and effectiveness?

EXTENSION ACTIVITY

Referring to the Snapshot at the beginning of this chapter, answer the following question:

1 Make a list of other ways in which Carmel could keep her team together, focused and engaged.

CASE STUDY 14

NEWCASTLE NERDS

Jake's start-up computing business, offering support and procurement for small businesses and website design and maintenance for SMEs, grew rapidly, averaging 25 per cent growth in revenue. Three years and three employees later, and buoyed by his success and his loyal customer base, Jake decided to expand further and bought another small computing business that subcontracted maintenance work mostly from larger government bodies and non-governmental organisations. Jake felt that the new company's client base would provide access to new business opportunities and that the skills of its employees would complement his own employees' skills.

The three employees of his acquisition joined his other three employees in new premises. Jake thought that the move to new accommodation would give them a chance to 'begin anew' together, and in a sense he was right. His new team got to know each other during the move, although it soon became clear that his 'acquired' employees had a somewhat different work ethic. In particular, they seemed reluctant to work weekends and what they considered to be 'out of hours'. This concerned Jake but he was unsure how to address it and, in any case, he was busy overseeing the additional business the acquisition brought.

Eight months after Jake's acquisition, the opportunity presented itself to merge his business with a similar business run by an old friend from his TAFE days. They felt that their combined client lists and business activities would give them the momentum they needed to take the business to a higher level and provide enough market share to become a significant force in the city. They rebranded the new company as Newcastle Computech and Jake's premises became its base.

Newcastle Computech prospered, gaining clients and recruiting additional employees and contractors as needed. The first 18 months flew by and now the company has a large and varied client list, 23 employees, including three part-timers, and a small group of contractors it regularly outsources work to, two of whom are based in Mission Beach in Queensland. At any given time, about half of the employees are likely to be out of the office either working from home or at a client's premises.

It's Friday afternoon and Jake leans back in his chair and looks around. He's just finished reading an article in the trade journal about building a business that stressed the importance of shared values, a shared vision and a shared working culture when building a business. He'd never thought about these matters, but off the top of his head he'd have to say that although everyone works well enough together at a professional level, he and the others probably have different views about vision and values. The employees from the two original companies tend to keep together, especially since the merger, and each group works a bit differently and, he suspects, thinks of Newcastle Computech's clients and their relationships to them in different ways.

According to the article, shared values give everyone clarity about what is expected of them and define what they can and cannot do – they cannot violate the values. A shared vision keeps everyone moving in the same direction and, like the values, guides their actions. A shared culture helps everyone work better together and sets them apart in the marketplace.

'We're a group of computer experts,' he thinks. 'We're fantastic at what we do, and we love our work. But I guess this stuff about culture and vision isn't just for business students; to really take the business to the next stage, we're supposed to become a team and look at things the same way. Fine. But how?'

CASE STUDY 14

Questions

1 What potential issues does Jake face in relation to the motivation and engagement of his employees who work remotely either all or some of the time?
2 Do you agree that Newcastle Computech needs to establish a shared set of values and a vision for the future of the business to take it to the next level? Why or why not?
3 Develop a plan to help Jake build his mixed, merged, semi-virtual team into a cohesive unit and build the type of culture it needs.

CHAPTER ENDNOTES

1 Australian Bureau of Statistics, 'Measures of a knowledge-based economy and society, Australia, 2003', 22 December 2004, http://www.abs.gov.au/Ausstats/abs@.nsf/46d1bc47ac9d0c7bca256c470025ff87/A46E142F20B029A9CA25719600166DFF, accessed 9 March 2015.

2 Matt Wade, 'Brains over brawn: Nearly two-thirds of jobs will be for knowledge workers by 2036', *Sydney Morning Herald*, 2 September 2016, https://www.smh.com.au/opinion/brains-over-brawn-nearly-twothirds-of-jobs-will-be-for-knowledge-workers-by-2036-20160902-gr76fd.html

3 Vadim Kotelnikov, 'Attracting people to opportunities, challenges, and growth', available at http://www.1000ventures.com/business_guide/cs_mgmt_kw_sv.html

4 Citrix, 'Remote work: The new normal?', 2020, available at https://www.citrix.com/en-au/news/announcements/apr-2020/remote-work-the-new-normal.html

5 Roy Morgan, 'Nearly a third of Australian workers have been "#WFH"', 29 June 2020, available at http://www.roymorgan.com/findings/8451-roy-morgan-working-from-home-june-2020-202006290638

6 David Braue, 'Working from home forever: More productivity and less stress', 6 April 2020, available at https://ia.acs.org.au/article/2020/working-from-home-forever.html

CHAPTER

15

PROVIDING FORMAL AND INFORMAL PERFORMANCE GUIDANCE

After completing this chapter, you will be able to:

15.1 identify the benefits and drawbacks of performance discussions and the types of formal performance review systems most commonly found in organisations, including an emerging trend in performance guidance

15.2 plan for and lead effective performance discussions

15.3 explain the importance of informal feedback and be able to effectively deliver it

15.4 make the most of receiving performance guidance.

TRANSFERABLE SKILLS

The following transferable skills are covered in this chapter:

2 **Critical thinking and problem solving**
- **2.2** Personal effectiveness

3 **Social competence**
- **3.1** Teamwork/relationships

OVERVIEW

To get the best out of the individuals in your team you have to ensure they remain motivated, engaged and feeling positive about what they do and what they achieve. While employing the strategies in Chapter 11 is a good place to start, as their leader, your team members need and will expect you to do more than that.

For a period, the word 'feedback' had negative connotations in many organisations and was viewed by staff simply as an opportunity for their manager to criticise them. As a result, some leader-managers were reluctant to provide it. Others provided it but made the mistake of only focusing on aspects of an employee's role that they were not doing well, leaving employees feeling discouraged and despondent. But with the adoption of a more holistic approach to providing feedback, the value of constructively provided feedback began to become more apparent. It gained traction because it provided an opportunity for employees to receive validation for the things they were doing well as well as a pathway for developing new skills in areas requiring improvement. Additionally, for their organisations, it provided a way of not only identifying gaps in their employees' skills but also a means of cataloguing their strengths. This meant tasks could be allocated more effectively, roles could be delegated with greater confidence and new market opportunities seized.

In today's workplaces, the provision of feedback forms an integral part of performance management and employees expect, and even feel entitled, to be provided with feedback on their work performance. In some organisations, this is a two-way street and employees also provide feedback on their leader-managers. Whether provided formally or informally, the performance guidance and performance planning that you provide to your team members is an important tool for building employee motivation and improving employee performance.

This chapter explains how to plan and conduct constructive, honest and supportive formal and informal performance discussions that will encourage staff, enhance working relationships and increase the value of employees to the organisation.

SNAPSHOT

A performance review 'train wreck'

'You simply can't keep rubbing people up the wrong way like you have been doing. You're arrogant, sarcastic and often racist in the comments you make. Your team members are also tired of covering for you with your customers and although the matter is still under investigation, everybody thinks it is you that has not been putting money in the honesty box to pay for the snacks in the kitchen. I mean, you just can't keep going on like that.' Serena sighed heavily. This is not how she had planned Sebastian's performance review but when the moment came, she just blurted it all out.

'Now hang on just a minute,' Sebastian retorted. 'You have no proof that I am the one not paying for the snacks. Also, I'm not arrogant, it's a fact that I am simply a lot better at my role than the rest of the team. It is me that is carrying them in relation to our customers, not the other way round. If you had any idea of what was really going on you would know that, but as you rarely leave your office you just let the others blind you as to how poorly they are actually performing and then they point the blame at me.'

'This is not about me,' Serena returned with quick fire, 'It is about your ...'

'It is about you Serena,' Sebastian interrupted. 'This whole thing is about you and the fact that you are not doing your job and I am the one being crucified for it. Oh, I'm sorry, I forgot, you don't make mistakes.'

How had it descended into this? Sebastian's formal performance discussion was supposed to provide Serena, his manager, with the opportunity to sort out some really important performance issues that were affecting the entire team but had degenerated into an argument and a blame game. With Sebastian now being patronising on top of all that, it seemed there was little that could now be salvaged from the 'train wreck' that the discussion had become.

15.1 Understanding the benefits, drawbacks and types of formal performance review systems

> Never mind who you praise but be very careful who you blame.
>
> Sir Edmund Gosse (writer), *Gossip in a library*, 1913.

Formal performance reviews are structured reviews of an employee's work performance conducted at periodic intervals where their performance is measured against predetermined criteria based on the person's role, responsibilities and expected behaviours and attitudes. They play an important part in organisational planning as well as providing a mechanism for ongoing workplace communication that helps employees perform well, keep improving and keep learning. They also provide an ideal opportunity for leader-managers to highlight the link between the organisation's strategic and operational goals and individual goals. When conducted well, they provide staff with positive affirmation of their value to the organisation and, as such, can form part of an effective employee retention strategy.

As formal performance discussions are structured and predictable, they help to eliminate subjective evaluations by leader-managers, which may be affected by their own unconscious bias, assumptions or stereotypes. The balanced consideration of performance that they provide means employees feel confident that their work performance is assessed fairly, impartially and objectively. They also provide a way to aggregate and analyse employee skill development and behavioural change over the long term, which is particularly important for large organisations. Considering how much they can help managers, organisations and employees, as summarised in Figure 15.1, formal performance discussions more than justify the time and effort you need to devote to them to maximise their effectiveness.

BENEFITS TO EMPLOYEES

- Air and clear up any concerns, irritations or uncertainties
- Ask for assistance in improving their performance and extending their skills and knowledge
- Clarify how they contribute to the goals of the team area and organisation
- Establish clear work expectations and goals for the next period
- Explain their work, training and career goals for future consideration
- Gain a better understanding of their strengths and development needs
- Gain a recorded commitment from their manager that certain actions will occur, for example training and support
- Gain a 'balcony overview' (see Chapter 9) of their roles
- Gain formal feedback and recognition for their performance and achievements over the previous period
- Hear how their manager views their performance
- Makes it easier to plan and prioritise work
- Protection from arbitrary decisions

BENEFITS TO LEADER-MANAGERS

- A chance to formally acknowledge and recognise employees' talents and achievements
- Agree areas of strength and improvement goals and opportunities
- Clarify expectations and employees' goals
- Improve morale through constructive feedback and clear direction
- Open communication channels and increase understanding of career aspirations
- Strengthened working relationships

BENEFITS TO ORGANISATIONS

- A permanent written record to support decisions regarding dismissals, promotions, redundancies, retrenchments, salary and wage changes, training, transfers, etc.
- A way to shift organisational culture
- Collate organisational training and development needs
- Ensure that employees are not poorly placed or misplaced in jobs and use employees' skills where they are most needed in the organisation
- Establish potential career paths for employees
- Establish succession plans
- Fill vacancies internally
- Identify, develop and nurture particularly talented people
- Identify employees for retrenchment and redundancy in the event of lack of work or restructuring
- Improved organisation performance through enhanced communication
- Inform salary and bonus reviews
- Link individual performance and behaviours with organisational strategy and values
- Monitor the effectiveness of selection or promotion procedures

FIGURE 15.1 Uses of formal performance discussions

Benefits to employees

When conducted in a constructive and structured manner, formal performance reviews provide employees with an opportunity to reflect on their performance, discuss it with their managers and start planning their future development. They also play an important part in confirming the context for employees' work efforts, which ensures that their own and their manager's expectations are both aligned and realistic. Aside from performance-related matters, performance discussions can be used as a chance to get things out in the open that might be difficult or too sensitive to bring up in other forums, such as meetings. Issues, questions or anxieties can be discussed, clarified and ideally resolved in a discreet and more comfortable environment.

Performance discussions allow employees to receive feedback on how their leader-manager perceives their performance via a comprehensive review of the period just passed. The review gives their manager a chance to recognise and acknowledge their good work by highlighting where their performance has excelled but also provides an opportunity for manager and employee to sit down together and set objectives for the upcoming period. This can include goals to achieve, ways to build on the employee's existing strengths and professional development options to learn new skills or address any gaps in existing skills. For an employee, a formal performance review should be a positive and constructive experience of reflection, discussion, problem-solving, learning, planning and goal-setting.

Benefits to leader-managers

Formally reviewing your team members' performance allows you to stand back from your daily routine and look clearly and objectively at each person's performance, potential, career aspirations, and training and development needs. It helps you monitor individual skills and past performance, set future performance objectives and motivate employees, and gives you an opportunity to show your interest in employees, their jobs and their training and development. Regular performance discussions also help you monitor team and individual competencies to confirm that the team as a whole is able to achieve its goals.

Benefits to organisations

Organisations need an objective way to calculate merit-based pay, pay for skills and general pay increases. When vacancies and other opportunities arise, many organisations look internally to find people suitable for promotions, special assignments and transfers and use performance reviews to place people in jobs that suit their capabilities. Organisations also use performance discussions to help shift their organisational culture by encouraging and acknowledging behaviours that reflect their values. Perhaps most important of all, formal performance discussions link individual performance with organisational values, strategies and goals.

Three main uses of performance reviews

Performance discussions are not intended to punish for misdeeds or provide a 'short, sharp kick', although they sometimes end up this way. They are intended to:

- *Look backwards:* to discuss employees' performances during the period under review. What did they do particularly well? What needs improving? What special skills or helpful behaviours do they have and do any need adjusting? What mistakes did they make and what can be learnt from them? This gives you an ideal opportunity to recognise good work, uncover problems, increase motivation and clarify any areas of misunderstanding.

- *Plan improvements:* to enable high performance and productivity, take the opportunity to review each of the **Five Keys** – What To, Want To, How To, Chance To and Led To (explained in Chapter 19) to make sure they are operating optimally. Discuss how to alter the job to make it easier, quicker or more economical to carry out. What problems has the employee run into? What prevents even better job performance? How can the job be streamlined and hassles eliminated? This can prevent misdiagnosing performance shortfalls, encourage innovation and continuous improvements, solve problems, improve your department's and the organisation's operations, and show employees that you value their opinion – provided you act on what you learn.
- *Look to the future:* align individual goals with the overall goals of the organisation and the department and discuss employee aspirations. What results do you expect over the forthcoming period and what new goals can the employee work towards? What training and development would the employee benefit from? What additional or delegated duties would increase job skills or job satisfaction? What direction would the employee like their job and their career to take? What other jobs in the organisation interest the employee?

Both parties need to think through these three topics in advance and be prepared to discuss them openly and honestly.

Other uses of performance reviews

Performance reviews can also be used for other purposes in addition to the three main uses just outlined. While there may also be other factors to consider, the following are additional uses for performance reviews:

- *Confirming ongoing employment following probation:* discussing a newly hired employee's performance during **probation** is the final and most important stage in the selection process. At this stage, you should be confident that the recruit meets or exceeds performance expectations, and if not, discuss your misgivings openly with the employee and the human resources (HR) manager if applicable. You want to determine whether the employee and the organisation are best served by further training the employee for the position, transferring the employee to a more suitable position or discontinuing the hiring process.
- *Determining remuneration bonuses:* some organisations include a remuneration review in performance reviews if the employee has met certain criteria over the preceding period to receive a bonus or increase in their remuneration.
- *Determining suitability for promotion:* this may be part of career and succession planning processes and can be particularly important in relation to roles that require highly specialised skills not readily available in the existing labour pool. Performance review is an especially important tool when ensuring there is an employee with the requisite skills ready to step up into the role when the incumbent leaves or retires.
- *Termination of employment:* while it should not be an intended use of formal performance reviews, it can on occasions be a necessary one. This is a permanent separation from the organisation as a result of a serious offence by the employee, continued poor job performance or because a position has ceased to exist, usually due to restructuring or changed market conditions. When it is due to continued poor performance, objective performance discussions documenting the employee's performance over a period and records of performance counselling interviews can show that dismissal was fair, justified and lawful. (How to terminate employment is explained in Chapter 16.)

Problems with performance reviews

Some problems are inherent in any performance review method, whether it be formal or informal. Some of these problems can be more about the reviewer than about the employee. This is known as the *idiosyncratic rater effect* and shows up as:

- a tendency to rate an employee's performance either too leniently or severely
- a tendency to rate people highest who are most like yourself and with whom you identify (see Chapter 32)
- basing assessments on arbitrary, imprecise and subjective 'evidence', in other words, your opinion, laced with your own biases, assumptions and stereotypes
- the halo/horns effect – allowing your assessment of one area of an employee's performance to influence how you assess the other areas.

The relationship between the leader-manager and employee can exaggerate the idiosyncratic rater effect due to the fact that the better they know each other, the more likely the chance the rating will be skewed. To some extent, a culture that values honest and helpful feedback, embraces diversity through training and acceptance, and emphasises and ensures a fair and objective performance discussion system can overcome these inbuilt problems. The extent to which organisations are prepared to devote limited resources to fund activities such as diversity training, however, is not assured.

There are also other problems that can reduce the accuracy and objectivity of formal performance reviews:

Transferable skills

3.1 Teamwork/relationships

- allowing recent events to be given greater importance over older ones as well as overemphasising non-typical events, which may more rationally be viewed as far less important due to the rarity of their occurrence
- stereotyping, or assuming that people who belong to certain groups (Generation Ys, Millennials, older workers, men, women, people from specific ethnic groups or cultural backgrounds, those identifying as part of the LGBTIQ+ community, etc.) are all the same and not viewing their performance objectively or on the basis of merit
- the temptation to give priority to keeping the team productive as a whole over providing accurate individual performance reviews.

Organisation-wide problems with performance reviews

Organisations themselves can create other problems with performance reviews by not applying the formal discussion process to everyone, including those at the top of the organisation, which invites cynicism. They might also develop a very clever performance review system that is, in practice, overly cumbersome, complicated, difficult and time-consuming to implement. This might ultimately invite people to avoid using it or take shortcuts, which compromises the integrity of its results. They may also develop performance review systems for the sake of having them but which are poorly designed, do not achieve the intended outcomes and end up being viewed by all who use them as a waste of time.

Ideally, every organisation should design or adopt a system that meets the needs of the organisation, where everyone's performance is discussed using objective, relevant and measurable criteria and which is relatively straightforward to administer.

Strategies to improve how you conduct performance reviews

Transferable skills
2.2 Personal effectiveness

There are many steps you can take to overcome the inherent problems in performance reviews yourself. You can base your discussion of job performance on the whole period under review, not just a small part of it or what has occurred most recently, and rate each aspect of performance objectively and independently of the others. Keeping a performance diary in relation to each employee throughout the review period will help you focus on the entire period, not just on what you can remember.

Being sensitive to cultural differences and treating each employee individually and on their merits is central to conducting performance reviews in an objective and fair manner. Self-awareness can alert you to any personal biases and blind spots that could affect your judgement, such as how easy or difficult a person is to manage, which can compromise your objectivity. Use mindfulness to concentrate your focus on an employee's work performance, not personality, or how you feel about them by distinguishing between personality traits and performance criteria. This strategy can also help you to avoid relying on hunches or intuition and over psychoanalysing an employee. You don't always need to understand 'why' someone does something or acts in the way they do, you only need to focus on their job performance. A mindful approach can help you focus on each person's typical job performance or behaviour rather than being unduly influenced by something they have done unusually well or poorly.

Always keep your rating standards fair and consistent and focused on results or work performance. Where employees are doing the same job, use the same standards to assess them. Also, don't allow your objective analysis of an employee's performance to be affected by their enthusiasm, motivated approach or bright personality. You should always rate a low-performing but highly motivated employee lower than an employee who is performing the job adequately but unenthusiastically. Another thing to watch for is confusing length of service with job performance. Being with the organisation for a long time doesn't guarantee high performance. Conversely, being new to a job doesn't automatically mean someone is unable to do a job just as well or better than someone who has been doing it for considerably longer.

Lastly, beware of negativity bias. Humans are hardwired to notice negative events more than positive events, so when reviewing someone's performance, guard against giving more weight to negative incidents than positive ones – but not so much that you swing the other way and rate people too leniently. When you do mention a negative event, do so carefully, because humans are also hardwired to hear criticism far more loudly than praise. Keep in mind when conducting a formal performance review how you want the employee to walk out feeling. With this in mind, when delivering negative feedback, make sure it is provided constructively, fairly and focuses solely on the person's performance, not the person.

Performance review systems

Formal performance reviews are part of the traditional performance management process, which includes clear job or **role descriptions**, performance standards and goals with measurable outcomes, and cascading objectives targeted to achieve the organisation's strategic and operational goals. Formal performance reviews are usually conducted on a six- or 12-month cycle or even more frequently in the case of some operator and customer service jobs. The employee's immediate leader-manager conducts them and, in many organisations, that manager's manager reviews them. Results are often collated and analysed for use with succession, training and other HR plans for the organisation.

The particular skills and abilities considered depend on the role and the organisation culture you're trying to support or create. Some typical areas for performance review are shown in **Figure 15.2**.

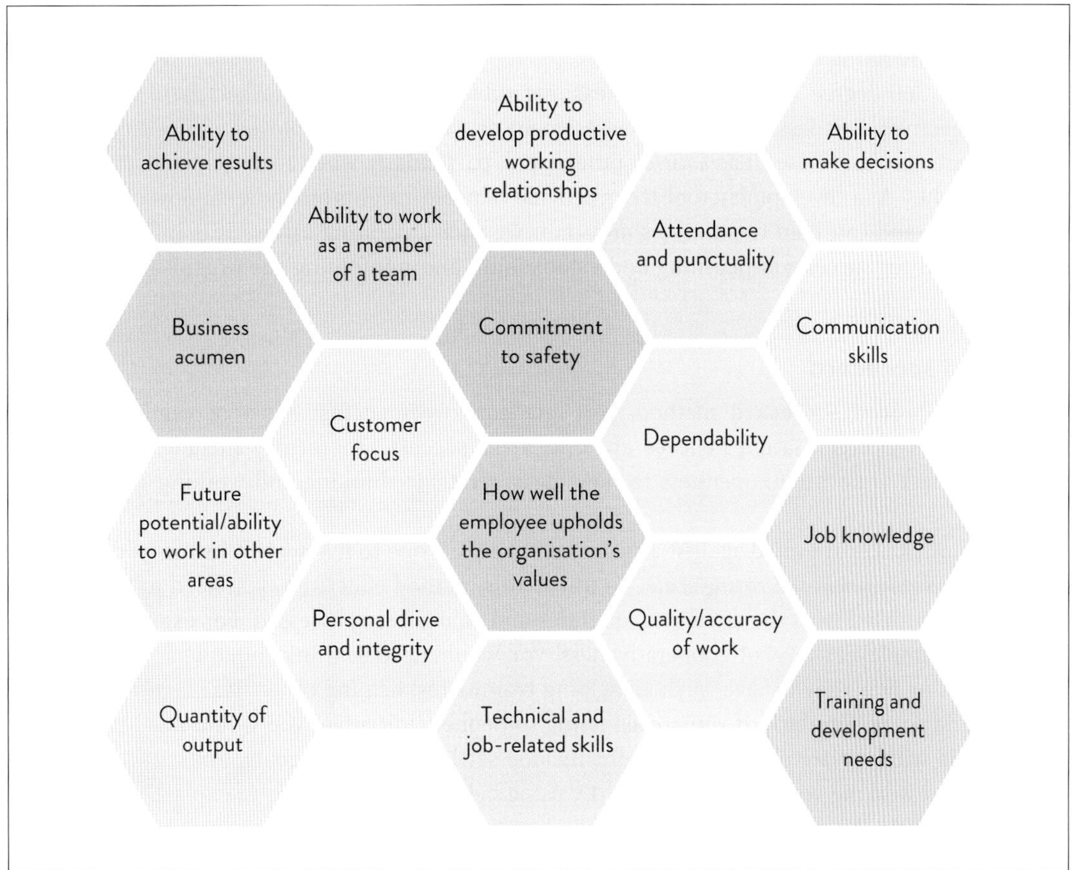

FIGURE 15.2 Areas for performance review

The main traditional methods for reviewing performance are described in the following sections. We then consider an emerging way to review performance – ongoing performance discussions. However, be mindful of the fact that every system can fall prey to the problems we have discussed so far.

360-degree feedback

Multi-rater feedback, or **360-degree feedback**, is often used to appraise leader-managers and members of high-performing work teams and project teams. This feedback provides anonymous information to employees from eight to 12 people who interact with them – direct reports, internal customers, their own manager, peers and sometimes external customers and suppliers. The person being rated also completes the feedback form for later comparison – 'This is how I think I perform, and this is how others think I perform.'

To be effective, 360-degree feedback needs to be completed in the spirit of generosity and honesty so that the feedback isn't more about the person giving the feedback than the strengths and weaknesses of the person receiving it. For example, in highly competitive organisation cultures, 360-degree feedback could be used to hurt, rather than help, colleagues. Another concern with 360-degree feedback is that it can be less objective than a leader-manager's feedback.

It is also important to remember that being effective and being liked aren't necessarily the same thing, and while raters – whether clients, direct reports, peers or suppliers – can probably offer relevant feedback on qualities such as trust and integrity, they may not know precisely what makes someone they're rating effective in their role.

Because 360-degree feedback often measures subjective attributes rather than performance against objectives, it is less useful as an assessment of whether an employee is meeting basic job requirements and more useful as a development tool, particularly when feedback is discussed with trained coaches. As a development tool, it can provide valuable insights into how employees' behaviour affects others and can help them assess and improve their operating styles. This information can also be useful for succession planning and establishing and reinforcing the organisation's culture and values.

Balanced scorecard

With the **balanced scorecard** method, you rate employees against a list of values, attributes and qualities the organisation believes are critical to success. These may include, for example, cooperativeness, innovation, openness to new ideas, strategic thinking and working as a member of a team.

When attributes are rated against a scale, for example a one to five scale, this method is known as a *behaviourally anchored rating scale*. To utilise this method effectively, you need to think about the behaviour linked with the attributes, qualities and values being assessed. For example, if you're assessing an employee's level of 'cooperativeness', you would need to think about what a cooperative person does or how they behave, such as helping teammates, helping others learn, going the extra distance and so on. Similarly, if you are assessing someone's 'initiative', you would need to consider what people with initiative do, which might include setting their own goals, finding ways around problems and working without supervision. By using behavioural examples to explain your ratings, you increase their objectivity.

Comparison or forced ranking

Devised by the US Army just before entering the Second World War to identify officer candidates quickly, the comparison, or ranking, method compares each job-holder with the others in the team or department against set criteria. This process ends up with, for example, a judgement made as to the most/least productive, the most/least innovative and so on. Because it is difficult to compare every individual with every other one, some ranking methods place employees only into the top third, middle third or lowest third instead of ranking each individually. Some organisations use a quota-based system known as *forced ranking* or *stacked ranking*, which forces employees' performance into a normal distribution, or 'bell' curve.

The variables being assessed are usually independent of each other, so an employee could rank, for example, in the top third of employees for planning and organising work and in the bottom third for accuracy of work. The collated results give organisations a quick, if only rough, assessment of employees' value to the organisation, a way to determine pay increases (e.g. the top employees receive a 3 per cent increase, the average employees 1 per cent) and a way to identify underperforming employees.

INDUSTRY INSIGHTS

Rank and yank

General Electric introduced forced curved ranking, or 'rank and yank', in the 1980s. 'Rank and yank' sees managers compare each employee's performance on a bell curve. The top 20 per cent are

'A players', the next 70 per cent are 'B players' and the bottom 10 per cent are 'C players'. If the performance of the C players doesn't improve, they are dismissed – even when they are performing satisfactorily. (See the Industry insights box 'Touchpoints' later in this chapter.) General Electric's then CEO Jack Welch claimed this method boosted their revenues from US$70 billion in 1995 to US$130 billion in 2000. As a result of GE's success, other large companies adopted versions of the system.

Critical-incident discussions

Critical-incident, or behavioural, performance discussions are based on a record of important (i.e. critical) incidents, both positive and negative, that have occurred during the review period. You maintain a record and employees often keep their own records as well. A shortcoming of this method is that people often record only negative incidents, seeing positive incidents as merely normal job performance.

Essay

With the essay method, you write a few paragraphs about each employee, usually according to set guidelines. This takes thought and care and can be quite time-consuming. Some managers can write more convincingly than others, which means that employees whose managers are not skilled writers may suffer by comparison with those rated by managers who write well.

Management by objectives

Management by objectives (MBO) compares an employee's results for the period under review against clear and agreed SMART targets. Goals are then agreed upon for the next review period and so on. Putting the focus on what is done rather than how it is done makes the MBO method ideal to use with knowledge workers, teleworkers and other off-site workers and people on project teams.

Here's how MBO works: your department's goal might be to reduce expenses by 3 per cent and increase output by 2 per cent during the forthcoming quarter. The administration assistant might suggest a personal target of producing 35 documents a day by the end of the next quarter and to begin at once to use recycled paper for all drafts and to print on both sides of the paper. If you and the admin assistant agree that this is reasonable, they become two of the administration assistant's targets. In a similar fashion, you would agree on personal targets with each team member that contribute to reducing expenses and increasing output to reach the department's overall goals.

Peer review

Some organisations include peer reviews as part of their performance evaluations. Team members review each other's performance against key criteria such as job knowledge, the ability to work as a member of and contribute to the team, to innovate and solve problems. This can be effective in productive teams where members work well together and value each other's contributions in achieving work-related objectives. When teamwork is not critical, peer reviews offer few benefits.

Performance diary

Sometimes called full-time performance reviews, employees and managers both make notes on performance-related matters throughout the review period. This means that when they review past performance, both are well prepared with a full record of achievements and development areas. This method links well with most other review methods, particularly the balanced scorecard, critical incident and MBO methods.

Rating scale

With the rating-scale method, you rate specific job-related skills and abilities of each employee according to a defined scale, as shown in **Figure 15.3**. This is an easy method to use and allows quick comparison between employees.

Role description or competency rating

An accurate, up-to-date job or role description that includes competencies and measurable standards of performance is the key to this method of performance review. In its simplest form, the role description method provides a list of duties that the job-holder performs, and you tick those performed adequately and put a cross against those needing improvement. This method is quick and easy and highlights training needs. It's particularly effective for routine jobs.

An emerging way to review performance – ongoing performance conversations

Traditional formal performance reviews are a heavy drain on an organisation's resources and there is little evidence that the time spent is cost-effective. In addition, they are increasingly seen as being irrelevant to the way we work and are being replaced by frequent or ongoing performance conversations.

Life in many organisations is different today than it was when traditional performance review systems were developed. Flatter organisation structures have dramatically increased the number of people who report directly to leader-managers, so asking a leader-manager to recall and appraise the

Employee ______________________________

Department ______________________ Section ______________________

Manager ______________________ Date ______________________

Please rate the employee on the skills or qualities listed below. Following each skill is a line with points along it to serve as a rating scale. The phrases beneath the line link the number of points that will be awarded to the rating. Rate the employee by marking at any point on the line the position that best describes the employee's ability in each area.

Job knowledge

0	5	10	15	20
Gaps in knowledge of a critical nature	Understands only routine aspects of job	Is well informed on all aspects of job	Has better than average knowledge of all aspects of job	Superior understanding of job; very well informed

Quality of work

0	5	10	15	20
Quality unsatisfactory	Quality not quite up to standard	Quality quite satisfactory	Quality superior	Quality exceptionally high

FIGURE 15.3 Part of an employee evaluation form used in the rating-scale method

behaviours and performance of numerous workers over six to 12 months is unrealistic, particularly when you consider their competing work priorities.

Team structures and composition have also changed and are often marked by large numbers of casual, contract and temporary employees who may leave a team prior to the six- to 12-month review period. More and more employees are working in multiple teams or on multiple projects, making it difficult for leader-managers to accurately assess an employee's performance. On top of that, not all leader-managers see or understand the work of their team members, especially when those team members are remote workers or knowledge workers.

Farewelling annual or biannual performance reviews in favour of frequent real-time performance feedback can help improve employee engagement and better align employees to organisation strategy. Regular performance feedback also aligns better with what younger employees want and suits today's more complex and rapidly changing jobs and roles.

Discussing team members' performance candidly, honestly and often can build or strengthen a culture of open communication. Frequent performance discussions become a habit and are much less threatening, more helpful and more constructive than traditional performance reviews. They lend themselves to a coaching approach and building an ongoing process and commitment to continuous improvement. (You can find out about coaching techniques in Chapter 29.)

Other benefits of frequent performance conversations include the fact that they are more likely to be done because they are less time-consuming and onerous and can be conducted more flexibly, making them more 'user-friendly'. They also reduce paperwork, keep the focus on improving current performance and can reduce underperformance because employees' performance is regularly monitored and coached.

For these reasons, we can expect to see more and more organisations joining Accenture, Adobe, Deloitte, General Electric (GE) and others in replacing traditional performance reviews with more frequent performance discussions.[1] Whether you call them debriefs, learnings, check-ins, development meetings, learning meetings or something else that fits the organisation culture, they are best based on the natural work cycle; for example, attaining a milestone, dealing with a challenge, completing a project or resolving an ongoing problem. By keeping the focus on outcomes (not activity), what the employee did well and how they can improve in the future, these short-cycle conversations follow the basic learning cycle shown in **Figure 5.7** in Chapter 5.

There are even apps available for frequent performance discussions that allow employees to request performance feedback and provide insights and feedback to their teammates. For example, GE uses PD@GE (PD stands for 'performance development') and Amazon uses Anytime Feedback. The latter, however, is based on anonymous feedback to a person's leader-manager and is combined with a yearly 'rank and yank', which may lead to less than honest peer feedback.[2]

Of course, frequent performance conversations can still suffer the same problems as traditional performance reviews and you still need to align the organisation's goals with employees' goals and develop performance improvement plans (as described in Chapter 16) for underperforming employees.

 INDUSTRY INSIGHTS

Touchpoints

Since the 1980s, General Electric was well known for its forced ranking appraisals and annual goals. In 2016, it replaced them in favour of shorter-term 'priorities' and short-cycle conversations called 'touchpoints'. Touchpoints focus on:

- What am I doing that I should keep doing?
- What am I doing that I should consider changing?

Touchpoints are intended to support General Electric's new business strategy based on innovation and cross-functional teams bringing new products to market rapidly. Leader-managers continue to have an end-of-year, formalised and documented summary discussion with each employee to supplement touchpoints. However, since the annual conversations are based on touchpoints, they are more objective, meaningful and future-focused, and less threatening because they are part of an ongoing dialogue.[3]

Individual meetings

You can initiate regular one-on-one meetings with each of your team members even if your organisation hasn't moved to more frequent performance discussions. They provide an opportunity to set expectations for the coming week or check-in period, review priorities, provide coaching and update your team members with any relevant or interesting information. Keeping these meetings about upcoming work and coaching rather than past performance increases engagement and role clarity.

Individual meetings are valuable communication and motivation tools, as well as a great way to ensure your team members are tracking towards their goals. Give them ownership of the meeting by asking each employee to set their agenda and send it to you a day or two in advance. They can cancel the meeting when there is nothing pressing to discuss. Let the employee do most of the talking.

Mixed method

Many organisations try to gain the advantages of all these methods by using a combination of them – the mixed method. Formal performance discussion documents are divided into several sections, each consisting of one or more of the methods discussed so far. In striving to retain a wide variety of features and benefits, however, document designers can fall into the trap of creating lengthy, complicated forms that take too long to complete and become ends in themselves.

Another 'best of both worlds' approach is frequent performance conversations plus an end-of-year formal wind-up using a more traditional performance review system.

The best method

Leader-managers and organisations will always need a mechanism to define performance and behavioural expectations, evaluate the degree to which they're being met and help employees develop their skills and therefore be of greater value to the organisation. 'Grades' and forced rankings, which make most people defensive, are being replaced by more frequent discussions. When determining the 'best' method to review and build performance, consider choosing one that:

- encourages open discussion and builds understanding between employees and their managers
- helps employees improve their performance and find ways to meet their personal goals
- managers and employees understand and will use willingly
- sheds light on organisational difficulties and problems and helps to fix them
- recognises the value of employees' work efforts and acknowledges this to them
- suits your organisation's culture and operations.

Whatever method of assessing and providing formal feedback on performance your organisation uses, it can be an important way to translate organisational goals into personal work goals and performance agreements and to encourage employees to take responsibility for meeting those goals (see Chapter 2).

15.2 Planning and leading performance discussions

We all need people who will give us feedback. That's how we improve.

Jana Kasperkevic, 'Bill Gates: Good feedback is the key to improvement', *Inc. Magazine*, 17 May 2013.

Whether you're leading annual, biannual or more frequent performance discussions, to lead them effectively, you need to combine your communication and interpersonal skills with a systematic approach. This approach consists of:

1 preparing for the discussion
2 conducting the discussion
3 undertaking any necessary follow-up actions after the discussion.

Figure 15.4 shows the overall cycle of individual performance discussions in the wider context of the organisation's goals. The information that follows considers formal performance reviews but also applies to the more frequent performance discussions considered previously.

Part 1: Prepare for the meeting

To ensure that both your organisation and the employee concerned maximise the value from a performance discussion, be organised and try to avoid the 'assembly line' approach – holding one performance discussion after another. Rushing the meeting can result in 'telling' rather than 'discussing' and is unfair to employees for whom the formal performance discussion meeting is

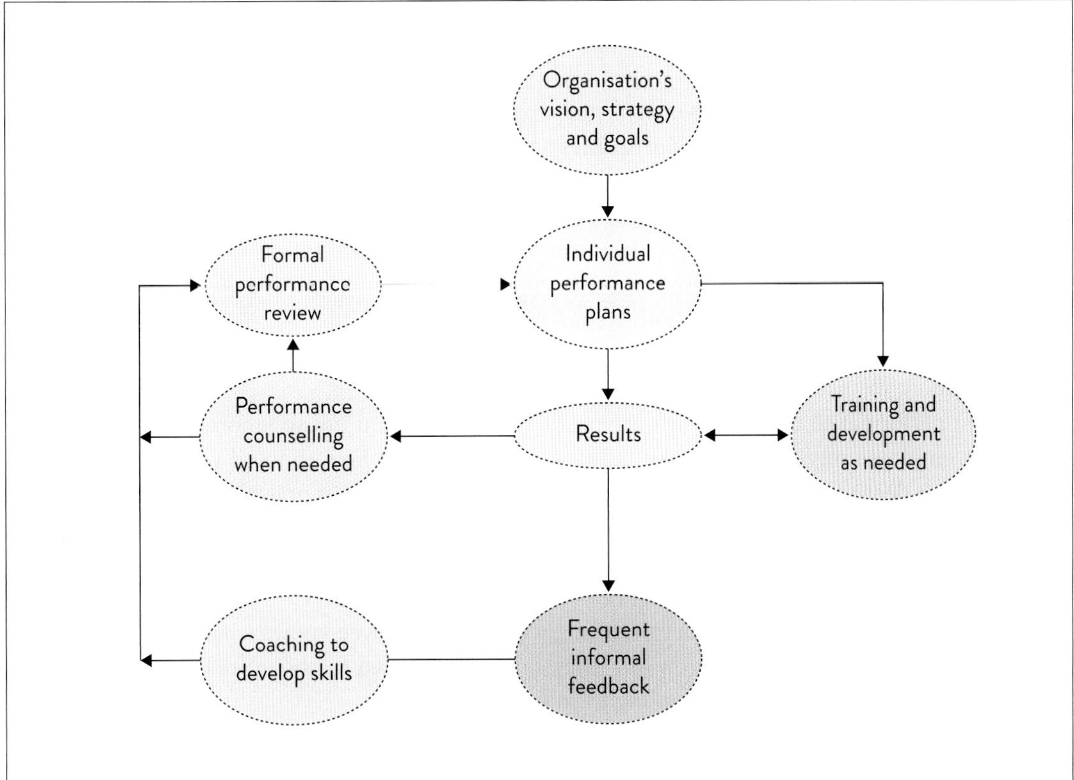

FIGURE 15.4 The cycle of performance discussions

their one opportunity for the year perhaps to have your attention solely devoted to them and their performance. Even with more regular one-on-one meetings, it helps to think of each meeting as 'the employee's meeting' because it is about their performance and development, not about ticking a box and filing away a report.

When choosing the location to conduct a review, ensure there is privacy and that there will be no interruptions from people, alerts and mobile phone calls so that both you and the employee can focus on the performance matters for review and discussion. Where possible, meet in a neutral area, such as a conference room, to help reduce employees' anxiety and make the discussion more constructive. Create a comfortable and non-threatening atmosphere to encourage the employee to speak their mind and be open to guidance and advice. For instance, you could sit in chairs by a low coffee table rather than facing each other from opposite sides of a desk. If setting up the room like this, make sure you have chairs of similar height and arrange the blinds so that light doesn't shine in the employee's face. Allow about an hour for the meeting when it's a formal annual or biannual performance discussion.

Organise to meet one or two weeks prior to the review to advise the employee as to how long you expect the meeting to last and how you plan to conduct it. Provide a copy of the discussion document or explain how to find it on your organisation's intranet. Ask the employee to consider:

- the successes, challenges, and most and least enjoyable parts of their job in the period since their last formal performance discussion, as well as where they have experienced problems, what the causes were and whether they have been able to resolve them
- what could be done to make their work easier, more efficient and more effective (see Chapter 19)
- the work goals they wish to achieve in the forthcoming period and career aspirations beyond that, as well as any support, training or professional development they need in relation to achieving or pursuing each of them.

To get the review off to a positive start, make your opening comments about what the employee does well and what development opportunities are available. But make sure you are authentic and provide accurate information by gathering as many facts and examples as you can to support your comments. This might include employee files, a summary of both on- and off-the-job training, their position description, the agreed targets from the last period and the extent to which the employee has met them, and any client comments. This information should be *naturally acquired* through sanctioned organisational processes rather than gossip or via the office grapevine. This ensures the information presented in relation to the employee is objective and doesn't leave them wondering who said what about them and why.

When performance improvements are needed, it is important not to ignore them because you think the employee might not react well. Think carefully about how to word your information so that you don't dent the employee's self-esteem but be honest in your appraisal of their performance. Identify areas of performance that require improvement as well as development needs in a way that is helpful, not hurtful, so the employee can take them on board. Aim to coach and advise rather than criticise by providing constructive guidance.

Acknowledge areas of satisfactory performance so the employee knows what to keep doing and highlight their strengths so they know how they can improve even further. (See Chapter 5 for more information on the importance of working to your strengths.)

When employees have reported to another manager during the period under review, for example because they recently transferred to your department or worked on a project during the period, ask the other manager(s) for their observations, assessments and feedback to include in the discussion. When their comments indicate a performance problem, find out whether it was discussed with the employee and what was agreed to. **Figure 15.5** shows information you and the employee need to obtain from each other and what you agree on together.

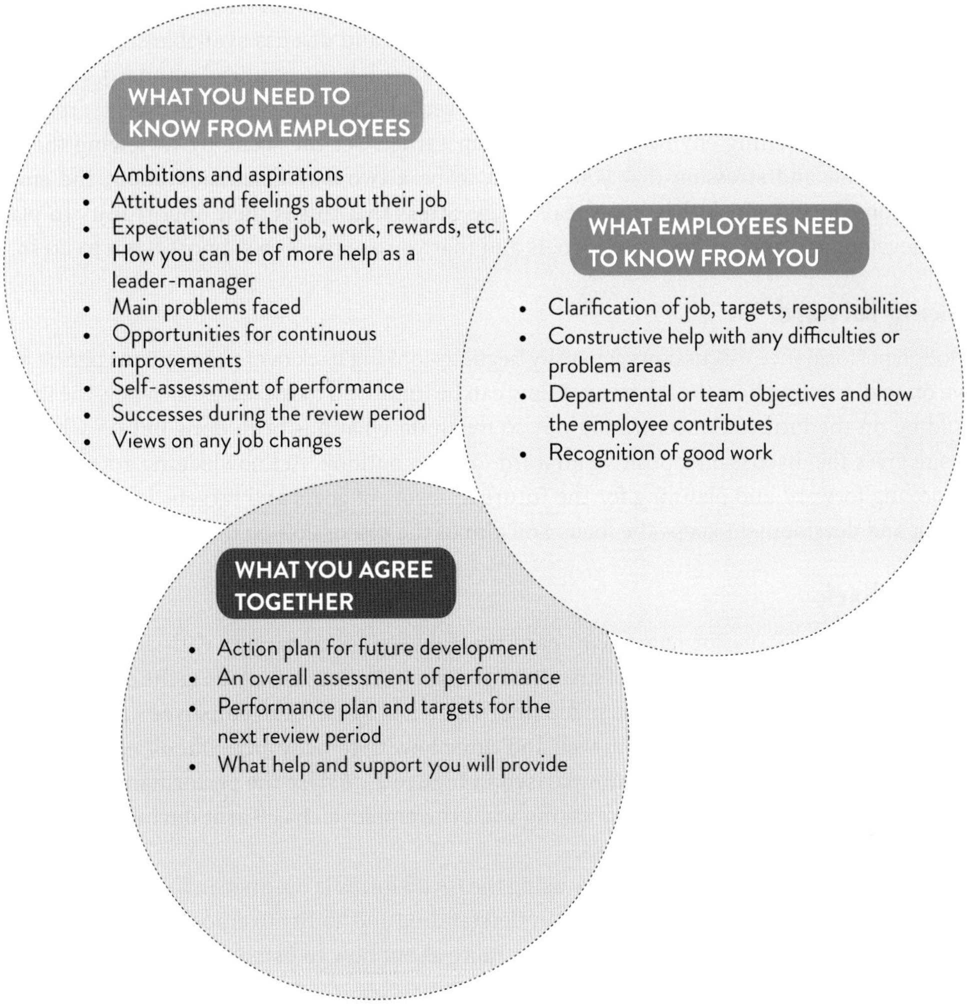

FIGURE 15.5 Information needed from performance discussion meetings

Part 2: The meeting

After creating the right environment, review past performance, plan performance for the following period and discuss development needs. You might also ask the employee for some feedback to help improve your leadership and management style, which shows them that you value their opinion and may also help you to improve your own performance. At the end of the discussion, summarise the main points and actions to be taken and end on a positive note by highlighting what might be achieved moving forward once the strategies outlined and agreed upon are implemented.

If you have been doing your job in monitoring your employees' performance and providing them with regular feedback, the formal performance discussion should contain no surprises. When an employee has performed better or less well than expected in some areas, you should have mentioned it long before the review in an informal feedback meeting (discussed later in this chapter). This is not the time to begin documenting performance shortfalls or counselling an employee for poor performance. (Chapter 16 explains how to counsel underperforming employees.) When discussing areas of performance that are below the expected standard, keep your input constructive in order to maintain or enhance the employee's self-esteem. Suggest and discuss available strategies as well as assistance and support you can provide so that they can reach the required standard.

Throughout the discussion, make sure your verbal and non-verbal messages are consistent with the non-threatening environment you set up earlier. Set the scene by reviewing the purpose of the interview and stressing that you want it to be a two-way discussion about the employee's contributions during which they can speak freely. Stress that this is their opportunity to plan their future development and job and career goals and that you are there to support them to do so.

Looking forward

Although performance discussions generally begin by looking back over the previous period and then move on to discussing how the job or workflow can be improved to increase efficiency, the main focus should be on the future. Concentrating not so much on what has been done but on what needs to be done gives the discussion a positive forward-looking outlook. Acknowledging good performance and looking forward and planning for the future in terms of goals and targets, job progression, and training and development keeps the focus and aim of the discussion on improving performance.

Looking back

When reviewing past performance, compare the deliverables or targets with actual performance, highlighting and appreciating areas of sustained performance that is exceeding the expected standard, and areas in which the employee has made improvements. Review the employee's progress since the last discussion to reinforce what went well and agree how to remedy any difficulties. Follow the Bat–Mice acronym for giving feedback summarised in Figure 15.6. Use the performance discussion as a way to reinforce a learning culture by asking what the employee has learnt during the period under discussion and how they've put it to use.

Listen to the employee's point of view using the EARS formula outlined in Figure 6.1 in Chapter 6. This reduces defensiveness, increases your understanding and ability to empathise, and sets the scene for collaborative problem-solving. (To find out more about how to listen well, see Chapter 6.)

Making improvements

Ask the employee whether they have experienced any problems since the last performance discussion, and whether they have resolved them or they are still ongoing. Use open questions rather than closed questions, as illustrated in Table 15.1 (see Chapter 6 for more information on asking questions).

Fully explore the 'Chance To Key' (explained in Chapter 19) and productivity to find ways that work could be carried out more easily, safely, quickly, reliably or cheaply and to remove obstacles to successful performance. This is a perfect opportunity to uncover and resolve problems and make continuous improvements. When there are opportunities to improve performance, employees generally respond better when you help them to figure out how to improve. Table 15.2 show ways in which you can frame your feedback to be positive, constructive and helpful rather than vague, personal and unhelpful.

Performance planning

As performance discussions are primarily aimed at the future, agree on future measures of success and timeframes for their achievement. Use SMART targets to help people do their jobs well by helping them concentrate their attention and energy on important matters. That's why it is necessary

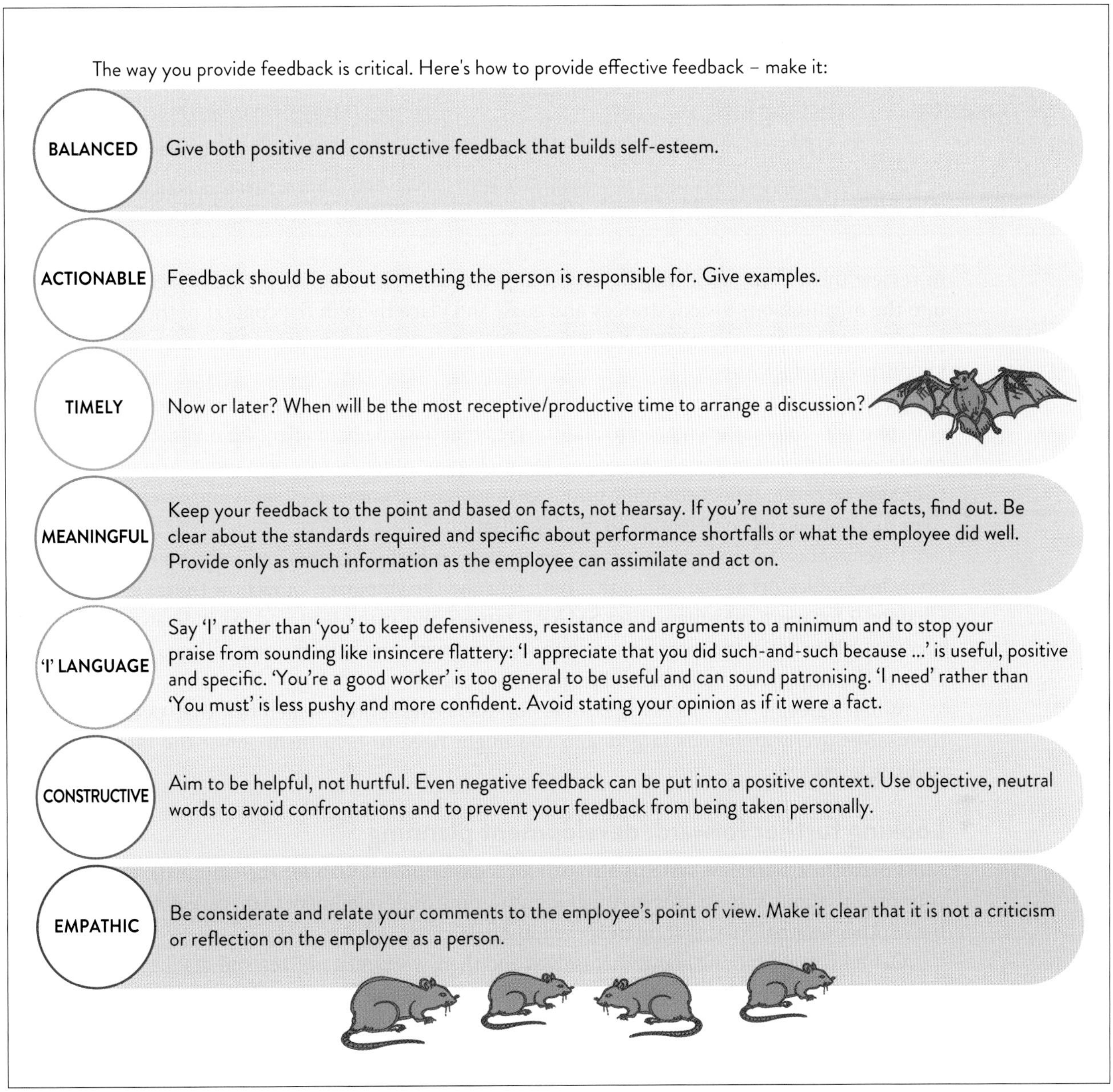

The way you provide feedback is critical. Here's how to provide effective feedback – make it:

BALANCED Give both positive and constructive feedback that builds self-esteem.

ACTIONABLE Feedback should be about something the person is responsible for. Give examples.

TIMELY Now or later? When will be the most receptive/productive time to arrange a discussion?

MEANINGFUL Keep your feedback to the point and based on facts, not hearsay. If you're not sure of the facts, find out. Be clear about the standards required and specific about performance shortfalls or what the employee did well. Provide only as much information as the employee can assimilate and act on.

'I' LANGUAGE Say 'I' rather than 'you' to keep defensiveness, resistance and arguments to a minimum and to stop your praise from sounding like insincere flattery: 'I appreciate that you did such-and-such because …' is useful, positive and specific. 'You're a good worker' is too general to be useful and can sound patronising. 'I need' rather than 'You must' is less pushy and more confident. Avoid stating your opinion as if it were a fact.

CONSTRUCTIVE Aim to be helpful, not hurtful. Even negative feedback can be put into a positive context. Use objective, neutral words to avoid confrontations and to prevent your feedback from being taken personally.

EMPATHIC Be considerate and relate your comments to the employee's point of view. Make it clear that it is not a criticism or reflection on the employee as a person.

FIGURE 15.6 The Bat–Mice feedback acronym

TABLE 15.1 Use open questions

Closed question	Open question
Can I help you?	How can I help you?
Do you want to give it more thought?	What other thoughts do you have?
Is there a better way to do this?	How else could you do this?

TABLE 15.2 Different types of negative and positive feedback

	Negative feedback	Positive feedback
Unhelpful/too general	'You're unreliable'	'You're a fantastic team member'
Better	'I need prior warning if your project is late'	'I can always count on you to meet your deadlines'
Best	'When you were late with that project, how do you think it affected the rest of the team?'	'I very much appreciated the way you pulled out all the stops to complete the XYZ project on time'

to review them even when they haven't changed much from the last period. Discuss how they fit into the organisation's vision, strategy and goals and place them in the context of the employee's job purpose and key result areas (KRAs). (See the 'What To Key' in Chapter 19 for more information on job purpose and KRAs.)

Keep targets flexible enough to accommodate changes in the marketplace and your operating environment. You may even need to alter targets that have been in effect for a long time when work conditions, different materials, processes, technology or other factors demand it. You may also need to change targets to reflect changing priorities or to develop employees' skills and extend and broaden their motivation and contribution to the organisation.

Discuss how you and the employee can track, or monitor, success and improvement. Identify as many lead indicators as you can so that both you and the employee know how things are going. (See Chapter 9 for more information on SMART targets and using lead and lag indicators to measure success.) Write down the measures of success, along with any agreed-upon actions, and distribute a copy to the employee concerned and keep a copy yourself.

When agreeing on success measures for the next period, remember that people often set themselves overly ambitious targets and you might need to help them adjust the targets to more realistic levels.

Looking further forward: development planning

Most performance review systems also call for a development plan for the employee. Depending on your organisation's system, this may include a training or development plan, career aspirations and a list of other internal roles that interest the job-holder.

Get employees talking about themselves and their work-related likes and dislikes. Discuss their short- and long-term career aspirations (remembering lateral moves as well as upward moves) and the learning and development opportunities that interest them most. Ask what assignments, projects and work they've found most enjoyable, what accomplishments over the last period they've felt good about and what aspects of their role makes for a great day at work. Ask what's most important to them and how they view themselves in relation to their team and the organisation. Getting an employee to think about how they can best contribute to the team helps them to not only recognise their strengths but also commit to improving the overall performance of the team.

Based on this information, draw up a development plan identifying any skills the employee could usefully learn or build upon. Set priorities by selecting two or three skills to concentrate on based on what is most achievable and what would be most useful to the organisation. Then identify the best approach (e.g. adding responsibilities to the current job, coaching, delegation, special assignments, training programs) and agree on the next steps in implementing the plan. Diarise to check in with the employee every few months to find out how their development plan is progressing and what help, if any, you can provide. (See Chapter 29 to find out how to encourage learning and create development plans and learning opportunities.)

As well as developing and retaining valuable employees, realistic development plans help match employees' skills and talents to the needs of the organisation and help employees ready themselves for changes and trends in their working environment. You benefit, too, by attracting the best people to work for you because of your reputation as a manager who builds people's skills and cares enough about them to help them build their careers.

Get some performance feedback yourself

It's a good idea to ask for some feedback for yourself, too. You may get useful ideas that help you improve your own job performance and gain employees' respect for your openness and willingness to listen and learn. Encouraging and listening to feedback also demonstrates the behaviour you expect of your team members.

A simple question like 'What can I do to make your job easier?' can start the ball rolling. Here are some other questions to try:

- Would you prefer me to be more or less involved in your work?
- Could I do anything to help you balance your personal and work commitments?
- Do I link the strategic direction of the organisation clearly enough with the team's goals?
- Do I provide enough information in relation to what's happening in the rest of the organisation?
- Do you feel comfortable making suggestions for improvement and do I ask you and the team for them often enough?
- How could I communicate my expectations of you more clearly?
- What could I do to encourage more creativity and innovation within the team?
- Are you comfortable raising work-related concerns with me?
- What would you like to see me do differently?

Summarise

Before closing the meeting, find out whether the employee has any questions or anything to add. Answer questions as fully, tactfully and truthfully as possible. Ensure the employee understands the performance agreement and has realistic expectations of career, pay (where relevant) and training prospects for the upcoming period. Confirm the main points covered and the actions and priorities agreed, and diarise a short follow-up meeting in about six weeks to discuss progress against targets and agreed actions.

Conclude the discussion constructively so that the employee leaves feeling confident that you have appreciated their strong points and contributions to the section or team.

You might try the timetable in Table 15.3 at your next formal performance discussion.

Part 3: After the meeting

In order to keep any promises or agreements you have made, put automatic reminders in your electronic task list so that you can check-in with employees. This also shows your continuing interest in the employee's performance and career. Keep up the two-way communication with regular informal feedback and continue to keep a written record of each employee's performance to which you can refer at their next performance review. Treat all performance discussions as confidential and store all documents securely where they cannot be seen or accessed by others.

TABLE 15.3 A typical agenda for a performance discussion meeting

	Agenda item	Time allocation
1	Put the employee at ease. They should be able to feel relaxed and speak freely. Do this by explaining how you are going to guide the meeting	2 minutes
2	Work through the performance review form and listen to the employee's thoughts. Explain your perspective. Discuss specific behavioural examples (that you have seen or heard) or refer to objective, measurable standards, such as agreed targets met or not met	15 minutes
3	Look for ways to make continuous improvements and improve the employee's job	10 minutes
4	Agree to SMART targets to drive performance for the next period	10 minutes
5	Agree to development goals and a development plan	5–10 minutes
6	Ask the employee to provide feedback for yourself	10 minutes
7	Finish by inviting the employee to ask questions. Review the actions you have mutually agreed to take and be sure to end on a positive note	3–5 minutes

15.3 Providing informal performance guidance

Employees rarely need to be reminded of their mistakes. However, they do need to be told how important and valuable they are.

Olivia McIvor (corporate culture adviser), *The business of kindness*, Fairwinds Press, British Columbia, 2006.

Employees want to know if they are doing a good job and most want or even need to have their efforts noticed and appreciated on a more regular basis than every six to 12 months. This is where providing regular informal feedback, in words and actions, about employees' performance fits in. Making it part of your everyday conversations builds motivation and morale and demonstrates your interest in your team members and their job performance. It keeps everyone's attention on what is important, builds good work habits and ensures that work standards are maintained. The more often you provide feedback, the more effective, expected and valued it is likely to be.

When your workload prevents you from providing informal feedback, or it is simply not something your personality lends itself to, schedule regular short sessions with each team member. This can easily be achieved by conducting one such session with a team member each week after your weekly team meeting for five or 10 minutes. It then only takes minutes out of your week, and over each two- to three-month period everyone in your team should get their 'turn'. If your formal performance reviews occur every six months, then with a team of 12, every team member will receive informal performance guidance twice between their formal reviews. This 10 minutes a week investment of your time is likely to repay you with interest in improved productivity, better team morale and more effective working relationships.

As these short sessions are to provide informal performance guidance, keep the meetings relaxed and let the employee do most of the talking. At the end of the conversation, provide a quick summary of the discussion and agree on an action plan, if you feel one is needed, that can be implemented and reviewed at the next meeting or during the next formal performance review. Record these actions, both for yourself and the employee, so that you can refer to them and follow up at the next meeting.

The 'informal performance guidance' meeting

While informal in nature, informal performance guidance meetings still need to have some structure to avoid them becoming opportunities for off-topic ramblings or whinging sessions. Preparing a list of discussion topics is therefore a good way to get the conversation started. These can include:

- a general update on the employee's progress
- an opportunity for them to raise any questions, problems or areas that they have identified for improvement
- areas or ways in which you could help the employee's productivity.

To open the discussion, you could ask how things are going generally with the employee's work, the team, clients (if relevant) and so on. Ask about the employee's working style, such as what time of the day they feel most productive, their biggest time wasters and roadblocks, the aspects of their job they feel most and least confident about, and the type of projects they most enjoy working on. Talk about their workload and their personal and professional goals. Your aim is to learn about each employee and how you can help them be more productive, to provide coaching and guidance where it would help, to agree on priorities until the next check-in, and to discover the employee's aspirations so you can help meet them with assignments and training.

Think of 'feedback' as 'guidance'

When the word 'feedback' is mentioned, many employees still think 'negative' and 'criticism'. It is important to stress, therefore, that informal performance guidance is not about finding faults or apportioning blame but rather about seeking and providing information that can help improve performance, build skills and add value. Effective guidance needs to be based on a solid working relationship built on trust where the employee knows your intentions are positive and directed at their development and future success. If done well, not only will your team members feel noticed, supported, valued and encouraged, it will help build a positive working climate and team culture based on open and honest communication.

Types of feedback

There are generally considered to be two types of feedback: positive feedback and **negative feedback**. Either can be general or specific, and specific negative feedback can be constructive or corrective. **Constructive feedback** is guidance that helps employees further improve already acceptable performance or to work out for themselves how to improve their performance. This is examined in the following paragraphs and discussed further in Chapter 29. *Corrective feedback*, given to assist underperforming employees bring their performance up to the required standard, is explained in Chapter 16. Only give corrective and constructive feedback on aspects of employees' performance that they can control; that is, behaviours they can change or skills they can improve or develop. Aim at changes in behaviour that can bring a measurable difference in results that both you and others can see.

Table 15.4 gives some examples of all of the types of feedback, with each discussed in more detail in the paragraphs that follow.

Positive feedback

General positive feedback is that which you give to employees just for being themselves. A cheerful 'Hello', a friendly smile or a 'Thanks, that's great' develops productive working relationships. General positive feedback makes people feel good and raises their self-confidence and self-esteem. It's

TABLE 15.4 Examples of feedback

Manager says	Type of feedback
'It's great to have you on the team'	Positive general
'You met all your targets again this week. I really appreciate your hard work and the contribution you make to our department's success'	Positive specific
'You'll need to try harder'	Negative general
'You're doing that the wrong way'	Negative specific
'Here, let me show you an easier way to do that'	Constructive
'That is fine, except for this one thing. Here's how to fix it'	Corrective
Walking past an employee's workstation and ignoring her	No feedback at all
Continually ignoring targets being met or not being met	No feedback at all

excellent for general motivation and morale and for maintaining a constructive working climate. It is best combined with positive specific feedback and negative specific feedback, so it doesn't lose its effect and you're not seen just as a jolly person, rather than as a helpful leader-manager.

Positive specific feedback, on the other hand, is helpful to ensure that people continue to meet performance standards and to increase employees' skills and willingness. Say what you appreciate as well as why you appreciate it: 'Thanks, that was great, particularly the way you presented the data in graphs – it made it much easier to understand'. Behaviour that is reinforced with positive specific feedback is repeated. Use it when people do something you want them to keep doing, such as meeting or exceeding a performance target, making a new team member feel welcome or keeping their work area tidy.

Negative feedback

Criticism, put-downs and sarcasm make people feel unimportant and unappreciated and lower morale and self-esteem. Messages like 'You again. What is it *this* time?' can be verbal or conveyed with just a look or a sigh. Avoid this type of feedback at all costs. There is never a good reason to use it.

However, specific negative feedback provides clear information regarding a particular action or result. Because it is specific, it can help reduce or eliminate the behaviour in question and improve results. The best specific negative feedback is corrective or constructive – it identifies precisely what is wrong and suggests an improvement strategy or explains what is wrong and why it matters: 'Thanks, this looks really good. The layout is fantastic – it's clear and easy to read. I think a great final touch would be to display the data in graph form. Would you have a go at that?' Feedback like this strengthens relationships and helps people perform tasks better.

Providing no feedback

If you don't provide any feedback, you create a feedback vacuum that implies that neither the employees nor their performance matter. Continually ignoring employees or walking by their desks each morning without saying 'Good morning!' creates an impersonal, tense and unpleasant work environment where performance, motivation and even self-esteem are likely to be adversely affected. If you remember that feedback is about enhancing performance, then not providing it means inviting poor performance.

Corrective guidance

Not all feedback can be positive. Where problems exist with an employee's performance, if they are ignored, they tend to grow worse. It is important, therefore, both for the employee's sake and that of the team to address problems of poor performance promptly when discovered, but this can still be done in an impartial and non-threatening way. Remember, though, that however tactfully you provide it, corrective guidance can still 'sting'. So unless it involves the whole team, provide it in private and plan carefully how best to phrase it. Think about how you would react to your words and if it is not the way you want your team member to react, think about an alternative way of expressing it. Also consider your tone of voice and body language as this can affect someone's confidence or enthusiasm just as much as your words.

Corrective guidance is more palatable when it is supported by facts and directed at behaviour and not at the person. Stick to facts and factual descriptions of behaviour, something employees do or say, and work performance – particularly outcomes or targets they are not meeting. Also, be careful to distinguish between a fact and your opinion and only offer your opinion if it is likely to be helpful, such as providing insight into some aspect of the person's performance or behaviour that might not be apparent to them.

Deal with one issue at a time because too much information at once is difficult to absorb. You can provide corrective guidance in the following way:

1 Explain precisely what you see or hear the employee do or say, giving one or two examples, or state the target that was not achieved and what was actually achieved.
2 Calmly and objectively explain how the behaviour or unmet target affects the team, the organisation or your customers. Stick to the facts and stay away from people's character or abilities. For example, telling someone it is rude to hold a side conversation during a meeting draws less cooperation than explaining that side conversations are distracting and make it hard for people to concentrate.
3 Offer an improvement suggestion – something the employee could start or stop doing in order to improve performance. Show how what you're asking meets the organisation's or team's needs or helps the employee in some way.

There are helpful and unhelpful ways to present the same information, so think about the words you use when offering feedback, as shown in Table 15.5.

TABLE 15.5 Choose the better feedback option

Poor ways to begin feedback	Better ways to begin feedback
'You don't seem to be able to ...'	'I see you're having trouble ...'
'You're not doing that properly ...'	'Let me run through how I'd like you to do this.'
'You didn't ...'	'You'll find it easier to ...'
'You shouldn't ...'	'It's faster to ...'
'You always .../You never ...'	'Next time .../From now on ...'

Notice that in these examples most of the instances of 'you' are changed to 'I'. This turns your information from a critical 'push' to a helpful 'pull'.

There are other ways to begin guidance tactfully. For example:

- Saying 'could' instead of 'should' creates less guilt about something the employee did that can't be changed and gives the employee a choice for next time. For example, 'You could have begun collecting the data last week so that you didn't have to rush through preparing the quotation.'

- Saying 'not wise' rather than 'bad' means you're not commenting on the employee's character but on the natural consequences of their actions. For example, 'The decision to wait to collect the data until the week the quotation was due was not wise. Not only did you need to rush the quotation's preparation, which I'm sure affected its quality, but the last-minute rushing affected the rest of the team.'
- Referring to a mistake as a 'valuable lesson' means that employees can learn from their actions. For example, 'Waiting to collect the data until the week the quotation was due was a valuable lesson for next time.'
- Say: 'You did a great job, and …' rather than 'You did a great job, but …' because people know when they hear 'but', bad news follows. 'You did a great job, and one thing you could do to improve it is …' is much more effective.

The way you deliver feedback is just as important as the feedback itself. People who receive constructive or corrective performance guidance accompanied by the positive emotional signals of nods and smiles feel better about their performance than people who are given positive performance guidance delivered in a critical manner, with frowns and narrowed eyes.

INDUSTRY INSIGHTS

Robyn: performance improvement plans – the last resort

I had been in my role for several years before being promoted from a back-office administration role to lead a team of 10 administration/reception staff in a community services organisation. Once in the role, I soon identified two staff members with performance issues that were negatively impacting on the rest of the team. With the team scattered in terms of location, working with each staff member individually to improve their performance was going to be a challenge.

Georgina was a mature-aged woman who had been in the same role for over 10 years and didn't welcome or embrace change. She felt overwhelmed with the recent management restructure that had taken place as well as technology upgrades that had affected the way she undertook her role. Amy was fairly new to her role and although she had excelled during her probationary period, it had become apparent to the rest of her team that she had stopped 'trying' once she had passed this milestone.

I initiated Performance Improvement Plans (PIPs) for both staff members, documenting the performance of each and conducting follow-up reviews. The PIP structure allowed me to identify and unpack where the roadblocks were with each staff member.

Georgina was provided with time each day to familiarise herself with the electronic file management system until she felt more confident. Spending time with her gave me valuable insight into her aspirations. She felt as though she had been overlooked numerous times for promotion and that her counselling degree skills were going to waste in her administration role. She was very skilled at managing clients who were agitated or in a heightened state of stress and, although it wasn't part of her role to manage those behaviours, she was a natural at defusing such situations. Through the strategies documented in her PIP, Georgina gained confidence and she was delighted when asked to develop an in-house training session for the team on managing difficult behaviours. Her presentation was well received by the team, and she became valued as the 'expert' in managing and defusing challenging behaviours. Eventually a new more client-oriented role opened up for which Georgina applied and was successful. She is now in her element undertaking more meaningful client-focused tasks and using her counselling and life skills with vulnerable clients on a daily basis.

Amy, on the other hand, had a different outcome. She was bored in her administration role and thought she was worthy of a role with more responsibility. While she had excellent technical skills, her attitude, mindset and demeanour in her public contact role did not meet the organisation's standards. She was abrupt with clients and was often late to 'open up' reception on her shift. She seemed unable to grasp that she needed to at least meet the basic requirements of her current role before she could be considered for one with greater responsibility. Amy's unwillingness to respond in a positive manner to the strategies in her PIP resulted in it being extended and HR becoming involved. Claiming she was being picked on, Amy lodged a workers compensation claim for stress and went on indefinite leave. She did not return, resigning six weeks later shortly after her compensation claim was rejected.

Using the keep–stop–start method to offer feedback and raise concerns

The keep–stop–start method is a good way to offer feedback:

- Keep doing these helpful things.
- Stop doing these unhelpful things.
- Start doing these things.

And then there's the 'more–less–keep' method:

- More of these actions that may be lacking or you would like to see more of.
- Less of these actions you do not need.
- Keep these effective behaviours and practices.

Be specific so that your comments aren't misinterpreted. When you have a concern, try these two ways to express your concern and suggest the solution. Use the prompts to fill in the gaps below.

- 'When you … (describe the action), it's a problem because … (describe the effect). Could I ask that you … (describe the solution)?'

  Or
- 'It would really help me achieve … (describe the goal), if you could … (describe the solution) instead of … (describe the current action).'

The sandwich technique

You may have heard of the 'sandwich technique' for giving feedback, where you 'sandwich' a negative piece of feedback between two positive pieces of feedback. It can work, provided you don't train employees to wait for 'the bad news' every time they hear some 'good news'.

For the sandwich technique to be effective, use it with bigger matters. In other words, don't say 'You handled that well, but you forgot to … But keep up the good work'. That's too small a matter. For small matters, coaching is more effective: 'Everything worked well there, except for this … Next time, try doing … instead. I think you'll find it a lot easier, and you'll get a better result'.

For bigger matters, you could say, 'Sasha, you're doing a great job. There is one thing I'd like to see you doing and it's this … When you do this, you'll be meeting all your key responsibilities'. (You can find more coaching techniques in Chapter 29.)

The hot-stove principle

The 'hot stove' is a particular type of specific negative feedback that you probably need to use only occasionally, and only with three types of employees:

- employees who are 'testing' rules to see how far they can go
- newer employees who inadvertently break a rule
- skilled and experienced employees who 'know better'.

As will be explained in Chapter 19, the hot-stove principle is particularly useful for safety and other straightforward infringements of the organisation's rules and policies. However, make sure you don't use this technique when performance drops for reasons outside the employee's control at the workplace or because of a personal problem. To do so under such circumstances undermines the spirit of integrity in which feedback is intended to be provided, is unfair to the employee concerned and will do more harm than good.

Turning criticism into guidance

You can't force people to change. You can only bring something to their attention and point out what they can do to improve their performance. Think of constructive and corrective guidance as sharing ideas and information rather than giving orders or advice. Think about how you would feel being given the same information. Work out how to make your guidance useful to the receiver and choose your words to show that you are both on the same side. Choose your time, too. Don't wait too long, but make sure the employee has the time to listen and is in the right frame of mind. Here are some other tips:

- Ask questions to guide the employee towards the suggestion or conclusion you want them to consider rather than telling them.
- Avoid vague statements and generalisations; when you use words like 'always' or 'never', you may be exaggerating.
- Describe behaviour and offer your observations rather than judge the person or attribute motives.
- Don't fix blame – fix the problem. Ask: 'How can we ...?' or 'What can we do to ...?'
- Focus on the future and on solutions and goals (what you *do* want), not on the past or on problems or mistakes (what you *don't* want). Paint the picture of the end result you're after.
- Think before you speak.

Offer improvement suggestions:

- 'I'll know you're doing a good job when ...'
- 'From now on ...'
- 'Here's another thought ...'
- 'Next time ...'
- 'That was good, and you could also ...'
- 'That was great and another thing you could do is ...'
- 'Try it this way ...'
- 'Would you please ...'

When you have trouble turning critical remarks into constructive remarks, ask yourself how the employee would describe their behaviours and results.

Positive guidance

Most people don't equate silence with approval – even employees whose work is always good need to hear it from you. Because each role contributes to the success of your team, each employee expects you to notice their contributions and provide feedback. Don't ignore performance that meets expectations. When your team or department is running smoothly, recognise work well done and encourage it to continue.

While general praise and 'thank yous' can help build morale and productivity, specific positive feedback is stronger and lets your team members know that you appreciate and value their good work. Positive specific feedback should also be offered for behaviours that fall short of expectations. Sometimes people try hard but events outside their control prevent them from reaching their targets. Similarly, when people try hard while they are still learning or building skills and experience and don't quite reach their targets, keep their motivation high by thanking them for their commitment to the goal. This reinforces the behaviour you want so that it continues. Acknowledge and appreciate extra effort and behaviour that supports the organisation's values too.

When you thank a member of another team for something they've done, do so in person when you can, and thank them again by email so you can copy-in their boss. Doing something as simple as this can cement a positive ongoing relationship and even gain you a supporter who may prove to be a useful ally in the future.

Provide positive balanced intermittent feedback

Monitor your feedback to make sure it is balanced because overusing any one type of feedback can quickly reduce its effectiveness. Even constantly saying 'Well done' can wear thin, so mix up your encouragement with 'Nice work', 'Good job' or even 'Awesome performance on that last report'.

To build or activate new behaviours (e.g. with new recruits or transfers or when training existing staff in something new) provide a lot of positive specific feedback and then gradually reduce it to maintain behaviours once they are established. Once people are doing a good job, the most effective feedback is intermittent (i.e. irregular or random), positive and specific.

15.4 Receiving performance guidance

> There are two things people want more than sex and money: Recognition and praise.
>
> Mary Kay Ash (cosmetics entrepreneur), quoted in Robert A. Eckert, 'The two most important words', *Harvard Business Review*, April 2013, p. 38.

It's disheartening having to guess how your boss thinks you're doing. Most people need guidance to figure out how to improve their performance and steer their careers. These are two good reasons to look forward to your own performance discussion. The following provides some tips.

If you haven't already done so, organise your job into KRAs and measures of success (explained in Chapter 9) and confirm them with your manager to ensure that you both assess your performance on the same objective, measurable criteria. Discuss which of your responsibilities are most important too. This gives you a clear basis for your performance discussion.

Between discussions, keep notes of your successes and achievements so if your manager has a short memory, you can jog it. Similarly, note any difficulties and review the Five Keys (explained in Chapter 19) to identify their causes so you can take and note remedial action.

Think about issues that need to be raised and how best to do so. You may like to prioritise issues where the solution or strategy to resolve them can also be applied to other issues. It invokes the old adage of 'killing two birds with one stone'. This may particularly be the case where delaying action will make a problem get worse or when the issue is complex or delicate and requires help or support from others.

Approach your performance discussion in a positive frame of mind and with the aim of gathering ideas on how to improve your performance, develop your skills further and enhance your contribution to the organisation. Don't make your manager fight every point; be open to advice and listen carefully to any suggestions and constructive feedback. When you're not clear about the feedback your manager gives you, ask for examples in a way that shows you want to understand.

When your manager asks for your feedback, concentrate on job-related areas where you interact with your manager. Acknowledge the ways your manager assists you to achieve your objectives and try the keep–stop–start or the more–less–same approach outlined earlier.

Don't shy away from asking for help or for changes in your working relationship that could help you achieve your goals more effectively (e.g. more easily, economically or quickly). Think about how to raise these issues sensitively and tactfully. (Chapter 5 provides more information on seeking informal feedback.)

STUDY TOOLS

QUICK REVIEW

KEY CONCEPT 15.1 

a List at least five ways that organisations and leader-managers use formal performance discussions and briefly describe the main systems that are commonly used. Which types of jobs does each seem best suited to?

b What role do informal and formal performance discussions play in performance management?

KEY CONCEPT 15.2 

a Briefly describe the three main parts of a formal performance discussion, stating what should be covered during each part and what is off limits.

b What is a SMART target? How do SMART targets fit into the performance review and planning process?

KEY CONCEPT 15.3 

a What do you believe are the key principles of giving feedback?

b How can formal and informal feedback encourage good performance and turn around poor performance?

KEY CONCEPT 15.4 

a List and briefly explain three things to do when receiving feedback, whether formally or informally.

BUILD YOUR SKILLS

KEY CONCEPT 15.1 

a Describe the main hazards to avoid when assessing employees' performance and discuss how you can overcome each.

KEY CONCEPT 15.2 

a Review five practices that leader-managers should follow when holding formal performance discussions.

KEY CONCEPT 15.3 

a Summarise the types of feedback and give three workplace examples of each.

b Turn the following critical comments into coaching comments:

i 'You should ...'

ii 'Why can't you ...?'

iii 'You'll have to ...'

iv 'I've told you before not to ...'

v 'You never ...'

vi 'You don't understand.'

vii '... but ...'

c Janeth consistently turns in quality work but, unfortunately, equally consistently, it is a day or two late. This creates a bottleneck as others rely on her work and can't carry on without it. You know that nothing in the work environment is holding her up. Apart from this, Janeth is a consistently good employee. What could you say to address this problem? Write down something you would feel comfortable saying that follows the suggestions in this chapter.

d You have spoken to Janeth about her work coming in late and causing hold-ups for others and she has tried to complete her work on time. Instead of being late 90 per cent of the time, she is late about 50 per cent of the time. Write down feedback that you would feel comfortable giving to Janeth and that follows the suggestions in this chapter.

KEY CONCEPT 15.4 

a Think of the last time someone offered you some unsolicited feedback. How did you respond? Did the manner of the feedback's delivery influence your response? If so, in what way? Could you have done anything to make the information you were given more effective?

WORKPLACE ACTIVITIES

KEY CONCEPT 15.1 

a Write a one-page synopsis of three types of performance reviews that you think would best suit your work group, explaining your reasoning.

b Describe your organisation's formal performance review and planning system and how your organisation uses it to manage its human resources strategically.

KEY CONCEPT 15.2 

a List and explain the steps you went through before conducting a recent performance discussion and the steps you took afterwards.

KEY CONCEPT 15.3 

a List the people in your work team and give an example of the last time you guided the performance of each. For each example, suggest how you could improve it the next time you guide an employee. You might consider, for example, timing, word choice, tone of voice and your mindset at the time. Select one of these examples and describe the extent to which your information helped improve their performance. (It's fine if these people don't report to you – employees give each other performance information all the time.)

KEY CONCEPT 15.4 

a If you have ever had your performance reviewed, describe the feelings you experienced before, during and after the performance discussion.

b Have you ever had a formal performance discussion? Discuss the system that was used, your feelings during the meeting, and whether and how it helped build your performance and morale. In your experience, what makes for an effective performance discussion?

c What reference to your ability to manage underperformance is likely to be considered in your next performance review?

EXTENSION ACTIVITIES

Referring to the Snapshot at the beginning of this chapter, answer the following questions:

1 Identify the things Serena did poorly in the formal performance discussion with Sebastian. How could she have raised the matters that required addressing in a more effective and constructive way? If Sebastian was in fact making racist remarks in the workplace, how should this have been specifically dealt with?

2 Should Serena place any importance on the feedback that Sebastian provided to her about her performance? What should she 'do' with the feedback he provided?

CASE STUDY 15

THE PERFECT OPPORTUNITY

Peter is thinking about the forthcoming performance discussion with Samantha. He is concerned about her ability to perform her job to the required standards, in terms of both quality and quantity of service. When she is assigned fewer tables to serve, her attention to detail, correct order delivery and customer service are first class. But when she is assigned the number of tables he expects her to serve, and that the others cope with adequately, her service level drops. She doesn't seem to be able to get the balance right, despite his feedback and coaching. Peter decides that the formal performance discussion next week is the perfect opportunity to warn her that her job is on the line unless her performance improves.

At the meeting, Peter explains to Samantha that her performance is unsatisfactory and outlines why, giving her several examples from the last few weeks, which, he is careful to point out, are representative of the way she has worked since joining the restaurant service team four months ago. He also explains that, as good as her service is when she serves fewer tables, he can't afford to keep her on unless she can find a way to deliver great service to the required number of customers.

Samantha seems to be truly shocked. While she knows that her productivity is lower than some of the others, she clearly hasn't realised how serious the problem is. She says that she is trying as hard as she can, and she really needs her job. She also indicates that she feels she has made progress over the last two or three months. With this, she bursts into tears, leaving Peter at a loss to know what to do.

Questions

1 Was the formal performance discussion the perfect opportunity to begin the termination of employment process? Why or why not?
2 What mistakes did Peter make with Samantha's performance discussion?
3 How could Peter have prepared before the meeting? What should he do now? In addition to his feedback and coaching, should he have made Samantha's performance shortfall clear to her before the formal review?

CHAPTER ENDNOTES

1 Marcus Buckingham, 'Trouble with the curve? Why Microsoft is ditching stack rankings', *Harvard Business Review*, 19 November 2013, https://hbr.org/2013/11/dont-rate-your-employees-on-a-curve, accessed 14 January 2018.

2 Madeline Stone, 'Amazon employees reportedly slam each other through this internal review tool', *Business Insider Australia*, http://www.businessinsider.com.au/amazon-employees-reportedly-slam-each-other-through-this-internal-review-tool-2015-8, accessed 14 January 2018; Graham Winfrey, 'Why Amazon's culture of competition could be right for your business', *Inc.*, http://www.inc.com/graham-winfrey/amazons-anytime-feedback-tool.html, accessed 14 January 2018; Phil Haussler, '4 ways to fix Amazon's Anytime Feedback tool', *Quantum Workplace*, http://www.quantumworkplace.com/future-of-work/4-ways-fix-amazons-anytime-feedback-tool/, accessed 28 December 2016.

3 Leonardo Baldassarre, Brian Finken, 'GE's real-time performance development', *Harvard Business Review*, 12 August 2015, https://hbr.org.2015/08/ges-real-time-performance-development, accessed 15 November 2016; Peter Cappelli, Anna Tavis, 'The performance management revolution', *Harvard Business Review*, Vol. 10, pp. 58–67.

CHAPTER

MANAGING UNDERPERFORMANCE

After completing this chapter, you will be able to:

16.1 think through poor performance before jumping into a performance counselling discussion

16.2 plan and lead a performance counselling discussion that helps employees improve unsatisfactory performance

16.3 correctly terminate someone's employment when performance counselling is unsuccessful

16.4 support employees who have a personal problem.

TRANSFERABLE SKILLS

The following transferable skills are covered in this chapter:

- **2 Critical thinking and problem solving**
  - **2.1** Critical thinking
- **3 Social competence**
  - **3.1** Teamwork/relationships
  - **3.2** Verbal communication
  - **3.3** Written communication
  - **3.4** Leadership

OVERVIEW

The ability to inspire and motivate, to communicate and coordinate, and to lead and delegate are some of the qualities and attributes that makes a great leader-manager. With performance-guided artillery such as this, surely transforming even the poorest-performing team member into a valued and productive member of their team would be assured ... not so. We can all think of individuals we have worked with or observed in the workplace who, for whatever reason, simply haven't been up to the job. Even when supported with training, guidance, instruction, direction and coaching, they still fell short of the mark. When this point is reached, performance management becomes managing underperformance.

Transferable skills
3.4 Leadership

Counselling, performance improvement plans and trying the person in other roles, if possible, are all courses of action that may need to be considered. But where an employee still continues to underperform, a leader-manager may be left with no other choice but to terminate their employment. There are few leader-managers that would take any joy in having to take this action, but it is a responsibility that sometimes must be acted upon. As difficult, confronting and sometimes emotional as it may be, it forms part of a leader-manager's role and, if delayed or ignored, can be debilitating or potentially devastating for the rest of the team.

Transferable skills
3.4 Leadership

Performance standards are 'ground zero' for every leader-manager and their team. They must be upheld and never compromised. It is the responsibility of every team member to know and understand them and of every leader-manager to support their team to attain them. This chapter explains how to turn poor performance around and what to do when this proves not to be possible.

SNAPSHOT

The beginning of the end

Jemima had tried everything she could to help Carmel perform to the expected standard. She had conducted several performance counselling discussions with her spanning over six months. At each session, she had identified Carmel's performance gaps as well as stating clearly what her performance needed to be to achieve the expected standard, and the timeframes in which this improvement needed to occur. Additional training had been provided and Carmel had been given ample time between each discussion to make the improvements agreed upon. Each counselling session has been carefully and accurately documented by Jemima and signed by Carmel.

But Carmel was nearing retirement age and was more intent on simply seeing out her final year with a minimal amount of stress ... and work! Everybody knew this was the case, including Jemima, and although Carmel was well liked, Jemima simply couldn't carry any 'dead weight' in her team, which had been given revised performance targets 15 per cent higher than in the previous financial year. Carmel said the right things at each performance counselling session but then went back to doing very little and biding her time in the weeks and months that followed. As a result, the counselling sessions were then followed by Jemima issuing Carmel with a verbal warning in relation to her performance, followed several weeks later by a written warning. With no improvement in the subsequent weeks, even after this, Jemima issued Carmel with a final written warning.

Jemima felt somewhat betrayed. She had worked with Carmel for six years and they had enjoyed a positive working relationship throughout this period. Jemima had believed there was a level of respect between them; however, Carmel's attitude and behaviour now seemed to indicate otherwise. Jemima knew what she had to do. The thought of it made her feel sick but it was part of her job as the team's leader, and she couldn't put if off any longer. She opened the organisational human resources (HR) manual to revise the procedure and sent Carmel a meeting request and copied the HR manager into the email. 'How did it come to this?' she thought. She shook her head and started preparing the necessary paperwork for HR to sign off on.

16.1 Thinking through poor performance

> **As all managers know from painful experience, when it comes to managing people, the 80:20 rule applies: The most intractable employees take up a disproportionate amount of one's time and energy.**
>
> Nigel Nicholson (London Business School), 'How to motivate your problem people', *Harvard Business Review*, January 2003.

Transferable skills
3.4 Leadership

When an employee's performance is unsatisfactory, it is the leader-manager's responsibility to recognise the problem and take the necessary corrective action. Most underperformance problems can be resolved if identified and addressed promptly and properly. But when it is ignored and allowed to continue, its effects on the rest of the team can be serious. Other team members may need to work extra hard to compensate but they'll only be willing to do this for so long. Eventually, tensions will rise to the surface, team morale will suffer, and the credibility and respect a leader-manager has built with their team can be lost in an instant. A very real danger then looms in overreacting to the poor performance and handling the situation poorly. It is better to act quickly and decisively and avoid allowing it to reach this point.

Poor excuses for failing to manage poor performance

Some leader-managers simply find conflict unpalatable so they shy away from providing honest and constructive negative feedback. They tiptoe around the performance issues and rationalise their actions, or inactions. Some of the poor excuses for avoiding managing poor performance can include:

- not wanting to disrupt the work environment
- using the excuse that managing poor performance should only be done as part of the organisation's performance review process
- waiting for the 'right time'
- believing that the person displaying the poor performance will resolve it themself
- being scared of handling it badly and 'losing it'.

Whatever the excuse, allowing poor performance to continue unchallenged is inexcusable. Always be alert to a team member's performance slipping and continuing on a downward trajectory. When observed or identified, plan your approach and tackle it swiftly. You'll be thankful you did and so most likely will the person, assuming they are able to turn their performance around.

Don't assume it's the employee's fault

A common misconception people have about performance problems is that they are solely the result of an individual's personal failure. Making this assumption ignores a factor just as important, if not more so – the context in which they are performing their work responsibilities. Does the person clearly understand what they are required to do? Have they been trained correctly? Are they placed in jobs that suit their skills, talents and interests? Do they have the information, time and tools they need to do their jobs well? Do they have a positive, productive relationship with their manager and other team members?

The **85:15 rule** tells us that 85 per cent of the causes of poor performance and low productivity can be found in the work environment. When these causes are found and fixed, productivity quickly gets back on track. This is not to say that poor productivity never results from personal factors or factors outside anyone's control. Figure 16.1 shows the main signs that indicate an employee's poor performance may fall into the 15 per cent category (part of the 'Chance To Key') or be the result of a regressed **task-readiness level**. Notice that some of the signs listed don't apply to knowledge workers or teleworkers.

When an otherwise strong performer goes 'off the rails':

- acknowledge the change in their performance so that they are aware of it and know that you are too
- explore and uncover any problems which might be causing the poor performance
- brainstorm solutions with them
- show them that you still have faith in them by expressing it verbally.

Given that the examples in Figure 16.1 account for a minority of performance problems, it makes sense to concentrate on improving productivity and performance where they are most likely to pay off. Employees often struggle on despite environmental barriers getting in the way of good performance and productivity, trying to do the best they can despite them.

'Bad person' or 'bad behaviour'?

When describing someone who is difficult to work with, it is easy and perhaps natural to describe their attitude or personality as being what makes them difficult rather than their behaviour. Focusing on who the person *is* rather than what the person *does* is not helpful and is more likely to escalate any existing problems than resolve them.

ABSENTEEISM	A higher absenteeism rate than other employees, excessive sick leave, frequent unscheduled short-term absences or multiple instances of unauthorised leave, particularly when absences follow a pattern, such as after a day off or when improbable reasons for absences are given.
DIFFICULTY WITH CONCENTRATION	Continually forgetting instructions, having to make a greater than normal effort to complete a task or taking too long to complete jobs.
FAILURE TO FOLLOW REGULATIONS	Lack of care of tools and equipment, not responding to emails and messages within expected timeframes. This applies when an organisation's standards are clear and the employee is aware of them.
LOWERED JOB EFFICIENCY	This can result in failing to follow safety or standard operating procedures, falling productivity or quality (e.g. due to excessive use of social media sites during work hours), lack of care for the customer's or the organisation's equipment, missed deadlines, mistakes due to inattention, poor judgement or wasting materials.
ON-THE-JOB ABSENTEEISM	Absenteeism (or presenteeism) while at work can result in erratic work quality, frequent trips to the rest area, long coffee breaks or more absences from the work station than the job requires.
POOR RELATIONSHIPS	This can apply to managers, colleagues, suppliers or customers, which can result in, for example, avoiding workmates or the manager, overreacting to real or imagined criticism or wide mood swings.
REPORTING-TO-WORK PROBLEMS	Examples include arriving at or returning to work in an obviously abnormal condition, arriving late and/or leaving early.
UNACCEPTABLE CONDUCT	Examples include bullying, harassment or racial vilification of colleagues either in person or via social media, using social media sites to defame the organisation, to disclose confidential information or intellectual property or to publicise workplace disputes.

FIGURE 16.1 Some signs of poor performance from the '15 per cent' category

Although 'attitudes', 'personalities' and 'personal characteristics' are a perennial nightmare, if the person is identified as the problem rather than their behaviour, there are only two alternatives: terminate or transfer (handballing the 'problem' to someone else).

Concentrating attention on changing a person's behaviour is far more likely to produce the desired outcome. The simple reason for this is because most people are able and often willing to change their behaviour, but few will be prepared to change the kind of person they are. Before raising the issue, consider the following questions:

- Has the person's unwanted conduct been reinforced in some way by you or others? For example, if you speak over the top of others in meetings, this sends a message to others that this type of behaviour is acceptable.
- Is the employee doing the best they can under difficult circumstances in the work environment or in their personal life? Is it actually their behaviour that is the problem or is that they are being allocated too much work or having to follow inefficient processes?
- What characterises the behaviour as difficult? Is there objective evidence to support that their behaviour is a problem? Consider whether the behaviour would be a problem for other managers and, if it wouldn't be, the problem may be yours, not the employee's.

Transferable skills

2.1 Critical thinking

However, when it is determined that the problem rests with the employee, the matter needs to be raised in relation to how their conduct affects their or their team's performance. Remaining clear, constructive and objective, and providing examples of their poor conduct or performance, will help the employee understand where they are going wrong and where they need to improve. Providing them with suggestions and strategies as to how they can improve may be enough in itself to turn their performance around. Generation X, Y and Z employees as well as Millennials are often described as having an 'entitlement mentality'. The reality is that people from all generations can have this mentality and develop a belief that work is all about them and their needs, not performance, productivity or customers.

Employees of any age who have this mentality need to have it explained in candid terms that their approach in not acceptable and needs to change. They need to be shown or made to see how their work contributes to both the team and the organisation and, when it isn't done correctly or on time, how it adversely affects their teammates and the way people think about them.

Think through the Five Keys

To address poor performance, explore its possible causes by working through the Five Keys. Psychoanalysing employees or 'second guessing' causes is unlikely to be helpful. A better approach is to work systematically through the Five Keys, asking questions like those shown in Table 16.1. When an answer is 'no' or 'possibly not' to any of these questions, consider implementing the strategies provided.

Role conflict

Sometimes a difference in perception or wanting to do two conflicting activities lies at the heart of underperformance. This is known as **role conflict** and there are two types that can cause performance problems – interpersonal and intrapersonal.

Interpersonal role conflict occurs when other people's ideas of how a job-holder should behave or what a job-holder should do differ from the job-holder's ideas. An example of this type of role conflict is the school-leaver who begins their first job wearing clothing or a hairstyle that conforms to their school peer group rather than to the role expectations of the organisation. A more serious example is the employee for whom wearing standard safety protection gear is not part of their role perception.

It is part of a leader-manger's role to determine when it is important that the role perception of an employee and the role expectations of the organisation match. In the wearing of safety gear, it is clearly important that they do, so the leader-manager needs to bring the employee's role perception into line with the organisation's role expectations. Sometimes, however, matching role perceptions and role expectations makes little difference to how well employees do their jobs.

Transferable skills
2.1 Critical thinking

TABLE 16.1 Diagnose and address poor performance with the Five Keys

1 What To	Is the employee aware of the standard? Outline the expectation or refer the employee to the applicable standard Is the employee aware that they are not meeting it? Explain how the employee's performance is not meeting the expected standard
2 Want To	Is the job well designed? Consider redesigning the job by removing or modifying some tasks or responsibilities Is the employee temperamentally suited to doing it? If not, think about assigning that part of their job they perform poorly to someone else who is better suited to it or has more interest in doing it
3 How To	Has the employee been fully trained in the job and done it enough to have built up the necessary experience and confidence? If not, revisit their learning or professional development plan and provide them with training, a mentor, coaching or other appropriate support
4 Chance To	Is there anything in the environment that makes good performance difficult, such as poor tools, insufficient information or time, substandard or unsuitable materials, awkward procedures, or poor team culture or group dynamics? Review and modify processes that may be hindering performance and ensure the employee can access the resources they require to meet the expected standard
5 Led To	Am I providing the right kind of leadership and setting the right examples? Do I think like a leader and act like a leader? Review your leadership approach, drawing on feedback from others, to identify where it might be contributing to employees' poor performance

Intrapersonal role conflict occurs when two or more of a person's several roles conflict with each other. A common example is when an employee's work–life balance skews too much towards their work. Working late, taking work home or always being in meetings while perhaps ignoring a partner back home or shirking parental responsibilities can create friction between the person's work life and home life. Staying sensitive to role conflicts like these, and helping team members balance their work and personal life roles, will help to keep them happy both at home and at work as well as to be productive.

16.2 Counselling unsatisfactory performance

Persons appear to us according to the light we throw upon them from our own minds.

Laura Ingalls Wilder (novelist), in Hines (ed.), *Laura Ingalls Wilder, Farm journalist: Writings from the Ozarks*, University of Missouri Press, Columbia, 2007, 1922.

When a **performance gap** becomes apparent, initiate discussion with the team member to address it as soon as possible. The longer the delay in doing so, the bigger the issue becomes and the more difficult it may be for the employee to change their behaviour. Plan the discussion carefully, thinking about the following:

- When is the best time to meet?
- How can the situation be raised tactfully but clearly without shattering the employee's dignity or confidence?
- What is the employee's task-readiness level in relation to the performance gap and the leadership style it suggests?

- How can the discussion be 'framed' so that it will be perceived by the employee as positive rather than negative?
- What contingency can also be prepared and turned to should the discussion go in a different direction from what is planned?

Figure 16.2 summarises the six systematic steps for improving an employee's work performance. When the situation calls for a formal **performance counselling** process to begin, inform the HR department, enlist their help, and follow the applicable organisational protocols to administer the counselling process.

FIGURE 16.2 Six steps to improving performance

Step 1: Analyse your information

The first question to ask is: what is the actual performance gap? A performance gap might be, for example, the employee's actual deliverables compared with targets, actual output, quality or sales figures compared with targets, the employee's actual time-keeping record or specific examples of undesirable conduct.

To establish the performance gap, there first needs to be a clear measure of success. This is the standard against which the employee's performance must be assessed. As shown in Figure 16.3, a clear deviation from the success measure, the performance gap provides concrete evidence of the performance issue to discuss with the employee so the reasons for the gap can be established and agreement reached on corrective action. Depending on the size of the gap, performance gaps can be 'steps', 'hops' or 'jumps' and discussions should be structured accordingly.

Transferable skills
2.1 Critical thinking

A performance gap can be from one of two areas:

1 *Work-related conduct:* for example, what an employee says or does. This should be observed or witnessed rather than interpreted. For example, observing an employee working in a customer service role who fails to greet customers with eye contact and a friendly greeting. This behaviour may appear to be 'rude' but should not be interpreted or described in the ensuing discussion as such. The behaviour should be described exactly as it was observed and then explanation provided as to how it clearly did not meet the expected performance standard.

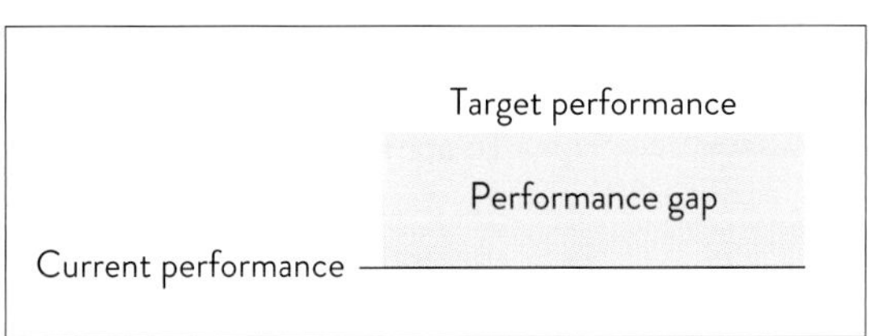

FIGURE 16.3 A clear performance gap

2 *A work target (or deliverable) that is not being met.* This target should be SMART (**s**pecific, **m**otivating, **a**mbitious yet achievable, **r**elated to the organisation's and team's goals, and **t**rackable). For example, employees may be expected to acknowledge and greet customers within 16 seconds. Taking longer than this, perhaps by leaving the customer waiting while they finish paperwork, is a performance gap.

Documenting and describing the performance gap clearly in specific behavioural or measurable terms is important because it:

- can be used as evidence should the employee take legal action (e.g. unfair or **unlawful dismissal**)
- ensures that the behaviour that has been observed has been analysed to determine and confirm its factual accuracy
- helps to clarify the counselling objectives and how best to go about achieving them

- helps provide specific examples to help the employee understand the detrimental effects of their underperformance on themselves and others
- helps set the scene for a productive discussion
- makes sure the gap is 'real' (i.e. objective and based on fact).

A clear performance gap relating to a specific work-related behaviour or a clear work target means the employee can be provided with clear and factual performance information without it becoming personal or critical. It provides an opportunity to remind the employee what 'right' looks like and present the performance information objectively. This reduces the employee's defensiveness and sets the tone for constructive and cooperative problem-solving. Table 16.2 illustrates performance gaps related to conduct and to targets not being met.

TABLE 16.2 Examples of performance gaps

Conduct	Targets not met
Keeping three out of five customers waiting for more than three minutes without acknowledging them	Arriving 10–15 minutes late two to three times a week for the past three weeks
Speaking briefly and curtly to 90% of customers or colleagues, especially during busy times	Producing the last three reports two days late
Once or twice a week, for the last two weeks, taking a break instead of helping team members complete their work	Producing an average of 80% accuracy in documents for the past two weeks, missing the 95% target
Having to be reminded two or three times a day to complete routine work	Not answering the telephone within four rings and not identifying the department and saying your name

Step 2: Give good information

Transferable skills
3.2 Verbal communication

When discussing underperformance the two main goals are to:

1. maintain or enhance the employee's self-esteem
2. help the employee accept and correct the performance shortfall.

To achieve this, it is critical to ensure that the underperforming employee clearly understands:

- the performance standard required (the measure of success) and why it's important
- the precise performance gap
- that they will be supported to achieve that standard
- that they must meet the performance standard and performance below this is not acceptable
- that the choice of whether or not the employee improves their performance is the employee's
- the consequences of continued poor performance.

Performance discussions should be conducted fairly, without hostility, and in private. Concrete evidence or examples of the performance shortfall, or performance gap, and any other relevant information that is required (discussed below) should be assembled prior to the discussion. The discussion should begin with clear explanation of the performance gap and the desire to explore the reasons for it. A framing statement can be used to introduce the discussion and communicate that its primary concern is satisfactory work performance. It can be an effective way to draw the person's attention to the main topic of the conversation; that is, their poor performance.

Transferable skills
3.2 Verbal communication

When developing a framing statement:

- clearly identify what will and won't be discussed so that the discussion does not stray onto other topics
- review the key events that have led to the discussion

- state the expectations of the discussion (i.e. what the discussion is intended to achieve)
- provide an outline as to how the discussion is to proceed
- clearly articulate the desired performance outcome
- summarise the information that will be discussed
- state the performance problem or issue, ensuring the description provided is factual and supported by examples and/or evidence.

After delivering a framing statement, describe the performance gap clearly and explain why it's important that the employee meets it. Separate the person from the problem so that the information, advice and strategies can be imparted to the employee in a way that builds their self-esteem and makes it clear that the sole purpose of the discussion is to improve their performance. Use language that demonstrates a 'we' approach – looking at and trying to sort out the problem together.

By adopting this approach, a hard line can be presented in relation to the problem without character-assassinating the person. Ideally, the desired outcome will be a joint effort between leader-manager and employee to address the performance gap. The employee should be left in no doubt, however, as to the seriousness of the issue and the ramifications should they not improve. They need to understand that the performance discussion provides them with a final opportunity to lift the standard of their performance, which will be necessary if they are to remain a part of the team.

Ways to give this information are:

Transferable skills

3.2 Verbal communication

- 'I' messages
- describe–explain–suggest (or specify)
- describe–explain–specify–consequences
- help me out here.

Showing a degree of empathy can help to ease the employee's emotions so they can focus on their performance. Avoid using intimidating language or an overly demonstrable posture as this can also distract the person from focusing on their performance. Two ways that can be used to describe an employee's unsatisfactory performance are:

1. The wrong way: 'Your work is shoddy and going to pot. You'll have to improve. And make sure you're in on time in the mornings, too – there's no room on my team for slackers'.
2. A better way: 'As you know, your output was down by 8 per cent over the last period and you were late four times this month. This isn't like you, and I'm concerned about what is happening'.

The first statement is non-specific and accusing and unlikely to lead to a fruitful discussion or change of behaviour, while the second one is more constructive and opens the door to joint and productive problem-solving.

'I' messages

Transferable skills

3.2 Verbal communication

'I' messages can be used to follow a framing statement. By accentuating the leader-manager's feelings in relation to the employee's performance, it makes it less likely for underperforming employees to counterattack or become defensive.

An 'I' message has three parts:

1. Clearly describe the performance gap. Be specific, factual and concise; for example, 'When you are 10 minutes late ...' is specific, while 'When you dawdle ...' is fuzzy. Don't guess; for example, 'You left work 15 minutes early' is a factual observed behaviour, while 'You don't seem to care about your job these days' is speculation. Avoid absolutes such as 'never', 'always' or 'constantly' and judgemental words such as 'lackadaisical', 'careless' or 'rude'.
2. Describe your own feelings regarding the underperformance – not what you think about it, but how you feel about it. For example, when an employee continually arrives at work 10 or 15 minutes

late, you might feel angry, annoyed or irritated, or you might feel worried about the effect it has on the rest of the team. (This is called *self-disclosure* and it makes your message powerful.)

3 Explain why the performance shortfall matters. What are the consequences of the underperformance? What effect does the performance shortfall have on you, the work team, the organisation and the employee?

Table 16.3 shows an example of an 'I' message.

TABLE 16.3 How 'I' messages can work for you

What you saw or heard	**Conduct** 'When you speak before I'm finished ...'
What you think the facts are	**Target not met** 'My records show that you have been absent for six Mondays out of the last 15 ...'
How you feel about it	**Your response** 'I am/get/feel ... angry/annoyed/concerned/irritated/uncomfortable'
Why it matters	**Tangible effects** 'This means ... or ...' 'Because ...'

The three parts of an 'I' message can be used in any order. For example:

- 'John, it annoys me when you speak before I'm finished because I lose my train of thought.'
- 'Carol, I'm concerned about your absences on Mondays, both because of the effect this may have on your own work and also because it may affect the team. Are you aware you've been absent for six Mondays out of the past 15?'

For straightforward performance gaps, where the solution is obvious, use corrective feedback to state precisely what needs to happen to correct the performance. For example, 'Jo, you're not wearing your safety goggles again. This really concerns me. I need you to always wear them when you come into this area. Can you ensure you do that from now on?'

When the solution is not obvious, indicate the need to resolve the problem together. For example, 'Karun, your last three reports have been up to a week late and that worries me because you're normally so dependable. Can you tell me what it is that's been holding you up?' or 'This is a real problem for me, and we need to figure out what needs to happen so your reports can be on time again.' In this example the conversation moves you from giving good information (Step 2) to gathering good information (Step 3). 'I' messages can also be used to turn positive general feedback into positive specific feedback, which ensures that the behaviour continues. See Figure 16.4 for some tips on describing a performance gap using 'I' messages.

Transferable skills
3.2 Verbal communication

DES: describe–explain–suggest (or specify)

The describe–explain–suggest (or specify) model is another way to follow up a framing statement. First, *describe* the performance gap using neutral, objective language. Then *explain* why performing to the required standard is important or highlight the effects of the poor performance. The explanation may involve, for example, how poor performance affects other team members or other **stakeholders**, or how it affects product or service quality.

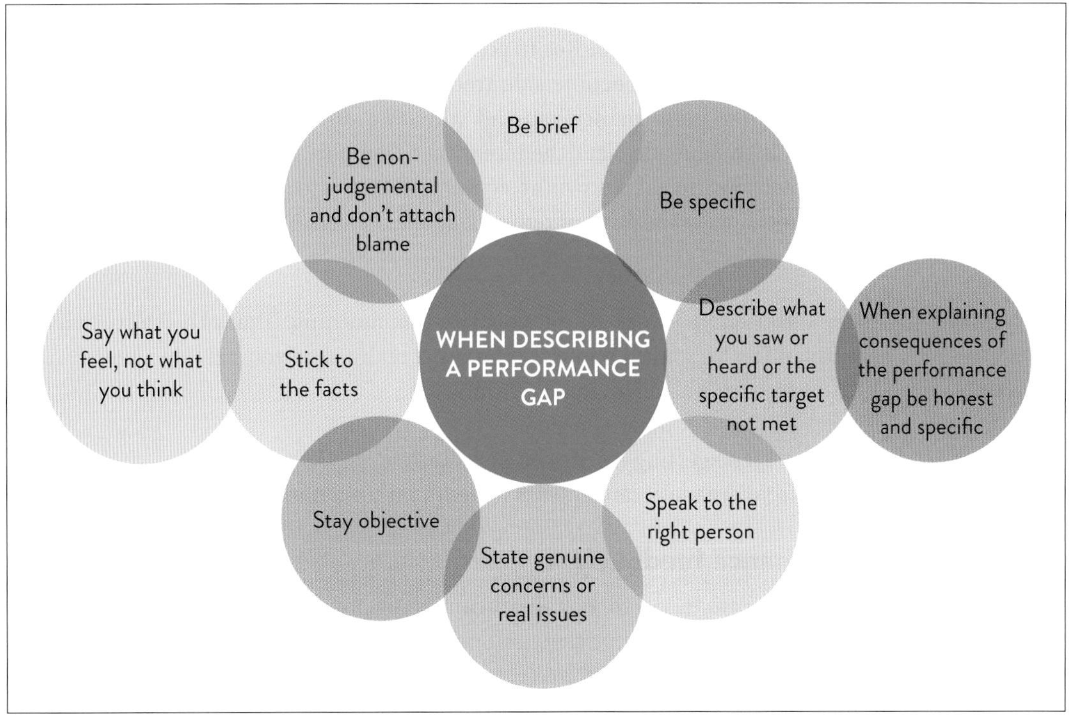

FIGURE 16.4 Tips for describing a performance gap using 'I' messages

When the performance shortfall is straightforward, *suggest* what the underperforming employee needs to do instead. When it is more complex, *specify* the performance goal that needs to be met and move on to discuss what might be preventing the job-holder from meeting it, and what could be done, including any support that is required to help the job-holder meet it.

DESC: describe–explain–specify–consequences

This model is slightly stronger than the describe–explain–suggest (or specify) model. Again, *describe* the conduct or target not met; *explain* why it matters or the effects it has on efficiency, service, workmates, and so on; *specify* the performance goal and the timeframe in which it must be achieved. Finally, state the *consequences* of not meeting the performance goal in the timeframe (e.g. termination of the employee's employment).

Transferable skills
3.2 Verbal communication

Help me out here

An employee has missed a deadline. Which approach do you think would work better: opening with, 'You missed the deadline' or 'Help me out here; I need to understand what stopped you from meeting the deadline'? The latter engages the employee to help you understand why the deadline was missed and opens the door to discussing next steps and how to prevent missed deadlines in the future. When it's suited to the performance gap, this is a non-threatening way to begin a fruitful discussion.

Transferable skills
3.2 Verbal communication

Dealing with denial

Situations will arise where an employee doesn't accept that a performance gap exists or that it presents a problem, makes continual excuses or tries to change the subject. When faced with this kind of 'denial', calmly remain focused on highlighting the performance gap with examples and evidence to back up your message until the employee accepts the reality of the situation. There is no point trying to progress to the solution-finding stage while the employee remains in denial. Stating the problem as a goal and then exploring ways with the employee to achieve it provides a slightly different approach.

Above all, avoid the temptation to become side-tracked. Until the employee accepts that the performance problem exists, the performance gap and why it's a problem needs to be repeated as often as is required. It can then be made clear the intention to support them to reach the expected standard. Repeating a stated position is known as echoing. It helps to prevent people from side-tracking a conversation, ignoring the message or redirecting the conversation elsewhere. An example of echoing might be:

Manager:	'Sam, I noticed you were 20 minutes late this morning. That's the third time this month and we've spoken about this before. I really need you here on time.'
Sam:	'Oh, it's my car. It's still giving me trouble.'
Manager:	'Well, I still need you here on time.'
Sam:	'Yes, well, I'll be getting it serviced next week.'
Manager:	'And have you made arrangements to get in on time until then?'

Reactions to performance feedback

Being prepared to provide performance feedback also means being prepared for the different reactions that may be received and having a follow-up response or plan for each. Here are some of the possible reactions that may be encountered:

- The employee might react with genuine surprise, indicating that they simply didn't realise there was an issue. Where this is the case, developing and working through strategies with the employee to improve their performance and with which they agree to will often be enough to address the performance issue (Step 5).
- The employee provides one or more valid reasons to explain their performance that may relate to problems with other team members, inefficient processes or problems in their personal life. As it is likely that these issues will be more complex to solve, you will need to spend time thoroughly exploring the problem(s) using the Five Keys (Steps 3 and 4).
- The employee comes up with a string of excuses that you know are not valid reasons for their poor performance. Acknowledge the points they put forward without actually agreeing with them. You can do this by paraphrasing or summarising what they have said; for example, 'So, Gordon, what I'm hearing is that other steps in the workflow process are taking longer to complete than the time allocated to them, which leaves you with insufficient time to meet your deadlines'. At this point, put this issue, which you know is not true, to the side to close it off. You can tell the employee that you'll come back to it later if they try to keep it in play. Ask for their attention and for them to focus carefully on what you are going to say. Make it clear from the outset that their performance or conduct is their responsibility. Describe the performance issue without allowing them to interrupt and make it clear that their conduct or performance is an issue that needs to be addressed independently of what they raised earlier. You may wish to return to the points the employee raised earlier to dispel them carefully and methodically, if required, but it is better to maintain yours and the employee's focus on the real issues … their performance.
- When the employee denies or does not accept that there is a problem, provide specific examples and evidence, or compare the actual performance figures with the performance targets, and reiterate how the employee's conduct, or failure to achieve targets, is adversely affecting the team or the department.

  Use the describe–explain–specify–consequences model; if that fails, switch to the change–time–consequence formula – if you do not make this *change* by this *time*, then there will be this *consequence*. The consequence is usually a formal **discipline** interview or termination of employment. Make the potentially impending consequence very clear to the employee and provide a strict timeframe in which improvement needs to occur. This puts the ball squarely back in their court and gives them the choice to improve. If they choose not to, they know what the outcome will be.

- Sometimes an employee will become angry and loud. If you are not already in a private space, such as an office, invite them to join you in the office where you can discuss any issues that they have. Shut the door, make sure they are seated and lower your voice so that they almost have to strain to hear you. All of these actions will help to take the wind out of their sails and defuse their aggression. You can then use reflective listening after they've taken a moment to calm down. Saying something like 'I understand that this is difficult but I'm here to help you improve' can show the employee that you are on their side. As soon as possible, get the employee to focus on solutions to address their performance. This will also help to keep their anger in check as they will see a 'way out'. It is important to always provide an employee with choices. Those choices may not always be the choices they want, but in the employee's mind, it transfers control of the situation back to them. Feeling like they have control will help to ease their anxiety and control their anger. However, if you back an employee into a corner and they have no choice, expect them to come out 'swinging'.
- If the employee becomes emotional and begins to cry, give them the time they need to collect their emotions. You might decide to arrange to meet later, for example, after a short break, later the same day or the next day. When you meet again, remember that it's better to be tactfully honest than nice. Let the employee know the discussion comes from your desire to help them develop and improve and that you are providing the feedback in their best interests. Ensure the meeting stays productive and professional and mention some of the positive things they have done to rekindle their confidence before the meeting ends.

You may want to take a break after explaining the performance gap to allow the employee to process what you've said. Most employees don't intend to perform poorly, and they may need some time to reflect on your feedback and reconcile how they will incorporate it into the way they go about their work. When you meet again, ask the employee to summarise the situation and then begin to explore what options they see to address it (Step 3).

The hot stove

It isn't always necessary to have a lengthy discussion with an employee about a performance shortfall, especially when the employee is clearly capable of performing at the required level and the required action is clear. Apply the **hot-stove principle** – point out the error straight away and remind the employee of the required conduct or performance.

Step 3: Gather good information

Having established the actual performance gap, the next step is to identify its causes. Unless the employee says 'Oh, I hadn't realised – I'll fix it straight away', switch to reflective listening and invite the employee to share their thoughts as to why they think the issue has arisen. Ask questions when you need to, so you can see the situation as the employee sees it. Remember, this doesn't mean you have to agree; you just need to understand the employee's perspective.

Providing employees with an opportunity to explain their viewpoint and to feel they've been given a fair hearing is known as procedural fairness. It is important to uphold this principle as it will be taken into consideration should the performance counselling process end in termination of employment and the employee claims unfair dismissal.

Step 4: Problem-solve

Transferable skills
2.1 Critical thinking

When you've each expressed your points of view and the employee accepts that the performance gap needs to be fixed, you can turn to problem-solving, structuring your discussion around the Five Keys to determine the source of the problem. What's preventing the employee from reaching the required standard? Perhaps there are circumstances beyond the employee's control that are easily fixed.

Once the source of the problem is known, it is best to work with the employee to come up with a solution. It might involve providing further training or coaching of some sort; job redesign to provide the employee with more challenges, delegation of one or two extra duties to develop the employee and increase motivation or lighten the employee's too-heavy workload; streamlining or rearranging poorly designed work systems or providing more accurate or timely information. The solution may of course lie with actions that the employee needs to take. As with any problem-solving, the more solutions that are considered, the better the chosen course of action is likely to be.

Step 5: Agree actions

Summarise what you have agreed upon – who is to do what and when, and how the performance improvement will be monitored. When the employee seems uncommitted or unmotivated to improve, run through your expectations once more before parting. Be specific and clear, and specify performance targets and timeframes, and why it's essential the targets are met. Explain the consequences of not improving using the change–time–consequence formula described earlier. Put the **performance improvement plan** in writing and have the employee sign off on it; this shows that you are serious about wanting to see an improvement and also makes it more likely that the employee will keep up their end of the bargain. Keep a copy of the performance plan in the employee's file.

Part on a positive note by reminding the employee about what they do well and why you value them. This maintains the employee's self-esteem and provides an incentive to improve this aspect of their performance. Shaking hands can be a good way to symbolically 'seal the deal', although it appears that at least for the time being, due to COVID-19, physical contact of any kind is off the agenda.

Step 6: Follow up

Once the performance counselling discussion has been conducted, the employee's progress needs to be monitored to ensure that they achieve the agreed improvement. How long this takes will depend on many factors. However, the timeframe for how long the employee has to demonstrate the improvement required should already have been agreed to, so this is the date to work towards.

When improvement is observed, offer specific positive feedback and encouragement to acknowledge the progress that has been made. This will help to keep performance moving in the right direction. If the employee doesn't make the expected improvement, return to Step 4, hold another conversation and delve deeper to identify the cause of the performance gap. If this happens several times with the same performance gap, it may be necessary to consider implementing the dismissal procedure (discussed in Section 16.3) or transferring the employee to a job better suited to their skills and abilities.

Document performance discussions

Transferable skills

3.3 Written communication

Ensure accurate and objective records of performance discussions are maintained. This can stave off disagreements and uncertainty about who said what and what was agreed upon. The following details should be recorded each time a performance discussion occurs:

- date, time and location of each performance discussion
- names of any other persons present (e.g. someone from the HR department or a union or employee representative)
- performance gap, how long it has existed, where and how often it occurs and any other evidence for the gap
- specific performance target
- performance plan that resulted from your discussion
- subsequent performance, which is indispensable in case the performance doesn't improve and you need to dismiss the employee.

The records should be kept in the employee's personal file and a copy sent to the HR department. A note should be made in a work diary or on a work calendar as to the next date to check the employee's progress.

Manage all performance

It is important to remember that some employees are generally high performers but occasionally underperform. Others are generally good performers who are high performers sometimes and underperformers at other times, while others underperform frequently with occasional good and even high performance.

While addressing chronic underperformance so it doesn't become 'toxic' is a high priority, as a leader-manager you are employed to manage the performance of all of your team members, so be careful not to spend all your time on problem staff members. Work at raising good performance to high performance and show you value high performance by acknowledging or celebrating it when it occurs.

16.3 Terminating employment

> An employer can only dismiss an employee if it would not be considered harsh, unjust or unreasonable. If a business has less than 15 employees, the termination needs to be consistent with the Small Business Fair Dismissal Code.
>
> 'Terminating staff', NSW Government, Office of Industrial Relations, http://www.industrialrelations.nsw.gov.au.

Dismissing employees is always unpleasant, but there are four reasons it might be necessary:

1. Their performance continually fails to meet the required standard over a reasonable period.
2. They engage in conduct that is in serious breach of organisational policy (e.g. theft), which can result in summary, or instant, dismissal.
3. Their job has become redundant.
4. There is insufficient work to keep them employed, making it necessary to retrench them.

Before moving on to termination of employment for the first two reasons, there are some general principles to bear in mind.

General principles

Always follow organisational protocol to ensure the employee is treated fairly and the rules of procedural fairness are adhered to. Because termination of employment is a serious matter, both in how it might affect the employee and also from a legal standpoint, many organisations take the precaution of requiring managers to talk it over with their own manager before beginning the termination process. Others require the manager's manager to be involved in each step along the way. Organisations with HR departments sometimes require a senior HR officer or manager to become involved at the verbal warning or first written warning stage. These sensible precautions safeguard the organisation as well as the employee. It is therefore good practice and, in almost all cases, mandatory to follow organisational procedures when instigating termination action.

Employees may request that a support person, for example their union or employee representative, attend any or all of these interviews, which is not unusual and actually helps to confirm that the employee has been treated fairly during the process.

When terminating an employee's employment, plan the process carefully by considering whether the employee should leave the premises immediately or at a different time. What items belonging to the organisation might the employee have that need to be returned (e.g. company car, computer files or documents, laptop, mobile phone) and how should this be done? Do the employee's computer files need to be backed up before they are advised of the termination of their employment?

It is good practice to avoid termination discussions on Fridays and before holidays, and it is better to meet towards the end of the workday so the employee can go home afterward. It is also recommended to arrange for an HR representative to be present to provide information about final payments and to ensure that the meeting follows the organisation's guidelines.

Always dismiss people in private and in person. Avoid skating around the issue because this only builds the tension and makes it harder to deliver the news. It is better to get right to the point by stating that the news is not good (e.g. 'I have some unpleasant news'). Should the employee become emotional, let them 'vent', within reason, but if there are any concerns with how they might react, take precautions, such as asking security to stand by.

Think through how the conversation should ideally proceed and how it might be made more palatable for the employee while still being honest, tactful and sticking to the facts. There is no point or advantage to sugar-coating the news. State clearly to the employee what is happening and why. Review how the decision was reached to show that a fair process was administered. Remain calm, choose words that deliver the news clearly but without malice and use reflective listening to acknowledge the departing employee's feelings.

Offer any assistance according to organisational policies and procedures, and, when appropriate, offer to provide contacts that might help the employee find another position. An act or gesture of goodwill such as this may even facilitate the person becoming a part of your extended professional network, which may come in useful the next time you are searching for a new position.

Once the details of the employee's departure have been worked through with the employee, and without going into details, let the team know that their colleague is leaving and be prepared for the effect that this may have (i.e. it may upset the team's balance and send it back into the 'storming' stage – refer to Tuckman's stages of team development in Chapter 13).

Termination for poor performance or misconduct

An employee's employment can be terminated based on the following:

- failure to conduct themself in a manner appropriate to the job (see the section on instant dismissal following)

- inability or continued failure to do the job adequately (provided you have discussed the problem with the employee, offered remedial training and given the employee an opportunity to improve)
- redundancy as a result of the introduction of new technology or organisational changes and the inability of the organisation to transfer the employee to another part of its operations
- retrenchment due to the operational requirements of the business.

It is not legal to terminate a worker's employment for any of the following reasons:

- absence from work due to carer or parental leave
- acting, having acted or seeking to act as an employee representative or other trade union activities
- discriminatory reasons, such as age, breastfeeding, carer status, colour, criminal record (except in some circumstances), disability, ethnicity, family responsibilities, gender, gender identity, intersex status, marital status, medical grounds, national extraction, nationality, physical or mental disability, political opinion, pregnancy, race, religion, sexual preference or social origin
- filing a complaint or participating in proceedings against an employer involving alleged violation of laws or regulations
- membership or non-membership of a union
- participation in union activities outside working hours, or with the consent of the employer within working hours
- temporary absence from work because of genuine illness or injury, provided the employee has given appropriate advice and the period of absence is not unreasonable in the circumstances
- time off work while on workers' compensation.

When all options have been exhausted to improve an underperforming employee's performance and the only choice left is to terminate their employment, it is important to do it right or risk legal proceedings. It is essential to follow the organisation's performance counselling procedure and ensure all discussions and agreed actions have been accurately documented. All organisations should have a warning procedure contained in their **workplace agreement**, which must be followed. If unsure, follow advice provided by the organisation's HR department or HR manager. Many organisations' guidelines are likely to have incorporated the three-step procedure detailed in the following sections. This procedure dovetails with the performance counselling procedure and legal requirements.

If the warnings given to the employee about their performance have been consistent, spaced out correctly to provide time for them to improve, documented factually, and appropriate support has been provided to them, termination of their employment should face no legal impediments.

Step 1: Verbal warning

When an employee's work performance is measurably or demonstrably below an acceptable level, the initial warning should take the form of a performance counselling meeting, described earlier. Even by this point, one or more performance improvement discussions should already have been held. For this meeting, have the notes from the previous meeting(s) on hand and refer to them. The tone and words used should be chosen carefully so as to demonstrate objectivity and a non-threatening approach. The conversation should at all times be directed to the employee's work performance and the need for them to improve so as to reach the required standards.

Provide the employee with an opportunity to explain their underperformance and request assistance. The performance plan to which the employee agrees should allow a reasonable amount of time for the performance improvement required to occur and include any help and support the employee needs. There is no hard-and-fast rule about how long they should have to improve to the level required but it should be long enough to realistically allow the employee to perform to expectations. During the meeting, ensure the employee understands that the consequence of continued poor performance is dismissal.

Some organisations require this first warning to be in writing; if your organisation doesn't, note the details of the discussion in the employee's personal file and maintain a separate record to refer back to later if required. At this and subsequent meetings, always document the discussion fully and carefully because these records may be used as evidence to determine whether the termination was legal or not if an unfair dismissal complaint is lodged.

Step 2: Written warning

Transferable skills
3.3 Written communication

When the agreed performance improvement does not occur within the agreed time, another performance counselling meeting needs to be held at which the employee is provided with an opportunity to respond. Listen carefully to the employee's views as there may be a valid reason to explain why improvement has not occurred.

But if the decision to proceed with the dismissal process is made, a second, written, warning must be given to the employee. The warning should refer to the date of the previous verbal warning and other performance counselling discussions and specify the performance gap and the time by which the improved performance should occur. The warning letter should be on the organisation's letterhead or a form specially designed for the purpose. Retain a copy and provide another copy to the HR department or HR manager.

Step 3: Final written warning

Transferable skills
3.3 Written communication

If, following the previous meetings, the employee's performance still does not improve, repeat the procedure outlined in Step 2, double-checking the Five Keys in case there is a valid reason for the continued poor performance that can be addressed. As the title suggests, this is the employee's last chance to explain or improve their underperformance and avoid their employment being terminated. Ensure, therefore, that the employee is clear about the required performance (What To), understands that it is important to meet it (Want To), has been trained correctly (How To), that nothing in the work environment is preventing acceptable performance (Chance To), and that appropriate leadership has been and is continuing to be provided (Led To).

When the employee's performance remains below the required standard after the final written warning, termination of employment results. This is done in a formal interview and is best followed by an exit interview, which can sometimes shed light on the reasons behind why the employee was not able or not willing to improve their performance.

How long does the termination process take?

The length of the dismissal process depends on the nature of the performance shortfall. When an employee refuses to follow safety procedures or adhere to the organisation's code of conduct, for example, it need take only two or three days to complete the dismissal procedure. When complex remedial training or coaching is needed, the process may take several weeks to complete. The golden rule is that the length of time allowed for the performance improvement must be realistic.

Instant dismissal

Instant dismissal is dismissal without notice or warning or pay in lieu of warning. It usually results from acts of serious misconduct, such as fraud, theft of or wilful damage to company or customer property. It may also be due to physical violence against other employees, customers or others on company property or while on duty, substance abuse while on duty, and blatantly unsafe conduct that endangers the employee, other employees or the public.

Many workplace agreements specify a 'cooling-off period' before dismissal, and legal precedent in Australia requires that the employee be provided with an opportunity to respond. For example, the employee may have to leave the premises immediately and not return until the next day to discuss the matter. Following that discussion, a decision will then be made as to whether to proceed with terminating the employee's employment.

For matters that are more complex and require investigation, interviewing other employees and checking email records may be required, and this process may take longer. In these cases, the employee will be sent home, suspended on full pay. Serious matters such as these should always be discussed with a more senior manager including the HR manager, someone in the HR department or the relevant employer organisation. It is important to always refer to the existing workplace agreement before taking any action as each agreement may contain slightly different procedures.

16.4 Assisting employees with personal problems

> To take care of your business, you first need to take care of your employees.
>
> Tim Rule, Instructional Designer, Swinburne University of Technology.

There would be few leader-managers qualified to provide counselling on issues such as mental illness, gambling, grief, post-traumatic stress, relationship breakdowns, substance abuse, terminal illness or other serious personal problems. However, there are workers across the country of different genders, ages, backgrounds and cultures who are facing these types of problems. As a result, they may experience reduced concentration, lower productivity, and sometimes their judgement may also be affected. This may also place them and those with whom they work at greater risk of suffering harm from accidents. Some will choose to hide their problems and 'soldier on' stoically but for others, their work and working relationships will be affected, sometimes profoundly. This may require them to take extended periods off work or be provided with additional support either from within or outside the workplace.

One of the most obvious signs of a personal problem is a reduction in work performance, which makes Step 3 (gathering good information) in the performance counselling process critical. There may be factors contributing to an employee's underperformance that have not yet come to light but that directly relate to a personal issue. In such cases, simply demanding the employee improve or allocating them additional tasks might not necessarily be the best approach! Even where their performance doesn't suffer, being attuned to changes in an employee's behaviour or demeanour may help to identify situations where factors outside of work are having a negative impact on them. This may mean they require additional support or understanding or sometimes greater privacy.

Offer assistance

Some leader-mangers take the approach that in their work environment it is not their responsibility or obligation to offer assistance to employees facing personal issues. While on one level this may be true, in practice it makes sense to offer assistance for a number of reasons. People who feel they're on their own or that they have been abandoned can begin to think and act erratically. Even if they are able to hold it together, they may become difficult to motivate and supervise as they simply 'go through the motions' and this can negatively impact other employees.

There are also many costs associated with losing an employee if that person resigns or ends up taking long periods of leave, requiring their position to be filled. Not only might the organisation lose valuable experience and skills, it may also incur significant costs associated with finding a replacement, such as the time taken for interviewing, providing induction and job training, not to mention the cost of errors that new recruits will inevitably make while learning and settling into their new job.

There is also the intangible but potentially serious cost of damaging an organisation's 'employer brand' should it become known for having an uncaring attitude towards employees. This will make it difficult to attract the employees it needs in the future and also adversely affect buying behaviour.

When an employee experiences a personal problem, no one expects their leader-manager to be a professional counsellor. Personal counselling from a leader-manager's point of view is really a listening activity. There may be ways to ease the employee's work pressure and, depending on the size of the organisation and its policies, there may be an option to offer the employee time off with or without pay. Many organisations also provide access to an **employee assistance program (EAP)**, which can be a source of support and referrals for employees tackling difficult personal issues. Some problems may not be resolved quickly, especially if they involve a long illness in an employee or one of their family members. Based on the employee's track record (including past performance reviews) and the value they add to the workplace, a decision will need to be made as to how long their reduced contribution can be accommodated.

When personal problems lead to underperformance, the performance gap needs to be discussed, as described above, and any professional counselling provided by the organisation offered at each performance counselling meeting. If the organisation doesn't provide an EAP, a referral may still be able to be made for the employee to a person more qualified, such as a professional counsellor. It is up to each employee whether to avail themselves of the offer of counselling.

When potentially serious psychological problems affect performance

Some mental illnesses can pose a more serious threat to both the person as well as those around them when not adequately treated or left untreated. Ensuring the safety of employees at work is a leader-manager's responsibility. Where a suspicion exists that an employee may be dangerous and needs professional help, but it is unclear whether it is safe for the employee to remain at work, an HR specialist should be brought in to assist in managing the situation. They may take over managing the situation in some cases. The employee might be asked whether they would consent to an independent medical assessment. If they agree, confirm their consent in writing. If they refuse, check whether the employment contract, company policy, workplace agreement or **award** that applies contains a clause allowing the organisation to direct the employee to attend a medical assessment.

When this is not the case, a further option is to seek legal advice based on concern for the employee's safety and the safety of other employees. It is preferable to use an experienced clinical psychologist or psychiatrist (rather than a general practitioner) to conduct the assessment. Provide the specialist with detailed background information, including the reasons for suspecting the possibility of psychological illness. Also provide a copy of the job or role description and a clear set of questions that need to be reported on by a medical practitioner, particularly whether the employee is currently able to safely perform the duties listed in the job description.

When an employee is found to have a psychological illness, the practitioner can recommend that the employee return to work on alternative duties until the condition is resolved. Allowing a person to remain at work often aids recovery.

If a personal problem is suspected to be the cause of an employee's underperformance, discuss it with the employee, minimising the employee's stress as much as possible. The focus of any discussion needs to be on assisting the employee to deal with their problem, if possible, and helping them return their performance to its previously high level.

The following are questions and statements that might be appropriate to use in such a discussion:

- 'Are you able to discuss whatever is affecting your work performance?'
- 'Do you know what is preventing you from doing the good work we both know you usually do?'
- 'I'm wondering whether there is a deeper issue affecting your performance. Would you like to discuss it?'
- 'I sense that there is something here that does not "meet the eye" and, while I don't wish to intrude, I have taken the liberty of making a list of the assistance options that the organisation makes available to employees. Assistance is completely confidential and whether or not you use it is entirely up to you.'

By using emotional intelligence skills, such as empathy and active listening, with the employee, they are more likely to offer information voluntarily without the need to ask them direct personal questions. The wisest approach, therefore, is to listen, be as positive as it is tactful to be in the situation and focus on the employee's welfare rather than on their problem.

STUDY TOOLS

QUICK REVIEW

KEY CONCEPT 16.1 

a What are the dangers of describing underperformance as a 'bad attitude'? What should you do when you believe an employee's attitude needs 'adjusting'?

b List the Five Keys and explain how they help you think through poor performance.

c How can role conflict result in underperformance? What can leader-managers do about that problem?

KEY CONCEPT 16.2 

a List and summarise the steps to take to help an employee improve their performance.

b What are four techniques you can use to explain an employee's underperformance?

c What should you do when an employee continually makes excuses or blames others or circumstances for their underperformance?

KEY CONCEPT 16.3 

a Describe the circumstances that make it necessary to terminate a person's employment and the process by which you should do this. What is the procedure and what documentation is necessary?

KEY CONCEPT 16.4 

a What avenues are open to you when you think an employee may have a personal problem that is affecting their performance?

BUILD YOUR SKILLS

KEY CONCEPT 16.1 

a If an employee's role requires them to maintain a certain standard of personal appearance, how might you address this issue if their personal presentation was not meeting the standard? If the employee's personal presentation continued unchanged because they believed that they were meeting the standard, outline the course of action you might need to take and highlight what you would need to be careful to avoid.

KEY CONCEPT 16.2 

a What should be your overall aims when counselling an underperforming employee? Describe the steps that you would work through to achieve these objectives and the skills you would draw on in each step.

b Below are four examples of how a manager might begin a performance improvement discussion. Explain why they are unsatisfactory and suggest an alternative for each one.
   i 'You've been coming in late. You've got a really bad attitude towards your work, and it had better change.'
   ii 'You made a mess of that last job. Obviously, you're not competent or you've lost your drive.'
   iii 'I was talking. You're rude to interrupt me.'
   iv 'You're not doing a good enough job. You need to boost your confidence.'

c Write a framing statement and an 'I' message, a describe–explain–suggest (or specify) message or a describe–indicate–specify–consequences message you could use to open a performance counselling session for each of the following situations when an employee:
   i Argues with a colleague in front of the rest of the team at least once a fortnight about non-related work matters.
   ii Fails to wear a hairnet in the food preparation area unless he is reminded. This has been going on since he transferred to your section (from a non-food area) three weeks ago.
   iii Has a pattern of absence on Mondays and Fridays. In fact, in the last six months, she has been absent on six Fridays and four Mondays.
   iv Is a very low participator in your virtual project team meetings; in fact, he doesn't contribute unless asked a direct question.
   v Shows work quality that is spasmodic. In the last six weeks her reject rate has been 30 per cent above average and this is costly in terms of material wastage.

KEY CONCEPT 16.3 

a Draft a first written warning letter to an employee who has been late seven times over the past 12 shifts and has been unable to provide a satisfactory explanation.

KEY CONCEPT 16.4 

a Rather than try to counsel an employee with a personal problem, why is it better to refer employees to a professional counselling service?

WORKPLACE ACTIVITIES

KEY CONCEPT 16.1 

a Identify one aspect of your team's performance that is often below the expected standard of performance. Diagnose the cause of this sub-standard performance by working through the Five Keys.

KEY CONCEPT 16.2 

a What are your organisation's policy and procedures regarding counselling underperforming employees? At what point does performance counselling end and dismissal proceedings begin?

b Describe the last time you counselled someone for underperformance and the steps you went through. What was the employee's reaction and how did you handle it? What made the discussion successful? What can you do next time a similar situation occurs to achieve an even better outcome?

KEY CONCEPT 16.3 

a What are your organisation's policy and procedures regarding termination of employment for continued poor performance and for summary dismissal?

KEY CONCEPT 16.4 

a What assistance does your organisation offer employees who are experiencing personal difficulties?

EXTENSION ACTIVITIES

Referring to the Snapshot at the beginning of this chapter, answer the following questions:

1 Why is this situation particularly difficult for Jemima? Could she have used the 'Help me out here' approach? Would it have been likely to be successful or not? Why or why not?
2 At what point and in what process is Jemima up to in relation to Carmel's employment? How would Jemima justify the action she is taking and what evidence does she have to back it up?
3 Outline the legal requirements of enacting the process that Jemima is about to commence.

CASE STUDY 16

A 'PERMANENT' UNDERPERFORMER?

Emily had not only been pleased with the performance of Caleb, she also felt vindicated because he had been hired predominantly on her recommendation. Employed as an intern proofreader back in February, Caleb had been enthusiastic, motivated and conscientious during his six-month probationary period, which had ended seven weeks ago with him being offered and accepting a permanent position.

But ever since he was made permanent, Emily had noticed an alarming change in Caleb. His productivity had fallen away sharply. Prior to becoming permanent, he would turn over 10 manuscripts a week but just three weeks later, this number had fallen to eight. Now it was just seven. His accuracy had also declined with two clients complaining about spelling errors that had not been corrected prior to final handover and incorrect referencing.

Caleb also seemed distracted and lacked the enthusiasm he had shown in Zoom meetings with the rest of the team during his probationary period. As the team was working remotely due to COVID-19 restrictions, Emily couldn't supervise him directly. When she first inquired tactfully about the backlog of unchecked manuscripts building up, Caleb just brushed it off, saying he'd get to them by the deadlines. When she made a more assertive inquiry two weeks later, after two deadlines were missed, Caleb became quite defensive, saying it wasn't his fault and that it was because seven of the last 15 manuscripts had been considerably longer and contained more errors than usual to fix. He had gone on to say to Emily: 'Why don't you raise this issue with the writers; after all, it's their fault everything is taking more time than it did before'.

But perhaps the thing that worried Emily most was the time Caleb had taken off in the seven weeks since being made permanent. In his first six months he had not taken any leave at all. But in the seven weeks that had followed, Caleb had already used up seven of his 10 days of personal leave. He had also finished work an hour early on three occasions to attend 'appointments', assuring Emily he would make the time up but was yet to do so. For six out of the seven days of leave he had taken, he did not provide medical certificates. However, for the other day of leave he had supplied a medical certificate. It was on letterhead from the local hospital with the box captioned 'Specialist Clinics Attendance' ticked. Emily wondered if this had anything to do with his underperformance. Should she ask him about it? He had been completely within his rights to take the leave he had taken, and his personal life was strictly his business. She knew she had no right to ask him about it. But what if it was something she could help him with? She decided not to ask.

Three weeks later Caleb's productivity had fallen even further to just five manuscripts a week. Clients were ringing demanding their files and the writers were also complaining that Caleb's edits were 'missing the mark'. Caleb had been absent for the past three days. Now Emily had to do something ...

Questions

1 Ignoring whether there is a medical reason behind Caleb's decline in performance, outline the process that Emily needs to follow in relation to his underperformance.
2 Outline the effects on the team, the organisation, its clients and Caleb that Emily's lack of action to address Caleb's performance have had so far.
3 How could Emily use 'I' messages to talk to Caleb about his performance? Provide three examples of what she might say.
4 If the reason for Caleb's underperformance is linked to medical reasons or personal problems, how should Emily handle this? What kind of help might she be able to offer?

PART

4

MANAGING OPERATIONS

The discipline of managing operations began with the move from the agricultural economy to the industrial economy. As the manufacturing era waned, managing operations encompassed service industries and added digital technology to its portfolio, further increasing the value well-managed operations can add to organisations. Managing and analysing information can streamline operations and supply chains, improve quality and better predict customer needs. Software has become essential to efficient operations, from innovation and design to managing finances and people.

Well-managed operations make an organisation viable. At its heart, managing operations is about designing and directing the way organisations produce and deliver their goods and services. It's about a streamlined, sustainable, safe, economical and efficient flow of information, materials, people and work. It's about converting raw materials, information and people's energy into quality products and services.

How well can you manage the three bedrocks of organisational success: sound finances, quality and customer service? Can you draw out people's most productive and innovative efforts? How solid are your skills at continuously improving ways of working to increase efficiencies? Do you know how to plan and protect your plans and lead and manage projects to a successful conclusion?

Then there are the myriad risks (and opportunities) to operations, people and the environment that you need to be able to spot and manage, all within a framework of sustainable operations that create value for customers, shareholders, society and the planet. And you need to do all of this in ever-changing external and internal environments, which means you need to be able to introduce, monitor and foster the changes, both large and small, upon which successful organisations depend.

As with any set of skills, you can learn them but you must also apply them. Applying any new skill can be difficult and even frustrating at first. But practice makes progress. By working with the skills explained in this part until you are familiar with them, you become a more effective leader-manager.

CHAPTER

MANAGING BUDGETS AND FINANCIAL PLANS

KEY CONCEPTS

After completing this chapter, you will be able to:

17.1 explain the fundamentals of finance
17.2 plan a financial management approach for your work team
17.3 put your financial management approach to work
17.4 monitor and control the money you're responsible for.

TRANSFERABLE SKILLS

The following transferable skills are covered in this chapter:

1 **Business competence**
- **1.1** Financial literacy
- **1.2** Entrepreneurship/small business skills
- **1.3** Sustainability
- **1.4** Business operations
- **1.5** Operations management

2 **Critical thinking and problem solving**
- **2.1** Critical thinking
- **2.2** Personal effectiveness
- **2.3** Business strategy

3 **Social competence**
- **3.1** Teamwork/relationships
- **3.2** Verbal communication
- **3.3** Written communication
- **3.4** Leadership

4 **Data literacy**
- **4.1** Data literacy

5 **Digital competence**
- **5.2** Technology use

OVERVIEW

Finances are more than columns and rows of numbers. As a leader-manager, you don't need to be able to perform all the tasks of an accountant or bookkeeper, but you do need to understand what those columns and rows of figures mean and how they show what's going on in an organisation, a unit and a team. You need to be able to evaluate and control those numbers, as well as talk about and present those figures so they make sense to others. And you need to use them to make sound decisions.

Transferable skills

1.1 Financial literacy

3.4 Leadership

The principles of managing a budget, whether it's for a government body, a registered company, a small business, a not-for-profit (NFP) organisation, a department or a work team, are similar to running a household budget – only there are more zeros on the end of the numbers. At home and at work, you plan your financial management approach, gain agreement for it, implement it, monitor and control it, and keep an eye open for ways to improve it.

In this chapter, you learn the language of finance and how to monitor and control the budgets (money) you are responsible for. You find out how to interpret, implement and manage budgets and financial plans with finesse. You might want to keep a list of definitions of technical terms – those in bold or italics – related to finance.

SNAPSHOT

Staying on budget

Miriam looks over her summary of consultations with the various heads of department and compares it with the calendar of training workshops she's drawn up for the coming year – one final check to make sure she's covered everyone's requirements.

Satisfied, she begins developing a budget for the head of human resources to approve. Which training sessions can her team develop and lead? The more she draws on the skills and knowledge of her staff and others in the organisation, the lower the cost of each program. Which sessions does she need to bring in external experts to lead? She needs to budget carefully for those workshops.

It's the same with venues – which workshops merit the cost of hiring an outside venue, and what level of venue, and which workshops can they run on-site? What sort of refreshments should she provide, and which programs need lunch organised? It all adds up. 'I'll plug in the high-end figures to give me some negotiating room', she thinks as she pulls out her file of preferred venues.

Careful planning is one thing. Staying on budget is another and that takes regular reviews. 'I think I'll involve the team a lot more in those reviews next year. Some of them may want to become leader-managers themselves one day and they'll need to know how to beat the budget blues.'

17.1 Understanding finance fundamentals

> Annual income twenty pounds, annual expenditure nineteen six, result happiness. Annual income twenty pounds, annual expenditure twenty pounds ought and six, result misery.
>
> Charles Dickens (1812–1870), *David Copperfield*, Bradbury & Evans, 1850.

In Charles Dickens' days, 20 shillings made a pound and 12 pence made a shilling. The maths is easier today, but the principles remain the same. Money. Money doesn't grow on trees, but it does make the world go round. Money is central to every organisation, from sole traders to huge international charities.

Even when your mission isn't making money, you need to make sure you gather enough, spend it well and keep your eye on it. This means monitoring your *income* (money coming in), *expenses* (the money you have paid and know you owe on a regular basis, e.g. rent and interest on loans) and *liabilities* (money you owe in the short term such as *accounts payable*, and longer-term debts such as repaying a bank loan). It means making sure your *assets* (what you own, such as land, buildings and equipment, and what you're owed – *accounts receivable*) can cover your liabilities. When you can do that, you are happy. When you can't repay what you owe, you become *insolvent* (unable to pay your debts) and miserable. Keeping your eye on the money is an important part of the due diligence that every organisation and every leader-manager, who is responsible for money in some way, owes their stakeholders.

The goal of management accounting is to provide financial and other information to all levels of management so that they can plan and control the organisation's activities and make sensible, evidence-based decisions. A number of strategies, such as capital budgeting, cost-volume-profit analysis, determining costs and costing systems, forecasting sales and producing various performance reports, provide the groundwork that allows good financial management.

As a leader-manager, understanding the financial management process and the accounting system used in your organisation, and communicating relevant financial information to your team, ensures everyone is on the same page. Let's see how **budgets** and the three main accounting statements – the **balance sheet** (or statement of financial position), the **income statement** (once called the profit and loss statement and now also known as the statement of financial performance) and the **cash flow statement** – help you understand your organisation and manage your team's financial resources.

Transferable skills

1.1 Financial literacy

3.2 Verbal communication

3.4 Leadership

Accounting systems

An *accounting system* collects transactions, including *source documents*, such as invoices and receipts for purchases and sales (discussed later in the chapter; see Figure 17.15), records them in a *chart of accounts* and stores them for future use; for example, for producing the financial reports and statements needed by the organisation's owners and managers, and other interested parties, such as the Australian Taxation Office and the organisation's auditors, bankers, creditors and investors. Figure 17.1 shows some examples of accounting reports used in the organisation and presented to outside parties in a chart of accounts.

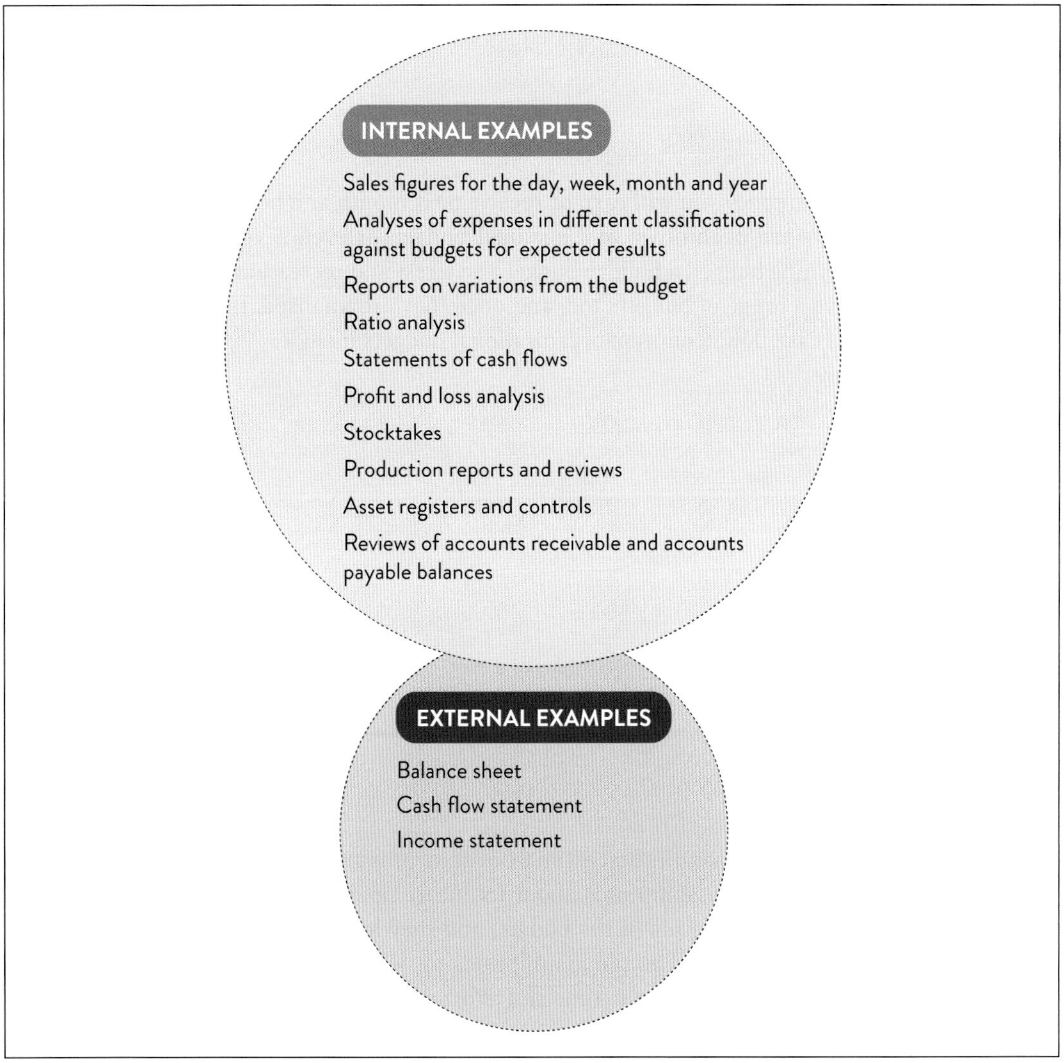

INTERNAL EXAMPLES

- Sales figures for the day, week, month and year
- Analyses of expenses in different classifications against budgets for expected results
- Reports on variations from the budget
- Ratio analysis
- Statements of cash flows
- Profit and loss analysis
- Stocktakes
- Production reports and reviews
- Asset registers and controls
- Reviews of accounts receivable and accounts payable balances

EXTERNAL EXAMPLES

- Balance sheet
- Cash flow statement
- Income statement

FIGURE 17.1 Examples of accounting reports for internal and external use

Accounting software systems organise every account in the accounting system into a numbered list that shows money received or spent, and budgets; for example:

- Asset accounts:
  - 100 Cash: Money in the bank or not yet deposited.
- 110 Accounts receivable: Money owed to the business by customers.
- Liability accounts:
  - 210 Accounts payable: Money owed to suppliers
  - 220 Wages payable: Money owed to staff.

Transferable skills

1.1 Financial literacy

Below is a list of the main terms you may use a lot:

- *Journal:* detailed record, or account of financial transactions, in date order, used for future reconciliations and transfers to other accounting records, such as ledgers.
- *Account:* a record of each type of asset, expense, liability, owners' equity and revenue.
- *Ledger:* a record that keeps economic transactions by account type.
- *Double entry* accounting or bookkeeping – recording every transaction in at least two accounts as a way to detect errors.
- *Trial balance:* compiling all ledgers into debit and credit columns that balance, which shows whether the ledgers are in balance (debits equal credits) and provides the basis for financial statements.

Budgets

Do you know how much money you will earn or receive next month and how much you will spend? When you do, you have the beginnings of a personal budget, or even several budgets, perhaps a groceries budget, a clothing budget, a holiday budget and a rest and recreation budget.

Organisations have a range of budgets too, and once they are finalised, the organisation is in a position to forecast its cash flow. Common organisational budgets include:

- capital expenditure
- cash flow projections
- cost of goods sold
- human resources
- inventory
- labour expenses
- marketing
- materials purchased
- operating expenses
- overheads
- plant and equipment
- production
- purchasing
- sales.

These budgets are the organisation's best estimate of its income and its expenditure over a specified period of time. They reflect its assumptions about its future operating (or external) environment as well as its ability to reach the goals of the budget, and they lead to action plans to reach them. Of course, budgets are only as good as the assumptions on which they are based and there is no guarantee of success. But they're worth the time and effort of producing because they provide a:

- way to measure performance
- way to identify trouble spots in time to act to rectify them
- framework in which to manage *contingencies*, or unexpected events.

Tables 17.1 and 17.2 show examples of a budget that restrains (sets targets to stay within) and a budget that sets targets to meet (attain). The type of budget you work to depends on your team's work. For example, in a *cost centre*, you are allocated money for various activities. This is a budget that restrains – you need to control expenditure and stay within budget, and you probably need to seek permission from the chief financial officer (CFO) to transfer funds from one 'line', or category of expenditure, in the budget to another. A budget that restrains is shown in Table 17.1. In a *profit centre*, you need to achieve the targets the budget sets. Table 17.2 shows a budget to attain, in which you are accountable for both the revenue from sales and the cost of sales, and therefore, for profit.

TABLE 17.1 A budget that restrains

Training unit expenses budget for year ending 30 June 2023				
	Quarter 1	Quarter 2	Quarter 3	Quarter 4
Payroll	$120 000	$120 000	$130 000	$130 000
Program costs	$100 000	$100 000	$110 000	$110 000
Accommodation	$ 30 000	$ 30 000	$ 35 000	$ 35 000
Catering	$ 20 000	$ 20 000	$ 25 000	$ 25 000
Consumables	$ 5000	$ 5000	$ 5000	$ 5000
Total	**$275 000**	**$275 000**	**$305 000**	**$305 000**

TABLE 17.2 A budget to attain

Sales budget, Ace Motor Scooters for year ending 30 June 2023				
	Quarter 1	Quarter 2	Quarter 3	Quarter 4
Projected sales Model A	40 units @	45 units @	45 units @	50 units @
Price	$12 000	$12 000	$12 500	$12 500
Total gross sales	$480 000	$540 000	$562 500	$625 000
Discounts and allowances	$40 000	$45 000	$48 000	$50 000
Total net sales	**$440 000**	**$495 000**	**$514 500**	**$575 000**

Table 17.3 shows the types of centres that might exist in an organisation. The more decentralised the organisation, the more of these centres you can expect to find.

TABLE 17.3 Types of centres

Cost centres	Are responsible for controlling both direct and indirect costs Don't contribute profit directly, but cost money to run Accounting, administration, human resources, IT, production, research and development departments are examples of cost centres One department might have several cost centres
Profit centres	Are responsible for earnings as well as costs (both direct and indirect) and the resulting profit Can make decisions about pricing and operating expenses Each store in a chain of stores, sales departments within large stores, and individually owned businesses are examples of profit centres

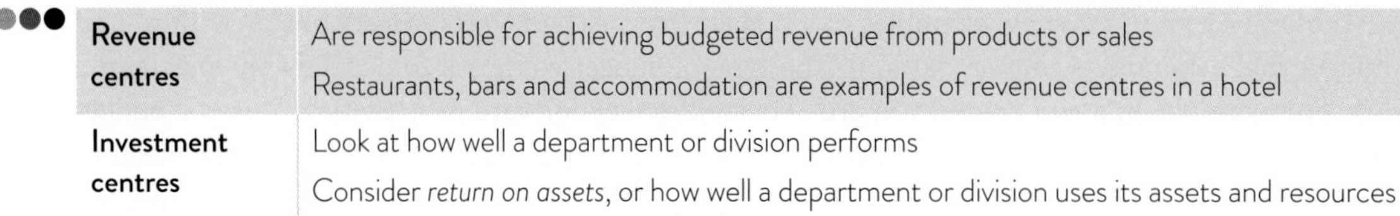

Revenue centres	Are responsible for achieving budgeted revenue from products or sales Restaurants, bars and accommodation are examples of revenue centres in a hotel
Investment centres	Look at how well a department or division performs Consider *return on assets*, or how well a department or division uses its assets and resources to generate revenue compared with its operating expenses

IN PRACTICE

Working through the numbers

Tony is considering buying a small lawnmowing business. He studies the sales figures:

July/August	$10 000
September/October	10 000
November/December	100 000
January/February	100 000
March/April	10 000
May/June	10 000

A few quick calculations tell him that, not surprisingly, summer is busy, and he may need to take on a casual employee to help him out. His teenage son could do it.

He also sees that 83.3 per cent of earnings occur over a four-month period and suspects those are the profitable months, and the rest of the year is less profitable. What would that do to his cash flow, in terms of paying his monthly expenses, he wonders? What could he do to compensate for the less profitable months?

Budgets are set for an entire organisation by top-level and senior management as well as for specific parts of an organisation, such as a department. Each department generally has its own budget that reflects its particular function. Budgets are also developed for specific tasks or activities and for individual projects.

However far a budget stretches – over an entire organisation or over a work team – it is a plan. Like any plan, budgets need to be communicated to people and people need to be committed to achieving them in order for them to work. We review budgeting principles and how to develop budgets in Section 17.2.

A dangerous promise?

Budgets are an offshoot of management accounting and are relatively modern in organisational terms. They became popular in the 1950s and 1960s when academics tried to show how managers could scientifically manage an organisation or a department by developing and monitoring financial targets.

Once simply a scorecard, budgets evolved into an all-embracing planning and monitoring mechanism – a promise managers make that translates into targets that cascade through the organisation. But when people's jobs depend on meeting targets, they will probably meet them – even when they have to destroy the enterprise to do it.[1]

Transferable skills

2.3 Business strategy

Budgeting methods

Different organisations budget differently. The key is to choose a process that suits the organisation's operations and mission, and its operating (external) environment.

Bottom-up and top-down budgets

Some organisations use a *bottom-up* process and others a *top-down* process. A bottom-up approach begins with individual departments budgeting revenue and expenses. These budgets are then *consolidated*, or brought together, as the corporate budget. The top-down method begins with top-level and senior management creating the corporate budget that cascades down through the organisation and is fleshed out in increasing detail by individual functions, departments and work teams.

Zero-based budgets

Another budgeting method is known as *zero-based budgeting*. This can be quite accurate because you start at zero (not last year or last month) and build your budget from there, asking a series of questions and identifying responsibility centres as you go. For example:

- What level of sales can we reasonably achieve?
- What do we need to purchase to achieve those sales (raw materials for production, inventory for a shop, etc.)?
- What fixed costs support these sales?
- How many people do we need to achieve those sales?

Zero-based budgeting can be time consuming, although considering budgets from previous years and comparing actual to budget can highlight any trends and give you some information to begin with. You can use zero-based budgeting along with a top-down or bottom-up approach.

Rolling budgets

Most budgets are fixed, covering a quarter or a *fiscal* (financial) year. Establishing them can be arduous, taking several drafts before they're approved. Continual change, market volatility, increased competition and so on all make setting annual budgets challenging, as some assumptions become irrelevant and other unknown factors enter the equation. In fact, some financial experts are questioning whether annual budgeting, which began in the 1950s, is even viable in the 21st century.

Some organisations have turned to *rolling budgets*, also called *continuous budgets* or *perpetual budgets*. These can easily reflect change because you add a new budget as each budget period (usually a month) ends; for example, at the end of June, you add a budget for the forthcoming June and adjust the intervening months as necessary. This way, you always have a budget that extends 12 months into the future and incorporates changes to the operating environment, revenue and expenses. You can continually revise your budgeting assumptions and budgeting model and keep your rolling budget up to date and realistic.

There is no such thing as a stand-alone budget. Imagine a production budget that is easily achievable, say 100 units a month. Now imagine a sales budget that is just wishful thinking, of 100 units a month, when the most the sales force can realistically achieve is 60 units a month. You would end up producing 100 units and perhaps paying a bonus to the manufacturing team but selling only 60 units. Think about what this would do to your cash flow!

Balance sheets

The balance sheet, or statement of financial position, shows the organisation's financial position at a specific date:

- *assets:* what it owns – buildings, cash, stock, etc. plus accounts receivable (accounts receivable is sometimes referred to as *debtors* or *trade debtors*)

- *liabilities:* what it owes – accounts payable, loans, etc.
- **equity**: the difference between assets and liabilities (i.e. assets minus liabilities), which are listed on its balance sheet; this means equity is the investment in the organisation by its owners.

In small businesses, the equity belongs to the owner(s) or partners; in government enterprises, the equity belongs to the government; and in an NFP entity, the equity is owned by the registered NFP company.

 IN PRACTICE

How equity grows

You borrow money from a bank (a liability) to purchase a house (an asset). Your equity (the difference between the value of the asset and the liability) is the deposit you contributed. As you pay off the loan and as the value of the house increases, your equity increases.

Assets include **fixed assets**, those that are expected to last more than a year, such as buildings and equipment, and **current assets** such as inventory, the money in your bank account and accounts receivable (since you can expect to receive them in less than a year); together, these are known as **tangible assets**. In many organisations, **intangible assets**, those that do not have a physical (tangible) presence, such as corporate image, capabilities, designs, goodwill and **intellectual capital**, are key **drivers of success** (in many countries – but not Australia – brand can be valued and is an important contributor to the value of an organisation's intangible assets). As important drivers of success, intangible assets also have value. However, they must meet strict criteria under accounting standards in order to have value reliably attributed.

Organisations are required to produce a balance sheet at the end of each financial year. Table 17.4 shows a simplified balance sheet. What does it tell you about Acme's financial position?

TABLE 17.4 Acme Services Ltd balance sheet

BALANCE SHEET FOR ACME SERVICES LTD 30 June 2023	
ASSETS	$
Current assets	
Cash and cash equivalents	30 000
Inventory	60 000
Receivables	10 000
	100 000
Non-current assets	
Buildings and land	2 000 000
Fixtures and fittings, equipment	100 000
	2 100 000
TOTAL ASSETS	2 200 000

BALANCE SHEET FOR ACME SERVICES LTD 30 June 2023	
ASSETS	$
LIABILITIES	
Current liabilities	
Creditors (payables)	50 000
Non-current liabilities	
Loan	250 000
TOTAL LIABILITIES	300 000
NET ASSETS	1 900 000
Represented by:	
OWNER'S EQUITY	
Shareholder equity	1 900 000

Income statements

An income statement, also called a profit/loss account and a statement of financial performance, shows income received as *gross income* or *revenue* (money earned), usually at the top of the statement, and expenditure (money spent) for a specific period. The difference is the *net income* (or loss). This shows the *profit* (or surplus), or loss, for the period (i.e. a week, month, quarter or year). The difference between money earned and money owed shows how much money is available, which assists in the planning and decision-making. Table 17.5 shows an example of an income statement.

TABLE 17.5 Acme Services Ltd income statement

ACME SERVICES LTD Statement of Financial Performance Year ended 30 June 2023		
Income	$	
Gross sales	4 562 500	
Less sales returns and allowances	2 500	
NET SALES	4 560 000	
Cost of sales		
Beginning inventory	80 000	
Stock purchases (including freight)	3 025 000	
Total goods available for sale	3 105 000	
Less stock inventory at year end	(60 000)	
Cost of goods sold	3 045 000	
GROSS PROFIT	1 515 000	33.2% of gross sales

ACME SERVICES LTD Statement of Financial Performance Year ended 30 June 2023		
Income	$	
Operating expenses		
Repairs & maintenance	40 000	
Consumables & office supplies	11 000	
Interest on loans	14 000	
Depreciation	20 000	
Wages	970 000	
Utilities expense	105 000	
Total operating expenses	1 160 000	
NET PROFIT before taxes	355 000	7.8% of gross sales
Income tax expense	(106 500)	
NET PROFIT after tax	**248 500**	

Most organisations use the *accrual accounting system* that shows income for sales (even when payment hasn't yet been received) and expenditure (even when the items incurring the expense haven't been paid for). In organisations using the *cash accounting system*, revenue is only recognised when it is actually received and expenses when they are actually paid.

Profit

We usually calculate profit in two stages:

1 *Gross profit:* sales revenue less the cost of the goods or services sold (COGS). COGS is the opening stock (or inventory) plus direct costs minus closing stock. This shows you how much you earn per dollar of sales and how well you are controlling purchasing and payroll costs.
2 *Net profit:* gross profit plus any other income after deducting operating expenses.

The comprehensive income statement

Comprehensive income includes net income (i.e. total earnings) plus other items not included in the income statement because they have not been realised, such as gains or losses from foreign currency transactions and unsold bonds.

Cash flow statements

We've seen that the balance sheet reports the assets, liabilities and equity at a point in time (usually the end of the reporting period), and that the income statement reports the sources of income and expenses over a period of time. The three financial statements, the balance sheet, income statement and cash flow statement, are related. Table 17.6 shows how Acme's cash flow statement, shown in Table 17.7, is built from its balance sheet and income statement.

TABLE 17.6 Sources of entries for Table 17.7

Entry	Source
Net profit after tax	Table 17.5
Depreciation	Table 17.5
Decrease in accounts receivable	Table 17.4 from $20 000 to $10 000 in 2023
Increase in accounts payable	Table 17.4 from $350 000 to $250 000 in 2023
Decrease in inventory	Table 17.4 from $80 000 to $60 000 in 2023
Acquisition of fixtures and fittings, equipment	Table 17.4 from $120 000 to $200 000 in 2023
Loan repayment	Table 17.4 from $350 000 to $250 000 in 2023

TABLE 17.7 Acme Services Ltd cash flow statement

ACME SERVICES LTD Cash Flow Statement Year ended 30 June 2023		
Cash flows from operations		
Net profit after tax		$248 500
Adjustments (for accruals and non-cash items)		
Add: Depreciation	$20 000	
Add: Decrease in accounts receivable	10 000	
Add: Increase in accounts payable	300 000	
Less: Decrease in inventory	(20 000)	310 000
Cash inflow from operations		558 500
Cash outflow from investing activities		
Acquisition of fixtures and fittings, equipment		(80 000)
Cash outflow from financing activities		
Loan repayment		(100 000)
NET CASH INFLOW FOR THE YEAR		408 500

Cash flow statements help you manage your cash because they tell you what the actual cash inflows (money coming in, e.g. through sales, money borrowed and money earned from investments) and outflows (money going out) were for the period. Cash flow statements also show any changes from previous periods.

Inflows and outflows are shown in the following categories:

- cash flows from operations
- cash flows from financing activities (sources of capital – taking or paying off loans or issuing shares)
- cash flows from investing activities (buying or selling assets such as furnishings and equipment but not stock for resale).

Cash flows from operations are relatively easy to determine with accounting systems that generate revenues received and expenses paid. Unfortunately, most don't do this. Instead, they report revenue earned and expenses incurred that took place at the date of the transaction.

INDUSTRY INSIGHTS

What do the figures tell us about Acme?

From **Table 17.5**, you can see that while Acme's net profit after tax was only $248 500, its cash flow for the year was a healthy $408 500. This shows the company made considerable progress in its financial situation during the year. Cash flow is critical in terms of a company's capacity to meet current expenses and to invest and repay loans. From **Table 17.4**, you can see that at year end 2023, there was $10 000 less in accounts receivable than at the start of the year; this is because money was received from customers who paid their accounts on credit. Accounts payable were $300 000 lower, indicating that trading conditions improved and the company was in a better position in 2023 to pay its creditors. In addition, $20 000 less was tied up in inventory. The major contribution to cash flow was from Acme's core operations ($558 500). Being a *trading company* (one selling a range of products) allowed it to invest $80 000 in fixtures, fittings and equipment and pay off $100 000 from its loan.

Working with cash flow statements

Transferable skills

1.1 Financial literacy

A strong cash flow is a sign of a healthy organisation. Some information you can interpret from cash flow statements includes:

- An increase in accounts receivable means you have increased your credit sales and decreased your cash sales; a decrease in accounts receivable means more customers are paying you in cash; an increase or decrease could also mean that your business has expanded or retracted.
- An increase in accounts payable means you've taken on more debt; a decrease in accounts payable means you've paid off debt.
- An increase in inventory means you have purchased more stock and have less cash; a decrease in inventory means you have more cash and have sold more stock than you purchased.
- An increase in non-current assets means you have less money due to acquiring assets; a decrease in non-current assets means you have more money from selling; for example, some plant and equipment.

Costs

Costs measure resources (usually in terms of money) given up to produce something or achieve an objective. Costs include effort, materials, opportunities forgone, time spent and utilities consumed. Cost is an important consideration for every leader-manager in every sector of the economy.

Understanding costs

Transferable skills

1.1 Financial literacy

You need to understand the components, or elements of cost, incurred in providing goods or services so that you can monitor and control finances. The three main elements of cost are shown in **Figure 17.2**. From this figure, you can see that costs fall into two categories:

- **Direct costs**: traceable to a specific cost centre, or item. You incur them when you make a product or deliver a service. They include labour and materials to produce the product or service plus the price of any products on-sold to customers.

- **Indirect costs**: not tied, or traceable to a particular cost centre, product or service, but are part of the ordinary running of an organisation and benefit the entire organisation. They include expenses like bank fees and charges, rent, stationery, utilities, and wages for administrative and other services staff. The total of all indirect costs is often called *overheads*.

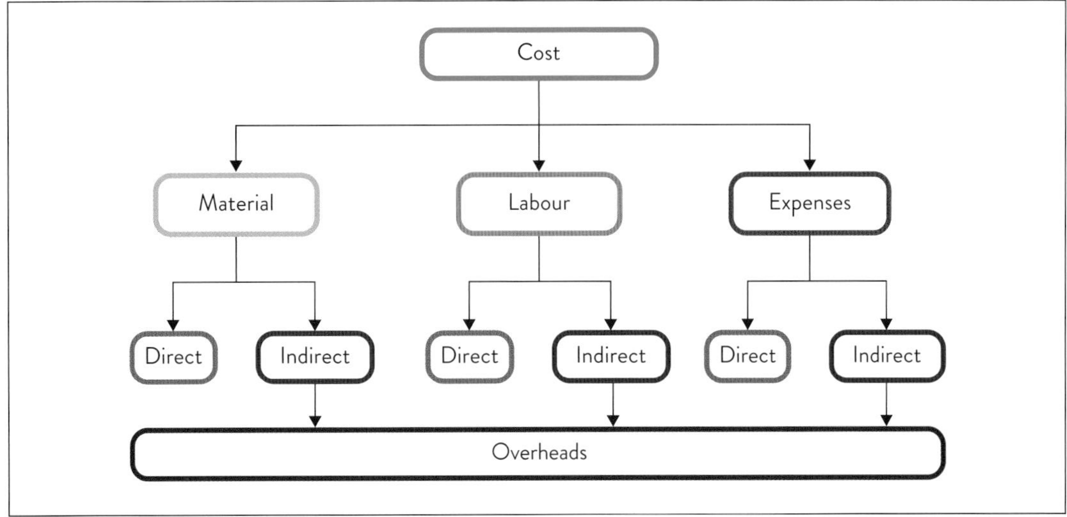

FIGURE 17.2 The three main elements of cost

Costs can also be fixed or variable. **Fixed costs** are fixed for a specific period of time – they don't change, no matter how many products or services you produce or however much revenue you earn (or don't earn). They are the price you pay for running an organisation. For example, rent is often set for a year and paid monthly; insurance covers a specified period, usually a year. *Depreciation* (the reduction in the value of an asset over time, due to obsolescence, 'wear and tear', etc.), is also a fixed cost. The higher your productivity and performance, the lower your fixed costs for each product or service you produce, which increases your profits.

You can't do much about fixed costs but you can really make your mark with the variable costs attached to your team or function. Unlike fixed costs, which are time related, **variable costs** are volume, or activity, related. Variable costs go up or down depending on how many products or services you produce – more output results in higher variable costs, less output lowers the variable costs. The wages of employees that directly produce the product or service and the materials used in the production of products or services are variable costs. You can reduce many of your variable costs by negotiating lower payments for them, which increases your profits.

Just to confuse matters, there are also *semi-variable costs*. These are costs that are fixed for a certain level of production or sales and become variable once that level is reached. (Think of your phone bill, where you might pay a fixed amount every month but if you use it too much, the variable cost kicks in.)

Spreading the costs – the advantages of sharing

An owner of a large café and a smaller delicatessen in different locations in the same street decides to merge operations on the advice of the accountant who reviewed the financial statement that follows.

	Delicatessen	Café	Total
Sales	$1100 000	$850 000	$1950 000
Cost of goods sold	$500 000	$350 000	$850 000
Gross profit	$600 000	$500 000	$1 100 000
Wages	$200 000	$300 000	$500 000
Electricity	$50 000	$70 000	$120 000
Administration	$50 000	$50 000	$100 000
Rent	$50 000	$75 000	$125 000
Other expenses	$25 000	$25 000	$50 000
Profit/(loss)	**$225 000**	**($20 000)**	**$205 000**

The market value of the two businesses is $1 000 000 for the delicatessen and $100 000 for the café. The owner had considered selling the café, but the accountant recommended relocating the deli to join the larger premises of the less profitable café. The accountant made the following projection of income and expenditure:

	Merged operation
Sales	$1950 000
Cost of goods sold	$750 000
Gross profit	$1200 000
Wages	$400 000
Electricity	$80 000
Administration	$65 000
Rent	$50 000
Other expenses	$40 000
Relocation and fit-out expenses	$75 000
Profit/loss	**$395 000**

Accepting the assumptions made by the accountant are correct, can you work out what has changed the financial situation for the owner?[2]

Types of costs

We can control some costs, such as direct labour and material costs, and some indirect costs, such as stationery, temporary employees and contractors. You want to pay attention to your *controllable costs* and any variances against your budget. *Uncontrollable costs* are those that you can't easily change, such as insurance, rent and other overheads.

Standard costs are estimated costs for producing goods or services under normal conditions for later comparison with actual costs. *Sunk costs* refer to costs incurred that you can't recover; rent paid, whether fixed or semi-variable, is an example of a sunk cost. *Non-monetary costs* are qualitative and can be difficult to put a dollar value on. They are sometimes called implicit costs, as opposed to the explicit monetary cost of a resource or action. **Opportunity cost** refers to the value of the benefits you give up by taking one course of action over another.

17.2 Planning your financial management approach

Performance stands out like a tonne of diamonds. Non-performance can always be explained away.

Harold S. Geneen and Alvin Moscow, *Managing*, Doubleday, 1984.

Financial plans help you predict what money will *come into* the organisation (income) and what it needs to *spend* to keep the organisation running smoothly (expenses). In this way, financial plans help you take control of your money so that you aren't caught out; for example, by not having enough money coming in to cover the amount of your bills, which can happen even to profitable businesses.

A financial plan includes a forecast (prediction, or estimate) of profit and loss or expenditure and income, a forecast of cash flow, a forecast balance sheet, and an understanding of where your expenses equal your income – your *break-even point*. These forecasts can be monthly, quarterly or yearly and once you have them, you can set sales targets, pricing and profit margins.

Organisations base their financial plans on past performance; on what they think is going to happen in the external, or operating, environment; and on market trends, industry benchmarks and market research. They task individual managers throughout the organisation with monitoring the forecasts that apply to their teams or departments to ensure they meet expectations.

What financial policies, procedures, goals and budgets should the organisation establish to help it fulfil its mission and meet its strategic goals? Developing financial plans falls to different groups in the organisation. Figure 17.3 shows an example of the hierarchical structure of a large manufacturing organisation focusing on people's financial responsibilities.

Financial planning involves a number of tasks, including those shown in Figure 17.4. The process is guided by accounting standards set by the Australian Accounting Standards Board (AASB) and the Australian Securities and Investments Commission (ASIC); various accounting organisations, such as Chartered Accountants Australia and New Zealand, CPA Australia and the Institute of Public Accountants, seek to uphold these standards by educating, training and supporting their members and by setting ethical and professional standards.

Transferable skills

1.1 Financial literacy

1.4 Business operations

2.3 Business strategy

3.1 Teamwork/relationships

3.2 Verbal communication

3.3 Written communication

3.4 Leadership

As a leader-manager, you probably establish plans and procedures to guide your team in dealing with finances and to help them achieve or stay within budgets. Make sure they're aligned to the organisation's mission, policies and strategies. You can also help your team members attain a broad understanding of financial management to ensure they are aware of and are able to work with relevant aspects of any financial plans that affect their performance. (When you need to, draw on your understanding of your organisation's structure for who to contact in relation to financial matters.)

You can plan your financial management approach at work much as you do your household budget:

- What money comes in (income) and what goes out (expenditure)?
- Which expenses does everyone share (indirect costs) and which relate directly to a specific person/department/team or activity (direct costs)?
- When does the money come in, when must expenses be paid and how should payments be made?

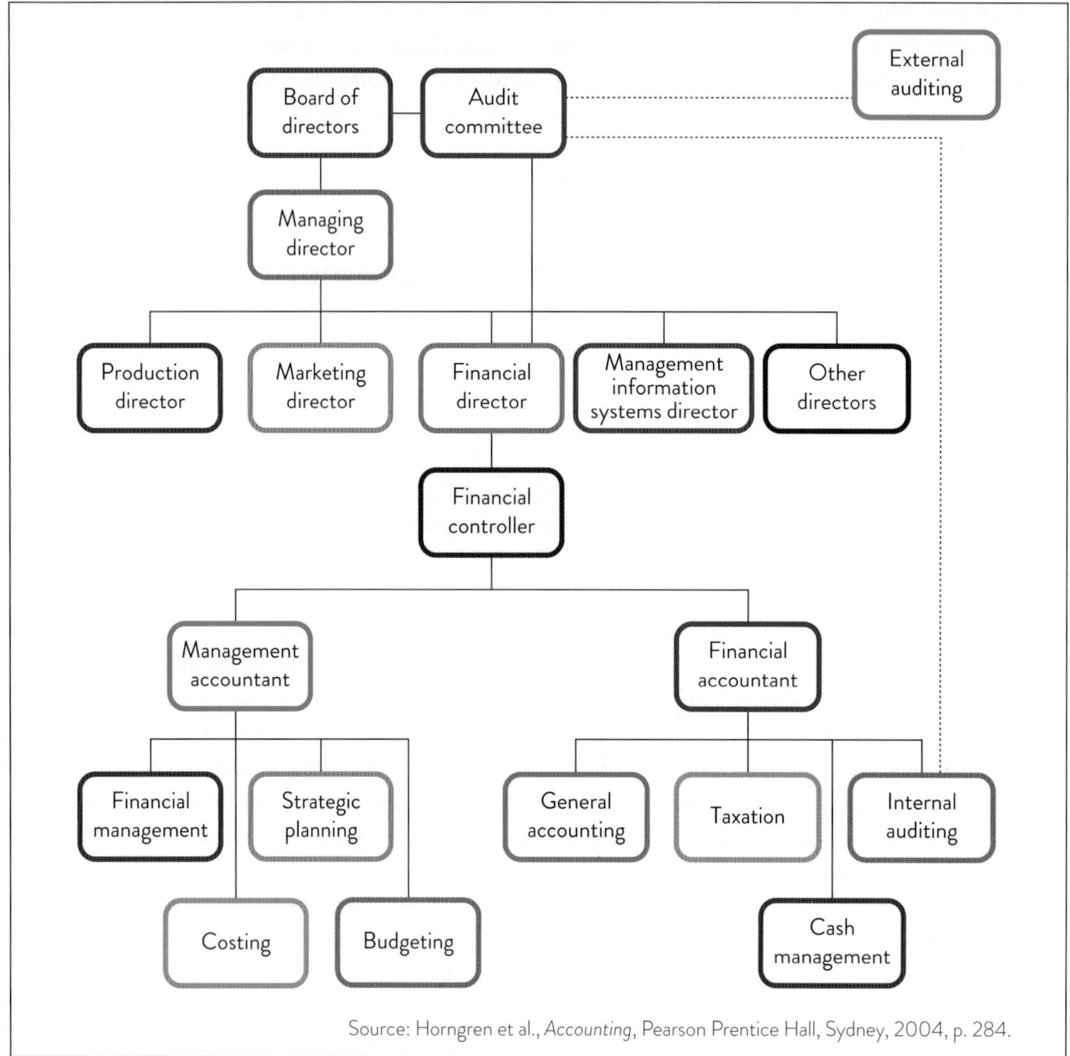

Source: Horngren et al., *Accounting*, Pearson Prentice Hall, Sydney, 2004, p. 284.

FIGURE 17.3 Organisational hierarchy showing financial responsibilities

- Which expenses are flexible and why, and which can be negotiated?
- How can you deal with unexpected expenses (contingencies) that arise?
- How should you share this budget information so that others know what is going on?

When you think through and carefully plan how you finance your operations, you help create stability for the organisation. Implementing, controlling and reviewing your financial plans ensures they serve their purpose. **Figure 17.5** shows some of the skills you need to do this, and **Figure 17.6** shows some of the tasks you and your team members apply these skills to.

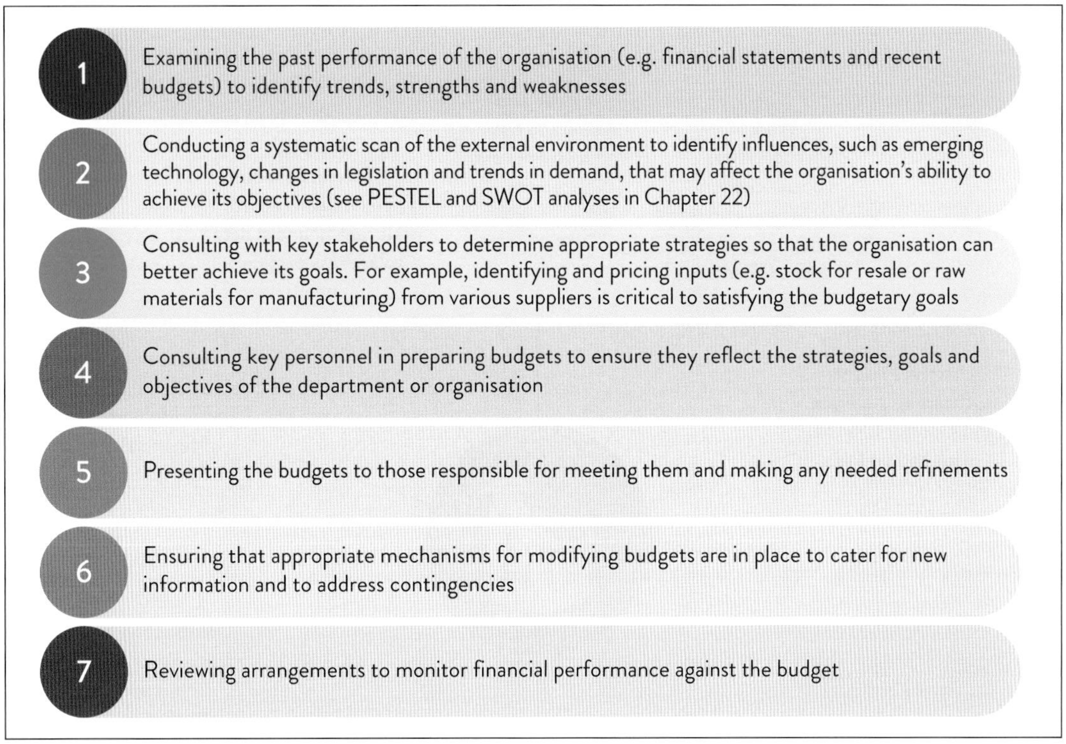

1 Examining the past performance of the organisation (e.g. financial statements and recent budgets) to identify trends, strengths and weaknesses

2 Conducting a systematic scan of the external environment to identify influences, such as emerging technology, changes in legislation and trends in demand, that may affect the organisation's ability to achieve its objectives (see PESTEL and SWOT analyses in Chapter 22)

3 Consulting with key stakeholders to determine appropriate strategies so that the organisation can better achieve its goals. For example, identifying and pricing inputs (e.g. stock for resale or raw materials for manufacturing) from various suppliers is critical to satisfying the budgetary goals

4 Consulting key personnel in preparing budgets to ensure they reflect the strategies, goals and objectives of the department or organisation

5 Presenting the budgets to those responsible for meeting them and making any needed refinements

6 Ensuring that appropriate mechanisms for modifying budgets are in place to cater for new information and to address contingencies

7 Reviewing arrangements to monitor financial performance against the budget

FIGURE 17.4 Seven elements of financial planning

The benefits, principles and steps of budgeting

Budgets guide people's actions by setting goals (e.g. a sales budget) or constraints (e.g. a wages budget). For example, in top-down budgeting, top-level and senior management decide what the organisation should achieve in financial terms over, say, the next three years. These strategic goals and plans flow through the organisation's various functions. Eventually, they are translated into operational goals and plans that cascade to each leader-manager: How much can my team spend on travel? How many employees can I engage, what can I afford to pay them and how much can I spend to train them? Can we buy or upgrade our equipment this year?

Good budgeting doesn't just answer questions. Some other benefits of budgeting are that it:

- gives focus to people's efforts
- helps people measure their performance
- helps you think about and plan your operations
- sets standards and targeted performance levels
- sets some planning and control procedures in motion
- helps you better understand your own organisation's performance
- motivates people to action
- helps you coordinate activities.

Above all, budgets need to be:

- achievable, so that people put in the effort needed to achieve them
- comprehensive, so that all aspects of the organisation's operations are covered
- coordinated, so that the entire organisation is pointing in the same direction.

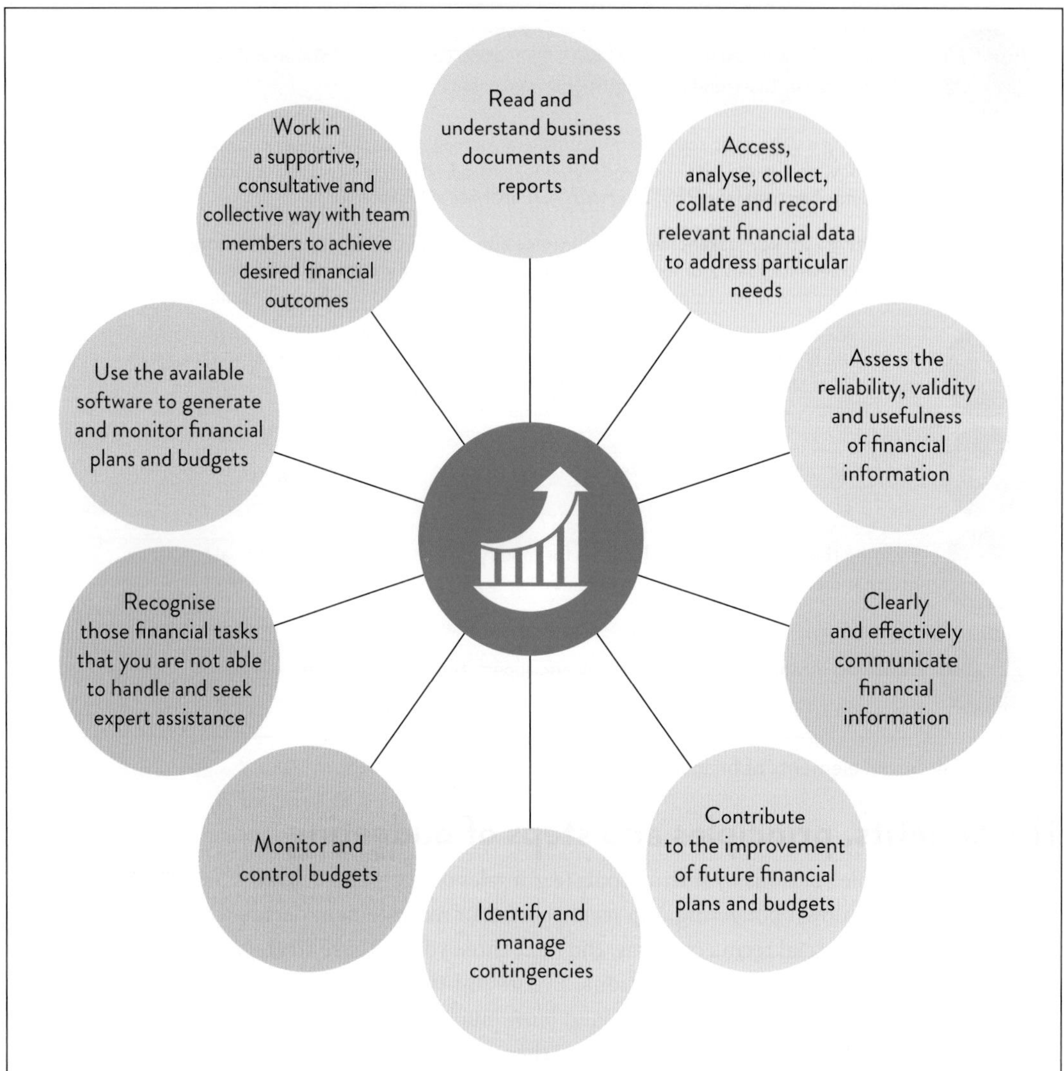

FIGURE 17.5 Do you have the financial proficiencies you need?

Let's look at preparing an achievable, comprehensive and coordinated sales budget as an example. You would first think about the main influences on sales, such as:

- the economic climate
- government influence
- your organisation's pricing policy
- seasonal variations in sales
- what you achieved last year and what has changed since then.

Then you might estimate:

- at what price units are to be sold
- revenue from sales
- sales commissions or fees.

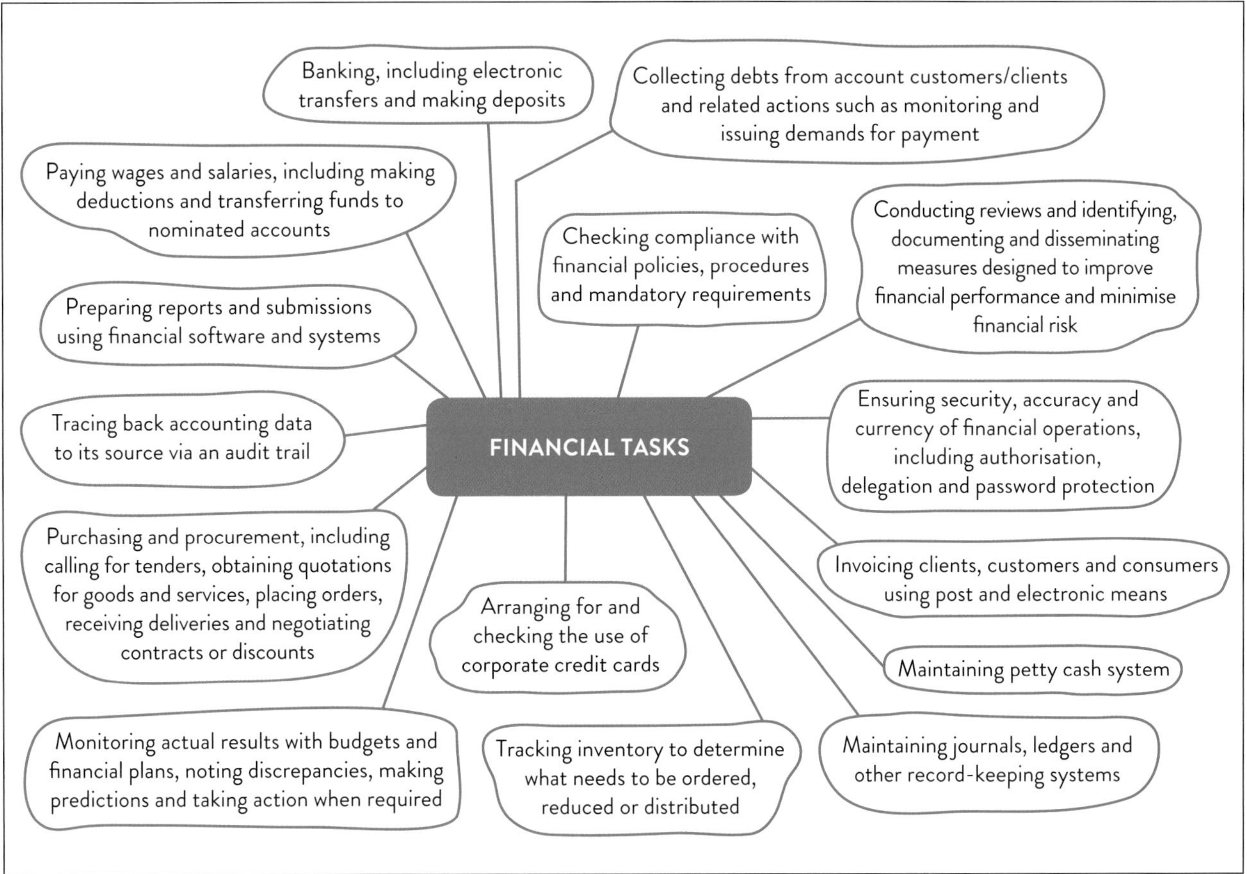

FIGURE 17.6 Some common financial and related tasks performed or overseen by leader-managers

You would also need to consider:

- the capacity of the business to produce what you sell
- advertising
- credit policy
- competition.

Once the sales budget is agreed, you can produce a production budget; when you have that, you can develop budgets for factory overheads, direct labour and direct materials. Then you could develop a cost of goods sold budget, reflecting those other budgets.

Of course, not all budgets are great budgets. They might be set by management without the input of the people who are to carry them out; they might be based on the last budget without taking into account changing circumstances; or they might be very optimistic (known as 'stargazing'). They might be inflexible or even invite waste ('We have to spend all our budget or we'll lose it next year').

Figure 17.7 outlines eight budgeting principles and Figure 17.8 illustrates the seven steps in the budgeting process.

FIGURE 17.7 Eight budgeting principles

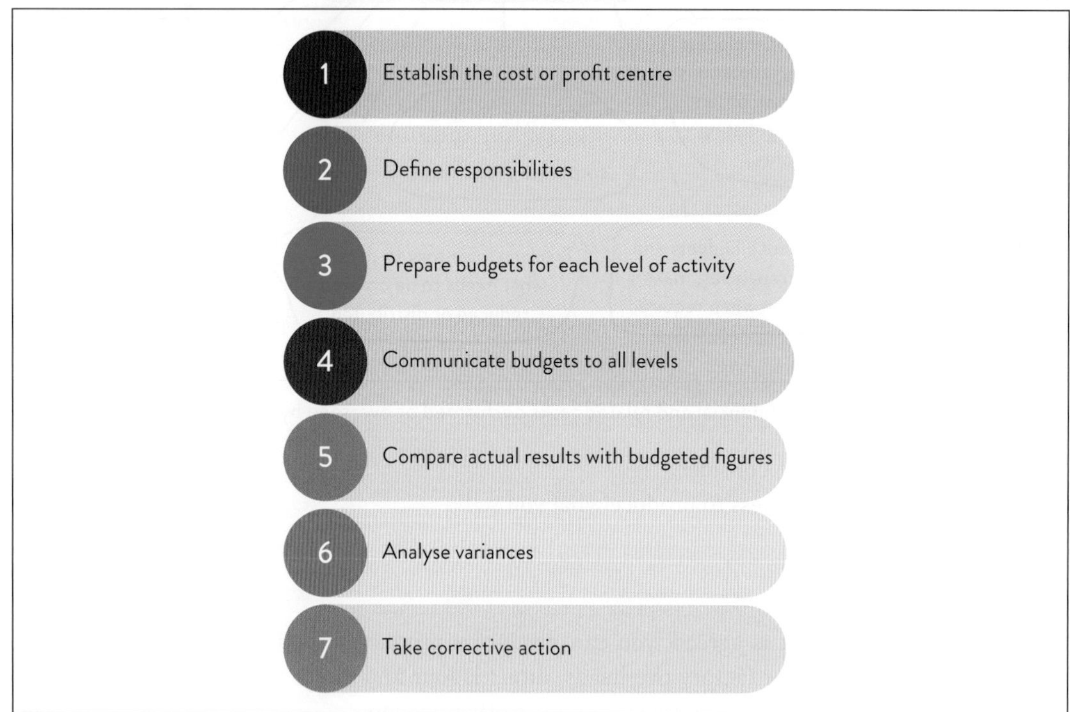

FIGURE 17.8 Seven steps to budgeting

Develop a budget

Transferable skills

3.1 Teamwork/ relationships

When you are tasked with developing or drafting budgets for your work team, consult with your team and others who can offer input, such as a budget committee. Feel free to use last year's figures – but only as a guide. You can also review the last few years' figures to see if you can spot any trends. Few things in organisations are static, as you learnt in Chapter 1, so don't just use last year's figures and add a percentage that you pluck from the air.

You might want to use some 'what if' questions to prepare two or three alternative budgets showing sales at 10 per cent higher and lower than anticipated, or if your costs are increasing or reducing by 10 per cent. (Know why you select a particular percentage, too.) Conduct a SWOT and/or PESTEL analysis, as described in Chapter 22, when you need to. Make sure you involve the right people and your budgets are realistic.

Think through the targets you are budgeting. When you set a budget that's easily achievable, you've lost your opportunity to motivate your team. On the other hand, the quickest way to deflate your team is to set a budget that's just wishful thinking. When you set a 'stretch budget', be sure to communicate this to your work team so they know that this budget is a little bit beyond their reach unless they 'stretch' themselves to achieve it.

Transferable skills

3.1 Teamwork/ relationships

Present your budget for approval

Use your organisation's budgeting templates or software and think about the person or people who approve them: how much detail do they want? Do they want 'what if?' scenarios? Would visual displays such as **bar charts**, graphs or **pie charts** help? What narrative describing how your proposed budget meshes with the organisation's strategy and goals would help your budget win approval? (You can find out more about presenting your ideas in Chapters 7 and 8.)

Transferable skills

2.3 Business strategy

Clarify budgets

Budgets and financial plans are usually prepared or finalised by the chief financial officer based on the draft budgets from each cost and profit centre and after a web of give-and-take discussions with managers across the organisation. The particular budgets and financial plans you and your team work to or work within depend on your team's purpose and objectives. A sales team needs different budgets and financial plans than marketing teams and distribution teams. A sales team's key budget, for example, is a sales budget that includes targets for sales over a specific period, which are used in the team's monthly performance reports comparing the actual with the target sales.

Make sure the expected outcomes are accurate, achievable and comprehensible. A plan that can't be easily understood has limited usefulness, so when reviewing budgets and plans, note any difficulties in understanding their precise meaning. A lot of questions can suggest that the plan needs more work.

To assess achievability, consider past performance, available resources and other constraints, and the anticipated internal and external operating environments. When assessing accuracy, check that all estimates of costs are current, that foreshadowed changes have been taken into account and that there are no omissions. The accuracy of forecasts can sometimes be critical; for example, trading companies need to consider changes in the value of the Australian dollar (AUD) because it affects the value of exported and imported goods and services.

Should you buy it?

How do you know whether a purchase (e.g. a software upgrade, an office refurbishment, new equipment) is worth making? You can put a dollar value on its expected benefits or anticipated profits and divide this figure by its cost and then multiply the result by 100 to show it as a percentage. This is known as *return on investment*, or ROI. Any positive ROI is usually considered a good return because it shows that returns exceed costs. A negative number means your investment costs you money. You then need to work out whether the non-monetary benefits are worth making the investment.

For example, you are wondering whether to purchase an indoor barbecue for your restaurant. It costs $2000 but you expect it can generate additional annual profits of $3000. Here's your ROI calculation:

$$3000 \div 2000 \times 100 = 150\% \text{ in the first year}$$

It looks like a good investment, provided you haven't been overly optimistic in estimating the additional profits it brings.

Changes, like office improvements that you think might increase motivation and productivity and reduce **absenteeism** and **attrition**, might not be easy to put an instant monetary value on, but the benefits will likely pay off later, and last for a long time.

Negotiate changes

Discuss any needed changes you identify with your manager and other relevant people in the organisation. The type of changes you believe you need determines who to consult; for example, financial concerns are usually discussed with the accountant or finance manager. When you need to discuss your budget, be clear on the manager's budget responsibilities – whether they have had a role in preparing the budget and whether it is a cost or a profit centre – because this may influence how they view the budget and therefore how you present your case.

Transferable skills

2.1 Critical thinking

2.3 Business strategy

3.1 Teamwork/relationships

Although there is usually pressure to negotiate changes within a timeline, take care to prepare your case by gathering supporting evidence and information. Be aware of the bigger picture and think about the upstream and downstream effects of any changes you request on other parts of the organisation. When your recommended variations affect other parts of the organisation, consult with the leader-managers of those areas; for example, if your team provides services such as marketing or information technology, you would want to discuss any changes with the managers of those areas.

Use the **ask 'Why?' five times** technique as you think through your reasons for requesting a budget change. This helps you to:

- make sure your request is objective
- make sure your request is accurate, relevant and realistic
- understand the effects on other areas of your requested changes
- develop a strong negotiating position.

When it seems unlikely that your negotiations for changes in your budget or other plans will succeed, begin planning how your team can best work towards achieving the financial plans. For example, when your expenses budget is reduced, actions might include reducing overtime, delaying purchases, running down inventory, identifying more efficient ways to work, and hiring more junior and less costly staff when filling vacancies. You could draw up a list of possible actions to discuss with your team or work with them to brainstorm some.

Approval for changes rests with a designated senior manager who must balance internal and external pressures and uncertainties and keep a range of stakeholders happy. The bigger the changes you request, the more difficulty you're likely to experience in having them accepted. Changes needed because of inaccuracy are more likely to be accepted than changes based on achievability. Different factors can all come into play when attempting to reach an acceptable decision, such as competing demands from different parts of the organisation; differing views of how the strategic directions of top-level management should be executed; difficulties in making accurate projections of the time needed to get new equipment and technologies up and running, and the amount of training staff need to operate new equipment and technology; and internal politics. (You can find out more about negotiating persuasively in Chapter 7.)

Senior management will approve and disseminate the final budgets and financial plans, once requests for changes have been discussed and reviewed for consistency with the organisation's overall strategy, policies and goals.

Develop plans and contingency plans

Plan how to achieve your budgets with the available resources and within the specified timeframes, as described in Chapter 20. The way you plan (and implement) your financial approach depends on the type of budget and plans you work with. Whether or not you involve your team, and the degree to which you involve them, depends on a number of factors, including the need for confidentiality and the team's skills and interest in becoming involved. (For more on when and how to involve your team, see Chapters 20 and 26.)

Transferable skills

1.4 Business operations

3.4 Leadership

Whether you are planning for and monitoring chargeable hours, customer numbers, productivity, profit, return on investment, sales, sales returns, wastage or any number of factors that come together to create a successful organisation, you also need to identify the many ways your plans can come unstuck and how you could deal with those possibilities. Some of the many events that can throw your plans and budgets off course are shown in Figure 17.9. The risk factors for your plans and budgets depend on the nature of your team's work. (For more on identifying potential problems, see the sections on force-field analysis in Chapters 20 and 27.)

Transferable skills

2.1 Critical thinking

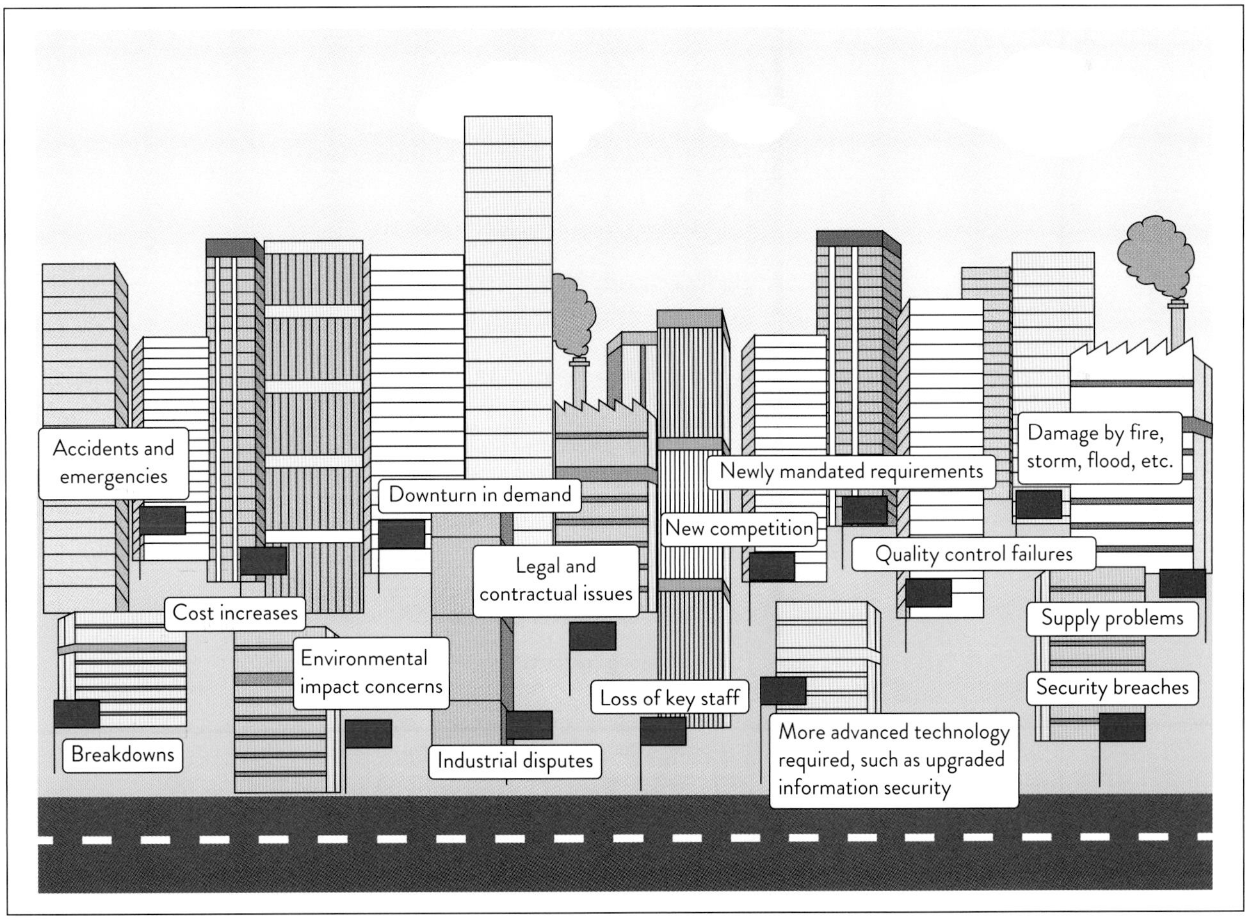

FIGURE 17.9 A multitude of risks

When you understand the organisation's internal and external risk environments, you can identify the risks that could throw your budget off course, analyse their likelihood and consequences and decide how best to deal with them. When you can't prevent them from occurring, develop contingency plans for the most significant risks. (This is explained in Chapter 22.)

Transferable skills

1.4 Business operations

Transferable skills

1.1 Financial literacy

2.1 Critical thinking

3.1 Teamwork/relationships

3.2 Verbal communication

3.3 Written communication

Contingency plans describe what actions to take should your monitoring show that you aren't meeting your budgets or your other financial plans aren't working as expected. Contingency planning is proactive. It enables you to take sensible action when the need arises. Knowing what to do, when and how to do it, who is to do what, and why, is your due diligence. It protects the organisation and gives you peace of mind. For example, when your team has essential deadlines to meet, you might ask all team members to report their progress at regular intervals and identify any risks of hold-ups and their likely impact; you might also develop a contingency plan to use temporary employees to cover an unexpected, short-term need for additional staff. In the finance area, you might arrange access to a bank overdraft should an unexpected cash flow problem occur. For your cash flow budgeting, you would develop and apply sound debt control policies and receive accurate, up-to-date information on who has not yet paid their bill so you can follow up payment. Figure 17.10 shows some other examples of contingency plans.

- Adopting proactive approaches to maintenance
- Coaching and mentoring
- Contracting out or outsourcing functions or tasks
- Diversifying range of services or products
- Finding cheaper sources of raw materials or consumables
- Increasing sales or production
- Negotiating new deadlines
- Recycling and reusing waste and other materials
- Reducing costs, wastage, stock or consumables
- Renegotiating contracts
- Rental, hire purchase or alternative ways to procure required materials, equipment and stock
- Restructuring to reduce labour costs
- Seeking further funding to cover shortfalls
- Specifying timeframes in service contracts
- Succession planning for key personnel

FIGURE 17.10 Examples of contingency plans

A close call

Meera, an accountant in a small enterprise, was reviewing the insurance policies the business carried. 'Let's just see,' she thought, picking up the phone to call her broker. 'What would it cost to insure for the cost of rewriting our financial records?'

Hearing the answer, she signed up immediately because she could fit the cost into her budget. When the office burned down three weeks later, Meera was a hero.

17.3 Implementing your financial management approach

> Finance is the art of passing currency from hand to hand until it finally disappears.
>
> Robert W. Sarnoff

Good planning is one thing; effective implementation is another. Figure 17.11 shows the three elements of effective implementation – circulate the plans to your team, support your team, and determine and obtain the needed resources.

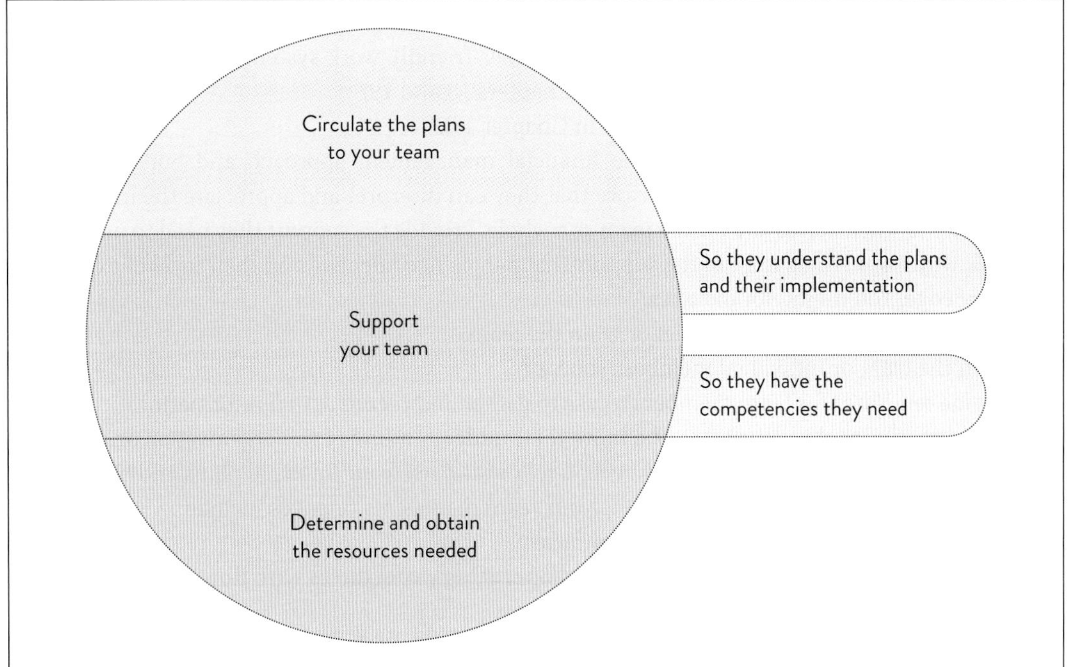

FIGURE 17.11 The three elements of effective financial implementation

Circulate the plans to your team

Transferable skills
3.1 Teamwork/relationships
3.2 Verbal communication
3.3 Written communication

Once you've decided what information is relevant in helping your team members work with the financial plans and budgets, you can decide how much detail the team needs; that is, who gets what information, how often and in what format. You can circulate the financial information to your team in several ways. You could, for example, hold a briefing meeting, send a team email, customise the information you are distributing for individual team members, or provide electronic access to the financial information they need.

Transferable skills

3.3 Written communication

5.2 Technology use

Discuss the format they prefer financial information to be provided in. This depends on the team's familiarity with financial planning and the types of plans you use. Select a format that is easy to understand at a glance. For example, you could show team targets as a bar chart, with current columns in one colour beside the targets achieved the previous period in a different colour; you could graph expected sales to reflect seasonal trends; and you could use a pie chart to show current against budgeted expenses. Your organisation's software may offer a variety of interesting and easily understandable options, which you can put into a dashboard of key financial information. (Creating dashboards is described in Chapter 21.)

Transferable skills

3.1 Teamwork/relationships

Support your team

Work through the Five Keys explained in Chapter 19 to ensure your team members have the understanding and knowledge they need to attain the performance you expect in their financial tasks. They need to be certain of their roles and responsibilities and understand why they're important, receive advice, guidance and training to carry out their tasks effectively and efficiently and have access to the necessary resources and systems needed to carry out their tasks well. This involves:

- building a team that works well together towards shared goals (discussed in Chapters 13 and 14)
- ensuring your team members have the skills, training and other developmental experiences they need to do their jobs well (discussed in Chapters 19 and 29)
- providing a clear understanding of priorities and how team members' financial duties fit into them (establishing and working to priorities is discussed in Chapter 9)
- providing safe, efficient, sustainable and customer-friendly work systems and procedures, and continually improving them (discussed in Chapters 18 and 19)
- providing well-designed jobs (discussed in Chapter 19).

Make sure everyone understands the financial management approach and budgets and the reasoning behind them. Follow up to ensure that they can interpret and appreciate the implications of the plan – for themselves and for the team as a whole. Provide the support they need to understand and work with them; the nature of the support that people need depends on their level of experience and knowledge. You might, for instance:

- bring in a specialist to advise, brief or train the team
- coach the team or individual members yourself
- provide templates for team members to use to gather and record actual information.

The more you involve your team, the more their understanding of the organisation and its goals increases and the more they are likely to accept, follow and use your financial plans and budgets.

Transferable skills

3.1 Teamwork/relationships

Some other actions you can take to help your team manage its finances include:

- clearly define the financial terms the team uses
- document financial procedures as **standard operating procedures** with **flow charts**, checklists or **job breakdowns**
- encourage team members to acquire relevant financial qualifications
- ensure that the team has a clear understanding of the budget's objectives and how to use and manage the budget
- explain the purpose of the data and record-keeping systems you use
- hold team meetings to gather ideas and share information, especially during the planning phase discussed above
- identify sources of help within the organisation, such as a help desk
- observe and analyse current performance of team members to identify any gaps to be eliminated through training, as described in Chapter 29.

Good training and communication help ensure the budget process is effective, that people receive relevant information and know their required roles, and that the team's financial processes are competently managed.

Determine and obtain the needed resources

You can find a range of information management systems software that can help with a variety of tasks, such as producing financial projections on a spreadsheet, and that help you manage duties such as compliance, finance, human resources and payroll. They can also extract details of financial performance to help you with benchmarking and to make decisions involving value for money for purchasing or using resources.

Good records help keep the wheels of organisations turning. You may find yourself responsible for a variety of records, including some of those shown in Figure 17.12. These are mostly electronic, although some paper-based financial records, such as cash register tapes, cheque stubs and credit card sales receipts, are retained for a limited time for data entry and checking. Many records and other documents that were once placed in suspension files in space-consuming cabinets are now scanned and stored electronically.

Transferable skills
4.1 Data literacy
5.2 Technology use

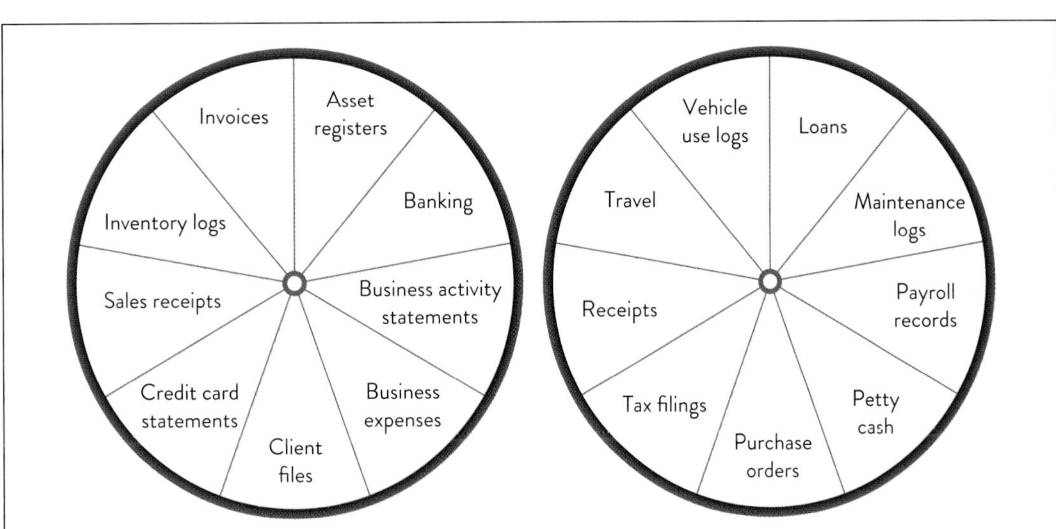

FIGURE 17.12 Types of records

However you keep your records, make sure they are accurate, convenient to access, store and update, comprehensive, cost-effective, reliable, well documented, transparent and able to be tracked. You also need to gather feedback from users and regularly review your record-keeping and storage systems to ensure they meet your organisation's current and emerging needs.

Remember that your team needs time and information to carry out their duties effectively. They also need safe, efficient and sustainable tools and equipment suited to the jobs at hand and amenities and furnishings, as well as appropriate software, record-keeping systems and storage space.

17.4 Monitoring and controlling finances

Watch the costs and the profits will take care of themselves.

Andrew Carnegie, US industrialist and philanthropist, quoted in R. Sobel and D. B. Silicia, *The entrepreneurs – An American adventure*, Houghton Mifflin Harcourt, 1986.

Monitoring and controlling finances revolves around cyclical (weekly, monthly, quarterly, yearly) checking of actual expenditure, assets, cash flow, income, sales and so on to compare what is expected, or budgeted, with the actual amounts. You then need to act on any significant variations you identify. In commercial organisations and government enterprises, the process of controlling finances helps ensure a profit. In NFP organisations, monitoring and controlling is designed to ensure funds are spent as planned and are not over-spent, so that the organisation at least 'breaks even'. (Of course, to ensure the organisation's viability in the short and long term, you need to do better than break even. You need a surplus, or profit, to invest in the business, assist with ongoing cash flow and pay any outstanding bills.)

IN PRACTICE

Cash is king!

Consider **Table 17.8**. What do the figures tell you about the cash flow of the business?

TABLE 17.8 Debtors

Monthly sales	Current (under 30 days)	30+ days	60+ days	90+ days
$302479	$143351	$82849	$52160	$24119
100%	47%	27%	18%	8%

Did you notice:

- 47 per cent of invoice values are less than 30 days old; if they're paid within 30 days, this is excellent
- 27 per cent of invoice values are over 30 days old
- 26 per cent (18% + 8%) of invoice values (over a quarter) are already over 60 days old, including some which are over 90 days old? This requires immediate attention; the money they owe should be in the bank account earning interest, not theirs.

Make sure you have processes in your team to prioritise following up that tardy 26 per cent. Don't just send out a letter; make it someone's responsibility to telephone the customers that owe you money and find out when you can expect payment.

Responsibility for managing, monitoring and controlling finances and budgets is spread across managers at various levels throughout the organisation. Some monitoring is likely to fall to you. What you monitor, and the budgets and reports you use, depend on your team's or unit's function in the organisation. You might provide services to other parts of the organisation and so have costs but no income, so you're a cost centre. In that case, controlling and monitoring your team's costs is an important contribution to your organisation's overall effectiveness. Or you might have both costs and income, so you're a profit centre. This makes continually improving your team's productivity and performance, as well as controlling and managing costs, critical.

Accurate, up-to-date information is essential to spot warning signs and protect your budgets. Use lead indicators rather than lag indicators whenever you can.

Identify team members who have specific roles and responsibilities in controlling finances and to whom you can allocate responsibility for particular financial tasks. For example, perhaps one or two team members could authorise expenditure within specified limits and someone else could undertake banking duties. Provide training and coaching when you need to (as described in Chapter 29).

Transferable skills

3.1 Teamwork/ relationships

Preventing fraud

Fraud is when someone uses false, misleading or deceitful practices in order to obtain money (or other objects of value), claim the accomplishments of others or gain power. Fraud is a risk that can occur in many organisations. There are a lot of ways organisations can control fraud:[3]

- cooperation with prosecution efforts
- customer feedback and complaints
- diligent fraud detection practices
- effective follow up and investigations
- effective oversight
- employee background screening
- fraud deterrent programs
- fraud reporting programs
- independent audits
- separating duties (e.g. authorisation for payments and accounts payable)
- zero tolerance fraud policies.

Control measures that you can take as an individual include:

- checking credit card statements with receipts
- checking purchase orders against stock received and invoices
- clearly communicating policies and procedures
- efficient and frequent recording of financial activities
- quarterly stocktakes
- regular reconciliations of petty cash.

Monitor and control costs

Transferable skills

3.2 Verbal communication

You need a comprehensive system to monitor expenditure and control costs in your team. Explain the system to the team so that everyone understands it and how it helps sustain the viability of the organisation.

To develop the system, work through steps 5 to 7 of the seven steps to budgeting shown in Figure 17.8. You might also want to review the financial procedures used to control finances in the organisation as a whole to make sure your methods are consistent and don't replicate any other monitoring activities.

Use your accounting software system to record the expenses and income relevant to your team and allocate the expenses and income to the relevant cost codes used in the organisation's chart of accounts (discussed in Section 17.1). When transactions are entered using the correct code, the software allocates it to the appropriate account.

Transferable skills

4.1 Data literacy

Measuring performance

Measure performance against controllable factors. A dollar budget is not the only performance measure; for example, hospitals measure bed days and hotels measure bed nights as well as their

financial performance. Other organisational effectiveness measures include corporate responsibility and environmental responsibility ratings, customer satisfaction and complaints, information contained in sick leave records, market share and returned products.

Measures of success or key performance indicators of effectiveness that leader-managers use include measures of absenteeism/attendance, accidents and incidents, attrition, customer satisfaction and productivity.

Use your budgets

Use your budgets – that's what they're there for. They help you:

- measure and report on actual performance
- compare actual performance with budgeted (planned) performance
- determine and implement appropriate action.

Comparing budgeted figures with actual figures gives you feedback on how you're doing and highlights any variances so you can decide whether, and what, corrective action you need to take. You compare what was expected with the actual 'line by line' on your budgets, and when the difference is large enough, you take action to bring the budget back into line. Figure 17.13 lists some ways leader-managers control budget costs and the Industry insights box 'Joan's Dress Shop' gives a retail example of monitoring and controlling finances.

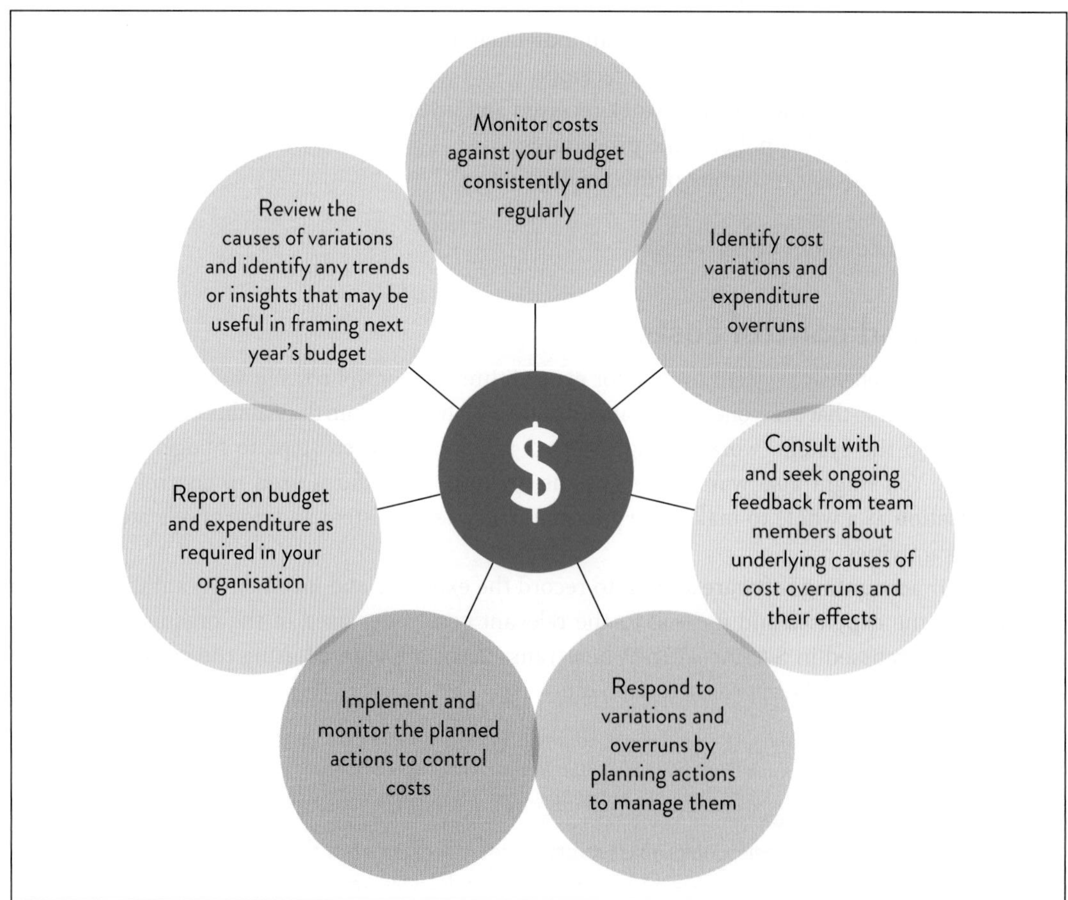

FIGURE 17.13 Seven ways to manage budgeted expenditure

Joan's Dress Shop

Joan owns a dress shop and dry-cleaning agency in a suburban shopping centre. She has set opening hours and permanent as well as casual employees. The shop stocks year-round clothing as well as seasonal fashion lines. We follow Joan as she monitors her financials.

Step 1: Access the relevant financial information

Joan begins by comparing actual expenditure against budget for the month, as shown in Table 17.9, and assessing variations.

TABLE 17.9 Joan's monthly performance report

Monthly performance report: May				
Data	**Budget $**	**Actual $**	**Variance**	**%**
Revenue				
Sales	730 000	680 000	-50 000	-5.5
Expenses				
Cost of goods sold	500 000	480 000	-20 000	-4
Labour	100 000	80 000	-20 000	-20
Overheads	80 000	70 000	-10 000	-12.5
Total expenses	680 000	630 000	-50 000	-7.35
Profit	50 000	50 000	0	

Step 2: Assess variations from budget projections

The budget variance in the May performance report differs between items in both size and significance. Sales are down and *cost of goods sold* (the cost of goods sold = beginning inventory + purchases – ending inventory) was less as a result. The reason the forecast profit was achieved was because Joan controlled her labour costs by reviewing the employee rosters regularly and reducing the hours worked by casual staff, and because overheads were less than budgeted. Joan had also delayed spending on consumables, such as store-branded bags, to lower her immediate outgoings as indicated in the reduced overheads. As retail sales were down by $50 000, the level of unsold stock at the end of the month, which Joan identified from her inventory control spreadsheet, was higher than Joan anticipated.

Step 3: Identify factors influencing the results

After discussions with her permanent staff, Joan notes that the month had been unusually warm and winter clothing was less in demand. Other traders in the shopping centre also had lower sales and felt this was due to a general downward trend in consumer spending. The drop in the volume of dry cleaning came at a period it usually increases, when lighter clothes are cleaned and stored away for winter. Warmer days required less heating and that probably helped reduce overheads, as did the drop in the turnover-based component of the rent, a semi-variable cost. However, payments by credit cards were up substantially, with fewer customers paying with cash, which resulted in higher credit card fees.

When Joan checks her bank statements, she worries about the possible cost of overdraft interest charged when her bank account is overdrawn, as cash flow could be a problem in June. She thinks she could mitigate that problem by delaying some new stock purchases.

Step 4: Pinpoint specific areas needing attention and identify possible actions

Joan considers what changes are most likely to bring performance in line with the budget. The most pressing problem she identifies is the need to sell the winter stock as soon as possible, because

otherwise it might not be sold or have to be heavily discounted to make room for new summer stock. She also thinks that increasing income from dry cleaning and reducing credit card fees would help.

Since sales are the greatest concern, Joan thinks through a range of possible actions, including advertising, creating customer interest by changing window displays more often, encouraging and mentoring staff to be more customer and sales focused, and offering discounts on second purchases as opposed to waiting and selling winter clothes at a significant discount at end-of-season sales. Joan also considers adding a surcharge for payments by credit cards or not accepting cards with higher merchant fees.

In previous years the dry cleaner had promotions that had increased the volume and she feels she might be able to negotiate another promotion. She also thinks about reducing the hours worked by casual staff but is reluctant to do that.

Step 5: Evaluate possible actions and decide which to take

Joan decides that the best immediate options from the point of view of cost, effort and time are contacting account customers and offering them discounts on second purchases, changing window displays more often to attract walk-in customers, not accepting payments by high fee credit cards as most customers have other lower-fee cards. (She believes that introducing a surcharge might decrease sales at a time when sales need to be increased.)

Step 6: Plan to implement the selected actions

Joan prepares and displays details of the actions required on the whiteboard in the staff lunchroom to explain them to her staff and assign responsibilities. She plans to spread contacting account customers among her permanent staff and to create a roster to change window displays more frequently. She plans to discuss the best timing at the staff meeting for changing window displays and to agree with them how best to explain their decision to not accept high-fee credit cards. She wants to make sure everyone puts a positive spin on that, along the lines of 'This is instead of increasing our prices, which we don't want to do'.

In practice, monitoring and controlling finances is more complex than in the example of Joan's Dress Shop for a variety of reasons. For example, Joan's monthly performance report didn't include a breakdown of the costs, and overheads were not itemised; knowing the cost of items such as taxes, office supplies, rent, interest on overdrafts, insurance and utilities would help Joan fine-tune her cost control.

Neither was the shop's cash flow detailed. Table 17.10 shows Joan's cash flow statement for April and May. Small businesses usually try to pay their running expenses from their revenue. The stock sold in May was ordered several months before and paid for in April; the dresses to be sold in June were ordered in March and paid for in May, and so on. Cash at the end of May is depleted due to lower than expected sales in May and operating expenses exceeded inflows from sales.

TABLE 17.10 Joan's cash flow for April and May

	April $	May $
Beginning cash balance	295 000	65 000
Cash in		
Cash sales	500 000	440 000
Credit sales (previous month)	250 000	240 000
Total cash inflows	750 000	680 000
Cash out		
Wages	100 000	80 000

	April $	May $
Stock purchases	500 000	565 000
Overheads	80 000	70 000
Total cash outflows	980 000	715 000
Ending cash balance	65 000	30 000

Analyse some ratios

There is other relevant financial information about the general health of Joan's business we could also consider, particularly her assets and liabilities. We could do what's known as the *quick ratio* (QR), or *acid test*, which measures a business' ability to pay its short-term debts (liabilities) through its 'liquid', or current, assets. Quick assets are *current assets* that can be converted to cash in less than a year. This ratio excludes inventory because of the difficulty in selling stock quickly and the likelihood of needing to offer heavy discounts to achieve quick sales. Some other useful ratios for monitoring an organisation's or profit centre's financial health are shown in Table 17.11.

TABLE 17.11 Some useful ratios: ratio analysis helps you examine how well an organisation is operating financially in a number of important areas. You can find out about its efficiencies, liquidity (ability to pay its bills), profitability and so on.

Transferable skills

1.1 Financial literacy

Name	Formula	Description
Acid test or quick ratio (QR)	(Cash + Marketable assets + Accounts receivable within 30 days) ÷ Liabilities	Measures an organisation's ability to meet its short-term liabilities with current assets. More robust than the current ratio, especially when there is a lot of money tied up in inventory (stock) because it ignores inventory and other non-liquid assets
Current ratio or working capital ratio (CR)	Current assets ÷ Current liabilities (debts due in a short timeframe)	Measures an organisation's ability to pay off its current liabilities with its current assets, indicating its liquidity
Gross margin ratio	(Revenue – Cost of goods sold) ÷ Revenue	Usually expressed as a percentage and indicates profitability
Net profit ratio (NP)	Net profit ÷ Revenue	Another indicator of profitability
Price-earnings ratio (P/E) or earnings multiple	Current share price ÷ Earnings per share (EPS)	A way to value a company; reported daily in the newspapers and on the ASX website
Price-earnings to growth ratio (PEG)	P/E ÷ EPS	Provides a more complete picture of listed companies' stock because it takes into account growth in earnings
Return on assets	Annual earnings ÷ Total assets	Expressed as a percentage, it indicates how profitable a company is relative to its total assets, which indicates how efficient management is at using its assets to generate earnings
Return on equity (ROE)	(Profit ÷ Equity) x 100%	Measures the net income returned (profit) as a percentage of the equity, or funds invested by the shareholders or owners

In Joan's case, we're looking for 1.0 or higher as a QR. We can't tell from our information what the QR is for her dress shop, but we do know that if she can't pay her bills when they fall due, she may have to borrow money and pay interest to avoid late payment fees or lose her discount for on-time payments. Since poor cash flow is the main reason that many small businesses fail in their first year or when the economy suffers a downturn, this acid test is critical.

Joan could use one of two main ways to improve her QR. She could attempt to bring in accounts receivable by offering discounts for prompt payment or make a few phone calls to urge late payers to honour their debts to her; this addresses the numerator, or above-the-line part of the ratio. She could also address the denominator, or bottom part of the ratio, by negotiating lengthier credit terms with her suppliers, which would delay her payment of stock purchases; should that fail, she could source alternative suppliers who are willing to offer her more favourable terms.

At the end of the last financial year, the balance sheet for Joan's Dress Shop showed assets greater than liabilities by $1 000 000. This value is the owner's equity in the business. If profit for the year was $100 000, then the return on equity (ROE) was 10 per cent, which is in line with the benchmark for similar retail clothing stores in Australia.

We could also calculate the ratio of wages to sales by dividing wages by gross sales and multiplying by 100. In April, wages were $100 and sales were $750, which gives us a ratio of 13.33 per cent. In May, wages were $80 and sales were $680, giving us a ratio of 11.8 per cent, both of which are satisfyingly below the benchmark of 15 per cent for similar retail shops. Joan seems to be effectively monitoring and controlling her labour costs.

Calculating Joan's gross profit margin, or gross margin ratio (GM), would also be useful, because margins often differ significantly between items. Seasonal stock often has a higher 'markup' to offset the risk involved if they are not sold during the season and need to be discounted towards the end of the season.

When Joan decides to retire, she would want to sell her business. Would you buy it? To decide you might consider her profit-earnings ratio or price-earnings to growth ratio. You would also want to consider the goodwill of her customers and other tenants in the shopping centre.

Use your reports

Think about the reports that can help you monitor and control costs, too. Monthly expenditure reports probably aren't enough, because by themselves, they don't tell you much. You want reports that help you monitor what else is going to help you control your costs and reports that give you information you can use to guide your decisions. The reports you use should also be timely and accurate. Figure 17.14 defines the most common types of financial plans and reports that leader-managers use.

Involve your team

Transferable skills

3.1 Teamwork/relationships

The more feedback you provide your team on its 'financials', the more you discuss ways to cut costs and the more you involve the team in monitoring costs, the more you can develop their awareness of the importance of following financial procedures and build a cost-conscious culture. Standard operating procedures and a general awareness of the importance of day-to-day financial procedures help ensure costs are controlled and budgets met. Making continuous improvements, as described in Chapter 19, is another important way to reduce costs and increase productivity.

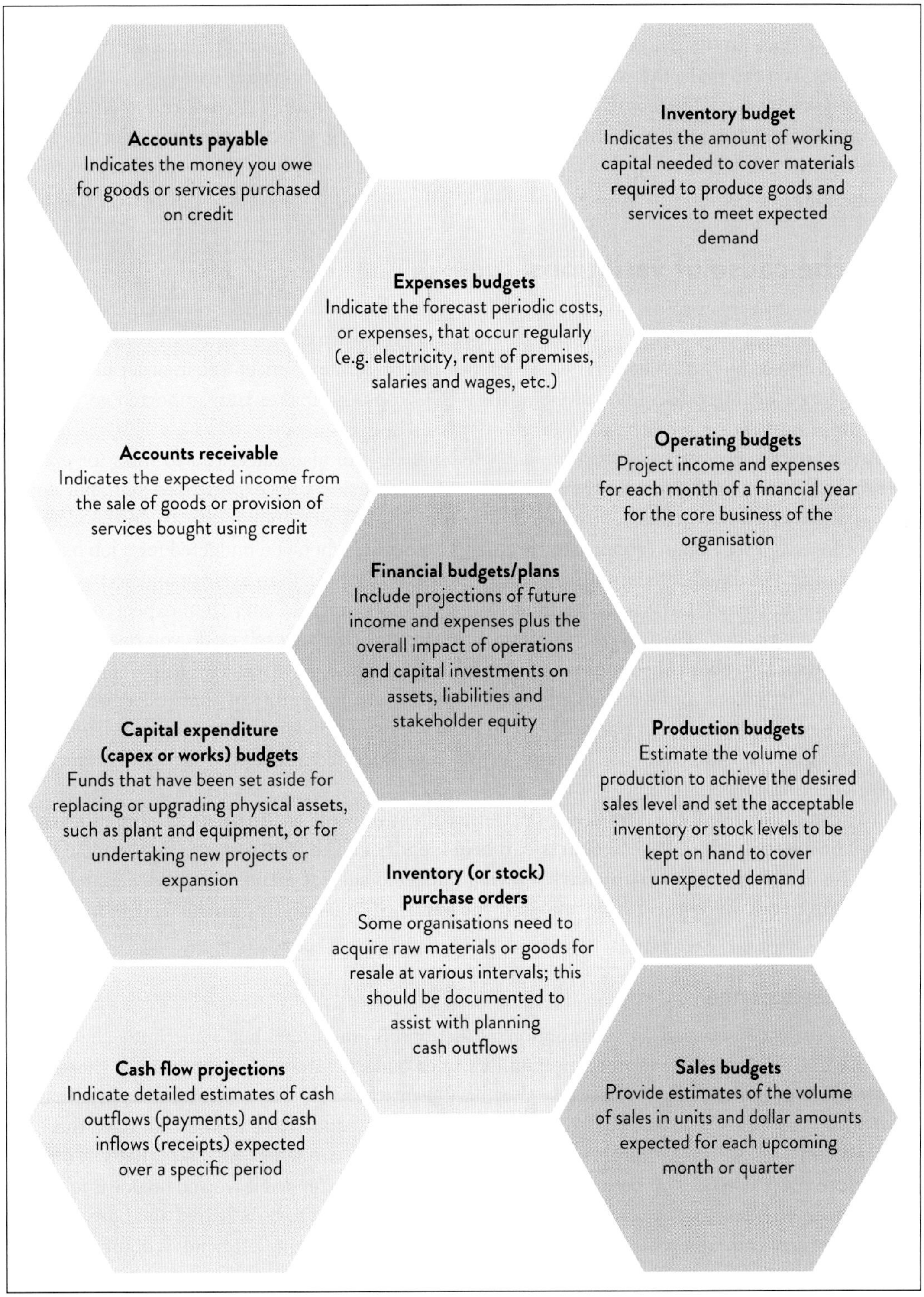

Accounts payable
Indicates the money you owe for goods or services purchased on credit

Inventory budget
Indicates the amount of working capital needed to cover materials required to produce goods and services to meet expected demand

Expenses budgets
Indicate the forecast periodic costs, or expenses, that occur regularly (e.g. electricity, rent of premises, salaries and wages, etc.)

Accounts receivable
Indicates the expected income from the sale of goods or provision of services bought using credit

Operating budgets
Project income and expenses for each month of a financial year for the core business of the organisation

Financial budgets/plans
Include projections of future income and expenses plus the overall impact of operations and capital investments on assets, liabilities and stakeholder equity

Capital expenditure (capex or works) budgets
Funds that have been set aside for replacing or upgrading physical assets, such as plant and equipment, or for undertaking new projects or expansion

Production budgets
Estimate the volume of production to achieve the desired sales level and set the acceptable inventory or stock levels to be kept on hand to cover unexpected demand

Inventory (or stock) purchase orders
Some organisations need to acquire raw materials or goods for resale at various intervals; this should be documented to assist with planning cash outflows

Cash flow projections
Indicate detailed estimates of cash outflows (payments) and cash inflows (receipts) expected over a specific period

Sales budgets
Provide estimates of the volume of sales in units and dollar amounts expected for each upcoming month or quarter

FIGURE 17.14 Financial plans and reports often used by leader-managers

Ask team members to keep track of and give feedback on events and situations that add cost or in other ways reduce productive outcomes. Ask them to remain alert for ways to increase productivity and savings. You can make this a standing item on your team-meeting **agendas**.

When you plan to take steps to control costs or make improvements, make sure you discuss them with any other upstream and downstream leader-managers whose teams could be affected. When your team has not been part of developing the improvement plans, brief them, and keep your own manager informed, too.

Find the cause of variations

A difference between an actual and a budgeted outcome is called a variation, or variance, which can be positive or negative. When you use more materials than anticipated, a *materials volume variance* means you missed budget. When you paid more for raw materials to meet a rush order because you couldn't access quantity discounts, or when the AUD drops and makes your imported goods more expensive, a *materials price variance* means you missed budget.

A *labour efficiency variance* or a *labour rate variance* can also cause you to miss (or exceed) your budget. For example, you may have budgeted for a job using your experienced staff, but due to a resignation (or two), you had to use new and untrained staff who took longer to do the work – a labour efficiency variation. A labour rate variation also occurs when you budgeted for a job based on average hours, but unexpected events meant the work took longer than average and you needed to pay overtime to complete the work on time. When invoices are paid later than expected, you may have a budgeted *cash flow variance*; the question is: will this correct itself or do you need to act; for example, by speaking with customers with overdue accounts?

Whether variations are in dollars, physical units, efficiencies, quality or some other unit, decide the nature of the variance. For example, if you miss your sales budget, is it a *volume variance* or a *price variance*? Then you could use the 'ask "Why?" five times' technique to work out the root cause of not achieving budget.

Transferable skills

1.2 Entrepreneurship/small business skills

You can analyse variations to identify patterns, a tendency of certain items to vary, or a general positive or negative trend. **Pareto charts** can help identify and display patterns and tendencies for certain items to vary while a **run chart** showing budgeted against actual is a good way to identify and display trends. When you have analysed the variance, you can implement and monitor your contingency plan.

A delicate balance

Keeping a balance between an organisation's functions is important but sometimes challenging. Take, for example, a sales team that meets all its sales budgets. The sales team are very happy and the production team is happy too because they have plenty of work. The accountant reports that the company's cash flow is bad and the business is struggling to pay its bills as they fall due. There are many potential sources for this problem: perhaps the salespeople are achieving their targets by offering generous terms to win sales, or perhaps the credit manager is on extended leave and no one is following up customers to ensure they pay on time. That is why it is important to be prepared and have everyone working towards common goals, with the 'right hand' knowing what the 'left hand' is doing and why.

Implement and monitor contingency plans

You developed contingency plans as part of planning your financial management approach. When things go wrong and threaten the achievement of financial objectives, it's time to implement those plans, adjusting them to suit the particular set of circumstances when you need to.

In the example of Joan's Dress Shop, Joan's contingency plans included:

- change window displays more often to attract more passing customers
- check the possibility of delaying the arrival of, and therefore payment for, new season's stock
- contact account customers and offer discounts on second purchases to boost sales
- continue to adjust the hours worked by casual staff
- no longer accept payments by high-fee credit cards.

We can't know whether Joan's contingency plans succeed until the next sets of financial figures are prepared in the following months. Assuming they work as anticipated, those actions can remain in place. Should sales still fail to meet budget, she may need to offer further discounts, resulting in decreased revenue and the need to modify her contingency plans by further reducing costs. And, since interest rates on overdrafts are usually about three times the deposit rate for small businesses, Joan might find she has cash flow problems that cannot be accommodated by her overdraft facility at an acceptable cost and may need to further modify her contingency plans as a result.

Initiating contingency plans often provides ideas for permanently improving the way you operate. Joan might decide to increase sales by offering online access to her store, for instance. She could also conduct a **cost–benefit analysis** (discussed in Chapter 20) to decide whether this is viable.

Keep improving

Don't forget that a key imperative of every organisation is continuous improvement. Here are some ideas:

- Can you reduce costs by using resources more efficiently or using fewer resources (e.g. electricity, stationery, water) or can you make fewer photocopies and retain electronic copies rather than printing copies?
- Can you improve efficiencies and therefore productivity by improving the way your work area (your own or your team's) is organised?
- Can you reduce costs through better inventory management? For example, can you identify more cost-effective ordering and storage methods or more economic order quantities? Can you reduce wastage or stock-holding procedures to prevent deterioration or pilfering?
- Can you improve labour use through training to improve productivity or improve efficiencies and reduce costs?
- Can you increase output by streamlining working methods, preventing the need for rework, providing more information, removing bottlenecks or removing backtracking?
- Can you reduce any of your operating costs without sacrificing the value they add?

Transferable skills

1.3 Sustainability

1.4 Business operations

1.5 Operations management

2.3 Business strategy

3.1 Teamwork/relationships

When your team develops intangible assets through continuous improvements and innovation and by expanding their know-how (whether for financial or other processes), document it and protect it. Inform your risk manager so it can be protected (e.g. through patents, licensing agreements or restricted access) and added to the organisation's intellectual property register. When your organisation has a knowledge management system, add these intangible assets to it so that others in the organisation can take advantage of it.

When you need specialist advice, ask for it. That's what specialists are there for. For specific advice on matters relating to budgets and financial plans, you could consult the chief financial officer. Sometimes, for example, when you need to update equipment, hardware or software, you may need to consult external specialists. Their timely and sound advice can help you achieve better outcomes and take advantage of emerging trends.

Report, review and recommend

Dates for submitting financial reports are published well in advance, usually at the beginning of the financial year. In small organisations, accountants often carry out this reporting. Whoever prepares these reports, the organisation uses them to gain a complete financial picture to assist in planning decision-making at the senior level.

The financial reports you provide depend on your role and your organisation's protocols. Project teams, for example, often produce reports containing descriptive and graphical information explaining their project's progress and report on their costs and other financial information. When you manage a cost centre, you might report on budget and expenditure, identifying any variances and how you have handled them. Use your organisation's accounting packages to prepare your reports in the format preferred by the organisation.

It isn't practical to review every item of financial data available. Mostly, you know from your ongoing monitoring and controlling of financial activities which data you need to gather and review. For example, a restaurant manager might be concerned about food wastage or the cost of laundering table linen; a leader-manager of a finance unit of a large organisation might undertake a wider review and consider data from many more sources. You might want to discuss the focus for each particular review with your team members.

Transferable skills
4.1 Data literacy

You also want to regularly evaluate the effectiveness of the financial management processes your work team uses and recommend or make improvements when you can. This entails:

1 identifying relevant data sources
2 collecting and collating data and information
3 analysing data and information to identify areas where financial performance is less than expected and the reasons for lower performance
4 documenting and recommending improvements to existing processes
5 implementing the recommendations and monitoring the outcomes.

Identify relevant data sources

Transferable skills
4.1 Data literacy

You can extract information from many sources, including bank statements, cash book accounts, credit card transactions, invoices, petty cash records, production records, purchase orders, taxation records and time sheets. These are called *source documents* and are often in paper form. **Figure 17.15** gives some examples of source documents and **Figure 17.16** shows the flow of data from source documents.

The accounting sequence described here and shown in **Figure 17.17** can help you track a particular financial transaction. All financial transactions should be traceable back to the original data source.

Source documents are generally carefully recorded in a *day journal* or *journal* that can comprise several *sub-journals* that relate to the form of sale or purchase (cash or credit). The journal data is then posted to the *general ledger*, usually through an accounting software package that shows an account for each type of revenue, expense, asset or liability. At the end of the reporting period (e.g. quarter, half year, financial year) the balance in each ledger account is extracted to produce a range of reports, such as a *trial balance*, balance sheet or profit and loss statement.

Collect and collate data and information

The time needed for a thorough review has an opportunity cost – you could be doing something else with that time. This means your reviews need to be both timely and cost-effective.

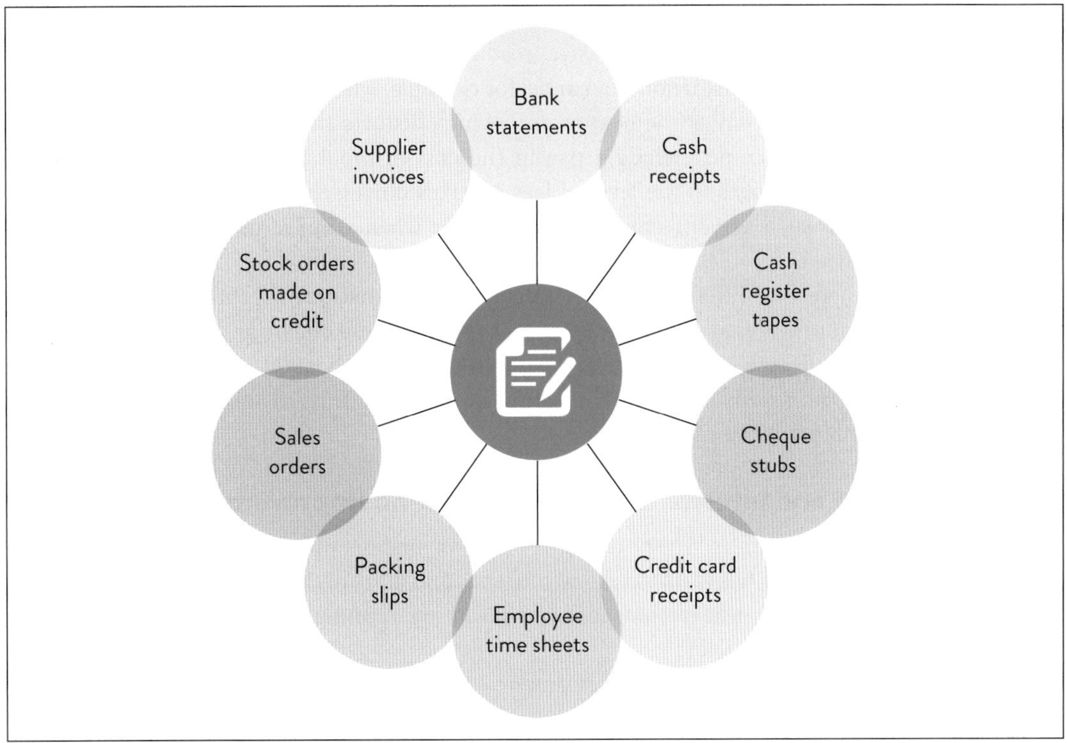

FIGURE 17.15 Examples of source documents

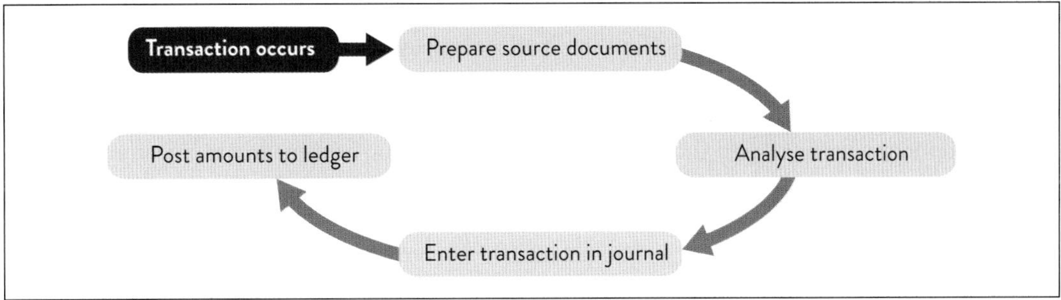

FIGURE 17.16 Flow of accounting data for a transaction

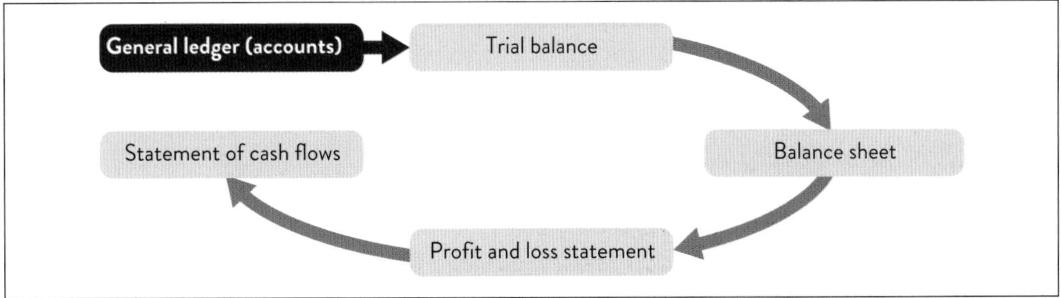

FIGURE 17.17 Using ledger information to produce reports

Many financial records consist of raw data in the form of numbers. Begin by systematically collecting data that is accurate, comprehensive, readily available and free of distortions, such as journals and ledger accounts. Distortions can arise, for example, when income derived in one month is not credited until the first day of the next month, which distorts the cash flow for both months. Other causes of distortion could include a rise in the cost of inputs, falls in the AUD affecting the value of exports, or changes in the level of fees or taxes during the reporting period. Seek the assistance of someone such as your chief financial officer when you are uncertain about how to obtain the data you need.

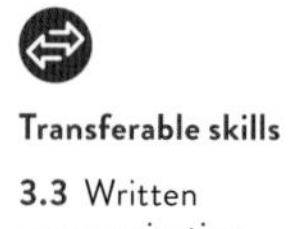

Transferable skills

3.3 Written communication

4.1 Data literacy

As you know, there is a difference between data and information. To obtain meaningful and valid information that provides as complete a picture as possible, you collate and display the data in a number of ways and study it to see what it tells you. Put it in formats that you and your team members are familiar with and can readily interpret. For example, you and your team are probably comfortable with spreadsheets and graphs of various kinds.

Analyse the data and information and recommend improvements

Once you've collated the data in a way that gives you an understanding of the finances you are studying, you can work with your team to review your data and information and look for improvement opportunities, or with other leader-managers when you are refining financial processes used by several teams. Your aims are twofold:

1 find performance gaps – areas where performance is better or worse than expected so that they can be capitalised on or rectified
2 find ways to make continuous improvements to the way budgets are prepared, how financial tasks are carried out, and the processes you use to manage financial and other resources.

Transferable skills

2.3 Business strategy

Make sure your recommendations are in line with the financial objectives of your work team and the organisation, and present them as a clear, well-structured business case. Present your recommendations as adjustments rather than major changes and provide supporting information regarding:

- how your recommendations will improve the organisation's finances and ability to meet its goals
- what options you considered and on what basis, or criteria, you have made your recommendations
- how cost-effective your recommendations are.

The following Industry insights box illustrates three different ways of reaching conclusions and presenting recommendations. (You can find out more about how to document your recommendations in Chapters 6 and 7.)

Three examples

Example 1: Streamlining systems

Phil manages a business that produces and delivers prepared meals. He asks the accountant how their bookkeeping costs compare with similar-sized businesses and finds they're higher. Phil thinks this may be a result of overtime usually required at the end of the month when customer invoices are prepared. The part-time bookkeeper often complains that she spent a lot of time collecting, searching for and checking source documents, particularly delivery notes.

Phil decides to follow this up as part of his financial management processes review and observe how source documents are handled. He finds that, indeed, many of them, especially delivery notes, are lost, misplaced or misfiled, requiring time-wasting sorting and shuffling by the bookkeeper. He decides that better systems, procedures and document storage facilities would cut back or eliminate these problems and reduce the overtime.

Phil documents his findings and improvement recommendations, including updating the bookkeeping software, and produces a list of costs and estimated savings to discuss with the owner of the business, making sure he presents them in a way that ties in with the owner's priorities.

Example 2: Balancing competing demands

The service department of a large regional agent for a popular brand of tractor holds a large inventory of replacement parts, which the owner believes ties up too much money. Some parts are expensive but seldom needed, others are low-cost and frequently required, and the rest of the stock falls somewhere in between. Holding spare parts incurs significant capital costs as well as costs for damage, insurance, shrinkage (or loss), storage and so on. On the other hand, farmers would lose a lot of money if they had to wait for parts to repair their tractors.

The owner asks the leader-manager of the parts section of the warehouse to determine the optimum level for the various parts they store. The leader-manager seeks expert guidance on how to analyse the information about the costs of parts and how frequently they are needed so that he can work out the most cost-effective and customer-friendly inventory levels. He also decides to think through some strategies to reduce the overall costs of the parts inventory.

He builds a well-founded recommendation that considers the issue in broader terms and uses that perspective to make accurate predictions that take into account the level of sales of different models, the average age of tractors serviced, the age at which parts are usually replaced and inventory turnover. The owner is delighted.

Example 3: The value of fresh eyes

Olivia is responsible for charging out the cost of items used in installing and servicing air-conditioning systems. She often finds it difficult to match the items with specific jobs because the technicians regularly purchase items they need locally.

To her, the solution is obvious – ask the technicians to write the job number on the tax invoice for items they purchase.

Implement and monitor the approved improvements

Since what one team does can affect other teams, you may want to discuss your intended improvements with your manager before implementing them. You may need to formally refer some recommendations to management; for example, when you are recommending a capital expenditure or when your recommendation materially affects other teams.

Transferable skills

2.2 Personal effectiveness

2.3 Business strategy

3.2 Verbal communication

The size and nature of your improvements affects the way you implement and monitor them, although you will follow the basic process described in 'Phase 3: Evaluate and act' in Chapter 26 and also information in Chapter 27. With significant changes, it may pay to test your changes with a pilot, or trial run, and follow the **P–D–C–A cycle** (Plan–Do–Check–Act).

Be aware that small changes to processes may at first appear to be straightforward. However, when changes involve working and thinking differently, team members may resist them, consciously or unconsciously. (See Chapter 24 for more on this.) And, as you will see in Chapter 29, it can take time to 'unlearn' an 'old way' and implement a 'new way'. Even an update to a financial management

Transferable skills

1.4 Business operations

2.2 Personal effectiveness

3.1 Teamwork/relationships

3.4 Leadership

package can result in competent employees initially feeling frustrated and incompetent. So, observe people's reactions and listen to their concerns.

However big or small your changes, plan them carefully, discuss them with your team (along with the reasons for the changes, when they haven't been part of developing them), clearly indicate the expected outcomes, or measures of success, provide the resources your team needs (including time and information) and support people with the positive feedback and coaching they may need as they adopt the change. Listen to their concerns and feedback, and celebrate success, as described in Chapter 24. Chapter 20 explains more about the monitoring process.

STUDY TOOLS

QUICK REVIEW

KEY CONCEPT 17.1 

a What does an accounting system do?

b List what constitutes each of the following and state their use:

i budgets

ii balance sheets

iii income statements

iv cash flow statements.

c What is the difference between gross profit and net profit?

KEY CONCEPT 17.2 

a What information is useful in preparing budgets and financial plans?

b How do budgets help control business operations?

c List the steps you would take if you wanted to negotiate changes to an expenses budget you have been allocated.

d What is the purpose of financial contingency plans?

KEY CONCEPT 17.3 

a Outline the key steps in implementing a financial plan.

b List 10 actions leader-managers can take to support their team in working with finances.

KEY CONCEPT 17.4 

a How could you go about monitoring and controlling finances in a work team?

b Why is it necessary to analyse variance between actual and budget forecasts?

BUILD YOUR SKILLS

KEY CONCEPT 17.1 

a What is a break-even point? Describe how you could use it as part of a business case for purchasing an automated appointment reminder system in a dental practice.

b Briefly describe your experience in financial planning and related tasks and your confidence and competence in this process. Then develop a plan to improve your competence and discuss it with your manager.

c How does your personal cash flow affect your own activities? What are your current and potential sources of cash?

d Arrange the following items into a statement of financial position using the layout demonstrated in this chapter or in your organisation:

Accounts payable	$35000
Accounts receivable – net	$17000
Cash	$25000
Depreciation on plant and equipment	$(56000)
Furniture, fixtures and fittings	$75000
Goodwill	$100000
Insurance – pre-paid	$2000
Intellectual property	$200000
Interest payable	$3000
Inventory	$36000

Loans outstanding	$80 500
Misc. assets	$5 000
Petty cash	$100
Plant and equipment	$208 500
Property and buildings	$950 000
Taxes payable	$7 200
Vehicles	$95 000

e Arrange the following items into a statement of financial performance using the layout demonstrated in this chapter or in your organisation:

Advertising	$15 000
Closing stock	$5 000
Consumables and supplies	$20 000
Depreciation	$20 000
Donations	$105 000
Interest earned	$7 800
Interest owed	$1 300
Misc. operating expenses	$15 000
Opening stock	$35 000
Rent	$40 000
Revenues from government	$90 000
Salaries	$89 000
Sales	$67 000
Stock purchases	$20 000
Utilities	$30 000

f Using the Australian Taxation Office (ATO) website at https://www.ato.gov.au/Business explain the following taxation requirements and how these are accounted for in an organisation:

i Goods and services tax (GST): consider under what circumstances GST is collected, and how businesses manage GST credits and the business activity statement (BAS).

ii Pay as you go (PAYG): consider under what circumstances this is charged and how a business pays the tax to the ATO.

iii Superannuation: consider an employer's obligations and how it pays superannuation.

KEY CONCEPT 17.2 

a What are the key principles to developing a sound budget?

b Develop a personal budget to cover the next three months. (You can find an example at http://www.skillstoolbox.com/financial-skills/basic-personal-budgeting/personal-budget-example) Then list the main risk factors that might cause you to not meet budget and develop contingency plans for each.

c Check through the Australian Securities and Investments Commission website (https://www.asic.gov.au), which has a range of information available for businesses, finance professionals and consumers. List how the resources it offers can help you manage budgets and financial plans.

d What is return on investment? Describe how you could use it as part of a business case for upgrading office equipment and the factors you would consider in calculating the return on investment. What qualitative factors might you also consider?

e Describe the steps you would take if your manager prepared a budget and you did not agree with the costings and the resourcing.

f Draft a personal expenses budget for the next seven days listing everything you plan to spend. Then put it away. During the next seven days, record your actual expenses and in eight days' time, compare your budget with your actual expenditure. What have you learnt?

KEY CONCEPT 17.3 

a What formats do you believe are most effective in communicating budgets and other financial information, and why?

b Why would you want your work team to understand basic financial principles and be aware of controlling costs? What are some ways you could develop your team's understanding in this area? How could you develop a culture of financial awareness in the team?

KEY CONCEPT 17.4 

a Using the information for a grocery shop that follows, develop a statement of financial position and calculate the owner's equity.

Accounts payable	$14000
Accounts receivable	$6000
Cash at bank	$16000
Bank loan	$24000
Motor vehicle	$30000
Cash in hand	$4000
Inventory	$22000

Now calculate the grocery store's profit or loss based on the following revenue and expenses:

Sales	$50000
Purchases	$24000
Salaries	$12000
Rent	$1800
Electricity	$300
Telephone	$450
Advertising	$800

Now conduct a ratio analysis on this store. Which ratios will you use, and why? What do you conclude from your analysis?

b Explore the ATO's website at https://www.ato.gov.au/Business/Small-business-benchmarks/In-detail/Benchmarks-by-industry and develop a list of benchmarks for the industry you are employed in, hope to be employed in or are interested in.

c Referring to the Industry insights box 'Three examples', how should Olivia put forward her idea? Should she simply ask the technicians or discuss her idea with the owner, who also costs jobs and acts as project manager, for example? How could she build a case for adopting her idea? Do you expect any resistance from the technicians and, if so, how could their resistance be overcome?

d Conduct an internet search for the annual report of a company you are interested in and complete some ratio analyses to determine its financial health. Prepare a short report for your class.

e What top five financial measures would you want to use if you ran a bank? What would you want to measure if you were interested in investing in a bank? What top five financial measures would you be interested in if you owned a sports store? What would you want to know if you were interested in investing in a sports store? What ratios might you look for in each of these businesses that could indicate its health, and why?

f List some contingency plans you could implement in the following circumstances:
   i a downturn in sales
   ii a sharp increase in water costs
   iii the introduction of a new business tax.

g How could you decide whether to do the following:
   i buy or lease
   ii close down or keep a department
   iii sublet a portion of your building or use the space yourself.

h Use the following information from a retail shop to:
   i complete a budget/actual performance statement
   ii produce a variance analysis report
   iii identify the variance amounts
   iv discuss whether the variances are favourable or unfavourable.

Sales	5000 units @ average sales price of $25
Cost of goods sold	30% of selling price
Equipment lease	$18600
Rent	$22500
Rates	$9300
Delivery costs	$18500
Marketing expenses	$3600
Administration expenses	$10300
Commission	$7900

Budget information for the month:	
Sales	4600 units @ average sales price of $28
Cost of goods sold	28% of selling price
Equipment lease	$18000
Rent	$8500
Rates	$9300
Delivery costs	$21600
Marketing expenses	$3000
Administration expenses	$18100
Commission	$7750

WORKPLACE ACTIVITIES

KEY CONCEPT 17.1 

a Diagram the accounting system used in your workplace.

b Obtain a copy of your organisation's annual report. Examine the financial statements (i.e. income statement, balance sheet and cash flow statement), the summary of financial results over a period of years, and read any discussion of the financial progress and trends across recent years. Use this information to form an assessment of the general health of the organisation. Then explain how this has increased your financial literacy and understanding of your organisation.

KEY CONCEPT 17.2 

a Draw a flow chart of the way your organisation goes about the process of developing its budget. Consider the type of budgets prepared, when the budgeting process commences, who is involved in it and their responsibilities in preparing the budget, when negotiation takes place during the budgeting process, how the budget is approved, and to whom and when the budget is communicated.

b Conduct a small-scale scan of the internal and external environments in which your team operates to identify influences that may affect your organisation's and team's operations, such as new technology, changes in legislation, and other trends and emerging developments inside and outside of your organisation.

c Draft a submission to the team preparing your organisation's budget that reflects your team's current operations and emerging needs and opportunities revealed in the scan conducted in the previous question.

d How does management in your workplace check that budgets are well understood? How could communication be improved?

e How do you communicate budgets and budget procedures to your work team? You can illustrate this as a flow chart if you wish. What steps could you take to improve your financial communication to your team?

f Summarise the key headings of the budget(s) for your work team and discuss how you monitor and control them.

g What significant financial contingencies do you consider in your work team? Are there others that could emerge in future?

h What aspects of contingency management have proved effective in your workplace?

KEY CONCEPT 17.3 

a What financial plans do you regularly access at work? How do you use the information they provide? Set your answer out in a way that might form part of your curriculum vitae.

b Develop a standard operating procedure or draw a flow chart showing the steps of a key financial task carried out by members of your work team.

c What financial records do you keep in your work team? How are they used? What steps do you take to ensure their accuracy?

KEY CONCEPT 17.4 

a Identify several ratios that could be useful in the analysis of performance in your unit, section or work team. Consider ratios that evaluate efficiency, liquidity, profitability and capacity to meet current financial obligations and to compare performance with like groups. Apply these ratios and discuss your findings with your manager.

b How are you involved in monitoring expenses and controlling costs? What training might you need to improve your performance?

c What elements of cost are most significant in meeting expected financial outcomes in your workplace?

d Review a recent report on budget and expenditure and describe how you can use this information to make improvements to the way your team works.

e What recommendations have you or other members of your team made for improving financial performance? Have they resulted in a change to work practices and significant improvements?

CASE STUDY 17

INVESTIGATING A DISTURBING TREND

Chailin is leader-manager of the finance team in a small business specialising in office design, fit-out and refurbishment. She has noticed that an increasing number of completed contracts have significant cost overruns. Chailin approaches the financial controller, Rod, and suggests identifying the underlying causes of the cost overruns in what she describes as a disturbing trend.

He agrees. In fact, he finds the trend so disturbing that he appoints an acting leader-manager to Chailin's role for a month in order to free her up to find the cause of the variances and recommend improved processes.

Chailin decides to follow the progress of three current contracts that are similar in many respects to those that had recently come in over budget. She reviews the entire process chain, from the initial contact, site visit, plans and specifications, detailed estimates of costs, quotations, profit margins, changes and revisions, delivery and installation, staffing, payments and any complaints requiring further work. She speaks at length with the staff involved to gain a clear picture of the way they carry out the various tasks, and asks about the challenges and frustrations they face on the job. Next, she examines the financial details associated with each stage and relates these to the earlier discussions and final costs.

Her analysis reveals a series of small events, oversights and other shortcomings, each relatively 'insignificant' on their own, but which come together to result in significant cost overruns. These include:

- accepting slim margins and building in small contingency allowances to secure work in a competitive market
- changes made as work progresses resulting in small, unbudgeted scope creeps
- deficiencies in timely and accurate monitoring of actual expenses against budget, making it difficult to take corrective action
- failure of staff to meet to discuss and record learnings at the end of projects
- floating membership of teams undertaking installations, resulting in time delays and poor communication
- lack of expertise in managing risks associated with fixed contracts
- small discrepancies in the estimated duration and cost of the jobs
- staff turnover issues, with new staff generally less experienced and requiring on-the-job training.

Chailin talks through her findings with Rod, who decides to work with the project managers to begin a process of continuous improvement in each of the identified areas. At Chailin's suggestion, he also plans to ask each project manager to report regularly about the changes they have made and the outcomes of those changes.

Questions

1. Do you think the reporting of a series of small events, oversights and other shortcomings is an appropriate outcome for Chailin's investigation? If not, what other outcomes might you expect?
2. What difficulties might Chailin have faced in undertaking this investigation? What steps could she take to lessen those difficulties?
3. What advantages might an insider such as Chailin have over a similarly qualified outside expert?
4. Can you think of any other ways the cost overruns on these projects could be overcome?
5. What further actions could Rod take to improve performance?

CHAPTER ENDNOTES

1. W. Edwards Deming, in Simon Caulkin, 'Escape from the budget straitjacket', *Management Today*, UK, January 2005.
2. By merging the two businesses, the owner potentially retains the income of both but considerably reduces fixed costs; after the costs of relocation and fit-out are absorbed, the profit increases further.
3. KPMG, 2006, *Guide to preventing workplace fraud*, http://www.chubb.com/businesses/csi/chubb5305.pdf, accessed 18 January 2018.

CHAPTER

PROVIDING QUALITY AND ENGAGING WITH CUSTOMERS

After completing this chapter, you will be able to:

18.1 monitor the quality of your products and services

18.2 identify your customers and what they want from you, and explain why providing what they want pays off

18.3 manage your relationships with your customers effectively

18.4 resolve customer difficulties and complaints in a way that maintains and improves your relationship with them.

TRANSFERABLE SKILLS

The following transferable skills are covered in this chapter:

1 **Business competence**
- **1.4** Business operations

2 **Critical thinking and problem solving**
- **2.2** Personal effectiveness
- **2.3** Business strategy

3 **Social competence**
- **3.1** Teamwork/relationships
- **3.2** Verbal communication
- **3.3** Written communication
- **3.4** Leadership

5 **Digital competence**
- **5.2** Technology use

OVERVIEW

Service has no shelf life; it is only as good as each customer perceives it to be right now. When a customer thinks you've done a bad job, you can't take it back – you can only try to make up for it. Customers can't hold service in their hands. Fleeting and insubstantial it may be, but customer service can make or break an organisation. Customer service, once a 'nice add-on', is now mandatory.

Of course, retaining customers depends on providing quality. What was once considered good in terms of both quality and customer service is now regarded as the bare minimum; what is considered good today is about to be surpassed, too, because customers are more demanding than ever before. They're better informed and have more choice. When they don't get what they want, they exercise their choice – with their feet, their tweets, their online reviews and so on.

Australia has moved from a supply-led service economy to a demand-led service economy and 88 per cent of Australians are employed in service industries.[1] This makes organisations vulnerable in another way – although they set the quality and service standards, they depend on each employee and each contractor, every day, to meet those standards. Every day, in every organisation, there are tens of thousands of individual points at which quality and customer service can break down.

In this chapter, you find out why quality is at the heart of your organisation's success and central to everything you, your team and everyone else in the organisation does. You find out how to identify your customers and what they want, and you find out how to provide it in a way that delights them enough that they keep coming back – even when there are occasional hiccups.

SNAPSHOT

The local newsagency

Laura runs a small business from her home and was in the habit of popping into the newsagency in a nearby Adelaide Hills village at least once a week. It stocks a large range of office supplies and was well laid out and clean. Most weeks, her purchases ranged from $8 to $20.

Despite the fact that she was in there so frequently, the owner never appeared to recognise her. However, the owner was always business-like and efficient and always gave the correct change. Laura didn't particularly enjoy going there but there was no other newsagency close to home.

Then another newsagency opened in her own village, just two minutes from her home, so Laura called in the next time she needed stationery supplies. The woman greeted her and introduced herself as Chris, asking whether she could help Laura find anything in particular. 'No thanks, I'll just have a look around first,' Laura replied.

Laura concluded that, although the shop wasn't quite as well stocked as the other newsagency, it could adequately supply her stationery needs. She paid for what she wanted and thanked Chris, who cheerfully said, 'Thanks. See you next time!'

Laura now purchases all her stationery items from the new shop. She enjoys going in there and having a quick chat with Chris while she browses and picks up supplies. Laura's weekly spending is now between $12 and $27.

18.1 Abiding by the quality imperative

Quality is free. But it's not a gift.

Phil Crosby (quality analyst), *Quality is free: The art of making quality certain*, Mentor, 1980, p. 7.

What is quality? It's something you have to work to attain. And once you've attained it, you actually *save* money. That makes it better than free. How do you measure quality in your job and at your workplace? How do you decide whether your product or service is a quality product or service? According to another pioneer in quality studies, Joseph Juran, 'Quality is whatever the customer says it is'.[2]

No one ever wanted poor-quality products, products unfit for their purpose or incompatible with products they already had, unreliable or dangerous products, or unfriendly service. But today's customers expect more in terms of service and quality than yesterday's customers. They can compare products and services from all over the world and read online reviews by real customers and from experts.

Customers typically make decisions on who they will and won't deal with based on the quality and service they and their friends receive. Even business-to-business (B2B) customers trust word of mouth and social media when making purchasing decisions.

What makes a product or service 'sensational', 'good', 'disappointing' or 'poor' is its quality. Even when you get your quality spot on, over and over again, you need to keep 'raising the bar' to meet changing customer expectations. This means you need to keep adjusting the way you produce your products or service. This, too, holds true for B2B transactions as well as business-to-consumer (B2C) and end user transactions.

Quality builds loyalty, attracts repeat business, generates word-of-mouth (free) business and boosts profits. Kaoru Ishikawa, another quality pioneer, believed that the drive for quality should flow through the entire organisation and that quality should be present in every part of a product's life cycle.[3] In today's highly competitive and global marketplace, where sustainability of operations and products is becoming a necessity, this is more essential than in the past.

INDUSTRY INSIGHTS

Quality: the Japanese miracle and the West's wake-up call

Continuous incremental improvements are a key feature of **total quality management (TQM)**. Although TQM originated in the US, few organisations paid attention to quality until the Second World War, when poor quality became a matter of life or death. Each manufacturing failure, however small, threatened the lives of thousands of soldiers and the freedom of millions of people. After the war, organisations seemed to forget about quality until the 1980s, when the West went into recession and, based largely on quality issues, nearly lost its manufacturing base to Japan – which had taken quality seriously.

Dr W. Edwards Deming, Armand Feigenbaum and Joseph Juran, leaders in the early Total Quality Movement, used TQM techniques and approaches to help Japan rebuild after the Second World War. In less than 40 years, Japan, a non-industrialised society with a low standard of living, became one of the world's manufacturing giants, the undisputed leader in quality and service, and one of the most economically developed and powerful nations on Earth.

The costs of poor quality

You can see how expensive 'doing things wrong' is when you calculate the costs of:

- customer allowances and other tactics to offset customer dissatisfaction
- investigating and processing customer complaints, returns and warranty claims
- lost customers and lost sales
- product recalls
- repairing or replacing damaged, faulty or lost goods
- scrap and other waste.

Then there are the more hidden costs, to name a few:

- correcting billing and other errors
- expediting late deliveries
- field service expenses
- late paperwork
- overtime
- premium freight costs
- redoing work, online returns or repeating a service.

When you 'do it right', those costs are not incurred. 'Doing it right' improves employee efficiency and productivity, reduces rework, scrap and costs and vastly improves customer satisfaction. A problem that costs $1 to fix in advance could potentially cost $20 to fix during a process, and $50 to fix afterwards. Building quality into systems saves money.

The four cornerstones of quality

Quality doesn't happen by itself. It takes effort to produce and maintain the four strong cornerstones of quality shown in Figure 18.1. These four cornerstones of quality give organisations the ability to provide goods and services that meet or exceed customers' expectations throughout their life cycle.

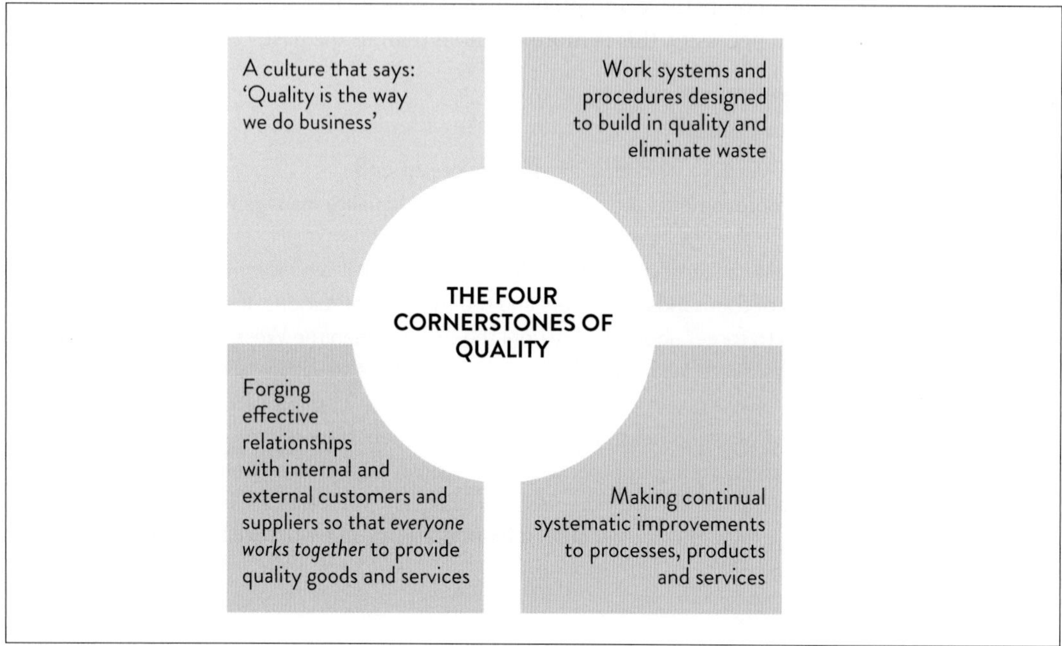

FIGURE 18.1 The four cornerstones of quality

Quality culture

Transferable skills
1.4 Business operations

In organisations with a **quality culture**, employees walk, talk and think quality, assist each other and hold each other accountable for producing quality work. They work with their customers and suppliers to streamline their work so that both benefit, and make a habit of systematic, continuous improvements, or enhancements, to processes, products and services.

There are no 'silos' in a quality culture – all functions in the organisation work together as service partners in one continuous **customer–supplier chain** (discussed later in this chapter).

A quality culture, where employees at all levels share the organisation's commitment to quality and meeting customer needs, takes commitment and time to build. Employees need to be well resourced. They need training in people skills, such as teamwork and participating in meetings (discussed in Chapters 13 and 25), and in the tools and techniques (explained in Chapter 27) to identify, analyse and solve problems (explained in Chapter 26) and continually innovate and refine systems and procedures (explained in Chapter 19). They need to be empowered and involved so they can keep finding ways to not only 'do it right' but also to 'do it better'.

In all their dealings with customers, organisations with a quality culture remain aware of and uphold their *customers' rights.* For example, their right to be told the truth, to be provided with a service or product that does the job you present it as doing and their right to confidentiality of information.

Customer service charters

Many organisations have a customer service charter, which states who the organisation considers its customers to be and explains how it intends to serve them. Many charters even state what customers can expect from the organisation when they contact it by email, post or telephone or visit it in person, and explain how customers can offer the organisation feedback.

Check out the following websites to view some customer service charters:

- Australian Red Cross' client service charter: https://www.redcross.org.au/publications/client-service-charter
- Australia Post's customer service charter: https://auspost.com.au/about-us/corporate-information/our-organisation/customer-commitment-and-service-charter
- ANZ's customer charter: https://www.anz.com/australia/aboutanz/customercharter/anzbra0010charterbrochure%20.pdf

To maintain a quality culture, you need all Five Keys to performance (explained in Chapter 19) in place. You need to walk your quality talk and deliver clear and consistent quality messages through constant communication via emails, tweets, newsletters, informal conversations and team meetings.

Quality systems and processes

What systems, or work methods, control the processes and activities that influence the quality of the goods and services your organisation produces? Total quality management (TQM) is the philosophy that guides organisations to build quality into their operations. Each organisation develops its own **quality systems** that reflect the nature and size of its operations, but whatever system they develop, the goal is the same: to do it right the first time and every time.

When an organisation's systems reliably and predictably deliver a quality product or service, they are *in control. Out-of-control* systems are haphazard – sometimes they produce good quality and sometimes they don't.

That's why it's important to design procedures and systems that reduce the chance of error and variation – the normal ups and downs in a process – so that you and your team consistently produce the quality your customers want. Your goal is to design all your systems so that mistakes and defects are virtually impossible; this eliminates the need for the traditional quality checking at the end of a process.

You also want your systems to streamline the flow of work and eliminate duplication and unnecessary work by reducing or eliminating activities that don't add value but needlessly take up effort, 'space' and time. This reduces costs and frustration. **Lean** production, **lean Six Sigma** and **Six Sigma**, explained in Chapter 19, are methodologies that help you do this.

Variation

There are two types of variation: *assignable-cause variation* and *chance-cause variation*. You can use a control chart to distinguish between the two. You then identify and remove assignable-cause variations to bring processes into 'statistical control', meaning there is only chance-cause variation. Chance-cause variation explains why no process can ever be 100 per cent perfect – things happen.

How reliably do your systems and procedures produce quality? Do they efficiently and consistently meet or exceed your customers' expectations and requirements? Are they simple and streamlined to avoid unnecessary activities and duplication of effort? Do they make it possible for people to 'get it right first time'? To make sure they do, concentrate on the five areas shown in **Table 18.1**.

Transferable skills

1.4 Business operations

TABLE 18.1 Five areas to check to support people's efforts

Suppliers	Do their inputs (information, raw materials, etc.) consistently meet your needs? Are they environmentally conscious?
Throughout each process	Where do things go wrong? Where are the bottlenecks? Where are the hassles? Where is effort duplicated or wasted? Where are materials wasted? How can you prevent this? How can you make each process more environmentally friendly? What is the user experience like; for example, how easy is your website or online ordering process to navigate?
Just before handover or delivery	Is the information, product or service packaged, or put together, in a way the customer appreciates? Does it contain everything the customer needs and wants? Is the packaging reusable, compostable or recyclable?
Post-sale or post-service support and follow-up	Are your customers happy three months later? How could you make them happier?
End-of-life	How can the product be disposed of easily for upcycling or recycling? Is the product sustainable, and can components be repaired or replaced?

When errors do occur, look for the causes in the right places – work systems and processes, not workers – and fix them quickly. Employees struggle to provide quality service and products unless their work inputs, systems and processes back them up. (Chapter 19 explains why poor training, inadequate and poorly maintained tools and equipment, substandard materials or clumsy production processes are the main causes of poor productivity and inconsistent quality and reliability.)

INDUSTRY INSIGHTS

The importance of systems

Sasha was so excited. She'd just found a terrific jacket on sale in an upmarket national retail chain. The sales assistant had been very pleasant and helpful and had provided great service!

When she took her jacket to the cash register, Sasha noticed that the sales assistant became a bit flustered as she searched first for tissue paper to wrap the jacket in, then for a bag in which to place it, then for the credit card machine. Clearly embarrassed at her seeming lack of efficiency, the sales assistant explained, 'I normally work in another shop and everything is different here.'

'Ah,' thought Sasha, 'we need some consistent systems here, so staff can change shops and do their jobs without holding customers up and being embarrassed by looking like they don't know what they're doing. It would be so easy to fix – I wonder if they'd hire me as a consultant?'

Monitoring quality to find problems

Many factors affect quality – employees' skills and morale, equipment, inputs (e.g. information, raw materials) and so on. Although there can't be 100 per cent perfection because of the natural variation in all systems, the constant operations challenge is to reduce variation as much as possible, keep it within acceptable limits and make quality highly predictable.

Rather than checking that everything is all right at the end of a process or service – traditional quality control – it's better to develop a system that builds quality in and check it's working throughout a process or service – quality assurance. You can check visually or use hard numbers, which is known as *statistical process control* (SPC): employees systematically measure and monitor the quality of their own work. (Using control charts, **histograms**, Pareto charts, **process capability charts**, run charts and/or **stratification charts** to monitor quality is explained in Chapter 27.) The point is, you want to know early about and quickly fix anything that is going wrong; this is easier and cheaper than waiting until the end of a process or service. When variations become too wide or too frequent, employees 'fix the process' using the tools and techniques explained in Chapter 27.

Involving employees – not experts and specialists – in monitoring and improving the quality of their own output or service is one of the keys to achieving quality and gives better outcomes than the more traditional 'inspection' quality control approaches.

Monitoring quality to make improvements

Quality isn't just about fixing problems. In a true quality culture, you're always looking for ways to improve what is already working just fine. We discuss the continuous improvement approach in Chapter 19.

Australian and international quality standards

Having quality systems is so important an internationally certifiable process can guide you to establish, supervise, maintain and improve your organisation's quality systems and processes. Most governments and major organisations around the world do business only with organisations that have been certified as conforming to the relevant **quality standards**.

The quality standards of the **International Organization for Standardization (ISO)** are developed by a panel of experts and reviewed and updated as necessary, at least every five years, to ensure they remain current, and more than 1000 new standards are introduced every year. The ISO has developed more than 18 500 standards. Nearly 1 600 000 organisations in 163 countries and more than 20 000 organisations in Australia currently implement the ISO standards.[4]

The ISO acronym

Because the International Organization for Standardization can have different acronyms in different languages (e.g. IOS in English, OIN in French), it is known as ISO, derived from the Greek *isos*, meaning 'equal'. All over the world, whatever the language spoken, the short form of the organisation's name is always ISO.

The standards help organisations to assure quality during the many stages needed to supply a product or service. Some studies have estimated that the benefits of reducing costs through quality can amount to about 10 per cent of sales. Other benefits of adhering to quality standards include:

- economically incorporating desirable characteristics of products and services, such as efficiency, environmental friendliness, interchangeability, reliability, safety and quality, and facilitating trade between countries
- making the development, manufacture and supply of products and services cleaner, safer and more efficient
- providing governments with a technical base for health, safety and environmental legislation
- safeguarding consumers and other users of products and services
- spreading good management practices, innovation, solutions to common problems and technological advances that save organisations 'reinventing the wheel'.

When organisations achieve **quality certification**, their customers can be sure that they have quality systems in place that ensure they are capable of reliably producing a product or service that meets customer requirements. To become certified, an independent external body audits the organisation's quality systems and verifies that they conform to the requirements specified in the relevant standard(s). The auditing body then issues a certificate, which it lists in its client register, making the organisation both 'certified' and 'registered'; the two terms can be used interchangeably, although the term most widely used is 'certified'. ('Accredited' has a different meaning. It refers to the fact that the auditing body has been certified, or accredited, as competent to carry out inspections and certifications in the specified sectors.)

To become certified, organisations must:

- define, establish, explain and guide the way they design, develop, produce, install and service their products and services. This entails analysing the processes and activities they carry out and improving them to eliminate waste in materials and effort, and to minimise the likelihood of errors and non-conformance (any product or service that fails to meet the agreed quality standard)
- document these processes and procedures explicitly, setting out in writing precisely how they achieve the specified quality throughout the entire manufacturing or service provision process (including design, inspection, measurement and testing)
- also document other procedures, including, for example, their procedures for dealing with customer complaints, maintaining machinery, purchasing, and training employees and contractors. Keep quality records that monitor and report on their quality performance to show that they are using their quality systems and that they have minimised variations in systems and processes
- provide other documents, including a quality policy that defines the organisation's approach to quality, a quality manual, work instructions that explain how each service or manufacturing process is to be performed, position descriptions and quality improvement plans that explain how the organisation intends to improve its quality.

The initial certification process usually takes 12 to 18 months. Once certification is awarded, regular 'check' audits, or surveillance audits, follow every six months, and a full and thorough audit is carried out every three years.

Certification is neither easy nor cheap. The costs include fees to the accrediting organisation and countless hours of internal staff time to develop, install and document the systems. Some companies say that certification hasn't really improved their business and they find it too costly to maintain for too few benefits; instead, they have kept their quality systems but given up their certified status. They say good systems, particularly with *traceability* (when a problem occurs you can trace back to find its source and fix it properly so it won't happen again), are what is required, and a company doesn't need certification to have these.

A great value chain

To offer the best quality to your customers and keep improving on it, you need reliable internal processes flowing through the organisation, reliable and sustainable inputs from outside your organisation, and – the icing on the cake – clever ways to work with other organisations to offer ever-better services and products. Together, these form a formidable value chain and a resounding competitive edge.

We discuss working internally, with your internal customers and suppliers, or service partners to refine and improve your processes and services below. We look next at working with your supply chain, or integrated *value chain* – the people and organisations who provide inputs for your products and services – to increase the quality you offer your customers. Then we look at **strategic alliances**, or working with non-competitive organisations, to increase the value that together you can offer your shared customers.

Internal customers

External customers 'pay the rent', but internal customers help you collect it. They are your service partners, the employees and contractors who are part of the internal customer–supplier chain that makes and supplies the goods and services your organisation offers.

Transferable skills

3.1 Teamwork/relationships

Seeing an organisation as a network of interdependent people, teams and functions working together to provide a quality service or product opens up the communication channels and builds a customer service culture. It builds bridges between design and manufacturing, administration, finance, purchasing and marketing, and integrates them into one mutually supporting chain, each playing an important part in adding value to the product or service. In this way, the entire organisation becomes a customer–supplier chain. Everyone works together to satisfy the customer.

To forge strong customer–supplier chains, you need to know who your service partners are. To find your internal customers, or quality and service or process partners, ask yourself:

- What do I produce?
- Who receives it?
- If I didn't do my job or didn't do it well, who would be affected?
- Who depends on my work or information to do their job well?

Next, ask yourself whose work and information you and your team depend on to do your jobs well. These are your **internal suppliers**. Together, they're your service partners in your organisation's customer–supplier chain. Work with them to find out how you can work together more effectively and efficiently to provide a quality service or product that the customer needs and wants. Discuss what you're doing well, what you could improve and how you could improve it. Listen to each other's insights and suggestions. Keep looking for ways to continuously improve your product or service in a way that aligns with the organisation's vision, values and goals and meets the external customers' needs.

Service and trading partnerships

Does your organisation have a cost-cutting mindset that gives contracts to the lowest bidder and forces its suppliers to the brink of bankruptcy? This can do long-term damage to the **goodwill** needed between customers and suppliers and ultimately harm both businesses.

Perhaps your organisation is loyal to its external suppliers, demanding high standards and helping them find ways to achieve them? Working with your organisation's external customers and suppliers to create a smooth and efficient supply chain needs a different approach from the old-fashioned 'adversarial' relationship between supplier and customer organisations. It's becoming progressively more important as organisations increasingly rely on suppliers to reduce costs, improve quality and develop new and sustainable processes and products.

Effective **supply-chain management** increasingly means going a step further and working in trading partnerships and committing to 'co-prosperity' and growing your businesses together. To do this effectively, you each need to understand how the other works and what you are each capable of. You can then work together to create compatible production philosophies and systems, build a common language, transfer knowledge and help each other improve. You need to give regular feedback on how well your trading partners are doing and meet regularly to share information. The trading partnership approach to supply-chain management often opens up a whole new way of doing business. It isn't easy, but it is worth the effort.

As the marketplace continues to be highly competitive and demanding, as global supply chains are hit by rising energy costs and as carbon costs increasingly need to be factored in, supply chain management and trading partnerships are destined to become increasingly pivotal to the success of many organisations. Fortunately, advances in technology are making it easier to streamline and optimise this complex and data-intensive activity.

Strategic alliances

The next wave of offering quality service and products is working with non-competitive suppliers to form a strategic alliance. This is when non-competitive organisations collaborate to grow their businesses together. Also known as *business collaboration,* combining strengths like this is cheaper and easier than buying a company with capabilities you need. As with trading partnerships, strategic alliances need good personal relationships, mutual trust and a commitment to co-prosperity, plus plenty of planning and feedback in order to work. You need to know what each partner is able to deliver and to understand each other's objectives so that each organisation benefits.

You also need to manage potential conflicts. These might be from different decision-making styles, different national or organisational cultures and ways of operating, different norms for social and business behaviour, the long-term aspirations of your alliance partner to enter your market and become a competitor, or competitors your alliance partner is aligned or otherwise involved with. When you understand potential risks like these, you can acknowledge and resolve differences and reduce and manage any remaining competitive and other risks effectively. (Chapter 7 explains how to manage conflict and you can find out about risk management in Chapter 22.)

Strategic alliances also offer important learning opportunities. You can learn, for example, how another organisation manages its research and development, how its information systems operate, how it manages overseas subsidiaries and how it determines remuneration packages. Some strategic alliance partners even set up internal seminars to share this information to further each other's development.

 INDUSTRY INSIGHTS

Clever alliances

Non-competitive suppliers are well down the road to working together to merge and streamline some of their processes. US food producer General Mills, for example, is working with a non-competitive supplier to supermarkets, butter and margarine producer Land O'Lakes, to improve its delivery efficiencies and costs by distributing Land O'Lakes' products with its own. The arrangement is working so well that the companies are now integrating their order-taking and billing processes, too.[5]

Other examples include:

- Starbucks partners with PepsiCo to bottle, distribute and sell Frappuccino and with Kraft foods to sell their coffee in grocery stores.
- Apple and IBM are partnering to produce and sell user-friendly analytics to business.
- Spotify and Uber are partnering to extend their customer base by providing stereo control to Uber Premium customers.

Systematic continuous improvements

Quality's fourth cornerstone is making continual improvements to your work systems and procedures. Chapter 19 discusses how to make continuous, systematic improvements and considers the creative and innovation abilities you need to make these improvements; and Chapter 27 explains the systematic analytical tools and techniques that support your continuous improvement efforts.

Transferable skills

1.4 Business operations

Australia's best

As well as keeping their own 'houses' in order, Australia's best companies look outward, too. They consider themselves connected to lots of other organisations, customers, governments, regulators, suppliers, unions and so on, and they build effective relationships and work with them to get what they want. They also think outside Australia, going overseas to find trends there and bring them back, where they'll be seen as real innovations (even though they aren't). For instance, in Europe organisations have successfully linked cheap petrol with groceries for decades so the partnering oil and grocery chains knew the formula was successful and likely to work in Australia, too.

Australia's best companies also have a '**kaizen** culture' of continuous incremental improvements. They find problems and fix them and find improvement opportunities to make what's working well work better. They expect to change and they can change – rapidly but with control. They value information, asking: what are our customers saying? What is the marketplace saying? How are we doing? Their culture is essentially humble and self-critical, which makes them willing to admit mistakes and learn from them. This rules out a 'blame' culture and creates a culture that supports a diversity of views. In essence, Australia's top organisations have the cornerstones of quality firmly in place.[6]

18.2 Reaping the rewards of caring for your customers

Take care of the customers and the profits will take care of themselves.

Soichiro Honda (founder, Honda Motor Company) in S. Caulkin, 'Why winners stand to lose', *The Guardian*, 4 March 2001.

When you're serious about engaging with and caring for your customers, you take four actions:

1 Find out who your customers are and identify what they expect from you.
2 Communicate precisely how to meet their needs and wants.
3 Build a team culture and procedures that support the desired behaviours and service levels.
4 Use relevant, reliable and verifiable information and data, and systematic analytical tools and techniques (explained in Chapter 27), to measure and analyse the level of service customers actually receive, and seek to continually improve it.

Transferable skills

1.4 Business operations

3.1 Teamwork/ relationships

Without customers, organisations can't survive. And this doesn't just apply to the private sector – hospitals heal patients, colleges and schools teach students. When these organisations can't do that, they cease to exist. How organisations go about satisfying their customers is what separates failed organisations, surviving organisations and thriving organisations. Satisfied customers drive profits, so satisfying customers is a primary concern.

Who are your customers?

Shops and hotels clearly have customers, but who else has customers? Does a mailroom assistant have customers? An orderly in a hospital? A garbage collector? A volunteer for a charity? Do HR and

IT teams have customers? What about finance and purchasing departments, or public servants – say, employees of the Australian Taxation Office or Centrelink?

Everyone has customers. Whatever sector of the economy they work in, whether they work directly with customers or behind the scenes with internal customers, every employee has customers and every work team has customers. In this section, we consider external customers; that is, customers outside the organisation who purchase or use its products or services. You might call them clients, users or patients, but, ultimately, they're still customers.

Know your primary customer

Customer is a loose term, but when you don't know who your primary customers are, you can put your efforts into satisfying the wrong customers. Your primary customers may not be those who provide the most revenue but those who unlock the most value in your business. The 530 million members of LinkedIn don't provide any revenue but they make the network attractive to LinkedIn's revenue providers – recruiters, who provide 54 per cent of LinkedIn's revenue, and advertisers, who provide 26 per cent.[7] That makes individual users LinkedIn's value creators and its primary customer group.

External customers

External customers may be individual customers, such as the shopper who purchases a box of cornflakes. Or they may be the organisations you supply, such as the supermarket chain that purchases the cornflakes in bulk or in pallets of pre-packaged retail boxes.

Whoever your customers are, they have a choice about where to spend their money. As summarised in **Figure 18.2**, you can think about, and deal with, your customers in the traditional way or in the customer-focused way.

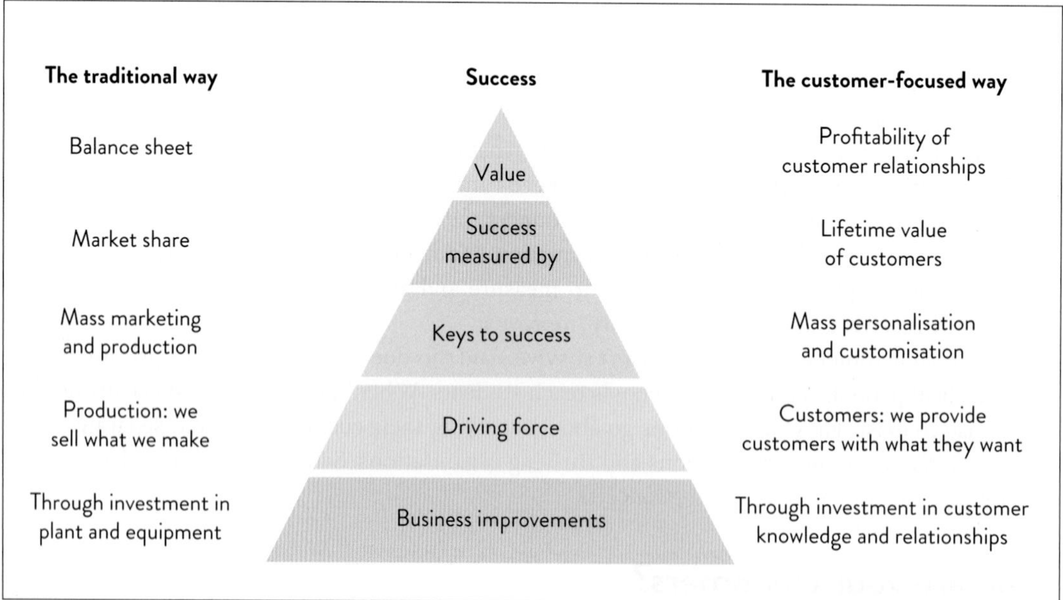

FIGURE 18.2 The way to success

When you analyse the profitability of various groups, or segments, of customers, you know which ones to treat so well they won't consider going elsewhere. You also know the profile of people to target as new customers and who you should not waste your time and money pursuing. When your customers are from multiple groups with different needs and expectations, you may want to build a customer register similar to the stakeholder register described in Chapter 22.

What are they worth?

Some customers are very profitable, some are moderately profitable, some are marginal and some cost you money. The lifetime value of existing and future customers is known as *lifetime customer value* (LCV). Calculating the sum of the value of current and future customers is one way to assess a company's value; many people believe that it is the only possible way to value many new internet and e-commerce businesses. It is also a key success measure in many businesses in high-growth sectors as well as in more traditional industries.

LCV is important because it costs money to win a customer. Since repeat business is free, you can think of happy customers who are 'regulars' as 'money in the bank'. Not for nothing do people say we should see our customers as appreciating assets, and we should appreciate those assets. Here is a simple way to calculate LCV. Take the average purchase value of your average customer per week (or month). Multiply this by 48 (weeks) or 11 (months) to allow for holidays. Multiply this by the number of years you normally retain a customer. The answer gives you their lifetime value.

Here are some ways to increase the lifetime value of your customers:

- extend the range of goods and services they buy from you
- retain their business longer
- sell them more expensive items than they are currently buying
- sell them more of what they're already buying from you.

And what about the value of lost customers, those who 'jump ship' to another organisation as a result of bad service? The more lost customers you have, the more they cost you, not only in terms of lost lifetime customer value but also in terms of the cost to replace them. That's why everyone needs to understand that service excellence must be upheld all the time, not just some of the time or when it's convenient. Figure 18.3 lists three quick tips to improve your quality and keep your customers.

As summarised in Figure 18.4, providing a service external customers value starts inside the organisation, with satisfied employees. This means training them well, rewarding them well with psychological as well as monetary rewards and offering career paths and other benefits. (For more

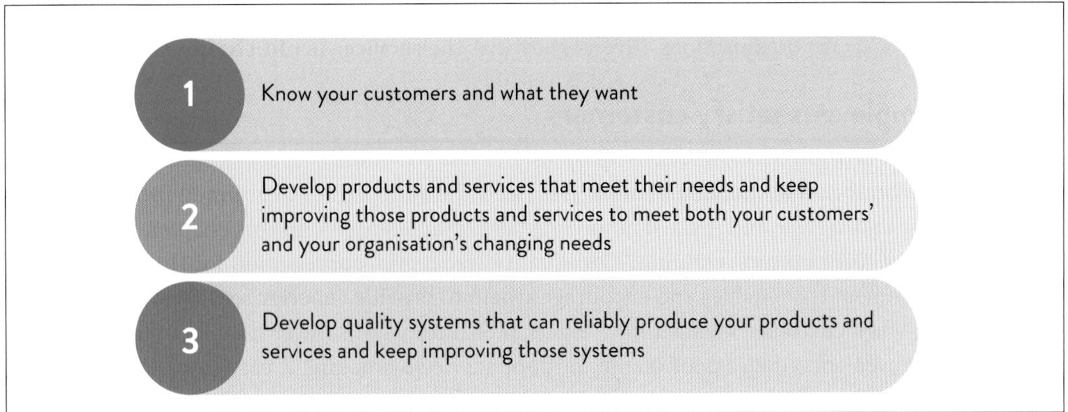

FIGURE 18.3 How to improve your quality and keep your customers

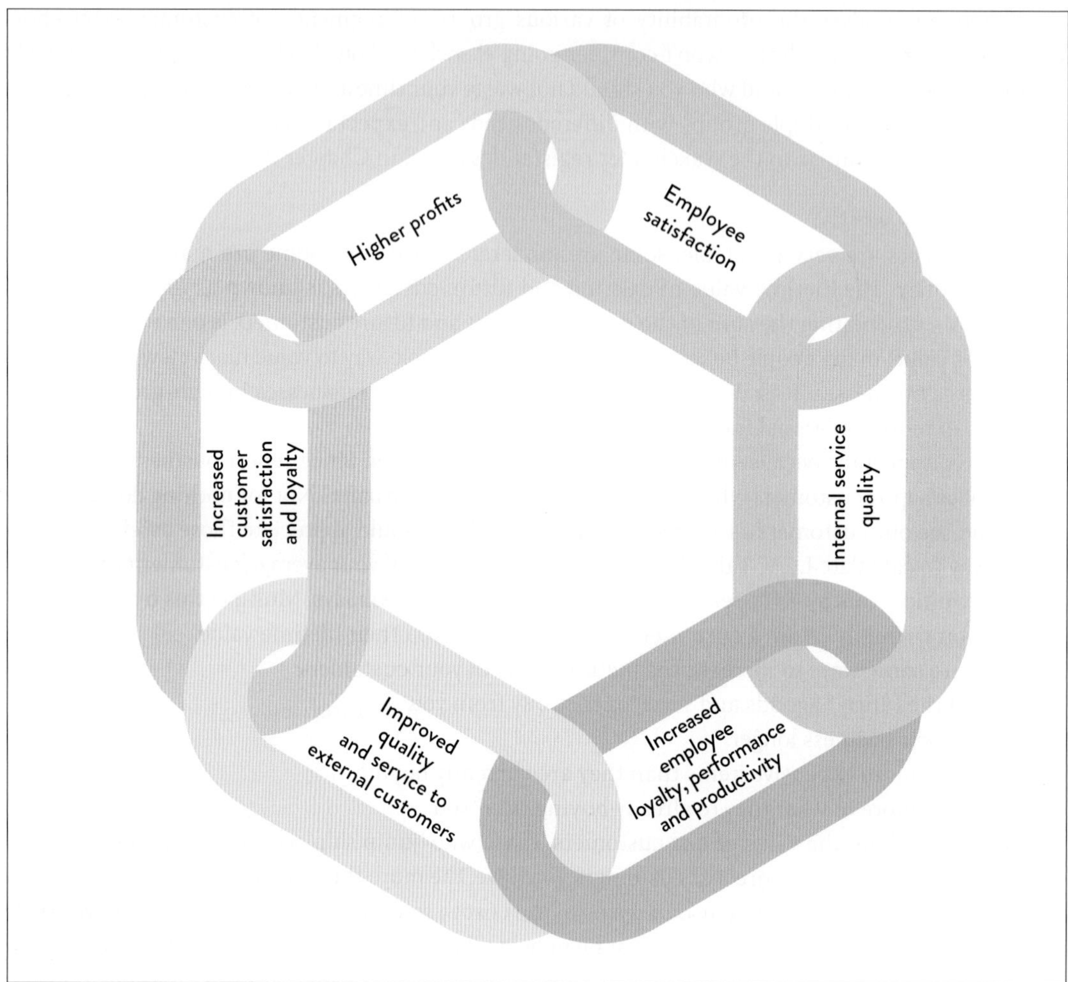

FIGURE 18.4 The service–profit chain

on this, see Chapter 11.) Satisfied employees are more willing to satisfy their internal customers than unhappy, grumpy employees, which boosts service to external customers, and ultimately increases their satisfaction and loyalty. The result is profits in the private sector and a fulfilled mission in public and not-for-profit sector organisations. This is known as the **service–profit chain**.

Satisfied employees satisfy customers

Satisfied customers begin with satisfied employees. But lest you think that service failures stem from individuals, remember that individual employees need the support of streamlined procedures that build in quality and service and make it automatic (as explained earlier in this chapter). They need a customer service team culture, training, high-quality leadership, appreciation for their work, and a working environment that enables and encourages them to provide superior service to their internal customers. So when customer satisfaction – external or internal – is lower than it could be, find out what allows or even encourages poor quality or poor service by making it easy to make mistakes or makes it easier to let quality and service standards slide than it is to maintain them.

Include satisfying or delighting your customers in your team purpose and make sure everyone understands what that means. Recruit the right people – people who will 'do it right' even when no one is looking, people whose skills, abilities and motivations are suited to their jobs and whose jobs can engage their loyalty and passion (this is explained in Chapters 10, 11 and 27).

There is good news, though; 60 per cent of Australians are willing to give a company another chance after two to four instances of poor customer service. After this they switch companies. That means, of course, that a rather high 40 per cent of customers switch immediately, and this is very expensive.[8]

Customer-driven, product-driven or cost-driven?

Identifying precisely who your customers are and exactly what they want from you, and working with your service partners to provide it, means you're *customer-driven*. Placing a high priority on identifying and meeting the needs of your external customers often requires a change in approach from the more traditional *product-driven* thinking, which says, in effect, 'This is what we produce. Do you want it or not?'

A product-driven organisation produces goods or services and then finds customers who want to buy them. It might say, 'We make cornflakes and we sell them in 500 gram retail packets supplied in pallets of 24 packs. Too bad if you want to buy 100 gram packets. We don't make them.' In contrast, a customer-driven organisation would say, 'Did you say you'd like to buy our cornflakes in 100 gram retail packets? Let me find out how soon we can adjust our manufacturing process to accommodate you.'

Customer-driven organisations are also different from *cost-driven* organisations, which concentrate mainly on reducing the costs involved in producing a product or service. 'Beat our competitors on cost' is their motto. A cost-driven organisation would say something like, 'Sorry, we don't do 100 gram packets. It would be too expensive to install the machinery.'

Until about 2000, internal cost-cutting was a good move. But once everyone started doing it, another competitive advantage was needed and it's this: working with your customers to give them exactly what they want and, when it's B2B, adding significant value to their business. This requires considerable innovation, optimising supply chain costs and efficiencies by, for example, joining some operations and sharing proprietary data with your external customers and suppliers (as discussed earlier in this chapter), and flexible manufacturing and/or service provision – something low-cost producers in emerging countries can't easily do.

Whether your customers are internal or external, here are the four steps to becoming a customer-driven work team:

1 Identify your customers, listen to them carefully and make meeting or exceeding their needs and wants your primary goal.
2 Develop work procedures that reliably satisfy your customers.
3 Build a culture that focuses team members on their customers and on providing what they want.
4 Use customer-friendly systems to build strong relationships with your service partners.

 INDUSTRY INSIGHTS

Serving your customers' needs

Reasoning that construction companies care more about the productivity they can achieve from using tools than about owning them, Hilti, the Liechtenstein-based maker of high-end power tools, introduced a fleet management program. Construction companies, its main customer group, pay Hilti a monthly fee. In return, Hilti manages customers' vehicle fleets to suit each customer's business

model and provides, services and repairs all tools. Hilti's slogan is: 'We manage your tools, so you can manage your business.'

This simplifies their customers' financial planning and reduces their administrative work and downtime. Customers also appreciate using high-quality tools.

Meet your customers' needs

Government agencies need to know who their customers are and what they want, and then develop services and other ways to meet their needs. So do not-for-profit service providers, retailers, and suppliers of utilities and commercial goods and services. Even sports teams, orchestras and colleges need to identify and meet the needs of their various customer groups. To survive, they all need to find better ways to do this than their competition. And to thrive, they need to keep improving their offerings.

The only reliable way to match your products or services to your customers' needs is to work with your customers to find out what is important to them and then provide it. The process is similar to the problem-solving and decision-making process summarised in **Figure 26.4** in Chapter 26. In fact, the more complex and sophisticated your offering, the more closely you should follow the seven steps described in Chapter 26. When your offering is complex and sophisticated, you may need to work through several options with your customers and assist them to evaluate which one best meets their needs.

Here are nine ways to better serve your customers and better predict and meet their needs:

1 Analyse complaints: track complaints and analyse them with a check sheet (explained in Chapter 27) or another quality improvement tool, to find what customers can be bothered to complain about most and remove the cause of those complaints; then look for suggestions for product or service enhancements that are disguised as complaints. (See the section 'Keep good records' later in the chapter.)
2 Analyse big data: with the right algorithms, you can accurately spot trends and patterns.
3 Ask the customer.
4 Ask your team: they can probably spot ways to better meet customer needs.
5 Eliminate: drop services and remove items that add no value or too little value for too few customers.
6 Look for 'hacks': find unexpected uses for your products on social media.
7 Observe your customers: iconic US jeans maker Levi Strauss saw customers ripping their jeans and brought out a line of ready-ripped jeans. Spotting and responding to trends and patterns can give you an edge in the marketplace and help you refine and improve your service and quality.
8 Tune into online forums: what are customers and potential customers asking about, complaining about and talking about online regarding your products and services?
9 Use customer relationship management software to manage your relationships with your customers, plan sales activities and so on; some can be used B2B as well as B2C.

Identify customer needs

Figure 18.5 shows some questions that you and your team members can ask each other. When you meet to get together, listen for people's different perspectives and ideas. Be careful when you think you know what your customers need and want, though. It's easy to make assumptions, to see what you want or expect to see. You and your team may think you know what your customers want, but you never know for sure unless you ask them. And you don't want to waste your time, energy

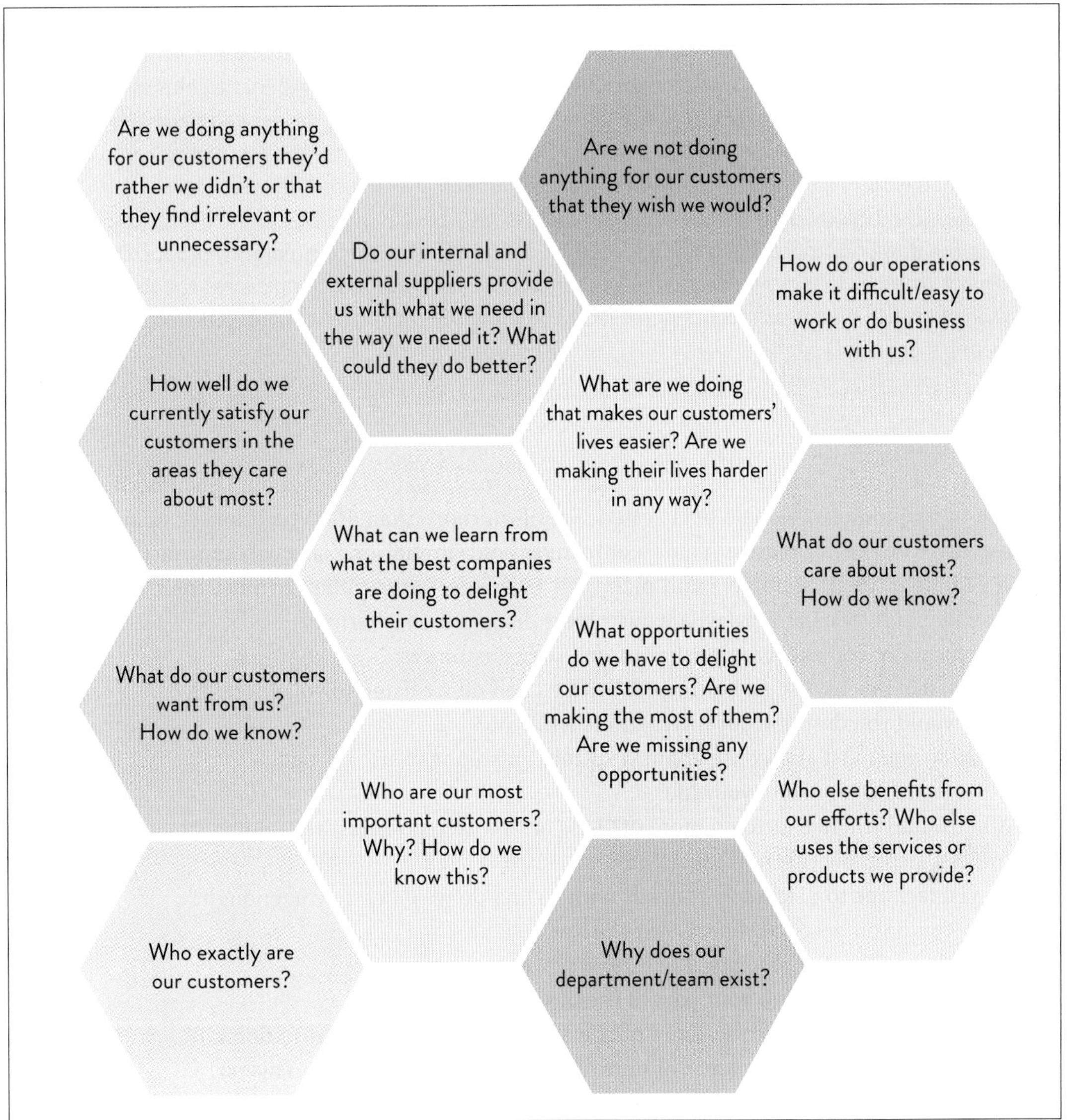

FIGURE 18.5 Identifying customer needs

and resources 'satisfying' customer needs that aren't important to them and alienate customers by ignoring needs that are important.

When you don't know what your customers really want, you could go out of business; when you do know, and provide it, you've got longevity and success.

INDUSTRY INSIGHTS

Partnering pays

Two European companies imbed valuable information into their offerings that only they can provide, binding them more closely to their customers and giving them the edge over cost-driven producers.

Schmitz Cargobull, a German truck body and trailer maker, supplies its customers with a range of support services, including telematics (sophisticated information technology) that track and transmit key information on any Schmitz Cargobull-produced trailer. Customers, drivers and freight agents can track, in real time, the location of a trailer, its maintenance history, the temperature of its cargo and the weight it is carrying. The information also helps reduce the risk of breakdowns.

In the oil and gas industry, fluctuating temperatures in pipelines cost money. It damages pipes, making the flow of oil more variable and reducing drilling efficiency, for example. By producing intelligent pipelines that monitor and level out temperatures throughout the pipeline, the subsea division of French company Technip increased its revenues by 35 per cent in one year and had operating margins 50 per cent higher than for the company overall.[9]

Ask the customer

Nestlé has a 'war room' where analysts monitor social media to find clues about consumer acceptance and use of its products. Google beta tested Gmail on more than 1000 technology opinion leaders for five years before its release. Some companies hold annual or biannual 'summits' where they host a sample of their customers and pick their brains for ways to better meet their needs. Other organisations run focus groups, where customers discuss their offerings.

Less formally, you can simply ask your end-user customers:

- Do you feel free to discuss your needs with us and do we listen to you enough?
- How would you describe our interactions with you?
- What do you most appreciate about your relationship with us?
- What value do we add to your life?
- What would you like us to do more of? Less of? To keep doing as we're doing it?

You can also apply this to B2B customers:

- Do you feel free to discuss your needs with us and do we listen to you enough?
- How would you describe the way we work with you?
- What do you most appreciate about the way we work with you?
- What value do we add to your part of the business?
- What would you like us to do more of? Less of? To keep doing as we're doing it?

Listen for three important areas of information in your customers' answers:

1. What they must have (their *needs*).
2. What they would like to have (their *wants*).
3. What would really thrill them (*delighters*).

Needs, wants and delighters

A *need* is what your customers require. A *want* is what your customers desire. A *delighter* goes surprisingly and wonderfully beyond your customers' wants, so much so that they'll probably tell others about it. Delighters multiply your customers' loyalty and goodwill towards your department, your organisation and their individual service providers.

When was the last time you sat down with one or more of your customers and discussed what they expect, want and need from you? What they expected, needed and wanted last year or six months ago may have changed. Keep records to highlight any changes or trends in your customers' expectations, preferences and satisfaction levels. Be certain that you fully understand their expectations. Don't just look for the negatives – give your customers a chance to give you positive feedback, too, so you know what to keep doing. The better you know your customers, the better you can serve and delight them.

What specific quality measures can you apply to your customers' needs? What time and cost specifications do you need to meet? When your customers' expectations are extensive, can you rank them in priority order? Of the possible ways you could provide the product or service that your customers want, which way would suit them best? In the largest ever study of chief executives, business leaders pointed to their own customer base as being the expected source of most of the important changes they would need to address. They identified two new demanding classes of customers that they expected to invest in most: the information omnivore and the socially minded customer.[10]

Another international study asked CEOs of top-performing organisations to identify the most crucial factor for their company's success. Getting closer to customers was nominated by 95 per cent of them as their most important strategic initiative. They plan to use the internet and interactive and social media channels to engage with customers and other stakeholders.[11]

Analyse big data

Transferable skills

1.4 Business operations

5.2 Technology use

Analytics, or **'big data'**, power consumer products and services in many companies. Every organisation that makes things, moves things, consumes things or works with customers has increasing amounts of data on these activities. Powerful data-gathering and analysis methods mean that organisations can gather and analyse huge data sets to predict consumer behaviour and trends, make sound decisions and take optimal actions.

Google analytics teams spend hours in their labs analysing customers' eye movements and other variables to assess their reactions to tiny changes in their products (display, maps, searches and so on). Property development company, Stockland, analyses billions of lines of data of credit card transactions and supermarket data to understand the purchasing behaviour of shoppers in the catchment area of a shopping centre it intends to build. This helps it to match the size of the centre to the needs of the local community and avoid over- or underdeveloping a site, and ensure the mix of retailers suits shoppers. AGL, Australia Post, the Commonwealth Bank, Wesfarmers and Woolworths all process big data for customer analytics, marketing strategies, risk management, audit reports and supply-chain management.[12] (For more information on analytics, see Chapter 1.)

Analyse your value chain

A technique called **value chain analysis** is another good way to pinpoint customer needs. Working with your customers, you identify and agree the 'critical few' outcomes that really make a difference to them. Once you've done that, you work with your team to examine how you deliver your service to your customers, step by step, to see where you can make improvements and find opportunities to 'delight' your customers. Then you set SMART targets to measure how effectively you make those improvements.

The mortgage journey

ANZ drilled down into its customers' home lending journey and found four critical points around which it redesigned its internal lending procedures: advising the customer of the initial credit decision, informing the vendor, the transaction and customer settlement. It then trained staff in the new procedures and in customer service.[13]

Keep good records

Transferable skills

1.4 Business operations

3.3 Written communication

5.2 Technology use

Tracking customer compliments, complaints and problems, and payment and purchasing histories and other behaviours for later study and analysis, can also help you better meet their needs. It can highlight important trends and risks and help you structure and improve your offering. Documenting, for example, the nature of compliments and problems, what led to them, how they were dealt with, how long problems took to resolve and how satisfied the customer was with the solution can provide valuable information regarding where problems are most likely to occur, isolate opportunities to improve your customer care and point to trends to manage before problems worsen. (Chapter 27 explains how to capture and display this data in a meaningful way.)

When the same type of problem repeatedly occurs, you can work with your team to fix it at its source so it won't happen again (explained in Chapter 26). Look for areas to make improvements, too (explained in Chapter 19). Look for ways to use customers' comments, complaints and suggestions to spot gaps in your service and add value to the way you serve your customers. (Chapter 20 explains how to monitor the results of your efforts.)

You can identify which customers you lose and compare their profiles with those of customers you keep to spot ways to improve your service, increase customer retention and identify which potential customers to target. Determining which customers are the most and least profitable can also help identify potential customers to target. You can use your customer data to benchmark important indicators of your ability to provide good service against all organisations as well as organisations in your industry, and to highlight improvement areas.

The rewards of quality and good service

What's most important to you when deciding who to do business with? Top spot for most consumers is good value for money (51 per cent), followed by excellent customer service (20 per cent) and better products (18 per cent). Few customers globally – 6 per cent and 5 per cent, respectively – care much about ease of doing business online and convenience. They would rather go out of their way to spend their money with businesses that offer quality and service.

For most Australians (81 per cent), having questions answered by knowledgeable people is part of an excellent service experience, although not that many of us need to be thanked for being a customer (34 per cent) or addressed by name (19 per cent), and being 'sold to' plays no part in excellent service, according to 95 per cent of us.

If you want us to spend more with your business, provide that good service, because 72 per cent of Australians spend more with a company because of a history of positive customer service experiences. And 95 per cent of us always or sometimes tell others about our good customer service experiences through a variety of channels, including face-to-face, texting and social networking sites.

And poor service? That results in lost sales – 58 per cent of Australians have chosen not to complete a transaction or an intended purchase because of poor customer service (only Indians, Mexicans, Singaporeans and Americans are fussier than we are in that regard).[14]

A difference of opinion ...

See your role as finding a way to meet your customers' needs. When this proves difficult, seek the assistance of your manager or other specialised staff in finding a way to provide what the customer requires. When your customer is internal, you can meet with them and redesign the workflow between you to overcome or compensate for the constraints you are facing. Don't automatically think or say, 'No, what you want is too hard, too difficult, too time-consuming, too expensive', or give any other excuse for not doing it. Ask questions to make sure you fully understand what your customer is after.

Cruise ship designer John McNeece once said:

> There is a problem trying to figure out what people want by canvassing them. I mean, if Henry Ford canvassed people on whether or not he should build a motor car, they'd probably tell him what they really wanted was a faster horse.[15]

What if your customers might think they need one thing and, based on your experience and knowledge, you believe they actually need, or indeed would be delighted, with another? This happens, particularly when you are more expert than your customers. For example, the customers of health professionals, IT service providers and vendors of complex products and equipment often don't know what is possible or what products even exist.

When you think you have a better way of meeting your customer's needs, you can offer your ideas. When you think your customer's expectations are unrealistic, you can help them adjust their expectations. When you have a hunch that something could be done more effectively another way, you can mention it and offer to investigate or test your theory.

18.3 Building customer relationships

> I told everyone, 'Be afraid of our customers, because those are the folks who have the money. Our competitors are never going to send us money.'
>
> Jeff Bezos (founder, Amazon), interview with Julia Kirby, Thomas A. Stewart, 'The institutional yes', *Harvard Business Review*, October 2007.

Transferable skills

1.4 Business operations

3.1 Teamwork/ relationships

Who would you rather buy from, someone you know, like and trust, or someone you hardly know at all? Who would you rather deal with over the counter, however briefly – someone who seems welcoming and friendly, or someone who seems cold and stand-offish? People deal with people, and most people want to deal with people with whom they feel some sort of connection or bond. Even when that connection is fleeting, people prefer 'feel-good moments' to those that leave them feeling dissatisfied or uncomfortable.

Whether the goal of service providers is to increase sales by offering friendly and appreciated advice or by providing information or assistance, the more quickly and thoroughly they can establish a professional yet cordial relationship, the better their results. Since the key to the success of many businesses is repeat business from loyal customers and word-of-mouth business based on recommendations from loyal customers (for 44 per cent of Australians, recommendations are the most likely reason we do business with a new company),[16] training your team to establish and build strong customer relationships makes sound sense.

You can take care of your customers *before* you provide the product or service, *while* you are providing it and *after* you have provided it. Each of these three opportunities contains six ways to delight your customers and make them feel special. You can:

1 communicate clearly and honestly
2 develop and maintain trust
3 meet or exceed your customers' needs and expectations
4 recognise their loyalty by offering a privilege they value
5 show that you can help your customers achieve their goals
6 show that you understand your customers.

Moments of truth

Have you ever noticed that it's the little things that delight people and build goodwill – or do the opposite? How do the little things that you and your team do build or destroy customer goodwill? Examining the moments of truth (MOTs) you and your team provide is a good way to find out.

A moment of truth is any contact a customer has with your organisation. Every contact gives customers information about the quality of service you provide and strengthens (or erodes) their loyalty. MOTs can occur without any contact between a customer and an employee, such as over an automated telephone system or a website, or they can involve direct contact, for example on the telephone or face-to-face.

One of the reasons MOTs are so important is that, however fleeting, they firmly establish how highly an organisation values its customers. This goes far deeper than logic. MOTs are strong and lasting because they involve emotions and, as we see below, emotionally satisfied customers are more loyal than those who are merely rationally satisfied.

Figure 18.6 shows five questions you and your team members can ask yourselves to build a picture of what the MOTs with your work team are like.

- ? Do your internal mechanisms – organisation culture, procedures, systems, training, tools and equipment – support employees to meet customers' needs and even help them delight customers?
- ? Do the MOTs with your team say, 'We care about our customers'?
- ? Do your team members feel empowered and supported to make on-the-spot decisions to meet customers' needs and make them feel valued and special?
- ? Does every team member treat every contact they have with customers as an opportunity to grow customer loyalty, win new customers and build the organisation's reputation?
- ? When team members talk to customers, do they realise they aren't just speaking for themselves – they are representing their team, their function and the entire organisation?

FIGURE 18.6 What are your MOTs like?

 INDUSTRY INSIGHTS

Magical memories

Disney's overarching vision is to provide 'magical memories'. At the Disney Yacht Club and Beach Club resorts, multifunctional teams of front-line 'cast members' (as service providers are called) service-mapped the arrival process. They identified the points of contact that guests experienced to check in: valet, front desk, guest services, bell services and housekeeping. They devised ways to make the entire process seamless and hassle-free and created a process known as the 'awesome arrival' – an integrated system that is swift, personalised and provides sensational service.

Make the most of every customer contact

When MOTs support customers' 'end-to-end' experience with your organisation, you have customer service that's hard to beat. Try mapping the total cycle, from start to finish, of dealing with your organisation or team that customers experience and see how you can make it hassle-free and delightful. Similar to the way a flow chart details the way work progresses through a department, a *customer service map* identifies each step customers take to accomplish their objective with you. First, list each step of your customers' experience, from when they first decide to deal with you through to after the transaction. Next, determine what most influences the customers' perception of value at each step. (Make sure you really know and are not just guessing.)

Once you and your team have created the map, look at each step to find opportunities to meet or exceed customers' expectations in a way that makes your organisation stand out from the competition. Set some SMART measures of success with your team – from your customers' points of view. Plan how to improve your performance in each one and track your improvements. Show you're serious by posting a graph of your improvements over time in the kitchen area or some other place where team members regularly gather. You might be able to benchmark your customers' start-to-finish experience with you, too, either within your own organisation or by identifying the organisations that excel at each of these factors, regardless of the industry they're in, and benchmarking your results against theirs.

Provide emotional as well as functional benefits

Transferable skills

2.3 Business strategy

3.1 Teamwork/ relationships

You can satisfy customers with functional benefits; for example, you can save them time or effort, or simplify their lives. The other way to satisfy customers is with emotional benefits; for example, you can reduce their anxiety, provide excitement, fun or nostalgia, offer them pride of ownership, provide an opportunity to help others or have a social impact by preserving the environment. Emotional benefits are the most powerful, although you want to provide functional benefits, too. The more of each type of benefit, the more loyal you can expect your customers to be.

There are many powerful emotional benefits. Here are some of them:

- feeling confident in myself or about the future
- feeling part of a group I admire or relate to
- feeling secure
- feeling successful
- showing my individuality
- reaching my potential or my ideal self.

To determine what emotional benefits you offer your customers, find out what they are hoping to accomplish with your product or service and target your appeal to that.

Offering functional and emotional benefits gives you two types of satisfied customers: *rationally* satisfied and *emotionally* satisfied. They differ in important factors, such as how many take their business elsewhere, how often they take their business elsewhere, how much they spend with you and how frequently they purchase your products or use your services. Emotionally satisfied customers contribute far more to the bottom line than customers who are primarily rationally satisfied, even though they may both score as satisfied with your offering.

The brains of emotionally satisfied customers actually behave differently; their brains, compared with rationally satisfied customers, have significantly more activity (measured with a functional magnetic resonance imaging machine) when thinking about a company. **Figure 18.7** shows the elements of emotional satisfaction in customers.

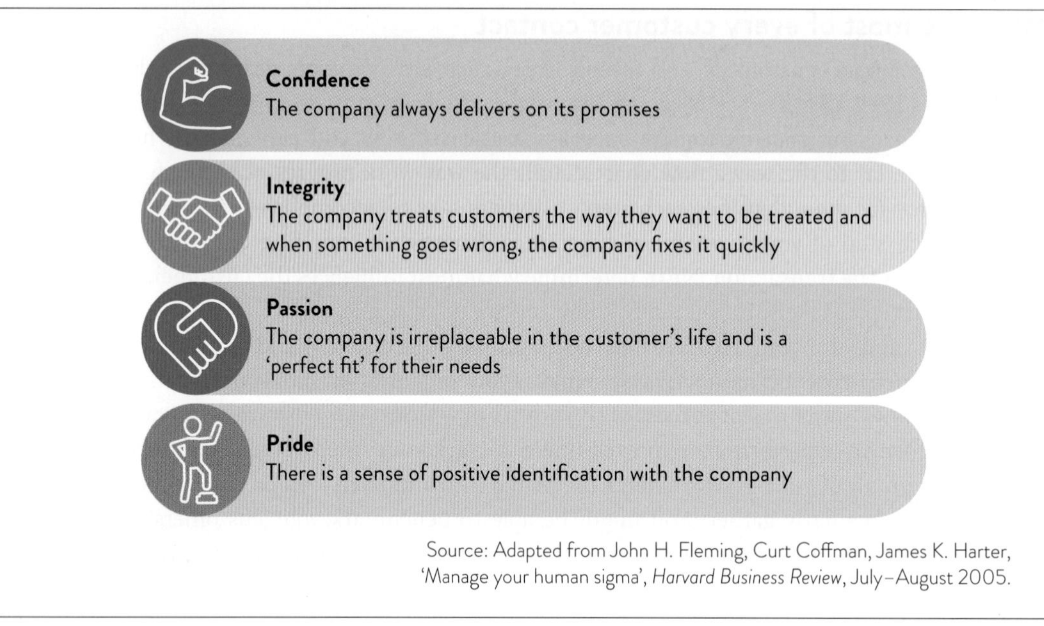

FIGURE 18.7 The elements of emotional satisfaction in customers

Look beyond your product or service to identify the emotional need you satisfy for your customers. Is it contentment? Peace of mind? Pride of ownership? Reliability? The relief of a problem easily solved? That's the big picture to keep in mind when working with your customers.

Moments of truth are one way to develop emotionally satisfying relationships with your service partners and external customers. Here are some other ways to meet their psychological needs:

- *Make customers feel welcome:* What first impression do you present? The way you and your team greet and respond to your customers tells them how pleased you are to see them. Train your team to know and use the visual and vocal elements of friendly service and to 'pass the time of day' with a bit of small talk. Ensure your premises are clean and well-lit and that customers can enter and find what or whom they want easily. This also goes to your online presence; how welcome do your customers feel when they visit your website?
- *Make customers feel important:* What do you do that makes your customers feel special? How do you and your team show you appreciate and value them and their business? Do your attitudes and actions show you respect your customers and their needs? Do you care enough about them to draw their attention to a product or service you think they might be interested in or suggest ways you can help them? How important do your customers feel when they visit your website?
- *Make customers feel understood:* Do you and your team really understand what your customers want and need and concentrate on meeting those needs, or do you just 'go through the motions' or do only what's easy? Do you listen to your customers and respond flexibly? Are you willing to customise for your customers so they get exactly what they want? Do team members have the authority to adjust what they're doing to suit customers' needs or must they blindly follow a prescribed system?
- *Make customers feel comfortable:* Do you and your team make your customers feel physically as well as psychologically comfortable? How secure and enjoyable does it feel to do business with you? How confident do you make your customers feel about how well you can take care of them and meet their needs? How easy is your website to navigate? How consistent is your social media presence?

The price of 'I don't care'

Why do you stop dealing with a company? Because a better offer or product comes along? Or a new company opens in a more convenient location? Maybe. But most people's motivation to move their business elsewhere begins with perceived indifference on the part of the customer service or sales staff. Poor service and poor attitudes lose business. Exceptional service engages the emotions and keeps business. The same holds true for dealing with not-for-profit and government organisations. People don't like being treated with indifference. Are your team members willing to 'think outside the square' and do that little bit extra for customers when they see the need or would that only result in reprimands?

Emotional needs in B2B

Purchasing managers are people too. What their emotional need often boils down to is finding a difference in your offering that would make a noticeable difference to their business. This is known as a *justifier*, and it provides a clear-cut reason for selecting one supplier over another. Think of it as the 'tie-breaker'.

The next time another business asks you for 'something else', look for something you can give that, while it would cost your company relatively little, would add a lot of value to your customer; or while it might involve a bit of extra work on your part, would save the customer much more work. For instance:

- A book publisher might offer to print books with a company's logo on the cover and include a message from the CEO as a foreword for a minimum order number.
- A company that leases vehicles to corporate customers might allow a customer to cancel contracts up to a specified number of vehicles prematurely without a penalty.
- A project management company might assign someone to manage a project that the client has worked with before and trusts to do a good job.

Once you've found that justifier, purchasing managers can present your offering for approval and show how they are contributing real value to their organisation. Helping them win means you win, too.

Look for justifiers in the following areas:

- How your customer actually uses the offering. Discuss how the customer uses your product or service from arrival to completed use and look for ways to make it easier, faster, more economical, safer and so on. (See Chapter 19 to find out how to do this and earlier in this chapter to find out more about trading partnerships.) Your basic question is, 'What can we do to be a better supplier?'
- Form a strategic alliance. You can work with another, non-competitive supplier to combine your offerings in a way that strengthens you both and adds value for your mutual customers. (See Section 18.1 for more information on building strategic alliances.)
- Cruise the customer's website. Most companies post their values, awards won, key initiatives in the areas of risk management, safety, sustainability and so on. Study these areas to find ways that you can add value.

Keep your tie-breakers fresh. Don't think that once you've found a justifier for a particular customer or industry, you can stop there. You need to keep moving to keep your advantage because customers' priorities and concerns change. On top of that, your competitors quickly catch on to what you're offering and offer the same or better.

Transferable skills

1.4 Business operations

3.1 Teamwork/ relationships

3.2 Verbal communication

3.3 Written communication

Explain in ways your customers can understand

You may have heard the advice 'sell the sizzle not the sausage'. It highlights the need to stress what matters to customers – the emotional benefits – when you communicate with them. Train your team to find out what emotional needs their customers want met and address that. Train them to use expressions and language customers understand, too; that usually means leaving out jargon and technical terms.

Often, what customers care most about is what your product or service can do for them, rather than its technical aspects. This means talking about *benefits*, not *features*. For example, imagine you are buying a smartphone and you want to take photos with it when you go bushwalking and sightseeing. You might want to know that it's light (not that it weighs 130 grams) and that it has a long battery life, making it the lightest and longest-lasting smartphone currently on the market, which means you can rely on it to take lots of photos over a long period. Or perhaps photo quality is more important; that would lead you to a different make and model that would help capture some great memories.

When you know what your customer is looking for and why, you can recommend products that best meet their needs and explain the benefits of those products, helping them to make a decision they will be happy with. (That means teaching your team to gather good information first, as explained in Chapter 6.)

To find the benefit of a feature, keep asking 'So what?' until you have found the core reason that a particular feature of a product or service would be useful to a customer. (The battery life is 27 hours. So what? It will last longer than other smartphone batteries. So what? You don't need to charge it as often. So what? That's really handy when you're bushwalking or on holiday.)

Some features have several benefits. Which should you mention? Listen as customers talk about what is important to them and note the terms they use to describe what they need and want. This helps you home in on what is most important to the customer, select which benefits to mention and then explain them in terms the customer can readily understand.

How are we doing?

Whoever and wherever your customers, service partners and trading partners are, keep the lines of communication open. Talking directly to them can show you what is important to them, what they're thinking and where they're heading. On top of that, people prefer to do business with people they have a relationship with.

Ask a few key clients and service partners to tell you what they think about the service you offer before, during and after delivery, what you do best and where you could improve. Ask them how easy it is to request your help and how satisfied they are with the promptness, quality and pleasantness of your and your team's responses. Listen for any patterns and stay alert to spot any trends. With social media you can do this by posting live feeds regularly and using polls in your online communication.

Get out and about with your customers, trading partners and service partners and see what they're doing and how they're using your products or services. Keep in touch through social media, informal conversations, formal feedback mechanisms and virtual meetings. Listen and act on what your customers are saying, particularly your most and least satisfied customers.

When customers provide positive feedback, it makes them more likely to purchase again, spend more money next time, feel more loyalty towards the company and increases their reported satisfaction with the company. It even works when customers aren't fully satisfied, perhaps because it reframes their experience more positively.

Recalling memories makes it easier to recall them in future, so it makes sense to ask customers to recall positive memories. People want to be consistent, so customers may be less apt to think poorly of a company after expressing a compliment. Saying nice things also builds positive relationships, too. Better still, paying a compliment to a company builds a virtuous cycle of mutual appreciation. When all employees hear are complaints and negative feedback, who can blame them for placing customers in the 'bad news' department? When employees also hear their fair share of customer compliments, they can take the 'good news' with them to their next customer interaction.[17]

Superconsumers

How many staplers do you have? Would it surprise you that some people own, on average, eight staplers each, even though they don't do more stapling than other people? They are the 'superconsumers', in this example the approximately 10 per cent of the stapler customers who want just the right stapler for each stapling occasion. Now, wouldn't you think their segment of customers would have no need to buy a ninth or a tenth stapler? You'd be surprised.

Superconsumers are similar to advocates in that they combine big spending with high engagement. Both love to use a product and use it as often as they can but superconsumers also want to find new uses for the product and variations on it. In many industries, including clothing, consumer durables, consumer packaged goods and financial services, this 10 per cent of customers provide 30 to 40 per cent of a product's or service's revenue and 50 per cent of the profits. Don't just keep this small valuable segment of your customers happy by treating them like VIPs. Find ways to increase sales to them – they're begging you to.

Fortunately, these superconsumers are easy to reach through social media and direct marketing. Social media is also a way to learn from your superconsumers and advocates how you can satisfy them even more and to pick up new product or service ideas and test them out.[18]

The ones that get away ...

Don't confuse satisfaction with loyalty. Even when you're providing quality service and products, satisfied customers may switch to another supplier when that supplier can do it better.

The truth is, you're always in danger of losing your customers. This makes feedback from lost customers valuable. When you learn why they left, you can often fix the cause before they begin a stampede.

18.4 Resolving customer difficulties and complaints

> The last of the human freedoms – to choose one's attitude.
>
> Viktor Frankl (neurologist and psychiatrist), *Man's search for meaning*, Washington Square Press, 1959, p. 86.

Transferable skills

1.4 Business operations

3.1 Teamwork/relationships

3.2 Verbal communication

3.3 Written communication

3.4 Leadership

Have you ever complained about a product or service and thought, 'Why did I waste my breath?' Even when complaints are made in the spirit of offering useful information to improve a product or service, they can be brushed aside, brusquely ignored or treated with disdain. Perhaps you have decided never to deal with a particular organisation again when, had your complaint or feedback been handled differently, you would gladly have kept doing business there. It's a pity when we let ourselves down by failing to handle complaints courteously, promptly and sensitively – especially since handling complaints properly isn't difficult, often strengthens customer loyalty and helps you improve your product or service for the future.

Yes, some customers are angry and rude. Some are tactless. Some are even abusive. Some lack the communication skills or emotional intelligence to word their complaint well or deliver it properly. Others are just having a bad day or have reached their daily stress threshold. Whatever the reason, when customers are difficult, guard against allowing the mirror neurons in your brain to 'respond in kind'. Take a deep breath and maintain your professionalism. Tell those difficult customers you need to write down what they're saying to encourage them to think about what they're saying and organise their thoughts; as a bonus, you have a written record to help you deal with the complaint. Then follow the steps described later in this chapter.

However they're delivered, here are three good ways to view complaints, whether they're from service partners or an external customer (or even one of your team members, for that matter):

1 as an opportunity to make amends for a problem
2 as feedback, or information, intended to help you improve
3 as a request in disguise.

When you receive a complaint or are alerted to a problem or difficulty by a customer, mentally translate it into a hidden request to provide something the customer wants but did not receive and try to provide it. Then use that information to ensure something similar doesn't occur again.

Welcome complaints

Here are four reasons to welcome complaints:

1 *Complaints are opportunities:* complainers are more likely than non-complainers to do business with you again. In fact, when you handle a complaint well, the complainer is more loyal to you than when everything goes smoothly.
2 *It takes time and effort to complain:* why should people bother when it's easier just to shrug and walk away? Unfortunately, that's what most customers do. More often than not, you don't even hear what went wrong or have the opportunity to fix it. The customer is lost and, quite likely, other customers are lost for the same reasons. Be grateful to the minority of unhappy customers who take the trouble to alert you to a problem.
3 *It's often your best and most loyal customers who care enough to complain:* after all, they have a vested interest in you 'getting your act together'. Customers who don't care about your organisation or their relationship with you, and those who don't expect to deal with you or work with you again, don't bother to complain. Why should they?
4 *Complaints are warnings:* when someone complains, it's seldom about an isolated occurrence: rather, it's usually about something that is symptomatic of the way you and your team operate. Whether customers complain in person, in writing, over the telephone or on social media, appreciate their comments as free information about what it's like to deal with you.

That's why it's important to treat complaints as important information from someone who cares and as opportunities to improve your service and build loyalty.

Manage complaints

Handling a complaint 'well' does not necessarily mean that every customer gets their way. Handling a complaint well means that the *way* you deal with the complaint satisfies the customer, and that means they're likely to deal with you again.

Nevertheless, even with a mindset that sees complaints as valuable information and as opportunities, dealing with them can be difficult and stressful. Here are some things to do, and to train your staff to do, when dealing with complaints:

- Manage your own emotions.
- Manage the customer's emotions.
- Manage the issue.

Manage your own emotions

Transferable skills

2.2 Personal effectiveness

However they may come across, complaints aren't generally intended as personal insults. They are seldom directed at a service provider personally, even when the customer's way of wording it makes it sound as though it is. Something has gone wrong and the customer wants it put right. Rather than taking a complaint personally, put up a mental 'serene screen' that lets the information through but not the emotions or any personal attacks.

In difficult situations, most people's natural tendency is to shallow breathe. Quick, shallow breathing causes panic, confusion and fuzzy thinking. It drains oxygen from your 'thinking brain' and switches on your 'reptilian brain', putting you into fight, flight or freeze mode. Out of breath means out of control – definitely not the way to earn points with unhappy customers.

When you feel yourself tensing up, relax and take a deep breath. This increases the flow of oxygen to your brain and heart, calms your nerves and helps you think clearly. Remind yourself to keep your cool and make sure your self-talk supports you: 'I can handle this', 'I'll do my best to help this customer' or 'We'll get to the bottom of this and sort it out'. In your mind's eye, see the customer leaving happy with the way you managed them.

When you still feel upset after dealing with a complaint, take a few minutes to destress and recover your equanimity. Go for a walk somewhere nice or, when that's not possible, close your eyes and spend two minutes visualising yourself in a calm, tranquil place. Breathe deeply, counting slowly to seven on the in breath and 11 on the out breath.

Looking after your team

Angry, demanding and rude customers can upset service providers. Some organisations take steps to prevent this by running staff training programs for dealing with problem customers and providing guidelines, such as how to respond to abusive customers. Some organisations also warn customers that abusive behaviour is not tolerated, with posters at key locations pointing out that threatening or aggressive behaviour towards staff is not acceptable.

Manage the customer's emotions

Transferable skills

3.1 Teamwork/ relationships

3.2 Verbal communication

3.3 Written communication

3.4 Leadership

No one can make you feel angry unless you let them. Professional service providers guide the conversation by modelling the behaviour they want from the customer. When you remain calm, helpful and polite, you encourage your customer to do the same. That's the boomerang principle – what a person sends out tends to bounce back. So be courteous, not curt, to customers with a problem. The more customers feel you aren't listening and are brushing aside their concerns or ignoring their needs, the further to the right on the 'unhappy customer emotions' scale they are likely to move (see Figure 18.8). The further to the right a customer moves on the scale, the more likely they are to become upset and even angry and abusive.

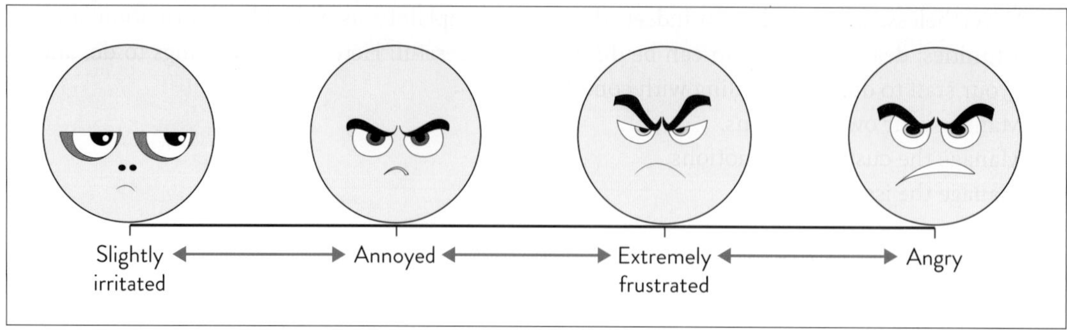

FIGURE 18.8 The complaining customer's scale of emotions

Don't make the people who are giving you valuable feedback feel you are pushing against them instead of working with them – that only encourages their emotions to escalate, creating a difficult situation for both of you and losing goodwill for your department or organisation.

Skills for dealing effectively with complaints

Below are some key qualities and skills, and related questions to ask yourself and consider if you are skilled enough in the following areas to achieve a successful complaints outcome:

- *Asking questions:* do you ask questions that uncover the real problem and the customer's expectations?
- *Attentive body language:* do you show the customer you're listening and trying to understand the difficulty?
- *Empathy:* do you see the situation from your customer's point of view so that you understand the customer's concerns and needs and take them seriously?
- *Interpersonal skills:* do you identify and meet the customer's basic psychological and emotional needs?
- *Reflective listening:* do you recap both the facts and the customer's feelings, removing the temptation for the customer to become upset or abusive?
- *Self-esteem and emotional intelligence:* do you manage your self-talk and your emotions well? Do you avoid taking complaints personally?

Manage the issue

When something goes wrong, the customer generally doesn't care whose fault it is or why it happened. What they want to know is that you're on their side in wanting to sort out the problem. This means taking a cooperative 'we' approach and seeing the situation as a problem to be resolved, not a situation to be excused. Once you've listened to the customer's description of the problem, gather any facts you need – timelines, major issues and so on. Take a 'helicopter' or 'big picture' view of the situation. Concentrate on the facts and on what you can do to try to put things right in the customer's eyes.

When you can't resolve the problem on the spot, explain that you will get back to the customer by a specific time with a solution, and do so. (Ensure your staff know the company line regarding what's possible and 'do-able'.) Never say 'This will never happen again' because you can't guarantee it; say you will do everything you can to see this doesn't happen again. When something goes wrong, diagnose the cause, develop options and advise your customer, as explained in Chapters 26 and 27.

Tips for dealing with angry customers

Even your best customers can get upset sometimes and how you handle the situation either strengthens or severs your relationship. It all depends on how and when you respond:

- When a customer requests help on social media, sends an email or leaves a voicemail, respond promptly and acknowledge there is a problem.
- When you're on the phone, let your tone of voice reflect your empathy; in person, be cordial and show your concern.
- Listen first. Take notes but don't offer explanations – they can come later.
- Show that you're listening and appreciate the practicalities of the problem as well as how the customer is feeling about it by acknowledging both the problem and the emotion.
- Agree they have a point (even when they're not totally correct) or say you can see why they would be upset. This dislodges a lot of the customer's anger because it's hard to be angry with someone who agrees with you.
- When the customer is right, say so and apologise. An apology is all many angry people want and the last thing they expect. It can knock the fury out of them.
- Let the customer know you care and intend to fix the problem. When appropriate, assure them you are beginning an inquiry into the problem; this makes them less likely to rant and rave and deflects their anger away from you.
- Once the customer has calmed down, you can manage the issue.

Three steps to a resolved complaint

It's easy to be helpful and courteous when all is going well. It's when they go wrong that your professionalism is tested. This is when your professionalism counts the most, too. Since unhappy customers spread bad news more quickly than happy customers spread good news, it's in your interests to deal with complaints properly. As stated above, it's the *way* they are handled – not their outcome – that matters most. Here's how to deal with complaints so that your customers spread good news about you instead of thinking, 'Why did I waste my breath?'

Step 1: Hear the customer out

Listening while the customer explains the situation from their point of view shows that you respect their experience. It helps you manage your own emotions and the customer's emotions. While you listen, put your own thoughts on hold so that you don't jump to conclusions, prejudge or evaluate the situation. Listen to find common ground so you can work with your customer to resolve the problem. Let the concept of trading partnerships remind you that you and your customer are on the same side.

Transferable skills

3.1 Teamwork/relationships

3.2 Verbal communication

3.3 Written communication

3.4 Leadership

The acronym ALARA can help you gather good information:

- **A**cknowledge the customer by making eye contact and using other attentive body language so they know you are listening. **Acknowledgement listening**, or 'nodding and grunting', shows you're following and helps bring out the full story. When a complaint is made over the telephone, use plenty of 'uh-huhs' and 'I sees'. Saying 'I understand', 'I see', 'I'm going to take care of this for you' allows the customer to continue and shows that you're listening. Saying 'I'm sorry this has happened' doesn't mean admitting guilt; it shows empathy and understanding, and that you care.
- **L**isten carefully to understand what your customer is trying to tell you. When you're tempted to cut them off because you think you know what they're going to say or you have the answer – don't. Letting customers have their say is essential to resolving complaints effectively.

- **A**sk the right questions so you can fully understand the problem. This might be 'How can I best help you now?', 'Can you explain that a bit more to me, please?' or 'When did that actually happen?' It depends on the situation.
- **R**ecap by summarising what you've understood using objective language, without adding anything or taking anything away. Review both the facts and the customer's feelings (e.g. annoyed, disappointed, inconvenienced). This helps calm down irate customers and gives them an opportunity to clear up anything you haven't fully understood.
- **A**ct by taking responsibility for putting matters right or for making sure someone else puts them right. Try to make all your sentences positive and helpful for maximum favourable impact. Say something like 'Thank you for telling me about this. I'm going to sort it out for you as quickly as I can.'

When the customer's facts are wrong, ask yourself whether correcting the customer would serve any purpose. Often, the facts are beside the point. Arguing back and forth about what happened is futile and certainly won't undo what's happened. Even when you can't agree, at least acknowledge how the customer is feeling: 'I can see that this has really inconvenienced you and I'm sorry about that. Let me see what I can do to get things back on track for you.'

Two other acronyms to help you remember how to hear a customer's complaint are:

1. LAST (**L**isten – **A**dvise – **S**olve – **T**hank): works well with straightforward customer complaints.
2. LEDO (**L**isten – **E**mpathise – **D**epersonalise – **O**ffer): is good for situations needing conciliation or conflict resolution and with angry customers. Listening to the complaint and empathising with the customer allows them to air their issue and feelings, while depersonalising the situation so you can look at it objectively helps you work together to find a solution that satisfies you both.

Step 2: Put matters right

Find out what the customer wants or offer a solution (depending on the issue and what you are able to do). Don't talk about what you *can't* do but what you *can* do and when. Avoid saying things like 'I'm sorry your order hasn't arrived; I can't get it for you until Tuesday now'; instead say, 'I'm sorry your order hasn't arrived; I can have it here for you Tuesday and once again, I'm so sorry you've been inconvenienced like this'. Say, 'There's something …' not 'There's nothing …'. Soften 'no' with 'I wish' or 'I hope' to show empathy and not apathy.

Concentrate on the future. Don't blame, deny, excuse or explain – customers aren't interested. Explain what you intend to do to sort it out: 'Here's what I'd like to do now … And I have made a note that this has happened so we can adjust our system to prevent something similar happening again.' (Chapter 19 explains how to adjust systems to prevent errors.)

Step 3: Agree and act

Ask 'Is this a good solution from your point of view?' Then once you've settled on what to do, do it. If you are unable to agree upon a solution, you can refer the problem 'up the line' to your manager or a customer advocate, if your organisation has one. Your goal is to have the complaint resolved and keep a customer, particularly your high-value customers.

When customers present you with several problems, prioritise them. Say something like, 'I'm sure I can help you with these concerns. Let's work on your biggest one first. Which is that?' Then respond to it following the three steps to resolve a complaint described above. After that, move onto the customer's next concern. When you run into one you can't answer or deal with straightaway, move it to the bottom of the list and deal with the next one. Say something like, 'I need to check with dispatch to find the answer to that. Before I do, can I help you with another question?'

STUDY TOOLS

QUICK REVIEW

KEY CONCEPT 18.1 

a Why is it cheaper to produce a high-quality product or service than to produce a poor-quality product or service?

b List and define the four cornerstones of quality.

KEY CONCEPT 18.2 

a What is the difference between an internal customer and an external customer? Are internal customers just as important as external customers? Why or why not?

b Why is increasing the lifetime value of a customer an inexpensive way to secure the future of an enterprise? List the four ways to increase LCV.

c Define and give an example of a service-profit chain.

d Why is it important to actually ask your customers what they want from your organisation? Does the need to ask them diminish the longer you have known them? Why or why not?

KEY CONCEPT 18.3 

a Define 'moment of truth' and give three examples of positive moments of truth (MOTs) and three examples of negative MOTs from your own experience. Could the positive MOTs be strengthened, and if so, how? How could the negative MOTs be made positive? Are those MOTs similar to competitor organisations' MOTs or do they differentiate it from their competitors?

b Explain the difference between customer satisfaction and customer loyalty.

KEY CONCEPT 18.4 

a List the steps to resolving a customer complaint.

b Why is the way you resolve a complaint so important?

BUILD YOUR SKILLS

KEY CONCEPT 18.1 

a Consider three examples of products you consider good quality at three price points: low, medium and high. What makes them 'good quality' in your eyes? Consider three examples of good-quality service at those three price points; what makes them good quality? How does quality relate to price? Does 'high quality' always mean 'high price'?

b 'People are an essential element of quality and service.' Do you agree? Why or why not? What else do you believe is essential to providing a quality product or service?

KEY CONCEPT 18.2 

a Explore Australian consumer rights at https://www.accc.gov.au/consumers/consumer-rights-guarantees, and summarise the three sections that most apply to your organisation's operations.

b Do you think customer service is more important to organisations in the private sector than in the not-for-profit and public sectors? Why or why not?

c Why is the threshold of what constitutes good customer service continually rising? Give some examples from your own experience.

d How do you rate your organisation's customer service or the customer service of another organisation you are familiar with?

e Investigate customer relationship management software and prepare a short report discussing their platforms, suitability to different industries and businesses of different sizes and costs.

KEY CONCEPT 18.3 

a Consider a product or service your organisation offers or one that you are familiar with. What are its features and what benefits to customers do those features offer? Which are functional and which are emotional benefits?

b For the next organisation you deal with, for example, your insurance company, a local café, greengrocer or bank, a government body or utility provider, list the moments of truth from the initial to the final interaction (e.g. entering the car park of the establishment to leaving it; making telephone contact to finalising the reason for the call; or visiting the retailer's website to receiving and using the product purchased for the first time). Then score each MOT on a scale of 1 to 5 for how well they were handled. Overall, how do you rate your satisfaction? Would you willingly use that organisation again? What would cause you to switch to another supplier?

KEY CONCEPT 18.4 

a When was the last time you complained about a product or service? How was the complaint handled? Will you continue to do business with that provider or company? Why or why not.

WORKPLACE ACTIVITIES

KEY CONCEPT 18.1 

a Describe the quality culture at your workplace. How does it correspond to the quality culture described in this chapter?

b What quality systems do you have at your workplace? How do they help you to reliably provide a quality product or service? Select one system and develop suggestions for improving it to help you produce a quality product or service every time; remember to consider the upstream and downstream effects of any changes you recommend.

c Diagram one of your work systems and analyse it to determine whether it is a quality system that builds quality in and eliminates assignable-cause variation.

d Why do quality standards matter? Investigate and report on the Australian or international quality standards currently used in your organisation.

e How is quality monitored at your workplace? Would you describe it as quality control or quality assurance?

KEY CONCEPT 18.2 

a List what your work team's internal or external customers want and need from you. Prepare a summary of your customers' wants and needs, by customer group if necessary.

b Who are your organisation's external customers? Do you and your work team have any direct external customers? If not, how far removed are your external customers? Calculate the lifetime value of a typical external customer of your organisation and list at least eight specific ways you could increase their LCV.

c Does your organisation have a customer service or customer rights charter? Summarise your organisation's approach to customer rights in 25 words.

d Diagram the internal customer–supplier chain for your own work team. Where are its weak points in terms of quality and service? How could they be improved?

e How customer-focused are you? How customer-focused is your work team? After answering these two questions, think about and note down the criteria you used to answer them. What does this tell you about what is important to you as a customer? Would all customers find the same things important? Why or why not? What are some factors other people might find important that you don't?

f Would you describe your organisation as cost-driven, customer-driven or product-driven? Why? Is it appropriate for its market? Why or why not? Would you describe your organisation's main competition as cost-, customer- or product-driven?

g What data do you collect concerning your customers' problems and concerns? How frequently do you collect it and how do you use it?

h How well are you and your team serving your customers? Once you know, develop a three-stage plan for improving your team's customer service.

KEY CONCEPT 18.3 

a Map the moments of truth your customers have with you and your work team. How well do you think you manage them? What is your evidence for this?

b Give three examples of how your work team rationally satisfies its customers and three examples of how the team emotionally satisfies them. What actions would turn the rationally satisfied customers into emotionally satisfied customers? If they are external customers, discuss how that might change their lifetime customer value. If they are internal customers, discuss how providing more emotional satisfaction might increase their job satisfaction, productivity and loyalty to the organisation.

c Give three examples of functional benefits and three examples of emotional benefits that your organisation offers its external customers.

d Seek out the 'grass roots', such as your organisation's receptionists, regular drivers from car hire firms, repair people, contractors, couriers – all sorts of people have insights into your organisation that they've gleaned while doing their jobs. Chat to them about their impressions of your organisation and prepare a short report outlining what you do well and areas for improvement. How closely do you think the views of the people you spoke with mirror your organisation's customers?

KEY CONCEPT 18.4 

a How does your organisation train people to deal with complaints from external customers? Prepare a short report to discuss with the class.

b Call your organisation's customer service or help line or contact it through social media and present a problem and see how it's handled. Write a short report outlining what was done well and suggesting how the service could be improved.

c What was the last complaint you received from an internal or external customer? Describe how you dealt with it. What constraints did you need to work within? How easy does your organisation or work team make it to complain?

d Create phrases that you could use when dealing with customer complaints in a face-to-face environment.

e Create phrases that you could use when dealing with a customer complaint in a letter or email.

EXTENSION ACTIVITIES

Referring to the Snapshot at the beginning of this chapter, answer the following questions:

1 Calculate Laura's lifetime value to the local newsagency that lost her business and to the newsagency she transferred her business to.

2 How did Chris meet Laura's psychological needs?

3 Discuss the importance of getting to know your customers in relation to the larger newsagency's lost business.

CASE STUDY 18

FEWER PROBLEMS, HAPPIER CUSTOMERS

With 14400 employees in 30 countries and sales of US$4.2 billion, Fujitsu Services is one of the largest providers of IT services in Africa, Europe and the Middle East. When other companies began outsourcing their customer services and internal technical support, Fujitsu put its hand up. After all, its helpdesks had been successfully servicing its own customers and providing technical support for its own products for many years.

Companies generally pay outsourcers per complaint handled – a business model that gives no incentive to reduce the number of complaints received and even discourages effective complaint resolution since fewer complaints mean lower revenue. Fujitsu approached the problem differently. It decided to eliminate the causes of the customers' complaints. This meant that instead of being paid for each call handled, it could bid for the business with a set fee based on the number of potential callers to the helpdesk – less than the current outsourcer's bid, yet still profitable for Fujitsu.

When Fujitsu took over the internal helpdesk contract for British Midland Airways (BMI), it immediately analysed the types of calls coming in from the employees and examined the problems that gave rise to the calls. Then it tracked the time and effort required to fix them and measured the impact on the client's business of failures or delays in fixing the problems.

More than half the calls were repeat complaints about recurring problems or repair delays. One of the most common reasons for calls – 26 per cent of the total – was malfunctioning printers, and check-in

CASE STUDY 18

staff couldn't print boarding passes and baggage tags for passengers. Clearly, solving the printer problem was critical to the airline's business as it could cause flights to miss their take-off slots – disastrous in Europe's crowded airports.

While BMI's previous contractor approached the problem by trying to get service technicians to respond more quickly, Fujitsu looked for the most cost-effective way to keep the printers working properly. The option it chose was to convince BMI senior managers to spend money up-front on better quality printers. It worked; the number of calls about faulty printers dropped 80 per cent in 18 months, resulting in major savings in flight operations that far exceeded the cost of the new printers. It also allowed the technician response time to fix printers that still failed to drop from 10 hours to three – a happy customer again. Continuing to identify and rectify the causes of the callers' problems, Fujitsu went on to reduce the total number of calls to the helpdesk by 40 per cent within 18 months. A very happy customer.

Fujitsu applied the same approach to its other customers that awarded it helpdesk contracts, analysing and optimising their IT response systems and delivering far beyond their customers' expectations. It doesn't stop at fixing defects, giving its customers only what it promises; it also goes a step further to create additional value by offering information about potential problems the customer hasn't experienced yet but will, without forewarning. More happy customers.

And the benefits flow both ways. While Fujitsu staff are working with customers to prevent current and potential problems, they learn about what problems the customers are trying to solve with their systems, which can lead to ideas for new products. The process builds customer loyalty while Fujitsu gains market intelligence and saves money by reducing calls to the helpdesks it is contracted to run. Fujitsu customers are so happy they give the company even more business.[19]

Questions

1 This case study is an example of trading partnerships. What element does trust play in the process? What risks might Fujitsu or its trading partners face as a result of their trading partnerships and what steps could they each take to manage them?

2 Discuss how Fujitsu's approach to implementing quality systems illustrates cost- and time-effectiveness, increases customer satisfaction and builds customer loyalty.

3 Describe how Fujitsu's approach to quality service resulted in satisfied customers.

CHAPTER ENDNOTES

1 Productivity Commission, 'Things you can't drop on your feet: An overview of Australia's services sector productivity', PC Productivity Insights, April 2021.

2 Joseph M. Juran, *Juran on planning for quality*, Free Press, New York, 1988.

3 Kaoru Ishikawa, *What is total quality control? The Japanese way*, Prentice Hall, 1985.

4 International Organization for Standardization, 'ISO Survey of management system standard certifications 2013', http://www.iso.org/iso/iso_survey_executive-summary.pdf?v2013, accessed 16 December 2014.

5 Robert Kaplan, Kathy Eisenhardt, Don Sull, Peter Tufano, Orit Gadiesh, *Harvard Business Review on Advances in Strategy*, Harvard Business School Publishing, 2002, p. 215; see also Barbara Grady, 'General Mills and Land o Lakes announce supply chain alliance', 1 September 2015, *Greenbiz*, https://www.greenbiz.com/article/general-mills-brings-supply-chain-emissions-goal

6 Graham Hubbard, Simon Heap, Delyth Samuel, Graeme Cocks, *The first XI: Winning organisations in Australia*, John Wiley & Sons, Brisbane, 2002.

7 LinkedIn, 'About us', https://press.linkedin.com/about-linkedin, accessed 23 January 2018.

8 'American Express Global Customer Service Barometer 2014', http://about.americanexpress.com/news/, accessed 5 January 2017.

9 Stephen E. Chick, Arnd Huchzermeier, Serguei Netessine, 'Europe's solution factories', *Harvard Business Review*, April 2014, pp. 111–115.

10 Amy Birchall, 'Mind the gap', *Management Today*, August 2008.

11 'Creativity selected as most crucial factor for future success', 18 May 2010, https://www-03.ibm.com/press/us/en/pressrelease/31670.wss??, accessed 20 December 2015.

12 Robert Simons, 'Choosing the right customer: The first step in a winning strategy', *Harvard Business Review*, March 2014, pp. 49–55; see also 'Fad or frontier: Is big data an under-utilized asset?', UNSW Business School, https://www.businessthink.unsw.edu.au/Pages/Fad-or-Frontier-Is-Big-Data-an-Under-Utilized-Asset.aspx, accessed 19 January 2018.

13 Milly Stilinovic, 'Hohn Harries: The face behind Australian banking', *Customer Service Excellence*, Australian edition, No. 55, 2011; and http//www.anz.com, accessed August 2011.

14 'American Express Global Customer Service Barometer 2014', http://about.americanexpress.com/news/, accessed 5 January 2017.

15 https://quoteinvestigator.com/2011/07/28/ford-faster-horse/, accessed 4 September 2017.

16 'American Express Global Customer Service Barometer 2014', http://about.americanexpress.com/news/, accessed 5 January 2017.

17 Sterling A. Bone, Katherine N. Lemon, Clay M. Voorhees, '"Mere Measurement Plus": How Solicitation of Open-Ended Positive Feedback Influences Customer Purchase Behavior', *Journal of Marketing Research*, February 2017, Vol. 54, No. 1, pp. 156–170.

18 Eddie Yoon, Steve Carlotti, Dennis Moore, 'Make your customers even better', *Harvard Business Review*, March 2014, pp. 23–25.

19 James P. Womack, Daniel T. Jones, 'Lean consumption', *Harvard Business Review*, March 2005.

CHAPTER

19

INCREASING PERFORMANCE AND PRODUCTIVITY WITH THE FIVE KEYS, CONTINUOUS IMPROVEMENT AND INNOVATION

After completing this chapter, you will be able to:

19.1 identify and take specific steps to unlock people's productivity and performance

19.2 lead improvement efforts with your team

19.3 identify the barriers to creativity and innovation and overcome them to become more creative and innovative.

TRANSFERABLE SKILLS

The following transferable skills are covered in this chapter:

1 **Business competence**
- **1.2** Entrepreneurship/small business skills
- **1.3** Sustainability
- **1.4** Business operations

2 **Critical thinking and problem solving**
- **2.1** Critical thinking
- **2.2** Personal effectiveness
- **2.3** Business strategy

3 **Social competence**
- **3.1** Teamwork/relationships
- **3.4** Leadership

4 **Data literacy**
- **4.1** Data literacy

5 **Digital competence**
- **5.1** Cyber security
- **5.2** Technology use

OVERVIEW

Many factors come together to improve (or reduce) productivity:

- government actions, through economic reform, the infrastructure it provides (internet connectivity, roads, transportation, etc.) and its policies (investment in the education and training system, policies that encourage innovation, etc.)
- corporate action, through investment (in employee training, research and development, technology, etc.) and the culture organisations develop (of innovation, learning, risk, quality, etc.)
- individual action, through people's health and their knowledge, skills and willingness to work smarter (to block distractions, delegate effectively, innovate, organise their workspaces, resist multitasking, work to priorities, etc.).

Productivity refers to quantity. It measures output against costs. Performance includes quality and measures how well work is done. Implementing five critical factors, or Five Keys, explored in this chapter will unlock peak performance, increasing both performance and productivity. Leading and managing through the Five Keys and helping your team make continuous, innovative improvements are two of the most important things you can do. Continually improving quality and efficiency is the opposite of the 'If it ain't broke, don't fix it' approach.

The 'leave well enough alone' approach only works in a world where nothing changes and when your systems and processes have reached the pinnacle of perfection. Neither can be true. Time passes, technology advances, a new competitor comes along and changes the rules ... there is no such thing as a steady state – you're either moving forward or falling behind. So if it ain't broke, it may soon be. The Five Keys are essential for productivity and performance, and innovating continuous improvements to all parts of the organisation is essential for organisational survival. This chapter explains how to lead people to deliver their best and live up to the continuous improvement imperative.

SNAPSHOT

Starting from scratch

Because of his track record in managing similar assignments on time and within budget, Damien is asked to lead a strategically important and highly visible project. He works out a rough plan of the logistics and thinks about the skills and knowledge he needs in the team itself. Damien sets to work putting the team together. He chooses most of the team members for their expertise in their fields, fully aware that quite a few lack experience of working in the type of tightly knit team this project calls for.

Next, Damien plans how to bring people on board and up to speed quickly. He makes a note to contact a couple of trainers he's worked with in the past to discuss the team's need for some workshops on communication and team-working skills.

He then schedules an inaugural briefing meeting to introduce the team members to each other and outline the scope of the project and his logistics. 'I'll get them working together to map out the milestones the team as a whole need to achieve to bring the project in on time and ask them to each begin developing their own deliverables', he mumbles to himself. 'Then I'll meet with them individually to agree on the details of each person's contribution before bringing the team together again to structure their project plan more tightly. That way, they all know what to do, as a team and as individuals. Because this is the first major project for most of them, I know they're all keen and want to participate, and technically, they all know how to do the jobs I'm bringing them in for. Their confidence will grow once they've had some interpersonal skills development. That leaves making sure they have the resources and tools they need to do their jobs ... the old chance to.' He flips the page of his notebook and begins brainstorming resource requirements.

19.1 Unlocking performance and productivity with the Five Keys

> Productivity growth is the only sustainable source of improvements in a community's or a nation's material well-being and that of its citizens.
>
> Saul Eslake and Marcus Walsh, 'Australia's productivity', Grattan Institute Report, Melbourne, February 2011.

The Five Keys – What To, Want To, How To, Chance To and Led To – work together to make it possible for employees to meet their measures of success, keep up their good work and improve on their work. As the leader-manager, you are primarily responsible for putting these Five Keys in place. By ensuring that each of them is working well, you can unleash both your team's willingness and ability to do their best. This virtually assures success for yourself, your team and each individual member. Figure 19.1 shows the Five Keys that unlock peak performance.

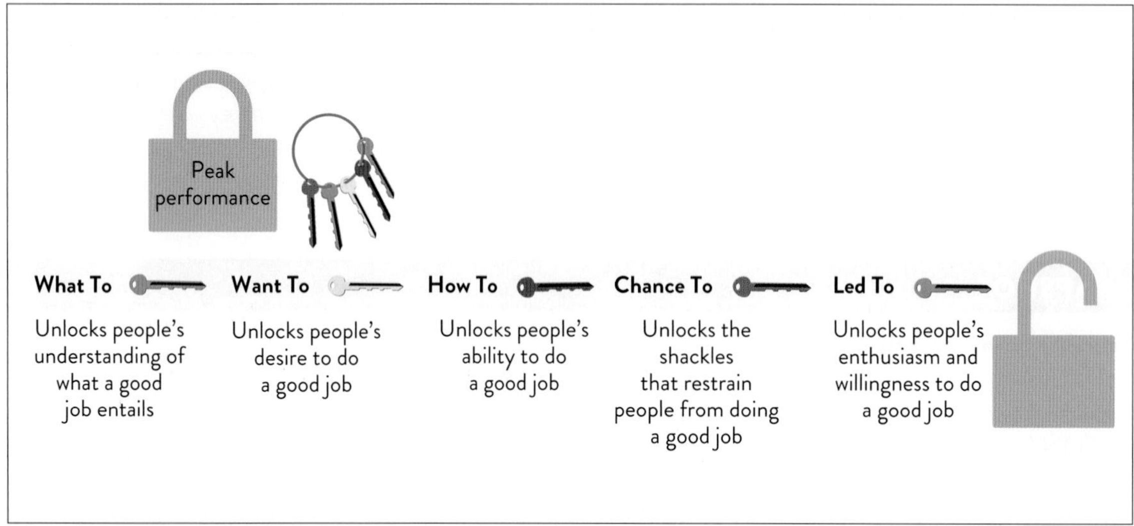

FIGURE 19.1 Unlocking peak performance

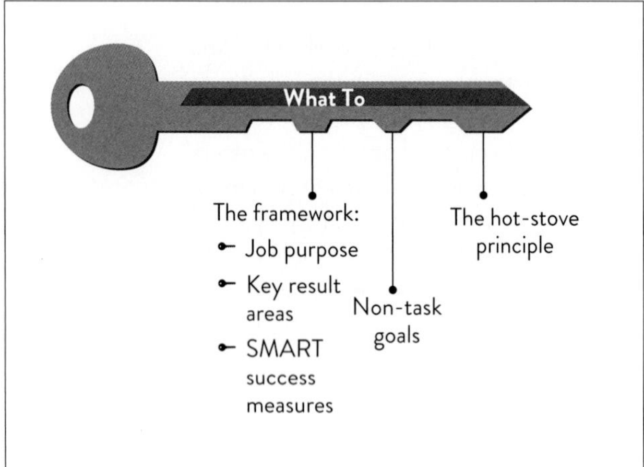

FIGURE 19.2 The three elements of the What To Key

The What To Key

The What To Key unlocks people's understanding of the expectations a task requires. It provides a structure, or framework, for employees. The human brain likes to find meaning. A framework will provide the guidance people need, taking out the guesswork.

The three elements of the What To Key (see **Figure 19.2**) are:

1 *The job framework:* made up of job purpose, key result areas (KRAs) and SMART measures of success. (Chapter 9 explains these in relation to your own job.)
2 *Non-task goals:* are often to do with behaviour expectations in the job environment.
3 *The hot-stove principle:* for the rules that apply to everyone, such as customer service standards and safety precautions (discussed later in this chapter).

Job purpose

When people know clearly and specifically what you expect of them, they have role clarity. Clear roles and responsibilities give people a point to aim their efforts towards and encourage people to monitor their own performance.

Discuss with your team the organisation's values, vision, mission and goals to ensure they have a broad understanding of the strategy, or overall approach, it intends to use to reach them. Emphasising the team members' personal roles and the team's role in helping the organisation reach its aspirations will draw attention to the connection individuals have to the organisation.

Highlight any other aspects of the organisation's overall operations that are of particular interest to individual employees; for example:

- *Employees interested in community:* explain how the organisation's vision and values support local involvement and how reaching its goals allows the organisation to participate in the community.
- *Employees interested in sustainability:* explain how the organisation meets its sustainability targets while achieving its goals.
- *Employees interested in flexible working:* explain that the organisation offers flexibility in return for high productivity and how flexibility helps people contribute to the organisation's vision and goals.

Now you're ready to write the employee's job purpose statement – the job-holder's personal mission statement. When you ask people to write the overall purpose of their job in one succinct sentence, their job becomes more than just a series of tasks. Employees can see that their job is worthwhile and, therefore, is worth doing well. The job purpose statement also gives employees overall guidance about the way to approach their job and describes the difference between doing a job well and excelling.

A job purpose statement generally follows this formula: 'To do ... (describe the job), so that ... (describe the outcome).' To kick-start a high-performance culture, ask every person in your work team to write their own job purpose statement like those shown in Figure 19.3, and share it with the rest of the work team. When new employees join your work group, help them to develop their own job purpose statement.

FIGURE 19.3 Two job purposes

Make sure that employees' job purpose statements support the team's purpose (discussed in Chapter 13) and the organisation's vision and goals. And make sure they're not too long – you want people to be able to remember them and 'carry them around in their heads'.

Transferable skills

3.1 Teamwork/relationships

REFLECT

What is your job purpose statement?

Key result areas

Key result areas (KRAs) describe an employee's main areas of accountability and responsibility. KRAs put tasks into context. They are not tasks or goals, but groups of tasks that together achieve results in important areas (see **Figure 19.4**). (Chapter 9 discusses how most jobs have five to nine KRAs. Fewer than five can indicate an 'underemployed' employee, while more than five can indicate an overstretched employee.)

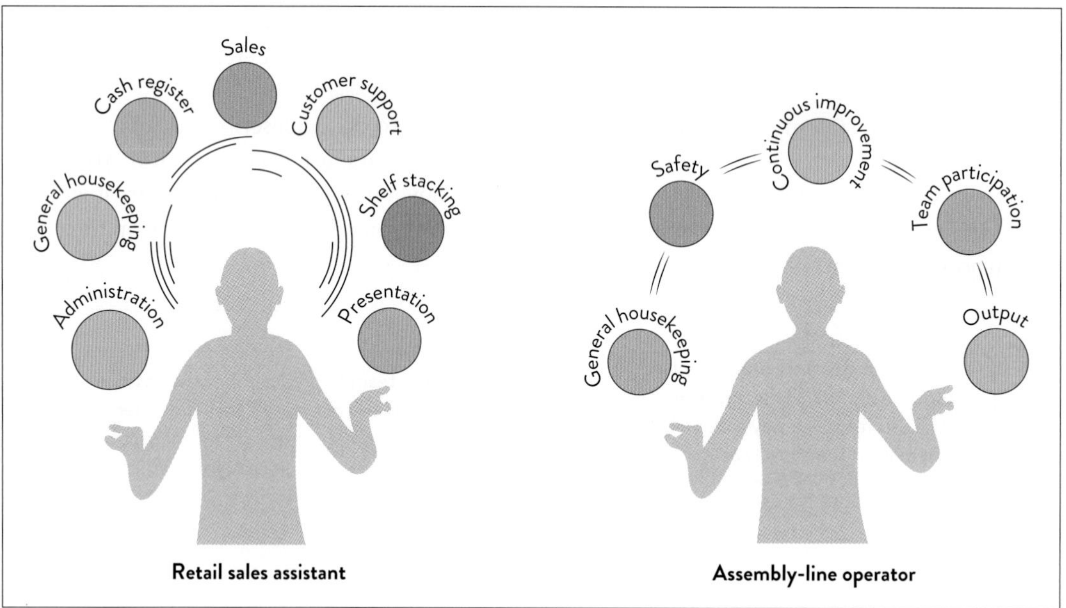

FIGURE 19.4 Two sets of KRAs

Even though employees may spend different proportions of their time on each KRA, each is equally as important. If someone has fewer than five KRAs, make sure that some of those listed aren't too big – they may describe more than one KRA and need to be broken down into separate KRAs. If someone lists more than nine, they have probably broken down one or more KRAs incorrectly. For example, an employee might divide a KRA of 'output' into 'quality' and 'productivity', when both should come under the umbrella of 'output'. When deciding on your KRA, consider the lead indicators for each (see Chapter 9 for information on lead and lag indicators).

REFLECT

Consider the main areas of accountability and responsibility in your role. How many KRAs do you have and what are they?

Measures of success

You've probably heard the truism 'What gets measured gets done'. Measures of success, also known as key performance indicators (KPIs), help people concentrate on what's important. Success measures strengthen the job framework by establishing the *performance standard*, or the result being strived for. Giving employees targets to aim for fosters individual accountability for productivity and results. Encouraging your team to take control over how they achieve their targets and review their progress towards their goals is known to increase job satisfaction.

There are many ways to measure people's success in achieving their goals; for example:

- measure one or two important indicators of performance
- select the most important or critical outcomes of each KRA
- reflect on the expectations of each stakeholder
- consider the business goals and strategies
- evaluate the outcomes that contribute most to the overall goals of the team.

Reject any measures that would not alert the employee to do something differently if the measure were not met and any that would be difficult, expensive or time-consuming to collect. Avoid any 'short-term thinking' measures that interfere with longer-term strategic goals. Also, ensure employees are fully aware of how they benefit from reaching their success measures.

Reject any that measure activity only – you don't want to confuse being 'busy' with achieving goals. Success isn't a numbers game and activity doesn't always equal results – results and success often come from working smarter, not harder. Consider, for example, a successful psychological testing salesperson who concentrates their efforts on a handful of leading human resources (HR) professionals; or a successful kitchen appliance salesperson who concentrates their efforts on only elite chefs. They sell to opinion-formers whose example other HR professionals and chefs follow. But what if their managers decided to monitor the number of sales calls they made instead of the number of overall sales? They'd have to increase their effort even though it would likely result in fewer sales.

Consider telling helpline staff that their goal is to answer a certain number of calls each day – what would happen to the quality of the way they deal with customers' problems when they focus on getting to as many calls as they can in their shift? Activity-based measures of success can warp the way people view their jobs.

Whenever possible, let people set their own targets or work them out together. Make sure they are motivating to the individual employee and that they align with the employee's experience and competence levels. Make sure success measures meet the SMART targets criteria:

- **S**pecific (which usually means measurable and time-framed) and concise
- **M**otivating in order to drive performance
- **A**mbitious (achievable yet challenging)
- **R**elated to the overall department and enterprise goals and therefore meaningful, which also drives performance
- **T**rackable (easily monitored).

Specific

An example of a poor measure of success is 'reduce returns to a minimum' because it is negative and not specific. How would you know whether or not the employee succeeded? Consider the following:

- Four purchases were returned last month because of cosmetic flaws to the product's surface.
- Six purchases were returned last month because they were unsuited to the purpose for which they were purchased.
- Three purchases were returned last month because they failed to work.
- Total returns fell by 14 per cent last month.

Did the employee succeed? You can't know because the success measure is not specific: it's neither measurable nor time-framed. There is no 'finishing line'. What is a 'minimum' number of returns? What number of returns is acceptable? By when should this minimum acceptable number be reached?

Now consider this success measure: decrease the number of returns to 2 per cent or less of sales per month by:

- discussing the intended use of the product with the customer to ensure the suitability of the product purchased
- inspecting and testing all purchases with the customer to ensure that the finish is acceptable and the product works before completing the sale.

Both you and the employee now know whether the goal is achieved and you can both track progress over the month, allowing the employee to take any necessary corrective action quickly. The employee has a specific goal to work towards (the outcome – to decrease returns to 2 per cent of sales or less per month). This particular measure of success indicates clearly not just *what* the employee should achieve (the *outcome*) and by *when*, but also *how* the employee can achieve it (*activities*). However, while every measures of success should measure outcomes, not every measure of success needs to indicate how a task is to be done. Keep the targets as concise as possible so they're easily remembered.

Motivating

There's no point setting goals that employees aren't motivated to achieve. To make sure goals are meaningful and motivating, link SMART targets to:

- the employee's job purpose
- the team's purpose
- the organisation's values, vision or goals.

Ambitious

Make sure the targets you set are achievable. It's fine to challenge people, but setting them up to fail by asking them to aim for an unreachable target demotivates them in the long run. Impossible goals don't motivate people to achieve outstanding performance; challenging yet achievable goals do. The best way to improve productivity is to combine small individual wins with incremental process improvements (i.e. continual small improvements to the way work is carried out, as explained later in this chapter).

Related

The success measures you agree upon with team members should help them succeed in their own KRAs as well as move the team and the organisation towards their goals.

Trackable

Selecting lead indicators that signal to employees how they're going with a task can alert them to make any necessary changes to the way they're operating and help lift both momentum and productivity. (Chapter 12 explains how to monitor performance, and Chapter 15 explains how to provide feedback on performance.)

Consider one of your targets or goals and apply the SMART targets criteria.

Measures of success for broad, ambiguous roles

Setting SMART outcome-based success measures for clearly defined, routine work can be straightforward; however, it can be more complex for knowledge and service work and the broad and multifaceted roles that organisations are creating as they build more flexibility and diversity into their job designs. Quality is often more important than quantity in these jobs: Someone can serve 50 customers in a day and leave them all dissatisfied or serve 35 and leave them all completely satisfied and intending to come back. Important behaviours, such as mentoring others or energising a team, don't fit easily into productivity equations, either.

The trick is to define the behaviours and results, or outcomes, that are most critical to performance and work out how to measure them, not just day to day but over the medium and the long term.

INDUSTRY INSIGHTS

Measuring success

A HR officer (HRO) who is responsible for designing and introducing a performance management system to the organisation, in order to create success measures, started by making a list of milestones and deliverables needed to complete the project.

Using the SMART criteria he determined the following:

1. research and report back on possible systems, by a certain date
2. create a draft design and pilot it with a representative cross-section of employees and managers by x date
3. submit final version for discussion and approval by x date.

These clear and definitive deliverables made it easy for him to measure success.

The HRO also considered the strategic compatibility of the performance management system with the organisation's overall vision and goals and the degree to which it is accepted and used throughout the organisation. While these last two criteria were difficult to measure, the HRO used careful judgement to assess effectiveness.

Productivity is a measure of outputs (goods, ideas and services) in return for inputs (labour, time, money, land, electricity, raw materials and other resources). Nations, organisations and people become more productive in one of two ways by:

1. producing or creating more value with the same resources
2. producing the same or creating the same value with fewer resources.

Consider a task your organisation, team or individual completes, and the input that is required to reach the output. Is there an opportunity where your organisation, team or individual can become more productive using one of the two ways listed above?

Improving performance with measures of success

Rather than treating any shortfall in meeting measures of success as a problem, treat them as an opportunity to improve, and work with the employee to help them reach the target. Discuss the reasons for the shortfall using the Five Keys as a guide; for example, something in the Chance To Key might be blocking success, or you may need to provide some coaching to strengthen the employee's skills or confidence.

Although an employee's job purpose and KRAs are unlikely to change substantially, you may want to periodically change some of the measures of success you monitor. For example, you could drop a measure of success that an employee consistently reaches and agree to a new SMART measure of success to boost performance in another area. You could do this during the performance review, or at any time between formal performance reviews when you want to shift an employee's attention to an improvement area.

INDUSTRY INSIGHTS

Improving performance

Jordan, a sales assistance for Made with Love Jewellery, is extremely knowledgeable about the various stock sold within the store. Jordan's performance is excellent in many areas; however, some customers complain about how queries are handled, commenting that Jordan's communication style can be a bit abrupt.

Rahul, the store manager, decides to implement coaching sessions for Jordan. Together Rahul and Jordan estimate that 40 per cent of queries lead to a sale, which is below expectations. Rahul and Jordan agree to try new techniques explored in weekly coaching sessions and to track customer queries weekly, with the aim to reach sales conversion of between 60 and 70 per cent within six weeks.

Rahul continues to coach Jordan and sees progressive improvement. Jordan enjoys trying out the new techniques and watching the sales conversion increase. Rahul and Jordan schedule a formal meeting every six months to review sales progress and continue to explore new measures of success to replace those Jordan meets consistently. This step gives both Jordan and Rahul a slightly different focus, ensuring continuous improvement.

Non-task goals

Employees also need to meet non-task goals. Non-task goals relate to the way people work. Here are some examples:

- Be cooperative, friendly and helpful to colleagues and customers.
- Clean up after yourself in our shared kitchen area.
- Find ways to improve the way you and the team work.
- Help out your teammates when you have a few spare minutes.
- Keep your work area tidy.
- Make our customers glad they deal with us.
- Share your knowledge.
- Try to finish one task before moving on to another.

Although some of these expectations are written down formally (e.g. in the role description or job contract), many are left as unspoken workplace norms that employees must infer, or pick up, for themselves. Problems can develop when team members fail to meet unspoken expectations and, when that happens, it's important to meet with the team or the individual employee and discuss your expectations openly.

Discuss these expectations with new team members on their first day or two. This helps them fit in more quickly and prevents bad habits forming. When you openly discuss expectations, you can be certain everyone understands them and can work towards achieving them.

The hot-stove principle

The hot-stove principle is about important rules and regulations that apply to everyone and involve matters such as customer service, housekeeping, safety, standard operating procedures and working with others.[1] Figure 19.5 shows how the hot-stove principle works.

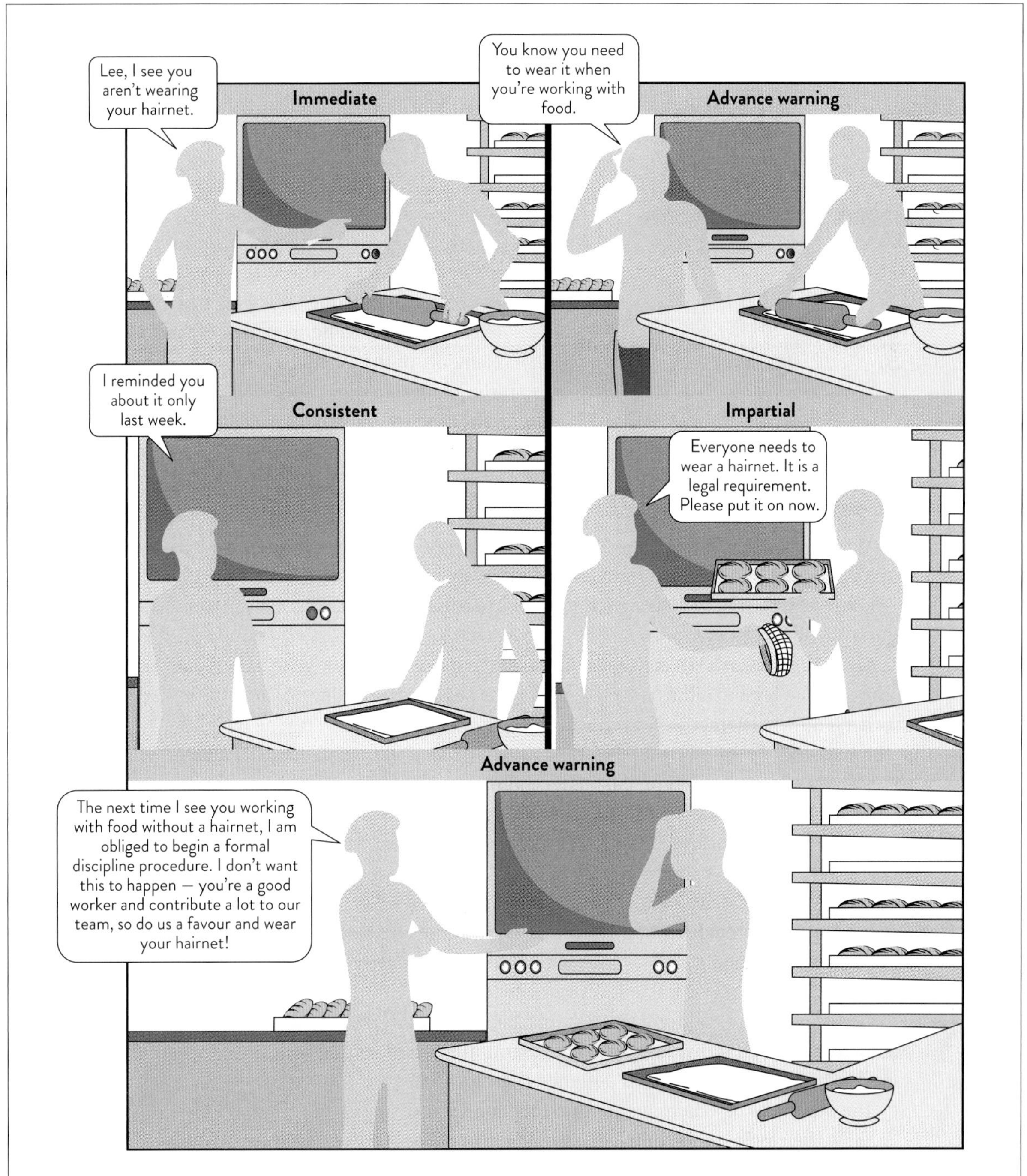

FIGURE 19.5 The hot-stove principle at work

Just as you can see from a distance whether a stove is hot and will burn you if you touch it, everyone should know your 'must-be-adhered-to' rules in *advance* and know they will be 'burnt' if they break or bend them. Just as when you touch a hot stove you are burnt straightaway, the consequence of breaking or bending a bottom-line rule should be *immediate*; if someone breaks a hot-stove rule, discuss it with the person at once (in private) to make sure it doesn't happen again. A hot stove is *impartial* – everyone who touches it is burnt. Hot stoves are *consistent* in that they always burn people who touch them, so don't 'play favourites' – bottom-line rules apply to everyone, all the time.

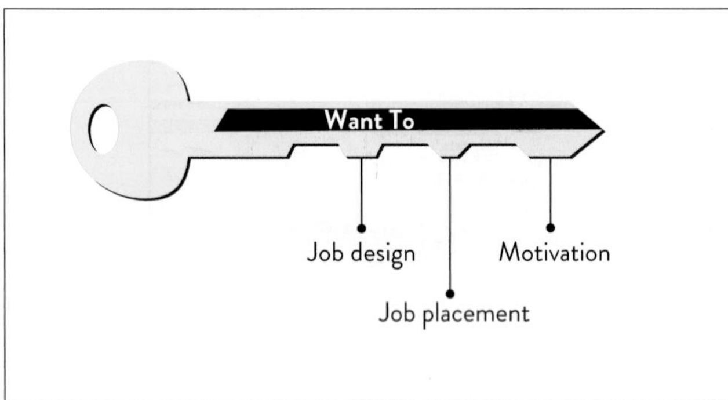

FIGURE 19.6 The three elements of the Want To Key

The Want To Key

As Henry Mintzberg pointed out, 'If you want people to do a good job, give them a good job to do'.[2] People can work hard when they *have to*, but they work harder when they *want to*. The Want To Key unlocks people's desire to do a good job. For this to happen, three elements need to be in place. Figure 19.6 shows the elements of the Want To Key:

- job design
- job placement
- motivation.

Job design

The Want To Key links with the What To Key because, in order to be motivated to perform well, employees must know their job is worth doing well. The Want To Key helps you to further motivate employees by offering well-designed jobs and putting people in jobs that match their interests and abilities – job placement.

Meaningful work is a concept that was unheard of only a few generations ago. Yet today it holds importance, at least in affluent societies. What is meaningful to one person may not be meaningful to another, and what someone finds meaningful at the age of 23 may not be what they find meaningful at the age of 53.

Meaningful work relies on balancing three sets of motives:

1. *Moral motives:* understanding that one's work is worthwhile.
2. *Compensation motives:* using one's skills and abilities; having authority, money, responsibility and status.
3. *Craft motives:* the desire to do a good job for its own sake.

It's up to individuals to find work that is meaningful for them. However, employers play a role by providing high-quality jobs – jobs with autonomy, security and variety, and a reasonable balance between effort and reward, skill level and job demands.

Good job design and correct job placement directly relate to motivation, performance and productivity. When individuals or whole teams aren't performing well, check whether they're really suited to their jobs and how well designed their jobs are.

The principles of job design are that each job should:

- allow the employee to complete a whole job or piece of work wherever possible
- allow the employee to have as much control over the work and work methods as technology allows

- contain a variety of tasks and activities requiring different levels of experience and training, and a minimum of repetitive, monotonous tasks
- contain variety in work pace and work methods
- contribute significantly to the organisation
- give the employee access to the resources needed to do the job
- have clear roles and responsibilities and a clear set of easily measured objectives that the employee can monitor
- offer a reasonable workload in terms of deadlines and demands (neither too much nor too little).

Job content often grows over time, sometimes haphazardly and often informally, which is why you should periodically examine the content of each job in your team to ensure each one makes the best use of people and resources.

Transferable skills
2.1 Critical thinking

The three Es

A 'good job' often involves the three Es – enlargement, enrichment and empowerment:

- **Job enlargement**: expanding a job horizontally by giving the employee more duties at the same level of responsibility; for example, **cross-skilling** and **multiskilling**. When additional duties are at a higher level of responsibility, multiskilling is also a form of job enrichment.
- **Job enrichment**: expanding a job vertically by increasing the depth of an employee's responsibilities through upskilling.
- **Job empowerment**: an expanded form of job enrichment. Empowered employees and teams take on many responsibilities previously carried out by leader-managers, particularly the ability to make on-the-spot decisions. But you can't just foist those responsibilities onto employees; empowerment grows as a result of a management style and an organisation's culture and climate.

When jobs are enlarged or enriched and employees empowered, the employees usually need training to expand their skills. Particularly with empowerment, training must include interpersonal skills, how to lead and participate in meetings, and problem-solving and decision-making skills and techniques. Just adding new duties and responsibilities to employees' workloads as a hierarchy flattens out isn't job enlargement, enrichment or empowerment – it's just more work.

The benefits of the three Es include:

- increased motivation
- increased organisational flexibility and responsiveness
- increased responsibility and job interest
- improved job design
- improved job performance and productivity
- strengthened customer and supplier relationships.

Empowerment often has the added benefit of enabling organisations to restructure their internal relationships and ways of working to increase efficiency and competitiveness and move towards a capabilities-based organisation (explained in Chapter 3).

While not every employee wants a job that excites and challenges them, the commitment, loyalty, productivity and motivation of most employees can be increased with good job design combined with correct job placement, frequent feedback and visible results from their efforts.

Consider your role or the roles within your team and how they measure against the three Es.

Transferable skills

1.4 Business operations

Job placement

Everyone has strengths. What are your individual team members' strengths? Exploring individual strengths can assist you with assigning tasks. Placing people in jobs they enjoy and that suit their temperaments and skill sets is essential to employee retention, motivation and productivity. It means that employees can complete work they enjoy and feel confident about what they do. Correct placement gives employees the opportunity to contribute fully, develop their skills and derive satisfaction from doing their jobs well.

Clearly, tasks and roles need to suit employees' skill and experience levels. Just as important, however, is meeting employees' motivational needs, temperaments and work-style preferences. For example, some people:

- are happy working on their own, while others want to be part of a friendly, cooperative team
- enjoy detailed work, while others prefer to take a 'broad brush' approach
- like a chance to move about, while others prefer to stay in one place
- need a lot of variety in their work, while others prefer a routine or predictable work environment.

Successful work placement allows people to have a sense of achievement in doing the work itself and a sense of using, stretching and expanding their skills. Giving employees the opportunity to work to their strengths – at work they enjoy and are good at – means they are six times more likely to be engaged in their jobs and more than three times as likely to report having an excellent quality of life than employees who are poorly placed in their jobs.[3]

Fortunately, as a leader-manager, you have a great deal of influence over placement. Naturally, there are aspects of everyone's role that they'd rather not have to do, but try to minimise this as much as possible. Remember, what one person finds difficult or dull, another finds interesting.

Improving the morale, motivation, satisfaction and productivity of the whole team may require:

- redesigning some tasks to make them more challenging or satisfying
- providing employees with opportunity to develop their skills
- transferring employees to a new working environment – either to work in isolation or to work within a group.

The important thing to remember is that people only do their best work when it closely matches their underlying interests and abilities. (For more information on matching people to jobs to build performance and productivity, see Chapters 8 and 28.)

INDUSTRY INSIGHTS

The right people, not the best people

Australia's top 11 companies select the 'right' people, not necessarily the 'best' people.[4] They pick people who are right for their culture and their strategy and who are enrolled for 'the cause' – and these organisations have queues of people wanting to work for them. They promote from within and spend a lot of money on in-house customised training and development. They set success measures and provide honest feedback on performance. This makes them tough to work for because they're tough on poor performers. When people don't do a good job, they're told so and they're helped to achieve their targets. Only when that doesn't work are they 'managed out' of the organisation.

Motivation

There is a fable about three labourers. One says, 'I'm breaking rocks'. Another says, 'I'm building a wall'. The third says, 'I'm building a cathedral'. Which of them do you think would be most motivated to do a great job? One form of motivation is to know why you are working hard. Worthwhile work encourages people to do their best. Without motivated employees, performance and productivity can never be more than mediocre. Naturally, people need to be satisfied with their pay and working conditions. But when these are the only rewards people get, they respond by doing only the bare minimum – just enough to get by. The work environment alone can't build better performance and productivity.

For this, you need to provide psychological rewards. Employees need to know that they are doing a worthwhile job and reaching their goals (which links back into the What To Key). They need to know you appreciate them and they need to feel proud of the contribution they are making. They need to use their talents, develop their potential and be treated with respect. (For more information on how to motivate people, see Chapter 11.)

The How To Key

When people know What To do and Want To do it, can you set them to work? Not unless they also know how to do the job. The How To Key unlocks people's ability to do a good job. Its elements, as shown in Figure 19.7, include:

1 training
2 experience
3 a learning environment.

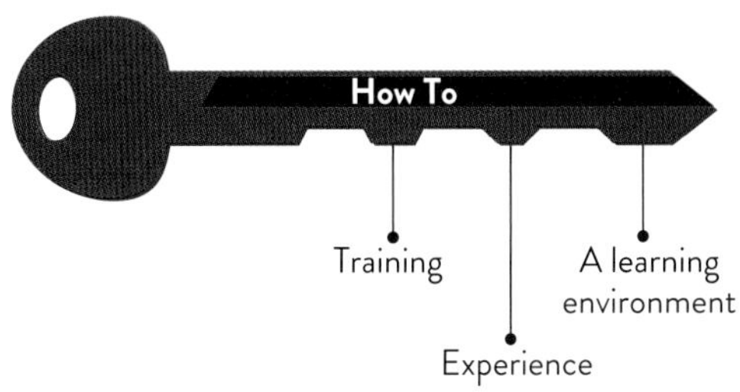

FIGURE 19.7 The three elements of the How To Key

Training and experience

People attain competence, or job skills and knowledge, through training and experience. You need to train employees to do their jobs and give them time to build their skills and gain confidence. Training and coaching provide ideal opportunities to let employees know that the things they do make a difference and how it fits into the organisation's, department's or team's operations. This is an important element in establishing positive attitudes, motivation and the desire to perform well, which strengthens the What To and Want To Keys. (See Chapter 29 for more information on how to coach people to improve or develop their skills.)

A learning environment

Transferable skills

2.2 Personal effectiveness

The third element of the How To Key is an environment that encourages learning and improving. Learning, sharing knowledge and continually finding better ways to work, builds teams and organisations. Training and continual learning are investments in your own future as well as the organisation's future. (Chapter 29 explains how to build a learning environment.)

The Chance To Key

When employees know What To do and How To do it, and Want To do it well, what can cause poor performance? This is where the Chance To Key comes in. It unlocks the shackles that restrain people from doing a good job. This Key helps you to create an environment for success.

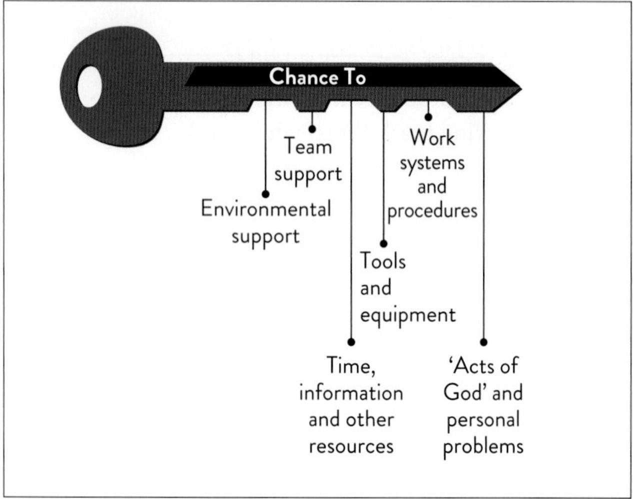

FIGURE 19.8 The six elements of the Chance To Key

Ensuring the team have access to what they need to achieve success within their roles can be helpful. However, sometimes these factors can also get in the way of people doing a good job. As will be discussed in the following sections, they slowly 'grind employees down' and sap their motivation to perform. Figure 19.8 shows the elements of the Chance To Key, which include:

- environmental support
- team support
- time, information and other resources
- tools and equipment
- work systems and procedures
- 'acts of God' and personal problems.

Environmental support

It's hard to do your work well when you're constantly distracted, don't have enough room to manoeuvre at your workspace or your back is aching from a hard, uncomfortable chair. It's hard to do your work well when you're constantly tripping over frayed carpets or cables strung across the floor or shivering from an overenthusiastic air-conditioning system.

When people are comfortable and feel they're being looked after, they work better. Steps you can take to support and energise your team and create a productive environment are shown in Figure 19.9.

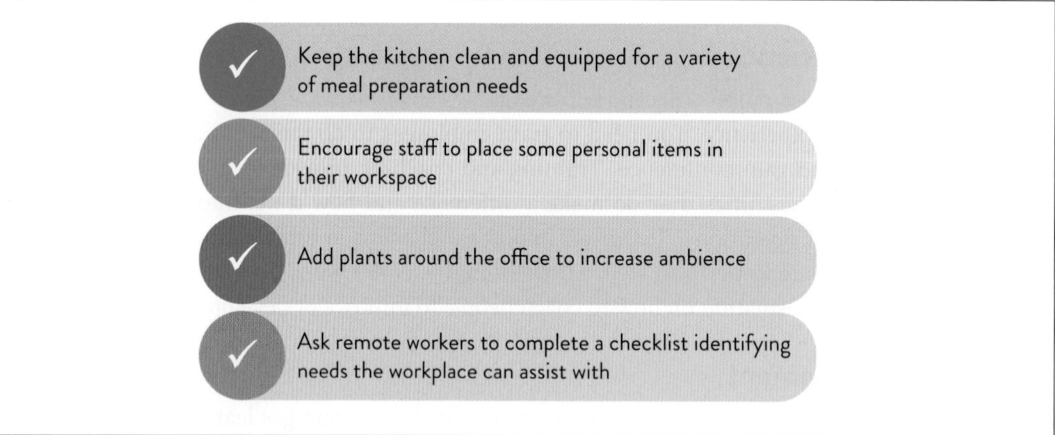

FIGURE 19.9 Steps to create a productive environment

Team support

Transferable skills
3.1 Teamwork/relationships

A high-performance team culture is one in which challenging goals are set and people are expected, and expect, to achieve them. The leader-manager coaches and helps team members to perform to the best of their abilities, and people learn from their experience and help each other out. Team members who work together will achieve more than they could by working on their own.

When team members don't understand what everyone else is trying to achieve, don't share common goals and purposes, and don't support or value each other's efforts, work becomes unnecessarily difficult. Major barriers to work performance and productivity can occur when there is a breakdown in working relationships, often leading to work becoming unpleasant.

Support teamwork through team building and team maintenance and build an enjoyable, collaborative working climate so that your team members remain willing to put in the effort required to do their jobs well. When people are having fun, they work harder, stay longer and are more engaged in their work. (For more on building productive teams, see Chapters 13 and 14.)

Time, information and other resources

When employees say they feel overloaded with work, they may have a valid point. Some organisations try to keep staffing levels down to save overheads but the result can be that people sometimes just don't have the time to do a job properly or to pass on complete information. Too many trivial tasks, duplication of work and inefficient procedures are other causes of running out of time to do everything that needs to be done and pass on needed information. People can be so busy 'keeping their heads above water' that they let important but non-essential tasks slide into oblivion. In the long run, productivity, quality and service suffer.

Doing jobs a second or third time because they weren't done correctly in the first place doesn't just cause annoyance and require effort. It also eats up huge chunks of time. Imagine saving 13 hours per person per week by eliminating rework. This one good habit alone – doing a task right the first time – is guaranteed to help people reach their targets consistently.

Time and information are intangible yet critical resources. Another habit to build among your team is passing on needed information and sharing helpful knowledge. Don't underestimate the importance of other resources, such as the working environment, supplies, access to a quiet place to meet and discuss work matters or to work on important tasks uninterrupted, and access to up-to-date technology that increases efficiency.

Tools and equipment

Faulty, inadequate, outdated or badly designed and maintained information technology systems, equipment, machinery and tools are a more common cause of poor performance than you might think. When everyone has limited time and lots to do, it's easy to let the important but not urgent tasks slip – tasks like carrying out routine maintenance. And as equipment, machinery and tools gradually become less efficient, often in incremental steps that people don't detect, they make it more and more difficult to get a job done well.

Similarly, without investing in updated IT systems, equipment, machinery and tools, perhaps due to budget constraints, it becomes harder and harder for employees to remain as productive as the competition and productivity falls behind, even when people's performance stays the same.

Transferable skills
5.1 Cyber security
5.2 Technology use

Tools and equipment

After nine years of operation, the CEO of an Australian research company decided to branch out internationally. As a part of the new global strategy, a revised recruitment strategy was drafted to include appointments of international consultants. To maintain a cohesive and collaborative team environment, in a hybrid working model, IT systems were expanded to include various communication and project management software, cyber-security systems and support services.

Work systems and procedures

Cumbersome work systems and procedures and out-of-date information management systems don't just discourage people from doing a good job – they can actually prevent them from doing a good job. Because procedures usually develop over time as additions and changes are made ad hoc, unwieldy work methods can mushroom unnoticed. This is an all-too-common cause of less-than-optimal performance and productivity.

Get together periodically with your work team or individual team members and examine work systems and procedures. Look for unnecessary steps and backtracking, bottlenecks, hiccups and hassles that make employees' lives difficult. Look for ways to streamline systems and procedures and redesign any awkward steps or processes so that employees can complete them in a more smooth, easy, quick or economical manner. Look for unnecessary red tape that you can eliminate, streamline or complete more quickly or efficiently to allow people to get on with their jobs.

Continually improving work systems and procedures makes a huge contribution to building performance and productivity. (Check out Chapter 27, which explains how to use flow charts and other techniques to help analyse and improve work systems and procedures.)

'Acts of God' and personal problems

The 85:15 rule says that, provided people know clearly what is expected of them and are trained to do it well, you can find 85 per cent of the causes of poor performance and low productivity in the work environment – the five aspects of the Chance To Key described so far. 'Acts of God' and personal factors account for the remaining 15 per cent of poor performance.[5] These are events you can't do anything about. When your workplace floods or loses its electricity, or a debilitating virus keeps a significant number of your work group home due to illness, it is difficult or impossible to get production or services out on time.

Personal factors can impact on your ability to concentrate fully on your work – from the occasional 'bad hair' day to more serious events, whether happy or unsettling. It makes sense to concentrate your efforts on improving productivity and performance in areas that will be of the most influence – in the work environment.

Transferable skills
3.4 Leadership

The Led To Key

The Led To Key is the most important Key of all because it is in charge of all the others. It unlocks people's enthusiasm and willingness to do a good job. You set the pace for peak performance and high productivity. The leadership you provide, setting clear goals and a good example, inspiring people with a compelling team vision and coaching them to bring out their best, provides the final touch to peak performance and productivity. Even when the other Keys are in place, poor leadership can spoil everything.

Do you practise what you preach, lead by example, and empower and help employees to do their jobs well? Six important characteristics of effective leaders that help build performance and productivity, shown in the Led To Key in Figure 19.10, are reviewed below (and discussed more fully in Chapter 5). They include:

- ambitious goals
- focus
- high standards
- interpersonal skills
- action orientation
- self-esteem.

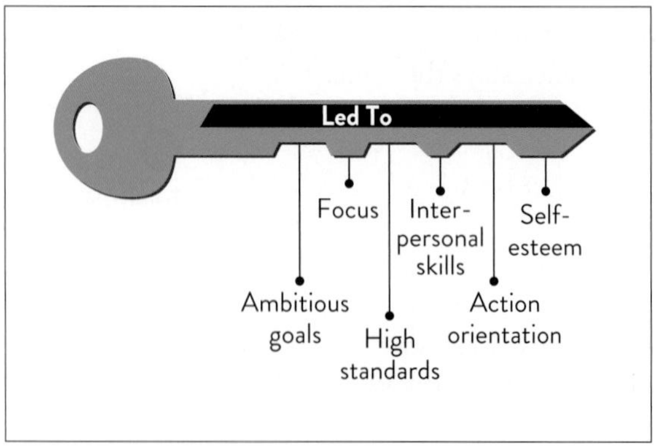

FIGURE 19.10 The six elements of the Led To Key

Ambitious goals

People with high standards and positive expectations set stretching (yet achievable) goals. By aiming high you can achieve more than by aiming low. Keeping goals to a manageable number will keep people motivated, challenged in a positive way and reduce consequences that stem from being overworked.

Focus

Keeping your goals clearly in mind helps you and your team meet the high standards and achieve the challenging goals you set for yourself and others. Encouraging your team to look at what practices they need to fine-tune or what distractions they need to remove will help them achieve maximum concentration.

High standards

The saying 'mediocrity is a choice; so is excellence' illustrates the importance of setting high standards and expecting the best. This approach is essential to building performance and productivity.

Interpersonal skills

To successfully build performance and productivity, you need well-developed interpersonal skills. Communicating and working effectively with others gives you the influence you need to encourage and guide people to lift their performance.

Action orientation

Leader-managers with a record for building performance and productivity are invariably proactive – they take responsibility for making things happen. Don't sit back and wait, blame others or find excuses for not achieving your goals or meeting high standards.

Self-esteem

Successful managers have high self-esteem. Valuing and respecting yourself gives you the confidence you need to develop effective working relationships, lead others and manage operations. The secure sense of self that comes from high self-esteem allows you to consistently build the self-esteem of people around you. Building self-esteem in others also builds performance and productivity. Offering recognition and praise for good work and opportunities for learning and personal growth are important for raising your team members' self-esteem.

Transferable skills

2.2 Personal effectiveness

If one of your team was asked to discuss your leadership skills and ability to inspire team vision, what do you think they would say?

Putting the Five Keys to work

The Five Keys, summarised in Table 19.1, guide you as you build your work team's performance. When people aren't performing to your expectations, you can use the Five Keys to analyse what is holding them back. You can also use the Five Keys to identify and rectify potential problems that could affect your team's performance, as shown in Table 19.1. Get used to thinking through the Five Keys to ensure your team members have and know what they need to do their best work.

TABLE 19.1 Using the Five Keys to find and fix performance problems

What To	Do team members understand what needs to be done, what is expected of them and why it's important?
Want To	Have you placed team members in well-designed jobs that suit their skills and interests? Is poor current performance rewarding in some way, perhaps even more rewarding than better performance? Does everyone understand how achieving the expected goals benefits them? (Remember that rewards come in many forms, not just money, and that the strongest rewards are psychological.)
How To	Have team members been properly trained and had enough time to build their experience and confidence?
Chance To	Might something be interfering with people's output? For example, are machines running properly? Are raw materials up to standard? Is the quantity of work unusually high? Is one team member's absence or lack of training or experience putting pressure on the rest of the team? What bottlenecks can you remove or cumbersome procedures can you smooth out? Might internal power struggles be hindering the group's effectiveness?
Led To	Is your leadership everything that it should be?

19.2 Prospering through continuous improvements

Practise the philosophy of continuous improvement. Get a little better every single day.

Author unknown

Many organisations must feel a bit like Alice in Wonderland when she said, 'It takes all the running you can do, to keep in the same place'.[6] The fact is, if you are not improving, you run the risk of being left behind. You don't need to look too far back to see that everything your organisation was doing is now outdated. Look forward: everything you're doing now is destined to become obsolete, too.

The intensity of competition has more than doubled in the past 40 years.[7] The operating environment is changing so rapidly and is so complex that while you continue to do what you've always done, the rest of the world moves on and leaves you behind; competitors eventually overtake you, no matter how good you are right now. It takes a lot of running to maintain your position and faster running to improve it.

Innovating **continuous improvements**, either to fix problems or to improve what is already working well, isn't just about processes, products and providing a better service. It's also for techniques such as sales (business-to-business as well as to individual customers), for user and customer experiences, for how customers and products interact, and for business propositions, such as packaging offerings with other businesses. Working with non-competitive suppliers to jointly take orders, deliver products and invoice for them, as Starbucks, Kraft Foods and PepsiCo; Google and Luxottica; Apple and IBM; and Spotify and Uber are doing (discussed in Chapter 18) is a whole new take on doing business. Innovations are often obvious – but only in hindsight.

Transferable skills
2.3 Business strategy

Innovating through integrated supply chains

Dutch company ASML, an imaging solutions provider for semi-conductor manufacturers, works closely with its customers and its own suppliers to develop the advanced micro-chips that the market demands. So closely, in fact, that three of its largest customers (Intel, Samsung and TSMC) are contributing €1.38 billion over five years to ASML's research and development program (R&D) to top up ASML's already-huge R&D budget of €78 000 per employee per annum (a sum more than most pharmaceutical or vehicle companies spend on R&D per employee).[8] (See Chapter 18 for more examples of working with your trading partners to innovate for quality.)

Thrive to survive

Transferable skills
5.2 Technology use

To stay in the race, keep getting better at what you do. You can improve your processes, your products or services, and your business models, and you can do this in the five ways shown in Figure 19.11.

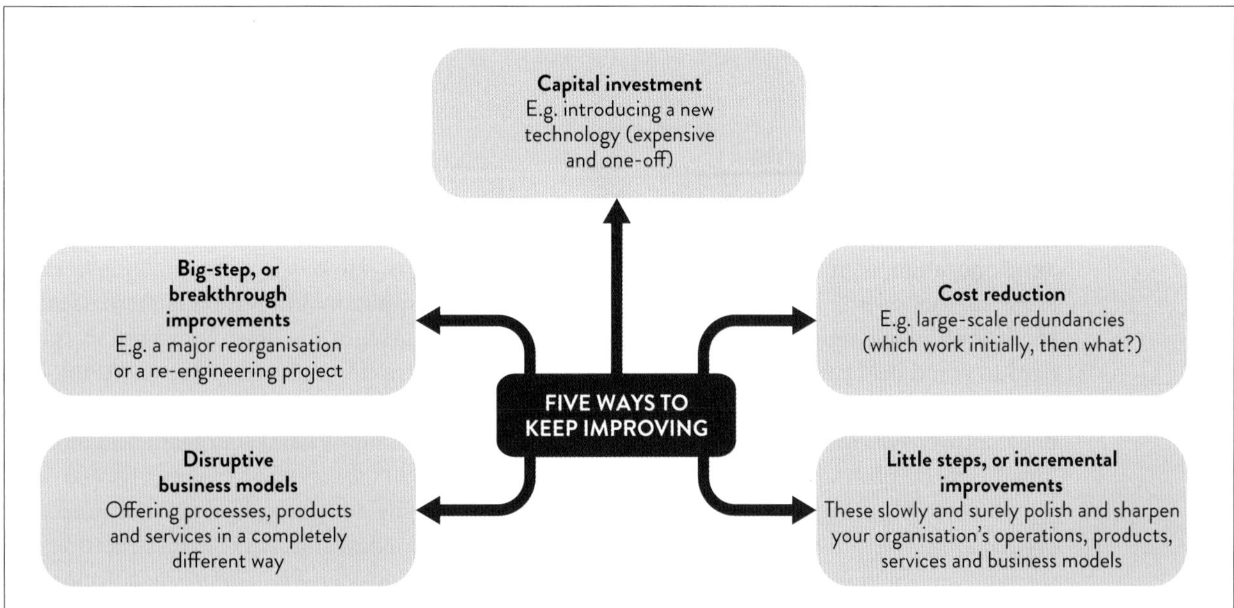

FIGURE 19.11 Thriving to survive

Most improvements come from making small adjustments and refinements to the way people do their work. Occasionally, a major redesign makes a 'great leap forward'. Both incremental (little-step) and breakthrough (big-step) improvements address the challenges of:

- achieving higher quality
- increasing efficiencies, saving time and reducing hassles through flexible and well-designed processes
- making the most effective use of people and information
- saving money through lower inventory and less waste.

Technology makes both big-step and little-step improvements easier. Collaborative systems technology and social media allow people to work together in real time, enabling learning and collaboration, rapid knowledge flows and finding answers fast – important elements of innovation and improvement. Multifunctional teamwork and quality-improvement projects, diversity, employee engagement, a learning culture and trading partnerships are also essential aspects of thriving to survive. (These aspects of innovation and continuous improvements are discussed in Chapters 3, 11, 18, 21 and 29.)

The improvement mindset can also change the way organisations do business. For example, confident that they can quickly match the cost of external suppliers and pocket the margin they pay them, many organisations are 'insourcing' previously outsourced activities, giving them greater control over their operations and the ability to spread overheads across a wider base.

INDUSTRY INSIGHTS

Innovation in practice

The Lego Group, nearly bankrupt in 2004, increased its profits by 400 per cent, revenue by 127 per cent and net profit after tax by 636 per cent in just five years through both breakthrough and incremental innovation. CEO Jergene Vig Knudstorp has often said that constant innovation led to Lego's success.

Finding improvements

Bionic ears, Hills hoists, in-vitro fertilisation, penicillin, polymer banknotes and wine casks are all world-beating Aussie innovations. Each year in Australia we celebrate the continuous improvement and innovation of many organisations and industry sectors. However, although innovation is essential, that doesn't mean it's easy. Rather than sudden inspiration, innovation is more usually a result of thinking and experimenting, trial and error. Of course, in the day-to-day rush, it can be hard to stand back and spot opportunities to make innovative improvements. But just think how much improved your operations could be if you spent just one hour a week finding a way to make one improvement. And what if everyone in your team did the same? What if your team held monthly 'improvement meetings' or 'innovation meetings'?

Start with looking at, and listening to, how things are being done now. Look at your processes, products, service provision business model, organisation strategy and work team structure, and see how you can polish them. Everything can be improved. Consider, for example, acquisition and suitability of materials, materials storage, product or service quality, rate of output or smoothness of operations or workflow. Look for problems, hiccups, hassles and irritations. Through innovative thinking, problems can either be improved or eliminated. (This is discussed further under the section 'Incremental improvements'.)

To gain an understanding of opportunities, listen to your customers, colleagues and other stakeholders. Analyse benchmarks, complaints, lost-time management reports, repeated work and other data.

Generally, innovation can take the following steps:

1. A problem or an opportunity for improvement is identified.
2. Potential solutions are generated with a selection chosen to develop further and test. (It's usually best to test early and often.)
3. The improvement that works best is implemented.
4. The improvement is monitored to see that it's achieving its objectives; when it isn't, remove it and return to Step 2. (See Chapter 26 for more information on solving problems and making decisions.)

These steps often loop back and forth, as ideas are refined and lessons learnt. Whenever possible, involve your team and anyone else who will implement and use the improvement.

Transferable skills
1.3 Sustainability

It is a good idea to get in the habit of considering risk and sustainability issues in your improvement plans and to liaise with relevant personnel when you need to (see Chapters 22 and 23 for more on this).

Benchmarking

Where are we currently? It's usually a good idea to know the answer to that question before you try to do anything so you can measure your success. Continually tracking your performance in key measures makes it easier to keep improving. Benchmarking is a reliable way to find out how you're doing; for example, in the areas of customer service, innovation, productivity and quality. To benchmark, establish meaningful key performance measures for important aspects of your operations. These become the benchmarks that you use to monitor your performance and compare with other organisations. Be cautious: it's easy to measure irrelevant benchmarks and miss the key factors that really drive successful operations; the latter is what you want to benchmark.

You can use benchmark measures in three ways:

1. To monitor and continually improve your own department's or team's performance and improvements over time; when a quality benchmark measure suddenly drops, it can warn you of a problem in the system that you can study and rectify. When a measure unexpectedly improves, you can study it to find out why and retain it.
2. To compare your performance with that of other similar departments in your own organisation. For example, you can adapt or copy the safety methods of the site with the most accident-free days and adapt or copy the delivery methods of the site with the highest number of orders delivered on time.
3. To compare your own organisation's key performance measures with the performance of other organisations in your own industry or in different industries. **Best practice benchmarking** allows you to compare your own performance with the world leaders' performance in a particular area that you are interested in. A finance department, for example, might set benchmarks for a number of key indicators of financial management (e.g. average length of time taken to invoice customers, errors per invoice, number of days for outstanding debts and interest earned on capital). It might find that a company in a different industry has reduced outstanding debts to 15 days and meet with that company to learn how it achieved this. Organisations can learn a lot from each other, and benchmarking makes this possible.

Transferable skills
4.1 Data literacy

When you benchmark, don't just collect data. Data is not the same as information and not all data is useful. Decide what information you need first; this tells you what numbers you need to gather. Also consider the best source for collecting data. You may need to engage with people and ask questions to ensure you gain the full picture. Benchmark often enough to keep abreast of what's really happening but not so often that measuring becomes an end in itself. At the other end of the extreme, annual or irregular benchmarking sends signals that what you're measuring isn't really important.

Be careful, too, about how you benchmark. For instance, it's virtually meaningless to benchmark customer satisfaction across an entire organisation. Company-wide figures may look good but hide the huge variation that can exist from location to location, customer group to customer group, product to product or shift to shift. Your stores may score nine out of 10 for happy customers, but what have you learnt if one or two locations are consistently scoring 2s and bringing down the average of the locations consistently scoring 10? A global score of nine doesn't give you the information you need to improve your operations. **Figure 19.12** shows how to avoid the most common mistakes of benchmarking.

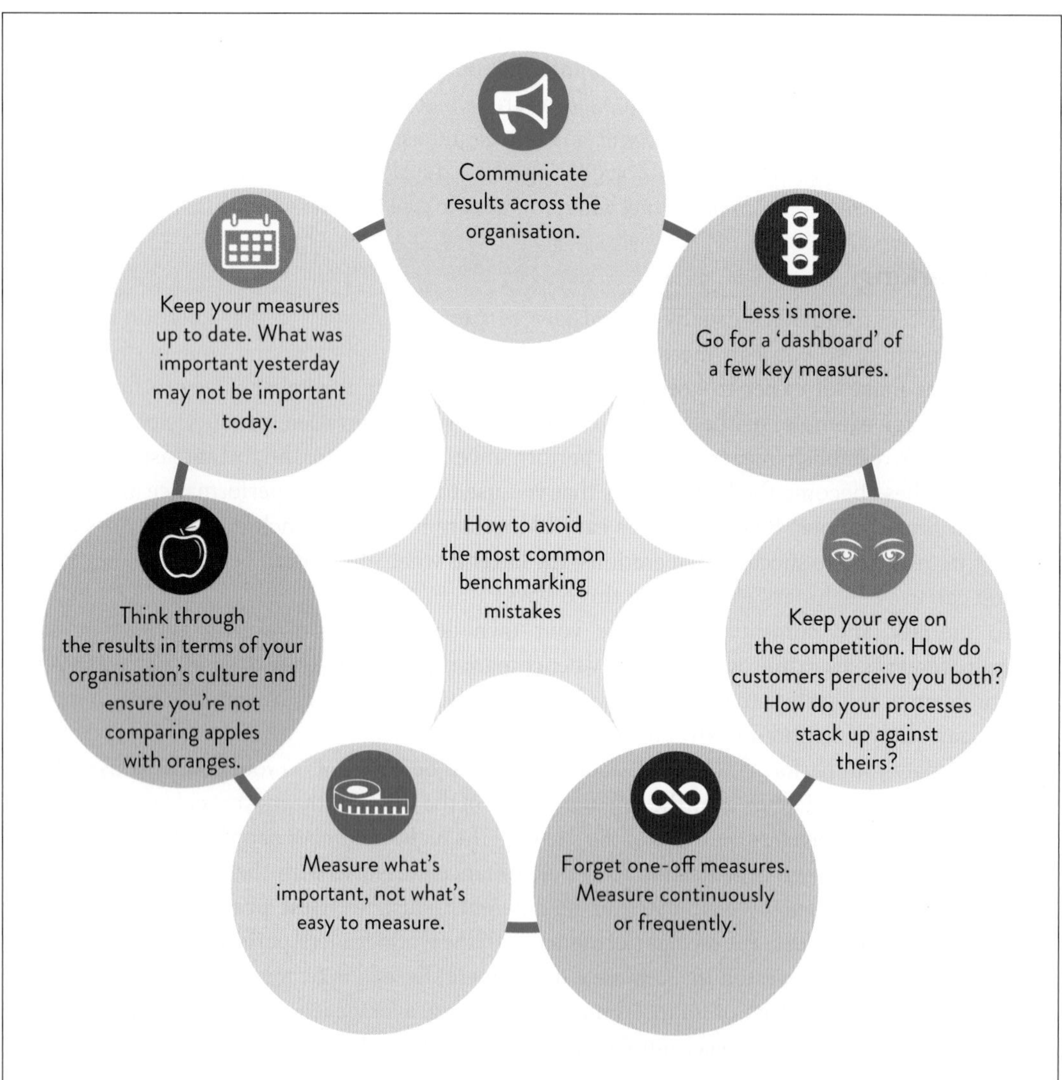

FIGURE 19.12 Avoiding the benchmarking blues

Incremental improvements

Online retailer Amazon concentrates on making incremental improvements in every aspect of the business, from order taking to speed of delivery. Little things count, and incremental improvements are about little things – doing 100 activities 1 per cent better, not one activity 100 per cent better. In fact, each incremental improvement averages a 10 to 15 per cent improvement, not a 1 per cent improvement, and they slowly but surely add up to big improvements in productivity and performance.

A quick-and-easy way to keep improving is through the measures of success you set for yourself, your team and individual team members. Once you are consistently achieving a measure of success, replace it with another one that lifts your performance still further.

Lean

The Japanese word for continuous incremental improvement is *kaizen* – change for the better. The **kaizen** approach is to keep examining everything you do to find ways to make small enhancements towards perfection. How can you do things a little bit better? How can you 'tweak' them, refine them and polish them? The changes you make don't need to be huge – kaizen results mostly in a small tweak here, or an adjustment there.

Lean is a methodology that encourages innovation to continually eliminate waste and improve processes so that each step adds value from the customer's perspective. Essentially, lean seeks to preserve or increase quality with less work, following key total quality management (TQM) principles:

- give employees responsibility to increase efficiency and eliminate waste in their jobs through continuous improvement
- commit to data-driven experiments using the tools and techniques explained in Chapter 26
- have uncompromising attention to detail.

Lean methodologies were pioneered by Toyota in Japan and have been called the most important innovation in operations since Henry Ford improved the assembly line by adding conveyor belts. Lean has since been used by other manufacturers and in service industries, such as finance, food production and health.

Although the lean approach isn't as rigorous and detailed as Six Sigma (discussed further later in the chapter) and business process management, introducing lean principles can nevertheless generate worthwhile results, including reduced costs, cycle times, inventory, lead times, materials handling, obsolescence, scrap, waste and work in progress, and improved productivity, quality and use of space. Lean Six Sigma, a combination of lean and Six Sigma, has been popular in Australia. It requires less employee training than Six Sigma (but more than lean) and overcomes the statistically 'light' nature of lean, resulting in quicker 'wins' than Six Sigma. Figure 19.13 shows lean Six Sigma's five 'Ss', or five core principles.

Eliminate waste

Waste is anything that doesn't add value, whether it's equipment, material, people or unnecessary steps in a process. You can remember the eight types of waste, shown in Figure 19.14, with the acronym TIM WOODS.

Look for small waste, not just big waste. For example, you might find and eliminate waste in:

- *unnecessary activities:* for example, looking for equipment, information or materials, rework (doing something a second or third time), unnecessary component or tool changeovers or unnecessary walking
- *layout:* for example, backtracking, distances travelled, unnecessary handling
- *other areas:* for example, damaged materials, faulty or poorly maintained tools and equipment, housekeeping and having incorrect information.

Improve processes

Process innovation aims to improve workflows and internal efficiencies by finding ways to make people's effort and work methods add value more cheaply, easily, reliably, safely, sustainably and quickly. When deciding how to improve systems, use a flow chart or job breakdown to break them

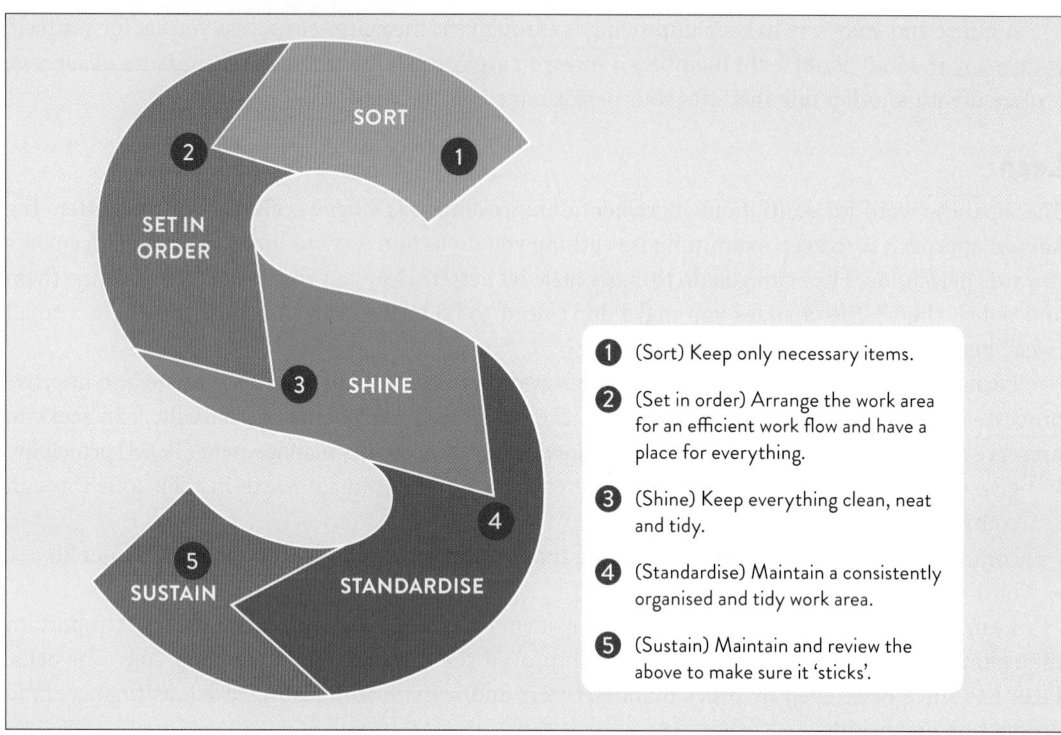

FIGURE 19.13 The five 'Ss' of lean Six Sigma

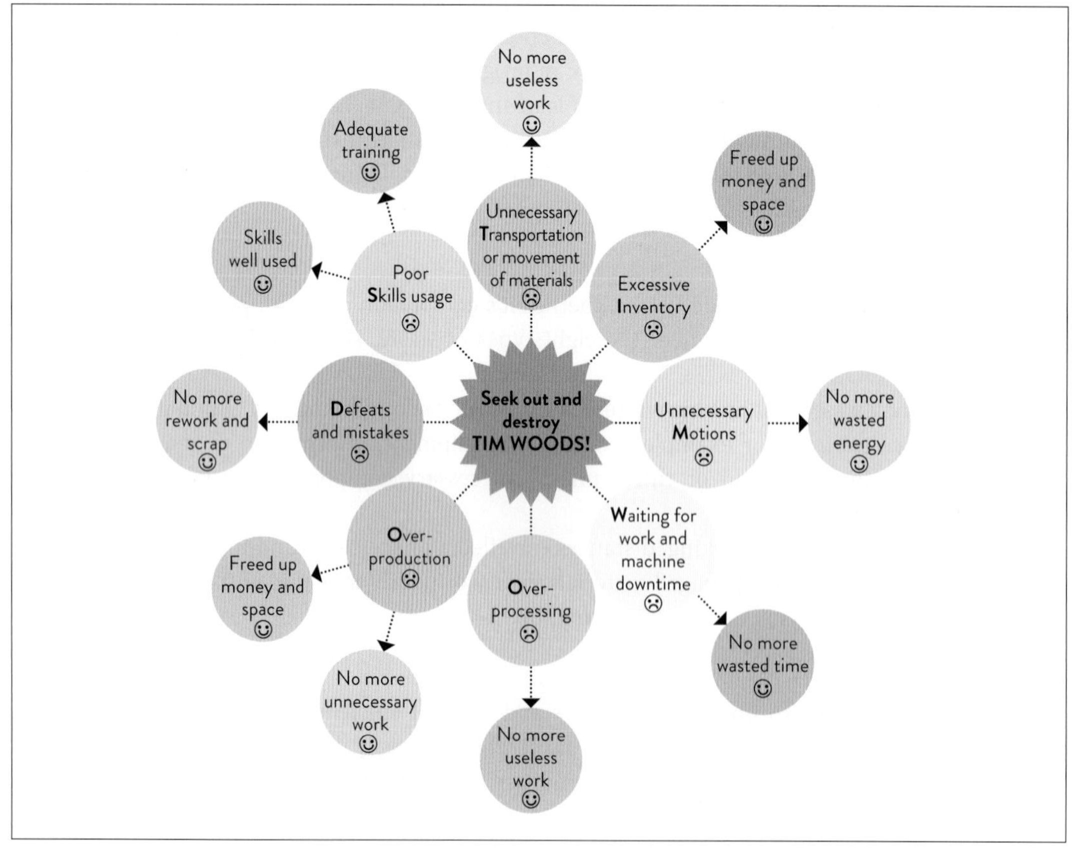

FIGURE 19.14 Eight types of waste

into their component steps. Then ask what value each step adds to decide whether the step is needed and why it's needed. When you're not sure whether a step adds value, ask:

- What would happen (really) if it didn't get done?
- When was it first done? Why? (It may have made sense once, but …)

The eight key questions for improving processes are shown in Figure 19.15. When you improve a step that adds value, ask more questions like those shown in Figure 19.16. Before you amend a work process, though, think through the potential impacts on people, resources and other organisational practices. When one aspect of a system is changed, there can be upstream and downstream effects. You may want to consult with stakeholders before implementing any alterations that affect them.

FIGURE 19.15 Tweak, polish and refine

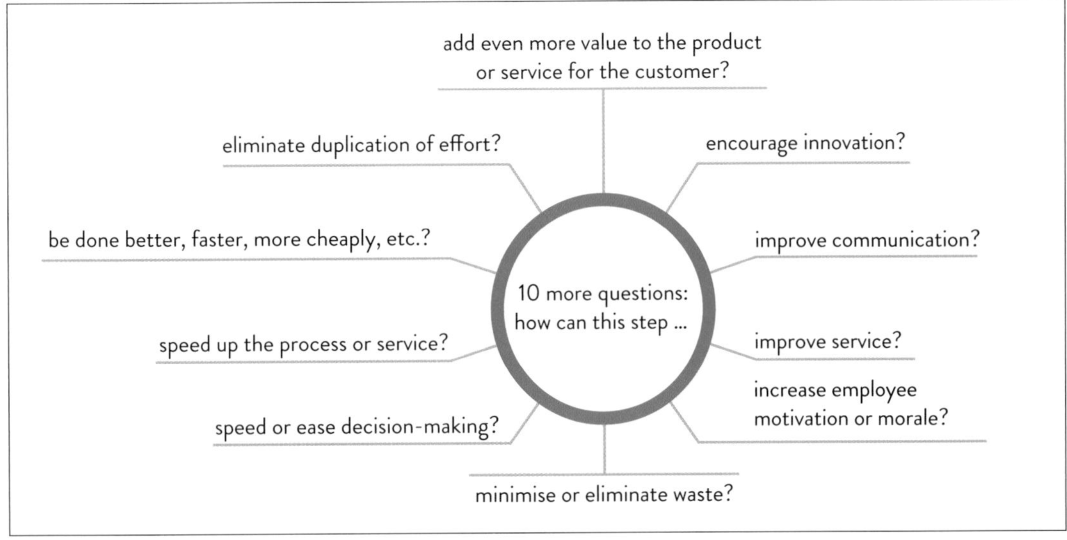

FIGURE 19.16 Keep improving

If you would like to know more about processes, Bill Peterson's 15-minute TEDtalk on YouTube, 'Lean applied to us', provides an overview of the lean process, available at https://www.youtube.com/watch?v=tfQiGDUBdD0.

REFLECT

As part of his job, Mauri prepared several reports each month. Along with 30 other leader-managers across Australia, he received a monthly reminder about one report that he thought was a waste of time. One busy month, Mauri decided to review his work priorities and 'accidentally' deleted the reminder, thinking to himself that if asked, he would apologise. In the meantime, no report was produced. The next month, the usual reminder arrived.

Oops! Deleted again! And again, for another two months. The sky didn't fall in and when Mauri travelled interstate to meet with his boss, he asked her, in passing, what she did with this report. 'She didn't know what I was talking about, so I explained, putting forward the argument that this report wasn't actually useful. That same week, we all received advice that a certain monthly report was no longer required!'

- Are all your tasks really necessary? What about your team members' tasks?
- How can you improve and streamline your work practices?

Improvement teams

A special improvement team or natural work group might be assigned a process to improve, or a work team might select its own issue to work on. The teams meet regularly and use a systematic process and the tools and techniques discussed in Chapter 27. (See Chapters 13, 14 and 21 to find out how to lead projects and project teams.) Not only do organisations benefit from improved processes and reduced waste, but those also involved in an improvement team experience, enhanced working relationships and more effective teamwork. Greater job involvement leads to employee motivation, and personal development for the team members.

Breakthrough improvements

In sport, rules can't be broken without a penalty. But Picasso broke the rules on how a face should look and Gaudi broke the rules on how a building should look. Airbnb broke the rules about renting a room, Amazon broke the rules about selling books and Uber broke the rules about hiring transportation. At work, it's good to break rules once in a while – especially self-imposed rules about how something should be done. That's what breakthrough improvements do.

There are two main ways to achieve breakthrough improvements: business process management (also known as *core process redesign*, *re-engineering* and *process re-engineering*) and Six Sigma (which is also used to achieve incremental improvements).

Core process redesign and Six Sigma attain breakthrough improvements through temporary cross-functional improvement teams using the systematic tools and techniques discussed in Chapter 26. Because their improvement projects generally relate to major improvements in key areas of the organisation, a management group usually selects the project, often targeting chronic problems. The teams aim to achieve a 50 to 90 per cent improvement within four to 12 months, depending on the project scope.

Business process management

Transferable skills

2.3 Business strategy

Business process management uses the concept of an enterprise as part of a web of relationships and information systems to dramatically improve the supply chain. It potentially results in far more than incremental improvements because it rethinks the organisation's processes, systems and procedures from top to bottom, aiming at great leaps forward in all measures of operating efficiency.

Redesigning business processes is a back-to-the-drawing board approach. Instead of doing what you've always done and refining the way you do it, you start with a blank piece of paper and ask, 'What is the best way to organise our activities?' (See also the information on capabilities-based organisations in Chapter 3.)

Begin with identifying the customers, internal and external, of the organisation's key processes, and what those customers need and want. Then work backwards, using technology and systematic analytical methods, to redesign – often radically – the workflows and operating procedures. The improvements in productivity and customer service that result can be dramatic.

Business process management aims to:

- increase productivity
- increase responsiveness
- reduce functionalism (silos)
- reduce non-value-adding activities
- reduce overhead costs
- reduce specialisation.

Unfortunately, in some organisations, business process management becomes synonymous with staff reductions, ill will and lowered morale among employees at all levels. When used correctly and the people aspects of the change are considered, however, core process redesign offers potentially significant gains in producing and offering products and services.

About 70 per cent of business process management efforts fail to achieve impressive improvements, largely because the fundamentals are ignored. An organisation may fail strategically by neglecting to examine the vision and strategic plan and identify how to help each arm of the organisation work towards achieving them. It may fail to examine the markets and customers before redesigning the organisation to meet their needs and wants. It may see core process redesign as a tool to achieve predetermined objectives, such as a convenient way to reduce the workforce, close a factory or shut down a department, rather than a way to provide quality products and services by building efficiency and quality into systems.

Some projects also neglect to recognise that organisations are complex and convoluted networks of multiple connections and relationships. Redesigning deeply embedded systems often fails because the old systems 'mysteriously' keep reappearing. 'Clean sheets' are tricky to make work in complex systems. In fact, it can take about five years or even more to embed improvements to the point where they become a way of life.

Six Sigma

Sigma is a statistical measure of variation used to measure defects per million. The greater the **sigma** number, the fewer the defects, as you can see in Table 19.2. A defect rate of three sigma is about 66000 defects per million; or four sigma is about 6000 defects per million. The Six Sigma level is considered to be virtually defect-free, with only 3.4 defects per million, resulting in 99.9997 per cent of products and services meeting quality standards or specifications. This translates into a huge leap forward in productivity, profits and customer satisfaction.

TABLE 19.2 The greater the sigma number, the fewer the defects

	4.3 Sigma (99.7% perfection)	4.6 Sigma (99.9% perfection)	6 Sigma (99.9997% perfection)
Incorrect drug prescriptions a year	54 000	4000	1 every 25 years
Incorrect surgical operations a week	5000	1350	1 every 20 years
Lost mail per hour	54 000	4000	1
Newborn babies dropped by doctors and nurses annually	10 000	3000	10
Unsafe drinking water: hours a month	2	1	1 second every 16 years[9]

A Motorola engineer coined the term 'Six Sigma' when the company decided to measure defects not per thousand but per million and saved more than US$16 billion as a result. BHP Billiton's Six Sigma program, called Operating Excellence, saved $US350 000, extending the life of tyres from 2000 to 6000 hours at its Saraji Mine in Queensland; Westpac saved $156 000 by reducing the time it takes to write letters about errors in deposits.[10] There is no doubt that Six Sigma projects can save significant sums of money.

Six Sigma identifies and eliminates problems and makes the most of opportunities in all sorts of companies and processes. It works in accounts receivable, call centres, customer service and support, finance, insurance, marketing, research and development, sales and supply-chain management as well as in highly standardised production operations.[11]

Six Sigma is usually applied after the organisation's core processes have been redesigned. It is a rigorous process centred on data gathering and statistical analysis that pinpoints where errors occur and eliminates them, seeking improvements organisation-wide, in customer relationships, design methods, investor relations, processes, products, recruitment, services, suppliers and training. D–M–A–I–C, or the five steps to Six Sigma improvement, is shown in Figure 19.17.

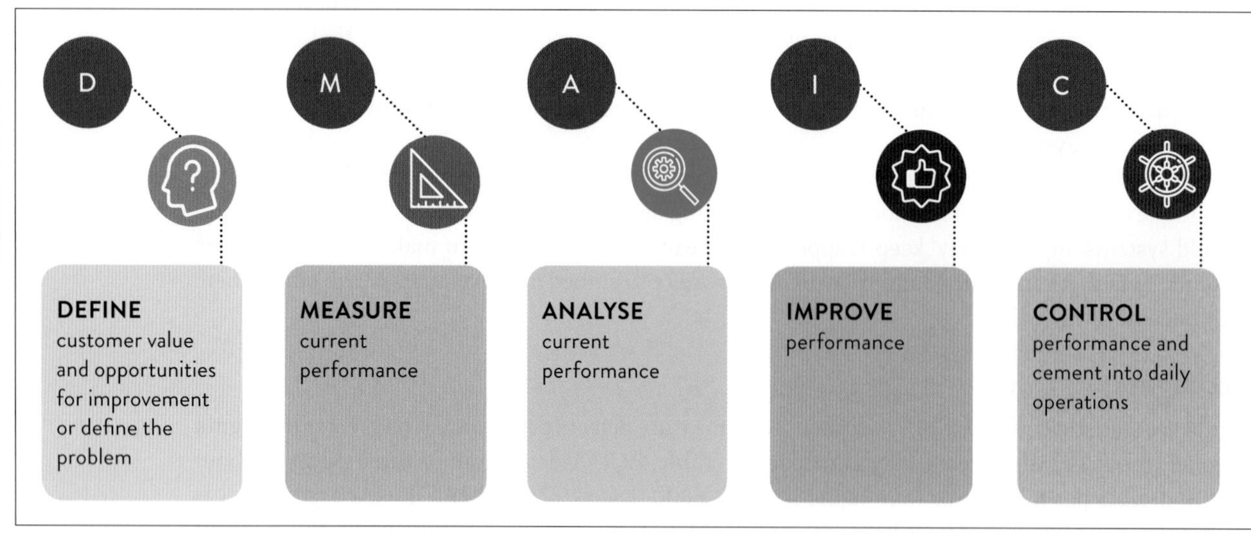

FIGURE 19.17 The five steps to Six Sigma improvement

Six Sigma projects typically result in:

- faster turnover of working capital
- fewer defects, rejects and errors and therefore less rework
- freeing up existing capacity and making new capacity unnecessary
- improved profitability
- improved response times
- increased employee empowerment, development, morale and motivation
- increased productivity
- increased reliability through decreased variation, achieving consistent, reliable quality (see Chapter 18 and engaging with customers to find out more about variation)
- increased sales
- optimised cycle time and equipment usage
- realising greater results from investments
- reduced capital spending
- reduced downtime
- reduced inventory levels
- reduced waste.

Six Sigma training

Employees need training to use Six Sigma techniques, progressing through five levels: from *white belts* to *yellow belts*, *green belts* and *black belts*, and finally, to the *master black belt* experts. Master black belts are qualified to teach analytical tools and techniques and coach black belts; they generally supervise multiple projects in parallel. Black belts have four to six months of training and work full-time, leading up to seven breakthrough improvement projects a year in temporary cross-functional project teams.

Green belts have about six days of training and are the grassroots practitioners in the operational level of the business, working on both little-step and big-step improvements. They spend at least 50 per cent of their time on their normal duties and the rest of their time working and driving projects in their functional areas. White and yellow belts are trained in the basic approach outlined in Figure 19.17 and undertake continuous incremental improvements, generally in their work teams.

In organisations committed to Six Sigma, all projects have a high profile and status – when you're trained to belt level, it's clear you're on the fast track. Six Sigma has been particularly successful in high-tech, mass market industries and other high-volume process areas, such as back offices and call centres. For example:

1. Dell emphasises incremental improvements with its Six Sigma projects. It streamlined its accounts payable department with Six Sigma, saving an estimated US$2.4 million a year; a team leader in Dell's server factory replaced coloured paper with white paper to print out parts lists, saving US$23 000 a year.
2. Six Sigma is well integrated into the Dow Chemical Company's operations, saving the company more than $1 billion in savings per year companywide. It first applied Six Sigma to environmental, health and safety services with a saving of US$130 million. The company was so impressed that it went on to apply Six Sigma to finance, information systems, HR processes, legal, marketing, public affairs and R&D and has used the technique to reduce capital costs, identify and implement best practice, forecast capital spending, predict market opportunities and much more.

3 Froedtert Hospital in Milwaukee in the US credits its Six Sigma standardising of intravenous drug procedures with there being only one incident of a patient being wrongly medicated. The hospital has also used Six Sigma to eliminate diverting emergency ambulances to other hospitals, reduce the length of patients' stay in the emergency department, optimise staffing levels and reduce patient waiting times.
4 Software manufacturer Honeywell uses Six Sigma as a critical strategy to accelerate improvements in processes, products and services, radically reduce administration and manufacturing costs and improve quality. Focusing on eliminating waste and reducing defects and variation, Honeywell has saved billions of dollars from tens of thousands of sustainable improvements across all areas of its activities and considers Six Sigma activities one of its principal growth and productivity drivers in all areas of its business. It expects its leader-managers at all levels and most professionals to become Six Sigma certified to at least the green belt level and gives new employees 12 months from their hire date to earn certification.
5 Raytheon Australia considers Six Sigma to be the 'vehicle through which we increase productivity, grow our business and build a new culture within our organisation'. A project team working on manufacturing helicopters for the Royal Australian Navy reduced unscheduled maintenance by 57 per cent, reduced supply lead times by 35 per cent and increased aircraft availability by 15 per cent.
6 Suncorp-Metway trained 60 black belts and 200 green belts who work on about 30 projects a year and have achieved, among other things, faster credit approvals, shorter queuing time for customers and tighter commercial lending practices.[12]

Benchmarking, customer service, lean, process re-engineering, Six Sigma, total quality management ... Are these fads? No. A competitor uses one of these techniques and gains a competitive advantage. So the rest use it too. Failing to use it is a disadvantage. Using it levels the playing field and the bar is raised. This is known as *competitive convergence*: a competitive advantage becomes mandatory and it is no longer a winning edge.

Organisations then need a new way to gain competitive advantage. The best way to achieve sustainable operational effectiveness as a competitive advantage is by preserving what is distinctive about an organisation – its culture.

19.3 Encouraging creativity and innovation

He was a bold man, that first ate an oyster.

Jonathan Swift (author, satirist), quoted in Henry Ashbourne, 'Polite conversation' in *The works of Jonathan* Swift, 1841, p. 344.

Are you bold enough to float an idea even when people might smirk at it or to test out an idea even when it may well fail? Are you willing to keep searching and trying until you find a better way to achieve a goal, complete a procedure, deal with a difficult team member or serve a customer? Are you able to put your experience and expertise behind you and see a situation from a completely different perspective? Do you take time to chill out and give your brain a rest so that ideas can incubate? Do you look beyond the obvious solution or one that has worked before for a different, even better way? If you answered yes to most of these questions, you demonstrate the fundamental behaviours of someone who is creative and innovative.

Kodak invented the digital camera but didn't commercialise it; Nokia 'owned' the mobile phone market but lost it when it didn't move into smartphones. Companies grow and plateau, at which point they either decline or jump to something new. This is known as the S-curve of change (shown in Figure 24.1) and that cycle of 'grow and plateau, die or jump' is happening faster and faster. In fact, right now is the slowest rate of change you and your organisation will probably experience in your lifetime.

In today's volatile, uncertain, complex and ambiguous environment, both organisations and individuals need to embrace change as the 'new normal'. They need to be nimble and adaptive and embrace the trial, test and learn approach. Organisations that don't recognise and work with what's happening around them and come up with new ideas are less likely to thrive. (The same applies to individuals who aren't proactive in fostering new skills; this is discussed in Chapter 29.)

How adaptive is your organisation? How adaptive are you?

Transferable skills

1.2 Entrepreneurship/ small business skills

Enterprising skills, particularly innovation and an entrepreneurial mindset, are as important as technical skills. Organisations need people who are curious and who have the courage to challenge the status quo. Leader-managers can support this essential mindset by being dynamic, encouraging collaboration and supporting flexibility. That's where creativity and innovation come in to support both breakthrough and incremental improvements.

When your mind is prepared and relaxed, ideas for changes and improvements can come serendipitously – seemingly (but not really) out of the blue. These 'eureka!' moments occur when you've pondered long and hard on an opportunity or problem and when you know enough about it that your subconscious can get to work on it while you relax and recuperate from the daily grind. That makes most innovative and breakthrough ideas far removed from pure chance and much closer to both creativity and hard work.

You can think of creativity as the ability to come up with novel ideas, and innovation as a bridge built through logic, creativity and, occasionally, serendipity, between old and new ideas, introducing those ideas and making them work. Innovations can be evolutionary (little step) 'twists', extensions of what we already know or do, or they can be revolutionary (big step) departures from what we currently know or do. Either way, innovations need to be made to work for the good of the organisation and its stakeholders.

Transferable skills

1.2 Entrepreneurship/ small business skills

Consider the following questions:

- Do you have enterprising skills?
- Are you eager to explore areas where you can incorporate innovation?
- Do you feel you have an entrepreneurial mindset?
- Are you creative?

Innovation inspiration

Systematically seek out innovative and creative ideas as sustained innovation and creativity can lead to a continuous stream of improvements. The innovator's motto, 'fail fast, fail forward', acknowledges that when you innovate, you make mistakes. Sometimes, it's the mistakes you make that you lead to innovate. Inventions that come from mistakes include:

- Post-it notes, which were created from mistakes while trying to create an alternative adhesive product.
- Goodyear accidentally combined and cooked rubber and sulphur, which ultimately was responsible for producing plastic.

- A sweetener called Saccharine was created because a scientist failed to wash his hands.
- Scotchgard was the result of a scientist trying to clean a mixture she was working with off her shoe.

Innovation is often derived from a pressing need. Ernest Hamwi's Syrian zalabia waffle stall wasn't selling much at the 1904 World's Fair, while the ice-cream stall beside him was doing so much business that it kept running out of plates and spoons. Hamwi twisted one of his waffles into a cone, passed it to the next stall, and the ice-cream cone was born.[13] Antoine Feuchtwanger's Bavarian sausage restaurant ran out of cutlery one busy day in 1880 and he had to serve the sausages in a bread roll. Snags in a roll are now a favourite in many countries, including Australia.[14]

Sometimes, what you think you're creating turns out to be something else. For example, a drug intended to treat the chest pain caused by angina had surprising side effects and is now known as Viagra. YouTube started out as a video-dating site.[15] Sometimes, you notice something unexpected and that leads to an innovation. Two Bell Laboratories technicians, trying to eliminate radio static, found to their horror that the bigger and better they made their equipment the louder the static became. They discovered the reason – they were picking up whispers from the Big Bang. It was 1931 and radio astronomy was born.[16]

Innovations can be counterintuitive. In 2003, Lebanese-Australian designer Aheda Aznetti realised the impracticality of wearing the Islamic hijab and veil to play sport and designed sportswear for Muslim women. Two years later, she created a two-piece, head-to-toe swimsuit – the burkini – that is now sold worldwide and worn by Muslim and non-Muslim women for modesty and for protection against the sun.[17]

Innovations can evolve over time. Icehotel's Yngve Berqvist started with an ice sculpture exhibit in a small town 200 km above the Arctic Circle called Jukkasjärvi. The next year, he built a big igloo. The next year, he built a large exhibition hall from snow featuring everyday objects made from ice. Some visitors asked if they could sleep overnight in the hall. The next year, Berqvist built the first Icehotel. That was 1991 and Icehotel is now a winter destination for 50 000 visitors from all over the world.[18]

Sometimes, you just innovate. Did you know that left and right shoes were only thought up just over a century ago? Strategic innovation means commercialising research; for example, thorough collaboration between universities and industry, and entering new markets. Think Aerogard, the Hendra virus vaccine, extended wear contact lenses, plastic banknotes and Wi-Fi, all invented here in Australia by the Commonwealth Scientific and Industrial Research Organisation (CSIRO). At the operational level, innovation means the little-step and big-step improvements discussed earlier in this chapter.

The three cornerstones of creativity and innovation

The three cornerstones of creativity and innovation – courage, accepting and learning from mistakes, and an open, 'beginner's' mind – are what allow you and your team to think of ways of doing things that haven't been thought of before.

A large-scale Australian study found that the most innovative companies are also ahead of the field in cash flow, customer satisfaction, productivity, profitability, revenue growth and other indicators of business performance that lead to long-term success. The study concludes that 'innovation performance is strongly linked to business performance' and that innovation is critical for Australia's future economic success, given that Australian wages are higher than many overseas competitors (creating a cost disadvantage) and that many overseas competitors are eating into our service and quality advantages (creating a competitive disadvantage).[19]

Creative people earn more, too. One third of the US workforce is made up of professionals whose primary responsibilities include designing, innovating and problem-solving – the 'creative class'. They take home nearly half of all wages and salaries.[20]

Courage

Creativity and innovation need boldness. Perhaps that's because when something is new or even improved, it can feel odd, and even seem absurd. For most people, odd and absurd aren't good. Take Daisuke Inoue, who invented and even sold a few karaoke machines in 1971. Most people chuckled; now millions of yen and dollars have been made on them. Discussing his work that led to the unique adhesive of Post-it notes, Spencer Silver later remarked that had he given thought to it, he wouldn't have done the experiment because the advice was you couldn't do it.[21]

Antibiotics from bread mould, light bulbs, the PC and refrigerators were all scoffed at. Wasabi-flavoured cough drops? Reckitt Benckiser markets them as 'Strepsils Warm Lozenges'. Marmite cashew nuts? Unilever markets them. An opera maestro and a rock band on the same stage? Pavarotti and U2 brought a new audience to each other's music. Ideas only seem strange, silly or absurd because they are creative – not thought of before.

Accepting and learning from mistakes

As Charles Darwin noted, mutations (read innovations) happen all the time, but most don't work out – just like creative ideas. With innovation comes failure, so as well as boldness, creativity and innovation need a mindset that accepts mistakes and learns from them. Not all innovations are instant successes or even successes:

- Apple has a 90 per cent failure rate in creating products.
- Einstein published hundreds of papers, many of which received no citations at all (a key measure of 'sound science').
- Dubsmash trialled and continually refined numerous apps based on feedback before becoming top of the Apple Store charts in 79 countries and being downloaded more than 100 million times in 193 countries.
- Finnish company Rovio developed 51 games before scoring with one of the best sellers of all time, Angry Birds, which added about US$10 billion to its value.
- The Virgin Group launched over 400 ventures but is known for only a few.[22]

(For more on using mistakes see Chapter 29.)

An open mind

Creative people see what everyone else sees, but they see it differently. They have the beginner's mind, meaning that when you see an everyday object, your mind doesn't automatically make the usual associations with it (e.g. pen → writing; hat → head). Instead, you can make other, innovative, associations (pen → plant stake; hat → container). There are lots of strategies to encourage strategic innovation:

- Google has 20 per cent time, where engineers get a day a week to work on whatever they want; it has led to products such as Google Now and Google's Transparency Report, AdSense (bringing in about 25 per cent of Google's revenue), Google Transit, Google Talk, Google News, Gmail and other innovations.
- Australian software company Atlassian pioneered programming marathons, or 'hackathons', where every quarter, engineers have 24 hours to work on projects that intrigue them; hackathons have now been adopted by Google, LinkedIn, Lonely Planet, NASA, the World Bank and Yahoo!, among others.

- LinkedIn also has The Incubator, where every quarter, engineers put small teams together, pitch an idea to an executive team and, if approved, have 30 to 90 days to develop it into a prototype, going through two rounds of judging to gain a further 30 days.
- You don't need to be a high-tech company to let employees get together, cross-fertilise ideas and let their creativity run wild.[23]

Innovation: the essential ingredient

What do the companies shown in Figure 19.18 have in common? Some are household names; others less so, but they've all appeared in the Thomson Reuters annual Top 100 Global Innovators League Table for six years running. The companies that top the League Table are innovative, creative and successful. (Although Australia ranks 23rd out of 131 countries on the Global Innovation Index, it ranks 6th among the 17 economies in South-East Asia, East Asia and Oceania.)[24]

Creativity and innovation are not just the engines that drive art. They are also the engines that drive science and business. They are increasingly key drivers of competitive advantage, and the pace required of innovation seems to be increasing. Your customers, the market, technology and the need to manage risks and increase the sustainability of operations, products, services and supply chains can all create the need to innovate. Ways you and your team can innovate include:

- *Combine:* blend existing ideas and features from one process, product or service into another process, product or service.
- *Extend:* enlarge or expand on your existing processes, products or services.

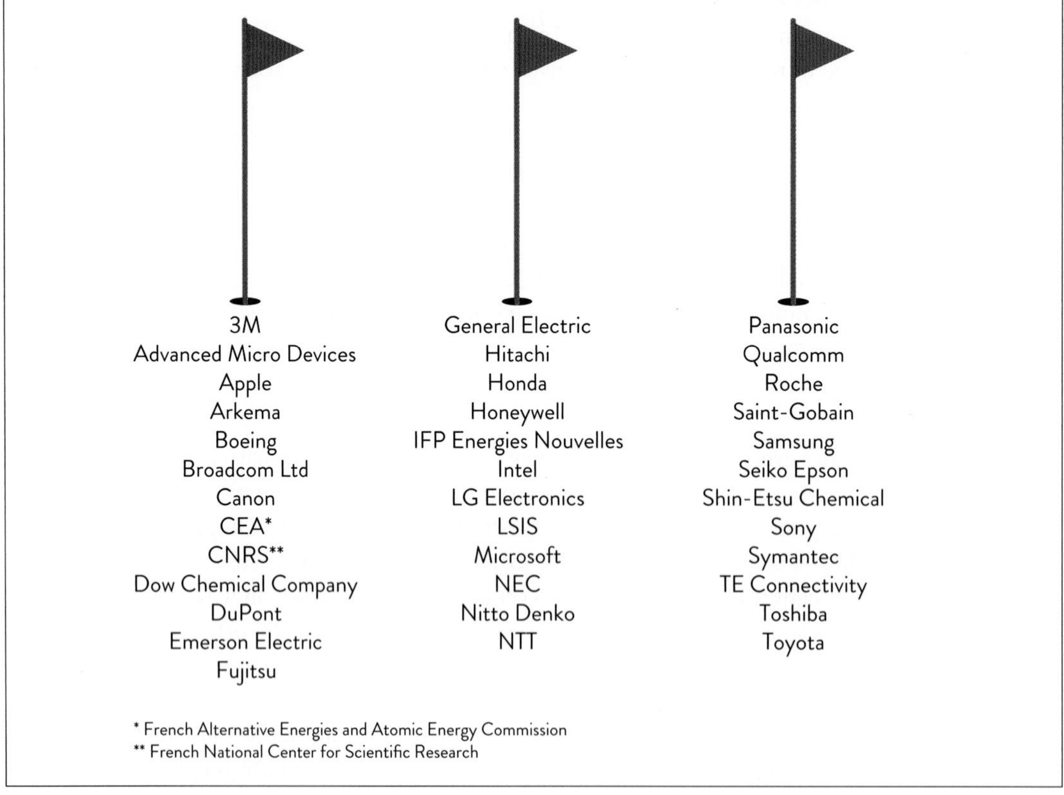

FIGURE 19.18 Global innovators

- *Improve:* make an existing process, product or service – your own or someone else's – better.
- *Invent:* dream up a completely new process, product or service.

On a strategic scale, your organisation can take advantage of advances in technology to innovate breakthrough improvements – not just communication and data transfer technologies but also innovating through robotics and automation (see Chapter 1 for more information on this).

Consider the processes and systems you follow or the tools, equipment and products you use. Which of these were saved, inspired or created from innovation?

Barriers to creativity

Everyone is creative to some extent but perhaps, like many people, your natural creativity and that of your team members has rusted through neglect. You may recognise some of the barriers to creativity shown in Figure 19.19. These creativity killers block your mind to 'absurd' and 'odd' solutions, encourage you to avoid possible criticism and mistakes, stick to the status quo and tempt you to stop at the first answer you think of rather than search for more and possibly better alternatives. (We discuss how you can help your team learn to innovate and be more creative in a following section titled 'Build an innovation culture'.)

FIGURE 19.19 Barriers to creativity

To combat the barriers to creativity, use these helpful tips to build a creative culture:

- Fire up people's brains with colour and other diverse stimuli, such as music and visual displays.
- Encourage surprises and give your team some freedom to sometimes make up their own rules and test ideas out.
- Schedule time for reflection, research and thinking.
- Provide opportunities for the team to experiment and learn from failure.
- Assist those who find it difficult working with creative people to see the positives.

Becoming more innovative

The world is becoming increasingly complex, uncertain and volatile, with changing government regulations, shifts in global economic power to developing markets, rapidly transforming industries, expanding volumes of data and rapidly evolving customer preferences. A survey by IBM of 1500 CEOs from 60 countries in 33 industries found that in order to successfully navigate these challenges, organisations need creativity and innovation at all levels.[25]

To innovate, you need to methodically apply various creativity techniques (discussed below). You need to put in effort and be persistent. You need to actively search for new ideas, opportunities and sources of innovation. One of the most important things you can do is to recognise the barriers to creativity and innovation within yourself and break them down (see **Figure 19.19**). You can also build adopting the five characteristics commonly found in creative people, shown in **Figure 19.20**, into your daily routine and into team meetings.

Although many creative people possess two or even three of the five creativity traits, it's unusual for even the most creative person to possess all five or even four of them. Which ones do you possess? Which do your team members possess?

Opportunities to innovate are everywhere. Start with what's there; that is, your processes, products or services, customer interfaces, supply chains and so on. Take a good look: how can you make it better, replace it or eliminate the need for it? Imagine what it would be like if it were slower, faster, bigger, smaller or different in some other way. How could you make it completely different? Or begin with your headaches. What bothers you is an opportunity to eliminate it or develop a way to turn it into an advantage. Here are some other ways to bring out the creative you:

- Chill out so that you can listen to your subconscious; creative ideas often 'bubble up from within' and you need to be able to hear them.
- Follow your passion – work in areas you enjoy and that inspire you to do your best.
- Keep learning.
- Learn to approach problems from different points of view.
- Stay open and curious and examine the unexpected.
- Use creativity techniques to promote creative and innovative ideas.
- Work at your cutting edge because boredom stifles creativity.

Scientists often think in analogies, using as many as 15 analogies in a one-hour laboratory meeting, and the most successful labs use the most analogies. For example, we know that X happens when A and B do this; let's see if X also happens when A and C do it. Scientists also use analogies to search for reasons and solutions when the unexpected occurs.[26]

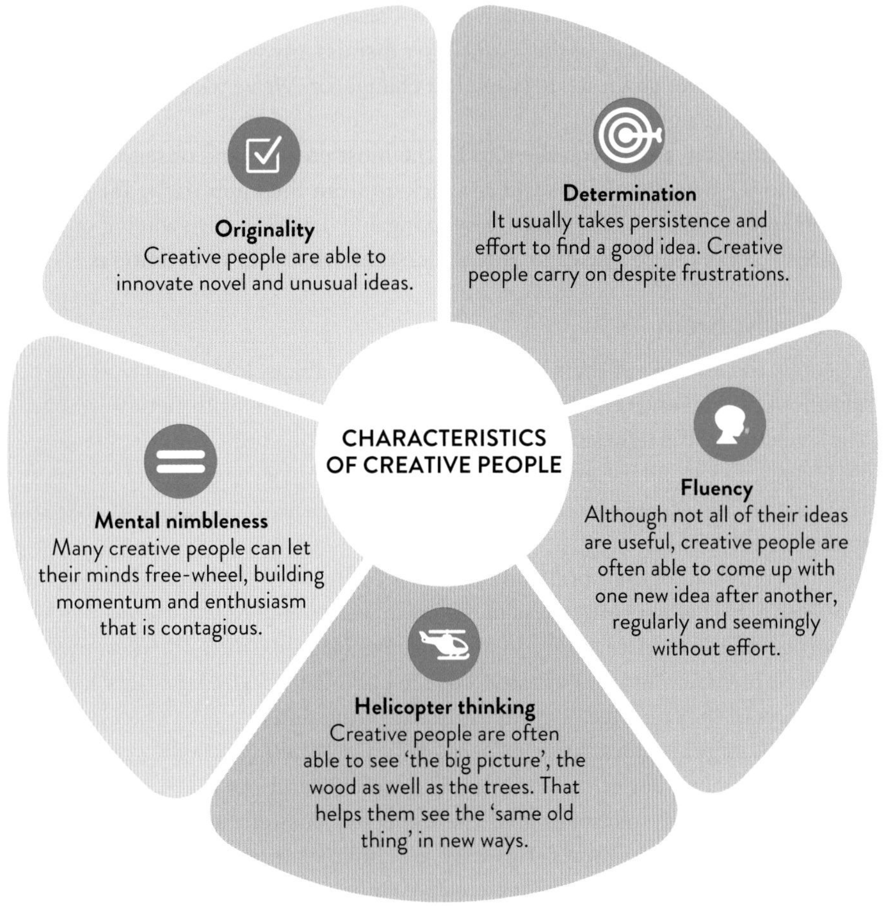

CHARACTERISTICS OF CREATIVE PEOPLE

Originality
Creative people are able to innovate novel and unusual ideas.

Determination
It usually takes persistence and effort to find a good idea. Creative people carry on despite frustrations.

Fluency
Although not all of their ideas are useful, creative people are often able to come up with one new idea after another, regularly and seemingly without effort.

Helicopter thinking
Creative people are often able to see 'the big picture', the wood as well as the trees. That helps them see the 'same old thing' in new ways.

Mental nimbleness
Many creative people can let their minds free-wheel, building momentum and enthusiasm that is contagious.

FIGURE 19.20 Characteristics of creative people

Try making an analogy to compare a situation you didn't expect or don't understand with something you do understand or a situation that produces what you do expect. First think about the thing you know about; that's your 'base'. Now you need a 'target', the event that is new, unexpected, different or you want to understand better. Your base and target need to be similar enough to let you build a useful bridge. You need to know the ways in which they are alike and not alike (so you know where the analogy breaks down).

Now look for similar patterns and other commonalities and for differences between your base and your target. Take some of what you know about the base and see how it relates to your target. This gives you something to test and helps you innovate. Finally, look for insights from the analogy. Then put it aside so that you don't get caught up in details – you want to work with general patterns.

Having a clear objective when you're searching for an innovative solution will make it easier for your creative subconscious to get to work. Your subconscious works even while you're asleep! Let your ideas emerge and grow. Then wait some more – 'sleep on them' a bit. Wait until you have a long list of possibilities before evaluating them and don't dismiss any without a good reason; 'It costs too much', 'The boss will never go for it', 'It's too big a change' or 'We've tried it before' are not sufficient reasons for abandoning a good idea.

Look for situations in which you seem to be the most creative and observe what you do. Watch creative people to see what good ideas you can pick up from their approach. Take a break when you feel 'stuck'. Pushing yourself stifles creativity; relaxing and daydreaming switch it on. When you have an idea, explain it simply so people can easily understand what your innovation is.

Left brain, right brain

For most people, the left side of their brain is better at language, logic, numbers and reasoning; it's linear and rational, literal and objective. You use your left brain for arithmetic, organising, planning, reading and scheduling. The right side of the brain is imaginative, intuitive and subjective. It specialises in colours, images, music and patterns, and is good at creating, developing and communicating ideas as well as seeing, and making sense of, the big picture. Creativity uses the right side of the brain to think outside the 'logic box'.

No one uses only half of their brain and the division between the two halves isn't as dramatic as it sounds. We work best when both halves of the brain work together and there are bundles of nerves called the corpus callosum that help us do just that. For example, the left half of the brain picks out the sounds that form words and how those words are put together while the right half picks up on the emotional features of the language – its rhythms and intonations.

Until recently, organisations have valued left-brain thinking, encouraging people to accept the 'obvious', evaluate any out-of-the-ordinary idea quickly and negatively, fixate on the usual and accepted assumptions and solutions, give the expected answers and see events, problems and decisions in the usual, accepted ways. However, it's different in many of today's capabilities-based organisations. Business complexity makes creative, innovative leader-managers and teams highly prized. You need both the linear, logical left brain to use many of the tools and techniques (discussed in Chapter 26), and you need your creative, intuitive right brain for others. And to light upon those innovative solutions – ah! – that takes both halves of your brain working together.

There are lots of ways to get your creative right brain working. Try writing your name as you usually do. Then write it backwards. Then upside down. Then in mirror writing (right to left). Then with your left hand. Check out http://www.mindtools.com and click on Skill Areas, and then Creativity Tools, to find some more useful ways to boost your creativity. You can also take a test on that site to see how creative you are.

Follow the five steps to creative innovation shown in **Figure 19.21** when you need to bring your creativity to bear on a decision or problem.

Creativity techniques

There are many creativity techniques, such as **brainstorming**, crowd sourcing, design thinking, forced analogy, incubation, problem reversal, scenario planning (explained in Chapter 22) and spidergramming (explained in Chapter 7). Or you can SCAMPER – substitute, combine, adapt, modify/magnify, purpose, eliminate, reverse/rearrange. A few other ideas are discussed in the following section.

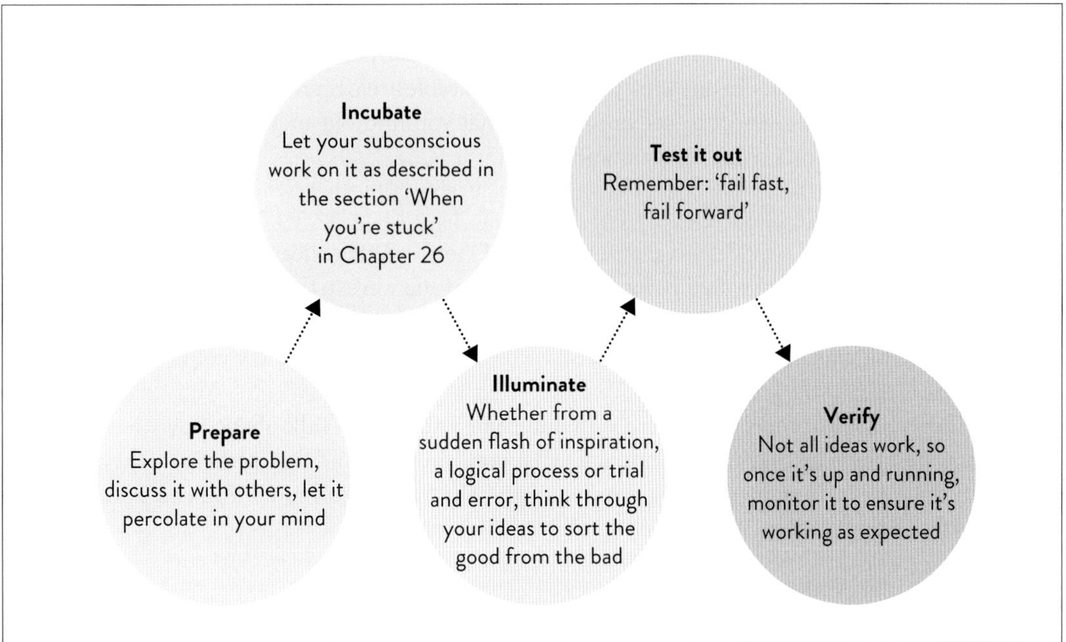

FIGURE 19.21 Five steps to creative innovation

Adapt other people's ideas

Put other people's ideas to use: did you know Henry Ford first saw a production line in a meat packaging plant? He applied the principles to automobile manufacturing and as a result of his innovation, he is now credited with 'inventing' the assembly line. Putting other people's ideas to good use explains why benchmarking is so popular, but you don't have to benchmark officially. Keep your eyes open, listen and learn from others in your organisation and networks. Good ideas can come from anywhere.

Ask crazy questions

Here are two examples of how effective short, simple, open questions can be:

- Once upon a time, a manager at the delivery giant UPS asked a crazy question: what if we avoid left turns? Today, routing technologies and strategies, including avoiding left turns, reduce kilometres driven and wasteful idling, saving 31.8 million litres of fuel a year.
- Managers at Adidas and Nike asked: how can we dye clothes without using water? Now, neither company uses water in its previously water-intensive dying processes.[27]

To get started, think through the five Ws and one H trigger questions (what? when? where? who? why? and how?).

Challenge your assumptions

Challenging your assumptions and self-imposed rules can open your mind to new possibilities. We can become so used to seeing things the way they 'are' that we assume that's the way they'll always be. Look for the assumptions that constrain you and develop the characteristics of creative people shown in Figure 19.20. Turn misfortune into good fortune and stumbling blocks into stepping stones by being open to new possibilities and seeing with 'new eyes'.

Study the unexpected

Examine the extremes to see what you can learn – high sales in one area, low sales in another, for example, or high productivity in one area, low in a comparable area. Study anomalies and surprises – results or behaviours you expect to see but don't. What you find out might lead to an insight that suggests an innovation or a completely new approach.

Think like other people

Study your products and services from other points of view – your colleagues, customers, suppliers and other stakeholders. What would you want and expect if you were in their shoes? What suggestions might they offer you? What might frustrate them most about what you provide them? What might they appreciate the most and would like increased or improved further? How could you make their lives easier?

Whether your customers are external or internal, visit them. Talk about how they use your products, watch them as they use them to see what you can learn and watch them as they go about their daily activities. You may discover ways you can help them even more. (You can find out more about this in Chapter 18.)

Think in other languages

Try thinking in other 'languages': make mental pictures or think in symbols instead of words. Use all your senses as you approach a problem. Find another way to describe the problem you're trying to solve, the improvement you're searching for, or the opportunity you're trying to make the most of. Look for another but similar issue or benefit to build on. Albert Einstein famously said that if he was given an hour to provide a solution, he would spend 50 minutes trying to understand the problem and five minutes solving it.

Build an innovation culture

Even the most creative people can be stymied by the wrong culture. The 'right' culture, an 'innovation culture', encourages and rewards experimentation and learning, and doesn't 'punish' mistakes, and has open communication and strong relationships with customers and suppliers. Guide your team to understanding why creativity and innovation are important to the organisation's future success and that most innovations result from a deliberate, determined search for a new or better way. Then motivate, inspire, encourage and empower them to think creatively and innovatively. Try building innovation into their KRAs. Use performance reviews to encourage continuous improvements (explained in Chapter 15).

'No mistakes' equals 'missed opportunities'. To innovate, your team members need to feel it's OK to make mistakes, suggest new ideas and try them out – even strange ideas. Replace the 'play it safe' song with 'fail fast, fail forward'. There is no need to 'get it perfect' before moving on; trial it often to find and work through the flaws and learn from your failures.

Provide the support that innovation needs, such as rewards, time to think, a collaborative, supportive working environment, and protection from paperwork and 'red tape' (although people do need to record important findings and learnings). While it's important to conform to the norms of the team and the organisation, make sure it's important norms that people conform to – norms that support the organisation's and team's values and purpose – and not norms that limit what people can bring to the team. People need the freedom to be themselves rather than conform to the average. Let people draw on their strengths to contribute ideas and produce results, and help them cultivate those strengths.

Some ways to help your team think more innovatively are as follows:

- Build a well-rounded, diverse team with different perspectives, backgrounds, expertise and thinking styles. Homogeneous teams may have less friction and reach solutions quickly, but they suffer from a lack of creativity and groupthink because everyone is so similar.
- Encourage collaboration and communication within the team and across the organisation.
- Give people autonomy over how to achieve goals.
- Greet new ideas with openness and explore them.
- Match people to jobs that take advantage of their expertise, interests and training; when you can, let people select the projects they want to work on to increase their motivation.
- Provide both positive and constructive feedback; without it, enthusiasm and creativity will wilt.
- Provide enough resources – money, people, psychological safety, space, support, time and so on – and opportunities for employees to interact with each other, face-to-face and electronically, to share ideas and learnings.
- See mistakes made in the interests of innovation as detours to good ideas.
- State goals clearly. People need to know where they're headed.

How are we doing?

What are the six most expensive words in any team? 'We've always done it this way.' You don't need extensive organisation-wide continuous improvement programs to continually find improvements in your own job and in your work team's procedures and work systems. Make sure everyone understands the importance of continuous improvement and include it on your agenda for team meetings. Find out what changes team members think would improve quality and service and what bottlenecks and hurdles they continually encounter. Don't worry that ideas may clash – respectful clashes and talking among yourselves lead to innovation. And the good news is that small groups generate ideas more easily than big groups.

After-action reviews

When did you last reflect on something you did and consider what went well and what you could have done better, with a view to improving your performance next time? Reflecting on what you've done and how you've done it to see what you can learn is a way to use the past to improve the future and undertake next week's or next month's tasks and projects more efficiently and successfully.

Building a daily habit of reflecting for 15 to 30 minutes about your day and what you can learn from it not only improves your performance but also helps you spot improvement opportunities. You can do this on your commute home from work, as you sit quietly at home unwinding from the day or even when you go to bed. With your team, you can meet informally at the end of the work week to reflect on events and what you can learn from them.

To debrief a specific activity, such as reaching a milestone or trialling a new procedure, ask yourself and your team these questions when events are still fresh in everyone's minds:

- What did we set out to do (your goals and measures of success)?
- What did we do? What actually happened? Review what you did and how you did it.
- What worked well, what worked better than expected and what didn't work as well as we'd hoped? Discuss and agree, not to blame anyone but to learn from experience. (Mistakes happen. When you don't learn from them, you're likely to repeat them.)
- What should we do next time? Decide on actions for the future and how to implement them – both successful steps to repeat and improvements to make.

Thinking and planning add tremendous amounts of value to any team. Think of after-action reviews as an important part of your team's learning and improvement efforts. Conduct them in the spirit of understanding, learning and improving. (For more about after-action reviews, see Chapters 4 and 29.)

INDUSTRY INSIGHTS

Fostering innovation and creativity in a team

Elizabeth, a Department Manager of a large retail organisation, added two new agenda items to the fortnightly team meeting:

- Reflection time
- Innovation time.

Reflection time required staff to consider two questions: what am I doing that is working well and what am I doing that is not? Innovation time required staff to share with the group one area where they felt change could be made or one new idea.

Once a month, the team selected an item on the innovations list and brainstormed creative ideas that would support change and innovation. This practice encouraged the team to consider new ways of thinking and after a while creativity increased and innovative culture was realised.

Lead by example

Your team members pay careful attention to what you do and say, so make sure you're a good role model for innovation. Set high standards because high standards encourage you to innovate and find better ways. Pay attention to what's going on around you, your customers' comments, your suppliers' ideas and your team's results (see Chapter 5). Make a habit of using creativity techniques and testing out new ones, and encourage your team members to do the same.

When you pass on a team's or team member's suggestion to another department or to your own leader-manager, let your team know the outcome. They need to know you pass on their ideas or they'll stop putting them forward. When an idea isn't taken up, explain why. It may be due to constraints, other priorities or other reasons. When it is taken up, measure the results, share them and acknowledge your team's role in the success.

Establish work practices that support innovation

Do your team members take enough breaks? Too few breaks actually reduce productivity and innovation. A relentless work pace leads to exhaustion and lack of time to reflect on ways to improve, and a team that consistently works flat out indicates you need to make some serious improvements to your work systems and examine people's workloads. Build breaks into your own and your team's workday and use any downtime that occurs as reflection time, because reflection is an important part of creativity and innovation. (For more on the value of rest and reflection, see the author's blog and read the post titled 'It's ok to daydream' at https://colemanagement.wordpress.com/2014/02/10/its-ok-to-daydream.)

Habit and routine are the enemies of creativity, so you may want to ensure all your standard operating procedures are necessary. When a specific order of steps isn't needed, try letting people do it 'their way'. Autonomy and discretion in the way work is carried out promote innovation because they lead to different approaches. That may sound slack and chaotic and it is, unless you periodically study those different approaches so that you can adopt those that work best and learn from those that don't.

A box is a box is a box. But it could be a lot of other things when you can shake off the functional fixedness trap that limits you to seeing an object only in the way it is traditionally used. Try instead describing or labelling objects differently, in a way that doesn't describe their traditional use, to crush your preconceptions and see objects with new eyes. (The brain traps and other traps discussed in Chapter 26 can all hamper your innovation efforts.)

Whether it's advertising, architecture, computer software design, entertainment, fashion, films, financial or legal services, media, music or publishing, creative people are the main 'raw material' for many of today's knowledge and service organisations. In manufacturing, too, 'making' often takes a back seat to creating and innovating as customers demand new features and good product design that uses less material and less energy. So you can expect to be leading creative people soon, if you aren't already.

Creative people are similar to knowledge workers in many respects – they are often able to produce more creatively when working in collaboration with other creative people; detest 'bureaucratic obstructionism', hierarchy and routine; and want to be trained and kept up to date with cutting-edge technologies and knowledge. They also respond better to intrinsic rewards and intellectual stimulation, loving challenge and craving the feeling of accomplishment that working creatively brings. Creative people enjoy their work and want to 'get it right' and they enjoy tough challenges. As with knowledge workers, it's important to provide SMART targets that engage their curiosity; however, leave how to reach those targets up to them. If you think about it, it's quite similar to motivating anyone.

Promote innovation

Innovation is doomed to evaporate unless you promote it. Work with team members' ideas quickly; support small experiments to test out 'new ways'; acknowledge and applaud innovations and innovators. Encourage your team to notice problems, own them and solve them. Help them see with beginner's eyes. Listen to your younger and less experienced team members, who may not be as constrained by what 'usually' works and what is 'usually' done. Experience doesn't necessarily equal expertise and, while experience can help make people more productive, it can also make them overly comfortable with the status quo, resistant to change and more likely to dismiss information and ideas that don't match their experience. Figure 19.22 shows some tips for promoting innovation for leaders.

Create a physical environment to support innovation

Picture yourself working in a still, windowless room, with a grey carpet and bland cream walls with no plants, paintings or posters and a bare, utilitarian workspace. Now picture working in a room with a large window overlooking a park, plenty of plants and colourful posters, one yellow and three green walls, colourful carpet tiles, a nicely decorated workspace and some pleasant background music. Which would make you feel more energised or more creative? There's no doubt that your surroundings affect you.

Large organisations may have 'skunkworks' (an experimental laboratory or department of an organisation) and other off-site areas and meetings where teams undertake innovative project work. But innovations have become so important to organisational success that continuous innovation is becoming part of everyday work. You can help by adjusting your work team's area to encourage it. Workspaces can be fitted out and decorated to encourage creativity and collaborative relationships, with social areas and areas for relaxing and letting ideas bubble. Innovation is often carried out in small groups, so your team also needs areas for collaborative work. Why not put up a poster of Einstein's opinion about innovation: 'If at first the idea is not absurd, then there is no hope for it'.

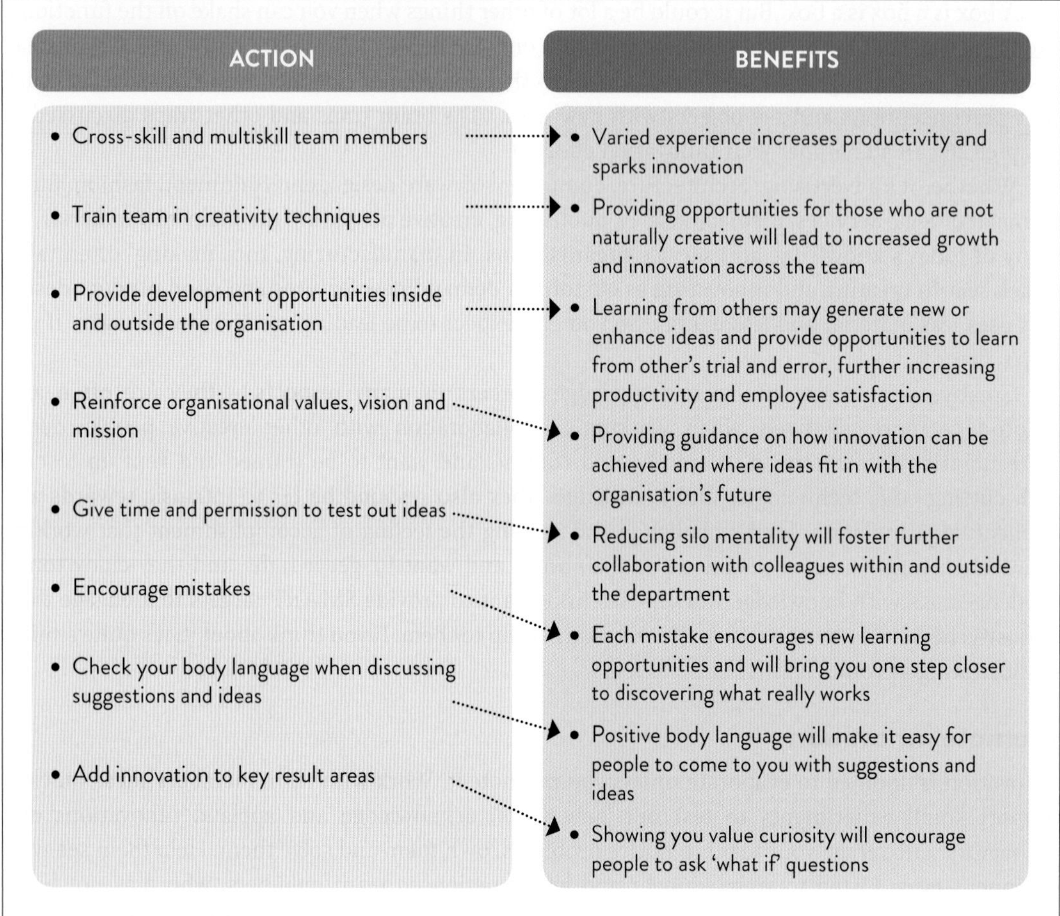

FIGURE 19.22 Promoting innovation – tips for leaders

Rounded furniture in rounded arrangements benefits creativity and productivity, too, just as sitting in circles encourages cooperation and communication. It's good to be able to adjust the light level to suit what you're working on, too; bright light helps with analytical and evaluative thinking, softer light with creative tasks. Blue, green and yellow have been shown to enhance creativity. Plants lower stress levels and the right plants keep the office air clean. In fact, looking at nature recharges your brain, even when that nature is on your screensaver or on a poster or painting.[28]

When designing workspaces for creativity and innovation, consider noise, collaborative work, individual work that needs concentration and social and communication needs. Why not give your team input into their surroundings, perhaps selecting plants and artwork of their choice? The more control people have over the way they do their work and their working environment, the more productive they can be.

Encourage your team to take some time with nature throughout the day. Taking a green microbreak by gazing at nature can increase productivity. One study found that gazing at nature for 40 seconds raised concentration levels by 6 per cent and performance held steady, while gazing at a concrete roof for 40 seconds, lowered concentration levels 8 per cent and performance grew less consistent.[29] And you know what? The 'nature' they gazed at was a screensaver! When you need to concentrate, take a nature microbreak.

STUDY TOOLS

QUICK REVIEW

KEY CONCEPT 19.1 

a Briefly explain the job framework and how it provides role clarity. Is it possible for an employee to perform well without role clarity, other than by chance?

b Explain the three elements of the Want To Key and how each contributes to people's ability and willingness to do their job well.

c How do the elements of the How To Key, individually and together, contribute to job performance and incremental improvement?

d How can factors outside an employee's control prevent them from doing their job well, even an employee who knows what to do, how to do it well and wants to do it well?

e How does leadership affect productivity? Briefly explain six actions effective leader-managers can take that build performance and productivity.

KEY CONCEPT 19.2 

a Briefly explain the following practices and how they help organisations provide quality products and services:

 i examining and streamlining processes and practices

 ii forming teams and involving people at all levels to identify and solve problems and make continuous improvements to work systems

 iii monitoring quality and performance and comparing it with other organisations' or departments' quality and performance

 iv working with your internal and external customers and suppliers to develop better ways of meeting customers' needs.

b Describe ways you can select benchmark measures. How can benchmarks be used?

c What is the difference between Six Sigma and lean Six Sigma?

d In what ways do the five Ss of lean Six Sigma help reduce waste?

KEY CONCEPT 19.3 

a Why is innovation becoming increasingly important?

b List and explain the three cornerstones of creativity and innovation.

c List eight barriers to creativity and suggest how leader-managers can overcome them in themselves and in their teams.

d Describe an innovation culture and discuss how leader-managers can build one.

BUILD YOUR SKILLS

KEY CONCEPT 19.1 

a Discuss why people need a vision or purpose statement for their job, and the role that clear targets play in motivating people and helping them monitor their own performance and build their productivity.

b Review each of the Five Keys that unlock peak performance, giving an example of each from your own experience. What happens when a leader-manager fails to manage one of these Keys properly? Describe what happens when one Key is 'deficient' to illustrate your point.

c Briefly explain corporate values, vision and mission and how they link to a team's purpose, goals and objectives and to an individual employee's job purpose, key result areas and measures of success.

d How well can you write SMART targets? Consider either one of your targets or a team target and rewrite it using the SMART principle.

e How well do you apply the hot-stove principle to build performance?

f Investigate the technology you can use to manage and monitor the planning, scheduling and completion of tasks and prepare a short report to discuss in class.

g Explain why we can expect job enlargement, enrichment and empowerment to become more common. How can becoming familiar with the principles of job design and job redesign and the Five Keys to unlocking productivity and performance benefit leader-managers and their organisations?

KEY CONCEPT 19.2 

a Explain the differences between breakthrough and incremental improvements and give an example of each from your own experience.
b Discuss the many places you can look when seeking to make improvements in a workplace.
c What are the last three improvements you have made to the way you do things, in either your private or working life?
d Conduct an internet search on creativity techniques. Select three that you find interesting and summarise them. Then test them out as often as you can over the next three weeks and prepare a short report on your results to share with the class.

KEY CONCEPT 19.3 

a Discuss the role of mistakes in creativity and innovation. What sort of mistakes can safely be encouraged and what sort are best discouraged?
b How much do you think organisational culture contributes to employees' innovativeness?
c Use an after-action review to analyse something you have recently done at work or in your studies; for example, preparing and delivering a presentation, studying for an exam, or researching and writing a report. Summarise your conclusions.

WORKPLACE ACTIVITIES

KEY CONCEPT 19.1 

a What non-task goals does your work team have? Is everyone aware of them?
b Give an example of how you have applied the hot-stove principle to ensure that people in your work team consistently follow rules.
c Assess your own job and the jobs in your work using the Want To Key. How well designed are these jobs? How well placed are you and your team members in your jobs? How well is your job designed?
d When did you last check that the tools and equipment in your department were well designed, properly maintained and suited to the job at hand? Does your team have the resources it needs, or quick and easy access to them? (If you're not sure, conduct your own research.)
e Are any systems or procedures in your workplace outdated, poorly integrated or just plain cumbersome? How do unwieldy systems and procedures sap people's motivation and their desire and ability to be fully productive? Provide an example to illustrate your thinking.

KEY CONCEPT 19.2 

a List at least 11 innovation opportunities that exist in your workplace.
b What have you done or what can you do to contribute to innovation at your workplace?
c List five measures you could use to benchmark performance and productivity in your workplace and explain:
  i why they are suitable benchmarking measures
  ii how you could use them to continuously improve performance and productivity.
d Thinking through the work procedures or processes used in your workplace, identify three examples of waste and discuss how each could be reduced or eliminated. Estimate the cost savings of each over 12 months.
e Depict a process or procedure you follow in your workplace as a flow chart and analyse it as described in this chapter. Where are the opportunities to improve it?

KEY CONCEPT 19.3 

a List five actions you can take to encourage creativity and innovation in your workplace and build an innovation culture.
b How can you rearrange your workspace to increase your productivity and creativity? How can you encourage your team members to do the same?
c Select a process or service you want to improve or a problem you want to solve, then apply two creativity techniques discussed in this chapter, as well as two other creativity techniques you know of, to innovate a workable new approach or solution.
d List some of the ways in which you lift your team members' performance and productivity, and ways you make continuous improvements to how your team works.

e Depict a process or procedure you follow in your workplace as a flow chart and analyse it as described in this chapter. Where are the opportunities to improve it?

EXTENSION ACTIVITIES

Referring to the Snapshot at the beginning of this chapter, answer the following questions:

1 How do the steps taken to create the new project team align with the What To Key and Want To Key?
2 What next steps could Damien take to support creating an innovative culture?

CASE STUDY 19

LEAN BELIEVERS

Custom Bikes R Us, a custom-made titanium bicycle company, recently undertook a complete review of business practices after receiving notification of upcoming price increases to a significant number of parts. Jordan, the owner, decided to look at where they could trim costs internally before having to offset the price increase onto the purchase price of the products.

A host of improvements followed in all areas of the organisation, from administration to ordering processes and workshop set-up. Nearly everything that didn't move had the five Ss applied to it, workflows were redesigned, and systems developed to improve time spent on administration tasks. Team meetings included discussion of new ideas for improvement and written communication kept everyone up to date with progress while ongoing collaboration ensured a consistent approach to how improvements were implemented.

Naturally, there were challenges, such as deciding on which improvement would give them the cost reduction they needed, and what to work on and when to stop working on something.

Custom Bikes R Us learnt a lot about the importance of:

- leading change
- gaining team support was important for overall success
- learning as you go
- having a clear goal
- small wins and going for big impacts.

Applying lean methodology helped Custom Bikes R Us tackle challenges and become a highly efficient organisation. The team were so effective at incorporating lean practices into their production process that what was usually an eight-week delivery-to-customer time frame reduced to just two days. The customers hated it. It seemed the process of acquiring a pricey cycle was nearly as important as the product itself. Some customers loudly complained that a true custom bike couldn't be built in two days; others complained that the two days didn't give them enough time to save up the US$5000 price tag. Still others complained that they didn't have time to enjoy musing about how to equip their new prestige bike.

The company listened to its customers and increased its delivery time to three weeks. The customers were happier and so was the company – it took the $500 deposit, sat on it for 19 days, then built the bikes. Then the company introduced a special expedite service and charged an additional $500 on top of the $500 deposit for an 'extra fast delivery' of 10 to 12 days. Customers were delighted.

Questions

1 Explain why each of the lessons Custom Bikes R Us learnt from efforts taken is important.
2 What specific work practices supported innovation and contributed to an innovative culture?
3 Did Custom Bikes R Us move in incremental steps? What could have been done differently?

CHAPTER ENDNOTES

1 Douglas McGregor, *The professional manager*, McGraw-Hill, 1967.

2 Henry Mintzberg, *The nature of managerial work*, Harper & Row, 1973, p. 38.

3 Michelle McQuaid, 'Tackling toxic bosses', *Company Director*, October 2012, pp. 50–51.

4 Gemma Robertson-Smith, Carl Marwick, 'Employee engagement: A review of current thinking', Report 469, Institute for Employment Studies, Brighton, UK, 2009; see also Tom Rath, Barry Conchie, *Strengths-based leadership*, Gallup Press, 2008; see also 'The state of the global workplace: Employee engagement insights for business leaders worldwide, 2011–2012', http://www.gallup.com/services/178517/state-global-workplace.aspx, accessed 27 January 2015.

5 W. Edwards Deming, *The new economics*, MIT Press, 1993.

6 Lewis Carroll, *Alice through the looking glass*, Bibliolis, London, 2012, p. 112.

7 John Hagel III, John Seely Brown, Lang Davison, 'The big shift', *Harvard Business Review*, July–August 2009.

8 Stephen E. Chick, Arnd Huchzermeier, Serguei Netessine, 'Europe's solution factories', *Harvard Business Review*, April 2014, pp. 111–115.

9 Craig Fontaine, 'Six Sigma and organizational culture', http://www.slideshare.net/Sixsigmacentral/six-sigma-and-organizational-culture, accessed 18 March 2015.

10 'The history of Six Sigma', http://www.isixsigma.com/new-to-six-sigma/history/history-six-sigma, accessed 13 May 2014 and 12 February 2017; Gillian Bullock, 'Secrets of the Six Sigma', Australian Institute of Management blog, 1 November 2005, http://blog.aim.com.au/secrets-of-the-six-sigma, accessed 12 February 2017.

11 Elizabeth Kazi, 'Six Sigma: Need to know', *Australian Financial Review*, 'Boss' section, July 2005.

12 Andrew Park, Peter Burrows, 'What you don't know about Dell', *Bloomberg Businessweek*, 3 November 2003, https://www.bloomberg.com/news/articles/2003-11-02/what-you-dont-know-about-dell, accessed 14 May 2015; 'Dow Six Sigma services', http://www.dow.com/dowservices/consulting/partners/sixsigma.htm, accessed 18 March 2015; and Michael Marx, 'Dow Chemical Company: Six Sigma', 17 May 2005, http://www.sixsigma.com/industries/chemicals/dow-chemical-company-six-sigma', accessed 14 May 2014; 'Froedtert Hospital improves ICU care', http://www.processmodel.com/resources/stories/Froedtert.pdf, accessed 14 May 2014; 'Inside Honeywell: New employee orientation – Six Sigma', http://www51.honeywell.com/hrsites/neo/howweworksixsigmaplus.html, accessed 14 May 2014; Kazi, op. cit.; Raytheon Australia, http://www.raytheon.com.au, accessed 18 March 2015; http://www.raytheon.com.au/ourcompany/ourculture/ accessed 26 January 2017; 'The Six Sigma primer', Six Sigma on line, Aveta Business Institute, http://www.sixsigmaonline.org/six-sigma-training-certification-information/articles/the-six-sigma-primer.html, accessed 14 May 2014.

13 See, for example, Jack Marlowe, 'Zalabia and the first ice-cream cone', Aramco World, July/August 2003, http://www.aramcoworld.com/issue/200304/zalabia.and.the.first.ice-cream.cone.htm, accessed 1 February 2015; Andrew Smith (ed.), *The Oxford encyclopedia of food and drink in America*, Oxford University Press, 2013, p. 3; Anne Cooper Funderburg, *Chocolate, strawberry and vanilla: a history of American ice cream*, Popular Press, 1995, pp. 117–119.

14 Snags in a roll, see Patricia Mitchell, 'Hot dogs: Baseball fans' convenience, traveler's salvation', http://www.foodhistory.com/foodnotes/leftovers/hotdog.htm, accessed 1 February 2015.

15 Viagra, see, for example, M. D. Cheitlin et al., 'ACC/AHA expert consensus document: Use of sildenafil (Viagra) in patients with cardiovascular disease', American Heart Association, http://circ.ahajournals.org/content/99/1/168.full, accessed 1 February 2015; Peter Wilson, 'Intelligent design', *The Australian Business Magazine, The Deal*, Vol. 5, No. 5, July 2012, p. 22.

16 Big Bang, see John Kennewell, Malcolm Wilkinson, 'The first 50 years of radio astronomy', *Amateur Radio Action*, Vol. 6, No. 8, 1983; see also 'Birth of radio astronomy', *Catalyst*, ABC, 17 February 2011, http://www. abc.net.au/catalyst/stories/3141255.htm, accessed 1 February 2015.

17 Peter Wilson, 'Intelligent design', op cit.

18 Icehotel, http://www.icehotel.com, accessed 27 January 2014.

19 Danny Samson, Marianne Gloet, 'Innovation: The new imperative', Department of Management and Marketing, University of Melbourne, 2013.

20 Richard Florida, Jim Goodnight, 'Managing for creativity', *Harvard Business Review*, July–August 2005.

21 Daisuke Inoue, Robert Scott, 'Voice hero: The inventor of karaoke speaks', *The Appendix*, 3 December 2013; see also http://theappendix.net/issues/2013/10/voice-hero-the-inventor-of-karaoke-speaks, accessed 31 January 2015; Spencer Silver, in J. Lynn, *The entrepreneur's almanac: Fundamentals, facts and figures you need to run and grow your business*, Entrepreneur Media, 2007, p. 130; Stephen E. Chick, Arnd Huchzermeier, Serguei Netessine, 'Europe's solution factories', *Harvard Business Review*, April 2014, pp. 111–115.

22 Frans Johansson, 'How to seize the opportunity', *Management Today* (UK), February 2013; 'The if at first you don't succeed award', *Management Today*, November 2016, p. 50.

23 See, for example, Christopher Mims, 'Google's "20% time", which brought you Gmail and AdSense, is now as good as dead', 16 August 2013, http://qz.com/115831/googles-20-time-which-brought-you-gmail-and-adsense-is-now-as-good-as-dead, accessed 1 February 2015; see also Christopher Mims, '20% time is officially alive and well, says Google', 20 August 2013, http://qz.com/117164/20-time-is-officially-alive-and-well-says-google, accessed 1 February 2015; Atlassian, see 'ShipIt days at Atlassian', https://www.atlassian.com/company/about/shipit, accessed 1 February 2015; see also Rohan Pearce, 'Hacking creativity: Making time for innovation', *Computerworld*, 8 July 2013, http://www.computerworld.com.au/article/490631/hacking_creativity_making_time_innovation/, accessed 1 February 2015; and 'What companies have regular hackathon/hack days?', http://www.quora.com/What-companies-have-regular-hackathon-hack-days, accessed 1 February 2015; LinkedIn, see Kevin Scott, 'The LinkedIn [in]cubator', http://blog.linkedin.com/2012/12/07/linkedin-incubator/, accessed 1 February 2015; see also 'The LinkedIn Incubator, LinkedIn Engineering, 20 December 2013, https://www.youtube.com/watch?v=WXippDHhxVw, accessed 1 February 2015; Ryan Tate, 'Google couldn't kill 20 percent time even if it wanted to', 21 August 2013, http://www.wired.com/2013/08/20-percent-time-will-never-die/, accessed 17 May 2014; see also Ryan Tate, 'LinkedIn gone wild: 20 percent time to tinker spreads beyond Google', 6 December 2012, http://www.wired.com/2012/12/llinkedin-20-percent-time/, accessed 17 May 2014; Kevin Scott, *The LinkedIn [in]cubator*, LinkedIn official blog, http://blog.linkedin.com/2012/12/07/linkedin-incubator/, accessed 7 May 2014.

24 World Intellectual Property Organization, 'Global innovation index', 2020, https://www.wipo.int/edocs/pubdocs/en/wipo_pub_gii_2020/au.pdf; The Global Innovation Index, 'Explore the interactive database of the GII 2021 indicators', 2021, https://www.globalinnovationindex.org/analysis-indicator

25 IBM Global, 'CEO study: Creativity selected as most crucial factor for future success', 18 May 2010, https://www-03.obm.com/press/us/en/pressrelease/31670.wss, accessed 20 December 2015.

26 Kevin Dunbar, 'How scientists think in the real world: Implications for science education', *Journal of Applied Developmental Psychology*, Vol. 21, No. 1, January-February 2000, pp. 49–58; Joel Chan, Susannah B. F. Paletz, Christian Schunn, 'Analogy as a strategy for supporting complex problem solving under uncertainty', *Memory & Cognition*, November 2012, Vol. 40, No. 8, pp. 1352–1356.

27 Andrew Winston, 'Resilience in a hotter world', *Harvard Business Review*, April 2014, pp. 56–64.

28 Oshin Vartanian et al., 'Impact of contour on aesthetic judgements and approach – avoidance decisions in architecture', *Proceedings of the National Academy of Sciences of the United States of America*, http://www.pnas.org/content/110/Supplement_2/10446.full, accessed 7 February 2017; Anna Steidle, Lioba Werth, 'Freedom from constraints: Darkness and dim illumination promote creativity', *Journal of Environmental Psychology*, vol. 35, September 2013, pp. 76–80; Stephanie Lichtenfeld, Andrew J. Elliot, Markus A. Maier, Reinhard Pekrun, 'Fertile green: Green facilitates creative performance', *Personality and Social Psychology Bulletin*, 16 March 2012; Ma D. Velarde, Gary Fry, Mari Tveit, 'Health affects of viewing landscapes – Landscape types in environmental psychology', *Urban Forestry & Urban Greening*, Vol. 6, No. 4, 15 November, pp. 199–212; Elizabeth Nisbet and John Zelenski, 'Underestimating nearby nature: Affective forecasting errors obscure the happy path to sustainability', *Psychological Science*, September 2011.

29 Nicole Torres, 'Gazing at nature makes you more productive', *Harvard Business Review*, September 2015, pp. 32–33; Stephanie Lichtenfeld, Andrew J. Elliot, Markus A. Maier, Reinhard Pekrun, 'Fertile green: Green facilitates creative performance', op cit.

CHAPTER

20

DEVELOPING, MANAGING AND MONITORING OPERATIONAL PLANS

After completing this chapter, you will be able to:

20.1 explain why planning is needed and relate your operational plans to strategic and business plans

20.2 prepare and present operational plans and estimate and secure the resources your plans need according to your organisation's guidelines and requirements

20.3 give your plans the best possible chance of success

20.4 monitor your plans easily, yet effectively.

TRANSFERABLE SKILLS

The following transferable skills are covered in this chapter:

1 **Business competence**
- **1.1** Financial literacy
- **1.2** Entrepreneurship/small business skills
- **1.3** Sustainability
- **1.4** Business operations
- **1.5** Operations management

2 **Critical thinking and problem solving**
- **2.1** Critical thinking
- **2.3** Business strategy

3 **Social competence**
- **3.1** Teamwork/relationships
- **3.3** Written communication
- **3.4** Leadership

4 **Data literacy**
- **4.1** Data literacy

5 **Digital competence**
- **5.2** Technology use

OVERVIEW

Planning happens a lot without you realising it. From setting the agenda for your weekend to what food to buy at the supermarket, many things require planning. The complex job of running an organisation, department or team, and having established goals and measures of success, requires a detailed written plan to achieve them. Since everyone needs to understand the plan and be willing to work towards achieving it, it makes sense to involve others in developing the plan, particularly those it affects and who will implement it. You may also need to gain approval for the plan from others in the organisation before setting it in motion.

Setting goals and thinking through how best to achieve them (yes, that's exactly what a plan is!) is worth the effort because it curbs chaos, missed deadlines, blown-out schedules, idle equipment and people scratching their heads wondering what to do. When a plan has been thought through and is under control, it fulfils the organisation's need to operate smoothly and helps employees feel comfortable and settled when undertaking the plan.

From simple plans like holiday rosters, to daily and weekly plans for a work group, to complex production and business plans, to plans involving just one project or those for an entire enterprise, organisations need all sorts of plans for both day-to-day effectiveness and long-term success.

SNAPSHOT

Plans within plans

Hamish sits back and draws a deep breath. This is big. His boss has just left his office, having dropped the bombshell that Hamish's section, which manages accounts payable and receivable nationally, is to take on all national administration – a task that was outsourced and offshored several years ago. The workload is set to treble and although there is a budget to expand staffing and other resources, trebling them is not on the cards.

As the section's leader-manager, Hamish will have a key role in the project team to plan and execute the transfer of operations. The project scope includes planning for the section's technical, communication and human resource needs; refurbishing and expanding the office; and risk and stakeholder management, assessment and planning. As his boss left, she stressed that the project transfer team would need to think innovatively in order to produce a viable plan within the time and budget constraints.

Hamish mulls over various scenarios. He'll need to reallocate duties and redesign some of the jobs, find and train additional staff, upgrade IT and communications systems, develop an office layout and design, and purchase the necessary equipment – at this point, his mind starts spinning. He'll need a project team himself.

As soon as the official announcement is made, Hamish can brief his team on the finer details. He begins listing what he wants to tell them and considers how best to present the news. He'll need their help and support to form subcommittees to work out subplans within the larger plans and he wants the team to be fully on board and conversant with the plans so they roll out smoothly when the time comes.

20.1 Understanding the context and components of operational plans

> When you fail to plan, you plan to fail.
>
> Reverend H. K. Williams, 'The church and the world', *Biblical World*, n.s. 53:81, 1919.

As the old saying goes, 'The right hand does not know what the left hand is doing'. The up-front time spent investing in planning saves time in the long run by keeping operations running smoothly and preventing emergencies. Up-front planning allows for focus on the critical work and to be proactive rather than reactive.

Like much important work, planning is mental work. It might look like idle work but being proactive and doing vital preliminary work when planning ensures success in the long run. Thinking through how best to achieve the desired result is the first step towards taking charge of events and circumstances.

Plans are projected courses of action aimed at achieving goals. They provide clear milestones and subgoals or targets and map the activities needed to reach them with a minimum of fuss. Plans can be long- to medium-term, like the strategic and business plans that guide entire organisations (discussed in Chapter 2), or they can be the shorter-term operational plans that guide the daily or weekly work of an individual, team, department or process. Strategic plans are the sails that steer the organisations in a chosen direction and operational plans are the rudders that guide and fine-tune their direction.

Transferable skill

1.5 Operations management

The benefits of planning

Don't be tempted to put planning into the 'too hard' category, and don't avoid it because the workload is high, it is difficult to find time to plan, or you would rather be 'out there', active and doing something. These are self-defeating excuses that actually make your job much more difficult.

Plans are foundations for the future. They are a reminder of what needs to be done, and in what order, help identify and concentrate on important issues, and give a way to track progress and assess achievements. They help coordinate people's efforts and skills, eliminate duplication of effort, minimise disruptions and put the necessary equipment, information, materials, people and systems in place. Because they provide a road map, plans help mitigate the need for crisis management – responding quickly and under pressure – and help achieve the goals more easily.

Thinking about what needs to happen in plenty of time reduces uncertainty and helps you anticipate and prepare for change. When plans are communicated well, everyone knows 'what, who, when, where, how and why'. It gives staff purpose and direction in their efforts; they can relax and perform better knowing that things are under control. Having a plan does not guarantee success, but it attracts success more often than thoughtlessly jumping into action. Forming the habit of thinking about the upcoming day and what you need to achieve means you don't just charge into the day but act with purpose.

Transferable skills

1.4 Business operations

2.3 Business strategy

3.3 Written communication

Developing operational plans that support strategic and business plans

An organisation's values, vision and strategic goals guide it in the same way that a team's purpose statement and measures of success guide the team. Similarly, an organisation's strategic and business plans explain how its vision flows through to functions or processes and teams. It helps to develop organisational goals and operational plans to enable the organisation to achieve its vision and realise its strategy. In this way, each team follows its own operational plan, each aiming at reaching the same overall strategic goals via a different path. (See Chapter 2 for information about values and vision and Chapter 13 for information about developing a team purpose statement and measures of success.)

From goals to plans

Goals are a glimpse of the future. They identify where you want to be, giving meaning and purpose to your actions and the actions of your team members. Like vision statements and team purpose statements, goals guide the choices you and your team make and help you to respond to change more easily because they give you a clear picture of where you want to be in the long term.

Break big goals down into shorter-term, more specific objectives or milestones. When objectives are still big or distant, chunk them down further into smaller, closer targets. Keep breaking down or refining the goals until the objectives and targets are meaningful, believable and specific enough to provide a sense of direction and drive performance. Goals will help fulfil the team's purpose to achieve the organisation's strategic goals.

Make them positive so that you know what you're aiming for (not trying to avoid), and remember the SMART acronym:

- **S**pecific so that they can provide clear measuring posts as you proceed towards your goals
- **M**otivating in order to drive performance
- **A**mbitious (but achievable) so that people won't give up before they begin
- **R**elated to the overall department and its goals
- **T**rackable so that you can monitor your progress along the way.

20.2 Preparing and presenting plans and estimating the necessary resources

Transferable skills

1.4 Business operations

1.5 Operations management

> If you are planning for one year, grow rice. If you are planning for 20 years, grow trees. If you are planning for centuries, grow men.
>
> Chinese proverb

While goals, objectives and targets focus on results, plans focus on activity – what people need to do to achieve the desired results. The operational plans that leader-managers develop generally look ahead one week to several weeks. As plans become more short-term or day-to-day, their precision increases in the detail provided.

Figure 20.1 shows a simple planning format that can be adapted to suit differing needs. Use the questions as triggers to help thoroughly think through the plan.

What results are we aiming for? (goals) or **What** do we need to do? (activities)	**Why** is this important? (strategic goal)	**When** or **by when** do we need to do it? (today, tomorrow, next month)	**Where** should we do it? (at the workplace, in the stockroom)	**How** should we do it? (steps to be taken)	**Who** is to do it? (list people by name or title)
Update our database	To enable us to access and retrieve current information on assistance programs in under three minutes in order to provide timely and helpful advice to the families and carers of people with Alzheimer's disease	By July 2023	Use the conference room as a project room	IT and marketing to plan and work on project together	IT technical support adviser, marketing officer and client services manager

FIGURE 20.1 A basic planning format

Expect to work with three different types of operational plans:

1. *Recurring plans:* such as holiday rosters, training plans and work schedules.
2. *Specific operational plans:* such as project plans. Project plans are for once-only activities or special occurrences. These can be very complex, and preparing them can be highly specialised, requiring computer applications and techniques. Diagrams generated by these applications include **PERT diagrams** (program evaluation review technique) and other types of flow charts and **network diagrams** to schedule the specific steps, highlight **critical paths** and tasks, and **monitor** progress.

   Special temporary project teams prepare and carry out these specific plans, requiring a range of tasks – from those straightforward to those so complex that they require external consultants and contractors to assist. (Chapter 14 explains how to lead and manage temporary project teams and Chapter 21 discusses how to lead and manage projects.)
3. *Standing plans* or **standard operating procedures**: set out procedures to follow in specific situations. These include evacuation procedures in the case of fire and the process to follow when counselling an underperforming employee. Also known as **programmed decisions**, these are established according to organisation policies and strategies.

A planning statement helps crystallise your thinking. Try the verb–what–why formula. For example: 'To develop and implement (verb) a plan to increase the team's output by 14 per cent by the end of the financial quarter (what) in order to ensure we meet our growth objectives and help achieve our corporate vision (why).'

The planning process

Sometimes, once a plan is developed, it is finished. More often, planning is iterative, as shown in Figure 20.2, which illustrates the six steps to planning as an ongoing process – always moving, always changing, and always being revised and updated. An iterative approach makes planning an ongoing process of adapting, adjusting and fine-tuning to meet changing circumstances and unexpected events. Iteration also means taking advantage of new ideas and technologies or incorporating new or modified customer needs or updated organisational or departmental goals. Achieving one plan can lead to launching another one.

Unless a plan is straightforward and people's input is completely unnecessary, or the plan is confidential because it involves, for example, yet-to-be-announced business initiatives, involve the

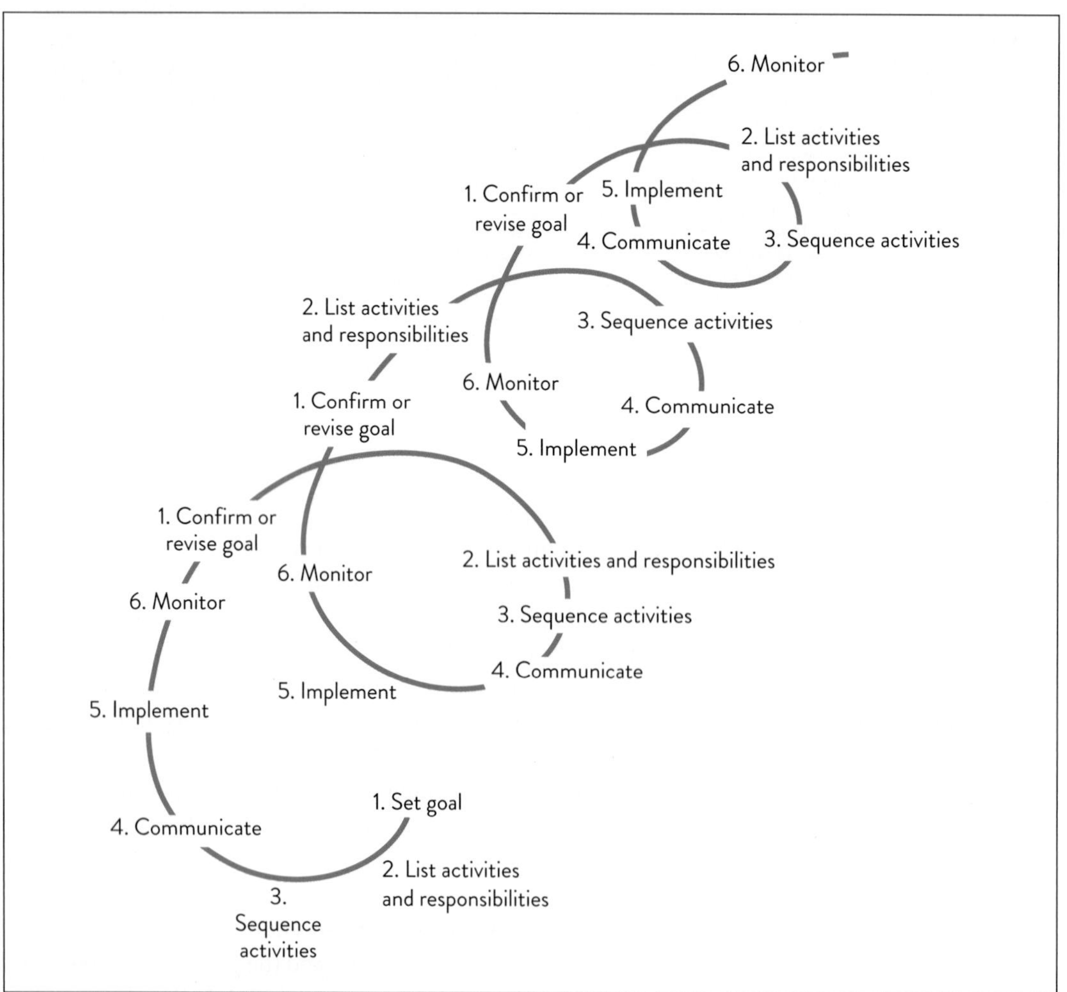

FIGURE 20.2 The planning process

team in developing plans and call in specialist staff to help when required. Involving people that the plan affects and who will be carrying it out ensures they understand it and are committed to its success. Involving others generally results in a higher quality plan because it draws on a range of skills, experience and knowledge. You can consult others informally (refer to Chapter 8 for information on who to consult 'politically', getting your ideas implemented and using your networks for assistance) or formally (see Chapter 25 to find out how to lead meetings).

No matter how informal a plan may be, write it down to study it, spot flaws and adjust it. Written plans are also easier to communicate to others, are there for future reference and make it easier to monitor progress. Once the plan is in writing, use it. A scribbled-on plan shows that it is being referred to and revised, and that it is a working document and not just a document taking up space in a filing cabinet, on a bulletin board or in Cloud storage.

Recurring and standing plans in practice

What sorts of plans would you want in a large suburban newsagency that sells a range of magazines, books, diaries, giftware, greeting cards and so on? Would you consider recurring plans entered into an electronic diary that shows daily duties for each day of the week? Not the obvious activities like opening the shop and tidying, restocking and dusting the shelves, but tasks that staff could easily overlook on a busy day, like magazine returns on Mondays, lotto ordering on Tuesdays, rubbish bin removal on Wednesdays and storeroom tidying on Thursdays.

Monthly reminders would be useful, too, for tasks that only need to be completed once a month, such as book returns, customer statements, end-of-month accounting figures, and stock valuation. Also, perhaps, a few annual recurring plans could be included so that orders of back-to-school stationery, calendars and diaries, seasonal gift items and similar are not overlooked.

Another thing to consider would be standing plans – listing the precise procedure to follow, step-by-step for each of these activities. These standing plans could be recorded electronically and saved on the computer to be changed as the need arises. Perhaps a printed copy could also be placed under the front counter or in a staff room, so casuals who don't work regularly and new staff who are learning can be kept up to date. While we're at it, we may as well include the procedures for opening and closing the shop and the end-of-year financial procedures.

Once the daily plans and standing plans – the 'how to' lists – are written, anyone can look at them and remind themselves how to complete an activity that pops up as a reminder. That way, nothing is forgotten and nothing is left to chance. Easy!

Six steps to planning

Transferable skill

1.5 Operations management

Below are six steps to planning in the workplace that will help to ensure successful outcomes:

1 Establish realistic goals. What is to be achieved? What indicators can show success? Use the verb–what–why formula described earlier in this chapter to set SMART success measures to aim for.
2 List all the activities that need to take place to achieve the plan's goals. Try brainstorming (explained in Chapter 26) and use the five 'W' and one 'H' triggers (What? Why? Who? Where? When? How?) shown in Figure 20.1 to determine what needs to be done, by whom, and all the other details.
3 Sequence the activities in the order in which they should occur and assign a target date to each activity. Network diagrams such as flow charts, PERT diagrams and Gantt charts (discussed later in this chapter) are useful tools for this because they provide a visual representation of your plan.

4 Communicate the plan to those it involves or affects. When people are aware of the goals and how they are to achieve them, they are more likely to help the plan succeed. When the plan involves a major change that affects many people, develop a communication strategy that covers all concerned stakeholders (as explained in Chapter 21).
5 Once satisfied that the plan is complete and communicated well, put it into action. Think about conducting a force-field analysis (explained later in this chapter) first. If the plan is sensitive or critical to the department or the organisation, test it first (as explained in Chapter 22).
6 Monitor the progress to see if the plan is working. Find out with plenty of time if the plan is failing to take effective corrective action. (Monitoring is discussed later in this chapter.)

Estimate the necessary resources

Transferable skills

1.1 Financial literacy

1.2 Entrepreneurship/ small business skills

2.3 Business strategy

For planning and successful outcomes, obtain the capacity, knowledge and systems the plan needs. Capacity and knowledge are mostly about the people required to carry out the plan and deal with its results. For example, the plan may be to develop a new sales area. Therefore, sales staff must make new contacts and work with customers to provide the service or make the product and process increased enquiries and sales results.

People with the knowledge to carry out the plan are also needed. In the previous example, people are required that know enough about the organisation's offering and values to develop the new sales area and answer the resulting enquiries. Consider the ability of current processes to support the plan and whether they need to be expanded, increased or redesigned. The plan may require more workstations, more equipment or a new way of working with internal or external suppliers. This is summarised in **Table 20.1**.

TABLE 20.1 Working out the details

Think through the resources your plan needs to succeed, such as:	
Equipment	Do you need to acquire, temporarily or permanently, additional equipment such as computers and workstations?
Facilities	Do you need to arrange facilities such as transportation or computer software?
Funding	Do you need to arrange for additional funds to cater for extra staff, professional development, new or hired equipment, overtime and any unforeseen events that arise?
Materials	Do you require additional materials, such as procedures manuals?
People	Do you need to bring in extra people to complete the plan? When your plan requires additional people, decide whether they should be casual, full-time, part-time, permanent or temporary employees or contractors, or whether you could second people (bring them in temporarily) from other parts of the organisation
Space	Do you need more space to set the plan in motion?
Time	Are people to undertake additional duties? You may need to free up some of their time from another project or duties
Training	Do people need additional training to carry out the plan?

Involve others to gain their ideas and their support. Consult other staff like line managers, your workgroup and other relevant stakeholders, or, more likely, a combination of all three.

Some other resource matters to consider include:

- Does the plan have enough support from management and key stakeholders? How can the support be increased?
- Does the plan make it necessary or possible to upgrade equipment or facilities?
- Does the plan support the organisation's strategic and business plans sufficiently?
- How will you allocate available human, physical and system resources most effectively and efficiently?
- How does your plan affect the resources you and your team have to hand?
- When the plan calls for a change, such as doing more or the same amount of work with fewer resources, with fewer people or less time, carefully refine your work procedures and practices.

Secure the necessary resources

Transferable skill

2.3 Business strategy

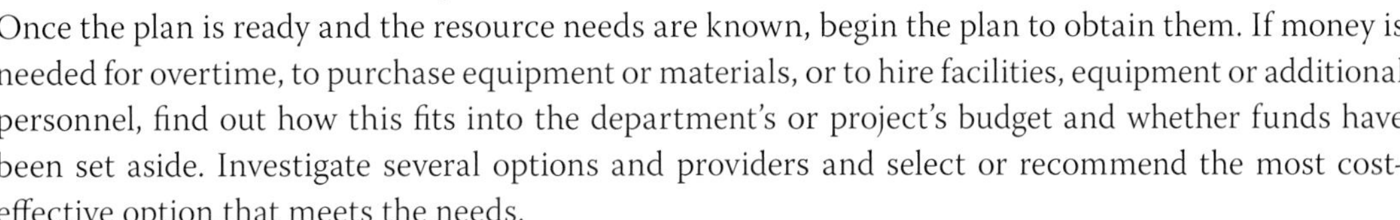

Once the plan is ready and the resource needs are known, begin the plan to obtain them. If money is needed for overtime, to purchase equipment or materials, or to hire facilities, equipment or additional personnel, find out how this fits into the department's or project's budget and whether funds have been set aside. Investigate several options and providers and select or recommend the most cost-effective option that meets the needs.

Follow the organisation's procedures for requesting funding and other resources. Begin by briefing the manager, project manager or other nominated people, either verbally or in writing, about the need and why it is needed, and provide an estimate of the costs involved. Support the estimates with actual quotes to clearly outline the benefits expected to be gained from investing in additional resources. Remember to secure people's commitment to the plan's success, too. The more you communicate with them and solicit their ideas, the better your chances of winning over their support for the plan. Failure to achieve the support of stakeholders, influential people in the organisation, your team and those implementing the plan, will mean it is doomed. (See Chapter 7 for some ideas on gaining support.)

Cost–benefit analysis

Transferable skill

1.1 Financial literacy

Are additional or improved resources worth the expense? Is a decision worth implementing or a change worth making? Is the solution to a problem worth the cost of fixing it? A cost-benefit analysis helps answer questions like these. It means to quantify, in dollar terms, the benefits and the costs one can expect from a purchase or course of action. When the benefits are worth more than the costs (e.g. increased productivity), it is a good indication that it is worth going ahead.

Some costs, such as capital costs and contractor costs, are once-off, while other costs, such as labour costs, are ongoing. Calculating these can be quite easy. Other costs, such as the opportunities-lost costs of not going ahead or environmental costs, are more difficult to quantify, and you may need to be subjective and prepared to defend your guesstimates. Some costs can increase or recur, too, for example, when once-new equipment ages and needs increasing maintenance or when technology becomes outdated and needs upgrading.

Like costs, some benefits are easier to quantify than others. Savings in energy, labour costs and time, for example, are easier to put a dollar value on than benefits to employee wellbeing, the environment or health and safety. Benefits often accrue over time and take a while to build up, and some can reduce when, for example, equipment ages and becomes less efficient. The benefits of some changes, such as continuous improvements to work systems or business processes, can deliver ongoing benefits once implemented, while other investments may provide only a once-off or short-term benefit.

The time it takes for the benefits to repay the costs is called the payback period, and the point at which costs equal benefits is called the break-even point. Many organisations look for paybacks on projects over a specific time; for example, three years.

Create a cost–benefit analysis as a graph by plotting the costs and the benefits (in dollars) on the vertical axis and showing them over time on the horizontal axis, sometimes called the return on investment, or ROI. The break-even point is where the two lines intersect, as shown in Figure 20.3.

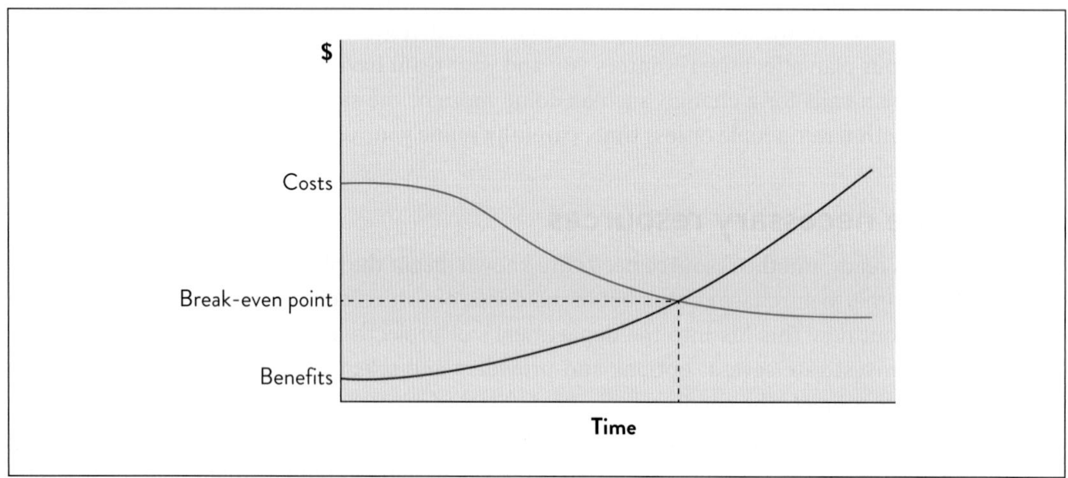

FIGURE 20.3 Cost–benefit analysis graph

Secure the right people

Most plans affect people – deploying people into roles, the actual jobs or tasks they carry out, the skills they need, even their working relationships. (To find out how to support people while introducing change, see Chapter 24.)

Here are some other staffing issues to consider:

- Is there any special expertise to help you implement the plan? If so, does it require internal or external people? If external, casuals or contractors?
- Is there a need for more or fewer people?
- Are the current team members in need of any training? Who should design and deliver it? When and for how long will it take? Who can cover for staff while they are in training? What will training and providing staff coverage cost? Which budget is to cover the costs? If it is within budget, are there sufficient funds?
- If there is a need for more staff, should they be temporary or permanent? If temporary, is it practical to use contractors or outsource the work? Is it possible to attract and train the additional staff required, and when should it begin? Are there enough people in the local area, or would it be better to retrain existing staff from other areas of the organisation?
- Should you adjust the mix of casual, contract, full-time, home-based, off-site, on-site, part-time, permanent and temporary staff in your team?
- Should you reallocate or redistribute duties to implement the plan more readily?
- Should you work towards cross-skilling, multiskilling or upskilling?

Present your plans

Most organisations have formats or templates they follow when setting out and presenting plans. When you're not sure what to do, get a template or an example of a previous plan of a similar type and follow the layout used.

Your aim is to make the plan clear and easy to follow – usually, the more simply you present something, the easier it is to understand. (Refer to Chapter 7 when you need to present a written plan to management and when you are presenting your plans orally.)

20.3 Protecting your plans

Transferable skills

2.3 Business strategy

3.4 Leadership

> Intellectuals solve problems. Geniuses prevent them.
>
> Albert Einstein, in Butler, *Navigating today's environment: The directors' and officers' guide to restructuring*, Beard Books, 2010.

According to Murphy's Law: 'Anything that can go wrong, will go wrong'. That is why you continuously monitor your plan as it rolls out to make sure that it doesn't go irretrievably off track when the unexpected happens at the most inopportune time. The more important it is that the plan works right from the start, the more important it is to monitor it critically and look for things that could go wrong. For highly critical plans, conduct a live trial run to identify hitches.

To prevent problems, once a risk plan has been developed, review this series of questions to assess the plan's viability:

1. What could go wrong? Brainstorm the events, people and problems that could turn the plan into a fiasco. Decide the most likely and those with the worst impact or repercussions to analyse. Unless it is a risk management plan, ignore any that are well outside the range of reason.
2. What would indicate it's about to happen? For each potential problem and adverse event, work out what the alert is to notify it is about to happen.
3. What could prevent it from happening? Consider how to prevent each possible problem from occurring; if that is not possible to prevent it, what can be done to mitigate or lessen its effects?
4. What should be done if it does happen? When a problem or an adverse event has occurred, have a contingency plan ready to implement.

Working your way through these four questions means that you have a preventative or mitigation plan to stop a problem from happening or reduce its impact. Have a contingency plan to know what to do if it does occur or an adaptive plan regarding how you will live with it if it happens. Refine the contingency plans with an interim plan, which describes what to do if something goes wrong until fixed with a corrective plan, which outlines the steps to take to put it right. These plans are summarised in Figure 20.4. (See Chapter 22 for more information on risk analysis.)

Force-field analysis

Transferable skill

2.3 Business strategy

As indicated in Figure 20.5, a force-field analysis is another way to spot people, problems and events that could prevent the plan from working – forces resisting the plan's success. It also helps identify factors working in favour of the project – forces driving the plan's success. Once you know what they are, look for ways to rectify, reduce or remove the resisting forces and make the most of the driving forces. Driving and resisting forces can come from many areas, including those listed in Table 20.2.

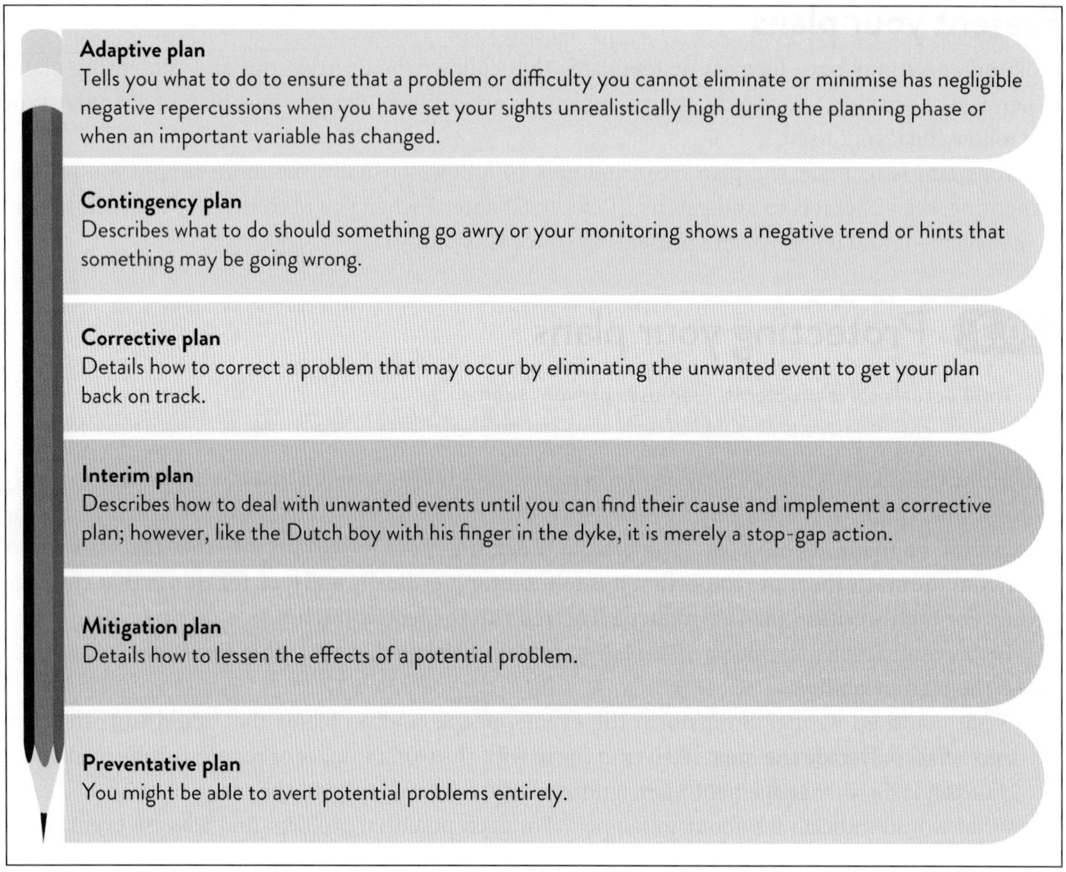

Adaptive plan
Tells you what to do to ensure that a problem or difficulty you cannot eliminate or minimise has negligible negative repercussions when you have set your sights unrealistically high during the planning phase or when an important variable has changed.

Contingency plan
Describes what to do should something go awry or your monitoring shows a negative trend or hints that something may be going wrong.

Corrective plan
Details how to correct a problem that may occur by eliminating the unwanted event to get your plan back on track.

Interim plan
Describes how to deal with unwanted events until you can find their cause and implement a corrective plan; however, like the Dutch boy with his finger in the dyke, it is merely a stop-gap action.

Mitigation plan
Details how to lessen the effects of a potential problem.

Preventative plan
You might be able to avert potential problems entirely.

FIGURE 20.4 Six protective plans

TABLE 20.2 Internal and external driving and resisting forces

Internal forces	External forces
Administrative practices	Changing government policies and regulations
Financial and other resources	Changing marketplace conditions
Individual employees	Climatic and pandemic events
Influential parties (e.g. management or unions)	Community pressures
Leadership styles	Competition
Organisation culture	Customers
Policies	Labour supply shortages
Procedures	Technology
Team culture	The economic environment
Time and information	The domestic supply chain
Tools and equipment	The international supply chain

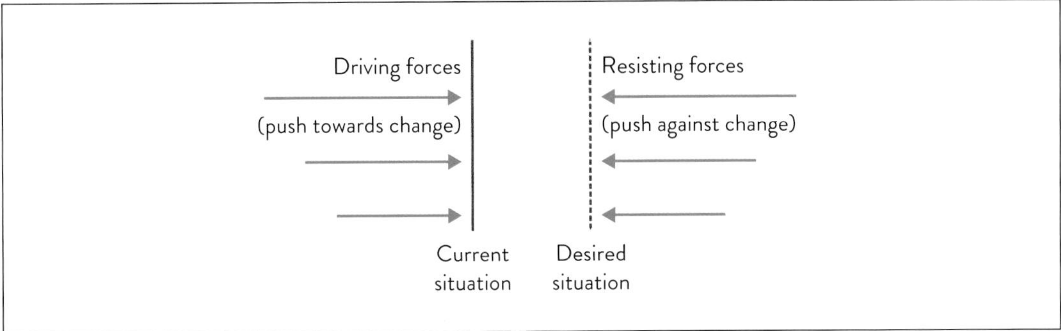

FIGURE 20.5 Force-field analysis

Force-field analysis can also help identify the implications of the plan and predict the effects on people, systems, procedures and so on, both 'upstream' and 'downstream'. See Figure 20.6 for the steps on how to conduct a force-field analysis.

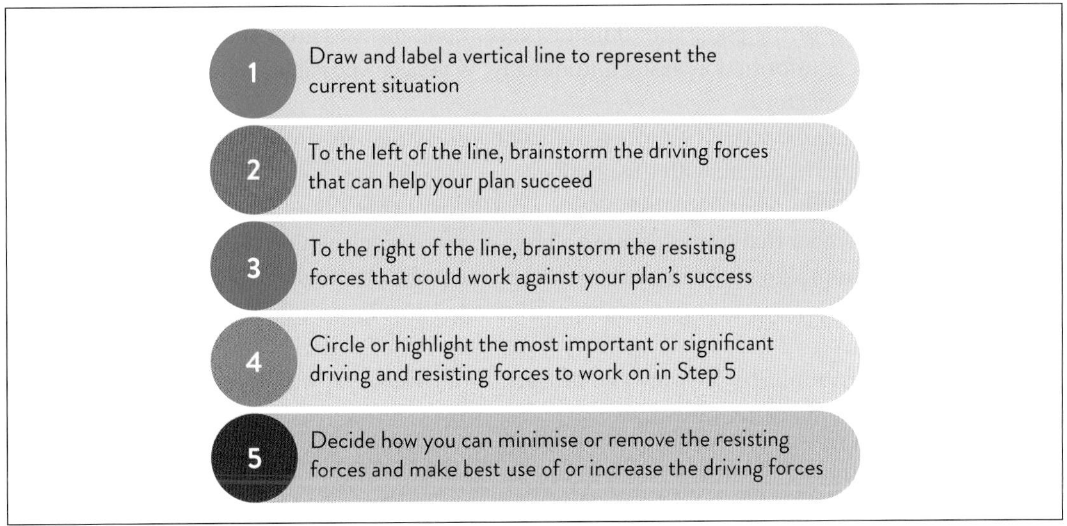

FIGURE 20.6 How to conduct a force-field analysis

20.4 Monitoring your plans

Transferable skills

1.4 Business operations

1.5 Operations management

> For if you stay there, disorders are seen as they arise, and you can soon remedy them; if you are not there, disorders become understood when they are great and there is no longer a remedy.
>
> Niccolo Machiavelli, *The Prince*, Harvey C. Mansfield (trans.), University of Chicago Press, 1998, p. 10.

The opening quote above is a long-winded way to say that you can spot problems quickly and fix them when monitoring a plan's progress. Problems can grow, and by the time they have been identified, it is difficult or even too late to fix them. Keeping track of the right measures and milestones can show how well the plan is unfolding. Think of monitoring as the partner of planning. The feedback provides an early warning of whether and where the plan is going off the rails so that corrective actions can be taken.

Monitoring also allows for quick adjustments to changing conditions. It may reveal the need to alter the way to give directions, modify the plan, reschedule activities, use the available resources differently or even change the monitoring methods themselves. But when monitoring, beware of confirmation bias. When you believe something or hope for something – in this case, hoping the plan works – it is easy to find the evidence you are looking for and to ignore contrary evidence. (Other traps to stay alert for are discussed in Chapter 26.)

Four steps to monitoring

To ensure plans succeed once they have commenced, follow these four steps:

1. *Decide what to monitor:* concentrate on what is most important to the plan's success, for example, delivering on time, improving quality, improving service levels, increasing output, increasing sales or reducing costs. Consider the danger points and what could cause the most damage should the plan go wrong. Think about the objectives and targets.
2. *Establish specific measures to monitor:* decide what counts the most; for example, in the customer service area, measure the most critical factors in satisfying customers – perhaps it is cost, product reliability, quality or time. Measure what supports the organisation's values, vision and strategy; for example, it is counterproductive to measure only individual contributions in an organisation that values teamwork.

   So as not to waste time by over-monitoring, look for the critical control points, the most important aspects of the plan, and monitor those. Look for measures that provide many data points and critical information easily and quickly. Whenever possible, measure lead indicators rather than lag indicators.
3. *Compare what is happening with what should be happening:* once you have identified what to measure, compare the actual with the planned.
4. *Take remedial action when required:* when what is happening isn't precisely what should be happening, remember that some variation always occurs. Decide which variations are important enough to warrant taking corrective action. Implement the contingency plans discussed earlier in this chapter or carry out a gap analysis (illustrated in Figure 20.7) to determine the best course of action.

Transferable skill
2.1 Critical thinking

When the plan is complete, see what can be learnt from the way it was developed, protected and implemented so it is done better next time.

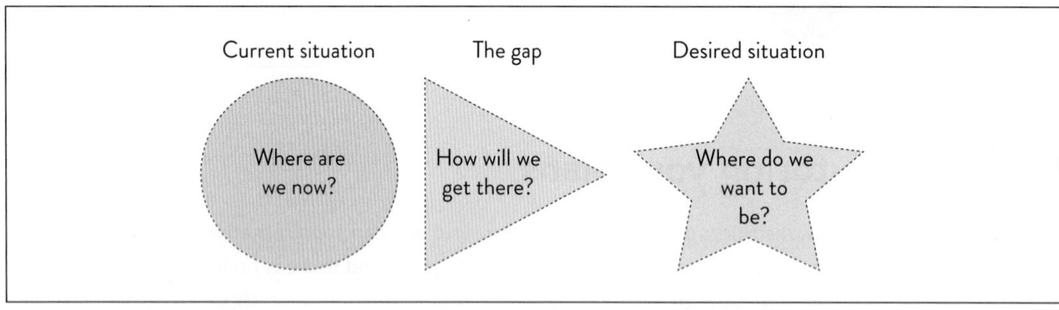

FIGURE 20.7 Gap analysis

Comparing current results with the desired results is called a gap analysis. Gap analysis can help decide how best to 'bridge the gap' or move from the current situation to the desired situation. Keep in mind that not all solutions have a measurable outcome; these may include results that are difficult or expensive to measure, are measured elsewhere, are not 'owned' by an individual or a team, do not demonstrate progress towards achieving your plan, or would be difficult to interpret or understand. Additionally, measures that would not cause individuals or teams to act differently or identify problem areas are not worth wasting time or resources on measuring. The resulting plan shows the steps to close the gap between 'where you are now' and 'where you want to be'.

Some common success measures to monitor

Customer satisfaction is important. Be sure to satisfy your customers by watching what's important. Perhaps it is:

- complaint response time
- on-time delivery
- percentage of enquiries resolved.

To keep tabs of your business' financial success and help it to continue thriving, you can watch:

- market share
- profit
- return on assets and on investment.

Growth, innovation and learning are important, and they keep your business from stagnating, so keep track of:

- number of new ideas generated and implemented
- percentage of revenue from new products and services
- research and development as a percentage of sales.

To ensure continued smooth operations, keep your eye on what's important to your organisation's operations. Perhaps it is:

- billing accuracy
- employee productivity
- tender success rate.

Employee engagement can help keep your employees committed and meet your organisation's strategic goals, so monitor:

- individual and group training needs are being met
- number of internal promotions
- number of training hours per employee per annum.

Common monitoring tools

It is common to interact with various tools daily to both plan and monitor recurring and occasional activities in industry. In a project manager's role, designing and developing these monitoring tools is part of the job. (Ways to monitor statistics are discussed in Chapter 27.) Four other common planning and monitoring tools are explained in the following sections: Gantt charts, network diagrams, financial tools and inventory controls. Then we take a look at the informal monitoring techniques.

Transferable skills

1.2 Entrepreneurship/ small business skills

1.5 Operations management

5.2 Technology use

Gantt charts

A Gantt chart is a horizontal bar chart designed to aid in operational planning and monitoring. It shows the anticipated start and finish dates for activities called for in a plan; as work starts and progresses, you fill in the actual line below the corresponding planned activity. This quickly shows whether the plan is on schedule.

Figure 20.8 displays a plan for painting a house. It shows that the plan calls for the scraping and sanding to be completed by midday Tuesday, but the actual time required to scrape and sand includes both Monday and Tuesday.

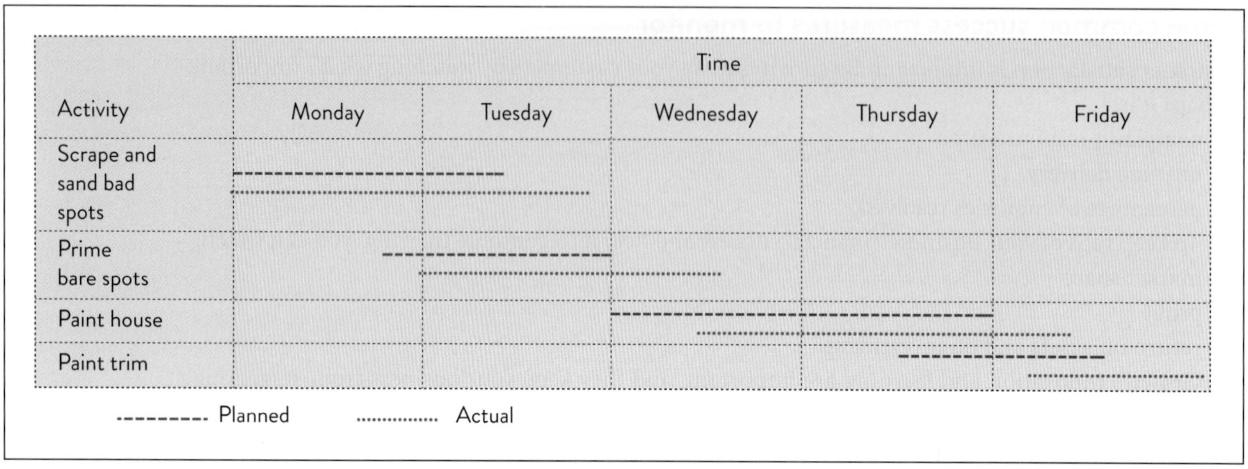

Activity	Time: Monday	Tuesday	Wednesday	Thursday	Friday
Scrape and sand bad spots					
Prime bare spots					
Paint house					
Paint trim					

--------- Planned .... Actual

FIGURE 20.8 Gantt chart for painting a house

Gantt charts also indicate where two or more activities can occur at the same time. The Gantt chart in **Figure 20.8** shows that some of the priming can be carried out while the scraping is still being done. Painting the trim can begin while the painting is being finished.

Constructing a Gantt chart can easily be done on a piece of paper or on a computer using a spreadsheet, or Microsoft Project or other programs, which can show activities in various formats, including alphabetical, date and numerical order. To make a Gantt chart:

1 List activities or tasks that need to be carried out, step by step, vertically down the left side of the chart.
2 Show when each task should start and finish horizontally (e.g. in hours or days).
3 Determine when the overall project should be completed.
4 As time passes, add the 'actual' lines to track how the plan progresses and see whether you are ahead of or behind schedule.

Gantt charts give the project team a visual overview of the plan. Adding the 'actual' lines helps you monitor the plan.

Network diagrams

Network diagrams and Gantt charts are powerful tools that help schedule, manage and monitor the tasks that must be completed to achieve the goals of the plans and projects. Network diagrams help identify the minimum time needed to complete a plan or project. The benefit of network diagrams over Gantt charts is that they provide an opportunity to identify which tasks can be delayed should there be a need to shift resources to catch up on other tasks.

Critical path analysis (CPA), or the critical path method (CPM), is a form of network diagram. CPAs show how various activities relate to each other, which cannot start until other activities are finished (known as dependent or sequential activities). They also show which activities can be worked on in tandem with other activities (known as parallel tasks or concurrent tasks). Specialised software can help develop a CPA by:

- identifying the tasks that need to be carried out
- estimating how long each task should take
- scheduling when the tasks should occur.

Program evaluation and review technique (PERT) is another type of network diagram. A simplified PERT diagram is shown in **Figure 20.9**. Time flows from left to right; circles represent events or activities, such as the start or completion of a task; and lines represent the tasks themselves.

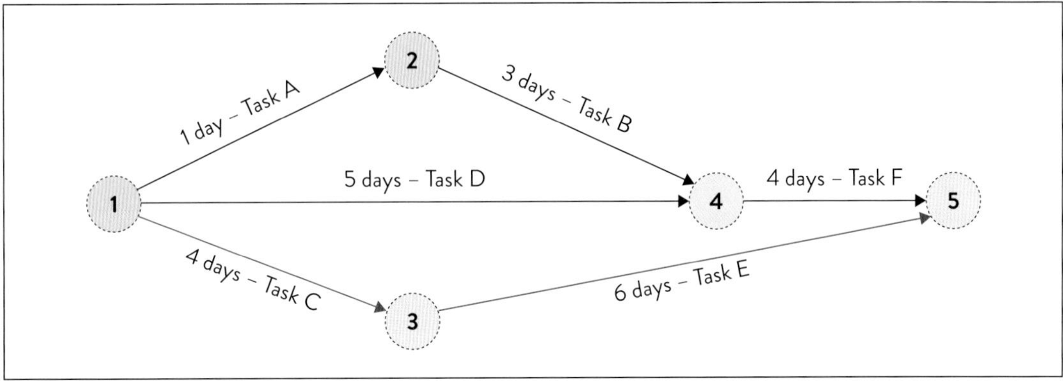

FIGURE 20.9 PERT diagram

Label each task line with the time it is expected to take, then add the times of task paths together to identify the critical path – the longest path through a plan or project. This critical path is the series of tasks to keep a close eye on because not completing them on time holds up the entire plan or project.

PERT charts take a slightly more sceptical view of time estimates for each project stage than CPA, which helps balance the optimistically short timelines people often estimate. They show an estimate of the shortest possible time each task could take, the most likely length of time and the longest time each might take. Then use the formula below to calculate the time to use for each project stage:

$$\text{Shortest time} + 4 \times \text{likely time} + \text{longest time} \div 6$$

Financial tools

Transferable skill

1.1 Financial literacy

Budgets are targets expressed in financial terms that forecast income and expenses over a specific period, most commonly a quarter (three months). Advertising budgets, purchasing budgets, salary budgets, sales budgets and training budgets are common types of budgets that projects and organisations deal with. The aim is to try to either reach budget (e.g. a sales budget) or stay within budget (e.g. purchasing, training or travel budget).

Budgets establish financial goals and show if the targets have been reached at the end of the period. During the period, interim budget reports can track progress. Where there is failure to reach or stay within the budget, it is best to find out why and fix it. For example, it may require a stop to all non-essential spending, freezing recruitment or selling more. Budgets can also help identify wasteful expenditure.

Balance sheets, cash flow statements and income statements are the three statements required in a financial report. Use them to spot and explain trends and to monitor the organisation's financial strength.

The balance sheet (or statement of financial position) describes the financial position of an organisation on a specified date, showing what it owns – its assets and reserves – and what it owes – its liabilities. It is like a snapshot of the organisation's affairs expressed in dollars and cents. The cash flow statement summarises the money the organisation has received, and the money paid out in its operating, investing and financing activities. It indicates an organisation's liquidity (assets that can be easily converted into cash) by showing how much working capital (money) is available; the more cash an organisation can quickly raise, the more liquid it is. The income statement, also called the profit and loss (P&L) account, describes the financial performance of a company by comparing the income from all sources with the expenses incurred to determine the net profit (or loss) made during the accounting period (e.g. one month, one quarter, one year). It shows what is known as the 'bottom line' – did we make money or didn't we? An organisation's accounting systems generate these and various other financial reports, making it easy to compare planned and actual results.

INDUSTRY INSIGHTS

What's a company worth?

Microsoft, Apple and Amazon are some of the world's largest and most successful companies, but you'd never guess it from their balance sheets. Like many modern companies, none of these own much that can be measured, weighed or counted, but both have a huge intangible worth based on their cultures, employees and systems.

In today's world, in which organisations need a sound employer value proposition and a positive public relations image, marketing may be an important investment, not an expense, as it usually appears on the P&L account. Today, many companies need 'smart' employees to succeed – are they an expense, as they have traditionally been, or an asset? Is training them an expense, as it has traditionally been, or an asset? New ways of doing business may require new ways of accounting for an organisation's success.

Inventory controls

Transferable skills

1.2 Entrepreneurship/small business skills

1.3 Sustainability

1.4 Business operations

1.5 Operations management

4.1 Data literacy

5.2 Technology use

Carrying too much stock is expensive while holding too little stock can lead to delays, inefficiency and even lost business. Any organisation or site that needs to keep track of goods coming in and going out uses some inventory monitoring and control system, be it factories, restaurants, shops or warehouses. At their most basic, they set maximum and minimum stock levels for inventory items and detail the most economical quantity of each item to carry.

More sophisticated inventory systems can also help employees locate items; for example, in transit or in a warehouse. The most modern systems also help organisations integrate inventory management across their functional subsystems and integrate the information with other control systems, such as accounts receivable, financial control and sales information, including customer purchasing patterns.

While many small businesses continue to track inventory manually, other small and medium-sized businesses use a computerised system to monitor and control inventories. These systems generally use barcode technology to track items in real-time and use wireless technology to notify an IT system that automatically alerts staff to place an order and advises how much to order. Some systems even place orders automatically.

Just-in-time and similar methods aim for inventory to arrive 'just in time' for use, minimising the need for expensive stock holdings and storage. Sophisticated computer techniques, such as product life cycle management systems, help by aiding planning, and coordinating and monitoring despatch, goods inwards, manufacturing and stores operations.

Vendor-managed systems use their customers' automated daily reports to replenish stocks as needed, using data analytics, giving the customer the savings of just-in-time inventory management. It gives the supplier the ability to anticipate production requirements more accurately; both customers and suppliers benefit from the stronger trading partnerships that can result. Table 20.3 shows the characteristics of an effective monitoring system.

Informal monitoring

Monitoring need not be impersonal, official and onerous. Being present, talking to people and listening to their comments are good ways to keep your finger on the pulse. Your diary and to-do list are also effective monitoring tools.

TABLE 20.3 The essentials of an effective monitoring system

Characteristic	Criteria
Accurate	The information is correct enough to provide the information people need to identify problems and take appropriate action
Easily understood	The information is clear to those it affects and those who use and act on it
Economical	The benefits of gathering the information outweigh the costs of gathering it
Timely	Information is available quickly and regularly enough to allow corrective or other action to be implemented
Useful	It meets the needs of the organisation and the people using it

Build in consultation mechanisms

Transferable skills

1.4 Business operations

3.1 Teamwork/ relationships

3.4 Leadership

When the plan involves people outside the project team, build in consultative monitoring mechanisms – perhaps a 'half-time review' – with stakeholders in a meeting, a survey or informal discussions. Information should be provided about improving project performance and the value you and your team add for your stakeholders. When the benefits to your stakeholders aren't as great as you had hoped, seek their input on how you and your team can better meet their expectations.

How to develop an effective monitoring system

You should aim to keep your monitoring system simple yet useful. Here are some tips to develop an effective monitoring system:

- Make it clear who is responsible for taking any corrective or other action that may be required.
- Make sure that people can produce, collect and use the monitoring feedback relatively quickly and easily. It must be worth the time and effort to collect, document and analyse it or use it in some other way.
- Track lead indicators rather than lag indicators.
- Try to incorporate management by exception, where 'no news is good news', and you are advised as soon as a critical activity deviates from the expected.
- When your monitoring system shows that things are going according to plan, thank people for their efforts.

Don't overmonitor

Monitoring might be ongoing but that does not mean it needs to take a lot of time. Coordinate what is to be monitored and by whom to avoid duplication. Monitor lead indicators for key success measures for those activities with the most significant bearing on the plans and productivity. Identify and measure important lead indicators at specific points where variations from plans indicate that performance is slipping or is in danger of doing so. Don't monitor too many indicators; as a general rule, if you regularly monitor more than 15 measures, go back to the drawing board and simplify.

Finally, involve the people whose performance or activities are being monitored as much as possible. Additionally, when establishing monitoring systems and procedures, let them monitor and control their own performance when possible. This ensures that those responsible for implementing the plan, meeting the targets and using the monitoring information understand and accept the measures and are aware of why they are needed.

STUDY TOOLS

QUICK REVIEW

KEY CONCEPT 20.1 

a Briefly explain how planning and monitoring can help organisations, leader-managers and individual job-holders achieve results.
b Explain the relationship between strategic plans, operational plans and business plans.

KEY CONCEPT 20.2 

a What distinguishes a good plan from a poor plan?
b List and explain the role that each of the six steps to planning plays.
c What do you need to consider when estimating the resources you need to make your plan work?
d What is a cost–benefit analysis and how is it used?

KEY CONCEPT 20.3 

a Why do plans sometimes fail? What actions can you take to safeguard the success of your plans?
b List the types of plans that leader-managers need to understand and describe how operational plans fit into the wider activities of the organisation.
c How does a force-field analysis help to protect plans?

KEY CONCEPT 20.4 

a How can you decide what to monitor in order to ensure your plans roll out effectively?
b Explain how Gantt charts, network diagrams, financial tools and inventory controls are both planning and monitoring tools.

BUILD YOUR SKILLS

KEY CONCEPT 20.1 

a It is often said that crisis management is a sign of poor planning. Do you agree? Explain why or why not, giving examples from your own experience. What advice would you offer a leader-manager who is caught up in dealing with crisis after crisis because of poor planning?

KEY CONCEPT 20.2 

a Should you stick firmly to your plans or consider them to be working documents that guide your actions?
b Describe a situation in which you invested the time and effort to develop a plan. Relate the plan you made to the six steps of the planning process described in this chapter. How did you estimate and secure the resources you needed? Was the time you spent in planning worth the effort? Why or why not? What conclusions can you draw about the usefulness of making plans?
c How do you rate your planning and organising skills? Which, if any, do you believe you need to strengthen? How could you do this?

KEY CONCEPT 20.3 

a What upcoming personal plans do you have; for example, for a holiday or completing your studies? Select one of these and conduct a force-field analysis on your plan and use it to strengthen your plan.
b Describe a time when you worked with others to plan and organise activities and when you communicated with others to coordinate the implementation of the plan.

KEY CONCEPT 20.4 

a Think of a plan you have made in the past. What kinds of things did you monitor as your plan unfolded? What tools did you use to monitor your plan?

WORKPLACE ACTIVITIES

KEY CONCEPT 20.1 

a Describe how developing and monitoring a plan helped you achieve an important work goal.
b How does your operational plan fit in with your organisation's strategic and business plans?

KEY CONCEPT 20.2 

a Describe the planning skills you use in your current role and the types of plans you develop and follow. How do you monitor these plans?

b What was the last activity you planned in detail at your workplace? Describe how you went about planning it and the steps you followed. How did you determine and secure the resources you needed to carry out your plan? How did you protect and monitor the plan? How do you know it was viable on a cost–benefit basis?

KEY CONCEPT 20.3 

a What standing plans and interim plans do you have in your workplace? Select one of each and conduct a force-field analysis on it with a view to making the plan more robust.

KEY CONCEPT 20.4 

a Describe the monitoring tools you and your work team use and explain how they conform to the characteristics of an effective monitoring system described in this chapter. How do they alert you to problems and help you work effectively?

EXTENSION ACTIVITIES

Referring to the Snapshot at the beginning of this chapter, answer the following questions:

1 Consider what information you would need to provide key messaging to the project teams.

2 What organisational and financial impacts might significant changes have on the operational workflows described in the Snapshot? You may want to consider the impact of:

- employee workplans
- rosters/allocation of duties
- new roles
- redundant/surplus roles and resources.

CASE STUDY 20

JOAN SIMON DISCOVERS THE NEED TO PLAN AHEAD AND KEEP TABS

Joan Simon has just been promoted to lead and manage the sales team of eight sales representatives, two key account managers and three merchandisers. As a key account manager before her promotion, all she needed to look after was herself. It was a matter of making sure she serviced her customers properly, that goods were delivered and they sold well, and her customers were up to date on payments and received the sales and merchandising support she deemed necessary. A simple spreadsheet system plus diligent use of her personal organiser had always sufficed.

Now that Joan is managing the whole team, she has people to look after and all the sales in the territory, product promotions, expenditure, business development and so on. Joan first decides to set up some planning and monitoring systems – systems that can quickly and easily give her the information she needs to manage the sales operation. How her predecessor had managed, she can't imagine – he must have kept track of everything in his head.

Her first move is to set up a spreadsheet for each sales representative and key account manager. The spreadsheet shows their sales to date against their budgeted sales so that she can monitor their results against targets and see who might need a bit of help. Joan then sets up a similar spreadsheet for each customer. The spreadsheet shows the customer's month-by-month and year-to-date purchases and compares both figures against previous months and years.

Joan discovers that she receives a monthly debtor statement for each customer. Upon looking it over, she finds that a number of customers, both small and large, are more than 90 days in arrears. Since the company policy is 30 days credit for small customers and 60 days credit for larger-volume customers, she realises she needs to remind the reps to push for payment. Joan suspects that some of these customers, and even some of the sales reps, may have taken advantage of the change in personnel (i.e. her appointment) to allow their payments to drift. Joan doesn't want to jeopardise the company's business relationship with these customers or her relationship with the sales reps (no rep likes reminding customers

CASE STUDY 20

to pay, as she well knows). Part of her responsibility as a manager is to ensure that their customers pay on time. And if one of those customers were to 'go under' with unpaid debts, management would be looking to her for an explanation.

With that gloomy thought in mind, Joan moves on to develop another spreadsheet to track her expenditure. The spreadsheet ensures that expenditure remains within budget. Joan then looks around to see where she should hang the large wall planner she has purchased to track her team's annual and personal leave.

When Joan meets with her manager at the end of the week to discuss how she's settling into her new role, he seems impressed with her planning and monitoring initiatives. He explains that he's a big fan of management by exception, and says that when she compiles her monthly reports to him, she only needs more than 10 per cent above or below target. This essentially gives him a summary of what is going well and what isn't. He advises her to apply management by exception principles with each of her staff and incorporate them into her department's weekly summaries for the management team to spend most of her valuable time poring over results.

On her way home, it occurs to Joan that she should also plan the year's promotions for their customers. 'I should probably get the team to help plan those, since they're the ones who manage the promotions,' she thinks.

Questions

1. What risks did Joan's predecessor take in not using any planning and monitoring systems?
2. How do you rate Joan's efforts so far in establishing effective planning and monitoring systems for her department? What should her next steps be?
3. What formal and informal planning and monitoring systems do you think would be the most suitable for Joan's needs, and why? Consider all the types of planning, including, for example, contingency and preventative planning.
4. Is Joan's idea of involving members of her team in planning the year's promotions for their customers a good one? Why or why not?

CHAPTER

21

PLANNING AND MANAGING PROJECTS

After completing this chapter, you will be able to:

21.1 scope a project and develop a project plan
21.2 lead a project to a successful conclusion
21.3 finalise a project and grow into your next project.

TRANSFERABLE SKILLS

The following transferable skills are covered in this chapter:

1 **Business competence**
- **1.1** Financial literacy
- **1.2** Entrepreneurship/small business skills
- **1.4** Business operations
- **1.5** Operations management

2 **Critical thinking and problem solving**
- **2.1** Critical thinking
- **2.2** Personal effectiveness
- **2.3** Business strategy

3 **Social competence**
- **3.1** Teamwork/relationships
- **3.2** Verbal communication
- **3.3** Written communication
- **3.4** Leadership

4 **Data literacy**
- **4.1** Data literacy

5 **Digital competence**
- **5.2** Technology use

OVERVIEW

A project by definition is a temporary venture with a beginning and an end. Projects are ideal for finding ways to capitalise on core capabilities, create a product or service, develop strategic alliances, increase productivity, reduce costs, refine supply chains, tackle unexpected problems, manage risks and take advantage of emerging opportunities. Every industry sector and every type of organisation has people working on projects that vary in duration and range from small and straightforward to large and complex.

Projects can involve a single department or work group or span an entire organisation, gathering expertise from far-flung divisions. Some projects might even involve two or more organisations working together to produce a joint product or service or develop an integrated value chain. However, what they have in common is delivering something that adds value to an organisation and usually to its customers and other stakeholders, and they must do this within identified constraints, particularly cost and time.

Many factors are involved in a successful project: a good project manager, effective project management tools, efficient work practices, experience, good teamwork and hard work, to name a few. In this chapter, you will find out how to manage a project to a successful outcome. Before you take on the task of leading and managing a project, you should also read Chapter 14. You might also want to keep a list of technical terms and definitions – those in bold or italics – related to project management.

SNAPSHOT

A project is born

Macy and Rosa are sipping a glass of pre-dinner wine as they discuss this afternoon's talk by Zheng Fang, from China's Sichuan University, and Michelle Andrews, from Temple University in the US. Both speakers presented at the conference on sensor networks the women are attending – finding out how they're going to change the way we shop, talk, work and have fun.

Wireless sensor networks, or WSNs to those in the know, are popping up all over Australia, making gathering all sorts of data cheaper and easier. The sensors, which can be as big as a shoebox or as small as a grain of dust, send information to a central location for analysis. They're a boon for traffic managers, farmers, fire fighters and other emergency services, and for businesses like shops, theatres and restaurants.

This afternoon's speakers told the audience about their research that combined GPS triangulation with WSN technology to alert customers to special offers. Just as airlines and hotels adjust pricing to fill seats and beds, retailers can use a similar approach to offer customers special deals. A Chinese study examined the best timeframes for offering promotions – come and buy today, tomorrow or in two days. Their research found that immediate offers work best for people within 200 metres of a business, increasing the odds of a purchase by 76 per cent compared to offers with a two-day delay. For customers 500 metres to two kilometres away, promotions for the next day worked best. Two-day delays were the least effective, no matter where customers were.[1]

'If we could find the best timeframes for offers here in Australia, imagine how powerful our direct marketing could be! We'd have an edge on our competitors and give our clients real value.' Macy runs through her mental project checklist. Related to an important business issue? Tick. Easily identified start and end points? Tick. Clear and measurable result? Tick. Realistically deliverable? Tick.

'I reckon, Rosa, we've got the makings of a project here. Let's investigate and if it's as promising as I think it is, I'll sponsor you to lead a project putting this technology to use. What do you say?'

21.1 Planning your project

Transferable skills
1.5 Operations management
2.1 Critical thinking
2.3 Business strategy
3.4 Leadership

Delivering a project isn't difficult. What's difficult is delivering a project without first taking the time to plan properly.

James Leal (author, project manager and CEO), 2014, http://projecttemplates.net/blog.

Someone recognises a need to improve a process, such as invoicing, developing people, improving patient care in hospitals, or receiving and registering guests. When considering the short-, medium- and long-term horizons, it is best to have options against each of them to redesign a **function**. Redesigning functions of a business could involve supply chains or improvement or redesign of logistics, such as storage or distribution. Perhaps a new business strategy is needed, or someone needs to guide and oversee a rescue operation. Alternatively, perhaps an organisation decides to develop new products or services, enhance its existing products or services, upgrade or overhaul its cyber-security infrastructure or software, or upgrade its assets (e.g. equipment, plant, premises or vehicles). Out of these a project is born.

The **project sponsor** or 'owner' writes up a proposal for approval (sometimes called the project initiation document) that answers the what, when, where, who, why and how questions. Once approved by the project's key stakeholders, this document becomes the project charter (sometimes called a project mandate) and acts as the project's terms of reference. Organisations that run projects often have templates for these and other documents, sometimes as part of a project software suite. Figure 21.1 shows a project life cycle from beginning to end.

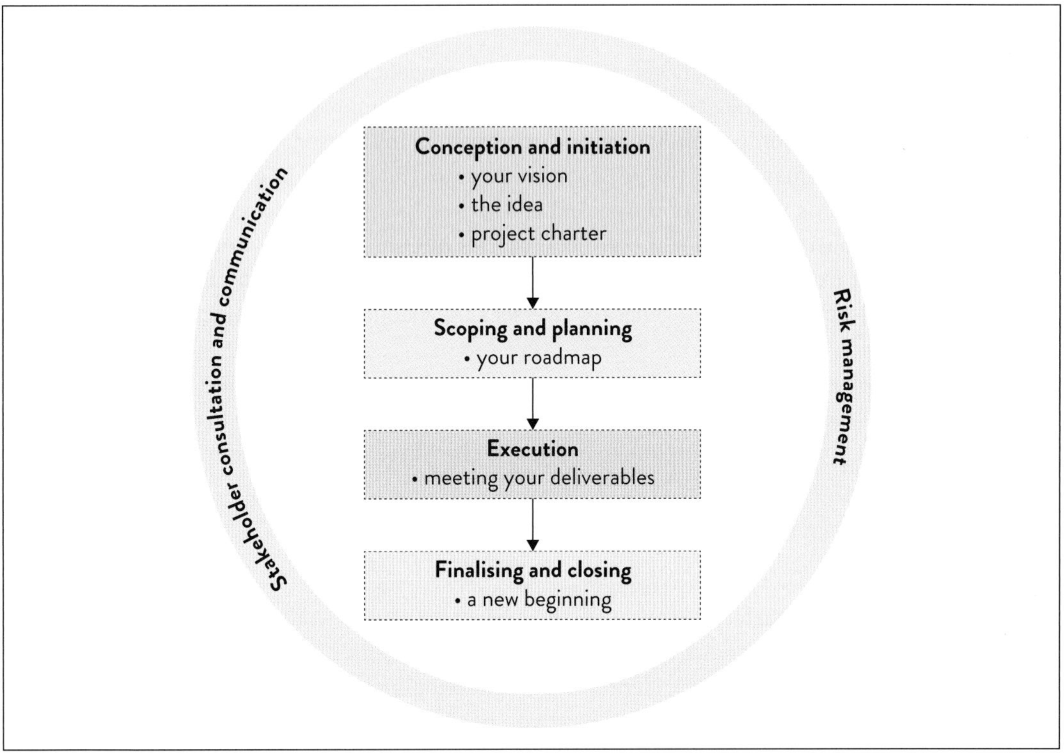

FIGURE 21.1 A project life cycle

The project charter

The project charter acknowledges the existence of a project and acts as the project's vision. It is the 'strategic overview' of the project and defines its boundaries – what it will and will not achieve – and the **project manager's** responsibilities: the person who guides the project through to its finalisation. The project charter generally outlines the following information:

- project title
- overall purpose and goals of the project
- background of the project, or what suggested the need for it
- who will use the results of the project (its customers or clients) and other interested parties or stakeholders
- the project's main deliverables, including a summary of the anticipated schedule, or main phases, of the project
- success criteria, including cost, time, quality and other critical factors, to guide decision-making
- business case, or justification for the project, explaining how the organisation benefits and how the project fits into the organisation's strategic plan
- approval requirements: an estimate of the financial and other resources needed and the person responsible for authorising cost and resource use
- main constraints within which the project must operate
- the project's major dependencies that affect the project during its life and interdependencies that exist after the project's implementation
- how the project relates to past or concurrent projects in the organisation
- associated documents and other useful information
- prospective project manager.

In the beginning ...

The project sponsor and project manager are mutually dependent roles. Except in small organisations and with relatively minor projects that do not require board approval, they are usually different people. The project sponsor, generally a senior executive, is the person who identifies and defines the project. The project manager is the person who executes the project or guides it to completion.

As well as conceiving the need for the project and setting its broad aims and outcomes, the project sponsor builds the business case for the project, carries out an initial **risk analysis** at a corporate level, seeks support from key players, establishes the funding and resources needed, appoints and supervises the project manager, and generally oversees the viability of the project, particularly from a financial viewpoint.

Should it become clear that the project cannot fulfil its purpose and meet the business case originally put forward, the project sponsor also cancels the project. (Better to end it quickly and kindly and put the effort, money and time to better use elsewhere. As explained in Chapter 26, do not keep throwing money at a lost cause.)

Find your feet

Once the project and its charter are approved, the project manager's work – your work – begins. It is primarily mental and iterative work at this stage – scoping or defining what the project will achieve and will not achieve (its deliverables), identifying and developing broad strategies for managing risks and stakeholders, and working out the resources you need. Develop an overall plan and schedule for what needs to be done to achieve the project's deliverables, and think about how best to monitor the project as it unfolds. Work closely with the project sponsor – in effect, your boss – in these initial stages of the project to ensure you are in harmony and that the project's outcomes align with the business strategy.

Commence the project process by reviewing relevant information (e.g. organisational documents, such as organisational hierarchy charts, previous project reports), establishing initial meetings with key stakeholders as defined in the project charter, and developing the project's initial timelines.

Transferable skills
2.1 Critical thinking

List constraints and assumptions

Constraints are the restrictions and resource limitations that a project has. Consider them to be unalterable 'givens' to complete the project. Adopting creative thinking approaches will lead to new and innovative ways to achieve the desired project outcomes. The project constraints are the operating guidelines you must work within or the limits of what can be done. To identify them, consider:

- deliverables (scope)
- resource limitations and resources available (including equipment, facilities, financial, funding and people)
- timeframes.

Be specific because you need to know what you're up against exactly. When you identify a constraint, note its source. Now compile a list of assumptions (factors taken to be true but that could change later) regarding cost, quality requirements, and risk, time and other factors that underlie the project. Assumptions usually include words like 'depends on' and 'relies on' and are not within your control (but could be within someone else's).

Check out your assumptions

Once upon a time, a project to create a yabby farm was proposed. A key assumption was the ability to sell yabbies into Europe at $25 a kilo. But when that assumption was investigated further, it turned out $25 a kilo was the price for 100 kilo lots, delivered weekly. Alas, the project was not feasible.

Always check out the project's assumptions carefully, particularly cost and quality, to prevent wasted time, effort and money. Otherwise, your project might become a 'thought bubble, unencumbered by any reality check'.[2]

Scope your project

Transferable skills

1.1 Financial literacy

1.4 Business operations

1.5 Operations management

2.1 Critical thinking

2.3 Business strategy

The project scope develops the information contained in the project charter. It describes the boundaries or parameters of the project. It establishes the work in terms of deliverables and SMART measures of success. It answers the what, when, where, who, why and how questions addressed in the project charter in more detail. Failing to scope a project entirely is one of the leading causes of unsuccessful projects. Think of the scope as a box, like the one shown in Figure 21.2, where what's inside the box is what the project will deliver; everything outside the box is not part of the project.

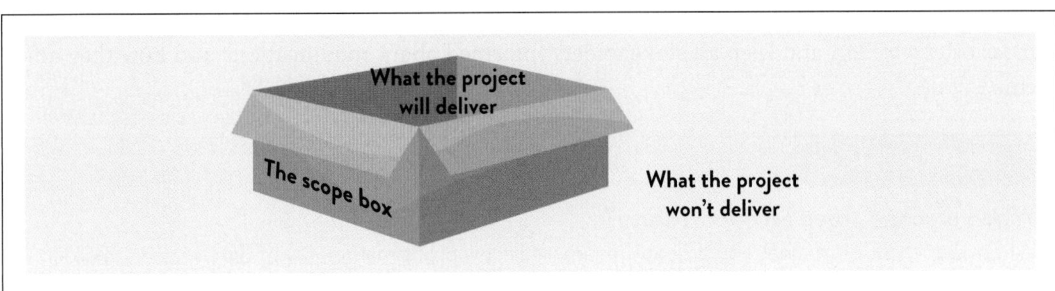

FIGURE 21.2 The scope box

Begin by writing a clear scope statement in 25 words or less along the lines of: 'This project will deliver this result by this time to ... (a clear business benefit).' A clear statement serves as your project purpose or vision statement. Next, list your deliverables (the product, service or results) and their SMART goals and measures of success (MoS). These define the success criteria or the conditions that must be met for the deliverables to be approved. Deliverables are the beginnings of your roadmap of milestones for your project schedule or timetable. Make these deliverables and success measures very clear because you don't want people wondering whether your project met its goals.

You might also want to generate a list of what is in scope or out of scope for each deliverable. The 'in scope' describes what your project will provide and the 'out of scope' states the exclusions – what it won't accomplish. (The more detailed project plan, which you begin to draft next, details how you'll deliver what's inside the scope box.) Your scope should also include:

- cost
- main risks
- people and other resources needed
- quality requirements
- stakeholder needs and communication arrangements.

This scope does two things:

1 helps you and your team stay focused on the task
2 provides guidelines for making decisions about any change requests during the project, helping to prevent 'scope creep'.

Review your scope document with the project sponsor and, when agreed, have it formally signed off. Consider this document as your contract. It spells out what the project's committed to achieve, by when and with what resources. You will present this project scope to your team members and stakeholders once you've drafted your project plan.

Transferable skills

1.5 Operations management

2.1 Critical thinking

Prevent scope creep

Knowing what's 'inside' the scope box and having clear deliverables and success measures helps prevent the project manager's perennial nightmare – scope creep. This is the tendency for deliverables to increase (or occasionally decrease) beyond initial expectations during the life of a project. Causes of project creep can include client or stakeholders requesting a change, or a team member identifying potential options. Including these changes without analysing the impact can put you over time and over budget.

Keep reinforcing your ultra-clear deliverables and success measures formally and informally. Explain that even minor adjustments to the scope mean that the project will take longer and/or cost more. Provide firm estimates of the additional cost or time a change to the scope would necessitate. If altering any of the deliverables, clear them with the project sponsor, add them to a *scope change register* or *change log*, and keep all stakeholders informed about modifications and how they affect them.

IN PRACTICE

When is scope creep an opportunity?

When your client is external, you probably estimated a low profit margin, say of 30 per cent, in order to win the job. This is when client-driven variations to the scope are an opportunity. You can cost the variation at say, 50 per cent profit, thereby increasing your overall profit margin.

Transferable skills

2.1 Entrepreneurship/ small business skills

Build a stakeholder register

Stakeholder and management engagement is an integral part of projects and begins with the stakeholder register. Stakeholders are people or groups with a vested interest in the project's success or (sadly) its failure. (See Chapter 8 to find out more about navigating organisational politics.) They include individuals or groups with a perceived direct or indirect interest in the project, directly or indirectly affected by the project's outcomes or its various phases or influence the project. The larger the project and the more it crosses organisational functions or operational areas, the more stakeholders you have. Think of your project's stakeholders like your customers.

Based on the project charter and discussions with your project sponsor, identify and list your project's stakeholders. Begin with the project sponsor, the project's clients (the people who will use the project's results), and the people with the specialist or organisational knowledge you need. List the people who control assets or resources you need, can advocate for the project, might oppose your project, and your organisation's management. Add any funding bodies, work teams, the general public and managers of part-time team members interested in the project. Identify the stakeholders methodically and logically so you don't miss anyone.

You can group stakeholders into the following:

- *Drivers*: who will use your project's results or who stand to benefit from your project.
- *Supporters*: who can help your project succeed.
- *Opposers:* who believe the project is detrimental to their interests.
- *Observers:* who are other interested people who may have a positive or negative influence on the project and its deliverables.

The *stakeholder register* tells you who to consider and who to consult with and how. When a stakeholder is an external body or group or a large group or department in your organisation, identify the person to communicate with and enter their details.

When appropriate, meet with stakeholders formally or informally to get a feel for what is important to them, what problems the project could help them overcome, how a successful project will affect them and so on. Use the feedback of the most powerful stakeholders to shape your project in its early stages; this makes their continuing support more likely (and can also improve your project planning). Work towards developing a matrix like the one shown in Figure 21.3.

Name	Contact details	Reasons for support/ opposition	Must haves	Desirables	Strongly against	Moderately against	Neutral	Moderately supportive	Strongly supportive	Likely influence – high	Medium	Low	Resources available or potentially available	Preferred mode of communication	Preferred frequency of communication	Last communication date	By (name of team member)

FIGURE 21.3 Stakeholder analysis

Transferable skills
2.1 Critical thinking

Analyse stakeholders

When you understand the 'stakes' of each stakeholder, you can determine the best way to work with them towards a successful project outcome. 'Stakes' might include the usefulness of your project's deliverables to them as well as their psychological stakes, such as power or prestige.

The stakeholder register is the basis for your *stakeholder analysis* (see Figure 21.3). You will probably complete both with your team soon after it forms, working out stakeholders' interests, whether they're supporters or opposers, and the strength and power of their support or opposition. Analyse stakeholders in as much detail as you can so you know what they need and expect from the project, the resources they can provide, and how and how often they want to hear from you about the project's status.

You can distribute the stakeholder register, but keep your analysis separate. You and your team are going to use it to develop a strategy to build effective working relationships with stakeholders (discussed in Chapter 8), manage their changing expectations, maintain their support and win over any stakeholders opposed to your team's work (discussed in Chapter 7).

Develop a stakeholder management strategy

Guided by the stakeholder analysis, begin developing a strategy to manage stakeholders early in the project life cycle. Aim to maintain or increase support from people in favour of the project, win over those opposed, manage their concerns and mitigate the risks they pose to the project. Use the guidelines shown in Figure 21.4 to prioritise stakeholders and plan any communication with them. Keep high-power/low-interest people happy, manage high-power/high-interest people closely, monitor low-power/low-interest people and keep high-interest/low-power people informed.

As part of scope management and stakeholder management, ask the various stakeholders to sign off on milestones (i.e. significant events in the schedule/plan) as they are completed to ensure the project meets everyone's needs. This two-way communication can be critical to the ultimate success of the project.

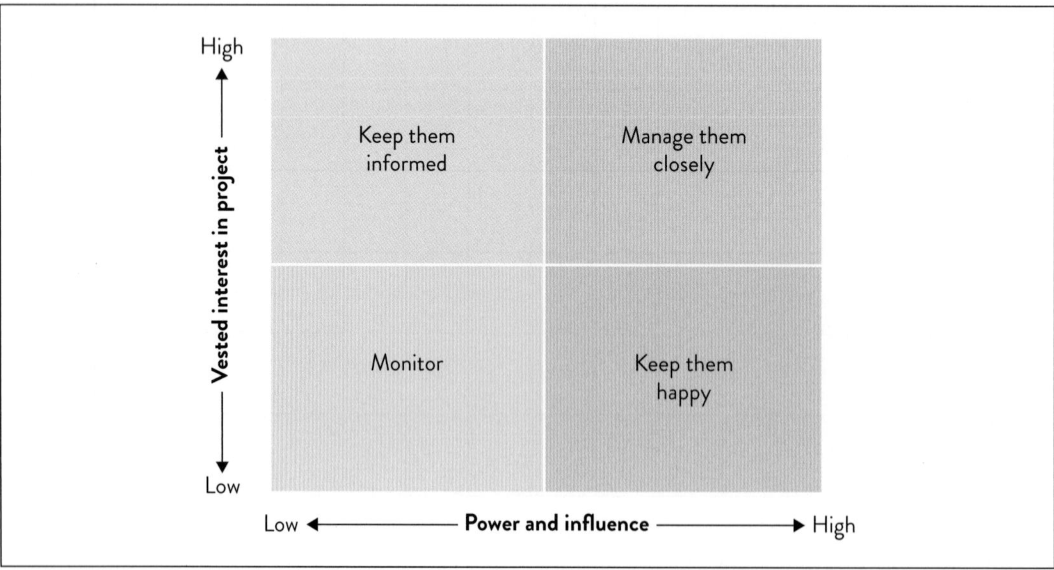

FIGURE 21.4 Managing your stakeholders

Develop a communication plan

Based on the stakeholder analysis, prepare a communication plan showing when, what, how and to whom to provide project updates and to help monitor the effectiveness of these updates. The goal is to communicate with stakeholders in an organised way, involving them as frequently as needed and providing the information they need in ways that suit them.

Schedule review meetings with key stakeholders or stakeholder representatives to keep them up to date. The frequency of these meetings depends on the nature and complexity of the project and how it affects stakeholders. Some stakeholders may only require one-page status reports at agreed intervals.

Stakeholder engagement

Transferable skills

1.2 Entrepreneurship/small business skills
2.1 Critical thinking
2.2 Personal effectiveness
2.3 Business strategy
3.1 Teamwork/relationships
3.2 Verbal communication
3.3 Written communication
3.4 Leadership

Extensive stakeholder communication and engagement is required for complex and sensitive projects, such as those that affect a local community, including building a library, developing land for commercial or residential use, improving a road, logging a forest or opening a mine. In this case, plan the engagement steps, summarised below, well in advance. These steps are often an iterative process; that is, revising upcoming steps in light of the new information and consulting and updating stakeholders. Large organisations often have protocols to follow, such as consulting with an internal corporate communications department, public relations department or similar while developing the stakeholder communication plan. Naturally, avoid creating unrealistic expectations about project timing and scope. Stakeholder engagement is an integral part of large government projects – so important, in fact, that communication specialists often develop and manage the communication plans.

Engaging with stakeholders assists in making decisions that better reflect community needs and widens the range of available expertise, knowledge and ideas. It helps identify and explore concerns while plans are being developed, helping to strengthen project plans, address concerns and provide a sense of ownership to the solutions developed.

Government guidelines for consulting with stakeholders ensure that the consultation and decision-making processes are transparent, logical and able to be understood by the stakeholders; give stakeholders a fair opportunity to express their views and concerns; resolve conflicting requirements constructively. These steps are good guidelines for any project:

1. *Identify stakeholders and the purpose of engaging them:* when stakeholders cannot influence the decision-making process, there is no point in seeking their opinion. The purpose is to keep them informed. When consultation seeks help to resolve a problem, the aim is to gather ideas and viewpoints.
2. *Determine the general approach to consultation:* the purpose of the consultation influences this. Creating awareness is different from inviting stakeholders to participate in the final decision. To determine the general approach, think about:
    a. *Degree of sensitivity of the project or its potential impact on a stakeholder or stakeholder group:* the higher the degree of sensitivity or impact, the more comprehensive consultation needs to be, which affects timelines and budget. The higher the degree of sensitivity, the more subject to scrutiny the project is likely to be, so think through the consultation approach carefully and plan it methodically.
    b. *Nature of feedback sought:* do stakeholders have an opportunity to affect the outcome significantly, or is consultation limited to comment about details?
    c. *Degree of technical difficulty:* highly technical projects may limit the number of feasible alternatives and may make communicating the issues more difficult.

3 *Identify who, how and how often to consult:* there are a variety of options including print media, community events such as open days, face-to-face and virtual meetings, media releases, public presentations, and social media and websites. High-impact, complex projects often have a community relations committee or advisory group liaison committee to plan and execute stakeholder engagement.
4 *Develop a communication plan:* set out in detail the steps described above; that is, who the stakeholders are, the proposed methods of consultation for each, the resources to be used (e.g. marketing or PR companies), a schedule and the estimated costs.
5 *Obtain resources and implement the plan:* the plan may call for engaging specialist contractors or consultants or using in-house experts, depending on the nature and level of the project.
6 *Analyse stakeholder feedback:* feed it into the decision-making process for consideration with other information and constraints. Always record statements and promises made by the project team to stakeholders and file these scrupulously. (Stakeholders may be sure a promise has been made regarding, for example, landscaping or noise levels, requiring a check of records to determine what was actually agreed to.)
7 *Follow up as necessary:* ensure that decisions about the project are readily available to stakeholders.

The motivation to keep doing well comes from the positive reinforcement of achieving your goals, not continually failing to achieve them – that's negative reinforcement, which dulls your desire. A series of achievable, realistic goals that develop into milestones provide the frequent positive reinforcement that comes with achievement and builds motivation.

Transferable skills

1.5 Operations management

Map the milestones and draft a schedule

Next is charting a path of reaching each deliverable as a series of milestones that the project team needs to complete. Begin by drafting a schedule, or timeframe, for reaching those milestones. Once the project team is in place, further project mapping is done by adding the tasks and subtasks needed to reach each milestone and adjusting and firming up the draft schedule.

First, list the deliverables. Then begin asking a series of questions to drill down to ever-greater detail about what tasks need to be done to achieve each deliverable, as shown in **Figure 21.5**. What do we need to do, or what needs to happen, to achieve or produce this deliverable? (Drill down as far as you need to but not to the end, as the team members responsible will finish it off.)

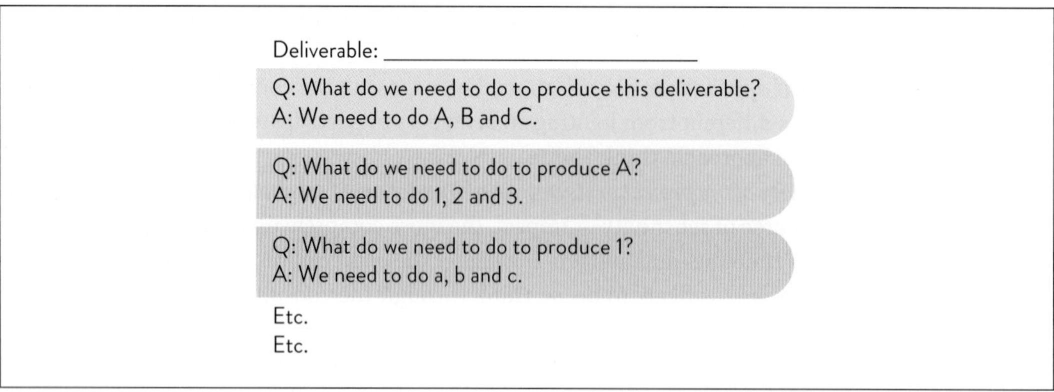

FIGURE 21.5 Mapping your deliverables

Once the milestones are broken down into tasks, a diagram can show what needs to be done. This provides a visual map of the project based on the deliverables, similar to the map shown in Figure 21.6. This project map is sometimes called a work breakdown structure (WBS). The WBS is not set in concrete but is open for continual revision to meet deliverables and timelines and gather more information. Keep the project's assumptions, constraints, deliverables and purpose in mind while mapping the project.

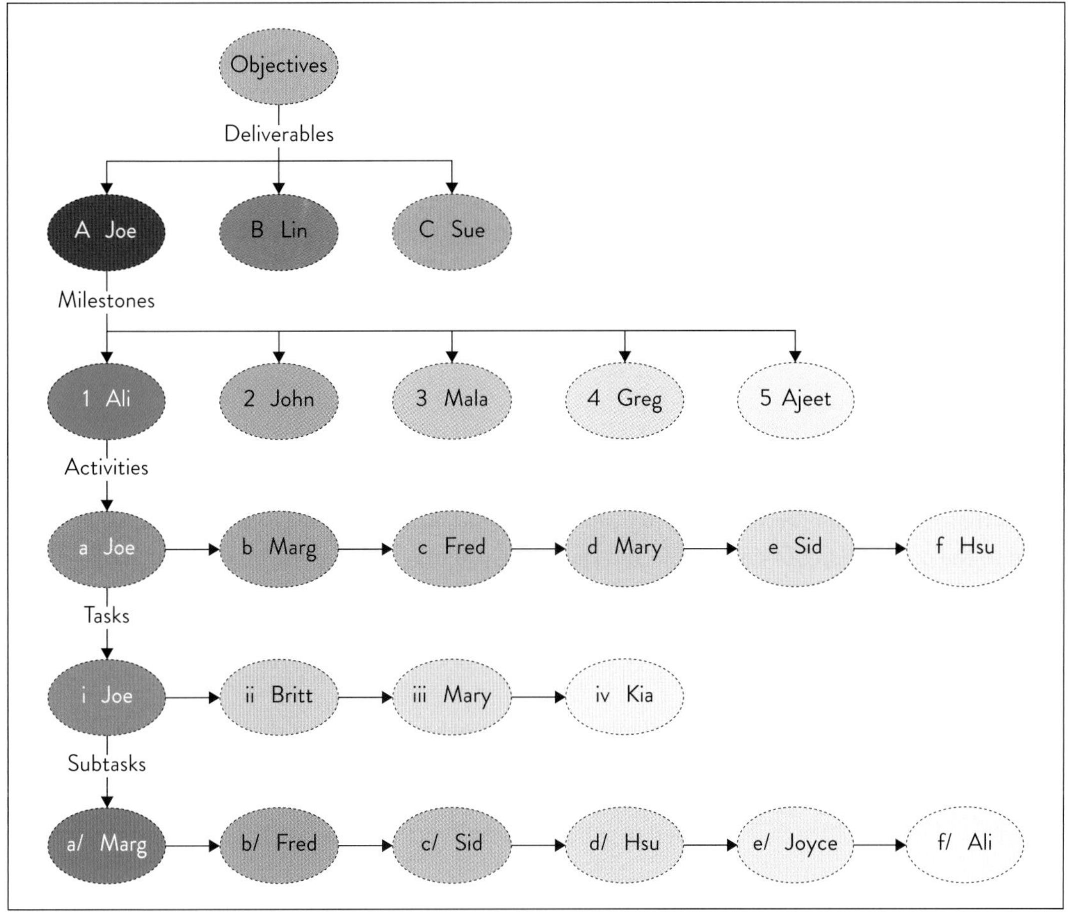

FIGURE 21.6 Your project map, or work breakdown structure

A project will not be successful without a clear WBS because when the project is in uncharted territory (which projects are by their very nature), you are lost without a good roadmap. A WBS can show how all the elements are logically connected and spot any unnecessary or duplicated activities and any omitted critical activities.

Keep the most important stakeholders informed of the development progress of the project plan and build in their ideas when possible so they feel more 'ownership' of the project.

Your planning and management tools

Transferable skills

1.5 Operations management

5.2 Technology use

You can use a range of planning tools to break your project down into manageable chunks and schedule them. Brainstorming, cause-and-effect (or fishbone) diagrams and gap analyses are good ways to begin structuring your project. You can use flow charts for less complex projects, but for more complex projects, Gantt charts and network diagrams and WBS show more detail, and are useful for scheduling and setting timelines and identifying and sequencing parallel and interdependent activities. Flow charts, Gantt charts and network diagrams are also good monitoring and reporting tools, and Chapter 27 explains a number of ways to monitor using statistics, including bar charts, control charts, histograms, Pareto charts, process capability charts, run charts and stratification charts. Financial planning and control mechanisms and administration controls are discussed in Chapter 17.

You can also use specialised software to estimate, plan, schedule, manage budgets, allocate resources, help make decisions, monitor quality and document progress. At the simple end of the spectrum, word processors and spreadsheets can create templates that you can use to plan, track and record expenditure. At the other end of the spectrum are dedicated project management tools to guide your project planning, management and closure, matching tasks and resources, scheduling tasks into a project timeline, tracking timesheets and expenses against timelines and so on. They also form the basis for reporting your project's progress.

Most project planning and management software tools are Cloud-based with various free or subscription-based options. Microsoft Project is both a desktop and Cloud-based service, with a range of other companies that provide different functionality, depending on the project's requirements. Asana, Monday.com, Basecamp, Atlassian's JIRA and Trello, Smartsheet and Wrike all offer varying planning and reporting tools and can be integrated into collaboration services such as Microsoft Teams and Slack.

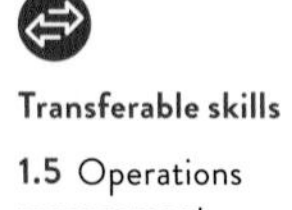

Transferable skills
1.5 Operations management

Milestones

Milestones mark the completion of a major stage or phase of a project. They are important control points that are easy for everyone to recognise. They should be in a clear sequence of events that slowly build to the completion of a deliverable and the whole project. A milestone in a project should occur roughly every two weeks for a project over several months in duration. Regular milestones prevent a loss of momentum and progress; too many milestones and they lose their lustre. When the team comes on board, review them to identify whom they affect and amend the stakeholder register as necessary.

Each milestone needs to be 'owned' by a team member or a subteam that appoints a task owner from its ranks – this task owner is ultimately responsible for the subteam achieving its goals. The team member or subteam breaks down each milestone into tasks, each with a start and end date; in subteams, these tasks are then assigned to subteam members.(See Chapter 13 to find out more about developing team performance plans.)

Give each milestone and task an identification number for long or complex projects. As a rule of thumb, tasks have a maximum duration of five to 10 days or 40 to 80 hours, but this depends on whether the team is full-time or part-time. Make milestones prominent in the project map and track them with a schedule, as discussed in the following section. If a milestone is missed, address it immediately and double-check that it has been allocated enough resources.

PMBOK and Prince2

Two most common project management tools are PMBOK and Prince2, PMBOK stands for Project Management Body of Knowledge and provides a generic approach you can use in a variety of projects and industries. Prince2 – PRojects IN Controlled Environments (version 2) – was developed by the British Government and is now widely used as a project management tool that guides you through managing a project. Both of these tools are complementary to one another – PMBOK is knowledge-based and Prince2 is a methodology-based program.

Timelines and schedules

Transferable skills

1.5 Operations management

Timelines allow the team to draft a schedule for the project map to provide a helpful overview. A visual schedule such as a Gantt chart, a calendar or project tracking software that depicts the flow of activities and tasks shows their timelines and how they relate. (For straightforward projects, add start and finish dates to each milestone chain.) A schedule shows what needs to be done and when, which helps with resource allocation, budget, quality assurance, managing risks and monitoring the project as it rolls out.

The team members and subteams can develop a detailed schedule, adding their start and finish times to the tasks and subtasks they are responsible for. For complex projects, subteams can also create network diagrams for their activity chains or use project management software to show the milestone's schedule.

When the project team have broken down the milestones into small enough chunks, estimating how long tasks will take is relatively easy. For complex and lengthy projects, it can be done with three estimates: an optimistic estimate (O), a pessimistic estimate (P) and a most likely estimate (M) and use the formula: O + 3M + P to arrive at a final estimate. (Keep a record of your initial three estimates for each task to work out a best-case and worst-case end date for your project.)

INDUSTRY INSIGHTS

Pull the plug when you need to (or fix your timelines)

Not pulling the plug nearly broke Atari, the once-premium maker of classic games, and caused the near collapse of the multi-million dollar US video game industry. In 1983, in a landfill in New Mexico, the company buried thousands, maybe millions, of what has been called one of the worst video games ever: *E.T.*

It seems the company tried to rush the project to cash in on the blockbuster film of the same name and the result was so bad they literally had to bury it. Having spent a rumoured US$20–25 million for the exclusive world rights, they gave the developer five weeks to design it – the same developer who spent over seven months developing *Yars' Revenge* and six months developing *Raiders of the Lost Ark*![3]

Estimate the resources required

Although the project charter may have begun to list the resources available, a review of the project's resources is required. Think about the project's needs regarding equipment, financing, information, office space, supplies and other consumable items, and people. What technology and project management tools are available or could be obtained?

Refer to past projects or discuss potential needs with people who have worked on similar projects. By definition, bearing in mind that projects are unique, look for information about the type and quantity of resources used, and how long tasks take, because these are linked. The number and quality of resources assigned to a task can influence how long the task takes. (Five people can paint a house quicker than two people, and quicker still with high-quality equipment.)

Identify any assumptions made about team members' skill sets and other resources; for example, office space. Figure 21.7 illustrates a way to work out the people and other resources the project needs. Estimating resource requirements is inherently uncertain. If unsure or inexperienced, have someone experienced in this area review the estimates. Depending on the nature of the project, team members can review and help revise the resource estimates. (See 'The estimating and forecasting trap' in Chapter 26.)

Work breakdown sheet	Task	Resources needed	Dates needed	Time (days/weeks)	Estimated costs	Actual cost

FIGURE 21.7 Resources requirements matrix

The time needed to reach a milestone or produce deliverables often depends on the available resources. Sometimes doubling the resources halves the time it takes. And sometimes it doesn't. Adding more resources to creative or knowledge work, for example, sometimes doesn't produce the deliverable more quickly.

People's skills and experience also affect the time it takes to produce deliverables. Generally, the more experienced and skilled team members are, the faster they can produce the deliverables. Team-building skills are highly valuable in helping the team work well together, which can affect how long it takes to reach deliverables. High-performing teams have **synergy** and their work flows smoothly.

Transferable skills

1.1 Financial literacy

Refine the project budget

Next, refine the budget in the project scope. Use the format that other projects in the organisation have used or that the finance department may recommend. It could be as simple as a spreadsheet or part of the project planning software.

Figure 21.7 and **Figure 21.10** (later in the chapter) can form the basis of the project budget. Be sure to include other expenses, such as project finalisation expenses, and perhaps an extra amount for contingencies. Review the budgets for similar projects and ask other project managers to get a sense of what funding the project needs.

Transferable skills

1.4 Business operations

2.1 Critical thinking

Build a risk register

Work through the project map and brainstorm the risks the project faces as it progresses. Deal with any issue that can affect the project's success – for good or ill – as a risk. A force-field analysis can also help you identify risks and opportunities. List the risks in a **risk register**, or *risk log*, to track and manage the project's risks throughout the entire project. Later, review and adjust the risk register with the team before analysing the risks and developing risk management plans that detail the best way to respond to each. Think about involving key stakeholders in identifying risks, too.

Risks may come from a variety of areas, including:

- *Deliverables:* what if deliverables fail to meet their success measures?
- *Environmental impacts and issues:* what if the project harms the environment or breaches the organisation's sustainability protocols?

- *External suppliers:* what if they don't deliver on time, go out of business or don't manage their own risks properly?
- *Finances:* what if your budget blows out due to unforeseen circumstances?
- *Organisational:* what if the promised support isn't delivered?
- *Safety:* what if a team member is physically or psychologically injured in the course of their work?
- *Security:* what if confidential information is inadvertently disclosed?
- *Stakeholder relations:* what if these deteriorate or are managed poorly? What if you lose the support of your supporters and some even join the ranks of the opposers?
- *Team members:* what if you can't bring the right people on board or bring them on board soon enough? What if a key member leaves? What if a team member consistently fails to meet deadlines?
- *Technical:* what if you can't get the right equipment soon enough or it costs more than you estimated?
- *Timeliness:* what if activities along a critical path are delayed, delaying an entire deliverable?

Figure 21.8 summarises the risk management process, which is explained in detail in Chapter 22.

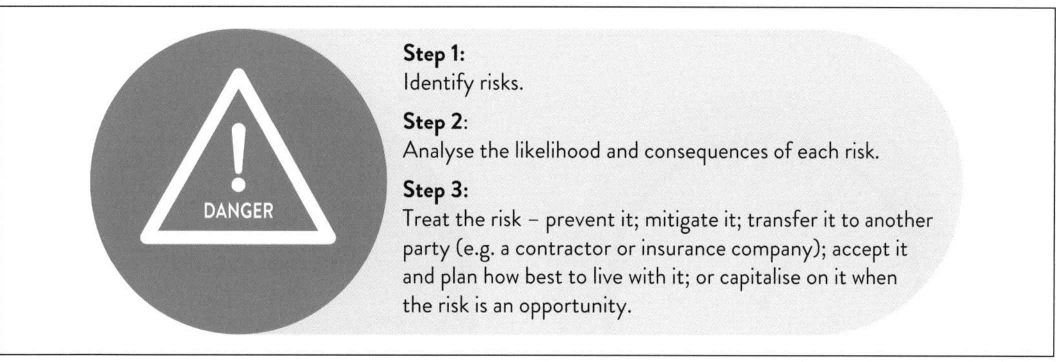

FIGURE 21.8 Identifying and managing risks

Assess the risks

Rate the risks and identify on a scale from 1 to 5 how *likely* a risk is to occur – 1 is very unlikely and 5 is very likely. Then rate their *impact* from 1 to 5 – 1 indicates little or no effect on the project and 5 indicates a catastrophic effect. Prioritise the risks by multiplying each risk's likelihood by its impact and pay the most attention to the risks with the highest number.

As the project progresses, the project team will identify additional risks, and some risks might disappear. Update the risk register as necessary and present it in any project status reports to the project sponsor and other stakeholders. Review the risk log regularly throughout the project and stay alert to early warning signs that risk is looming and action as required. Highlight identified risks on the WBS and timeline map to pay special attention to that activity.

Select your project management software

Transferable skills
5.2 Technology use

Selecting the right software is important; using a sledgehammer to crack a walnut only bogs projects down with red tape. Technology is there to help, not overwhelm, and the right computer-based tools can ease life of a project manager. The graphs, charts and templates created with them help plan, organise and schedule the project; estimate resource requirements; allocate resources; identify problems and risks; and build a dashboard to monitor progress, health and safety, and resource use. The tools that best suit the project depend on its complexity, duration and nature, and the number and location of team members. (See Chapter 14 for more information on using technology in teams.)

Transferable skills
1.5 Operations management
2.1 Critical thinking
4.1 Data literacy

Create a dashboard

In the early stages of the project, create a dashboard of indicators that shows whether the project is on track and highlights areas that need attention. (A variety of software is available to help you create the perfect dashboard.) A good dashboard lets everyone in the project team and stakeholders monitor the project's progress 'at a glance' by consolidating, arranging and summarising key performance measures in visual representations. A dashboard is also the basis for progress reports and highlighting any risks, success measures and tasks that need attention.

Dashboards show actual against planned achievements. They typically include visual indicators, such as those shown in Figure 21.9, for various key performance indicators, such as milestones started and completed against planned timelines, and progress towards the next milestone for each subsection of the project. It can indicate the workload of each team member, performance to resource budgets (e.g. hours worked, money spent) and the current state of risks that could hinder or enhance performance.

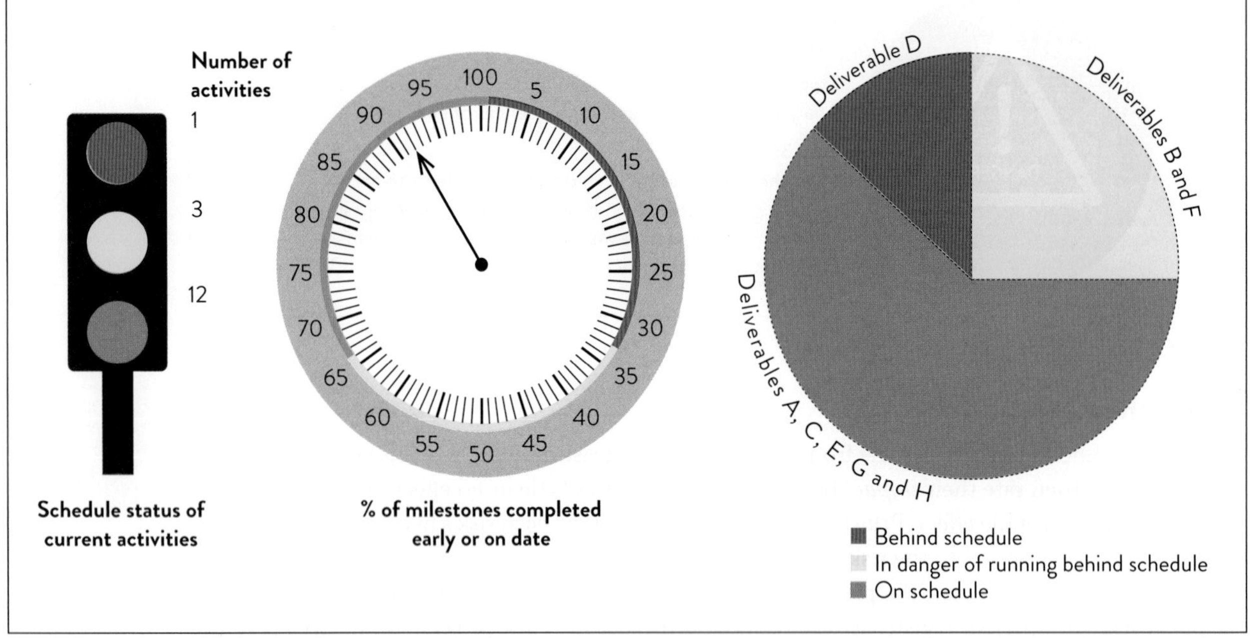

FIGURE 21.9 Dashboard indicators

Involve the team and key stakeholders in finalising the categories, indicators and their display formats. First, decide the categories to monitor. Then select the indicators, or measures of success, for each category. Finally, choose a format for each indicator, such as traffic lights (green is going according to plan, yellow for one or more problems, red for serious situations needing attention). Keep the dashboard front and centre in the team members' minds by posting it in the project workspace (as described in Chapter 14).

Write up your project plan

Transferable skills

3.3 Written communication

The team will spot things missed in each of the above areas, and together everyone will add further levels of detail and continually adjust and fine-tune the roadmap once the project gets underway. Meanwhile, write up the project plan for the project sponsor's and stakeholders' comments and endorsement. Once the necessary approvals and commitments are received, begin to obtain the management tools and operational resources needed and gather the team, confident that the project has the support it needs.

21.2 Leading your project

Transferable skills

1.5 Operations management

3.4 Leadership

How does a project get to be a year late? One day at a time.

Frederick Brooks (computer scientist who developed IBM's System/360 computers), *The mythical man month: Essays on software engineering*, Addison Wesley, 1995, p. 153.

Once the project plan is approved, finalise the stakeholder and risk registers, and distribute tasks and resources. Then it is a simple matter of managing and monitoring the performance of the team and the risks surrounding the project to ensure the plan stays on track, and then adjusting it as needed. The project plan describes the intention and the WBS visually represents how the project is to roll out; however, the reality might be quite different.

Remember, too, that the P in *project* management is also about *people* management. The project lives and dies by the work done by the project team. The leadership provided by the project manager is to make the project's pathway as smooth as possible by navigating risks, roadblocks and other issues.

Hold a stakeholder alignment meeting

Transferable skills

2.2 Personal effectiveness

2.3 Business strategy

3.1 Teamwork/relationships

3.2 Verbal communication

3.4 Leadership

The first major cause of unsuccessful projects we discussed (above) was failing to scope the project entirely. The second major cause of unsuccessful projects is that the scope and goals are not understood in the same way by all the stakeholders. This can also lead to scope creep (described above). The stakeholder alignment meeting (or project kick-in meeting) aims to prevent scope creep and misunderstandings regarding the project's goals.

The more far-reaching, important and complex the project, the more critical it is to present an overview of the project plan to key stakeholders. This one-off meeting, held early on, ensures everyone is clear about the project's outcomes. It need not be a long meeting, and it is not about the nuts and bolts of the project – it is to ensure that everyone understands the scope and goals of the project and their role in the project's success. Provide an opportunity for stakeholders to air any concerns, although this should all have been covered in advance, in individual stakeholder consultation meetings.

Depending on the project and the organisation's protocols, other team members can participate in the stakeholder alignment meeting or hold a kick-off presentation as a joint meeting of team members and stakeholders. The latter would be the team's introduction to the project. (In addition, frequent interim checks with stakeholders will be part of your communication plan.)

Put your team together

Transferable skills

3.1 Teamwork/relationships

Gathering the right people together and leading them to meet the project's constraints, timelines, quality standards and other requirements takes thought and skill. If done incorrectly, the project is at risk of failing. The team might be virtual or bring people with different expertise from the same worksite together. It might include external contractors and advisers who might bring people in as and when needed. The team might have constantly shifting membership, and members might work full-time on the project or they may remain part of their own work teams and work part-time on the project in addition to their other duties. Whichever it is, think about the knowledge and skills the team members need to meet the deliverables (see **Figure 21.10**) and go for a diversity of experience, expertise and personality styles, including people who are:

- action-oriented
- creative and can come up with ideas for others to take forward
- good at implementing and executing
- nurture the team and the project along
- willing to search for information and investigate options.

Work breakdown sheet	Activity	Skills and knowledge needed	Skill level needed	Name of team member	Deliverable	Days estimated	Schedule		Days actual	Cost estimated	Cost actual
							Start	Finish			
Activity A Task A 1	Develop research study	Market research design: high-tech and WSN	Expert	Joe	Research ready to trial	3	3/7	6/7		$2000	
A 2	Trial research	Conducting research analytics	Expert	Britt	Results, conclusions and recommend-ations	10	8/7	20/7		$6000	
A 3	Conduct research	Conducting research and applying analytics	Intermediate	Mary	Results and conclusions	35	12/8	23/9		$18 500	

FIGURE 21.10 Best fit for the project?

When the project is for a specific user group, include one of their members on the project team, if not as a full member, at least as someone to regularly liaise with and review the progress. This person's insights into the user group's culture, informal working relationships, power structures and working styles helps ensure the end product is perfect for its users' needs.

(See Chapter 28 to find out about determining the attributes, experience and skills you need, Chapter 8 to find out why personality styles are important and Chapter 32 for more on the importance of diversity in teams.)

Transferable skills

3.1 Teamwork/ relationships

3.2 Verbal communication

3.4 Leadership

Kick-start your project team

It isn't every leader-manager that has the opportunity to build a team from scratch and help them move quickly through the full team life cycle, from the storming stage, to the performing stage and, finally, the adjourning stage. However, project managers have that opportunity and need to make the most of it. (See Chapter 13 to find out how to develop a team through predictable stages.)

For a project team in which members can get together in the same location, set up an actual team room supported by the adopted technology. When the team is virtual, set up a virtual team room (as described in Chapter 14) and ask members to familiarise themselves with it before your launch meeting. The launch meeting, or kick-off meeting, generally lasts a half to one day and is the first opportunity to work with the team to gain their buy-in to the project and its objectives. A typical agenda is shown in **Figure 21.11**.

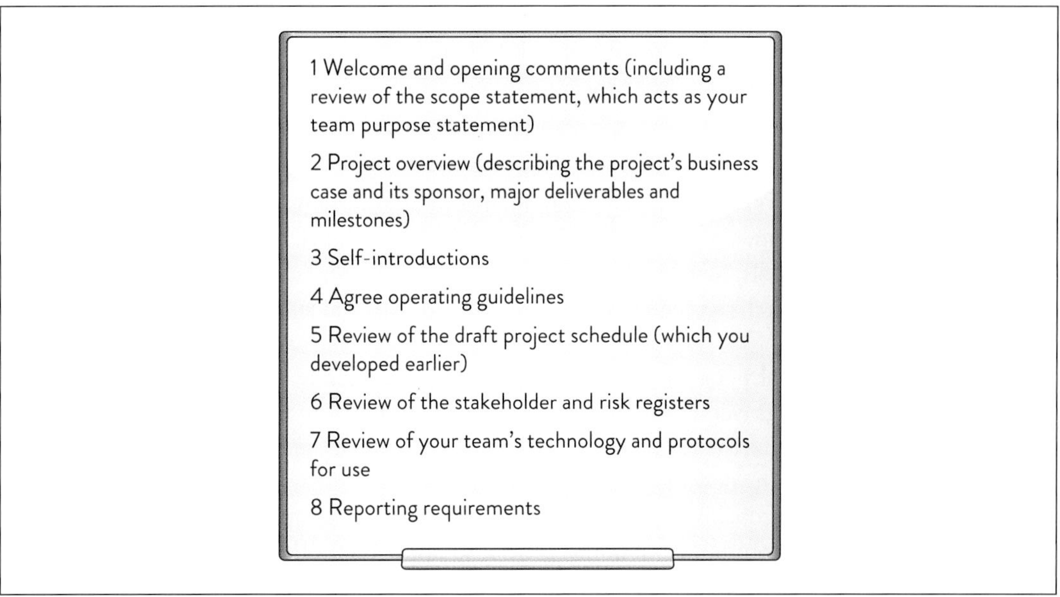

FIGURE 21.11 A team kick-off meeting agenda

Share the agenda for the team's kick-off meeting and any pre-meeting documents required by the team to read (e.g. the project charter, scope and project plan) and advise team members what you want them to cover in their self-introductions to their teammates.

To help make sure people's knowledge is used and the team does not defer to the person with the loudest voice or to the most articulate person, self-introductions should include members' areas of expertise. Ask members to comment on how they believe they can add value to the team, their working style and other projects they have worked on and what they have learnt from them that might help this team.

To help team members find out what they have in common and help people bond and build working relationships, ask people to say a few words about themselves, such as their interests outside work. Figure 21.12 shows why these introductions are so important.

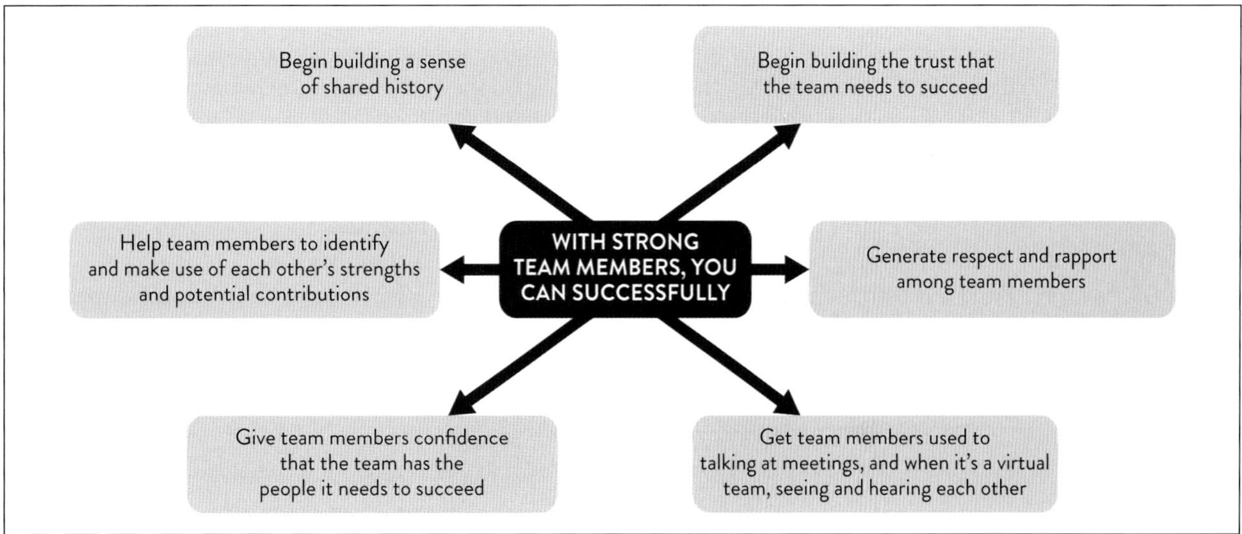

FIGURE 21.12 The importance of introductions

After members have introduced themselves, develop a team operating agreement that describes how the team works together and communicates. It is a big mistake to save time by working out the 'rules of engagement' as the project progresses.

Your team operating agreement

Transferable skills
2.3 Business strategy
3.1 Teamwork/relationships
3.2 Verbal communication
3.3 Written communication

Team operating agreements (TOAs) manage team members' assumptions and behaviours about such matters as confidentiality, how to share information and make decisions, how and when to use which types of communication tools, how quickly to respond to requests and queries, how to air problems and concerns and deal with disagreements and conflict, and where meetings are to be held and who should attend.

TOAs should also cover personal courtesies, such as use of mobile phones or interrupting and overtalking during meetings (see **Figure 25.1** in Chapter 25). These are the operating guidelines for working together and become the team's norms after a while. Update them as the need arises and use this information to orient any new members joining the team.

Although the team is probably expected to start producing results quickly, the time spent laying the groundwork for clear communication and getting to know each other pays off in the long run. However, keep the meeting moving so as not to get too bogged down in the 'getting to know you' part, otherwise you may be left with no time to turn to discussions of the task.

Leading innovative project teams

Transferable skills
2.2 Personal effectiveness
3.4 Leadership

When leading a team on complex, innovative projects that require team members from cross-functional areas, they generally require members from different industries, disciplines, suppliers, customers and competitors. The usual broad mix of experiences, different technical languages, and so on that create gulfs between norms and values can be even more significant in these teams.

These teams need particularly skilled leadership. Four leadership practices help these teams work through the storming to performing steps (explained in Chapter 13), the first two focusing on the people and the second two on task:

1 Encourage an adaptable vision, not just a compelling vision (which every team needs) – one that invites collaboration to adapt and improve the initial vision continually. The vision needs to evolve as the team grows and members learn what they each can bring to the project, which keeps people engaged and motivated. So that people do not become confused and disconcerted from changes to the vision, put them in a positive light and explain and discuss the rationale. Because the vision changes, the values must act alone as the team's unchanging foundation.
2 Let team members get to know each other to build a culture where people know they will not be ridiculed for coming up with unusual solutions and ideas or have different points of view. Support making mistakes or 'failing fast' so that people can take risks needed to support innovation; otherwise, expect people to put only the standard ideas forward.
3 Promote learning by doing. Test, learn and adapt as the team innovates.
4 Build a learning culture where people can share their expertise and knowledge. Get people to think out loud, explain their reasoning, share their thought processes and so on, to counter the potential for misunderstanding and conflict due to different backgrounds and specialisations.

Your first few meetings

Transferable skills

1.4 Business operations

1.5 Operations management

2.2 Personal effectiveness

2.3 Business strategy

3.1 Teamwork/relationships

3.2 Verbal communication

3.3 Written communication

3.4 Leadership

Plan actual meetings carefully (as described in Chapter 25). Initial objectives for the first few meetings include:

- help members bond
- agree and follow TOAs
- establish team and individual performance plans (see Chapters 13 and 19) by your third meeting.

Review the WBS and timelines and begin taking them to the next levels of detail. Assign individual roles, responsibilities and deliverables so that team members can complete the WBS for their areas of responsibility and start developing their performance plans. The WBS and timeline form the basis of the team's work, provide role clarity, and assess the team's and individual members' performance and progress. Discuss and agree on each team member's performance plan privately, as you may or may not want to share each performance plan.

Also, ask team members to review the stakeholder and risk registers, particularly regarding their areas of responsibility, and begin detailing the risk management plan and stakeholder communication plans during the next meeting. The goal is to have the WBS and risk and stakeholder management plans fleshed out as quickly as possible so the team can get on with their work while avoiding the omissions and mistakes caused by rushing.

Ask members to keep a learnings log for the post-project lessons-learnt review and request weekly work updates, or project status reports, from all team members summarising:

- work accomplished
- work planned
- risks identified
- any problems
- any requests.

Working together on the operating protocols, team performance plan, and risk and stakeholder management plans ensures everyone understands the team's important issues and feels ownership and accountability for achieving the team's goals.

Try a project pre-mortem

A project pre-mortem helps identify what could cause your project to fail. Since forewarned is forearmed, it's a good way to safeguard your project's success. It tempers excessive optimism, encourages a more realistic assessment of risks, and helps prepare risk management strategies, or back-up plans.

At the team's second or third meeting, announce that the project has failed spectacularly. Then ask them to spend five or 10 minutes individually listing plausible reasons for the failure on a sheet of paper. Then go around the team asking for one reason each, listing each on a whiteboard. When all the reasons have been recorded, review the list to find ways to strengthen your WBS and risk register. For more complex projects, ask team members to write one reason per index card. Then gather and shuffle the cards and sort them into themes for reviewing and finding ways to strengthen your plan.

Execute and monitor your project

Transferable skills

1.4 Business operations

1.5 Operations management

Now it's time to get to work as the project manager, guiding, facilitating, coordinating and controlling the project. Manage it from the following perspectives:

- *Business:* covers the organisation's strategic goals and vision and the project's goals.
- *Political:* covers the organisation's and stakeholders' issues and constraints.

- *Team:* ensures team members fully understand their deliverables and timelines and remain focused on, committed to and able to achieve them.
- *Technical:* covers the work that must be done to deliver the project successfully.

As shown in **Figure 21.13**, your project management activities fall into six areas. Consider these as your key result areas.

FIGURE 21.13 Keep your project rolling by managing these activities

Transferable skills
1.5 Operations management
3.1 Teamwork/relationships

Coordinate project work

While team members work on the tasks they are responsible for, individually and in subteams, the project manager's role is carrying out the essential work of monitoring milestones and deliverables. It is essential to pay particular attention to the critical paths and critical control points so that delays do not hold up other work. It is critical to monitor the quality of team members' output and ensure that needed resources (equipment, information, etc.) reach them in a timely manner so they can achieve their deliverables. Avoid getting caught up in the day-to-day, unimportant urgent activities, as explained in Chapter 9.

Keep the project schedule up to date and posted in the project workspace. Doing so is an excellent way to keep everyone on track and working on the priority tasks, and reminding them of upcoming tasks and milestones. If a milestone is missed, address it immediately, reallocating resources as necessary.

The nature of some projects means that testing at various phases is needed. It is generally best to test early and often. To save trouble further down the track, do not take shortcuts with tests, even when budgets and time are tight.

Keep up with administration

Transferable skills

1.4 Business operations

1.5 Operations management

Set time aside for administrative duties, such as updating expenditure records, resource use and timesheets, managing scope change requests and completing project reports. Track changes to the project scope, cost and schedule variances. Alert the project sponsor at the first sign of a timeline or budget overrun. Demonstrate problem-solving skills by identifying options for getting back on track. If the project needs more time or more money, explain the benefits that can accrue and present the request as an alteration or adjustment to the plan, not a crisis.

Support your team's task

Transferable skills

1.5 Operations management

3.1 Teamwork/ relationships

3.4 Leadership

A team's process is how team members interact and conduct themselves, and their task is their actual work. Pay attention to both. (Chapters 13, 14 and 19 expand on the information below.) Ensure that team members know what is expected of them when mapping the project and assign deliverables. Provide training to team members to use any of the team's project management tools and techniques they are not familiar with early on; learning 'on the fly' is inefficient.

Hold regular status meetings with the team to review progress-to-date, current status against plans and forecast completion estimates, and discuss any decisions to be made, corrective actions to be taken, looming risks and the need for additional resources.

Status meetings can range from daily stand-up meetings or 'team huddles' to regular weekly or biweekly meetings; try to hold them at the same time on the same day(s). The intention is to keep everyone up to date without wasting time. If an issue or questions arise, schedule a follow-up meeting for further exploration.

There is a saying that 'if everything seems to be going well, you have obviously overlooked something'. In project management terms, this means you should expect to be adjusting the schedule as the project unfolds – adding and removing activities, altering timelines and so on.

Introduce a 'pause and learn' discussion after each milestone to identify mishaps and successes and see what you can learn from them and to look for ways to work better, faster and smarter (see Chapter 19 for ideas on how to make small improvements).

Use meetings to help pull the project together. As with all meetings, prepare for them in advance and send out a clear agenda with notice of any needed reference material and preparation. (Chapter 25 explains how to prepare for and lead actual and virtual meetings.)

Support your team's process

Transferable skills

3.1 Teamwork/ relationships

We have considered two main causes of failed projects: partial scoping and stakeholders not being clear on the project's scope and goals. A third major cause of unsuccessful projects is poor working relationships within the team. Hidden agendas, lack of trust, poor interpersonal skills and strong personalities can quickly push a project off course.

Building and maintaining a good working environment takes effort but is essential to a project's success. Take particular care to monitor team dynamics and keep morale up when members leave and join the team. (See Chapter 13 for information on what happens when people join and leave teams and Chapter 4 for information on working with group dynamics.) Address any concerns, disagreements and disputes early on because minor issues can quickly become full-blown problems.

Don't let people's hard work go unrewarded. Recognise accomplishments and small wins and celebrate milestone completions in a fun and energising way.

Transferable skills

3.2 Verbal communication

3.3 Written communication

Communicate

Plan to spend up to 80 per cent of the time during the project's execution phase communicating with the team, the project sponsor and the project's stakeholders. When team members are part-time and retain responsibilities in their usual roles, check in regularly with their managers to make sure they know the project's progress and their team members' contribution to it.

When the team are working in the same location, check-in daily with team members individually, however briefly, to see how they are going. When in different locations, meet virtually with team members individually at least weekly to discuss progress, concerns or anything that might be holding them back. When an activity is not on track, work out what corrective action to take. Remember the small talk, too. Find out what each team member is enjoying about the project and their contribution to ensure they are motivated and keep their motivation high.

Keep in touch with the project sponsor and update stakeholders on the project's progress according to the communication plan. Distribute one-page status reports to stakeholders with a brief overview of accomplishments and successes, key milestones, top five risks and issues, dashboard information and anything else important to the project and stakeholders. Copy the team in on these regular, formal written communications to stakeholders or place them on the team notice board.

Discuss any risks or decisions that require the sponsor's and stakeholders' input. Do this face-to-face or by telephone rather than email, and check informally to make sure everyone is happy with the way the project is unrolling.

Transferable skills

1.5 Operations management

2.1 Critical thinking

2.3 Business strategy

Monitor and manage risks

Keep a constant eye on whatever can endanger or assist the project, to remove or mitigate the former and capitalise on the latter. There are lots of ways to manage risk; for example, develop more efficient working methods, redefine or renegotiate project parameters when necessary, reduce costs when this does not adversely affect quality, seek further resources to meet deadlines, or multi-skill and cross-skill team members. Lastly, set reminders so that important activity is not forgotten, which is explained in detail in Chapter 22.

Transferable skills

1.5 Operations management

21.3 Completing your project

'Begin at the beginning,' the king said gravely, 'and go on till you come to the end; then stop.'

Lewis Carroll, *Alice's adventures in Wonderland*, Macmillan, 1865.

Once the team has achieved its deliverables, there is still work to do. It is important to complete the project correctly – so important that large and long-lived projects often have specialist closure managers.

Begin finalising the project by identifying work that still needs to be completed, so it is not forgotten. Thank all the team members for their energy, effort and contributions, and formally mark the end of a successful, and hopefully rewarding, part of their working lives; when appropriate, hold a closing ceremony – silly or serious – and hand out small tokens of appreciation. When the project is lengthy and major, compiling a scrapbook (described in Chapter 14) can make a nice parting gift from you to team members.

Thank team members' managers and begin releasing those who have completed their assigned deliverables, ensuring they transition smoothly to their next role or back to their previous role. Offer private individual feedback and encouragement and, when appropriate, to the managers whose team members were 'on loan'.

Finish administrative tasks, such as finalising the budget and other necessary documentation, writing team member performance reviews and organising a formal project closure meeting with the sponsor and stakeholders. Preparing a project closure document to send to them after the meeting marks the end of all project activities and the acceptance of the project's deliverables. Store all documents produced during the project in the organisation's knowledge base for future use. Closing a project is as important as its planning. Figure 21.14 presents a handy checklist for closing a project.

FIGURE 21.14 Project closure checklist

Prepare a project evaluation, or close-out report. Follow the format used in the organisation or use the following headings:

1 Project scope and deliverables (outline the original objectives of the project).
2 Project evaluation (compare the project's actual achievements in terms of costs, deliverables, timelines and managing risks with the original plan; explain any deviations from the plan; suggest actions to realise or improve benefits).
3 Team member appraisals.
4 Lessons learnt (add this after your team lessons-learnt meeting).

Here are some questions to consider when writing the close-out report (you can find out more about preparing reports in Chapter 7):

- Is everything in place and working properly?
- Are the users or clients, the project sponsor and stakeholders happy?
- Are there any problems and how will they be addressed?
- How will any areas of dissatisfaction be addressed?
- Does this project lead naturally to other projects to build on its success and extend the benefits delivered?

Learn from the project

Transferable skills

1.5 Operations management

2.1 Critical thinking

2.2 Personal effectiveness

2.3 Business strategy

Lessons learnt are an important way to reflect on the outcomes of a project. Invite the team to join in once more to celebrate the project's successful completion and review it to capture lessons learnt. Do this while the project is still fresh in everyone's minds and see whether the organisation has benefited from the project as expected. Consider inviting the project sponsor and key stakeholders to the celebration and project review too.

The purpose of this kick-out meeting is twofold: to officially acknowledge the end of the project, providing closure for team members, and to thank them for their hard work. Moreover, it can be used to identify lessons that can be applied to other projects. Remember to consider successes as well as shortfalls.

Think about the following:

- How efficiently and effectively were the outcomes achieved?
- How well did team members work together?
- What went well in this project?
- What would you make sure you do again next time?
- What didn't go as well as expected and how can that be prevented next time?
- What you would do differently next time?
- How well did you and the team manage the risks and how could you do this better next time?
- How well did you and the team manage other issues and how could you do better next time?
- How well did you and the team handle any unforeseen problems and how could you do better next time?

Take some time to look for insights about customers, markets, future trends and the organisation itself, too.

Figure 21.15 shows an example outline for a debrief meeting. As with any review, focus on the future and keep blame out of all discussions. Document successes and capture the lessons learnt to make sure they aren't forgotten. A word of caution: make sure the potential benefits are worth the time and effort you put into the review.

Think about what you learnt as project leader too: what discoveries did you make? How did people work together at the start of the project? What accounts for that? How well did you work with your sponsor? Did you select team members with the skills and attributes the project needed? What would you do differently next time and what improvements to your leadership could you make?

Debrief meeting agenda

1 Welcome and thank people for attending. Review the purpose of the meeting and the agenda.
2 Members reflect and make notes on these questions:
i What went exceptionally well in their own work that they would want to repeat in future projects?
ii What went exceptionally well in the project as a whole that they would want to repeat in future projects?
iii What went less well in their own work than they hoped and how could that have been prevented?
iv What went less well in the project as a whole than they hoped and could that have been prevented?
v What surprises – pleasant or unpleasant – occurred and how are they better equipped to handle similar occurrences in the future?
3 List responses to the above questions on flip charts (no discussion; questions for clarification only).
4 Select a few specific learnings to act on in the future and to add to the organisation's knowledge management system.
5 Thank the team once again for their efforts on the project and for attending this meeting.

FIGURE 21.15 Agenda for a debrief meeting

STUDY TOOLS

QUICK REVIEW

KEY CONCEPT 21.1 

a What is the difference between a project charter and a project scope? Which one does the project manager develop?
b Explain the function of a project scope and list the information it should contain.
c Explain the uses of a project plan and list the information it should contain. At what point should the project manager stop adjusting it?
d What is the difference between a milestone and a deliverable?

KEY CONCEPT 21.2 

a What is the purpose of a stakeholder register and what should it contain? How can a stakeholder analysis be carried out?
b List the four perspectives from which to manage projects and explain why each is important.

KEY CONCEPT 21.3 

a What does finalising a project entail?

BUILD YOUR SKILLS

KEY CONCEPT 21.1 

a Develop a project scope for this chapter's opening Snapshot.
b What happens when a project manager and project team are not clear about their project's constraints and assumptions?
c Why should project managers not complete project planning, stakeholder analysis and risk analysis in too much depth?
d Investigate the technology you can use to manage and monitor the planning, scheduling and completion of tasks. Prepare a short report to discuss in class.

KEY CONCEPT 21.2 

a Draw a flow chart of the approach to setting up a project team and review your approach with a classmate. What are the next steps in leading the team? If your project team were virtual, what additional advice would you need to consider?
b What is the purpose of stakeholder communication and engagement?
c Discuss the following statement: Managing projects is mostly about planning, managing risks and managing people.
d List the three major causes of unsuccessful projects mentioned in this chapter and discuss how each could doom a project. Give specific examples.
e How would a careful project charter and project scope, and proper project execution, prevent project failure?
f List and discuss the key considerations in putting together an effective project team. Explain how you can build a high-performing project team and what should happen when the adjourning stage is reached.
g Prepare generic agendas for a project kick-off and close-out meeting.
h What is the purpose of a team operating agreement and what should it contain?

KEY CONCEPT 21.3 

a What should a project's close-out report contain?

WORKPLACE ACTIVITIES

KEY CONCEPT 21.1 

a Find and review two or three examples of project charters in your organisation and discuss how they get a project off to a good start and guide its execution.
b Investigate how projects are scoped in your organisation. Is there a template or a format to follow?
c What documentation does your organisation require to plan, execute and finalise a project?
d How was scope creep prevented in the last project you worked on? If it wasn't prevented, how did scope creep occur and what were its results?
e Obtain a copy of the risk register for a project you have worked on to share with the class and explain how it was used to identify and manage risks.

KEY CONCEPT 21.2 

a Describe your day-to-day activities as you led a project through to its conclusion in terms of the project management activities shown in **Figure 21.13**.

KEY CONCEPT 21.3 

a What information from after-action reviews, or project learnings, are held in your organisation's knowledge base? Review the last few documents and summarise the main lessons learnt.

b What steps did you take to finalise the last project you led?

EXTENSION ACTIVITIES

Referring to the Snapshot at the beginning of this chapter, answer the following questions:

1 What might be some of the constraints and considerations of using location data for targeted marketing and how might this impact the scope of the project?

2 Should Macy and Rosa initiate the project, as part of the project charter what would be the purpose and goals of the project and the potential deliverables?

CASE STUDY 21

THE EXECUTION BLACK SPOT

Paul sits pondering his close-out report for the traffic black spot improvement project he has just managed. He's noted a few learnings for future projects: don't use the traffic management contractor I used. They were hopeless. Contact electricity earlier because their timelines are long and complex. That held the project up for a good three weeks, which I could have avoided by earlier liaison. Keep the community better informed and updated more regularly so we're not inundated with complaints and questions.

And what about me personally? I worked hard to get this gig, he thinks. My first as a project manager – putting in my time working on project teams for huge, billion-dollar road projects undertaken by the department, convening subteams, networking with the bosses to keep my visibility high, always positive, always 'Can do'. But did I get as big a kick out of managing this project as I expected?

I enjoyed the whole scoping and project planning part. Nice and logical – think it through carefully, just as I learnt to do. Get that right and the project flows pretty smoothly, which basically it did, apart from the odd gentle hiccup. The risk assessment was interesting and taught me to be wary of quotes given during a busy period when the contractors have enough work on. They just pull silly numbers out of the air, I reckon. That's something to add to the learnings too, maybe. But I nailed the bitumen supply – always tricky. I don't know why there's such a shortage of the stuff.

The sponsor was great, I checked in every week with a progress report. They were supportive and understanding when I nearly ran over budget (even though we'd built in an extra 10 per cent for contingencies). They knew exactly how to get me back on track. That was a valuable learning experience.

Yeah, loved the scoping and planning. Execution – that's another story. I felt like a pure administrator. During execution, my job was hassling people all day. Have you done this? Have you done that? When will this be finished? All that endless following up. Once the project got underway and I handed over work to the contract administration department, their site engineer took over monitoring the contractors and I hardly even got on-site to see what was happening.

Perhaps I should go into professional landscaping – then I could plan the project and when it comes to execution, get in there with a shovel and really get my hands dirty. Best of both worlds.

Ah well. Back to the close-out report.

Questions

1 What other learnings might Paul have taken from scoping and managing the project?
2 How do learnings in a close-out report help organisations and project managers?
3 What sort of attributes do you think a good project manager needs? Does Paul have the necessary skills and attributes, or does he need to develop any?

CHAPTER ENDNOTES

1 Zheng Fang, Xueming Luo, Michelle Andrews, Chee Wei Phang, 'Mobile discounts: A matter of distance and time', *Harvard Business Review*, May 2014, p. 30.

2 Stephen Hartley, *Project management: Principles, processes and practice*, Pearson, Sydney, 2009.

3 Delia Paunescu, 'Atari's failed E.T. game found in New Mexico landfill', Vulture.com, 27 April 2014, http://www.vulture.com/2014/04/ataris-et-game-found-in-new-mexico-landfill.html, accessed 28 April 2014; Juan Carlos Llorca, 'Diggers find Atari's E.T. games in landfill', Yahoo! News, 27 April 2014, http://news. yahoo.com/diggers-ataris-e-t-games-landfill-193256509.html, accessed 28 April 2014; Adario Strange, 'Legend confirmed: Atari 2600 'E.T.' game discovered at New Mexico dig', 27 April 2014, http://mashable.com/2014/04/26/legend-confirmed-atari-2600-e-t-game-discovered-at-new-mexico-dig/?utm_cid=mash-com-Tw-main-link, accessed 28 April 2014; and Liam Martin, 'Atari US files for Chapter 11 bankruptcy', 21 January 2013, http://www.digitalspy.com.au/gaming/news/a452483/atari-us-files-for-chapter-11-bankruptcy.html#~oCG0G5mwRjPK5Y, accessed 28 April 2014.

CHAPTER

IDENTIFYING AND MANAGING RISKS

KEY CONCEPTS

After completing this chapter, you will be able to:

22.1 identify what constitutes a risk and the types of risks your organisation is exposed to

22.2 apply the principles of risk management to develop a cost-effective risk management plan

22.3 identify and manage the risks at your workplace and ensure the continuity of operations should the worst occur.

TRANSFERABLE SKILLS

The following transferable skills are covered in this chapter:

1 **Business competence**
- **1.1** Financial literacy
- **1.2** Entrepreneurship/small business skills
- **1.3** Sustainability
- **1.4** Business operations
- **1.5** Operations management

2 **Critical thinking and problem solving**
- **2.1** Critical thinking
- **2.2** Personal effectiveness
- **2.3** Business strategy

3 **Social competence**
- **3.1** Teamwork/relationships
- **3.2** Verbal communication
- **3.3** Written communication
- **3.4** Leadership

4 **Data literacy**
- **4.1** Data literacy

5 **Digital competence**
- **5.1** Cyber security
- **5.2** Technology use

OVERVIEW

Risk management is a discipline that enables individuals and organisations to remain resilient when faced with significant uncertainty. Some risks are hard to predict, like the volcanic eruption on the island of La Palma in the Canary Islands in 2021, but that doesn't mean we can't assess and manage them. Some risks are clear but ignored and horrendously mismanaged, like those leading up to the global financial crisis that began in 2007 and the Volkswagen emissions cheating scandal that unfolded in 2015. Some risks are complex and evolving, like the COVID-19 pandemic, and may require us to rethink many aspects about the way we live, work, communicate and interact with one another. Some risks, such as a large passenger cruise ship sinking, are unlikely but would be catastrophic should they occur. Many risks, such as earthquakes in Japan and New Zealand or bushfires in Australia and California, are ever present and need to be managed continuously.

When negative risk events strike, business and operational plans can go out the window. Organisations can lose customers, income and future business, and can even collapse. People can lose their livelihoods and even their lives. Towns, cities and economies can be ravaged. And what about the cost of ignoring positive risks – opportunities? That can cost an organisation dearly, too. This makes identifying and managing risks, both positive and negative, and building a strong risk culture, essential elements of sound corporate governance and operational management that should involve stakeholders at all levels across the entire value ecosystem in which organisations operate.

Risks can come from outside the organisation, such as the marketplace, technology, the political and social environment and from natural hazards. Then there is the array of risks that come from inside that can damage an organisation when managed poorly and strengthen it when managed effectively. And just as organisations are at risk from damage to their reputation, and even shareholder value, from poor environmental management and sustainability practices, unethical behaviour on the part of employees, or unsavoury human resource practices, they also stand to benefit when they excel in these areas.

We have moved from a prescriptive model to a principle-based approach to managing risk. This means adopting a set of risk management principles and a continuous improvement framework for managing risk, and developing and implementing sound risk management processes. This also means predicting what could occur, assessing the potential causes and outcomes of those future events and the likelihood of their occurrence, establishing overall priorities for removing or controlling the possible causes of negative risk events, planning how to deal with them should they occur and planning to capitalise on positive risk events.

This chapter explains how to apply risk management practices so that your organisation can develop the ability to resist, absorb, recover and adapt to the ever-changing and increasingly complex environment in such a way that will enable it to achieve its objectives, rebound from setbacks and prosper.[1] There are technical terms to come to grips with and some terms have similar meanings. Try keeping a running list of risk management terms and their definitions (words in bold and italics), showing words that mean the same or link with other terms and their synonyms.

SNAPSHOT

Unforeseen events

Susan is the national operations manager for a mining supplies and equipment company. Susan goes down to breakfast reflecting on the challenges of managing three teams: her local customer service and sales team in Sydney (made up of telecommuters, part-timers and casual workers), a team in Perth that looks after the accounts receivable function that she manages, and a national distribution centre for their products based in Adelaide.

She switches on the news while having a quick breakfast. A report on major fires overnight in several suburbs in and around Perth shows the area where the offices are located and images of the ensuing chaos gradually pierce her thoughts. The next story tells of unprecedented floods in Adelaide with the potential for major rail and road connections being cut for up to several weeks.

Having heard enough, Susan decides that breakfast is over and it's time to login to Teams to find out whether the staff are okay, if the offices have been damaged and how business can continue. After logging-in, she finds a message from the team leader in Perth from the night before saying that while everyone's safe, the fires continue to burn out of control and the area around the Perth office has been closed off and some suburbs are without power. While Susan knows not to expect anyone from the Perth team to turn up to the office to work for at least the rest of the week, most of them have the ability to work from home, although with the ongoing fires it's doubtful they'll be at anything more than 50 per cent capacity. How much damage the nearby fire has caused remains to be seen.

Susan now turns her attention to South Australia. It looks like the distribution centre itself is okay but the road and rail have been cut west of Port Augusta through to Western Australia, and north all the way to the Northern Territory. While these aren't the largest number of customers, the mining customers in those areas are some of the largest and account for 40 per cent of the company's business. The government is saying that these routes are likely to be cut for at least two weeks and possibly longer.

It is most important that accounts receivable keep up with the workload and therefore the company's cash flow. There is no way the Sydney team can do all their own work as well as all of the Perth team's work, even if they all worked double shifts. If the Perth centre loses that much productivity for more than a week, the company will be in serious strife. Meanwhile, Susan needs to find a way of getting the orders to key customers in Western Australia, northern South Australia and the Northern Territory. Who in the world could have foreseen this, she thinks, as she puts her head in her hands. Who indeed?

22.1 Understanding risk

I cannot imagine any condition which would cause a ship to founder. I cannot conceive of any vital disaster happening to this vessel. Modern ship building has gone beyond that.

Edward John Smith (ship's captain who died in the *Titanic* tragedy), 'Disaster at last befalls Capt. Smith', *New York Times*, 16 April 1912.

Transferable skills
1.4 Business operations
2.1 Critical thinking
2.2 Personal effectiveness
2.3 Business strategy
3.4 Leadership

Organisations, like ship's captains, can't afford to pretend **risks** don't exist. Organisations face ever-present risk from dependence on, and vulnerability to, communication and information technology, globalised competition, increasing occurrences of natural disasters, and rapidly evolving business models. Disruptive change is accelerating to the point where there is no 'new normal' but a continuous series of 'not normal' times.[2]

A risk event can threaten an organisation, a nation and even the planet. What steps would you take should any of the events shown in Figure 22.1, or a similar event, occur? How would you look after your employees? How would you protect your organisation's physical and intangible assets? How could you and your team keep your work flowing to your internal or external customers?

Here are some more questions to ponder:

- How could you prevent or reduce the likelihood of adverse events such as those shown in Figure 22.1 from occurring?
- Should your organisation insure for any of these or similar events?
- What contingency plans and accountabilities does your organisation need to deal with these and similar emergencies should they occur and how should you test those plans?
- How can you keep abreast of the continually changing risk landscape?
- How can you continuously strengthen your organisation's *risk resilience*?

Organisations need increasingly sophisticated and swift risk management processes with stronger controls and better risk warning mechanisms. Reactive risk management is just too risky and is a sign of poor corporate and operational governance.

Transferable skills
1.4 Business operations
2.1 Critical thinking
2.2 Personal effectiveness
2.3 Business strategy
3.1 Teamwork/relationships
3.2 Verbal communication
3.3 Written communication
3.4 Leadership

What is a risk?

The ISO defines risk as 'effect of uncertainty on objectives', where *objectives* can be strategic or operational and relate to any function of an organisation, such as production, service delivery, people and culture, information technology, marketing, communications and finance.[3] *Effects* are deviations from the expected or intended situation and can have a positive or negative consequences or both, and can address, create or result in opportunities and threats. *Uncertainty* is a measure of just how likely such deviations are or how often they could occur. Risk is usually expressed in terms of risk sources (or causes that give rise to risk), potential events, their consequences and their likelihood. For example, a key objective of an organisation may be to create and maintain a safe working environment. Risk sources might include a lack of effective induction or skills training,

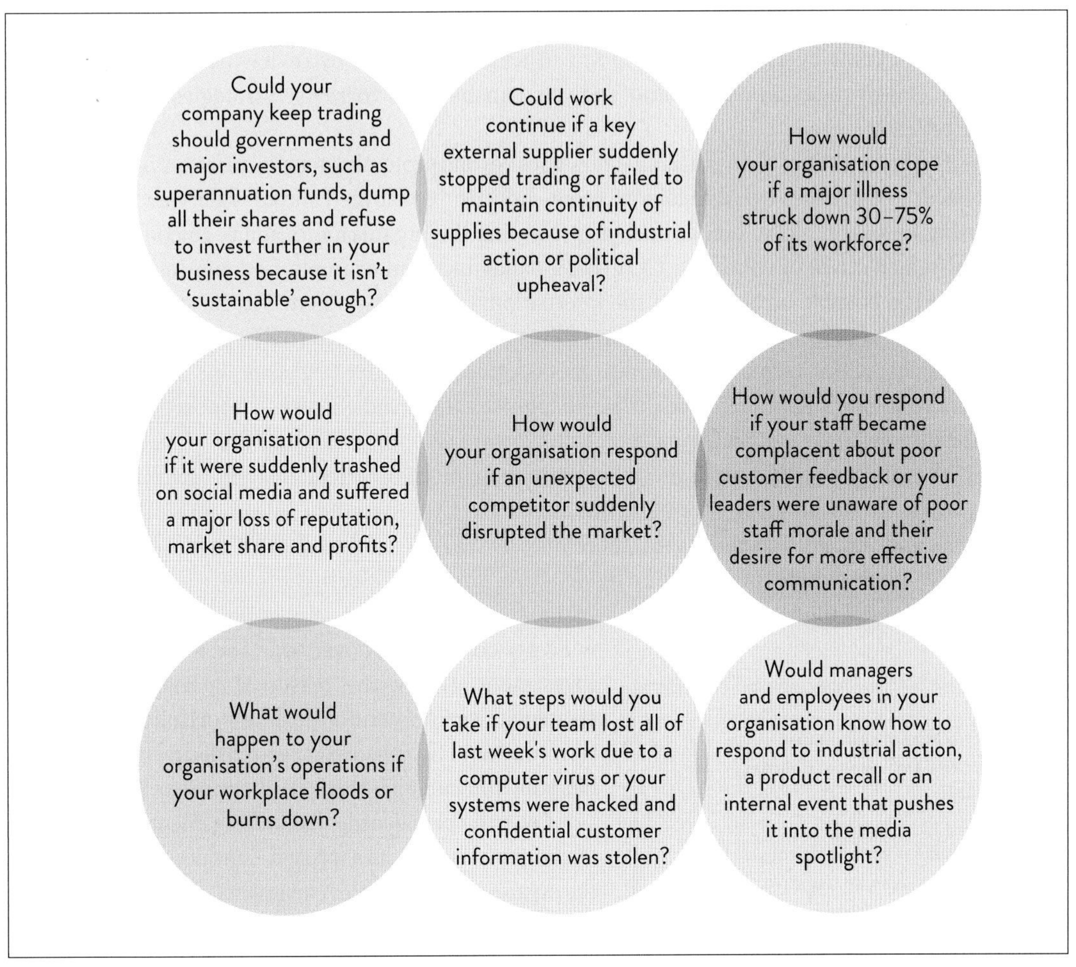

FIGURE 22.1 What steps would you take if faced with these questions?

poorly documented procedures, ineffective cleaning and inadequate supervision. A risk event could be that an employee falls because they slipped on an oil spill in the workplace, resulting in a broken arm and lacerations to their leg.

So the starting point for understanding organisational risk is to begin by understanding the organisation's objectives – strategic, business and operational. We can then start to examine areas of uncertainty that may have an effect on these objectives. This uncertainty could exist in the objectives themselves if they are unclear, ambiguous or haven't been communicated well. Uncertainty may also be due to changes in the external or internal environments beyond expectations. With areas of uncertainty determined, managing risks then involves identifying potential risk events, analysing the likelihood and consequences, and then deciding whether or not to implement plans to deal with them.

The way we think about risk has evolved in the last few decades. Traditionally, risk management was all doom and gloom, concentrating on dangers, hazards, perils and threats. It was focused on business **contingency planning** and it was about identifying and minimising negative outcomes for the organisation. In practice, this meant protecting the organisation's infrastructure against fire, riots and natural disasters, such as earthquakes and floods, and having recovery plans detailing what to do should they occur. Greater emphasis is now placed on the iterative nature of risk management. We simply can't know everything at any point in time, but rather, by reviewing the results of new activities or endeavours, knowledge and analysis can be used to revise strategies, processes and controls after each stage.

At the operational level, risk management now goes beyond protecting the organisation's infrastructure from isolated occurrences to developing more holistic, employee-centred safety-aware cultures; incorporating unfolding global events, such as protecting the organisation's ability to conduct business during a sustained crisis, of which the COVID-19 pandemic is an example, and continuing operations in the face of the possible breakdown of the international monetary system. At the strategic level, risk management is used to identify and respond to evolving changes in the external factors – changes in local and international politics, technology, business models, the competitive landscape and the environment.

This contemporary approach to risk also recognises the upside of risk – opportunity, as well as the relationship between risk and reward. While greater risk may lead to greater reward, the pursuit of greater rewards can still be achieved through management practices that effectively identify and manage risk. It would be an oversimplification to state that there is a linear positive relationship between risk and reward. In some cases, there may be no relationship at all. Take a superannuation account, for example, where there will be a tendency for shares to offer higher rewards (returns) as well as higher risk (losses) than other forms of investment, such as cash, bonds or property. However, this will vary considerably over time and with the individual investment. Hence the reason that many investment strategists recommend a diverse portfolio and a long-term outlook. So when you read 'risk' in the rest of this chapter, you can also think 'and opportunity'.

Over the past decade, risk management has tended to be more inclusive in its approach, considering the ways that the organisation's activities can impact different stakeholder groups. By seeking stakeholder input at the early stages of activities or projects, not only can we come up with greater diversity of perspectives and ideas, but we can also increase buy-in to new ideas through effective engagement, thus reducing the risk of stakeholder resistance. This approach, summarised in Figure 22.2, acknowledges that a risk can be negative, positive or neutral.

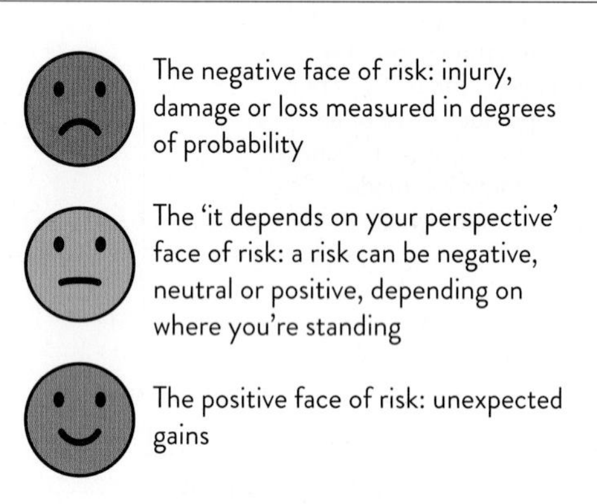

FIGURE 22.2 Three faces of risk

Two sources of risk

Transferable skills

1.4 Business operations

2.1 Critical thinking

2.3 Business strategy

3.4 Leadership

Risks can result either from an organisation's activities or come from outside the organisation. Those that come from outside the organisation are known as external, or *extrinsic risks*, while those that arise within the organisation itself are known as internal, or *intrinsic risks*. Together, they form the *risk context* and are the basis of your risk management strategy (see Section 22.3). Some (but by no means all) internal and external risks are summarised in Figure 22.3 and others are listed below. Risks from these external and internal areas can affect organisations in a variety of ways.

Extrinsic risk

Extrinsic risks abound. They include all the external parameters and factors that influence the organisation as it works towards its objectives, including trends and changes in:

- competitor activity
- the cultural, economic, financial, legal and regulatory, political and social environments

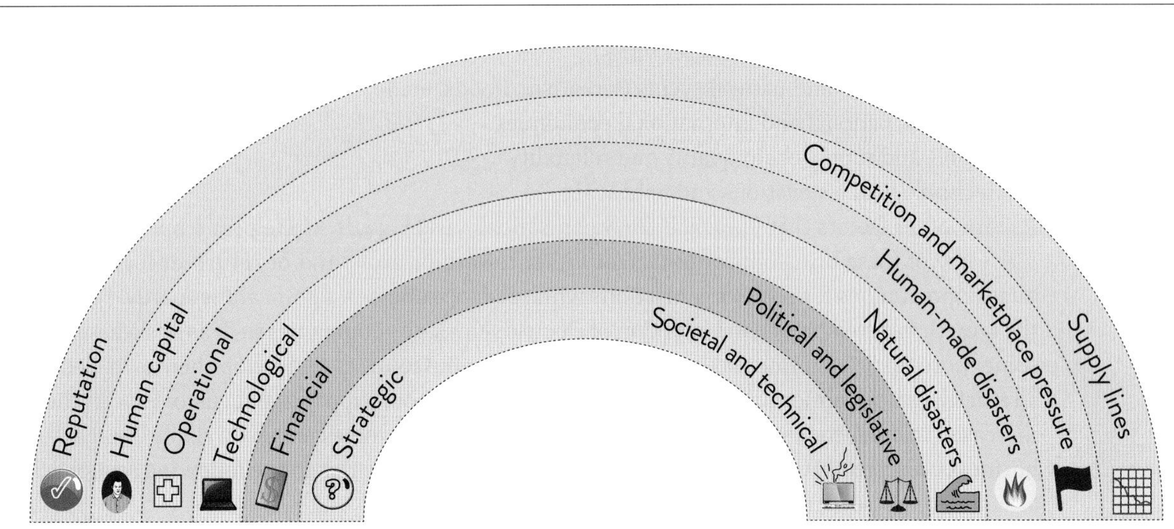

INTERNAL RISKS

Reputation:
Image of responsibility and integrity, brand damage, sabotage

Human capital:
Contract management, culture and values, ethical behaviour, actions and inactions of employees, the departure of key staff, training, performance management and career-pathing systems, human error

Operational:
Equipment control and quality, insurance costs, workplace health and safety, (e.g. asbestos, carcinogens, stress, accidents, environmental pollution, equipment failure, sabotage), product and service quality, recurring problems and near misses

Technological:
Security of information, data and intellectual property, communications and IT systems failure, equipment failure, computer viruses, lost and corrupted data, information, systems and processes

Financial:
Fraud, loss on investment, theft, cash flow, capital management and controls, ability to attract investment

Strategic:
Risk flowing from strategies, plans, projects and policies

EXTERNAL RISKS

Supply lines:
The collapse of a key customer or supplier, variable fuel and raw material availability and costs, a sudden shortage of a key commodity, loss of supplies of energy and other utilities

Competition and marketplace pressure:
Industrial action, national and international economic pressures, rapidly evolving business models, skills shortages, unpredictable capital markets, changes in consumer and public expectations

Human-made disasters:
Fire, nuclear plant power leakage, oil spillage, sabotage, security and supply of energy and utilities, terrorism, transport shutdowns, wars

Natural disasters:
Earthquakes, fires, floods, storms, tsunamis, climate change, epidemics and pandemics

Political and legislative:
Civil unrest, political instability, new legislation and regulations

Societal and technical:
Technical advances, technology-related accidents, changes to demographics, consumer trends, social unrest, social media, changing work patterns

FIGURE 22.3 Risks (and opportunities)

- external stakeholders (those affected by or who perceive themselves to be affected by the organisation's decisions and activities)
- human-caused and natural events (terrorism, floods, etc.)
- the local, national and international economies
- supply and supply chain quality and reliability
- technological innovations and upheavals
- any other factors that influence the organisation's vision, goals, strategy and operations.

Some of these bring opportunities for either reward or profit and/or return or loss. Some bring huge opportunities for some organisations while placing others in significant jeopardy. For example, the growth in development and adoption of electric vehicles by companies such as Tesla has prompted some more traditional internal combustion vehicle manufacturers to develop their own electric and alternative energy options. Globalisation allows access to more suppliers and customers yet the vastly increased interdependence means that a small disruption anywhere can have a ripple effect across the business ecosystem. We review eight common areas of extrinsic risk in the following sections. Many are interconnected and all have flow-on effects.

The competition

What if your competition develops a strategic alliance or strengthens its value chain ecosystem in a way that you just can't match, at least in the short term, resulting in declining sales and profits? Or what if a strong competitor launches a price war that you can't afford to win, or someone you've never heard of develops a new digital platform business model that competes head-to-head with your business while skirting around regulations and laws that your organisation must comply with (to its cost)? The potential for losses due to competitor pressure are a daily reality. You can be caught on the back foot and respond tactically or you can predict, in a loose way, various scenarios and plan your response to each.

The economy

Companies doing business overseas face exchange rate volatility, business interruption due to geopolitical risks (e.g. wine tariffs imposed on Australian wines in 2020 due to worsening diplomatic tensions), societal risks (e.g. large-scale involuntary migration and food and water crises), supply chain risks and market changes (volatility or stagnation). Economies going pear-shaped can lead to election upsets, nationalisation of resources and unpredictable regulation, particularly in countries or regions considered to be unstable. In extreme cases, political regimes can be destabilised, as evidenced by the regional unrest of the Arab Spring of 2011, carrying consequences for organisations with investments and operations in those countries.[4]

One event often leads to another. The lockdowns and border closures in many countries due to the COVID-19 pandemic led to the suspension of the tourism industry globally and heavy restrictions on the hospitality sector. This resulted in the grounding and mothballing of whole airline fleets. Non-essential service organisations were forced to shift to virtual operations.

Nationally, the state of the Australian economy, be it boom times, deflation, depression, inflation or recession, affects organisations' costs, customers' purchasing power for organisations' products and services and the availability and mobility of the workforce. A period of high market volatility, brought about by, for example, economic uncertainty, natural disasters, pandemics and/or political instability, could increase the number of mergers and acquisitions and make forecasting profits difficult. This in turn could spook investors and affect the value of corporations.

Risky cities

With more than 70 per cent of Australians living in cities,[5] Australia is highly urbanised and reliant on infrastructure, making our cities vulnerable. As we have seen, communicable diseases can spread very quickly in highly urbanised environments during a global pandemic. Populations living along coastal areas are at risk of rising sea levels and flooding, extreme weather events, earthquakes and tsunamis. And it isn't just Australian cities at risk. The United Nations forecasts the number of people in large cities exposed to cyclonic winds, earthquakes and floods will more than double in the first half of this century.[6]

The government

Changes in government and government policy, legislation and regulations are ever-present, with significant repercussions to organisations in all three sectors. The more reforms that government introduces, the bigger the risks.

For example, banking and financial systems faced increased legislation and regulation in the aftermath of the global financial crisis (GFC). The passing of the *National Disability Insurance Scheme (NDIS) Act 2013* and its subsequent rollout led to a significant restructuring of the disability services sector and fundamental changes to the way that services are provided to people with disabilities. The Australian Government's 2021 plan to achieve net zero emissions by 2050 is intended to reduce the cost of low-emissions technologies and enable these to be deployed at scale, while seizing opportunities in new and traditional markets and fostering global collaboration.[7] As governments around the world come to terms with the implications of reaching net zero emissions, much uncertainty will exist and many positive and negative risks will arise.

Information technology and artificial intelligence

Information technology (IT) provides wonderful opportunities as well as dangers. It lets us perform millions of calculations in a fraction of a second, provides us with the tools to design buildings, simulate complex weather patterns and make forecasts, fly pilotless aircraft and even perform surgery. Computers are even parking cars and assisting us to more safely drive them. Artificial intelligence (AI) mimics the problem-solving and decision-making capabilities of humans, where virtual assistants like Siri respond to the questions we put to them, and allows us to automate business processes. But what is the danger if they fail? One example of failure was the case with the Boeing 737 MAX aircraft, where a new feature in the flight control computer triggered flight control movements that placed the aircraft into a dangerous nose dive attitude and contributed to the crash of two aircraft in the space of just five months in October 2018 and March 2019 with the loss of 346 passengers and crew.

Transferable skills
5.1 Cyber security
5.2 Technology use

Another threat to IT systems is if they are deliberately compromised. Since 1997, when IT security was more about making sure the computer room was locked, threats to corporate information security have exploded in volume, sophistication and the degree of nastiness – email and web threats, denial of service, hacking and other security breaches, data fraud or theft, ransomware, and viruses and worms, to name just a few. Hackers are looking to steal specific intellectual property (IP) to sell for profit or to use for a politically or socially motivated purpose.

The COVID-19 pandemic has significantly increased our dependence on the internet and with it has come a corresponding increase in cybercrime. The Australian Cyber Security Centre (ACSC) reported that during the 2020–2021 financial year it received over 67 500 cybercrime reports, an increase of 13 per cent on the previous year, with a higher proportion classified as 'substantial' in impact. The losses reported in Australia for that same year due to cybercriminal activity totalled more than A$33 billion. The increasing frequency of cybercriminal activity is compounded by the increased sophistication of their operations. Cybercrime services, such as ransomware-as-a-service (RaaS), are now accessible via the dark web and increasingly open the market to a growing number of malicious actors who no longer require significant technical expertise and financial investment.[8]

The valuable information that organisations hold in a variety of formats and places must be protected, or they face anything from a financial or proprietary information loss to denial of access and a major disruption in business activity. Automated attack tools, exploitation of unprotected software and misconfigured operating systems, applications and network devices are common attack methods. Because their large storage capacity makes them portable computers, unlocked electronic notebooks and smartphones are other common weak points, and when used in a wi-fi environment, such as an airport lounge or coffee shop, these devices are easy pickings for hackers. Backing up regularly and installing an antivirus package is no longer nearly enough.

Meanwhile, digital disruption, together with techniques such as analytics or 'big data' and the internet of things (IOT), are changing business models and altering logistic possibilities, offering both threats and opportunities. Public Cloud computing (as differentiated from the more secure private Cloud environment) has become a dominant paradigm in software development and usage and is also an important risk area as organisations store their data in the Cloud.

CERT can certainly help

The Australian Government has established the Computer Emergency Response Team (CERT), which you can find at https://www.cyber.gov.au/acsc/view-all-content/glossary/cert-australia. It provides free advice and support on cyber threats and helps organisations identify where they're vulnerable. You can partner with CERT before an incident occurs and you can report all incidents to them.

Transferable skills
1.3 Sustainability
1.4 Business operations
2.3 Business strategy

Mother Nature

The sixth assessment report of the Intergovernmental Panel on Climate Change (IPCC) makes it clear that science shows, with 95 per cent certainty, that human activity has been the main cause of global warming since the middle of the 20th century.[9] Human-induced climate change is already affecting many weather and climate extremes in every region across the globe. Increased frequency and severity of bushfires, cyclones, floods, hailstorms, rising sea levels, shortage of drinkable water and warmer temperatures all present risks and opportunities. In addition to climate-related events, natural disasters, such as earthquakes, tsunamis and volcanic activity, also pose significant threats to human habitation and economies.

Natural disasters and climate change affect organisations' and nations' abilities to obtain resources and to operate effectively. The results of climate change may also require organisations to alter the way they operate and have already presented lucrative new opportunities to some organisations. (Chapter 23 has more information on this aspect of risk management.)

Pandemics

The COVID-19 pandemic has had a devastating effect on human populations globally, with over 293 million reported cases and over 5.4 million deaths at the time of writing. It has overwhelmed many health systems, led to the virtual shutdown of entire industries, the lockdown of whole cities and the disruption of global supply chains. Yet, while nations were struggling to control the pandemic, scientists warned that deadly outbreaks of other viruses are inevitable. Since 1918 there have been six distinct influenza pandemics and epidemics. Ebola viruses have spilled over from animals about 25 times since 1970. Expecting to avoid another spillover is not possible, so being prepared is the key.[10] Biosecurity experts have been outlining preparedness plans for over 20 years. The core components consist broadly of surveillance to detect an outbreak; data collection and modelling to see how they spread; improvements in public-health guidance; and the development of therapies and vaccines. Despite the millions of dollars that both governments and private funders have poured into these plans, COVID-19 has demonstrated that the world was less prepared than most imagined. So how can we improve our preparedness?

In answer to this question, infectious-disease researcher Jeremy Farrar, director of the UK biomedical funder Wellcome, says: 'Everything starts with smarter surveillance. If you don't look, you don't see. If you don't see, you will always respond too late'.[11] If you respond too late, outbreaks get exponentially harder to contain. With better surveillance comes improved access to data. Better data drives smarter decisions. Another key strategy is to improve communication, and combat misinformation and biases against the scientific establishment. Other strategies include improved vaccination capability to develop vaccines for novel diseases within 100 days and creating prototype vaccines against known families of viruses to speed up development in case of emergency.

So while these strategies can be developed by the health and biosecurity sector, all sectors need to review their pandemic preparedness and response strategies. This will enable them to reduce the negative impacts on their operations, while allowing them to adapt or pivot to new modes of operation, as many organisations have done successfully during COVID-19.

Reputational

Transferable skills
5.2 Technology use

Although it is has only been around for about two decades, social media is considered to be one of the biggest risks to reputation; in fact, it can shred an organisation's reputation in minutes. While it allows organisations to be transparent and connect with stakeholders, it also allows real-time, unverified, hashed and rehashed environmental, social and shareholder activism. With no 'truth test', misinformed and misinforming social media can do huge damage to organisations and their brands. It's the speed and loss of control that cause the biggest headaches.[12] Many high-profile companies take their risk to reputation from social media so seriously that they constantly scan social media and top-level management reviews dashboards summarising views on their products and the strength of their various brands.

Yet, despite all the money and effort thrown at managing reputational risk, reputational trashing regularly occurs. That's where culture and processes come in. Volkswagen's autocratic management style that squashed debate and disagreements and made sure blind eyes were turned to the emissions cheating software, cost it the biggest settlement by far in the US auto industry (US$53 billion). The company is still defending itself against compensation claims in Australia and Europe.[13] This shows how risky it can be to have insufficient checks and balances, or due diligence (as it's known in the finance industry), that allow people to behave badly. Functionalism, or silos, that allow people to pass the responsibility buck for anything from poor customer service to risky risk management, doesn't help, either.

The chances that your organisation, product or service is currently being discussed, evaluated, recommended or trashed is high – and people believe what their contacts say. Nielsen research, for example, found that 78 per cent of people believe their contacts' negative and positive comments about a company, product or service (versus 16 per cent who believe advertising).[14] Moreover, while organisations could once train one or two key people to be their 'face and voice' to the public via the media, every employee now has that ability.

Utilities

A variety of risks relating to the security and supply of energy and other utilities hover in the background, including broken water mains, electrical blackouts, gas field explosions, power grid failure and telecommunications failure. The 2019–2020 bushfires in Australia caused key electricity infrastructure to be impacted across the east coast, resulting in power outages for tens of thousands of homes and many businesses.[15] Slow recovery times across the electricity network highlighted its lack of resilience, with thousands of customers still without power weeks later. The bushfires highlighted the importance of whole-system thinking. Additional state-to-state connections, strategically located energy storage, more distributed renewable generation sources, and burying power lines where possible could all contribute to wider system resilience.

Drinking water quality is also under threat from bushfires. Impacts to catchments from bushfires and subsequent erosion can have long-lasting effects, potentially worsening untreated drinking water quality for many years.

Organisations across all sectors should review their risk exposure in the event of significant short- to medium-term disruption in utility supply. Where business continuity or product quality may be impacted, organisations should consider developing or enhancing strategies for improving organisational resilience.

Transferable skills

1.1 Financial literacy

1.2 Entrepreneurship/small business skills

1.4 Business operations

1.5 Operations management

2.1 Critical thinking

2.2 Personal effectiveness

2.3 Business strategy

Intrinsic risk

There is an element of risk in every activity an organisation undertakes. It is inherent in every strategy, every decision employees make and every action they take or fail to take. Risk is part of every organisation's commercial, legal and supply chain relationships and obligations, contractual expectations and liabilities, management shortcomings and excesses, product design and safety, work systems and processes and their controls and equipment – all the internal parameters and factors that influence the organisation as it works towards its objectives. The internal risk context also includes its:

- approach to and governance of risk
- decision-making processes (both formal and informal)
- internal stakeholders and their view of and behaviour towards risk
- organisation structure, capabilities, culture and standards, policies and guidelines.

Obviously, we have more control over the internal risk context than the external risk context. Take information governance, an area of critical importance. Managing massive amounts of information and storing it for ease of access when needed (e.g. for compliance, internal investigations or litigation) is only the beginning. IT data breaches, downtime, equipment failure, theft or loss, and recovery from a server failure are all risky but arguably more easily controlled than external IT risks.

Many investment funds use a framework of environmental, social and governance criteria, known as *ESG*, to assess potential and current investments, making these other key internal risk areas. Other areas to monitor and actively manage include:

- strategic planning
- brand, image and reputation management and protection
- project selection, planning and management
- compliance and legal requirements
- employee wellbeing
- workforce planning and retention
- organisational culture and values, including its norms and practices
- technology and technological issues.

When identifying internal risks, don't just think about potential crises and disasters; include less visible risks too, such as the *ongoing risks* (also known as *business-as-usual risks* and *operational risks*, which are discussed later in this chapter). Remember, too, to look for and capitalise on the array of opportunities arising from employee behaviour. We consider three (of the many) categories of intrinsic risks in the following subsections.

Employee wellbeing and expectations

Transferable skills

3.1 Teamwork/ relationships

3.2 Verbal communication

3.3 Written communication

3.4 Leadership

Changes in how we work, where we work, who we work with, why we work and the technologies we use are in continual flux. Although these changes started prior to the COVID-19 pandemic, they have been accelerated subsequently, and are now commonly seen in the workplace. The future of work is now seen as *employee wellbeing*, which has five key levers – financial, mental health, social, physical and career wellbeing. Unless organisations develop the capabilities and culture to support these elements they are likely to face the risk of significant turnover in their people. Hybrid work is here to stay and is what the majority of workers want. One of the key risks for organisations is how to develop the leadership, communication and technology practices, skills and structures that will support a 'productivity anywhere' workforce model. Beyond wellbeing, employees also expect their employer to be a force for good in society. Research indicates that half of the knowledge workers surveyed would quit their job if their organisation's values did not align with their own.[16]

BHP's Samarco tailings dam collapse in Brazil, James Hardie's asbestos liability, Rio Tinto's destruction of the Juukan Gorge cave sacred site, unethical sales practices by major banks, governance breaches leading to corporate collapses, such as ABC Learning, and other corporate disgraces, are all examples of how important it is to monitor and manage environmental, social and governance risk – or face the consequences.

Employee acts and omissions

You can no doubt think of executives in all sectors who have had to step down following behaviour considered to be 'unbecoming' to their positions. Employee acts can result in huge financial and reputational damage, making employees themselves a large risk area. In fact, many adverse events that have affected companies have had employee acts and omissions at all levels at their core; for example:

- breaches of compliance with workplace health and safety (WHS) and other legislation
- complacency about risks
- corporate fraud
- failure to manage creditors
- lack of vigilance regarding IT and IP security
- reputational damage from internal disputes and legal claims
- theft or poor treatment of key equipment
- unconscionable behaviour, including providing false and misleading information.

Corporate fraud, particularly asset misappropriation, bribery and corruption, cybercrime and procurement fraud, costs the Australian economy billions of dollars a year and affects 52 per cent of Australian businesses, far higher than the global average.[17] (However, more fraud is detected and reported in Australia because of a higher awareness of and low tolerance for fraud, and strong regulatory and **corporate governance**.)[18] **Figure 22.4** lists some measures organisations can take to pre-empt bribery and corruption.

Whether intentionally or inadvertently, employees can cause IT and IP security breaches and while most organisations guard against external violations, it's difficult to guard against breaches originating inside the organisation. Unless employees are careful with their downloads, they risk

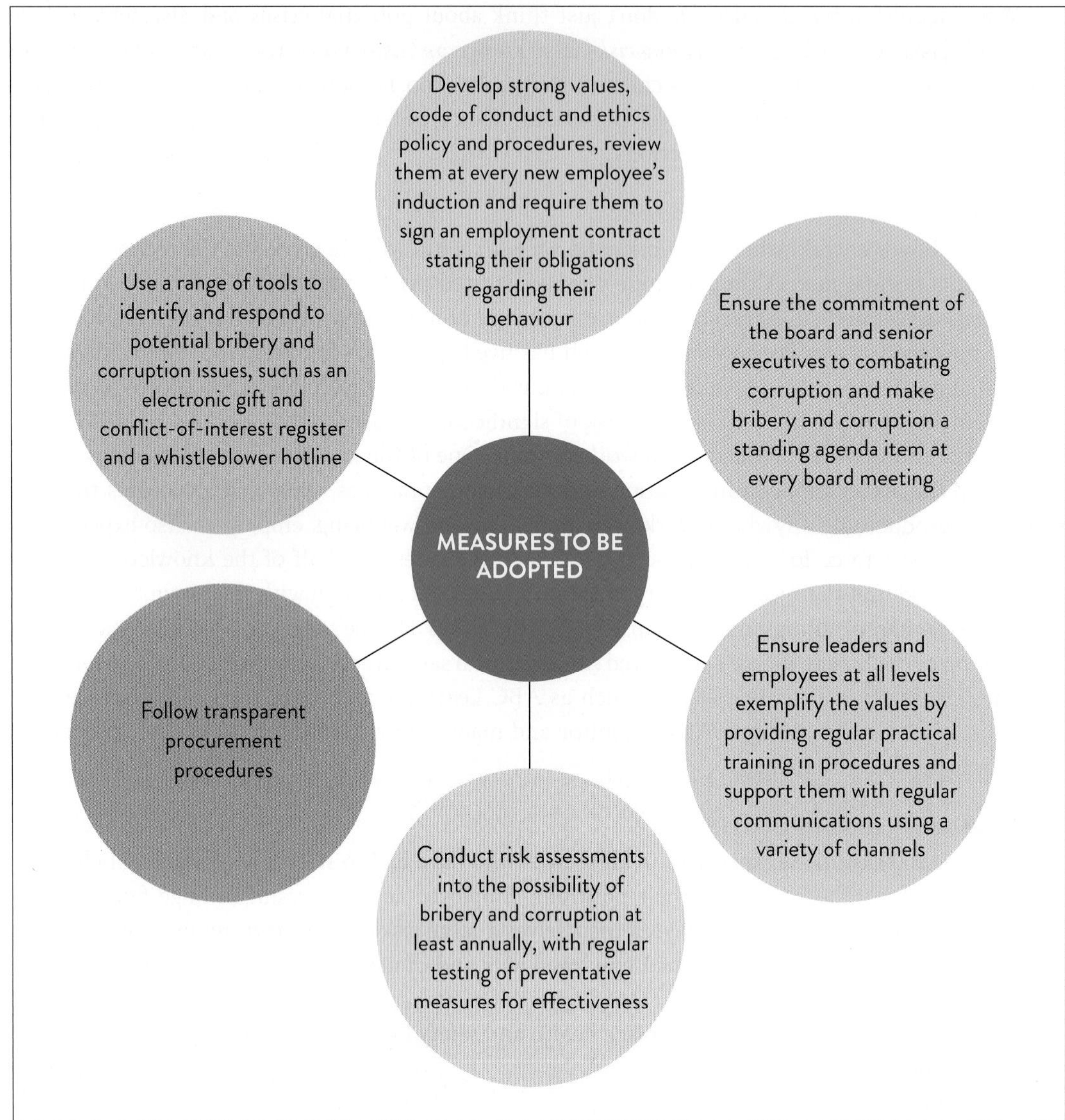

FIGURE 22.4 Blocking bribery and corruption

trojans, viruses and worms entering the organisation's IT network and the risks heighten with 'bring your own device' policies. USB sticks are also a main cause of infection.

The risks arising from employee misuse of social media, magnified by the speed it spreads information and the fact that it's unstoppable, are too great to ignore. Social media risks include:

- cyber bullying, harassment, e-discrimination and religious discrimination
- defamation
- improper disclosure of confidential information and market-sensitive information
- misrepresentation or breaches of trade practices legislation
- reputation damage.

The real cost of cost-cutting

When an organisation cuts costs, the bottom line quickly benefits. But it's important to look further down the track. BP didn't, when years of cost-cutting through reduced maintenance and training at their Texas City refinery, following years of cost-cutting by Amoco, the site's previous owners, resulted in an explosion in 2005 that killed 15 and injured 180 people.[19]

The 2013 European horse meat scandal is similar. Continued price pressure from supermarkets produced small cost savings that included padding out beef, lamb and pork products with (cheaper) horse meat. Predictably, suppliers were found out and suffered cancelled orders, their food pulled off supermarket shelves, followed by lawsuits and police raids.[20]

Intellectual property

Transferable skills
2.3 Business strategy
5.1 Cyber security
5.2 Technology use

How does your organisation protect its **intellectual property**? Once upon a time, it was difficult to steal IP, the intangible assets resulting from creativity, such as brand names, copyrights, designs, images, patents, processes, methodologies, symbols, trademarks, formulas and recipes. Proprietary and confidential information, such as insider knowledge, know-how (a body of knowledge built up over time), names, tender documents and pricing, customer and supplier lists, also form part of an organisation's IP. But storing these assets on the Cloud, manufacturing goods offshore, selling products and services online – 21st-century life – makes pilfering IP all too easy. This is worrying for all organisations and particularly those whose value lies largely in intangible assets and who have operations in the developing world, where IP is often not recognised or is ignored.

Intellectual property – a risky area

Did you know that companies can borrow money against their IP and license and assign it to others? Knowledge isn't just power – it's also value. Between 2011 and 2020, standard patent applications in Australia increased by 15 per cent. Most standard patent applications in Australia are filed by non-residents. In 2020, this trend continued with Australian residents responsible for only 8 per cent of the total applications filed in Australia (out of a total of 29 293). Of these, 45 per cent were US applicants followed by China with 8 per cent and they exist across technology classes, such as telecommunications, medical technology, pharmaceuticals and biotechnology.[21]

Operational and strategic risks

Some risks are operational and arise through the organisation's day-to-day work; they include capacity problems, cost overruns, earnings shortfalls, employee issues and fraud, WHS, IP and IT security, non-compliance, projects, security and supply chain issues. These risks can generally be managed by active prevention (e.g. internal control systems such as standard operating procedures), documenting a comprehensive risk management framework, effective training and skills development, diligent monitoring, establishing clear values and codes of conduct to guide employee behaviour, building strong risk and safety cultures, and effective leadership.[22]

Operational risks are at the top of the risk manager's to-do list when an organisation first embraces risk management. As its risk management matures, these become business-as-usual risks that are satisfactorily managed and monitored by their 'owners'. At some point, these current, or business-as-usual risks, only need annual or biannual audits (with quarterly audits for severe risks) to make sure all is well, although for project-based organisations, every project has potential risks that should be identified and assessed.

Once your organisation is 'mature' in operational risk management terms, the next level of maturity will be to consider strategic risks. *Strategic risk management* involves scanning the external environment, looking for future opportunities and threats that could increase or reduce value to the organisation and its offerings. Strategic risks may affect the entire organisation and its ability to meet its vision and overall goals; these are very 'high-stake' risks and are generally managed at senior executive and board level. Some arise internally and others externally. Strategic risks include competition, corporate governance, customer losses, demand shortfalls, pricing pressures and research and development.

Banks take a risk when they loan money; oil companies take a risk when they drill for oil; organisations take a risk when they merge with or acquire another organisation. These are *internal strategic risks* that result as the organisation executes its strategy. Organisations accept these risks because the potential gains outweigh the potential losses from the risk, but they need to manage them well to reduce the likelihood that they occur and to reduce their effects should they occur.

Events such as depressions and recessions, industry disruptions, technology shifts, natural disasters and pandemics are *external strategic risks*. Because they are beyond an organisation's control, you can only identify their possibility and have contingency plans to mitigate, or lessen, their impact.

Strategic risks need different treatments than operational risks. Think about the worst-case scenario and how your organisation could survive it. Use this information to guide your decisions regarding the extent to which, and how, to manage the risk, aiming to remove it when possible and when that's not possible, to reduce the likelihood that it occurs and its consequences if it does.[23]

The nature of risk

Transferable skills

2.1 Critical thinking

2.3 Business strategy

Some risks are risks of *scale* – for example, what is the number of people testing positive to COVID-19 and those being hospitalised? Others are risks of *timing* – for example, more earthquakes will occur in Japan and New Zealand, but when? Other risks relate to *structure* – for example, computers are bound to be attacked by a virus, but what sort of virus? What could happen? Where could it happen? When could it happen? Why would it happen? How could it happen? How would you know it was about to happen? These are *future risks* and they can be extrinsic or intrinsic; other risks are *current* or *ongoing*. Some are *strategic*, others *operational* (as just discussed). Some are lurking, or looming, but you don't yet know their precise cause or nature; others arise from current problems and trends that have the potential to worsen, such as:

- abusing stakeholders' goodwill (e.g. by taking short cuts for short-term profits)
- attending to low-priority areas and working on low value-adding tasks instead of important work
- capital availability, credit and liquidity problems
- difficulties in attracting, engaging and retaining staff
- failures and near-failures in routine operations that could be prevented or designed out
- a hostile takeover bid
- letting cumbersome systems that make people's work difficult continue, unimproved
- loss of key personnel
- missed opportunities (e.g. using assets or resources poorly or letting them languish)
- operational exposure to changing regulations
- **outsourcing** that results in loss of customer goodwill and reputational damage
- patchy regulatory compliance
- poor organisation culture

- poor product design (e.g. when customers don't understand how to use your product, they may hurt themselves or may not buy it again and tell others of their frustration, harming your organisation's reputation and costing it sales)
- poor relationships with a key business partner or stakeholder
- a public relations disaster
- shareholder activism.

These are often not recorded in registers of potential risks but in a separate risk register and assigned to a *risk owner* to control and review.

Types of risk

The **inherent risk** is the risk before treatment (i.e. before you establish controls). **Residual risk** is the risk remaining after treatment and needs to be taken into account in your **risk management plans** (RMPs). Your risk reduction and control efforts may have risks of their own, which are known as *secondary risks*; for example, an automatic fire sprinkler system might go off mistakenly, resulting in property damage. List these secondary risks in your ongoing risk register.

Risk appetite and tolerance

Organisations have to take some risks and they have to avoid others. The big question that all organisations have to ask themselves is how much risk are they prepared to take? **Risk appetite** is the amount of risk an organisation is willing to accept in order to pursue its objectives and, as such, sets the tone for risk taking in general.[24] Risk appetite will differ according to an organisation's internal and external contexts and will change over time. It will often take the form of a statement or series of statements that describe the organisation's attitude towards risk taking, and is generally aligned to categories of risk; for example, financial, people and reputation risks.

You can think of risk appetite as a continuum that varies within organisations depending on the activity – low in some areas and higher in others. It is a scale ranging from low to high, as shown in Figure 22.5.

Risk appetite statement

In many organisations, the board risk management committee develops a *risk appetite statement* that states how much risk they are prepared to accept in strategically important areas without reference to the board and without compromising good governance. These *boundaries*, or *risk limits*, can be expressed as averages (e.g. one in five tests successful); frequency of occurrence (e.g. one negative event every five years); percentages (e.g. plus or minus per cent of estimated cost); or time limits (e.g. security systems checked daily).

Since risk appetite is dynamic and needs to be adjusted as the external and internal environments change, risk appetite statements are normally reviewed by the board annually and by the risk management committee more frequently. The organisation's risk appetite forms the basis for establishing its risk culture, risk management policies and risk treatments. Some examples of risk appetite statements are:[25]

- *WHS:* our organisation is committed to providing a safe workplace for all employees, visitors and contractors and there is very low appetite for death, permanent disability or time lost because of inadequate safety protocols.
- *System and infrastructure:* there is moderate appetite associated with manual systems and outage of non-critical internal systems, accepting that some inefficiency may exist and non-critical errors may occur, provided they do not result in breach of regulation, privacy and/or result in litigation.

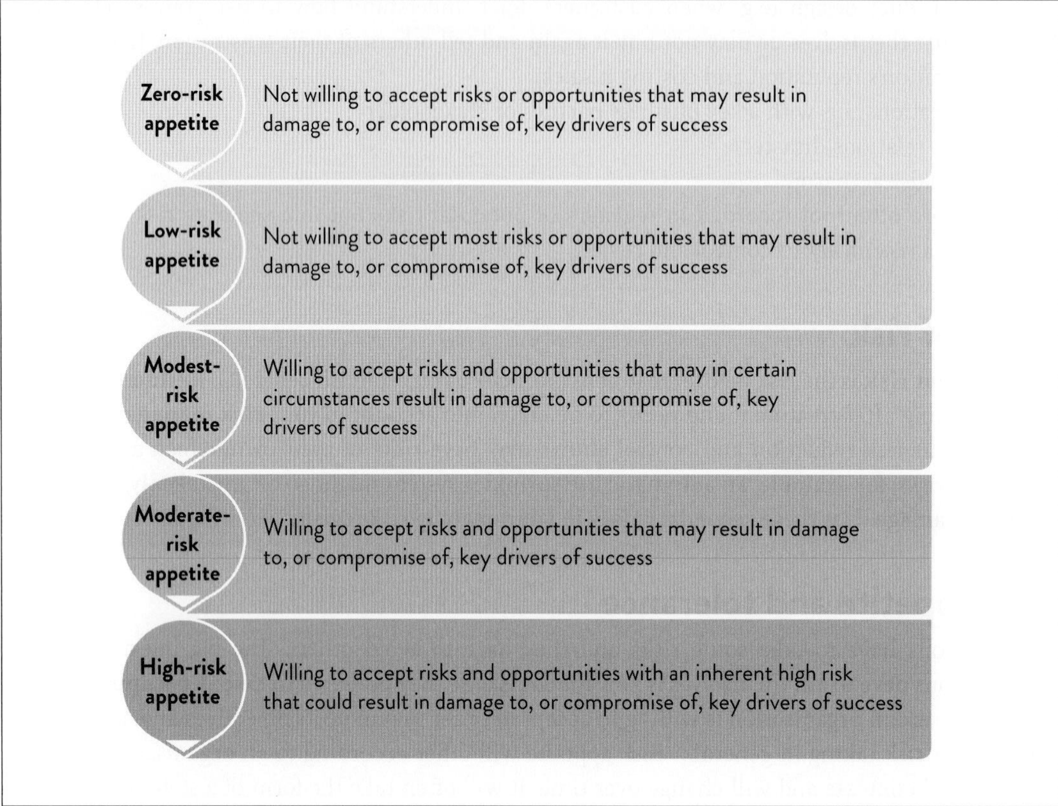

FIGURE 22.5 Risk appetite scale

Risk tolerance defines the levels of risk taking acceptable to achieve a *specific* objective or manage a category of risk and represents the practical application of risk appetite. Risk tolerance informs expectations for mitigating, accepting and pursuing specific types of risks, boundaries and thresholds for acceptable risk taking and actions to be taken for acting beyond approved tolerances. Example risk tolerance statement and measures may include the elements in **Table 22.1**.

TABLE 22.1 Example key risk indicators and associated tolerance limits

Specific risk area	Key risk indicator		Tolerance
	Metric	Timeframe	
Employee safety	WHS compliance training completion	Annual	Not more than 10% not completed
Systems and infrastructure	Number of outages for system B	Quarterly	Not more than 5% allowance

Adapted from Department of Finance, 2016, 'Defining risk appetite and tolerance', p. 5, accessed February 2022, https://www.finance.gov.au/sites/default/files/2019-11/comcover-information-sheet-defining-risk-appetite-and-tolerance.pdf

REFLECT

You know that going through a red light greatly increases the likelihood of causing an accident. Have you ever gone through a red light? Under what circumstance, if any, would you take this action?

You also know that the faster you drive, the greater your risk exposure. Crowded roads, narrow streets, the presence of pedestrians, rain, fog, an uneven road surface and winding roads all dramatically increase risk. What steps do you take when driving to mitigate (reduce) these risks?

Do you ever intentionally introduce risks while driving by doing things like eating, not fastening your seatbelt, texting or talking on the telephone, or driving after drinking alcohol? Under what circumstances would you be willing to add further risk to an already dangerous activity by taking these actions?

Take the example of a bank or credit union making a loan – both a risk and an opportunity. Without taking some risks such as this, banks and credit unions wouldn't have a business. The key is to manage risks and know how much risk you're willing to accept.

You want to have a clearly articulated risk appetite because when risk management processes, or ways of identifying and dealing with risks, are poor, employees may make their own assessment of how to deal with each risk as it crops up. As a result, the same risk may be dealt with differently in different parts of the organisation or one area may unintentionally undermine the efforts of another area. Eventually, a sticky end is reached and the organisation's ability to achieve its goals, and probably also its reputation, is damaged.

Risk or opportunity?

A first-year teacher was once offered a six-month contract for teaching in a rural town. No bank would lend him a loan for a reliable car. But a credit union had a higher risk appetite and thought that teachers were a good risk. Seeing the loan as an opportunity, they lent the young man the money. They also offered him a savings account and a credit or debit card. That young teacher was one happy customer. Some years later, he came back to the credit union for his first home loan. Now retired, he's still a satisfied customer.

Determine risk appetites

Transferable skills

1.1 Financial literacy

1.2 Entrepreneurship/ small business skills

2.3 Business strategy

Organisations determine their risk appetites based on their overall strategic objectives and set risk appetite levels for different drivers of success, operational areas, risk categories or strategic imperatives. An organisation might have a low appetite for risks relating to governance, legislative compliance, reputation and brand, and WHS, and a high risk appetite for research and development of new products as well as business models, where the failure rate might be high but the returns are great. Table 22.2 shows one organisation's risk appetite for different risk categories, but another organisation might have different risk appetites for these categories.

To determine the risk appetite for a particular success driver, operational area, risk categories or strategic imperative, weigh up how critical it is to the organisation against what could happen should something compromise it, and whether, and to what extent, the organisation is willing to accept those consequences. For opportunities, weigh up how much an opportunity would strengthen a business area or success driver against the effort (e.g. in terms of cost and time) of optimising it.

TABLE 22.2 Risk appetite matrix

	Willingness to accept risk			
Risk category	**Low**	**Medium**	**High**	**Very high**
Compliance		X		
Environment		X		
Financial		X		
Workplace health and safety	X			
Intellectual property	X			
Quality	X			
Reputation	X			
Research and development				X
Security of tangible assets		X		
Strategic			X	

Answering questions like the following for both operational and strategic risks can help you balance risks against rewards and create an appropriate risk culture:

- Are the risks we pay most attention to consistent with our overall strategy and goals?
- Is the organisation too comfortable with risk, putting itself in excessive danger? Or too risk averse, missing opportunities?
- What level of risk exposure requires a formal strategy to mitigate it? Why?
- What level of risk exposure requires our immediate action? Why?
- What risks are we willing to take? Why? Where is our boundary between acceptable and unacceptable risk? Why?
- Where should we allocate our time and resources to minimise risk exposure? Why?

The 'Why?' questions help you state the qualitative or quantitative basis for the level of risk appetite selected.

Risk culture

An organisation's **risk culture** describes how aware of risks and opportunities, and their potential effects on the organisation, employees at all levels and in all parts of the organisation are, and how conscious they are of the role they play in controlling and optimising those risks and opportunities. Ambiguous or weak risk cultures lead to inappropriate behaviours towards risk. Some serious risks might be treated too lightly some of the time or all of the time, while other far less serious risks consume inordinately large amounts of effort, money and time.

The elements of a risk culture are shown in Figure 22.6. In strong risk cultures, risk management isn't placed in a separate 'silo' of isolated, stand-alone programs. It is an integral part of an organisation's daily routines, processes and practices, and it is incorporated into strategic, business and operational planning and decision-making as well as the organisation's various management systems. This protects the organisation from the beginning and through all stages of an asset acquisition, operational area, product, project, process and supply chain.

Like all cultures, risk culture starts at the top and is built on a healthy risk philosophy and policies, a clear risk appetite and a trained workforce that is well aware of risks and their roles and individual

FIGURE 22.6 Elements of a risk culture

responsibilities in avoiding them and bringing to management's attention any budding risks. The risk manager monitors and guides the risk culture by, for example, offering interesting and informative risk management training and working with senior management and the board to establish clear risk management processes and guidelines.

Since people pay attention to what is measured, risk management metrics are included in performance reporting systems and individual measures of success and are continuously monitored. This also eliminates the possibility of duplication when measuring and monitoring organisational activities.

The diversity advantage

Diversity is a key cultural risk management tool. People with truly different perspectives, knowledge, skills, and work and life experiences help organisations avoid groupthink, challenge assumptions, spot opportunities, recognise decision-making biases and connect the dots to spot emerging risks. Companies lacking in diversity risk missing out.

Transferable skills

1.4 Business operations

22.2 Understanding the risk management principles and framework

Call on God, but row away from the rocks.

Indian proverb

Risk management refers to the coordinated activities and systems that identify and manage the many risks that can affect an organisation's ability to achieve its objectives. It is part of the overall **duty of care** and responsibility the organisation's board of directors and senior managers owe to the organisation and its stakeholders and is part of the organisation's corporate governance structure. The principles-based approach of AS ISO 31000:2018 (replaces AS/NZS ISO 31000:2009) highlights the importance of leadership by top management and the integration of risk management, starting with the governance of the organisation; and places a greater emphasis on the iterative nature of risk management, noting that new experiences, knowledge and analysis can lead to revision in process elements, actions and controls.

A solid **risk management framework** (RMF), shown in Figure 22.7, provides the arrangements needed to identify, prioritise, treat (but not 'overmanage') and monitor the way an organisation identifies and deals with the risks in all aspects of its operations. The best RMFs also strengthen your risk maturity and risk resilience. RMFs rely on the commitment of senior management and are made up of policies and objectives, and arrangements, such as the RMPs, accountabilities, resources, processes and activities that manage risk.

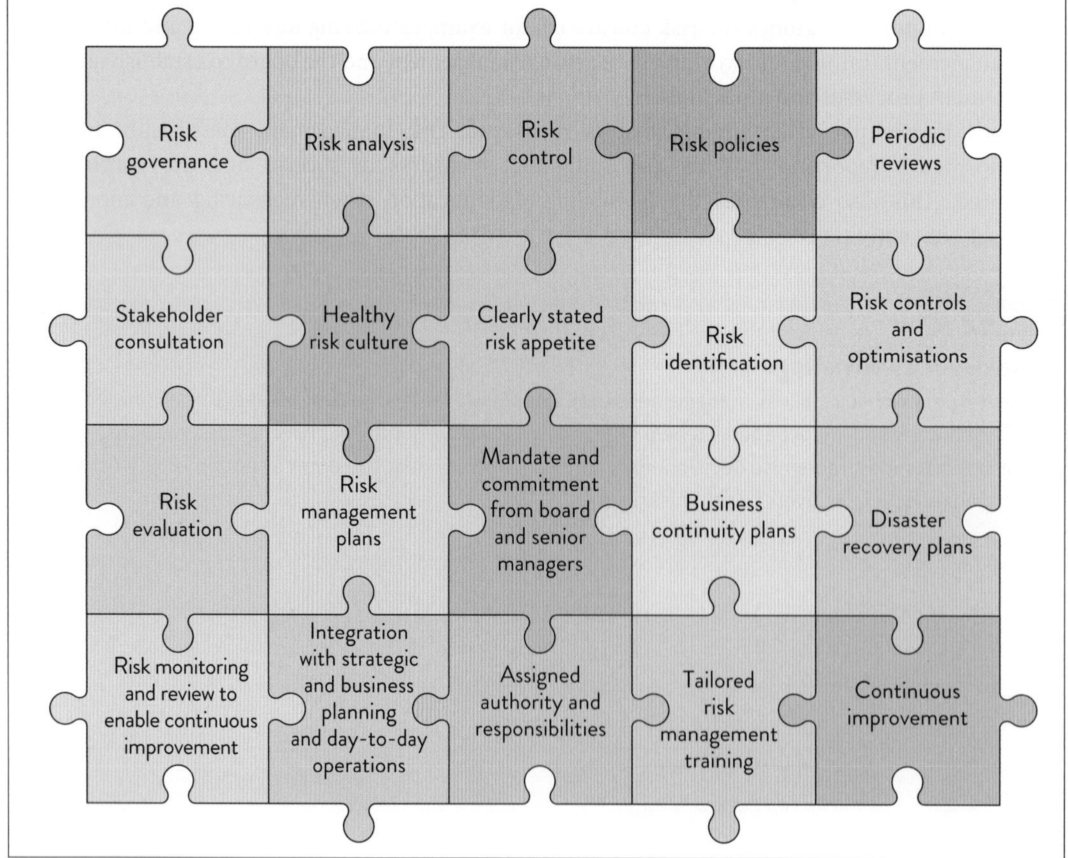

FIGURE 22.7 The risk management framework

Stakeholder communication and consultation is an ongoing feature of the RMF, as is continuous improvement. The framework needs to be continually monitored and reviewed so it can evolve and be continually improved as the organisation, its circumstances and its operations and operating environment change.

Risk management software

Transferable skills
5.2 Technology use

Risk management software systematises your RMF and uses automation technologies to make managing risks and incidents easy. It can, for example, alert you when risks reach a certain threshold and provide reporting information. When it comes to risk management software, there are many choices available. You can have three types of risk management software packages: bespoke, generic or industry specific. Aim for:

- software that includes dashboards, remediation strategies, reporting templates
- risk registers with links to incident logs that send out automated emails alerting the risk owner (the individual or committee members) of a reported incident
- step-by-step planning for a range of RMPs (e.g. plans targeting business continuity and disaster recovery, operational risks, reputational risks and strategic risks)
- graphics showing how various risks link to each other
- tools that can establish whether or not an event reflects an organisation's risk appetite and needs treating.

Automated tools like these are readily available, making your job as a risk manager so much easier.

IN PRACTICE

Empty rhetoric

One of the world's worst human-made risk events was the explosion of BP's Deepwater Horizon oil rig and resulting oil spill in the Gulf of Mexico in 2010. Investigators blamed the disaster on what amounts to a flimsy risk management framework that impeded the ability for those involved to determine what the risks were and thus to sufficiently evaluate, communicate and address them.[26]

Why manage risk?

Waiting until you have time to attend to risks or until a negative event threatens operations before deciding how to respond to it may mean you respond too late or inappropriately and your organisation may never recover. Waiting for an opportunity to tap you on the shoulder is more likely to result in it whizzing past you before you've noticed it, leaving you scratching your head and wondering how you could have been so blind.

Identifying and managing risks reduces the chance of serious error, omissions, shocks and unwelcome surprises and helps organisations deal with interruptions to operations and threats to customers, employees,

A foreseeable and preventable human-made disaster ignored

It is a well-known pattern since ancient times – a fault line runs through the north-east coast of Japan and about every 100 years an earthquake hits, generating a tsunami. A 2100-year-old monument on a hill in Fukushima prefecture states, 'Beware the great tsunami; do not build below this level.' Yet far below that hill, at ground level where the land meets the ocean, the Fukushima Daiichi nuclear plant was built, where sooner or later, a massive earthquake and tsunami would strike

and destroy the plant. It seems the Japanese Government spent a lot of time, effort and money to convince the country of the 'absolute safeness' (meaning zero risk, which can't exist) of nuclear power and nothing could go wrong. The real risk became a taboo topic and was ignored.[27] However, Kiyoshi Kurokawa, chair of the Fukushima nuclear accident independent inquiry, was blunt when he said, 'It was a profoundly man-made disaster that could and should have been prevented'.[28]

information, IP and public image, as well as identify and grasp opportunities quickly. Paradoxically, effective risk management also allows higher risks to be taken in pursuit of opportunities and goals.

Transferable skills
2.1 Critical thinking
3.4 Leadership

Risk management principles

Adhering to risk management principles encourages proactive risk management, improves organisational resilience and increases the likelihood of the organisation achieving its objectives. It helps organisations meet their legal and regulatory responsibilities and international norms, work effectively with stakeholders, and control and allocate resources to treat risks. Effective risk management:

- is an integral part of all organisational activities
- takes a structured and comprehensive approach
- is customised and proportionate to the organisation's context and objectives
- includes appropriate and timely involvement of stakeholders to enable their knowledge, views and perceptions to be considered
- is dynamic as it anticipates, detects, acknowledges and responds to changes and events in a timely manner
- is based on the best available information, including historical and current information as well as future expectations while accounting for limitations
- recognises that human behaviour and culture significantly influence aspects of risk management at each level and stage
- is continually improved through learning and experience.[29]

Who is responsible for managing risk?

Every employee and contractor is responsible for following the organisation's risk management policies and procedures, and for remaining aware of the risks they and the organisation might be exposed to and the risks to which they themselves might expose the organisation. However, the ultimate responsibility for identifying and managing risk and establishing a robust risk culture lies with the board, which establishes the organisation's risk appetite and risk management policies and monitors the effectiveness of the various programs and measures that flow from the policies.

The *board risk management and audit committee* oversees the development, implementation and continuous improvement of organisation's risk management framework and processes. Their role is to satisfy themselves regarding the adequacy and appropriateness of the organisation's entire risk management framework. At least once, and sometimes twice a year, committee members audit the organisation's RMPs to ensure they are up to date and meet the needs of the organisation. They examine the risk register and the policies and programs for each risk. They may test the effectiveness of risk management arrangements by, for example, asking how a risk assessment was carried out, examining the effectiveness of controls to eliminate or reduce the risk, and identifying improvement areas. They also confirm that 'further actions' identified in the RMPs by *risk event management teams* or individual risk owners have been taken.

At a more strategic level, the board risk management and audit committee monitors the risk culture; considers the extent to which risk management is built into the organisation's normal decision-making, planning and reporting procedures; and identifies areas where it is weak or unhealthy and how it could be improved. It ensures that all key strategic organisational objectives are mapped for risk and that early warning indicators are in place where appropriate.

It examines the *business impact statements* (periodic monitoring reports) on significant risks made by risk event management teams, and also examines the processes that identify new or emerging risks and ensures that positive aspects of risk are assessed so that the organisation can benefit from opportunities that arise.

Risk management committees, made up of a cross-section of employees, stakeholders affected by the risk and experts in the area of the risk, assist the board in carrying out its risk management responsibilities. These committees develop and test RMPs for individual risks; monitor and report risks; communicate and consult with employees; keep abreast of changing legislative, regulatory and other requirements; and monitor project risk registers. *Risk owners*, risk event management teams or individual managers are tasked with monitoring individual risks.

What makes a good risk manager?

Good risk managers are strategic thinkers who are able to look beyond risks and appreciate broader trends. Yet they're strong on detail, too. They know how to build effective working relationships, communicate clearly and translate risk metrics so management and stakeholders can understand the organisation's risk exposure. They can think outside the box and they've mastered the technical aspects of risk management, especially the models. They're risk takers, too, because when you keep saying 'No', nothing can ever be achieved and you doom the organisation to fail in its mission. Perhaps, most importantly, they seek to raise awareness and engage the whole organisation and its stakeholders to take responsibility for effective risk management.

The fatal price of complacency

Perth-based Sundance Resources Company, an international iron ore company, lost its entire board of directors and, ironically, a risk management consultant, in a plane crash in West Africa in June 2010. Instead of smaller groups shuttling to the company's mine, they all flew together, in breach of company travel policy. To make matters worse, they flew on an airline and on a type of aircraft specifically banned by their specialist risk management insurance firm.[30]

Risk management policies

A risk management policy sets the organisation's commitment to risk management and its general approach to managing risks. It states:

- the organisation's goals and overall approach to identifying and managing risks
- the principles for considering the interests of, and communicating with, each stakeholder group when managing risk
- how and when RMPs and programs are trialled, reviewed and updated
- the roles and accountabilities of the board, management, risk committees and any internal risk management specialists.

The international and national benchmarks for risk management

The benchmark, AS ISO 31000:2018 (see **Figure 22.8**), provides general standards on risk management. Covering the principles, framework and process for managing risks, it can be used by associations, groups and individuals, and community, private and public enterprises. The standard applies to a wide range of activities, including asset management, functions, operations, processes, products, projects, services, strategies and decisions, and can be applied to any type of risk.

Risk management plans

More significant risks can be managed to acceptable or tolerable levels using risk management plans (RMPs). To develop RMPs, you first identify, assess and prioritise the risks based on their likelihood of occurrence and level of impact on the organisation's operations or stakeholders. An RMP describes a specific risk and what the organisation is doing to improve it, remove it or control it (risk management systems), and/or *contingency plans* to deal with it should it occur. It describes the procedures, resources, responsibilities, and sequence and timing of activities in managing the risk event. RMPs need to reflect and support the organisation's overall strategy and business plans while also aiming to meet the expectations of its stakeholders. (Section 22.3 details how to develop an RMP.)

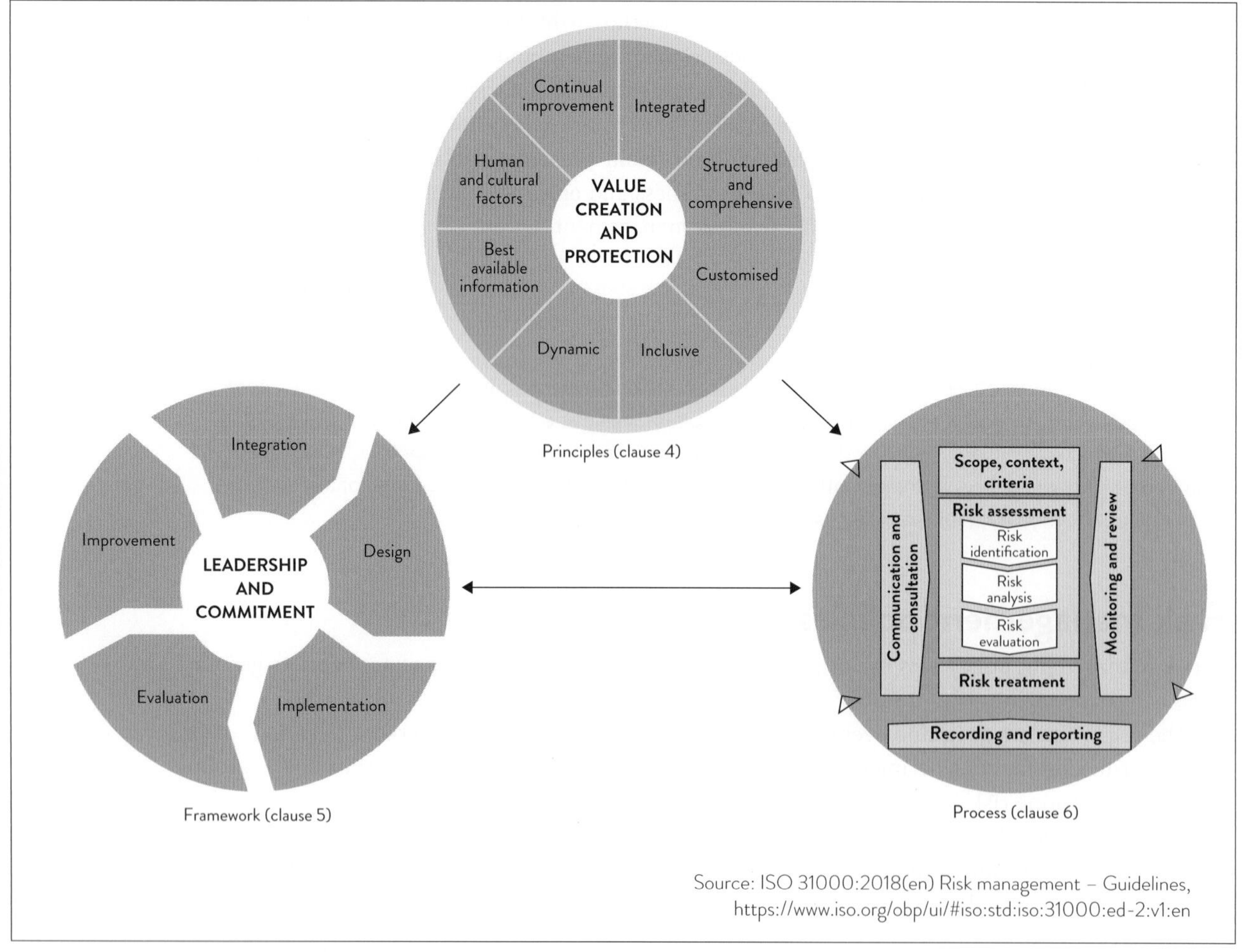

Source: ISO 31000:2018(en) Risk management – Guidelines, https://www.iso.org/obp/ui/#iso:std:iso:31000:ed-2:v1:en

FIGURE 22.8 AS ISO 31000:2018 Principles, framework and process

Business continuity plans and disaster recovery plans

Transferable skills

1.3 Sustainability

1.4 Business operations

3.1 Teamwork/relationships

3.4 Leadership

A **business continuity plan** (BCP) outlines exactly how an organisation will continue operating *during* and *following* a disaster or significant disruption to its operations. The aim of the BCP is to minimise the impact that a catastrophic event might have on an organisation's ability to reliably deliver its products and services. A **disaster recovery plan** (DRP), a subset of business continuity planning, details the steps to be taken following the event to return to safe, normal operation as soon as possible. Both plans state how employees are to communicate, and how and where they are to carry out their work.

The starting point is a *business impact analysis* that identifies the organisation's most essential operations, who performs them and how losing them would affect the organisation. The more damaging those effects, the higher the priority to develop a business continuity plan. When developing business continuity plans, it's wise to anticipate interruptions of essential government services and work out how to ensure core business activities can be sustained over months; you don't need to state why, just that this has occurred and take it from there. Factor in the psychological effects that traumatic events, such as bushfires, floods and pandemics, may have on employees, clients and their families, and on the local community, and decide the action you can take to ensure adequate care for the mental and physical health and wellbeing of employees and to provide assistance to the general community.

A BCP or DRP might include, for example:

- alternatives to essential supplier activities (e.g. transportation systems to provide essential materials, backup generators and fuel for power)
- arrangements for regular business continuity exercises with other key parties, such as emergency services, fire brigade and police
- arrangements to keep contact lists up to date
- arrangements to secure the premises during periods of vacancy
- measures to ensure knowledge and skills are distributed across interstate or geographically dispersed branch offices
- measures to ensure security in the event of multiple demands on the security provider(s)
- multiskilling employees on critical activities and tasks
- nominated off-site crisis meeting points and crisis communication plans for key staff
- off-site storage of copies of all critical information
- providing police and emergency services with a contact and alternative contact in the organisation
- succession/stand-in plans for key personnel
- the procurement of a second IT system to have on stand-by to get your IT systems running immediately after a crippling disruption
- working with emergency services, such as the fire brigade and police, to develop your plans.

The more severe the risk, the more detailed your plans need to be. For extreme and high risks, nominate understudies to the risk owner in case the risk owner is unavailable. Make arrangements such as trial runs to ensure that everyone involved in the contingency plan remains familiar with their duties.

Your plan should aim first to stabilise the situation and deal with the immediate consequences of the event, perhaps by making arrangements to work with emergency services and other specialists, and nominating a trained person to work with the media. Next, it should plan how to resume the most critical activities and operations, and in what order, showing a series of milestones that return the organisation to normal operations. Then you can tackle the underlying cause of the event or figure out how to survive (and thrive) in the new reality.

Once your BCP or DRP plans are developed, carry out full-scale tests, perhaps twice a year, to ensure they remain current. You need to act quickly and decisively when a disruptive event or potentially disruptive event occurs. It's easier to pull back from implementing your BCP should a potentially disastrous situation not eventuate than to begin implementation on the back foot once an emergency situation or disruptive event is underway.

When the time comes, inform employees and customers that your BCP or DRP has been activated, and advise them about what you know and what you don't know about the situation and what they should and should not do. It's better to overcommunicate than to undercommunicate. A 1800 number, the organisation's intranet, mobile networks, SMS and social media are all effective ways to reach stakeholders. Bear in mind that during times of disaster, like cyclones and bushfires, regular communication networks may be rendered inoperable, so backup forms of communication may be required.

22.3 Managing risks

> Those who triumph compute at their headquarters a great number of factors prior to a challenge. Those who are defeated compute at their headquarters a small number of factors prior to a challenge. Much computation brings triumph; little computation brings defeat. By observing only this, I can see triumph or defeat.
>
> Sun Tzu (c. 400 BCE), *The art of war*, cited in R. La Monica, *Protecting your assets: The art of strategic business intelligence*, Tertiary Press, Melbourne, 2005.

Risk management isn't about avoiding risks but understanding them and dealing with them in a systematic way. As seen in Figure 22.8, this is a continuous process that helps you identify and develop suitable risk management procedures and position your organisation to respond to risks and disruptive events. We review that process in the following sections.

Transferable skills

2.2 Personal effectiveness

3.1 Teamwork/relationships

3.2 Verbal communication

3.3 Written communication

3.4 Leadership

Consult and communicate with stakeholders

The AS ISO 31000:2018 standard explains that the 'purpose of communication and consultation is to assist relevant stakeholders in understanding risk, the basis on which decisions are made and the reasons why particular actions are required'.[31] By communicating effectively with stakeholders we can promote awareness and understanding of risk, then through consultation we can seek their ideas and feedback. Often one of the biggest risks that organisations contend with is a lack of stakeholder support for decisions made and actions taken. Effective communication and consultation with stakeholders can help us to identify risks previously not considered, understand different perspectives on existing risks and, most importantly, gain their support and commitment to decisions that are made and actions taken.

Communicating and consulting with stakeholders is an ongoing and iterative process that begins when we start to identify risks and then continues throughout the entire event or operation. In Victoria, community consultation is now a statutory requirement for all councils when decisions are being made with respect to a range of matters, including the adoption of the council plan and making of local laws.[32]

You might invite stakeholder representatives to join the risk management committee and risk event management teams, and consult other stakeholders as you identify and evaluate risks, develop risk management treatments and develop and review the RMP. When the risk is organisation-wide, include representatives from all operational areas. Involving stakeholders is important, but remember that consultation is about informed discussion. Ensure that all decisions are based on factual information, knowledge and experience. (Chapter 26 has more information on involving others and Chapter 25 explains how to prepare for and lead meetings.)

Even when the events that would trigger the plan seem remote, communicate the plan to the workforce so that everyone is aware of the plan and its contents and their own related duties and responsibilities. Design and provide any necessary training and education so that people understand the risk and what to do should it happen. Ensure that the plan is readily available and that people know where and how to access it.

Develop and institute rolling communications campaigns to make sure that the RMP's principles and procedures remain fresh in people's minds. Articles in the organisation's newsletters and intranet, periodic drills and trial runs, posters and training are all good ways to keep people aware of RMPs and of their own roles in preventing and mitigating risk events. The precise frequency and nature of communication depends on the attrition at your workplace and the nature of the risk event itself.

Establish the scope, context and criteria

The purpose of establishing the scope, context and criteria is to customise the risk management process, and to enable effective risk assessment and appropriate risk treatment. Defining the scope involves being clear about the levels to which the risk management activities will apply (e.g. strategic, operational, program or project) and their alignment with organisational objectives. The ISO states that scope considerations should include:

- objectives and decisions that need to be made
- outcomes expected from the steps taken
- time, location, inclusions and exclusions
- risk assessment tools and techniques
- resources required, responsibilities and records to be kept
- relationships with other projects, processes and activities.[33]

Earlier in this chapter we looked at a variety of potential internal and external risks; that is, the organisation's risk context. Many organisations establish the context at a strategic planning workshop, during which the organisation's vision is reviewed and adjusted as necessary, an environmental scan is undertaken and its risk appetite is reviewed and agreed upon. Together, these form the basis for formulating strategy. From there, priorities and targets to achieve the vision and strategy are agreed and incorporated into the strategic plan as strategic imperatives or strategic goals. This allows the risk manager to develop a strategic risk and opportunity register to ensure that all uncertainties are addressed so that the organisation can meet its strategic imperatives. The risk management committee reviews the register, which then goes to the board of directors for approval. A senior manager or risk management team – the risk owner – is then allocated responsibility for each strategic risk.

Two common frameworks for beginning to understand the risk context are *PESTEL* (political, economic, societal, technological, environmental and legal) and SWOT (strengths, weaknesses, opportunities and threats) analyses, both of which are explained in the following sections. You can also use a **cause-and-effect diagram** to scan key areas (explained in Chapter 26). This groundwork helps you identify risks and define whether a risk is acceptable and, in this way, sets the scene for managing risks.

Transferable skills
1.3 Sustainability
2.1 Critical thinking
2.3 Business strategy

Do a PESTEL analysis

Brainstorm the risks (and opportunities) in the PESTEL areas in which your organisation operates. You might begin with an overview of each area and then move on to more specific risks by area. While there are usually recurring risks in each of these areas (e.g. political; change of government may mean change of policy), it is important to identify the specific trends (or risks) that are emerging and their impact on your organisation (e.g. political; government and opposition have strengthened their policy on climate change and commit to a whole-of-economy plan to achieve net zero emissions by 2050).

Ask these questions:

- What has happened in this area over the last two to three years?
- What will, or is likely to, happen over the next few years?
- What could happen over the next few years?
- What is the impact on our sector, industry or organisation if it does happen?
- What aspects of our organisation and its strategy and operations will be affected?

Do a SWOT analysis

While PESTEL helps you find risks and opportunities in the external environment, SWOT looks both externally and internally for risks and opportunities. As illustrated in **Figure 22.9**, it examines the organisation's internal strengths and weaknesses, and the opportunities and threats in its external environment. (SWOT analyses are also used to develop strategic and business plans.)

INTERNAL	
STRENGTHS Consider your organisation's internal strengths, derived from its capabilities, employees, intellectual property, stakeholder goodwill, strategies, drivers of success and so on that distinguish it from its competitors.	**WEAKNESSES** Consider your organisation's weaknesses, posed by its ability to innovate, financial position, infrastructure, knowledge base, processes, strategies and so on that make it vulnerable.
THREATS Consider the risks posed by your organisation's operating environment, such as new or emerging business models and technologies, its competition, geographic location, supply chains and so on that you can avoid, minimise or turn into opportunities.	**OPPORTUNITIES** Consider trends in your organisation's location, socioeconomic trends, technological trends and so on that you can capitalise on.
EXTERNAL	

FIGURE 22.9 SWOT analysis

Internally, and in the context of your organisation's strategies and objectives, key drivers of success and the basic parameters in which risks must be managed, consider factors such as:

- culture (including risk culture) and values
- customer loyalty and unfolding needs
- employee profiles in terms of engagement and flexibility; also their ability to meet the organisation's current and future objectives in terms of their current skills and potential
- financial security and stability, security of cash flow, effectiveness of asset distribution, relationships with key creditors, debtors and trading partners
- the growth potential, profitability, range, sustainability and quality of the organisation's products, packaging and services
- the organisation's reputation for quality and reliability
- the quality and reliability of work processes and systems (e.g. administration and information systems; production management; customer service and delivery systems; WHS and training systems)
- the quality, soundness and sustainability of buildings, plant and equipment, particularly regarding their age and ongoing supportability and how they compare with the competition.

Any of these can be strengths or weaknesses. Also consider the organisation's ability to:

- adapt and respond flexibly to changes in the marketplace and to competitor activity
- build effective working relationships with stakeholders
- empower and develop individuals and teams to meet its goals
- innovate and make continuous improvements
- make sound and timely decisions
- manage costs and information
- nurture a learning environment
- recruit and develop the employees it needs
- think and manage strategically
- reward performance.

In the external environment, ask:

- What do trends in regard to climate, the economy, and politics, society, technology and other key areas hold in store for the organisation?
- What is likely to happen in the organisation's industry and marketplace, particularly changes and trends in consumer patterns and government regulation, opportunities for expansion, technology and threats from new or existing competitors?
- Is the cost, supply and quality of our raw materials reliable?

Think more broadly, too:

- What is likely to happen in the national economies you operate in and in the global economy?
- What is happening in the world political arena?
- What technological threats and opportunities might develop?

Identify risks

Transferable skills

1.4 Business operations

2.1 Critical thinking

3.1 Teamwork/ relationships

Rather than deal with the organisation as a whole, it's often easier to consider the organisation's strategic goals and functions, operational areas and risk areas (e.g. brand risk, financial risk, HR risk, IT risk, reputation risk, supply-chain risk, etc.) or, for capabilities-based organisations, its capability streams, and identify risks for each in separate brainstorming workshops (as shown in Figure 22.10 identifying business functions, and Figure 22.11 risks identified for supply chain function). Your goal is to find, recognise and describe the risks that could affect the achievement of the organisation's objectives.

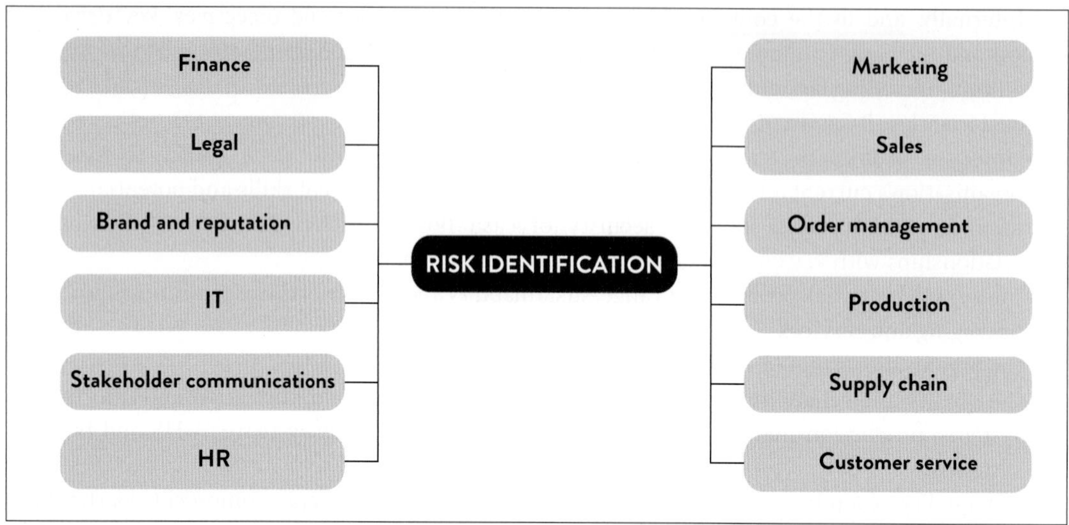

FIGURE 22.10 Begin by identifying business functions

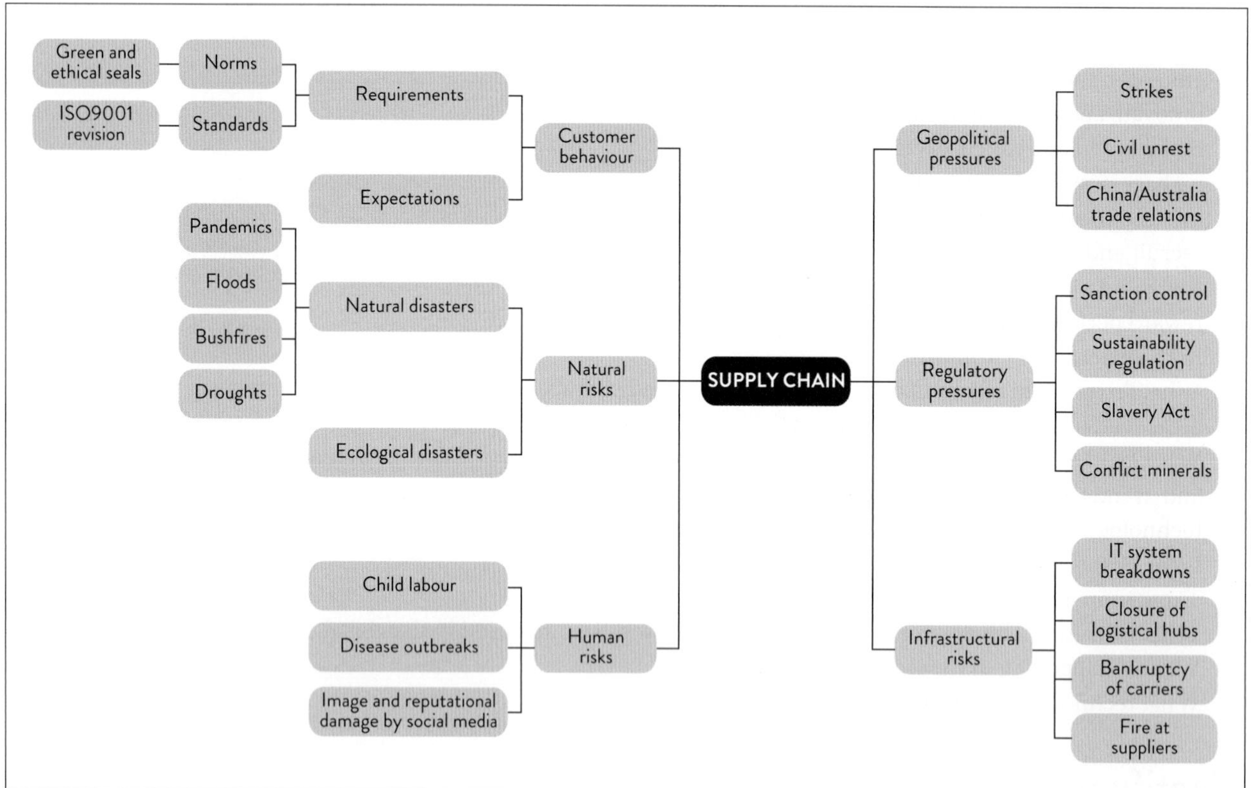

FIGURE 22.11 Mind map of risks identified for supply chain function

Based on the risk context you have established earlier, identify the key risks and opportunities facing the organisation. Begin by preparing a comprehensive list of possible extrinsic and intrinsic *risk circumstances*, *risk events* and *risk sources* that could affect the organisation's normal operations, their possible causes and their potential consequences. Risk events and circumstances could be tangible or intangible occurrences that alone or in combination have potential to give rise to a risk. They could be one occurrence or several, or even a non-occurrence, when something doesn't happen that you expect to happen. One risk event (which you identified when you established the risk context) can generate a range of positive and negative consequences that can escalate through knock-on effects. Think widely so that you include even those with a remote likelihood of occurring when they would significantly harm (or help) the organisation.

Some other ways to identify risks that can be used alone or in combination, and can supplement or replace the brainstorming workshops, include:

- analyse accident statistics and **near misses**
- conduct scenario planning
- examine contracts with external organisations and individuals
- identify risks for capability streams, critical activities, drivers of success or strategic imperatives
- inspect organisational performance reports (e.g. customer feedback, income and cash flow records)
- inspect safety audits
- interview key people and stakeholders for their informed opinions and expert advice
- map your supply chains
- use questionnaires and written surveys
- work through your critical resources.

We examine five of these below. Whichever methods you use, verify *every* significant assumption when listing (and later, analysing) a risk. Obtain relevant data whenever possible to analyse and help you spot peaks and troughs, recurring problems and incidents, and trends that could provide valuable insights. (Chapter 27 explains how to plot and gain useful information from data.)

Conduct a stress audit

Is stress a problem in your organisation? If you think it might be, conduct a stress audit to find out who is feeling stressed. You could ask a representative sample of employees about their work-related stress levels, what they believe to be the source of any stress they feel (e.g. lack of control over their work, organisation change, organisation culture, overworking, poor relationship with manager, poor work–life balance) and how they feel the organisation helps them handle stress.

Then analyse the results. Are employees who feel stressed clustered in a particular area or at a particular level? Are the numbers higher than you would expect? If so, your organisation has a duty of care to take measures to control stress (find out more about this in Chapter 31).

Analyse near misses

Do you know that nearly all mishaps at NASA have resulted from a series of 'small signals that went unnoticed at the critical moment'?[34] Many adverse events are preceded by recurring problems and near misses – close calls that would have been worse if not for chance. It's easy to come to see these as 'normal' and brush them aside. But in a healthy risk culture, people are alert to near misses and deviations from the norm.

A series of small, often seemingly minor mishaps, human errors, technical failures and poor decisions can eventually combine to produce a significant failure. So rather than seeing a near miss as evidence that the system is working well and breathing a sigh of relief, see these incidents as warning signs. Look for the cause and fix it, and review your risk controls (Chapter 26 explains how to spot and analyse deviations, problems and near misses).

Identify risks for critical activities

List the activities, capabilities, operational areas, outcomes, processes, projects and roles critical to the organisation's performance and achieving its strategic imperatives, or main goals. These are your high priorities. Work through them one by one, listing the risks, risk sources and events that could affect them (e.g. through brainstorming or undertaking a SWOT analysis).

Conduct a key position audit

Employees with skills and knowledge that are uniquely valuable to an organisation's success may represent *key person or key position risk*. The impact of losing a key person may be felt across all success factors: profitability, response time, productivity, image, reputation and confidence. Identify the organisation's most critical job roles and how they might be at risk. For example, if the role-holder left the organisation, how easy or difficult would it be to attract, recruit and train a replacement? What knowledge and information might the role-holder take with them and is this information and knowledge captured elsewhere in the organisation? Are internal successors available for key roles? Are role-holders and potential successors kept up to date with technical and other advances in their area? One aim should be to spread the knowledge across a team rather than just a key person. Having people document and systematically create checklists for what they are working on helps to manage the risk, as does mentoring co-workers.[35]

Transferable skills
2.1 Critical thinking
3.1 Teamwork/relationships
3.4 Leadership
4.1 Data Literacy

Use scenario planning to predict the future

Steve Jobs, founder of Apple Inc., said of the future, 'The web will be one more area of significant change and those who don't pay attention will get hurt, while those who see it early enough will get rewarded'.[36] Implausible as this statement sounded at the time, in hindsight Jobs was stating the obvious. But imagining a future that isn't an extension of today isn't easy and it's made harder by groupthink and *heuristics*, the brain's unconscious thought processes. (Groupthink and heuristics are explained in Chapter 26.) In fact, there are lots of possible futures, some more plausible than others, but each possible. This is where scenario planning can be useful. Scenario planning is traditionally used to help identify threats, but it's now increasingly used to generate ideas for innovation.

Scenario planning taps into people's imaginations, intuition and knowledge bases to describe plausible futures and develop 'stories', or scenarios, about how they might unfold three, 10 or even 20 years from now; appropriate responses to each can then be developed. These imagined futures aren't meant to be definitive, but they help organisations anticipate and plan for future risks and opportunities, including the black swan events, that are otherwise difficult to imagine.

To develop possible scenarios, follow these six steps:

1 Work with your organisation's top decision-makers, key stakeholders and thinkers, and gather their views about future developments with questions such as: which decisions are likely to make or break the organisation over the next few years? What trends are most important to our operations and customers now and in the future? Which potential developments in the industry and marketplace excite you the most?
2 Gather and analyse relevant developments and trends and compile a list of external forces that seem most likely to affect your organisation.
3 Weave together the information from Steps 1 and 2 to sketch out plausible future scenarios. Some authorities recommend aiming for three scenarios: your worst nightmare, a different but better world, and a world that is basically an extension of the current world. Give each scenario a name that makes it vivid and memorable.
4 Assess the implications of each scenario for your organisation.
5 Identify the real-life developments and signs that could indicate each scenario is unfolding. These might include competitor activity, demographic changes, environmental trends, regulatory trends and technological trends.
6 Develop appropriate RMPs and put a risk event management team in place for each scenario.

Map your supply chains

Transferable skills

1.1 Financial literacy

1.4 Business operations

2.1 Critical thinking

3.1 Teamwork/relationships

3.4 Leadership

There are everyday risks and exceptional risks along every organisation's supply chain. One is putting all your supply eggs in one basket. What if the supplier has a fire in its factory or the transport chain is broken or compromised? You're left scrambling around looking for another supplier, while months of production and sales evaporate. You can avoid that by identifying the suppliers you depend on most and working out whether it makes sense to create a second supplier partnership.

Work through your organisation's supply chain from beginning to end to identify risks in terms of, for example, environmental, social and governance criteria of suppliers; their reliability and flexibility; and the transportation routes and sustainability of their supplies. Sourcing from lower-cost suppliers in developing economies puts you at risk of accusations of labour exploitation and negative environmental impacts arising from poorly enforced labour and other laws, and poor WHS and human resource management practices. Even when these risks are not in your first-level suppliers but buried deep in the supply chain, they can damage your organisation's reputation, image, brands and, ultimately, its profitability.

You can avoid this outcome by mapping your supply chain in depth. Supply chain software, for example, compiles data about contractors, suppliers and sub-suppliers and you can alter the parameters so you only do business with companies that have similar values and standards.

Risk events may be outside your organisation's control, so you may need to work out how to become aware of and respond to them. Remember that supply chains that are lean and low cost may look good on paper but can be extremely expensive should the unexpected occur.

IN PRACTICE

How the world ran out of everything

The COVID-19 pandemic led to global shortages of many goods due to decades of pursuing industrial efficiency through just-in-time manufacturing, where parts are delivered to factories right as they are required, hence reducing the cost of inventories and their associated management. Pioneered by Toyota more than 50 years ago, this approach has been embraced by industries beyond the automotive sector, from fashion to food processing to pharmaceuticals, allowing them to adapt to changing market demands while cutting costs.

But as the pandemic hampered factory operations and delivered chaos to global shipping and transportation, many countries and sectors suffered from shortages in materials and lengthy delays in deliveries – from medical supplies to personal protective equipment to electronics, timber, clothing, paints and sealants.

So while just-in-time and lean operations have generated innovations and savings, and will no doubt continue to do so after the problems associated with the pandemic have abated, it does raise the question whether organisations have been too aggressive in harvesting savings by slashing inventories, hence leaving them unprepared for supply chain disruptions.[37]

Some questions to help you think through how much at risk your supply chains are include:

- How financially stable are companies in your supply chain?
- How prone are they to extreme climatic events because of their location?
- How adversarial/cordial are their industrial relations?
- Are they located in politically stable areas?
- Who do they source their raw materials from? How secure are those sources? What risks might they pose, for example, in terms of corporate responsibility?

- How easily and quickly could your organisation source those supplies elsewhere?
- How dependable is the quality of what they supply?
- Are companies in your supply chain located in the same geographic area, meaning that one event, such as a flood, tsunami or pandemic, would affect the entire chain?
- What would be the cost to your organisation if your suppliers' operations were disrupted?

Work through your critical resources

Brainstorm risks by key drivers of success and the resources the organisation needs to have working optimally in order to achieve its goals. Think about, for instance:

- *Capabilities:* how the organisation creates value, for example, through design and marketing, delivery and invoicing, the ability to bring new products or services to market quickly, information systems and work flows.
- *Cost:* for example, direct and indirect, and economies of scale and scope.
- *Culture and values:* for example, customer focus, learning, improvement and innovation orientation, problem-solving and communication methods, responsibility and accountability, risk culture, trust and the way people work together.
- *Resource velocity:* the rate at which value is created from applied resources; for example, asset use, inventory turns, lead times, throughput.
- *Revenue:* for example, sales, market size, price structure.
- *Staff:* for example, the organisation's employer value proposition, the way it attracts and retains staff, employee engagement, motivation and competencies, succession and quality of leadership.
- *Structures:* for example, the buildings, organisation structure and physical layout.
- *Systems:* for example, administration and information systems; customer service and delivery systems; financial and budgetary control systems (e.g. cost and debt control); WHS marketing and corporate relations; performance management and productivity systems; training systems; and waste and energy management systems.

Record the risks and opportunities your organisation faces once you've identified them. You could begin with a simple matrix by adapting the one shown in **Figure 22.12**, to risk events and risk areas that suit your organisation, grouping risks into categories and locations. You can also group risks into areas such as brand risk, financial risk, HR risk, IT risk, reputation risk, supply chain risk and so on. Notice that in **Figure 22.12** some risk events are both threats and opportunities. A matrix like this, however, doesn't indicate how various risks interact, which is where good risk management software comes in.

Another way to group risks is shown in **Table 22.3**. (The categories in this table are also useful for reporting and tracking incidents.)

TABLE 22.3 Categories of risk

Risks	Risk name/number
Current	Business-as-usual risks; e.g. health and safety of staff and customers
Operational risks	Business-as-usual risks, financial processes, project risk, unethical conduct
Looming risks	Risks you can see coming in, say, two to three years but are not sure of the precise nature of the risk; e.g. potential regulatory changes, changing customer patterns
Strategic risks	Fundamental shifts in customer preferences, technology changes that affect the organisation's viability, and so on

Risk areas	Internal risks				External risks				
INTERNAL AND EXTERNAL RISKS	**Accidents and hazards**	**Information security**	**Product or service quality**	**Staff**	**Competitor activity**	**Natural disasters**	**Supply lines**	**Pandemics**	**Political and legislative**
Buildings	✓		✓	✓O		✓			
Extended supply chain		✓O	✓O	✓O	✓	✓	✓	✓	✓
Financial stability	✓	✓O	✓O	✓O	✓	✓	✓	✓	✓
Image and reputation	✓O	✓	✓O	✓O	✓O	✓O	✓	✓O	
Plant and equipment	✓		✓	✓O		✓			✓
Proprietary information systems, data		✓		✓			✓		
Staff	✓O		✓O		✓	✓O		✓O	

Prepared by: Risk management committee, 26 November 2021; Reviewed by: GHJ, 6 May 2022

✓ = threat

O = opportunity

FIGURE 22.12 Risk/opportunity matrix

Analyse risks

Now that you have recognised and described the risks your organisation faces, you can begin to examine them and any controls that currently exist. Follow the three-stage procedure described below.

Transferable skills

1.4 Business operations

2.1 Critical thinking

3.1 Teamwork/relationships

4.1 Data literacy

Stage 1: Define the risk

To analyse each risk, begin by defining it in three parts. The first part defines, or names, the risk event, and the second indicates a possible or likely cause or source (e.g. supply chain breaks due to storm activity or IT system crashes due to a virus). These are columns 2 and 3 in the risk register shown in Table 22.5 later in this chapter. This allows you to determine the initial result of the risk, which is the third part of the risk definition – how it would affect the organisation (shown in column 4 in Table 22.5). This indicates who and/or what is at risk; for example, life, ongoing operations, people, property, reputation, and why (e.g. 'supplies dry up and work cannot continue', 'work cannot continue efficiently and some records and data are irretrievable').

You then have a risk definition in this format: 'This event could happen due to ... and this is what it would mean and why'; for example, 'The supply chain breaks due to violent storm activity, which interrupts our operations and means work cannot continue'. Or another example, 'The IT system crashes due to a virus, so work cannot continue efficiently and some records and data are irretrievable'.

Stage 2: Determine the risk's consequences

Next, think about the risk's duration and the severity of its initial consequences to the organisation. This is the *inherent level* of risk. Then think about the longer-term effect and knock-on effects of the risk to the organisation. This is known as the risk's *consequences* or *impact*. Think through possible worst-case scenarios. Be thorough in this, as this information allows you to aim *preventative* risk treatments at the sources of risks and reactive or *contingency* treatments for the results of the risks.

Two scales for assessing consequences are:

- Catastrophic–Major–Moderate–Minor–Insignificant
- Disastrous–Severe–Moderate–Minimal.

You can develop a matrix like the one shown in **Table 22.4**.

Some factors to consider when thinking about consequences include:

- degree of damage or injury to critical activities, equipment, key capabilities, operations, people, property, stakeholders or systems
- degree of reversibility of harm to the organisation or its stakeholders
- effect on financial stability and systems
- effect on goodwill, image, reputation
- effect on supply chain
- financial costs
- legal repercussions (e.g. civil, criminal or industrial lawsuits, legal costs)
- opportunities from, for example, investments, commercial relationships and technology to mitigate (reduce), reverse or even benefit from the consequences

TABLE 22.4 Risk consequence matrix

Impact area	Catastrophic	Major	Moderate	Minor	Insignificant
Environment	Serious effect. Recovery >10 years	Serious effect. Recovery <10 years	Moderate effect. Recovery in 6–12 months	Minor effect. Recovery in 1–6 months	No damage or residual impact but some clean-up required
Legal	Significant prosecution and fines	Major breach of regulation, major litigation	Serious breach of regulation with investigation or report to authorities and prosecution	Minor legal issues, non-compliance and breaches of regulation	Minor legal issues, non-compliance and breaches of regulation
Reputation	Government inquiry	Heavy negative national media coverage	State media coverage	Local press coverage	Incident form filed
Service	1–4 weeks or revenue loss $2 000 000.01	1–7 days or revenue loss $0.5–$2 million	2 hours–1 day or revenue loss $50 000.01 –$0.5 million	30–120 minutes or revenue loss $5000–$50 000.01	<30 minutes or revenue loss of <$50 000

- opportunity-lost costs
- technological consequences (e.g. breakdown, damage to information and communication systems, or theft).

Stage 3: Determine your exposure to the risk

You also need to estimate the risk's *likelihood of occurrence*; this is also known as *exposure*. You have a high exposure to risks with a high probability of occurrence and a low exposure to risks with a low probability of occurrence. Depending on the nature of the risk, this may be in terms of:

- *frequency of exposure:* frequently, often, occasionally or seldom
- *likelihood of occurrence:* highly likely, probable, possible or unlikely.

You can assess frequency by how often an event occurs over a particular time period and likelihood by deciding how certain or unlikely it is the event will occur. You need to be realistic so you can make an informed decision. Figure 22.13 summarises the two dimensions of probability and consequences, which together determine a risk's *significance* (see Figure 22.15).

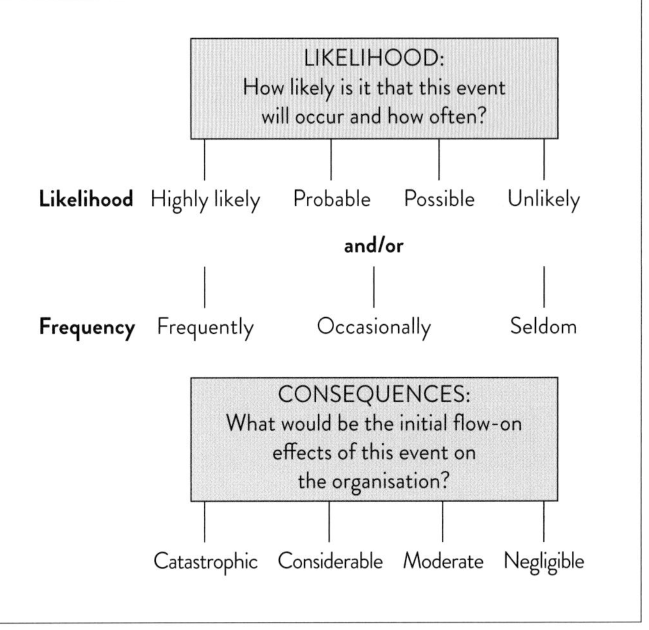

FIGURE 22.13 Dimensions of risk

Another scale of likelihood is:

- *almost certain:* expected to occur once a year or more frequently in most circumstances
- *likely:* expected to occur in one to three years in most circumstances
- *possible:* expected to occur in one to 10 years
- *unlikely:* expected to occur in one to 30 years
- *rare:* expected to occur in one to 100 years in exceptional circumstances.

This chapter shows several scales for likelihood and consequences. You should choose the scale that best suits the risks in your organisation.

Evaluate risks

Weigh up each risk against your *risk criteria* to evaluate the significance or importance of a risk to determine which risks are acceptable and which are unacceptable and need treatment. Think about how each risk event would affect your organisation in the areas shown in Figure 22.14. Choose risk criteria that reflect your organisation's values, policies and objectives; your external and internal risk context; and that conform to laws, policies, accepted standards and other requirements. Bear in mind the views of stakeholders when selecting risk criteria and ensure they are flexible enough to accommodate changing circumstances. Also consider whether there are already some controls in place and their effectiveness.

Transferable skills
1.4 Business operations
2.1 Critical thinking
3.1 Teamwork/ relationships
4.1 Data literacy
5.2 Technology use

When it helps, you can combine a number of risks into one risk to develop a more complete understanding of the overall risk. This is called *risk aggregation*. What you want to do is sensibly balance risks and rewards according to your organisation's appetite for various categories of risk.

FIGURE 22.14 Evaluating risk events

Prioritise the risks

Prioritise the risks by considering their *significance* (also called *level* and *magnitude*). Significance is a function of your *exposure* to each risk (its frequency or likelihood of occurring) and its *consequences* (impact).

When probability is high and consequences low, you might evaluate the risk's significance as moderate. But when consequences are high and probability low, the risk is significant because even a remote chance of a catastrophe warrants more attention than a high chance of a hiccup, so give it a high priority. After all, Qantas has never had a fatal air crash (low probability) but the company still has a major risk to manage due to the enormous consequences of a fatal crash.

To help rank risks according to their significance, you can visually summarise the risks under consideration with a matrix like the one shown in Figure 22.15, writing the risk description, name or reference number in the appropriate area.

FREQUENCY

CONSEQUENCES	**Frequently**	**Occasionally**	**Seldom**
Catastrophic			
Critical			
Moderate			
Negligible			

FIGURE 22.15 Risk significance

A 'heat map', shown in Figure 22.16, is another way to illustrate how risks are prioritised. Risks falling into the red and pink zones are the extreme- and high-level risks. Give them the highest priority for treatment because their likelihood is high and/or consequences significant. Closely monitor those falling into the yellow zone because either their outcomes are serious or their likelihood is high; treatment is recommended and if you choose not to treat a medium, or yellow-zone, risk, you must be able to state your reasons. You probably don't need to treat low, or blue-zone, risks but keep a watchful eye on them, looking particularly for adverse trends.

A team of people from diverse levels and functions should develop heat maps because no single perspective can give you the full picture. The maps should represent consensus about the financial, operational, regulatory and reputational impacts of risks.

Document and file your risk assessment for each risk and the reasons for your evaluation to provide a record of how the decisions were reached. You could summarise your evaluation as a heat map, as shown in the example in Figure 22.17. Always show the date risks were identified, analysed and evaluated and by whom, and the date risk analyses and evaluations were reviewed and by whom.

Likelihood	Insignificant 1	Minor 2	Moderate 3	Major 4	Severe 5
A (Almost certain)	M	M	H	VH	VH
B (Likely)	M	M	H	H	VH
C (Possible)	M	M	M	H	VH
D (Unlikely)	L	M	M	H	H
E (Rare)	L	L	M	M	H

FIGURE 22.16 Heat map

Risk	Probability	Frequency	Consequences	Current risk level
A	Highly likely	Frequently	Catastrophic	Extreme
B	Probable	Often	Critical	High
C	Possible	Occasionally	Moderate	Moderate
D	Unlikely	Seldom	Negligible	Low

Prepared by: Risk Management Committee, 21 December 2021
Reviewed by: CLM, 6 January 2022

FIGURE 22.17 Summarising risk levels

Prioritising IT and IP risk

To manage information and IP risks, identify important information and IP and categorise it according to its value and sensitivity. Four key questions in this exercise include:

1 What 10 pieces of data/information/IP do we rely on most? For each of the 10 pieces, ask these three questions:
2 What would happen if we lost it entirely?
3 What would happen if we lost it but could only recover it with difficulty?
4 What would happen if the competition acquired it?

The answers will indicate the priority areas.

Transferable skills
3.3 Written communication
5.2 Technology use

Build a risk register

Having analysed and evaluated the risks you've identified, you can list them in a risk register and use it to monitor risks. A risk register is a record of information about active risks in the organisation. It may include:

- risk name, identification number and description
- risk impact (consequences)
- date identified, date reviewed, date updated and by whom
- cause of risk
- risk controls pre-event: measures to prevent or mitigate (i.e. lessen by reducing or transferring) the risk, showing where the paperwork is located (e.g. a document file name or number)
- risk controls post-event: contingency plans and business continuity/disaster recovery plans, showing where they are located (e.g. a document file name or number)
- risk evaluation, or likelihood of occurrence and the consequences or severity of its effects (used to determine whether a risk is acceptable or tolerable)
- risk owner, or the person or team with accountability and authority for managing and monitoring the risk
- risk score, or current risk level
- risk trends, or performance measures for risk.

Date risk registers to show the name of the person or committee who prepared or updated each one. Also note the date it was examined and by whom, along with any recommendations.

A risk register often takes the form of a matrix summarising identified risks. Risks are listed vertically and identified by name or a phrase describing the risk; sometimes an identifying number is used. The matrix lists information about each risk horizontally. One form is shown in **Table 22.5**. Notice that this part of the risk register has a built-in 'heat map' showing each risk's inherent and residual risk level and that it summarises the RMP for each risk.

Most organisations have enough risks that a spreadsheet won't do. Electronic risk registers make life easy, especially those linked to reported incidents and to legislation and regulations and that list all the policies, procedures and so on that may help either to mitigate or tolerate the risk. They can also work out how good risk management measures are and show a control effectiveness rating. Electronic risk registers can automatically advise the board of incidents that could become crises. They also provide automatic version controls and are auditable (neither of which are possible with a spreadsheet).

You might want to develop an *intellectual property register* showing your organisation's existing IP, where it's stored, who has access to it and how it's protected, as well as IP 'in the pipeline' – who is developing it, where it is kept and when it's expected to be realised. You could also develop a list of the organisation's information and knowledge, graded for sensitivity and showing where it is stored, who has access to it and how it is protected. Contracts with employees and contractors should also state clearly that IP created for the organisation or during work time belongs to the business.

TABLE 22.5 Part of a risk register

Reference no.	Risk	Cause	Result	Risk owner	Inherent level*	Residual level*	Action required
RO-MGTG 00 1317	Loss of market share	Outdated products, services and strategies, impacting our ability to achieve our financial targets	Gradual loss of revenue threatens business viability	CEO, marketing director	D	S	Invest in R&D; institute service enhancement project; research market trends and drive offerings accordingly; develop more robust measures of customer satisfaction
RO-HR 00 117	Incorrect staffing levels	Skill shortage and inability to attract and retain the people we need; inadequate training and succession planning	Loss of productivity (quantity and quality) leading to erosion of customer base	HR director, general manager	S	Mod	Recruit training manager; undertake gap analysis of skills required versus current skill levels; update recruitment framework, including policies and procedures
RO-OP 00 2217	Critical activities interrupted	Extreme weather, terrorism or similar incident	Operations interrupted, disrupting supplies to the customers	Operations manager	S	Min	RMP to be developed and to include discussions with emergency services and utilities providers. Investigate use of scenario planning

* Disastrous (D), Severe (S), Moderate (Mod), Minimal (Min) Risk register prepared by George Hinos, 4 May 2021, Head office.

Only register 'real' risks

Are the risks in your risk register really risks? It's easy, but a mistake, to list as risks things you can't analyse or manage properly, such as:

- a broad statement, such as compliance failure, environmental damage, fraud or reputation damage
- the cause of a risk, such as inaccurate records, lack of resources, lack of time, poor inventory management or poor project management
- the consequence of a risk, such as overspending a budget, a project coming in late or not reaching strategic goals.

To prevent this, ask yourself whether you could conduct a *post-event risk analysis*. When the answer is yes, you have a risk – one that is worthy of listing in your risk register and one you can plan to mitigate, monitor and manage. Keeping non-risks out of your risk register keeps the numbers down and makes the real risks easier to manage and monitor. Table 22.6 shows a summary of pre- and post-risk event analysis.

TABLE 22.6 Pre- and post-event risk analysis

Pre-event analysis	Post-event analysis
What could happen?	What happened?
Why would it happen?	Why did it happen?
What would the consequences be?	What were the consequences?
What could we do to prevent it happening?	How could we have prevented it happening?
How can we reduce the consequences should it happen?	How could we have reduced the consequences? What can we do to prevent it happening again?

Treat risks

In large organisations dealing with many risks or when dealing with extreme- and high-level risk events that are costly to remove or mitigate (reduce), it can be very complex to treat, or modify, them. A risk management specialist is often employed to supervise this function.

Risks are normally assigned to an individual or a risk event management team (assisted by a risk management specialist as necessary) to develop (and test, when appropriate) a risk treatment. These individuals and teams are the risk owners who then monitor their risk and respond as necessary.

In deciding the best way to deal with each risk, follow the problem-solving and decision-making steps outlined in Chapter 26. When the risk is complex, break it down into its component parts, or sub-risks, and deal with each individually.

When you decide to share risk with a contractor, identify, assess and treat the risks of the contractor failing to meet requirements and build them into the contract. Proactively monitor the contractor's performance, not just accept their reports.

Risk treatments

You can consider a range of responses to various events:

- Avoid it by not starting or continuing with the activity that gives rise to the risk and finding another way to achieve the particular objective.
- Take or increase the risk to pursue an opportunity.
- Remove the source of the risk.
- Reduce the risk to an acceptable level through controls or preventative measures to lessen its likelihood or its consequences; these might be devices, policies, practices or other actions to modify the risk; but remember – they don't always succeed.
- Share the risk with a third party, such as an insurance company or contractor (remember to take into account the consequences of a subcontractor going out of business or performing the work poorly, and that you can't really transfer a risk because you still own the consequence).
- Retain the risk by informed decisions and devise contingency and business continuity/disaster recovery plans to deal with it should it arise. This might be, for example, when the effort and expense to mitigate it is not worthwhile or when the risk level is low. Accepting the risk can also include risk financing – setting aside funds to meet or modify the financial consequences should the risk occur.

Transferable skills

1.4 Business operations

2.1 Critical thinking

3.1 Teamwork/relationships

Follow the risk treatment process flow

The *risk treatment process flow* is shown in Figure 22.18. (Note that there is a different process for risk prevention in Chapter 30, designed specifically for WHS matters.) First, direct your attention to the source of risks and search for solutions to *prevent* them from occurring. Can you *eliminate* the

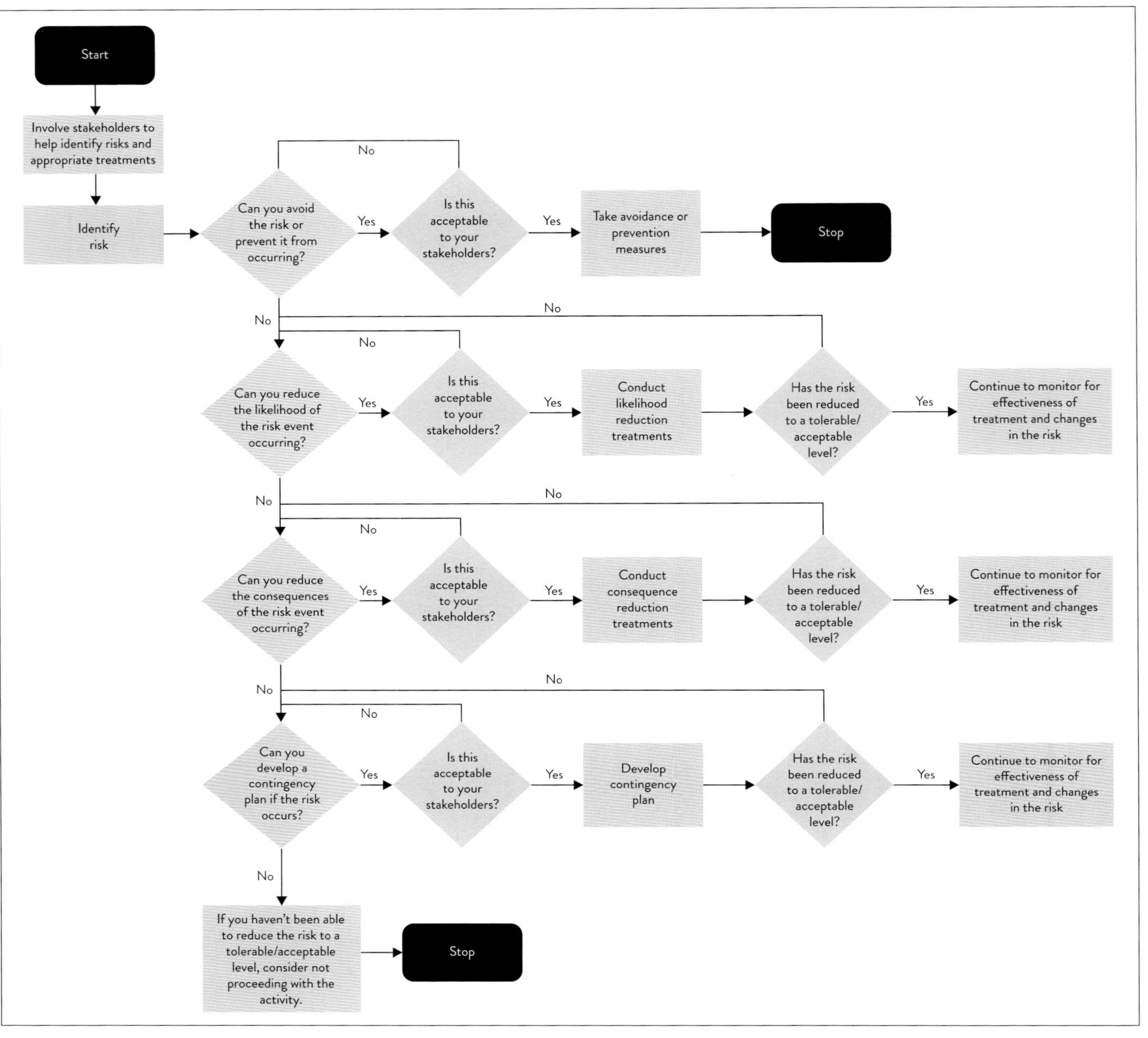

FIGURE 22.18 The risk treatment process flow

risk by, for example, altering your extended supply chain, changing suppliers or redesigning a job or process? Or is it better to *reduce* the risk by sharing it with another party through insurance or contracting the job out?

Organisations generally retain low and moderate risks, especially when their risk culture supports ongoing risk management and risk identification, assessment and monitoring as part of its normal reporting procedures. When robust RMPs are in place, organisations can retain even higher levels of risk. Organisations must retain some risks because insurers do not cover them or make covering them an expensive option. For example, insurance cover for natural disasters, such as earthquakes, fire and flood, and non-natural disasters, such as nuclear accidents, terrorism and war, may be available, but it is expensive.

When you can't avoid or prevent a risk from occurring, try to *reduce the likelihood of it occurring*; for example, you might increase the use of virtual meetings, institute working from home or limit business travel to reduce the likelihood of employees contracting a severe virus, or redesign a procedure to reduce the possibility of an accident. One of the most important ways to manage risk is to involve and train employees in risk awareness, identification and assessment so they see it as a natural part of their jobs.

When it is not possible to reduce your exposure to a risk, or when the residual risk (the exposure that remains after treatment) is unacceptable, move on to your third and least preferred option – reducing the consequences of the risk should it occur. Your goal is to *reduce the risk level* from unacceptable to acceptable or at least tolerable; this is known as the *target risk level*. An example is shown in **Figure 22.19**; although target risk levels vary depending on the risk and how much, if any, control over the risk the organisation can take.

To reach a target risk level, you might decide to retain the risk and develop a contingency plan to *mitigate* its consequences should it occur; for example, you might develop and test a pandemic management program that includes a hybrid of in-office and work from home, together with the adoption of a virtual collaboration platform, or guard against a loss of power by installing a generator. Or you might *share* residual risk (by contracting out that aspect of your operations or developing a joint venture) or *spread* the risk across multiple locations. Remember, though, that when you share or spread a risk, you may still need to develop contingency plans for any remaining risk. Develop several options from which to select based on your goals.

A series of measures is often effective in minimising and managing a risk. For instance, to protect your premises from fire, you might enforce strict housekeeping throughout the premises to reduce the amount of combustible material and install sprinklers that engage automatically in case of fire to make it practically impossible for a fire to cause damage. You would then need to manage the risk of

Risk	Probability	Frequency	Consequences	Current risk level	Target risk level
A	Possible	n/a	Catastrophic	Extreme	Moderate
B	n/a	Often	Critical	High	Low
C	n/a	Occasionally	Moderate	Moderate	Low
D	Unlikely	Seldom	High	Moderate	Low

Prepared by: Ngaire Ho, 6 September 2021. Location: Main factory.

FIGURE 22.19 Target risk levels

the sprinklers going off unnecessarily and dealing with any water damage; to minimise those risks, you might institute a program of regular testing and maintenance of the sprinklers.

After taking these measures to minimise the risk of fire, you may then decide to share the remaining risk with an insurance company, or you may decide you have minimised the risk of fire so effectively that it makes financial sense to retain the risk yourself, saving the expense of fire insurance premiums over a period of years.

Work through your goals, timelines and so on when selecting risk treatment measures. Consider the cost of their development and implementation (and possibly maintenance) and their ease of execution against their effectiveness. A SWOT analysis or a **force-field analysis** can help you choose the most effective treatment plan.

Document your risk management plan for approval

Transferable skills

2.2 Personal effectiveness

3.3 Written communication

3.4 Leadership

Document the RMP following your organisation's usual protocol. Begin with the risk definition and its inherent, residual and target risk level that the plan addresses. Outline the treatment(s) selected and explain the rationale behind it. Identify the management and control structures needed to execute the RMP and any other resources the program needs; for example, funding to consult with experts, to develop and roll out a communication program to the workforce, to purchase equipment, to train employees or to trial treatment options.

List the action items needed to implement the plan and assign responsibilities for executing each step and overall responsibility for the plan's operation to a risk owner. Nominate deputies for each role in case the primary role-holder is not available. Your goal is to practically be able to go on automatic pilot so that you do not need to think your way through each step under extreme pressure and have people running off in different directions.

Finally, establish a review process that involves stakeholders and encourages continuous improvement, innovation and learning. When the plan is approved, the risk owner takes ongoing responsibility for monitoring, reviewing and improving the RMP. Depending on the risk event, you may need to develop a communication network and a network of cross-functional employees who can coordinate responses, monitor unfolding events and adapt the organisation's responses as the risk unfolds.

Test your plan

Until you've tested your plan, you have no idea whether it works or will worsen the situation. When your plan is long and complex, test each part separately. (Depending on the risk and your organisation's protocol, testing may be before or after the plan is approved.)

The more serious the risk event, the more important rigorous testing is, so plan the test properly. With large plans or major risk events, such as the need to evacuate a building or to have a substantial portion of the workforce work from home, hold a trial run. (Regular trial runs also develop a risk culture and skill level of the participants, which is essential should the plan be needed.)

When an actual trial run is not possible, arrange to test the plan in an environment that reproduces authentic conditions as much as possible. When you can't do that, conduct a round-table theoretical run, or a table-top scenario. Involve a cross-section of the people who would be involved in the actual event, including some devil's advocates. Look for areas in the plan that may fail and for ways to improve the plan. Document and store the test procedures and the results with the RMP. When you are confident the RMP works, draw up a procedures manual, a checklist of steps to follow or a diagram, such as a flow chart or a PERT diagram, and incorporate the plan into your organisation's standard operating procedures.

IN PRACTICE

Honing flexible response skills

Large global firms often find it worthwhile to establish a virtual team with shifting membership that meets virtually for half a day every second month to simulate various crises (e.g. 30 per cent of the workforce is absent for a lengthy period due to a pandemic or the US closes its borders). The goal isn't to create specific contingency plans for these events but to practise problem-solving disastrous scenarios in unpredictable and fast-changing environments.[38]

Transferable skills

1.4 Business operations

2.1 Critical thinking

3.1 Teamwork/relationships

4.1 Data literacy

5.2 Technology use

Monitor and review your risks and management plans

As shown in **Figure 22.18**, continual monitoring and review of the risk management process is essential. The risk management committee should periodically review the organisation's risk management framework and risk management process to determine their adequacy, effectiveness and suitability for achieving the organisation's strategic objectives. The committee should also review extreme- and high-level risks with the risk owner approximately every six months to ensure the controls remain appropriate and adequate for the level of risk, and review moderate-, low-level, tolerated, mitigated and transferred risks, generally annually. The risk management committee should also review reported incidents against KPIs for each department monthly.

Regular reviews also allow you to proactively re-examine risks and your evaluation of them, analyse the strengths and weaknesses of the RMPs, and identify opportunities to improve and update the plans so that they reflect changing circumstances inside and outside the organisation.

While regular reviews are proactive, monitoring is more reactive. At its regular (probably monthly) meetings, the risk management committee should monitor:

- accident and incident statistics in a variety of categories that suit your organisation
- legislative and regulatory updates
- project risk registers
- risk and incident logs
- 'works requiring attention' or similar, to alert you to pay attention to a particular area or activity.

Link these daily with your automated risk register so that you can spot any trends and patterns, investigate them as necessary, and make sure the risk is at the level you think it is – risk management is something of a moving target. When there is an increasing trend of incidents or a pattern emerges, consider reassigning the risk(s) to a more severe category. Present this information to the quarterly board audit and risk committee for review.

Risk owners monitor the risks for which they are responsible through continual checks, supervision and observation, and conduct regular reviews (generally annually for low- and moderate-level risks, six-monthly for high-level risks and quarterly or even monthly for extreme-level risks) to ensure the control measures are in place, working and used correctly, and to compare the goals specified in the RMP with the actual results. The review also includes an assessment of the effectiveness of employee and contractor education and training programs and communication strategies, and any communication strategies with the local community and other stakeholders.

Risk owners send or present a report of their findings, often called a *business impact assessment* or a *business impact statement*, to the risk management committee, which sends reports for extreme and high risks to the board audit and review committee. They also regularly scan the external and internal environments to monitor events and keep abreast of trends that indicate a risk level may be changing and note relevant matters to incorporate in the RMP when it is next reviewed; for instance, any changes to operations, key processes, materials or supply lines reflected in the plan should be fully tested, documented and communicated. When any increased level of risk or a new risk is identified, it should be incorporated into the RMP immediately and stakeholders notified of the change and the treatment measures.

External reviews help keep the organisation's risk management processes sound, too. Insurance companies and government insurers (e.g. the Victorian Management Insurance Authority and other state-nominated risk insurers and advisers) should periodically review an organisation's risk arrangements and recommend improvements. (You can find out how to set up effective monitoring systems and use common monitoring tools in Chapter 20.)

Monitoring severe risks

Some risks, such as risks from extreme climatic events, are higher at certain times than at others. When the level of risk is extreme or even high, monitoring might include continual or regular scanning of the environment, opening lines of communication with official sources of information, instituting a communication program with employees and other stakeholders, initiating precautionary measures, and participating in local or national strategic response committees.

Recording and reporting

Transferable skills

2.2 Personal effectiveness
3.1 Teamwork/relationships
3.2 Verbal communication
3.4 Leadership
4.1 Data literacy
5.2 Technology use

Recording and reporting is a new element included in the risk management process in the current standard.[39] The risk management process and its outcomes should be documented and reported as part of good corporate governance. It helps to show all stakeholders that the organisation in general, the board and senior executive in particular, are all serious about their responsibilities with respect to risk. This helps to ensure that risk management activities and outcomes are communicated throughout the organisation. It also provides support for effective, well-informed decision-making at all levels. It also provides a framework to support organisational stakeholders with responsibility and accountability for risk, and in recording and reporting about risk in a clear yet consistent way. Such a framework provides guidance on what information needs to be recorded and reported, when and by what methods. This improves the quality of dialogue about risk and, in turn, the agility of the organisation to foresee and respond to risk events.

STUDY TOOLS

QUICK REVIEW

KEY CONCEPT 22.1 

a Briefly explain what constitutes a risk and the types of risk that can affect organisations.

b List the main risks posed by Mother Nature in your geographic region. Are there any opportunities as well as threats to some organisations?

c Human nature being what it is, what do you think are the main areas of risk most organisations face from their employees?

d What is the difference between inherent risk and residual risk? What is risk tolerance and why is defining it for different categories of risk important?

e How does understanding an organisation's risk appetite for different categories of risk help it establish a satisfactory target risk level?

f How can a risk present both an opportunity and a threat?

KEY CONCEPT 22.2 

a What does risk management mean to you? What is the difference between proactive and reactive risk management and the likely short- and long-term consequences of each approach?

b Explain the responsibilities of directors, managers and employees in risk management, and the roles of board risk and audit management committees and risk owners. Who should be on risk management committees and how often should they meet?

c How often should risk management plan for high-, medium- and low-level risks to be reviewed and tested, and who should do this?

d What is the difference between business continuity plans and disaster recovery plans?

e List 10 ways to identify risks and five ways to prioritise risks.

KEY CONCEPT 22.3 

a List the information a risk management plan should contain.

b Prepare a diagram (e.g. a flow chart or a Gantt chart) illustrating the steps to take in managing risks, indicating timeframes where relevant.

c What is the purpose of a risk register? What should it contain?

BUILD YOUR SKILLS

KEY CONCEPT 22.1 

a Explain the relationship between risk and reward.

b Using the SWOT framework explained in Section 22.3, form into small groups and brainstorm the intrinsic and extrinsic risks your university faces. Which are risks of scale? Of timing? Of structure? Which are future risks and which are ongoing, or business-as-usual, risks? Which are strategic and which are operational?

c Consider the Reflect box in Section 22.1. Which risks are external and which are internal that arise from your own actions? How would you describe your own risk appetite in relation to driving?

d List and discuss at least six steps first-line leader-managers can take to build a strong risk culture in their work groups.

KEY CONCEPT 22.2 

a Explain how the elements of a risk culture shown in **Figure 22.6** contribute to an organisation's risk culture.

b Briefly define and explain the purpose of each of the elements of the risk management framework shown in **Figure 22.7**.

c What do you believe are a first-line leader-manager's responsibilities regarding risk? List at least five actions leader-managers can take to fulfil these responsibilities.

KEY CONCEPT 22.3 

a Identifying and managing all the possible risks in an organisation or a workplace can be daunting. What measures can you think of to make the process less so?

b Brainstorm the intrinsic and extrinsic strategic risks and the operational risks at your workplace or another workplace you are familiar with. Select two from each group that you estimate to be the most likely to occur and the most serious if they did occur. Define each of these risks, identifying their nature and source, and initial and longer-term consequences. Then apply the risk management hierarchy to each.

c Prepare risk management plans for two risks from each group identified in the previous question with the highest current risk levels. Then discuss which of the three ways to assess their effectiveness you could use and how you could use it.

d In small groups, write three scenarios about the future of education, the use of cash or the distribution of music following the guidelines in this chapter.

e Discuss why it is important to pay attention to incidents or near misses.

f Explain how mapping an organisation's supply chains to identify risks can help the organisation avoid some of the many difficulties in supply chain management.

WORKPLACE ACTIVITIES

KEY CONCEPT 22.1 

a What are the biggest cyber risks in your industry? Who would benefit from gaining access to your organisation's information systems and databases and how might they gain that access? How much do you estimate it would cost your organisation to respond to and recover from a cyber incident that compromised your organisation's files and accessed its databases?

b What are your organisation's critical digital assets, the information and systems it must keep operating in order to survive a serious disruption to its activities? Where are they located and who has access to them? What would happen to the organisation's continuity if they were compromised?

c Explore the Australian Government's Australian Cyber Security Centre at https://www.cyber.gov.au and prepare a short report on how your organisation or your work team can improve its IT security.

d List the five most significant extrinsic risks and five most significant intrinsic risks affecting your organisation, function, business process or work team. Explain why you consider them to be high priority in terms of their likelihood and consequences and illustrate them in a risk appetite matrix and a heat map.

e List five risk mitigation strategies your organisation applies or that you and your work team, function or business process apply, and any secondary risks (or opportunities) resulting from them.

f What is your organisation's risk appetite for its various activities and drivers of success?

g How would you describe the risk culture of your organisation? Of your work team, business process or function? What is your evidence for this?

h What are the main risk factors in your industry? What is their likelihood of occurring and what might be their consequences should they occur? Consider operational and strategic consequences as well as stakeholder consequences.

i What current problems and trends that meet the definition of risk (see the text under the heading 'Only register "real" risks' in Section 22.3) that your organisation, function, business process or work team faces have the potential to worsen?

j What risk metrics do you use in your work team? What risk metrics does your organisation monitor?

KEY CONCEPT 22.2 

a Describe the risk management frameworks and processes at your workplace. How do these operate in your own work team?

b Do you have a business continuity plan to keep your work team going should your team members not be able to attend work due to, for example, illness resulting from a pandemic or the destruction of your workplace from a flood or fire? If not, prepare a flow chart to illustrate the steps you could take.

KEY CONCEPT 22.3 

a What organisational information, including intellectual property, do your external suppliers and Cloud providers hold? What steps do they take to safeguard this information? How regularly do you monitor their systems for safeguarding your organisation's information? What are the risks involved in them holding that information? Do you consider that the risks outweigh the benefits? If so, explain your reasoning, quantifying your thinking if possible.

b What risk management training do you or your organisation provide to your work team?

c One of the two measures of risk is consequence (the other is likelihood). What are the consequences of various risks to your organisation?

d Referring to 'Workplace activities' question, Key concept 22.1(d), are the risks your organisation or your work team pays most attention to consistent with the organisation's overall strategy and goals? What evidence do you have to support your assertion?

EXTENSION ACTIVITIES

Referring to the Snapshot at the beginning of this chapter, answer the following questions:

1 The events portrayed in the Snapshot at the start of this chapter may seem a little extreme, but both scenarios have happened in Australia in the last few years. They've just been brought together at the same time to affect Susan's business. Imagine you are in Susan's role. Work through the steps that you would take to maintain business continuity during the crisis period through to resumption of normal operations once the crises have passed. Give consideration to:
   - employee safety and wellbeing
   - customer relationship management and satisfaction
   - asset repairs and management
   - company cash flow and profitability
   - communication and reporting
   - roles and responsibilities.

2 Consider the value chain of your own organisation or one with which you are familiar. Identify three scenarios of potential vulnerability to extreme climate or terrorist events that may not have been considered fully. For one of those aspects, recommend the steps that should be taken by your organisation to reduce the risk and improve business continuity in the event of an emergency situation arising.

CASE STUDY 22

BOEING 737 MAX CRASH INVESTIGATION[40]

On 29 October, 2018, Lion Air flight 610 crashed into the Java Sea 13 minutes after take off from Soekarno–Hatta International Airport in Jakarta, Indonesia, killing all 189 passengers and crew. Less than five months later, on 10 March 2019, in strikingly similar circumstances, Ethiopian Airlines flight 302 crashed six minutes after take off killing all 157 passengers and crew, including eight US citizens.

While certain facts and circumstances surrounding the accidents differed, a common component in both of the accident airplanes was the new flight control feature: the Manoeuvring Characteristics Augmentation System (MCAS). Boeing developed MCAS to address stability issues in certain flight conditions induced by the plane's new, larger engines, and their relative placement on the 737 MAX aircraft compared to the engines' placement on the previous model the 737 NG.

The Committee's investigative findings identified five central themes that affected the design, development and certification of the 737 MAX and the Federal Aviation Administration's (FAA) oversight of Boeing. Acts, omissions and errors occurred across multiple stages and areas of the development and certification process of the 737 MAX. These themes include:

1 *Production pressures:* there was tremendous financial pressure on Boeing and the 737 MAX program to compete with Airbus' new A320neo aircraft. Among other things, this pressure resulted in extensive efforts to cut costs, maintain the 737 MAX program schedule, and avoid slowing the 737 MAX production line. The Committee's investigation has identified several instances where the desire to meet these goals and expectations jeopardized the safety of the flying public.

2 *Faulty design and performance assumptions:* Boeing made fundamentally faulty assumptions about critical technologies on the 737 MAX,

CASE STUDY 22

most notably with MCAS. Based on these faulty assumptions, Boeing permitted MCAS – software designed to automatically push the airplane's nose down in certain conditions – to activate on input from a single angle of attack (AOA) sensor. It also expected that pilots, who were largely unaware that the system existed, would be able to mitigate any potential malfunction. Boeing also failed to classify MCAS as a safety-critical system, which would have attracted greater FAA scrutiny during the certification process.

3 *Culture of concealment*: in several critical instances, Boeing withheld crucial information from the FAA, its customers, and 737 MAX pilots. This included concealing the very existence of MCAS from 737 MAX pilots and failing to disclose that the AOA Disagree alert was inoperable on the vast majority of the 737 MAX fleet, despite having been certified as a standard aircraft feature. The AOA Disagree alert is intended to notify the crew if the aircraft's two AOA sensor readings disagree, an event that can occur if one sensor is malfunctioning or providing faulty AOA data. Boeing not only concealed this information from both the FAA and pilots, but also continued to deliver MAX aircraft to its customers knowing that the AOA Disagree alert was inoperable on most of these aircraft. Further, Boeing concealed internal test data it had that revealed it took a Boeing test pilot more than 10 seconds to diagnose and respond to uncommanded MCAS activation in a flight simulator, a condition the pilot found to be 'catastrophic'. While it was not required to share this information with the FAA or Boeing customers, it is inconceivable and inexcusable that Boeing withheld this information from them.

4 *Conflicted representation*: the Committee found that the FAA's current oversight structure with respect to Boeing creates inherent conflicts of interest that have jeopardized the safety of the flying public. The Committee's investigation documented several instances where Boeing Authorised Representatives (ARs) – Boeing employees who are granted special permission to represent the interests of the FAA and to act on the agency's behalf in validating aircraft systems and designs' compliance with FAA requirements – failed to disclose important information to the FAA that could have enhanced the safety of the 737 MAX aircraft. In some instances, a Boeing AR raised concerns internally in 2016 but did not relay these issues to the FAA, and the concerns failed to result in adequate design changes. Some of the issues that were raised by the AR and not thoroughly investigated or dismissed by his Boeing employees, such as concerns about repetitive MCAS activation and the impact of faulty AOA data on MCAS, were the core contributing factors that led to the Lion Air and Ethiopian Airlines crashes more than two years later.

5 *Boeing's influence over the FAA's oversight structure*: multiple career FAA officials have documented examples where FAA management overruled a determination of the FAA's own technical experts at the behest of Boeing. In these cases, FAA technical and safety experts determined that certain Boeing design approaches on its transport category aircraft were potentially unsafe and failed to comply with FAA regulations, only to have FAA management overrule them and side with Boeing instead. These incidents have had a detrimental impact on the morale of FAA's technical and subject matter experts that compromises the integrity and independence of the FAA's oversight abilities and the safety of airline passengers. A recent draft internal FAA 'safety culture survey' of employees in the agency's Aviation Safety Organization (AVS) drew similar conclusions. 'Many believe that AVS senior leaders are overly concerned with achieving the business-oriented outcomes of industry stakeholders and are not held accountable for safety-related decisions', the survey observed.

These five recurring themes point to a troubling pattern of problems that affected Boeing's development and production of the 737 MAX and the FAA's ability to provide appropriate oversight of Boeing and the agency's certification process. These issues must be addressed by both Boeing and the FAA in order to correct poor certification practices that have emerged, reassess key assumptions that affect safety, and enhance transparency to enable more effective oversight.

Questions

1 For each of the five themes identified in the report, consider the potential for a similar theme to occur in your organisation or industry. How could it happen, what risk events might ensue and what would be the potential consequences?
2 For three of the risk events identified, what measures are currently in place to prevent this from happening? Are these adequate? Identify any additional measures you believe may be needed to treat these risks.

CHAPTER ENDNOTES

1 Matt Kunkel, 'Why enterprise risk management is key to organisational resilience', *Forbes*, 30 April 2021, https://www.forbes.com/sites/forbestechcouncil/2021/04/30/why-enterprise-risk-management-is-key-to-organizational-resilience/?sh=12e0ebb03bea

2 Jim Collins, Morten T. Hansen, *Great by choice*, Random House, 2011.

3 Australian Standards, ISO 31000: 2018 – Risk management – Guidelines, Section 3.1.

4 Ian Bremmer, 'Inflation + subsidies: An explosive mix', *Harvard Business Review*, December 2008; Matt Kunkel, op cit.

5 Committee for Economic Development of Australia, 'Australia's future workforce?', June 2015, https://www.ceda.com.au/ResearchAndPolicies/Research/Workforce-Skills/Australia-s-future-workforce

6 Tom Wilson, 'The demographic constraints on future population growth in regional Australia', *Australian Geographer*, Vol. 46, 2015, pp. 91–111.

7 Commonwealth of Australia, 'Australia's long-term emissions reduction plan', October 2021, https://www.industry.gov.au/sites/default/files/October%202021/document/australias-long-term-emissions-reduction-plan.pdf

8 Australian Government, Australian Signals Directorate, 'ACSC annual cyber threat report 2020–21', p. 8, https://www.cyber.gov.au/sites/default/files/2021-09/ACSC%20Annual%20Cyber%20Threat%20Report%20-%202020-2021.pdf

9 IPCC, 'Climate change 2021: The physical science basis, Sixth assessment report of the Intergovernmental Panel on Climate Change', https://www.ipcc.ch/report/ar6/wg1/

10 A. Maxmen, 'Has COVID taught us anything about pandemic preparedness?', https://www.nature.com/articles/d41586-021-02217, accessed 5 January 2022.

11 Ibid.

12 Tammy Buckley, 'Risk management focus changing', *Risk Management Magazine*, 10 December 2013, http://www.riskmanagementmagazine.com.au/news/risk-management-focus-changing-182281.aspx, accessed 11 December 2013.

13 Carl Rhodes, 'Volkswagen's record settlement payout', *The Conversation*, 4 July 2017.

14 Domini Stuart, 'Staving off cyber criminals', *Company Director*, December–January 2012, pp. 50–51.

15 Helen Civil, 'The whole system impact of the Australian bushfires', *The Resilience Shift*, 23 January 2020, https://www.resilienceshift.org/bushfires-resilience/, accessed 5 January 2022.

16 Jeanne Meister, 'Top ten HR trends for the 2022 workplace', *Forbes*, 5 January 2022, https://www.forbes.com/sites/jeannemeister/2022/01/05/top-ten-hr-trends-for-the-2022-workplace/?sh=69959b173006

17 'Rats in the ranks: Collusion and white-collar crime', *BusinessThink*, University of NSW Business School, 19 November 2014, https://www.businessthink.unsw.edu.au/pages/rats-in-the-ranks-collusion-and-white-collar-crime-.aspx/?Keyword=rat&PageNumber=1; PricewaterhouseCoopers, 'Global Economic Crime and Fraud Survey 2020, http://www.pwc.com.au/publications/cyber-global-economic-crime-survey-2016.html

18 'Fraud epidemic: Revealing the corporate underbelly', *Knowledge@Australian School of Business* (online resource), 18 May 2010, http://knowledge.asb.unsw.edu.au/article.cfm?articleid=1118, accessed 31 March 2015.

19 CSB US Chemical Safety Board, 20 March 2007, http://www.csb.gov/u-s-chemical-safety-board-concludes-organizational-and-safety-deficiencies-at-all-levels-of-the-bp-corporation-caused-march-2005-texas-city-d-isaster-that-killed-15-injured-180/, accessed 18 June 2014.

20 See, for example, 'Q&A: Horsemeat scandal', 10 April 2013, BBC News, UK, http://www.bbc.com/news/uk-21335872, accessed 18 June 2013.

21 IP Australia–Australian Government, *Australian Intellectual Property Report 2021*, Ch 2 Patents, https://www.ipaustralia.gov.au/ip-report-2021, accessed 7 January 2022.

22 Robert S. Kaplan, Anette Mikes, 'Managing risks: A new framework', *Harvard Business Review*, June 2012, pp. 49–60.

23 Ibid.

24 Department of Finance, 'Defining risk appetite and tolerance', 2016, p. 1–2, https://www.finance.gov.au/sites/default/files/2019-11/comcover-information-sheet-defining-risk-appetite-and-tolerance.pdf, accessed February 2022.

25 Ibid, p. 3.

26 Robert S. Kaplan, Anette Mikes, 'Managing risks: A new framework'.

27 'Lessons from the Fukushima nuclear disaster', knowledge@Australian School of Business, published and accessed 15 October 2013.

28 'Fukushima report: Key points in nuclear disaster report', BBC News, 5 July 2012, http://www.bbc.com/news/world-asia-18718486, accessed 7 December 2014.

29 Standards Australia, AS ISO 31000:2018.

30 David Humphries, 'Sundance executives breached protocol by flying in same plane', *Sydney Morning Herald*, 22 June 2010, https://www.smh.com.au/world/sundance-executives-breached-protocol-by-flying-in-same-plane-20100621-yse5.html

31 Standards Australia, AS ISO 31000:2018, p. 9.

32 Know Your Council, 'Guide to councils', https://knowyourcouncil.vic.gov.au/guide-to-councils/consultation-and-complaints/consultation-and-objections, accessed 4 January 2022.

33 Standards Australia, AS ISO 31000:2018, p. 10.

34 NASA's Edward Rogers quoted in Catherine H. Tinsley, Robin L. Dillon, Peter M. Madsen, 'Learning from failure: How to avoid catastrophe', *Harvard Business Review*, April 2011.

35 Anslee Wolfe, 'How to manage key-person risk', *Financial Management*, 4 January 2019, https://www.fm-magazine.com/news/2019/jan/how-to-manage-key-person-risk-201819925.html, accessed February 2022.

36 Gary Wolf, 'Steve Jobs: The next insanely great thing', *Wired Magazine*, 1 February 1996, https://www.wired.com/1996/02/jobs-2/, accessed 5 September 2017.

37 Peter S. Goodman, Niraj Chokshi, 'How the world ran out of everything', *The New York Times*, 1 June 2021, https://www.nytimes.com/2021/06/01/business/coronavirus-global-shortages.html, accessed 9 January 2022.

38 Nohria Nitin, 'Survival of the adaptive', *Harvard Business Review*, May 2006.

39 Standards Australia, AS ISO 31000:2018, p. 14.

40 Committee on Transportation and Infrastructure, 'Final committee report – The design, development and certification of the Boeing 737 Max', September 2020, https://transportation.house.gov/imo/media/doc/2020.09.15%20FINAL%20737%20MAX%20Report%20for%20Public%20Release.pdf, accessed 11 January 2022.

CHAPTER

23

MANAGING FOR SUSTAINABILITY

After completing this chapter, you will be able to:

23.1 develop, communicate and implement a workplace sustainability policy

23.2 help your organisation select suitable sustainability programs

23.3 monitor, review and continuously improve sustainability policy and programs.

TRANSFERABLE SKILLS

The following transferable skills are covered in this chapter:

1 **Business competence**
   1.1 Sustainability
2 **Critical thinking and problem solving**
   2.3 Business strategy
5 **Digital competence**
   5.2 Technology use

OVERVIEW

When the concept of sustainability first came to prominence in Australian workplaces three or so decades ago, the impacts and potential threats of runaway climate change and other environmentally damaging consequences had not yet been fully experienced, investigated or understood. Sustainability was considered to be more of a 'feel good' action for organisations and, for the most part, was left to be administered by staff at a workplace level. Popular sustainability strategies included turning off computer monitors during lunch breaks, turning off lights in toilet blocks after leaving and making sure taps were turned off properly. It was a start, but while other organisational activities were rapidly increasing their impact on the climate and natural environment through pollution of the land, air and waterways, waste creation and disposal, carbon emissions, salinification, habitat destruction and species extinction, such measures had little or no real impact.

Fast-forward 30 years and the role and context of sustainability in saving our planet is now front and centre for organisations, governments and individuals. We have entered the age of the Anthropocene, where human activity is the main influence on climate and the environment and global warming is accelerating at an unprecedented speed. As a result, we now face more extreme weather events and more often; a loss of ecosystems, rainforests and viable cropland; decreased biodiversity and species extinction; ocean acidification and overfishing; rising sea levels and surface temperatures; a shortage of clean water ... the list not only goes on but is increasing. In the context that these challenges present for the global human population, sustainability is not only critically important, it is perhaps the key to our survival.

Sustainability is no longer just concerned with finding and harnessing sustainable sources of power, ensuring a sustainable clean water supply, or replenishing the Earth's natural resources as we remove them from the ground, forests, rivers and oceans. It is now a planetary prerogative that must be pursued with urgency and a single-minded focus by both governments and organisations alike. It requires an understanding and acceptance of the vulnerable position in which we have placed our planet and that sustainable work policies and practices must be embedded in all organisational operations at all levels if we are to change the current course of climate change. The Holocene extinction, also referred to by scientists as the sixth mass extinction, has seen the loss of many families of plants and animal species in a relatively short space of geological time. If we are to ensure our own existence on our planet and avoid a similar fate, we not only need to get sustainability right, we need to get it right now!

SNAPSHOT

A sustainable solution

Forever Floating Floors, a medium-sized manufacturer of bespoke composite laminate aluminium floating floors, which sells direct to the public and through major retail department stores, was haemorrhaging financially. The costs associated with its energy usage, raw materials, transport and logistics, packaging, water use and waste disposal were all soaring. It was also spending large sums on recruiting new staff, many of whom resigned in their first 12 weeks, forcing the business to conduct the recruitment process all over again. Its factory, built over 40 years ago, was not fit for purpose, resulting in inefficient production processes compounded by outdated equipment. By producing a jaw-dropping 41.4 KT (kilotons) of CO_2 emissions per year, the business was further impacted by having to comply with reporting requirements imposed upon it by Australian legislation (NGER). Something had to change.

Owners Victor and Juanita Reinhard decided to engage a business consultant, Henry Nguyen, to assess every aspect of the business as part of a complete overhaul to increase efficiencies, reduce costs and halt its slide into liquidation. After spending a month reviewing the business' policies, practices and financials, Henry submitted his report containing a raft of recommendations, including:

- Construct a new purpose-built production facility designed according to the latest 'green' design principles and using 'smart insulation' materials that would reduce energy consumption by 30 per cent.
- Utilise thermal plasma technology to ionise the previously discarded composite flooring off-cuts, turning the laminate into paraffin and recasting the aluminium into ingots, which could be rolled into new foil stock. Recycling the off-cuts would not only save the business \$250 000 a year in disposal costs, the sale of the recycled products would generate additional revenue of \$350 000.
- Introduce just-in-time agreements with retailers, meaning product orders would be filled in 'real time' as received and then transported directly to retailers and customers, reducing warehousing costs by 90 per cent.
- Replace the warehouse with a small, low-cost holding depot and outsource transportation, which would save the business a further \$310 000 in vehicle maintenance, government charges and fuel costs.
- Install a new water recycling system to halve the business' water usage and costs by 40 per cent.
- Replace carcinogenic Styrofoam packaging with eco-friendly potato packaging, which would save \$50 000 and enable the company to spruik its commitment to environmentally friendly practices as part of a new marketing campaign.
- Model a new sustainable workforce development strategy where the recruitment, selection, induction, onboarding, employee engagement, learning and development, and succession planning processes are linked together and rolled into one interconnected holistic strategy with the aim of not only recruiting the best talent available, but retaining them in the longer term.

Victor and Juanita addressed their staff: 'We have before us a number of recommendations, which if implemented strategically have the potential to transform our business into a modern, efficient, lean and sustainable producer of high-quality eco-friendly flooring. You will all play a vital part in its implementation and in embedding a culture of sustainability and continuous improvement in all work practices across the organisation as we reduce our costs, improve our efficiency, and create an eco-friendly and sustainable business that continues to produce the highest-quality flooring. So, let's get started ...'

23.1 Develop, communicate and implement a workplace sustainability policy and strategies

> As I see it humanity needs to reduce its impact on the Earth urgently and there are three ways to achieve this: we can stop consuming so many resources, we can change our technology and we can reduce our population. We probably need to do all three.
>
> 'How many people can live on planet earth?', 2009.

Governments, organisations and individuals are taking action against climate change across the globe to instil a new more sustainable model of living and conducting business. Yet the failure of climate-change mitigation and adaptation still ranks as number one by impact and number two by likelihood over the next 10 years in the World Economic Forum's top 10 risks facing our world.[1]

The organisations spearheading these new ways have changed their approach to sustainability. Rather than being solely about saving the planet by adopting more sustainable business practices, sustainability is now also viewed as an opportunity for enhanced brand value, an improved corporate image and higher profits. The organisations that get it right may be able to attract and retain the workforce they need, increase sales and customer loyalty, and attract supportive stakeholders. In an ironic twist, the very thing that placed us in the position we're now in may also be the very thing that pulls us out of it.

Once a series of tokenistic and reactive measures, sustainability is now a key strategic issue for many organisations. Clean greener operations can generate income and reduce costs through the design of more sustainable processes, products and services. By **upcycling**, recycling, reusing, repurposing and utilising the **continuous manufacturing model**, organisations can now be more profitable than when they produced products for obsolescence. Expanded markets, new industries and a new category of jobs, known as 'green-collar jobs', have been the result.

For sustainability to deliver its suite of benefits to both an organisation's bottom line as well as to the environment, it needs to be built into an organisation's decision-making and planning processes and then integrated into its operations across the organisation. It needs to be measured, reported on and become a central and ongoing component of continuous improvement. Every strategic business and investment decision an organisation makes, therefore, needs to be automatically examined for its long-term impact on both the environment and the organisation.

Scope the policy

Policies articulate an organisation's intentions in different areas of their operations. When implemented as procedures, they become commitments that guide an organisation's activities and decisions. Policies set goals without stating specifically what actions need to be done. It is left to an organisation's strategic, business and operational plans to provide the details in relation to implementation.

The first step in creating a sustainability policy is to define its *scope*, or boundaries. This establishes the framework for developing the policy and ensures that stakeholders who might be affected by the policy are identified and consulted. As many organisations embed the principles of sustainability across multiple areas of their operations, defining its scope brings with it a broader context than perhaps just focusing on reducing carbon emissions or striving to achieve a neutral **carbon footprint**. Sustainability is now being applied to production, procurement, human resource management, supply chain, financial management, marketing, sales, administration and pretty much any aspect of a business.

Because sustainability inevitably always comes back to (responsible) resource usage, when defining a sustainability policy's scope, identify what, from where and how resources will be used.

This information can then be moulded into a purpose statement that outlines why the organisation is issuing the policy and what its desired effects or goals are. Additionally, constraints and limitations must be identified along with any underlying assumptions upon which the policy is predicated. As with any policy, there also needs to be reference to how the policy will be managed and monitored, how its success will be measured and finally evaluated to identify improvements.

The policy should include the business activities and stakeholders covered or affected, while expressly excluding those that are not. Like any other policy, an implementation date or rollout schedule of dates will inform stakeholders of when it comes into effect and the broad responsibilities of those positions administering the policy should also be listed. It can be useful to include any terms or definitions that might be outside of mainstream understanding as well as sustainability concepts relevant to the policy, such as economic or social sustainability and their application to the policy.

Refer to the example of a scope document in **Figure 23.1** as a basis for the structure when developing your own policy or follow your organisation's preferred format.

XZY Pty Ltd

Policy title: ______________________

Date prepared: ______________________

Prepared by: ______________________

1. **Background or reason for policy:** Why have a policy on this subject? What are the goals of the policy? What compliance requirements does the policy address? The purpose of this policy is ...
2. **Responsible persons:** Person or persons responsible for developing the policy for approval and for implementing, managing and monitoring the policy once it is accepted and released.
3. **Policy outline:** An outline of what the policy is to cover, subject to later revision, and the target date for the policy to come into force.
4. **Consistency with other organisational policies:** Set a context for this policy in terms of the organisation's goals and related policies and state what procedures may be required.
5. **Impact on the organisation:** The resources (financial, human, operational, physical, technical, etc.) expected to be needed to implement and maintain compliance with this policy; the stakeholders and operational activities that the policy may affect, including any systems changes and changes to technical and other procedures anticipated as necessary to comply with the policy.
6. **Assumptions and constraints:** These underline all policies.
7. **Stakeholders:** The interested parties to consult with when developing the policy.

FIGURE 23.1 Policy scope statement

INDUSTRY INSIGHTS

Transferable skills
1.3 Sustainability

Wake up and smell the sustainability!

Hundreds of millions of people across the globe start their day with a cup of coffee and many of them choose Nespresso. However, the discarded coffee pod capsules used in Nespresso coffee machines were ending up in landfill, which began to raise the ire of many people, including Nespresso coffee drinkers themselves. In response, the company embedded sustainability into the DNA of every part of its business through its positive cup framework. The framework outlines its commitment to sustainability on numerous fronts including:

- teaming up with the Rainforest Alliance, whose mission is to conserve biodiversity and ensure sustainable livelihoods, to produce sustainable quality through the Nespresso Sustainable Quality Program™
- supporting vulnerable coffee-growing communities such as those in South Sudan through its Reviving Origins concept
- making 100 per cent of the aluminium used in the production of Nespresso capsules infinitely recyclable
- teaming up with the Colombian Ministry of Labour, the Aguadas Coffee Growers' Cooperative and Fairtrade International to launch a pilot pension scheme to support coffee farmers in Colombia to save a pension on which they can live when they retire
- forming long-term partnerships with Fairtrade US, Technoserve, PUR Projet and many others, including those listed above, to make a real, lasting and positive impact on the environment and society.[2]

Research sustainability strategies

Researching sustainability policies and strategies can help you to decide which strategies are most suited to achieving the goals and needs of your organisation and its stakeholders. There are many on the internet to which you can refer, and a good starting point is to visit https://www.corporateknights.com/rankings/global-100-rankings, which lists the top 100 most sustainable corporations in the world for each year, with links to their websites. You can also explore the website of the World Business Council for Sustainable Development (https://www.wbcsd.org), an association of about 200 major international corporations, including 3M, Coca-Cola, DuPont and Sony.

Create files for the various strategies and programs you come across, and collect, codify and consolidate the information that may be of relevance to your organisation's sustainability approach. (Sustainability programs are explored further in Section 23.2.)

Find out where you are now

As with any policy, to determine its value, it needs to have measures of success attached to it. However, before you can measure the success of a sustainability policy, you need to identify or create a starting point, or baseline measurement. This will depend on the focus and direction of your organisation's policy but considering your organisation's current impact on the environment is a good place to start. You can calculate your organisation's **ecological footprint** at sites such as https://www.footprintnetwork.org. You can use the figures produced as your baseline or invent your own measuring system. A measurement system is useful for determining whether or not your sustainability policy is working if it provides a baseline measurement of the relevant areas of sustainability and figures for consistent future comparison.

Specific environmental measures that best apply to your organisation, such as usage and trends for energy and water, **life cycle analysis**, value chain analysis, and the use of sustainable and non-sustainable materials, are good areas about which to gather data that can give you meaningful information. Many industry associations also provide benchmark information and guidelines on what to measure and how to measure it. The Doughty Centre for Corporate Responsibility provides an excellent resource for identifying a company's major impacts, including how to manage them via the following link: https://www.cranfield.ac.uk/-/media/images-for-new-website/centres/school-of-management-centres/doughty-centre/pdfs/how-to-guides/how-to-identify-impacts.ashx. This resource can help you to not only look 'inside-out' to understand the impact of your organisation's activities on the environment but also 'outside-in'. Government regulations, resource availability, factors in the supply chain and so on can also all have an impact so they must be taken into account.

Looking 'outside-in' as well as 'inside-out' helps you think broadly when assessing your organisation's overall carbon exposure and sustainability opportunities. Thinking through the major risks and opportunities that affect your organisation and thoroughly exploring them in this way will provide you with a more thorough and meaningful picture of your organisation's impact than if your analysis only consisted of looking 'inside-out'.

Transferable skills
2.3 Business strategy

When outside-in is inside-out

An inside-out effect to one organisation is an outside-in effect to others. For example, the price of oil and cost of emissions affect industries dependent on oil (e.g. transport industries, such as airlines, couriers, road freight and taxis) and may drive down consumer demand for oil, affecting oil producers, refiners and sellers. The effect on those industries in turn affects others, such as the hospitality industry, which then affects other industries, such as laundry services and food and beverage producers and wholesalers.

The price of oil also affects the cost to restaurants of storing food that needs to be kept cold and restaurants may have difficulty sourcing food supplies as the productivity of various regions that have traditionally supplied agricultural and farming products changes and as the cost of transporting food over long distances increases. The upstream and downstream effects of climate change, increasing legislation and public demand can therefore be far-reaching.

Climate change

Organisations can no longer simply ignore climate change. As global temperatures continue to rise, floods, bushfires and droughts are becoming more prevalent and more severe. They wreak havoc on property, livestock and infrastructure, contribute to rising insurance premiums, the costs of which may be passed on to consumers, and can even affect financial markets. Of perhaps even greater concern is the damage caused by rising sea levels and changes to rainfall patterns that may well overtake these disasters in the near future. Even organisations that experience only minor direct effects from climate change still face indirect flow-on effects, including employee migrations; increases in disease; rising electricity, fuel and waste disposal prices; shortages of energy; and supply-chain breakdowns. Harm caused to the reputations of large-scale organisations who are acting in a sustainable and responsible manner is also a collateral cost that they must endure as a result of being lumped into a category with those that aren't.

The effect of climate change on an organisation can be considered from the outside-in, in three broad ways. The first is changing temperature and weather patterns. More frequent drought, flooding and storms might directly affect various aspects of an organisation's operations and the environments it operates in. These effects are more likely to be felt in countries or areas where the government's ability to respond is limited, where the local ecosystem is fragile and where water supplies are already stretched. Availability of supplies, consumer demand, supply chain operations and other aspects of an operation can all be affected.

The second outside-in area to consider is regulations and public opinion that increase the financial and image costs of unsustainable operating practices. Australia has already made one attempt at placing a price on carbon with a carbon pricing scheme introduced by the then Labor government in 2011, which took effect in 2012. Although repealed by the Liberal government in 2014, it brought into the public consciousness both the legal and ethical obligations of the 'big polluters', as they were called, and planted the idea that the days of uncontrolled and irresponsible carbon emissions was over. Australia now has the Emission Reduction Fund (ERF) where carbon credits can be earned and then sold by organisations that achieve emissions reductions. Although the punitive provisions introduced under the carbon pricing scheme are no longer present, as each ecological tipping point is reached and passed, and wholesale carbon emission reduction or even elimination becomes the last remaining strategy, the situation may change once more. By the time this point is reached, everyone will have already paid the price of carbon emissions and the next and final regulatory step may be their total abolition. To this end, the recently elected federal Labor government has set a target of zero net emissions by the year 2050.

In terms of corporate image and reputation, organisations need to think very seriously about whether the way they conduct their operations attracts or repels customers, shareholders and the type of employees they require now and in the future. They need to think about the impact on sales, whether suppliers will continue to work with them if they fail to act in a sustainable manner and, more obviously, the cost of increasing fuel and energy prices.

When considering how much carbon emissions and other forms of waste are costing your organisation now and what they are likely to cost in the future, it is important to think in both financial and corporate image terms.

Consult stakeholders

No organisation operates in a vacuum. Every business has a variety of stakeholders that influence the organisation's actions and behaviour. Customers, shareholders, employees, suppliers, lending institutions, and government at local, state and federal levels are some of the main ones. Determining what is important to them can help direct the development of a sustainability policy and strategy options. Do existing products and services need to be replaced with new ones with drastically reduced environmental impacts? Can products or services be produced using less energy and materials that last longer? A growing number of stakeholders are now going beyond the organisation's operations in relation to the production of their goods and services and demanding that they actively protect or even regenerate the Earth's natural resources.

Because the most effective sustainability policies will be those that are embedded across all business practices, careful thought needs to be given when developing the policy to which roles and processes it will affect. Consultation with a range of representatives from different areas of an organisation will be necessary so as to take their knowledge, opinions, experience, ideas and needs into account.

External stakeholders, such as those referred to above, also need to be consulted as part of an ongoing process to enlist stakeholder support; provide ideas, information and initiatives; and prevent a policy from unintentionally harming stakeholders.

The rapid increase in shareholder activism concerning environmental, social and governance (ESG) issues is now on the radar of most listed companies. Investment funds and institutional investors are becoming increasingly vocal on ESG matters and are divesting shares in fossil fuel and other companies seen to be harming the environment. Litigation against listed companies is increasing, and not-for-profit organisations are running increasingly sophisticated campaigns targeting not only companies whose operations harm the environment but also institutions that fund those companies.

Speaking at a symposium on risk management in Melbourne, the Vice Chairman (Australia and New Zealand) of Deutsche Bank, Steven Skala, had this to say, 'In my view, the objective of the modern corporation is not to make a profit but to live profitably forever. In order to live forever, different considerations must be taken into account apart from the sheer notion of making a profit.'[3]

Set goals and targets

Once you know where your organisation is and where it wants to be, it's time to confront the 'elephant in the room' – how much change and how quickly? The battle against climate change is a race and one where there is no medal for second place. Having said that, each organisation needs to weigh up its capacity in terms of the degree to which it can implement sustainable work practices and the pace at which it can do so.

Refer back to the scope of your workplace sustainability policy to provide guidance in creating a 'dashboard' of specific measures of success or key performance indicators (KPIs) that you can apply to the activities that have the greatest impact on the sustainability of your organisation's operations. Waste, emissions and natural resource depletion easily spring to mind. Reviewing and relaying these measures quarterly to the board, senior management and other stakeholders will enable them to track improvements and suggest further improvement initiatives. Ultimately, senior management and organisational policy makers will determine how much they want to shift the 'elephant' and how quickly they are able to do so.

Setting ambitious sustainability targets and goals

In 2016, the Australian Centre for Corporate Social Responsibility (ACCSR) acknowledged global resources company South32 for its commitment to achieving the United Nations' Sustainable Development Goals (SDGs).

The company has not only outlined 11 of the 17 SDG goals it was committed to achieving but also the actions it was undertaking to meet them. Below is a snapshot of how the company went about implementing the SDGs into its operational framework:

- SDG 1 (No poverty) – 'reduce poverty through direct employment, local procurement and the payment of taxes and royalties which enable the development of essential social and economic infrastructure'.
- SDG 3 (Good health and wellbeing) – 'work to eliminate exposures to safety and health risks, while running wellness programs to promote a healthy workforce and include community investment projects on malaria and tuberculosis reduction'.
- SDG 4 (Gender equality) – 'have set ambitious targets that focus on gender and ethnicity. To achieve these targets, a number of initiatives have been implemented, including attraction of female engineers, closing the gender pay gap, redesigning work and a flexible work environment'.
- SDG 6 (Clean water and sanitation) – 'recognise we are a significant user of water resources and have a responsibility to utilise water appropriately within the context of each catchment. Our material water-related risks are assessed and managed through our risk assessment, planning and projects group'.[4]

Four shades of green

Transferable skills
1.3 Sustainability

Returning to that 'elephant', how green should an organisation go and how quickly? Should you leave your systems as they are? Should you invest in technologies to reduce pollution? Some more ambitious companies are now aiming to go *carbon neutral* – producing no net contribution to carbon emissions, which requires significant planning and may involve significant expenditure in the short term. Or you may want to aim even higher, for *carbon negative* – producing more clean energy than you use and storing and/or selling the surplus to the grid. Figure 23.2 summarises these options. You can decide how green you want to go on a financial basis, on a philosophical basis, in response to stakeholder demands, or a combination of these rationales. You may even want to run various scenarios to see which path delivers both on a sustainability as well as a profit front.

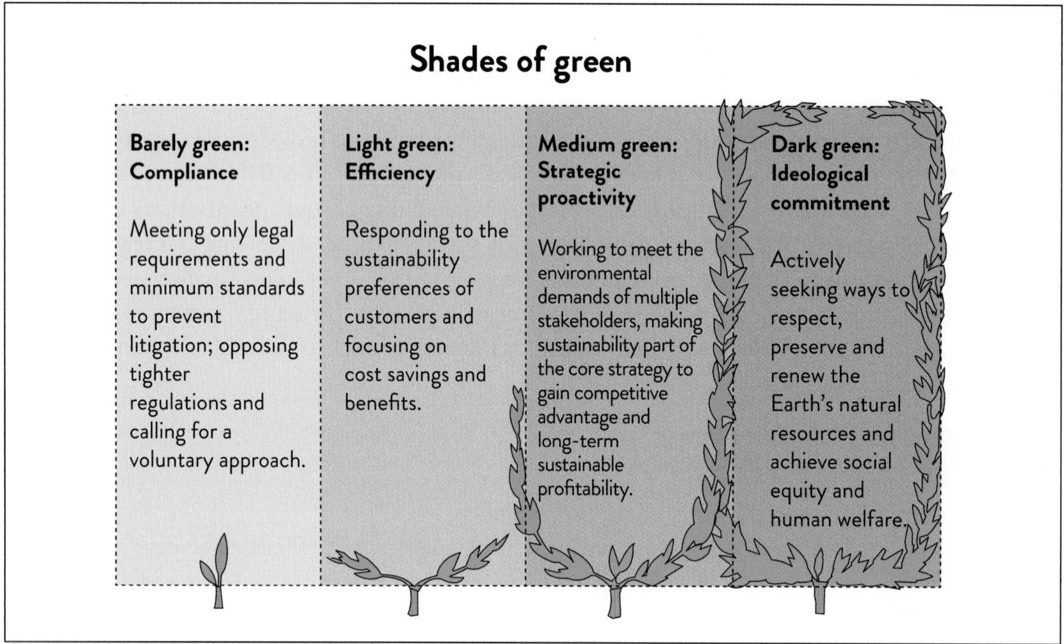

FIGURE 23.2 Shades of green

Being 'barely green' may be cheap and easy in the short term, but for organisations that pollute more than minimally, the costs of mere compliance are likely to increase steeply. Organisations that depend on the goodwill of their customers and repeat business may need to go 'light green' at a minimum to respond to the environmental preference of their customers. Organisations at this level concentrate on the cost savings that result from efficiency.

Many organisations find it worthwhile to go 'medium green' and meet the environmental demands of multiple stakeholders, including the community, employees and suppliers, and make sustainability part of their core strategy. They might, for example, invest time and effort in re-engineering a function or capability in a way that is difficult for competitors to copy, replace printed product manuals with electronic versions, or develop or purchase virtual meeting technology that allows technicians to troubleshoot problems at a customer's premises remotely, saving on travel costs and the resulting carbon emissions. The COVID-19 pandemic has already forced most organisations across the globe to implement virtual meeting strategies, at least in part, purely as an operational solution. Many are now seeing not only the environmental benefits of doing so but are also questioning why for so many years they have been shelling out large amounts of money to rent floors in city office buildings, pay for power and force their employees to waste time and money travelling to and from work each day. The cost and time savings to both organisations and their employees have suddenly become apparent and many are now reluctant to return to the 'old ways'. Any strategy that results in a smaller ecological footprint can also improve an organisation's corporate and brand image, increase profitability and help to recoup investments more quickly.

Some organisations may decide to go beyond operational effectiveness and choose the 'dark green' option, actively looking for ways to protect, preserve and restore the Earth and its natural resources. For instance, they might make strategic changes that allow them to benefit from climate change and move further towards sustainability, or they might enhance or extend their competitive positioning by creating products such as electric cars, water filtering systems or window glass that can capture and store the sun's energy for later use.

Determining how green an organisation wants to go helps with two other important considerations: whether to adopt the International Organization for Standardization (ISO) 14001:2004 environmental standards and whether to undertake voluntary *sustainability reporting*. The ISO 14004:2004 provides guidelines on the principles, issues and elements of an environmental management system and how to implement such a system. It specifies the requirements for an environmental management system and discusses how to provide objective evidence for audits. These standards can help organisations to minimise the effects of their activities on the environment and continually improve their environmental performance. (The ISO's standard on corporate social responsibility is ISO 26000: 2010.)

Sustainability reporting is not mandatory in Australia, although many organisations choose to do so voluntarily. Australian companies are, however, obliged to disclose sustainability-related information under the *National Greenhouse and Energy Reporting Act 2007* (Cth) and the National Pollutant Inventory. Also, under the *Corporations Act 2001* (Cth), directors of public companies, large proprietary companies, registered schemes and disclosing entities are required to publicly disclose information relating to the company's environmental performance.[5]

The input–output–outcome–impact framework

The *input–output–outcome–impact framework* is a useful way to set goals and measure progress in each of those four areas:

1. *Inputs* could be, for instance, financial or technological, or they could be initiatives such as a green office program or research and development for new green products, services or systems.
2. *Outputs* consist of what is produced or done with the inputs. They allow you to see the immediate results of your inputs, or how they have been used or applied.
3. *Outcomes* are short-term results from the outputs.
4. *Impacts* are the longer-term results of your efforts.

For example, to reduce the carbon footprint of your organisation's delivery chain, you might decide to spend a specific sum of money (*input*) on installing dual engines in your delivery vehicles (*output*). You would then measure the monthly reduction in vehicle emissions (*outcome*) and, say, 24 months later, then measure the total reduction in vehicle emissions over an annual cycle and find out what portion of your company's total emission reductions it represents. The *impact* of reduced emissions might be improved air quality and a reduction in asthma and other respiratory complaints along your transportation route, a lower carbon footprint and resulting financial savings. Work with your organisation's finance specialists to calculate the cost–benefit of various inputs.

Develop strategy options

Once you have determined where your organisation is and where it wants to get to, it's time to identify strategies which will get it there. This is known as a gap analysis.

You will need to assemble a cross-functional team comprised of personnel from finance, legal, operations, procurement and other function areas to develop strategy options. 'Recruit' anyone who has knowledge or expertise in the area of sustainability because this will give your team added credibility and get influential senior people on side or in the team, which will help gain executive support when it comes to having your strategies ratified.

Begin by taking a broad approach to achieving sustainability goals by identifying which strategies your organisation could feasibly adopt. Large organisations with varied operations, particularly those spread over more than one geographical area, may need different strategies to address different aspects of their operations and/or locations.

Relatively simple, eco-efficient defensive actions might be your starting point and then you can move on to offensive strategies. Consider the following approaches:

Transferable skills

2.3 Business strategy

- *Do what you've always done – but better.* Go for small, quick wins by reducing costs, risks and waste of resources (e.g. energy, materials, water) by using them more efficiently and showing customers proof of value. (You can find some ideas in the first part of Section 23.2.) At the same time, begin planning for longer-term eco-effectiveness measures and consider the impact of all decisions on eco-efficiency and eco-effectiveness.
- *Do new tasks in new ways with innovative approaches.* Select functions, operations, products and supply chains to redesign for sustainability by optimising their eco-effectiveness and eco-efficiency, and contribution to human welfare and social equity, and invest in technologies to make an even greater impact on the sustainability of your organisation's operations.
- *Build sustainability into the organisation's core activities and supply chains.* This way, sustainability becomes the source of new income and growth; for example, through new products and developing new capabilities.
- *Build new business models and platforms that use your innovations.* This can enhance your organisation's culture and offerings and secure its future.

There may be opportunities within your organisation and its supply chains to significantly lighten the footprint their activities have on the planet. This is the 'look inside-out and outside-in' approach. Some activities your organisation controls while other activities it can indirectly influence, such as those carried out by suppliers, that occur within distribution channels and can even extend to the way customers use and dispose of your products. Look at all three areas to maximise the impact of your strategies.

Encouraging and supporting innovative thinking within your organisation can also lead to new ways and ideas in relation to sustainable work practices and approaches. There are numerous examples of 'unusual ideas' that ended up being environmental and financial successes, such as drones being used to plant tree seeds, solar panel roads, harvesting power from raindrops, and robotic bees that can pollinate crops. These are just a few examples.

Emissions-intensive activities and low-sustainability activities that add little value are candidates for outsourcing to more eco-efficient and eco-effective organisations. Those that add value are candidates for keeping in-house and re-engineering to reduce their impact on the environment. Finding sustainable ways to perform key activities in ways your competitors can't match gives your organisation a valuable competitive advantage, too.

Improving your resource productivity and reducing waste saves money as well as the environment. Identifying and managing environmentally driven risks is sound risk management and can help you design more sustainable and environmentally friendly operations. Examining and managing your supply chain to reduce your organisation's footprint and finding ways to reduce regulatory burdens and your organisation's impact on the environment are other ways to strategically increase your organisation's sustainability.

Here are seven other strategies to achieve more sustainable operations:[6]

- *Acquire, or buy, someone else's green brand* or a **B corporation** to gain access to knowledge and sustainable systems. L'Oréal bought The Body Shop, Unilever bought Ben & Jerry's. Beware of culture clash and lack of strategic fit when going for this option. Consider your brand portfolio when adopting this strategy, too. How will the rest of your products look when compared with your wonderful green product? Too big a gulf can undermine your sustainability claims.

Transferable skills
2.3 Business strategy

- *Build green offerings from scratch.* This is particularly suited to organisations with a track record of innovation. It can be slower and more costly than the other strategies, but the organisation builds valuable, transferable competencies that can extend to profitable platforms along the way; Toyota produced a hybrid version of Lexus, for example, forcing Mercedes-Benz and BMW to introduce their own hybrid models.
- *Improve resource productivity and reduce waste* to save money as well as the environment.
- *Make the most of your organisation's existing or latent green attributes.* Struggling Brita was about to be sold off by Clorox but saved itself by showing how its water filtration systems could keep millions of plastic water bottles out of landfills.
- *Manage environmentally driven risks* and be sure to find them before they find you.
- *Manage your integrated value chain* to reduce your organisation's footprint.
- *Reduce environmental costs and regulatory burdens.*

When selecting strategies, consider which best meet your organisation's mission and goals, taking into account their cost-effectiveness, ongoing expenses, timeframes, and economic, social and stakeholder impacts. Consider any underlying capital expenses and the cost of developing any new methodologies. These need to be weighed up against the cost of polluting and other non-financial costs, such as those relating to your organisation's employer brand and market reputation. When the numerical calculations involved are large, enlist the help of experts. You can also use data-mining, forecasting and optimisation techniques to cost and analyse various options and run simulations on different scenarios to select the strategy.

Carry out a risk analysis on any investments; for example, if you invest in a **carbon sink** forest and it burns down, your investment is lost. Conduct a force-field analysis on each strategy option. You may also want to do some scenario planning for the strategies that seem most promising.

You can apply a problem-solving process to help guide you to identify, assess and develop the policy and strategies. This might involve:

- identifying the problem clearly
- establishing the desired outcomes
- analysing the problem to determine its cause
- generating alternative solutions
- evaluating the effectiveness of the solution options and selecting the most suitable.

Make sure the policy and strategies you recommend are integrated with the organisation's overall strategy and that they address stakeholder, environmental and social imperatives; decreasing pressure on natural resources; increasing expectations regarding corporate environmental performance; and lowering costs of introducing sustainability measures.

Recommend policy and strategy options

Bearing in mind your organisation's goals and the objectives of its key decision-makers, put forward your policy and strategy recommendations for consideration. Ensure the policy reflects the organisation's commitment to sustainability, aligns with your organisation's business planning and decision-making processes and can drive a sustainability culture throughout the organisation. Presenting a sustainability policy in positive terms is critical so that it is seen as a business opportunity and part of the organisation's corporate responsibility measures rather than as a burden. Identify the positions that will be responsible for overseeing and arranging the policy's implementation, reviewing it and monitoring its effectiveness.

It is also important to link the sustainability strategies you recommend with your organisation's vision and mission, its other strategies and policies, and how it reflects the expectations of the organisation's key stakeholders. Explain the rationale behind each and any downsides, and suggest their expected cost, effectiveness and timeframes.

Finalise the policy and strategies and agree on introduction methods

After obtaining, considering and incorporating feedback from the decision-makers, where applicable, write up the policy for final approval. Pay particular attention to getting the estimates of costs and revenues associated with the implementation of the policy as accurate as possible. You will need to build in some flexibility as well as contingency plans to fall back on if, for instance, costs blow out or the expected benefits don't materialise. You will also need to factor in the resources needed to communicate the policy and its associated strategies, which may involve training for employees as well as other professional development activities. Ensure that any required compliance training is also provided so that all employees understand their personal obligations in implementing the policy.

Use a range of communication channels to promote the policy and the expected outcomes to stakeholders. Your aim is to create awareness, develop a sense of enthusiasm and generate support for the organisation's sustainability commitment. Build in regular communication mechanisms with stakeholders and include ways to keep the policy 'living' to maintain its profile and encourage continuous improvements. Ideally, you want the policy and its strategies to become part and parcel of everyday operations and work practices and second nature in the way that employees incorporate them into their work roles.

23.2 Developing and implementing sustainability programs

> In the end, our society will be defined not only by what we create, but by what we refuse to destroy.
>
> John Sawhill, President and CEO of the Nature Conservancy, quoted in 2014 *Nature Conservancy Annual Report*.

While a sustainability policy might be an overarching policy to be applied across all levels and areas of an organisation, for it to be understood and implemented successfully, the tasks and responsibilities need to be broken down into areas, with different teams working on different areas simultaneously.

Although there is no 'one size fits all' formula for developing and implementing a sustainability policy, there are some general guidelines that can be applied when selecting and implementing suitable sustainability programs.

Begin by identifying specific categories in which to execute your sustainability strategies. Some common examples applicable to most organisations include the areas of energy consumption, water usage, recycling and upcycling, investing in energy-efficient equipment and production technologies and redesigning processes. Once you have identified the relevant areas, select specific programs and narrow down the choices until you have found the most suitable.

The next step is to identify in what areas both within and outside of the organisation the strategies are relevant and can be applied; for example, production or energy used for heating and cooling. A close examination of your organisation's supply chain is likely to highlight processes that could be streamlined or even eliminated, and selecting or changing suppliers with low carbon footprints can also make a significant difference to the organisation's ecological footprint. 'Dark green' organisations might investigate ways to create a negative footprint.

Measuring and valuing natural capital

Natural capital, the sources of the services that nature provides, including fresh water, flood control, clean air, **biodiversity** and forest products, should also be taken into account and assigned a value. Natural capital has for a long time been considered free by organisations with the inevitable consequences of not being valued and, therefore, not being used or preserved judiciously.

Transferable skills
1.3 Sustainability

The more organisations understand the economic value of nature's resources, the smarter and more sustainable decisions can be made to use them wisely. By valuing natural capital, nature's economic role can actually be measured. Once governments and organisations can see its numerical economic value, and it is included within their accounting methodology, like any decision in relation to resource usage, they will be more likely to make decisions involving the use of natural capital with efficiency, risk management and sustainability outcomes in mind.

Linking sustainability to performance

The leading public body for protecting and improving the environment in England and Wales, The Environment Agency, includes sustainability objectives in individual performance plans for its project managers within its overall construction function. The project managers must use a carbon calculator during the design and construction of all new flood risk management schemes, which provides them with choices in relation to the embodied carbon dioxide emissions of materials, their transportation, site energy use and waste management.[7]

Eco-efficiency programs

There are a number of tried, tested and relatively cheap, easy and quick eco-efficiency initiatives that you can employ in the short-term while your organisation develops longer-term, more significant eco-effective strategies. Some of these easier, short-term innovations are reviewed in the following sections. They can be used as 'thought starters' to help you identify practices that suit your own organisation. As you develop options and programs, facilitating as much employee involvement as possible will help to generate ideas as well as build their support and enthusiasm.

Build-wise

Transferable skills

2.3 Business strategy

Green buildings with substantially reduced footprints are springing up in most cities. They capture and utilise fresh air, cooling breezes and warming sunshine; generate electricity; harvest roof water directly or indirectly (e.g. through roof gardens); treat grey and black water for recycling; provide natural lighting (reduces eye strain when working on computers, increases productivity, and saves energy and money); and use building panels that clean smog. These measures can increase productivity while reducing carbon use and energy bills. Other initiatives include improving glazing and shading; investing in monitoring equipment and control systems to improve a building's energy efficiency; upgrading office air-conditioning, heating, lighting and ventilation; and installing chilled beams, movement detectors and solar shading for lighting and heating/cooling.

Buy-wise

Transferable skills

2.3 Business strategy

Known as green purchasing, many organisations are choosing to purchase products and services that have minimal or reduced environmental and human health and welfare impacts; for example, alternative-fuel vehicles, bio-based products, energy-and water-efficient products, furniture made from recycled or upcycled materials and non-toxic finishes, green cleaning products, locally made and fair-trade products, and recycled paper. This is as simple as sourcing a reputable supplier, and it is visible and popular with employees, and encourages the market for eco-friendly products to grow.

When buying green, factors such as longevity and life cycle are important, so it is important to consider:

- how equipment and products were manufactured (their environmental and human impact)
- what happens to the product at the end of its life cycle
- whether products contain harmful chemicals or toxins (ingredients that are toxic to life and can leach into waterways when dumped)
- whether recycled or, better still, upcycled materials (which reduce their environmental impact) were used
- whether you really need it, since the best way to conserve is not to consume in the first place.

Some useful websites that can help with green purchasing include:

- https://info.australia.gov.au/information-and-services/environment/environment-friendly-products
- http://www.geca.org.au (Good Environmental Choice Australia or GECA)
- http://www.greenfinder.com.au.

Energy-wise

Transferable skills

2.3 Business strategy

Power prices have risen a massive 117 per cent since 2008,[8] so reducing energy consumption is not only good for the environment, it also makes good business sense. There are many easy ways to reduce and make energy use more sustainable.

Air-conditioning is quite literally a 'gas guzzler', accounting for 39 per cent of energy consumption in most buildings, with lighting making up a further 25 per cent.[9] That's a lot of greenhouse gas emissions. Simple actions to reduce energy use by 10 to 15 per cent include fine-tuning existing systems, cleaning air-conditioning ducts, keeping air-conditioning and plumbing systems in good working order, and using energy-efficient light bulbs and natural light when possible. Most of the traditional ways of saving energy are also still applicable, such as turning off lights and computer monitors when not in use, and setting thermostats on air-conditioning.

If your organisation wants to get creative, it can save more than 30 per cent of its energy costs through efficiency strategies, such as capturing waste heat from electricity generation to use for heating and cooling, and variable-speed motors and voltage optimisation (VPO) technologies to reduce power use.[10] As well as the obvious renewable energy options of rooftop solar and wind energy there are also many others, including advanced batteries, biofuels, fuel cells, LED lighting, collecting and burning methane from landfills and photovoltaics (converting light into electricity using semiconductors).

Reducing demand on traditional systems through relatively simple engineering actions is another way to reduce emissions. For example, using hybrid air-treatment systems, such as mixed-mode ventilation (combining natural and mechanical ventilation), natural ventilation or cross-ventilation, improves indoor air quality and provides an oxygen-rich air supply that is better for people's health, and boosts both productivity and energy efficiency. Building control technologies and high-efficiency central energy plant and modern lighting systems garner more energy savings.

The next step might be to purchase 100 per cent accredited **green electricity** (aka **renewable energy**) or convert to cleaner-burning fuels. When your organisation is ready for more sophisticated measures, which also reap higher returns, think about measures such as:

- *green manufacturing*
- *generating renewable energy*
- *geosequestration:* injecting greenhouse gases directly into underground geological formations)
- *biosequestration:* harvesting (i.e. capturing and removing) greenhouse gases using biological processes; for example, practices that enhance soil carbon in agriculture and using vegetation to help offset greenhouse gas emissions, such as commercial tree plantations, forests and woodlands, which take up (i.e. *sequester*) carbon dioxide from the atmosphere and release oxygen as they grow; vegetation releases that CO_2 again only when it decomposes or is burnt
- *cogeneration:* reducing greenhouse gas emissions by generating electricity on-site; for example, with natural gas-fired generators, and using the recovered heat from in-house electricity generation to provide heat for the building
- *trigeneration:* which takes cogeneration one stage further by converting waste heat from cogeneration to help cool the building interior using absorption chillers.

The choices an organisation makes about energy consumption do not only influence its energy costs. They also influence employee engagement, and how the market, and its customers, perceive it, and those choices can all contribute to improved employer brand and reputation.

Office-wise

Transferable skills
2.3 Business strategy

Green office programs incorporating the more straightforward measures of eco-buying and that are energy-, travel-, waste- and water-wise are good ways to involve all employees. Promoting wellbeing and work–life balance, and teaching staff to make continuous improvements, are other common elements of green office programs. Other quick and easy ways to green-up your office include investing in bike racks and showers, promoting carpooling, recycling bottles, glass and paper and making double-sided printing the default. Small actions accumulate.

You can take green office programs further by setting challenging environmental and carbon-management targets. More sophisticated strategies, such as green construction and refurbishment programs, and developing or investing in data collection, management and reporting tools to measure your progress, are two other ways to ramp up green office programs.

Pack-wise

Transferable skills
2.3 Business strategy

Whether it's cardboard, plastic or Styrofoam, packaging uses up natural resources, damages the environment in its manufacture (e.g. through excessive water use and emissions) and causes disposal problems. Replacing these with mushroom and potato packaging is an eco-friendly, sustainable alternative. When you're considering packaging alternatives, ask these three questions before making a decision:

1 What is it made of and could it be made with something more sustainable?
2 Is the size of the box or packaging it comes in necessary or could it be smaller?
3 Is the packaging material easily recyclable?

INDUSTRY INSIGHTS

Reuse, recycle, reduce and renew

As part of Dell Technologies' Advancing Sustainability Moonshot Goal, by 2030 the company will reuse or recycle an equivalent product for every product a customer buys from it. It also aims to use 100 per cent recycled or renewable material in its packaging and more than 50 per cent recycled or renewable material in its products. It is also aiming to reach net zero greenhouse gas emissions across direct and indirect emissions and purchased goods and services by 2050. Lastly, 75 per cent of its electricity across all facilities will be sourced from renewable sources by 2030 – and 100 per cent by 2040. These are just some of a raft of sustainability initiatives the company has put into place.[11]

Resource-wise

Transferable skills
2.3 Business strategy

Auditing the categories of waste produced by your organisation and selecting other materials you don't need to waste is a good place to start to be resource-wise. Substituting the wasted materials with more sustainable materials that can be upcycled or reused, using less of the materials you waste to begin with and segregating waste at the point of use for reuse or recycling are other strategies to consider, especially if your organisation is a big waste producer.

The resource-wise pecking order, summarised in Figure 23.3, provides a possible solution to the current imbalance between the products and services we need to satisfy our wants and needs and the area required to absorb the resulting waste. The more we can satisfy our demands from existing products through upcycling, reusing and recycling, or reduce our demand through avoiding and reducing, the less the imbalance will be. Think it through at every opportunity and visit the following websites for more good ideas for using resources wisely:

- http://www.agriculture.gov.au
- http://www.environment.gov.au
- http://www.environment.sa.gov.au
- http://www.sustainability.vic.gov.au
- http://www.wastewise.wa.gov.au
- http://www.wmaa.asn.au.

Travel-wise

Transferable skills
2.3 Business strategy

Prior to the COVID-19 global pandemic, the concept of travel-wise went little beyond encouraging employees to walk or cycle to work, carpool or use public transport. But with organisations forced to allow employees to work away from the office and mostly at home, travel-wise has taken on a whole new dimension. With work and meetings now being largely undertaken remotely using videoconferencing software, employees are enjoying the extra time and costs saved from avoiding travel to and from work, employers are benefiting from lower energy costs in the office and reduced fleet vehicle costs, and the planet is perhaps enjoying the greatest benefits of lower emissions, less pollution and cleaner air. The following are some travel-wise websites that can provide a few more ideas:

- http://www.carbonneutral.com.au
- http://www.greenvehicleguide.gov.au.

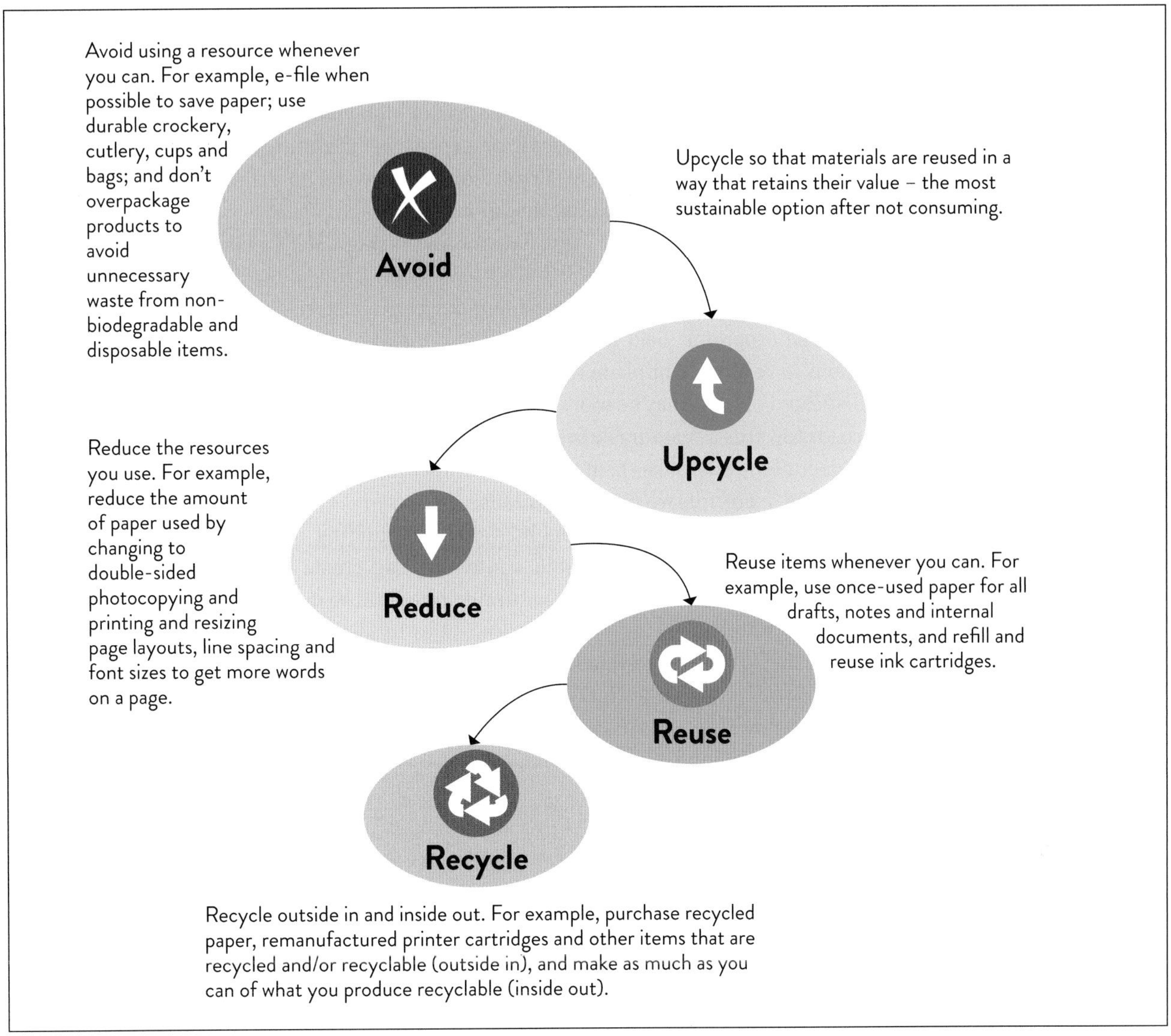

Avoid using a resource whenever you can. For example, e-file when possible to save paper; use durable crockery, cutlery, cups and bags; and don't overpackage products to avoid unnecessary waste from non-biodegradable and disposable items.

Avoid

Upcycle so that materials are reused in a way that retains their value – the most sustainable option after not consuming.

Upcycle

Reduce the resources you use. For example, reduce the amount of paper used by changing to double-sided photocopying and printing and resizing page layouts, line spacing and font sizes to get more words on a page.

Reduce

Reuse items whenever you can. For example, use once-used paper for all drafts, notes and internal documents, and refill and reuse ink cartridges.

Reuse

Recycle

Recycle outside in and inside out. For example, purchase recycled paper, remanufactured printer cartridges and other items that are recycled and/or recyclable (outside in), and make as much as you can of what you produce recyclable (inside out).

FIGURE 23.3 The resource-wise pecking order

Water-wise

Transferable skills

2.3 Business strategy

When you look at a photograph of the Earth from a certain angle, it looks like the entire surface of the planet is covered by water. In fact, water covers 75 per cent of the Earth's surface, but only 2.5 per cent of water on Earth is fresh, and most of that fresh water is locked up in polar ice caps and glaciers, leaving just 0.075 per cent of the Earth's total water available for the world's animals, people and plants. Water is one of our scarcest resources. More than 30 per cent of the drinking water produced worldwide never reaches the customer due mostly to leaky pipes.[12]

In most countries, industry, not people, consumes the most water. For example, in agriculture, it takes 1000 litres of water to produce one cup of coffee and it can take 15 000 litres of water to produce one kilogram of beef (while at the same time, producing substantial amounts of the greenhouse gas methane). It is estimated that each person living in developed Western nations uses 3000 litres of water per day, 2500 litres of that being used to water crops to produce the food they eat.

It is predicted that by 2025, 1.8 billion people will be living in countries or regions with absolute water scarcity and 66 per cent of the world's population will be living in water-stressed areas – areas that suffer chronic or recurring water shortages. Add the increasing effects of climate change and almost half the world's population will be living in areas of high water stress by 2030.[13] Fortunately, saving scarce water doesn't need to be difficult or expensive. There are many ways to store and transport water, make existing water safe to drink, convert seawater to drinkable water and reduce the existing water footprint of organisations' operations.

Fixing leaks and installing water-efficient fixtures and fittings, such as flow restrictors and tap aerators, are quick, cheap and easy to do. Infrared sensors on urinals, replacing conventional taps with spray models and installing water-displacement devices in cisterns are other easy ways to save water. Many of these programs yield important, if incremental, returns with quick paybacks, and many organisations have already implemented them.

More sophisticated options may be more complicated but can yield even bigger returns and make even bigger inroads towards a sustainable future. These call for strategic changes to an organisation's philosophy and operations but make them more resilient, even in the face of extreme events, and can even create new value. Here are two of those options:

1 Site ecology renewal projects take thought, time and funding but make large impacts. For example, where sufficient land is available, companies can create wetlands and water run-offs that allow organisms to treat wastewater naturally in the soil so it can be reused.
2 On a larger scale, water metering systems allow cities to identify leaks and changes in water-use patterns so they can respond quickly to water waste and loss in homes, offices or the water distribution network. Kalgoorlie, for example, has reduced its water loss by 10 per cent by monitoring water flows.[14]

For some more ideas and information, check out these water-wise websites:

- http://www.awa.asn.au
- http://www.environment.gov.au
- http://www.natureaustralia.org.au/celebrating-australia/water-saving-tips
- http://www.ourwaterfuture.com.au
- http://www.savewater.com.au
- https://www.watercorporation.com.au/save-water.

Oh, and next time you think about buying a bottle of water, remember that the energy it takes to make one small bottle of water is equivalent to the energy spent driving a car 500 metres.[15]

Eco-effectiveness programs

Transferable skills
1.3 Sustainability

Since the Industrial Revolution, products have been designed and manufactured by taking raw materials from the Earth, making them into products and then throwing them out when their useful life is over, often damaging the environment as they deteriorate or break apart. This is known as **cradle-to-grave** production. **Cradle-to-cradle** production offers a sustainable alternative and a way to deliver us from our current overshoot situation where we no longer have the biological productive area to meet the world population's resource demands and to absorb the waste we generate. The **circular economy**, designing products to be reused, not wasted, provides an answer to the problem. Cradle-to-cradle production takes us from cradle-to-grave 'take, make, waste' to 'make, use, return', as illustrated in **Figure 23.4**. South Australian Government research estimates that following circular economy principles could create an extra 25 700 full-time equivalent jobs by 2030 compared with business as usual, and reduce GHG emissions by 27 per cent.[16]

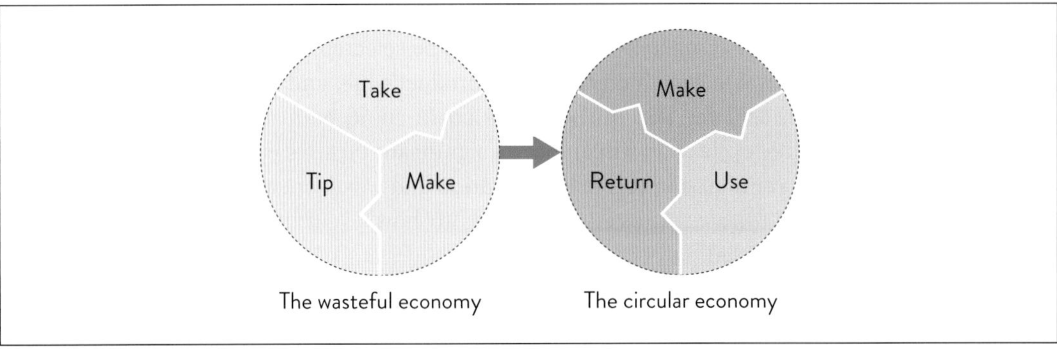

FIGURE 23.4 The circular economy

The additional benefit that the circular economy offers is that it can save more money than it costs. For example, cleaning up pollution after creating it, fines for mismanaging environmental issues, money spent on pollution control equipment and so on are generally more costly than reducing pollution or not polluting in the first place. Some other eco-effectiveness strategies are described in the following sections.

The internet of things

Transferable skills
2.3 Business strategy

The internet of things (IoT) is providing a range of different ways for us to use resources more efficiently and effectively as well as connect to and interact with suppliers across the globe. For example, sensors connected to the internet can help by making resource use more controllable, such as detecting moisture levels in soils and turning on watering systems automatically, which helps to prevent overwatering.

These smart, connected sensors have given rise to the continuous manufacturing model, part of the circular economy, where software upgrades and updates can continue long after a product is purchased. This means that a sale isn't just a once-off transaction anymore but the beginning of an ongoing relationship where the product improves over time. This can be an important profit generator and can allow more sustainable manufacturing because the products themselves have longer life cycles. They can also allow organisations to collaborate and produce joint offerings.

Life cycle analysis

Transferable skills
2.3 Business strategy

Analysing the life cycle of products and services from cradle-to-grave, from extracting their raw materials to disposing of their packaging and remanufacturing, distributing, disposing of or reusing the products themselves when they are no longer needed or working, provides an array of opportunities for using resources more wisely. The analysis can be as simple or as complex as you need. You can go from a quick screening to a full ISO-compatible, peer-reviewed analysis.

A life cycle analysis includes:

- measuring the energy and other resources associated with materials extraction and the production of goods
- measuring the environmental emissions (acidification, eco-toxicological and human-toxicological pollutants, GHG, smog) that result from the manufacture, assembly, distribution, use and disposal of purchased and produced goods
- considering the impact on the environment (e.g. depletion of fossil fuels, desertification and land, minerals and raw materials used in the production, distribution, use and disposal of purchased and produced goods)
- considering all intervening transportation steps needed and resources used for a product or service.

From the outside-in, life cycle analysis helps to identify which resources or materials to use so the least environmentally damaging item or material can be selected. By considering the pollution, disposal of packaging and waste generated through a product's life, and looking at how the actions and processes of suppliers and the rest of the supply chain could be made more environmentally friendly and sustainable, life cycle analysis can have a significant positive environmental impact.

From the inside-out, a similar analysis of the pollution and waste created during the production process can be conducted with consideration given as to how it can be disposed of responsibly, upcycled, repurposed or recycled.

Value chain indices (VCI) are a more sophisticated form of life cycle analysis because they are developed jointly by the integrated value chain (supply chain). VCIs provide information at brand, factory and individual product level and can be used to compare businesses within a sector to track business performance over time. This helps designers select materials and suppliers with the lowest environmental impact and it helps investment funds select sustainable companies.

Avoid

Transferable skills

2.3 Business strategy

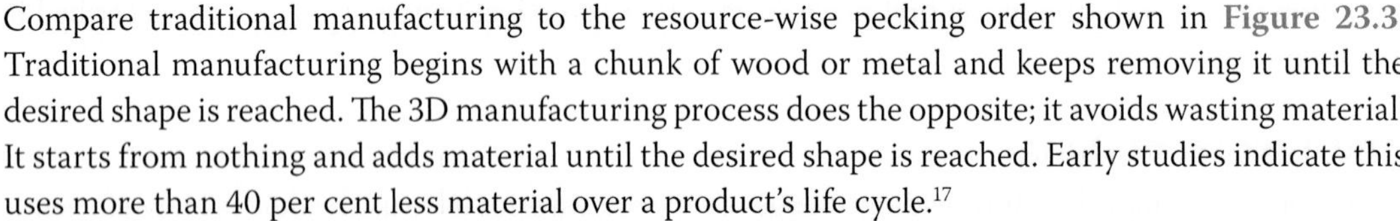

Compare traditional manufacturing to the resource-wise pecking order shown in Figure 23.3. Traditional manufacturing begins with a chunk of wood or metal and keeps removing it until the desired shape is reached. The 3D manufacturing process does the opposite; it avoids wasting material. It starts from nothing and adds material until the desired shape is reached. Early studies indicate this uses more than 40 per cent less material over a product's life cycle.[17]

As with many sustainability initiatives, several benefits flow from one action. With **additive manufacturing**, the amount of material needed to make a product is not only reduced, but it also enables manufacturing on demand, which localises supply chains. This, in turn, reduces the need for long distribution chains and cuts delivery times and emissions.

INDUSTRY INSIGHTS

3D in practice

Transferable skills

5.2 Technology use

Many companies, large and small, are embracing 3D manufacturing as a way to operate more sustainably and serve the customer better. BMW uses 3D manufacturing to make lighter tools for its assembly lines. Nike uses it to make some shoe models, reducing waste by 80 per cent. Siemens uses it to create industrial gas turbines, reducing GHG emissions and resource use throughout its production processes.[18]

Upcycle

Transferable skills

2.3 Business strategy

Although most companies begin their sustainability journey by using less, the logic turns on its head when designing (or redesigning) how to produce a product based on upcycling. Upcycling principles include designing methods to recover the materials used to produce the product when it is at the end of its useful life. Ironically, this means not having to worry about using less. In fact, it's better to use more, because when only small amounts of a material are used, it's difficult to recover for recycling or upcycling. Using less only makes sense when the product is to be dumped.

Natural products can decompose and be reused in an endless cycle of renewal. Upcycling, or cradle-to-cradle production, achieves the same cycle of renewal. Assessing every material used in a product to determine whether it is safe for the ecosystem, and how it can be reused in a way that retains its value, creates a 'virtuous cycle' of materials, making upcycling a far better alternative to destroying, **downcycling** or dumping products.

Companies that take this route find a new meaning to the adage 'stay close to your customer' because their customers also supply their raw materials. This means they need to forecast future demand as well as future returns, which depends in part on the anticipated life cycle of the product. Products with long life cycles may require manufacturers to plan for interim material supplies for the first few years.

Cradle-to-cradle producers also need to work out the logistics of getting their used products back to the factory for reprocessing. Depending on the product, customers could, for example, post it back or drop it into a retail outlet; for other products, the company might need to arrange collection of used products and organise routes and timings to use transport efficiently. This may involve extra work, but virtually guarantees repeat sales and dramatically increases an organisation's sustainability.

Reduce and simplify

Transferable skills

2.3 Business strategy

Many companies begin by weeding out toxic materials and/or hazardous chemicals from what they purchase and produce. There are two ways to do this: one is to send a list of prohibited chemicals to suppliers and the other is to collect detailed information from suppliers about the chemicals in their products and then evaluate the impact of those chemicals on environmental and human health. However, working backwards like this is painstaking and slow.

Redesigning products using *eco-design* principles is often quicker and more effective. The ultimate goal is to design products that can be upcycled and to ensure that any materials that can't be upcycled can be cost-effectively recycled so that it is cheaper to buy those materials reprocessed than new. For instance, up to 75 per cent of steel and more than 50 per cent of aluminium is recycled, mostly because this uses a fraction of the energy needed to produce new metal.[19]

As a producer, when you can't avoid using a material or you can't redesign a product for upcycling, your next best option is to minimise the number and types of materials used. But there is a caveat: reducing resource use should be carried out in a way that doesn't make the product more difficult or impossible to recycle; potato chip bags, for example, are composed of so many ultrathin layers that they are impossible to recycle economically.[20]

Using fewer materials reduces both supply-chain complexity and the number of suppliers you need to deal with. When you reduce the number and types of materials you use, you generally use more of the remaining materials, making it easier to negotiate volume discounts and keep costs down. It also improves the service of suppliers because of the increased volume of business you give them, and it makes the product easier to recycle.

Reuse or recycle

Transferable skills

2.3 Business strategy

Reusing and recycling are the next best options. Recycling bottles, cans, cardboard, furniture, paper and old equipment is common. Several national recycling programs have been operating for a number of years, making it relatively straightforward to organise recycling for items such as batteries, computers, mobile phones and printer cartridges. Some offer the choice of using commercial or charity-based recycling programs. In either case, the resources are recycled or reused and saved from ending up in landfill.

But here is another caveat: a lot of recycling is actually downcycling. Although this is preferable to dumping or burning these items, recycling is energy-intensive and usually water-intensive, too. That's why avoiding and upcycling are the most sustainably desirable choices, followed by reducing and simplifying, thus minimising waste produced at the source.

There is also a serious cost associated with dumping. Arsenic, asbestos, cadmium, chromium, lead, polychlorinated biphenyls and polyvinyl chloride can all seep out of computers, mobile phones, personal digital assistants, tablets and TVs and other electronic waste in landfills, seriously damaging ecosystems. In fact, e-waste is being sent to landfill at three times the rate of general waste and is responsible for 70 per cent of the toxic chemicals found in landfill. Japanese landfill now contains three times the gold, silver and indium (used in coating LCD – liquid crystal display – screens) and six times the platinum the world uses in one year.[21]

The European Community Waste Electrical and Electronic Equipment Directive (WEEE Directive) 2012 sets collection, recycling and recovery targets for electrical goods. It makes electrical and electronic equipment manufacturers responsible for collecting (at no charge to private users) and disposing of their equipment by ecological disposal or reuse/refurbishment. It aims to recycle 85 per cent of electrical and electronic waste – that's a lot of harmful metals being saved from going into landfill.[22]

Collaborate

Transferable skills

2.3 Business strategy

Working with your supply chains to ensure they provide clean, green products, and finding out what your downstream customers want from you regarding sustainability, also forms an important part of an organisation's commitment to sustainability.

Sometimes it is also possible to work with competitors. Surprising as this may sound, it's an excellent strategy for sustainability. Coca-Cola, for instance, has teamed with its suppliers, the Consumer Goods Forum, Greenpeace and its arch-rival PepsiCo to find substitutes for hydrofluorocarbons, the dangerous GHG used in refrigeration. Where you identify areas of common concern with competitors that you can work on together, even while competing elsewhere, an opportunity to collaborate may present itself. The Coke and Pepsi collaboration is a good example because although they may compete on taste, distribution networks and marketing, no one picks either product ahead of the other based on how their vending machines work![23]

Collaboration makes sense because new technology can be expensive in the early stages until economies of scale are reached. Collaboration can help spread the development cost and the cost of building the market.[24]

Implement your sustainability programs

Once the programs to adopt have been agreed upon, plan their implementation and include contingency plans as a backup. Assign activities, responsibilities and success measures to those involved in implementing the programs and make sure everyone involved in the implementation process understands their deliverables.

Think about whether it might be helpful to develop an education program for employees, external customers and suppliers on sustainability matters and how they can help you protect the environment. A program like this can prove to be an important marketing tool and another way to increase consumer loyalty.

The process of developing the sustainability policy, identifying, developing and implementing sustainability programs, and consulting and communicating with stakeholders is summarised in Figure 23.5.

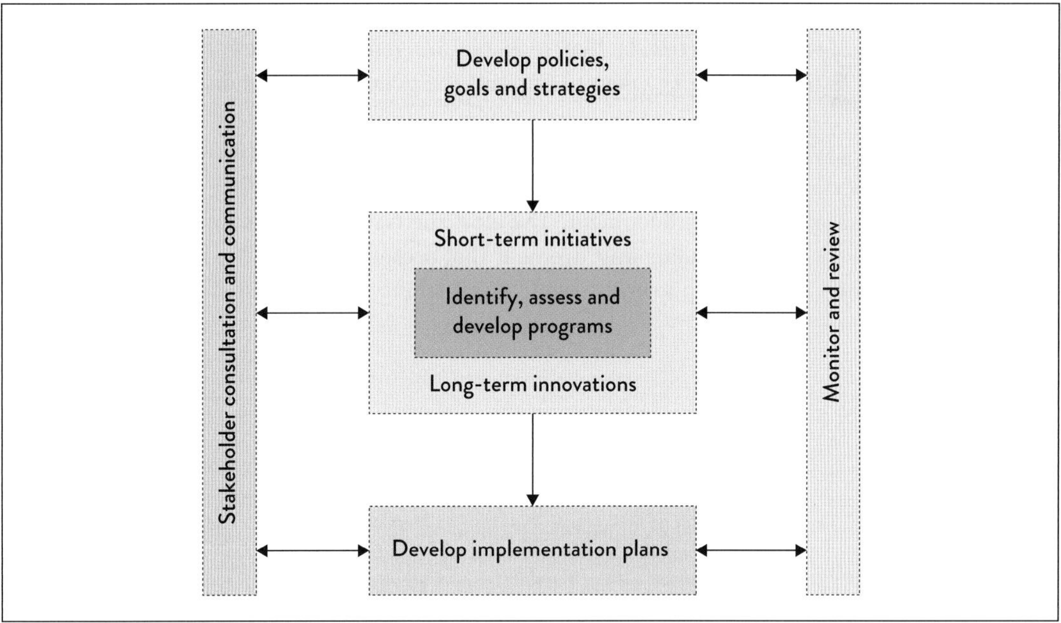

FIGURE 23.5 Increasing sustainability

Involve employees

The more your employees are involved in the organisation's sustainability efforts, the more success you will have. Communicate where you are now, where you want to be and how you plan to get there. Involve employees in developing and implementing your organisation's sustainability strategies and programs as much as you can. Provide regular updates about achievements and link them with both the benefits they provide to the environment as well as to the organisation. Aim to make sustainability an everyday habit and a consideration of every decision and action.

23.3 Monitoring and improving your sustainability policies and programs

> Unless we stop now, we will really doom the lives of our descendants. If we just go on for another forty or fifty years faffing around, they'll have no chance at all, it'll be back to the stone age. There'll be people around still. But civilisation will go.
>
> James Lovelock, in T. Flannery, *The weather makers: The history and future impact of climate change*, Text Publishing Company, 2005, p. 203.

In addition to regularly monitoring your key measures of sustainability success, you should formally review your sustainability policy and programs at least annually in order to:

- ensure their ongoing relevance
- incorporate any changes required by legislation, public demand or best practice
- make best use of current and emerging technologies and approaches
- use the information to provide feedback to stakeholders as part of your ongoing communications on sustainability matters.

Follow the 'four steps to monitoring' and use the Plan–Do–Check–Act (P–D–C–A) cycle (monitoring is the 'check' in this cycle) or Ishikawa's expanded six-step cycle to ensure your plans achieve the desired results and to identify areas for improvement.

Gather and display relevant monitoring information and devise a dashboard showing key performance measures. Look for trends that may require remedial action and investigate any disappointing results so action can be taken to improve the policy programs or procedures as soon as possible.

Investigate the causes of any surprisingly good results also, so you can ensure the success continues and replicate it in other areas. Like any other organisational policy, your sustainability policy should be treated as a living document. Therefore, be on the lookout for and ready to seize upon any opportunities for continuous improvement that present in either the internal or external environments because this will help to ensure your sustainability efforts don't stagnate.

STUDY TOOLS

QUICK REVIEW

KEY CONCEPT 23.1 

a What is the function of a sustainability policy?
b List or diagram the steps in developing a sustainability policy and strategies, and briefly describe each step.
c What do 'inside-out' and 'outside-in' mean in terms of designing sustainable organisations?
d Who should be consulted when developing a sustainability policy and strategies? What should it contain?

KEY CONCEPT 23.2 

a Explain the resource-wise pecking order and why it is ordered as it is.
b What is the circular economy?
c Why is upcycling a preferred option to recycling?

KEY CONCEPT 23.3 

a Discuss the role of monitoring in increasing an organisation's sustainability.

BUILD YOUR SKILLS

KEY CONCEPT 23.1 

a Develop an electronic file of information on sustainability using sub-file titles relevant to your organisation, such as 'benchmarks', 'green providers', 'policy development' and 'recyclers'.
b Dr Goran Carstedt, the former president of Swedish Volvo and former head of IKEA Retail Europe, said in an interview:

> Corporations have a tremendously important role in our future, almost more important than nations in terms of how to create value and wealth and distribute it. If we want to have a future that is financially viable, socially viable and ecologically viable, that has to be part of the corporate agenda.[25]

Do you agree? Why or why not? How do these comments fit in with corporate responsibility and sustainability?
c Discuss how climate change affects organisations and how organisations can help prevent further climate change.
d Review the four shades of green and discuss how organisations can decide which shade to adopt.
e Discuss how the input–output–outcome–impact framework can help organisations select which strategies and sustainability measures to adopt.
f List at least 15 strategies discussed in this chapter that organisations can use to increase their sustainability.

KEY CONCEPT 23.2 

a Discuss why it is often cheaper to prevent environment-harming activities than to address them after the fact.

b Give an example of the circular economy from your own experience.
c Discuss the resource-wise pecking order.
d What does a life cycle analysis involve?

KEY CONCEPT 23.3 

a Describe how an organisation's sustainability efforts can be monitored in a way that maintains employee involvement and interest.

WORKPLACE ACTIVITIES

KEY CONCEPT 23.1 

a Discuss how climate change could affect your organisation over the next 10 to 15 years; consider its supply chains in your discussion.
b What issues matter most to your stakeholders?
c Which shade of green is your organisation? Provide evidence for your answer and discuss how appropriate you believe this strategy is, given your organisation's customers, employee profile and shareholder base. Suggest what is needed to move to the next shade of green.
d Select one of your organisation's sustainability measures and discuss it in terms of the input–output–outcome–impact framework.
e Review each of the four approaches to sustainability outlined in the chapter. Which best suits your organisation's current circumstances and why?
f How well positioned is your organisation in terms of sustainability? Use your findings to begin setting improvement goals and, later, for tracking improvements.
g List as many ways as you can think of that your organisation could make money from sustainability and discuss your ideas with the class.
h List the key elements and intentions of your organisation's sustainability policy.
i What benefits to the organisation itself and its shareholders and other stakeholders are expected to result from your organisation's sustainability initiatives?

KEY CONCEPT 23.2 

a List and summarise your organisation's programs for sustainable operations and the goals of each program. What might your organisation's next steps be to increase its sustainability? Explain your rationale behind each recommendation in terms of ease of application and estimated costs versus benefits.
b How sustainable are your organisation's premises? What could be done to improve them?
c What procurement strategies does your organisation use to buy wisely?
d How do you rate your organisation's energy use in terms of sustainability? Explain your thinking. Where is there room for improvements?
e Discuss your organisation's measures for operating sustainably in terms of its day-to-day operations and ability to make continuous improvements.
f What innovations that differentiate your organisation from its competitors has your organisation introduced to operate more sustainably? Can you suggest any others?
g Select one service or product your organisation provides and discuss how it could reduce the resources required to produce it. Then redesign it from cradle to grave to move it towards zero impact on the environment.
h How sustainable are your organisation's supply chains? What measures could your organisation take to reduce the negative impact of its supply chains?
i What actions do you take to involve the employees in your work team to help the organisation operate sustainably?

KEY CONCEPT 23.3 

a What metrics does your organisation use to measure its progress towards reaching its sustainability goals?
b Display the results of your organisation's programs.

EXTENSION ACTIVITIES

Referring to the Snapshot at the beginning of this chapter, answer the following questions:

1 Identify the goals of the recommendations provided by the consultant Henry Nguyen.
2 Describe the level and nature of involvement required from its employees in implementing the recommendations that Forever Floating Floors would have needed to make the strategies successful.

CASE STUDY 23

KEEPING CARPETS OUT OF THE TIP

Shaw Industries, a large company based in Georgia, US, made nylon carpet tiles for commercial customers around the world. When they reached the end of their life, 95 per cent of these carpet tiles went to landfill. When Shaw decided to make virtuous recycling its goal, it went back to the drawing board to rethink its production processes.

The designers searched for a more sustainable solution and eventually chose an eco-friendly polyolefin backing to replace the traditional PVC plastic (a potentially toxic material that is difficult to recycle). Both the new backing (which holds the carpet tiles flat) and the nylon face fibre (the walking surface) can be recycled endlessly without losing performance or functionality.

Shaw then developed a production system that could take the carpet back at the end of its life, separate the backing from the walking surface, grind it up and reuse it as backing for new carpet tiles. The company also found a way to upcycle the nylon that used 20 per cent less energy and 50 per cent less water than using brand-new nylon, making it cheaper than new nylon.

As well as giving Shaw a fully sustainable product, upcycling also freed the company from price fluctuations and shortages of raw materials. Petroleum, the main input for both the backing and the nylon face fibre of traditionally made carpets, is both non-sustainable and subject to wide price fluctuations.

Radically redesigning its production process wasn't easy and it took courage – the unproven technology required a US$2 million investment and, if it worked, it would make the rest of Shaw's production facilities obsolete. In addition, the company had no concrete evidence that customers would value sustainability in carpeting.

But the gamble paid off. Oil prices rose dramatically after Shaw's move to upcycling and the company has grown its business by leveraging its technology to move into the broadloom carpet market, which accounts for more than 70 per cent of the entire carpeting market.[26]

Questions

1 Summarise the principles of upcycling illustrated in this case study.

2 Shaw's investment seemed like a huge gamble. What five points would you have made to convince Shaw's directors to make the investment? Would these same points persuade your organisation's directors to take such a big risk to move towards virtuous recycling?

CHAPTER ENDNOTES

1 Charlotte Edmond, 'Global risks report 2020: These are the top risks facing the world', World Economic Forum, 15 January 202, https://www.weforum.org/agenda/2020/01/top-global-risks-report-climate-change-cyberattacks-economic-political/

2 Helen Shariatmadari, 'How many people can live on planet earth?' BBC, 2009.

3 Philip Cenere, 'Back to school', *Company Director*, February 2015.

4 South32, 'Sustainable development goals', https://www.south32.net/sustainability-approach/sustainable-development-goals

5 Charmian Barton, 'Trends in sustainability reporting and carbon risk disclosure', HWL Ebsworth Lawyers, 4 September 2017, https://hwlebsworth.com.au/trends-in-sustainability-reporting-and-carbon-risk-disclosure

6 Daniel Esty, Andrew Winston, *Green to gold: How smart companies use environmental strategy to innovate, create value and build competitive advantage*, Wiley, New Jersey, 2009; and Gregory Unruh, Richard Ettenson, 'Growing green', *Harvard Business Review*, June 2010.

7 Dean Bartlett, 'Going green: The psychology of sustainability in the workplace', *The British Psychological Society*, 2011, https://www.bps.org.uk/sites/bps.org.uk/files/Member%20Networks/DOP%20Going%20Green%20The%20Psychology%20of%20Sustainability%20in%20the%20Workplace.pdf

8 J. Byrd, 'Chart of the day: Something has gone terribly wrong with electricity prices', *ABC News*, 18 July 2018, https://www.abc.net.au/news/2018-07-18/electricity-price-rises-chart-of-the-day/9985300?nw=0&r=HtmlFragment

9 Australian Department of Industry, Science, Energy and Resources, 'Factsheet: HVAC energy breakdown',

https://www.environment.gov.au/system/files/energy/files/hvac-factsheet-energy-breakdown.pdf

10 Phillip Lawrence, 'Becoming clean and green', *Company Director*, November 2013.

11 Dell Technologies, '2030 goals: View year-over-year progress on our social impact goals', https://corporate.delltechnologies.com/en-au/social-impact/reporting/2030-goals.htm#scroll=off&#advancing

12 US Geological Survey, 'The world's water', http://ga.water.usgs.gov/edu/earthwherewater.html, accessed 5 April 2015; see also Kathy Miles, 'Questions and misconceptions about the Earth', http://starryskies.com/articles/2003/08/earth.facts.html, accessed 5 April 2015; and Stephen E. Chick, Arnd Huchzermeier, Serguei Netessine, 'Europe's solution factories', *Harvard Business Review*, April 2014, pp. 111–115.

13 D. Heinke, D. Gerten, I. Haddeland, et al., 'Multi-model assessment of water scarcity under climate change', *Proceedings of the National Academy of Sciences of the USA*, http://www.phas.org/content/111/9/3245.short, accessed 26 December 2015; United Nations, 'Water scarcity', http://www.un.org/waterforlifedecade/scarcity.shtml

14 Chick, op. cit.

15 'Just stop buying it', The Hoopla, 18 January 2013, http://thehoopla.com.au/just-stop-buying-it, accessed 26 June 2014; and Rachel Browne, 'Battle of the bottle', *Sydney Morning Herald*, 11 May 2008, http://www.smh.com. au/lifestyle/homestyle/battle-of-the-bottle-20090403-9p4a.html, accessed 26 June 2014; and 'Bottled water', *Choice*, http://www.choice.com.au/reviews-and-tests/food-and-health/food-and-drink/beverages/bottled-water.aspx, accessed 26 June 2014.

16 Narelle Hooper, 'Rise of the B. Corps', *Company Director*, November 2017.

17 Luke Heemsbergen, 'What price our fascination with cheaper 3D printing?', *The Conversation*, 20 January 2014, http://theconversation.com/au/business, accessed 5 April 2015.

18 Marc Gunther, 'Nike and Levi's pile on for fast fashion: Culture reform', *GreenBiz*, 20 September 2016, https://www.greenbiz.com/article/nike-and-levis-pile-fast-fashion-culture-reform, accessed 19 May 2017.

19 Gregory C. Unruh, 'The biosphere rules', *Harvard Business Review*, February 2008.

20 Ibid.

21 Dave Waller, 'Recycle your kit', *Management Today* (UK), November 2008; see also Clean Up Australia, 'E-waste fact sheet', November 2009, http://www.cleanup.org.au/PDF/au/clean-up-australia–e-waste-factsheet-final.pdf, accessed 6 April 2015.

22 Waste Electrical and Electronic Equipment (WEEE), *Environment*, European Commission, http://ec.europa. eu/environment/waste/weee/index_en.htm, accessed 6 April 2015.

23 Andrew Winston, 'Resilience in a hotter world', *Harvard Business Review*, April 2014, pp. 56–64

24 Ibid; see also Ram Nidumolu et al., 'The collaboration imperative', *Harvard Business Review*, April 2014.

25 Dr Goran Carstedt, quoted in 'Follow the leader', Australian Human Resources Institute, 7 October 2004, http://www.highbeam.com/doc/1G1-122888493.html, accessed 7 April 2015.

26 Stephen E. Chick, Arnd Huchzermeier, Serguei Netessine, 'Europe's solution factories', *Harvard Business Review*, April 2014, pp. 111–115. See also Jan H. Schut, 'Close-up on technology: Big German plant may relieve US bottleneck in recycling carpet nylon', *Plastics Technology*, May 2002, http://www.ptonline.com/articles/big-german-plant-may-relieve-us-bottleneck-in-recycling-carpet-nylon, accessed 6 April 2015; and Shaw Sustainability, http://www.shawfloors.com/shaw-sustainability

CHAPTER

INTRODUCING AND LEADING CHANGE

After completing this chapter, you will be able to:

24.1 explain why change is a continuing process and discuss the six phases of change that continually cycle in all organisations

24.2 plan, resource and monitor the introduction of change

24.3 promote change with empathy and understanding

24.4 overcome people's resistance to change.

TRANSFERABLE SKILLS

The following transferable skills are covered in this chapter:

2 **Critical thinking and problem solving**
- **2.1** Critical thinking
- **2.2** Personal effectiveness
- **2.3** Business strategy

3 **Social competence**
- **3.1** Teamwork/relationships
- **3.2** Verbal communication
- **3.3** Written communication
- **3.4** Leadership

OVERVIEW

If you don't like change or find change difficult, then being a leader-manager or even simply working in an organisation in any role may not suit you because change is here, and it's here to stay. As organisations constantly face changes in the external environment, they must adapt or transform their internal environment if they going to survive.

Laws, international borders and the views and expectations of society change; the natural environment is changing at its most rapid rate in its history and then along comes a global financial crisis followed just over a decade later by a global pandemic. While we may not necessarily be able to predict the next big change, one thing is certain, it will come. When it does, those organisations that embrace it as an opportunity and are flexible and agile enough to adapt will be the ones that not only survive, but flourish.

To do so, organisations must be prepared to change the way they organise and manage their operations and the way they organise and manage their employees. With change occurring at an increasingly rapid rate, organisations need to reinvent themselves every few years if they are going to keep up. As a leader-manager in today's organisational climate, you not only need to be able to manage your employees and operations, you also need to regularly change the way you do so. Change management has become an essential skill for all leader-managers.

Managing change is, however, a delicate balance. Leave it too long or do it too slowly and you'll 'miss the boat', but do it too quickly or too often and you'll face burnt-out employees who have lost trust and faith in you. When change occurs too often and too fast, people's tendency is to fight, flee or freeze. This can lead to employee reluctance, refusal, resignation or paralysis, none of which are going to be helpful reactions, especially when you are trying to manage a potentially challenging change. This makes leading change well both essential and yet at the same time incredibly difficult.

Leading change involves making adjustments and changes, both large and small. The skills you will need to successfully manage change include knowing when, how, how quickly and to what degree these adjustments and changes are required. This chapter aims to show you how.

SNAPSHOT

The change challenge – pandemic or endemic?

Servicing the financial services, manufacturing and telecommunications industries GROW's senior management team needed to come up with a plan to keep the business operational throughout the early years of the COVID-19 pandemic.

One proposal included reallocating resources to the area of the business that had suffered the least and then back again once time had passed. The team identified that re-establishing relationships post-pandemic would take more time and money than would be financially viable so decided against it. Several options were explored and dismissed as the pandemic worsened.

Fazal, one of the executives, proposed moving into sectors that had not suffered as much as others and expanding the organisation's recruitment operations outside of the international market to capture the domestic recruitment market. Many organisations associated with supply chain operations, such as transport and warehousing businesses, were doing extremely well out of the pandemic as online shopping boomed. Similarly, many of the medium-sized online retailers had undergone rapid expansion and now were ready to start competing with the big players like Amazon. But Fazal's plan didn't end there.

He identified that while the pandemic had certainly impacted the business, it was in fact the organisation's internal structure and processes that lay at the core of its problems. Inefficiencies and duplication of tasks, processes and roles was rife across the organisation. Rather than having each recruitment department perform each stage of the recruitment process from start to finish, the new client relationship-based divisions would each be responsible for a particular stage of the recruitment process. This allowed for greater specialisation of tasks and the removal of much of the duplication that existed with the previous structure.

Training, mentoring relationships and coaching would be provided to help support management and staff during the change and performance measures would be analysed on a monthly basis to monitor their effectiveness.

A consultation process involving existing staff and key external stakeholders would form part of the implementation plan and invite suggestions and feedback for how the new process could be refined and improved.

The new strategy not only recognised the existing opportunity provided by the pandemic but also included provision for capitalising on post-pandemic opportunities. Now the challenge for Fazal and the executive team – how to sell the vision to the management, staff and organisation's key stakeholders.

24.1 Accepting change – the new normal

Nothing endures but change.

Heraclitus (ancient Greek philosopher), quoted in Plato, *Cratylus*, see F. Shapiro, *Yale book of quotations*, Yale University Press, 2006, p. 356.

When we think of organisations as living systems, we can see change as a normal ever-present cycle that every individual and every organisation goes through. Caterpillars become butterflies; seasons change; babies grow to adulthood. Organisation change, once occasional, is now the 'new normal'.

As a living system, an organisation can be viewed, as a *sigmoid*, an S-shaped curve of growth, prosper, plateau and decline. This process is depicted in the shaped curve of growth shown in **Figure 24.1**.[1] Systems need to make 'great leaps' and jump the plateaus to the next S-curve of change in order to escape the decline that is the natural order of life. These 'great leaps' may involve expanding their markets, changing their products or services, reconfiguring their supply chains or overhauling their organisational structure. This ongoing procession of change demands that leader-managers come up with new and creative ways of managing their operations and employees while at the same time finding ways of exploiting the opportunities that present in both the internal and external environments.

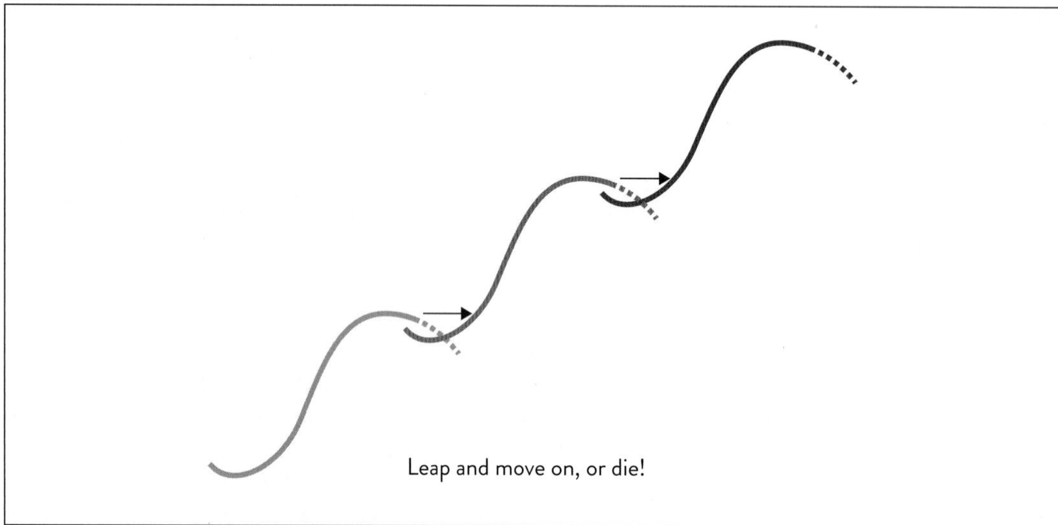

FIGURE 24.1 The S-curve of change

The continuous cycle of change

Whether you're thinking about families, organisations or societies, change is a continuing process, not a one-off event. The six phases of change shown in **Figure 24.2** continuously cycle around all systems, although the rate at which they cycle differs from one system to another.

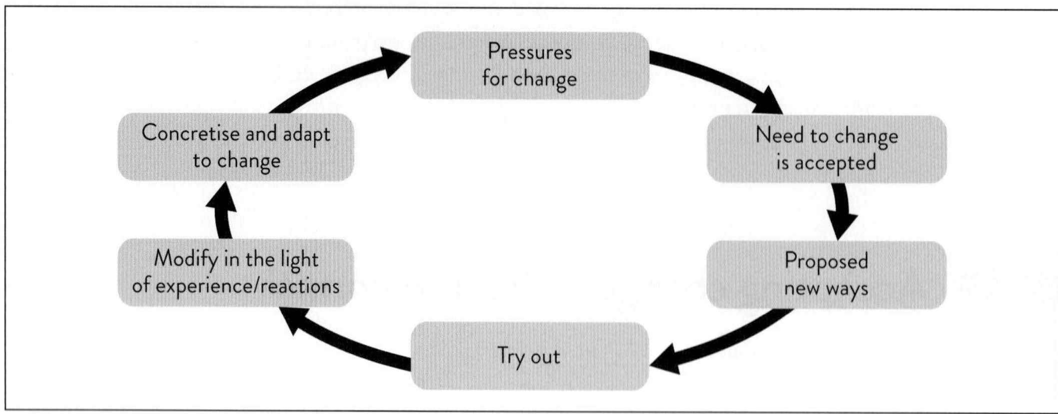

FIGURE 24.2 The continuous cycle of change

Phase 1: Pressures for change

Pressures for change can arrive suddenly or build slowly. Organisations may be forced into change (e.g. by a change in legislation) or they might gradually realise the need for change (e.g. because of a steadily declining share price or declining profits). Whatever the pressures for change and how they arrive, the need to change becomes increasingly noticeable as time passes. Figure 24.3 shows some of the many external and internal pressures that force organisations to change.

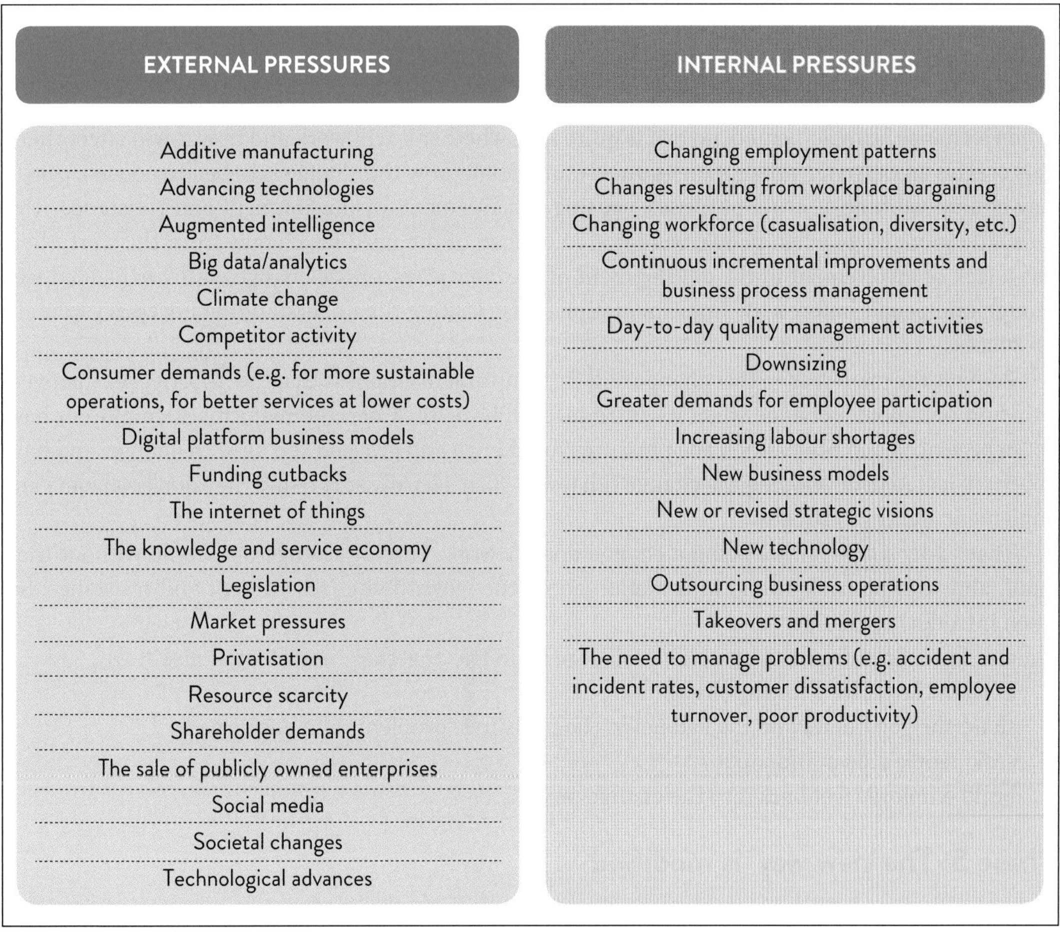

FIGURE 24.3 Pressures driving change

Phase 2: The need for change is accepted

As the pressures for change build, some within the organisation will recognise the need for change and begin the process of convincing others. The reactions they receive are often not what they had hoped for. Blinkered thinking, confusion, opposition and uneasiness are not uncommon. However, as the signs become more pronounced and the reality harder to deny, eventually there are enough people who accept the need for change and from this point the momentum gathers speed. The more that accept the need for change and the quicker this occurs is a key factor in a smooth transition to the new ways. But if resistance is resolute, the pressures for change may need to become quite strong before the need is widely acknowledged and accepted.

Phase 3: New ways are proposed

Once the need for change is accepted, people can start to think about how it will affect them and what they can do to prepare for it. Discussion revolving around the goals for change and possible alternatives will ensue, and these will be reviewed and revised until enough people are satisfied that a proposal or combination of proposals meets their needs.

The more people that are involved in creating or contributing to the 'new ways' based on their understanding the reasons for change, the greater the 'buy-in' to the change is likely to be. Resistance to change is often due more to a lack of **consultation** rather than genuine opposition.

Phase 4: Change is introduced

When a change is implemented, no one is quite sure whether it will work and how it will affect them. This creates anxiety and where there is uncertainty about how the change is to be introduced, people may end up working at cross-purposes, causing disagreement, disillusionment and resistance. This is usually more likely when people were not convinced of the need for change from the start, there was a lack of involvement in the development of the 'new ways' or the change wasn't explained well enough and people entered the implementation phase lacking the understanding necessary to make it a success.

Perhaps the main reason that change fails in many organisations is that the majority of employees only find out about a change when it's introduced (Phase 4). When the majority of employees have not experienced and understood the pressures for change and grasped the need to change, and have not participated in developing the change (Phases 1–3), it's hardly surprising they don't welcome and implement it enthusiastically.

That's why simply announcing a change doesn't work. Forcing change on people without their input, and with no background information about the whys, invites resentment and resistance. So, when introducing change:

- aim for cooperation, not compliance: 'We're all in this together', not 'Do it or else'
- explain the reasons for the change
- share the good news and the bad news, the pressures, problems and concerns
- seek people's ideas and input
- build employee feedback into the change process.

Phase 5: The 'new way' is modified

Once the changes have been implemented and taken effect, they are monitored, and adjustments and refinements are made as it becomes apparent what is working and what isn't. The more people involved in adjusting and improving the new ways, the faster and better progress is likely to be, both in acceptance and quality.

Phase 6: The 'new way' becomes 'our way'

Once all of the 'bugs' have been ironed out and everyone knows what they are doing and how it fits in with the bigger picture, the change eventually becomes the norm – that is, until pressure for change builds again and the cycle of change continues.

24.2 Introducing change

> **The reinvent-or-die challenges that used to be rare catastrophes in business have practically become the new normal – but without much direction about how to meet them.**
>
> William McComb (CEO, Fifth & Pacific Companies), 'Transformation is an era, not an event', *Harvard Business Review*, April 2014, p. 34.

Despite change being natural and even essential, with every change there are winners and losers, vociferous resisters and indifferent bystanders. It is not surprising therefore that the main barrier to genuine change is people. Unless all those within an organisation are prepared to change, there is little chance that organisational change will occur and, even if it does, it is unlikely to last for long. While it's true that change management is about goals, new systems and structures, and technical practicalities, it's equally true that change is about people's behaviours, hearts and minds. Failing to address the people issues means that your entire change initiative is likely to run out of steam and inevitably fail.

To capture people's hearts and minds, you need personal credibility so that people buy into your vision and the reasons for a change. You need to inform them in ways they understand why change is needed and how it affects them. Involving them as much as possible in designing and/or planning the change also allows you to influence people's attitudes and understanding and build their long-term commitment to 'new ways' so that the change 'sticks' rather than having things revert to the way they were after just a short period.

Table 24.1 considers the problems that create difficulties in introducing change and Figure 24.4 summarises the main reasons changes succeed or fail.

TABLE 24.1 The problems that create difficulties in introducing change

Problem	Reason
A quick start that fizzles	No clear shared vision
Anxiety and frustration	Insufficient resources allocated to implementing the change
Cynicism and distrust	Leaders not 'showing the way' or 'walking their talk'
Haphazard efforts and false starts	No clear action plan
People go back to the 'old ways'	Changes not reinforced and rewarded
Scepticism	No serious evaluation of the change program's results
No forward movement	No attempts to improve upon the changes

Source: © Ron Cacioppe, http://www.integral.org.au. Used by permission.

Think about a change that has been introduced that impacted your life, personal or professional. How was this change introduced? Thinking back to this situation, do you recognise any of the problems from Table 24.1? Do the reasons resonate with you?

Why change succeeds		Why change fails
Adequate rewards for those adopting the change	C	Authoritarian direction, or pushing people into changes they don't understand or feel ready for or are not committed to
Appropriate strategies to introduce and manage the change	H	Expecting too much, too soon
Clear and measurable objectives and outcomes	A	Failing to integrate the change into the day-to-day operations and the system as a whole
Competent staff support	N	Failing to involve a representative cross-section of employees in planning the changes
Constant, honest and clear communication about the change and its progress	G	Fuzzy, grandiose, idealistic or unrealistic objectives
Continuing modification and adaptation of the 'new ways' in the light of experience	E	Half-heartedly introducing change due to lack of commitment from managers, critical power groups and key stakeholders
Drawing on support from the existing formal and informal power structures		Ignoring or glossing over resistance
Employee involvement and participation in designing and planning the change		Inadequate information about the whys and wherefores of change
Good timing (i.e. fast enough to give a sense of progress yet not exceeding people's ability to absorb the change and feel in control)		Inappropriate strategies (e.g. inadequate resources or pre-packaged programs)
Integrating the change with the rest of the system and the formal and informal rewards structure		Insufficient staff support or other resources
Maintaining momentum as the change rolls out		Introduced suddenly
Majority support for the change sufficient to keep it moving forward		Introduced in a climate of poor morale and distrust
Realistic and limited scale of the change		People finding it hard to give up the old ways, or falling back into them, because there is no incentive to keep moving forward with the change
Support from key formal and informal power groups		People perceiving that the changes impose additional work without removing any work
Visible successes throughout the organisation resulting from the change		Poor timing (e.g. introducing change too quickly, causing people to feel out of control, or too slowly, inviting cynicism and disillusionment)
		Unclear implementation plans that result in people not knowing precisely how to make the desired changes happen

FIGURE 24.4 Why change succeeds or fails

Helping your team understand change

Campaigns and slogans don't create commitment – involvement and understanding do. So, begin with the broad goals and move on to the more detailed and personal aspects of change:

- This is the 'big picture' for our organisation.
- This is the change that needs to happen.
- This is why it needs to happen like this – how the change fits into the 'big picture'.
- This is what we think would happen if we didn't make these changes or if we don't make them successfully.
- Here's how our team fits in.
- This is how the change affects each of us individually.
- This is our new operating plan and these are our new systems, processes, policies and procedures.
- This is our transition plan.
- Here is how we plan to monitor progress and measure success.
- Here is how to get more information about the change.

Transferable skills
3.1 Teamwork/relationships

INDUSTRY INSIGHTS

David Marriott: MLC Group Reboot 2.0

David Marriot, The MLC Group

When the COVID-19 pandemic hit, many international borders closed with little or no warning. This left Managing Director of the MLC Group, David Marriott, facing a dilemma. Based in Tokyo, but operating throughout Asia, MLC specialised in executive recruitment in healthcare, information technology and automotive. With operations in the automotive industry shutting down almost overnight, the industry was brought to a virtual standstill. One option was for the company to reallocate its resources from automotive to the other two sectors until the pandemic was over. However, to do so would mean having automotive consultants learn healthcare or information technology and then re-establishing their relationships in automotive once the pandemic subsided. The risks of such a decision seemed to outweigh the rewards. 'It takes months to learn a new industry and would take as long to reheat relationships in a post-pandemic world'. The decision was taken to persist with candidate relationship management in the current sectors until the hiring restarted.

As the pandemic worsened rather than improved, the company's outlook remained challenging. Performance was stable, however, there was room for significant change at an organisational level. 'I realised that I couldn't blame the pandemic wholly for the business' position. COVID was more the catalyst which highlighted existing deficiencies within the business itself. The consultants worked hard and did their jobs but in such a climate, the urgency, ownership and accountability that was needed to thrive had to improve.'

Marriott launched the MLC Group Reboot 2.0 in April 2021, which focused on how the company would adapt to the increasing competitive environment moving forward. He redeveloped and formalised the company's values together with the team, which included defining core behaviours to reflect the values and providing a suite of new tools to support the team. Personnel changes that

were necessary were made but as other businesses were shedding staff and cutting costs, MLC actually took on new staff. It also made a significant financial investment in LinkedIn enterprise over three years to expand the scope of its operations with a focus on improved branding. Professional development opportunities were provided while monthly one-on-one discussions were implemented. 'Although the staff are recruitment professionals with most in senior roles, there was still a real need to invest in them so we could facilitate the changes we wanted to achieve. But it had to start at the top; I had to start the change process. By acknowledging that and then making the changes I needed to make, I was then in a position to lead the team through the change process individually.' The business has already recovered significantly and continues to perform strongly despite the pandemic showing little sign of slowing.

Seven steps to introducing change

People often see change as a surprise, a crisis and a sign of poor planning and clumsy leadership. But if introduced well, this needn't be the case. Change advances in stages, each building on the previous stage. The bigger the change, the longer it takes and the more stages there will be. There are no short cuts. The seven steps summarised in Figure 24.5 and explained in the following sections can be used when you introduce change. These steps apply whether you are initiating the change yourself or facilitating it on behalf of your organisation.

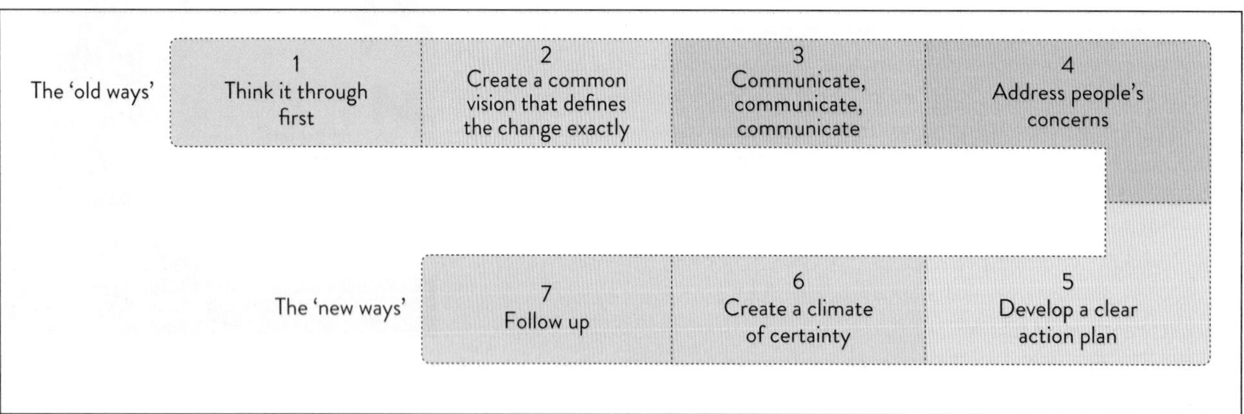

FIGURE 24.5 Seven steps to change

Transferable skills

2.2 Personal effectiveness

Step 1: Plan change carefully in your own mind

If you are unsure what a change will involve and what results it will deliver then your team is likely to have even less idea. It is therefore important to use a tool such as gap analysis to help you get clear in your own mind precisely what the change is meant to achieve and what support and actions you expect from your team when the change is introduced. You might then use a force-field analysis to explore the forces favouring change and those resisting it. This helps you create a clear, strong and straightforward vision to direct the change effort and develop strategies for realising it.

Is there a change you are wanting to implement at work? Using one of the tools listed in Step 1, explore your idea for change and create a well-considered plan in your mind.

Step 2: Create a common vision

Until you help people accept, adapt and develop new ways of working, they're likely to resent you and your attempts to introduce change. People want to know precisely how the change affects them and how you intend to help them prepare for and implement it. They can probably figure out what they stand to lose as a result of the change, so make sure they have a clear understanding of what they stand to gain, too. But perhaps your biggest selling point is making your team understand what they stand to lose if change isn't made. This can be a powerful motivator, especially if it means jobs will be lost or team members will need to be redeployed to other parts of the organisation. It is certainly not a good idea to support your change with arguments like this unless they are valid, and an even worse idea is to deliver them as an implied threat. Instead, use them as a positive way of reinforcing the change by pointing out how the new ways will keep the team together, galvanise team members' cooperation and unity and drive new business and opportunities.

Provide frequent and enthusiastic communication on these topics:

- The purpose and reason for the change; that is, why it is necessary.
- An understandable and convincing picture of the desired outcome, including where precisely the organisation and the team are headed, how the change affects employees individually and as a team, and how their working lives will improve as a result of the change.
- How the change is to take place in clear, small steps.
- What you expect each team member to do and how much effort is required.
- How much support (e.g. training and time to settle in and learn and apply new skills) you plan to provide.

Step 3: Communicate clearly, honestly, accurately and often

Transferable skills

2.3 Business strategy

3.2 Verbal communication

3.3 Written communication

Avoid the temptation to think that you can push a change through by withholding information or misrepresenting what the actual change will involve and its impact on the team. When you don't communicate effectively, employees fill in the blanks themselves, often in ways that are not only incorrect but which form conclusions that are far worse than the actual reality. Communicate clearly, regularly, honestly and accurately and use a variety of communication modes so that you reach as many of your team as possible and as often as you can. These might include the following:

- an internal change bulletin website
- corporate breakfast sessions
- informal chats
- newsletters
- other employees who have experienced this or similar change
- posters
- videos.

Providing frequent progress can help build enthusiasm and avoid misinformation being communicated via the organisational grapevine. Even when you don't have anything to report, keeping contact with regular communication can help to reassure your team and provides opportunities to reiterate the change goals and vision for the future. It also gives your team members the chance to ask questions which they might not have thought of in earlier updates.

Communicating regularly, honestly and clearly will help to build trust with your team by demonstrating your integrity as a leader. It will also reinforce to your team your belief in the change being implemented, which will in turn reassure team members that the change is beneficial and will succeed and that they will be an integral part of that success.

Thinking about the change idea and plan you created in your mind at Step 1, consider the communication strategy you would apply to inform others about your idea.

Step 4: Address people's concerns

Introducing change can be a delicate balancing act between managing operations – the 'organisation journey' – and addressing employees' needs – the 'employee journey'. The former is logical, procedural and tangible, while the latter involves the emotional impact of change on individuals. Manage both 'journeys'. When you forget about the people, you lose their trust and generate fear and scepticism just when you need loyal, productive and enthusiastic employees.

While it is important to convey optimism about a change, you should not ignore the difficulties your team members are facing, whether they are real or perceived. Acknowledge when problems and challenges arise and offer strategies and support for dealing with them. Remember that the other side to communication is listening, so make time to listen to your team members' concerns and anxieties and do your best to reassure them by offering honest, practical and realistic solutions and strategies.

Think carefully about what you say and the messages you deliver as you can expect that your words will be remembered and potentially revisited down the track, especially if you contradict them later on. Speak to your team as a whole but also speak to individuals one-on-one. Referring to each team member's role and importance in the 'new ways' will help, over time, to demystify the change and make each person feel a part of it. If, after all of this, you still encounter resistance, don't ignore it and let it continue unchallenged – implement the strategies outlined later in Section 24.4.

Think about a time where you have been involved in change, in relation to Steps 2, 3 and 4 explored in this section:

- Were you provided with a clear vision of the purpose and reason for the change?
- Did you receive regular, honest, clear and accurate communication?
- If you had any concerns, were they recognised and addressed, leaving you feeling reassured?

Taking time to reflect on situations you have been a part of can help remind you to think about what might be happening for your team members and guide you towards making positives steps that support your team through the change.

Step 5: Develop an action plan

Transferable skills
2.1 Critical thinking

Once you've explained the need for change and created a common vision, it's time to turn the vision into action. Invite ideas and suggestions and involve those affected by the change as much as possible. It gives them a stake in its success and allows the conditions, the new relationships, the ways of thinking and strategies for implementing the change actions to come together organically, helping to cement new bonds between people as the new ways come into effect.

Ensure that you develop clear plans about who is to do what, when and how, in order to achieve your goals and see that the actions needed to make the change come to fruition. Brainstorm all the action steps you can think of and then review them, sequence them, and assign start and finish dates. Some activities need to be completed before others can begin while sometimes two or more activities can be done at the same time. Using a Gantt chart or critical path analysis to create a visual 'path of progress' for yourself and your team can help you track the progress of change and actions, and provide advance warning if it begins to veer off track.

When you're sure team members understand their roles and responsibilities, empower them to take the actions required to make the vision a reality. This may involve removing any obstacles so that the 'new way' is easier than the 'old way'. If the reverse is true, there will be the temptation for people to slip back into old habits. Some processes may require standard operating procedures to achieve consistent and predictable outcomes.

Plan for and acknowledge early successes no matter how small because a sense of progress and achievement is heartening and creates its own momentum. Recognise and reward employees who contribute to the wins and develop measures of success and a monitoring system that quickly and easily track your progress.

Step 6: Create a climate of certainty

Our brains are programmed to consider new circumstances in terms of their familiarity. When you've come across a similar situation before, your brain relaxes: 'Ah ... I've survived this before, so I probably can again'. Without the comfort of familiarity, you go into full alert: fight, flight or freeze. That's why British consultant Alastair Dryburgh reminds us 'that we experience benefits in the head, but risks in the gut', and advises us to 'speak to the caveman' when helping people accept change.[2]

The sooner you can establish a sense of familiarity for your employees, the sooner they will 'relax' and be less concerned with the change and more focused on their work roles. Explaining what *will* change and why gives people something specific to aim for. Making sure they are clear as to what will not change is also important as this calms the fight, flight or freeze instinct. Build as much psychological certainty around the 'new ways' at every opportunity, since it's the uncertainty of what change might bring that causes the most anxiety and resistance.

Some other ways to reduce people's anxiety and reassure them about change are as follows:

- Celebrate successes whenever progress is made.
- Demonstrate the changes you want.
- Give people a clear path to follow in terms of action steps to help the change move forward.
- Give plenty of individual and team feedback about how the change is progressing and how their efforts and support are helping.
- Involve people; for example, through training, discussions, and question and answer sessions to help them develop new attitudes and knowledge and adapt to the change.
- Maintain as much consistency as you can, including in your leadership; people tolerate change and uncertainty more easily when their leader is calm and clear-headed.

- Provide clear direction to overcome any inertia or apathy and to keep up the momentum for change.
- Set short-term goals for individuals and groups to work towards and to provide a sense of achievement when they reach them.
- Stay enthusiastic.

It may also be beneficial with some teams to provide a way for team members to officially cut their ties to the 'old ways'. An afternoon tea or similar gathering and some carefully chosen words to welcome the new and farewell the old can help people to separate, let go and move on.

Have you ever felt the fight, flight or freeze response? Explore one of those situations in relation to the following questions:

- What was the catalyst that invoked the response?
- What strategies did you, your organisation or others put in place to support you and were they effective?

Step 7: Monitor your progress

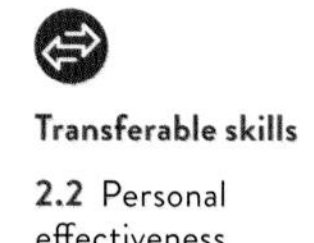

Depending on the depth of the change, you may need to hold regular change briefing meetings to keep your team abreast of how the change is progressing across the organisation. Collect feedback from employees about what is working well and what needs improving and work with them to incorporate their improvement ideas. If some team members are still resisting, find out why and see what you can do to ease their reservations.

Maintain enthusiasm and a sense of engagement with the change by making sure your team can see how well the change is progressing and go out of your way to express your appreciation of individual and team efforts. This underscores the benefits of change and helps any remaining resisters see some positive results.

Identify ways to consolidate improvements and reinforce them by integrating them into the system and anchoring them in the team's culture. Stay optimistic and keep promoting the change, even when you face bumps along the way. Eventually, the change becomes the status quo.

INDUSTRY INSIGHTS

A culture reversal

A doom and gloom culture nearly finished off the children's cancer charity Camp Quality in the early 2000s. A decade later, it had transformed its culture into positivity and hope, not just for recipients but also its staff. High employee absenteeism and attrition, low morale and a A$1.5 million operating loss due to declining donations turned into a 40 per cent reduction in sick leave and a 560 per cent increase in income.

Key to the cultural about-face was implementing change in a variety of ways across the organisation, including redefining values, mission and image, and instilling a positive culture that extended to activities with parents, children and volunteers – all with the complete commitment of senior management.[3]

When the news is mostly bad

Some changes can't be couched in positive terms. For example, a factory, shop or bank branch might close, or people might be subjected to **redundancy** due to outsourcing or the introduction of new technology. When announcing such changes, avoid blaming anyone or anything for the bad news and don't pretend that the change is good for everyone when you know that it's not. Do make it clear that you support it, nonetheless. Be as transparent as you can about what's going on and when you know the rationale behind the bad news, share as much of it as you can without breaking confidentiality.

Transferable skills

3.1 Teamwork/relationships

3.2 Verbal communication

3.3 Written communication

3.4 Leadership

Present the information neutrally and objectively, without trying to make it sound better than it is. Avoid trying to 'spin' it as a positive and urging people to see 'the big picture' as people will quickly see through this and you will lose their trust and respect.

Offer empathy and support as much as possible and offer whatever assistance you can on behalf of the organisation (e.g. outplacement counselling or further training). Acknowledge people's feelings and concerns but avoid giving false hope while doing so. Some people will react emotionally, and this is okay, to a degree, but don't allow it to develop into prolonged complaining. Provide some form of closure to help people say 'goodbye' and allow them to move forward at their own pace.

It's all about communication

The merger between Western Australian-based Challenge Bank and Westpac is an example of discontinuous change introduced well and successfully. Their approach to the change included:

- being open about the bad as well as the good, right from the beginning
- communicating informally (person to person) before communicating formally (role to role)
- explaining the reasons for the change and the bridge that would take people to the merged organisation
- explaining the value to the community
- helping people shift their identity, not just their roles or skills
- no-fail first steps
- no sense of crisis
- no spin – helping people make their own decision to buy into the change and foregoing any 'We'll be bigger/better/best' exhortations
- showing care and respect for employees and their families.[4]

Predicting resistance to change

Figure 24.6 shows a simple model you can use to predict the success of your change efforts. It considers how deep the change is and how much it affects the culture of your work group or organisation. The bigger the change and the more it affects the way people work together, the more resistance you can expect. Conversely, small changes with little cultural impact are relatively easy to implement.

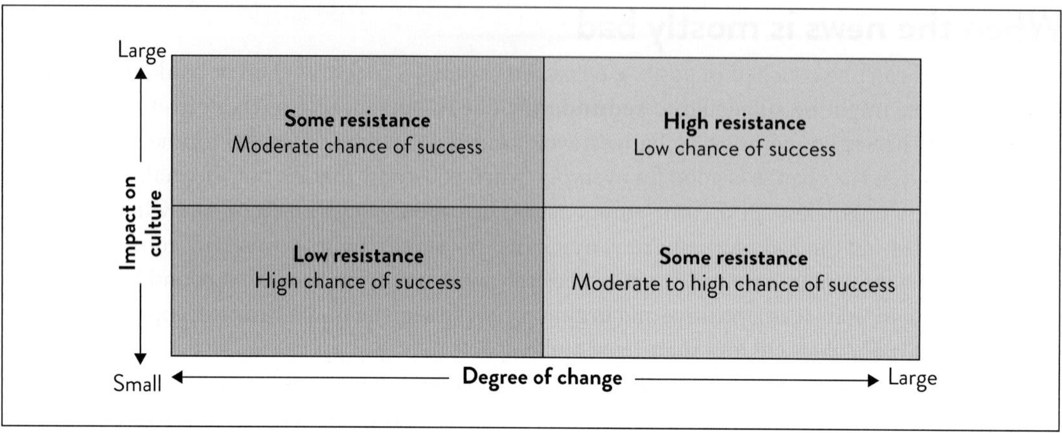

FIGURE 24.6 Predicting resistance to change

24.3 Promoting change

> Nothing is more difficult to handle, more doubtful of success, nor more dangerous to manage, than to put oneself at the head of introducing new orders. For the introducer has all those who benefit from the old orders as enemies, and he has lukewarm defenders in all those who might benefit from the new order.
>
> Niccolo Machiavelli, *The Prince* (Mansfield trans.), University of Chicago Press, 1998, p. 23.

Transferable skills
3.4 Leadership

As a leader-manager, you sometimes instigate and lead a change; at other times, you respond to and manage a change. The changes may be minor, such as small improvements to work methods or workflow, or transformational, which fundamentally alter the way your organisation operates internally or relates to its external environment. Whichever type you're promoting, to initiate that new order you need a well-developed package of skills and personal credibility. Conceptual skills help you to analyse the proposed change to see how it affects your operations and your work team. This, in turn, will help you lead your team to devise a sound action plan for introducing and monitoring the change that makes good use of the resources and other supports available to you from the rest of the organisation.

You will also need interpersonal skills to promote the change in a way that boosts its chances of gaining acceptance and cooperation from all stakeholders and resource providers. As there will almost always be some resistance to a change, having conflict-management skills to deal constructively with any conflict that arises during the change is essential.

Perhaps most importantly, you need to understand how and why people respond to change as they do, the questions they want you to answer and the order in which they want them answered. Armed with those skills and that information, you can ease people through the three stages of adopting change explained below – letting go of the 'old', transitioning to the 'new' and stepping forward into a new beginning.

There are two types of change: incremental, step-by-step change, which builds slowly and is based on current practice; and discontinuous change that turns things upside-down. Incremental change fits nicely into a linear, progressive, predictable world because it's logical. This makes it relatively easy to communicate and to accept. Discontinuous change comes from transformative organisational change, introducing new equipment or technology, and major reorganisations, such as those resulting from takeovers, mergers and **re-engineering**, for example. It breaks with the past, requiring dramatic shifts in habits and beliefs about how things are done, taking people into the unknown and making them uncomfortable (to say the least).

Responses to change

Why is it that when the winds of change blow, some people build walls and others windmills? People respond differently to change – some see change as loss, misery, uncertainty and vulnerability and this creates anger, anxiety, confusion, doubt and frustration. Others, however, see change as a challenge and an opportunity for growth, innovation and learning that creates benefits, better ways, excitement and even enjoyment.

Reactions to change

As change is about taking people from the known, predictable and comfortable to the unknown, frightening and threatening, it is perhaps no wonder it can make people uncomfortable. Employees who welcome change with open arms are rarities, even when the change makes their work more challenging and interesting. Consciously or unconsciously, most people think, 'Better the devil we know'. This is because change, particularly discontinuous change, hits people at core levels. Change to work groups, for example, usually means both formal and informal changes; the unofficial group leadership might change and other internal relationships, including the unofficial 'pecking order' and established networks, may shift. Change often destroys cherished group norms and routines, making people anxious about having to become used to new routines or work areas, learn new skills or work methods, or having to work harder.

People may fear the loss of their old job or that their new job will be less skilled, less interesting or too demanding. They may resent the implied criticism that the way they have been doing their job isn't good enough. They may dislike the thought of outside interference in their job or fear loss of control. Change can also contradict people's mental model of 'how the world works'. When a person's belief system is challenged, they can feel untethered and out of control. The result can be a dramatic decline in morale and motivation, which can have a serious impact on the working environment.

Not surprisingly, the uncertain future that change creates produces varying degrees of anger, apprehension, bewilderment, confusion, dismay and a whole host of other emotions. Everyone experiences this discomfort differently and acts in different ways to address it. But their aims are the same: to protect themselves and preserve their identity. Table 24.2 shows some of the reasons people baulk at change.

TABLE 24.2 Concerns sparked by change

Challenges to group norms and culture	Groups strongly resist any changes to their norms or culture
Disrupting habits	Many people prefer their well-known, familiar and predictable routines and don't give them up easily, especially when the routines work for them and they don't know whether the new ways will work
Disturbing existing social networks	Change may disband friendships and informal networks. The stronger the group ties being threatened, the greater the resistance
Losing existing benefits	Change may bring costs that outweigh its benefits. People resist change that threatens the continuity of their environment, their employment, their career prospects, wages or benefits, or that looks likely to increase job demands

Threats to position, power and security	People resist any change that causes them or the group they're part of to lose status, or power prestige. Those with the most to lose resist the most strongly
Uncertainty about the change and its results	People try to avoid uncertainty – no one enjoys walking in the dark where unknown dangers may lurk. Lack of understanding or insufficient information about a change leaves a vacuum that attracts anxiety, insecurity, rumour and speculation

Health implications

Change is a psychosocial risk factor that, when introduced and managed poorly, can lead to physical and mental health problems (for more information see Chapter 31). You (and your organisation) have a legal responsibility to be sensitive to the concerns that change can spark and to help team members deal with them effectively. Feeling unsettled or concerned about change can lead to stress responses, such as sleep disturbance, absent-minded behaviour, gloominess and restlessness. When people go into the fight, flight or freeze response, the brain produces the hormones adrenaline and cortisol. Too many of these hormones can lead to long-term health damage. That's why it's important to make change tolerable at worst and energising at best.

Positive reactions to change

The other view of change is that some people are attracted to novelty and the lure of the new, unexplored, different and even exciting. Those who sit in this camp love to try new fashions, new foods and new restaurants. But even these people may not necessarily love change at work. The reason as to why seems to lie in the fact that the word 'change' is interpreted as code for something that is unpleasant or onerous. Another factor affecting the way people respond to change is whether it's done *to* you or *by* you. Few people warm to things that are imposed upon them and about which they have little or no say. When you consider these perspectives, it isn't surprising that even people who love change outside work may hate it at work.

This doesn't apply to everyone, though. The kind of employees who don't mind change at work include those who:

- are comfortable with uncertainty and willing to step out of their comfort zones and try out new ways of working
- have an open mind
- trust their manager and their organisation to 'do the right thing'
- understand why change is needed and what it entails for them personally, for the organisation and for its stakeholders
- want to learn and develop their skills.

People who possess the characteristics above are lifelong learners who work in a climate of trust and support. You may not necessarily have a say as to whether your team is made up of lifelong learners, but you may have the power to at least create a work environment that offers and cultivates trust and support among team members.

The information people need to accept change

When you consider all the questions people have at each of the seven stages of adopting a change, it's clear why communication is so important. People need information, but more than that, they need certain types of information at certain times – and the timing will be different for different individuals.

Hall's hierarchy for adopting a change

Drawing on extensive research, Dr Gene Hall developed a seven-level hierarchy (from 0–6) that describes the stages people go through in adopting any change, shown in Figure 24.7. When a change is introduced, people are at the bottom of the hierarchy. Before they can move up to the next level, their current (and predictable) questions must be answered in order to alleviate their concerns so that they can move up to the next stage. The more quickly you help employees move through each successive level, the more quickly and easily the change can progress.

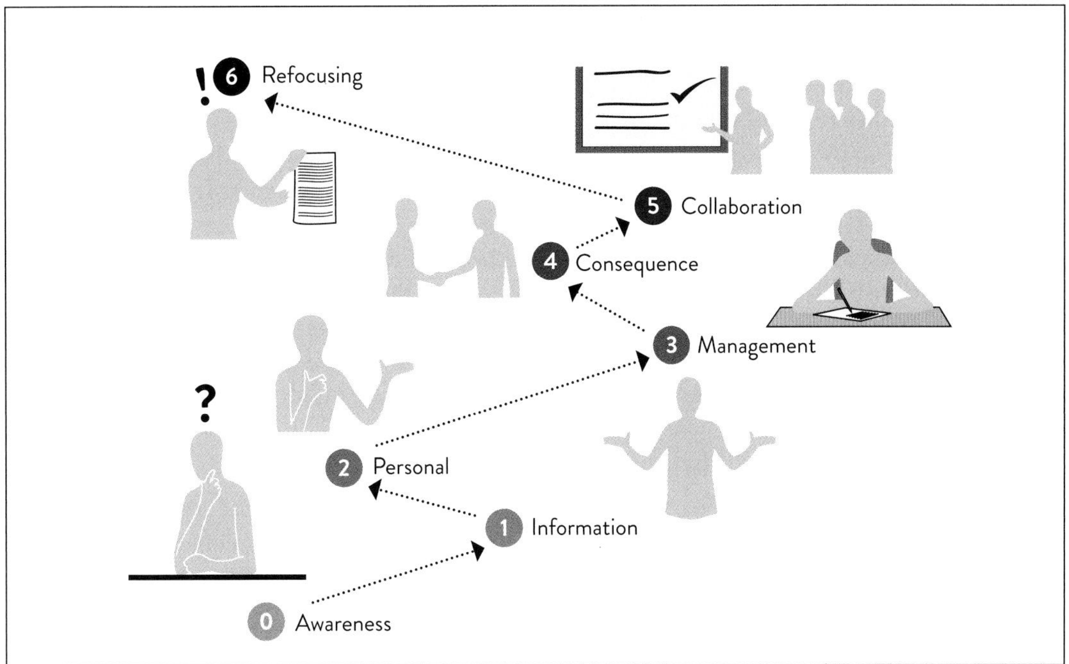

FIGURE 24.7 Hall's hierarchy for adopting change

Here are people's mindsets at each level of adopting change:

0 *Awareness:* 'Change? What change?' 'I'm not aware of any change.' People's behaviour and comments indicate little concern about, or involvement with, the change.

1 *Information:* 'I would like to know more about the proposed change.' People indicate a general awareness of the change and an interest in learning more about it. They seem not to be worried about themselves in relation to the change and are more interested in the substantive aspects, such as the reasons for the change, its general characteristics or the effects of the change.

2 *Personal:* 'How does the change affect me?' 'Will you train me and give me enough time to learn?' 'Will you support me until I master the change?' People want to know how the change affects them and their job, what it requires of them and whether they can meet the demands of the change. They want to know how their existing benefits, formal and informal routines and networks will change.

3 *Management:* 'I am working hard at doing what this change requires of me.' People turn their attention to implementing the change. They're concerned about building their skills and efficiency, organising and managing themselves and scheduling their time properly in order to efficiently carry out the tasks the change requires.

4 *Consequence:* 'How are our customers being affected?' Employees begin to consider the impact of the change on their customers and others in their immediate sphere of influence. They want to make sure the change is benefiting them and achieving what it is supposed to achieve.
5 *Collaboration:* 'I want to work with others to smooth out the process.' People want to coordinate and cooperate with others to implement the change effectively.
6 *Refocusing:* 'I have an idea about something that might work even better.' People begin to see ways to refine the change further and extend its benefits. This may include minor or major modifications.[5]

Understanding where your team members are at any point as change rolls out means you can provide the information they need to move through the hierarchy. This helps them come to terms with the change more quickly and implement it more smoothly.

You can identify where people are on the hierarchy from the questions they ask and from their behaviour. For example, when an employee is at Stage 2 and concerned about how the change affects them personally, it's no good telling them how much the customers will love it. The person wants to know things like how much training you plan to provide, how much time they have to learn the new skills required, whether you plan to support them if they encounter trouble learning them, whether they need to move their workstation and whether you expect them to take on additional duties.

Without pushing too fast, acknowledge which phase team members are in and help them into the next by providing the type of information they need. Remember: people change only when they're ready to believe that the change won't make life worse for them, and that it may even make life better.

Hang on to your best and brightest through change

When change strikes, it's often your top performers who stand to lose the most. They probably have more options than your other employees and less patience with changes that could jeopardise their success. Give them a good reason to stay by finding them an equally rewarding role and a chance to shine once the change takes hold. Explain how their role can continue to provide the things they value despite the change.

Think about meeting with them individually to explain the change and why it's needed to show you value them. Give them a role in helping launch the change and involve them in implementing the change as much as you can, too. This increases their buy-in and gives you access to their good ideas.

The three stages of accepting change

As you answer people's questions so they can move up Hall's hierarchy, you're also helping them move through the three stages of accepting change. First, they 'let go' of the 'old', which propels them into the uncomfortable 'transition' phase. Eventually, they reach a point where they can release the past entirely and move into the future, the 'new beginnings' phase.

Stage 1: Letting go

To embark on change, people first need to make a break with the 'old ways'. Letting go of the past can be painful, especially when people have a big investment in what they are losing or strongly identify with it.

Anthropologists have discovered that a ceremony is one of the most powerful and satisfying ways to achieve closure. Closure enables people to let go psychologically of the 'old' and gives them permission to do so, allowing them to begin the 'new'. Find a way to help your team say goodbye to the past. It might be a tea party with silly hats or a solemn ceremony, but whatever you choose, help your team let go. See Steps 2 through 4 of the seven steps to change in Section 24.2 to help employees let go.

Stage 2: Transition

When important ties are broken, the world can be a confusing and uncomfortable place. People experience a sense of bewilderment, unreality, emptiness and even horror once they let go and enter the in-between phase. They often 'go through the motions' as if in a state of shock, swinging between hopefulness that the change will work out well and worry that it won't. Gradually, a sense of hope begins to emerge.

Use Hall's hierarchy to provide the appropriate information to help your team move through this painful and largely unproductive transition phase and explain your action plan so that people know where they're going and how they'll get there (see Steps 5 and 6 of the seven steps to change).

Stage 3: New beginnings

People enter the third and final stage, discovering a new beginning, when they're ready to adopt new goals and start thinking about and planning for the change and the future. The energy they previously spent worrying about and resisting the change is now available for dealing with it constructively. Remember to follow up to make sure the change is working and that it sticks (Step 7 of the seven steps to change).

24.4 Overcoming resistance to change

> We can never be really prepared for that which is wholly new. We have to adjust ourselves, and every radical adjustment is a crisis in self-esteem; we undergo a test, we have to prove ourselves. It needs inordinate self-confidence to face drastic change without inner trembling.
>
> Eric Hoffer (US longshoreman and philosopher), *Between the devil and the dragon: The best essays and aphorisms of Eric Hoffer*, Harper & Row, 1982.

Some people resist change because their leader-manager hasn't clearly explained why it's needed, what their working life will be like after the change or their own role in making the change a success. Sometimes an individual's make-up or skills incline them towards resistance: they may have negative mindsets about change; they may lack the necessary skills for responding to change and coping with the stress change often produces; or their personality structure might make them wary of change. Then there's the 'proactive inhibitory interference', the brain's in-built program to reject the new and preserve the old; we don't even realise when it kicks in.

Resisting change can take the following main forms:

- *Malicious compliance:* people comply, but in a way that they know isn't really what you want, which is likely to result in an outcome you don't want.
- *Passive compliance:* people just 'give up' and go through the motions, without commitment, effort or energy.
- *Vocal resistance:* people air their concerns openly, either clearly and constructively or negatively and destructively. They may air them to you, making your life easier by giving you the opportunity to deal with their resistance, or behind your back to their workmates, which can seriously undermine your change efforts.

Whatever form resistance takes, ignoring it only strengthens it and delays your change efforts. It's far better to get resisters talking about their concerns so you can deal with them. Listen carefully, with your heart and your eyes as well as your ears, and use the SHEER (surface, honour, explore, explain, recheck) formula, shown in Figure 24.8, to bring their worries into the open. This way, you can try to allay their concerns so they can accept the change and help make it work.

S

Surface
Invite people's thoughts, concerns and questions. They may be reluctant to air them at first, so you may have to ask: 'Here's what we need. Do you see any problems? What concerns do you have?'

Honour
Listen to people's concerns and feelings

Explore
Find out why people feel the way they do. Ask questions and help them state their misgivings as specifically as possible. This helps you provide the information they need to feel more comfortable with the change and come to terms with it

Explain
Answer people's concerns and questions as fully and honestly as you can, giving both the 'good' and the 'bad' news

Recheck
Make sure you have fully addressed people's concerns and questions and satisfied them with your answers. If they still have doubts, go back to the beginning: 'Anything else?' Otherwise, their doubts will fester

FIGURE 24.8 The SHEER formula

Show resisters you value them and their skills. Involve them as much as you can in designing and building the new ways. Sometimes you can nurse them along; sometimes you need to lay down the law. If a team member simply refuses to adopt a change despite all your best efforts, you may need to support them to find employment elsewhere!

The main causes of stalled change efforts include the following:

- A leadership vacuum allows resistance to mushroom.
- The team gets tired and loses energy and enthusiasm. Change, after all, is hard work. Beginnings are a lot of fun, then reality sets in and spirits lag. Energetic leadership is the antidote.
- Time and resource shortages, which are often due to poor forecasting and planning and compounded by the fact that it can be difficult to go back and ask for more resources.
- Trying to move too quickly.
- Unexpected obstacles. When you've never been down this particular track before, naturally you can't foresee all the hurdles.
- A crisis in energy that can result from apathy, which can develop as a stress response and cause the change to lose its momentum, or from accumulated negative energy that stops the change moving forward.
- Vested interest. People who have a lot to lose increase their efforts to block change or combine their efforts to prevent the change going through.

These snags are godsends to serious resisters, who are most likely to attack when the change is nearly a reality (rather than at the beginning when it may never eventuate). Time-wise, resistance generally occurs either:

- early on, when people are struggling to come to grips with the change and are trying to avoid the real or perceived personal losses that they fear accompany the change
- when everything seems to be going well, often when implementing the change is at about the halfway point or towards the end, when the change is nearly a reality.

Using your personal power can help move stalled change along. A personal appeal – 'Just give it a go for me', 'Help me out and try this' – can often be just what's needed. Use the boomerang principle, too: when you can, make a small concession to engage the team's willingness to reciprocate and carry on with the change.

Leaders can reduce the risk of a breakdown in the change process by:

- building change into key systems, such as performance reviews and operating procedures so that the change doesn't slide and eventually evaporate
- identifying any conflict and resistance at an individual or group level and managing it well so that group or individual relationships aren't eroded and goodwill towards the change lost
- 'keeping the ball rolling' so that inertia, or lack of energy, doesn't hold change back
- providing enough, and the right type of, equipment, information, money, people, time or other resources to make the change workable
- helping people find a way to move forward so they don't become 'stuck' in the letting go or transition phase of accepting change
- rewarding people who adopt the change quickly so they don't give up; let others see the benefits of adopting the change so they join in
- communicating the change congruently and wholeheartedly and actively supporting it
- monitoring and evaluating progress to ensure the change works and remains in place.

- Have you ever felt resistant to change? Explore what key drivers were influencing the resistance.
- Looking back at the three forms of resistance – malicious compliance, passive compliance or vocal resistance – where do you think your actions sit?

Transferable skills

2.2 Personal effectiveness

Tips for dealing with persistent resisters

Following the seven steps for introducing change discussed earlier in this chapter helps reduce opposition and makes the change easier for employees to accept. For whatever reason, though, some people may seem determined to oppose change. Figure 24.9 offers some tips for working with people who insist on resisting. Notice that, with all the responses, you clearly communicate the required change; listen to, respect and examine the resistance; and then plan with the employee what action they can take to cooperate. Once people state their agreement to trying something out, they're less likely to renege.

Resistance to change can be reduced by eliminating or lessening people's urge to resist in the first place. The following small steps can support you in reducing resistance to change:

- Build a 'critical mass' of supporters for the change to help it 'take hold' quickly.
- Commit the necessary resources to the change (e.g. budget, communication, time, training).
- Detail the change clearly in terms of both the 'what' (e.g. goals, success measures, standards) and the 'how' (e.g. vision, behaviours, culture).
- Ensure that key people fully support the change.
- Ensure visible signs of early progress to encourage people and build momentum.

The road-blocker	This vocal resistance is a nice, clean type of resistance where the employee just says 'No' in one form or another, usually without giving reasons.	Help them to be specific about their objection by asking, 'What specifically worries you?' or 'What in particular do you object to?' Their answer tells you what you are dealing with and gives you a starting point for exploring the resistance using the SHEER formula outlined earlier in this chapter or suggesting a trial: 'Give it a go for a couple of weeks, just to see'. Before you part, ensure that the employee has clear change-related goals to achieve and that the goals have clear timelines.
The passive 'complier'	This is a hidden form of resistance where the resister says, in effect, 'Tell me exactly what you want me to do'. When you fall for that, the resister can comply with the bare minimum, but not the spirit, of what you want.	Explaining what you need from the resister and asking, 'Are you quite clear about what I need from you?' or 'Let's talk about how you plan to approach this; what is your first step going to be?' can encourage the resister to accept more responsibility for good performance.
The malicious 'complier'	This is another hidden form of resistance where the resister appears to comply with the changes, but in a way that clearly is going to make the changes fail to work properly.	Discuss the steps the malicious complier took and together work out how to make the change work more effectively. Then seek commitment to making the agreed changes work.
The delayer	'I'll get onto it first thing Monday morning' says the delayer. And then, of course, something more important crops up.	When you think this is a resistance tactic rather than an honest response, try asking, 'Is there anything preventing you from beginning now?'
The reverser	This can be a tricky form of resistance. When you find yourself surprised by someone's enthusiastic response ('Wow! What a great idea!'), followed by a quick delay, you can be fairly sure the employee is telling you what you want to hear but intends to do nothing about it.	Say something like, 'I'm really glad you think it's a good idea. What in particular do you like about it?'
The dodger	'Let Jane do it' switches the responsibility to someone else or even another department.	When your request is reasonable, let dodgers know that it is from them that you are expecting action.
The threatener	These resisters imply that 'the boss' (or someone else) won't approve. This may or may not be true, but don't discuss it now.	Say something like, 'I appreciate your concern and I'll check it out. Meanwhile, what I'd like you to do is ...' or 'I'll bear that in mind. What objections do *you* have?'
The sympath seeker	These resisters try to make you feel guilty for asking them to alter their ways and try something new.	Hear them out, empathise with their concerns and, unless their reasons are sound, repeat your request.
The traditionalist	This resister says, 'But we've always done it the other way'. Sometimes the old way is the best way, but more often the appeal to tradition is straightforward resistance of the 'better the devil we know' variety.	Try saying, 'I understand the old way worked very well; however, we need to adapt to changing customer expectation/market needs' or 'Yes, the old approach worked well – how can we adapt it to this new way?'

FIGURE 24.9 Tips for dealing with resisters

- Explain how the change links with the organisation's values, vision and strategy.
- Explain what successful change will 'look like' and how it benefits people.
- Involve your team in designing and implementing the change as much as you can. Make sure everyone is 'engaged' and has a common understanding of what you're trying to achieve.
- Keep communicating and listening.
- Manage the transition from the old to the new carefully; look after people and help them through the uncomfortable transition zone that bridges 'where we are now' and 'where we want to be'.
- Monitor progress so you know what is and what is not working and where the blockages are that you need to remove.
- Provide training and other opportunities for learning and developing from the change.
- Publicise the successes.
- Thank, support and reward the supporters.

STUDY TOOLS

QUICK REVIEW

KEY CONCEPT 24.1 

a In the chapter, change is described as the 'new normal'. Why is this the case and what does it mean for leader-managers?

b Summarise the continuous cycle of change that all systems seem to go through.

KEY CONCEPT 24.2 

a Summarise or show as a flow chart the steps to take before introducing a change, listing any key factors to bear in mind at each point in the change planning process.

b Why is communication such an important part of any successful change effort?

c Summarise how leader-managers should deal with change that negatively affects their work team.

KEY CONCEPT 24.3 

a What is it about change that makes people uncomfortable? What are some steps leader-managers can take to ease people's discomfort?

b Review the three stages of accepting change and explain how leader-managers can help people through them.

KEY CONCEPT 24.4 

a Describe the ways leader-managers can handle team members who resist change.

BUILD YOUR SKILLS

KEY CONCEPT 24.1 

a The organic view is that organisations need to change and people need to be involved in change at their workplace. What are the implications of this for leader-managers?

b From your own experience, describe a situation that illustrates the continuous cycle of change.

KEY CONCEPT 24.2 

a Is change positive, energising and uplifting, or is change challenging and stressful? The answer depends on whether the change is done to you or by you. Discuss.

KEY CONCEPT 24.3 

a Why do you think some people embrace and adapt to change more readily than others, and why do all people resist change to some extent? Discuss the process of adapting to change and illustrate this process with a personal example.

b Briefly explain Hall's hierarchy of adopting a change and discuss how you can use it to be ready for the questions that your work team will ask and when you should provide certain answers.

KEY CONCEPT 24.4 

a Describe the strategies you may apply that will support those who demonstrate malicious compliance, passive compliance or vocal resistance throughout the change process.

WORKPLACE ACTIVITIES

KEY CONCEPT 24.1 

a What changes have you experienced over the last three years at your workplace? Review these changes, describing how they were introduced and how you and your work team felt about them.

b Select one of the changes from question (a) above and discuss it in terms of the continuous cycle of change.

c For the change you selected in question (b) above, discuss how, in retrospect, it could have been introduced more effectively.

d Considering all that you have learnt in this chapter, what strategies could you, your organisation or others have put in place that would have limited the resistance you experienced with the change you discussed in questions (b) and (c) above?

KEY CONCEPT 24.2 

a Interview someone who has experienced a major change at work. This might have been, for instance, the result of a change in funding, job redesign, a merger or an acquisition, a move to a new location or restructuring. Find out all you can about the impact of this change on the person, the person's work group and the organisation's culture. How was the change introduced and managed? What were the obstacles to this change? What resistance to it occurred? Prepare a report analysing this change in terms of how well the seven steps to introducing change were followed. From your analysis, draw conclusions about how effectively the change was managed. What, if anything, could have been done to help the change take effect more smoothly and quickly?

KEY CONCEPT 24.3 

a What changes have you been involved in implementing at your workplace? Select one to review, from beginning to end, using the information from this chapter about the cycle of change, the seven steps to change, predicting and dealing with resistance to change, and helping people accept change.

KEY CONCEPT 24.4 

a What forms of resistance to change have you encountered and how have you dealt with them? On reflection, could you have dealt with them more effectively and, if so, how?

EXTENSION ACTIVITIES

Referring to the Snapshot at the beginning of this chapter, answer the following questions:

1 Develop a plan for informing GROW's management, staff and key stakeholders of the changes that are to be implemented.

2 What resistance and other stumbling blocks to successfully introducing the changes might be expected?

3 Identify strategies for dealing with those who might resist the changes.

CASE STUDY 24

A MAJOR CHANGE

Chan strides out on the treadmill at the gym, thinking long and hard. As part of the latest workplace agreement, the organisation is about to introduce multiskilling for all non-salaried employees. The goal is to enhance efficiency, flexibility and job satisfaction and help the organisation recruit the people it needs.

Section managers are responsible for developing and implementing a learning plan for the employees in their sections. They are to ensure that all employees can benefit; that dignity, equal opportunity and health, safety and welfare issues take top priority; and that a net 3 per cent gain in productivity results in the six months after the training is completed. Measures of each section's success also include attendance rates, labour retention rates, number of grievances registered and output to costs ratios.

As Chan rolls this around in his mind, he can see some obvious benefits to the employees. A greater variety of tasks and increased skills should provide more job satisfaction, and the flexibility resulting from multiskilling should increase efficiencies and productivity. The career opportunities should improve, too. Depending on how the multiskilling takes shape, employees may have the opportunity to undertake complete projects and take on more responsibility and decision-making in their jobs.

And Chan can see plenty of other benefits to the organisation, too, apart from those stated in the workplace agreement: multiskilled staff, improved workplace health and safety, improved and easier recruitment and retention due to increased levels of job satisfaction, more effective use of technology, improved staff morale – it sounds too good to be true!

He narrows his eyes as he thinks of Newton's third law: for every action, there is an equal and opposite reaction. What is the downside of all this?

Questions

1 How might the move to multiskilling affect individuals in Chan's department and the work team as a whole? What are his team members' concerns likely to be? How would you advise Chan to deal with their concerns?

2 What do you predict will be the major resistance points or obstacles to this change and why? Discuss how Chan could handle them.

3 If you were to coach Chan on how to plan, introduce and manage this important organisational initiative in his section, what steps would you recommend he follow and why?

CHAPTER ENDNOTES

1 Jonas Salk, *World population and human values: A new reality*, Harper & Row, 1981.

2 Alastair Dryburgh, *Akenhurst Newsletter*, 3 July 2012 (akenewsletter@aweber.com).

3 Amy Birchall, 'Good culture, great results', *Management Today*, June 2013.

4 Department of Education, Skills and Employment, 'Australian cultural imprints at work: 2010 and beyond', March 2011, *Industry Skills Councils*, Australian Government, Department of Education, Employment and Workplace Relations.

5 Gene E. Hall, Shirley M. Hord, *Change in schools: Facilitating the process*, State University of New York Press, Albany, 1987.

PART

5

WORKPLACE PRACTICE

An organisation's workplace practices establish the working environment it provides for its employees. This is more than restrooms, workstations and equipment. It relates to the entire package the organisation and individual leader-managers provide – how employees are recruited, managed, trained and developed and looked after as people.

Do you recruit people carefully, people who are naturally inclined to do the type of work you offer and who can contribute to your organisation in a variety of ways? Do you include a range of people on your team – from different age groups, backgrounds, cultures, experiences and lifestyles? Do you induct and train employees properly and provide opportunities to continually develop their skills and potential? Do you provide a safe and healthy workplace that affords people dignity? Do you have systems that help employees balance or blend their private lives with their working lives and afford them the dignity every human being deserves? Do you give them opportunities to get together to share ideas, keep up to date with the organisation's events and results, make improvements and solve problems? These activities influence how good a job people want to do and are able to do. They influence the type of people organisations are able to attract to work for them and how long organisations are able to retain them. They influence whether organisations are able to make the best use of employees' skills and abilities and draw on their ideas and experience. In short, they influence how successful an organisation is and how well it is positioned for the future.

Part 5 helps you develop a working environment that attracts, develops and looks after the employees who can help your organisation succeed.

CHAPTER

25

LEADING AND ATTENDING MEETINGS

After completing this chapter, you will be able to:

25.1 call the right type of meeting at the right time

25.2 carry out your responsibilities when leading a meeting and avoid the common mistakes that meeting leaders make

25.3 lead virtual meetings

25.4 participate effectively in meetings

25.5 adhere to the different requirements of formal and informal meetings.

TRANSFERABLE SKILLS

The following transferable skills are covered in this chapter:

1 **Business competence**
   - **1.4** Business operations

2 **Critical thinking and problem solving**
   - **2.1** Critical thinking
   - **2.2** Personal effectiveness

3 **Social competence**
   - **3.1** Teamwork/relationships
   - **3.2** Verbal communication
   - **3.4** Leadership

5 **Digital competence**
   - **5.1** Cyber security
   - **5.2** Technology use

OVERVIEW

People are social animals. Since we first walked the Earth, we have come together in small groups to plan, make decisions, learn from and help each other, and have fun. With the workforce becoming more and more digitally resourced, holding meetings has never been easier. Modern technology allows people in different cities, states and countries to meet in real time.

Meetings are a way to share and work with information and help people do their jobs better. They also help people work together and build a sense of belonging, shared responsibility, shared goals and team spirit. Meetings, if carried out unsuccessfully, can also take up too much time and give the illusion of progress when, in fact, none has been made. This chapter explores the ins and outs of meetings and will support you in leading successful meetings, both actual and virtual.

SNAPSHOT

The stand-in

Grace's boss has asked her to chair the quarterly team leaders' meeting in four weeks' time. He has delegated everything to her – the choice of venue, the time and duration of the meeting, the agenda, the whole works. This is a major event in the team leaders' calendar and an opportunity for her to show her organising and leadership skills, so she wants to make sure she gets everything right.

Where should she begin? What should she do first? What should she say when she opens the meeting? How can she keep order and stop babbling Ben from talking too much, and how can she get Anh, who is really smart, creative – and quiet – to contribute? How can she make sure people don't interrupt each other and prevent a cacophony of voices with no one able to listen?

When he handed her the assignment, Grace's manager gave her a few words of advice. 'Grace,' he said, 'do your preparation for the meeting well in advance. Once you have everything planned and thought through, everything falls into place.'

'Preparation?' thought Grace. 'What and how should I prepare?'

25.1 Calling the right type of meeting at the right time

Meetings are a great trap ... They are indispensable when you don't want to do anything.

John Kenneth Galbraith (economist), *Ambassador's journal*, Houghton Mifflin, 1969, p. 84.

When properly planned and run, meetings can make a significant contribution to a team's effectiveness. They can be a good way to give people information on a more personal basis than, say, sending a group email. They can help you identify, explore and solve problems; gather information, opinions and ideas; and allow full and open discussion on important matters and, through discussion and analysis, reach agreement.

While the objective of meetings can relate to direct operational matters, meetings have other indirect advantages that help establish a friendly and supportive work climate. Meetings can clarify the aims of the group as a whole, and help members understand where their own work fits in. They can define the team and make people feel part of it. Everyone can look around and clearly see the group of which they are a part. This can help make a group more *cohesive*, or unified, and build people's attachment to it. This is particularly important with the increase of remote workforces.

Meetings also show who the official team leader is; in many work groups, a meeting is the only time the leader is clearly seen as the leader of the group, rather than as a person doing a job or the person to whom people report individually.

When everyone contributes, meetings can create a pool of shared knowledge and experience and an opportunity for a group to revise, refresh and add to its collective understanding. This helps teams grow and develop, increases the speed and efficiency of communication between members, enhances their work performance and helps the team achieve its goals. Of course, it's also true that meetings can be big time wasters. Figure 25.1 shows some ways to maximise meetings.

FIGURE 25.1 Make your meetings matter

INDUSTRY INSIGHTS

Recently, Max's team underwent two major changes, the appointment of new roles and the implementation of a new working from home policy, which many staff embraced. The new appointments were from individuals living on opposites sides of the country and a restructuring of roles enabled two new team members to job share.

Max's communication strategy included formal meetings and informal check-ins through the week. The formal team meetings held at the start of the week invited all staff to attend and usually included a large agenda that covered the morning. Informal briefings occurred through the week among the staff members present with the understanding that the information provided would be passed on to those not present. Max came to realise that this structure was unreliable, at times inefficient and starting to impact on team dynamics.

He reflected on his leadership goals and the team itself and their needs and went to work on developing a new team meeting strategy. His manager suggested he consider virtual platforms and the different ways information could be communicated to the team. He said, 'Maybe not everything has to be covered in the one meeting at the start of the week'. Then he started to think about the various ways information could be shared and what meetings were needed and when.

Types of meetings

Meetings can serve a variety of purposes and knowing why you're calling a meeting will reduce participant confusion. The following sections introduce you to four main types of meetings that you can expect to attend or to lead.

General update meetings

Many leader-managers find that monthly team meetings, interspersed with fortnightly individual meetings with each of their direct reports, keep the channels of communication open, strengthen working relationships and keep people's attention on organisational direction and immediate task parameters and purpose.

Time your meetings

It generally takes about 30 minutes of team time to bring everyone 'up to speed' with team results, review progress on goals and long-term organisational and work plans and generally check in with team members.

To prevent team meetings from digressing, give each team member specific timeframes to update the others on what they're working on, what problems they've resolved or are facing, any improvement suggestions and so on. Then allow up to three minutes of questions from the others.

The week before the team meeting, post an agenda on a noticeboard and ask people to add any topics to it they want to discuss or questions they would like answered. Asking for topics to be added prior to the meeting will allow you to seek further clarification on any topics that could be considered sensitive or ambiguous.

Try mini-meetings

Mini-meetings are also useful for work groups in which people work more as individuals but still want to be aware of what others are up to. Everyone is given 60 seconds to say how they're doing and what is urgent or important for them that day or week.

Leader-managers who need to direct team activities, discuss changes or make announcements related to the day's or week's work often begin each day or week with a quick mini-meeting, or 'huddle', that lasts only five or 10 minutes.

Information-giving meetings

Call an information-giving meeting when you need to pass on information to a group of people. Use demonstrations, slides, videos or other aids to reinforce your verbal message. Allow some discussion and questions but keep the focus on providing information.

Do you need a meeting?

Before calling an information meeting, be sure you cannot get the information across more cheaply and effectively in other ways, such as one-to-one, virtually or in writing. Information-giving meetings are useful when the information to be shared:

- has major implications for the meeting attendees
- has symbolic value in being given personally
- is complex or controversial
- needs to be heard from a particular person
- requires clarification or comments to help people make sense of it
- requires some discussion or information exchange.

Meetings to introduce change

These meetings allow you to introduce and explain forthcoming changes in order to help your team understand the reasons for the changes and to gain their support. For example, this is the type of meeting to hold when intending to announce and explain an organisation restructure or merger, or a change to procedures or a policy.

Since change is unsettling to most people, it is beneficial to explain the change fully and clearly and allow time for questions, discussion and dissent. The bigger the change, the more unrealistic it is to expect people to accept it quickly. Be prepared to discuss the issues involved and allow people time to air their thoughts and opinions. (You can find out more about introducing change in Chapter 24.)

Information-seeking and information-exchange meetings

When you want to gather opinions, facts and other information or give people the opportunity to discuss and exchange information and ideas, information-seeking and information-exchange meetings are the answer.

Innovation meetings

Holding an innovation meeting is a great way to bring the team together to generate ideas, develop new offerings or discuss more efficient ways of working. Creative solutions are more easily conceived when everyone is contributing.

Brainstorming sessions are the best-known type of new-ideas meeting. Brainstorming helps to generate ideas quickly. Later, the participants explore, refine and develop those ideas. (Brainstorming is explained further in Chapter 26.) Questions like 'What are our options?' and 'How could we ... ?' help people exchange information and ideas.

Information-seeking and innovation meetings combine the knowledge, skills, ideas and experience of several people at once. You can encourage this by guiding discussions rather than dominating them.

Planning meetings

When you want people to help plan something, perhaps because they'll be involved in executing the plan or to draw on their expertise, call a planning meeting. Members can decide or offer suggestions on what is to be done, who is to do it and where, and when and how it is to be done.

Guide participants to decide or suggest action steps, distribute responsibilities and tasks and set priorities. Begin with a clear outcome or goal to be accomplished and aim to finish with a clear action plan to achieve it.

Problem-solving and decision-making meetings

Call this type of meeting when you need to discuss, consider and agree solutions, and make or recommend a decision. Explain how the final decision is to be made; for example, by you after consultation with the meeting participants or by consensus among the participants. Aim for a free and lively discussion that builds on the diverse talents, backgrounds and experiences of all the participants.

Before reaching the decision, ask, 'What information are we missing?' and 'Does anyone have any information we need that we haven't discussed?' Once the decision is reached, discuss how success will be measured so everyone can look for possible signs that the decision is working and possible signs that it is going wrong.

In problem-solving meetings, you are looking for solutions. What may seem at first to be wild ideas can turn out to be excellent ones after a little polishing and refining. Problem-solving meetings typically aim to explore the problem with key stakeholders and work together to search for solutions (as shown in Chapter 26, **Figure 26.4** 'The problem-solving and decision-making process'). When the problem is complex, this may take several meetings.

Quality improvement meetings

Originally called *quality circles*, quality improvement meetings now go by various names, but they all share the goal of identifying and solving problems, gathering ideas, and deciding and planning how to improve work systems and provide better service to internal and external customers.

Consider the team meetings you have either attended or led. What worked well and what didn't?

Team-briefing meetings

The purpose of team briefings is to:

- allow questions and suggestions to be fed back from all staff to senior management
- create a culture of open communication by clearing information blockages, reducing misunderstandings and increasing commitment
- develop a shared sense of what the organisation is; what its values and objectives are; mission, vision, collective aims; and reasons why things are being done as they are
- develop greater awareness and understanding of key organisational and workplace issues and results and encourage involvement at all levels
- enable and improve downward, upward and lateral (sideways) communication through the organisation
- explain financial, commercial and strategic issues
- prevent guesswork, rumour and 'the grapevine' from gaining influence
- strengthen clarity of direction and information from senior management.

When briefings are face-to-face, team leaders can ensure that people understand what is happening, and why, and can ask questions and explore issues that affect them directly. Briefings can also be held virtually or electronically, with online discussion forums accessible for staff to ask questions and organisations to collect feedback.

For larger organisations, the managing director, chief executive officer or board of directors are in charge of guiding the organisation's operations; issuing a *core management brief* or *core brief*; and covering the main commercial, financial, people, policy and strategic issues. This information is cascaded through the organisation as every manager and team leader incorporates the core brief points into their own *local brief*, which contains issues relevant to their team, generally working through these headings:

- *People*: matters concerning people in the company and the team, new appointments and visitors.
- *Progress*: how the organisation/division/team has performed overall in relation to key measures in areas such as customer satisfaction, finance, safety and quality.
- *Policy*: any new policies, procedures or changes to corporate or workplace policy or procedures that need to be explained or reinforced.
- *Points for action*: priorities over the next month for the team and the organisation; what's coming up and the team's or organisation's response.
- *Any general information*.

Team briefings are weekly or monthly, depending on the organisation's needs, with dates set well in advance. People meet in teams of four to 15 people, led by the team's leader-manager, and the meetings usually last around 30 minutes. A feedback form captures questions that arise at briefings and questions the team leader can't answer are passed upwards so that they can be answered at the next briefing meeting.

Prior to presenting a brief, have a clear understanding of the key messages and information to present and take the time to collect further information, pre-empting questions. Successful briefing presenters apply the following:

- provide information clearly and concisely, minimising misunderstanding
- use familiar words and terms, avoiding jargon and rambling repetition
- look and sound confident, showcasing positivity
- use effective pausing techniques, allowing key points to resonate and time to breathe
- deliver messages with tact, considering the needs of others
- consider own body language
- provide plenty of time for team members to ask questions, making note of the questions that cannot be answered directly with an intention to provide the answers at the next meeting.

INDUSTRY INSIGHTS

Every three months Priya's organisation holds a meeting referred to as a 'Town Hall' meeting, where the department is briefed on various activities occurring across the organisation. Priya looks forward to these meetings as she enjoys hearing her General Manager speak. Priya, given the opportunity to speak directly with the General Manager, decided to ask her if she would share with her a few tips to use when speaking in meetings with larger audiences such as this. Priya's General Manager, Linda, gave her the following tips:

- Even if you are in a large room of people, speak to the group as if you were all sitting around a kitchen table.
- Identify what your audience feels is the most important piece of information you are sharing by picking up on key body language. While most of the time we have a list of points we would like to share, read the room and be willing to change your agenda to meet the needs of the audience.
- Be authentic, positive and considerate.
- Take deep breaths and don't rush.

Figure 25.2 shows what you should do and avoid doing when preparing and presenting a local brief.

DO	AVOID
• Have a clear objective • Keep communications open, allowing time for questions • Emphasise key points, pausing to allow the point to sink in • Use positive words and phrases • Consider the audience and their individual needs	• Repetition • Using unfamiliar technical terms • Using ambiguous language • Not making eye contact with each participant and only looking at notes (in a virtual meeting try to look into the camera) • Cramming in to much information

FIGURE 25.2 Preparing and presenting a local brief

When to call a meeting

Hours in the week can be easily filled up with meetings. How can you predict a meeting is worth the time and trouble? Figure 25.3 shows when to call a meeting and when to use an alternative.

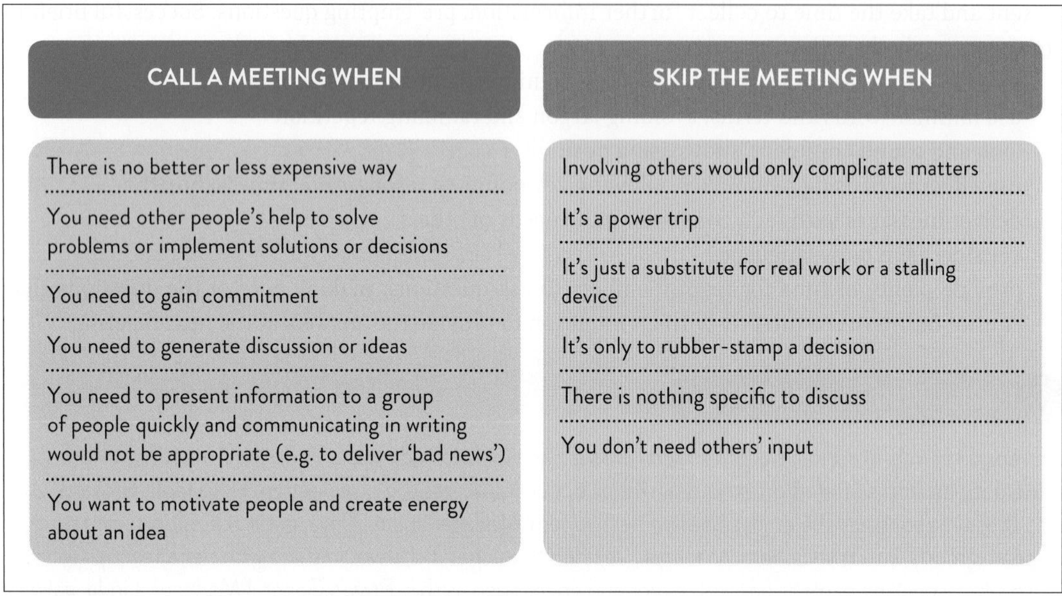

CALL A MEETING WHEN	SKIP THE MEETING WHEN
There is no better or less expensive way	Involving others would only complicate matters
You need other people's help to solve problems or implement solutions or decisions	It's a power trip
You need to gain commitment	It's just a substitute for real work or a stalling device
You need to generate discussion or ideas	It's only to rubber-stamp a decision
You need to present information to a group of people quickly and communicating in writing would not be appropriate (e.g. to deliver 'bad news')	There is nothing specific to discuss
You want to motivate people and create energy about an idea	You don't need others' input

FIGURE 25.3 When to call a meeting and when not to bother

25.2 Planning and leading meetings

> **In meetings, I try to be sure that everybody has an opportunity to speak … A successful meeting depends on how much everybody participates – not on how long it goes on.**
>
> John D. deButts (former chair, AT&T), in W. Fletcher, 'On the way up: How to keep cool in the hot seat', *Management Today*, 1 November 1999.

Any meeting worth holding is worth planning. Planning and leading meetings are each important skill sets for leader-managers and they each require a different set of competencies. Planning a meeting involves establishing the key aims of the meeting objectives, planning the agenda, selecting participants, choosing a time and place, and distributing the agenda. Let's begin there.

Transferable skills

1.4 Business operations

Establish objectives

Ask yourself the following three questions:

1 What do I need this meeting to achieve?
2 How can I know whether it has succeeded?
3 What do I want the atmosphere of the meeting to be like?

The answers should form a clear picture in your mind and provide the explicit objectives that every successful meeting works towards.

Here are some other questions to think through beforehand:

- How can I best convey my objectives to the meeting participants?
- Do we need to make any decisions at the meeting? If so, what information do we need?
- What topics do we need to cover?

- What issues or concerns are likely to come up?
- What needs to happen before the meeting can take place?

Plan the agenda

Some meetings have only one objective; for example, to give information or to reach a decision. Others have several objectives and cover several topics. When that is the case, list the topics in writing; these form the basis of your agenda. When listing the topics, keep them results-oriented by using a verb to begin each: Decide ... Plan for ... Generate ideas for ... Gather opinions on ... and so on. This emphasises the purpose of a discussion and indicates what is (and isn't) relevant to discuss.

Without making the agenda so rigid that it can't be adjusted, it's also a good idea to state the start and finish times for the meeting and indicate the time you've allocated each topic, keeping in mind the number of topics need to fit within the allocated timeframe for the meeting. Some topics can take more or less time to discuss than expected and others may arise that were not anticipated, but at least you have a plan for what you want to discuss, why you want to discuss it and for how long. Even small informal meetings benefit from agendas like this because they provide a sense of direction.

Start with a topic that is brief and easy to deal with and that you expect participants to receive positively. Even when you have some information to pass on, put items requiring discussion and active input first, because once people have sat quietly in listening mode it's hard to make the switch to contributing mode. Put routine matters, 'FYI' items and items you want to deal with briefly towards the end and make the final topic one that gives members a sense of unity or achieves a positive outcome.

Here are some other ideas for ordering agendas:

- Put the most important item second on the agenda and use the first item to warm participants up.
- Schedule items of great interest to everyone for the lull in the meeting that seems to come 15–20 minutes after its start.
- Sequence the topics logically so that they build on each other, or from the easiest to the most difficult or controversial, or the most to the least urgent. Separate the information exchange and problem analysis from problem-solving.
- Since people tend to be more lively, creative and attentive during the early part of a meeting, put items that require a lot of mental work first.

Be aware of your options and the group itself and consciously select the most suitable approach. At the top of the agenda, indicate where and when the meeting will be held.

Try to keep meetings to less than an hour to avoid people becoming restless. When a meeting must go on for longer than one hour, schedule a short break every 50 to 75 minutes and encourage people to stand up and walk around to rev up their blood flow. A study at Wellington Hospital in New Zealand found that employees who sit for several hours without getting up (e.g. at a meeting or even at their desks) are more likely to develop deep-vein thrombosis than those who move about more often.[1]

Distribute the agenda to participants, giving them enough time to prepare for the meeting. Two or three days before the meeting is usually enough for informal team meetings; formal meetings often specify how many days or weeks prior to the meeting the agenda should be sent out. Invite participants to suggest any changes to the agenda before the meeting.

Agendas can be brief, such as Figure 25.4(a), or more detailed, such as Figure 25.4(b) and (c).

TEAM MEETING – AGENDA		
Agenda items		
	Agenda item	**Comments**
1		
2		
3		
4		

FIGURE 25.4(a) On-site small business team meeting agenda

MEETING AGENDA			
Date:			
Attendees:			
Apologies:			
Item	**Brief description**	**Deliverable**	**Presenter**

FIGURE 25.4(b) Virtual meeting agenda between two project teams across two organisations

MEETING AGENDA			
Date:		**Duration:**	
Location:			
Attendees:			
Meeting chair:			
Apologies:			

Item	Time allocated	Presenter	Brief description	Deliverable	Action/ responsibility

FIGURE 25.4(c) Off-site meeting agenda for department leaders from multiple stores

Select participants

Transferable skills

3.1 Teamwork/ relationships

More is not merrier – more than 12 participants makes a meeting difficult to control and hold everyone's attention, and harder for each participant to contribute fully. Large numbers also mean that the meeting is likely to last longer. Four to seven participants are ideal, 10 is tolerable.

When you can't limit the numbers, try holding two smaller meetings, or form subgroups to discuss topics in advance. Each group can then send a representative to the main meeting. Failing that, structure the agenda so that some members join at half-time and others leave, or invite people in for the specific sections of the agenda that they are concerned with or can contribute to.

Sometimes the decision of who to invite is made for you – it might automatically be your whole team, for example. At other times, you need to think through who should attend. Invite people who can best contribute to the discussion – people with the relevant knowledge, skills or experience.

You probably want to invite people affected by the outcome of the meeting and leave the decision of whether to attend up to them.

You might want to include people who you can count on to support you, people whose commitment you need or people who have resources that you need, such as budget, influence, other staff or time. You might want to include specialists from different areas of the organisation in order to get broad representation and a balanced group. You should also consider how diverse your group is. Diversity makes a team smarter. Research by the Victorian Equal Opportunity and Human Rights Commission and Deloitte found that organisations that have greater gender, ethnic and racial diversity experienced an increase in innovation and ability to be responsive to changing needs.[2] Teams that include people from various backgrounds challenge thinking and offer varied opinions and experience.

When you're not sure whether to invite someone, think about their role and whether they need to be present or simply be advised of the outcome. When people need to be kept 'in the loop' but don't need to attend, make the **minutes** available to them and pass on any essential information. The two-thirds rule is a good rule of thumb to follow when deciding who should attend – each person attending a meeting should be directly concerned with two out of three, or two-thirds, of the agenda items. This prevents the meeting from wasting anyone's time.

Use your intra-office communications to invite people to meetings and take RSVPs. State the main meeting objective in the title and attach the agenda. There are many meeting schedulers on the market. You can compare the key functions of these through websites such as Board Room Comparison – https://boardroompro.org/ or try http://www.doodle.com, which is a free meeting scheduler.

Decide when and where to hold the meeting

Select a time during working hours convenient to everyone. Meetings held outside working hours work in some organisations, but when a meeting isn't held during working hours, people may reason that the topics can't be too important and may resent having their personal time taken up by what is essentially work business, even when the outcome affects them. Out-of-hours meetings also disadvantage people who have home responsibilities and other personal commitments. When you schedule a meeting over lunch, provide food.

What time of day is best? People are generally fresher early in the day and have less on their minds. They may also be more eager to get on with the meeting so they can get on with the rest of their work. A meeting may take on a more leisurely tone late in the afternoon. When you think a meeting may drag on too long, avoid scheduling the meetings near lunch or at the end of the day as people may have personal errands to attend to at lunchtime or carer commitments at the end of the day.

When considering where to hold the meeting, think about the main objectives. A small informal meeting with your direct team could be held in the main work area, your office or out in the sun at the park while taking the daily team walk. For meetings that may take more than 20 minutes or require the team to work in groups, discuss strategies and problem-solve. You may opt for a well-lit, temperature-controlled conference room so that everyone can see and hear each other. Look for comfortable seating, temperature and ventilation, freedom from distractions and relative quiet. Also consider seating arrangements, which can subtly affect the way people participate in a meeting, as summarised in **Table 25.1**.

TABLE 25.1 Seating arrangements

Seating arrangement	Effect on the way people participate
Circles, hollow squares and U-shapes	Encourage collaboration, cross-talk and ideas sharing
Semi-circles	Direct people's attention on to the meeting leader
Chairs in rows	Good for information-giving meetings; add tables so that people can take notes when you provide technical or procedural information
Boardroom style or around a conference table	Sends the message that the meeting is serious and important
Stand up	When time is tight and for short, sharp meetings

Transferable skills

2.1 Critical thinking

3.1 Teamwork/relationships

Meeting roles

The leader-manager usually leads team meetings, although you could occasionally rotate the chair among team members to give everyone valuable experience in leading meetings. You might also act as *recorder*, or secretary, jotting down important points raised by meeting members. Again, this role can be rotated among meeting members.

The recorder can keep individual notes for later posting or distribution, or take the notes on an electronic whiteboard or a laptop projected onto a screen or the wall, or as a shared document. This way, meeting members can see what is being recorded and no one has to worry that their point has been missed. Visible minutes also help meeting members keep to the topic at hand.

Another useful role is that of *meeting facilitator*. This is different from the leader's role. The meeting leader is formally in charge of the meeting, whereas the facilitator's job is to lead the *process* of the meeting, staying away from *content* (i.e. meeting facilitators don't normally contribute any ideas themselves). For example, in a brainstorming session, the facilitator ensures that everyone is contributing, no one is criticising and points out when meeting members are not following the agreed meeting ground rules (see Figure 25.5). You could also usefully rotate the role of facilitator among group members.

- Accept differences in personal styles
- Ask what's wrong, not who's wrong
- Be factual (not personal)
- Be open
- Check out what people mean
- Focus on team development
- Go for win–wins and consensus
- Have fun, too
- Keep lines of communication open
- Listen
- Make team time belong to the team
- No multitasking
- No shouting
- Practise what we preach
- Raise real issues
- Share understanding
- Speak one at a time
- Speak up
- Treat each other with respect
- Work to resolve conflict

FIGURE 25.5 Meeting guidelines

Lead an effective meeting

Transferable skills

3.4 Leadership

To lead meetings effectively, you need the ability to:

- be assertive
- be sensitive to group dynamics
- guide and maintain a balanced discussion that stays on track and moves towards the desired outcomes
- listen carefully and summarise accurately and clearly

- open and close the meeting well
- engage participants' attention and energy.

Of course, meetings are about more than listening and talking. They are called to achieve specific goals and tasks, as set out in the agenda. An effective meeting process is beneficial for all involved in completing the task. Task meetings provide an opportunity for participants to clarify points, gain ideas and benefit from others' experiences and knowledge, collaborate and explore issues, gather information and define action points.

Some meetings are cooperative, cordial and relaxed while still being professional. Others can be stiff and awkward, filled with embarrassment, gameplaying, ill will and undercurrents. Which better describes the meetings you lead and attend? These dynamics can make or break a meeting's success.

Transferable skills

3.2 Verbal communication

To gain important information about how well meeting members are working together, how involved they are and how committed they are to achieving the meeting's objectives, take note of the communication patterns between participants, such as:

- who talks to whom, for how long and how often
- communication styles being used (e.g. aggressive, assertive, passive)
- tones of voice being used
- questions and the manner in which they are being asked
- type of language (e.g. formal and stilted or friendly and informal)
- body language.

Additionally, notice who supports whom, whether there are cliques or factions developing, because this indicates internal tension in the group and prevents it from working optimally. You might also pay attention to who members look at when they talk because this can show you who the informal leader is; that is, the person who wields the most influence in the group. By contrast, note who is often interrupted because this can show you who wields the least influence in the group – yet, remember, this does not make their contributions or opinions any less useful.

INDUSTRY INSIGHTS

After four months of implementing a new team meeting structure, Ahmed decided to survey the team to gain an understanding of their satisfaction levels of the strategies applied. The following points outline the survey results.

Overall, the team were highly satisfied with the meeting structure and resources used throughout meetings, such as Zoom, Microsoft Teams, Miro and shared documentation. Key positives noted in the survey include:

- meetings, while professional, are somewhat informal and everyone's input is encouraged
- atmosphere lightened with a little humour
- participants are thanked for their contribution
- clear meeting objectives established.

Areas for improvement identified include:

- address side conversations held by individual team members
- provide further opportunities for all staff to contribute as it is identified that some staff are passive participants
- further summarising after each point will be beneficial.

What group norms are apparent in your meetings? For example, do people arrive early, on time or late? Prepared or unprepared? Do they hold side conversations or text during the meeting or does everyone pay full attention to whoever is speaking? The group norms can give you an insight into the priorities of the group. When you're paying attention to the meeting group's norms and dynamics, you can address behaviours that seem to be harming the meeting's effectiveness. In fact, you can prevent any harmful norms and processes from developing by asking participants at the start of the meeting to develop or refer to previously developed ground rules for the meeting. Figure 25.5 shows an example of the ground rules one team agreed to. (Find out more about these aspects of people working together in Chapter 4 and Chapter 13.)

You or other meeting members may support a smooth meeting process by adopting the following roles:

- *gatekeeper:* ensures everyone has the opportunity to speak
- *coordinator:* summarises progress and leads to the next step
- *compromiser:* helps people who disagree to build on their viewpoints and reach agreement
- *clown:* relieves tension and provides a quick mental break through humour.

Creating a climate that values everyone's opinions, ideas and experiences will lead to open and honest conversation and establish a friendly and supportive atmosphere where everyone feels comfortable to contribute freely. Simple gestures, such as thanking people for their contributions, asking questions and even lightening the atmosphere with a little humour, can make a significant impact.

Open the meeting

Arrive early so you can greet people as they arrive. This sets the scene and establishes a friendly atmosphere. Making people feel comfortable from the start promotes open discussion and cooperation.

Transferable skills

2.2 Personal effectiveness

Begin the meeting on time. Starting late sets a bad precedent and penalises those who were on time while rewarding the latecomers. Open the meeting by welcoming people, thanking them for attending and saying a few words about what you expect the meeting to accomplish. Briefly review and confirm the agenda, which gives people a chance to ask questions and generally orient themselves to the meeting's task. It also ensures that everyone has the same understanding and signals the importance of the agenda, making participants less likely to drift away from it. Meeting participants keep their eyes on and take their cues from the leader, so keep your posture erect and positive and your facial expressions alert, attentive and encouraging.

When leading a meeting of a merged, mixed, project or virtual team (discussed in Chapter 14), you might want to begin the meeting with 10 minutes of unstructured discussions to talk about matters not directly related to the meeting's purpose. This gives team members an opportunity to catch up and build their relationships, which they might not otherwise have a chance to do, and which is crucial to the team's functioning.

Transferable skills

3.1 Teamwork/relationships

Lead discussions

Transferable skills

3.4 Leadership

Your success in gathering information and ideas or in reaching a decision depends on how effectively you invite free and open participation. Keep discussions balanced by tactfully curbing the talkative people to ensure that all sides of an issue get equal 'airtime' and that all participants have the opportunity to contribute. Make sure comments are on topic and listen carefully to ensure that ground already covered is not repeated and that discussions don't drag on. Reduce opportunities for futile, ineffective or irrelevant discussions.

Stay neutral and avoid aligning yourself with any participants or ideas – people need to know you're not taking sides. Treat everyone equally; for example, don't say 'good idea' to some but not others – respond to ideas and contributions, not individuals. Explore issues fully, clarifying and asking the right questions so that discussions don't disintegrate into confusion or become aimless. Summarise often, to help people keep on track and on the 'same page'.

Asking the right question of the right person at the right time isn't hard, but it does require careful listening and practice. When you get it right, everyone's views and information are aired, discussions flow and people stay on topic. **Figure 25.6** reviews the main types of questions that encourage discussions (you can find out more about helpful questions in Chapter 6).

Hold your own ideas until last to encourage more open contributions since your team may not want to openly disagree with you or challenge your opinions. This also helps to avoid anchoring your opinion in people's minds. When meeting members reach a decision, summarise it clearly and, when appropriate, discuss how to implement it (Chapter 26 explains anchoring and groupthink). Encourage all members to participate in discussions. Some attendees may be less inclined to speak up; however, to maintain inclusion and ensure you have gained insights from everyone, take the time to encourage contribution from everyone. You never know what valuable information you may miss out on if you don't. Five ways to encourage participation can be seen in **Figure 25.7**.

When you feel people have unspoken reservations, encourage them to air their genuine concerns, but stay alert for any 'hidden agendas' (ulterior motives) and self-interest. Don't stifle disharmony when participants are exploring an issue, but make sure debate is respectful so it doesn't collapse into poisonous conflict. Make sure all participants respect every speaker's right to be heard so that only one person speaks at a time and people keep their voices down.

When you're not able to reach agreement, ask the experts, because people listen to topic experts; the informal leader, because people listen to them, too; or offer your own opinion, because your opinion can be equally valuable.

Close a discussion only when it is clear that:

- consensus has been reached
- events are changing rapidly and are likely to alter the basis of discussion quite soon
- more facts are required before further progress can be made
- participants need more time to think about an issue or discuss it with colleagues not present
- the meeting needs the views of people not present
- there is not enough time to discuss the issues fully
- two or three members can settle the topic being discussed outside the meeting without taking up the time of everyone present.

When all the points have been covered or agreement has been reached, summarise once more and move on to the next agenda item. Draw participants' attention to it by briefly explaining the background of the topic and confirm the purpose of the discussion. Should energy wane or enthusiasm wilt, **Figure 25.8** suggests some ways to get the meeting back on track.

INDUSTRY INSIGHTS

Amina likes to use the Edward de Bono six hats thinking when conducting meetings that require a problem to be solved or looking for innovative ideas. Amina believes that the highest creativity can be achieved when a group of people spend time thinking the same way together.

When implementing this form of meeting structure Amina wore the blue hat as the director. While each hat represented a particular stage of the thought process, Amina was careful to ensure that all members of the team had an opportunity to share their thoughts and asked all participants to follow three basic meeting guidelines:

1. Each person needed to allow four seconds of quiet to occur after each person spoke, before sharing their thoughts.
2. No participant was to comment in a negative way to an idea.
3. Each person had to contribute to each stage.

CLOSED	Use closed questions when you want direct and specific information or facts. Follow with a probing question when you need to.
CLARIFYING	Ask a clarifying question to make sure you have understood someone's comment or to summarise in the form of a question.
CONSENSUS-SEEKING	These questions ask for the meeting's confirmation that everyone is in agreement and you can move on.
CONSE-QUENCES	These questions ask participants to consider the consequences or implications of their decision, solution or suggestions.
DIRECT	These are questions aimed at a specific meeting member. Take care not to make people feel like you're putting them 'on the spot'. Use them mostly to direct a question to someone about their particular expertise or when you see a non-verbal cue that someone has something to say.
GENERAL	These are questions you ask to everyone at the meeting, leaving it up to individuals to respond or not. They can be open or closed questions, consensus-seeking questions or consequences questions.
OPEN	Because they allow so much latitude in the way people respond, open questions are the best for finding out what people think and know, and for drawing out ideas.
PROBING	Ask a probing question when you want more information or detail, an example or the reasoning behind what someone has stated.
REDIRECTED	When someone asks you or another meeting member a question, you may want to direct it to the entire meeting or a particular person to keep meeting members participating and to prevent a discussion between only two people.
UNSPOKEN	Use your body language, for example, a raised eyebrow, to ask someone to elaborate or repeat their last few words.

FIGURE 25.6 Questions that help discussions

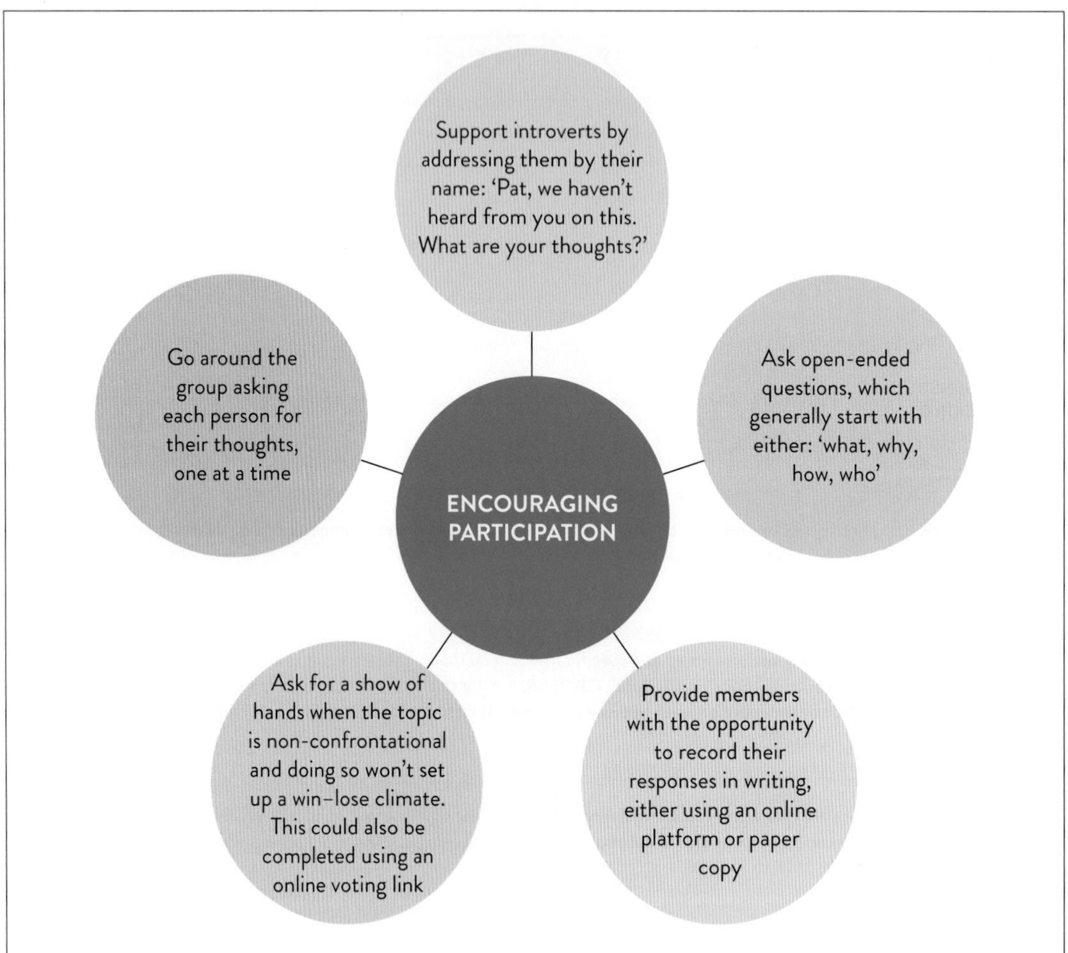

FIGURE 25.7 Five ways to encourage participation

From planning the meeting to closing the meeting, the actions leaders take will influence the level of success a meeting can achieve. Table 25.2 lists the most common mistakes meeting leaders make and how to avoid them.

Close the meeting

Clarify the next steps, particularly who is responsible for doing what and by when. Double-check that all decisions and actions to be taken have been recorded and confirm that these will be distributed to all meeting members. When you're tempted to ask, 'What else do we need to discuss?', change the question to 'What do we need to put on the agenda for the next meeting?' When appropriate, agree on the time and place of the next meeting.

Finally, thank everyone for their participation and spend a few minutes talking about how well the meeting went. Always try to end a meeting on a positive note and with a sense of accomplishment. You can do this, for example, by summarising a major achievement of the meeting.

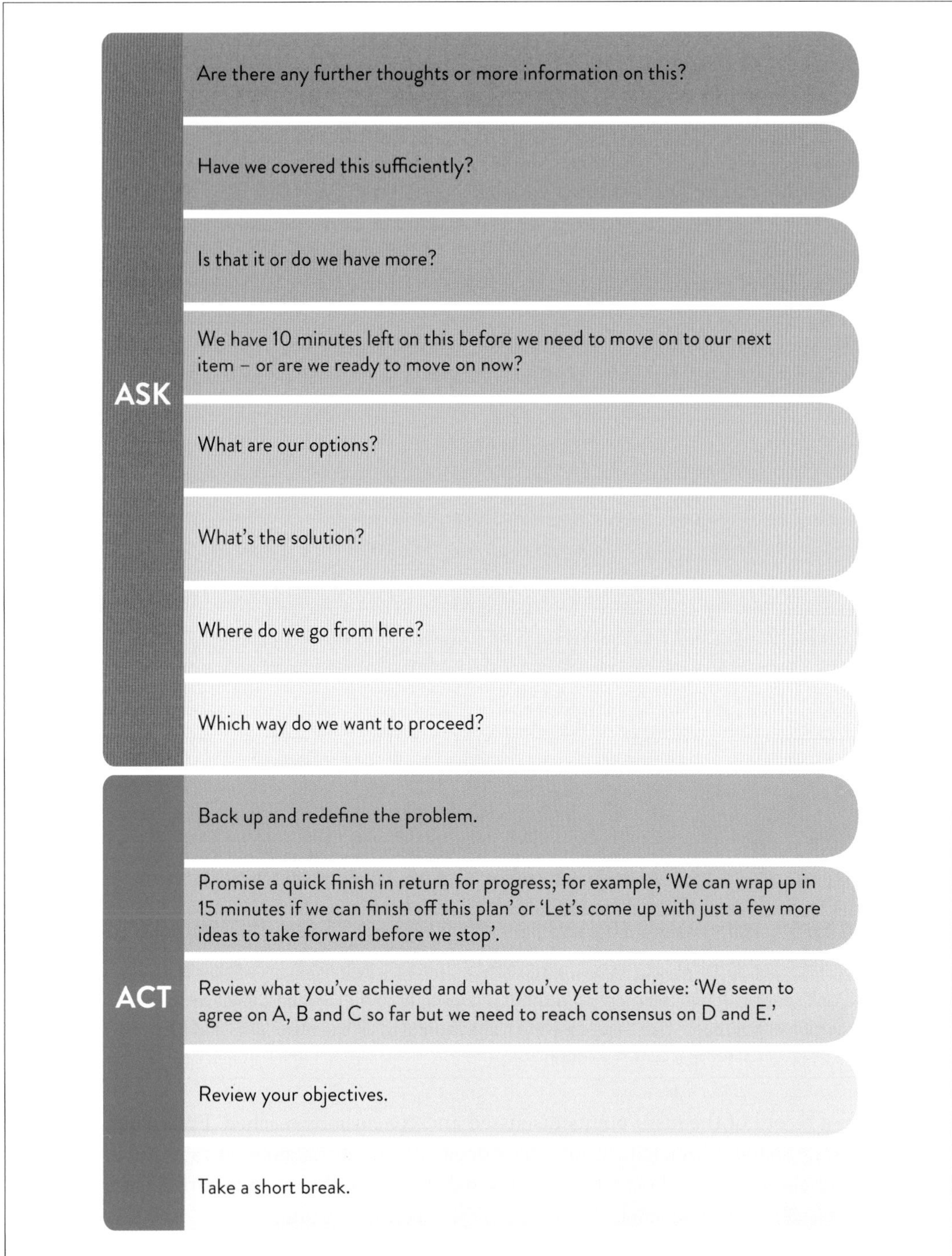

FIGURE 25.8 What to do when a meeting strays or gets stuck

After the meeting

Gourd's axiom states that meetings are events where minutes are kept and hours lost.[3] When you lead the meeting well, the time isn't lost and you have something worthwhile to write up in your minutes.

TABLE 25.2 Avoiding the most common mistakes meeting leaders make

Arriving or starting late	Yes, you're busy, but when the meeting leader is late it encourages everyone to turn up late next time. Similarly, delaying starting a meeting until everyone is present sets a bad precedent. Starting on time encourages everyone to arrive on time
Being too controlling or too relaxed	Chairing a meeting doesn't give you a licence to do all the talking yourself and force your ideas onto everyone else. Learn to lead discussions and reach consensus. The opposite mistake is being too *laissez-faire* and letting everyone talk at once, whether or not their comments relate to the agenda, and paying more attention to making the meeting 'enjoyable' than to the meeting's goals. Keep the main purpose of your meeting in mind and balance maintenance and task issues
Failing to inform others in plenty of time	Meeting participants need to prepare too, even when it's only to study the agenda and do a bit of thinking about it beforehand. Give participants the agenda early enough to allow them to prepare for the meeting, but don't schedule the meeting so far in advance that people misplace the agenda or forget about the meeting
Failing to prepare	Remember the adage 'prior planning prevents poor performance'. Think through your objectives and the issues that the meeting needs to address, and gather the information you need beforehand
Failing to record decisions and agreements	Keep a note of all action items, responsibilities as signed and decisions reached; then diarise to follow them up
Inhibiting free discussion	This happens when you ask leading questions, state your opinion before hearing others' opinions, and defend rather than explore. Don't fall into the trap of cutting off anyone who disagrees with your conclusions, ideas and opinions. Instead, use different points of view as opportunities to explore issues more deeply. See yourself as the gatekeeper, coordinator and compromiser
Launching straight into the agenda without attending to maintenance issues	Establish the right climate and help people orient themselves to the meeting before moving on to your first agenda item. Open the meeting on a pleasant note; welcome people and thank them for coming. Say a few words about what you intend the meeting to achieve and, when you have meeting guidelines, draw people's attention to them
Permitting the group to wander from the point and failing to finish on time	Allowing digressions and rambling shoptalk kills any meeting. Keep discussions on track and to the point and don't let the meeting drag on
Poor sequencing of agenda	A good agenda is important because it anchors the meeting. Follow the guidelines for preparing an agenda outlined earlier
Rushing	Don't speed through the meeting without providing time for members to develop their own solution or approach. See that everyone has a chance to air their thoughts and hear everyone else's so they can develop a joint resolution

Minutes are a record of the main points discussed and conclusions reached. Even when your brief summary is only a handwritten note in your diary or electronic journal notes, it's a useful memory aid. When appropriate, write up a short set of minutes to distribute to the meeting participants or post on your team's noticeboard or intranet team room in the meetings section.

Head the minutes with the date, time and place of the meeting and who attended. You can set out the minutes in one of the following ways:

- Show each agenda item in order, with a brief summary of the discussion, conclusions and decisions reached, tasks assigned and timelines for any action or follow-up action agreed, and those responsible for taking action.
- Organise the minutes into 'information shared', 'items discussed', 'decisions made', 'actions to be taken', 'pending issues' and so on, to make it easy for people to scan them.

Just include the facts, key points, important decisions, and actions to be taken by whom and by when. They should accurately reflect the meeting's tone and main themes. Show the time the meeting ended and the date, and the time and place of the next meeting. Transfer actions to be taken and responsibilities to the agenda for the next meeting so you can follow through on them.

Keep control

A clear agenda, experience and self-confidence are your best tools for making sure your meetings stay on track. Observe other good meeting leaders to see what tips you can pick up from them. You may notice that they use more direct control than usual when strong and potentially disruptive feelings are present, when the group is moving towards a decision or when time is tight.

Short of formal parliamentary procedures (described at the end of this chapter), two of the more common, less intrusive techniques for keeping control are making a short summary after each contribution and using an electronic whiteboard, flip chart or collaborative software such as Miro, Trello or Microsoft Teams chat channels to record these summaries (this is handy for writing up the minutes afterwards, too). Non-verbally, a glance at the clock can help keep the meeting focused and moving forward.

Don't use control techniques to smother differences of opinion and strong feelings – this would probably strengthen them and increase tension or lead to groupthink.

Disruptive behaviours

Transferable skills
2.1 Critical thinking

What do you do when someone argues over every point, continually distracts people with whispered side conversations, dominates the discussion, moves away from the topic under discussion, sits in silence or talks over everyone else? Behaviours like these present problems for meeting leaders.

We examine some common disruptive behaviours below and offer suggestions for dealing with them during the meeting. After the meeting and in private, calmly, assertively and politely speak with the participant concerned, using an 'I' message (explained in Chapter 16). Name the behaviour you want to stop and say what you would like instead. For example, you might say to someone who held side conversations, 'Alex, when you talk while someone else is addressing the meeting, I get quite distracted. I need to have just one person speaking at a time. Can you help me out with that?' Alternatively, describing the effect the behaviour has on the team can encourage the person to also reflect on their behaviour.

Arriving unprepared

When a meeting participant repeatedly turns up to meetings unprepared and without the information that the rest of the meeting participants need to get on with the agenda, address the behaviour sooner rather than later. Remind the participant of meeting requirements, identify if there are any other factors that may be impacting the person's ability to achieve what is required and discuss actions the person is to take to attend meetings prepared.

Constantly criticising

Some people seem to criticise every idea, every point of view, every helpful suggestion, pointing out the downsides but seldom offering alternatives or positive suggestions in return. This behaviour saps a meeting's creativity, energy and goodwill. Don't allow it.

You could gently point out that unconstructive criticism doesn't move the meeting forward, ask what they do like about a suggestion or ask for their thoughts on how to improve it. This might refocus them on the positive.

You could try treating comments and criticisms as though they were normal and routine by rephrasing and restating them so they appear to be conforming to the approach you want, and then asking for a response from other members. For example: 'Terry isn't convinced this approach is feasible. What could we do to make it work?'

Daydreaming and hesitating

Some people let their minds wander. Others may be shy or become self-conscious when speaking before a group and, even when they have a good point to make, they just can't seem to find the words. Others prefer to wait to be invited to contribute. Be patient and supportive to help their thoughts and ideas to see the light of day.

Encourage people to speak when you think they have a contribution to make, but don't embarrass them by asking a difficult, direct question. Instead, invite them to respond to questions you know they can answer or let them know in advance that you'll be directing a specific question to them. For example, 'Sonya, I'd like to ask you for your thoughts on this in a minute, after we've heard from Stan.' (When Stan is a bit of a digresser or a dominator, this serves the dual purpose of warning him to limit his comments.)

Summarise when the daydreamer or hesitator is finished and thank them for their contribution. You want to encourage them to speak so that the rest of the group can hear their worthwhile contributions.

INDUSTRY INSIGHTS

Sam, a new intern, recently joined Janine's team, his very first employed position. Lin noticed that while Sam is confident in his skills and knowledge and speaks confidently when communicating with Janine, he is an introvert and doesn't seem to contribute to discussions within team meetings. Janine is also mindful that Sam started work just before the COVID-19 lockdowns occurred in Melbourne and had limited time to get to know the team in the office before moving to working from home full-time.

Janine recently met with Sam to have a general one-on-one meeting about his first month with the team and she took the opportunity to open up a discussion about team meetings to find out how he feels about them. Janine wanted to confirm with Sam that her strategy of using his name and asking him questions throughout the team meeting has been beneficial for him.

Sam advised that he does enjoy the strategy and appreciates it when Janine uses his name. He advised that everyone has been very welcoming, and he likes the regularity, agenda and style taken to conduct the various team meetings. He advised that providing him with an opportunity to speak is increasing his confidence.

Further strategies agreed upon included Sam leading one of the agenda items that most related to his role in the formal Monday morning meetings.

Digressing

Questions and comments that lead the group astray are sometimes referred to as 'red herrings'. They impede progress, side-track meetings and test the tact of even the best meeting leader. Thankfully, there are several useful techniques to keep the meeting on track. Try to link the off-point comments to the topic at hand. If that doesn't work, try summarising what has been said so far to return to the topic under discussion. Failing that, you can say, 'That's an interesting observation. How does it fit into our topic?' to highlight the digression and encourage the digresser to return to the topic. You may have to be even more direct: 'This discussion is interesting, but I suggest we postpone it until next month's meeting when I can put that topic on the agenda'.

Dominating

Some people just talk too much. Others keep pushing their point of view until everyone folds and sees it their way. Monopolising discussions wastes the meeting's time and destroys its sense of purpose. When you know in advance that someone is likely to dominate a discussion, try seating them to your extreme left (or right if you are left-handed); this makes it easier to avoid seeing their attempts to get the floor. When they do get the floor, let them have a reasonable amount of time, then interrupt by saying something like, 'You've got some good points there. Now let's hear what others think and then you're welcome to respond.' Another strategy is to provide time limits for each person to state their opinion or provide information before moving on to other participants.

Interrupting

Some people interrupt so much that other participants just give up and yield the floor. Help them out by signalling to the chronic interrupter that talking over people is not acceptable. You could say something like, 'Hang on, Ian, let's hear the idea Kim is explaining', or 'Kim, you were starting to suggest something. Could you finish please?' Including etiquette norms to the meeting, such as raising a hand in virtual meetings or signalling with the placement of a number, may encourage the constant interrupter to pause, knowing that they will have the opportunity to speak again.

Failing to follow through or speak frankly

When you suspect someone may not complete an assignment, after the meeting or informally over coffee during a break (to avoid taking up the meeting's time) ask them what might prevent them from completing the accepted assignment on time; then ask how they can prevent that and confirm that they can take the action they've agreed to.

You may occasionally sense that someone isn't expressing their true opinion or is holding back from providing information. Bring any concerns to the surface by directly asking for their opinion or what information they can add to the discussion.

Reiterating

Someone may continually repeat the same point, even when the subject has moved on. Gently remind them that their views have been heard. When you're making summaries on a whiteboard or groupware, point to the chart as visual evidence that their point has been noted.

A good general technique, especially when a meeting member is inclined to dominate a discussion, veer off point or repeat a point unnecessarily, is to nominate three or four people at a time, selecting the speakers who need to be restrained to speak first: 'John, let's hear from you first, then Jane, then Jacob, and after that Jenny'. This puts pressure on the earlier speakers to be succinct because the people after them are waiting their turn. You may also like to include that each person is to share their one best idea or point and include a time limit.

Side conversations

While people whispering together or having separate individual virtual chats can indicate good morale and team relationships, they can also be distracting. You can ignore them for a while but not to the point where they irritate those near them. Some ways to deal with the problem are:

- Break in and say, 'Excuse me. I want to have one discussion at a time. (Whisperers), are you ready to join us now?'
- Look at the speaker (not the chatterboxes) and say, 'Excuse me, (Speaker), let's wait until we have everyone's attention'. When everyone is silent, invite the speaker to continue.
- Look at those involved and ask them whether they have any comments they would like to share with the rest of the meeting.

When you don't allow disruptive side conversations, you soon won't have to worry about them at all.

Reflect on disruptive meeting behaviours observed in meetings you have either participated in or discussed with others. What strategies were used to address these behaviours? Do you think they were successful?

25.3 Leading virtual meetings

Imagine yourself as a tour guide charged with keeping everyone in the meeting oriented and engaged.

Shani Harmon, 'Three rules for holding virtual meetings that people don't hate', *Fast Company*, 7 February 2016, https://www.fastcompany.com/3061260/three-rules-for-holding-virtual-meetings-that-people-dont-hate.

Teams consist of individuals from within the local area, various places interstate and from outside of Australia. Office structure is now more mobile, with many people taking advantage of 'hot desk and hot offices' and working from home. Virtual meetings are crucial to the new way we work. Virtual meetings – particularly web meetings – are cheaper and easier to organise than traditional meetings, giving team members, customers and suppliers greater access to each other. You can meet more often, increasing efficiencies in communication, decision-making, discussion and information sharing. Many teams now converse more often virtually than in a room together. The meeting strategies include daily catch-up meetings or check-ins several times a week or ad hoc calls online. Essentially, virtual meetings allow for interaction and immediate feedback. See **Table 25.3** for more information about virtual meetings.

TABLE 25.3 Virtual meetings unpacked

Type of meeting	Resources/tools	Benefits	Challenges
Instant messaging	Mobile text Yammer	Quick and efficient way to ask quick questions or to communicate short messages	Written text only – may impact interpretation and tone of message
Teleconference	Internet Suitable telephone	Easy to arrange Cost-effective	Verbal communication only – may lead to misunderstandings and ineffective interactions
Videoconferencing	High-quality videoconferencing hardware (camera, microphone) Zoom Slack Teams Skype Google Hangouts Webex	Great visibility and interaction with smooth communication Real-time conversation between people at multiple locations Ability to utilise other collaborative software to interact	Expense Poor internet connectivity can impact interactions

Type of meeting	Resources/tools	Benefits	Challenges
Web conferencing (Webinars)	Zoom Skype Google Hangouts Webex	Present to large audience with the host taking control	Poor internet connectivity can impact interactions Unable to ask questions directly to presenter or ask for clarification (unless specific time is allocated for this function) Presenter unable to see body language of participants (where function disabled) and gauge engagement

INDUSTRY INSIGHTS

Oskar had established clear protocols for virtual meetings, and proposed a new meeting structure to the team, with the aim to align virtual meetings with agile project management methodologies. Now, his new strategy includes four meeting types shown in the following:

Meeting title	Aim	Duration/Time	Attendees
Project brief	Outline project details and discuss scope of works in detail	One hour on commencement of a new project	Project leads and personnel assigned to the respective project
Spring planning	To discuss each project	One hour at the beginning of each week	All staff
Stand-up scrum	Staff check-in – identify progress with projects and any situations impacting successful completion	15–30 minutes Tuesday to Friday	All staff
Project review	Showcase progression, celebrate milestones, gain feedback	30 minutes	Staff assigned to respective projects

Organising virtual meetings

When you're organising a webconference, videoconference or teleconference, be considerate of those in other time zones when deciding on the time. Send out the agenda and supporting documents far enough ahead to allow people to prepare. Include a list of participants by location, balancing the number of participants from each location when possible. Attach any other pertinent information, such as the start and finish times of the meeting in local times (emphasising that the meeting will start on time), locations and contact details of participants, and their job titles if applicable. (PDFs display and print more predictably than other document formats.)

Detail any information or material that participants need to have at the meeting. For example, when participants don't know each other, ask them to be ready to give a 30-second general background introduction of themselves. This helps participants know how the other members can contribute and gets everyone used to speaking and to hearing the sound of others' voices and, when it's a video or videoconference, seeing them. Confirm that everyone can hear (and see, when it's a videoconference or webconference) clearly. This groundwork helps people settle in comfortably and sets up good dynamics for the rest of the meeting.

When a video director isn't assigned to you for a videoconference, familiarise yourself and the participants with the equipment when you need to. Know where the controls are, how to zoom in, pan out and sweep from side to side, where to position your documents or diagrams for participants to refer to and so on. Ask someone to operate cameras, microphones and lights because it is difficult to lead the meeting and act as technician at the same time. Depending on your organisation's protocol, you may decide to email a reminder to participants a few days before the conference, confirming the details.

Virtual meeting etiquette

Etiquette in meetings produces a common level of courtesy, which is essential when people come together for any reason. It can be a little easier for members who attend a virtual meeting to become distracted or tune out of topics they are not particularly interested in and continue on with other work. Discussing basic etiquette and establishing meeting norms will assist in leading and holding successful virtual meetings. Figure 25.9 shows some tips for achieving positive meeting etiquette.

It is important when preparing for a virtual meeting to test your equipment and your environment with a co-worker prior to the meeting. Testing is not only about if your camera, video, microphone and Wi-Fi are working correctly, it also allows you to assess what other people will see when they are meeting virtually with you. You may like to opt for an organisational image, use an image or background effect provided within the software, or blur your background.

DO	AVOID
• Speak slowly and clearly • Encourage 10-second pause time between comments • Use the 'raise hand' function to signify that you would like to make a comment or ask a question • Ask the speaker for further clarification or to repeat what was spoken if you didn't hear the comment • Show more tact and be courteous in the absence of body language cues • Select 'mute' if your environment is noisy • Smile and maintain eye contact with the group	• Unnecessary extraneous noise that the microphone can pick up (e.g. shuffling feet, tapping pencils) • Interrupting someone who is speaking • Jargon and expressions that may not be familiar to everyone • Holding side conversations

FIGURE 25.9 Tips for achieving positive meeting etiquette

Think about the virtual meetings you have been involved in personally or witnessed on a TV show. Have you seen anything that you would rather have not seen? For example, up the nose of the presenter or someone being interviewed or an item such as a piece of laundry. How distracted were you by these situations?

Teleconferences

When a teleconference lasts more than 30 minutes, assess the mood of the participants occasionally. Hear from each site ('Location A, how are you going?' or 'Location B, do you have any questions?'). If someone hasn't said anything for a while, ask them to contribute: 'Sam, we haven't heard from you for a while. Can you add something at this point?'

Until people get to know each other and can recognise each other's voices, ask them to say their name when they speak and the name of anyone they may be addressing a question to; for example, 'This is Graham. I'd like to ask Pat ...' Lengthy teleconferences that cover several agenda items can be trying. Because people avoid making distracting 'uh huh' sounds that could replace non-verbal nods and eye contact, it can sometimes feel like you're speaking into empty space. And without the visual element to anchor people's attention, minds can wander.

Tips for teleconferences and audio-only web meetings

All you need to have for a webconference are an internet connection, microphone, speakers and software to facilitate the conference. Here are some 'To dos' for basic, audio-only meetings:

- Let people know if you leave the room so they don't address comments to you and get no response.
- Sit up straight and wear a pleasant expression on your face; your voice reflects your posture and expression.
- When some people are face-to-face and others virtual, the virtual people can fade out as the face-to-face people start talking to each other and the virtual participants find it difficult to follow them. So when some meeting members work at the same site, ask them to sit in different rooms rather than cluster around a speaker. This 'levels the playing field' and encourages equal attention from everyone.
- When you can't see everyone, it's easy to forget who is actually 'present'. Draw your own 'map' to keep fully tuned in. Write the names of those present on a piece of paper and put it in front of you. If it helps, draw it as you would if people were sitting around a conference table.

Videoconferences and webconferences

Transferable skills
5.2 Technology use

Videoconferences and webconferences let you bring people together in real time, where they can see each other as they work their way through the agenda. They can see slides and videos and work on documents together using interactive features, such as screen-sharing.

There are several videoconference options to select from:

- *Chair controlled*: one site is designated as the 'chair' site and all sites see the chair.
- *Continuous presence video*: the video is segmented into four quadrants, each displaying a different site simultaneously.
- *Leader controlled*: the meeting leader can see, and be seen by, all meeting members.

- *Telephone-only participation:* when someone can't get to a site with the necessary equipment or is delayed in transit, they can still participate using audio-only capability. That is, they can hear and be heard but cannot see or be seen by the other participants.
- *Voice-switched video*: everyone sees the current speaker and the current speaker sees the image of the last speaker.

Webconferencing using collaborative systems technology allows you to have a totally interactive meeting in which meeting participants can share documents online, simultaneously exchanging, viewing and working on them. For example, team members can collaboratively edit a document or spreadsheet of any file type and receive emails or Really Simple Syndication (RSS) alerts when changes or comments are made on documents or a project. An additional window displays the data file, which can be moved around when it obstructs the view of any of the other quadrants showing other conference participants. Collaboration tools also let you:

- create a virtual team room where you can conduct real-time brainstorming and problem-solving sessions, meetings and training
- make 10 to 15 participants at a time visible during team meetings (depending on the software)
- record a meeting or a presentation
- share files
- share software applications
- take live minutes 'on screen'
- use a 'whiteboard' interactively to diagram, capture and share ideas
- use audio controls to mute or 'unmute' participants and control their volume levels.

You can even gauge the mood of meeting members with mood indicators!

Your organisation might own its own equipment and software or it might go through a webconference hosting company or videoconferencing provider. Some organisations use webconferencing for online project team meetings between, for example, an engineering head office and its engineers in the field, speeding up problem-solving, troubleshooting and decision-making. Teams can meet securely to discuss sensitive documents and can view and revise complex technical drawings and plans.

Transferable skills
5.1 Cyber security

Webconference security

During a webconference, data is stored temporarily on an internet server that belongs either to the organisation or to the company providing hosting services in the Cloud. It is at this time that the data is most vulnerable to hackers. Even when your organisation uses its own in-house network that doesn't use the internet, all conferencing and collaboration tools should defend the traffic that flows between the participants through encryption (data scrambling) with Secure Socket Layer (SSL) technology to make the data unreadable.

Ideally, each computer involved in the conference should have a digital security certificate that is used to authenticate the computer to the conference host computer. You can assign longer-term security certificates to permanent team members, provide contractors with security certificates that last the length of their contract and give temporary team members (e.g. external consultants or specialists) certificates of a shorter duration that you specify.

Tips for videoconferences and webconferences

Cameras and their speakers are turned on all the time in videoconferencing and webconferencing, so be aware of what you're doing and how you can make your colleagues comfortable in this environment. Here are some tips:

- Avoid side conversations because the voice-activated microphones pick them up and the camera refocuses on you.
- When your facility has a third monitor that allows you to preview your image, use it.
- Keep in mind that there can be a lag between the spoken word and when it's heard.
- Keep reasonably still and refrain from hand gestures to avoid creating distractions. Use slower and smaller movements than you would in a face-to-face meeting and avoid jerky movements, which the video exaggerates.
- Mind your body language. People may be able to see you even when you aren't the one talking.
- Sit face-on to the camera rather than at an angle, and when you have a choice, go for full- or wide-angle shots rather than close-ups.
- Smile and maintain 'eye' (camera) contact. Look at the monitor to see others and at the camera to make eye contact with them.
- Stay two to three metres away from the camera and don't lean into it or towards the listeners because it can look aggressive.

Run effective virtual meetings

Leading virtual meetings is the same as leading actual meetings. It's normal to connect with other meeting members, chatting about what's going on in their lives, sharing stories and so on, before a meeting begins. It's good for productivity because people are more willing to help each other out when they know and like each other as people. A group of independent workers can always achieve more results or innovate further when working as a team. When people are in the same place, it's also easy to connect on a more personal level.

The informal chitchat and banter can be somewhat difficult in virtual meetings, so creating opportunities for increased personal connection can support productivity. It's a good idea to begin the meeting by checking in with everyone in turn and asking them to share something that's happened in their lives since the last meeting, either personal or work related, or having 10 minutes of open general discussion. This makes people feel part of the team and helps them get to know each other and build bonds. You can hold a virtual lunch every once in a while, too.

As with any meeting, prepare and post the agenda online or send it by email. At the beginning of the first meeting, agree meeting protocols like those shown in Figure 25.5. Some meetings may also benefit from being recorded, particularly if the meeting is with a client or there are multiple components to work through. Having a recording of the meeting to go back to can also assist with completing minute meetings and recalling key elements of the meeting and action points. Always ask for permission to record the meeting prior to doing so.

It is particularly important that participants agree not to multitask, which can be common in virtual meetings. People need to be fully mentally present and engaged and not working on another task or checking emails. Set that as an expectation from the beginning and involve everyone in contributing to the meeting frequently to reduce the multitasking temptation. Also agree how meeting members should gain the floor when someone has something to contribute.

Open by welcoming everyone and confirming what the meeting is intended to achieve. Include something unexpected or some interesting news in your opening comments to make your virtual meetings special, so no one wants to miss them. Then move on to your first agenda item. Make it a topic that gets people talking.

Keep to the agenda and for meetings that run longer than an hour, remember to schedule short breaks. End the meeting as you would any meeting: summarise the key points and confirm decisions and action items. Acknowledge what the meeting has achieved. Thank participants for their time and attention. And confirm when you will post the minutes (if you don't put up live minutes on screen).

Follow up as you would with any meeting. Post the minutes showing key information, such as actions and responsibilities that team members can check off as they complete them, discussion points and issues, decisions and next steps. Make a checklist of action items to follow up on before the next meeting.

25.4 Attending meetings

Meetings ... are rather like cocktail parties. You don't want to go but you're cross not to be asked

Jilly Cooper (British author), *How to survive from nine to five*, Random House, London, 1970.

Meetings can take up a significant amount of your week, so before agreeing to attend, find out specifically what the meeting is intended to achieve. You can then decide whether you could achieve the same goal differently or whether someone else could or should attend in your place. Negotiate the length of short informal meetings in advance so they don't devour all of your time. Ask people how much time they think they'll need and agree when the meeting will begin and end. Open-ended meetings can go on forever; prevent this by asking the person to send you a short, specific agenda estimating how long to spend on each topic. When a meeting has several agenda items and will take considerable time, you may be able to arrange with the chairperson to drop in and out so that you're present only for the items that directly concern you.

Before attending a meeting, decide what you need to achieve from it. You may want to contribute important information, find out where others stand, make a suggestion that is accepted, network and make allies, provide information that changes the participants' way of looking at an issue or even impress someone. Then decide how to achieve your goal. When you have a clear goal and a plan to achieve it, you can make meetings work for you.

Participate professionally

Whether you are leading a meeting or participating in one, how effectively you participate is an important factor in how you are perceived in the organisation (and hence in your career success). Here we will discuss how to be an effective meeting participant.

Before the meeting, think about the items on the agenda and do any research that would help you make a worthwhile contribution. Bring any information and paperwork you might need with you, along with copies for others when this would be helpful. Arrive fully prepared and on time – tardiness is disrespectful to others. Bring some work to do while you wait for a meeting to start to give you a choice between spending time getting to know others either inside or outside of the organisation networking or getting on with other work. Unless you're expecting an important call or message, turn off your mobile phone, or switch it to silent and explain to the meeting leader why you need to leave it on; should you need to take an urgent call, leave the room.

Speak up when you can contribute and take care to use only your share of the speaking time. To project a professional impression and avoid rambling, organise your thoughts in your head or on paper before speaking. Except in formal meetings where you address the chair, speak to the entire meeting. Keep your contributions relevant to the subject under discussion. Make your point succinctly; you can pull out some of your detailed information when people have questions. Omit personal stories unless they make a point and avoid 'inside jokes'. Make all your comments clear and loud enough to be heard and make eye contact with everyone, not just one or two other meeting participants.

Encourage good ideas suggested by others and don't play devil's advocate for the sake of it. To disagree without being disagreeable, paraphrase the other person's point before expressing your reservations, concern or confusion in a way that shows you're open to alternatives, and offer an alternative or a way to make the idea work better. Don't set a pattern of always disagreeing or seeing the negative side; offer solutions and encouragement too.

When you're asked to contribute and you don't have anything to say, it's fine to say, 'I can't add anything to what's been said' or 'I don't know anything about that and I don't want to confuse the issue'. Don't explain other people's remarks: 'I think what Bill is trying to say is ...' When someone interprets your comments incorrectly, correct them: 'Actually, Bill, that isn't quite what I meant. What I meant was ...'

When you let people interrupt you, they will continue to do so. Keep the floor by saying: 'I have three points I'd like to make. First ...' Keep numbering as you go so that people know you haven't finished when you pause to draw breath. Keep your points brief, though!

Follow through on any promises you make, tasks assigned to you or actions you agree to take. Unless you have a good reason, avoid accepting tasks that do not properly belong to you or your work group. Otherwise, you could end up being too snowed-under to get your own work done.

Use the chat function of virtual meeting software platforms to add or share information. You can also use this to ask questions of the group or use the raise your hand function. Remember to use the mute button wisely. Before speaking, check that you are not on mute, and when you are passively participating click the mute button again.

25.5 Understanding meeting protocol

> Robert's Rules provides for constructive and democratic meetings, to help, not hinder, the business of the assembly. Under no circumstances should 'undue strictness' be allowed to intimidate members or limit full participation.
>
> Henry M. Robert, *Robert's Rules of Order* (1915).

Meetings can vary greatly in their degree of formality. Some meetings are very informal and seem more like a conversation among colleagues. Don't let the relaxed and casual atmosphere fool you. People discuss some very significant matters and make important decisions in informal meetings. Most work team meetings and many other meetings that managers attend are run informally. This is particularly so with smaller groups and people who meet together regularly. At the other extreme are formal meetings that follow parliamentary protocol. The meeting's *constitution* is the list of written rules that guide how the meeting is conducted and how many members must be present before the meeting can take place; this is called a *quorum*.

Official meetings between employer and employee representatives (e.g. workplace bargaining) and many workplace health and safety and risk management committees and teams, and committees made up of people who don't know each other well and are brought together temporarily for special purposes, often use formal procedures. So do professional bodies and associations, local councils and boards of directors.

Formal meeting roles and protocol

When you first join a committee or an organisation that follows formal meeting protocol, find out the rules, the terms of reference they follow, and a bit about the other members, the informal power structure and 'pecking order' of members. Try to gain an understanding of the 'politics', or informal alliances between members, too. Find out if there is a certain dress code for the meetings and follow its lead. Aim to observe the way the meetings work for your first two or three meetings so that you gain a good understanding of expectations.

A *chairperson* may be elected or appointed to carry out various duties on behalf of the meeting. This may include:

- developing an agenda before the meeting, often inviting participants to submit agenda items for it and including them when they are appropriate for that particular meeting
- ensuring that everyone who is necessary to the meeting is invited to attend
- leading the meeting, ensuring that the constitution of the meeting is followed, maintains a sense of order and direction, opens and closes the meeting, introduces each topic on the agenda, calls on members to speak and calls for votes
- dealing impartially and objectively with all sides of the issues being discussed
- giving each participant the opportunity to speak and ensuring that no one dominates or in any other way disrupts the meeting. Participants of formal meetings make remarks only when invited to do so by the chairperson and these remarks are usually made 'through the chair' – that is, they are directed to the chairperson.

The first item on the agenda of most formal meetings is a call by the chairperson for members to approve the minutes of the previous meeting. This means they agree that the minutes accurately reflect the previous meeting. The chairperson then signs the minutes and places them in a special minutes file for storage and future reference.

Before members can discuss or vote on a topic, someone must *propose* it as a *motion*. Another member must then *second* it. This ensures that two people (at least) agree that the matter is worth discussing. In very formal meetings, the chairperson gives the floor alternately to people speaking for the motion and people speaking against it.

A meeting member can propose an *amendment* to the wording of a motion before it is voted on. Another meeting member then needs to second the amendment. After the discussion and before the group votes on a motion, the chairperson gives the original proposer the right of reply to say a few final words about it.

Meeting members then vote *for* or *against* the motion or they can *abstain* (refrain) from voting. Voting can be by ballot, verbally or by a show of hands. When a majority of meeting participants vote in favour of a motion, it is *carried* and becomes a *resolution*. The minute taker records this, as well as the key points of the discussion (who said what), in the minutes.

STUDY TOOLS

QUICK REVIEW

KEY CONCEPT 25.1 

a Review the useful task and maintenance functions meetings can serve and determine whether these apply to actual and virtual meetings alike. Which task and maintenance issues do meeting leaders need to be most alert to in actual meetings? How about in virtual meetings?

b What should you consider before calling a meeting?

c Review the main types of meetings found in most organisations and explain when they can usefully be called.

KEY CONCEPT 25.2 

a List seven steps you can take to lead a productive meeting, whether actual or virtual, and explain why they're important.

b Briefly explain the purpose of agendas and minutes and what they should include.

KEY CONCEPT 25.3 

a List the differences and similarities between virtual and actual meetings from the leader's point of view.

KEY CONCEPT 25.4 

a What are the main responsibilities of people attending a meeting? How does honouring these responsibilities help a meeting succeed and how does failing to honour them hamper a meeting's success?

KEY CONCEPT 25.5 

a What is the function of formal meeting protocol?

BUILD YOUR SKILLS

KEY CONCEPT 25.1 

a What types of meetings have you participated in? Consider meetings with your family, friends and fellow students, clubs and organisations to which you belong, as well as work meetings. Describe four of these meetings, commenting on their degree of formality and their effectiveness. Discuss the skills needed by the leader and the participants in each. In retrospect, what could the meeting leader and the participants have done to make the meetings more effective?

b Consider how your organisation or work group could change (e.g. introduction of a casualised workforce, working from home or job share). With this change of working structure, what meeting strategy would you put in place to ensure your work group maintains effective relationships, shares information and collaborates on areas of importance.

KEY CONCEPT 25.2 

a Outline an agenda for the first meeting of a team that you have just joined as its leader-manager.

b Thinking about both the task and the maintenance needs of a meeting, discuss the steps that leader-managers can take to ensure that their work group reaches consensus at a meeting.

c What is the difference between 'railroading' and reaching genuine consensus? Give an example of each from your own experience.

d What unhelpful meeting behaviours have you observed in classes or in meetings you have attended? Select three and discuss how a meeting leader can firmly and tactfully prevent them from occurring and how they can be dealt with should they occur.

KEY CONCEPT 25.3 

a Discuss the role of virtual meetings in modern organisations from a sustainability and cost point of view.

KEY CONCEPT 25.4 

a Thinking of the last three meetings you attended, including meetings of your class, how well prepared were you? How did your behaviours and contributions help and hinder the meeting's effectiveness?

KEY CONCEPT 25.5 

a Attend a formal meeting at your university or local council and observe the protocol followed. What helpful and unhelpful meeting behaviours did you observe? What was their effect? How did the chairperson respond to those behaviours? Prepare a short report summarising the meeting in terms of its leadership, effective and ineffective meeting behaviours and the protocols followed.

WORKPLACE ACTIVITIES

KEY CONCEPT 25.1 

a Thinking of a meeting you recently led, answer the following:
   - i Was the type of meeting selected suitable to meet your objectives?
   - ii Were the strategies you used to encourage the meeting processes successful?
   - iii What went well and what could you have done better?
   - iv What will you remember to do during the next meeting you lead?

KEY CONCEPT 25.2 

a Thinking of the last meeting you led, how well did you prepare for it? How can you improve your preparation for the next meeting you lead?
b Develop and distribute an agenda for a meeting at your workplace.
c Take, prepare and distribute minutes for a meeting at your workplace.
d Collect feedback from a minimum of two participants who attended a recent meeting you led, to gain an insight as to how they felt you led the meeting. Based on their feedback, what areas did you do well in and what areas do you need to further develop or consider for the next meeting?
e Prepare a plan to develop your skills at leading meetings.

KEY CONCEPT 25.3 

a What virtual meetings are held in your organisation? Attend one as a participant or an observer and note the main differences and similarities between these meetings and actual meetings to discuss in class. How is the leader's role altered in virtual meetings?

KEY CONCEPT 25.4 

a From either participating in meetings, leading meetings or discussing meetings with others, compile a list of helpful and unhelpful meeting behaviours. For each of the unhelpful behaviours, consider how you could address these and how the helpful meeting behaviours could be reinforced (e.g. positive specific reinforcement for helpful behaviours and 'I' messages for unhelpful behaviours).

KEY CONCEPT 25.5 

a List the committees in your organisation that follow formal meeting protocol. Attend one of their meetings as a participant or an observer, and note down which of Robert's Rules of Order, mentioned in the quote at the start of Section 25.5, were followed, and how this helped all members to be heard.

EXTENSION ACTIVITIES

Following on from the Snapshot at the beginning of this chapter, Grace, acting on her boss' request to organise the next quarterly team leaders meeting, started to formulate a plan that would lead to a successful and engaging meeting.

The first step she took was to create a meeting plan. This included identifying the following:

- key stakeholders attending the meeting and their individual needs
- selecting the most appropriate meeting venue (either virtual or on-site), time and duration
- identifying the equipment and software needed.

The second step involved preparing for the meeting, which included:

- establishing meeting objectives
- creating a draft agenda and sending it to applicable parties for input
- sending out meeting invites
- finalising the agenda and forwarding to all attendees.

The third step involved preparing to present which involved:

- deciding and creating any materials that would be used
- acknowledging characteristics of the group and making notes of solutions to support handling situations that may arise.

For your organisation and industry, work through the process Grace is taking above for a meeting of your choice and complete the steps outlined.

This will involve producing a:

- meeting plan
- draft and final agenda
- meeting invite
- materials to support meeting objectives.

CASE STUDY 25

GATHERING GOOD IDEAS

You manage a department with 26 employees divided into three work groups, each with a team leader. Your organisation recently completed an analysis of its quality management processes, which included observation of work practices, desktop analysis of completed documentation and collection of staff feedback through staff surveys.

From this analysis, the organisation established that employees both wanted and needed further professional development in three key areas – customer service, critical thinking and the new inventory software program.

Prior to organising professional development programs, the organisation has asked you to coordinate the following activities:

- Schedule a meeting where the senior team can take the employees through the analysis process and give an overview of key findings.
- Congratulate personnel on completing various successful projects.
- Invite internal and external suppliers to meet the three work group leaders.

Your manager has encouraged you to organise the meeting structure in a way that you feel would suit the objectives and the teams.

Questions

For each of the three activities outlined above:

1 What type of meeting would you hold and how would you organise it?
2 Where would the meeting occur?
3 What structure would you implement?
   a Would you have key speakers?
   b Would you include a presentation – what information would you share?
   c How long would the meeting go for?

CHAPTER ENDNOTES

1 Peter Gahan, Mladen Adamovic, Andrew Bevitt, Bill Harley, Josh Healy, Jesse E. Olsen, Max Theilacker, *Leadership at work: Do Australian leaders have what it takes?*, 2016, Centre for Workplace Leadership, University of Melbourne, http://apo.org.au/node/64175, accessed 10 April 2017.

2 Deloitte and Victorian Equal Opportunity and Human Rights Commission, 'Waiter, is that inclusion in my soup? A new recipe to improve business performance', 2013, https://www2.deloitte.com/content/dam/Deloitte/au/Documents/human-capital/deloitte-au-hc-diversity-inclusion-soup-0513.pdf

3 Cited in Arthur Block, *The complete Murphy's Law*, Price Stern Sloan, 1991, p. 4.

CHAPTER

26

SOLVING PROBLEMS AND MAKING DECISIONS

After completing this chapter, you will be able to:

26.1 make a range of problems and decisions while avoiding the common decision-making and problem-solving traps

26.2 apply a seven-step process for solving problems and making decisions

26.3 apply the correct decision-making style and avoid using inappropriate decision-making methods.

TRANSFERABLE SKILLS

The following transferable skills are covered in this chapter:

2 **Critical thinking and problem solving**
  2.1 Critical thinking

3 **Social competence**
  3.4 Leadership

OVERVIEW

If you want to be a leader-manager in today's organisational environment, you're going to have to make decisions and solve problems – lots of them! How you approach these two core functions will, to a significant extent, determine your success leading and managing your team. Treat problems as opportunities and use your decision-making authority to transform them into improvements and you and your team will thrive. Ignore them, hesitate, or make rash and reactive decisions and your tenure as a leader-manager is likely to be short-lived.

As you scan both the internal and external horizons, you will be able to see many problems looming before they materialise. Where this is the case, deal with them swiftly and decisively and they will be vanquished before any significant harm is done. But there will also be problems you don't see coming, both big and small. You'll need to deal with these also. The more complex problems will require your analytical and critical thinking skills to solve, but you'll still need to address them in a timely manner to prevent them causing damage.

Flatter organisational structures, rapidly changing technology, dynamic market conditions and an ever-changing organisational landscape has made the need for sound problem-solving and decision-making skills at all levels more important than ever. Not everyone will agree with or support your decisions, and some will miss the mark, but if your decisions are carefully thought-out and taken with both organisational and team objectives in mind, you're going to get more right than wrong. This chapter shows you how to recognise and solve problems properly and make sound and timely decisions.

SNAPSHOT

Decisions ... decisions ...

Khalid Bibi, the leader-manager of the local council's Sports and Recreation Centre, is returning from the weekly management meeting when he passes the chief aerobics instructor. She says that her team of casual instructors is becoming more vociferous in their complaints about the ventilation in the gym and the problem needs to be sorted out quickly. Then Mattie Smith, one of the best receptionists he has ever worked with, catches up with him to say that she has been offered another job with an increase in pay and responsibilities, and she wants to speak to him about opportunities at the council.

When he gets back to his desk, Khalid finds himself faced with a number of additional issues. An email from the general manager of the centre asks for his thoughts about whether, and how, to implement a proposed customer service program. There is a message from his partner requesting that he phone home immediately, and another from the maintenance contractor warning that problems seem to be developing with the pool filtration system. A quick check of the monthly costs analysis shows a trend towards increased chemical and cleaning costs for the pool and, to top it all off, there is a candidate for a job opening in the cleaning staff waiting to be interviewed.

Everything always seems to happen at once, thinks Khalid, as he considers which problems to tackle first, and which can safely wait.

26.1 Understanding the range of problems and decisions and the traps to avoid

> Anyone can hold the helm when the sea is calm.
>
> Publilius Syrus (freed Roman slave), *Sententiae*, C. J. Clay, London, 1895.

Making decisions and solving problems is central to your role as a leader-manager so your first decision needs to be to tackle them head on as they arise rather than procrastinating and trying to skirt around them. You'll need to rank each problem based on its complexity and urgency and allocate your time accordingly to find a solution. There will be a number of factors you'll need to take into account as you do so, including stakeholder feelings, opinions and situations, the needs of your team, and your organisation's vision, values and strategic goals.

Whether your problems and the decisions you need to make relate to customers, employees, processes, products, technology or the service you provide, they all need to be approached in the same or a similar manner. The golden rules for approaching problems are:

- Refrain from immediately reacting to a problem. A panicked decision or one made based on an emotional response can cause emotional or physical harm to staff, compromise customer relationships, lead to a waste of organisational resources or cause damage to equipment.
- Remain calm and then, with a clear head, gather information and diagnose the cause of the problem. Once you know the cause, you can work on finding a solution.

Decide now or later ...

Transferable skills
2.1 Critical thinking

Problems don't improve with age and rarely just disappear. The best time to solve a problem is in its early stages before it builds into something bigger and becomes a serious threat to your organisation's operations. When a problem or decision comes to your attention, assess how serious a threat it poses and how soon that threat, if realised, will cause harm. Give those that are serious (i.e. pose significant harm or damage) and urgent (i.e. will cause harm in the near future) a high priority. Give those that are serious but not urgent a high priority as well because if you don't, they can quickly become urgent and then you'll need to come up with a decision under pressure. Place any that might take care of themselves or pose little threat aside and check on them later.

You also need to ask yourself whether the situation really requires your involvement. If it doesn't and you're confident it can be handled competently by someone else, don't be scared to delegate decisions that you don't need to be involved in and any that are urgent but not important. It goes without saying that you probably don't need to waste your time and effort on those that are neither important nor urgent.

... or pay the price

A number of unfortunate outcomes affect leader-managers and teams that don't follow systematic problem-solving procedures. Ironically, one of the worst results is a lack of time to solve problems properly because people are too busy putting out 'spot fires', dealing with crises and implementing 'quick fixes'. As a result, many 'solutions' that are applied are actually 'patch-ups', which do not provide a long-term solution. Failing to solve the original problem means it will resurface at some point later on and by that time it will have created new problems.

To avoid this type of situation from occurring:

- Don't patch a problem. When you can't fix it properly, leave it until you can, but if it's important, make sure it's added to your high-priority list.
- Keep investigating a problem until you diagnose its real cause. A diagnosis based on your gut feeling can work but utilise the systematic analytical tools and techniques outlined later in this text to provide evidence-based backup to support your diagnosis.
- Address the most urgent problems first: when you have many competing problems, prioritise them and work on them in priority order. Tick each off your list as you resolve it.
- Remove solutions that don't work: when your first attempt doesn't fix the problem, remove the solution. Once it's removed, try an alternative approach.[1]

Thinking about any current problems in your life or decisions you are required to make, how would you assess these in terms of importance and urgency: high or low?

Variations in complexity

One of the many facets of good management is the ability to solve problems of varying degrees of complexity. For some decisions and problems there is clearly one best action to take and it's obvious what that action is. That's when you need a programmed decision or a standard operating procedure that provides a consistent solution so time and energy are not wasted figuring out how to fix the same problem over and over again. Standard responses also make dealing with routine matters easier, faster and more reliable. When there is more than one possible action but those actions are predictable, you can apply algorithms such as the Five Keys to help you think through the potential solutions.

Sometimes an automatic, computerised response can be put in place. Computers can use decision rules and algorithms – a series of logical steps – to make and process many programmed decisions without any intervention by people. Although automation can be difficult to develop and the decision criteria may change, it is accurate and quick. Take, for example, automated inventory control and purchasing; once you have determined the minimum and maximum levels of stock to be carried and worked out the optimal order size, a computer keeps track of the use of each inventory item and automatically prepares and transmits an order when levels drop below a specified point.

At the other end of the complexity scale are problems and decisions that aren't linear and logical because they involve unpredictable events and ever-changing activities and relationships. Consider the following:

- What is the best way to distribute work to the team?
- What is the best way to divide scarce resources between users?
- What is the best way to improve services to customers and win their loyalty?
- What is the best way to deal with a major environmental disaster or an epidemic that severely compromises your organisation's ability to operate?
- What is the best way to reach your customers through social media?

In an increasingly complex and demanding business environment, where predictability is far from common and no one can forecast the future with any degree of certainty, when the unexpected keeps happening and leaves people scratching their heads, the importance of making wise non-programmed decisions is increasing. The variations in complexity of problems and decisions call for different approaches, as illustrated in Figure 26.1 and summarised in Table 26.1.

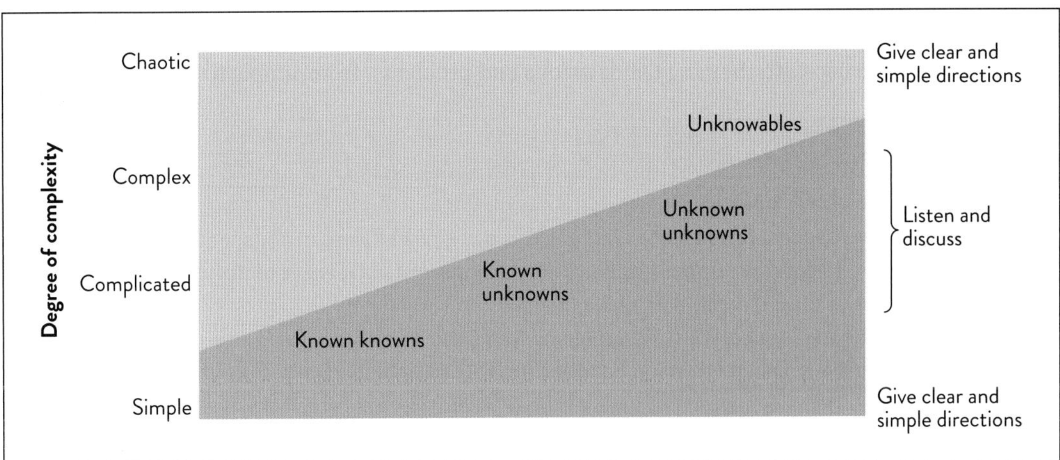

FIGURE 26.1 Gradations of complexity in problems and decisions

TABLE 26.1 Approaching problems and decisions of varying complexity

Situation	Description	Response called for	Action
Simple situations	Straightforward situations, predictable circumstances, clear cause and effect, same patterns repeat, many *known knowns*	Programmed decisions, best practice procedures, established policies and practices, standard operating procedures, computerised response	Communicate clearly and directly

Situation	Description	Response called for	Action
Complicated situations	Several possible right answers, a cause and effect takes expertise or time and patience to see, *known unknowns*	Programmed decisions, find the cause of the problem with an algorithm that points to the correct action, work with experts and others to analyse, diagnose and probe the situation	Listen and discuss, investigate several options before reaching a decision, but beware of analysis paralysis
Complex situations	The whole is greater than the sum of its parts, the situation is dynamic and unpredictable, there are no right answers, *unknown unknowns*	Creativity and innovation	Probe the situation, look for patterns and let solutions emerge through investigation and discussion
Chaotic situations	Constantly changing, no 'rules' and no right answers, little time to think, many *unknowables*	Act quickly, establish control, then assess the effectiveness of your actions and fine-tune or try something different	Communicate clearly and directly

The seven steps to solving problems and making decisions described in the next section of this chapter are ideal to use with the range of decisions and problems, from simple to complex.

INDUSTRY INSIGHTS

Automated decision-making

Cemex, a Mexican-headquartered global cement company, paints pipes in all its factories with the same colour code. Transferring employees don't need to figure out the way a factory is set up and don't make expensive or potentially dangerous mistakes.[2]

But with more complex decisions and problems, you need to put your brain into gear. The thornier the problem, the more you need to stand back and look at the underlying principles that are operating. Considering only surface, or superficial, parts of the problem prevents you from making a sound decision or finding a really workable solution to the problem.

The traps to avoid

There are, however, some traps that you need to be on the lookout for and try to avoid. With awareness and practice, you can avoid falling into the first four traps described in the following sections and you can avoid the final seven 'brain traps' when you learn to recognise them and consciously override your brain's programming.

The reluctance, haste and hesitation traps

The reluctance, haste and hesitation traps speak for themselves and we have all seen at some stage or another those who have fallen into them. These include the conflict avoiders who hesitate to upset anyone, those who would worry or agonise over every decision no matter how small, and the escapists who shuffle their facts, feet, figures and papers, trying to fool themselves and others that they are 'working on it' rather than face the problem head on.

Two more traps to avoid are being too hasty or too slow at reaching decisions and solving problems. Quick decisions and problem-solving frequently fail to consider people's feelings or the facts, while hesitation and endless 'research' can cause unnecessary bottlenecks, delays and frustration, and opportunities slip past. See Figure 26.2 for tips on what you should do and avoid doing when decision-making.

DO	AVOID
Decide whether the decision is a big or small one	Deciding in haste through impatience
Focus on what you want rather than what you don't want	Putting off decisions or solving problems until it becomes a crisis

FIGURE 26.2 Tips for effective decision-making and problem-solving

The ignoring near misses trap

Don't ignore everyday small failures that cause no immediate damage – these are warnings and are often the precursor to something major happening that causes significant harm, hurt or damage. Rather than turn a blind eye to near misses, treat them as problems to be investigated and solved before the failures become more serious.

Researchers investigating near misses in dozens of companies in a variety of industries have concluded that multiple narrow escapes preceded and foreshadowed every disaster and business crisis they studied. The problem is twofold:

1 *Normalisation of deviance bias:* over time, people become oblivious to problems and accept them as normal.
2 *Outcome bias:* when a glitch doesn't cause damage, people focus on the 'successful' outcome rather than the (often) pure good luck that allowed the narrow escape.[3]

The well from hell and bad apples

Statistically speaking, when you give an accident enough opportunities to happen, it happens. Take, for example, the series of ignored near misses and poor decisions that resulted in incalculable damage to the environment and BP when, in April 2010, the Deepwater Horizon oil well blew out. The resulting fire killed 11 people, sank the rig and triggered a massive underwater spill that took months to contain.

Warning signs, rather than prompting investigations, were taken as an indication that safety and operating procedures worked (outcome bias), and the fact that many wells in the Gulf of Mexico suffered similar problems enticed BP employees to view the problems as routine (normalisation bias). In fact, there had been dozens of minor blowouts but disaster had always been averted by sheer luck, such as a favourable wind direction and no one welding near the gas leak at the time of the blowout.

In another example, when Apple launched its iPhone 4 in June 2010, complaints about dropped calls and poor signal strength poured in almost immediately. Customers complained loudly in social and mainstream media while CEO Steve Jobs described the dropped calls as a 'non-issue' and blamed the users for holding the phone incorrectly. Eventually, customers filed class action lawsuits, including a suit alleging fraud by concealment, negligence, intentional misrepresentation and defective design.

Like the problems with BP's Deepwater Horizon well, the problems underlying Apple's crisis had long been present. The flaw allowing a drop in signal strength had been present in earlier iPhones, as well as in competitors' phones, for years and came to be seen as increasingly acceptable (normalisation bias), and the lack of outcry over shortcomings with previous models was seen as evidence of a clever strategy rather than good luck (outcome bias).[4]

The excessive optimism trap

Some people tend to be overly optimistic about the outcome of a decision or plan and to underestimate its potential negative outcomes. Adopting an approach where you not only critically analyse the potential outcomes of a decision or solution but do so with a focus of 'what is the worst thing that could happen?' means you are more likely to anticipate negative outcomes and be ready for them with contingency plans if they arise. When you're feeling completely confident, find a devil's advocate to bounce your decision or solution off or use a force-field analysis to identify any weak spots in your decisions or solutions. Think about events related to the success of your decision or plan that you can't control, too, and have your 'Plan Bs' ready just in case.

Brain traps

These next seven traps are more treacherous. They arise not because you haven't followed the seven steps described below, are reluctant, hasty or hesitant, blindly biased, optimistic or overconfident, but because your brain sabotages your decisions. The human brain is wired with unconscious programs, called *heuristics*, to help us deal with complexity. These heuristics are meant to rule out the seemingly irrelevant and help people think problems and decisions through quickly and easily. But the irrelevant is sometimes relevant and speed and ease aren't always a good thing.

In evolutionary terms, our mental programs made sense. Today, it means that we go with the mental programming that's served us well over 200 000 years, especially when we don't have the inclination or the time to work out a decision logically and methodically. But it doesn't necessarily mean the resulting decision is a good decision.

Each of the following seven heuristics can work in isolation or in combination with the others. They lurk in every stage of the problem-solving or decision-making process. High-risk decisions leave people particularly prone to them. Forewarned is forearmed. The key to beating the tricks of the mind listed in **Figure 26.3** is to stay alert and recognise when you're succumbing to them.

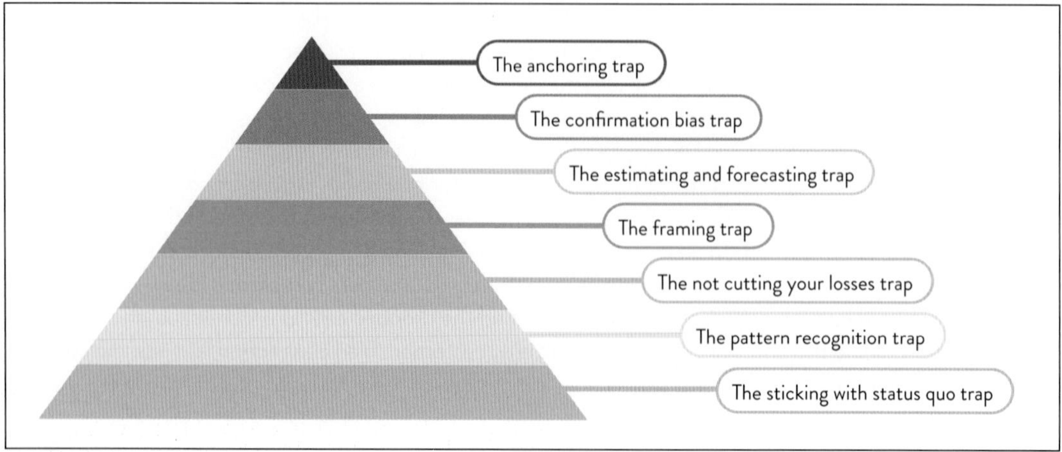

FIGURE 26.3 The seven brain traps

The anchoring trap

It's easy to give too much weight to what you see or hear first and last, whether it's estimates, evidence, ideas, information or opinions. An off-the-cuff comment, prejudice, previous similar experiences and stereotypes can also act as anchors, even in the face of strong counter-evidence. Anchors influence the way you think about a problem or decision and can even set the terms on which a decision is made.

You can't avoid this trap, but you can reduce its impact. Be aware, and beware, of your first and last impressions, and the first and last pieces of information you receive, and make a conscious effort to allocate fair weight to what you learnt in between. Take the trouble to view problems from different perspectives and don't automatically stick with whatever occurs to you first. Be open-minded and seek a variety of views, opinions and information. Also make sure you hold back your own opinions and ideas until last so that you don't unintentionally anchor your team members with your own views and create a leader-influenced groupthink mentality.

The confirmation bias trap

Your brain seeks evidence that confirms and supports your opinion or preferred decision and avoids information that contradicts it. This affects both where you go to collect information and how you interpret it, and it causes you to put too much weight on supporting evidence and too little on opposing evidence.

The best way to avoid this is to make sure you never decide first and then figure out how to justify it later. Always gather your facts and conduct your research first, objectively analyse the evidence it produces and allow this to guide your decision. Asking someone to play devil's advocate and argue against your preferred decision is also a good checking mechanism. When asking others' opinions, avoid leading questions which will direct the other person to provide you with the answer you want or expect.

The estimating and forecasting trap

The accuracy of your estimates and forecasts depends largely on the feedback and data on which you base them as well as the predictability of the event. Where you have little data or previous similar events to look back at, or where uncertain and unfamiliar events present, this becomes more difficult.

Regardless of whether the event to be forecasted is familiar and predictable or not, don't become overconfident or, alternatively, overcautious. Be wary of relying too heavily on past events or trends or on dramatic events that have left a strong impression.

Be disciplined when you need to make forecasts or assess probabilities. Consider the extremes first; this also means you won't be anchored by your initial 'best guess'. Examine all your assumptions and try not to be guided by impressions. Use accurate facts and figures when you can, and when you can't, make the best decision you can with the evidence in front of you and be prepared to be wrong, cut your losses and change course as may be required.

The framing trap

The way you frame, or describe, a problem or decision is important. It guides you down one path or another, towards the status quo or away from it, towards taking a risk or towards a position of safety. For example, losses loom larger in our brains than gains, and, especially when the stakes are high, our brain automatically errs on the side of caution.

The thing to remember is that frames cause distortions. The more important the decision or problem, the more important it is to word it in different ways. Don't automatically accept the way problems or decisions are presented to you. Restate them in neutral ways that combine gains and losses and reflect different reference points. Ask yourself how your thinking would change if you word, or frame, the problem or decision differently.

The not cutting your losses trap

Sometimes, even when we know we have made a decision that is wrong, we are reluctant to abandon it, cut our losses and change course. This is where you need to be honest with yourself, admit that you, or at least your decision, was wrong and set it aside. Known as a 'sunk cost' this cost has already happened and is not recoverable. You can't change what has happened but you can take mitigation actions to prevent it from becoming any worse. Your decision may have caused loss of time, effort or even money but trying to turn a poor decision into a good one is a 'fool's errand', so pick yourself up, dust yourself down and start again. Look to the future and think about what you have to *gain* by cutting your losses, rather than looking backwards and seeing what you're *losing*.

The pattern recognition trap

The brain is hardwired to recognise patterns and, to do so, it pulls together information from up to 30 different parts of the brain. When faced with a new situation, we make assumptions based on prior experiences. People tend to believe that they can safely act on their experience, even where that experience is limited. Whether it's new leader-managers facing unfamiliar situations or old hands facing decisions or circumstances not often encountered, the belief that what has held true in the past will continue to hold true can lead to unwarranted confidence and incorrect assumptions. Given the rapidly changing operating environment, this heuristic is a bigger trap for the current generation of leader-managers than for previous generations.

Making assumptions based on previous experience can work well but it can also mislead you, particularly when you're dealing with seemingly familiar situations that turn out to be out-of-the-ordinary. You may think you understand what's going on, but in reality, you don't. Relying on previous experience can also mislead you when your past experience is no longer relevant. There is barely an hour in a day let alone a day itself where change doesn't occur. This means that what worked well last year, last week or yesterday may not necessarily work now. Conditions, technology, people and economic situations all change, and these changes influence what works and what doesn't.

To avoid this trap, look for differences between the current situation and previous similar situations and think about whether you're seeing patterns that you want to see because the resulting decision suits you. Involve people who could challenge your thinking and gather a range of opinions and ideas before acting.

The sticking with the status quo trap

It often seems easier to continue with things as they are. When we are unsure of what might happen, the conventional wisdom is often to 'wait and see'. Doing nothing when faced with tough choices can be very tempting, while taking action requires courage and conviction. The less action you take, the less responsibility you may feel and the less criticism you are open to. The pull of the status quo becomes even stronger when you are faced with several options.

Maintaining the status quo may actually be the right choice but don't submit to it just because it's easy, comfortable and abdicates you from responsibility. Keep your objectives clearly in mind and ask yourself whether the current situation is working well or would another alternative work even better. A good question to ask yourself is: 'Would I select the status quo if it were just another alternative?'

When you're stuck

When you're having trouble solving a problem, take some time to let your mind wander and daydream a bit. This activates problem-solving areas of the brain – the 'executive network' associated with high-level, complex problem-solving.[5]

'Subconscious incubation' works well, too. As you're falling asleep, think about a problem you are trying to solve or a decision you need to make. What do you know about it already? What do you need to know? What do you want the solution to offer? Then go to sleep and let your subconscious work on it. More often than not, you have your answer within a few nights of incubation – it pops into your mind upon wakening or during the next day.

Thinking about the current problem or decision you reflected on earlier, is there a trap holding you back from taking action?

26.2 Using seven steps to solve problems and make decisions

> When you give a problem some thinking time, it's amazing what you can come up with. You just need to make people feel comfortable about having a conversation and thinking through a difficult problem.
>
> César Melgoza of Geoscape, 'Seeing potential in every pause', The Corner Office, Adam Bryant, *New York Times*, 22 December 2015.

Whatever difficult problems you may have solved recently or sensible decisions you have made, you probably followed similar steps to the seven steps discussed in the following. Notice the three distinct mental processes that those seven steps, summarised in Figure 26.4, go through: analysing, imagining and evaluating.

As you apply these seven steps, remember that the more complex the problem you're dealing with, the more important it is to intervene at a higher level, where your actions can have the greatest impact. Table 26.2 shows what to consider from the highest to the lowest level. For instance, training people isn't helpful when the incentives to use the training are missing. Providing incentives can't help when the procedures are flawed. Designing sophisticated systems isn't much good when they're aimed at achieving a poor strategy. When you're tempted to use an easy solution, remember H. L. Mencken's advice: 'There is always an easy solution to every human problem – neat, plausible and wrong'.[6]

Phase 1: Analysing – explore the problem

In Phase 1, you draw on your patience, clear and logical thinking, and a bit of intuitive insight to analyse the problem. You need to start by determining where you are now and why, where you want to be and then look for the source of the problem.

Step 1: Identify the problem clearly

Here's what Albert Einstein said about the importance of knowing precisely what the problem is: 'If I were given one hour to save the planet, I would spend 59 minutes defining the problem and one

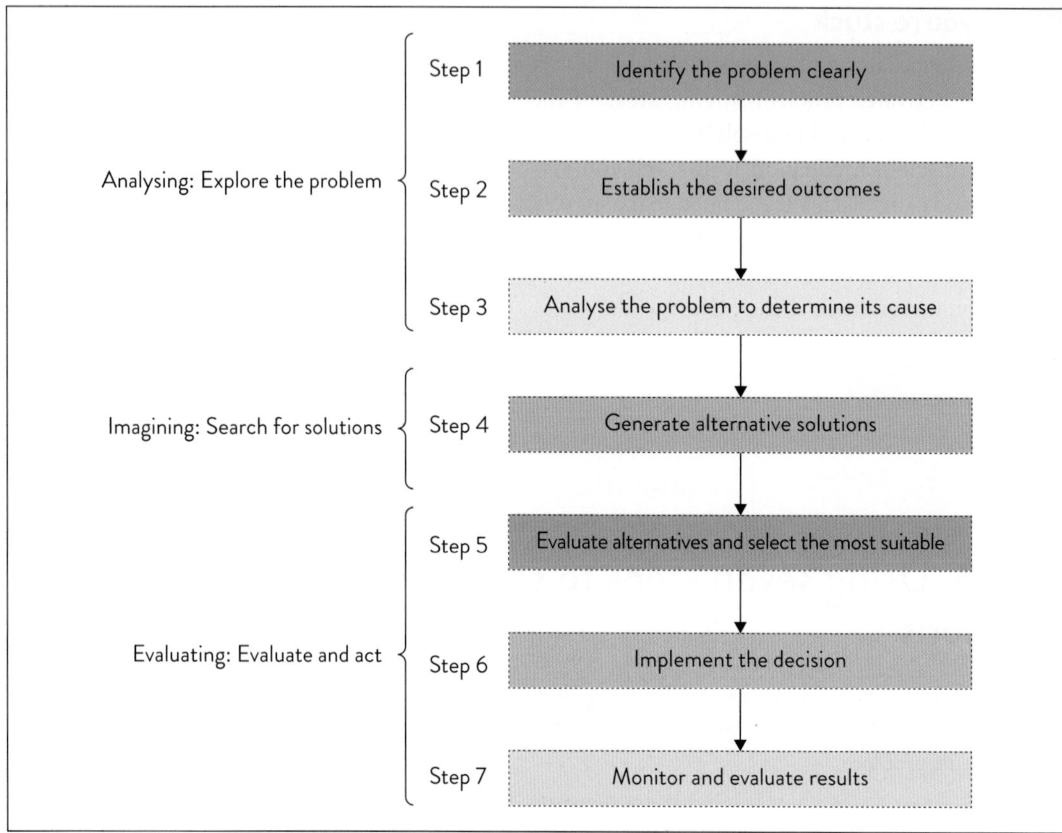

FIGURE 26.4 The problem-solving and decision-making process

TABLE 26.2 Intervene at the highest level you can

Strategy or objectives	Are these appropriate?
Systems	Is there something awkward or wrong with the procedures or with the allocation of responsibilities?
Incentives and information	Do the rewards (psychological as well as monetary) support your objectives? Do you have enough information?
Individual performance	Is the problem a 'people problem' that training or motivation could help?

minute resolving it.'[7] Take Einstein's advice – it's well worth spending time on this step. Say, for example, that you notice your team's equipment seems to be breaking down more than usual, or someone comments that 'our equipment is less reliable than it used to be', or your work team has brainstormed a list of problems and decided to work on fixing the problem of equipment breakdowns first. However, 'too many equipment breakdowns' doesn't describe the problem precisely enough to work on. After asking and answering a number of questions, your problem statement for 'too many equipment breakdowns' might become: 'For the past three quarters, 60 per cent of portable equipment over two years old used in the vans and in home offices has been failing before its service warranty expires; in previous quarters, the failure rate was 40 per cent.'

A clear problem statement like this tells you what to work on and why. No matter how pressing the need for a solution seems to be, don't move on to Step 2 until you have clearly described the problem you intend to solve. Using the example of two problems, Table 26.3 shows you some questions to help you define the problems clearly.

TABLE 26.3 Using detail to clarify problems

General problem	Questions to ask
Too many equipment breakdowns	How many breakdowns? Which equipment? What is the nature of the breakdowns? When do they occur? What is happening when they occur? Who is involved? How regularly has the equipment been serviced? Has anything changed?
Too many accidents	Are the number of accidents increasing, decreasing or staying the same? What is the specific nature of the accidents? Where do they happen? When do they occur? Who is involved? Exactly how many accidents of each type are there and how does this compare with previous periods and similar workplaces? Has anything changed?

Step 2: Establish the desired outcomes

Alice in Wonderland asked: 'Would you tell me, please, which way I ought to go from here?' 'That depends a good deal on where you want to get to', she was advised. 'I don't much care where', Alice replied. 'Then it doesn't matter which way you go'.[8] This highlights the need to think about the results you want from the decision or solution to the problem. What position do you want to be in after you have taken action and how can you tell whether your action is working?

A clear outcome helps you concentrate your thinking and direct your aim, and helps you in Step 5 when you select the most suitable solution and Step 7 when you evaluate the effectiveness of your decision or action. Reaching a perfect decision or solution to a problem may not always be possible but at least when you have clearly defined goals, you have something concrete to aim for that you have identified as the best possible outcome. This helps you and your team concentrate on what you are trying to find answers to and keeps you on track.

Try making a 'how to ...' statement to set goals. For example:

- how to ensure availability of raw materials to the front line when they are needed without tying up extra working capital in stockholding
- how to get more storage space in the administration section
- how to increase battery sales in stores
- how to reduce the failure rate of portable equipment over two years old
- how to respond to 80 per cent of inquiries for quotations within three working days

- how to serve customers more quickly during the lunch hour
- how to speed up the invoicing process at the checkout.

For complex or very important problems, divide your criteria into *musts* and *wants* – what must your decision achieve and, ideally, what other outcome or outcomes would you also like it to produce? Clearly establishing musts and wants puts you in a good position to select the best alternative when the time comes and to then determine how well it is working.

Step 3: Analyse the problem to determine its cause

Now that you've defined the problem clearly and know what you want the solution to achieve, it's time to analyse the problem. 'Analyse' comes from the Greek verb meaning to undo or loosen, and that's what you do with problems – you pull them apart (staying alert to your brain traps) and break them down into their smallest elements.

Analysing problems helps you identify *symptoms*, which result from problems but are not the problem itself. Symptoms can alert you that a problem exists, but until you know its cause, you can't fix it. If you only focus on solving symptoms, the real problem will remain unsolved and as it recurs again and again, it will often bring with it a bunch of new problems.

The only way to fix a problem is to find its cause and remove it. You can achieve this by analysing the problem and untangling it from its symptoms. Once you've pinpointed the cause, you can look for a solution that removes it. When you can't remove the cause of the problem in order to fix it, try looking for a solution that minimises the cause.

INDUSTRY INSIGHTS

The cost of treating symptoms

As the US$200 million Mars Climate Orbiter headed towards Mars to study the Martian weather and atmosphere, it drifted slightly off course four times. Each time, managers treated the symptom with small trajectory adjustments but didn't investigate the reason for the drifting.

When it neared Mars, the spacecraft disintegrated rather than entering into orbit. That's when NASA looked for, and found, the cause of the problem – programmers had used imperial rather than metric units in their software coding. The ignoring near misses trap resulting from the apparent success in treating the symptoms lulled some of the world's best brains into thinking they had rectified the problem.[9]

Just as with the brain traps discussed earlier, guard against jumping to conclusions about the cause of a problem. Examine the problem from all angles – competitors, colleagues, customers, management, the public, suppliers and so on. Conducting a thorough analysis in the first instance saves you a lot of time and trouble in the long run because you won't waste time 'solving' symptoms. In fact, a clear and accurate analysis of a problem sometimes points directly to its solution.

Gather facts, ideas and the opinions of others that may help your analysis. Test your theories before you act on them. You may not be able to get all the facts to help you with your analysis, but use those you have as well as those you can get without too much trouble or expense. Table 26.4 shows you how to analyse and then solve a simple problem.

TABLE 26.4 Analysing and solving the problem

Analysis	Problem
Step 1: Analyse the symptoms	Home computer suddenly switches off
Step 2: Identify possible causes	Loose wire to terminal Power failure Blown fuse
Step 3: Test these possible causes to see whether one caused the problem	Check the wires to the computer Check the power by switching on a light Check the fuse board

Thinking about the current problem or decision you reflected on earlier, can you identify any symptoms?

Cause-and-effect diagrams

A cause-and-effect diagram, also known as an *Ishikawa diagram* (after its creator) and a **fishbone diagram** (because of its appearance), allow you to 'see' a problem from its various aspects and identify its most important features. They are especially helpful with complicated problems that require you to sort out a maze of facts to isolate the most likely cause(s).

To make a fishbone diagram, put the problem in the square at the 'head' of the fish. Then decide the possible categories of causes of the problem and show them as major 'bones' off the central 'spine' of the fish. It is usual to break a problem down into four components, but don't let this constrain you – use three or five categories when you need to. Always note who prepared the diagram and the date. See Table 26.5 for some categories you can use to break problems apart.

TABLE 26.5 Categories to use to break problems apart

Clear goals	Job design	Rewards
Customers	Machinery, equipment, tools	Systems and procedures
Efficiency	Materials	Team culture
Employees	Methods	Time
General public	Money and funds	Training
Information	Policies	Work environment
Internal policies	Procedures	

Figure 26.5 shows a cause-and-effect analysis for the problem of employee turnover. You can see that four possible causes of the problem are considered: employees, rewards, work environment and equipment. These possible causes may not suit every problem.

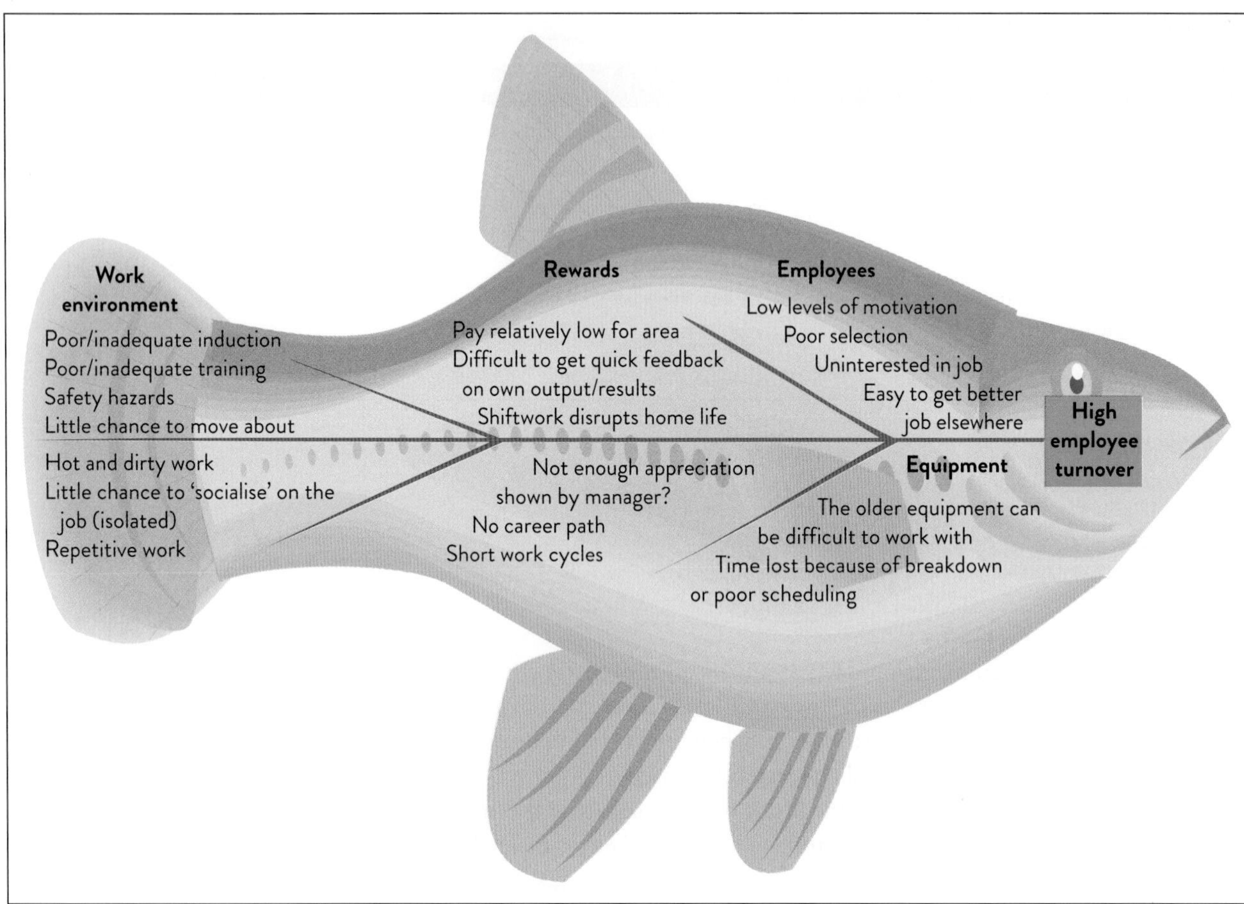

FIGURE 26.5 A cause-and-effect diagram

When you think of a possible cause of a problem that could go under more than one category on your diagram, just add it somewhere. The important thing to remember here is that you are looking at the problem from all angles, which is essential to a thorough problem analysis. When you've brainstormed as many possible causes of the problem as you can, stand back and consider each. Identify which seem most important to you and circle those that warrant further investigation.

Ask 'Why?' five times

Asking 'Why?' five times helps you to drill down to the cause of a problem. Follow these steps:

1 Define your problem clearly.
2 Brainstorm or use a fishbone diagram to determine possible causes.
3 Decide the most likely cause(s).
4 Ask 'Why?' five times for each likely cause to work out the real reason.

Here is how the technique of asking 'Why?' could work to determine the most likely cause of costly employee turnover in your team. You have defined your turnover problem clearly as employee turnover being consistently 20 per cent higher than comparable local sites over the past 24 months.

From your fishbone diagram you decided that the two most likely causes are poor selection and poor induction. Your 'Why?' chain for poor selection might look like this:

- *Why* have I hired the wrong people?
- *Why* am I not applying effective recruitment and selection techniques?

- *Why* am I not confident in my ability to use these techniques?
- *Why* do I need more training?

This is the logical end to this 'Why?' chain. Four 'Whys?' were enough to arrive at a possible solution – get more training. But what happens when four whys are not enough? You need five whys. Here is the 'Why?' chain for poor induction:

- *Why* aren't new employees learning key skills and fitting in properly?
- *Why* isn't induction providing the right information and motivation?
- *Why* is it too ad hoc? Nothing is written down.
- *Why* haven't I approached it in a disciplined and systematic way?
- *Why* don't I know enough yet about developing induction programs?

As you can see, by the time you've reached the end of the 'Why?' chain, the solution often becomes clear.

Phase 2: Imagining – search for solutions

In Phase 2, you let go of assumptions, longstanding beliefs and preconceived ideas and put yourself on high alert for your brain traps. Look beyond the obvious and use your creativity, innovativeness and imagination to generate viable and novel solutions.

Step 4: Generate alternative solutions

The more possible solutions you have to choose from, the greater the chance of fixing a problem properly. When you have several desired outcomes, compare one against another to determine which option would best achieve Objective 1. Objective 2? Objective 3? Then you can develop a matrix or checklist of ideas and see which solution occurs most often.

Here are some things to remember about finding suitable solutions:

- The best solutions are often the most difficult to find and will require you to develop several possible solutions and keep an open mind to all of them. This means you will need to let go of your fixed ideas about what caused a problem or how it should be solved and refrain from jumping to hastily formed conclusions.
- Don't frame your search for solutions as a Yes–No; for example, 'Should we upgrade our equipment?' Instead, ask something like, 'What benefits and risk would come from upgrading our equipment?' or 'Which equipment would be worth considering upgrading?'
- The best solutions sometimes come not from logical thinking but from creative thinking. Seemingly 'wild' or 'crazy' solutions can lead to some great ideas. This makes it essential to keep Step 4, generating solutions, completely separate from Step 5, evaluating them.
- Don't settle for the first solution that occurs to you – keep looking. You need plenty of options to select from. When you're tempted to choose the first (or last) action you think of, remember the anchoring heuristic. Brainstorming is a good way to tap into your creativity and develop lots of options.

Some guidelines to remember when it's time to come up with possible solutions include:

- bring underlying assumptions out into the open, which ensures you're aware of them and can change them or drop them when they're unrealistic
- review the big picture because this helps you assess your options and check that the one you select is best for the organisation

- don't waste effort, money and time by gathering data indiscriminately. Seek information that is useful and relevant and find out only what you need to know
- seek help when you need it by asking other people what they think, especially informed people whose judgement you trust or experts
- work on eliminating the cause of the problem rather than just covering up its symptoms. Band-aid solutions don't work in the long term and are likely to make the problem worse when it resurfaces later.

Brainstorming

Done correctly, brainstorming boosts creativity and generates lots of ideas quickly. You can brainstorm alone or with a group of people. Six to nine people is a good number because smaller groups have trouble generating enough ideas and some participants can be left out in larger groups.

When brainstorming in groups, seat people informally – in a circle of chairs, for example. Use a flip chart, whiteboard, butcher's paper or an electronic whiteboard to record the ideas that are generated so they can be saved for future reference. Write up the ideas as people call them out without changing, editing or 'improving' the words. Everyone should be able to see the ideas list being generated so they can build on each other's ideas. Write clearly and large enough for everyone to read the ideas easily.

Make sure the topic is specific and everyone understands it as well as the goal of the brainstorming session; that is, not just 'to brainstorm' but, for example, 'to brainstorm possible causes of a particular problem' or 'to brainstorm possible solutions for a particular problem'. Make sure everyone has a say; use the 'round-robin method' (explanation following) when necessary.

Here are some more brainstorming guidelines:

- Don't expect to come up with a great idea every time. When you have this expectation, the pressure can stifle your brain's ability to freewheel.
- Go for quantity. Forget normal constraints and limitations. Ideas can be 'sensibilised' later. Wait until Step 5, when you evaluate alternatives and select the most suitable, to consider quality.
- Have some fun. Laughter and fun encourage creativity.
- Let your thoughts freewheel. Let them hop easily from one line of thinking to another, so that a continual flow of ideas streams out. Don't constrain your thinking in any way.
- Suspend judgement. New ideas are delicate and easily killed by a frown, a sneer or a wisecrack; don't worry about whether they are good or even workable. Aim to produce as many ideas as you can before evaluating them, because even the silliest idea can spark off a great one through a process known as 'cross-fertilisation'.

There are two ways to generate ideas in a group brainstorming session. The first is to let everyone call out their ideas as they come to mind. This works well with enthusiastic and involved groups who are experienced at brainstorming. The second is known as the *round-robin* method. Here, each person calls out their idea in turn, one after the other, or says 'pass' when they have nothing to contribute when their turn comes up. Keep going until everyone has 'passed' on the same round.

Whether brainstorming on your own or with a group, don't give up at the first sign of ideas running out. When you wait a minute or two, more ideas are sure to come. A good rule of thumb is to keep going through three 'dry periods' before stopping to evaluate the ideas.

INDUSTRY INSIGHTS

How three heavyweights make decisions

Amazon founder Jeff Bezos believed that informed decisions were so important that his senior executives read a six-page narratively structured memo (one written in full sentences and carefully thought through) for about 30 minutes, in silence, before meetings began. This guaranteed the group's attention and promoted clear thinking on the part of both the readers and the writers. Bezos also kept in mind how things might change and spurned the conventional wisdom about how things were typically done, preferring to reinvent everything, even small things.

Stephen Borg, global director of strategy and market development at electronics manufacturer AOPEN, emphasises consultation throughout the decision-making process and leaves difficult decisions until after his morning exercise, which gives him clarity and takes away some of the emotion.

Co-founder of travel search website Adioso, Tom Howard, says he thinks about which of the alternatives can deliver the biggest upside and looks for the best outcome with the fewest downsides.[10]

Phase 3: Evaluating – evaluate and act

In this final phase of problem-solving and decision-making, you evaluate the possibilities, select the one likely to work best and implement it. It is a good idea to test it first if you have the opportunity. Problem-solving now morphs into decision-making, and to be a good decision-maker you need the ability to think clearly and logically, and to implement and follow through your decision with attention to detail.

Step 5: Evaluate alternatives and select the most suitable

Every potential solution you developed in Step 4 is likely to have some good points and some bad points. Evaluating them helps you select the one that can achieve the objectives you set in Step 2 in the best way possible.

Some other factors to consider when choosing between alternatives are shown in Figure 26.6. An increasingly critical factor to consider is the rapid changes in the marketplace, society, the economy, technology and the workplace, and, of course, how the world and individual countries have responded to the COVID-19 pandemic.

Follow the principle of *Ockham's razor*: go for the simplest alternative that will work or the one that makes the fewest untested assumptions. Other decision-making aids are cost–benefit analysis and force-field analysis, which were covered earlier in this text.

When you have reached the decision, attend to the finer details. When is the decision to be implemented? Who is accountable for implementing it? Who is affected by it that you need to bring on board? Who has to be informed about it? Who has to understand and approve it? What would indicate this decision is not working?

Don't be too quick to settle on an option. When you think you've identified the right one, assume you can't implement that option and ask: what else could we do? This approach will help you to generate more alternatives.

Step 6: Implement the decision

Now it's time to implement your carefully thought through solution. To do this, you need to complete three important tasks:

1 *Plan:* decide what must be done, by when and by whom. Use the who, how, what, where, why and when prompts to develop your plan.

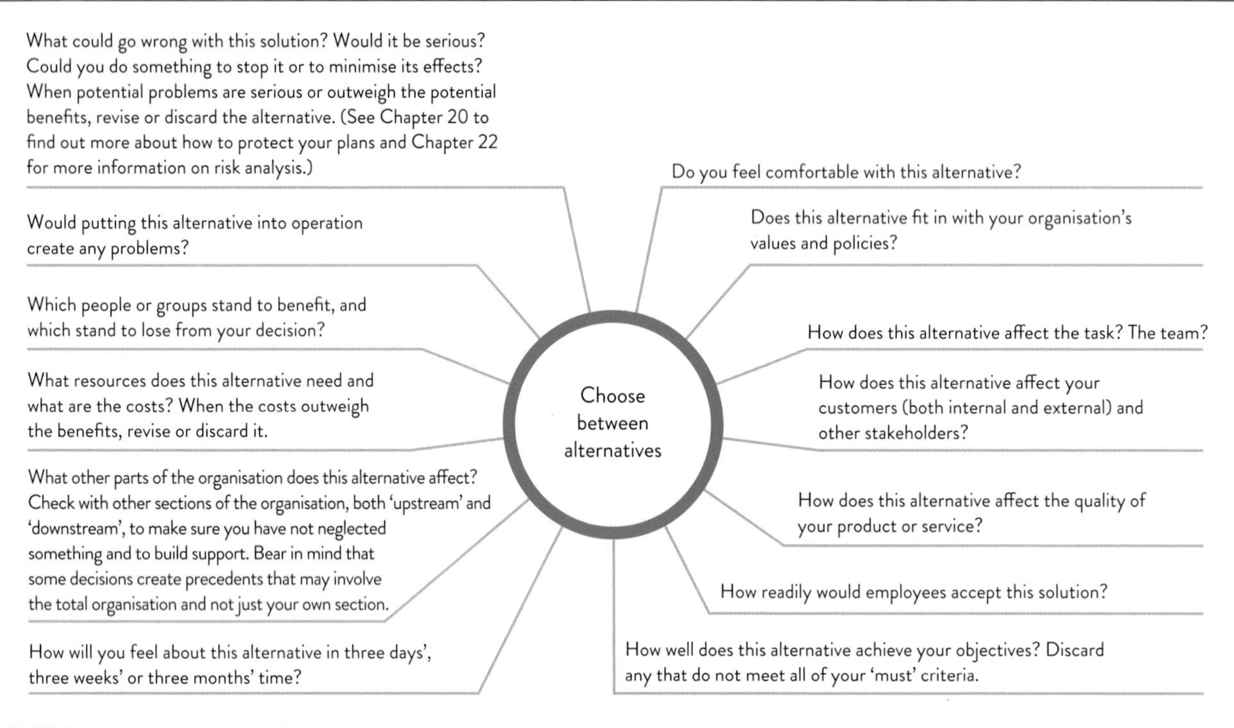

FIGURE 26.6 Which solution to choose?

2 *Safeguard:* adopt a pessimistic outlook for this step and ask yourself: What can go wrong? How would you know it is about to happen? What action could you take now to prevent it happening? What could you do to recover if it does happen? What can you monitor and how can you ensure your decision is working?

3 *Communicate:* how and to whom should you communicate your decision or solution? Include everyone who is involved or affected. How can you motivate people to accept your decision or solution and help make it work? Communicate promptly to gain people's support and answer any questions carefully and fully. No matter how good your solution is, if the people around you don't support it, it is unlikely to succeed.

Transferable skills
2.1 Critical thinking

Step 7: Monitor and evaluate results

This step is important because no matter how carefully you have thought through your implementation plan, unexpected events can interfere with its success. Monitoring is your insurance. You don't have to be involved in every aspect of implementation, but you do need to track whether or not it's working out as expected and, if it isn't, make the necessary adjustments to get it back on track.

Make routine checks, and diarise them if necessary, so you can catch and fix small deviations before they grow into major problems. You also need to be prepared to 'let it go' and try something else when it is not achieving its objectives and the adjustments you have made aren't working. Figure 26.7 shows how you might monitor and evaluate the results of your decision or solution after it has been implemented.

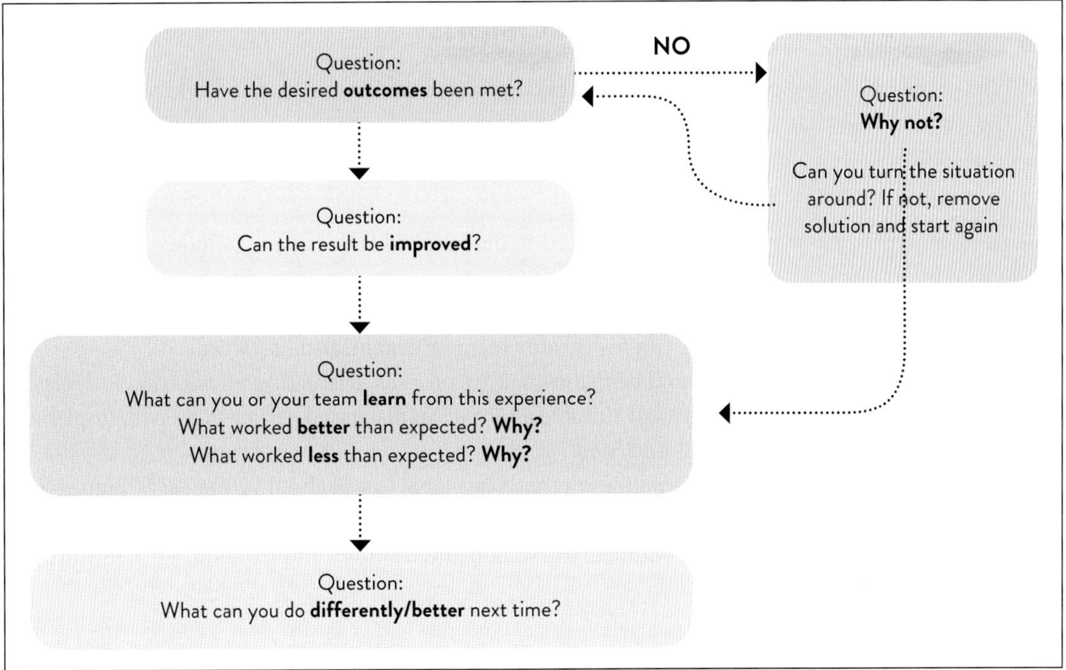

FIGURE 26.7 Monitoring and evaluating results

Helping others solve problems

The maxim 'Bring me solutions not problems' doesn't mean you shouldn't be interested in problems. Disasters like the *Challenger* space shuttle explosion in 1986, the BP Texas City Oil Refinery explosion in 2005[11] and the chaotic opening of Heathrow Airport's Terminal 5 in 2008[12] were all linked to management's reluctance to consider or hear about problems.

While you need to listen to reported problems and assess their validity, you don't need to personally solve them all. Help people benefit from your experience by showing them how to solve their own problems using the seven steps described above. Ask questions to help them think their problem through with a 'beginner's mind'. Help them pinpoint what they want to happen and to concentrate on solutions and finding a way forward. Help them establish a timeline for solving their problem.

If you hear 'Yes, but …' when you suggest a possible solution or offer advice, stop – your help is being butted away. Switch to asking questions, listening and summarising. When 'Yes, buts …' really mean someone doesn't want to solve their problem, but just wants to moan about it, it soon becomes clear. Adopt the approach from the leader-manager's prayer, adapted from the 'Serenity Prayer' by Alcoholics Anonymous, which says: 'Grant me the serenity to accept the things I cannot change, The courage to change the things I can, And the wisdom to know the difference'.[13]

26.3 Reaching sensible decisions

No sensible decision can be made without taking into account not only the world as it is, but the world as it will be.

Isaac Asimov, 'My own view' in *The encyclopedia of science fiction*, 1978, edited by Robert Holdstock; later published in *Asimov on science fiction*, 1981.

Situations in which leader-managers are required to make sensible decisions include:

- in a crisis
- to solve a problem
- when an opportunity arises that can move your team or organisation forward.

Phase 3 of the problem-solving and decision-making process, evaluating and acting, is decision-making. This is where you select the most suitable alternative (discussed earlier in Step 5), implement it and monitor it (discussed in Step 6 and Step 7).

But how? Which of the decision-making methods available to you should you use? Which style of decision-making should you use? Should you involve your team and, if so, how much? What are the traps to be alert for, so you don't kid yourself you've consulted others and gained their commitment when, in reality, you haven't?

Six ways to make decisions

There are six possible decision-making procedures to choose from, ranging from decisions that you reach yourself to those you agree with your team. We begin with two that are never useful, move on to two that are seldom useful and conclude with two participative methods that are useful in most cases.

1 Factional decisions

Factional decisions are those that a minority push through using their influence or by having the loudest voice, or even a few articulate people who speak persuasively. A leader-manager might announce a decision after consulting 'the clique', so it may look like a unilateral decision but it is really a factional decision. Or 'the clique' might railroad a team into reaching the decision it wants, maybe even fooling the rest of the team into thinking they've had a voice and actually participated in the decision.

Factional decision-making does happen, but it is not a great way to make decisions because you lose out on the potentially valuable input and insights of the whole team, especially when you listen to the same people all the time. Also, when a decision is made by a select few, those whose voices were ignored or overruled are bound to harbour resentment, which threatens the long-term viability and success of the decision.

2 Groupthink

Transferable skills
2.1 Critical thinking

While new ideas and challenging the ways of the past are welcomed in many organisations and teams, sometimes people feel that the approval of their colleagues is more important than stating their reservations or an opposing viewpoint. This can occur even when the idea or viewpoint might add new information or provide a better perspective.

A team may think it's reaching a joint decision, but when individuals aren't prepared to speak up with an alternative point of view, groupthink is probably occurring. Conforming to group norms overrides members' desire to develop new and better ways and innovative approaches, and anyone who dares to disagree is viewed as not being a team player.

As a result, the group ignores negative aspects of its decisions and fails to test its decisions. Task-oriented and goal-driven groups are particularly vulnerable to groupthink when they are under pressure to make a good decision. As a result, a team can reach poor and even dangerous decisions, or develop policies or strategies that harm a department or an entire organisation.

The main symptoms and consequences of groupthink are:

- An illusion of invulnerability, which creates excessive optimism and risk-taking, ignoring obvious danger and consequently failing to develop a contingency plan.
- An unquestioned belief in the 'rightness' of the group, whereby members are inclined to ignore the moral or ethical consequences of their decisions and to fail to ask experts outside the group for input.
- The 'common knowledge effect', whereby information 'known' by all group members has a greater influence on their judgement than information held by one or only a few.
- Discounting or rationalising warnings or signs that the team is operating under false assumptions, making a poor decision or developing a faulty plan, which prevents it from searching for more information or more alternatives.
- Limiting discussion to only a few alternatives, possibilities or solutions, looking mostly at its good points instead of gathering a wide range of information, thereby reaching quick agreement on a decision or course of action.
- Not criticising or questioning each other's ideas and an absence of devil's advocates to bring to the group's attention any information or evidence that does not conform to the group's expectations and stereotypes, or that might shatter its complacency about its correctness and effectiveness.
- Rationalising, or 'explaining away', contrary information and decisions or plans not working as expected, rather than reconsidering decisions, plans and strategies.
- Shared stereotypes of 'enemies' outside the group, leading to a reluctance to negotiate and to underestimating the enemies' ability to counter the group's plans or strategies.
- Strong pressure on group members to conform to group norms and adhere to the group's commitments, illusions and stereotypes, making members unwilling to state their true thoughts and feelings and to air any discomfort, doubts or uncertainties they have about the group's decisions or plans in order to avoid appearing 'disloyal' and to maintain an illusion of unanimity.

Mariano Sigman and Dan Ariely's TED talk provides some useful information on making good decisions in a group and can be viewed at: https://www.ted.com/talks/mariano_sigman_and_dan_ariely_how_can_groups_make_good_decisions?language=en

Avoiding groupthink

To avoid feeling like you and your team are in an echo chamber, take a lesson from Alfred Sloan, former chair of General Motors, who closed his meetings this way:

> ... I take it we are all in complete agreement on the decision here. I propose we postpone further discussion until our next meeting to give ourselves time to develop disagreement and perhaps gain some understanding of what the decision is all about.[14]

A participative or democratic leadership style discourages groupthink whereas an authoritarian leadership encourages it. Here are some other ways to ensure that your team does not fall into the groupthink syndrome:

- Actively look for the weak points in your decision or chosen course of action.
- Assign at least one team member to play the role of 'devil's advocate' when evaluating alternatives.
- Be wary of reaching agreement too quickly and too easily. Be sure that people have yielded to other opinions for objective and logically sound reasons and are not changing their minds simply to avoid conflict. Confirm that everyone genuinely accepts the decision or solution.
- Brief the group impartially and objectively, without advocating your own preferences.
- Develop the habit of open inquiry and careful consideration of alternatives; help the team to explore alternatives impartially and view honest differences as a healthy sign of progress.
- Have subgroups discuss and then report back.

- Inform the group that everyone has different and relevant experience and information to contribute.
- Invite and consider opposing opinions, objections and doubts.
- Invite experts within the organisation to share their thoughts and ideas and encourage them to air views contrary to team members' views.
- Know the warning signals that might indicate your decision is failing, keep alert for them, have a contingency plan ready and reconsider your decision when necessary.

Transferable skills
3.4 Leadership

3 Unilateral decisions

Leader-managers sometimes make a decision and announce it to the team. While this is appropriate in some circumstances – for example, in an emergency or when there is no other possible course of action – consultation and participation usually result in not only a better decision but also one that is backed by greater understanding and commitment.

Pretending to consult people before reaching a decision when you have already decided generally fools no one and invites cynicism and mistrust. Guard against this should you ever feel obliged to consult your team but really know the outcome you want. It is actually probably better to simply announce you have made the decision alone and explain the reasons why.

4 Voting

People often think that voting is a democratic and quick way to reach agreement. Voting is quick and certainly guarantees that a decision is reached. To the uninitiated, it can even look like consensus decision-making. However, voting has the following big drawbacks:

- It accentuates the differences of opinion between people and produces 'winners' and 'losers', which can create a confrontational atmosphere and make some people uncomfortable – especially those in the minority.
- It commits people publicly to a position, making it difficult for them to change their minds later without appearing weak and indecisive.
- Those who 'lost' the vote usually feel bad about losing and may carry out the 'winning' decision with little commitment or enthusiasm and may even undermine it.

No matter how impatient you are to reach a decision, unless the vote is about something straightforward and in which people have no emotional or vested interest, it's usually better to work towards consensus than to take a formal vote.

5 Participation

If you think you're the best person to make a decision or that it is your responsibility and you should make it because you are accountable, think again. Research shows that teams make better decisions than even the brightest individual in the group, provided the group is diverse, harmonious and cohesive, and clear about its purpose and goals.

Consider how a group of people can inspire each other and build on each other's ideas, and how involving people means more brains, more experience, more information and more knowledge will go into the decision. This inevitably will yield better results. Additionally, don't forget that people are more committed to decisions they helped make and solutions they helped design because their involvement gives them a more complete understanding of why and how the decision or solution was reached. This, in turn, assists and encourages them to make the solution or decision succeed.

Consultation

People work harder to ensure the success of a decision they have had a part in reaching than when they are merely complying with someone else's wishes. Ask team members for their ideas and opinions when a decision or solution to a problem affects them, when they are involved in implementing a decision or solution to a problem and when they have relevant experience or expertise. Then, taking their views into account, make the decision and explain how you reached it.

6 Consensus

When you reach a decision by consensus, the group reaches it together. During discussions, everyone hears everyone else's point of view and explains their own. Team members explore differences of opinion and use diverging points of view to clarify issues, gather more information and polish their ideas. Gradually, consensus, or general agreement, is achieved.

Although consensus requires skilled communication, meeting management and problem-solving and decision-making skills from both the leader and the group members, and although it can take time, consensus usually results in better decisions and solutions and greater commitment. As an added bonus, the process of participating in and achieving consensus is usually both instructive and motivational for team members.

The beauty of consensus is that, even when people don't agree 100 per cent with the decision or solution, everyone can say, 'It may not be exactly what I would have done, but I understand why it has been agreed to, and I agree with it enough to support it and help make it work.'

Reaching consensus takes time, skill and patience, and will require meeting management and participative leadership skills. It also takes practice because as groups become more experienced in participative methods, they usually get better at them. You need to be able to help others think of their own point of view as one piece of the puzzle and understand that others have other pieces based on their experience, their area of expertise and so on. Then you need to be able to lead a discussion that helps put all the pieces of the puzzle together.

Invite discussion once you have stated the purpose of the meeting and provided the necessary background information. Create an atmosphere that treats what everyone says as important and that values everyone's participation. Try to lead the discussion without entering into it so that all team members are afforded the opportunity to freely express their points of view.

Other factors to help a group reach consensus include:

- Clarify the issue under discussion and what the discussion is intended to achieve; for example, to solve a problem, to come up with a range of options, to analyse and explore a problem, to determine its cause, to reach a decision and so on.
- Ensure participants understand and agree with the desired outcomes.
- Frequently summarise, particularly each time a major conclusion or decision is reached.
- Keep the discussion to the stated topic: avoid unnecessary diversions or digressions onto other topics.

Discussion is a key ingredient of consensus, yet, ironically, meeting participants often report a feeling of going 'round in circles' until a point is reached when 'suddenly' consensus is achieved and a decision made. Until members become used to it, this feeling can be frustrating and disheartening. Clear signs that consensus is approaching include people:

- asking for specific information
- beginning their sentences with 'Yeah ...'

So, for your team to become skilled in reaching decisions via consensus, they need to be able to:

- communicate empathically
- give and receive feedback

- listen to others and admit that another approach is better
- respect and value diversity and various points of view and look for ways that differences can complement each other
- state their points of view clearly and coherently
- support and encourage team members
- understand and use the problem-solving and decision-making steps and tools
- use creativity techniques and think innovatively
- work in a collective spirit, putting the interests of the group before their own.

When to involve your team

Should you involve your team in every decision? No. Involving your team generally takes more time and more skill on your part, so don't involve them in making decisions or in solving problems that have no real effect on them or that they have no real interest in. When this is the case, make the decision yourself, and then announce or explain it.

Here are some important guidelines regarding when to involve your group in problem-solving and decision-making:

- If the issue affects the group, involve your team in solving it; the more the problem or decision affects the group, the more necessary it is to involve them.
- If the group members are able to and want to become involved, where you can, let them. This is particularly the case when they have sufficient knowledge of, or expertise in, the issues involved. Even when they don't, though, remember that involving people can provide a useful training and development opportunity.
- If the group will be involved in implementing the decision, it makes sense to involve team members in making it. Not only will they have a vested interest in making a good decision, but due to the understanding developed from their involvement in reaching it, the transition to implementation should be considerably easier.
- If you need your decision to be accepted and supported, the more you need your team involved in making it.

When you decide that you want your team involved in decision-making:

- Don't force the group into agreeing with you.
- Don't let people become competitive.
- Don't make early, quick, easy agreements and compromises; these are often based on flawed assumptions resulting from groupthink.
- Don't vote – this divides people into winners and losers.
- Encourage people, particularly the quieter ones, to offer their ideas.
- Include the major stakeholders in the outcome of the problem or decision as well as anyone concerned with or affected by the solution or decision. Seek their information, ideas and suggestions and pay attention to what they say (see Chapter 8 for information on who to involve).
- Keep everyone's attention on the objectives and on solving the problem or reaching the decision. Don't dwell on past mistakes.
- Take your time so that the group takes ownership of the whole process.
- Treat differences of opinion as a way to gather additional information, clarify issues and force the group to seek better information.
- You can also consider using the stepladder technique (outlined in **Figure 26.8**), which can help your team avoid anchoring, confirmation bias and groupthink, and encourage everyone's full participation.

STEP 1	Present the decision or problem and ask group members to form their own ideas about the decision or solving the problem
STEP 2	Pair two members together and ask them to discuss their thoughts
STEP 3	Add a third group member to the pair and ask the third member to present their ideas to the first two members *before* hearing the ideas they have already discussed
STEP 4	Repeat Step 3 by adding a fourth member and so on to the group, allowing time for discussion after each additional member has presented their thoughts
STEP 5	Once everyone has been brought in and presented and discussed their ideas, the group is ready to reach a decision

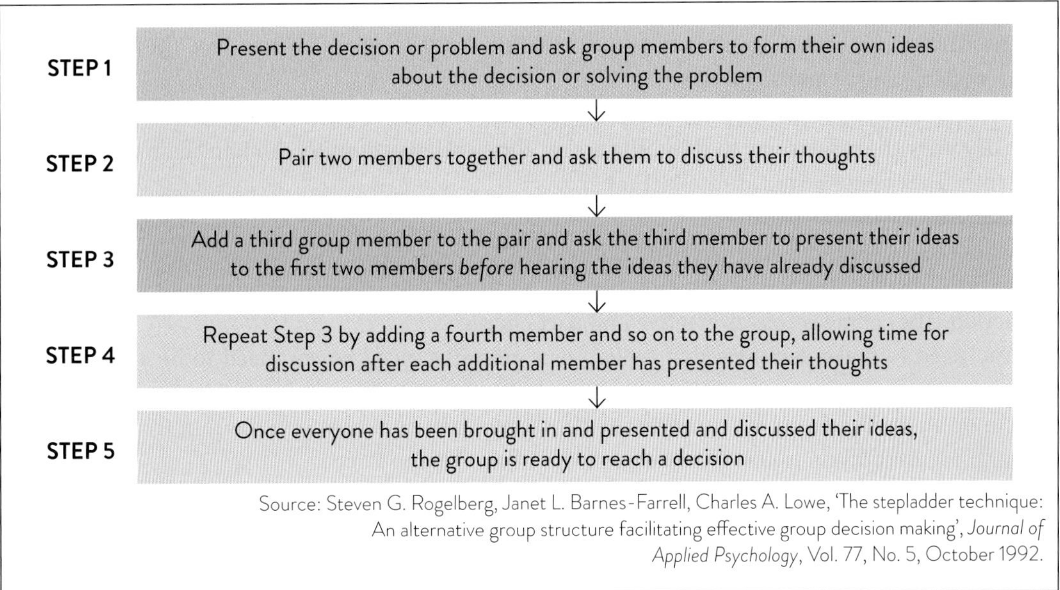

Source: Steven G. Rogelberg, Janet L. Barnes-Farrell, Charles A. Lowe, 'The stepladder technique: An alternative group structure facilitating effective group decision making', *Journal of Applied Psychology*, Vol. 77, No. 5, October 1992.

FIGURE 26.8 The five steps of the stepladder technique

Decision-making styles

Research shows that decision-making styles change over the course of successful leader-managers' careers.[15] So you might start as a 'satisficer' where you learn the key facts, leap into action and perhaps test it as you go along but then later on become an 'optimiser', where you mull over reams of data and keep looking until you think you found 'the best answer'.

Satisficers and optimisers are just two examples, but there are also 'single-focus' decision-makers who want to take one course of action and put their energy into making it work, and 'multi-focused' decision-makers who prefer to pursue multiple courses of action and who adapt to changing circumstances.

That gives us the four decision-making styles shown in **Figure 26.9**:

1 *Decisive*: these are the action-oriented, speedy decision-makers. Once their decision is made and their plan in place, they stick to it and move on to the next decision. Time is precious to them and they value brevity, clarity, honesty and loyalty. They come across as task-oriented.

	Single-focus	Multi-focus
Satisficer	Decisive	Flexible
Optimiser	Hierarchical	Integrative

FIGURE 26.9 Four decision-making styles

2 *Flexible*: flexible decision-makers are speedy, too, but they're also adaptable. They get just enough information to reach a decision and quickly change course when they need to. They come across as sociable and responsive.
3 *Hierarchical*: if anyone is going to suffer analysis paralysis, it's the hierarchical decision-maker. They want their decisions to stand the test of time and expect others to join their search for the truth. They come across as intellectual.
4 *Integrative*: you can't rush these decision-makers and they like lots of input, even from people whose views conflict with their own. But rather than looking for the one best solution, integrative decision-makers frame the situation broadly and reach decisions that have multiple courses of action. They come across as creative and participative.

You need to make decisions that reflect your circumstances, so you need to be able to use all four styles. As we have seen, circumstances can change rapidly so, sometimes, there just isn't enough time to be an optimiser. At other times, the operating environment is so uncertain that you need to be multi-focused, while in a stable operating environment you can be more single-focused in your decision-making style.

Interestingly, research suggests that successful leader-managers adjust their decision-making style as they move up the hierarchy, and failing to do so can derail their career quite quickly. In general, most first-line leader-managers use a decisive decision-making style, middle and senior managers use an integrative style, and directors and others in senior management roles use a hierarchical style in public.

When leader-managers mull matters over on their own, though, the most successful are integrative decision-makers throughout their careers, and many use increasingly more hierarchical (lots of data, one option) and less flexible decision-making as a secondary style as they move up the hierarchy.

When you have an emergency or too many decisions

Whatever decision-making style you use, don't feel the need to rush. Few complex problems require immediate action. While decisiveness is an admirable leadership trait, you still need to take whatever time is available to consider the options. Remind yourself that you can think your way through the problem and draw confidence from this knowledge. Gather facts and opinions, analyse the situation, challenge and check assumptions and generate and assess your options before making your decision.

Some signs you need to improve your approach

When you and your team spend more time responding to problems and emergencies than preventing them, this could signal a problem. You may need to build your own and your team's skills in identifying and preventing potential problems and in planning ahead. When team members continually bring you their problems to solve and you spend more time fixing up their work than working on your own priorities, you may need to teach your team to solve their own problems.

When your plans tend to stray off course, you may not have spent enough time protecting your plans or monitoring them; or maybe you didn't develop a workable plan in the first place. When team members seldom or never come to you with concerns about something that 'might' happen or alert you to something that 'might' be a problem, it might be because you unwittingly discourage this open approach, creating a reluctance in your team members to bring problems forward. When you find yourself looking back and saying 'I had a feeling ...', this is another sign you may need to work on your problem-solving and decision-making skills.

If you find your decisions are creating more problems than they solve, it may be because you have ignored legal or ethical considerations. If you suspect this is the case, check your organisation's policies and procedures, which should reflect regulatory requirements and be based on ethical ways of doing business. Ask yourself if your decision could affect your own, another person's or the organisation's reputation, if you would be comfortable for it to be announced on the front page of the news or whether you would be happy being on the end of the decision had someone else made it. If your team, others in the organisation, your network contact or even your family disagree with your decision, this should signal alarm bells. You should at least take another look at it with fresh eyes and ask those people why they disagreed with it.

When you've made a poor decision ...

The only way never to get anything wrong is to do nothing. You'd be safe – like a ship in a harbour – but, as American author John Augustus Shedd said, '... that's not what ships are built for.'[16] Doing nothing may be safe, but you won't make any improvements, learn anything, and you won't be doing one of the things you are being paid to do.

Since no one can be 100 per cent right all the time, you're bound to make a few poor decisions. This fact is compounded by the rapid rate of change: today's leader-managers are facing situations they've never faced before. The COVID-19 global pandemic is a prime example as it has turned the world upside down and meant that leader-managers have found themselves in an environment that none of them have ever experienced. This makes generating new ideas and testing new approaches mandatory, and when you do this, you are bound to make the odd mistake. When you get a decision wrong, have the courage and self-confidence to own up to it and then go back to the beginning and do your best to fix it.

STUDY TOOLS

QUICK REVIEW

KEY CONCEPT 26.1 

a Summarise the types of problems and decisions leader-managers face in terms of complexity and the best way to approach each.

b List the more easily avoidable and less easily avoidable traps when solving problems and making decisions and summarise how to avoid them.

KEY CONCEPT 26.2 

a List and explain the seven steps to solving problems and making decisions and the role each step plays.

KEY CONCEPT 26.3 

a Summarise the six ways to make decisions described in this chapter.

b How can you recognise groupthink? What steps can you take to avoid it?

BUILD YOUR SKILLS

KEY CONCEPT 26.1 

a Thinking through the last important problem you solved or decision you reached, which traps might have been present? Did you fall into them? If not, how did you avoid them?

KEY CONCEPT 26.2 

a Describe the three distinct mental processes involved in solving problems and making decisions and explain why each is important.

b Why is it critical to focus on the cause of a problem rather than its symptoms?

c Imagine that you are going to rent or buy a home or a car. Develop a list of 'must' and 'want' criteria for it. How would this list help you in identifying possible homes or cars and making your decision?

d Discuss the following quotation in relation to problem-solving: 'Every problem has in it the seeds of its own solution. If you don't have any problems, you don't get any seeds.'[17]

KEY CONCEPT 26.3 

a Which of the two participative problem-solving and decision-making techniques discussed in this chapter did you last use? Describe the process you went through and its outcome. On reflection, what can you do differently the next time you use this approach?

b Thinking of the signs that indicate you need to improve your approach to decision-making and problem solving, develop an action plan for improving your skills.

c Describe a time when you worked with others to solve a problem or reach a decision. What helped people work well together? What lessons did you learn for next time?

WORKPLACE ACTIVITIES

KEY CONCEPT 26.1 

a Give some examples of programmed and non-programmed decisions used in your workplace.

b Thinking of a recent problem-solving or decision-making discussion or meeting you attended or led, which traps did you recognise? How were they avoided? If any were not avoided, what was their effect?

KEY CONCEPT 26.2 

a Think of a current or recent problem you have experienced at work that had many possible causes. Analyse it using a cause-and-effect diagram to determine its most likely cause. Discuss how this technique can help you identify the cause of the problem and explain why knowing the cause of a problem helps you solve it.

b List your last 10 workplace decisions and review the criteria you used to reach your decision. Which decisions deserved a lot of time and which didn't? Which did you make as quickly as possible, which did you wait to make and which did you delegate? Explain your reasoning.

c Think back over the last few days and make a list of all the problems you solved and decisions you made (however major or minor). Select a suitable problem (i.e. a fairly substantial problem, one that was not a programmed decision and one where you wanted to fix the cause of the problem to stop it recurring) and apply to it the seven-step problem-solving and decision-making model described in this chapter.

KEY CONCEPT 26.3 

a Do you and your team have the necessary skills to reach consensus? Develop a three-stage action plan to develop your skills further.

EXTENSION ACTIVITY

Referring to the Snapshot at the beginning of this chapter, answer the following question:

1 How should Khalid tackle each problem and decision to avoid falling into the decision-making traps discussed in this chapter?

CASE STUDY 26

NIPPED IN THE BUD

Alma and her small web-design team recently acquired a new client. While the small business had an adequate supply of work, the forward-thinking managing director strategically responded to tenders that were a good fit for their organisation.

On signing the project contract and creating a project plan, Alma came to the realisation that they had approximately 16 weeks to prepare for the start of the project. To increase capacity, Alma engaged Quickstart recruitment with offices all around Australia. Alma's team grew considerably, and within four weeks she had appointed the correct amount of staff to fulfil the requirements of the contract, albeit from all over the country.

Two months into the contract, at a monthly project meeting, several team members expressed concern with the communication and collaboration processes used within the business, stating they were ineffective. Most of the feedback referenced 'old-fashioned approaches' and 'unsupportive software'.

Alma often said that she felt quite challenged when it came to technology and that she lacked experience with leading remote teams, so she decided to engage an expert.

Questions

1 Develop a step-by-step plan showing what Alma and the expert should do based on the seven-step problem-solving and decision-making process described in this chapter.

2 Should Alma involve the design team? If so, in what way and for what purpose? What level of input from the team (including those working remotely) would you recommend and why? Should Alma involve anyone else?

3 What signs should Alma look for throughout the problem-solving process that will help her recognise if the approach she is taking needs to be revised?

CHAPTER ENDNOTES

1 Roger Bohn, 'Stop fighting fires', *Harvard Business Review*, July–August 2000.

2 Rosabeth Moss Kanter, 'Transforming giants', *Harvard Business Review*, January 2008.

3 Catherine Tinsley, Robin Dillon, Peter Madsen, 'How to avoid catastrophe', *Harvard Business Review*, April 2011, p. 90.

4 Ibid.

5 Media release, 'Brain's problem-solving function at work when we daydream', University of British Columbia, 11 May 2009, http://www.sciencedaily.com/releases/2009/05/090511180702.htm, accessed 17 March 2015.

6 H. L. Mencken, 'The divine afflatus', *New York Evening Mail*, 16 November 1917.

7 Albert Einstein, quoted in A. Bingham, Dwayne Spradlin, 'Are you solving the right problem?', *Harvard Business Review*, September 2012, p. 85.

8 Lewis Carroll, *Alice's adventures in Wonderland*, Oxford University Press, 1865.

9 Catherine H. Tinsley, Robin L. Dillon, Peter M. Madsen, 'Learning from failure: How to avoid catastrophe', *Harvard Business Review*, April 2011; and 'Mars Climate Orbiter', NASA Science Missions, National Aeronautics and Space Administration, 30 April 2013, http://science.nasa.gov/missions/mars-climate-orbiter, accessed 6 May 2014.

10 Adam Lashinsky, 'Amazon's Jeff Bezos: The ultimate disrupter', *Fortune*, 16 November 2012, accessed 17 May 2015, http://fortune.com/2012/11/16/amazons-jeff-bezos-the-ultimate-disrupter; see also Max Nisen, 'Meetings with Jeff Bezos may start with 30 minutes of silence', *Business Insider Australia*, 17 November 2012; Amy Birchall, 'The decision makers', *Management Today*, September 2013.

11 Andrew Hopkins, *Failure to learn: The BP Texas City refinery disaster*, Wolters Kluwer, 2008.

12 Dan Milmo, 'Passengers fume in the chaos of Terminal 5's first day', *Guardian*, 28 March 2008.

13 Reinhold Niebuhr, *The essential Reinhold Niebuhr: Selected essays and addresses*, Robert McAfee Brown (ed.), Yale University Press, 10 September 1987, p. 251.

14 Alfred Sloan, quoted in D. Chorafas, *The management of equity investments*, Butterworth-Heinemann, 2005, p. 217.

15 Kenneth R. Brousseau et al., 'The seasoned executive's decision-making style', *Harvard Business Review*, February 2006.

16 John Augustus Shedd, *Salt from my attic*, The Mosher Press, Portland, 1928, cited in *The Yale book of quotations*, Fred R. Shapiro (ed.), Yale University Press, 2006. Author's note: Information as to whether J. A. Shedd is the original author of the quotation is not conclusive.

17 Norman Vincent Peale, *The power of positive thinking*, New York: Prentice Hall, 1952.

CHAPTER

27

USING SYSTEMATIC, ANALYTICAL TOOLS AND TECHNIQUES

After completing this chapter, you will be able to:

27.1 use a range of qualitative and quantitative tools to help identify and prioritise problems and opportunities

27.2 choose the right qualitative and quantitative tools to help analyse problems and opportunities

27.3 choose the right qualitative and quantitative tools to help resolve problems and opportunities

27.4 choose the right qualitative and quantitative tools to help implement and monitor solutions and opportunities.

TRANSFERABLE SKILLS

The following transferable skills are covered in this chapter:

1 **Business competence**
- **1.2** Entrepreneurship/small business skills
- **1.3** Sustainability
- **1.4** Business operations

2 **Critical thinking and problem solving**
- **2.1** Critical thinking
- **2.3** Business strategy

3 **Social competence**
- **3.4** Leadership

4 **Data literacy**
- **4.1** Data literacy

OVERVIEW

Real information and numbers are the most reliable ways to solve problems, make decisions and abide by the quality, innovation and continuous improvement imperatives. The tools and statistical techniques reviewed in this chapter give you and your work team objective and systematic ways to identify, analyse and resolve problems, and also provide ways to streamline and build quality into systems and processes. Together, these tools are an indispensable part of your continuous improvement, innovation, problem-solving and quality efforts.

Although you can apply these tools and techniques on your own, they work best in a team environment because those involved in doing a job know it best and are more likely to develop workable solutions. Drawing on the skills, experience and ideas of a range of people also increases their commitment to the resulting improvement efforts. (Chapter 13 explains how to build your team's group dynamics and help its members work together effectively.)

SNAPSHOT

The improvement team

Jess is preparing to meet her team of four travel consultants and a trainee administration assistant in the boardroom. They are about to continue with their series of weekly Customer Care Circles. Jess is pleased with how they are responding to their latest challenge – utilising quality management tools and techniques to improve their work systems. Their overall goals are to keep finding ways to make work flow more smoothly and serve their customers better.

In the first meeting, they brainstormed a list of 'job hassles' and used the nominal group technique to prioritise the issues to work on them. In their second meeting, the circle used the fishbone technique to analyse the problem they decided to work on first. The fishbone technique highlighted that there was a lot more to the issue than first met the eye. In the third meeting, they finished 'fish boning' their problem and began to flow-chart how the process is currently done. In their fourth meeting, they plan to finish flow-charting the current system and look at the check sheets that two of the consultants started keeping at the third meeting. These will help them analyse the nature of delays in the process so they can design and flow-chart a more streamlined and effective system.

The circle is making good progress, and although they are still analysing the problem, Jess feels that they will soon be ready to design and test a new, improved system. Whatever it is, Jess knows it will make everyone's life easier and allow them to offer a faster and more reliable service to their customers. She also knows that the business will benefit enormously from the improved teamwork that has already resulted from the Customer Care Circles.

27.1 Identifying and prioritising problems and opportunities

> It is a capital mistake to theorise before one has data. Insensibly one begins to twist facts to suit theories, instead of theories to suit facts.
>
> Arthur Conan Doyle, *A scandal in Bohemia* (1895).

Transferable skills
2.1 Critical thinking
2.3 Business strategy

Whenever you want to solve tricky problems, find ways to improve or identify opportunities to make the most of them, you need facts. They help you find the real cause of the issues and innovate solutions. Figure 27.1 summarises the tools and techniques you can use. Notice that some tools and techniques can help you in several ways, such as identifying problems and analysing them. Four of these techniques – force-field analysis, cause-and-effect diagrams (or fishbone diagrams), ask 'Why?' five times, and **brainstorming** – are also discussed in Chapters 20 and 26. **Circling**, the nominal group technique, flow charts, **is/is not comparison**, **checkerboard analysis**, and the P–D–C–A cycle – are systematic techniques. The others we examine in this chapter are statistical techniques that rely on gathering and analysing samples large enough to be reliable, or statistically significant.

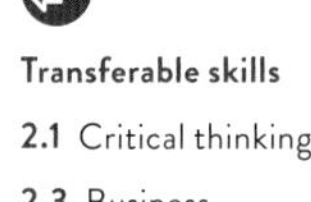

With statistical techniques you're looking for a '*p*-value', or probability value, of less than 0.05. When you have that, you can rely on the data; when you have a higher *p*-value, gather more data or make sure your sample is homogeneous, or similar enough, to give you accurate data. (You don't need to worry about calculating statistical significance because most computer packages report the significance along with the results; if yours doesn't, there is a formula in Microsoft Excel and several online tools that can calculate it for you.)

Identifying problems and opportunities and deciding which to address

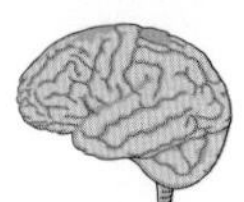
Brainstorming

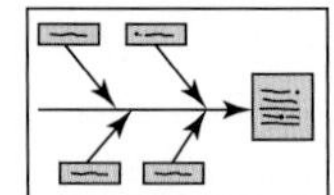
Cause-and-effect diagram

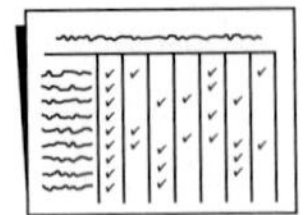
Check sheets

Circling

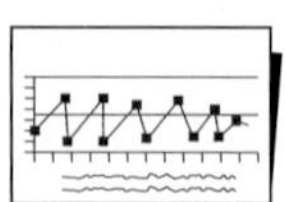
Control charts

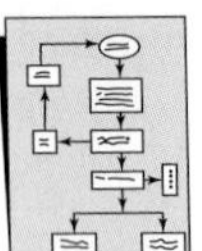
Flow charts

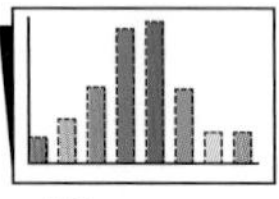
Histograms

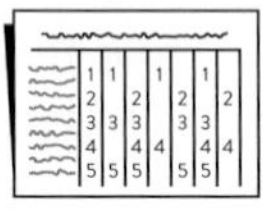
Nominal group technique

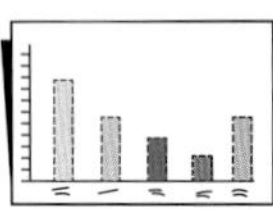
Pareto charts

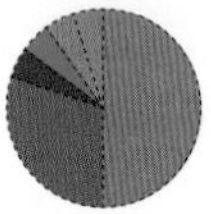
Pie charts

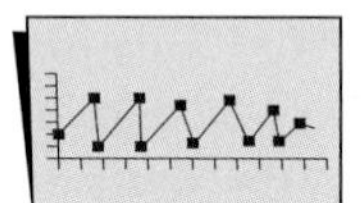
Run charts

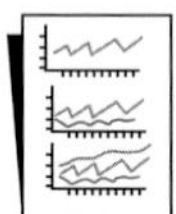
Stratification charts

Analysing problems and opportunities

Ask 'Why?' five times

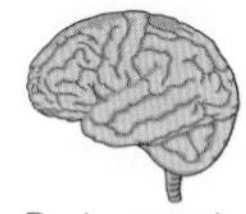
Brainstorming

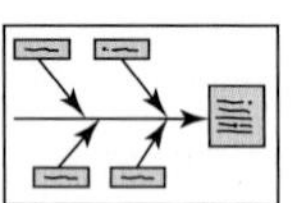
Cause-and-effect diagram

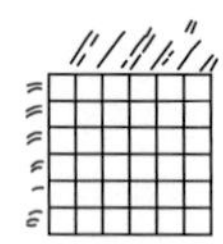
Checkerboard analysis

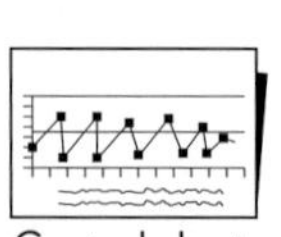
Control charts

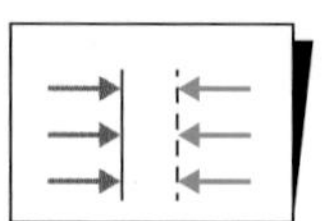
Force-field analysis

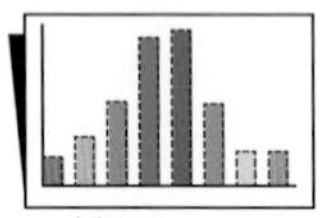
Histograms

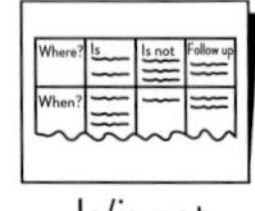
Is/is not comparison

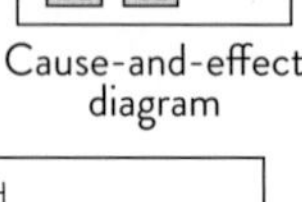
Pareto charts

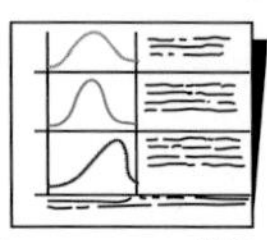
Process capability charts

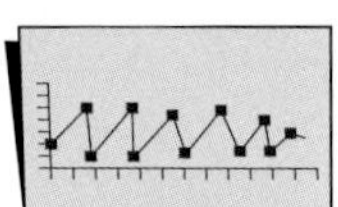
Run charts

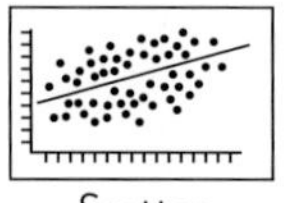
Scatter diagrams

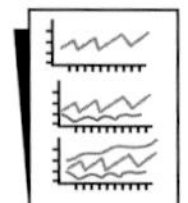
Stratification charts

Resolving problems and capitalising on opportunities

Ask 'Why?' five times

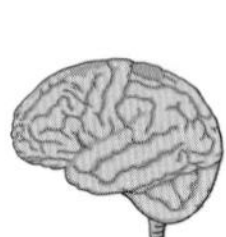
Brainstorming

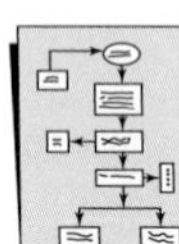
Flow charts

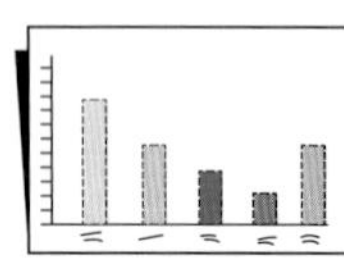
Pareto charts

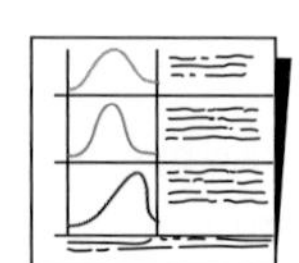
Process capability charts

Implementing improvements and solutions

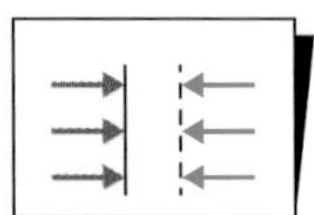
Force-field analysis

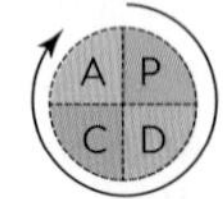

P–D–C–A cycle

Monitoring processes

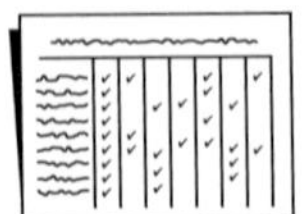
Check sheets

Control charts

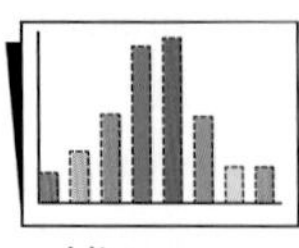
Histograms

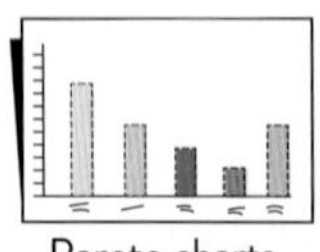
Pareto charts

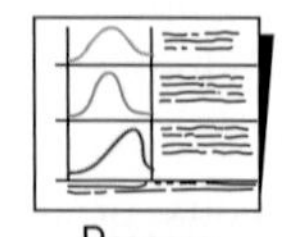
Process capability charts

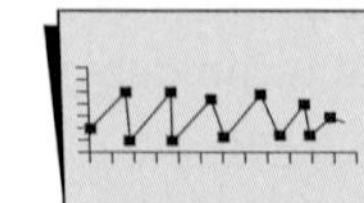
Run charts

Stratification charts

FIGURE 27.1 Using the systematic analytical tools and techniques

With all of the techniques in Figure 27.1, label each chart clearly. Show who collected the data, how (e.g. by instruments, observation), where and when (e.g. time of day, shift) and the period covered. With the analytical techniques, show who carried out the analysis, precisely what was analysed and when. Someone may need to refer to them in the future, so be meticulous in the way you label your charts.

Where to begin?

You might have identified a specific problem or perhaps you want to prevent an unexpected failure from happening again. Maybe an unexpected success has occurred that you want to ensure continues or there is a gap between a result you're getting and the outcome you want. Perhaps there has been a change in the way you engage with a customer or supplier that you want to capitalise on or make sure doesn't adversely affect you. Perhaps you have so many 'headaches' that you need to prioritise them so you can work on the most critical problems first.

Brainstorming is a common way to begin your analysis. A work team or improvement team brainstorms regarding things like problems or bottlenecks that need to be worked on, and, when necessary, uses the circling technique (discussed in the following section) to describe the issue clearly. They can then prioritise the issues using the *nominal group technique* (explained further on) or use a cause-and-effect diagram to prioritise the causes of a problem. Or they might construct a flow chart to spot backtracking, repetition or other inefficiencies in a process to find ways to improve it.

You might also use statistics – check sheets, control charts, histograms, pie charts, run charts or stratification charts – to collect relevant information about current performance and trends in performance. Pareto charts allow you to identify the most critical problem to work on first.

Once you have decided which problem to work on, you must gather more information about it, which you then display and analyse using the tools and techniques discussed in this chapter. Following that you develop and test options to improve the situation and select and implement the most effective solution. (You can find the seven steps to problem-solving explained in Chapter 26.)

These tools and techniques help you address today's key challenges of:

- achieving higher quality
- improving customer satisfaction
- increasing efficiencies, saving time and reducing hassles through flexible and well-organised processes
- making the most effective use of people and information
- making continuous improvements and innovations
- saving money through lower inventory levels and less waste
- solving a wide range of problems.

Circling

Transferable skills
2.1 Critical thinking

When you want to tighten up a broad or complex issue, write it up on a flip chart and then circle the key words, as shown in Figure 27.2. Each time you clarify, you sharpen your problem definition. When there is an 'and' in the description, check whether you're trying to solve two problems at once (as in this example). Split them and solve each separately.

Nominal group technique

Transferable skills
2.1 Critical thinking

Often the person with the loudest voice in the group, the most articulate person or the most senior person gets their way. The rest lose heart and interest because it seems their point of view is never 'heard'. The nominal group technique gives everyone an equal say in deciding which problems to

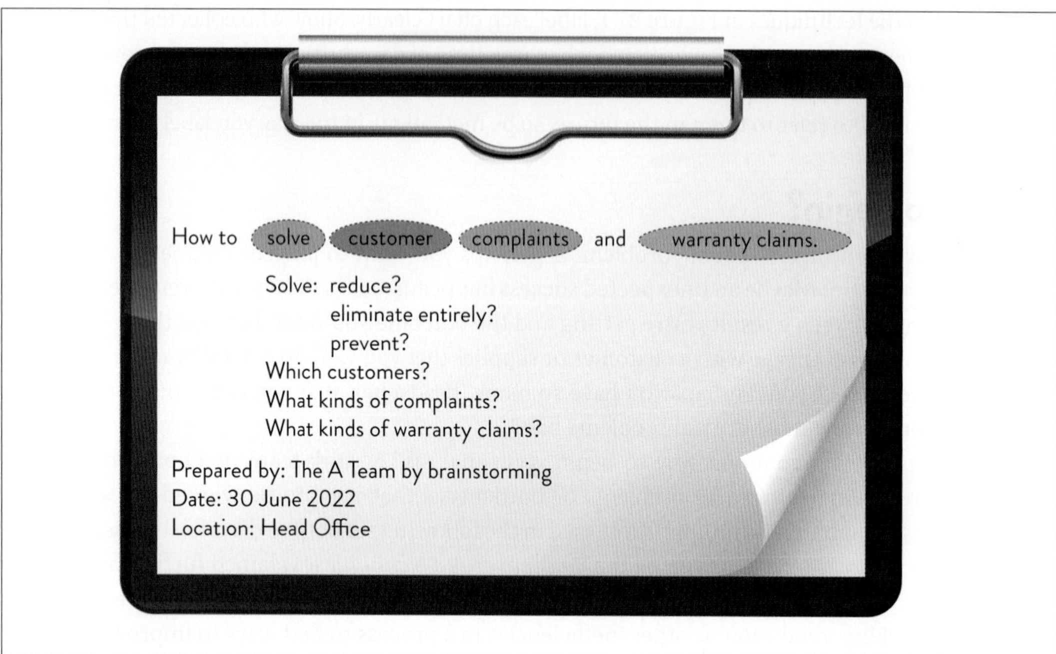

FIGURE 27.2 The circling technique to specify broad or complex issues

work on and in what order, clearly showing the group's wishes without the divisions caused by straightforward voting (discussed in Chapter 26). Giving everyone a say increases interest and commitment.

The steps to using the nominal group technique are as follows:

1. Brainstorm problems that need to be resolved. A list of problems that a work group might brainstorm is shown at the top of **Figure 27.3**.
2. Word each problem clearly so that everyone has the same understanding of it. Examples are shown at the bottom of **Figure 27.3**. Double-check that you have listed each problem only once and not repeated a problem using different words.
3. Assign a letter to each problem, as shown in **Figure 27.4**.
4. Each team member then votes on which problem they believe is the most important. In **Figure 27.4** there are five problems. Each member assigns a 5 to the problem they believe is the most important, a 4 to the next most important problem, and so on, ending with a 1 next to the least important problem. One team member's vote is shown in **Figure 27.4**.

   When you are discussing a large number of problems, follow the 'half plus one' rule. Instead of ranking each problem, rank only half plus one of the problems listed. For example, if 22 problems are listed, rank 12. Each member would assign a 12 to the problem they believe is most important, an 11 to the next most important, and so on.

   Another way to 'see' the opinions of the group, after brainstorming and recording ideas on a flip chart, is to give everyone coloured dots to rank problems. Then count the coloured dots beside each problem.
5. Tally the ratings. For example, the results from a team of five voting on how to rank problems to decide which to work on first might look like the ratings shown in **Figure 27.4**. Problem C, safety procedures not always followed, has the highest score. This team thinks that this is the most important problem to work on first. They will work on Problem B, people not putting tools away, next, and so on.

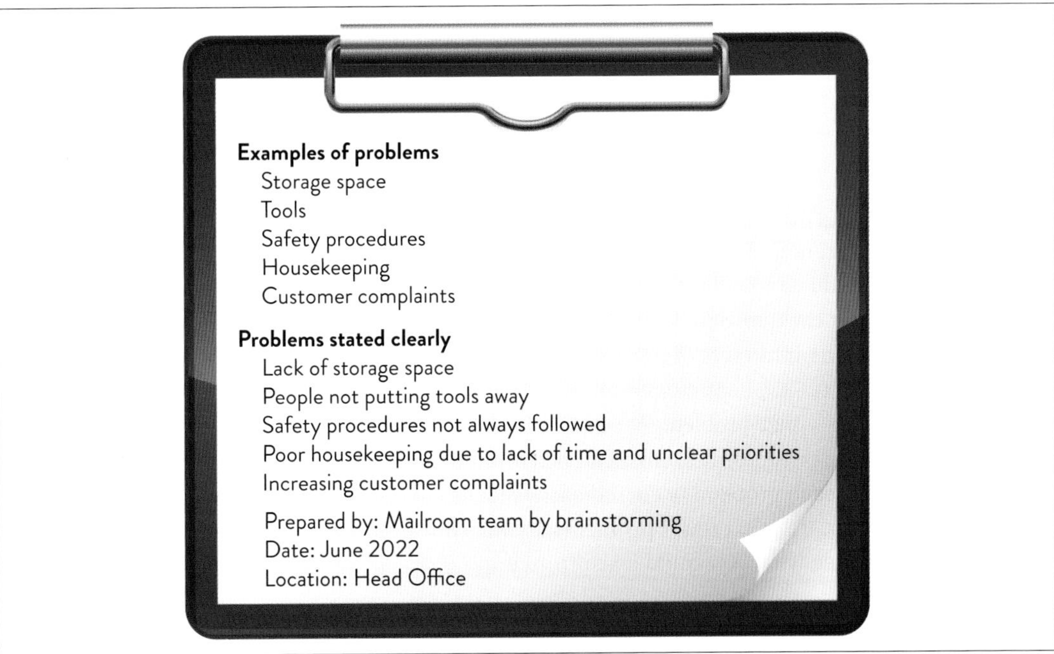

FIGURE 27.3 Stating problems clearly

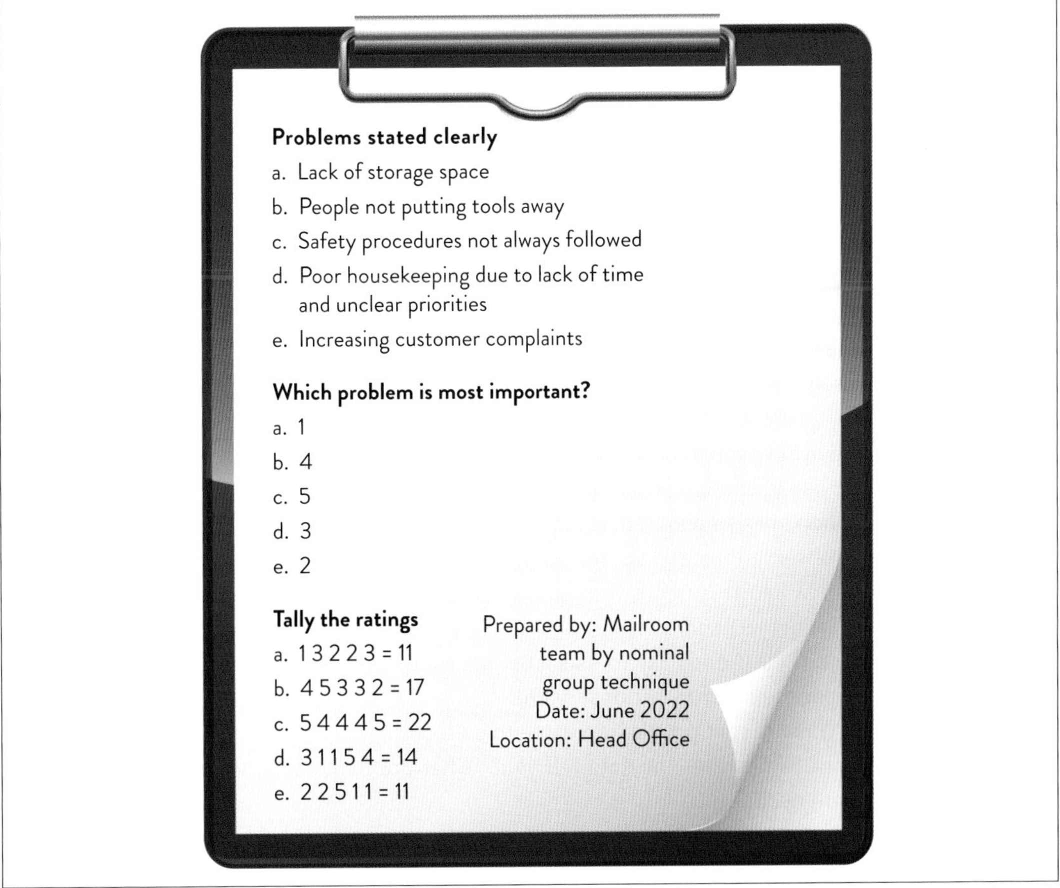

FIGURE 27.4 Problems labelled and rated

Once you know where to begin, you can launch the problem-solving process described in Chapter 26.

Check sheets

Check sheets help you gather data based on sample observations so that you can detect and isolate patterns of non-conformance and variation – in other words, check sheets highlight where work is going wrong. They are a good starting point because they help you identify problems and build a picture of them, so you can see which occur most often, which happen when and so on. They are a simple way to answer the question 'How often are certain events happening?' and begin the process of translating opinions into facts. You can also use them to monitor a process to make sure it is working as you expect.

Figure 27.5 shows that problem A occurred seven times, problem B occurred 13 times and problem C occurred six times. It seems that attention should focus on problem B, particularly as the number of times each problem occurred each week is consistent. If one week stood out from the others as having far more or far fewer problems arising, you would want to examine what happened during that week to see what you could learn from it.

Problem	Week			Total
	1	2	3	
A	II	III	II	7
B	IIII	~~IIII~~	IIII	13
C	II	I	III	6
Total	8	9	9	26

Data collected and compiled by T Tree by observation. Period: 30 June–14 July 2022.

FIGURE 27.5 Check sheet

The steps to using a check sheet are:

1 Agree and precisely define the events you want to monitor so that everyone is looking for the same thing.
2 Decide the period over which to collect data; this might be several hours or several weeks. Collect enough data over a long enough period to be as representative as possible, but not so much data that collecting it becomes an end in itself.
3 Check that your observations and samples are homogeneous; that is, from the same machine, person and so on. When this is not the case, stratify, or group, the samples (see stratification charts later in this chapter) and then sample each one individually.
4 Design a form that is clear and easy to use, labelling each column clearly and making sure that there is enough space to record your observations.
5 Collect the data. (Ensure that people have time to collect it.)
6 Examine your data. What does the data tell you? What points need actioning or what further information do you need?

Meaningful data

Having tools doesn't necessarily mean that people use them well. Thanks to technology, readily available information can result in an abundance of meaningless information. How can you assess what's important and what isn't?

Consider the goals you wish to achieve, what information you need, and what you want to do with it (e.g. spot trends, isolate problem areas, pinpoint where and when certain events occur). Think what data can provide the information you need, how to ensure the data is accurate, the size of the sample you need and any possible biases (e.g. from poorly gathered data). You need to collect good data for it to be useful. Then think about how best to arrange or display your data to make understanding it more straightforward.

Control charts

Transferable skills
2.1 Critical thinking
4.1 Data literacy

You can use control charts to monitor quality continuously and identify and analyse looming problems. As you can see in **Figure 27.6**, a control chart is a type of run chart that shows the upper and lower statistically acceptable limits of results drawn on either side of the average. Note that these are statistically acceptable limits that may or may not be the same as customer requirements or specifications. They may be tighter than you need or than the customer requires (are you putting too much effort into this?) or they may be looser than you need or than the customer wants (you'd better fix what you're doing or risk losing a customer).

Calculating the upper and lower control limits requires the use of complex statistical formulas and is usually done by specialists. Again, don't confuse the upper and lower limits of a control chart with specification limits. The former tells you what a process can do consistently, and the latter tells you what you or the customers think is needed.

After establishing the control limits, you can plot the sample averages onto a control chart. Operate the process following standard procedures (without any 'tweaking' or adjustments) and

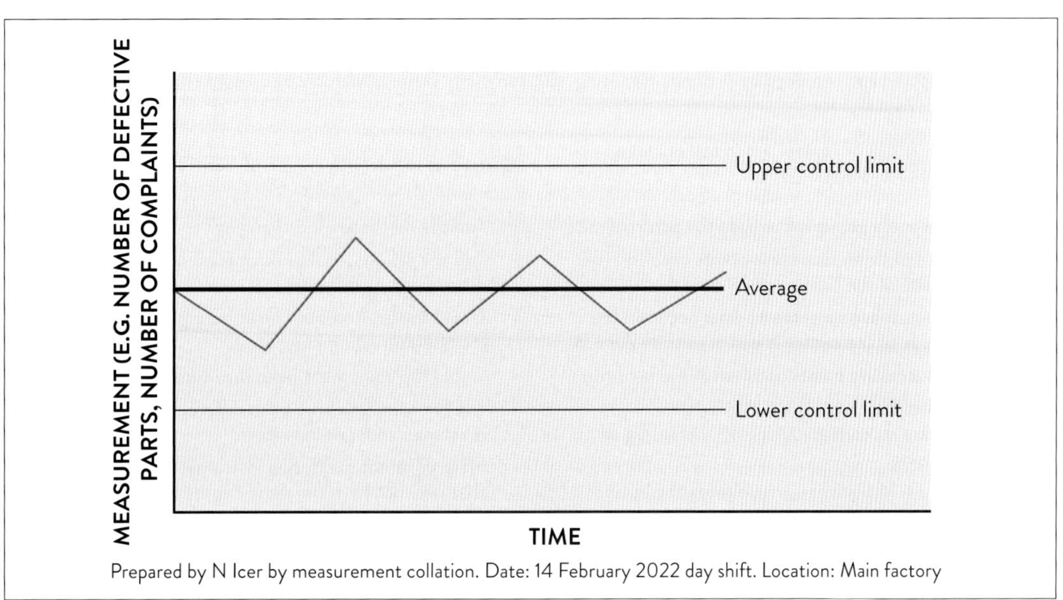

FIGURE 27.6 Control chart

check **key performance indicators (KPI)** either randomly or continually and keep records plotting variations of output so they can spot problems early on.

When the averages fall within the control limits, your process is 'in control'. Although there is always some variation in any system, you can probably improve your system (in this case, make it more reliable and predictable) by bringing the control limits closer to the average.

When any of the points fall outside the control limits or form unlikely patterns, your process is statistically 'out of control' – you need to examine and fix it. Find out what event or events caused the result to be outside the control limits (check out the 85:15 rule discussed in Chapter 16) and fix it to bring the process back into control. Ideally, you want a permanent 'fix' so that it doesn't happen again. Figure 27.7 gives some indications of processes that are 'out of control' and suggests questions you could ask.

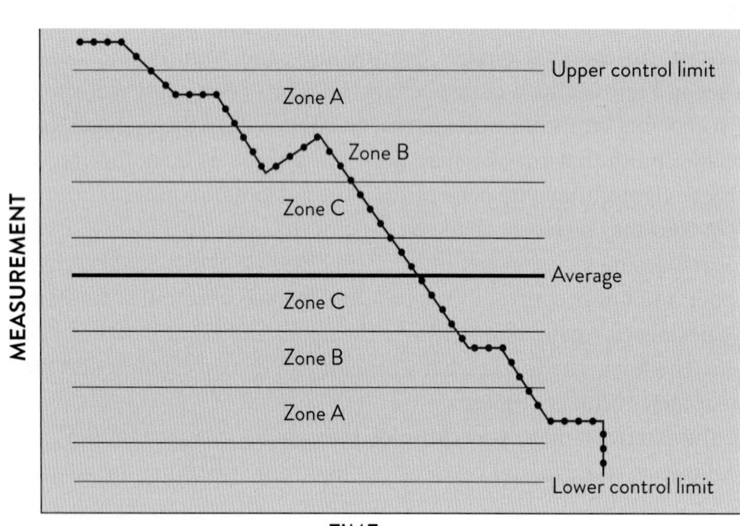

Data collected and compiled by A Bundance, using 50% sampling. Date: 3 March 2022, night shift. Location: Main factory

A process is 'out of control' when one or more of the following happens:

1 One or more points fall outside the control limits.
2 Two out of three successive points occur on the same side of the centre line in Zone A.
3 Four out of five successive points occur on the same side of the centre line in or outside Zone B.
4 Nine successive points occur on one side of the average line.
5 There are six consecutive points increasing or decreasing.
6 There are 14 points in a row alternating up and down.
7 There are 15 points in a row within Zone C.

Questions to ask with an out-of-control process:

- Are the methods used changing?
- Are the raw materials, information or other process inputs different?
- Could the environment be affecting the process (temperature, humidity, etc.)?
- Could the equipment need maintenance?
- Did the samples come from different methods, machines, shifts or operators?
- Have different measuring instruments been used that may not have the same degree of accuracy?
- Is everyone trained in how to carry out the process?
- What has changed in the process or the environment (e.g. maintenance procedures, training, overtime levels, raw materials)?

FIGURE 27.7 Out-of-control systems

When variations become too wide or too frequent, you 'fix the process' to identify and correct the causes of low quality. While this doesn't guarantee perfection, it helps to identify and correct the causes of below-standard performance quickly and prevent substandard products from being used again in the production process or being dispatched to customers.

Remember that every process and system has natural variation, but too much variation results in unreliable quality and increased costs. Control charts show you how much variation exists in a process, whether this variation is random or follows a pattern, and whether or not the process is in statistical control. Thus, they indicate whether a problem exists and help you implement and monitor solutions. For example, control charts show you:

- how long it takes to complete a process (produce a product or service; e.g. answer a customer query, make a sale, resolve a customer complaint, send out an invoice)
- how machine A's productivity and quality compares with machine B's
- the running speeds, temperature, pressures and other factors in a process.

You can also use control charts as a monitoring tool by taking samples at regular intervals and plotting them on the control chart. Monitoring this ensures that the process doesn't change and remains reliable. It also highlights any non-conformance or variations outside the control limits that you need to investigate.

Histograms

Transferable skills
4.1 Data literacy

Histograms are bar charts that show the number of units in each category you are studying. It's best to display these bar graphs showing the frequency with which certain events occur; this is called a *frequency distribution*. Whereas Pareto charts display characteristics of a product or service, called *attribute data* (e.g. complaints, defects, errors), histograms show the distribution of *measurement data* (e.g. dimensions, temperature). Histograms can reveal the amount of variation in a process and help you discover and describe a problem, analyse it and monitor its solution.

Figure 27.8 contains a typical histogram. It shows the greatest number of units in the centre with a roughly equal number of units on either side. Statistically, a *normal distribution curve*, or bell shape, is what you can expect from any process because every process varies over time. Repeated samples of any process that is 'under control' follow this pattern. When a histogram does not show this pattern, you need to investigate. Figure 27.9 shows an out-of-control process where the data is 'piled up' at points to the left of centre. A distribution like this is referred to as *skewed*.

You can use histograms to identify and analyse problems and monitor a process. When examining histograms, look at the shape of the distribution for surprises. For example, a distribution that you would expect to be 'normal' (a centred curve) is skewed. Are most measurements skewed on the 'high side' or the 'low side'? Look for whether the 'spread' of the curve (variability) falls within specifications; when it does not, how far outside the specifications is it? Analyse the process further to find out what you can do to bring it back to specifications. Table 27.1 shows you how to calculate the number of classes according to the data points.

TABLE 27.1 Calculating classes

Number of data points	Number of classes
Under 50	15 to 7
51 to 100	16 to 10
101 to 250	17 to 12
Over 250	10 to 20

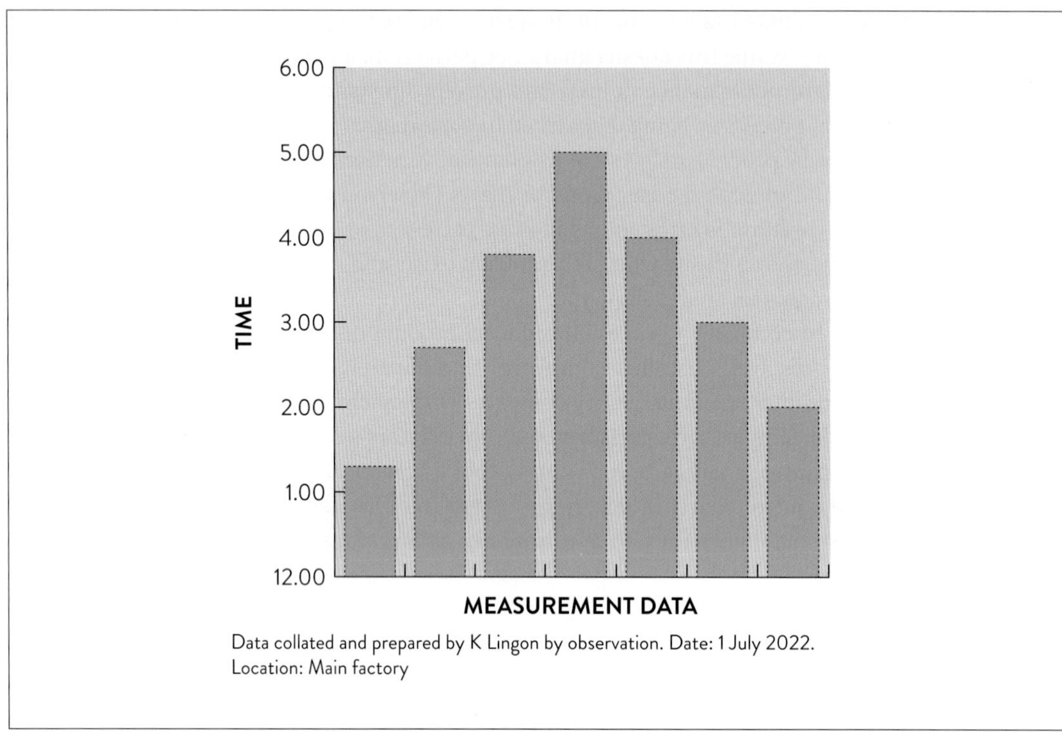

FIGURE 27.8 A histogram of a process that is 'in control'

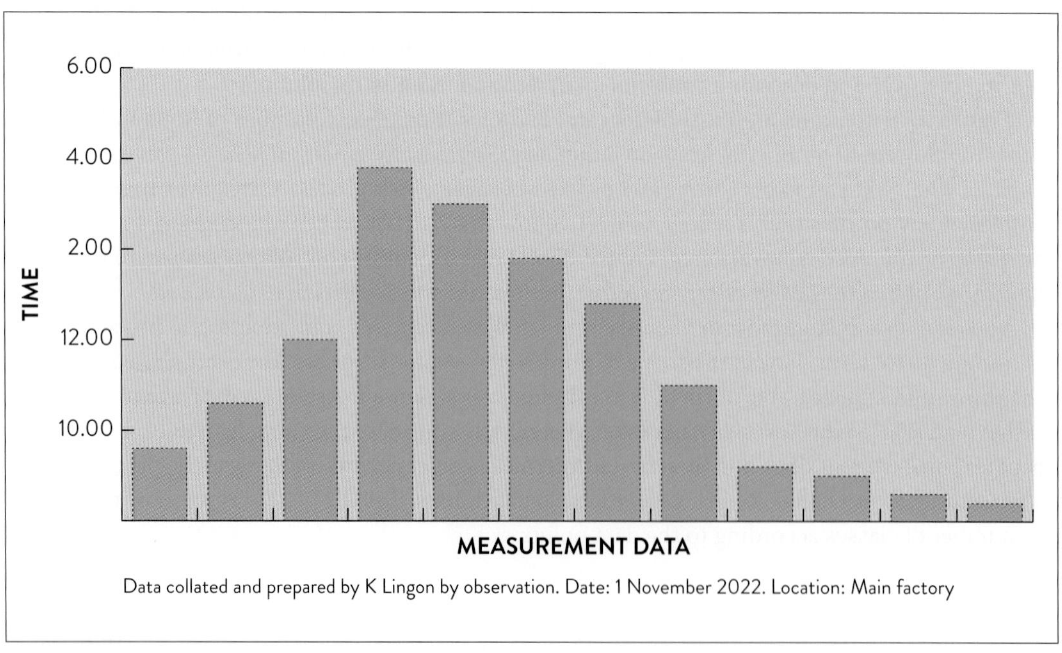

FIGURE 27.9 A histogram of a process that is 'out of control'

To construct a histogram, follow these steps:

1. Gather your data (*data set*) and count the number of data points in your data set.
2. Determine the range (R) value for the entire data set. The range is the smallest data point subtracted from the largest.
3. Divide the range value into a certain number of classes (K) or *bars* on the chart.
4. Determine the class width (H) using this formula:

$$H = \frac{R}{K}$$

5. Decide where each bar on the histogram should begin and end by determining the class boundary, or end points. Take the smallest measurement in the data set and use that number (or round it down to an appropriate lower number) as the lower end point for your first class boundary. Then add the class width to your lower end point, and this number becomes your next lower class boundary, as shown in this example:

$$\text{Smallest measurement in the data set} = 7 = \text{lower end point}$$
$$\text{class width} = 0.20$$
$$7 + 0.20 = 7.20 = \text{next lower end point}$$
$$7.20 + 0.20 = 7.40 = \text{next lower end point}$$

Therefore, the first class (or bar on the histogram) would be 7 and would include all data points up to but not including 7.20. The next class would start at 7.20 and include data points up to but not including 7.40. The third class would start at 7.40 and stop just before data point 7.60, and so on. Keep adding the class width to the lowest class boundary until you obtain the correct number of classes containing the range of all your data points. This process makes each class mutually exclusive – each data point fits into one and only one class (or bar) – and gives you an accurate histogram.

6. Construct a frequency table based on the number of classes, class width and class boundary, calculated above. A frequency table is a histogram in tabular form.
7. Construct a histogram based on the frequency table, as shown in Figure 27.10.

Use the histogram to diagnose variations and problems in a system. In the example shown in Figure 27.10, the data centres on 7.80 to 7.99, which is close to a normal curve. If the specification for the temperature were 5.5 to 8.5 with a target of 7, the histogram would show that the process was running high and producing too much unacceptable product. If, on the other hand, the temperature specification were 7 to 9 with a target of 8, the process would be in control.

When studying histograms, remember that some processes are naturally skewed – not all follow a natural bell-shaped curve. When a class suddenly stops at one point without a previous decline in number, check your data for accuracy; someone may have made a mistake. When a histogram shows two high points, check whether two or more sources provided the data; if so, go back and get homogeneous data.

Pie charts

Transferable skills
4.1 Data literacy

As Figure 27.11 shows, pie charts are circular graphs in which the entire circle represents 100 per cent (not 360 degrees) of the data. You divide the circle, or pie, into percentage slices that clearly show the relative sizes (e.g. amounts, frequencies) of the data you are studying. A pie chart can indicate where to begin your problem-solving efforts. Be sure to mark the subject matter clearly, showing the percentages within the slices and what each slice represents.

Class	Class boundaries	Mid-point	Frequency (number of data points falling into this class)	Total
1	7.00–7.19	7.1	I	1
2	7.20–7.39	7.3	HH IIII	9
3	7.40–7.59	7.5	HH HH HH II	17
4	7.60–7.79	7.7	HH HH HH HH HH II	27
5	7.80–7.99	7.9	HH HH HH HH HH HH I	31
6	8.00–8.19	8.1	HH HH HH HH I	21
7	8.20–8.39	8.3	HH HH II	12
8	8.40–8.59	8.5	III	3
9	8.60–8.79	8.7	IIII	4
10	8.80–8.99	8.9		0

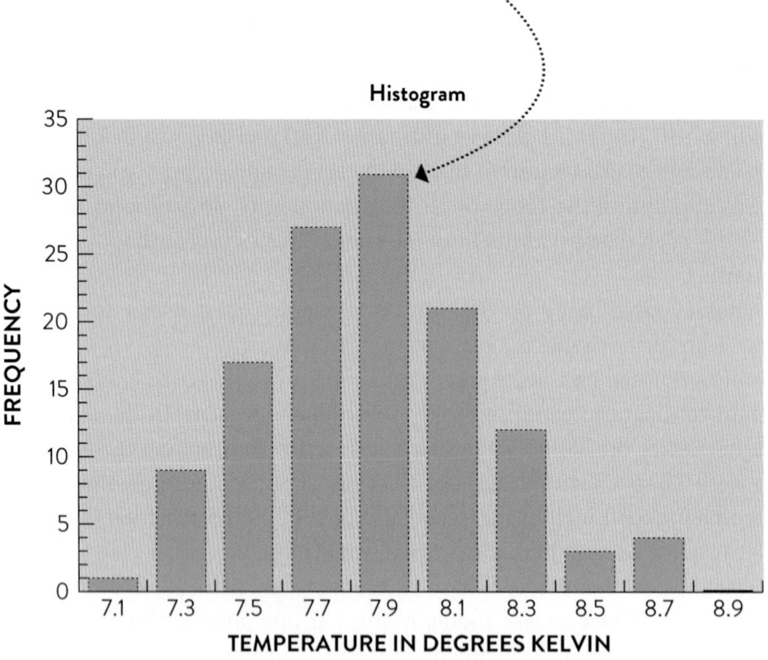

Data collated and prepared by L Ninio, based on thermostat readings. Date: 2 December 2022. Location: Main factory

FIGURE 27.10 Constructing a histogram from a frequency table

Transferable skills
4.1 Data literacy

Run charts

Run charts are a simple way to show trends in processes such as administrative errors, customer complaints, machine downtime, productivity, scrap or yields. Seeing how things vary over time (are they getting worse, staying the same or improving?) can help you to identify, describe and analyse a problem as well as monitor a process.

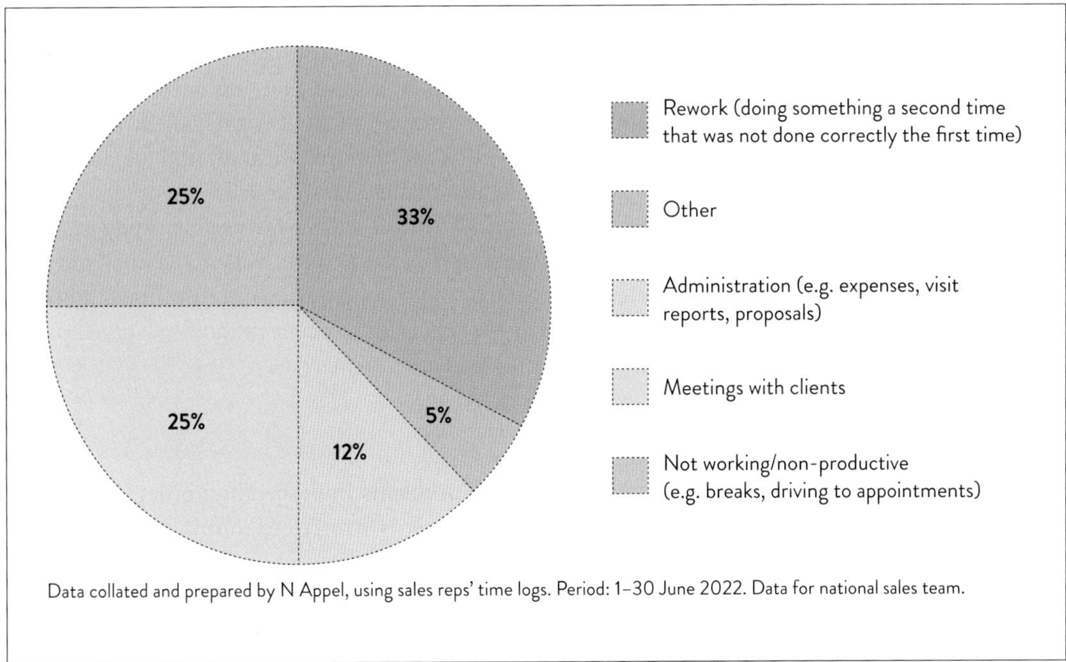

FIGURE 27.11 Pie chart: time usage of sales representatives

Run charts are simple to construct and interpret. To make a run chart, plot what you measure as points on a graph and then connect the points. Plot the measurements in the order that you made them since you are tracking them over time (see Figure 27.12).

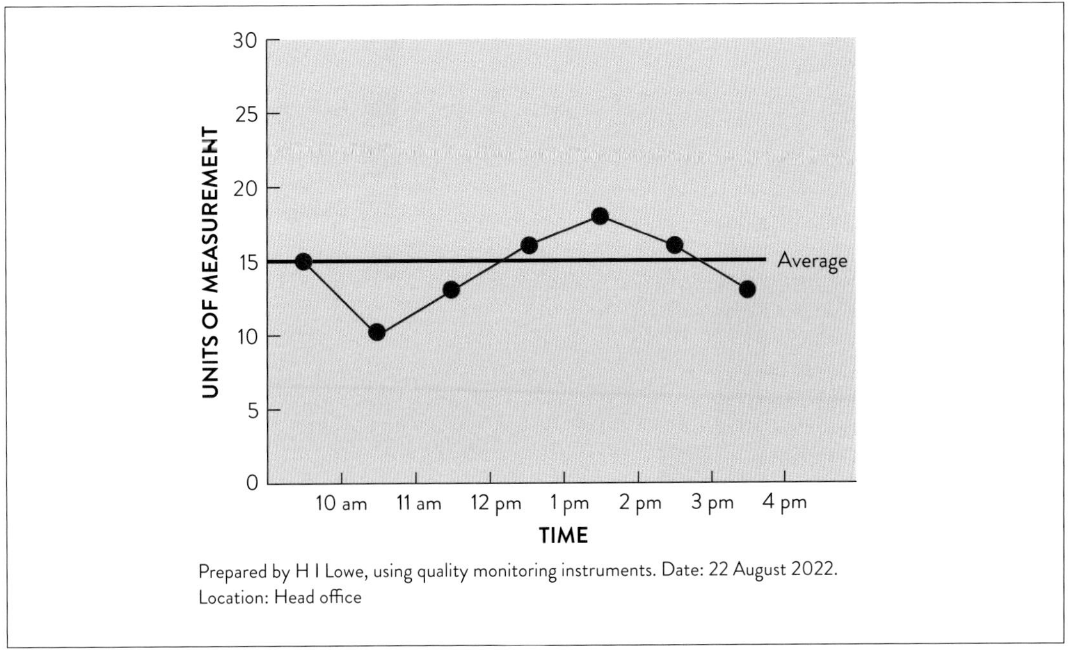

FIGURE 27.12 Run chart

Not every variation that shows up in run charts is important. Pay attention to any wide variations, significant variations and meaningful shifts in the average that are unlikely to occur by chance. Variations might point to a problem or looming problem in a process that you need to investigate and eliminate (or when the change is positive, see how you can make it a permanent part of the process). For example, when monitoring a system, an equal number of points should fall above and below the average. When this does not happen, it indicates that either an unusual 'event' or a change has occurred in the system or the average has changed. When the shift is favourable, study it to find out why, so that you can make the change a permanent part of the system. When it is unfavourable, find out why it has occurred and eliminate the possibility of it happening again. Examine any steady increase or decrease in a trend, too; since you would not expect this to occur randomly, it can indicate a necessary change that you need to investigate.

Transferable skills
4.1 Data literacy

Pareto charts

Pareto charts are vertical bar charts that plot events or problems in descending order of quantity, showing you the relative importance of all the issues or events you are examining. Pareto charts direct your attention and efforts to the critical problems and help you choose a starting point for problem-solving. Pareto charts can also help you to identify and describe a problem or its basic cause, plan to resolve it and monitor your success.

From the information shown in **Figure 27.13**, you would want to investigate the causes of raw materials run-outs to try to stop this occurring. Then you would want to find the causes and sources

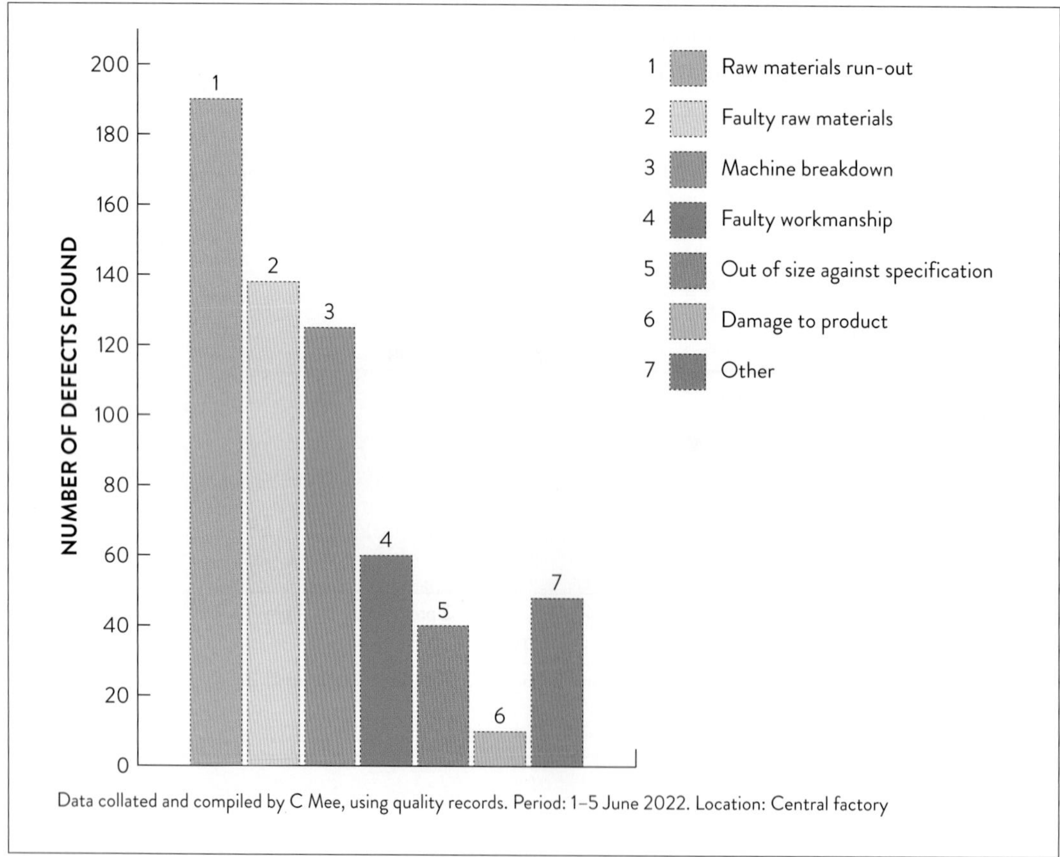

FIGURE 27.13 Pareto chart: defects found at in-process inspection

of faulty raw materials and discuss this with your suppliers; you might even consider changing to a more reliable supplier. Next, you would want to investigate the types and causes of machine breakdowns and see what you could do to stop or reduce them.

You can compile Pareto charts from check sheets or other forms of data collection. To construct a Pareto chart, follow these steps:

1 Select the problems to compare and rank.
2 Select the unit of measurement (e.g. cost, frequency, percentage) and the period to study (e.g. hours, days, weeks).
3 Gather the data.
4 Plot the data by listing the units of measurement vertically and each category (problem or event) from left to right horizontally in decreasing order. Mark the measurements and categories clearly. Combine the categories with the fewest items into one category called 'other', which goes at the extreme right as the last bar. (This final bar is often 'higher' than the bars to its immediate left because it contains several categories.)
5 Draw a vertical bar above each category with the height representing the unit of measurement in that classification.

Pareto charts can provide surprising insights. For example, the two charts in Figure 27.14 illustrate the importance of examining a problem from different perspectives – resolving the most frequently occurring problems first might not be the most cost-effective way to proceed. But, as Figure 27.15 shows, you sometimes need to use your imagination when measuring problems and information. Showing defects by type and by machine doesn't give you very much information but showing defects by shift really gives you something to investigate.

Figure 27.16 shows how you can use Pareto charts to measure the impact of change, with 'before' and 'after' comparisons. In the example shown, the number of complaints drops markedly after the introduction of a revised process flow. Pareto charts can also help you to break down a problem, as shown in Figure 27.17. This can help to isolate the causes of problems from their symptoms.

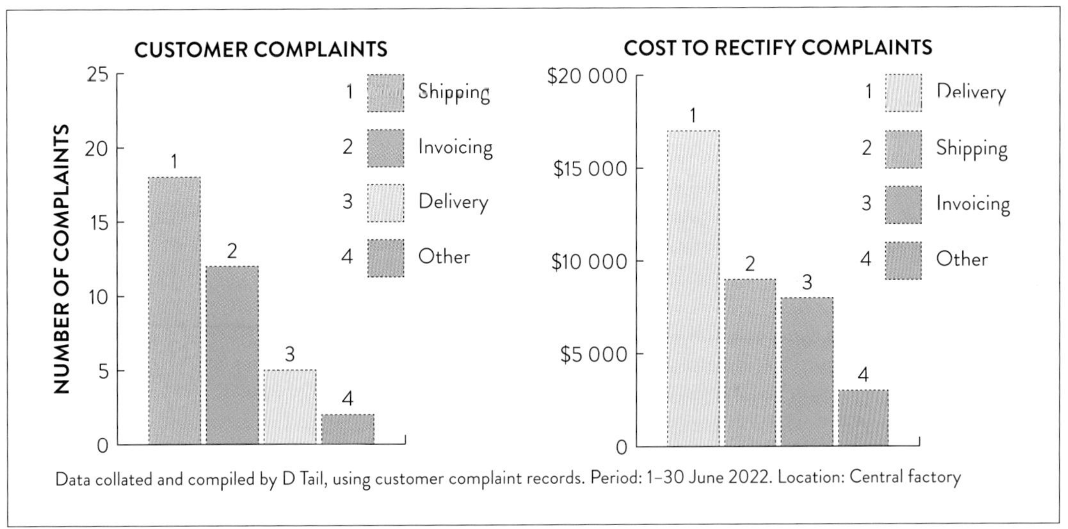

FIGURE 27.14 Using Pareto charts to identify the most important problems through different measurements

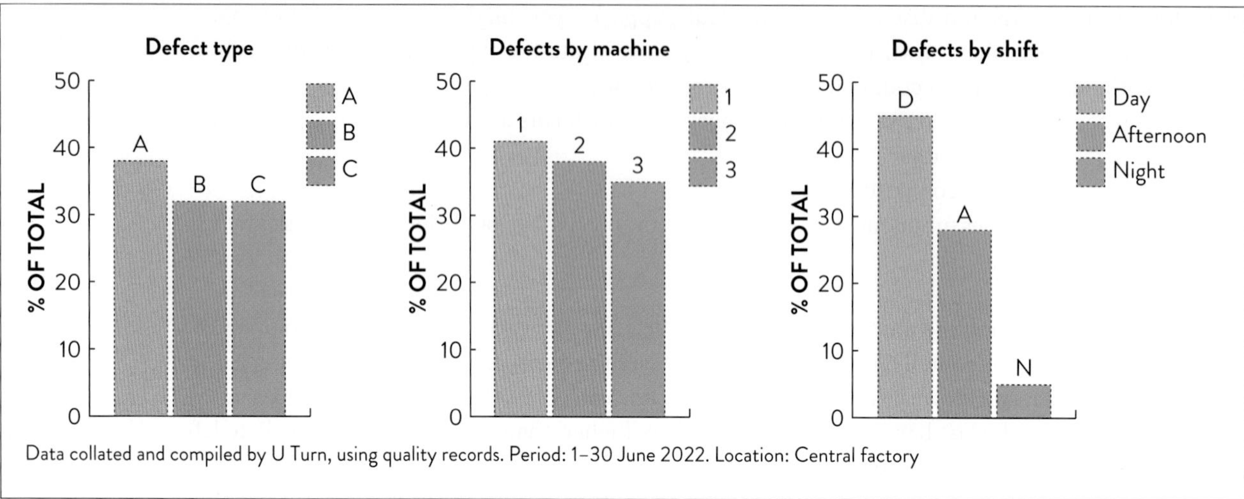

FIGURE 27.15 Using Pareto charts to analyse information in different ways

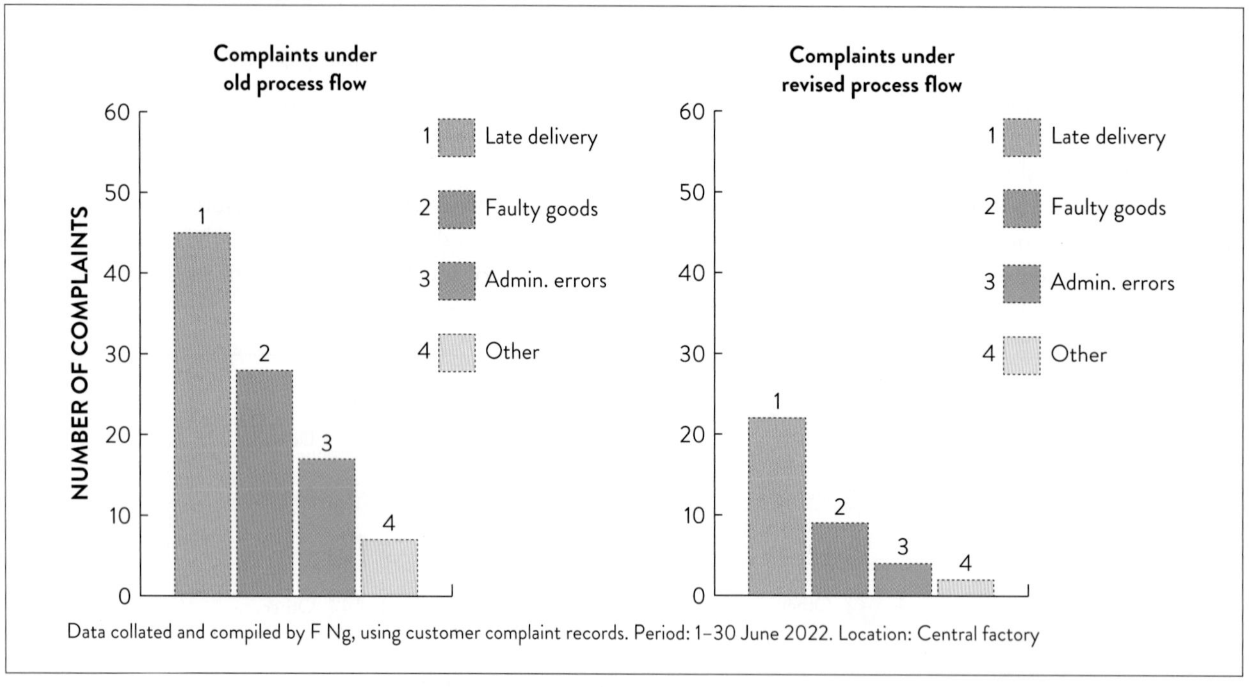

FIGURE 27.16 Using Pareto charts to measure the impact of change

Use common sense when constructing and analysing Pareto charts. For example, it may pay to resolve a recurring complaint from a major customer before resolving numerous other complaints from small customers.

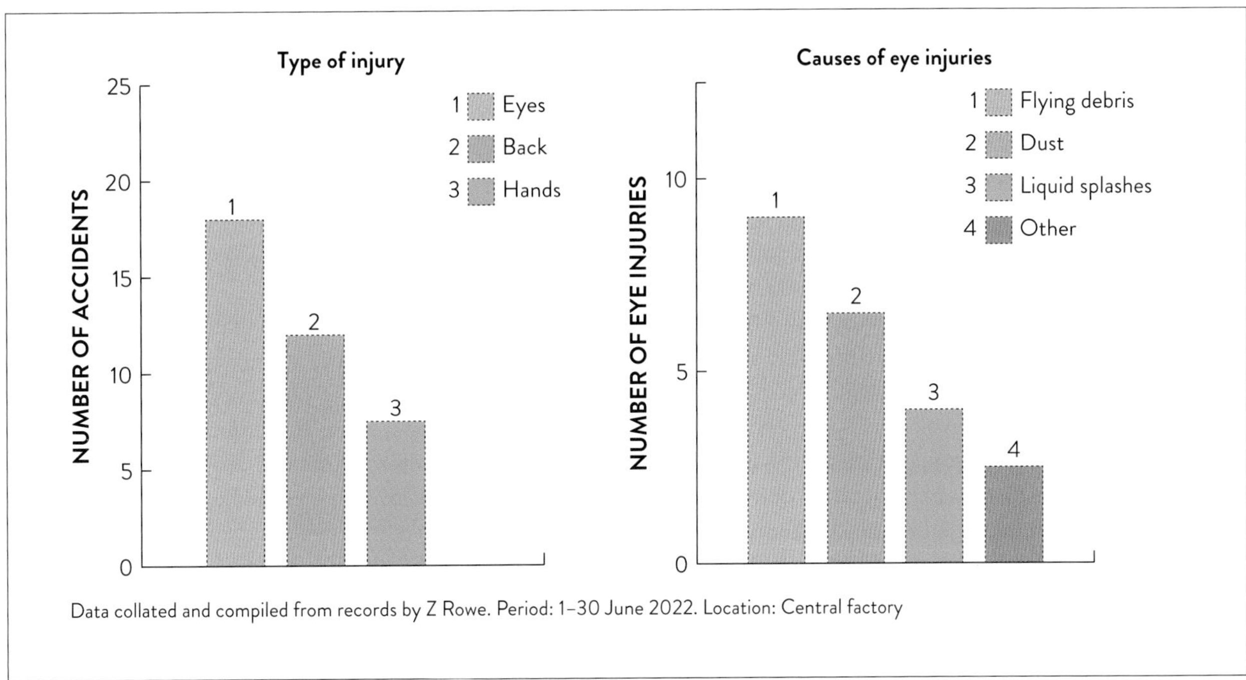

FIGURE 27.17 Using Pareto charts to break down a problem

Tips on charting

Here are some tips to help you get the most from your charts:

- Base the data you use on random representative samples taken from homogeneous groups and gather it consistently (in the same way each time) to ensure that it is not biased.
- Don't make decisions based on just one piece of evidence. Gather other information to ensure you have it right.
- Get help from experts whenever you need it; that's why they're there.
- Keep it simple. Use the most appropriate tool or technique possible, and don't overcomplicate your graphs.
- Label every chart clearly.
- Remember that the point of charts and graphs is not to collect and display just *any* numbers. The point is to collect and display *meaningful* numbers – information that helps you to analyse and improve your services and processes.
- Use your common sense when interpreting graphs and charts.

27.2 Analysing problems and opportunities

> Quod gratis asseritur, gratis negatur: What can be asserted without evidence can be dismissed without evidence.
>
> Christopher Hitchens, *God is not great: How religion poisons everything*, Twelve Books, New York, 2007, p. 150.

Transferable skills
2.1 Critical thinking
2.3 Business strategy
4.1 Data literacy

Now you can get to work analysing the situation. You can use the techniques already discussed: ask 'Why?' five times, brainstorming, cause-and-effect (or fishbone) diagrams, control charts, force-field analysis, histograms, run charts and Pareto charts. We consider four other systematic techniques in the following sections – checkerboard analysis, is/is not comparisons, **scatter diagrams** and stratification charts. You can also use process capability charts to analyse problems and opportunities; we discuss these in Section 27.3.

Transferable skills
2.1 Critical thinking

Checkerboard analysis

Checkerboard analysis uses a matrix to analyse a situation. Elements of one key aspect of a problem or opportunity are placed down one side of the chart and elements of another aspect across the top. Concentrate your analysis on where they intersect.

The example shown in Figure 27.18 is from a chain of wholesale shops that serve mainly trade account customers but also sell to the general public. The shops have experienced problems with delayed invoices sent from head office, primarily to general public customers. The preparation of these invoices is based on information sent in by the shops. From this information, you would probably concentrate on the form itself and the number of interruptions occurring in the shops as the forms are being filled out. How could the form be improved? What could be done to reduce the errors caused by interruptions in the shops? This might lead you to consider changing the system of information gathering itself. You would probably also want to clarify why the shops are providing insufficient information and the cause of the processing difficulties at head office.

Problem: 'How to speed up the invoicing process to non-trade customers'

Problems within accounts / Problems at source	Insufficient information	Inaccurate information	Details incorrect	Processing difficulties at head office	Accounts staff not clear about procedure	Total
Form for collecting information confusing and repetitive	×	×	×		×	4
Staff too 'hurried' to collect details correctly and/or fully	×	×	×			3
Too many interruptions	×	×	×	×		4
Correct pricing information unavailable	×			×	×	3
Forms not passed on to accounts quickly enough				×		1
Forms not batched correctly at source				×		1
Total	4	3	3	4	2	16

Data collated and compiled by J Cob by analysing head office invoices and information provided by shops.
Date: 1 July–31 July 2022. Location: Head office

FIGURE 27.18 Checkerboard analysis

Is/is not comparison

Transferable skills
2.1 Critical thinking

To do an is/is not comparison, write down what you *know* about the problem in one column and, in a second column, write what you know is *not* part of the problem. Use the 'Where?', 'When?', 'Who?', 'How often?', 'How much or how bad?' and 'What?' triggers to guide your thinking.

Then compare the *Is* and the *Is not* columns, looking for differences and changes. The *Is* and *Is not* columns give you points to follow up, which could lead you to identify the source of the problem. An example is shown in Table 27.2, which shows an is/is not comparison of absenteeism among office staff to identify points to follow up in order to improve the situation.

TABLE 27.2 An is/is not comparison of absenteeism

	Is	Is not	Points to follow up
Where?	General office	Accounts, public relations, sales and marketing, finance, human resources	Working conditions, hours of work, supervision What is different about the general office?
When?	Most days	No obvious patterns (e.g. Fridays or Mondays)	Complete a check sheet to identify any hidden patterns
Who?	Mostly newer staff	No absenteeism from longer-serving staff	Make a histogram of age groups to check this Check ages and profiles for 'job fit' Check training and induction given to new recruits Check their jobs for job interest; are they different from jobs of longer serving staff?
How often?	About 17% on any given day		Benchmark with local organisations to see how bad this problem is for them
How bad?	Problem may be increasing	Not getting better or staying the same?	Check this year's absenteeism rates against those of previous years
What?	Mostly one-day absences	Seldom longer than two days	

Prepared by: General Office team from internal records, covering 1 April–30 June 2022. Date: 21 July 2022. Location: Head Office

Scatter diagrams

Transferable skills
4.1 Data literacy

Does overtime affect quality? Does training improve results? Does placing an advertisement on the right-hand side of a screen create more sales than placing it on the left-hand side of a screen? Does a new way of greeting customers affect their reported satisfaction with the interaction? To know the answers to these questions for sure, construct a scatter diagram. A scatter diagram reveals any relationships between one variable and another and possible cause-and-effect relationships. Scatter diagrams can't prove whether one variable causes another, but they clarify whether a relationship exists and how strong it is. In this way, scatter diagrams help you analyse a situation.

In scatter diagrams, the horizontal axis measures one variable and the vertical axis the second variable. Figure 27.19 is a typical scatter diagram showing a positive relationship or correlation between two variables. Notice that the plotted points form a clustered pattern. The direction and tightness of the cluster indicate the strength of the relationship between the two variables. The tighter the cluster and the more it resembles a straight line, the stronger the relationship between the two variables. Figure 27.20 shows other scatter diagrams and how to interpret them.

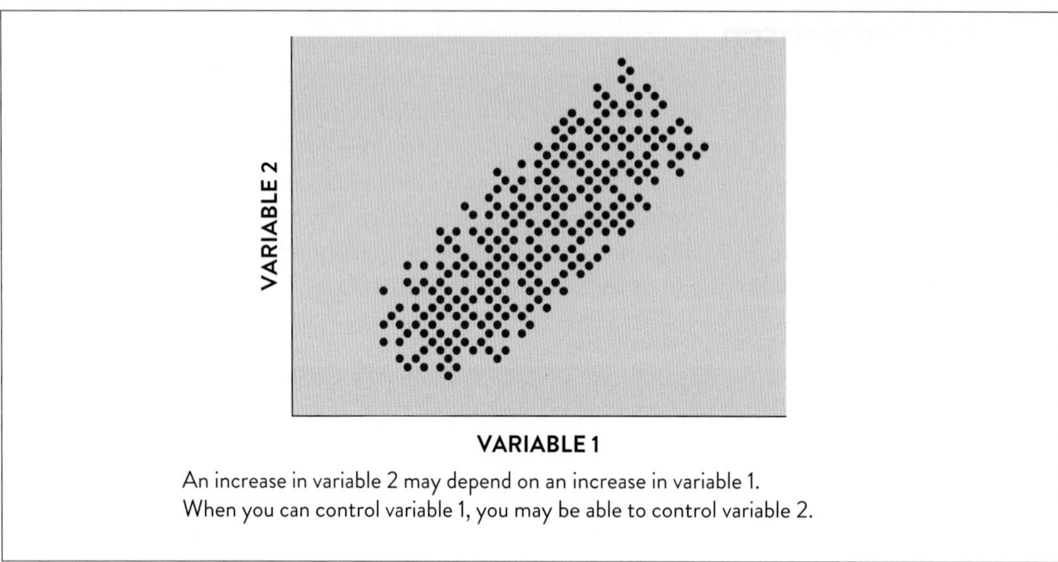

An increase in variable 2 may depend on an increase in variable 1.
When you can control variable 1, you may be able to control variable 2.

FIGURE 27.19 Scatter diagram: strong positive correlation

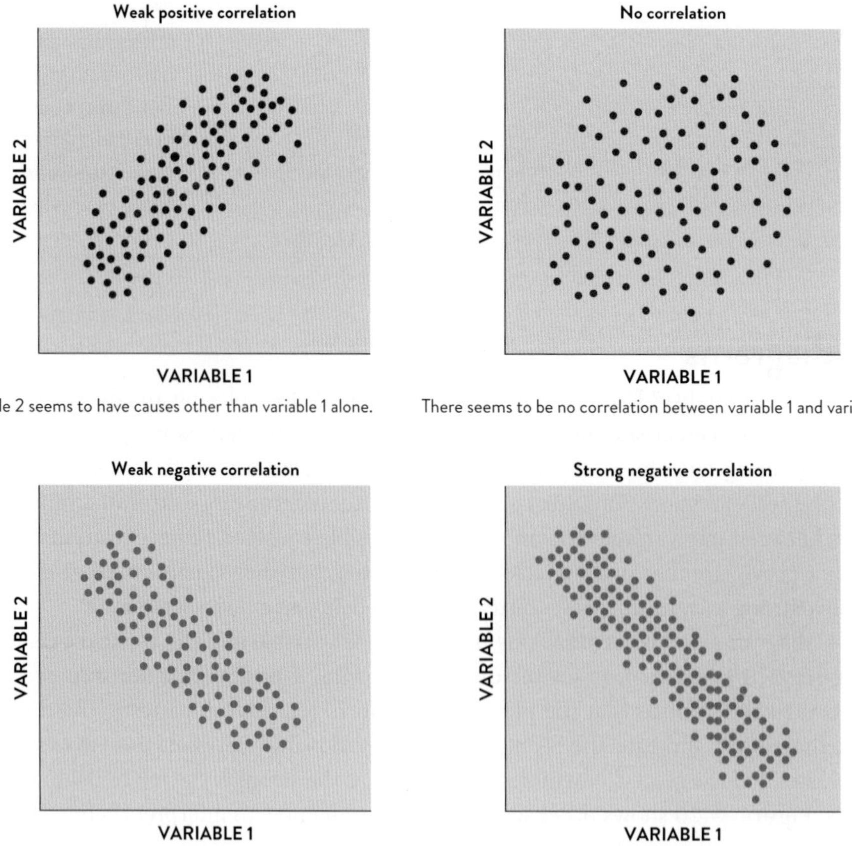

Weak positive correlation

VARIABLE 2

VARIABLE 1

Variable 2 seems to have causes other than variable 1 alone.

No correlation

VARIABLE 2

VARIABLE 1

There seems to be no correlation between variable 1 and variable 2.

Weak negative correlation

VARIABLE 2

VARIABLE 1

An increase in variable 1 may cause variable 2 to decrease somewhat.

Strong negative correlation

VARIABLE 2

VARIABLE 1

An increase in variable 1 seems to cause a decrease in variable 2. You may be able to control variable 2 by controlling variable 1.

FIGURE 27.20 Scatter diagrams and their interpretations

Here are the steps for making a scatter diagram (persons 4 to 49 have been omitted here for space reasons, but you would fill them in on your diagram):

1 Collect 1 to 50 paired samples of data that you think may be related and construct a data sheet, as shown in Table 27.3.
2 Draw the horizontal and vertical axes of the scatter diagram, with the values increasing as you move up on the vertical axis and to the right on the horizontal axis. Put the variable you are investigating as the possible cause on the horizontal axis and the effect variable on the vertical axis.

TABLE 27.3 Data sheet example

Person	Weight (kg)	Height (cm)
1	73	178
2	65	155
3	100	191
...	...	...
...	...	...
...	...	...
50	82	155

Remember that negative relationships are as important as positive relationships, and that scatter diagrams show only relationships – they do not prove cause and effect.

Stratification charts

Transferable skills
4.1 Data literacy

Stratification helps sort out confusing data that masks the facts; as might happen, for example, when the recorded data is non-homogeneous (from many sources but treated as one number). Stratification is also useful for identifying problems and analysing data. To find improvement opportunities, break the data down into more meaningful categories or classifications to help you describe a problem and focus on and monitor corrective action. Stratification charts can also help you monitor a process.

The stratification charts in Figure 27.21 begin with a run chart showing that the number of minor injuries has been steadily increasing over the last 12 months. However, this is the total of all minor accidents – we don't know what type of accidents they are (bumps, burns, cuts, scratches), where they are occurring (which department, which machines, which processes), when they are happening (which shift or day of the week) or any other potentially important information. We need to examine the data more closely, so the run chart is broken down into two stratification charts, making it easier to isolate the real problem and act to resolve it.

The first stratification chart in Figure 27.21 shows that you should probably investigate the cause of falls first and try to reduce them, and then move your attention to strains. The second stratification chart shows that distribution seems to be a particularly bad area for minor injuries, and you should focus your attention there, at least initially. It also indicates that the main factory had a far higher than the average number of minor injuries in September and December, which you should investigate.

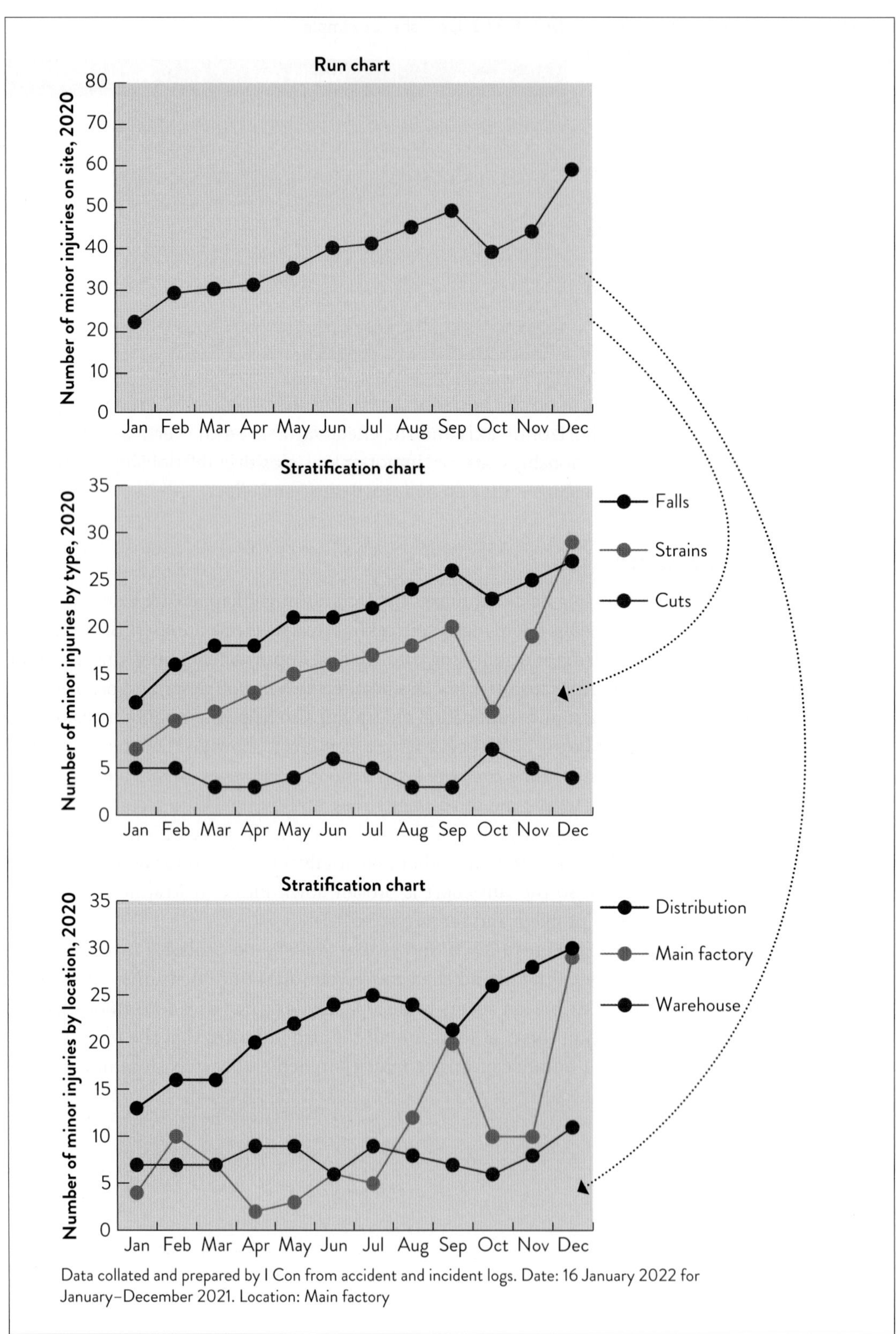

FIGURE 27.21 Stratification charts

27.3 Resolving problems and capitalising on opportunities

> He uses statistics as a drunken man uses lampposts – for support rather than illumination.
>
> Andrew Lang, Scottish historian and author, 1903.

Transferable skills

1.2 Entrepreneurship/ small business skills

2.1 Critical thinking

2.3 Business strategy

3.4 Leadership

4.1 Data literacy

You now have a sound basis to begin resolving problems and taking advantage of opportunities. But don't go mad with data – use your common sense. As the saying goes: 'Not everything that can be counted counts, and not everything that counts can be counted.'[1] Keep your thinking cap on.

Flow charts

Transferable skills

1.2 Entrepreneurship/ small business skills

2.1 Critical thinking

4.1 Data literacy

A flow chart is a graphical representation of an algorithm, a detailed sequence of simple steps that helps you work through a situation to decide what to do. By helping you 'see' each step in a process and how it relates to the other steps, flow charts can also help you:

- analyse a process to find out where value is (or is not) added
- design and refine procedures and processes and train people to use them
- identify deviations from the ideal path a process should follow and sources of problems
- identify problems in a process by highlighting backtracking, duplication of effort, hassles and wasted effort
- resolve problems and inefficiencies.

Flow charts are useful for relatively straightforward problems and operations; with more complex problems and decisions, use the problem-solving and decision-making steps explained in Chapter 26. With very complex problems, include creative thinking (discussed in Chapter 19).

As shown in Figure 27.22, show all the steps of a process inside boxes; when a decision needs to be made, use a diamond instead of a box. Use circles or ovals for the first and last steps of the process being charted and arrows to connect the boxes, decision diamonds and circles to show the sequence of activities. Each activity has one arrow leading into it and one arrow coming from it, leading to the next activity or decision. Decision diamonds have two arrows, one leading to a 'yes' action and the other to a 'no' action.

You can make a flow chart of any process – from administration to customer service to production – showing the flow of materials or the steps involved in, for example, producing an invoice, serving a customer, making a sale or making a product.

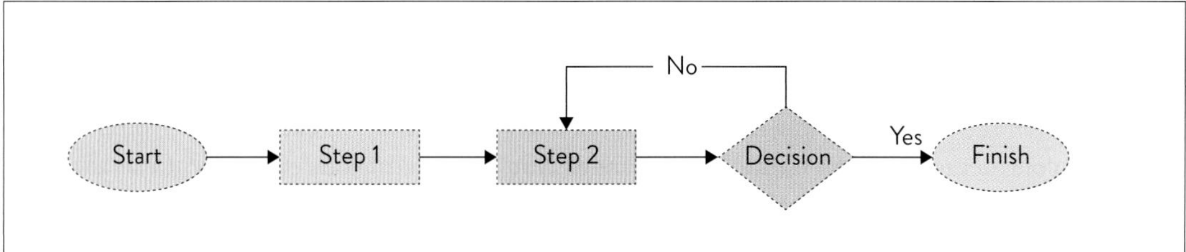

FIGURE 27.22 Flow chart symbols

To develop a flow chart, follow these steps:

1 Gather together the people who work in the system or process being charted.
2 Discuss and agree on the steps the process entails and diagram the process as it is currently followed.
3 Agree on how the process should ideally occur when everything is working right and diagram this.
4 Compare the two charts to find out where you can improve the process.

Make sure that everyone is clear about the process they are flow-charting, including where it begins and ends. See that every feedback loop in the chart has an escape.

Transferable skills

1.2 Business operations

2.1 Critical thinking

2.3 Business strategy

Process capability charts

A system may be 'in control', but that doesn't mean it meets your needs; it only means it is consistent – it may be consistently bad. This is where process capability charts come in. They show you, given its natural variation (established by control charts), whether a process is capable of meeting the specifications and helps you find ways to improve it. You can also use process capability charts to monitor a system and check that your improvements are working. Capable systems meet customer requirements every time because they are 'in control' and the controls match the specifications.

As Figure 27.23 shows, capability charts show graphically whether or not your system is meeting requirements by illustrating how your process performs within its specification limits. A process capability index is calculated from the upper and lower specification limits, the measured natural variation in the process and the standard deviation in the process using formulas you can find online or in your organisation's software. When the process variation exceeds the specification, you know that there are too many defects or that services are not being provided satisfactorily. Even when the process variation is within specification, defects could still occur when the process is not centred on the specified target.

Test and learn

Once you've developed options, test them one at a time; when you test more than one at a time, you don't know which one worked if there's an improvement, and you don't see how the different options affected each other. So the only way to find out what drives results, positive or negative, is to change one thing at a time. When there is no improvement, remove the change and either refine it or try another option.

Have a large enough test group to offer statistically significant results; this is known as the scientific method. When you can, have a control group or control site, where there is no change. The control ensures that any change in your test group or test site wouldn't have happened anyway. For instance, when sales go up in your experimental, or test, group, that's great. But when they also go up in your control group, where nothing has changed, you can't claim your experiment was a success since sales would probably have risen without your intervention.

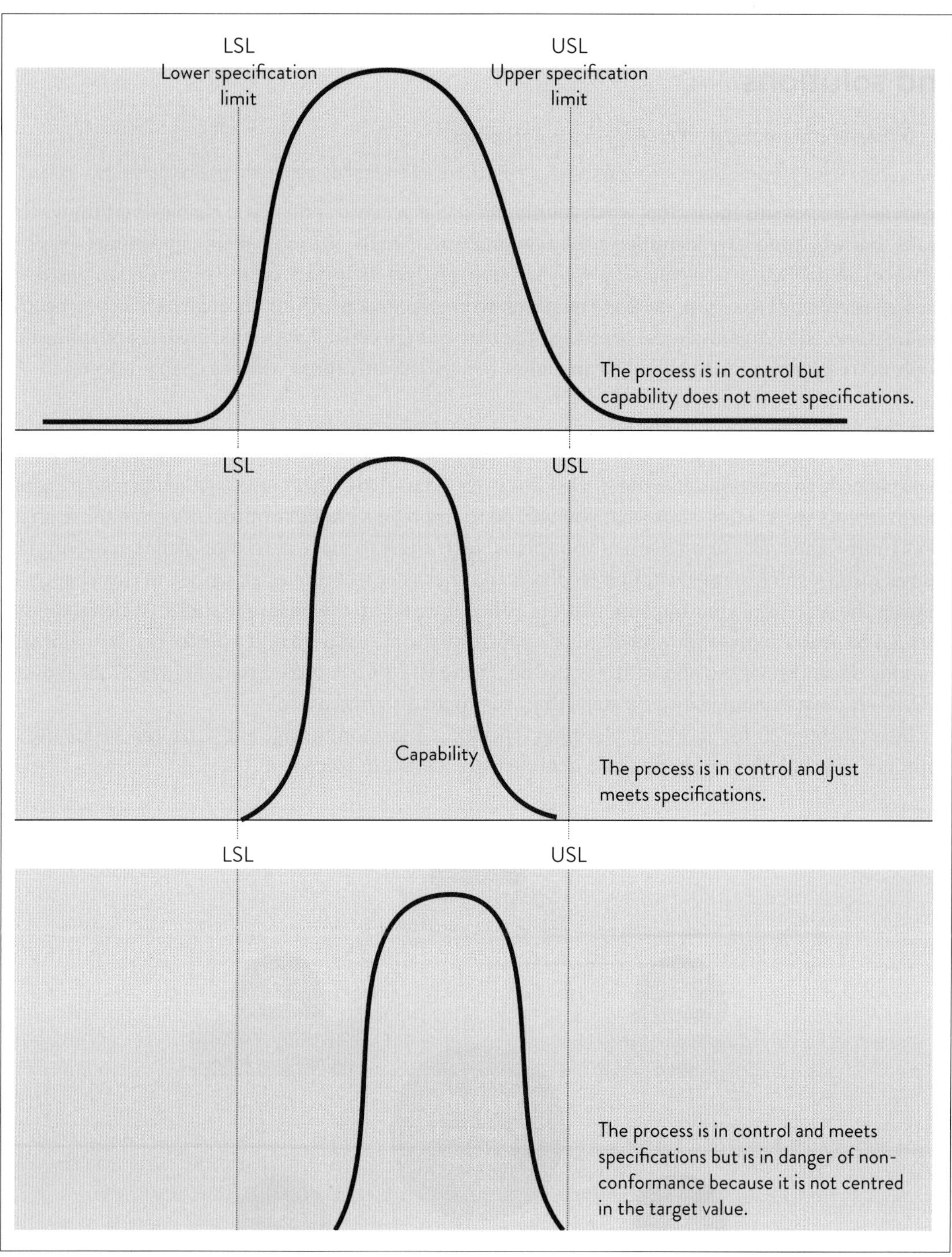

FIGURE 27.23 Process capability charts

27.4 Implementing and monitoring improvements and solutions

When you are through changing, you are through.

Percy Barnevik, Swedish former CEO of ABB Group, quoted in *Financial Times handbook of management* (Stuart Crainer, ed., 1995).

Transferable skills

1.2 Entrepreneurship/ small business skills

1.3 Sustainability

1.4 Business operations

2.3 Business strategy

We know from systems theory that when you change one aspect of a system, you change everything. This means that when you have identified a solution or a way to make the most of an opportunity, you still have work to do. Before implementing your solution, analyse its impact on the organisation upstream and downstream to make sure there are no unwanted repercussions. Think through its effect on people, resources and other organisational practices. You may want to consult with stakeholders and influential people in the organisation to hear their thoughts, too, particularly those who the change affects.

The P–D–C–A cycle

To implement your actions, use the P–D–C–A cycle (Plan–Do–Check–Act), which can help ensure improvements work. First, *plan* what you will do to improve a system or process or capitalise on an opportunity. Then *do* it or implement your plan. Next, *check* to make sure your plan is achieving the desired results; you can use customer feedback and the other techniques explained in this chapter to evaluate the success of your implementation. When it works, *act* to ensure it 'sticks'. When it doesn't work, go back and analyse your problem or opportunity some more to find a better resolution or way of taking advantage of the opportunity, and begin the P–D–C–A cycle again. Figure 27.24 shows a P–D–C–A cycle expanded into six steps that you might also find useful.

(See Chapter 20 for more on planning, checking and monitoring, and Chapter 24 for *do*, or introduce your solution or change, and *act* to ensure it stays in place.)

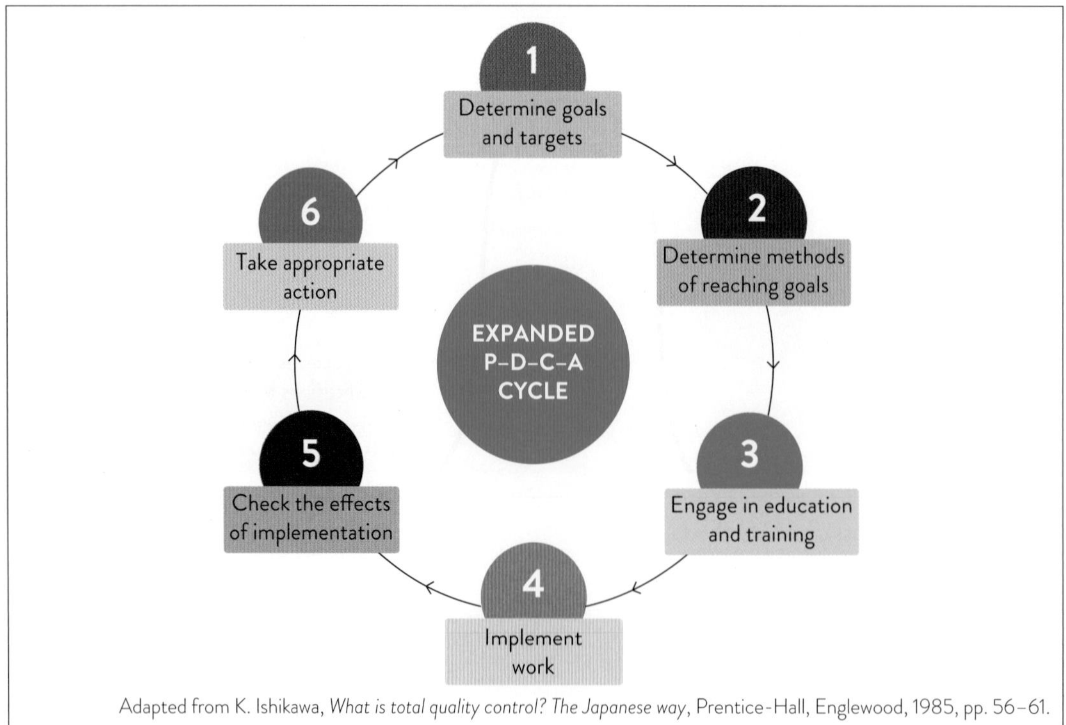

Adapted from K. Ishikawa, *What is total quality control? The Japanese way*, Prentice-Hall, Englewood, 1985, pp. 56–61.

FIGURE 27.24 An expanded P–D–C–A cycle

STUDY TOOLS

QUICK REVIEW

KEY CONCEPT 27.1 

a What is the difference between systematic techniques and statistical techniques?

b List the analytical and statistical tools and techniques you can use to help identify problems and opportunities, and define each one in your own words.

c When would you use a Pareto chart?

d What are the benefits of using solid statistical information to examine problems and measure performance to improve quality and service and make continuous improvements to all aspects of a team's and an organisation's operations?

KEY CONCEPT 27.2 

a List and in your own words define the analytical and statistical tools and techniques you can use to analyse problems and opportunities.

KEY CONCEPT 27.3 

a List the analytical and statistical tools and techniques you can use to resolve problems and capitalise on opportunities, and define each one in your own words.

KEY CONCEPT 27.4 

a What are the steps in implementing and monitoring improvements and solutions?

b What monitoring tools and techniques can you use to ensure processes remain efficient and effective?

BUILD YOUR SKILLS

KEY CONCEPT 27.1 

a Data is made up of numbers. Some data is useful; some isn't. What are some ways you can ensure that the data you collect is useful?

b Consider a problem you face. Write it down clearly, using the circling technique if you need to. Then gather data to understand it further and prepare a plan using the P–D–C–A cycle to implement a solution.

KEY CONCEPT 27.2 

a Consider the problem you might face in Build your skills question 27.1(b) and consider, is there a checkerboard analysis or is/is not comparison that could help extrapolate the problem?

KEY CONCEPT 27.3 

a Consider an opportunity you have, analyse it and prepare a plan to capitalise on it.

KEY CONCEPT 27.4 

a Considering the problem you worked on in Build your skills question 27.2(a) and the opportunity in Build your skills question 27.3(a), what monitoring methods can you use to show whether your plans are succeeding?

WORKPLACE ACTIVITIES

KEY CONCEPT 27.1 

a Give two examples of each of the tools and techniques you could use or have used in your workplace to identify problems and opportunities, explaining how you used them.

KEY CONCEPT 27.2 

a Give two examples of each of the tools and techniques you could use or have used in your workplace to analyse problems and opportunities, explaining how you used them.

KEY CONCEPT 27.3 

a Give two examples of each of the tools and techniques you could use or have used in your workplace to resolve problems and make the most of opportunities, explaining how you used them.

KEY CONCEPT 27.4 

a Give two examples of each of the tools and techniques you could use or have used in your workplace to implement improvements and solutions, explaining how you used them.

EXTENSION ACTIVITIES

Referring to the Snapshot at the beginning of this chapter, answer the following question:

1 Jess and her colleagues are at the point of designing and testing a new improved system for managing their customers. Consider what the P–D–C–A cycle is for this situation and what measures Jess can use to assess the proposed improved system.

CASE STUDY 27

KEEPING THE CUSTOMERS SATISFIED

Shelly Sanders has just been promoted to supervise the home furnishings department of the large department store where she works. The store manager made it clear to her that her first challenge was to turn around the poor showing of the department, particularly in customer satisfaction and also in sales, which were below budget. The department receives more complaints than any other in the store (although it rates about average in the chain).

Reasoning that dissatisfied customers contribute to a poor reputation in the community, which translates into poor sales, Shelly decides she needs to learn about the department's current customers and find out how they feel about purchasing from the department. Her first move is to check the department's information on repeat business. There isn't any.

Next, she hunts out the department's customer suggestions and complaints records to analyse, and finds a notebook of scrawled customer comments and queries – all negative. Wondering how valid the information is, but realising she probably won't find anything better, she draws up a check sheet to break down complaints and suggestions by frequency and type. Then she transfers the data onto Pareto charts and finds that the most common cause of customer dissatisfaction is problems with the delivery of furniture they have ordered.

On investigation, she finds that, when furniture is ordered, the manufacturer quotes a lead time, which sales staff pass on to their customers. The manufacturer is often late with delivery. In turn, manufacturers often blame their suppliers for late delivery of raw materials.

However, because the store has no tracking system, the first the staff in the furnishings department hear of a problem is when customers ring up to complain that their order is overdue and to ask when they can expect delivery. The staff then have to search through back orders, check with the supplier to find out the new delivery date and ring the customer back. This is time-consuming and creates ill will between customers and the store. It's also difficult for the staff to find the time to track down late orders and phone the customers, since their priority is meant to be serving customers and ensuring the display area is well presented.

Shelly realises that the problem is too big for her to fix on her own. She gathers her team to brainstorm all the problems they experience. They then prioritise the problems and plan to resolve each of them in turn. They decide to assign some problems to 'working parties' so that they can work on more than one problem at a time. They're keen to get the ball rolling and see some results. As it happens, the problem that the team decides to work on first is the customer delivery problem.

Questions

1. What seems to be the most important issue – the one that could significantly diminish or remove the others? What would be your objectives for resolving the major issue? How could you measure your success?
2. What are some possible approaches to resolving the major issue? What might the teams' next steps be to resolve the issues they're working on?
3. Should the staff involve their suppliers at any stage? If so, how could they best do this?
4. Do you think Shelly should have involved the staff from the beginning? Why or why not? What can she do to ensure that their motivation remains high as they improve their customers' satisfaction with the furnishings department?

CHAPTER ENDNOTE

1 William Bruce Cameron, *Informal sociology: A casual introduction to sociological thinking*, Random House, New York, 1963, p. 13.

CHAPTER

28

RECRUITING, INDUCTING AND ONBOARDING EMPLOYEES

After completing this chapter, you will be able to:

28.1 use the six tools at your disposal to make the best possible match between candidates, your vacancy and your organisation

28.2 launch and complete a recruitment process when a vacancy arises

28.3 plan and lead an effective competency-based interview in order to make a sound selection decision

28.4 induct and onboard people who join your team, monitor how well they are doing and help them to reach the required standards of performance quickly.

TRANSFERABLE SKILLS

The following transferable skills are covered in this chapter:

3 **Social competence**

- **3.1** Teamwork/relationships
- **3.2** Verbal communication
- **3.3** Written communication
- **3.4** Leadership

OVERVIEW

Consider the following scenario: your team is motivated, engaged and highly skilled; you manage them effectively and provide each team member with the resources, support and work environment to excel in their role – all the ingredients needed to be a high-performance team. So why is the team not performing at the expected level? In fact, it is performing very poorly. How can this be? The explanation may actually be a simple one; you simply don't have the right employees.

Even when you apply all of the most effective strategies for managing and motivating your employees, if you don't have the right employees to begin with, the task of moulding them into a high-performance team becomes near impossible. This makes recruiting the right employees in the first place essential for achieving team success.

However, even when the right employee is recruited, retaining them is just as important. When a newly hired employee leaves shortly after commencing, not only are their desirable skills, attributes and experience lost to the organisation, the recruitment process has to start all over again. This can be very costly to an organisation, with some recruitment processes costing tens of thousands of dollars to administer. Add to this the time spent to readvertise the position, sort through applications, shortlist candidates, conduct interviews and contact referees, and the costs keep mounting up. But it doesn't end there. While a position is vacant, the potential loss of productivity can be the highest cost of all. Properly inducting new employees, and then supporting them with an onboarding process that allows them to build and nurture ongoing relationships through organisationally based programs, systems and arrangements, is therefore a vital component of an organisation's long-term employee retention strategy.

A successful recruitment process begins with identifying the skills needed by the organisation, and clearly articulating them together with the attributes, experience and/or qualifications required by potential candidates into a position description. If the **remuneration** and employment conditions offered are appropriate, and the labour market favourable, it is likely that suitable candidates will apply. However, this can all be brought undone if the organisation has a weak employer brand and questionable employer value proposition. Competition for high-quality talent is fierce and if all other factors are equal, the deciding factor may well come down to the organisation's reputation and whether it has a good name, both in the community and in the industry in which it operates. Organisations that pay little or no regard to acting ethically, operating sustainably, acting in a socially responsible manner, offering attractive work–life balance options to their employees, and so on, risk being left to squabble over the employees left after all of the best ones have already been snapped up.

This chapter explains how to develop and use a positive employer brand and employer value proposition to attract the right candidates and then follow up with appropriate strategies to retain them.

SNAPSHOT

A virtual induction

Marlow hung up the phone, excited about the new staff member who had just accepted the quality manager position and would join the team in just a few weeks. The role was pivotal in ensuring that the learning resources developed for students enrolled in the university were meeting the expected standards. The quality manager position involved working closely with the writing teams for each faculty, providing them with both guidance and feedback. Also, final sign-off for all resources required the quality manager's approval. Working with 12 faculties comprising almost 250 staff, an effective induction was crucial to getting the new quality manager off on the right foot. But with all staff and students working and learning remotely due to the COVID-19 restrictions, how would Marlow facilitate the building of these important relationships between the staff and the new quality manager?

Marlow decided that after going through the induction basics, such as policies and procedures, safety, organisational structure, the university's facilities and the like, he would send the new quality manager on a university 'scavenger hunt'. The new quality manager would be provided with the names of the heads of each faculty and the writers working under them and would need to contact each to answer a list of questions developed by Marlow in conjunction with each faculty. The questions covered a range of different aspects relating to both the university and each faculty, including processes, facilities, technology, staff roles, on-campus services, student demographics, organisational values and much more. Using videoconferencing software, the new quality manager would contact each faculty, introduce themself to the head of faculty and writers who would do the same in return, and learn how each operated and fitted into the overall university structure. Marlow advised each faculty that the new quality manager would be contacting them to join one of their team meetings and provided them with the questions that would be asked so they could prepare and be ready with their answers.

Marlow also organised an extended quality team meeting on the quality manager's first day. To be conducted virtually, introductions to the team's members would take place and an icebreaker activity would also be conducted where each team member would write a question and the quality manager would ask that question of a different team member. As no team member knew what they were going to be asked, their answers would provide both an insightful and potentially humorous context to the meeting.

Marlow organised one other thing for the quality manager's first day. The university already had a virtual campus tour that was accessible on its website. Marlow obtained permission to go on campus and took additional video footage of rooms, offices and facilities relevant to the quality manager position and organised with the IT department to splice the footage into the existing video.

When the quality manager subsequently 'arrived' for their first day, they were taken on a personalised virtual tour of the campus, met their team, had some fun with the icebreaker activity. Over the course of the rest of the week, found out about the other faculties and got to know their staff members as part of the scavenger hunt. 'Not quite job done,' thought Marlow, but a pretty good start to induction considering they didn't step foot on campus. Now, for their onboarding.

28.1 Making the best match

Hire for attitude. Train for skills.

Herb Kelleher (co-founder, US South West Airlines), 'Hire for attitude, train for skill', *Harvard Business Review*, 1 February 2011.

Recruitment is really both a 'buying' as well as a 'selling' exercise. On one hand, it is about finding the person best suited to carrying out the work (i.e. the buying part); on the other hand, it is also about promoting the position that needs to be filled and attracting suitable candidates to apply for and accept it (i.e. the selling part).

The three 'buying' tools are the job or role analysis, the job or role description and the **person specification**. Together, they identify the specific duties and tasks attached to a vacancy and build a profile of a candidate who would be suitable to fill it.

The 'selling' tools that can be used to attract suitable applicants to an organisation are an organisation's employer brand and its employer value proposition (EVP). These are designed to attract candidates who are suited to the organisation, align with its vision and values, and believe in how the position for which they are applying can positively contribute to what the organisation is trying to achieve.

But an organisation's reputation and image are only as good as the way in which its people represent it. That makes you the third 'selling' tool, and possibly the most important. Everyone wants to work for a boss who is fair, supportive, trustworthy, competent and reasonable. Alternatively, no one wants to work for someone who micromanages them, doubts the talent of their team members, or is inflexible, incompetent and unreasonable. You may think you have all of the good attributes and none of the bad ones, so it is merely a case of being yourself. But, remember, people from different cultures, generations and backgrounds, and with different genders and motivations, will be looking for different qualities in the person they work for. Being able to convince them that you understand them and will represent and manage them in an authentic manner will go a long way to making both you and your organisation a marketable and desirable employer of choice.

Position analyses

As an organisation's needs and goals change over time, so too do the requirements relating to each position. Changes in both the internal and external environments can alter the way tasks need to be carried out and render some tasks redundant. The responsibilities attached to a position may also change. Reviewing whether a position's goals, tasks and responsibilities remain aligned with the organisation's strategic goals is therefore an important part of an effective recruitment strategy. A position analysis should therefore be carried out each time a role becomes vacant. The exception to this would be if the position was reviewed very recently and subsequently vacated by the incumbent employee after only a short tenure. Unless during this period there were significant changes in either the internal or external environment, redrafting the position analysis so soon after would not be needed.

The first step in conducting a position analysis involves reviewing the organisation and team goals to determine if they have changed and, where changes have occurred, whether they have impacted the position. Next, review the purpose of the position – what essential function does it provide to the team or organisation? If there is difficulty in establishing a clear purpose, ask how the organisation would be affected if the position didn't exist. If no negative impact is determined, the position may be obsolete and therefore no longer need to be filled. But if a clear purpose can be established, identify the goals that are linked to it and check whether the tasks associated with the position continue to support the achievement of those goals. If the position is still filled, it can also be useful to ask the position-holder about any new tasks or responsibilities that have become part of the role since they took it over. If the position is vacant, check exit interviews, which may also provide further information in relation to the position.

The purpose of conducting a position analysis is not only to realign a position with the organisation or team goals, if required, but also to identify opportunities where tasks and duties can be consolidated, changed or removed to allow team members to work more efficiently and effectively. It can also highlight where additional resources, such as equipment, might be needed.

Position descriptions

Once the position analysis is complete, the position description should flow naturally from it. **Position descriptions** provide clear, concise outlines of the tasks, duties and responsibilities of a position. An effective position description contains specific language so that candidates know exactly what skills and attributes are required to undertake the role and the outcomes they would need to deliver were they to fill it. For example, a position description may state that the successful candidate 'must be able to communicate technical and complex information in a manner understandable to relevant stakeholders as part of an effective consultation process'. If a position description simply states that the candidate needs to have 'good communication skills', this does not provide any insight or understanding of what communication skills are required and for what purpose, or what good communication skills might include.

Position descriptions help an organisation and its employees in several ways, including:

- acting as reference points for training and developing position-holders
- allowing remuneration scales to be structured fairly, logically and transparently
- clearly articulating the organisation's expectations of position-holders
- helping attract and match people with the right skills and attributes for the position
- providing an objective and fair basis on which employee performance discussions can be conducted.

Position descriptions generally list the internal and external relationships, responsibilities and accountabilities of position-holders and any other information that is relevant to the position. Additional information might include the requirement to work overtime, to lift heavy loads or to travel away from home regularly. In light of the recent COVID-19 pandemic, many position descriptions now contain reference to 'flexible working from home arrangements'.

A position description should not refer to specific targets because targets can change. It is also important to remember to comply with equal opportunity requirements by ensuring that the language used in a position description does not favour some groups over others.

Job descriptions

Job descriptions are more prescriptive than position descriptions and provide greater detail relating to the position's tasks and duties. However, there is no need to write a job description like an instruction manual. For instance, the job description may contain something like 'answer phones and address customer enquiries' but it would be unnecessary to extend this to 'pick up and answer phones, greet customers warmly, establish rapport, establish the customer's needs, offer options to meet the customer's needs' and so on.

Competency-based job descriptions

In addition to listing a job's duties, **competency-based job descriptions** also list the essential knowledge and skills needed to successfully perform those duties. These are the mandatory requirements that a candidate must be able to demonstrate to be considered for the position. Because competency-based job descriptions may contain the knowledge and skills required of the job-holder that would otherwise be listed in the person specifications, a further person specification may not be required.

Role descriptions

Organisations building a performance-focused work culture have moved away from the traditional 'narrow' job descriptions specifying the duties and tasks people are expected to perform towards broader role descriptions describing value-adding behaviours and outcomes rather than tasks. Value-adding behaviours might be, for example, continuous improvement of work systems and processes, proactive teamwork, or problem identification and resolution. Outcomes might be prompt customer service, policy development or generating positive publicity through electronic media.

Role descriptions identify the areas or groups that a position serves and focus on end results that are important to the organisation, often in terms of key result areas (KRAs), or areas of responsibility and accountability. In effect, role descriptions articulate:

- the overall outcomes that a role is designed and expected to achieve
- some of the ways in which the role can add value (KRAs) to the organisation.

Results-driven feedback can provide role-holders with useful insight into how to add value to help an organisation achieve its goals. One framework that can be used to develop role descriptions includes:

- *Inputs:* the resources, systems and processes that a role-holder will normally have at their disposal.
- *Outputs:* strategies for adding value to these inputs.
- *Outcomes:* the expected short-term achievements.
- *Impacts:* the desired longer-term contribution to the organisation's strategic goals.

Describing roles this way allows role-holders to adopt an innovative approach to their work and gives them the scope to take on new responsibilities. It also provides organisations with the flexibility to adjust employees' roles to respond to changing operational needs.

How to write role descriptions

The key to writing role descriptions is for employees, managers and internal customers and suppliers to work together. Different approaches that may be considered include:

- A pair of employees who perform similar roles completing a form or questionnaire in relation to their responsibilities and performance expectations, checking with the other employees and managers concerned and modifying them as required.
- The same approach as above except that a team of three or four employees complete the role questionnaire. This method is effective when a number of people perform similar roles or the same role in several departments
- A leader-manager and role-holder work together to complete the role questionnaire. This approach works well when employees are new to a role, when there are performance or role clarity concerns or when a role is undergoing major changes.
- A single employee or manager completing the role questionnaire. This method can be used when only one employee carries out a role or when the position is vacant or new but, being the least collaborative, this is the least preferred approach.

Person specifications

Once the position description has been updated, analysis of the skills, knowledge and attributes that an employee needs to perform the role successfully can begin. The results of this analysis underpin the selection criteria by developing a person specification or profile of the ideal candidate, both from the perspective of someone who would not only enjoy the work and perform the role competently, but who would also engage with the company and its culture and values. This is important for both attracting employees in the short term and retaining them in the long term.

To develop the person specification, refer to:

- *The position description:* what must the position-holder know or be able to do in order to perform the role competently and effectively? What attributes, knowledge and skills would complement those that currently exist in your team?
- *The organisation's employer value proposition and employer brand:* what sort of person with what sort of attributes would find the work engaging and be suited to the organisation's culture and values? Do they need to have a high level of energy, be committed to achieving high standards, display a high degree of honesty and integrity or be self-disciplined with a strong work ethic?

Ensuring the position description and person specification accurately reflect the requirements of the vacancy will help to avoid recruiting someone with more skills than are needed to do the work well or the even bigger problem of recruiting someone lacking the skills or motivation needed for the role.

With the person specification completed, consider adding a 'T' to any skills and knowledge that can be provided through training and an 'M' to any knowledge, job and performance skills that are considered mandatory for the employee to have. This may be because they are not easily 'trainable' or the organisation does not provide training in that particular area. For example, a 'cheerful disposition' would be hard to train someone to develop who is naturally sullen; a payroll clerk would need basic numeracy skills and someone who is naturally shy and withdrawn is probably not going to suddenly become outgoing and gregarious because it is in the person specification relating to their role! Candidates who don't possess those mandatory skills must be automatically ruled out. Job and performance skills that are desirable, but which would not rule out a candidate who didn't possess them can be marked with a 'D'; if there are no candidates ranked above them or they provide some extra value in some other area, then they will come into consideration.

'Selling' the organisation

An organisation that assumes there will always be the number of employees in the **labour market** with the requisite knowledge and skills to fill their available positions is likely to be in for a shock. Even where this is the case, there is no guarantee that those employees searching for a job will choose that particular organisation unless they are provided with a compelling reason for doing so. Labour market volatility is nothing new, and periods of labour oversupply and undersupply driven by a range of factors can create labour market conditions where filling available positions can be extremely difficult. For example, as many economies emerge from lockdowns as a result of the COVID-19 pandemic, jobs in industries in Australia, such as hospitality, fruit picking, cleaning and the care sector, are all experiencing severe labour shortages. Organisations therefore need to be proactive in not only providing their prospective employees with an attractive work environment, competitive pay rates and desirable work conditions, but also in developing a positive reputation which will attract the calibre of employees needed. Whether an organisation's brand and value proposition, as discussed below, is based on a commitment to corporate responsibility, adhering to a strict ethical code, promoting diversity and inclusivity, adopting sustainable work practices, or something else, one or more of these can be the key to establishing a reputation in the labour market, which will attract the best and brightest employees capable of delivering industry-leading results.

Employer brand and employer value proposition

To attract top-end talent, an organisation needs a strong employer brand and employer value proposition. They are the package of the organisation's reputation and practices concerning how it treats its people, its customers and the environment, and how it delivers on its promises. They need to convey an authentic commitment to their stakeholders and be in harmony with each other.

An organisation's EVP consists of five dimensions:

1. *Characteristics of the organisation:* such as its culture and values, market position and policies, and the nature, size, sustainability and locations of its operations.
2. *Characteristics of the organisation's people:* such as the degree to which people treat each other with respect and the quality of its managers.
3. *Opportunities that the position or organisation offers employees:* such as interesting career paths, mentoring, training and development, work on interesting projects, and the chance to work with and learn from interesting and knowledgeable people.
4. *Tangible rewards that employees receive:* for their work (compensation and benefits).
5. *The work itself:* such as the way positions are designed and the extent to which the work matches employees' interests.

The right EVP benefits an organisation in two important ways:

- It helps it attract the employees it needs, which means it can put the right people in the right positions.
- It helps it attract more engaged employees who know something about the organisation they are joining and join it for the right reasons, which improves both performance and retention.

Just as organisations have cultures and subcultures, roles and departments can have their own 'sub-EVPs'. This means that a leader-manager not directly associated with the human resources (HR) management department may have the opportunity to draft their team's or department's sub-EVP to attract people to a vacancy within the team. It allows that extra level of detail or inside knowledge to be communicated to potential candidates, although it must be in tune with the organisation's overall EVP and consistent with its employer brand.

Organisations depend on everyone who leads and manages people to understand and support the package they offer employees and use it correctly to recruit employees. The EVP must genuinely reflect employees' experience of the organisation and recruits must find the culture they were promised when they join. When that doesn't happen, they leave, usually after only a short tenure in their position, and the organisation's investment in attracting and recruiting them is wasted.

Selling yourself

You are the third selling point in recruitment. Understanding your organisation's employer brand and EVP, and using it to help you recruit, ensures that the people who join your team can feel engaged with the organisation.

Transferable skills
3.4 Leadership

Even when the employer brand and EVP help attract the right employees to your vacancy, you cannot retain those 'right people' for long when you fail to live up to the EVP promise or offer employees the management style they want. When you adapt your leadership style in order to lead people from different cultures and generations and with different levels of experience and skill, you motivate and engage employees, which brings out their best efforts. When an employee is performing well, is motivated and is engaged, their affinity with the organisation increases and this makes them far more likely to stay.

28.2 Understanding the recruitment process

When I find an employee who turns out to be wrong for the job I feel it is my fault because I made the decision to hire him.

Akio Morita (founder, Sony Corporation), quoted in Robert Heller, *In search of European excellence*, HarperCollins Business, 1997.

In smaller organisations, leader-managers are usually involved in the recruitment process from the beginning. In large organisations, a HR specialist might turn to leader-managers to develop a position analysis, update the position description and prepare the person specification. Alternatively, they may choose to discuss the vacancy and update those documents themselves. Where this option is chosen, HR then sources and shortlists candidates but will usually delegate the interview process and final decision to the relevant leader-manager or department.

Some organisations outsource the entire recruitment process to recruitment consultants who manage the recruitment process up to the final interview and appointment stage, including checking references. This is known as *recruitment process outsourcing*. The consultants present a shortlist of candidates containing those they consider most suitable for the leader-manager or a panel to interview and make the selection decision.

Using specialists can save time and effort in sourcing candidates, conducting the initial interviews, checking references and so on. In addition, agencies can provide advice in relation to the competitiveness of an organisation's employer brand, EVP and salary scale. But preparing the position description and a person specification remains the responsibility of the organisation itself.

The interview process can be used as an opportunity to promote the organisation's brand by effectively treating each candidate as a potential customer and referee. Returning phone calls, processing electronic applications promptly and replying to emails within 24 hours is a start, but backing this up with a follow-up call within 48 hours after the interview, thanking candidates for their time and keeping them in the loop as to when a final decision can be expected are all small things that can boost the organisation's image as one that cares for, respects and values its employees. Failing to make the effort when candidates have can potentially derail an interview process and also result in negative publicity for the organisation. In fact, around 40 per cent of candidates have turned a position down because of a bad interview experience and 81 per cent tell 10 people about their poor interview experiences. Two of the biggest mistakes are not responding to applications and not contacting candidates after an interview.[1]

Reaching potential candidates

The days of placing a job advertisement in the weekend newspaper are long gone. There are now a range of different ways to reach potential candidates for organisations to consider. Many organisations advertise positions internally before advertising them externally or bringing in recruitment consultants. Some encourage and even reward employees who successfully refer a friend or person in their professional network for a vacancy. Traditional advertising methods, such as newspapers and specialist journals, are still used by some organisations but most vacancies, one way or another, end up appearing on an online platform. This can include being posted on an organisation's website, intranet and noticeboards, online job boards, social networking sites and Twitter streams. E-channels are cheaper than newspapers and are especially important in attracting tech-savvy Generation Ys and Millennials. However, care still needs to be taken when selecting the mode of advertising so as to not unintentionally cut out groups of potential candidates. For instance, exclusive use of social media may not reach older candidates who may well be the most suited to fill the vacancy.

Local radio stations popular with candidates you want to target can also be a good way to attract applications. Schools, tertiary education institutions and other training providers can put forward candidates, especially where specialist training is required, but be sure to brief them clearly on the type of employees that are required.

Most recruitment agencies, dedicated internet recruitment sites and large employers have automated interactive websites listing employment opportunities that accept and sort e-applications. Where a specific skill set is required, a targeted campaign may be the best option to access candidates from the relevant talent pool. Various agencies also specialise in mature-age workers, people with disabilities, mothers re-entering the workforce, the long-term unemployed, and professionals with specific functional skills or knowledge in particular areas, such as accounting, IT and marketing.

Transferable skills

3.3 Written communication

If a job advertisement attracts a lot of unsuitable candidates or, conversely, few suitable candidates, the mode being used to advertise it may need to be reconsidered. When advertising or announcing a vacancy, be careful not to choose language or include requirements that directly or indirectly exclude members of a particular group. The language you use can subtly encourage some candidates and discourage others from applying; for example, using the words 'nurturing' and 'supportive' may be interpreted as: 'We're looking for women' while 'competitive' and 'assertive' may be interpreted as: 'We're looking for men'. Avoid age- and gender-linked position titles; that is, those that describe the position or occupation in terms of one particular age or gender (i.e. office junior, draftsman, waitress, etc.); instead, use titles with no age or gender attachment (i.e. office assistant, draftsperson, waiter, etc.).

When designing the vacancy announcement, cover both the 'selling' and the 'buying'. Keep the people you want to respond to the ad in mind as you write it. **Figure 28.1** shows the information that should be included.

XZY Pty Ltd
Position vacant

Title of position (reflecting duties and responsibilities):
....
....

Salary range and benefits:
....
....

Location:
....
....

Relevant EVPs (culture, values, work environment):
....
....

Reason for position and its main duties and responsibilities:
....
....

Applicant's essential skills, knowledge and attributes:
....
....

How to apply:
....
....

FIGURE 28.1 What to include in a vacancy announcement

Passive candidates

There are several ways to reach passive candidates – people who aren't actively looking for another position. When you have an established, engaged group of employees, you can encourage them to mention the vacancy through their professional networks or recommend people that they believe would be suitable candidates. Because they're familiar with the nature and requirements of the work and the workplace culture, existing staff generally recommend suitable people, making it more likely that recruits fit in well and engage with the organisation.

People who are, or have been, employed satisfactorily in a casual or part-time capacity within the organisation can also be a good avenue of recruitment. They are familiar with the type of work and the organisation, and you know their work standards and capabilities, which makes it easier to assess their suitability for the vacancy.

Some organisations maintain close connections with former employees through 'alumni newsletters' and make vacancies known through this network. Former employees may wish to apply or to recommend people from their own networks.

Approaching people known to have the required skills but who are not actively seeking a new position (called *head-hunting*) is becoming more common at all levels. Regular check-ins and catch-ups with former colleagues as well as those within your own organisation can be an effective way of building a pool of suitable candidates to approach directly when the right vacancy occurs.

Screening applicants

Standardised application forms are used by many organisations in their recruitment processes. As they can be designed to collect specific information in relation to applicants' qualifications, work history and experience, they make it easier to compare applicants.

Determining which candidates will make it through to the next stage can be done manually by reading through each application and forming a judgement as to which applicants meet enough of the selection criteria to merit an interview. Alternatively, software can be used to perform this function, which can save a lot of time, especially when a large number of applications have been received. Assigning numerical values to each applicant's key skills, knowledge and attributes can be an effective way to differentiate between suitable and unsuitable candidates. Using a ranking system like this also helps to promote objectivity in the recruitment process while guarding against unintentional discrimination.

Adopt an approach that focuses on whether the skills and attributes that an applicant possesses, as well as what they have done in the past or are doing currently, matches the position being offered. This approach is more likely to identify a suitable candidate than placing emphasis on job titles or length of experience. Build a profile of the person by looking at their career progression and whether they have been given increasing responsibilities in their previous positions, taken on challenging roles or managed projects. Where there are gaps in their work history, check elsewhere in their application for volunteer or freelance work, travel or education that corresponds with those periods. Think about transferable skills or new perspectives that they could bring across to your organisation from these experiences. Many outdoor pursuits, such as mountaineering, trekking, white-water rafting, sailing, rock climbing, cycling and kayaking, to name a few, require attention to detail as well as planning, problem-solving, trouble-shooting and teamwork skills.

The presentation and structure of an applicant's résumé or curriculum vitae (CV) and covering email or letter can also provide insight into various aspects about the person. Have they laid out their information clearly, concisely and logically? Are there formatting errors that might point to the person lacking attention to detail? Where written and presentation skills are crucial to the position, is their information presented professionally and their application well written?

Being thorough and having a robust screening process means that even when there is no 'perfect fit', it is likely that those applicants who 'best fit' the person specification will be identified. Appropriate training to address the competencies that each lack can always be provided later.

Using social media to screen applicants

Is it a good idea to use social media to gain further insight into a person, where the person has not protected their personal information? This is a matter of choice but there are some things to consider before playing social media detective:

- If you decide to view their personal information or posts on sites such as Twitter and Facebook, you are essentially conceding that you do not trust the information provided in their application to give you their 'full story'. This then brings into question whether you can rely on or trust your own recruitment process to achieve the same.
- By 'snooping' on the person you are starting the relationship off on a bad footing. If you are going to emphasise trust as being an important part of the employer–employee relationship, then it might be a good idea to start by 'practising what you preach'.
- It is illegal to take information about a person, such as their age, carer status, marital status, political views, religious beliefs, sexual orientation, unsavoury personal opinions and behaviour into account when making an employment decision. If this was to occur, the person would have the right to bring forward an action for discrimination.

Even when you find out information about a person that may not be to your liking, does it really define the person in their entirety? If you accept that everything a person puts or says on social media is true and is a wholly accurate representation of who they are, their values and what they believe, perhaps you need to consider the different purposes for which people use these sites – you will likely find that escapism in the form of making flippant, contentious or silly remarks without being held to account for them (except in the limited social media court of public opinion) is one of the main reasons. However, cyberbullying, trolling or making statements that discriminate, marginalise or denigrate particular groups in society are completely unacceptable regardless of the person's intent and should raise a red flag about whether the person will be a good fit for your organisation, or any organisation for that matter.

Selection tests

Pre-employment testing falls into three categories: aptitude and skill tests, medical tests and psychological tests. There are many tests from which to choose, with most requiring a qualified person to administer them, and some the supervision of a registered psychologist.

Candidates should be briefed on the purpose of the tests and the applicable policy for distributing and storing the results. It is a legal requirement that the results of such tests be kept confidential. When providing the results to the candidate, it must be done so in a private feedback session. Organising ahead of time any special arrangements that need to be put in place for candidates with particular needs (e.g. for those visually impaired or requiring an interpreter) is required so that you are not discriminating against them.

Aptitude and skill tests

Aptitude tests measure abilities such as abstract and verbal reasoning, literacy, mechanical comprehension, numeracy, spatial skills, how quickly a candidate is able to assimilate new information and the ability to check detailed information. These tests are usually given at the screening or preliminary interview to help determine whether an applicant has the basic skills or aptitudes to do the work.

Medical tests

Medical tests, conducted by the organisation's nominated medical practitioner, should assess only the applicant's current health status to determine whether they are physically capable of doing specific work. For example, a position that requires the successful candidate to work in a boiler room, foundry or glass factory would need to confirm that the candidate is medically fit enough to withstand high temperatures. Some organisations also carry out drug and alcohol screening.

Refusal to employ a person whose medical examination discloses a disability or an impairment unrelated to their ability to do the work they've applied for is discriminatory and therefore illegal. For example, if a person with a disability is capable of doing the work, the organisation needs to provide them with the facilities or services they would reasonably need, such as wheelchair ramps and suitable toilet facilities. A person's predicted future health or deterioration in health also cannot be used as a reason to refuse to employ them. The same applies to their past injuries, unless it can be demonstrated that the injury will have a direct bearing on the candidate's ability to do the work applied for and that in doing that work, their own or others' health and safety would be at risk. Similarly, a person's previous and current workers' compensation claims should also have no bearing as to whether they are employed or not.

Psychological tests

Psychological, or psychometric, tests have become very popular in recent decades to ascertain particular information in relation to a person's intelligence, personality, behaviour and motivations. Psychometric tests (literally meaning *mental measurement*) are particularly popular when recruiting leader-managers, and are used to probe decision-making ability, emotional intelligence, leadership potential, intelligence, interests, motivation and values, and personality traits such as extroversion/introversion and sociability.

When used correctly, these tests can provide useful information to compare with the person specification and, when considered with the candidate's résumé, the interview and comments received from referees, can help ensure a good match between the candidate and the vacancy.

Interviews

Despite all of the available ways of obtaining information and forming an opinion about the suitability of a person, interviews are still the most commonly used selection method. They provide an opportunity for both parties to learn about each other; the candidate can get a feel for the work environment, climate and culture of the organisation, while the interviewer can gain more detailed information about the candidate's skills and overall fit for both the position and the organisation.

Some organisations hold three selection interviews:

1. *Screening interviews:* to eliminate those applicants who are obviously unsuitable (sometimes conducted over the telephone).
2. *Preliminary interviews:* to select a shortlist of suitable candidates.
3. *Final interviews:* to decide which candidate to appoint.

Employment interviews can be structured or unstructured. Unstructured interviews are more like a series of meandering questions aimed at getting a general 'feel' about the person by asking them: 'What are your strengths and weaknesses?' and 'What do you like doing outside of work?'

Structured interviews ask all candidates the same questions and rate the candidates on the same criteria. They provide a much better chance of reaching successful selection decisions, reduce the possibility of bias and are more positively viewed by candidates, who experience them as more relevant and thorough. **Competency-based interviews** are the most reliable type of structured interview as they focus on determining whether the candidate possesses the knowledge, skills and attributes needed to perform the work role to the expected standard.

Panel and group interviews

Common types of interviews used in selection processes include panel interviews and group interviews. Group interviews, where several applicants are interviewed together at the same time by several interviewers, are popular when the person specification requires 'people skills', such as good communication, poise, tact, resourcefulness, leadership and the ability to cope with stressful situations. Panel interviews, in which two or more people conduct the selection interview and make a joint decision about which candidate to appoint, allow interviewers to both ask questions and, when not doing so, observe the body language, demeanour and skill with which the candidate handles the pressure of answering questions from multiple interviewers.

When conducting both group and panel interviews, meet with the other interviewers beforehand to determine who will chair the interview and to review the position description and person specification. Agreement should be reached on the selection criteria to be used and the relative weighting or ranking of each (see Figure 28.2). The interview agenda and the approximate time to spend on each area should also be determined and then a section of each interview agenda item allocated to each interviewer to cover. In other words, one person opens the interview, another explains the vacancy and the EVP, another probes the candidates' work history, and so on. It is worth considering assigning the note-taking role to one person only, since it can be very distracting to candidates to have several people scribbling down notes and can make it difficult for them to choose with whom to make eye contact when providing their answers.

Selection criterion	A	B	C	D	E	Total
Weight / Candidate	1	3	3	4	5	
Candidate 1	3 / 3	3 / 9	5 / 15	5 / 20	2 / 10	57
Candidate 2	1 / 1	2 / 6	4 / 12	4 / 16	5 / 25	60
Candidate 3	5 / 5	5 / 15	2 / 6	3 / 12	2 / 10	48

FIGURE 28.2 A weighted ranking system for candidates

To conduct group and panel interviews professionally, the interviewers should avoid talking over one another, be organised as to who will ask what and proceed at a steady, orderly pace. Sufficient time should be allocated to cover the desired areas while providing the candidate with the necessary time to think about and provide their responses. When interviewers interrupt each other to ask questions, ask questions that are unrelated to the position or the candidate, or move from one topic to another rather than follow a clear interview outline, they give a poor impression of the organisation and are less likely to make a sound selection decision. The candidate might also leave the interview and pass on bad publicity about the organisation to contacts within their network. Rather than diminishing the organisation's EVP, an interview can be used to promote it by providing a positive experience to the candidate, who then spreads the word about the employer's brand and EVP to their contacts, family and friends. When the next position is advertised, it may be from one of these groups that the ideal candidate then applies.

The drawbacks of interviews

Everyone likes to think they have good 'people sense' and a rare ability to pick the right person. Unfortunately, most people don't. Unless you take great care in the employment interview, research has shown that you could make just as good a selection decision by choosing at random from among the applicants.[2] This is because everyone has their own biases and prejudices and own ways of sifting and filtering information so that it fits in with what they expect or want to hear. As most of this occurs subconsciously, only those with an acute sense of self-awareness have even the slightest idea of how pronounced their biases or prejudices are and the impact they can have on their decisions.

This is illustrated by a study conducted by Australian National University researchers Alison Booth, Andrew Leigh and Elena Vargonova. They sent out 4000 fake job applications to employers who had posted job advertisements on the internet for entry-level hospitality, data entry, customer service and sales jobs. The same applications were sent to the same employers with only the racial origin of the supposed applicants' name changed. The results were damning. Applicants with Chinese names had only a one-in-five chance of being invited for an interview, compared to applicants with Anglo-Saxon names, whose chances were better than one-in-three. The study found that a Chinese-named applicant would need to submit 68 per cent more applications than an Anglo-named applicant to receive the same number of calls back. For those with Middle Eastern or Aboriginal and Torres Strait Islander names, the figures were 64 per cent more and 35 per cent more, respectively. Even those applications containing an Italian-named applicant needed to submit 12 per cent more applications to receive the same number of calls back.[3]

In addition, the halo/horns effect means that, unless you're careful, one or two positive or negative attributes of candidates can influence you to see candidates in a generally positive or negative light. Interviewees who put themselves in a positive light, project confidence and give a firm handshake combined with eye contact are offered more jobs than those who don't.[4] That's why it's important to assess each candidate on one selection criterion at a time with a matrix like that shown in Figure 28.2.

Then there is the fact that the first impression, although often incorrect, is a lasting one. This means that an interviewer might make up their mind about a candidate during the first few minutes of an interview and spend the rest of the interview noticing 'evidence' that confirms their first impression. Other common interviewing mistakes are not asking each candidate the same questions, not basing questions on the requirements of the position, not knowing what an 'acceptable' answer is, and asking questions in a way that makes the 'correct' answer obvious.

The selection decision

While there is no guaranteed way to tell which candidate will best suit a job vacancy, the chances of hiring the right person can be increased significantly by comparing how each candidate meets each selection criterion objectively.

Numerical 'scoring' systems, like the one shown in Figure 28.2, are used by some organisations, whereby each selection criterion is given a weighting from 1 (less important) to 5 (very important) and each candidate is rated according to what degree their answers match those criteria from 0 (no match) to 1 (poor match) to 5 (excellent match). (The candidates' results in any selection tests that have been conducted as part of the recruitment process should be used as well.) Multiplying the rating by the weights and adding up the sums for each candidate will give them a total rating. The candidate with the highest total rating is the one that best matches the selection criteria.

Since it's unlikely that any one candidate will match the person specification perfectly, remember that building skills and providing knowledge is one thing but it is much harder (if not impossible) to teach people values and attributes. It is therefore wise to avoid hiring candidates unless there is a good 'fit' or alignment between their values and the organisation's values and their working style and the work requirements.

To make the best possible match, good rules to follow are:

- *Never settle for the best of a bad bunch:* review the job or role description and person specification, see whether you can adjust them, and think about starting again when you're not happy with the first group of candidates.
- *When in doubt, the answer is 'no':* your subconscious has probably picked up some evidence that you can't put your finger on. Listen to any 'nagging doubts' – a wrong decision is too costly in terms of time, money and morale.

Reference checks

Reference checking protects the organisation's interests by endorsing the selection decision reached and validating the candidate's main claims. The more harm to a team's morale or productivity that can occur as a result of hiring the wrong person, the more thorough should be the reference checking process. Reference checks may be conducted by the organisation's HR department or by the employment agency if one was used. However, they are often undertaken by one or more members on the interview panel, which often includes the team's leader-manager.

Some organisations have a policy of confirming only basic factual information, such as dates of employment and job title. When this is the case, confirm those details and move on to the next referee. It's best to speak with two or three people who directly managed the candidate. Most reference checks, in the case of external candidates, are conducted by calling the referee directly. When the candidate is internal, meet with their current manager (and previous manager when possible) and follow steps 3 and 4 below.

The procedure is as follows:

1 Telephone the organisation's reception, not a direct line or mobile phone, so that you can verify the person is in the role the candidate said they are.
2 Provide the referee with your name, position and organisation and explain the reason for your call. Some referees may want to ring you back to ensure that you are who you say you are. (This is good practice, and you should do the same when you are approached to act as a referee, again, ringing back through the reception.)
3 Briefly explain the key tasks of the position and the main selection criteria (from the person specification). Ask open questions directly related to the position's requirements and to clarify and substantiate the information you obtained from the candidate during the interview. Pay attention to what referees say and how they say it. Lukewarm comments and half-hearted praise speak volumes. What is not said is often just as, if not more, insightful than what is said.
4 Thank referees for their time and the information they have provided.

In short, reference checks are mostly concerned with:

- confirming factual information provided by the candidate regarding the employer in question, such as dates of employment and the nature of duties performed. Avoid volunteering this information yourself – ask the referee
- probing important areas of the person specification to determine areas of match and mismatch.

Some sample questions that can be used when conducting a reference check include:

- What were the candidate's dates of employment, position title (any other important details)?
- Did X have any contact with the public? (when relevant)
- Did you form any opinion of the work for which X is best suited?
- How closely did you need to manage X?
- How did X get on with people/teammates?
- How much potential/initiative did X show?
- How well did X perform the job? How well does X compare with the person currently doing the work?
- How would you rate X's general conduct?
- Was X dependable regarding quality of work? Attendance? Timekeeping?
- What did you/X's manager think of X?
- What were X's main responsibilities?
- What would you say are X's strong points? Weak points?
- X mentioned working on a project with you; how did X contribute to that project?
- Why did X leave?
- Would you re-employ X? Why or why not?

Make an offer

Once the decision on the successful candidate is made, act quickly. Contact them to offer them the position and follow up with a written offer as quickly as possible. Inform relevant others in the organisation as required, ensuring that the letter of offer and contract of employment are sent to the new employee's home. Once you have confirmation that they have accepted the position, inform them as to where they should report on their first day, to whom and at what time.

Include a probationary period, or trial period, of one to six months for new recruits when organisational policy allows this. An alternative is to 'audition' the candidate with real work or a simulation of the type of work they'd be doing if they got the job. This is outlined later in this chapter.

Contact the unsuccessful candidates and tactfully advise them they have been unsuccessful on this occasion, thanking them once again for their interest and wishing them success in their careers. This is quick and easy to do via email, so there is no excuse not to. Wrapping up loose ends like this is vital to maintaining the organisation's reputation.

Legal requirements

No discrimination, overt or implied, intended or unintended, against or in favour of candidates, must be involved in the recruitment process. Attributes such as candidates' age, ethnicity, marital status, physical or mental impairments, religion, sex or sexual preference must not factor into a recruitment decision. For example, you cannot ask:

- Are you married?
- What clubs and organisations do you belong to?
- When do you plan to start a family?
- Where were you born?

Ask the same core questions of each candidate and be certain that these questions relate directly to the position's requirements. Be aware of any underlying assumptions that may be made about people from particular groups. Do not imply unfair or partial attitudes to, for example, race or sex in the questions asked and give each candidate the same information about the position in the same way.

The following provides some guidelines as to what questions are legally acceptable to ask and what aren't:

- Don't ask questions of applicants from a particular group (e.g. females, minorities or people with disabilities) that you don't ask of all the others. Ask the same position-related questions of all applicants.
- Don't ask about childcare arrangements, family circumstances, family planning, partners' situations or other relationships.
- Don't state, imply or take into account that certain groups of people have traditionally held or never held particular positions.
- Don't treat candidates from one group differently from candidates from other groups.
- Only ask questions that relate directly to the position's requirements.
- Recognise any biases you may have and guard against letting them cloud your judgement.
- Avoid using Mr, Mrs or Ms unless the person has introduced themselves using one of these titles.

Standardise the forms used during interviews to record questions and answers to help maintain an unbiased record and to impartially compare candidates' skills, knowledge and attributes to the person specification. When a vacancy has special requirements, address these directly. For example:

- This position frequently requires working overtime at short notice. Are you able to do that?
- This position involves working on Saturday mornings from 8 a.m. to noon. Are you able to do that?
- This position requires overtime most Tuesday and Thursday nights until 7.30 p.m. Are you able to do that?
- You would need to spend three days a month travelling in this position. Are you able to do that?

Questions such as these should relate specifically to the position's requirements and be put to each candidate.

Keep the details of all applicants and interview notes taken on all candidates confidential and in a locked file. They may need to be referred to later if a candidate complains that they have been treated unfairly. Don't discuss applicants with anyone other than your manager or the HR department.

28.3 Conducting competency-based interviews

You're only as good as the people you hire.

Ray Kroc (former CEO of McDonald's), quoted in L. Harris, *Surrender to win*, Greenleaf, Austin, 2009, p. 147.

Competency-based interviews aim to uncover more than simply what a person knows or what they can do. They delve deeper into the person's personality and way of thinking to help develop an understanding of why, in the past, they acted in a particular way or made a certain decision. By finding out about a candidate's position-related personality traits, how they apply their skills and knowledge and why they act or respond in certain situations, a more accurate assessment can be made as to how closely they match the person specification. It can also help to predict how they will perform in the role and engage with the organisation, both important factors in determining their longevity in the position.

This type of insight can be gained by asking the candidate questions about not only what they have done in the past but exploring these experiences further by asking how they acted or responded and, most importantly, why. Providing the questions asked directly relate to the position being applied for, their answers should indicate how closely the person matches the job specification.

Competency-based interviewing has distinct advantages:

- Asking about past behaviour and thinking processes helps ensure that candidates base their answers on fact and provides a reliable insight into their experience, knowledge, motivation, thought processes and values.
- Asking each candidate the same series of questions helps to ensure that a fair and objective comparison is made between the applicants.

The five steps of employment interviewing are summarised in Figure 28.3 and described in the following sections.

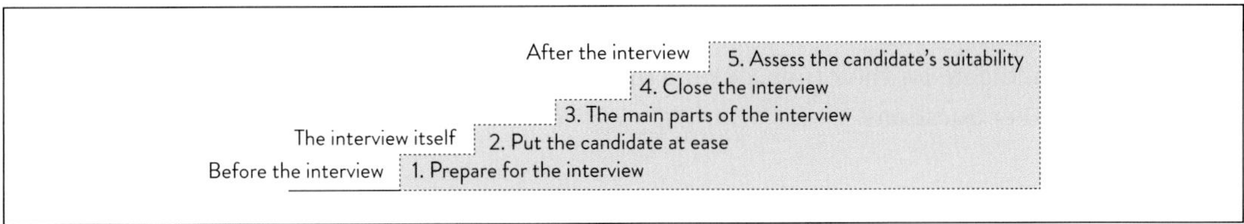

FIGURE 28.3 The five steps to recruitment interviewing

Step 1: Prepare for the interview

Transferable skills

3.2 Verbal communication

Set aside 30 to 40 minutes for the interview and a further 10 minutes to think about and note down how the candidate matches your selection criteria afterwards. When scheduling interviews, leave time between each one to attend to other matters that crop up and to reflect on what the candidate has said and what their answers tell you about them.

Having an interview agenda to follow helps each interview run smoothly and professionally. Prepare opening remarks to welcome the candidate and briefly describe the position and the opportunities it presents. Then develop a list of questions that target information about the skills, experience and attributes needed to succeed in the position.

There is no hard-and-fast rule about whether to talk about the organisation or the position first. However, regardless of the order chosen, be careful about speaking for too long as the danger may be that the candidate switches to 'listening mode' and may then find it difficult to find their 'talking groove' once you have finished. Punctuating the information that you provide with questions can be a good way to keep the interview conversation flowing from both sides. Consider following the approach below:

1 Welcome the candidate and make them feel comfortable. You can do this by starting the conversation about something unrelated to the position like the weather or current topics of interest.
2 Review the organisation's EVP and describe the work environment, position, purpose, key duties and responsibilities of the position. You can then ask the candidate a broad opening question, such as what attracts them to the position and why they feel they would excel in it.
3 The response candidates provide to the above can then be used to launch into more specific questions about their skills, experience and attributes. For each question asked, get the candidate to back up their answer, if they haven't already, with examples from their experience, including behavioural examples such as why they acted in a particular way or responded in the way they did. When asking them to provide detail, make it clear that you want to find out the detail of what they did and how they did it rather than simply a detailed description of the duties and responsibilities of the position they were in. Asking them how they solved particular problems or would approach certain situations relevant to the position applied for is a good way to start finding out whether they are 'right' for the role.

4 Don't make the mistake of ruling out a candidate just because they don't have specific work experience relating to the role on offer. They may have recently finished study, which has provided them with the skills and knowledge needed to do the role, or have worked in other roles or industries with transferable skills. Also, as referred to earlier, other activities done outside of work, such as volunteering, leading, being part of sports or other teams, or engaging in pursuits requiring problem-solving skills and resilience, can provide great insight into their aptitudes, attitudes and behavioural traits.
5 If there are specific requirements relating to the position, such as the need to work overtime, be on call or stand for long periods, take the time to outline each and confirm that the candidate can meet these requirements.
6 Thank the candidate for their time, outline the next steps in the process and check to see if they have any further questions.

The details

Gather any information you need, such as pay, conditions and hours of work, and when necessary, book a suitable interview room that gives a favourable but realistic impression of your organisation and is reasonably private and free from distractions. If conducting the interview via videoconferencing software from home or some other location outside of the organisation's premises, think about your background and, where possible, use one that replicates the usual work environment. Many organisations can provide you with such a background.

If utilising the traditional face-to-face interview method, consider the seating arrangements. You could use a meeting room or your office and sit behind your desk; or you could be less formal and invite candidates to join you at a low coffee table if you have one in your office. Make sure that the sun or artificial lighting won't blind candidates and that your chairs are the same height. Ensure that telephone calls or visitors do not interrupt you and that others in your organisation who need to know are aware that you are conducting interviews, as well as the position for which you are interviewing .

Review each candidate's application, initial letter and completed application form *before* the meeting and scan the information they have provided for potential follow-up questions that you could ask and list any additional points to cover.

Prepare the sell

Consider how you can best sell your organisation and present your EVPs to interest and enthuse candidates in your vacancy and the organisation. Decide how best to describe the job purpose, key duties and responsibilities of the position and how to paint a positive picture of the work environment or team in which they will be working.

Be aware that candidates from different generations and different cultures may be interested in different aspects of the organisation's offerings. For example, some people are more likely to be concerned with work–life balance and your organisation's green credentials than their long-term prospects with the organisation.

Ensuring that your 'sell' matches the reality is critical to securing the right person for the position, so be honest and factual. New employees enter into a psychological contract, or set of mutual expectations, based on the interview process, their position description and a range of discussions that take place as the employment relationship begins. Therefore, 'overselling' or 'underselling' your organisation or the position, and presenting an unrealistic picture, is likely to result in a dissatisfied employee within a short period or that you lose a potentially excellent prospect.

Prepare the buy

We have already looked at some general questions to ask that are followed up with more specific ones, such as:

- Tell me about your most important duties in your last position.
- What attracts you to our industry?
- What made you decide to become an engineer/operator/trainee accountant?

Ensure follow-up questions can't be answered by 'yes' or 'no' so that the interviewee is encouraged to provide more expansive answers.

Transferable skills

3.2 Verbal communication

Avoid leading questions that flag the answer you're looking for or that lead candidates into answering what they think you want to hear. Also avoid multiple questions, where you ask a string of several questions, leaving the candidate to guess which one you want answered. When asking a hypothetical question, present it in the form of a typical scenario they're likely to encounter on the job, such as 'You are likely to have to deal with competing work tasks, team member problems, customer-related issues and delegated tasks from senior management on a daily basis, which are all important; so how would you prioritise your workload on any given day?'

Think about using the two types of questions below:

1. *Behaviour-based questions:* target information about candidates' competencies relating to the position's requirements. These seek examples of candidates' past performance and conduct that you can use to predict their behaviour in your vacancy.
2. *Verbal simulation questions:* discover the candidate's thinking process and likely future behaviour in a similar situation. These present a typical work-related scenario and ask the candidate to explain how they would deal with it, and provide an opportunity to ask follow-up questions to uncover their thinking process when you need to.

Competency-based questions

Table 28.1 gives some examples of competency-based questions that bring out examples of candidates' experience in various areas of your selection criteria. Their answers build a picture of how their competencies relate to the vacancy for which they are applying. Be cognisant, however, of how a rapidly changing world can mean that what they did in the past is not always relevant, so choose your questions carefully.

Transferable skills

3.2 Verbal communication

TABLE 28.1 Examples of competency-based questions

Adaptability/flexibility and ability to learn	Give me an example of a change in your work that you had to adapt to – how did you feel about it? How did you manage that change? What did you learn from that experience?
Communication skills	Tell me about a time when, as a team member, you had to use spoken communication skills to get a point across. Were you successful? Did you use any other forms of communication to achieve your desired outcome? Tell me about a time when someone misunderstood something you said or wrote – how did you make your meaning clear? What was the result? Were you able to influence them?
Customer service orientation	Tell me about a time when you felt you went beyond the call of duty to help a customer. How do you know it was appreciated? Describe a time when a customer requested something that was outside of your organisation's policy or guidelines and how you handled it. What was the result?

Innovation	Tell me about a time when you found a way to improve a procedure or the way something was normally done. Was your improvement successful? How do you know? Describe a problem you faced where the usual solutions wouldn't work and how you dealt with it.
People skills/team working and ability to learn	Describe a situation in which you were able to 'read' another person accurately and deal successfully with them. How did you measure your success in that instance? Give me an example of a time when people were disagreeing about how to proceed and you were able to influence them to work together effectively – what did you say or do? What effect did you have on the group? Describe the most difficult customer/co-worker/manager you have ever encountered and how you handled them. What would you do differently next time?
Planning/time management	Tell me about a time when you were under pressure to get a lot done quickly – how did you decide what to do and in what order? Was your call correct? How do you know? Describe a lengthy or time-consuming project you have undertaken and how you approached it. Tell me about a time when you were working hard to meet a deadline – how did you manage your time and work with others to finish on time?
Problem-solving and ability to learn	Describe a time when you needed to identify the cause of a problem in order to resolve it – how did you go about it? How do you know you identified the correct cause? Describe a difficult problem you have recently confronted and how you handled it. What did you learn from that?
Results orientation	Tell me about the most difficult task you have ever tackled. What was so difficult about it? How did you go about solving it? What was the outcome? Was it successful? How do you know? Tell me about your greatest success/biggest achievement so far. (Ask probing follow-up questions to uncover more detail.) Why do you consider it to be your greatest success? How did that come about? Which of your achievements make you most proud and why?
Self-motivated/ self-disciplined	What was the most helpful feedback you have received? How did it change your behaviour? Give me an example of a time when you had to 'dig deep' into your personal qualities and attributes to complete something.
Work without supervision/self-starter	Describe a time in your last position when you needed to work without supervision. In what areas would you like to expand your skills? How would that help you in your career or personally? What steps have you taken to expand those skills?
Working style	Describe the most frustrating/enjoyable part of your current position (probe into reasons and ask for examples). Describe what you liked and disliked about how you were managed in previous positions. Tell me about what you dislike(d) about your current/last position (probe into reasons and get examples). Tell me about the most rewarding position you have held. What in particular made it so rewarding (ask for examples)? What triggered your decision to leave your last position?

When asking probing or follow-up questions, maintain an expectant silence and eye contact. Examples of probing questions you can use in an interview are:

Transferable skills
3.2 Verbal communication

- Can you outline exactly what happened?
- Can you explain how you responded?
- What was the outcome of your response?

Prevent candidates from straying onto matters that are irrelevant by asking them questions to find out exactly what they did and said and what the outcomes were. Here are some questions to draw out results:

- What measures or indicators did you use to determine how successful your response was?
- How did your strategy improve your team's work process?
- How did your team benefit from the measures you put into place?
- Considering the lessons learnt, how would you change your approach in future and how would you expect the outcomes to change as a result?

Verbal simulation questions

Verbal simulation questions are the next best thing to tryouts. Ask candidates to describe precisely how they would handle a particular situation they are likely to face in your vacancy. For example, you could describe a problem the successful candidate is likely to face during their first month in the position and ask them to tell you how they would handle it; or you could give them a typical work-related problem and ask how they'd analyse it. Table 28.2 gives some other examples.

TABLE 28.2 Examples of verbal simulation questions

Transferable skills
3.2 Verbal communication

Ability to learn	Outline the steps you would take to learn about our customer base.
Flexibility/innovation	Walk me through your options when faced with an unexpected change in customer requirements.
Logical approach	What steps would you take during your first weeks with us to identify the most current problems or opportunities in your work?
Planning ability	Can you outline what your goals and action plan for your first two or three weeks with us would be? (Listen for key actions, goals, who they would consult with, etc.) How would you know your plan is working?
Problem-solving	Here is a typical problem you will face in your first week with us ... Talk me through your general approach and the precise steps you would take to solve it. (Know what you're looking for here, e.g. consulting the team, identifying success criteria, looking into past precedents.) Here is a flow chart of an existing process. Can you look at it and identify three areas where problems are likely to occur? (Know what the main problem points are.)

Make sure candidates provide considerable detail in their answers. Listen for what is important in the position as they answer. For example, you might listen for the ability to handle stress; the ability to consult, coordinate or work with others; consideration and tact; problem-solving ability; and whether they included following up to make sure the solution they propose is effective. Ask *follow-up* and *probing* questions, such as the ones already explored, to overcome vague or incomplete answers and bring out the information you need.

Their answers will provide you with considerable detail and give you a window into candidates' thinking processes and likely future approach in a similar situation. Because your verbal simulation questions contain considerable detail, they invite a detailed response, rather than 'flights of fancy' and 'creativity' as with hypothetical questions.

Tryouts

You can put candidates into typical work situations to see how they respond and even ask them to work alongside the people they would be working with if they get the job. When recruiting a chef, you could ask candidates to cook a meal. When recruiting a computer programmer, you could ask them to write some code. When you're recruiting a sales representative, you could ask them to prepare a presentation they might give to a potential customer. If the tryout is going to take a considerable amount of time or they have to travel a long distance to undertake it, consider remunerating the candidate even if it is with a supermarket voucher or equivalent non-monetary reward.

Step 2: Start by putting the candidate at ease

Relaxed candidates are always more forthcoming than nervous ones, so help them relax as quickly as possible. Give them your full attention and have a brief conversation about something unrelated to the position before commencing the formal questioning to build rapport. Throughout the interview, show the person that you are genuinely interested in them and their responses. Maintaining eye contact, displaying positive body language and picking up on cues are all ways to authentically demonstrate your interest.

When interviewing people from other cultures, think about the following:

- Avoid acronyms, abbreviations and slang, and if using metaphors, keep them relatively easy to understand.
- Be aware of culturally based body language and eye contact.
- Don't speak louder to candidates with accents or hearing impairments (unless they specifically ask you to).
- Provide them a list of what will be discussed before they attend the interview so they can prepare adequately.
- Check carefully to make sure the questions you ask are free from bias or are skewed to a particular culture.
- Be aware that in some cultures people may prefer to describe the 'group's achievements' rather than their own.
- Allow extra time for candidates from non-English-speaking backgrounds to formulate their responses and process what you have asked them.
- If you are unsure how to pronounce a name, research it beforehand or make it the first thing you politely ask the person when they arrive for the interview.
- As much as possible, make interview panels culturally and generationally diverse.
- If you do not understand an answer, ask the person to repeat their answer but in a way where you accept responsibility for not understanding. Then, if required, summarise what they have said to confirm your understanding.

Step 3: The main parts of the interview

Now comes the 'selling' part of the interview, where you explain the position, the organisation and your EVP, and the 'buying' part, where you find out how well the candidate meets your needs. Allow plenty of time for the interview, based on the importance of the position and the number of questions that you plan to ask, and avoid rushing through it. This is your chance to find out how suitable candidates are for the position, and their chance to find out whether they want to work with you, so give the process the time it requires.

Probing the candidate's suitability

Effective questioning and listening skills develop with practice, but some guidelines you can follow are:

- Question with a purpose: gather specific evidence of each candidate's ability (or lack of it) to meet your selection criteria.
- Give the applicant enough time to think and respond to your questions – don't jump in to fill the gap of a thoughtful silence. Show that you are listening with eye contact, periodic summaries, reflective listening responses and so on. Don't jump to conclusions and don't forget to ask some questions whose answers could challenge your assumptions, first impressions and the halo/horns effect.
- Whatever you think about a candidate's answer, remain neutral.

Table 28.3 summarises some key dos and don'ts when finding out about candidates.

TABLE 28.3 Some dos and don'ts when learning about candidates

Do	Don't
Aim for a conversational flavour to the interview, not a rigid question-and-answer session	Don't allow interruptions or distractions, such as telephone calls, to spoil your interview
Allow candidates enough time to answer	Don't ask 'cute' or trick questions such as: 'Tell me about yourself' or 'Why should I give this position to you?' These don't draw out specific information related to your requirements except by chance
Ask competency-based and verbal simulation questions using neutral language	Don't ask hypothetical questions ('What would you do if ... ?')
Ask questions that draw out specific behavioural information that relates to the position's requirements	Don't ask illegal or discriminatory questions geared around, for example, age, disabilities, gender, nationality or race
Encourage candidates to provide details	Don't ask leading questions ('You will be able to work overtime, won't you?')
Find out whether candidates are motivated to do the work as well as whether they can do it	Don't do all the talking
Keep the flow of the interview moving smoothly	Don't make snap judgements
Keep concentrating and listening	Don't unduly pressure candidates or put them under contrived stress to 'test' their tolerance

As the interview progresses, you probably need to jot down a few brief notes or key words to jog your memory after the interview, but keep them short so you can give every candidate your complete attention. Cluttering up an interview with distractions, such as shuffling papers, writing or taking telephone calls, should be avoided at all costs because it disrupts your train of thought and announces that you don't think the candidate is worth your undivided attention.

Step 4: Close the interview

Before winding up, find out whether the candidate has any questions. Be ready for questions like 'What's your sustainability policy?' Your response could make the difference between a 'yes' and a 'no' to a job offer. Think about what the questions candidates ask tell you about how much research they've done into your organisation and what they find important in a job.

Before you part, explain the next step (perhaps another interview or that you will make the selection decision after meeting with a few other candidates) and when and how you will be in touch. Thank candidates for coming in and for their interest in the position and your organisation and check whether they are still interested in the vacancy. If the interview is being conducted face-to-face, briefly show them around the work area on the way out. If your interview is conducted virtually, check to see if there are virtual tours that you can provide of the workplace or URL links to pages of your organisation's website that can provide the candidate with some idea of what their work surroundings look like.

Step 5: Assess the candidate's suitability

After each interview, gather your thoughts, list your overall impressions of the person, including their strengths and weaknesses, and where the candidate matched or didn't match your person specification. It's easy to confuse candidates without clear notes to jog your memory, so note down anything that can help you recall each candidate (remembering they can ask to see your interview notes).

Don't overrate the last person you interviewed. That candidate might look better simply because your own interviewing skills have improved with practice or you are glad to have finished the interviews, which put you in a better frame of mind. When all the interviews are completed, review the candidates as described earlier in this chapter.

As with one-on-one interviews, document the process of group and panel interviews so that, should it be necessary due to a challenge or an appeal, you have an accurate audit trail and can clearly show that the interview was fair.

28.4 Helping recruits fit in and do well

> I want all our people to believe they are working for the best agency in the world. A sense of pride works wonders.
>
> David Ogilvy (founder, Ogilvy and Mather advertising agency), *The unpublished David Ogilvy*, Profile, London, 2012.

After being successful in a recruitment and selection process, you would expect new recruits to be enthusiastic and eager to do well. For most, this is probably the case. But enthusiasm doesn't last forever and will in time be replaced with deadlines, responsibilities, problems and challenges. Providing new recruits with a comprehensive induction can string that enthusiasm out a little longer and help them successfully navigate their way through the initial period of their employment. Induction helps new recruits 'find their feet' and sets them up so that they can begin contributing as soon as possible.

Induction consists of more than just introducing new employees to their duties and their workmates. It involves anything and everything that helps them settle into their new surroundings and their new position, work team and organisation as smoothly as possible. A well-thought-out induction anticipates and answers questions new staff members might have but don't know who to ask or don't feel sufficiently confident to ask them. It also shapes their approach to their new position by establishing clear expectations about their duties and how to carry them out, as well as their behaviour in the organisation by familiarising them with key policies and expectations and how these apply to their role.

But the importance of induction extends even further. Just as employers often take on a new employee on a probationary basis, employers are also on trial. New employees determine, generally during their first few weeks, whether the position and the organisation meets their expectations. Induction, therefore, needs to quickly build engagement and make new employees feel as though 'this is an organisation that is right for me and which I can be proud to be part of'. If it fails to create this feeling and connection, the likelihood of a new recruit withdrawing their efforts and looking for other work increases dramatically.

However, like a toddler needing to burn up boundless energy, the initial enthusiasm that new employees possess may also need a release valve. It is, therefore, important in their first few days and weeks not to solely focus on explanation and information. They need to be given something to do – preferably something with a tangible outcome that they can see at the end and that is of value to their team or the organisation. Giving them a goal and checking on their progress in this initial period is an effective way of harnessing their enthusiasm, creating engagement and producing an outcome which will benefit their team or the organisation.

A good induction has other benefits, including:

- It shows new employees how the EVP works in practice, which can help reinforce their positive impression of the organisation and maintain their sense of enthusiasm.
- It can reduce the time spent by new employees being ineffective by giving them a project or task to work on while being inducted.
- It helps to build trust and rapport and link with the **onboarding** (discussed later in this section) process so that the new employee can establish positive working relationships, learn the group norms and feel like a valued member of the team.

What should induction cover?

New employees, whether recruited externally or transferring over from another area within the organisation, need to receive induction. It needs to cover aspects relating to the organisation as a whole but also those specific to the employee's department or team.

Transferable skills
3.4 Leadership

The HR department often carries out induction to the organisation or provides leader-managers and new employees with the relevant checklist for accessing information in booklets or electronically. It should be completed soon after employees join the organisation and cover, for example, the organisation's key policies and programs (e.g. corporate responsibility, risk management and sustainability policies, flexible working and wellbeing programs), and general items, such as protecting the organisation's intellectual property and maintaining confidentiality, reporting lines, pay arrangements and employee benefits and activities. It should also explain the organisation as a whole: how it is structured, where the recruit and their team fits into the structure, the organisation's history, and its products, services and customers. For organisations with no HR function, leader-managers will need to cover both the organisation and the departmental induction. Developing an induction checklist that can be referred to when inducting each new employee can help ensure that nothing is missed.

Transferable skills
3.1 Teamwork/relationships

Involving other members of the team in a new employee's induction helps to make them feel welcome and accepted. It also provides an opportunity for the new staff member to not only learn about the official organisational rules and regulations, but also the non-written ones. These are the norms that develop within a team or organisation and form the basis for how team members interact, work together, meet informally and communicate. The quicker the new recruit understands their team's norms, the sooner they will be able to engage positively with other team members and cement their place as an accepted member of the team.

Other aspects that need to be covered in induction that are no less important include safety hazards and procedures, any special duties and responsibilities attached to the recruit's position, where to find or how to requisition necessary equipment and tools, and other policies and processes of which the recruit needs to be aware (e.g. organisational code of conduct or code of ethics, diversity policy).

The induction process

Transferable skills
3.4 Leadership

The induction process begins before the new recruit arrives for their first day of work. It is the responsibility of their leader-manager to inform them about the expected dress code or style, security procedures, start time, where to park and where to report on arrival. These details are normally emailed, although some organisations might still send them via post. Other documentation that needs to be provided to new employees can include the organisation's annual report, employee handbook, terms of employment, a copy of the organisation's latest internal newsletter or magazine, the organisation's code of conduct or code of ethics, and so on. The new employee can be encouraged to explore the contents of some of these documents via links to the organisation's relevant intranet sites, although they may need to be provided with a temporary password to be able to do so. The more information they find out about their new place of work, the more comfortable they are likely to feel when they arrive on their first day.

Email internal suppliers and customers, reception, relevant managers and security announcing the new employee's imminent arrival, where appropriate. Providing existing staff members with the recruit's name, title, phone extension and a little bit of background information can make it easier for them to initiate conversation when they first meet the new team member.

Personally greeting and welcoming the new team member on their first day can help to put them at ease, establish rapport and get the work relationship off on a good footing. Prior to their arrival, their workspace should be cleared and cleaned, including desk drawers and cabinets, and access organised to email, the organisational intranet and the building. When new recruits have to wait a week or more to receive a password to access their work email it can create a very poor first impression. Provide them with a schedule of the briefings that have been arranged on different aspects of the organisation and an outline of their induction program.

Transferable skills
3.4 Leadership

Use the Five Keys, particularly the 'What To Key', to make sure recruits understand their role and responsibilities and how they contribute to the team. Take the opportunity to clearly outline any 'hot-stove', or bottom-line, rules and allocate some time to get to know the new team member so that the 'Want To Key' can be managed effectively.

Welcoming new employees with an informal team lunch or morning tea, or inviting them to bring their lunch and join other team members at a nearby park, are all possibilities to consider to help make them feel at home. If they are working from home or some other location other than the office, set up a virtual meeting with the rest of the team and have each team member introduce themselves and outline their role in the team.

When a new member joins the team, it also provides an opportunity to hold a mini team-building meeting during the first week or two. Give team members, including the new member, a few days to think about things, such as:

- My special skills and abilities are ...
- My working style is ...
- The unique knowledge I bring to the team is ...
- The benefits my unique knowledge, skills, style and interests bring to the team are ...
- Three things I'm most interested in (inside or outside work) are ...

Meet over an informal lunch or during a regular team meeting and ask team members to take turns answering the first point, then the second, and so on. In this way, the team and their new colleague quickly learn about each other and how everyone can best contribute to the team's results.

Setting up an induction program

To create an induction program, begin by making three lists: a list to remind you of the actions you need to take before a new employee's first day, a list of the topics to cover for organisation induction and a list of topics to cover for department induction. Order the actions and topics into a suitable sequence and add a column for target completion dates and another to sign and date when you've covered the topic.

Be careful not to bombard new employees with too much information at once. Information given in one big 'hit' is difficult to remember so it is better to provide information in 'bite-sized' chunks and stagger it through their first few working weeks. For example, you might spread organisation induction over several weeks, with one activity scheduled for each day. Throughout the induction program, use what you learnt during the selection interview to emphasise how the organisation's policies and other arrangements relate to what the new employee values and is interested in.

Provide information that is of most direct relevance to new employees first, such as where the toilets are, where they can park and how their pay is calculated. Once they begin to settle in, you can move on to more general information, such as the overall structure of the organisation, who the senior managers are and what they're responsible for, reporting lines and so on. Set them short-term goals to achieve in their first few weeks so they become quickly engaged with their work and provide plenty of positive feedback to boost their confidence.

A great place to work

Melbourne-based OBS is an IT services company that emphasises work–life balance, health and wellness, a culture that provides empowerment, a sense of family and pride, and staff who stay 'for the long term'. It begins before a new recruit joins, when they're sent a large OBS gift box including OBS shirts, a 'hitchhiker's guide' to OBS, lollies and material relating to their role.

Induction is designed to give recruits the best possible first impression of the organisation and make them feel like part of the family from day one, when they participate in a detailed induction. The rest of their induction, which continues over the next three months, is carefully planned and monitored by their manager.[5]

Transferable skills

3.1 Teamwork/ relationships

The 'cobber' system

You might have so many new hires that carrying out the entire induction program yourself would leave you little time for your other duties. That's when the Australian Army's 'cobber' system comes in. Cobbers, or mates, should be experienced, organisation-minded people who are fully conversant with the organisation's benefits, EVPs, procedures, regulations and rules, and who can answer most questions new employees ask. Try appointing a 'cobber' – an experienced workmate – to assist new employees during their first few days or weeks of employment. This gives them an additional, and appreciated, point of contact and someone to go to with questions, taking some of the load off your shoulders.

E-induction

Some organisations use technology to ease and speed induction. New team members are sent a tablet a few weeks before they start, with downloads on everything from who's who in the workplace to safety procedures and the best places to eat lunch.

With a bit more investment, some organisations develop online induction modules that new employees can access on the organisation's intranet. Topics such as the organisation's structure and culture, its history, policies, products and services, and messages from the CEO, other leaders and key people such as employee and health and safety representatives, are all suited to e-induction. Compliance modules can also be included for new employees to complete covering areas such as intellectual property, conflicts of interest, emergency procedures, manual handling and so on.

While technology can never fully replace the personal contact that face-to-face induction provides, it can streamline the induction process, save money and time and promote consistency across the organisation. It can also offer an engaging 'edgy' option that some recruits may appreciate and that can reinforce the organisation's branding, culture and values. Perhaps the biggest advantage, especially when workers are working remotely, is its portability; recruits can access e-induction when and where it suits them and digest the important information it provides at their own pace.

Employees with special needs

Members of disadvantaged groups are more at risk than others, so identify and take their specific requirements into account when designing or delivering their induction (and other training programs). For example, while you should always pay special attention to health and safety matters and workplace hazards, accident rates are higher and tend to be more serious for young workers, so consider assigning an experienced worker or 'cobber' to ease them into their new position.[6] While young people are not all the same, many lack workplace experience, which can lead to accidents when they don't fully understand the potential dangers and the need for special precautions.

Induction information, safety signs and operating instructions for machinery printed only in English can disadvantage and place at risk people from non-English-speaking backgrounds. To help them, obtain health and safety publications printed in a variety of languages from the workplace health and safety authority in your state or territory. Encourage these employees to participate in committees and make sure they have access to all information that affects their employment. Using symbols in the workplace can be an effective way of highlighting hazards or precautions without using a specific language, but ensure that everyone understands what each symbol means, including existing staff members.

Provide assistance to people with disabilities to the degree that they require it. The assistance required may differ widely, so don't make assumptions. Allow people with disabilities who require additional assistance to ask you for it or offer it when it appears obvious that it is required. The main goal in inducting and training people with intellectual disabilities is to create independence. Use the 'show me' technique throughout their induction and training to ensure you have provided them with sufficient explanation. People with movement restrictions may have difficulty walking upstairs or reaching or grasping objects. Adjustments to the workplace can assist people with motor impairments and those who are amputees. Work through their individual needs with them carefully. Providing these supports is a legal obligation so, when required, make sure you put them into place to avoid your organisation falling foul of regulatory authorities.

Be careful not to assume that every worker can read and write proficiently. Some employees may not have received the education necessary to develop these skills or may have a learning or developmental disorder such as dyslexia. This can make it more difficult for them to complete forms and understand their workplace rights and responsibilities, including those relating to written emergency procedures, machine operation manuals, and safety instructions and precautions. Take particular care to induct and train them fully, providing instruction where required, and information in verbal or their other preferred format.

Performance reviews for new team members

Conduct fortnightly or monthly performance discussions with new team members for the first few months and regularly chat with them informally. Provide them with feedback to let them know how they are progressing and fitting in. Ask whether the position is what they had expected and whether they are enjoying it. Guided by the Five Keys, highlight and explain any concerns and analyse with the employee the possible causes. Follow this up by developing an improvement plan. Address any misunderstandings that they have and summarise any important discussions you had with them in writing, then add them to the employee's personal file. Should it become clear you've made a mistake in hiring the person and no amount of coaching, cajoling or training can transform their performance to the required level, terminate the employment before it's too late, invoking the provisions of the probationary period where applicable.

Onboarding

Many organisations do not differentiate onboarding from induction or simply include it as an extension of their induction program. This can make sense where there is obvious overlap between the two. But the process of onboarding stretches a little further out beyond the boundaries of induction. While, like induction, it is concerned with familiarising new employees with the requirements and responsibilities of their position, it places greater emphasis on integrating them into the organisation's culture via the building and nurturing of ongoing relationships through organisationally based programs, systems and arrangements. Onboarding is also the responsibility of the new employee's leader-manager rather than being a function of the HR manager or department.

Transferable skills

3.1 Teamwork/ relationships

Focusing on the relationship building aspects of onboarding, it begins with the initial introductions of the employee to their new team members. Simply going around the circle of team members and having them introduce themselves, or having each team member on screen say their name and give the new employee a cursory wave, falls short of effective onboarding. As outlined in the section 'The Induction process', organising an informal lunch or morning tea or partnering other team members with the new employee to 'show them the ropes' provides a better opportunity for the new recruit to start building workplace relationships even at this early stage in their tenure.

Involving the recruit in a new project where they can work closely with existing team members on exploring new ideas and initiatives is a good way for them to see team processes in action, involve themselves in planning and decision-making and gain exposure to the team culture.

Consider assigning a mentor to the new recruit from whom they can not only seek guidance on aspects of their work role, but who can also instruct them in the ways in which the internal systems and machinations of the organisation operate. A good mentor can help them understand who wields the real power and influence in the organisation, how to go about getting the things they need and connecting them with networks both within the organisation and externally.

Transferable skills

3.1 Teamwork/ relationships

Depending on the size of the organisation, there may be subgroups that the recruit can join. Organising representatives from these groups to come and meet the new employee and outline what each group offers can also be a good way to connect them with members of other teams and departments and form new networks. Some organisations also provide links to affinity groups combining people both from within and outside the organisation who share common interests. Others take it one step further and form arrangements with local businesses, such as fitness centres, where employees receive a discount or other benefits and can meet other members of their organisation outside of their usual work setting.

With the COVID-19 pandemic and accompanying widespread lockdowns, many of these options have not been available. As a result, leader-managers have had to put in place contingency plans to facilitate these relationships virtually, where possible. Virtual team rooms, social chat channels, one-on-one and group meetings, and links to social media-based groups, have become possible options to consider. Have new employees undertake a virtual scavenger hunt where they have to contact people in different roles within the organisation via videoconferencing, email or phone to obtain information or answer questions. This is a great way for them to not only meet others across the organisation but also to learn about the organisation all in the one activity.

Regardless of whether a new recruit is connected physically or virtually, facilitating the building of long-term relationships that provide them with support, engagement and opportunities to increase their knowledge and further their careers is a critical element of a successful employee recruitment, engagement and retention strategy.

INDUSTRY INSIGHTS

Onboarding at Netflix

Streaming giant Netflix has an onboarding process that begins even before a new employee turns up for their first day. When the new recruit arrives for their first day on the job, they already have a desk set up for them with an accompanying laptop. Their orientation begins with an explanation of the technology behind the Netflix success story, then new recruits spend time with the company's executive management, which provides them with the opportunity to learn about the organisation's culture, ethos and future aspirations. While each new employee is allocated their own mentor to provide them with help and guidance, they are also assigned to one of the company's large projects and given a role commanding significant responsibility. This allows them to undertake meaningful work from the day they walk in the door and make a solid contribution to the company's fortunes from the outset.

STUDY TOOLS

QUICK REVIEW

KEY CONCEPT 28.1 

a Briefly explain why recruitment is both a selling and a buying activity. In what way is recruitment a public relations exercise?
b What are the six tools you can use in recruiting and what purpose do they serve?
c Explain the role an organisation's employer brand and employer value proposition serve in recruiting the people the organisation needs.

KEY CONCEPT 28.2 

a List six ways to reach potential candidates.
b What is covered in a reference check?
c Explain the legal requirements you need to be aware of when recruiting.

KEY CONCEPT 28.3 

a Describe the five steps of a recruitment interview. What should interviewers do before and after the interview?
b List and briefly explain the three ways you can assess candidates' suitability for a vacancy when you invite them for an interview. How else can you assess candidates' suitability?

KEY CONCEPT 28.4 

a What is induction intended to achieve? What are a leader-manager's responsibilities in induction?
b List five onboarding strategies that a leader-manager could implement to help a new recruit form relationships both within and outside of their organisation.

BUILD YOUR SKILLS

KEY CONCEPT 28.1 

a Develop a job or role description for a position you are familiar with, or interview someone who works part- or full-time to find out about their duties and develop a job or role description for their job.
b Explain why a clear person specification is essential to recruit a suitable person for a vacancy.

KEY CONCEPT 28.2 

a Discuss the sources of information about candidates and the role each plays in building a better understanding of them.
b Develop a short planning agenda for a meeting between members of a panel interview.

KEY CONCEPT 28.3 

a The next time you are in a fast-food outlet or department store, carefully observe the people who are serving customers. Is anyone particularly good at the job? Is anyone not very good? Based on your observations, develop some criteria for selecting customer service staff for this establishment. Develop six questions you could ask to determine candidates' suitability for a position there.
b Manager A says she hires only those people who have the experience and competencies she is looking for, because she doesn't have the time to carry out a lot of on-the-job training. Manager B says she would rather hire a person with the right 'approach' and train them herself, so the duties are carried out just the way she wants. Who do you agree with? Why? Which approach would save more time in the long run? Why?
c Discuss the merits of competency-based questions, 'tryouts' and verbal simulation questions.

KEY CONCEPT 28.4 

a Discuss the benefits of thorough induction and training to: (i) the trainee, (ii) the manager, (iii) the work team and (iv) the organisation.
b Referring to Case study 10 'Management by filing cabinet', discuss how new members are introduced to this team. Would this work at all workplaces? Why or why not?
c Outline three ways in which onboarding helps to retain a new employee in the long term.

WORKPLACE ACTIVITIES

KEY CONCEPT 28.1 

a Check out the 'Pre-employment checks: An employer's guide' at https://www.cipd.co.uk/knowledge/fundamentals/emp-law/recruitment/pre-employment-checks-guide and summarise how you can use this information when recruiting.

b List the key features of your organisation's employer brand and employer value proposition and discuss how you can use them when recruiting.

KEY CONCEPT 28.2 

a What is your organisation's policy regarding using social media to research candidates? What are its implications for you when recruiting for a vacancy?

b Which sources of recruitment are best suited for the positions at your workplace? Why?

c How can you overcome the drawbacks of interviews?

KEY CONCEPT 28.3 

a Develop a series of behavioural questions to target key aspects of a position that reports to you. Refer to the position description and, if there isn't one already, develop a person specification to refer to.

b Develop a telephone reference check for the position mentioned in the previous question. Note what you would say at the beginning of the call and list the questions you would ask. Finally, prepare a general outline to use in a monthly performance review with a new employee in this position during their probationary period or first eight weeks with you. Be sure to include key deliverables or measures of success in key result areas.

c Would 'tryouts' work in recruiting people to your work team? What about in the rest of your organisation? Why or why not?

KEY CONCEPT 28.4 

a Design an induction program for your work team following the guidelines in this chapter, and explain how it could best be conducted.

EXTENSION ACTIVITIES

Referring to the Snapshot at the beginning of this chapter, answer the following questions:

1 Explain what Marlow was trying to achieve with the scavenger hunt and icebreaker activity? Why was what he was trying to achieve important?

2 Develop a possible onboarding program for the new quality manager.

CASE STUDY 28

EAST-WEST OIL

The East-West Oil Company is a growing company with a progressive management team. Brian Vawn is in charge of the company's retail outlets (service stations). In general, the company tries to locate a service station in towns with a population of 15 000 or more, but location also depends on business potential, competition and a suitable site.

East-West employs a local manager on a profit-sharing basis in its service stations. The managers operate within broad company guidelines and with minimum direct supervision. Every station is required to sell batteries, oil, tyres and related products as well as petrol and diesel. They can sell additional products at their discretion and many stations carry lines such as confectionery, fast food, grocery items and soft drinks. With company encouragement, most stations operate a service centre that carries out minor car repairs. Most of these centres, for example, balance and align wheels, correct minor electrical troubles, give motor tune-ups and reline brakes.

The manager of the Vancetown station has notified Brian that he intends to retire. Located in an area with a population of 88 000, Vancetown is one of East-West's most profitable and best-equipped stations. Situated at the intersection of two main highways, it attracts a great deal of passing trade as well as local trade. The station has eight pumps and operates two wash pits, two lubrication bays and a large service centre employing four full-time mechanics. With the exception of the service centre, the station is open 24 hours a day. Turnover has climbed steadily in the last 10 years.

Finding the right person to replace the station manager won't be easy, but Brian is encouraged by the background and record of one applicant, Ralph Lewis. Ralph is a first-rate motor mechanic who has been employed for the past 12 years with a local transport firm. He has a good record with that company and at present is in charge of a fleet of 12 trucks. He has also worked as a front-end specialist, a transmission mechanic and a tune-up specialist.

Questions

1 On the basis of the information presented in the case study, develop a brief role description and person specification for the vacancy.
2 If you were interviewing Ralph Lewis, what would you need to know to make a decision about hiring him?
3 Prepare an interview outline, including several behavioural questions to use at each stage of the interview.

CHAPTER ENDNOTES

1 Craig Donaldson, 'Interviewers get thumbs down', *Human Resources Magazine*, 30 October 2007. (Refer p. 17 – content under deliberation.)

2 See, for example, Jason Dana, Robyn Dawes, Nathanial Peterson, 'Belief in the unstructured interview: The persistence of an illusion', *Judgment and Decision Making*, Vol. 8, No. 5, September 2013, pp. 515–520.

3 Peter Martin, 'Australian bosses are racist when it's time to hire', *Sydney Morning Herald*, 18 June 2009, accessed August 2021, https://www.smh.com.au/national/australian-bosses-are-racist-when-its-time-to-hire-20090617-chvu.html

4 Juan M. Madera, Michelle R. Hebl, 'Discrimination against facially stigmatized applicants in interviews: An eye-tracking and face-to-face investigation', *Journal of Applied Psychology*, Vol. 97, No. 2, 2012, pp. 317–330.

5 OBS, http://www.obs.com.au, accessed 6 April 2015.

6 Safe Work Australia, 'Work-related injuries experienced by young workers in Australia, 2009–10', March 2013, http://www.safeworkaustralia.gov.au/sites/SWA/about/Publications/Documents/764/work-relatedinjuries-experienced-young-workers-Australia-2009-10.pdf, accessed 8 December 2014.

CHAPTER

29

ENCOURAGING A LEARNING ENVIRONMENT AND DEVELOPING EMPLOYEES

After completing this chapter, you will be able to:

29.1 establish a learning environment that creates and supports meaningful learning and development opportunities for employees and that helps them improve their learning effectiveness

29.2 identify your own and your team members' learning and development needs, and develop and gain approval for learning plans

29.3 facilitate and promote learning and monitor and assess the effectiveness of learning activities

29.4 plan and conduct one-on-one and small-group skills training.

TRANSFERABLE SKILLS

The following transferable skills are covered in this chapter:

1 **Business competence**
- **1.4** Business operations

2 **Critical thinking and problem solving**
- **2.1** Critical thinking
- **2.2** Personal effectiveness
- **2.3** Business strategy

3 **Social competence**
- **3.1** Teamwork/relationships
- **3.3** Written communication
- **3.4** Leadership

5 **Digital competence**
- **5.2** Technology use

OVERVIEW

The Australian Aboriginal word 'Birimba', meaning 'forever learning', is apt for today's employees who, by 2030, are expected to spend one-third of their working hours learning.[1] The only way to survive is to thrive, to keep improving and to move with, or better still, ahead of the changes. To do this, organisations need to keep developing their capabilities, and teams and individuals need to keep learning and developing their skills. That can't happen without a learning environment and a learning culture where building skills and knowledge is part of the way individuals and teams work.

Are the people in your team willing to get out of their comfort zones and try new things? Are they encouraged to make and learn from mistakes? Are there opportunities where your team can learn from each other or from you? Today's fiercely competitive and volatile global economy means that establishing a workplace climate that encourages and facilitates learning is an important part of every leader-manager's job. Why? Because the skills and knowledge of the workforce are an important resource and a worthwhile investment. Just as worthwhile an investment as marketing and technology, but unlike other resources, the value of knowledge doesn't lessen when it's used – it increases. This chapter explains how to build a working environment that keeps people effective and up to date to meet your organisation's needs now and in the future.

SNAPSHOT

A conducive learning environment

After graduation, Dallin's and Alicia's careers saw them working for two different organisations situated in the same building in the city. Over lunch one day, Alicia and Dallin discussed their careers and goals for future learning and development. Alicia commenced further study with her organisation and discussed how her manager encouraged her to integrate study time away from routine tasks into her weekly work plan. Alicia described her organisation as being a learning organisation. She boasted about even having access to an internal mentor with whom she met fortnightly. She aligned her professional development goals to her course learning outcomes, and she implemented concepts she was learning directly to her work.

Dallin's experience was quite different. While he worked for an organisation that understood the value of education, the head of the department believed that any further development should be completed in an employee's own time. Dallin recognised that he had a gap in his skills and knowledge, and because he loved his role and where he worked, he signed up for an online course. Dallin's routine consisted of studying on the train to and from work and spending a minimum of 15 additional hours per week studying at home. Dallin enjoyed what he was learning; however, with little children at home and inconsistent study quality during transit, his situation was not a conducive learning environment.

29.1 Establishing a learning environment

Transferable skills

1.4 Business operations

3.4 Leadership

> It isn't enough to take responsibility for your failures. It's important to create a culture that turns failures into learning and leads to continual improvement.
>
> A. G. Lafley, CEO of Procter and Gamble, 2000–10, quoted in Karen Dillon, 'I think of my failures as a gift: An interview with A. G. Lafley', *Harvard Business Review*, April 2011.

Few companies survived the Industrial Revolution of the 1800s. Few even survived electrification. Why? Because they failed to grasp the need to change the way they made and sold things in a changing world. As we saw in Chapter 1, we're in the midst of another revolution – the information revolution. How many of today's companies will live to tell the tale?

The central challenge of industrial-age work was efficiency; for knowledge-age work, it's learning. In today's **knowledge economy** and **service economy**, you're not just trying to do the same things you've always done, you're trying to do it better, cheaper or faster, while continuously improving and innovating different operations and offerings.

Encouraging and supporting learning, capturing what people learn, and making it widely and easily available to others, are essential in order to avoid organisational (and career) extinction. In fact, without a skilled and adaptable workforce, Australia's competitiveness and economic future will erode. We need to be able to learn, unlearn and relearn in order to innovate, recognise and take the right risks, and make the most of our changing environment.

Do you know that every dollar's worth of plastic in LEGO bricks sells to the customer for $75?[2] That's the value of knowledge. With knowledge being such an important asset, it doesn't make sense to leave its development to chance. The more your team or your organisation depends on knowledge and cooperative, innovative, smart employees, the more you need to nurture and manage their learning and experience methodically and deliberately, and more than that, help them put what they've learnt into practice. Hardly a day goes by without Google introducing a new product or feature that moves it along the road to fulfilling its mission.

Transferable skills
2.1 Critical thinking
3.4 Leadership

Surmount the obstacles

Before you can create learning opportunities, you need to know what the hurdles are and how to jump them. Figure 29.1 lists seven common hurdles with suggestions for overcoming them.

'IT'S NOT MY JOB'

Impact: Focusing only on what their job description requires limits the person's role. They lose the 'big picture' – the role's purpose, goals and responsibilities

Solution: Develop a job purpose statement with each team member and empower them to take responsibility within agreed parameters

'IT ISN'T MY FAULT'

Impact: Blaming something or someone else when something goes wrong prevents the person from taking responsibility or rectifying the situation

Solution: Turn the 'blame game' into 'What can I do to fix this?' Encourage your team to have a solution-focused mindset

'I'M IN CHARGE'

Impact: Failing to see your own contribution to a problem or thinking your 'taking charge' actions are helpful when they aren't, can lead to bigger problems or solutions that don't actually fix problems

Solution: Encourage each team member, and remind yourself, to think through their contributions to difficulties and the results of their actions. Effectiveness is more than action – it's helpful action

FIXATING ONLY ON THE URGENT

Impact: Revolving actions and conversations around 'urgent', attention-grabbing issues blinds a person to the real threats to the organisation and their job, which tend to instead sneak up gradually

Solution: Spend less time in the short-term thinking space and make the time for more long-term thinking

COMPLACENT THINKING

Impact: Neglecting thinking about the long term and becoming relaxed may allow for threats to creep in unnoticed

Solution: Stay up to date on potential threats and emerging trends that may impact your career or organisation

SILO THINKING

Impact: Failing to notice the direct consequences of decisions and actions, and not taking the opportunity to learn from them, can weaken the organisation's ability to improve

Solution: Reflect on decisions and spend more time analysing and solving complex problems. Build networks with your team and encourage both 'upstream' and 'downstream' thinking before and after actions or decision-making

'DON'T ROCK THE BOAT' THINKING

Impact: Failing to encourage different viewpoints and wanting to appear as a cohesive group increases the risk of crushing innovation

Solution: Encourage and reward innovative thinking and unusual ideas and solutions. Evolve work practices that support innovation and thinking 'outside the box'. Help people accept and learn from mistakes and keep an open mind

Adapted from Peter Senge, *The fifth discipline: The art and practice of the learning organization*, Doubleday, Sydney, 1990.

FIGURE 29.1 Identify and overcome hurdles

You have probably noticed that these learning hurdles are linked, which means you need to be aware of them all. Removing one or two, or even three, might help, but you're still hampered until you remove them all.

Create learning opportunities

Transferable skills
3.4 Leadership

With the seven learning hurdles addressed, you can more easily help team members gain and improve their skills, develop a range of skills and build learning into your team culture. Learning opportunities are everywhere. For example, you can:

- extend employees' skills and experience through additional responsibilities
- empower the team to consider their own learning goals
- guide new skill development
- provide opportunities for teams from other areas or departments to work together
- work with your team to redesign roles
- assign special projects that will expand existing skills and knowledge
- make time to mentor and coach.

Here are some everyday ways to create an environment where picking up knowledge and skills is something that occurs all the time.

Make time to reflect

Make time for yourself and your team, alone and together, to reflect, diagnose problems and learn from experience in a stable and anxiety-free environment. When planning for this time, ensure you have access to an environment that is physically, psychologically and socially comfortable. Throughout this process, demonstrate a willingness to explore different points of view. Air ideas, ask questions, seek out dissenting views and pay attention to them. Look for underlying assumptions that may be holding back improvements or acting as a flawed basis for decision-making and problem-solving. Encourage adaptability, curiosity and innovation so that team members see new ideas and opinions as valuable for developing novel approaches and solutions to make continuous improvements.

Help people listen to minority viewpoints and learn from mistakes. As they say, experience is a great teacher, but only when you learn from it. Teach your team to use the learning cycle shown in Figure 5.7 in Chapter 5 to identify and put to good use what they learn as they go about their jobs.

INDUSTRY INSIGHTS

End-of-year team performance review

Before the summer break, Alita scheduled some time out with her team to reflect on the past year. The scene was set for a relaxed and constructive meeting with a well-appointed meeting room and perhaps some coffee, tea and sandwiches or finger food. In preparation for the review, Alita sent the following list of questions to the team so people could have the opportunity to reflect and contribute thoughtfully about last year's performance:

- What are you and we as a team proud of?
- What worked well last year for you? For the team?
- What are the three biggest lessons you learnt this past year?
- What are the three biggest lessons we, as a team, learnt this past year?
- How would you describe the team's energy at this point?
- What projects or processes do we need to improve?

- Who are three people you should thank for their help in making the past year successful for you? (Call them or send a card, or similar, over the next couple of weeks or early in the new year.)
- Who are three people or other teams we as a team should thank for their help in making the past year successful for us? How can we thank them?

Alita aimed to encourage the team to congratulate themselves on what went well, and work together to plan what the team and its members could do to make the next year an even better one.

Alita asked each team member to write down one 'to do' idea along the lines of 'From now on I intend to ...' and share their commitment with the others during the review meeting. Alita plans to then ask the team to brainstorm ideas for working better as a team next year. The team would then select the top five ideas, which will be reviewed when the team meets in new year.

Learn from others

Learning from others can be a rewarding experience for all involved. Learning from others can be an informal event or a structured formal arrangement. Table 29.1 shows some examples.

TABLE 29.1 Examples of informal and formal knowledge-sharing activities

Examples of informal knowledge-sharing activities	Examples of formal knowledge-sharing activities
During a meeting a team member explains a problem and requests assistance. Other team members share their experiences with similar problems and explain their applied solutions	An organisational policy requires team members who participate in approved professional development activities to share a recount of the activity and key learnings
Use of a virtual board or chat space for team members to communicate challenges and request support from each other. This space is also used for sharing information discovered throughout the course of team members' roles	A formal mentor relationship that meets regularly to discuss learning needs of the mentee
Time spent with customers to find out how they operate, find and solve problems and approach innovation and continuous improvement	External networking events, which include industry socialising and presentations
Liaising with contractors and suppliers to gain product and industry knowledge	Formal development programs with groups from within and outside of initial departments

Use mistakes to learn

When you let them, mistakes and failures are all about learning. They are part of growth and improvement, not just for individuals but also for organisations. To learn from mistakes, you need to work through the process of reflection and analysis, and openly discuss the negative consequences. Without carefully examining the mistake to learn from it, the brain isn't sure what to store or how to rewire itself, so it does nothing. This means that you need to 'force' your brain to learn from mistakes.

When your mind looks for precedents among past actions when deciding what to do, it doesn't consider whether an action was successful or not. This means you can end up repeating your mistakes unless you've thought through what went wrong and what to do instead. Without taking this time to analyse the mistake and learn from the experience, you run the risk of making the same mistake again. Some of your more important and insightful learning is more likely to come from failures than successes; that is, as long as you worked out what went wrong.

Rather than ignoring, covering up, making excuses or finding someone else to blame for the mistake, it is much better to analyse what went wrong and to act on whatever corrective you decide to do. When it's appropriate, explain (not excuse) where you went wrong, how you've rectified it and, most important of all, what you intend to do to make sure it doesn't happen again. The more you try out new things, the more mistakes you're bound to make; and the more successes you're bound to have, too. The old cliché, 'Out on a limb is where the fruit is', is a useful one. People who score a lot of goals also kick a lot of misses. People who achieve anything worthwhile make more mistakes than most because they try out more things than most.

INDUSTRY INSIGHTS

Valuable mistakes

Thomas Alva Edison once said: 'Results! Why, man, I have gotten a lot of results! I know several thousand things that won't work!'[3] That prolific inventor also knew that mistakes can give you valuable information and golden opportunities when you let them.

Here are some other worthwhile mistakes:

- In 1894, the Kellogg brothers developed Corn Flakes after leaving out a sticky, doughy mess of wheat, which then went stale. Rather than throw it out, they processed the mess and baked it. Their customers loved the cooked flakes that resulted.
- In 1961, meteorologist Edward Lorenz' weather simulation was going terribly wrong. When he looked for the reason, he discovered that rounding off his figures by dropping the last three decimal places had a spectacular impact on complex systems. He had discovered chaos theory.
- Paying attention to mistakes was how the cholera vaccine, dynamite, penicillin, photography, Post-it notes, radium, Scotchgard™, shatterproof glass, silly putty, vulcanised rubber and X-rays were discovered.

It must be said that while mistakes can be learning opportunities, we also learn from achieving success. We learn more from success when success leads to a reward, because that strengthens the relevant neural pathway. This means that the successful behaviour is repeated more efficiently the next time.

Build learning mindsets

People's beliefs about knowledge deeply affect how well they learn. You can support your team members to develop mindsets that will help them learn effectively and become lifelong learners. Lifelong learners are ambitious, curious and self-aware. They ask good questions, focus on what they gain from learning (not the challenges of learning), tolerate mistakes and want to understand and learn new skills. To find out about developing learning mindsets, see the author's blog 'What do you believe knowledge is?' at https://colemanagement.wordpress.com/2015/06/05/what-do-you-believe-knowledge-is/.

Transferable skills
3.1 Teamwork/relationships
3.4 Leadership

Work with people's learning styles

How do you learn best? By doing, laughing, listening, making mistakes, reading, talking, watching and writing ... Learning in a way that comes most naturally can enhance your learning. There are more than 100 accredited learning style models, although research has shown that, while people may have preferences about how to learn, possibly based on what they're used to and feel most comfortable with, they can learn just as well whether information is presented in their preferred learning style or another. In fact, the most effective modality for teaching and training tends to vary according to the nature of the material. In addition, most scales for measuring learning styles are unreliable in that they produce different results on each testing, and they often fail to correlate with people's actual learning performance.[4] Nevertheless, it's a good idea to tweak the way you coach and train people to their preferred learning style when you can. And there is no doubt that presenting information in a variety of ways helps engage learners, if for no other reason than variety holds people's attention.

The Honey and Mumford learning style model, shown in **Figure 29.2**, describes four learning styles:[5]

- *Activists* like to roll up their sleeves and get 'stuck in', learning as they go. They enjoy trying new things, having new experiences and prefer relatively short learning activities and competitive team exercises. When helping them learn, say 'Explain what you're doing as you try out this procedure.'
- *Pragmatists* want to know how to apply the techniques and processes they are learning 'in the real world' and to their current job. Make the immediate relevance of your training clear to them. When helping them learn, ask 'How can you use this to improve your productivity and make your job easier?'
- *Reflectors* prefer to listen and observe others before having a go themselves. Give them a chance to collect information and time to review and think about what they are learning before trying it out. When helping them learn, ask 'What did you find easy/difficult in using this procedure?'
- *Theorists* learn well from concepts, models and theories, and prefer to think about what they are learning in abstract and systems terms. Stretch them and let them work in structured situations with a clear purpose. Give them time to explore associations and interrelationships, question assumptions and logic, analyse and generalise. When helping them learn, ask 'What conclusions can you draw from ... ?'

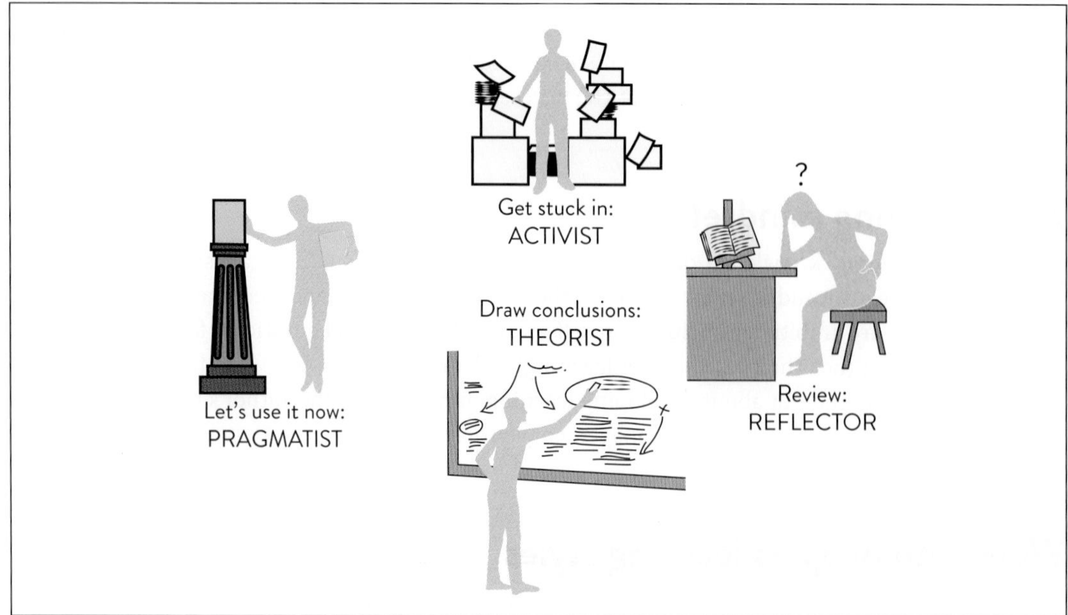

FIGURE 29.2 Honey and Mumford's learning styles

Here is a summary of other ways you can present information to learners based on three other learning styles models: David Kolb's learning styles, the Felder-Silverman model and the Herrmann brain dominance. Become familiar with the various ways you can help people learn so that you can add some spice and variety to your instruction, coaching and mentoring sessions.

- *Expressive and symbolic:* present information in a creative, meaningful, interesting, personal, representational way. Try to incorporate as many senses as you can: seeing, hearing, touching, feeling and doing are easy; smell and taste take a bit more thought and aren't always possible.
- *Holistic, big picture:* present information from a big-picture perspective; explain the entire system and how what you're explaining fits in.
- *Logical, analytical:* present information factually, logically and quantitatively, in an ordered fashion and in small steps. Zoom in on the details and provide evidence.
- *Pragmatic:* provide concrete, practical information and learning activities that concentrate on facts and procedures. Move from the specific to the general as you present information.
- *Relevance*: provide plenty of reasons to learn what you're explaining and the benefits derived from learning it.
- *Sequential:* present information chronologically or step by step, in an organised, structured manner.
- *Show:* demonstrate or model the skill or behaviour and give learners time to think it through on their own and work out how they can apply it or become comfortable with applying it.
- *Theory to practice:* explain the theory or concept and how it applies to what you're explaining. Move from the general to the specific as you present information.
- *Try it for yourself:* provide guidance on how to do a task and let learners practise, or let people learn by doing or even by discovery (within health and safety constraints).
- *Verbal:* provide written and spoken explanations.

VAK is another popular way to think through how to help people learn:

- *Visual:* learning by seeing. Use bar charts, diagrams, images, maps, pictures and so on to make your points; verbally 'paint a picture' that learners can see in their mind's eye.
- *Auditory:* learning through language, whether hearing or reading. Discuss learning points, give explanations, tell an illustrative story, think out loud and so on.
- *Kinaesthetic:* learning through doing, moving and rhythm. Physically walk people through a process or procedure, let people touch materials and so on to get a 'feel' for them; supervise people while they have a go.

Whether these various styles actually make learning easier is heavily disputed, but they certainly can make it more interesting.

Work with the three domains of learning

Figure 29.3 depicts the three types of learning: affective, cognitive and psychomotor, or attitudes and emotions, knowledge and skills. These are known as domains, or categories, of learning and include how people approach learning as well as the subject matter.

1. The affective domain includes the way people learn emotionally (e.g. with enthusiasm or apprehension) and covers topics like dealing with difficult customers, emotional intelligence and offering feedback.
2. The cognitive domain involves awareness of how people think and covers the development of conceptual skills and knowledge, including recognising and recalling specific concepts, facts and procedures and being able to apply them.

FIGURE 29.3 Three domains of learning

3 The psychomotor domain includes physical movement, coordination, and manual or physical skills. Developing psychomotor skills requires practice and is measured in terms of distance, precision or accuracy, speed, and correct execution of procedures and techniques.[6]

Understanding which domain people feel most comfortable in – feeling, thinking or doing – helps you present information in a way that can more readily be taken on board. You can also incorporate all three domains when learning and helping others to learn to provide a fuller, richer, learning experience and deepen understanding.

Transferable skills

3.1 Teamwork/relationships

The learning generations

Generational characteristics stem from the era that people were born into and grew up in. This leads to differences in the way people from different generations tend to prefer to work and be managed and also differences in the ways they prefer to learn.[7]

Don't ignore the development needs of your Baby Boomers and traditionalist team members (roughly, people over the age of 60). Training shows that you and the organisation are interested in them and their future. While Baby Boomers and traditionalists can learn from the time-honoured classroom and lecture-style methods, your youngest team members, Gen Z (roughly teens to early 20s), are likely to be strong visual learners who like to learn in short, sharp bursts that provide specific job skills. When appropriate, let them learn by discovery (under supervision) rather than simply telling them what to do or how to do it. Those in between, Millennials, also demand exciting, fast-paced learning, with the bells and whistles of graphics, bullet lists and hands-on activities. They understand that knowledge and skills increase their marketability, which makes them motivated learners.

Many from Gen X (aged in their 40s to mid-50s) appreciate small bits of information and lots of graphics to convey key points. Most Baby Boomers aren't as open to continual learning and they dislike the role-plays that those from Gen Y and Gen X enjoy, but they do like interactive discussion. The notion about not being able to teach old dogs new tricks is a myth. Older workers can learn as well as younger workers and once they have acquired the skills, they can apply them effectively. Older people's strengths are in their experience and brainpower. This is partly due to their experience and partly to their brainpower. Inductive reasoning (moving from the specific to the general) and spatial orientation (awareness of the space around you and where your body is in relation to it) peak around 50 years of age, and verbal abilities and verbal memory peak around 60 years of age. In terms of performance, research shows that, until people reach their 80s, age accounts for less difference in performance than individual differences.

Most people from Gen Y (aged in their mid-20s to 40) appreciate coaching, guidance and mentoring support (rather than 'teaching') and expect continuous learning and development. Help them develop their skills and show them what they need to work effectively in your team with an entertaining, active and interactive approach. You may find that difficult customers and authority figures intimidate them, so show them how to overcome objections and how to deal with difficult people.

They may be aces at instant messaging, but you may need to help some Gen Y and Gen Z team members with more traditional forms of communication, such as writing business documents in full sentences and using vowels and correct punctuation, how to organise and present evidence that supports their ideas, and with verbal presentations. You may also need to teach them basic corporate manners (e.g. turn off the tablet and silence the smartphone at meetings).

Keep your younger team members involved as they learn. Many in Gen Y and Z grew up with gaming and are active as well as pragmatic learners (see Figure 29.2). They are interested in learning conceptual and physical skills that are immediately relevant and increase their job opportunities, so ensure they can use the skills you help them learn straightaway. Forget the theory, facts and figures (which they can Google when the need arises) and concentrate on the practical 'how tos' they need to succeed in their jobs.

Think about the people you know and work with. How do your learning needs and preferences differ from others around you?

29.2 Identifying learning needs and planning to meet them

Transferable skills
2.1 Critical thinking
2.2 Personal effectiveness

> Learning is like rowing upstream: not to advance is to drop back.
>
> Ancient Chinese proverb

Picture this:

- A department suffers excessive turnover, with staff complaining their leader-manager has 'no idea'.
- A fire in an office spreads while employees work out how to use the fire extinguisher.
- A high-value customer is lost because a query is poorly handled by a new employee who has not yet been trained in customer-service skills.
- A promising young employee resigns because he feels he isn't receiving the coaching he needs from his leader-manager.
- A woman takes stress leave because she feels she isn't keeping up with her workload; her doctor suggests this could easily have been prevented with basic training and coaching on working to priorities.

Why is it that poor training is at the heart of so much angst, lost productivity and accidents? Strong training, coaching and mentoring programs that target organisational needs are how you keep and motivate good staff, increase morale and job interest, keep valued customers and build strong teams.

Effective learning and development (L&D) is an important part of many organisations' **employer value proposition**, essential to attracting and retaining the people they need. L&D makes sense as an investment in other ways, too. As well as boosting productivity, learning can boost morale because it helps to meet people's needs for recognition and development. It is generally reflected in indicators of employee satisfaction, such as absenteeism, **employee engagement**, retention and timekeeping.

INDUSTRY INSIGHTS

'L&D – a good investment'

A newly appointed human resources (HR) manager of a medium-sized financial management business learnt that the company had recently stopped investing in staff training and development. Management viewed training to be expensive, and they couldn't see sense in investing in L&D when:

- productivity was lost when employees were in training
- the company was experiencing high attrition
- new recruitment strategies were adopted, which saw more part-timers and casuals employed
- many of the team were over 40
- return on investment was not measured.

The HR Manager spent the next year implementing a new L&D strategy, which saw a range of development opportunities conducted with the team, including:

- *Structured induction:* a two-week induction program introducing task and organisation fundamentals.
- *Monthly workshops:* small one-hour monthly workshops inviting discussion and exploring new techniques to complete various components of the team's roles. The HR manager measured the success of each workshop before the next.
- *Product training:* an industry specialist highlighted the benefits of key financial products on the market and explained how to introduce them to clients.

Within six months, staff engagement was at an all-time high. The team's productivity was high, and revenue had increased by 12 per cent.

The organisation achieved these positive outcomes because employees felt more invested in their roles. They also found that understanding the benefits of the products made it easier to communicate these to clients.

Learning isn't just about providing, updating or upgrading technical skills; there are also the all-important people skills. Training and coaching in people skills improves employees' abilities to work cooperatively with others, to communicate clearly and to be part of high-performance, high-productivity teams.

The question is not should we train people, but rather how should we do it? Planned, systematic training can help people work together better and show them how to do their jobs more efficiently. Training can also reduce accidents, minimise customer complaints, contribute to a positive employer brand and employer value proposition and enhance an organisation's global competitiveness. It reduces the length of time it takes new employees to reach what is known as experienced worker standard, saving time and money, reducing waste and increasing quality. Training targeted to meet the strategic needs of the organisation can also increase employees' ability to take on other roles, positioning the organisation to meet its future challenges. When combined with a learning culture, managing employees' learning properly greatly strengthens an organisation. **Figure 29.4** shows four types of knowledge on which to concentrate.

To reap the benefits of knowledge, you don't necessarily need to employ really smart people or people with a lot of qualifications. You need to employ people with the ability to learn and to share and use what they've learnt. Once you have these people on your team, you need to provide opportunities for them to share their built-up knowledge, insights and experience. The aim is to build an organisation of committed and dedicated people and support them with the culture, equipment, facilities, tools, training and other resources they need to do their jobs well.

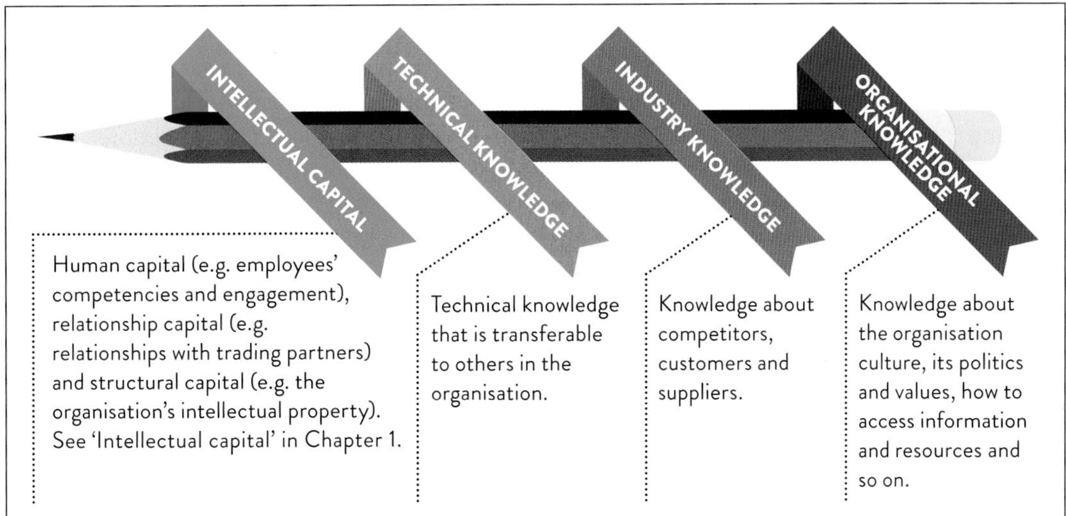

FIGURE 29.4 Four important types of knowledge

Identify learning and development needs

You can think of 'training' as short-term, formal and semi-formal instruction of basic skills and knowledge; for example, how to operate equipment and machinery, how to complete a document or prepare a spreadsheet, or the implications of a new policy or procedure. Training may be instigated by identifying a specific area that needs addressing. Figure 29.5 shows individual employee and team training needs and leader-manager training needs.

'Development' has a longer-term flavour and involves deeper and more complex knowledge and skills; it may include formal training, guided experience and mentoring. Organisational changes, job changes and individual and team performance shortfalls can all indicate a need for training and development. They aren't just about plugging gaps, though. They are also about strengthening existing skills and developing employees for the future.

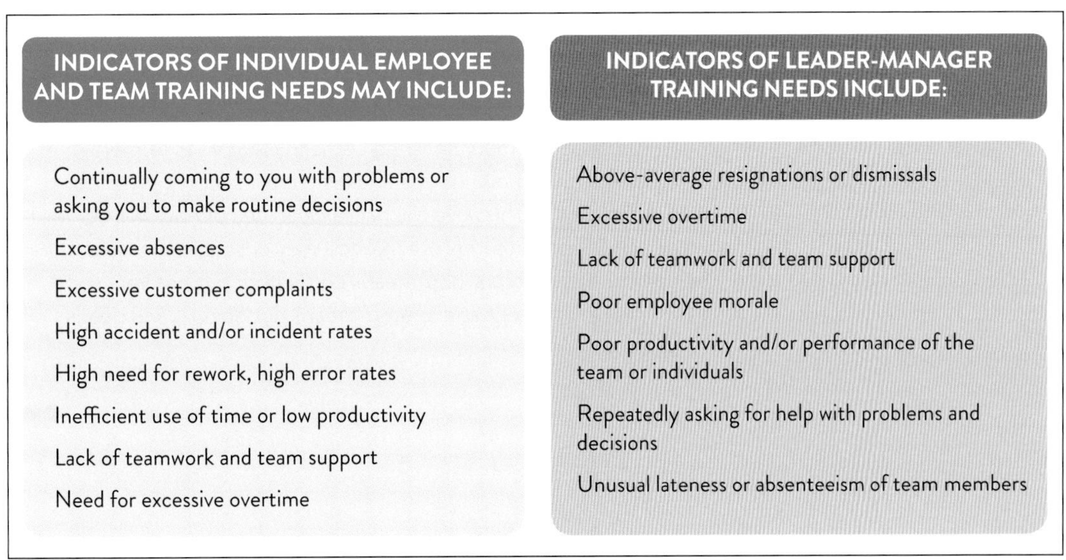

FIGURE 29.5 Individual employee, team and leader-manager training needs

Learning needs analysis

You don't want 'plug-in' training solutions that don't work. A thorough learning needs analysis ensures training and development activities are targeted to the precise needs of your team and organisation. Knowing the precise requirements of your team helps you identify the best training option.

You may want to begin a learning needs analysis by thinking about the organisation's goals and strategies and how prepared your team is to contribute to achieving them. Then you can pinpoint the learning needs of your team. The two most popular ways to pinpoint learning needs are to complete *learning needs analysis* (LNA) and invite each employee to identify and discuss their own learning needs. These discussions can be either informal or formal. Both approaches aim to identify opportunities to extend or improve already strong skills and add new skills.

The more you involve employees in identifying their own learning needs, the more readily they accept the need for and look forward to extending their knowledge and skills. Be aware, though, that some people overestimate their skills and underestimate their need for training while others do the opposite; that's where competencies and a good learning culture can help. Once you've identified your team's learning needs, ensure they link back to the organisation's strategy and plans and key organisation objectives.

Figure 29.6 shows six other ways to identify learning needs. Customers, peers, other leader-managers and mentors can also shed light on people's training needs. Be mindful not to just accept third-party reports as gospel.

Analyse records, e.g. accident and incident statistics, customer feedback, exit interviews, performance reviews, quality measures.	Compare performance against benchmarks or measures of success.	Consider your organisation's plans, e.g. for expansion or introducing new technology.	Have employees complete learning questionnaires or competency checklists.	Hold group meetings where the team brainstorms its training needs.	Observe employees as they carry out their duties.

FIGURE 29.6 Other ways to identify learning needs

INDUSTRY INSIGHTS

Steps, hops and jumps

Michael is a member of a customer service team in a medium-sized company that visits farmers to advise on products and services. At the end of his first year, he and his team leader reviewed his performance, which they summarised in **Table 29.2**. This gave Michael a clear idea of how well he was performing and where and how much he needed to improve. Notice they describe Michael's learning needs in terms of steps, hops and jumps, where a 'hop' means competent but not yet proficient, a 'step' means doing it but not yet competent and a 'jump' means not doing it and needs to begin to develop it.

TABLE 29.2 Michael's development needs

Area of competence	Gap size	Comments
Managing time	Step	Not able to prioritise
Delivering high level customer service	Step	Few issues
Evaluating and improving customer service	Jump	Has not gathered customer satisfaction data
Managing own development	Jump	Has not made use of available opportunities
Making effective use of available technology	Hop	New technology is a challenge
Demonstrating leadership within work team	Step	Few opportunities to do this
Managing stress in the workplace	Hop	Mainly in very busy periods
Industry and related technical knowledge	Nil	Well qualified, experienced and informed
Knowledge of new products	Jump	Missed recent presentations, demonstrations and conferences

A learning needs analysis identifies gaps between the current job knowledge and skills of an employee or a group of employees and those required for the future (see Figure 16.3 in Chapter 16). The skills and knowledge possessed and needed can vary from the 'bare minimum' to 'expert', shown as the six levels of competence, summarised in Figure 29.7.

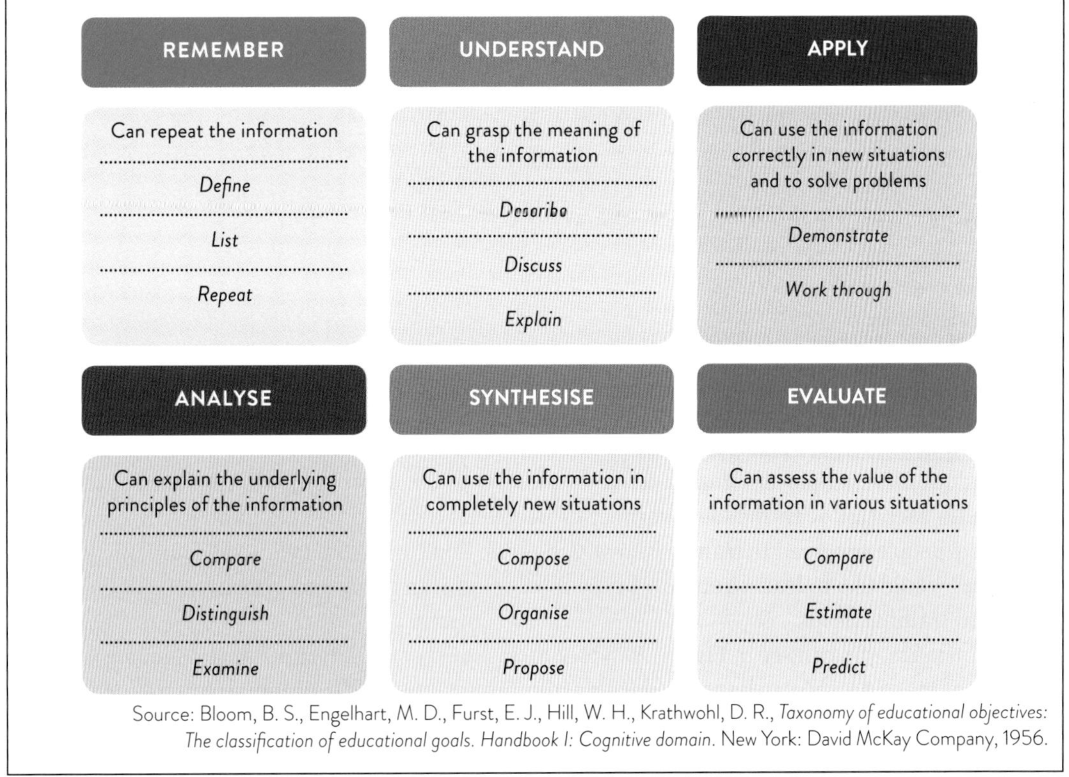

Source: Bloom, B. S., Engelhart, M. D., Furst, E. J., Hill, W. H., Krathwohl, D. R., *Taxonomy of educational objectives: The classification of educational goals. Handbook I: Cognitive domain*. New York: David McKay Company, 1956.

FIGURE 29.7 Six levels of competence

When you're assessing gaps and how large they are, think about, for example, whether the employee has the skills to:

- prioritise their work in this area
- organise tasks related to this competency
- communicate key aspects of it to others as needed
- deal with problems and contingencies that arise
- transfer knowledge, skills and attitudes to new situations
- work effectively with others as part of a work group.

Once you have pinpointed the performance gaps, you can develop a learning plan showing which individuals or groups of employees are to be trained in which task or skill, by when and by whom. This information can be recorded with a matrix (see **Figure 29.8**). List the key tasks and duties of your team across the top of a spreadsheet and the names of the employees down the left-hand side. You can also include any tasks or duties that are not done now but will be in the near future. At the bottom, show the ideal number of people that should be available at all times to carry out each task.

	A	B	C	D	E	F	G	H	I
1					TASK DUTIES				
2 3 4		Stock shelves	Price goods	Order goods	Take inventory	Make change	Operate cash register	Answer customer queries	Resolve customer complaints
5		1	2	3	4	5	6	7	8
6	Jean	✓	✓	+	+	✓	✓	+	✓
7	Yunhua	–	–	✓	✓	✓	✓	✓	✓
8	Alf	+	✓	X	X	+	+	–	+
9	Morgan	✓	✓	✓	✓	✓	✓	✓	✓
10	Terry	✓	+	+	+	✓	+	+	✓
11	Actual number able to perform task	3	3	2	2	4	3	2	4
12	Ideal number able to perform task	5	3	2	3	4	4	5	4

Key

✓ can do well

\+ can do but needs more training/experience

× cannot do and does not need to do

– cannot do and should be trained to do

Prepared by Melanie, 19/6/22

FIGURE 29.8 Learning needs analysis and a learning plan for a convenience store

Place a tick (√) where employees carry out a task or duty competently and a cross (×) against any tasks or duties that employees don't need to know how to do. Then compare the number of people who can do each task with the ideal number of people who should be able to do it. This shows you how many people you need to train and in which tasks. You can also take into account any jobs that employees would like to learn. You now know the degree of urgency and priority you should give to individual training needs.

For instance, you can see in **Figure 29.8** that all tasks except 1, 4, 6 and 7 have adequate job cover and that, of these, 4 and 6 can be covered with a minimum amount of training, so you should probably give special attention to training for tasks 1 and 7. In addition, you can see that Morgan, a very able employee, can do all the required tasks. Perhaps you should think about additional training and development for her so that she does not become bored and her performance level drops as a result.

To turn your learning needs analysis into a learning plan, add target dates to each person's square showing when you intend to begin or complete training for that task. For instance, to have Jean fully trained in task 7 by 4 September, you would write 4/9 in that box.

Your own learning needs

Transferable skills

2.2 Personal effectiveness

Einstein said, 'Life is like riding a bicycle. In order to keep your balance, you must keep moving.'[8] You probably agree that your own L&D is a never-ending investment in your future. Think about your strongest skills and how you can develop them further. Think about the path your industry and your organisation are on and what skills you need to develop for the future. You may need to update or upgrade your skills to meet future organisational needs. Decide what you want to learn over the next six months, plan how to do it and set time aside to ensure you complete your plan.

Employees take their cues from you – your attitudes and the way you approach your work and the people you work with. To encourage the people in your team to see learning as a lifelong journey and to take responsibility for their own L&D, you need to do the same. As a bonus, acting as a positive role model also makes you a more valuable employee, because as organisations continue to develop and change, people are valued as much for what they can learn tomorrow as for what they can do today.

Career pathing

A career path charts a course for an employee, showing the various positions they can take up. Today's career paths often look more like a lattice than a ladder, with people making vertical and horizontal moves as well as cross-functional moves. Fewer organisations (even large organisations with more positions and places for employees to move) offer formal career paths to employees, even though it can help retention and grow their own talent and promote from within. Organisations that still offer career pathing begin by identifying the core roles and levels in the organisation and setting clear criteria to reach those roles in terms of formal education required, leadership qualifications, personality profiles and other capabilities. This gives employees a sense of where their career in the organisation could take them and a way to identify their L&D needs and plan to meet them, and it allows the organisation to develop succession plans that identify employees who can replace people in key positions when they leave or retire.

You may need to encourage your team members to make their own career map by listing the roles they have fulfilled, identifying goals and positions inside and outside the organisation they aspire to, analysing their skills and preparing a development plan that may include establishing networks and finding a mentor.

INDUSTRY INSIGHTS

Alicia's career path

Alicia's career aspirations included achieving team leader status within three years. Before Alicia gained employment in her chosen field, she finished VCE and started as a part-time receptionist in her chosen industry. Alicia's manager, Graziano, was impressed with her commitment to her role and the team. While Alicia was recognised for her performance, Graziano noted that Alicia does not recognise the value of her skills. Graziano decided to discuss career pathing with Alicia.

Throughout an informal conversation, Alicia indicated that she wished to become a fully qualified senior consultant. Over the next four years, Alicia remained employed part-time and commenced working full-time as a senior consultant once she completed her degree.

Six months into her new position, Graziano and Alicia met to formally review her role, identify new goals and complete a development plan that met her career path. Graziano upgraded Alicia's position to 'cadet team leader' and agreed to suitable training. The training Graziano arranged recognised both the need for the training to be aligned to organisational requirements and for the organisation to receive value from costs incurred in the form of enhanced performance in Alicia's upgraded position. Alicia was happy to build the knowledge, skills and experience to be a team leader and made full use of her opportunity.

Transferable skills
2.1 Critical thinking

Decide on the learning method

Once you have identified learning needs, your next step is to determine the precise outcomes you want by answering these questions (which also apply to fulfilling your own professional development plan):

- How do you want your team members' behaviour – what they say and do on the job – to be different?
- What specific outcomes do you want to achieve as a result? For example, do you want the people who attend a spreadsheet workshop to be able to design and maintain spreadsheets so that they can track sales by customer and type of sale, order size, order frequency and payment status?

Once you answer these questions, you will identify whether providing learning opportunities is the right solution. Providing learning opportunities is a good solution when learners don't know, when they don't know how and, sometimes, when they need to improve at something. It's also great when people need to learn specific pieces of information and when there is one correct answer. Training is not the answer when people lack motivation, when inefficient systems are causing poor performance, or when it's the tools, equipment and other resources, not the people, that aren't up to the job. Training is not the answer when you're short-staffed and there aren't enough hours in the day to do everything that needs to be done or when people aren't clear about what you expect of them. It also isn't the answer when the organisation's leadership or the team's leader-manager is setting such a poor example that people are completely cynical about their jobs and their organisation. Nor can training 'fix' people who are temperamentally unsuited to the job or who are in the wrong job to begin with.

If training is the answer and you have gained the information you need, you can decide whether to provide formal or informal training or whether there is a better alternative to training. You can select the most appropriate from the types of training shown in **Figure 29.9**.

When you need to update, extend or develop business, interpersonal or technical skills, formal training, either on the job or off the job, is one of many possible solutions. Some others are shown in **Figure 29.10** (see also Chapter 5).

The learning method or methods you choose depend on how much time and money you have, the nature of the training and the number of people you want to train. Consider employees' varying abilities and take special needs into account. You may need to be quite creative in the way you design and offer L&D so that it appeals to the various people in your work team.

Type	Examples
AWARENESS TRAINING	Equal employment opportunity and workplace diversity, risk management, sexual harassment and bullying, sustainability
BASIC SKILLS TRAINING	Business writing, English as a second language, remedial training in literacy, maths, reading comprehension
IT TRAINING	How to use computer software and groupware, spreadsheets, databases and graphics (both off-the-shelf and company-specific), how to use sophisticated aspects of your devices to manage time, information security
CUSTOMER SERVICE TRAINING	Call centre operations, dealing with and learning from customer complaints, maintaining and improving customer relations
EXECUTIVE DEVELOPMENT	Creativity, due diligence, global marketing, leadership, strategic planning
INDUCTION TRAINING	Information about the organisation and its operations, functions, mission and policies, compensation and benefits, work requirements, standards and rules
JOB-SPECIFIC TECHNICAL SKILLS TRAINING	Equipment, procedures, products, service delivery, technology
LEADER-MANAGER DEVELOPMENT	Budgeting, conducting performance reviews, implementing regulations and policies, managing projects and processes, performance management, planning
WORKPLACE SAFETY AND COMPLIANCE TRAINING	Safety hazards, procedures, regulations
PRODUCT KNOWLEDGE TRAINING	Product specifications, repair, upgrading, maintenance for sales and service professionals
PROFESSIONAL SKILLS TRAINING	Specialised knowledge and applications in accounting, consulting, computer science, engineering, information systems management, law, project management
QUALITY, COMPETITION AND BUSINESS PRACTICES	Benchmarking, business fundamentals, business process management, quality management and continuous improvement
SALES TRAINING	The attitudes, skills and habits needed to influence the purchasing decisions of prospects and customers for franchisees, dealers and salespeople
TEAMWORKING SKILLS AND TEAM BUILDING	Individual and group training to improve

FIGURE 29.9 Types of training and development

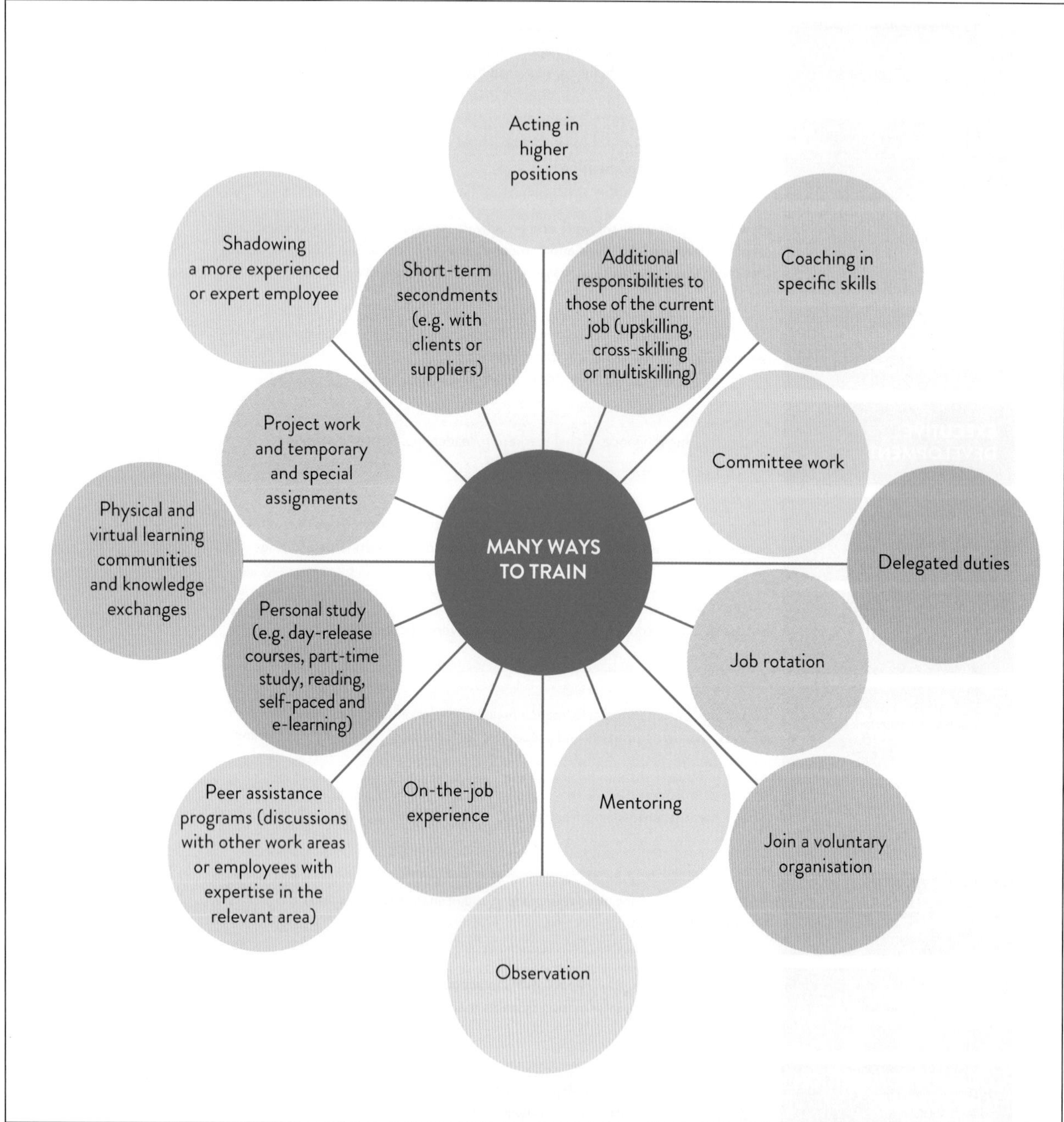

FIGURE 29.10 Many training solutions

Discuss possible strategies with the learners and choose those that suit them best and are the most cost-effective. The more you involve learners in identifying their learning needs and planning to meet them, the more effective their learning is likely to be. After all, they are the customers in the process.

Table 29.3 summarises the strengths of 12 common delivery methods. Whichever method you select, it is essential to agree on clear learning objectives with the learners prior to the training and to debrief them during and after the learning process to ensure the learning objectives are met. The following sections review the main types of training and other learning methods to choose from.

TABLE 29.3 The strengths of common delivery methods

Delivery method	Strengths
Attending conferences, seminars and information sessions	Provides current information from experts and may provide an opportunity for networking
Coaching	Provides opportunities for skill development and ongoing feedback on performance of work tasks
Demonstrations and practice	Effective for passing on skills
E-learning/online learning	Useful for developing new knowledge and refreshing knowledge at a time and place suitable to the employee
Induction	Required to provide new staff with an appropriate workplace orientation
Job rotation/exchange	Helps in multiskilling and developing wider perspectives
Mentoring	Assists longer-term professional and career development
Networking	Can provide ideas, help solve problems, give support and aid career development
On-the-job learning	Usually involves informal training, feedback from other work group members and individual reflective practice
Role-plays and simulations	Safe ways to develop management skills dealing with analysing situations and making decisions
Team meetings	Provide opportunities to share ideas, raise issues and solve problems when well facilitated
Training sessions, on-the-job or external	Valuable in developing expertise when objectives are well defined

Off-the-job learning

Parts of induction programs, product training and other conceptual and physical skills training often take place off the job, particularly when the training takes longer than two or three weeks and a number of employees need to be trained. Training for technical aspects of a job generally takes place in a training room that duplicates work conditions as much as possible; for instance, it might be equipped with machines, telephones and other task-related tools. Off-the-job training is beneficial because it allows people to learn and make mistakes in a safe environment.

The wide range of off-the-job learning options includes:

- corporate, or in-house, seminars and workshops on specific topics
- distance learning, such as satellite or videoconferences and virtual seminars (useful for reaching large numbers of people dispersed geographically)
- evening classes on various work-related topics
- external courses, conferences, lectures and training programs organised for the public or by professional bodies and industry associations for their members and guests

- formal study, such as day-release for tertiary studies and updating qualifications (e.g. post-trade training)
- plant visits (can open trainees' eyes to other ways of doing things and extend their general knowledge)
- secondments and study tours; however as they can be time-consuming and expensive, target learning needs carefully, and thoroughly brief and debrief participants
- self-paced online learning, or e-learning
- team-building workshops.

The main advantages of in-house training programs are that they are generally less costly per person and can be designed specifically to meet the organisation's learning goals and to support its culture, strategy and values. Participants can extend their knowledge of how the organisation operates and their networks within it, which is motivating. Public courses, although generally costlier, can expose participants to a range of experiences, opinions and thinking. Both allow participants to share and learn from each other's experiences as well as from their course leader.

When lasting longer than a day, off-the-job programs can be residential, which allows the learners to work on into the evening, study in the evening or strengthen their working relationships over a meal and a relaxing get-together. The choice depends on the nature and the objectives of the program.

Winston Churchill once said: 'Personally, I am always ready to learn although I do not always like being taught.'[9] This applies to many learners, which is why experienced trainers use a variety of techniques to engage learners and develop their skills and understanding. The following techniques can make learning more enjoyable and help learners retain the knowledge more easily:

- *Experiential learning activities* where people learn by doing rather than talking about something.
- *Problem-based learning activities* are also used to engage learners and provide opportunities for teams to collaborate with each other on 'real life' situations and issues.
- *Games* are active learning experiences that extend learners' skills, knowledge and experience. On the surface, some may seem to have nothing to do with the learners' jobs. However, with skilfully guided discussions afterwards, participants can learn about themselves and each other, how to more effectively work in groups to achieve goals, how to improve their own work style and how to develop useful working procedures. Many indoor and outdoor team-building activities use such games and learning experiences, and e-learning often uses games to provide learning experiences. Specially designed 'games', case studies and role-playing also assist with practising the techniques and concepts.
- *Simulations* allow trainees to perform tasks under virtual conditions. This hands-on virtual practice in a range of technical and interpersonal skills allows learners to build their skills in a situation that is nearly live without their mistakes having serious repercussions.

To ensure learning occurs, and for easier application back on the job, the learning cycle needs to be used to help learners reflect on their insights and actions and the consequences of their actions.

Well-designed and facilitated off-the-job training workshops can effectively provide in-depth knowledge and an understanding of principles and how to apply them in practice. They can:

- develop conceptual skills in areas such as decision-making, planning, problem-solving and time management
- develop 'soft' skills in areas such as communication, leadership, performance management and teamwork
- extend technical understanding of aspects of employees' jobs in areas such as business writing, computer applications, health and safety training, sales and negotiation skills.

Self-paced, e-learning and blended learning

When it's difficult to release employees for blocks of training, bringing training to employees through self-paced and e-learning is a possible solution. Even when large numbers of learners are involved, organisations save money in travel and accommodation costs and employees spend less time away from their jobs.

Self-paced workbooks with study guides and e-learning modules are transportable and flexible, so people can learn wherever and whenever suits them best. They can accommodate different rates of learning, and learners can review and repeat learning points in a way that is not possible with traditional conferences, seminars and training workshops. Well-designed **self-paced learning** and e-learning stimulates thinking throughout the learning process, as well as after it. The most engaging e-learning products are fully interactive.

A variety of media can be used for e-learning, including audio and video, podcasts, blogs, chat rooms and discussion boards, online learning programs, web-based courses and wikis. An increasing number of tools are being used to access e-learning media, including tablets, smartphones and other portable media players, and Voice over Internet Protocol (VoIP) services, such as Teams, Zoom or Webex. Private and secure networks use internet technology to link organisations with their customers, suppliers or other organisations with shared goals or common learning needs. Many of these platforms take advantage of interactive capabilities for learning and assessment, with some providing dedicated chat rooms with a tutor available at specified times.

With so many options, the only way to make the right choice is to establish your objectives, consider your learners and your budget and see whether self-paced or e-learning can meet your needs. When looking at e-learning solutions, consider selecting a resource that can be updated where information will change regularly and think about the needs of your employees.

The following are some of the ways you can encourage e-learning:

- Discuss what will be covered before the training begins and ask trainees to think about real work problems the training could help with so they can relate what they're learning to the job.
- Explain how the training links with their job and personal goals.
- Let people know how well it's worked for other individuals and teams.
- Check in regularly as the training progresses to discuss how it's going and how the learner is using it.
- Encourage trainees to complete the e-program, and when they have, discuss how they have used it and plan to continue using it on the job.

Informal learning with technology

Transferable skills
5.2 Technology use

People have always learnt opportunistically, by osmosis – the gradual, often unconscious assimilation of ideas, knowledge and understanding. Observing someone as they do something or manage their time or a difficult situation, listening to workmates think out loud and chatting problems through during a lunch break – all builds people's competencies.

Technology can now make that natural learning mobile and 'just-in-time', too. People can easily and quickly find the information they need and capture, retrieve and share experience, information and insights – regardless of geography and hierarchy. Smartphones can access information as employees need it for a specific project or task. Social media can engage younger generations of learners through micro blogs, shared workspaces, social networks and wikis, supplementing traditional training with collaboration and co-creation, and bringing distant employees together into communities of learning. Networking sites can also support employee development programs and help employees coach each other remotely. However, make sure people are aware of, and know how to guard against, 'fake news', false 'information' and dodgy websites.

Wiki software is being used increasingly. Organisations are setting up wikis on their intranets to allow employees to add or edit content, ranging from product specifications to explanations of complicated acronyms and procedures, saving hours unearthing or re-creating information, and to brainstorm new products and processes, document best practice and plan meetings. Some organisations invite their customers and suppliers to contribute to and use their wikis, too. Open source learning platforms such as LinkedIn, accessible either individually or through organisational credentials, also offer a variety of learning opportunities.

What if off-site, less-experienced workers wore a video camera to show highly experienced workers back at the base what they're seeing; for example, workers repairing a power line? The expert workers can coach them through the repair. What if people doing a physical job wore a device that alerted them to when they're working unsafely? For example, people who lift a lot might be alerted to an incorrect lifting position. Wearable technology is beginning to expand the ways we can coach and train employees.

Learning by doing

Acting in higher positions, becoming a committee member (e.g. of a health and safety committee or a risk management event team), rotating jobs, secondments (temporarily transferring to another role in the organisation), shadowing a more experienced employee, and undertaking delegated duties, special assignments and projects, are all ways for employees to develop skills and knowledge on the job and add value to the organisation at the same time. Learning by doing can be an effective, enjoyable and inexpensive way to build knowledge, skills, attitudes and experience. The following sections review two of these methods: action learning and undertaking special assignments and projects.

Transferable skills

2.1 Critical thinking

3.1 Teamwork/relationships

Action learning

With problems and challenges that are complex or have many possible answers, people need to think critically, explore issues and reflect on possibilities. Action learning encourages discussion, analysis, evaluation, synthesis, reflection and insight by helping people learn from each other. Learners then transfer the process they learn to use to other situations.

Action learning brings a group of people together in an action-learning team, who meet with a facilitator or adviser who supports them, particularly in the early meetings. Team members are selected based on both the skills and the knowledge they can bring to the team and their learning needs. (This dual focus makes action-learning groups different from teams that focus only on improvements and project teams that work on a specific project.)

Groups can work on either an organisational problem or a member's work problem, with members taking turns to present a work challenge they are currently grappling with. These problems provide learning opportunities and, at the same time, improve the organisation's performance when resolved. The groups usually meet once a fortnight for several months, with meetings generally lasting a half day or full day.

Advisers begin by establishing the ground rules for working well and productively together. They help group members replace bad habits, such as jumping in to give advice too quickly or not exploring and analysing a problem sufficiently, with skills such as effective listening and questioning. They model the questioning process, help group members to develop their own questioning skills and promote other 'learning to learn' behaviours. Facilitators also create a safe space for open discussion, advise on resources and models, act as timekeepers, and provide training in problem-solving and decision-making as required. The result is 'double-loop learning', a deeper form of learning than, for example, trial and error, or 'single-loop learning'.

In single-loop learning, life and learning are a series of episodes. People learn from their mistakes and change their day-to-day behaviour as a tactical response, without questioning or altering their underlying assumptions and beliefs. In double-loop learning, people think over and adjust their assumptions, beliefs and/or guiding principles based on their results, which gives them a profound grasp of what happens in a situation and lets them rethink their entire strategy. The difference between these two types of learning is illustrated in Figure 29.11.

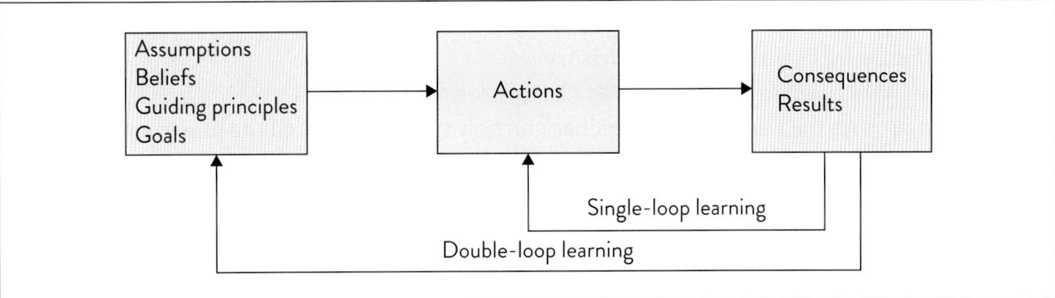

FIGURE 29.11 Single- and double-loop learning

Figure 29.12 summarises the process used when action learning groups work on an individual member's issue or problem. (The process is similar when groups work on an organisational problem.)

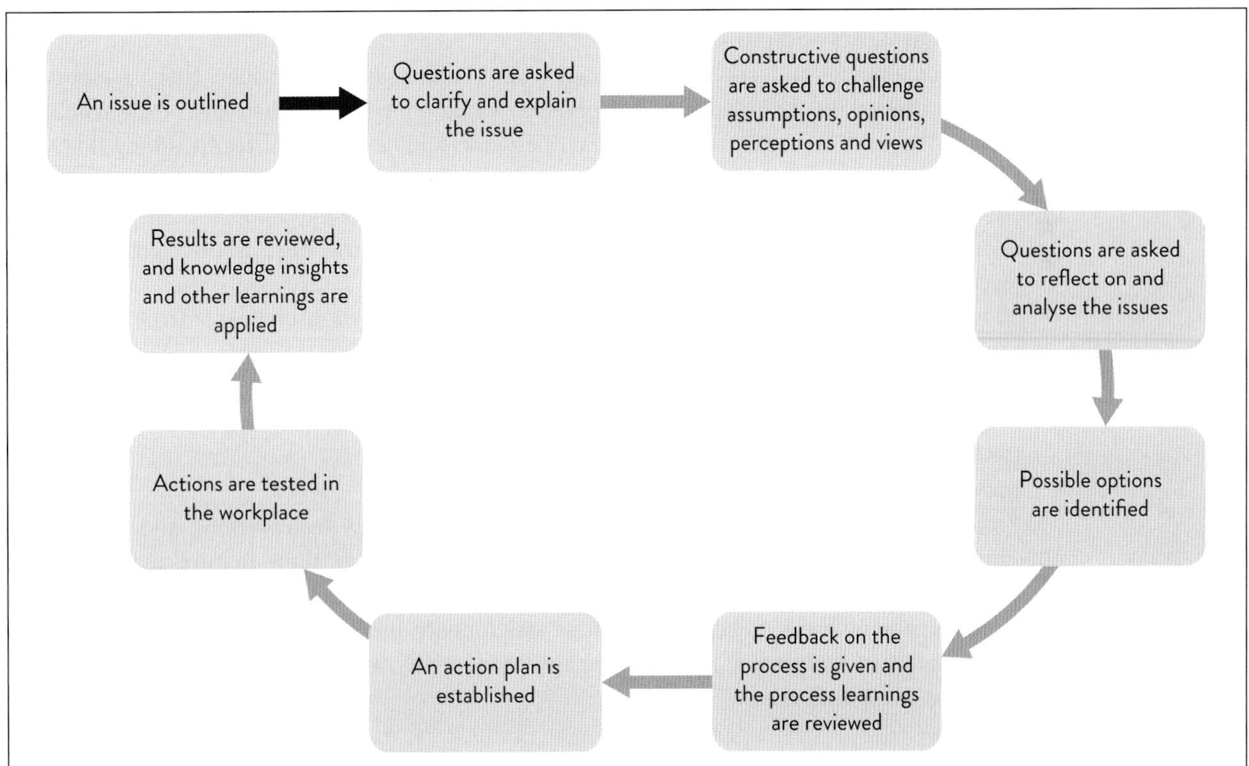

FIGURE 29.12 The action learning process

Throughout the action learning process, the following 10 steps are common:

1. The group member is allocated five to 10 minutes of uninterrupted time to outline a challenge, issue or problem, or question or decision they need assistance with.
2. Members are given the opportunity to ask exploratory questions. These questions may aim to:
   - seek clarification
   - challenge assumptions, opinions, perceptions and views.
3. Members will move to asking reflective and analytical questions.
4. Final questions directed towards future action are asked. The facilitator intervenes if the questioning becomes adversarial or advisory.
5. The group works together to explore and clarify possible actions.
6. The member with the issue provides feedback on how they experienced the process and what was learnt.
7. Other group members offer their observations and learning on both process and content. These first steps usually take about two hours.
8. The group member outlines an action plan for dealing with the issue until the next meeting.
9. After the meeting, the group member trials the plan and reports the results back to the group when it next meets – what worked, what didn't work and possible explanations.
10. The group learns from the implementation and discusses any corrections or refinements needed, draws conclusions, notes what has been learnt, and discusses how to put its learnings and new knowledge into practice.

Special assignments and projects

Projects, secondments and special assignments allow employees to broaden their perspectives and expand their skills, knowledge and experience while contributing their own experience and knowledge. They also let employees extend their networks and develop their teamworking skills.

Like action-learning projects, special assignments and projects should be directed at improving the organisation's performance. Equally, they should meet the following important criteria:

- allow employees to build important networks throughout the organisation, encouraging a learning culture
- allow employees to work with a variety of people in a variety of disciplines, further improving their interpersonal skills and extending their knowledge
- challenge and extend employees' technical and interpersonal skills
- help employees learn more about the organisation in a holistic sense, making them more valuable to the organisation
- provide lateral career paths.

Projects like these go a long way towards offering the L&D, teamworking and networking opportunities that younger employees, especially, want. They also allow mature-age employees, whether as full- or part-time employees or contractors, to share their knowledge and coach and mentor younger employees. When you get these assignments, projects and secondments right, they increase employees' motivation, performance and productivity, as well as organisational flexibility, knowledge and responsiveness.

INDUSTRY INSIGHTS

'Knowledge share because you care'

The owner of four Cheap as Chips retail stores across regional Victoria decided to bring all the team leaders from the different locations together to share ideas and success stories with each other. Virtual monthly knowledge-sharing meetings were conducted. Each meeting addressed a new topic, such as cost control, customer relations, stock management or merchandising. A representative from the team who excels in each area presented ideas on how they achieved success and gave others the opportunity to ask questions.

The store owner then provided further guidance to the group on how they could apply what they learnt into their own teams. Individual stores were encouraged to also share their time with follow-up coaching and mentor sessions.

Coaching

Transferable skills
3.4 Leadership

The Chinese have a proverb that says, 'A single conversation with a wise man is better than 10 years of study'. Coaches and mentors are more experienced or skilled people who strengthen the skills and understanding of the employees they are working with. They also share their experience and ways of thinking to extend employees' job skills and personal and professional development. Both are personalised, one-on-one ways to develop employees. To ensure a valuable experience for all parties, the coach, mentor and employees need to know their overall goals from the relationship. Coaching and mentoring can prepare someone for a higher position as part of career pathing and succession planning, help improve underperformance or further improve already good performance. Although the terms are often used interchangeably, there is a difference.

There are two types of coaches – expert coaches and generalist coaches. Expert coaches are usually from inside the organisation, but sometimes from outside it, and they help employees hone and polish a specific job skill. Leader-managers and selected professionals or specialists are the most common expert coaches. Expert coaches are not necessarily experts but use a process to meet a specific learning or development need and improve performance. They can be employees, often from the L&D or HR departments who have been trained in coaching, or people who work independently.

Some generalist coaches are well trained in effective coaching techniques, others less so or not trained at all. Some independent coaches have purchased a franchise and trained in that franchise's methods; others have paid for training in a particular coaching system from one of many coach training schools worldwide. Unfortunately, there is little consistency in coach and coaching standards, and therefore, it's important to choose a generalist coach carefully. Generalist coaches might use tools such as the 360-degree review and psychological tests to identify employees' strengths and weaknesses, pinpoint L&D needs, and help the people they're coaching uncover underlying mindsets that may limit their effectiveness.

Coaching sessions usually take place over several meetings. Whether the coach is an expert or a generalist, they should encourage winning behaviours and confront negative attitudes and beliefs. The best coaches are experienced with finding people's potential and honing it. (You can find out more about coaching techniques later in this chapter.)

Mentoring

Transferable skills
3.4 Leadership

Mentors are usually experienced and respected people who support the mentee's personal as well as professional goals. Opportunities for people to interact and get to know each other, such as interdepartmental projects, company-sponsored conferences, seminars and social events, can help people forge their own mentoring and networking relationships.

By offering advice, guidance, information and support, and acting as a sounding board and wise guide, mentors can open doors to new information and perspectives. Approachable and empathic mentors can explain how the organisation works and help mentees navigate the informal organisation. Mentors assist in networking and help mentees deal with difficult or negative experiences and feedback. They also offer guidance to the people they mentor. They can listen to personal challenges and offer encouragement, different viewpoints and ideas, and provide support in times of crisis and change. Most of all, mentors share valuable experience, knowledge and accumulated wisdom, and teach by example.

Although mentoring is generally an informal, voluntary process, some organisations have formalised it as part of the career planning and performance review process. Employees complete personal development plans, stating their development goals, and then either select a mentor or a mentor is assigned to them. The mentor and the mentee meet informally or semi-formally at agreed intervals, for example, once a month, to discuss progress, difficulties, plans and so on. To work well, employees need to know what they want to gain from meetings and provide this information to the mentor. When that fails to happen, they fail to make the most of the opportunity. Formal mentoring programs have mixed results, possibly because successful mentoring is based on positive chemistry between people, and you can't predict the affinity people have for one another.

What's the difference between instructing, coaching and mentoring? Instructing works best for straightforward cognitive and psychomotor skills and activities. Mentoring works best in complex situations, for affective and complex cognitive thinking and reasoning; for example, in situations where many answers are possible and when the skills to be learnt involve interpersonal relations. Coaching falls somewhere in between. Table 29.4 summarises the differences in the three activities.

TABLE 29.4 Instructing, coaching and mentoring compared

Instructing	Coaching	Mentoring
Teaching	Supporting	Enabling
Showing	Guiding	Encouraging self-development
Telling	Explaining	Listening, questioning, sharing, advising

Transferable skills

2.3 Business strategy

3.3 Written communication

Prepare a learning and development plan

A learning plan answers the *who* is to receive *what* learning support, and the *when, where, how* and *why* questions. It generally contains the following information:

- a summary of an individual's or a team's learning needs and an indication of any priority areas. What (the specific skills, knowledge or attitudes to be taught or developed)? Why (the learning objectives)?
- the learning method and when and where the learning is to occur
- how the effectiveness of the learning will be assessed
- the links with the organisation's vision, mission and business plan.

When establishing timelines and learning methods, think about constraints, such as the availability of any resources the L&D plan needs and your team's busy periods and peak holiday periods. Ensure that learners agree with the learning needs and objectives.

Prepare a business case when needed

Transferable skills

1.4 Business operations

3.3 Written communication

You probably need to make a sound business case for any off-the-job training you want to provide, following your organisation's usual procedures. You might want to begin by stating the objectives of the training and the benefits to the organisation in a well-defined sentence. Show that the training you propose is relevant, timely and targeted to meet identified learning needs that can lead to performance improvements that benefit the individual, team and organisation. For example:

- The goals of this learning support are to ... so that ...
- These intended learning outcomes are ... which will help us to ...

The key is to identify strategic benefits and convert them into hard numbers. How can you calculate the *return on investment* (ROI)? How can you demonstrate, preferably in measurable terms, how the training can positively affect the organisation's vision, mission and business plan? The business plan needs to clearly show how the proposed training activity can contribute to the overall improvement of the organisation.

When training addresses an identified problem, you can measure the cost of the current situation against the cost of the expected situation after the training. The difference shows you how much the training, assuming it works, can save the organisation, quantifying your ROI. The more persuasively you can show, in factual and objective terms, that your department and the organisation is likely to benefit from the training you propose, the more likely it is that scarce funds can be made available to pay for it.

Here is a commonly used equation:

$$\text{ROI\%} = \frac{\text{Total benefit in \$} \times 100}{\text{Total training cost}}$$

Provided you can make a case for ongoing savings, you can also calculate the *payback period* for the training. This is the time it takes for the training to cover its costs through increased performance and productivity. The point at which the training has covered its costs is known as the *break-even point*. After that point, the training is saving the organisation money. Naturally, the sooner the training pays for itself, the more likely senior management is to agree to it.

Similarly, when training is intended to result in a general improvement in something – for instance customer satisfaction, leadership or teamwork – you can develop a range of measures to track its effectiveness. For example, to measure the value of leadership training, you could measure absenteeism, attrition and productivity before and after the training. When training relates to compliance to government regulations, you can compare the cost of the training to penalties for non-compliance.

Remember that L&D can do more than improve work performance in the short term. Although it can be difficult to quantify, regular, high-quality training and learning interventions can make your organisation a more attractive place to work, improve people's ability to innovate, reduce overheads through greater flexibility and multiskilling, and reduce costly staff **turnover**.

29.3 Helping people learn

Transferable skills

3.4 Leadership

> The most important skill you will need in your careers is the ability to acquire new skills.
>
> Rupert Murdoch, 'Who's afraid of technology?', ABC Boyer Lectures, 9 November 2008.

Understanding the basic principles of how people learn makes it much easier to help people put what they've learnt to good use. People of all ages and intellectual capacities can learn new skills and behaviours – provided they *want* to. The motivation, or desire to learn, can take many forms, including financial incentives, increased promotional prospects, personal development, personal satisfaction or the respect of teammates.

Set clear learning goals

Set clear learning goals and measures of success that trainees can work towards and use to track their progress. Discuss how learning goals may be achieved and monitor their progress along with them. This shows you're interested and are there to help when needed. Remember to positively reinforce correct behaviours so they continue.

Build on existing knowledge

People have different levels of ability in different areas, different interests, different levels of motivation to learn and different background knowledge. You need to take them all into account when deciding the best way to help people learn. For example, you wouldn't teach someone advanced accounting methods before they had a sound grasp of basic arithmetic or put someone in charge of an organisation before they had a sound grasp of strategic thinking, leadership, communication and other core management skills.

Learning is a process of gradually building knowledge, skills and understanding. You can help learners build mental bridges of understanding and put what they've learnt to good use by:

- asking, for example, whether learners know anything that relates to the learning goal or have done anything similar in the past, or how the learning content is similar to and different from what the learner already knows or does; this gives them something to 'attach' the new information to
- encouraging learners to combine what they're learning with other concepts they already know into patterns and a connected whole. You can ask, for example, in what other situations they can use what they've learnt.

Building bridges like this results in deeper learning and understanding. It differs from rote learning (memorisation), which can provide a piece of information or a skill but without the understanding of the 'why' behind it.

Involve learners and provide variety

The more you involve learners so that learning is active, rather than passive, and uses as many senses as possible, the better. And particularly with conceptual skills and understanding, the more you help people reach their own conclusions, the better. As the saying goes, 'Tell me, and I will forget. Show me, and I may remember. Involve me, and I will understand'.

Good training materials and teaching aids are always important. Use job breakdowns, examples, diagrams, Socratic questions (explained later in this chapter) and other techniques appropriate to the skill and knowledge you're teaching, and try to use a variety of techniques to stave off boredom and suit people's preferred learning styles.

Learning plateaus

People learn at different rates and almost everyone has periods when their performance doesn't improve, regardless of how much effort they are putting into the job or the quality of the training.

This is called a learning plateau. It is as though the learner is saturated with new skills and knowledge and subconsciously 'switches off' in order to consolidate what they have recently learnt.

Most people experience plateaus when learning something new. They occur at different times and last for varying lengths of time for different people and different tasks. Try to recognise this difficult part of learning when you're coaching, mentoring or training people. Slow down and stop pushing when you suspect a learner has 'hit the wall' and reassure them that it is only temporary.

Which of the following types of learner are you?

- Surface learners, who do as little as possible to get by.
- Strategic learners, who go for top marks rather than true understanding.
- Deep learners, who go for deep and genuine understanding.[10]

Ensure learning is used

The best training in the world is useless unless it's used. This applies to both on-the-job and off-the-job L&D as well as to the various structured and unstructured learning activities you organise. When your team or any team members undertake any type of learning activity, you want to make sure it is effective. The two things that most influence the effectiveness of any learning are what you (the learner's leader-manager) do before and after the learning activity. Both are critical, and both are up to you.

Before the training takes place, discuss it. Develop, for example, three clear learning goals and discuss how meeting those learning goals can assist them on the job. This helps trainees concentrate on the learning content and is your base to monitor and evaluate the effectiveness of the training. (When training is on-the-job, monitor learners while they're learning to determine any additional support they may need and any workplace health and safety issues.)

Here are some other ways to protect your investment in employees' learning and assist them to become better learners when they attend off-the-job training programs or courses of study:

- Advise them to arrive early, introduce themselves to the trainer and express their interest in the program.
- Advise them to sit near the front in order to be more involved and hear and see better, and to take notes of the main points for later reference. Taking notes can also reinforce learning.
- Work out who is to cover their critical duties while they attend the training program so they are free to concentrate on the training without worrying about work piling up while they're away.
- Explain that reviewing the training materials within 72 hours after the session improves retention by 50 per cent and ask them to schedule some review time during that period.

After the learning activity, or periodically during it when the learning is over an extended period, set some time aside to discuss it. Encourage your employees to reflect on what they have learnt. The process of reflection deepens and extends learning opportunities. Questions you can encourage them to ask themselves include:

- What have I learnt from this?
- What were my actual compared with intended outcomes?
- What principles can I extract from this?
- What did I learn about myself?
- How can I use this in other situations?

Reflecting on your own and with others helps people learn, consolidate what they've learnt and put it to use, particularly when the reflection links current learning and experience to previous learnings and experience. Reflection leads to discoveries, insights, self-understanding and double-loop learning.

People also learn better when they expect to share what they've learnt or teach it to others. They need to reflect on what they've learnt, look for the key points, think about how to explain them and organise them in a logical way – all vital elements of learning. You may even like to create a team training notebook – electronically or on paper – in which everyone who attends a training session enters a one-page summary of what they've learnt, how they can use it and how it can help the team.

Identify any barriers in the work and team environment that may prevent them from applying what they've learnt and, once discussed, removed them. Show employees that you notice them using their newly acquired skills and knowledge. Acknowledging employees using their new skills is important and may prevent them from going back to their old ways. Showing your support for training is essential and reminds people that the time and effort spent on learning is valuable.

Don't forget the all-important administrative functions. Follow your organisation's systems for keeping records of training and learning activities undertaken by people in your team, for logging any certificates of competency they earn, and for reporting progress to management. This important information helps you at performance review time, when you undertake further learning needs analyses and when you update learning plans.

Transferable skills

2.1 Critical thinking

2.2 Personal effectiveness

Evaluate learning effectiveness

How do you know whether an L&D activity has effectively met the learners' needs? The best training and learning activities are enjoyable, but learners also need to put what they've learnt to use and the organisation needs to benefit in some way.

There are five levels to evaluate training, which are commonly used all over the world:

Level 1 *Reaction:* how satisfied are the learners with the content, trainer and facilities?

Level 2 *Learning:* can learners prove that they have learnt; for example, by pre-training and post-training skill tests or skill assessments, or by their action plans?

Level 3 *Application:* even when learning occurs, transferring it to the workplace can be prevented or avoided for many reasons, so it's important to determine whether learners are using what they've learnt. You can assess this through observation, self-reports, surveys, action plan monitoring and discussion.

Level 4 *Results:* are the new behaviours leading to the expected improved results? There are many ways to measure this, depending on the learning content and objectives.

Level 5 *Return on investment:* what was the ROI, particularly in terms of performance measures and business results?[11]

Having established the current skill levels and learning goals when you identified learning needs and prepared the L&D plan, you can now measure the change. To measure the effectiveness of the training you may adopt one or more of the following strategies:

- Ask learners to fill out a post-workshop evaluation at the end of the workshop, and another at a time where they have had adequate opportunity, to put what they've learnt to use and what results they've achieved.
- Interview participants individually or in groups of five to seven about the extent to which they realised their learning objectives and are putting them to use.
- Use a survey to seek participants' views on the program and the extent to which the targeted performance has improved.

- Collect quantifiable data.
- Put some hard numbers on learners' achievements whenever you can. You can measure their performance after the training and compare it with their performance before the training. You can directly measure whatever results the training is targeting or you can measure a range of generic results, such as absenteeism, employee turnover, output, overtime, quality, timekeeping and waste. You can easily convert most of these measures into dollars to assess the cost-benefit of the training.

While these strategies will provide you with a variety of valuable information to measure the effectiveness of training, you cannot always be sure that improved performance is due to learning. For example:

- When salespeople sell more after a sales training program, is this because of the training or would sales have increased anyway? Or when they sell less after sales training, does this mean that the training failed? Maybe the competition ran a special offer during the period for which you measured sales.
- You might train leader-managers to run induction courses for new employees with a goal of reducing their staff turnover. When turnover drops after training, how can you prove that your training was responsible? It could also have been due to altered employment practices, a downturn in the local economy, improved recruitment practices, recent wage increases or the time of year.

One way to find out is to compare the group of employees who were trained with another group who were not trained (i.e. a control group). This might show, for example, that the group who received training increased their sales by an average of 12 per cent, while the average sales of the control group declined by 8 per cent. This would strongly indicate that the training was worthwhile.

The many variables, or factors, that can affect results make it difficult to isolate the precise benefits of training. This means that you often can't get incontestable proof that learning has been effective and must go for evidence instead. Objective observation and self-reports plus any objective measures you can apply are generally considered sufficient evidence.

It is easier to measure the effectiveness of manual skills training; for example, you can measure keyboarding speed and accuracy before and after keyboarding training. When competency-based training methods are used, assessors can determine whether and how well each trainee was able to apply the skills learnt on a training program.

It can be more difficult to assess the effectiveness of training in topic areas such as communication, decision-making, leadership or teamwork. Tests might show that employees have learnt something, or they may say that they enjoyed a workshop and benefited from it, but that doesn't guarantee they put what they've learnt to use in their job. (But as discussed earlier, you can help to ensure that employees put their learning to use on the job by discussing it with them beforehand and, afterwards, by asking how they are using it.)

Be sure that the cost of evaluating the results of training is justified. When a training program is to be run only once or twice, or when small numbers of learners are involved in various learning activities, it might not be worth spending much time and effort on evaluation. Nor is it always practical to implement a full-blown evaluation effort.

Imagine a company pursuing a level 3 evaluation, asking learners to complete a survey reporting how they used the training. Say the total hourly pay of the 50 respondents is worth $1500 (at $30 an hour each) and it takes 30 minutes to complete the survey. The cost of the survey would be $750. But have you learnt anything worthwhile, such as how to improve the transfer of knowledge gained on the training program back to the job? Would that evaluation be worth the time and money involved? Or could the leader-managers of the participants judge the effectiveness of the training through observation and discussion equally well, and strengthen working relationships at the same time as a bonus?

Here are some tips for measuring the effectiveness of training:

- Allow time for changes in behaviour to occur and the results to be realised.
- Compare results against a control group not receiving the training when you can.
- Compare the costs against the benefits of the training.
- Look for evidence when proof is not possible.
- Measure before and after results when possible.
- Seek either a 100 per cent response or use a large enough sample so that the results are meaningful.

Transferable skills
3.4 Leadership

Coaching and mentoring techniques

Coaching and mentoring – sharing your experience, expertise and insights – is an excellent way to support team members and strengthen their skills. It also contributes to a learning environment and helps attract quality people to work with and remain in your team.

It's a good idea to begin coaching and mentoring relationships by discussing the scope, or boundaries, and ground rules of the relationship so that you both have realistic expectations. Also make clear the confidentiality of discussions so that you can both speak freely. The coachee/mentee should also keep an action step summary for each meeting (and other learning activities in which they participate) and complete evaluation and review processes along the way.

Using questions and discussion will help you come to an agreement on the coaching and mentoring goals. For example:

- What do you think needs to happen?
- Can you state this as a goal?
- What sort of assistance has helped you achieve your goals in the past?
- How would you like to go about achieving this goal?
- What will work best?
- What difficulties might you face?
- What will be your first step?
- When will you do this?
- When can we meet to review your progress?
- When you achieve the goal, how will you feel?[12]

The following techniques may be used when coaching and mentoring. Remember to take people's preferred learning methods, prior knowledge, experience and confidence level into account when you're mentoring and coaching.

- *Gap analysis:* this is a good way to begin a coaching session. Ask the person you're coaching three questions: 'Where are you now (in this skill) out of 10?'; 'Where would you like to be?'; and 'How can you get there?'
- *Flag–example–benefit model:* specific positive feedback encourages behaviours you want to continue. By flagging what you're about to comment on, giving an example of it and explaining why it works, your feedback becomes very powerful. For example, if you were coaching an industrial sales representative, you might say:
  - Flag: I liked your use of open questions with that customer.
  - Example: and I thought it was great when you asked about his goals for the business.
  - Benefit: because that gave you a lot of useful information to build on.

This model also works with constructive feedback. For example, you might say:

- Flag: I thought you began well by asking the customer how business was going.
- Example: I think you could learn even more useful information by following up with some probing questions. For instance, when she said business was going well, you could ask where she sees the business in two or three years' time.
- Benefit: That would give you further information about her needs so that you could select the best products for her and explain them to her in the light of her goals, which would make you more persuasive and increase your chances of closing the sale.

(To find out more about the types of feedback and their uses, see Chapter 15.)

- *Intent–outcome model:* when helping people understand the effects of their behaviour on other people or situations, ask what they intend their behaviour or action to achieve. Then ask what actual outcome they are getting. When the two don't match, help the learner develop alternative strategies (making suggestions when necessary) to bring their intention and outcome closer together. When appropriate, you can explore their *espoused theory* and their *theory-in-use* (explained in Chapter 5).
- *Overuse–appropriate use–underuse model:* strengths can be double-edged swords. When you're highly skilled at something (e.g. at asking Socratic questions – discussed next – when coaching), you might use that skill even when using another skill would provide a better outcome. As a result, you underuse other skills; in this example, you might keep asking questions when you should tactfully put forward your experience, knowledge or opinion for consideration.

  No matter how useful a skill is, overusing it leads to an unwanted outcome. When coaching people who overuse one skill, help them discover when to use it appropriately and when a different skill would work better. When coaching a salesperson who excels at listening, for example, you might help her pinpoint when to stop listening to the customer's needs and begin explaining what she recommends; when a salesperson overprovides clear and compelling explanations of a product's features and benefits, you would help him understand when to stop explaining and ask for the order.
- *Socratic questioning:* asking questions and suggesting points to consider in order to guide people to work out the answers and ideas for themselves is known as the Socratic method. Skilful questioning, based on the 'tell me more' approach, invites people to consider the accuracy and completeness of their thinking and explore the implications of their positions; it draws out new ideas and perspectives and helps people think matters through.

  Helping people find their own insights and solutions is a powerful way to help them increase their effectiveness. Linking an important value of the person you're helping with the skill you're helping them strengthen makes your support even more effective because when values lead, behaviour follows.

When you have reached your coaching or mentoring goals, close on a positive note, reflecting on the benefits gained for both you and the person you are assisting, as well as the organisation.

For a successful coaching and mentoring relationship, consider these top tips:

- Find fixes, not faults.
- Highlight the positive, so people feel good about themselves and can do their best work.
- Include everyone, not just your best people – everyone has unique talents and contributions to make.
- Talk about subtly shifting or adjusting, rather than changing, behaviour – it's much less daunting and it doesn't take a complete overhaul to boost someone's performance.
- Use phrases like 'I've noticed that …', 'I realise that …' or 'I'd like to suggest something that can make this easier/that can deliver an even better result' to take the sting out of constructive feedback.
- Work on one area at a time to avoid overwhelming the learner; when someone needs coaching in more than one area, set up separate meetings for each area.

29.4 Delivering training

The illiterate of the 21st century will not be those who cannot read and write, but those who cannot learn, unlearn, and relearn.

Alvin Toffler (futurist), in *Future shock*, Random House, 1970, p. 414.

Training is more than lectures, lessons and lifting weights. You can expect to train individual employees and small groups of employees for many reasons, including cross-skilling, multiskilling and upskilling. You may need to train people for job rotations or secondments, or to be placed into acting positions or newly delegated duties. People may also need training to operate new equipment or adapt to organisational change and new technology and procedures.

To train properly, you need to be able to develop a job breakdown and apply the four systematic steps to instruction described in this section. In large departments where there might be several trainees, you might delegate this training to another experienced worker who should also be trained to break a job down and teach it following the four-step instruction method.

You will avoid the frustrations of trial and error by providing appropriate levels of guidance and time for learning. Without guidance, inefficient and dangerous work habits, misunderstanding or even reaching incorrect conclusions and using unsafe practices may occur.

Use the principles of primacy and recency to strengthen your training. People remember what's said or shown first and last as most important, so that information is most likely to reach the long-term memory. The middle can become a blur – a good reason to keep training sessions short and sweet, followed by practice to make it stick, then more information. Learning tasks that need deeper understanding can benefit from a 'try it and see' approach, even when it doesn't work the first time. Learners can try it out individually, under guidance, or work in small groups to find several solutions. This produces deep learning because thinking about a task and drawing on what you already know fires up your brain circuits and gets you ready for deep learning.

Actual learning represents a change in behaviour and all changes require adjustment, so give people time to adjust, internalise and assimilate what they've learnt. Let them practise and build their experience, because with repetition and experience comes confidence and long-term retention.

Remember that learning requires attention and concentration, so when people are learning and practising new tasks, provide a quiet area as free as possible from distractions. Snatching minutes of practice between normal job tasks seldom works.

Know people's comfort zones and don't push too hard, too fast. When you need to repeat an instruction or explanation, try something different – the next way might work when the first one didn't. Consider each trainee's motivations and remember to allow for individual differences in learning.

Prepare job breakdowns

Job breakdowns help you instruct correctly and thoroughly by ensuring that you teach the job in the most logical sequence (stages) and that you include all the important considerations (key points). They reduce training time, discipline your training, and speed up learning by making sure you don't give too much information for the learner to master but only cover what is important to do the job correctly and safely.

To ensure you use only relevant information always develop a job breakdown and follow it whenever you give on-the-job training. Once developed, you can file it and use it repeatedly. There are two steps to preparing a job breakdown – determining the stages and determining the key points.

The acid test of a good job breakdown is being able to do the job using only the stages you have written in the job breakdown. First, do the job and break it down into stages. Physically do the job so that you don't miss anything important, making notes as you go. Don't just think about how you would do the job or how you have done it in the past. Stages are usually natural breaks in the action, activity or process of the job. A job breakdown should have less than seven stages; more than this is too much for learners to remember all at once. When a job has seven or more stages, break it down into separate units and teach each unit separately.

Once you've determined the stages, do the job again to establish the key points for each stage. Key points are actions that make each stage easier for the learners to remember and carry out correctly, efficiently and safely. Key points are anything about a stage that might:

- affect safety
- affect quality
- cause injury
- make the work easier
- provide any special information (e.g. special knacks or know-how).

Safety factors are always key points. When a stage contains more than five key points, break it down into two stages.

At the top of the job breakdown, list any tools or materials needed to do the task. List the measures of success, or results learners are aiming for, at the bottom. When necessary, add a series of 'if/then' instructions: 'If this happens, then do this'. When there are a lot of 'ifs' and 'thens' or several choice points, develop a flow chart from the job breakdown stages. Table 29.5 shows a job breakdown for scheduling a meeting.

TABLE 29.5 Job breakdown: schedule meetings

Tools and materials required	
• Meeting agenda template • Meeting invite script • Attendees list and contact details • Computer, internet, outlook	
Stages	**Key points**
Set up equipment and tools	• Set up workstation following safety ergonomics • Collect documentation and information
Define meeting objectives	• Set the meeting goals • Establish attendees list and contact details
Prepare agenda	• Confirm key points for discussion (aligned to the meeting objectives) • Use the meeting agenda template • Record attendees to invite
Prepare meeting invite	• Collect relevant materials to assist attendees prepare for the meeting • Use the appropriate email invite script
Send meeting invite with all attachments	• Use confirmed email addresses • Send email

You can easily adapt job breakdowns into standard operating procedures (SOPs). These step-by-step guides are handy references for employees to turn to when they need to confirm how to do a task. When turning your job breakdowns into SOPs, make sure you use the active voice (e.g. 'Grease the pan', not 'The pan should be greased') and use the same terms throughout the SOP (e.g. don't say 'pan' in one place and 'saucepan' in another).

You can also give a copy of the job breakdown to the learners to refer to while their confidence builds. For long and complex jobs that are broken into several training units with a job breakdown for each unit, some units will be easier than others. Sometimes, you can teach the easiest units first, gradually moving on to the more difficult ones. This may not always be possible. For example, a job may need to be completed in a particular sequence, in which case, complete the job in its correct sequence – teach the trainee the easiest units as you come to them and complete the more difficult ones yourself. As the trainee masters the easier units, begin teaching the more difficult ones. This allows trainees to build their skills gradually until they can complete the entire job.

Think about a more complex task in your own job. How many training units would this task take?

Instruct systematically

Once you have your job breakdown, all you need to do is use it to follow these four steps to good training:

1 *Prepare for the training*: before beginning, tidy the workspace so there are no distractions and to present a professional, welcoming area to the trainee. Remove any equipment or materials you don't need and lay out the equipment and materials you need. Place the job breakdown where you can easily refer to it.

2 *Present the training*: explain what you are going to show the learner, why the job is important and how it fits into the team's or department's work. State what you expect the learner to be able to do after training and make sure the trainee can see what you're doing clearly.

   When you begin training, complete the job with slow and deliberate movements. State the name of each stage as you come to it and stress each key point with examples, exaggerated movements, repetition or changes in voice tone or speed (i.e. louder, slower, softer, quicker). Don't make the mistake of instructing too fast – let the trainee digest each stage before moving on to the next one. Look at the trainee when you finish demonstrating each stage and watch for a nod or some other sign of understanding before moving on.

3 *Confirm understanding*: after slowly demonstrating how to do the job, it's time to make sure that the learner has understood what to do. Ask the trainee to go through the job, naming each stage as they come to it and stating each key point. Let the learner concentrate – this is not the time to make small talk to fill a silence. Provide opportunities for the trainee to perform the job. When you are satisfied that the trainee can continue practising the job without your supervision, ask something like 'What else can I tell you?' to make sure there are no questions.

4 *Consolidate practice within the real world*: added to a desire to learn, repetition builds competence. Keep in touch while trainees practise on their own. Learning a new skill or mastering a new task takes time – the more complex the skill or task, the more time it takes to become proficient. Allow time between practice sessions to let the brain consolidate the new information and actions. Implement a regular follow-up program to ensure that the trainee continues to do the

job in the required manner and to the required standard – you don't want any bad habits to creep in. Your follow-ups can become less frequent as the trainee gains experience.

These four instruction steps are written as a job breakdown in Table 29.6. Although it is written with sentences under key points for clarity, strictly speaking, you need only key words rather than sentences as key points because your job breakdown is your 'memory jogger'.

TABLE 29.6 A job breakdown of the four steps to instruction

Step 1 Prepare for the training	
Stage	**Key points**
Gather materials	• Set out job breakdown and other training aids • Ensure workspace is clean, tidy and free of tools and equipment that are not required
Relax the learner	• A nervous person cannot learn effectively
Explain	• Explain what you are going to show the learner how to do and explain your aim – what you expect the learner to be able to do after their training
Can they do it?	• Ask the learner what they know about the job. Have they ever done anything like this? • If yes, build on existing knowledge and make associations with the learner's past experience to make learning easier • If learners say they can do the job, ask them to demonstrate their method. (You may not need to teach it, or you may find gaps in skills and knowledge that need filling)
Motivate the learner	• Give the learner a good reason to learn. People who want to learn are the easiest to teach • Explain why the job is important, how it fits into the overall purpose of the organisation and the benefits of learning it to the learner
Ensure correct position	• The learner must be able to hear what you are saying and have a clear view of the job you are about to demonstrate
Step 2 Present the training	
Stage	**Key points**
Create understanding	• Use your job breakdown as a guide • Carry out the job yourself stage by stage, emphasising the key points • Instruct patiently, clearly and slowly, not too fast
Step 3 Confirm understanding of the training	
Stage	**Key points**
Ask the learner to do the job	• Have them do the job exactly the way you have just demonstrated
Ask the learner to tell you, out loud, what they are doing	• Listen to make sure the learner repeats the key points back to you • If any key points are missed, ask the learner what they have just done, in order to draw out all the key points

●●●

Step 3 Confirm understanding of the training	
Stage	**Key points**
Stop learners if they make a mistake, or if you can see that a mistake is about to be made	• Tell the learner they did something that was not quite right and ask if they can identify it. It is better for learners to work out their mistakes than for you to tell them
Continue until satisfied	• Have the learner continue doing the job for you, explaining to you what they are doing, until you are satisfied they have learnt it correctly
Step 4 Put the trainee to work	
Stage	**Key points**
Application	• Leave the learner to practise their newly acquired skills and gain experience and confidence • Indicate precise measures of success by explaining what you expect the learner to do. For example, to complete 12 forms over the next 2½ hours • Always provide a job goal for learners to aim for to help them assess their own performance
Problem-solving	• Indicate to whom the learner can go should a problem arise and you are unavailable
Check back	• Go back and check as often as necessary to ensure that the job is being done as you have taught it: safely, efficiently and correctly

Avoid teaching too much at once

Like most people, you may believe that you can keep seven pieces of information in our short-term memory at a time. But research shows it's really a lot less – more like two to four pieces of information.[13] That's why it's important to allow for modest short-term memory when you're teaching someone new material and not try to teach too much at once.

You can distinguish between must know, should know and could know information in order to target only the most important information. That way, you don't give learners too much information to absorb. 'Must know' refers to the stages and essential key points of a job, all the basics that learners must know in order to do the job correctly. Your job breakdowns should contain only 'must knows'. Once the learner has mastered the basics of the job, after Step 4 of the training process, you can explain the 'should knows'. This is information that learners really should have but which is not essential in the early stages of learning. And finally, when the learner has become skilled in the job, it is time to add the icing on the cake, to explain the 'could knows'. These details add job interest and round out a person's job knowledge.

With the example of scheduling a meeting used earlier, the 'must knows' are all contained in the job breakdown. 'Should knows' might include communication methods and how to use outlook. 'Could knows' might include individual attendee preferences and the filing format and location for meeting agendas.

Training can mean 'less is more'. You guide rather than lead. Try these tips to help you along the way:

- Ask learners to record how they are doing against their learning goals and review their results with them regularly.
- Build learners' confidence with lots of specific positive and constructive feedback related to the learning goals and measures of success.
- Don't step in and take over when learners make a mistake. Let them figure out what they did wrong and how to correct it and offer guidance when they need it.
- Explain and reinforce basic workplace terms as you train.

- Follow your job breakdown strictly.
- Frequently review what you've covered; since people tend to recall what they've heard first and last, pay special attention to emphasising, reinforcing and reviewing the middle bits.
- Have frequent breaks so learners can refresh themselves and you can check your messages and deal with any urgent matters that have arisen.
- Keep learners involved and active, not just sitting there watching you. Most learning takes place by doing, not watching.
- Make it clear what learners should do once they've finished the task that you've set them, so they don't just sit there. For example, should they come and ask you to check what they've done, ask for another task or read a product manual?
- Relate the training to the learners' prior experience and knowledge.
- Smile, use a friendly voice and watch for signs of understanding or confusion.

Instructing small groups

Group instruction is broadly similar to individual instruction. You still use your job breakdown and instruct following the four steps described earlier. However, when you come to the third step (show me), give each learner a turn at doing a stage of the job. Ask them to say out loud what they are doing while you and the other trainees watch and listen for key points.

The other important point with group instruction is to ensure that the whole group can hear and see what you are doing in Step 2. This isn't always as easy as ensuring that just one trainee can see you.

STUDY TOOLS

QUICK REVIEW

KEY CONCEPT 29.1 

a Why is it important that employees at all levels in today's workplaces have the ability and willingness to learn a key skill?
b List the various ways that employees can learn as they work and give an example of each.
c How can effective formal and informal learning activities benefit organisations?
d What are some actions leader-managers can take to encourage and reinforce learning in their teams?
e What is meant by learning styles?
f Define the three domains of learning and explain how they can aid multisensory learning.

KEY CONCEPT 29.2 

a What might alert you that individual team members or your team as a whole need training? How can you ensure that training really is the answer?
b List and briefly explain eight ways to identify learning and development needs. How can you ensure the identified needs support your organisation's strategic goals and longer-term plans?
c What learning methods have you experienced? What do you see as the advantages and disadvantages of each?
d In general, when would you lean towards providing off-the-job training and development for your team members and when would you opt for on-the-job training? When choosing on-the-job training, what options would you consider?

KEY CONCEPT 29.3 

a Why is it important to develop precise learning objectives? What can you do with those objectives once you have developed them?
b How can building on a trainee's existing knowledge assist their learning experience?
c What are the two most important things leader-managers can do to ensure learning is used?
d Describe how the effectiveness of training and learning activities can be assessed.
e List 10 coaching and mentoring techniques and give an example of each.

KEY CONCEPT 29.4 

a Discuss the benefits of systematic on-the-job training to a team, the learner, a department and the organisation. Which, if any, of these benefits overlap?

BUILD YOUR SKILLS

KEY CONCEPT 29.1 

a Explain how each of the seven learning hurdles limit learning, give an example of each from your own experience, and suggest how leader-managers can overcome each in their work teams.
b How have you used reflection to enhance your own learning and the learning of your team members?
c Describe how you could build your team's skills, both formally and informally. What sort of learning environment will you build?
d What steps can you take to encourage an innovative and learning culture?
e Explain your role as a leader-manager in terms of the coaching, mentoring and guidance you need to provide.
f Find an online learning style questionnaire to discover your preferred learning style. How do you believe you learn best?

KEY CONCEPT 29.2 

a Compare, contrast and discuss the following two statements: 'Learning is a cost to the organisation and should be invested in carefully.' 'Learning is of such benefit to modern organisations that investing in building a learning culture, sharing knowledge and formal and informal training is essential to success.'
b Compare and contrast the six levels of competence shown in Figure 29.7 with rote learning and discuss how you can help learners build mental bridges of understanding to learn more deeply.
c How did you identify your learning needs for your current study program? Did you undertake a self-assessment? Assess how well you match the required competencies and whether any gaps are a step, hop or a jump.
d Describe the steps you would take to assess a new employee's learning and development needs.
e Design your own learning plan with consideration to your top three priority learning and development goals for the next 12 months.
f What e-learning and blended learning have you experienced? What were their advantages and disadvantages? How can the advantages be built on and the disadvantages mitigated?
g What is the best training you've been involved in? What made it good? Contrast it with a training 'disaster'. Reflect on your own experience to identify the factors in the training and development programs you have undertaken that are critical for success.
h Conduct your own research and reflection to discover if you are a coach or a critic. What are the strengths and weaknesses of each?
i What points would you bring up to help another leader-manager decide whether to invest in a training program for their work team?
j Review the Industry insights box 'Steps, hops and jumps' about Michael and Table 29.2 and develop a learning and development plan for Michael's high-priority needs (jumps). Set your plan out as a table with the following columns – Need, Action, Comments – and make use of a variety of learning methods in your plan. Then discuss how Michael might improve his ability to prioritise his work in small steps over the course of a year and create a development plan for Michael with the following columns: Learning need, Goal, Objective, Method. The goals should help Michael and his leader-manager evaluate the outcomes of the development plan as the year progresses.
k Develop a training plan for your work team like the one shown in Figure 29.8.

KEY CONCEPT 29.3 

a Some members of your team have returned to work after an off-site training day. How can you determine whether their time, the cost of the training and the opportunity cost of those team members not working that day were well spent?

b When evaluating the effectiveness of training, explain what you would do in the following situations:
   i feedback is critical of on-the-job training you delivered in terms of your knowledge, explanations, timing and so on
   ii feedback is flattering of on-the-job training you delivered in terms of your knowledge, explanations, timing and so on
   iii feedback is critical of the external trainer you arranged to deliver a workshop, including that there was too much up-front input, not enough facilitated learning, staff felt they know more than the trainer in 'real life' and training 'missed the point'
   iv feedback is flattering of the trainer you arranged to deliver to staff
   v feedback is good, but monitoring performance indicates no progress
   vi nine of 10 attendees give 'good' feedback, but one gives 'bad' feedback.

c You are setting up an evaluation of customer service training for retail staff using the five levels outlined in Section 29.3. How can you set this up?

KEY CONCEPT 29.4 

a Prepare a job breakdown for a task you do regularly, following the layout shown in this chapter, and use it to instruct someone who doesn't know how to do that task. Then ask for feedback on how clear your instructions were and what you could do to improve.

b Why is it important to not teach too much at the one time? Provide an outline of how you can avoid this.

WORKPLACE ACTIVITIES

KEY CONCEPT 29.1 

a What steps have you taken to build or strengthen a learning environment in your work team? List 10 other actions you can take to promote a learning culture.

b Discuss the formal and informal learning opportunities that exist in your organisation. How do you take advantage of them and encourage your team members to take advantage of them?

c Describe three effective techniques you use for facilitating learning and encouraging team development and improvement.

d List three actions you regularly take to act as a role model for learning.

e What informal learning arrangements have you introduced in your work team? Conduct an analysis of these arrangements to see how you can make them even more effective.

f What have you recently done to 'spread knowledge around' in your organisation or work group? How can sharing knowledge help an organisation?

KEY CONCEPT 29.2 

a Develop a learning plan showing suggested training methods for your work team to meet its current and anticipated needs, indicating priority areas. Then build a business case for your high-priority areas.

b Discuss the ways you act as a role model for continuous and open learning in your work team.

c Describe the training needs of a member of your work team, how they were met and how you evaluated the outcomes. How did this team member's learning link to their career path?

d Develop a coaching plan for a member of your work team and list the specific coaching techniques you plan to use. How do you plan to commence and end the coaching?

KEY CONCEPT 29.3 

a Discuss how you approach coaching or training team members on the job. For example, how do you work with their learning styles, build on their existing knowledge, create generative, double-loop learning and associative learning, and use mistakes to aid learning?

b Describe how you assess and record the learning outcomes of team members to determine the effectiveness of development programs, coaching, mentoring and other support, and what you do with your assessment of the effectiveness of development programs.

c Write a brief account of how you elicit and use feedback from individuals in your work team to identify and implement improvements in future learning arrangements.

KEY CONCEPT 29.4 

a Prepare a job breakdown and use it to instruct someone in your team to meet a learning need identified in the learning plan developed in Workplace activities question 29.2(a). Then ask for feedback on how clear your instructions were and what you could do to improve.

b Describe a training program you have designed and delivered or plan to deliver. It could be formal group training or one-on-one training. Describe the changes you would make to improve your design and delivery for next time.

EXTENSION ACTIVITY

Referring to the Snapshot at the beginning of this chapter, answer the following question:

1 Detail the strategies Dallin's organisation could adopt to create a supportive learning environment.

CASE STUDY 29

CUTTING-EDGE LEARNING

Rachael is stoked! The company is launching an extensive series of in-house, just-in-time learning packages this week. Employees can access state-of-the-art training, covering technical as well as interpersonal and customer service skills on the company's intranet and on their tablets and smartphones. Learning – anywhere, any time. When employees successfully complete a learning module that is part of their approved development plan, they receive a specified number of hours pay, depending on the training package.

As the leader of a team of front-line customer support staff, Rachael knows this is a huge help. No more downtime during slow periods – just learning time. When it suits them, employees can log onto the intranet on their home computers and learn or sit on the bus and learn – great for the contractors and part-timers and great for the company because now they'll be as well trained as the full-time staff.

When a new or modified product is introduced, which on average is once a month, everyone can plug into the training system and learn the product details at their own pace, whenever it suits them. Or they can brush up on their soft skills. Rachael has already worked out personal development agreements with most team members, targeting the packages to work on first.

This training is more than just self-paced learning on a computer screen. It is high-tech and interactive. Each time a learner uses a program, it is different from the last time, so learners can use each learning package many times without becoming bored. Along with core scenarios and examples, the programs randomly deliver a range of additional examples and scenarios each time a learner logs on. Best of all, the software monitors each learner's strengths and areas needing further development, and selects examples and scenarios targeted to provide practice in areas they need most. Learning is automatically tailored to each person's needs.

This makes learning by doing safe. When people make a mistake, there are no red faces or adverse customer consequences – learners can just try again and keep trying until they are competent and confident.

Rachael and her team members can also request a summary of their strengths and development needs from the system whenever they want to, and when learners successfully complete a module they and Rachael both receive a printout summarising the learner's scores and suggesting areas for further development. This gives Rachael information about individual coaching and other development opportunities she should provide for each team member. And she can quickly spot who might be having problems in which areas, who is up to date with their learning and who might need a gentle reminder. Rachael can also print out a summary for her entire team to get an idea of other training she should plan for them as a group.

Rachael's mind is buzzing. Because she can see who is strongest in which areas, she can pair up team members to coach each other. She can use the software to help her select people and place

them in jobs that suit them best. People can learn by themselves or in small discussion groups – great for the interpersonal skills programs. Best of all, these interactive training packages put people in charge of their own learning. Isn't technology glorious?

Questions

1 Rachael is very clear about the benefits her company's new learning packages offer her work team. How important do you think her enthusiasm and support for the packages is to encourage her team to make the best use of them?
2 What pitfalls does Rachael need to be aware of that could prevent her team from making best use of the new learning packages?
3 How could Rachael maintain the momentum once the learning packages have been up and operating for several months?
4 How could Rachael monitor and evaluate the effectiveness of the packages and ensure training doesn't become 'hit or miss' but is targeted at individual learning needs and the needs of her team?

CHAPTER ENDNOTES

1 Foundation for Young Australians, 'The new work smarts: Thriving in the New Work Order 2017', https://www.fya.org.au/report/theh-new-work-smarts

2 Fact box, *Management Today*, UK, October 2014.

3 Frank Lewis Dyer, Thomas Commerford Martin, *Edison: His life and inventions*, Harper & Brothers, New York and London, 1910.

4 Cedar Riener, Daniel Willingham, 'The myth of learning styles', *Change*, September–October 2010, http://www.changemag.org/Archives/Back+Issues/September-October+2010/the-myth-of-learning-full.html; see also Harold Pashler, Mark McCaniel et al., 'Learning styles: Concepts and evidence', *Psychological Science in the Public Interest*, December 2008, pp. 105–119.

5 Alan Mumford, Peter Honey, *The manual of learning styles*, Ardingly House, Maidenhead, Berkshire, 1986.

6 Benjamin S. Bloom (Ed.), Max D. Engelhart, E. J. Furst, Walker H. Hill, David R. Krathwohl, *Taxonomy of educational objectives. Handbook I: The cognitive domain*, David McKay Co Inc., New York, 1956.

7 See, for example, Thomas C. Reeves, Eunjung Oh, *Handbook of research on educational communications and technology*, University of Georgia, Athens, Georgia, 2013, pp. 819–828.

8 Albert Einstein, quoted in W. Isaacson, *Einstein: His life and universe*, Simon & Schuster, London, 2007.

9 Winston Churchill, *Hansard*, UK Parliament, House of Commons, 4 November 1952.

10 Ken Bain, *What the best college students do*, Harvard University Press, 2012.

11 Jim Kirkpatrick, 'Productive methods to increase return on training investment', *Training and Development in Australia*, August 2005; J. J. Phillips, *Return on investment* (2nd edition), Butterworth-Heinemann, Boston, 2003.

12 John Whitmore, *Coaching for performance* (4th edition), Nicholas Brealey, Boston, 2009.

13 Nelson Cowan, 'The magical number four in short-term memory: A reconsideration of mental storage capacity', *Behavioral and Brain Sciences*, February 2001, Vol. 24, No. 1, pp. 87–114; Fernand Govet, Gary Clarkson, 'Chunks in expert memory: Evidence for the magical number four ... or is it two?', *Memory*, November 2004, Vol. 12, No. 6, pp. 732–747; René Marois, Jason Ivanoff, 'Capacity limits of information processing in the brain', *Trends in Cognition Science*, June 2005, Vol. 9, No. 6, pp. 296–305.

CHAPTER

30

ENSURING A SAFE AND HEALTHY WORKPLACE

After completing this chapter, you will be able to:

30.1 explain and comply with workplace health and safety legislation

30.2 apply the consultative arrangements required by workplace health and safety legislation and consult with employees to promote a safe and healthy workplace

30.3 identify potential causes and effects of accidents and investigate accidents

30.4 identify and control hazards to foster a safe workplace.

TRANSFERABLE SKILLS

The following transferable skills are covered in this chapter:

1 **Business competence**
   - **1.2** Business operations

2 **Critical thinking and problem solving**
   - **2.1** Critical thinking
   - **2.2** Personal effectiveness
   - **2.3** Business strategy

3 **Social competence**
   - **3.1** Teamwork/relationships
   - **3.2** Verbal communication
   - **3.3** Written communication
   - **3.4** Leadership

4 **Data literacy**
   - **4.1** Data literacy

5 **Digital competence**
   - **5.2** Technology use

OVERVIEW

Of the 13.4 million Australians who were employed during 2017 to 2018, 563 600 people were injured at work – this equates to 4.2 per cent, or 42 out of every 1000 workers – and 54.4 per cent of people injured were men. Most work-related injuries are not serious, coming from sprains, strains, cuts and chronic joint and muscle conditions. About 53 per cent of injured employees received some sort of financial assistance, and of those who received financial assistance, 52 per cent received workers' compensation.[1] However, many injuries are serious. In 2018 to 2019, 114 435 serious workers' compensation claims (9.4 per 1000 employees) and 144 workers' compensation fatality claims were accepted. (The figure for fatality claims is underestimated because some fatalities involved no dependants to lodge a claim and others were self-employed workers.)[2]

The median time lost through workers' compensation claims in 2017 stands at more than six weeks off work. Injury and musculoskeletal disorders accounted for 87 per cent of serious claims in 2018 to 2019. Of these, the most common were traumatic joint/ligament and muscle/tendon injuries, accounting for 45 per cent of all injury and musculoskeletal disorders claims, and 39 per cent of serious claims overall. Diseases were responsible for 13 per cent of serious claims, with the most common being mental health conditions (68 per cent of disease claims and 9 per cent of claims overall).[3]

Work-related injuries, illnesses and deaths impose costs on employers, workers and the community. These include both direct costs and indirect costs. Direct costs include items such as workers' compensation premiums paid by employers or payments to injured or incapacitated workers from workers' compensation jurisdictions. Indirect costs include items such as lost productivity, loss of current and future earnings, lost potential output and the cost of providing social welfare programs for injured or incapacitated workers. Their social and economic costs are immense. For 2012 to 2013, the cost to the Australian economy of work-related injury and disease amounted to $61.8 billion (4.1 per cent of GDP). A massive 95 per cent of this cost was borne by individuals and society. Broken down, this equates to workers 77 per cent, the community 18 per cent and employers 5 per cent.[4] It literally pays to keep safe.

This chapter concentrates on workplace health and safety (WHS) legislation and your day-to-day responsibilities for protecting employees' physical safety. Chapter 31 examines your responsibilities for protecting employees' dignity and wellbeing – the psychological aspect of WHS. You may want to keep a note of terms in bold and italics and what they mean.

SNAPSHOT

Health and safety in the office

After thanking everyone for their time, Michael opens the monthly staff meeting: 'As you know, I've spoken with most of you, as well as our cleaning contractors, and studied our accident and incident books. I've now completed my risk assessment. I'll give each of you a copy in a minute and I'll also post one on our noticeboard. First, I'd like to say that we're doing a great job and as you know from the injuries run chart posted on the noticeboard, we've reduced our injuries by 40 per cent, which I think is fantastic, although I know we'd all like to have zero injuries. Let me go over the hazards I think we need to pay a bit more attention to.

'Slips and trips are still on the agenda, even though our housekeeping is generally excellent, and Ben has done a terrific job making sure there aren't any trailing cables or leads, and everyone is doing their bit keeping work areas clear. The key thing we still need to improve is our housekeeping in the kitchen, like wiping up spills immediately so no one can slip and fall. That's up to everyone so let me thank you in advance for doing the right thing there. And let me now unveil the safety poster I bought us as a reminder: "A spill, a slip, a hospital trip."

'And one more reminder. The trolley is there to be used, so please use it whenever you're moving boxes of paper and other heavy items. Back injuries hurt and they just aren't worth the risk.

'The next item on my checklist is workstations. Everyone seems happy with our ergonomics campaign, and I'm pleased to say that since we've been paying more attention to posture, glare and so on, the injury book is satisfyingly empty of those type of injuries. So keep it up, keep taking regular breaks and keep changing your activities regularly – standing up and moving every 30 minutes or so – maybe walk up and down the stairs rather than take the lift. I'll hand over to Amy now so she can brief us on the ergonomics checklist for the induction program that she's prepared. Amy?'

30.1 Understanding the legislative framework

Transferable skills

2.2 Personal effectiveness

3.4 Leadership

> Creating a safe work environment is critical to the success of your business, and is one of the best ways to retain staff and maximise productivity.
>
> Australian Government, 'Workplace health and safety (WHS)'.

How would you feel if someone on your work team was badly injured or killed? How would you like to be the one to take the bad news to the family? No one wants this. The Commonwealth *Work Health and Safety Act 2011*[5] (the Act) came into force on 1 January 2012 and was last updated in 2018. Administered by Comcare, the Act seeks to protect Australian workers from workplace death, disease and injury. It covers people at any workplace, including state and local government premises, private offices and home offices, mobile worksites, workshops and factories. That is, everywhere people work and anywhere people go while at work. When employees leave their employer's premises in the course of their duties, their workplace goes with them.

The Act places a duty of care on employers to ensure, so far as is reasonably practicable (i.e. realistically possible), the health, safety and welfare of employees and other people on their premises, including self-employed people, contractors, voluntary workers and visitors. Employers must also protect the WHS of people in the vicinity of their premises from risks arising from their activities. They must also consult with employees to determine how best to reduce risks arising from work activities and comply with their other WHS responsibilities. Health means psychological as well as physical.

Detailed *regulations* and *codes of practice* and a system of advice, compliance activities, education, inspection and, where appropriate, fines and prosecution, support the Act. Table 30.1 shows the relationship between the WHS Act and its supporting regulations and codes.

TABLE 30.1 Workplace health and safety obligations in Australia

Act	Sets principles and philosophy – the general duties of care applying to employers, self-employed persons, employees, etc. It enables codes of practice to be approved
Regulations	Pick up particular aspects of the Act
Codes of practice	Give practical guidelines for complying with a general duty under the Act or putting a specific duty under the relevant regulation into effect to eliminate or reduce risks to health, safety and welfare. Although codes are not mandatory, because you can comply with the Act or a regulation in some other way, if you comply with the code, you are probably complying with the provisions of the Act or relevant regulation
Australian standards	Provide details of how to comply with regulations and codes of practice. Safe Work Australia develops Standards (e.g. for atmospheric contaminants in the occupational environment, classifying hazardous substances, manual handling, manual tasks, noise, safe working in a confined space, the storage and handling of workplace dangerous goods, and for construction work). They are intended to guide organisations in their operations and are non-prescriptive models that detail not what to do but focus on the desired outcome or standard to be achieved

Serious stuff

The Act imposes penalties on individuals and organisations who, by their acts or omissions, put others at risk. Companies and individuals found to be negligent in WHS matters can be fined and/or prosecuted. For example, an employee engaging in reckless conduct can be fined $300 000 or given five years imprisonment, or both. A person conducting a business who acts recklessly can be fined $600 000 or given five years imprisonment, or both; a body corporate acting recklessly can be fined $3 million. Failing to comply with a WHS duty that exposes someone to a risk of death, serious injury or illness brings fines of $150 000 for employees, $300 000 for persons conducting a business or $1.5 million for a body corporate.[6]

Employers cannot discriminate against employees who exercise their rights under the Act. This includes, for example, acting as, having acted or proposing to act as a WHS representative or a member of a WHS committee, or raising a concern about WHS with management, an inspector, a WHS representative, a WHS committee member or another employee. Discriminatory conduct includes dismissal or termination of employment or a contract for services, altering the duties or position of an employee to the employee's detriment, refusing or failing to offer to engage someone, or treating someone less favourably due to their WHS activities.

It is also unlawful for employers to assist, authorise, encourage, induce, instruct or request another person to engage in discriminatory conduct. To do so carries an individual penalty of $100 000 and a penalty to a body corporate of $500 000.[7]

As with any legislation, WHS legislation can make a workplace only as safe as its **safety culture** determines. Every leader-manager is important in setting a good example in upholding not only the law but also the spirit of the law. As the safety slogan goes: 'Safety is about doing the right thing – even when no one is looking'. And that's what a safety culture is all about.

Management commitment

Transferable skills
1.4 Business operations
2.3 Business strategy
3.4 Leadership

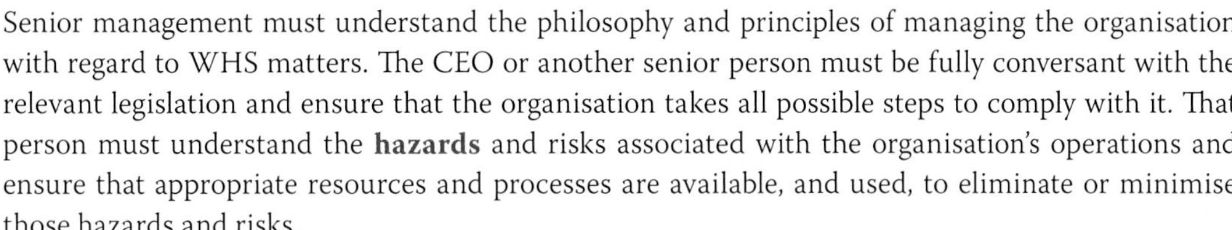

Senior management must understand the philosophy and principles of managing the organisation with regard to WHS matters. The CEO or another senior person must be fully conversant with the relevant legislation and ensure that the organisation takes all possible steps to comply with it. That person must understand the **hazards** and risks associated with the organisation's operations and ensure that appropriate resources and processes are available, and used, to eliminate or minimise those hazards and risks.

Senior managers must assess the effectiveness of WHS measures, ensure that employees adhere to them and ensure that information about **accidents** is properly recorded, considered and acted on. They should give safety matters the same degree of attention as functional areas, such as finance, production and supply. This is part of their duty of care.

Employers must provide a sufficient number of employees to do a job safely and not expect people to work beyond the bounds of reasonable human effort. They must also provide appropriate WHS consultative mechanisms.

Inspectors and notices

Transferable skills
1.4 Business operations

Inspectors can enter any workplace, with or without notice and with or without permission, to assess compliance with the legislation; all employees are required to provide reasonable assistance. Hindering or obstructing an inspector or inducing someone else to do so is an offence carrying a penalty of $10 000 for an individual and $50 000 for a body corporate. Assaulting, threatening or intimidating an inspector carries penalties of $50 000 and/or two years imprisonment for an individual and a fine of $250 000 for a body corporate.[8]

When inspectors believe a provision of the Act is contravened or likely to be contravened, they issue a written *improvement notice* to remedy the contravention or prevent it from occurring, stating the date by which this must be done. Inspectors can verbally issue a *prohibition notice* for activities they believe involve a serious risk to health or safety with later confirmation in writing. *Non-disturbance notices* are given to preserve a site at which a **notifiable incident** has occurred for up to seven days. Inspectors can also issue an *infringement notice* based on reasonable belief that a person has contravened the Act. The notice explains the contravention, the maximum penalty, when and where the contravention occurred, the amount payable under the notice and an explanation of how the payment is to be made. When an infringement notice is paid within 28 days, there is no admission of guilt or liability, and no prosecution is made. When a difference of opinion arises between employees and management on WHS matters (e.g. concerning membership of WHS committees or paying for WHS training) inspectors can act as **mediators**.

Notifiable incidents

Notifiable incidents involve one of the following:

- a death
- serious injury or illness (one that could be considered to require treatment as an inpatient in a hospital or medical treatment within 48 hours of exposure to a substance)
- a dangerous **incident** (one that exposes someone to a serious risk to WHS, such as an uncontrolled escape, spillage or leakage of a substance; an uncontrolled implosion, explosion or fire; or an electric shock).

Preserve the site of any notifiable incidents. Whether they involve an employee, contractor or member of the public, notifiable incidents must be reported to the regulator within seven days after becoming aware they have occurred; failing to report is an offence. When requested to do so, written notification of the incident must be provided within 48 hours.

Employers' responsibilities

Transferable skills
1.4 Business operations
2.3 Business strategy
3.4 Leadership

Safety begins at the top. The ultimate responsibility for the health, safety and welfare of employees and others at the workplace ultimately rests with employers. As Figure 30.1 shows, employers' responsibilities for providing safe systems of work can be grouped into nine interconnected areas. (Apart from employee welfare, which is explained in Chapter 31, these areas are reviewed in this chapter.)

Middle management should act in the same way with regard to their departments as the chief executive acts on behalf of the entire organisation. They should organise processes and workflows safely and efficiently, plan safe procedures and work systems, set up WHS systems of education and training, and ensure that they are carried out.

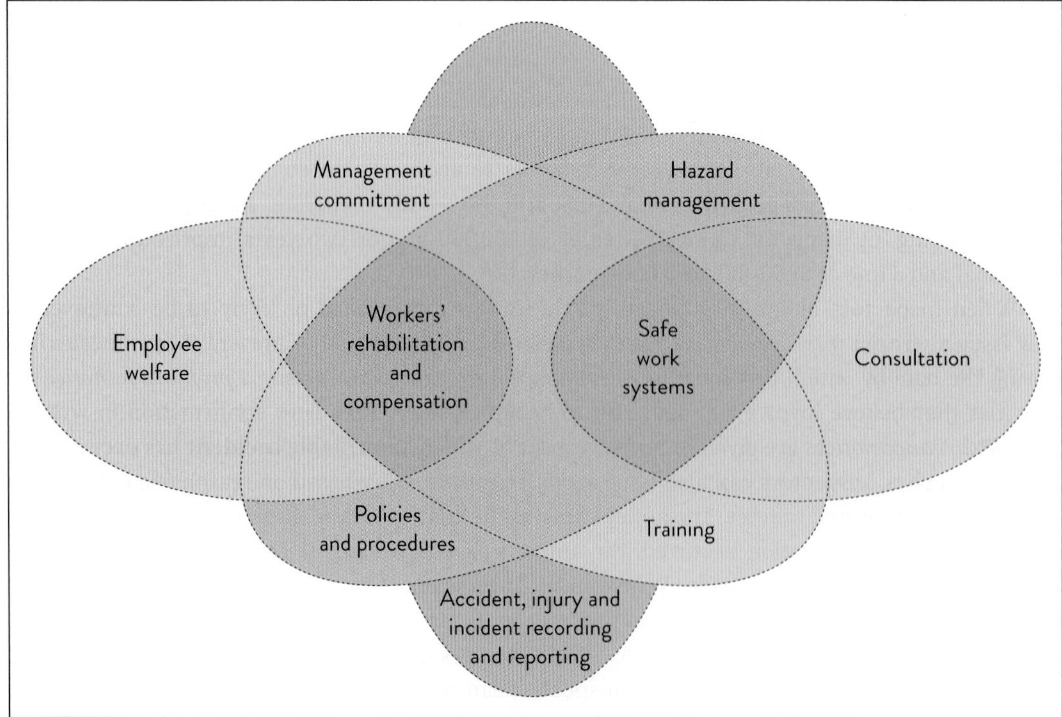

FIGURE 30.1 Employers' responsibilities for providing safe systems of work

Middle managers should become more directly involved in the detailed activities of WHS programs than senior managers. This includes, for example, ensuring that chairs are ergonomically suitable, work areas are adequately lit, dangerous machines and equipment are guarded, photocopy rooms are properly ventilated and workplace temperatures are comfortable.

Policies and procedures

Transferable skills

2.3 Business strategy

Senior management must develop written WHS policies, programs and procedures, make them available to all concerned and monitor their effectiveness. They should contain considerable detail about how the organisation ensures a healthy and safe working environment and describe its overall arrangements for health, safety and welfare. For example:

- specific types of hazards and risks associated with their particular industry and their worksites
- how accidents are prevented and investigated
- how employees and others on or near the employer's premises, including members of the public, are protected from, for example, electricity, explosions, exposure to harmful substances such as asbestos and lead, falling objects, fire, noise and radiation
- how the buildings and land, and the equipment, operations and processes carried out at the workplace, are made safe
- improvement targets in key WHS areas
- mechanisms to review the effectiveness of policies, programs and procedures
- procedures to remove or reduce specific hazards in the organisation
- resources available to put the policies into action
- safety reporting and recording procedures followed
- type of safety training and education provided
- how employees can contribute to the improvement, development and/or implementation of WHS policies, procedures, systems and training methods.

Always remember, 'Safety rules are your best tools'. Like all policies and procedures, those relating to WHS apply to every employee, at every level and function, equally. They need to clearly state what is and is not acceptable behaviour and the consequences of unacceptable behaviour. The best tool you can equip your staff with is knowledge.

Common law

Common law is not written in statutes but built up over time through judges' rulings. It reflects the way judges have interpreted legislation and is based on precedents, and also sets them. When common law isn't enough, or is outdated or inequitable, an Act of Parliament makes a new law, after which the process of interpretation and precedent setting begins again.

Employers have basic WHS duties under common law. They must do everything practicable to provide and maintain:

- a safe system of work
- a safe workplace
- competent staff
- safe plant and equipment.

Drug and alcohol testing

Drugs and alcohol impair people's coordination, motor control, alertness and judgement. Affected employees and those around them are at risk, particularly those operating machinery and driving forklifts, trains, vehicles and so on. Drugs and alcohol also affect the performance of people whose jobs require concentration. A co-worker 'under the influence' affects nearly one in 10 other employees and the cost to Australian workplaces is estimated at $6 billion a year in lost productivity.[9]

The Building Code (Code for the Tendering and Performance of Building Work 2016) requires principal contractors on federally funded projects to test employees as part of their Fitness for Work policy. Many large companies in other industries have also introduced random drug and alcohol testing for all levels of employees, including managers. The Fair Work Commission supports testing in order to eliminate the risk of employees being impaired by drug and alcohol when this poses a risk to health and safety.

Employers must have a clear policy on testing, respect employee privacy and have a valid safety or other reason for introducing and conducting testing. They should take a three-tiered approach of providing information and education, developing a policy and procedures for dealing with affected employees and create opportunities for affected employees to return to their usual work. Any disciplinary action resulting from positive tests should reflect the circumstances of individual employees.

Safe work systems and training

Following safe and correct procedures shouldn't be an added burden or create additional steps. Rather, performing tasks safely and correctly should be part of the normal systems of work and integrated into all aspects of operational planning and execution.

Employers must provide adequate, industry-specific safety training and ensure that employees understand and follow safe and correct procedures. Training needs to be ongoing and consistent to be effective.

Workers' rehabilitation and compensation

Employers are required to insure their employees against workplace disease and injury so that employees injured at work can receive weekly payments to cover loss of earnings, medical and rehabilitation expenses, and, when an injured person has to establish a new career, retraining costs. These payments are made regardless of whether the injury was the fault of the employee or the employer. When it is not possible for an injured worker to return to work because of death or disablement, lump-sum compensation payments can be made.

Employers must have a rehabilitation and return-to-work program for employees injured on the job. The aim is to get them back into the workforce as quickly as possible after suffering a work-related injury.

Workers' rehabilitation and compensation covers employees at work in any workplace. Employers can self-insure or insure through an approved insurer. Premiums are calculated according to the following factors:

- industry category of the employer – the more dangerous the industry, the higher the premiums.
- individual employer's safety record – the better the organisation's safety record, the lower its premiums.

As we've previously mentioned, the requirement for provision of insurance also applies to employees working from home offices or vehicles. The only way to have peace of mind is to check with your insurance provider that your policy covers all employees, particularly as we continue to move into a more flexible and mobile working world.

Environmental hazards

Pandemics and biological, chemical, nuclear and radiological incidents have WHS implications as well as the business continuity implications discussed in Chapter 22. You must not expose employees to disease-causing agents, such as asbestos or radiation, and you must take reasonable steps to ensure employees' work activities do not expose them to the risk of contamination from infection and disease. If you know or even think an employee has been exposed to a serious virus and continue to allow that employee to come to work and come into contact with other employees or customers, you are potentially breaching your duty of care.

Your responsibilities

Transferable skills

1.4 Business operations

2.2 Personal effectiveness

3.1 Teamwork/relationships

3.4 Leadership

3.2 Verbal communication

3.3 Written communication

Leader-managers are crucial in establishing a safety culture. You represent the organisation in health, safety and welfare matters to non-management employees and you set the safety climate for your area. It's your responsibility to make sure people work safely at all times and to hold them accountable for safe work practices.

Your WHS responsibilities begin with inducting new employees, contractors and temporary employees when you explain the organisation's WHS policy and the role of others in the organisation regarding WHS matters. This is also where you must demonstrate the emergency procedures, safety procedures (e.g. incident reporting) and safety requirements of the work area. You must ensure all employees understand their own WHS responsibilities and that safety procedures are followed meticulously at all times.

Identify the WHS training needs of your work group, and develop and implement training plans to meet those needs through formal and informal on- and off-the-job training as required. When you develop new procedures and processes, keep WHS at the top of your mind and periodically review all procedures and processes to ensure they are as safe as possible. Don't ask employees to achieve more than they can safely and comfortably achieve, because haste leads to mistakes, fatigue and clouded judgement, all of which can (and do) cause accidents and injuries.

Transferable skills

2.2 Personal effectiveness

3.4 Leadership

Keep a tidy workplace. Good *housekeeping*, the standard of cleanliness and tidiness of a workplace, is a reliable indicator of how well managed a workplace is and how safety conscious the people working there are. Creating and maintaining a clean, safe working environment is a good way to save money, and boost morale and productivity as well as reduce accidents.

Good housekeeping means a good workplace

A large aluminium foundry in the United Kingdom had too many slips and trips, mostly due to poor housekeeping and poorly maintained machinery leaking oil onto the floor. The company implemented the '5S Philosophy': *sort*, *set* in order, *shine*, *standardise* and *sustain* to keep up the good work. The result:

- obvious improvements to housekeeping by marking pedestrian routes and introducing non-slip surfaces, keeping walkways clear, removing trailing floor cables and removing clutter (by giving all items and tools a 'home' and putting them 'home' when not in use), which reduced slipping and tripping hazards and lost-time injuries and meant fewer lost items thanks to improved, more 'visible' storage
- avoiding duplication of work and purchasing unnecessary equipment by making each team responsible for its own equipment
- keeping plant and equipment clean and identifying maintenance problems at an earlier stage, which reduced production downtime and saved money
- positioning tools and equipment ergonomically, which reduced strains and fatigue.

Once hazards were under control (impressing customers, visitors and employees alike), morale and productivity improved.[10]

Transferable skills

2.2 Personal effectiveness

5.2 Technology use

3.1 Teamwork/ relationships

When new equipment is installed, familiarise yourself with its operations and safety requirements and train your team to use the equipment correctly and safely. Keep a log of all accidents and incidents and track both. Use systematic, analytical tools and techniques, to identify trends and patterns you need to address to improve employees' WHS.

Develop good working relationships with safety committee members, safety officers and safety representatives so that you can draw on their expertise, ideas and support. Diarise reminders to conduct regular safety audits to identify hazards and to ensure standard safety procedures are working. You can do this on your own, with your team members or with your safety officer or representative.

Transferable skills

3.1 Teamwork/ relationships

3.2 Verbal communication

Consultation and participation are part of your WHS role, too. Ask employees about the problems and hazards they experience in the course of their work and ask for their ideas on how to rectify them. Keep communicating about WHS matters so they remain in the forefront of people's minds. You want to act as a positive **role model**, because your team members derive their impressions of the meaning of 'safety' from what you say and, more importantly, what you do. Safe working practices are only as good as you insist they be.

Transferable skills

2.3 Business strategy

Off-site workplaces

Modern workplaces are no longer the traditional office-based, 'cubicle and computer' spaces. Many factors have contributed to far-reaching and probably long-term changes in working environments. Longer commuting times, more user-friendly and adaptable technological advances and, without doubt, the COVID-19 global pandemic, have all compelled business owners and managers to implement rafts of new policies and procedures with regard to working from home – not just for their employees, but for themselves too. This has significant WHS implications for employers. Although, in practice, you have little control over these workers, your legal duty of care, which includes providing WHS training and information, safe work systems and a safe workplace, extends to home offices. When employers cannot assess remote or off-site workplaces for risk, they should train their employees to assess the risks themselves and keep them aware of the need for vigilance in safety matters with regular updates and reminders. Home offices and mobile worksites of employees who work from a vehicle should be equipped with the same safety and emergency equipment, such as fire extinguishers, first aid kits and personal protective equipment (PPE), that is found at the employees' main workplace or base. In short, employer responsibility extends to wherever they have the capacity to act or control matters related to WHS.

Here are some steps you can take to look after **teleworkers and remote workers**. Ensure that:

- teleworkers and remote workers are encouraged to create a separate work area at home
- home offices are made safe by, for example, removing lifting and tripping hazards, set up in an ergonomically correct way, have adequate heating, lighting and ventilation, and that there are sufficient power points to avoid overload and the resulting fire hazard. Ask for photographs of the work area from a number of angles, which can be analysed and approved by a WHS officer if a home visit is not feasible
- teleworkers and remote workers report WHS concerns and incidents to you
- emergency plans for medical treatment are in line with those for employees in the office and home workers are aware of them
- smoke detectors are installed where appropriate
- a first aid kit is provided and the teleworkers are asked to keep it readily available
- compliant fire extinguishers are provided for work vehicles
- a self-assessment checklist is created for home workers to use to check for hazards periodically or conduct periodic safety audits with them when practical.

Employees' responsibilities

Employees have a legal duty to cooperate with their employers in ensuring the WHS of their workplaces. This involves taking reasonable care to protect themselves and others around them: employees must not, through their acts or omissions, endanger themselves, their colleagues or members of the public.

This means, for example, that employees must ensure that they are not affected by alcohol or other drugs while at work, they must follow safety procedures and use the equipment provided for WHS purposes, they must also follow reasonable instructions concerning WHS. Employees should not carry out or continue with work when they have a reasonable concern that doing so would expose them to a serious risk to their health or safety. In such situations, they must notify management and remain available to carry out suitable alternative work.

30.2 Consulting with employees

Safety is a cheap and effective insurance policy.

Safety slogan

The Act requires employers and employees to agree procedures for ongoing consultation on WHS matters. This gives employees an opportunity to influence matters affecting their health, safety and welfare, and gives organisations access to the detailed knowledge that employees have of the risks related to the work they perform. This is valuable for identifying and assessing risks and in working out effective and economical control measures.

Consultation is not one party making a decision and limiting discussion to when and how to implement it. Employees and their representatives must have access to relevant information on, for example, hazards and potential hazards; work conditions; work organisation; and plant, equipment and materials used in the workplace. They must also contribute to the decision-making process relating to WHS matters.

Consultation should begin when workplace changes are contemplated and continue as they are introduced so that employees' experience and expertise can be taken into account when it can most effectively be used. Employees should be given a reasonable opportunity to express their views and raise workplace WHS issues, and should be advised of the outcome of consultations in a timely manner.

Consultation can take place directly with employees, with WHS representatives, or with WHS committees. The penalty for failing to consult employees is $20 000 for an individual and $100 000 for a body corporate.[11]

Consultation should also occur with other interested stakeholders, such as contractors, suppliers and the owner of the building where work is carried out. The Act requires that employees be consulted in the circumstances outlined in Figure 30.2.

WHS officers

Many organisations employ a specialist WHS officer to advise on and oversee WHS matters and to take responsibility for safety and accident prevention programs. WHS officers are knowledgeable about the Act, regulations, codes of practice and Australian standards, methods of investigating and preventing accidents, and the best ways to protect the organisation's workforce. Smaller organisations often appoint an existing manager to take on the responsibility of managing the safety program.

Safety officers usually report to a senior and influential person in the organisation who can help achieve its WHS goals. Although safety officers act in a support role, when they discover an imminent

- Assessing the risk of a new process or procedure
- Deciding how to consult with employees
- Deciding how to eliminate or minimise risk
- Deciding how to implement regulations
- Deciding how to monitor the health of employees
- Deciding how to monitor working conditions
- Deciding how to provide information and training for employees
- Deciding how to resolve WHS issues
- Identifying hazards and assessing their risk
- Making decisions about the adequacy of welfare facilities for employees
- Proposing or planning to change work or work processes that may affect the health or safety of workers
- Reviewing the effectiveness of control measures

FIGURE 30.2 The WHS Act requires that employees are consulted in these instances

and serious danger during a routine hazard inspection, they usually have the authority to stop the work until the problem is rectified.

Other common duties of safety officers include:

- advising and guiding line staff
- conducting safety audits
- examining plant, equipment, processes and working methods for safety
- helping leader-managers to develop safety plans for their areas
- investigating accidents and incidents
- keeping and monitoring accident and incident records and statistics
- organising the circulation of safety information
- preparing safety instructions and advising on safe working practices
- reporting to and advising management and individual leader-managers on all safety matters
- serving on the safety committee as technical advisers
- testing fire and other emergency protection activities through drills and exercises
- training management and employees in safety matters.

Transferable skills

1.4 Business operations

3.2 Verbal communication

3.3 Written communication

WHS representatives

An employee can request the organisation's assistance in conducting an election for one or more WHS representatives and deputy representatives to represent employees in WHS matters. Elections are carried out in work groups and representatives and deputy representatives must be from that work group. The term of office is three years, at which time representatives and deputy representatives can stand for re-election.

Deputy WHS representatives carry out the duties of WHS representatives when they are not available or are no longer able to carry out their duties. This might be because they resign in writing before the end of their period of office, leave their work group, are disqualified by a court because of improper use of their power as a representative or are removed from their position by a majority of the members of the work group.

The powers and functions of WHS representatives are generally limited to their work group. An exception is when, for instance, a member of another work group asks for the representative's assistance or there is a serious risk to WHS from an immediate or imminent exposure to a hazard that affects or may affect a member of another work group. As the need arises, they can:

- inquire into anything that appears to be a risk to the health or safety of workers in the work group
- investigate complaints from members of the work group relating to WHS

- monitor the effectiveness of measures taken by the organisation to comply with the WHS legislation in relation to their work group.

In order to carry out these duties, WHS representatives may:

- accompany inspectors during workplace inspections
- assist in investigating accidents and near misses (incidents)
- attend interviews concerning WHS between leader-managers or inspectors and one or more employees they represent with the consent of those employees
- inspect the workplace for hazards and compliance with WHS regulations
- receive information concerning the WHS of employees in the work group in a form that does not identify or lead to the identification of the employees (they can access personal or medical information concerning an employee with that employee's consent)
- request the establishment of a WHS committee.

When WHS representatives identify unsafe work, they should consult with management to remove the hazard or protect the employee. Only when consultative attempts fail and when representatives have completed their initial training may they direct employees to cease the unsafe work. However, when the risk is so serious and immediate or imminent that it is not reasonable to consult or attempt to remove it, they may direct the unsafe work to cease and consult with management as soon as practicable afterwards.

WHS representatives can issue a written provisional improvement notice (similar to the improvement notices inspectors issue, but without legislative powers) after consultation with management, and display it as soon as possible in a prominent place near the work area affected by the notice. An inspector then reviews the notice and confirms it, confirms it with changes or cancels it.

Employers have a number of responsibilities regarding working with WHS representatives. They must:

- allow representatives access to discussions with inspectors on WHS matters
- consult them on WHS matters
- give them access to information relating to hazards and associated risks
- give them access to information relating to the WHS of employees in the work group
- give them time off work to attend approved WHS courses with their normal pay and pay the course fees and other reasonable costs associated with attending the training
- let them accompany an inspector during an inspection of their work group's workplace
- provide resources and facilities to help them perform their role as a WHS representative.

Employers must also make a list of WHS representatives and deputy representatives for each work group. They must keep it up to date and display it at the workplace where it is readily accessible to workers in the relevant work groups.

WHS representatives are key players in workplace consultation and are valuable allies for leader-managers. They should be your first point of contact in sounding out employees on WHS issues. Think of them as an extra pair of hands, ears and eyes to help you identify and control hazards, and consult them on any changes to the workplace that might affect the health, safety or welfare of the employees they represent.

Because of the nature of their responsibilities, it is recommended that WHS representatives have certain qualities, including:

- listening skills
- communication skills

- empathy
- a trustworthy nature
- approachability
- an eye for detail (for when conducting inspections)
- cultural sensitivity
- a willingness to represent all employees, not just those with whom they share affiliations or friendships.

WHS representatives should be selected from a diverse pool of employees. Nobody should be excluded from volunteering for a WHS representative role for any reason, including gender, sexuality, cultural or socio-economic background.

What's the difference between practical and practicable?
Practical means usable. However, *practicable* is a more specific term – it means doable, feasible or possible.

Transferable skills
1.4 Business operations

WHS committees

Organisations that don't already have one or more WHS committees must establish a committee within two months of being requested to do so by a WHS representative or five or more employees, or when regulations require them to do so. Membership of the committee is agreed between employees and management, aiming to ensure that members represent a cross-section of employees from all levels and areas of the organisation.

Although there is no ideal number of committee members, at least half must be employees who are not nominated by the organisation. Elected employee members, elected WHS representatives, a WHS officer and nominated members of the management team (including leader-managers) generally participate on WHS committees. Because these committees can be an effective way to involve people in WHS matters, many organisations rotate committee membership every year or two so that as many people as possible have a chance to learn and serve in this capacity.

The number of WHS committees should be kept to the minimum required to provide the necessary coverage of the workplace and work performed. WHS committees should meet at least every three months and at any reasonable time at the request of at least half the members of the committee.

Transferable skills
1.4 Business operations

The main aim of WHS committees is to help management and non-management employees work cooperatively towards shared safety goals. They tend to consider strategic health, safety and welfare issues that relate to the organisation as a whole and consider policy matters that have an organisation-wide impact rather than becoming involved in departmental or work group matters. This means they may instigate, develop and carry out measures designed to ensure WHS at work and assist in developing WHS standards, rules and procedures for the workplace. More specifically, they:

- assist employees who have suffered work-related injuries to return to work and find suitable employment for employees who suffer from any form of disability
- assist in formulating, reviewing and distributing (in appropriate languages) WHS policies and procedures
- assist in resolving WHS concerns that arise
- consult on any proposed changes to WHS policies and changes to workplace practices and procedures that may affect workplace health, safety or welfare

- develop purchasing policies for new plant, equipment and substances that address WHS issues
- develop and monitor an injury reporting system
- develop and monitor methods for conducting regular safety audits of the workplace
- develop procedures to ensure compliance with new and existing regulations and approved codes of practice
- establish a priority list of WHS issues to address
- encourage effective cooperation between management and employees when initiating, developing, carrying out and monitoring measures designed to ensure workplace health, safety and welfare
- review the availability of resources for health, safety and welfare
- review progress in rehabilitating employees who have suffered work-related injuries.

Employers must let committee members spend the time that is reasonably necessary to attend meetings and carry out their duties as a member of the committee and pay them at their normal rate of pay. They must also provide information relating to hazards and their associated risks and the WHS of employees (but not personal or medical information without the employee's consent unless it doesn't identify or lead to the identification of the employee).

Transferable skills

3.2 Verbal communication

3.3 Written communication

Effective safety committees

A number of practices contribute to the effectiveness of safety committees:

- carefully preparing an agenda for every meeting to ensure that discussions don't ramble or become confused
- encouraging a climate of openness and trust so that members feel free to express their opinions
- holding regular meetings – many organisations have found that once a month is suitable
- providing the safety committee with necessary information (e.g. accident statistics) so that it can base its recommendations on full knowledge of a situation
- providing training in WHS matters for committee members
- receiving the full support of senior management by, for instance, allowing members time off work to attend meetings and safety training seminars, and providing a comfortable, well-furnished meeting room and secretarial assistance
- selecting members based on a genuine interest in WHS matters.

30.3 Understanding accidents

> The model *Work Health and Safety (WHS) Act* sets out certain types of workplace incidents that need to be notified to regulators. Only the most serious safety incidents are intended to be notifiable and they trigger requirements to preserve the incident site pending further direction from the regulator.
>
> Safe Work Australia, 'Workplace incident reporting', http://www.safeworkaustralia.gov.au.

Accidents hurt – safety doesn't. Accidents cost, too; they destroy efficiency, interfere with people's work and make everyone's job harder. They are symptoms that something is wrong. They signal a lack of control over people, materials and/or processes and point to inefficient operations. It isn't just serious accidents that cause trouble; a series of minor accidents indicates inefficiency and can drive a workplace into a state of uncertainty. The following FYI box shows who is most at risk of serious injury, what industries are most at risk and the most common causes of injury. But a safe workplace is more than just the absence of major and minor accidents. It's an attitude of mind and a way of approaching jobs, day in and day out.

Who is most at risk for serious injury, and where?

In 2017 to 2018, 63 per cent of all serious workers' compensation claims were lodged by males. Labourers are the most injured compared to employees in other industries. Industries with the next three highest injury rates are community and personal service workers, professional workers and sales workers.

Overall, 41 per cent of claims were for traumatic joint/ligament and muscle/tendon injury, followed by wounds, lacerations, amputations and internal organ damage (16 per cent) and musculoskeletal and connective tissue diseases (14 per cent). Fractures accounted for 11 per cent of serious claims, and mental health conditions 7.5 per cent.[12]

Transferable skills

1.4 Business operations

The high price of accidents

There's a safety slogan that says, 'Slip, trip and fall are four-letter words'. Accident isn't a four-letter word but it might as well be. Suppose an employee is injured at your workplace. Work is likely to be held up. Property, machinery or equipment may be damaged, which you may need to arrange to have replaced or repaired. Other employees are affected; people rushing to assist and sympathetic onlookers mean further lost output. You are called away from whatever you are doing, for minutes or maybe hours. You may need to reorganise staff and their work, and find and possibly train a replacement for your injured team member. You spend time investigating the cause of the accident and preparing an accident report. Medical expenses (e.g. for hospitalisation, doctor's visits and rehabilitation), legal costs and the cost of hiring a replacement worker may be high.

Apart from these obvious costs, there are further hidden costs, such as lowered morale. There are also human costs. Pain and suffering, loss of enjoyment, permanent disability or death, loss of earnings, the psychological effects of an accident and its consequences, and disruption to the victim's private life are only some of them.

There are costs to the community, too, which must, for example, provide hospitals in which to treat the injuries and support facilities for permanently injured workers. And there are costs to society. Not only could millions of dollars be wiped off the national debt through improved WHS practices, but the number of productive working days in Australia could be increased.

Although the total costs of a particular accident or injury are difficult to measure precisely, we can estimate them. The direct costs to the organisation are workers' compensation costs and associated administrative costs. But that's just the beginning. Table 30.2 shows the hidden financial costs of accidents and injuries. Figure 30.3 shows how the other costs and effects of workplace accidents continue spreading, like a pebble dropping into a still pool of water – the repercussions can go on and on.

TABLE 30.2 The hidden financial costs of workplace accidents and injuries

Employee costs	Production costs	Other costs
Costs of rehabilitation	Damage to property, materials, equipment and resulting loss of production	Damage to public and employee relations
Costs of replacing and training injured worker	Delays and interruptions to products and services	Fines

Employee costs	Production costs	Other costs
Medical costs	Losses due to general disruption	Increase in WorkCover levy
Time for investigation of accident	Loss of production due to worker absence and less skilled replacement worker	Legal/witness fees
Time lost due to curiosity	Other work not being completed	Lowered morale
Time lost due to sympathy	Repair, replacement and disposal costs of damaged products and material	Transport to hospital
Time lost clearing up and repairing damage		
Wages		

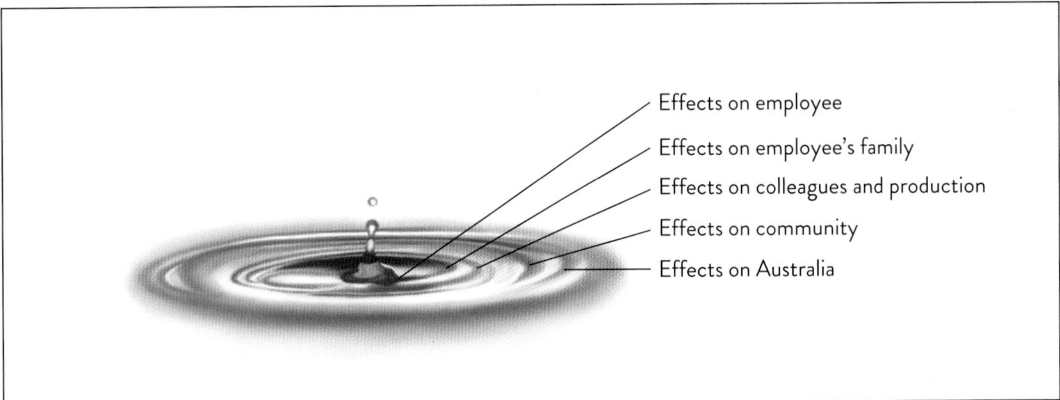

FIGURE 30.3 The ripple effects of injuries

Lost-time injuries

Lost-time injuries are events that result in a fatality, permanent disability or time lost from work of one day/shift or more.[13] They are broken down into three categories:

1. damage that permanently alters a person's life, including death, paraplegia, amputation of a limb and severe psychological damage
2. damage that temporarily alters a person's life; for example, a fractured leg or a deep cut that repairs with no lasting damage
3. damage that inconveniences a person's life.

The *Lost-Time Injury Frequency Rate* (LTIFR) is the number of lost-time injuries within a given accounting period relative to the number of hours worked in that same period. To calculate the number of lost-time injuries per hour worked during a period, divide the number of lost-time injuries by the total hours worked in a period. That always results in a tiny number, so it's multiplied by one million and reported as the number of lost-time injuries per million hours worked. (Because of the difficulties of collecting nationally consistent workers' compensation data for time lost, Safe Work Australia uses only workers' compensation claims of one or more weeks of lost time to calculate LTIFRs.)[14]

What causes accidents?

As the nature of work has changed in Australia, so has the pattern of work-related injuries. The expanding service sector and changing workplace technology, combined with high workloads, poor job design and tight deadlines, have resulted in an increase in stress and stress-related issues leading to *psychosocial problems* (the interaction of psychological and social factors that affect people's physical and mental wellbeing and that can result in mental health problems as well as physical injuries).

Health concerns related to computer use include *musculoskeletal disorders* (injuries affecting the soft tissues of the body – tendons, ligaments, muscles and nerves), such as carpal tunnel syndrome, tension or motion strain from mouse usage, and eye fatigue, blurred vision, and headaches from glare and poor lighting. Prolonged sitting can result in back and neck pain from poor seating posture, while the overuse of personal digital devices has led to an increase in sprained thumbs. New and emerging technologies, for example, nanotechnology, also have WHS implications.

Whatever the nature of the work, however, the fact remains that accidents don't happen by themselves – they are not 'acts of God' or bad luck. All accidents have a cause and at the root of every accident is a failure in a system of work, a machine or a piece of equipment.

This is why you should treat all accidents and near misses seriously and investigate them, whether or not someone has been injured. You need to determine the chain of events that led to the accident or incident and take steps to eliminate or minimise the hazards, acts or omissions that contributed to it.

Figure 30.4 shows the most common factors contributing to accidents. How many of these are present at your workplace? In deciding whether an organisation or a person has been negligent or failed to meet their duty of care, several factors are considered:

- Was the accident foreseeable?
- Was it preventable?
- Was it reasonably practicable to provide methods to prevent it?
- Was there causality, or a direct link between the negligence and the injury?

When the answers to these questions are 'yes', the person or the organisation is legally accountable and penalties are imposed.

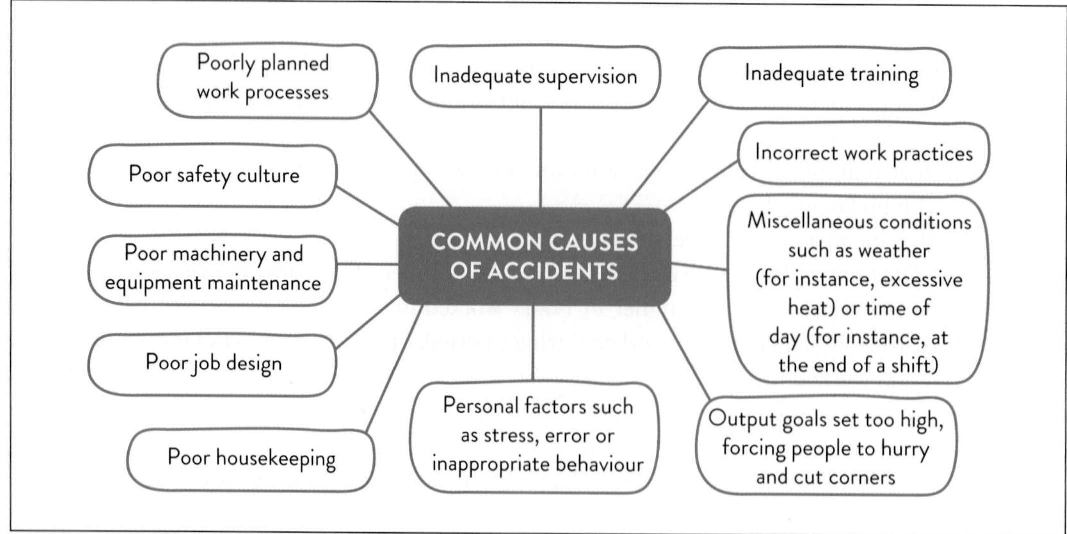

FIGURE 30.4 Common causes of accidents

Poorly designed work processes and faulty machinery and equipment cause many accidents. You and your work team should be in the habit of regularly checking the condition of equipment machinery and tools and fixing any defects promptly. The same applies to regularly checking methods, procedures and systems of work, and looking for ways to improve them (see Chapter 19 for more information on making continuous improvements).

Transferable skills
1.4 Business operations

Human error also causes accidents but there should, in most cases, be no attachment of blame. An error is generally an act that is inappropriate and which the system of work allowed to be taken; after all, people don't usually injure themselves intentionally. Human error includes unsafe or inappropriate behaviour by an employee, such as absent-mindedness, forgetfulness, ignorance of risk or tiredness, which can often be traced back to poor job design, supervision or training.

Accident-prone employees

Partly due to genes and partly to experience, high-risk people (e.g. risk-takers, stress addicts and closet thugs) exist. They are more likely than others to have accidents, even when placed in safe, low-risk environments. When you look at the accident and incident statistics, you see patterns, the same few people with multiple entries, year after year.

Some employees have attitudes, beliefs and habits that lead to taking risks – even with their own safety. They may have an external locus of control and believe that chance, fate or luck have more to do with injuring themselves than their own behaviour or lack of caution, so why pay attention to safety? As a result, they may behave in an unsafe manner and suffer more injuries. Some employees may seek sensation and be willing to place themselves in the path of risk for the thrill they experience. Others may have trouble paying attention. They, too, are likely to suffer more accidents and injury at work.

But labelling people as 'accident-prone' is flippant; it doesn't help them or the organisation and simply blaming accidents on employees is clearly no answer. Any control or measure that depends solely on individual behaviour for its success is guaranteed to fail sooner or later. You can see how few accidents are solely the employee's fault in Table 30.3, which summarises circumstances and the contributing factors that might place so-called accident-prone employees at risk.

TABLE 30.3 Risk circumstances and contributing factors

Cause of accident	Contributing factors
Carelessness and lack of concentration	Lack of mindfulness, poor training, poor supervision
Dislike of the job or the leader-manager	Poor job placement, poor job design, poor supervision
Existence of hazards	Unsafe work systems, poor supervision
Failure to follow safe work practices	Poor training, poor supervision
Insufficient manual skills to perform the job correctly	Poor job placement, poor training, poor supervision
Level of intelligence too low for the job they are required to do	Poor job placement, poor training, poor supervision
Poor sight, poor hearing or lack of stamina	Poor job placement
Poor use of plant and equipment	Poor training, poor supervision
Stress, fatigue	Poor supervision, poor work systems allowing for long or double shifts

Transferable skills

1.4 Business operations

You can often correct a systems failure that leads to accidents. Your first step is to investigate whether unsafe behaviour is easier or faster than safe behaviour; when it is, rectify it. Then assess your safety culture and work towards improving it when necessary. Make the safety slogan 'No safety, know pain; know safety, no pain' top of everyone's mind. Design jobs properly, place employees in jobs that suit them, train them correctly and supervise them properly. Establish clear, safe and efficient work systems and procedures and see that employees consistently follow them and use equipment properly. Improve work systems as necessary so that the possibility of unsafe behaviours is reduced or removed altogether.

Transferable skills

3.4 Leadership

Ensure that carelessness is not seen as acceptable practice and work targets are realistic. Conduct a job safety analysis and develop a critical behaviour checklist, then use it to observe employees and give feedback and remedial training as necessary. Teach people to practise mindfulness (explained in Chapter 5) as a way to improve their concentration.

Transferable skills

3.4 Leadership

When employees don't respond to training or your other interventions and continue to engage in risky behaviour, they remain liable to injury. Placing them under hazardous conditions is a threat to themselves and to others and contravenes your duty of care. When you can, place at-risk employees in jobs where their efforts are more likely to be safe and effective. Should they continually disregard safe working procedures or behave inappropriately, manage their performance as explained in Chapter 16.

 IN PRACTICE

Protect employees who can't protect themselves

Many organisations have a zero-tolerance policy regarding illicit substances in the workplace. If yours doesn't and you suspect that an employee is under the influence of drugs or alcohol and you do not take steps to protect them, you could be failing in your duty of care.

Treat drug and alcohol misuse as a WHS risk and support the employee as far as possible; for example, through employee assistance programs (EAPs).

Transferable skills

1.4 Business operations

3.4 Leadership

What to do in the event of accident, incident or injury

Although WHS issues can have serious ramifications, they can also provide opportunities for improvement. You can learn something from every accident, incident and injury. Investigate each one as soon as possible after it occurs, while the event is still fresh in people's minds. Reconstruct the chain of events leading up to it so you can pinpoint the factors that contributed to it. Once you know why your policies, procedures or practices failed, you can take measures to prevent a recurrence.

While several factors may contribute to an accident or near miss, concentrate on those you can actually do something about. When appropriate, involve others, such as the safety officer or WHS representative, in your investigation and in taking steps to ensure that the event never happens again.

 IN PRACTICE

Should a serious accident occur ...

If a serious accident occurs, executives of the organisation may need to deal with the media and minimise any adverse market and community responses that may harm the company in the longer term. Efficient organisations have crisis management policies in place to deal with this. It's important that only appointed representatives speak to the media.

As a leader-manager, employees feeling vulnerable may look to you for information and reassurance. This places you in a perfect position to keep them updated on what is happening and how they may be affected. Set a schedule to update employees and stick to it.

The object of your investigation is to:

- find the facts, particularly which system failure, for example, faulty equipment or poorly designed work systems, led to the accident or incident
- identify and analyse the circumstances involved
- select remedies to eliminate the hazard or, when this is not possible, to reduce and manage the risk it presents.

Interview any witnesses to the event and the person involved to gather facts and hear their views on what led up to the event and any contributing factors. Carry out these interviews in a friendly, informal atmosphere; they are not cross-examinations. You're not looking to find fault, just reasons, so that you can identify why policies and procedures failed in order to prevent a similar accident.

Conduct your investigation at the site of the accident or incident. Leave everything exactly as it was when the event took place, especially in the case of serious injury. When necessary, take steps to prevent further injury to people or damage to equipment (e.g. by switching off the power supply to an unguarded or dangerous machine).

Afterwards, record the incident or accident and injury, write a report summarising your investigation and findings, and file it according to your organisation's protocol. When someone was injured, inform your team about what occurred and what is happening to the injured person. Explain what action is being taken to ensure that a similar accident does not occur and discuss how best to make interim workplace arrangements and adjustments. Periodically analyse accident, incident and injury information (as described in Chapter 27) to resolve problems and capitalise on opportunities, and to alert you to patterns and trends that need special attention.

Transferable skills

1.4 Business operations

3.1 Teamwork/ relationships

3.2 Verbal communication

3.3 Written communication

4.1 Data literacy

What to do when an employee has a lost-time injury

While injured employees are at home, phone to ask how they are and update them on workplace news. Find out what you can do to help them get better and back to work. When injured employees return to work, make every effort to accommodate any restrictions caused by the injury, aiming to provide ongoing employment where reasonably practical.

Minor accidents and near misses

Employees should report all accidents and near misses, however minor, to you. This ensures you can take remedial action before an incident ultimately causes injury, ill health or worse. It is a good idea to have a special form to complete to give to the safety committee, safety officer or another nominated person.

Minor accidents

In the case of minor accidents in larger organisations, the injured person would report to the first aid centre for treatment and be asked to take a report form back to you. In other organisations, you should ensure the employee's injury is treated appropriately and then complete your report after discussing the circumstances of the accident with the injured employee and conducting any necessary investigations. The form normally then goes to the safety officer or another nominated person, who may decide to investigate further or simply file the form and record the details for statistical purposes and later analysis. This form may be distributed by hand or electronically. Some organisations keep their entire reporting and recording systems in an online system, which collates data, creates reports and provides statistics when required. This type of innovative system is becoming more and more prevalent.

Transferable skills

3.2 Verbal communication

3.3 Written communication

5.2 Technology use

Investigating and analysing near misses helps you to catch and prevent injuries before they happen. As you can see from **Figure 30.5**, near misses are lucky escapes that foreshadow larger accidents and injuries, so always investigate them as well as actual accidents, no matter how minor. Both can damage morale and are symptoms that something is wrong.

For every major injury or fatality, there are:	
10 minor injuries	𝍸𝍸
30 lost-time accidents	𝍸𝍸𝍸𝍸𝍸𝍸
100 minor accidents	𝍸𝍸𝍸𝍸𝍸𝍸𝍸𝍸𝍸𝍸𝍸𝍸𝍸𝍸𝍸𝍸𝍸𝍸𝍸𝍸
600 near misses	𝍸𝍸𝍸𝍸𝍸𝍸𝍸𝍸𝍸𝍸𝍸𝍸𝍸𝍸𝍸𝍸𝍸𝍸𝍸𝍸
	𝍸𝍸𝍸𝍸𝍸𝍸𝍸𝍸𝍸𝍸𝍸𝍸𝍸𝍸𝍸𝍸𝍸𝍸𝍸𝍸
	𝍸𝍸𝍸𝍸𝍸𝍸𝍸𝍸𝍸𝍸𝍸𝍸𝍸𝍸𝍸𝍸𝍸𝍸𝍸𝍸
	𝍸𝍸𝍸𝍸𝍸𝍸𝍸𝍸𝍸𝍸𝍸𝍸𝍸𝍸𝍸𝍸𝍸𝍸𝍸𝍸
	𝍸𝍸𝍸𝍸𝍸𝍸𝍸𝍸𝍸𝍸𝍸𝍸𝍸𝍸𝍸𝍸𝍸𝍸𝍸𝍸
	𝍸𝍸𝍸𝍸𝍸𝍸𝍸𝍸𝍸𝍸𝍸𝍸𝍸𝍸𝍸𝍸𝍸𝍸𝍸𝍸

FIGURE 30.5 'Lucky' this time but maybe not next time

Transferable skills

3.2 Verbal communication

Near misses

Employees don't always report incidents. This could be because of embarrassment about making a mistake, fear of criticism, not realising its significance, peer pressure, not wanting to spoil a good safety record, or falling into the trap of ignoring near misses, where near misses come to seem 'normal'. To uncover near misses and prevent them from becoming serious injuries, ask employees to recall how many incidents with potential for injury they have been aware of over a certain period, say six months. Assure them that you intend to keep all statements confidential – and stand by your word. Use the information to develop specifically targeted programs to manage the hazards uncovered.

Transferable skills

1.4 Business operations

3.4 Leadership

30.4 Preventing accidents

> A hazard is anything that could hurt you or someone else.
>
> Government of Victoria, Department of Education and Training, 'Hazard identification, risk assessment and risk control'.

To prevent workplace death, disease and injury, you need to find hazards and remove them or minimise their risk. Known by the acronym *HIRAC: Hazard Identification, Risk Assessment and Control,* this is a proactive approach. You *prevent* problems, rather than react to them after they occur. Two organisations in a similar business may prevent accidents in different ways and this is fine as long as each approach works.

Identifying and controlling hazards is your main occupational WHS obligation. Work with your team, safety representatives and committee members to identify and manage hazards and make the workplace safer. Follow these three steps:

1 *Identify hazards*: things that could cause an accident or injury, or harm health or property.
2 *Assess their associated risks*: the *probability* of the hazard causing harm and the *consequences*, or severity of the hazard's potential illness or injury to people or damage to the environment or property.
3 *Control hazards*: follow the chart in **Figure 30.6**. Begin with the most serious hazards and eliminate them. When you can't eliminate them, minimise the risks they present in the order of preference shown.

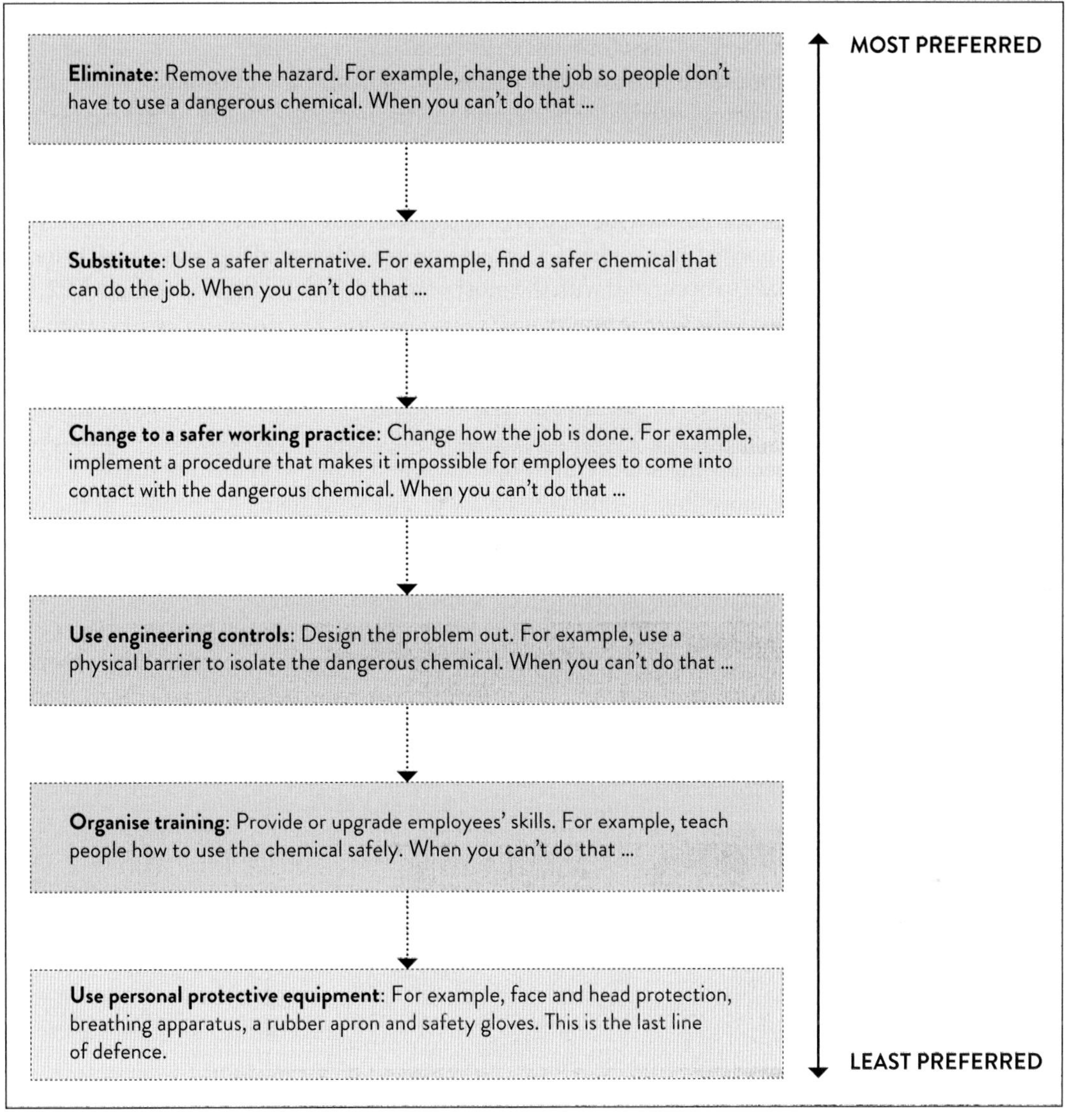

FIGURE 30.6 How to control hazards

For instance, it is hazardous to cross a road – a passing vehicle might hit you. Before crossing a road, you probably assess the risk of being hit. The risk is higher at peak hour, in the dark, the more slowly you cross and/or the faster the traffic moves. The greater you assess the risk to be, the more important it is that you take steps to eliminate it by, for example, using a pedestrian bridge or tunnel. When you can't eliminate the risk, you might minimise it by crossing the road at a brisk pace and only when the traffic lights indicate you can do so, looking carefully in both directions before crossing and wearing light-coloured clothing after dark.

Step 1: Identify hazards

A hazard is anything with the potential to harm life, health or property. Ways to identify hazards include:

- complete a safety analysis
- conduct a safety audit (or hazard inspection)

- observe the way jobs and procedures are carried out to make sure they are completed following safe work practices
- study the accident and incident statistics (as explained in Chapter 27) to resolve problems and capitalise on opportunities, so that you understand the hazards, who could be harmed by the hazards, and how.

First, we'll take a look at where most hazards are found and then turn to each of these four methods of identifying hazards. Use each method periodically because they are an indispensable part of controlling hazards and preventing accidents. Correct any hazards you identify as a high priority, beginning with the most likely to occur and with the most potential to cause harm (see **Figure 22.13**).

Where are most hazards found?

A popular safety slogan is, 'Safety never takes a break'. That's because hazards are everywhere, particularly:

- around machinery, especially machines run by operators and those with moving parts
- wherever people lift or move items, especially heavy or awkward items (or people, in the case of carers), regardless of whether cranes, forklift trucks and hoists are used or the lifting is done manually
- wherever people stand or sit for long periods
- wherever people use hand tools
- wherever people use hazardous substances and chemicals
- wherever people walk – on aisles, ladders, ramps, scaffolds and stairs.

Once you know what the hazards in your work area are, you can set priorities and concentrate first on those with the highest risk.

Complete a safety analysis

Transferable skills
1.4 Business operations
2.2 Personal effectiveness
3.2 Verbal communication
3.3 Written communication

Take a look at the rules and regulations and your checklists, manuals, standard operating procedures (SOPs) and other systems and procedures of work for the jobs and tasks people carry out. Do they sufficiently emphasise health, safety and welfare? If not, amend them. Consider job design, measures of success, workloads and the working environment, too. Use your own experience and consult with your work team and WHS practitioners to identify hazards in work procedures. Consider occasional activities, too, and listen to employees' concerns and opinions.

Examine the controls currently in place to manage each hazard and ensure they are written into the relevant document(s). When they are not sufficient, note down what else needs to be done and set a target date; check your plans with the safety officer (if your organisation employs one) and your safety representative. You could also delegate responsibility for some actions to team members or your safety representative, when appropriate.

Transferable skills
1.4 Business operations

At the very least, every hazardous procedure (such as carrying awkward, bulky or heavy items, handling hazardous materials or operating machinery) and important safety measure (such as correct lifting methods or caring for tools and equipment) should have written instructions readily available for employees to refer to, in the languages of the workforce. These are supplements to safe working methods, and never the only means of reducing hazards.

Writing safety instructions

Transferable skills
3.3 Written communication

Follow these three steps for writing safety instructions:

1 Break the job down into its component parts.
2 Identify any hazards. Deal with them as shown in **Figure 30.6**.

3 Clearly list any precautions for the hazards you can't remove under key points. Print these precautions in red, highlight them or draw special attention to them in some other way.

Perform the job as many times as necessary to ensure that you don't overlook anything, and examine any drawings, equipment, tools, work permits and other factors associated with the job. When a job is particularly hazardous, list any necessary safety precautions separately as shown in Figure 30.7, which shows a typical safety instruction form.

Safety instruction form

Job ______

Prepared by ______ Approved ______ Date ______

Stage	Key point	Hazards	Safety precautions	Skills/training/ licence/other requirements

Skills and qualifications required ______

FIGURE 30.7 Safety instruction form

Your safety analysis and safety instructions should list any special skills or qualifications that someone doing the job needs. For example, certain manual skills or dexterity, special coordination, special training or a licence to perform high-risk work. You should also incorporate these requirements into the person specification (discussed in Chapter 28) to avoid putting the wrong person in a job, since a poorly selected or placed employee is more at risk of injury than one whose capacities match the job requirements.

Preparing safety instructions is neither difficult nor time-consuming. The challenge lies in keeping them up to date and ensuring that people always follow them. One way to do this is to involve the people who use the instructions in writing them. Make your safety instructions part of the induction process for people joining your work area and diarise to review your safety analysis at least annually, or immediately when there are major changes in the workplace.

Conduct a safety audit

It's amazing how many hazards surround us – Figure 30.8 shows seven common hazards, but these are just the tip of the iceberg. To spot hazards, walk around with a safety audit form and when you identify a hazard, tick the box and note the location so you can follow up later with appropriate action.

Transferable skills

1.4 Business operations

Accidents waiting to happen
Among the most common accidents are slips, trips and falls, which may not lead to major health problems but can cause broken bones and worse.

Air quality
Air quality is affected by air movement and changes, temperature and humidity, and contaminants such as chemical fumes, dust and other particles.

Dangerous chemicals
These include adhesives, cleaning products, fuels, heavy metals, paints and paint thinners, pesticides, petroleum products and photocopier toner. Label all dangerous substances with a warning for users and attach a material safety data sheet (MSDS) that explains the health effects, instructions for safe use and emergency instructions.

Drugs and alcohol
Employees under the influence of alcohol or prescription or illicit drugs can cause accidents and incidents.

Manual handling
Carrying, holding, lifting, lowering, pulling, pushing or moving cause up to one-third of work injuries. Particularly hazardous are bending, reaching or twisting; heavy work requiring forceful movements; poor posture; repetitive movements; and sudden, jerky or hard-to-control movements. The three most common types of injuries are back and muscle injuries due to manual handling and overuse injuries due to repetitive movements. Workers in the cleaning, hospitality and manufacturing industries are most at risk.

Needlestick injuries
Every year, thousands of Australian healthcare professionals suffer needlestick injuries from, for example, discarded needles and sharp or pointed objects used to treat patients. These are a major, and growing, occupational hazard, especially for health and community service employees.

Stress
Stress at work is a serious issue and can potentially lead to burnout, depression and even addiction and suicide. An Australian Council of Trade Unions (ACTU) study found that one in four employees regularly takes time off work due to stress. Excessive workloads, insufficient training, long work hours, poor job design and poor-quality supervision are common causes of stress.

FIGURE 30.8 Seven common hazards

Two pairs of eyes are generally better than one, so think about inviting one of your team members, a safety representative or safety officer to accompany you when you go hazard spotting. When you see the same hazards every day, you often stop seeing them, so fresh eyes are a bonus.

Sign and date your safety audit or summarise it in a report like the one shown in Figure 30.9, discuss your findings with your team and post the audit in a prominent place. Sign and date identified

Safety inspection report

Date of inspection ______
Department/section ______
Inspector/s ______

Hazard found	Location	Person notified	Action taken	Date	Initials

FIGURE 30.9 Safety inspection report

actions to be taken as they are completed. Diarise to review and update your safety audit at least annually, or immediately when there are major changes in the workplace.

Before inspecting your own workplace, have a practice session by going to https://www.comcare.gov.au and search for 'virtual office'. Here you can explore the many hazards lurking in an office environment and discover some effective ways to control them.

Observe people as they work

Transferable skills

2.2 Personal effectiveness

3.1 Teamwork/relationships

3.4 Leadership

Keep your eyes and ears open for hazards all the time, not just when you're conducting an audit. You can spot accidents and incidents waiting to happen and flaws in working procedures and methods by noticing how people work, particularly in high-risk areas and on high-risk tasks, and when new equipment or work is introduced. When you notice, for example, people cutting corners, not following safety procedures or developing unsafe habits (e.g. sitting incorrectly or carrying heavy items rather than using the trolley) step in and take appropriate measures. As they say, 'Alert today; alive tomorrow'.

You might provide training or coaching to respond to gaps in behaviour or knowledge, give a gentle reminder or have a chat with someone to adjust their perception of risk. You might find out why someone isn't following safe working procedures and work with them to make it easy to do so – easier than working unsafely. Should someone continually breach safety protocols that could lead to dangerous incidents or accidents despite your interventions, use the hot-stove principle to begin managing their performance. Now is *not* the time to turn a blind eye.

Desk bound? Stand up and move

Sitting, compared to even just standing, makes the body 'go to sleep'. There's nothing for the muscles to do, which slows down metabolism. But the problem is worse than that. People who work at computers for long periods experience high levels of arm, back, neck and shoulder pain, despite ergonomics education and better workstation and seating design. This includes teleworkers (more prevalent since the COVID-19 pandemic and working from home arrangement), secretaries, data entry and call centre workers, or professionals and managers. The long-term results of prolonged sitting and lack of physical activity can include blood clots, cardiovascular disease, diabetes and obesity. It can even reduce life expectancy by an estimated three years.[15]

There are measures people can take to prevent this, including performing some work while standing, walking to a colleague's desk rather than sending an email, holding standing and walking meetings, and placing telephones and in-trays away from people's desks. Organisations can encourage healthy lifestyles that include exercise, but even with regular exercise, spending long hours in a sedentary position increases the risk of neck pain, chronic disease such as diabetes, heart disease and mental health issues.[16]

Transferable skills
2.1 Critical thinking
4.1 Data literacy

Study the stats

The fourth way to identify hazards is to collect accident, incident and injury information, present it in a usable way (see **Figures 27.17** and **27.21** in Chapter 27) and periodically analyse the numbers to see what they can tell you. You can use graphs of lost-time injuries, medical treatments, positive performance indicators and workers' compensation claims to facilitate continuous improvements and identify looming problems.

Look at lost-time injuries (explained earlier in this chapter) and look for patterns and trends, such as:

- *What types* of accidents, injuries and incidents occur most often? For example, are they mostly falls, back injuries, or cuts and abrasions?
- *Where* do most occur? Does one location stand out among all others as having a higher rate of accidents, injuries or near misses?
- *When* do accidents, injuries and near misses occur? Is there a particular time of day – for example, the beginning or end of a shift – during which they tend to happen?
- *Who* is involved? Is it mostly new employees, old hands, people under training or some other identifiable group who seem to be most at risk?
- *What types* of equipment, machinery or processes are involved?
- *Which hazards* and incidents are the most likely to result in an accident or injury? Which would be the most serious?

Answers to questions like these can give you valuable information about particular areas and jobs to monitor or investigate for the cause in order to correct it. (You can find out how to analyse and present data in Chapter 27.) **Figure 30.10** shows which information you should include when building a WHS file.

Transferable skills
1.4 Business operations
2.1 Critical thinking

Step 2: Assess risks

Risk estimates the likelihood and severity of potential illness or injury, or damage to the environment or property, resulting from a hazard. You can attach a degree of risk, such as high, medium or low, to all hazards.

When assessing a hazard's degree of risk, consider these factors:

- *Frequency*: how often is a person exposed to the hazard? You would deal with frequent, say daily or weekly, exposure differently from infrequent, say once-a-year, exposure.
- *Probability*: how likely is the hazard to result in an accident? The higher the probability, the more urgent it is to eliminate or minimise it.
- *Severity*: how potentially serious would an accident caused by this hazard be? You would deal with the risk of a paper cut differently from the risk of death.

FIGURE 30.10 Components of good WHS files

- *How the above factors combine*: for example, even when a hazard has a very low chance of occurring (frequency) you would treat it as a high priority when it has a catastrophic outcome (severity). Draw up a matrix, as explained in Chapter 22, to see whether the way the factors combine changes a hazard's priority.

Based on your risk assessment, determine priorities for dealing with hazards, starting with those with the highest risk.

Stop that noise!

When it comes to hearing damage, workers (and customers) in clubs, gyms and pubs are at risk. Gardeners are at risk. Maintenance staff are at risk. Construction and road workers are at risk. In fact, the risk of hearing damage is present in a surprising number of workplaces, not just the obvious heavy engineering ones. There are 4700 noise-induced hearing loss claims made annually, with males between the ages of 60 and 64 making more than any other group. For example, in 2015 they made 1070 claims.[17]

Providing ear protection isn't enough. Codes of practice for noise management and hearing protection at work promote:

- developing a noise policy covering noise goals
- funding a noise-control program
- implementing a program of action, which should include a noise assessment, hearing tests, a plan to replace noisy machinery and equipment, ongoing training for employees and reducing exposure time to noise
- purchasing machinery and equipment that is as quiet as practicable
- hearing protection for individual workers is the last resort.

Transferable skills

1.4 Business operations

2.1 Critical thinking

Step 3: Control hazards

Use the flow chart for hazard control shown in **Figure 30.11** or follow **Figure 30.6** to manage hazards. Select and implement appropriate control measures in consultation with employees, engineers (when appropriate) and WHS specialists.

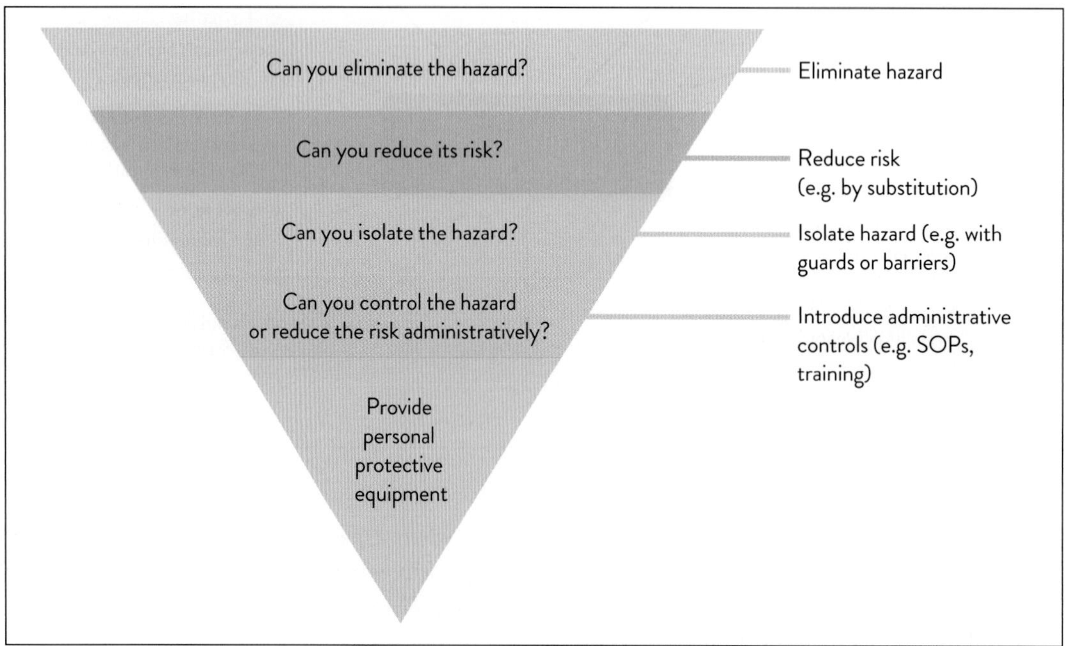

FIGURE 30.11 Hierarchy of controls

Think of the possible actions to control risks as a series of preferred steps. The best remedy is to *eliminate* the hazard. When you can't, *reduce* the risk it poses by substitution or isolation. When neither of those options is possible, introduce *administrative controls*.

Personal protection or PPE is your last resort because it is usually the least effective. PPE includes aprons and overalls, earmuffs and earplugs, gloves, hairnets, hard hats, hoods and shields, safety goggles and glasses, safety shoes and boots, and self-contained air breathing apparatus and filter respirators.

The main drawback of PPE is that it doesn't eliminate, reduce (provide a safer alternative or safer working practice) or isolate (through engineering or well-designed workflows) the hazard. PPE is only a thin line of defence between the employee and the unsafe condition. That's why it's better to remove the need for PPE by eliminating, minimising or isolating hazards.

The other drawback to PPE is that it can be unsightly, restrictive or cumbersome to use and employees often prefer not to use it, despite the danger of not doing so. People can also become so familiar with a job that they become careless in their use of safety equipment, which increases the risk of an accident. When PPE is the only option, though, you must ensure that employees use it. When it comes to safety, there is no excuse for lenient management. Think 'tough love' instead.

INDUSTRY INSIGHTS

Soft sensors

You can find soft sensors, or wearable technology, everywhere, from doors opening automatically to cars providing auditory alerts to put on your seatbelt. Soft sensors can be placed in clothing or in equipment to detect and measure a body's movement without inhibiting it.

You can use them to measure and optimise the posture of office workers or to adapt chairs to the preferred seating of employees so the chairs adapt to them rather than the other way around. You can use them to signal employees when picking up a heavy object to alert them to use correct lifting techniques or to send an alert telling them they're not lifting correctly; they can even automatically compress the employee's midriff to ensure correct lifting techniques.

Staying safe

Once hazards are identified and controlled, you still have work to do. This includes:

- carrying out preventative maintenance and corrective actions to prevent hazards multiplying
- continuing to communicate the safety message to ensure hazard control measures are used and that they work
- developing safe working procedures for hazardous jobs, documenting them and checking them regularly
- ensuring any PPE is appropriate, maintained and used correctly
- providing job instruction, information and ongoing training so that employees automatically perform work safely
- recording and analysing data to help identify hazards
- supervising employees to ensure they always follow safe working procedures
- working with employees to identify hazards and keep refining hazard control measures.

Manage for safety

Transferable skills

1.4 Business operations

3.1 Teamwork/relationships

3.2 Verbal communication

3.3 Written communication

3.4 Leadership

It has been said, 'If you can't manage for safety, you can't manage'. You need to promote a safe workplace constantly and consistently. Begin by setting a good example. The more safety conscious you are, the more safety conscious your work team should become. As we've discussed, this starts at induction – the moment an employee starts working for your organisation.

Use positive and constructive feedback to build and reinforce safe work habits. Train and supervise new employees, contractors and temporary employees carefully to correct any unsafe work practices early before they become hard-to-break habits. Provide regular training and information on safety rules, regulations, work systems and procedures. When people know what the safe work method is and how important it is to work safely, they are more likely to follow the safety procedures.

Communicate safety messages regularly and hold mini training sessions three or four times a year; invite the safety officer in, show a safety video or ask a team member to give a short talk on safety relating to their particular role, or to share real-life experiences where things have gone wrong (or right). Hold emergency drills for evacuating the work area and for giving first aid, and include safe work practices and safety consciousness in your regular performance reviews. Think about making safety a regular item on team meeting agendas.

Consult employees for their ideas on how to improve WHS. Inspect new items (e.g. chairs, chemicals, equipment and machines, and tools) for hazards and ask employees for their thoughts. Employees are usually well aware of what can go wrong and why, so listening to them is an easy and effective way to identify workplace hazards. Their observations and suggestions are likely to be good, since they are involved in the day-to-day operations and work processes.

Respond to employees' concerns and questions on WHS, whether they make them directly to you or through their WHS representative. Act on, and provide, prompt feedback on the issues they raise. This encourages employees to report hazards and incidents and to remain safety conscious.

Transferable skills

1.4 Business operations

3.4 Leadership

5.2 Technology use

Innovation in risk management

The world around us is rapidly changing, whether we like it or not. Innovation and automation are moving at an incredible pace across all areas of the working environment – including WHS. New work technologies are already making work tasks safer, improving productivity and streamlining processes.

Automation is being used in a number of WHS-related areas, including:

- induction
- service delivery
- reporting (incidents, near misses, hazards and risks)
- risk assessment
- wearable safety technology
- smart PPE.

All of these new innovations are designed to make your job, and the jobs of your team, easier and safer, and should be embraced with gusto if and when they are introduced to your workplace.[18]

STUDY TOOLS

QUICK REVIEW

KEY CONCEPT 30.1 

a Employers, managers and employees all have responsibilities under the Commonwealth *Work Health and Safety Act 2011*. Outline the senior and middle managers' responsibilities, leader-managers' responsibilities and employees' responsibilities.

b What is the role of safety inspectors and what powers do they have?

KEY CONCEPT 30.2 

a What are WHS committees and who are WHS representatives? How do they differ from WHS officers?

b Why is it important to involve employees in health and safety matters?

KEY CONCEPT 30.3 

a Describe the steps to take should an accident or incident occur in the work area you are responsible for. Draw this as a flow chart if you prefer.

b What is the significance of near misses? How should they be reported and dealt with?

KEY CONCEPT 30.4 

a What is the difference between a hazard and a risk? Refer to **Figure 30.11** to explain what to do when you become aware of a hazard.

b Describe how to estimate the cost to the organisation and society of a serious injury at a workplace.

BUILD YOUR SKILLS

KEY CONCEPT 30.1 

a List the actions you should take as a leader-manager regarding workplace health and safety.

b Obtain information on your state or territory's workers' compensation and rehabilitation program and requirements, and prepare a short report summarising how the system works.

KEY CONCEPT 30.2 

a In smaller organisations that don't employ a safety officer, discuss how health and safety representatives and health and safety committees can assist in keeping employees safe.

KEY CONCEPT 30.3 

a Are some people accident prone? Discuss what leader-managers should do about employees who seem to have more accidents than others.

KEY CONCEPT 30.4 

a Look around you and spot three hazards. Then choose one and describe how best to deal with it.

b Conduct a safety audit in your home and present your results in a summary document.

c Write safety instructions for a task you are familiar with that contains one or more hazards, such as changing a bicycle tyre or lighting a campfire.

WORKPLACE ACTIVITIES

KEY CONCEPT 30.1 

a Develop a plan for keeping your work team abreast of safety procedures and regulations in your organisation.

KEY CONCEPT 30.2 

a If possible, attend a safety committee meeting as an observer and report on the proceedings and what the meeting achieved.

b Interview a WHS officer or a WHS representative. What are their duties in relation to health, safety and welfare matters? What support does their organisation provide them in carrying out their duties? What are their main sources of information? Their main challenges?

c Describe how you consult with the people in your work group about health and safety matters.

KEY CONCEPT 30.3 

a Who was the last person who had a lost-time injury at your workplace? Estimate the cost of that injury to the organisation. Diagnose the cause of the accident and what led up to it. Were near misses involved?

KEY CONCEPT 30.4 

a What are the main causes of accidents at your workplace? Display this as a chart or graph (see Chapter 27 for examples).

b Explain how you prevent accidents and injuries in your work area and give examples of the steps you take to prevent a physical injury with respect to two hazards. Explain how you assess the risk in the examples.

c Write safety instructions for a task carried out by members of your work team that contains one or more hazards.

d Join a leader-manager, a WHS officer or a WHS committee member in a safety audit. Learn as much as you can about the potential hazards in the area being inspected and how they can be spotted. How is the inspection documented and acted on?

e Find out what WHS records your organisation keeps, where it keeps them and for how long it keeps them. Prepare a report summarising these records and how they are used.

EXTENSION ACTIVITIES

Referring to the Snapshot at the beginning of this chapter, answer the following questions:

1 How does Michael manage to get his message across clearly? Do you think he can improve on his delivery of the key messages?

2 Michael hasn't given his audience the opportunity to ask questions or give feedback. Is this appropriate at this point, or should he leave an open forum situation until the end of the meeting? Why do you feel this way?
3 Reflect on your own experiences with WHS meetings in the workplace. Have you ever been a WHS representative? If so, what were the pitfalls, and did you enjoy the job? If not, is it something you'd consider putting your hand up for in the future?
4 In your own workplace, find out if you have a WHS committee. If so, reflect upon its effectiveness, and the process that was followed when forming the committee. If there is no committee in your workplace, should there be one?

CASE STUDY 30

WORKING FROM HOME INJURIES

Alex runs a team of e-learning designers in an educational institute. Since an international pandemic broke out, the entire team has been working remotely. In the 18 months since this situation began, the team has hit a real groove. They work collaboratively using innovative technology, communicate extremely well via online tools, and their productivity has increased by 20 per cent. Alex is extremely pleased with the performance of both the team and the individuals within it.

However, he has gradually noticed that instances of personal leave have increased. Although some of these absences have been because of colds or viruses, the number of neck and back-related issues has increased, and Alex believes that the team members have relaxed on their vigilance regarding ergonomic safety.

Because the working from home arrangements were implemented in such a hurry, the issue of WHS was skirted around somewhat, in an attempt to keep the momentum of the team going. Now Alex knows that something has to be done in order to minimise injuries to his team. Although the performance of the team is important, he is more concerned with their health and wellbeing, and is determined to take action. It's time for him to set up some meetings.

Questions

1 Alex is determined to share his concerns with a number of people in his workplace in order to improve the situation. Who might this include?
2 What could the costs be if these injuries and absences continue to rise?
3 Could the organisation have prevented this situation from arising, and how?
4 What could happen if Alex doesn't act immediately?

CHAPTER ENDNOTES

1 Australian Bureau of Statistics, 'Work-related injuries, July 2017–June 2018', http://www.abs.gov.au/ausstats/abs@.nsf/mf/6324.0, accessed August 2021.
2 Safe Work Australia, 'Australian workers' compensation statistics', https://www.safeworkaustralia.gov.au/collection/australian-workers-compensation-statistics, accessed 23 August 2021.
3 Ibid.
4 SafeWork Australia, 'Cost of injury and illness statistics', https://www.safeworkaustralia.gov.au/statistics-and-research/statistics/cost-injury-and-illness/cost-injury-and-illness-statistics, accessed 23 August 2021.
5 Australian Government, *Work Health and Safety Act 2011*, https://www.comcare.gov.au/scheme-legislation/whs-act, accessed 23 August 2021.
6 Ibid.
7 Ibid.
8 Ibid.
9 Alcohol and Drug Foundation, 'Alcohol and other drugs in the workplace', 16 February 2017, https://adf.org.au/insights/alcohol-and-other-drugs-in-the-workplace/, accessed 23 August 2021.
10 Japanese 5S management system, 'Japanese "5S system" in an aluminium foundry – better control, fewer injuries', *Health and Safety Executive*, https://www.hse.gov.uk/slips/experience/japanese.htm, accessed 23 August 2021.

11 Australian Government, *Work Health and Safety Act 2011*.

12 Australian Institute of Health and Welfare, 'Worker's compensation', 23 July 2020, https://www.aihw.gov.au/reports/australias-health/workers-compensation, accessed 26 August 2021.

13 Safe Work Australia, 'Lost time injury frequency rates (LTIFR)', https://www.safeworkaustralia.gov.au/statistics-and-research/lost-time-injury-frequency-rates-ltifr, accessed 26 August 2021.

14 Ibid.

15 Karin Lindgren Griffiths et al., 'Prevalence and risk factors for musculoskeletal symptoms with computer based work across occupations', *Journal of Prevention, Assessment and Rehabilitation*, IOS Press, Vol. 42, No. 4/2102, p. 533, April 2012, http://www.ncbi.nlm.nih.gov/pubmed/22523044, accessed 26 August 2021.

16 Be Upstanding, 'One of the biggest factors impacting your health when working from home is prolonged sitting', https://www.lp.beupstanding.com.au/wfh01e, accessed 26 August 2021.

17 Industrial Deafness Australia, 'Industrial Deafness and Hearing Loss Claims in Victoria', August 2010, https://www.industrialdeafnessaustralia.com.au/industrial-hearing-loss/vic-legal-services

18 Rapid Global, 'How risk management technology is changing the work health and safety landscape', December 2019, https://www.rapidglobal.com/knowledge-centre/how-risk-management-technology-is-changing-the-work-health-and-safety-landscape, accessed 26 August 2021.

CHAPTER

31

MANAGING FOR PSYCHOLOGICAL SAFETY AND WELLBEING

After completing this chapter, you will be able to:

31.1 identify forms of harassment and assaults to people's dignity and create a culture that appreciates and respects everyone

31.2 investigate complaints concerning dignity violations

31.3 encourage employee welfare and wellbeing.

TRANSFERABLE SKILLS

The following transferable skills are covered in this chapter:

1 **Business competence**
- **1.1** Financial literacy
- **1.4** Business operations

2 **Critical thinking and problem solving**
- **2.1** Critical thinking
- **2.2** Personal effectiveness
- **2.3** Business strategy

3 **Social competence**
- **3.1** Teamwork/relationships
- **3.2** Verbal communication
- **3.3** Written communication
- **3.4** Leadership

4 **Data literacy**
- **4.1** Data literacy

5 **Digital competence**
- **5.1** Cyber security
- **5.2** Technology use

OVERVIEW

Transferable skills

3.1 Teamwork/ relationships

3.4 Leadership

Have you ever felt uncomfortable, anxious or fearful? It's hard to do your best when you're always looking over your shoulder, protecting yourself physically or psychologically, or attempting to tune out unpleasant or cruel comments and remarks. It's hard to reach your true potential at work or in your personal life when you feel like an 'outsider' and your contributions aren't appreciated or even understood, or when your mind continually returns to other events in your life. Some common themes of these thoughts include guilt about things you have done in the past, people you feel you have wronged, situations where you might have done things differently, or any number of occasions where your actions could have resulted in a more palatable outcome. The seriousness of such situations may vary. They could be work related: 'Why didn't I speak up when I felt that a colleague was being bullied?' or more personal: 'Why did I have to shout at my children yesterday?' An anxious person may dwell on these types of situation for days, weeks, months or even years.

Psychological safety is part of the workplace health and safety domain. Employers have a legal and moral responsibility to ensure their employees, customers and others on their premises are treated with dignity and respect. Many organisations have grasped the benefits of helping their employees, and often their families, to maintain physical and mental fitness. As a result, they have extended their efforts beyond merely preventing harm to employees' physical and psychological safety to actively encouraging their physical and psychological health. This is known as employee wellness, or wellbeing.

This chapter deals with psychological health and safety and explains how to protect employees' psychological health and encourage their wellbeing. (Chapter 30: Ensuring a safe and healthy workplace, explains the health and safety legislative framework and how to identify and manage hazards.) To complete your understanding of dignity and psychological safety, you should also read Chapter 32: Moving from diversity to inclusion.

SNAPSHOT

The consequences of procedural unfairness

Lee has returned from a Fair Work Australia Hearing in the CBD and calls the entire human resources (HR) team into the boardroom. From the glum look on his face, the team members can tell that the outcome of the hearing is not a favourable one.

'Hi everyone. I'm going to lay it on the line. We've lost the case against Alex and, quite frankly, Justice Allingham explained to me very well why the decision went against us – and I'm sorry to say that I actually agree with him. Hindsight is, as they say, 20:20.'

The team look apprehensive and worried, but intrigued.

'Alex had every right to ask for working from home and flexible working arrangements during the COVID-19 pandemic. Our defence that it would affect the performance of the business was completely rejected. The fact is, the staff who were available to work on-site were more than capable of dealing with on-site needs, and Alex was easily contactable at all times. We didn't fully take into consideration that she is the single mother of twin toddlers, that childcare was limited and that Alex was suffering diagnosed mental health issues because of this.

'To be honest, we as a team and as a company should have supported her more in her situation. We've failed her, and the consequence is that she has refused our renewed offer of working from home and flexible hours. She has now resigned from her position and is claiming constructive dismissal and bullying, a case I'm afraid she is likely to win.

'One of the matters that Justice Allingham brought up was that the analysis of Alex's situation was unfairly biased, particularly as she was not invited to view any documents or to be meaningfully involved in the process. This is, with the aforementioned hindsight, completely unacceptable.

'Our case has backfired on the company spectacularly, and the consequences could be far-reaching – not just financially, but in terms of our policies and procedures. The Justice examined them and said they were antiquated, skewed towards the company and should have been swiftly updated when it became clear that the pandemic was going to be a long-term issue. It has been further complicated by the fact that we allowed some other staff to work from home, and they were not in as challenging a position as Alex. The refusal given to her was blunt and stoic, with no real empathy. That's on me.'

The team as a whole look downcast, and Lee, in an attempt to reassure them, continues: 'It's OK; none of you are at risk; you followed our polices and procedures. We need to treat this as an opportunity to learn from our mistakes, and we need to make an apology to Alex, regardless of the ongoing legal situation. Please don't contact her personally; that could complicate things. Leave that to the executive team.

'Ok, that's all. Let's all reflect on what we did, how we did it, and what went wrong. We'll have a team meeting next week to look at what we do next. I've got the unenviable task of taking this to the board. Wish me luck!'

Lee leaves the room, and the rest of the staff, visibly shocked, go back to their duties.

31.1 Managing for psychological safety and employee dignity

> Keep away from angry, sore-tempered men, lest you learn to be like them and endanger your soul.
>
> Proverbs 15:18, *The living Bible*, Tyndale House Foundation, 1971.

Transferable skills

1.1 Financial literacy

2.3 Business strategy

3.1 Teamwork/relationships

3.4 Leadership

Organisations have a clear duty of care to ensure that employees are psychologically safe. **Harassment**, **racial** and **religious vilification,** and **occupational violence** are significant workplace hazards and should be measured, monitored and treated in the same way as physical hazards.

It's important that you read and understand your organisation's policies on psychological safety and know how to deal quickly with any instances of unacceptable behaviour and treatment of others. It's also critical that you model appropriate behaviour in your own work and set clear expectations of others regarding what behaviour is acceptable and what is unacceptable.

Harassment, vilification and workplace violence can seriously undermine the victim's **performance**, **mental health** and wellbeing, motivation and enjoyment of work. Harassment and violence make their victims miserable and can trigger physical illness from the stress they produce. The emotional and psychological costs can be far-reaching, and may involve any or all of the following:

- depression
- loss of self-worth and self-respect
- headaches
- lowered creativity
- poor concentration
- sleep disruption
- feelings of anxiety
- insecurity
- shame.

Transferable skills

1.1 Financial literacy

Although the financial costs are often hidden, organisations pay in terms of **morale**, productivity and reputation. Victims may take sick days or stress leave, or leave the job altogether, particularly when they feel they have no other recourse. For example, a study from Human Rights.gov found that almost one in five people who did report harassment, were labelled a troublemaker (19 per cent); were ostracised, victimised or ignored by colleagues (18 per cent); or resigned (17 per cent).[1] In these times of a higher awareness of mental health, psychological injury claims are often more expensive than physical injury claims, often because they have longer recovery times.

Transferable skills

1.4 Business operations

2.3 Business strategy

3.4 Leadership

The majority of victims do not come forward. Anecdotally, many perpetrators show a charming face to others, especially those higher up the hierarchy, and their victims are often reluctant to speak up for fear they won't be believed. Some may not come forward because of fear of reprisals, of sounding weak, affecting promotion prospects, or even because they don't believe anything will change when they complain. A safety culture with clear policies, training, and open communication and support can lessen victims' concerns about making a complaint. A very common reason that victims do not want to come forward with complaints about **bullying** or harassment is that their employment may be at risk, particularly if the person they are complaining about is in a position of power, or a person who could have an effect on the future of the victim. These issues are more prevalent when there are outside issues, such as a poor economy or a natural disaster, such as the COVID-19 pandemic.

What is 'wellbeing' or 'wellness'?

Transferable skills
1.4 Business operations
2.2 Personal effectiveness
3.1 Teamwork/relationships
3.4 Leadership

Wellbeing is defined by the Oxford English Dictionary as 'the state of being comfortable, healthy, or happy'. However, you must also consider the fact that the concept of wellbeing is far broader than 'in the moment' happiness. Of course, happiness is a large part of wellbeing, but there are other facets, which can include happiness and satisfaction regarding:

- personal life
- relationships
- parenting
- work–life balance
- sense of purpose and meaning
- self-worth
- anxiety and depression levels
- susceptibility to mental illness (general brain health).

Who is most at risk?

Transferable skills
1.4 Business operations
3.1 Teamwork/relationships
3.4 Leadership

Although harassment, vilification and violence can be directed at anyone, some groups of workers are more at risk than others. Casual employees, trainees, young employees and employees lower down the organisational hierarchy are most at risk. Others might become victims because they lack social skills or have a disability, their appearance, gender identity, personality style, physical characteristics, race or nationality, or sexual orientation. A person can even become a victim because they are perceived as more competent than their persecutors.

Transferable skills
1.4 Business operations
2.3 Business strategy
3.4 Leadership

However, the most sensible and realistic view to take, known as the **universal precautions approach**, is that harassment, vilification and violence can happen to anyone in any workplace. It can also occur away from the workplace; for example, at off-site business-related functions (e.g. business trips, conferences, social events, trade shows, etc.), in clients' workplaces, and even over the telephone and electronically. Wherever it takes place, employers have a duty of care to take the initiative in identifying the risks their employees and people who come into contact with their employees face and to remove or reduce those risks. When they don't, the costs can be steep – to the victims as well as to the organisation.

Create a safety culture

Transferable skills
1.4 Business operations
2.3 Business strategy

There is a famous quote from the late Lieutenant-General David Morrison 'The standard you walk past is the standard you accept.'[2] That is, when you ignore and walk past harassment or violence, you condone it. In organisations with weak safety cultures, abusive behaviour is tolerated; infringements of people's dignity are brushed aside, ignored or joked about. These organisations are typified by aggressive behaviour and overly competitive organisation cultures of fear and insecurity. They often have different conditions of employment for different groups of workers, poor job training, and lack clear and transparent **grievance** procedures.

Uncompromising performance-related pay schemes, poor performance management systems, unclear or unreasonable performance measures, targets and timeframes combined with pressure to get the job done, regardless, and toxic, often authoritarian leadership styles are common in organisations in which harassment and violence – verbal and/or physical – are allowed to occur.

In organisations like these, position and power are abused, and demanding customers or clients, personality clashes and personal prejudice are allowed to dictate the work climate to the detriment of dignity and productivity.

In contrast, organisations with robust safety cultures do not tolerate attacks on people's dignity or damage to people's wellbeing. It is every employee's responsibility to treat other employees, customers and suppliers with respect, and respect is a core organisational value. What constitutes unacceptable behaviour is clear and everyone knows how unacceptable behaviour will be dealt with should it occur.

Transferable skills

1.4 Business operations

2.3 Business strategy

In strong safety cultures, induction programs must explain the organisation's policies and this information is informally reviewed periodically during the working year, such as at team meetings. Policies should also be examined and amended during high-stress situations, such as corporate takeovers, rounds of redundancy or the external factors we have discussed, such as economic downturns or natural disasters. Ongoing communication, regular workforce awareness training and other training (e.g. in assertiveness, communication, conflict resolution and other interpersonal skills) are part of the organisation's normal routines. Literature on the various aspects of a dignified workplace, such as government pamphlets in English and in the languages of people from non-English-speaking backgrounds, and the organisation's policies covering dignity, diversity, safety and stress management is readily available and understood.

Transferable skills

2.2 Personal effectiveness

3.1 Teamwork/relationships

3.2 Verbal communication

3.3 Written communication

3.4 Leadership

5.2 Technology use

Everyone must know what harassment, vilification and violence mean in practice, how to make complaints and where to go for advice and support. Everyone must know the relevant incident recording procedure, detailing what was said and done so that it can be used should they need to make a formal complaint. They also know what to do should they become stressed in the course of their work and how the organisation can help.

REFLECT

In a culture where humour and 'getting a joke' is valued, people sometimes think they can get away with passive-aggressive humour, sarcasm and 'harmless' put-downs. They may be acceptable when aimed at yourself or others in your 'in group', but when someone in the 'in group' aims a 'joke' at someone in the 'out group', it is not acceptable. In workplaces where 'just joking' is the norm and 'get over yourself' is the response to someone not finding it funny, we have covert or even systemic discrimination at work.

Put-downs and 'humour' based on negative stereotypes have no place in the workplace. Call it out. And should you be called humourless for saying so, call it out again. And remember: 'The standard you walk past is the standard you accept.'[3]

If you're called out for an unfunny barb, your response should be something like: 'I'm sorry I offended you, thank you for telling me.' (Not 'I'm sorry *if* I offended you.')

Can you think of times when this has happened in your workplace, and the reactions from others?

Transferable skills

1.4 Business operations

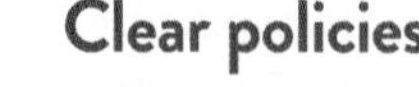

Clear policies

A formal policy or policies on bullying, sexual harassment, occupational violence, and racial and religious vilification is the first step in proactively creating an organisation culture that values and respects people's dignity. When the nature of the work performed is itself stressful, the organisation's measures to reduce stress and programs to help employees suffering from stress should be explained in its health and safety or welfare policies.

Policies should explain how complaints are addressed confidentially, fairly, impartially and quickly. The policies should be administered by a trained person and widely circulated, and all managers should be trained in implementing them.

Transferable skills

3.2 Verbal communication

3.3 Written communication

Dignity policies and the procedures that support them are part of the organisation's health and safety package. They should be available and explained to all employees and reviewed regularly for effectiveness. Best practice is for an initial round of training for all staff, followed by quarterly updates and annual refresher training. Some ways to ensure that the policies are visible include to post them where people meet; for example, in kitchen areas, meeting rooms and rest rooms; display them on computer screen pop-ups or tabs; and make them easily accessible on the organisation's intranet.

Clear policies show the organisation takes these issues seriously and can ensure that trouble is addressed quickly and effectively. They should serve to alert the organisation to patterns of unacceptable conduct and the need for training and other prevention measures in particular areas.

From a purely practical standpoint, this makes it less likely that complaints escalate to government authorities, which can be costly, time-consuming and damaging to the organisation's public image. From a morale and productivity standpoint, they help maintain a positive working climate and positive working relationships, reassure victims and minimise victims' stress. When widely promoted, understood and supported, these policies are the foundation for a culture that values everyone's contributions and respects individual differences in styles and abilities.

Transferable skills

1.4 Business operations

2.3 Business strategy

What should I include in a dignity policy?

Dignity policies must follow the principles of procedural fairness and be understood and supported by all employees at all levels. They must include:

- definitions of bullying, sexual harassment, workplace violence and racial and religious vilification
- a statement that these behaviours are unlawful
- the complaints process, including how to make a complaint and how investigations and resolutions are to be conducted
- the consequences for any employee who engages in these unlawful behaviours.

Other common ingredients of dignity policies include:

- a clear range of responses to deal with offenders, beginning with performance counselling and ending with termination of employment
- a clear undertaking that people who make complaints will not be disadvantaged or victimised and that complaints and discussions are confidential
- a commitment to a workplace environment that values people's safety, dignity, welfare and wellbeing
- a commitment to prompt action, generally within three days
- a list of people to approach to discuss the problem (including union representatives, when appropriate)
- accessible supporters who are from all levels of the organisation and who have been trained to give confidential emotional support to victims considering taking action and to the alleged offender(s)
- an outline of the responsibilities of all management and non-management employees in applying the organisation's dignity principles
- champions of the policies at senior level throughout the organisation, to promote and give credibility to the policies
- clear guidance on internal investigation procedures and record-keeping
- clear standards regarding acceptable behaviour, with the stated objective of ensuring dignity for everyone and creating a positive working environment

Transferable skills

1.4 Business operations

2.3 Business strategy

3.1 Teamwork/relationships

3.2 Verbal communication

3.3 Written communication

3.4 Leadership

- formal and informal internal complaints procedures and access to an independent external investigator – with no requirement that the informal complaints path should be followed first or that internal procedures be followed before approaching the relevant government authority – and a clear statement that employees may at any time pursue a formal approach with the Australian Human Rights Commission or, if it appears to be a criminal matter, the police
- incorporation of dignity-at-work issues into training programs.

Stay alert and observant

Merely dealing appropriately with a complaint is not enough. You must also take steps to prevent harassment. Be alert to your own unexamined assumptions and actions based on these assumptions and to the actions of others that may cause unnecessary discomfort, embarrassment or unpleasantness. Create a climate in which people's beliefs and feelings are respected and that rejects offensive behaviour and language. Make it possible for employees to raise concerns informally with you.

Train yourself to recognise early signals of harassment, vilification and violence so you can step in quickly. Early signs include:

- a change in demeanour or mood; for example, an employee becoming withdrawn and isolated or looking tired
- an employee experiencing a number of minor workplace injuries
- higher than usual, unexplained absenteeism
- new employees, particularly those most at risk, resigning suddenly and without explanation
- reduced productivity
- regularly damaged personal effects or work tools
- regularly torn clothing or uniforms.

When employees take stress leave, think about the possibility that workplace abuse might be the cause; medical certificates are unlikely to mention harassment, but merely state that the employee is unwell due to emotional stress at work.

Transferable skills

1.4 Business operations

3.1 Teamwork/ relationships

3.4 Leadership

Find it and fix it

In your workplace, use statistics to help spot problem areas and potential problem areas. Proactively monitor patterns in key indicators for signs of harassment and violence; for example, high levels of **attrition** or absenteeism associated with particular shifts, departments or teams. Other indicators and patterns to monitor are accident and incident statistics, use of employee assistance programs, employee satisfaction surveys, exit interviews, grievances, lost productivity, personal leave, reported incidents of bullying, harassment, racial or religious vilification and workplace violence, as well as **workers' compensation** claims.

These types of indicators of employee satisfaction and productivity help organisations to identify problems early on, investigate them and respond quickly with appropriate support and assistance.

Harassment

Harassment is unwelcome and uninvited physical or verbal conduct that is offensive to its recipient. Whether it's based on ability, age, gender identity, marital status, pregnancy status, race, religion or sexuality, it leaves the harassed person feeling angry, frightened, humiliated, intimidated, offended, resentful or trapped.

Harassment has to do with dominance and the exercise of power, real or perceived, in the workplace. This is why the most common (but not the only) victims of harassment are young people and women employed in positions lower down the organisational hierarchy. These people generally find it awkward, difficult or embarrassing to make complaints about the treatment they are receiving. Leader-managers of young people need to be particularly alert to the possibilities of harassment taking place.

Transferable skills

2.2 Personal effectiveness

3.1 Teamwork/relationships

3.4 Leadership

Some harassing behaviour may be based on unexamined assumptions and be unthinking rather than malicious. Whether or not harm is intended, however, harassment creates an unpleasant working environment and reduces the victim's job satisfaction and their ability to complete their duties effectively.

The cost of claims

Transferable skills

1.1 Financial literacy

1.4 Business operations

Harassment claims are generally more costly than physical injury claims because employees typically need more time off work. Like physical injury, the impact of harassment stretches beyond the victim to their family and colleagues through damaged morale and lowered productivity.

- An employee must not harass another employee in the same organisation. For example, a manager must not harass an employee; a group of employees must not harass another employee; one employee must not harass another employee.
- An employee of one organisation must not harass an employee of another organisation during the course of their work. For example, a technician servicing a client's equipment on the client's premises must not harass that client's employees.
- An employee or a group of employees of an organisation must not harass an employee of another organisation who visits to provide goods or services. For example, the employees at the client company must not harass the technician in the previous example.
- A person must not harass another person when providing goods or a service. For example, a hairdresser must not harass a customer.
- Employees must not be harassed by the people to whom they are providing goods or services. For example, a customer must not harass a hairdresser.
- Should any of these types of harassment take place, employers have a responsibility to protect the victim from harassment and to prevent their employees from harassing others.

Bullying

Bullying is a form of harassment. It is repeated and unreasonable behaviour directed towards a person or group of persons at a workplace and creates a risk to health and safety. It can include threats, violence and abusive language, or the opposite – shunning – and it degrades, embarrasses, humiliates, intimidates or undermines the victim(s).

Safe Work Australia's 'Australian Workplace Barometer' is an evidence-based project monitoring work conditions in Australia. It shows that Australia rates as having the sixth-highest rate of bullying in the workplace in comparison with 34 European countries. Its research shows that the national average rate of bullying in the workplace has risen by 40 per cent. In addition, independent research conducted by mental health charity Beyond Blue suggests that almost 50 per cent of Australians experience workplace bullying at some point in their career.[4] Experts believe that between one in four and one in two employees are bullied at least once during their career; it is estimated that between 400 000 and two million Australians are bullied at work every year and 2.5 to five million will experience bullying at some time during their career.[5]

Until 2014, victims could only claim compensation for mental stress from bullying – after the damage was done. Since then, they've been able to apply to the Fair Work Commission for a 'stop bullying order' against an organisation, individual or group of individuals.

Bullies invalidate and demean their victims, gradually wearing them down and eroding their self-esteem with hostility, ridicule and petty fault-finding. Unlike physical abuse, psychological bullying doesn't leave marks that you can see, but it's just as painful; in fact, it can be even more painful because it's so easily hidden and bottled-up. It is intended to make the victim feel miserable. It drains the victim's self-confidence and leaves them unable to perform effectively; meanwhile, the perpetrator feels superior and dominant.

Here is how some victims have described being bullied:

- 'She would time me when I went to the toilet.'
- 'He would tear strips off me at meetings, in front of my peers.'
- 'People used to cower when he entered the room. Some people literally jumped.'
- 'My work was never good enough, no matter how hard I tried. And I know I was doing what I was expected to do, and as well as everyone else.'
- 'She'd set an impossible deadline and then say something like: "Just remember. Jobs are no longer for life."'
- 'He regularly and deliberately used inappropriate or incorrect pronouns when addressing or referring to me, even though I had expressed my identity.'
- 'They would laugh at the pitch of my voice, and imitate me regularly. I felt that if I didn't laugh along then I would be seen as a "bad sport" or as having no sense of humour – but it really hurt me.'

Some bullies repeatedly target one individual, while others spread their aggression and intimidation around. Some offend, demean or put people down in private, some in front of colleagues, clients or customers. Some bully openly (*overt bullying*), others in more subtle ways (*covert bullying*). Some bullying is done electronically (*cyberbullying*) and some is done by groups (*mobbing*). Some bullying is through exclusion or *ostracism*. Some people even harass their manager (*upwards bullying*) by spreading rumours, skipping meetings and ignoring the manager's opinions and views. There really is no limit to the lengths bullies will go to achieve their aims, and there are countless methods they employ to do so.

In the workplace, bullying is generally seen to come under two categories:

1 Unreasonable and inappropriate acts of *commission* – a pattern of repeatedly doing or saying something.
2 Acts of *omission* – a pattern of repeatedly failing to do something that should reasonably be expected to be done.

Table 31.1 shows examples of the two forms of bullying.

TABLE 31.1 Bullying in the workplace: acts of commission and omission

Acts of commission	Acts of omission
Adjusting rosters and work allocation so the victim is near the leader-manager/bully and isolated from the team	Deliberately withholding information, support or access to needed information, resources or training
Approving leave for the victim only when the manager has leave scheduled	Denying opportunities (e.g. for promotion, secondments, training)
Belittling/humiliating the employee through derogatory comments, graffiti, personally offensive remarks, sarcasm or teasing	Exclusion from social events
Blocking promotion	Failure to pass on messages or supply the correct or necessary information

Acts of commission	Acts of omission
Constant fault finding and put-downs	Pointedly ignoring the victim while speaking to others
Constantly changing targets or guidelines	Regularly delegating interesting work and assignments to everyone but the victim
Intimidating the employee (e.g. glaring at the employee, invading their personal space, making threats)	Unfairly allocating work benefits
Making threats (e.g. about job security)	
Making unwelcome remarks (e.g. about a person's dress or appearance, or more subtle embarrassing comments)	
Micromanaging or supervising in an overbearing fashion	
Persistently questioning a person's beliefs, gender identity, customs, racial or ethnic origin or religion	
Providing uncomfortable furniture and poor-quality equipment that continuously breaks down, with no technical assistance available	
Taking away interesting work and giving it to others, and replacing it with boring, demeaning duties	
Sabotaging the victim's work (e.g. by hiding important documents or supplying incorrect information)	
Setting impossible assignments, deadlines or unreasonable workloads	
Shouting and screaming at employees	
Spreading malicious rumours	
Telling jokes and stories of a humiliating nature	
Verbally abusing people	
Undermining by constant public criticism, ridiculing the victim's opinion and work contribution in front of the team	

Euphemisms for bullying

Have you heard any of these 'spins' for episodes of bullying?

- 'It's a personality clash.'
- 'There's nothing wrong – she just needs to adjust her attitude.'
- 'That's just old Brucie complaining again.'
- 'We have a robust management style in this company.'
- 'We're tough here – but it works.'
- 'She's a very strong woman.'

Transferable skills

1.4 Business operations

2.2 Personal effectiveness

3.1 Teamwork/relationships

3.4 Leadership

Identifying bullies

Bullies often use strength of physicality, personality or power to coerce and dominate others through fear. Some bullies are socially inept, whose lack of interpersonal skills is revealed in often menacing and unprofessional behaviour. However, many bullies are also devious, clever, competent, sophisticated manipulators who take delight in making others feeling uncomfortable. Because they have had so much practice at it, they are masters of using verbal hostility to wield power over others and even to terrorise them.

There can also be a more surprising explanation for people who have bullying tendencies. They may have low self-esteem and/or low emotional intelligence and will try to enhance their own sense of self-worth by demeaning that of others. Their need to dominate and humiliate leads them to deny or ignore the accomplishments, experiences, feelings, opinions, plans and values of those around them. While many bullies attack people with less power who are likely to feel powerless to complain, other bullies target more competent, successful people who might make them feel inadequate or threatened in some way.

While some bullies are their victim's peers, studies in Australia and overseas show that it's mostly leader-managers, both male and female, who are the bullies. Many bullies began their careers as bullies in childhood and carry the behaviour over into adulthood and into their working lives. Others become bullies when they feel under pressure. Intense work pressure leaves less time to develop the healthy working relationships that can prevent bullying and can increase the occurrences of bullying.

Overloaded bullies may be becoming more common due to stress resulting from increasing automation, restructuring and downsizing and the need for fewer people to achieve more with less. These bullies may not have a deep-seated need to humiliate others but lack the skills to deal more effectively with the stress job demands put on them; bullying is how they cope. They have the age-old 'Dog eat dog' mentality.

Don't confuse strong, directive management with bullying. Most managers occasionally need to put pressure on people to achieve results, but bullies can be relied on to pile on the pressure. This can be made clear when an employee feels comfortable approaching a manager or not.

Table 31.2 shows the difference between professional leader-managers' behaviour and the way bullies behave. Figure 31.1 gives some examples of bullying.

TABLE 31.2 Professional behaviour versus bullying

Professional leader-manager	Destructive bully
Constructive criticism	Personal attack
Build employee's self-esteem and confidence	Tear down self-esteem and confidence
Use their influence	Abuse their power
Find ways to draw on people's talent and treat everyone the same	Single people out
Deal productively with underperforming employees	Attack even high-performing employees

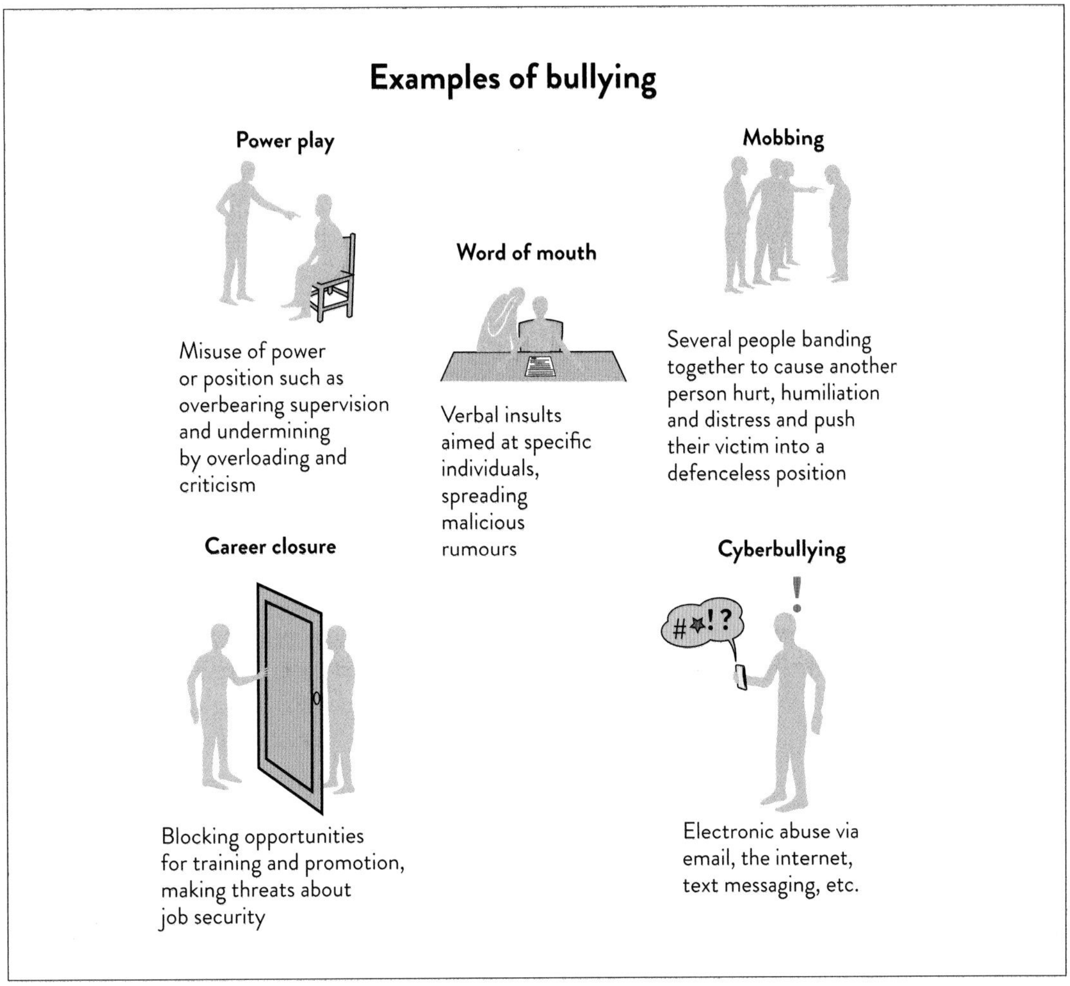

Examples of bullying

Power play

Misuse of power or position such as overbearing supervision and undermining by overloading and criticism

Word of mouth

Verbal insults aimed at specific individuals, spreading malicious rumours

Mobbing

Several people banding together to cause another person hurt, humiliation and distress and push their victim into a defenceless position

Career closure

Blocking opportunities for training and promotion, making threats about job security

Cyberbullying

#✱!?

Electronic abuse via email, the internet, text messaging, etc.

FIGURE 31.1 Examples of bullying

Cyberbullying

Transferable skills
5.1 Cyber security
5.2 Technology use

Enabled by the universal use of smartphones and the prevalence of social networking sites, cyberbullying in the workplace can cause major problems. These technologies allow cyberbullies to be even more aggressive than people who bully face-to-face due to the anonymity that they afford. Cyberbullying is particularly insidious because only the most astute of people will recognise it, many people don't know about it unless the victims report it, and the victims have no escape from it, since it doesn't need to be confined to working hours.

Mobbing

Transferable skills
3.1 Teamwork/relationships

People have always gossiped. In fact, gossiping may even have been an important survival skill during human evolution and, as a result, may be hardwired into the human brain; 'human nature', if you will. Gossip can have positives – it can help employees exchange information quickly, keep up to date on corporate news and, provided it's harmless, gossip strengthens relationships.

But gossip can also have a nasty side. When a number of people band together and unleash intense, destructive, vicious gossip that causes another person or group of people hurt, humiliation and distress, it becomes mobbing. A lone individual, or sometimes a small group of similar individuals, may be bullied, called names, made the brunt of 'pranks' or 'practical jokes', ridiculed and even physically assaulted. The intent is to force the target out of their employment or to behave or perform in ways they are not supposed to for the benefit of the 'mob'.

Targets are commonly enthusiastic employees, such as those who often volunteer; high achievers; employees from gender, religious or cultural minorities; employees who don't join in with the destructiveness of a larger group; employees with family responsibilities (especially women); employees with integrity, such as those who don't condone theft of company property or refuse to engage in inappropriate behaviour; and whistleblowers.

Transferable skills

3.1 Teamwork/relationships

Ostracism

The same people targeted by bullying may instead be targeted by ostracism, which is often viewed as a more acceptable form of social control compared to the more active, direct and overt forms of bullying. Ostracism is silent bullying that involves the absence of wanted behaviour whereas harassment is the presence of unwanted behaviour. It is notable that this type of bullying is extremely prevalent in schools, and is therefore a learnt behaviour if not dealt with swiftly when the bully or bullies are young.

Bullying by exclusion is different in that it requires no effort from the bullies, and has the added effect of making the victim(s) feel as though they are not even worth the effort of 'actual' bullying. Rather than instilling a *fear* of rejection, ostracism *is* rejection and so is often more psychologically devastating to the victim; in fact, it's experienced much like physical pain. This is because shutting a person out of conversations, leaving the area when they enter, not responding to their questions, comments or emails, and generally behaving as if the person does not exist, violates a person's basic human needs for belonging and acceptance.

Recent research has found that being ignored is more common and more damaging than other forms of harassment in the workplace. It's also more likely to lead to anxiety, depression and stress, and lowered self-esteem. Not only does ostracism seem to be more harmful to the victim, it also may be more harmful to the organisation because it reduces job satisfaction, commitment and performance even more than other forms of harassment and causes more resignations.[6]

Transferable skills

2.1 Critical thinking

2.2 Personal effectiveness

3.1 Teamwork/relationships

3.4 Leadership

Thwarting a bully

Never ignore bullying of any sort or turn a blind eye – bullies continue to bully as long as people let them. When bullying is reported to you or hinted at, or when you suspect it is occurring, tackle it quickly. Don't take the common (and cowardly) way out by forcing the victim to address the bullying themselves, resign, suffer in silence or take stress leave. Tactfully find out whether others are being bullied and are willing to speak up.

As a leader-manager, you are the most likely person to spot the isolation of a team member. Treat the situation seriously and intervene quickly. Explain the deep pain it can cause and make it clear that ostracising a co-worker is not professional behaviour, is not harmless and is not acceptable, and that you will deal with behaviour that excludes teammates as you would with any other harassment issue. Bullies in all situations need to know that their behaviour is unacceptable, will not be tolerated, and is potentially illegal and can result in harsh penalties. Regardless of these legal and ethical considerations, a person who gains a reputation as a bully will find future work options limited due to personal reputational damage.

Because bullying is often a long-established habit, one discussion is usually not enough. Address the bullying behaviour each and every time it occurs – set clear boundaries and clearly explain consequences – following through with these consequences when it's required. Use the hot-stove principle (as described in Chapter 19) and begin managing the behaviour. Since many bullies lack the interpersonal skills to deal with people differently, name the bullying behaviour and tell the bully what to do instead. Be clear – there must be no room for ambiguity in such a serious position, particularly when the health and wellbeing of your team members is at stake.

To counteract a culture of bullying of any sort, if possible, you should try to build a diverse team in which people are respected as individuals and for the roles they carry out. (This must, of course, be counter-balanced with the fairness of employing people because they are the right person for the role.) In the course of your management of a team, make sure everyone is aware of your organisation's workplace health and safety, HR and wellbeing policies through regular discussions and team meetings.

Sexual harassment

The Commonwealth *Sex and Age Discrimination Legislation Amendment Act 2011* defines **sexual harassment** as a person making a sexual advance, requesting sexual favours or engaging in other conduct of a sexual nature that is unwelcome, and takes place in circumstances that a reasonable person would have anticipated *the possibility* that the person harassed would be humiliated, intimidated or offended (see Figure 31.2).[7] This includes the unacceptable 'grab and grope' as well as less overt but unwelcome touches and pats, verbal and non-verbal behaviour, and innuendo. Sexual harassment can even be electronic.

Here are some examples of sexually harassing behaviour:

- displaying or distributing offensive messages or material (including cartoons, 'girlie' posters and lewd jokes) on hard copy or electronically
- irrelevant and unnecessary references to sex
- leering or staring
- persistent unwelcome emails, instant messages, social invitations, telephone calls, text messages and so on, at work and/or at home
- physical contact ranging from, for example, unwanted and unwarranted 'patting', pinching and touching to criminal assault
- general or perceived discrimination based on sexual orientation, gender identity or intersex status, including (but not limited to) remarks or jokes about a person's alleged sexual activities or private life
- sexually explicit communications through emails, text messages and so on

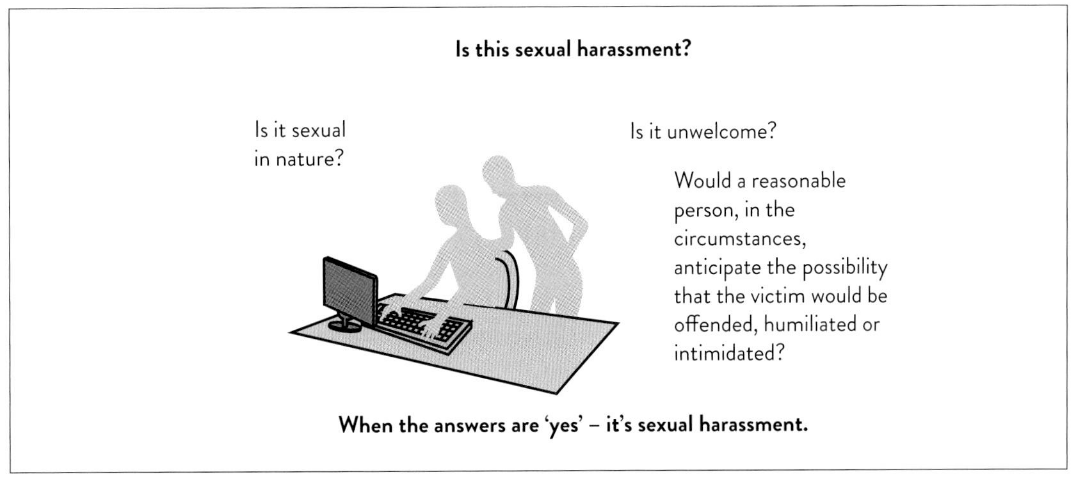

FIGURE 31.2 Is it sexual harassment?

- sexually suggestive comments, jokes or remarks
- unwelcome sexual advances.

In 2018, Australia's Sex Discrimination Commissioner Kate Jenkins announced an enquiry into sexual harassment in the Australian workplace.[8] The results show that a majority of Australians over the age of 15 have experienced some form of sexual harassment at some point. Although women are more likely to be harassed, men are also increasingly harassed. The survey showed:

- in their lifetimes, 71 per cent of Australians have been sexually harassed
- almost a quarter of all women have experienced rape or sexual assault
- 70 per cent of people who identify as straight or heterosexual have experienced sexual harassment over the course of their lifetimes, compared with 83 per cent of people who identify as gay or lesbian and 90 per cent who identify as bisexual
- 90 per cent of women and 68 per cent of men with disability have been sexually harassed in their lifetimes.

In the last five years:

- 39 per cent of women and 26 per cent of men have experienced sexual harassment at work
- people aged 18 to 29 were most likely to have experienced workplace sexual harassment
- people from the LGBTQI+ community were more likely than people who identify as straight or heterosexual to have experienced workplace sexual harassment
- Aboriginal and Torres Strait Islander people were more likely to have experienced workplace sexual harassment than people who are not Aboriginal or Torres Strait Islander (53 per cent and 32 per cent, respectively)
- people with disability were more likely to have been sexually harassed than a person without disability (44 per cent and 32 per cent, respectively).

The survey results indicate that, based on the most recent incident of sexual harassment experienced at work in the last five years:

- perpetrators of workplace sexual harassment are ordinarily male
- although more than 30 per cent of people witnessed or heard about the sexual harassment of someone else in their workplace, only one in three of them actually took some kind of action to intervene
- when bystander action *was* taken, in 71 per cent of incidences the action taken by the bystander was to talk or listen to the victim regarding the incident. Astoundingly, in less than half of witnessed cases, the bystander reported the harassment to the employer
- the most common reason for bystanders not reporting the harassment was the knowledge that others were supporting the victim. In a quarter of unreported cases, the bystander's reason for taking no action was to spare the victim from further unpleasantness.

The survey also found that when people made a formal complaint of harassment, usually to their manager or boss, the harassment stopped in 48 per cent of cases involving females and 37 per cent involving men. The majority of complainants were satisfied or extremely satisfied with the complaint process and 78 per cent of complaints were finalised in less than a month.

Male and female employees and managers in information, media and telecommunications are the most likely groups to be harassed; however, other industries follow very closely. The majority of sexual harassment continues to be experienced in workplaces of all sizes: large (39 per cent), medium (33 per cent) and small (19 per cent) organisations.[9]

Occupational violence

Occupational violence is defined as any incident during which an employee is physically attacked or threatened with violence in the workplace. It need not be repeated – once is enough. Violence can include both physical and psychological harm. Physical violence in the workplace can result in minor or serious injury, and sometimes even death, particularly where a workplace has common hazards, such as a building site. It includes the direct or indirect application of force to the victim's body, to equipment or to clothing worn by the victim that places their health and safety at risk. Grabbing, indecent physical contact, kicking, pushing, striking, spitting, throwing objects, tripping and use of weapons (whether they are designed as weapons or simply other items used as such) are all included.

Psychological violence can include ostracism (as discussed earlier), verbal abuse, personal insults, stalking and other forms of unwanted communications and intrusions into a person's private life, whether in-person or electronically. Sexual, racial and religious harassment and all forms of bullying are types of occupational violence, as is any physical action directed at inanimate objects (e.g. banging a table or throwing objects), vandalism and destruction of another employee's or the organisation's property, and rude or offensive gesturing.[10]

What constitutes a threat?

A threat is a statement or behaviour that causes a person or persons to believe that they are in danger of being physically attacked, regardless of the attacker's intent. For example, a customer may become so verbally abusive towards a sales assistant that it seems likely the customer will become physically violent. Or perhaps a colleague threatens 'I'll see you in the car park', or an employee repeatedly draws a finger across his throat while looking menacingly at another team member. These unsettling and frightening acts are rightly considered workplace violence, and when behaviours like these occur, they must be stopped and prevented from recurring.

Of course, a method used by violent people to excuse their behaviour is attempts at dismissal or minimisation – 'But I didn't mean it', 'I was only trying to scare her' or 'I was just joking'. These are not valid defences, and, in fact, in our modern, progressive world, they are an insult to the societal efforts made towards preventing such disgraceful attitudes. They display ignorance, disrespect and arrogance, and a leader-manager must deal with this type of reasoning swiftly.

Transferable skills
3.4 Leadership

Workplace violence: who is most at risk?

Transferable skills
1.4 Business operations
3.1 Teamwork/relationships
3.4 Leadership

Workplace violence occurs in all industries and occupations although it's more common in some workplaces than others. Employees who face a greater risk of violence are those who:

- carry out inspection or enforcement duties, such as government employees, police officers and prison officers
- handle money, prescription drugs or valuables, such as doctors' surgery staff and retail staff
- have a mobile workplace; for example, a taxi
- provide advice, care, education or services, such as healthcare workers, social services employees and teachers
- work alone or in small numbers, such as meter readers, petrol station cashiers and real estate agents, or in isolated or low-traffic areas, such as storage areas, utility rooms and washrooms
- work during periods of intense organisational change or conflict; for example, during downsizing or industrial action
- work in community-based settings, such as nurses, social workers and other home visitors
- work in premises where alcohol is served (e.g. food and beverage staff)
- work near businesses at risk of violent crime, such as pubs and banks
- work with the public; for example, Centrelink employees and insolvency and trustee officers
- work with unstable or volatile persons, such as social services or criminal justice system employees.

Racial and religious vilification

The Commonwealth *Racial Discrimination Act 1975* and the Commonwealth *Racial Discrimination Amendment Act 1980* make any behaviour that belittles, denigrates, humiliates, insults or maligns a person or group in public based on their colour, race or national or ethnic origin, illegal. Inciting or encouraging hatred, revulsion, serious contempt or severe ridicule against a person or group of people because of their race or religion includes drawings, gestures, graffiti, images, spoken words and written material. People who are subject to vilification feel harassed, humiliated, intimidated or physically threatened.

Transferable skills

1.4 Business operations

2.2 Personal effectiveness

3.4 Leadership

No self-respecting organisation or leader-manager allows that to happen to any employee. Again, organisations need to respond with clear policies supported by senior executives, strong HR teams and leader-managers, ongoing awareness training and communication, well-known and easily accessed complaints procedures, regular monitoring of key measures and a complete zero-tolerance approach – the only appropriate approach in civilised society if the scourge of racial and religious vilification is to be minimised, if not eliminated from the workplace.

Sexual and gender identity vilification

It is important to take into account the fact that sexual and gender identity and expression has become a far more respected area of human rights in recent years. It may be understandable (if not entirely forgivable), that some organisations or employees with them may not be aware of the multitude of sexual and gender identities and the issues that may arise should a perceived discriminatory event occur. Employers have a duty to educate themselves, their leader-managers and all other employees on this important subject in order to achieve equality for all in the workplace.

Sexual and gender identity can be a divisive and misunderstood area. Most of us know the term LGBTQIA+, but not all of us are aware of some of the more complex areas. LGBTQIA+ is an evolving acronym that stands for lesbian, gay, bisexual, transgender, queer/questioning, intersex, asexual. Gender identities represent the 'unknown' for many people, who are then made fearful by it. As we've discussed, bullies can be driven by fear, which makes the LGBTQIA+ community another group at high risk of vilification.

Transferable skills

3.4 Leadership

A good leader-manager will never be made to feel uncomfortable with these identities; in fact, they should be valued, as with any diverse group. If there are areas a manager does not understand when it comes to gender identity, they can research the topic, or discuss with HR. But the easiest way to understand a person's gender identity is to simply ask! The LGBTQIA+ community are keen to raise awareness of gender identities, and welcome respectful and open-minded questions and conversation.

This brief list will give you an idea of just some of the different types of gender identities there are:

- *Cisgender:* the person's gender identity matches their assigned sex at birth.
- *Transgender:* the person's gender identity does not match the sex they were assigned at birth.
- *Non-binary:* the person does not identify exclusively as male or female, regardless of the sex they were assigned at birth.
- *Intersex:* the person is born with some combination of both biological sex characteristics.
- *Gender-fluid:* the person can express either maleness or femaleness or a combination of both on a varying basis.

It is important to note that, in short, biological sex is physical, while gender is psychological, behavioural, cultural and social. Regardless of how a person identifies, everyone should be treated equally and fairly, and this includes in incidences of bullying or vilification. People of all genders are protected by the *Sex Discrimination Act 1984* and the *Sex Discrimination Amendment (Sexual Orientation, Gender Identity and Intersex Status) Act 2013*.

31.2 Investigating complaints

Transferable skills
3.4 Leadership

> If you have made a complaint to your manager or others in your workplace and there have not been adequate steps taken to stop the bullying, there are a number of options that you can take to get help.
>
> Australian Human Rights Commission, 'Workplace bullying: Violence, harassment and bullying fact sheet'.

Investigating authorities take the way an organisation treats complaints into account as much or more than the details of the complaint itself. This makes it essential to follow your organisation's policies and procedures. People who are upset by unwelcome conduct normally complain to their leader-manager first. Never attempt to skirt around a complaint or pressure complainants to drop their claim.

Early intervention is the key. All complaints concerning harassment, violence or vilification require a prompt (within three days) formal investigation by discussing the incident(s) with the complainer and the subject of the complaint.

Take immediate steps to prevent any further occurrence of the illegal behaviour, offer the victim any necessary assistance and, when allegations are serious, suspend the alleged perpetrator. Report allegations and incidents of workplace violence to the police for investigation. Harassment and vilification allegations can be investigated and dealt with in-house unless the complainant prefers to go to an external authority. Equally, deal quickly with any behaviour that puts others at physical or psychological risk, even when you only suspect that harassment, violence or vilification may be taking place in your work group.

Conducting an investigation yourself

If your organisation hasn't nominated someone to investigate complaints, do so yourself – promptly. Determine whether the complaint is serious enough to bring in an external independent mediator. When you investigate the complaint yourself, interview the people concerned. Advise everyone you interview of the need for total confidentiality and that breaches are a disciplinary issue. This is to prevent gossip and claims of defamation. Either or both the complainant and the person accused can have a support person attend the interviews with them. Make full notes of your investigation, including the dates and times of interviews and of writing your notes.

Use the communication skills described in Chapter 6. Speak with the victim and document the allegations fully, including dates, times and any witnesses. Then put the allegations to the alleged offender and hear their version of the events. Let both the complainer and the alleged offender know about any support systems available to them, such as employee assistance programs (EAPs), harassment or violence contact officers, and peer support systems.

When there is a dispute over facts, interview any firsthand witnesses, and gather any relevant information or evidence. Evidence might be a lack of evidence where you would logically expect it to exist; complaints or information provided by other employees about the behaviour of the alleged perpetrator; records kept by the victim; personnel records that may show, for example, unexplained requests for transfer or a sudden increase in sick leave; and the complainant having discussed the matter with a counsellor, friend, medical practitioner or relative.

Try to keep the two sides apart until the issue is resolved because it can distress victims to have to carry on working with someone they feel is harassing, threatening or vilifying them. Don't move either party into a less important or less senior role, however. You may need to supervise the work group more closely while you are investigating the complaint to make sure that the behaviour does not continue, and you need to maintain the confidentiality of both the victim and the alleged offender while doing this.

Remain neutral as you look for what is actually happening. The fact that there are no witnesses is not sufficient to dismiss a complaint on the grounds that it can't be substantiated. Remember that, because of the nature of workplace violence and harassment, the matter is unlikely to be clear-cut and you may have to form an opinion based on probabilities.

Transferable skills

1.4 Business operations

2.2 Personal effectiveness

3.2 Verbal communication

3.3 Written communication

3.4 Leadership

Substantiated complaints

If you believe the complaint is substantiated, meet formally with the alleged offender to discuss the misconduct, then meet with other relevant staff (e.g. your manager) to discuss the next steps. Inform the victim of your finding and the options for addressing the matter. Do not require the victim to 'negotiate' an outcome or enter into a dispute-resolution process with the perpetrator.

Take disciplinary action with the offender in line with the seriousness of the matter so that the 'punishment' fits the 'crime'. Never excuse the behaviour or overlook it but take into account factors such as disciplinary history, including any prior similar incidents or complaints; the desired outcome of the victim; and the severity and frequency of the proscribed (illegal) behaviour.

Transferable skills

1.4 Business operations

2.2 Personal effectiveness

3.2 Verbal communication

3.3 Written communication

3.4 Leadership

Unsubstantiated complaints

When the complaint is not substantiated, possibly for lack of evidence or witnesses or on the balance of probabilities, notify both parties of the outcome. The fact that the complaint cannot be proven does not mean that harassment or violence has not occurred or that the complainer has lied. Your finding may be that the harassment, threats of violence or vilification may or may not have occurred and that it is impossible to make a conclusive finding. When that is the case, consider whether to provide further training to the work team and monitor the situation closely.

Let the complainant know about avenues for support. Employees who are dissatisfied with the outcome can complain to an independent body, such as the Australian Human Rights Commission.

Transferable skills

1.4 Business operations

2.3 Business strategy

3.2 Verbal communication

3.3 Written communication

Officially appointed investigators

Most organisations nominate a senior person formally trained and highly skilled in workplace investigations, such as the equal employment opportunity manager, health and safety manager, HR manager or workplace diversity manager, or an external expert consultant, to receive and investigate complaints relating to workplace bullying and vilification.

The investigation must be clearly impartial and independent in order to avoid allegations of cover-up or favouritism. Investigators begin by agreeing specific terms of reference with senior management and asking for the complaint to be put in writing. They then review all relevant awards, workplace agreements, legislation, policies, procedures and personnel files, prepare interview questions and arrange for a quiet, private room to meet separately with the parties concerned.

Generally, the complainant is interviewed first to obtain full details of the allegation, including the names of witnesses, if any. The subject of the complaint is then interviewed, told the exact nature of the complaint and provided with full details. The investigator obtains the alleged perpetrator's response, concentrating on the facts (not rumour or hearsay), and provides an opportunity to respond in writing. When necessary, any witnesses are then interviewed (this is not normally required when there is no dispute between the parties concerning the facts) and the investigator reinterviews the complainant, the accused person and witnesses.

The next step is usually **mediation**. The mediator should ask what the complainant's desired outcome is and advise the parties of the process and its likely duration. When the complainant is not satisfied with the outcome, a **conciliation** phase generally begins. A representative from the appropriate government body or another independent **conciliator** listens to both sides and then tries to help the parties reach an agreement or a compromise that is satisfactory to both parties.

When agreement is not reached, or if either party is unhappy with the outcome, **arbitration** is the next step. This involves tribunals and then courts, which, in most cases, have powers to enforce their decisions. Findings in favour of the complainant may include paying compensation, reinstating the complainant (when the complainant has resigned or been transferred) or other action that is felt appropriate. Hearings by a government body are in private and are relatively informal. Tribunals and courts tend to be public and more formal.

31.3 Managing for employee welfare and wellness

> There are over seven million Australians in full-time employment, each of whom spends over half of their waking hours in the workplace, so there can be no doubt the workplace has a role to play in employee health.
>
> Craig Bosworth, Industry Affairs Manager, Medibank Private, 'Physical inactivity costs billions', HRD online, 26 November 2008, http://www.hcamag.com/hr-news/physical-inactivity-costs-illions-115108.aspx.

Since 1984, employers have been required to prevent psychological as well as physical harm to employees and provide not just a safe, but also a healthy, working environment. The latest move in the health and safety arena, summarised in Figure 31.3, is to actively encourage physical and psychological health and wellbeing.

Transferable skills
1.4 Business operations
2.3 Business strategy

The organisations at the forefront of managing for employee welfare and wellness are those keenest to attract and retain a high-quality, engaged and productive workforce. The working environment they provide isn't just neutral, it actively seeks to promote employees' physical and psychological health. The best programs continuously improve their health promotion activities.[11]

Although organisations are still learning how to quantify the benefits of employee wellness programs precisely, those that have introduced them have both quantitative and qualitative evidence that well-targeted programs work. Wellness programs can help to counteract the skills shortage and boost the bottom line by:

- increasing return on learning and development investment
- improving employee engagement
- improving employee morale, satisfaction and motivation
- improving employee retention
- improving employer brand and employer value proposition
- improving work performance and productivity
- improving workplace relationships
- reducing absenteeism and sick leave
- reducing the cost of workers' rehabilitation and compensation
- reducing presenteeism.

Employees benefit too. Apart from living longer, they also gain:

- a greater capacity to enjoy life both at work and away from work
- increased health awareness and knowledge

- increased physical health and mental wellbeing
- improved morale, job satisfaction and motivation
- improved opportunities for a healthier lifestyle.

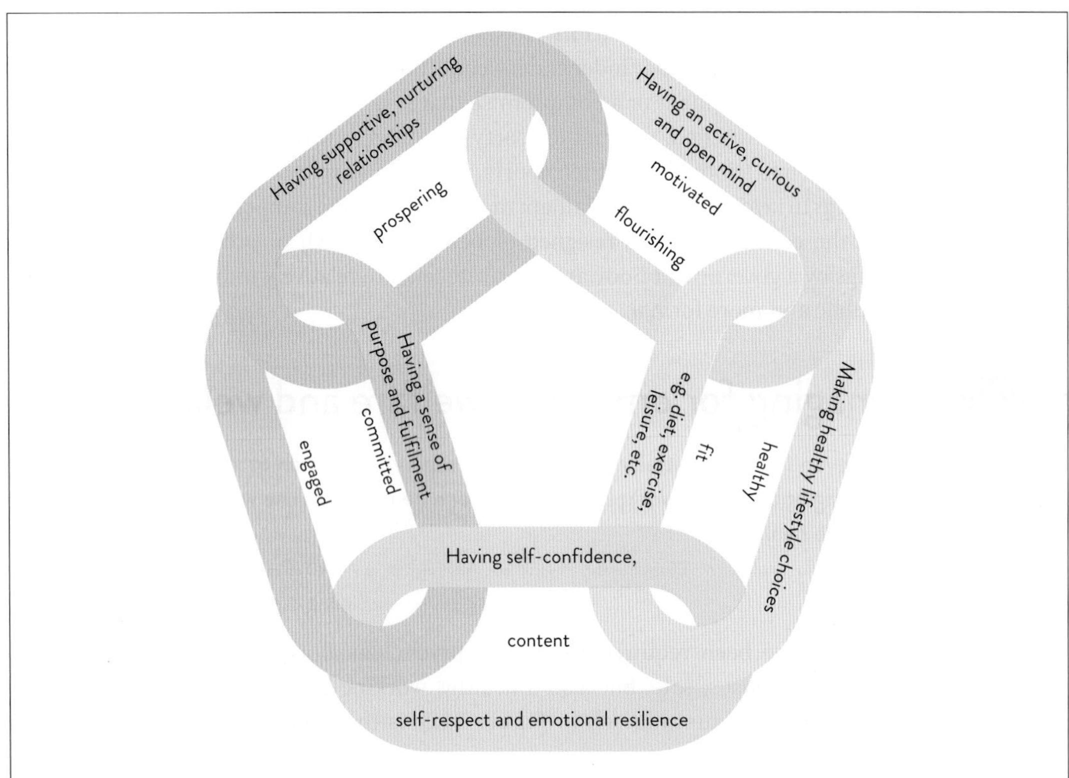

FIGURE 31.3 From preventing to encouraging

Transferable skills

2.2 Personal effectiveness

FYI

Stay at home when you're ill

Absenteeism directly costs organisations about A$578 per employee per absent day, and the Australian economy over A$44 billion a year – and that's just the direct costs. But lest you think going to work, even when you've 'just got a cold', is a better option, think again. As well as risking infecting your workmates, it costs the economy over A$34 billion a year in lost productivity. On top of that, employees who come to work when they're ill are more prone to injury.[12]

Employee welfare

Providing a working environment that is healthy begins with ensuring the workplace is well lit and ventilated and providing amenities and facilities, such as adequate drinking water, hot water, space for eating meals and toilet facilities.

IN PRACTICE

Better lighting or the Hawthorne effect?

The artificial lighting in most offices may not be the most effective in terms of maintaining employees' alertness. Research involving 104 office workers, carried out at the Surrey Sleep Centre at the University of Surrey in the UK, found that replacing traditional white-light with blue-enriched lighting helped the workers stay more alert and feel less sleepy during the day. The workers also subjectively reported improvements in concentration, mood and work performance, less eye strain, irritability and fatigue in the evening, and improved sleep quality.[13]

The Hawthorne effect, named after the Hawthorne plant of the Western Electric Company in Illinois, illustrates why experiments can have falsely positive results. A research team led by Professor Elton Mayo of Harvard University found that even minute changes in illumination levels in a factory, which at one point were as low as bright moonlight, resulted in improved productivity. During five years of experimentation between 1927 and 1932, the researchers made other refinements to the work environment, such as clearing floors of obstacles, maintaining clean workstations and relocating workstations. Productivity increased after each small change.

The researchers finally realised the actual source of the improved productivity: the relationship they had developed with the workers – one of respect and camaraderie. This type of relationship was certainly not a part of standard worker–management relations in the early 1900s. The researchers concluded that people produce more when they feel appreciated, when people pay attention to them and seek their opinions, and when their expertise is being studied. It may sound like a no-brainer today, but it was revolutionary at the time.[14]

Psychosocial factors

Transferable skills
3.4 Leadership

Psychosocial factors, the interaction of psychological and social factors, can harm or help employees' physical and psychological health, thereby affecting an organisation's effectiveness. Table 31.3 shows how much there is to be aware of, as a leader-manager, in looking after the welfare of your team members. The factors listed can cause stress and weaken the immune system to varying degrees, depending on personality attributes, such as the ability to cope with pressure, as well as factors in the work environment.[15] They open the door to physical illness and stress-related disorders. As discussed earlier, they can lead to bullying, reduced productivity and an increase in the organisation's costs through increased attrition, compensation and time off. Good employers aim to limit all of these factors. (Notice how many of these factors leader-managers can directly influence.)

TABLE 31.3 Psychosocial risk factors

Career development	Insufficient recognition and rewards; job insecurity; lack of pay and/or status, opportunities for growth and development; lack of promotion prospects; unclear or unfair performance evaluation systems; work of low 'social value'
Interpersonal relationships	Bullying, harassment and violence; customer aggression; inadequate supervision; high staff turnover; inconsiderate or unsupportive supervision; isolated or solitary work; no agreed procedures for dealing with complaints or problems; poor relationships with colleagues
Job content, poor job design	Lack of clarity of roles and responsibilities, lack of control of the work and working methods, lack of variety, monotonous and meaningless tasks, unpleasant tasks

●●●

Organisational culture	Excessive competition, incivility and lack of respect; not feeling able to ask questions, report mistakes and problems; organisational change, organisational politics, poor communication; poor leadership; unclear organisational objectives and structure
Organisational role	Suitability to job, conflicting roles within the same job, continuously dealing with other people and their problems, responsibility for people, unclear role and responsibilities, job insecurity
Participation and control	Lack of control over, for example, work environment, working hours, work methods and work pace; lack of involvement in decision-making; not feeling involved and able to influence decisions and events
Working hours	Badly designed shift systems; excessive work hours; inflexible work schedules; long and unsocial hours, and shift work; unpredictable working hours
Work–life balance	Conflicting demands of work and home life, lack of support for domestic problems at work, lack of support for work problems at home
Workload and work pace	Having too much or too little to do, excessive time pressure such as tight deadlines, unreasonable performance demands

Transferable skills

1.4 Business operations

3.1 Teamwork/relationships

3.2 Verbal communication

3.3 Written communication

5.2 Technology use

You can see that it isn't just physical risk factors, such as noise, poor seating and lighting, poor posture or repetitive movements that disrupt concentration, harm the body and lead to physical and mental problems. People's work environment, working relationships and the work itself can cause harm, too.

This means you need to identify and control both physical and psychosocial risk factors in order to provide a healthy workplace. Providing well-designed jobs and placing the right person in the right job, building strong teams and engaging employees with your leadership style and organisation culture are not just good management but part of the organisation's duty of care and part of your duty of care as a leader-manager.

Mental health

Every year, one in six people in the workforce experience a mental health problem, so it's likely that organisations of every size and in every sector need to know how to provide suitable support.[16] Employers are required to take all reasonably practicable steps to protect the mental health of their employees.

People experience mental health problems in a range of ways, from mild or moderate to severe and debilitating disorders.[17] Organisations have a duty of care to employees suffering from mental illness under the Commonwealth *Disability Discrimination and Other Human Rights Legislation Amendment Act 2009* and the Commonwealth *Privacy Act 1988*.[18] Moreover, under the Commonwealth *Disability Discrimination Act 1992*, the burden of proof is on employers to show they have taken all necessary and reasonable steps to adjust their workplaces so that employees suffering from any form of health concern or disability can work safely.

Many biological, environmental and psychosocial factors affect people's mental health. With positive mental health, or psychological wellbeing, you can interact with others and the environment in ways that you feel good about. Without it, you might develop behaviours and symptoms that distress yourself or others and interfere with your social functioning, productivity and ability to negotiate daily life.

While many organisations manage for physical safety, and support employees with physical disabilities and injuries, mental health issues are not yet as widely covered. Employees may hesitate to speak up for fear of being stigmatised and it can be difficult for leader-managers to identify problems, and to address them and offer support when they do.

Transferable skills

1.4 Business operations

3.2 Verbal communication

3.3 Written communication

3.4 Leadership

Organisations and leader-managers can help meet employees' mental health needs by creating a culture in which mental health issues are not unmentionable and by raising awareness of how people can look after their own and others' mental wellbeing. Many organisations also offer confidential assistance and support through EAPs.

Depression and stress are the two biggest mental health issues in organisations. You should also be aware of the possibility of other psychological problems, such as grief and loss, obsessive-compulsive disorders, pathological bullying, personal trauma, poor anger management, and self-esteem issues, and know your organisation's procedures for offering assistance with these.

Depression

Depression is a mood disorder characterised by feelings of loss of interest or pleasure in most activities, hopelessness and sadness, and suicidal thoughts or self-blame. It is a condition that generally comes and goes and is driven by biological or genetic factors or is a response to a major life event. Depression is linked with a range of health risk behaviours, including alcohol misuse and dependence, eating disorders, tobacco use and illicit drug use.

In Australia, 20 per cent of people suffer from depression every year. It has the third-highest burden of all diseases in both Australia (13 per cent) and globally. Rates of depression decline with age, with people aged 16–24 experiencing the highest rates.[19]

Mental illness costs the Australian economy around $60 billion each year in lost wages and reduced productivity.[20] Although it is the leading cause of non-fatal disability, and despite effective treatments, less than 50 per cent of sufferers seek professional help.[21]

Transferable skills

1.1 Financial literacy

Transferable skills

1.4 Business operations

2.3 Business strategy

3.4 Leadership

Signs that mental health support is needed

When an underperforming employee raises a psychological reason to justify poor performance or misconduct, or is repeatedly absent from work and exhibits one or more of the signs listed below, draw on your organisation's wellness programs to assist the employee and manage the underperformance (only) through counselling, as described in Chapter 16:

- aggression, bullying, boundary issues
- attendance problems (constantly arriving late, frequent absenteeism or presenteeism)
- breaks with reality, confused thoughts, odd behaviours
- difficulties following directions or following through on tasks and projects
- increased anxiety
- increased interpersonal conflict
- injuries that may be self-inflicted
- lack of emotional control
- lethargy
- poor concentration
- signs of intoxication or hangover
- social withdrawal
- tearfulness.

Stress

While a manageable level of stress is motivating, too much stress can cause productivity to deteriorate, and is a growing concern for employers and employees alike. According to the World Health Organization, 'Workers who are stressed are also more likely to be unhealthy, poorly motivated, less productive and less safe at work. Their organisations are less likely to be successful in a competitive market'.[22]

Psychosocial hazards are factors in the design or management of work that increase the risk of work-related stress and can lead to psychological or physical harm. Examples of psychosocial hazards might include poor supervisor support or high job demands.

Employees are likely to be exposed to a combination of psychosocial hazards. Some hazards might always be present at work, while others only occasionally. There is a greater risk of work-related stress when psychosocial hazards combine and act together, so employers should not consider hazards in isolation.[23] Symptoms include anxiety, cynicism, depression, excessive distrust, fatigue, headaches, loss of concentration and memory, mood swings and tiredness. The Commonwealth *Work Health and Safety Act 2011* requires organisations to manage stress-related illnesses and disorders and the return to work of employees suffering from such illnesses.

Psychosocial factors can lead not only to stress, a hazard in its own right, but also to musculoskeletal disorders. For example, stress-related changes in the body, such as increased muscle tension, can make people more susceptible to injuries, arthritis and back problems.[24]

As well as physical problems, stress, when not addressed, can lead to mental health problems such as burnout or more serious disorders like depression and anxiety. There is significant evidence that people under stress are also more vulnerable to illness. And although many employees who suffer from stress keep quiet about it, their work and morale suffer.

Transferable skills
3.4 Leadership

The first step is identifying the original cause of the stress or, when the source of the stress is outside of work, determining the conditions at work that worsen the stress. When you or the organisation can control any of the contributors to the employee's stress, you should do so. There is a range of options available to manage these situations.

Transferable skills
3.1 Teamwork/relationships
3.4 Leadership

Conducting a stress audit

To conduct a stress audit you should gather information by undertaking the following:

- Ask team members to list their main problems and sources of frustration at work and whether they feel they may be adversely affecting their health.
- Ask team members to list the three 'best' and three 'worst' aspects of their job and whether they think any of these place them under too much pressure.
- Ask more detailed questions, based on the causes of stress, asking whether any of those possible problems apply to your team members' own jobs.
- Regularly monitor absenteeism, accidents, incidents and mistakes, attrition and performance levels and look for changes, excesses and patterns.
- For organisation-wide audits, ask a representative sample of employees. This information can alert you to 'at-risk' work and work groups.

Once you have gathered information, analyse the results. Are employees who feel stressed clustered in a particular area or at a particular level? Are the numbers higher than you would expect? If so, your organisation has a duty of care to take measures to control stress. (You can find how to analyse the results of your audit in Chapter 27.) Based on the results, decide the best approach for your work group. Record what you decide to do and your reasons for choosing that approach.

Work–life harmony

Transferable skills

2.2 Personal effectiveness

Australia rates above average in all but two of 11 dimensions of quality of life. What are the out-of-kilter ones? Personal security and work–life balance. That's a concern, because, as George Eastman (inventor of roll film and founder of the Eastman Kodak Company) pointed out, 'What we do during our working hours determines what we have; what we do in our leisure hours determines what we are'.[25] (The remaining nine dimensions of quality of life are civic engagement and governance, education and skills, environmental quality, health status, housing, income and wealth, jobs and earnings, social connections and subjective wellbeing.)[26]

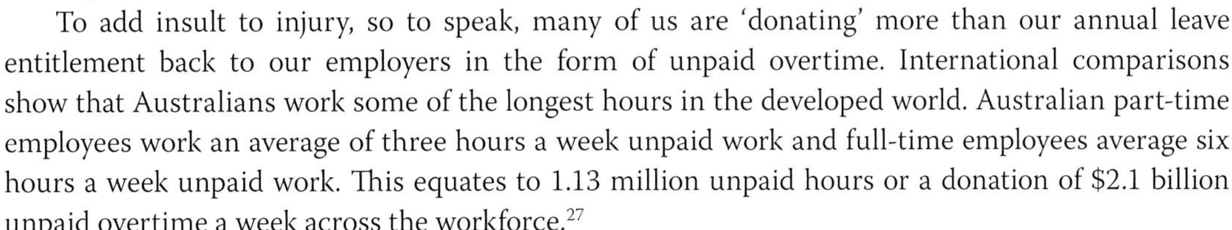

To add insult to injury, so to speak, many of us are 'donating' more than our annual leave entitlement back to our employers in the form of unpaid overtime. International comparisons show that Australians work some of the longest hours in the developed world. Australian part-time employees work an average of three hours a week unpaid work and full-time employees average six hours a week unpaid work. This equates to 1.13 million unpaid hours or a donation of $2.1 billion unpaid overtime a week across the workforce.[27]

We know that a rich life is a rounded life; maybe that's why the adage 'All work and no play makes Jack a dull boy' has stuck around for so long. So why do we work long hours? Some say that if they didn't put in the extra time the work wouldn't get done, suggesting that organisations are placing excessive demands on employees. Then there's the organisation culture, whereby unpaid overtime is often 'compulsory', 'expected' or 'not discouraged'. In some workplaces, taking advantage of work–life balance and **work–life blending** measures is a career-limiting option, despite the fact that we know that people work better and more productively when they lead balanced lives, as shown in Figure 31.4.

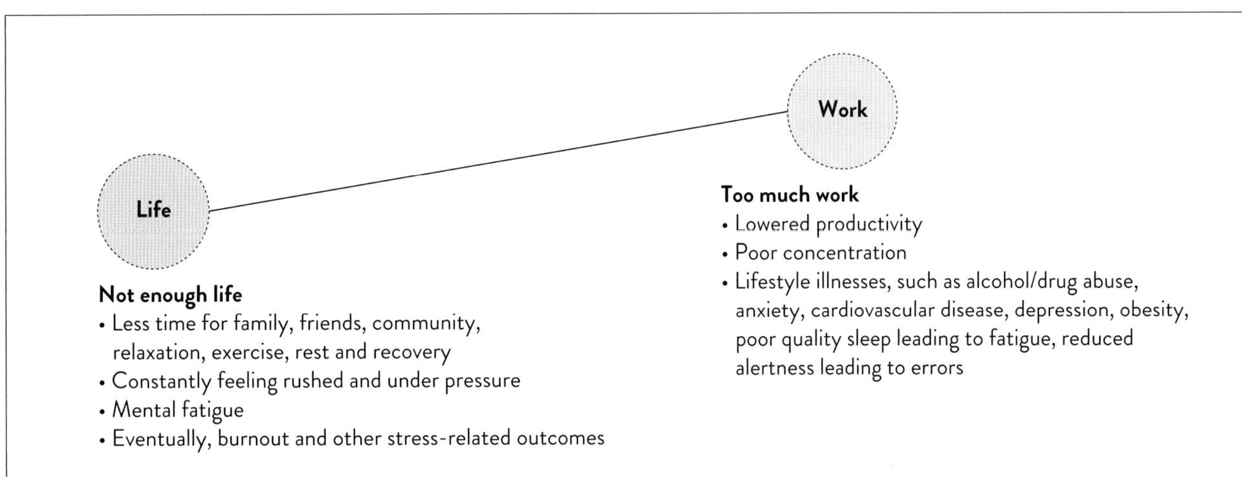

FIGURE 31.4 The results of work–life imbalance

Take a break

Studies suggest that constant connectivity wreaks havoc with people's ability to concentrate and that regular downtime leads to greater productivity. To this end, some companies insist employees take breaks. Lloyd's Bank banned all employees from travelling during the third week of every month, not only improving employees' work–life balance but also significantly reducing costs – 70 000 fewer trips were taken during the first six months after the ban.[28]

Transferable skills

1.4 Business operations

2.3 Business strategy

3.1 Teamwork/ relationships

3.4 Leadership

Why should work interfere with personal responsibilities or prevent the active enjoyment of family life? Similarly, why should home responsibilities, for example, looking after a sick child, interfere with getting our work done? We can find ways to do both. Measures such as care referral services, carer's leave and breaks, emergency childcare assistance, family rooms, on-site, near-site or work-based subsidised childcare and seasonal childcare programs suit many groups of employees and contribute to employee welfare and work-life harmony.

Here are some quicker and easier options that take less thought and administration, yet are appreciated by busy workers leading full lives:

- Extend your organisation's cafeteria hours or arrange with a local caterer to fill orders for healthy take-away meals to eat at home.
- Have a dry-cleaner collect from and deliver to your workplace.
- Invite people on personal and parental leave to attend relevant functions, meetings and training programs.
- Keep people on personal and parental leave up to date with what's happening at work.
- Negotiate with a cleaning company to provide discounted household cleaning.
- Provide technology that allows people to work from home when children are sick, to stay home for a tradesperson, to accept a delivery and so on.

Your actions as an individual leader-manager count, too. You can probably offer some of the options in the previous list to your work team. You could also do the following:

- Allow make-up time so employees can make up hours when they need time off to attend needed medical procedures, court hearings or a partner or a child's university graduation, for example.
- Allow team members to take annual leave in single days.
- Allow team members to use work mobile phones for emergency family reasons.
- Consult staff on rostering arrangements.
- Discourage regular weekend working and staying back late.
- Include your organisation's welfare and wellness policies in letters of offer to new employees.
- Introduce 'keep in touch' arrangements for staff on parental or extended sick leave.
- Negotiate flexible start and finish times.
- Schedule meetings within normal working hours.

Provide support like this to everyone equally and encourage everyone to make use of it.

Flexible working

Technology lets people work anytime, anywhere, so rather than fight it, why not make the most of it? For many employees of all ages, work–life balance has morphed into work–life blending, made possible by flexible working arrangements and communications technology. Add to this the effects of the COVID-19 pandemic, which have led to a discernible shift in executive-level perceptions of flexible working, moving it from distrust and unease to productivity and inclusion.

Transferable skills

2.2 Personal effectiveness

3.1 Teamwork/ relationships

Flexible working arrangements are becoming virtually mandatory for employers depending on a capable, engaged and productive workforce, and those wanting to retain knowledgeable older employees and other valuable employees. They are also an important way for organisations to reduce work-related stress and, along with cross-skilling and multiskilling, to respond rapidly to changing market conditions. They also multiply the other benefits of looking after employee welfare, including reduced absenteeism, attrition and presenteeism, and increased motivation and productivity.

Flexible working reflects the reality of modern Australian society by acknowledging the non-work responsibilities and outside interests of all employees. Flexible working isn't just for women with young families. In fact, offering flexible working only to women or allowing it to be seen as supporting only female employees backfires because it results in women being seen as different and more costly to employ.

Flexible working can benefit everyone, male and female, employees without families and employees with families – whether those families are traditional nuclear families or extended families and whether the family members are young, old or in between. They benefit people who want to combine work with study or community service, and people who want to downshift towards phased or permanent retirement.

A wide range of flexible working measures exists to accommodate individual needs and improve job satisfaction and family lives. Some flexible working options are shown in Table 31.4.

Transferable skills

1.4 Business operations

3.4 Leadership

TABLE 31.4 Ways to work flexibly

Annualised hours	Specifying working hours for 12 months and agreeing how best to fill the yearly quota allows employees to work flexibly and organisations to organise work around an annual cycle to meet peak demand periods as well as cover for unforeseen events such as short-term surges in demand or abnormal absenteeism
Banked time	Allowing employees to save accumulated worked time up to an agreed total of hours or weeks to 'cash in' later for time off in single days or as part of another form of leave, gives them more control over the way they blend their working and private lives and allows them increased flexibility to deal with planned or unexpected events in their private lives
Career break opportunities and sabbaticals	Extended leave from work for two to 12 months lets employees rejuvenate, study, travel, undertake carer responsibilities – whatever they want, knowing their job is waiting for them when they return
Compressed working weeks	Condensing the standard 40-hour week into fewer days; for example, nine-day fortnights or four-day weeks, lets employees work fewer days for the same pay and retains their productivity levels
Flexitime	Staggered start and finish times and a wider spread of ordinary hours, generally with mandatory attendance during specified core hours, can help employees avoid stressful and time-consuming rush hour commuting and arrange their working day to suit their personal needs
Job-sharing	Splitting a full-time job between two or more part-time workers, each receiving the relevant proportion of pay and leave and other benefits, gets the job done and allows employees to contribute part-time
Part-time working	Offering people the option to work shorter weeks extends the employment pool you can tap into
Phased retirement	Allows employees to prepare for retirement while continuing to contribute by working successively shorter days or hours over an agreed period
Purchased leave	Also called reduced work time, flexible working years and 48/52, this allows employees to have periods of up to, for example, four weeks of unpaid leave in addition to their paid leave
Teleworking	Working from home, from a satellite office or workplace hub near home or from a mobile office, such as a caravan, for all, most or some of the time, linked to the employer's office through information and communications technology offers many employees the flexibility they crave
Term-time working	Sometimes combined with temporary or on-call contractors to cover for employees needing to take time off during school holidays

Flexible working myths

Some previously held perceptions regarding flexible working are now known to be myths. They include that:

- being 'present' equals being productive and hours at work equals results
- flexible working is for non-management employees
- flexible working is for women
- flexible working means management loses control
- flexible working means productivity suffers
- flexible working is unfair to employees without children
- people should leave their personal lives at home
- people who take up flexible working options aren't serious about their jobs.

Employee wellbeing

Transferable skills

2.2 Personal effectiveness

2.3 Business strategy

Employee wellbeing goes beyond making sure employees aren't injured or have their health damaged on the job. That's health and safety management. Wellbeing is about finding ways to make work more engaging and enjoyable and helping employees manage their physical, mental and social health, as shown in Figure 31.5. This is in the organisation's as well as the employees' best interests.

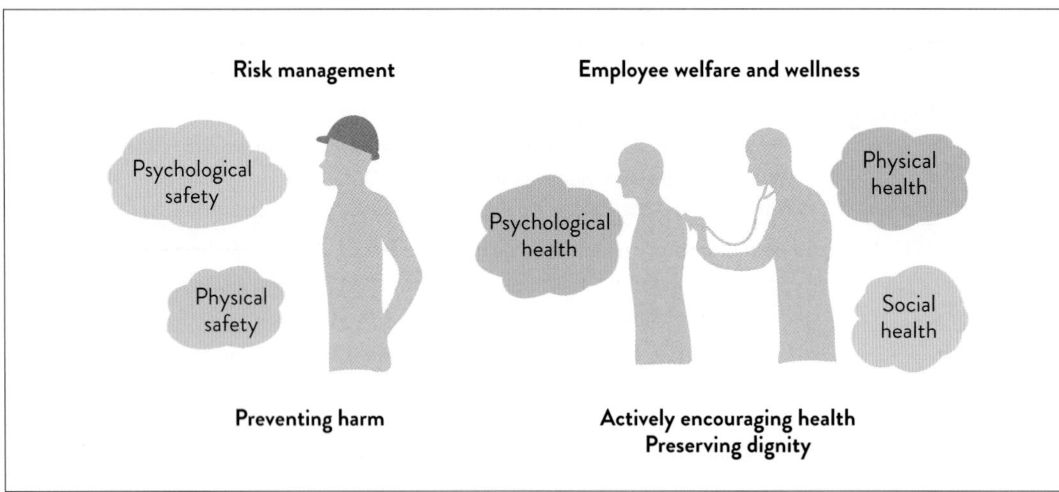

FIGURE 31.5 Components of wellness

A 'thriving' workforce – one whose employees have feelings of wellbeing – is one in which employees are not just satisfied and productive but also engaged in creating the future – their organisation's and their own. Wellness policies and programs don't just improve employees' health and wellbeing, they can also bolster the organisation's bottom-line; fit, healthy, happy people are more attentive, creative, innovative, productive and service-oriented than their out-of-sorts counterparts.

Wellness programs

Transferable skills

1.4 Business operations

Employee wellness is more a management approach than a checklist of benefits. A fair balance between effort and reward goes beyond money. It includes a good boss, good relationships with colleagues, interesting jobs, knowing how you fit into and contribute to the organisation, and procedural fairness so you know you're being treated justly. With these elements in place, you can start looking at more specific wellness programs. These might include:

- an on-site visiting nurse
- corporate gymnasium

- fitness and lifestyle packages
- flu injection subsidy
- fruit in the tearoom
- gym membership subsidy
- health and wellbeing education and promotions
- health assessments
- massage rooms
- posture improvement and ergonomics coaching
- prayer rooms.

Most people know that measures of health, such as blood pressure, cholesterol levels, glucose levels and height–weight ratios, are indicators of risk factors, but few people actually know their personal measures and risk levels. Personal health assessments can make it easy for employees to act effectively to improve their health, and the aggregate data can help organisations identify health and wellbeing risks across their workforce and develop suitable programs to address the risks. This can be done with a mixture of face-to-face checks for some of these health measures and online programs that let employees self-assess other measures. Online programs can also provide a range of follow-up tools, such as diet plans, exercise programs and a health information library.

Transferable skills
1.1 Financial literacy

Wellness programs don't have to cost a lot. When you want people to increase their fitness, give a trophy to the team or department that improves the most. Some ideas that are free and need minimal time to organise include articles in the newsletter, short emails with tips for healthy eating, brain-boosting activities and fitness, a list of health and lifestyle smartphone apps, and so on.

Evidence indicates that successful health and wellbeing programs are an excellent return on investment, decreasing disability management costs by 24.2 per cent, sick-leave absenteeism by 25.3 per cent and workers' compensation costs by 40.7 per cent. In fact, for every dollar invested in employee health and wellbeing, organisations save $5.81.[29]

To begin employee wellness efforts, identify the particular health issues affecting your own employees and design campaigns and programs to target them. Educate employees so that illnesses don't go undiagnosed, and provide information on lifestyle management to prevent and manage illness.

Employee assistance programs

Transferable skills
1.4 Business operations
2.3 Business strategy
3.1 Teamwork/relationships
3.4 Leadership

Few people go through life without a personal crisis, difficulty or problem. Perhaps that's why a huge number of Australia's top companies have implemented (or are designing) employee assistance programs (EAPs) that offer external counselling services. A large Australian study found that about twice as many women as men avail themselves of EAPs (66 per cent and 34 per cent, respectively) and nearly half of them are from Generation X (perhaps not surprising as this age group also has the highest divorce rate and highest levels of personal debt). Personal issues, mostly concerning family/relationship (35.4 per cent) or psychological difficulties (29.4 per cent), are the most common reasons for taking up the counselling, with work-related issues making up a much smaller percentage.[30]

EAPs offer confidential, short-term counselling to employees (and often their immediate families) with personal problems that affect their work performance, regardless of whether these problems are caused by workplace issues. The aim is to restore their wellbeing and return the employees to previous levels of performance. These programs have been invaluable during the COVID-19 pandemic, where employees have suffered from the negative impacts of isolation and lockdowns.

Most organisations refer employees to professionals or agencies or subcontract to EAP providers that can deal with a range of issues, such as aged care and parenting difficulties, balancing work and family, depression, eating disorders, family violence, financial difficulties, gambling, grief, legal problems, retirement planning, separation, stress and substance abuse – areas where leader-managers should rarely venture. Some EAP providers can provide crisis counselling and work with employees on disability issues and long-term illnesses.

Contact details of EAP providers should be readily available to employees. Some organisations allow employees to approach EAP services directly and receive an annual or biannual statement showing only numbers of employees counselled and the areas worked on. Other organisations request employees to approach a nominated person in the organisation, such as the HR manager or a health professional in the medical department, for referral to the appropriate professional or agency.

Transferable skills

3.1 Teamwork/relationships

3.2 Verbal communication

3.3 Written communication

3.4 Leadership

Using EAPs is generally voluntary, although leader-managers can refer or request that employees in difficulty obtain assistance when they believe it could prevent their performance from deteriorating significantly. These are considered informal referrals and generally no record appears on the employee's file. When performance has deteriorated and you believe that assistance could sufficiently improve the employee's difficulties so that performance could return to previous levels, you can make a formal referral, based on job performance. This referral may or may not appear in the employee's file, depending on your organisation's policy. What is discussed during counselling sessions of EAPs is not reported to the employer in any of these situations.

Without this strict confidentiality, employees may not avail themselves of assistance. As with any health and safety program, it is important to have senior management support, management and employee training in how the EAPs work, promotion of the EAPs and encouragement to use them, and periodic evaluation to ensure the needs of employees and the organisation are being met.

Steps you can take

Transferable skills

3.4 Leadership

What leader-manager doesn't want to increase their team's performance and productivity, their customers' satisfaction and their team members' creativity? One of the many ways is to pay attention to easing the psychosocial risks to employee welfare and wellbeing listed in Table 31.3 earlier in this chapter. How to manage to reduce or remove these risks is discussed throughout this text. The following sections look at four other ways to look after your team members' wellbeing.

Build a balanced and healthy culture in your team

Transferable skills

2.2 Personal effectiveness

3.4 Leadership

Teach your team individual wellness strategies; for example, taking short active breaks is energising; and putting your hand up for projects that engage you expands your experience, knowledge and skills, job interest and networks. Hold walking meetings with team members and short standing meetings with your team. Walking meetings can even be performed when working remotely; a video or phone call is just as effective for short, sharp communications. Get team members into the habit of walking to another team member's work area to discuss something or pass on information and taking the stairs instead of the lift, or make a pact with yourself to walk to the *next* bus stop instead of the closest one at the beginning and end of the day to get some fresh air and gather your thoughts.

Develop effective working relationships in your team

Transferable skills

2.2 Personal effectiveness

3.1 Teamwork/relationships

3.2 Verbal communication

3.3 Written communication

3.4 Leadership

Happiness is more related to moment-to-moment experiences, routine interactions with colleagues and daily contributions to projects than to job title or salary.[31] This highlights the importance of providing meaningful work and establishing a strong, respectful, high-performance team culture. Make it a pleasant work culture too – people work best when they're enjoying themselves.

Create opportunities for people to work collaboratively together on projects that use their skills and talents and to share their ideas and experience. Employees who provide lots of support to other employees, by developing good working relationships, helping out a teammate who is overloaded with work and so on, are far more likely to be engaged at work than people who provide little support to colleagues.[32] Should you witness behaviour or a conversation that disrespects someone, intervene promptly.

Help people concentrate

Transferable skills

3.1 Teamwork/relationships

3.2 Verbal communication

3.3 Written communication

3.4 Leadership

Have you ever noticed how often your mind wanders? In fact, we concentrate about 50 per cent of the workday and our minds wander – almost always to personal concerns – the other 50 per cent. But mind-wandering lowers people's spirits and productivity. People are much happier when they are *mindful* – fully engaged in what they're doing. To optimise employees' emotional wellbeing, find ways to help them concentrate. As a bonus, selective attention drives up your intelligence. The more you concentrate, the more you *can* concentrate. For example:

- Encourage people to set a goal for the task they're engaged on; working aimlessly pulls you in different directions.
- Greasy, heavy meals overload your digestive system, robbing your mind of energy; light fresh food helps you concentrate. Be a good role model and have a healthy, light lunch at work to encourage team members to do the same.
- Make sure people understand *why* their work is important; without knowing how tasks fit into the bigger picture, it's hard to concentrate on them.
- Multitasking and distractions kill your concentration – encourage people to clear their desks, silence email and other electronic alerts and work on their high priorities.
- Pent-up energy makes you mentally distracted; exercise, particularly first thing in the morning when you can sweat out impurities and reflect on the day ahead, clears your mind and uses up distracting energy.
- Regular breaks clear your mind, too, which helps you concentrate.
- When you haven't had enough rest, it's hard to concentrate. Discuss how important getting enough – but not too much – sleep is.[33]

Keep in touch

Transferable skills

3.1 Teamwork/relationships

3.2 Verbal communication

3.3 Written communication

3.4 Leadership

Have regular, informal conversations with each team member on how they're performing. Every day, send a quick email or verbally praise one team member on their work, their contribution to a larger effort or to the team, or something they did that puts the organisation's values into action. When people work with a positive mindset and know their contributions are valued, their creativity, engagement, work quality and productivity improve.

Transferable skills

1.4 Business operations

4.1 Data literacy

Measuring wellbeing

Wellbeing is about being happy and healthy, and physically and psychologically fit. You can measure employees' wellbeing by:

- *health:* physical and mental health and capacity
- *skills and experience:* the alignment of competencies to the demands of the job
- *values and motivation:* personal and professional motives and drivers, alignment of personal and professional values
- *work environment:* the physical environment, social support, nature and structure of work, and leadership quality
- *family and wider community:* the influence of relationships with others.[34]

STUDY TOOLS

QUICK REVIEW

KEY CONCEPT 31.1 

a Why should organisations be concerned about harassment, occupational violence and vilification?

b Who is most at risk of assaults on their dignity? Where does the universal precautions approach come in?

c What are some steps leader-managers can take to prevent bullying, sexual harassment, occupational violence, racial and religious vilification and gender identity vilification? What responsibility does the organisation have to protect employees?

KEY CONCEPT 31.2

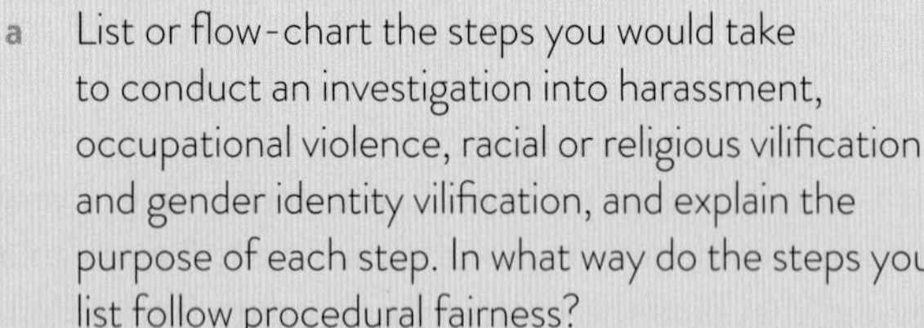

a List or flow-chart the steps you would take to conduct an investigation into harassment, occupational violence, racial or religious vilification and gender identity vilification, and explain the purpose of each step. In what way do the steps you list follow procedural fairness?

b If a complaint is unsubstantiated, does it mean the complainant was lying?

KEY CONCEPT 31.3 

a Discuss the concepts of employee welfare and wellness and why they are becoming increasingly important.

b What is meant by employee welfare? How does it differ from employee wellness? How does each affect an organisation's bottom line?

c What are the two biggest mental health issues in Australian organisations? What other employee mental health problems do you expect to cross your path as a leader-manager?

BUILD YOUR SKILLS

KEY CONCEPT 31.1 

a Discuss the factors that may lie at the heart of harassment, occupational violence and vilification.

b What's wrong with saying 'I'm sorry if I offended you' when someone objects to a remark you've made?

c Discuss the elements of a culture that values and respects people's dignity.

d Conduct an internet search for the consequences of burnout and make a list of symptoms and results. Thinking of yourself and people you know, do any seem familiar? (You could start your search with the Mentally Healthy Workplace Alliance.)

e Review three cases each of bullying, sexual harassment, occupational violence, racial and religious vilification, and gender identity vilification on the internet, and develop guidelines based on the judges' findings. Based on one of the cases you reviewed, discuss the difficulties the victim may have faced in coming forward with a complaint.

KEY CONCEPT 31.2 

a Flow-chart the procedure that an officially appointed investigator is likely to follow in dealing with a dignity complaint.

KEY CONCEPT 31.3 

a Discuss how the work environment can affect people's physical and psychological health and welfare, and feelings of wellbeing, and the measures organisations and leader-managers can take to promote employee wellbeing.

b Does your organisation have an officially appointed investigator to deal with dignity violations? If not, who do you think employees would approach to air a grievance, and why would they go to that person? (Or would they not go to anyone and suffer in silence, and if so, why?)

c Discuss and provide examples of psychosocial factors that can put employees' welfare and wellbeing at risk. Which of them can leader-managers affect?

d Work and the workplace affect people's mental health for better or for worse and employees' health problems affect the workplace. Discuss.

WORKPLACE ACTIVITIES

KEY CONCEPT 31.1 

a Who in your organisation is most at risk of dignity violations and why?

b How would you describe the culture of your workplace and your work team with respect to valuing and respecting people's dignity?

c Does your organisation have a policy regarding employee welfare and dignity? If so, how fully does it address the criteria given in this chapter? How might it be strengthened?

d What do your workplace statistics on harassment, occupational violence and vilification indicate about its dignity culture? Do low numbers of complaints mean that your organisation is 'in the clear'?

e Develop a plan for keeping your team members abreast of employee welfare and wellness initiatives in your organisation.

f Draw a Pareto chart, for the main categories of dignity injuries (harassment, occupational violence, vilification and mental illness). If harassment numbers are high, prepare a stratification chart breaking bullying down into the types of bullying and do the same with vilification. Draw another Pareto chart showing the groups of workers affected in your organisation (e.g. males, females, employees in various age groups, employees by area and by occupation). Break this down further by charting specific dignity injuries by groups of workers. What do your charts tell you about who is most at risk in your organisation, where and from what? Establish priorities and a target for improving the situation.

KEY CONCEPT 31.2 

a Why might employees in your workplace be reluctant to come forward with a dignity grievance?

b Flow-chart your organisation's procedure for dealing with complaints regarding assaults on employee dignity. Do you see any areas where it could be strengthened?

KEY CONCEPT 31.3 

a What employee welfare and wellbeing measures does your organisation take? Build a case for increasing programs in these areas. List the actions you have taken as an individual leader-manager to enhance the welfare and wellbeing of the people who report to you.

b Investigate the concept of 'mindfulness' and discuss how it can help leader-managers perform their own role better and how it can help the productivity and satisfaction of their team members.

c Make a persuasive case for introducing wellbeing practices in your organisation.

EXTENSION ACTIVITIES

Referring to the Snapshot at the beginning of this chapter, answer the following questions:

1 How would you rate Lee's performance at delivering the news to the HR team?
2 What does the constant use of the word 'we' create an assumption about regarding who was responsible for the failures identified – the entire company, just the decision-makers or just the members of the team?
3 How would you, as a leader-manager, have delivered this message and outcome to the team, and how do you think your method would have made it more effective?

CASE STUDY 31

CARMEN'S PROBLEM

'Come in, Carmen, and sit down. I want to talk to you about how you're getting on here. You seem a bit nervous and edgy lately and I'm worried that it seems to be affecting your work performance. Is anything wrong?'

'No, everything's fine ... (pause) ... It's just, well – oh, it's nothing, really. Not important.'

'I'd like to hear what it is, Carmen, although of course I'll understand if it's personal and you'd rather not tell me.'

'It's stupid – you'll think I'm just being silly ...'

'It seems to be bothering you, whatever it is. Why don't you tell me about it?'

'Well, you know how the men fool around and make jokes and things.'

'Yes, I know they all get along well together. What is it you mean, Carmen?'

'Well, they tease us a lot. It doesn't seem to bother the other girls much, but it makes me upset. I'm not used to that sort of thing. I don't know what to do about it.'

'What do you mean, they "tease" you?'

'For instance, when we have to climb up those ladders to get at the things stored up high, they make remarks. I don't always understand what they say, but they always laugh loudly and I get embarrassed. I sometimes drop things and they laugh even louder.'

'Is this only with you, or does this happen with the other women too?'

'Oh, no, it isn't just me – they tease them, too. I don't think they really like it much either, but they pretend to laugh back.'

'I see ...'

Questions

1 If you were Carmen's manager, what would you say now?
2 What action would you take?
3 How difficult do you think it was for Carmen to talk about this?

CHAPTER ENDNOTES

1 Australian Human Rights Commission, 'Industries where sexual harassment occurs', 2018, https://www.humanrights.gov.au/chapter-6-working-without-fear-results-sexual-harassment-national-telephone-survey-2012, accessed 14 September 2021.

2 David Morrison, transcript of speech to Australian Army personnel, http://vividmethod.com/transcript-the-standardyou-walk-past-is-the-standard-you-accept, accessed 14 September 2021.

3 Ibid.

4 HRM Solutions, 'Workplace bullying in Australia – is it happening in your workplace?', https://www.hrmresolutions.com.au/workplace-bullying-in-australia

5 Australian Human Rights Commission, 'Fact sheet: Workplace bullying', https://www.humanrights.gov.au/info_for_employers/fact/workplace.html, accessed 14 September 2021.

6 Andrew Riley, 'Ostracism more damaging than bullying in the workplace', *University of British Columbia media release*, 29 May 2014, https://news.ubc.ca/2014/05/29/better-to-be-bullied-than-ignored-in-the-workplace-study, accessed 14 September 2021; Lynn Stuart Parramore, 'The social death penalty: Why being ostracised hurts even more than bullying', *Truthout*, 5 June 2014,

http://truth-out.org/news/item/24158-the-social-death-penalty-why-being-ostracized-hurts-even-more-than-bullying, accessed 14 September 2021; Jane O'Reilly, Sandra Robinson, Jennifer Berdahl, Sara Banki, 'Is negative attention better than no attention? The comparative effects of ostracism and harassment at work', *Organization Science*, 4 April 2014, http://pubsonline.informs.org/doi/10.1287/orsc.2014.0900, accessed 14 September 2021.

7 Australian Government, *Sex and Age Discrimination Legislation Amendment Act 2011*, http://www.austlii.edu.au/au/legis/cth/num_act/saadlaa2011427/sch1.html, accessed 14 September 2021.

8 Camilla Gebicki, Alexandra Meagher, Gabrielle Flax, 'Everyone's business: Fourth national survey on sexual harassment in Australian workplaces', Australian Human Rights Commission, 2018.

9 Australian Human Rights Commission, 'Everyone's business: Fourth national survey on sexual harassment in Australian workplaces', 2018, https://humanrights.gov.au/our-work/sex-discrimination/publications/everyones-business-fourth-national-survey-sexual?_ga=2.242075393.2006761046.1631930058-1486070698.1631581693

10 WorkSafe Victoria, 'Occupational violence and aggression in your industry', https://www.worksafe.vic.gov.au/occupational-violence-and-aggression, accessed 16 September 2021.

11 World Health Organization, 'WHO Healthy Workplace Framework and Model', https://www.who.int/occupational_health/healthy_workplace_framework.pdf, accessed 14 September 2021.

12 Australian Industry Group, 'Absenteeism and presenteeism survey 2015', https://www.aigroup.com.au/policy-and-research/industrysurveys/absencesurvey/; Lucy Carter, 'Presenteeism costs economy $34 billion a year through lost productivity, report shows', *ABC News*, 12 April 2016, http://www.abc.net.au/news/2016-04-12/presenteeism-costing-the-economy-billions/7318832, accessed 14 September 2021.

13 Vitality Works, 'The importance of work wellbeing and how it can affect your bottom-line', https://vitalityworks.health/work-wellbeing, accessed 21 September 2021.

14 Rob McCarney, James Warner, Steve Iliffe, Robbert van Haselen, Mark Griffin, Peter Fisher, 'The Hawthorne effect: A randomised, controlled trial', *BMC Medical Research Methodology,* Vol. 7, p. 30.

15 Health and Safety Executive, 'Manual handling assessment chart (the MAC tool)', http://www.hse.gov.uk/msd/mac/index.htm, accessed 14 September 2021; see also Consortium for Organizational Mental Healthcare, 'Guarding minds at work', 2010, http://www.guardingmindsatwork.ca, accessed 14 September 2021.

16 Domini Stuart, 'A mental health check', *Company Director*, January 2017, http://aicd.companydirectors.com.au/membership/company-director-magazine/2016-back-editions/december/a-mental-health-check, accessed 14 September 2021.

17 Australian Government, 'Department of Health and Ageing, National Mental Health Report 2013: Tracking progress of mental health reform in Australia, 1993–2011', https://www.health.gov.au/internet/publications/publishing.nsf/Content/mental-pubs-n-report13-toc, accessed 14 September 2021.

18 Commonwealth of Australia, 'Explanatory Memoranda, Disability Discrimination and Other Human Rights Legislation Amendment Bill 2009'; also see Australian Government – Office of the Australian Information Commissioner, *Privacy Act 1988*, https://www.oaic.gov.au/privacy/the-privacy-act, accessed 21 September 2021.

19 Australian Government, 'National Mental Health Report 2013', Department of Health, op. cit.

20 Peter Ryan, 'Mental illness costing Australian economy $60b a year, research shows', *ABC News*, 4 October 2019, https://www.abc.net.au/news/2019-10-04/mental-illness-costing-australian-economy-60-billion-a-year/11573966?utm_campaign=abc_news_web&utm_content=link&utm_medium=content_shared&utm_source=abc_news_web, accessed 14 September 2021.

21 Ibid.

22 World Health Organization, 'Work organisation and stress', accessed 14 September 2021.

23 WorkSafe Vic, 'Psychosocial hazards', https://www.worksafe.vic.gov.au/psychosocial-hazards-contributing-work-related-stress, accessed 14 September 2021.

24 Health and Safety Executive, 'Manual handling assessment chart (the MAC tool)'.

25 Elizabeth Brayer, *George Eastman: A biography,* University of Rochester, 2006, p. 346.

26 Organisation for Economic Co-operation and Development, 'How's life in Australia?', November 2017, https://www.oecd.org/statistics/Better-Life-Initiative-country-note-Australia.pdf, accessed 14 September 2021.

27 David Baker, Molly Johnson, Richard Denniss, 'Walking the tightrope: Have Australians achieved work/life balance?', 2014, The Australia Institute, http://www.tai.org.au/content/walking-tightrope-have-australians-achieved-*worklife-balance*, accessed 15 September 2021.

28 Michael Burd, James Davis, 'Workplace rights: Email emancipation', *Management Today* (UK), March 2012; see also 'Flipping the switch: Who is responsible for getting employees to take a break?', Knowledge@Australian School of Business, 20 February 2012, http://knowledge.wharton.upenn.edu/article/flipping-the-switch-who-is-responsible-for-getting-employees-to-take-a-break, accessed 14 September 2021.

29 2TwoHands, 'Employee Corporate Wellness Program Statistics', https://www.2handsmassage.com.au/corporate-massage/corporate-wellness-program-statistics, accessed 14 September 2021.

30 K. Kind, 'Coping strategies', *Sydney Morning Herald: My Career Supplement*, 30 October 2011, p. 5.

31 Shawn Achor, 'Positive intelligence', *Harvard Business Review*, January–February 2012.

32 Ibid.

33 See for example, Healthline, '12 tips to improve your concentration', https://www.healthline.com/health/mental-health/how-to-improve-concentration, accessed 14 September 2021.

34 Smart Company, 'The EY Australian Productivity Pulse', https://www.smartcompany.com.au/finance/ey-australian-productivity-pulse-nsw-workers-most-productive-but-businesses-missing-out-on-latent-potential, accessed 14 September 2021.

CHAPTER

32

MOVING FROM DIVERSITY TO INCLUSION

After completing this chapter, you will be able to:

32.1 spot discrimination when it occurs and explain how diversity and inclusion benefit organisations, employees, customers and the country

32.2 develop and implement strategies to build a diverse and inclusive workplace

32.3 promote inclusion in your work team.

TRANSFERABLE SKILLS

The following transferable skills are covered in this chapter:

1 **Business competence**
- **1.1** Financial literacy
- **1.4** Business operations

2 **Critical thinking and problem solving**
- **2.1** Critical thinking
- **2.2** Personal effectiveness
- **2.3** Business strategy

3 **Social competence**
- **3.1** Teamwork/relationships
- **3.2** Verbal communication
- **3.3** Written communication
- **3.4** Leadership

4 **Data literacy**
- **4.1** Data literacy

OVERVIEW

Perhaps a few of your team members look too young to shave and some are old enough to be your grandparents. Maybe one or two sport a nose ring while another dons a hijab and yet another a turban. Maybe one is an athlete and another is in a wheelchair, and some have parenting responsibilities while others care for elderly relatives. This shouldn't be too surprising in a country made up of people of varying abilities, ages and responsibilities, and who come from diverse backgrounds and heritages. We vary in aptitudes, education, ethnicity, family status, generations, personality styles, political leanings, physical and mental abilities, race, religion, gender identities, sexual orientation and socio-economic status. Australia truly is one of the most diverse nations in the world.

Transferable skills

2.1 Critical thinking

2.2 Personal effectiveness

3.3 Written communication

3.4 Leadership

Can you work with, include, motivate and bring out the best in a changing and diverse workforce, not just as groups of employees but also as individuals, each with their own unique needs and preferences? Organisations and work teams that reflect the diversity of the general population, their customers and other stakeholders can have a distinct advantage over homogeneous organisations and teams. That is, as long as they don't try to apply one set of rules to today's wide range of employees, and provided they're well led and everyone has the same opportunities to contribute and develop their skills.

In this chapter, you will find out how to tap the vast Australian reservoir of potential. But a word of warning – don't become so aware of differences that you ignore similarities. What people hold in common provides the basis for building a strong work team. Finding a way to include everyone's diverse attributes is what makes diversity – and teams – powerful.

SNAPSHOT

Transferable skills
3.4 Leadership

I have your back

Former Army Lieutenant-Colonel Malcolm McGregor, a cricket-loving, rugby-playing member of the Order of Australia awarded for exceptional service to the Australian Army, had felt like an 'out of tune orchestra'. Something was not right. Conflicted about his gender from childhood and on the brink of suicide, he finally stopped fighting his inner feelings and transitioned to Lieutenant-Colonel Catherine (Cate) McGregor.

What would her boss, David Morrison, with whom, as Malcolm, she had served as an infantry soldier many years before, make of the transition? Morrison said to her, simply, 'I'm with you.' Morrison remained true to his commitment to stamp out the Army's grim record as a place of bullying and sexual harassment and transform it into a place where respect is a core value.

His support, acceptance and affirmation of Catherine's value as a human being and as a soldier became a contributing factor to her life as a woman: 'It's a wonderful feeling to be alive and be me,' she said in an interview in 2014.[1]

32.1 Understanding diversity and inclusion

> **.... but that's the point – women have to be exceptional to succeed, while even the average man can expect to earn at least 18 per cent more and occupy at least 70 per cent more of the leadership roles in business and politics.**
>
> Denise Kingsmill, 'What glass ceiling?', *Management Today*, March 2016, p. 29.

Australia is a vast country, filled with an eclectic mix of people, each with the potential to make meaningful contributions to our economy and to society. But it's easy to unwittingly close doors to people and exclude them from opportunities, based on misconceptions and stereotypes.

There is no doubt that the members of particular groups experience higher levels of unemployment than the population in general, and many face barriers and other disadvantages in their employment throughout their working lives. The groups most at risk of discrimination in Australia are:

- Aboriginal and Torres Strait Islander peoples
- immigrants
- people with disabilities
- women
- people of a more advanced age.

This doesn't mean that every person who belongs to one or more of these groups is disadvantaged, but they are more likely to be disadvantaged than those who do not. Statistically, for example, individuals who are members of these groups tend to be:

- concentrated in a limited range of occupations
- concentrated in low-paying, low-status jobs
- excluded from the labour force for reasons not related to their ability to perform a job
- limited in their opportunities for career progression
- more likely to be unemployed
- more likely to face prejudice when applying for a job and throughout their working life.

Some of the workplace barriers people from disadvantaged groups face include:

- a shortage of affordable childcare, which particularly affects women
- a conscious or unconscious bias in recruiting, assignments and promotions, pay and bonuses, and in other employment-related decisions
- exclusion from informal networks
- lack of mentoring and sponsorship opportunities
- lack of role models (e.g. fewer people from disadvantaged groups are on boards of directors or work at management level)
- perceptions that cultural or religious practices, family responsibilities and so on interfere with work.

As a result, organisations aren't making full use of the talent available. What a waste.

Not a pretty picture

Australia has the lowest percentage of women in management and one of the most gender-segregated workforces in the industrialised world. Women are employed in a narrower range of industries and occupations than men, are clustered lower down the organisational hierarchy and are offered less training than men. The national gender pay gap is 22.8 per cent.[2]

Similar patterns are found in other groups of Australians, such as immigrants, older workers and people from culturally and linguistically diverse backgrounds.

Recognise bias

Have you ever experienced or seen any of the following behaviours:

- an idea you put forward being met with silence or ignored yet, when brought up later by someone else, is taken up enthusiastically
- assumptions being made about your abilities, commitment and dedication to your career because of 'who' you are
- being accorded low informal status in a group because you speak less than others
- having to prove yourself over and over again
- having to provide an abundance of evidence to show you're competent in order to be seen as equally competent
- your mistakes being noticed more readily and remembered for longer
- your success being put down to luck rather than skill?

People from minority groups experience these behaviours frequently but unless they happen to you, you may not notice them when they happen to others. But they happen nevertheless. They are the result of biases.

We all have biases, both for and against things. Biases can be a handy shorthand for quickly evaluating events, people and situations. But when they're based on stereotypes, they prevent us from seeing people as they really are and limit our ability to interact successfully with them. When biases rule people 'in' or 'out' based on irrelevant characteristics (gender, schooling, wealth), they harm the people who hold them, the people they are aimed at, work teams, organisations and society.

When biases put people at a disadvantage, the result is discrimination. When you disadvantage (i.e. discriminate) against people from some groups (let's call them the 'out groups') you automatically advantage people who aren't in those groups (let's call them the 'in group'). And the opposite holds true – when you advantage people from the 'in group', you automatically disadvantage those who aren't in the 'in group'.

Transferable skills

3.1 Teamwork/ relationships

3.4 Leadership

Because biased thinking leads to two-dimensional thinking, there is a tendency to see people in the 'out groups' in either–or terms: black–white, creative–not creative, female–male, straight–gay. But people are much more than a simplistic either–or. People are a complex package of characteristics, skills and abilities. What we need to do is acknowledge differences but not let them define a person or blind us to what's important; that is, their values and integrity, ability to contribute or innovate, their self-understanding and communication skills.

Anti-discrimination legislation

Transferable skills

1.4 Business operations

3.2 Verbal communication

3.3 Written communication

3.4 Leadership

4.1 Data literacy

Discrimination is against the law. Outlawing a behaviour doesn't make it stop, of course, but at least when you know the law, you know the obvious pitfalls to avoid. Known collectively as anti-discrimination legislation, state and territory legislation closely mirrors the following federal Acts:

- *Workplace Gender Equality Act 2012* (updating the *Equal Opportunity for Women in the Workplace Act 1999* and renaming the Equal Opportunity for Women in the Workplace Agency the Workplace Gender Equality Agency)
- *Fair Work Act 2009* with amendments up to 2017
- *Australian Human Rights Commission Act 1986* (formerly the *Human Rights and Equal Opportunity Commission Act 1986*)
- *Age Discrimination Act 2004* with amendments up to 2020
- *Disability Discrimination Act 1992* with amendments up to 2018
- *Sex Discrimination Act 1984* with amendments up to 2018
- *Racial Discrimination Act 1975* with amendments up to 2015.

These Acts are the key legislative mechanisms for achieving diversity and equality in employment and in other areas of life. They prohibit discrimination based on any of the factors shown in Figure 32.1. They are based on common sense and fair play and aim to ensure everyone has equal opportunity. The legislation covers full-time and part-time employees, temporary employees and contractors. These laws describe how and to whom people can make complaints concerning discrimination and provide a means to rectify or compensate for acts of discrimination.

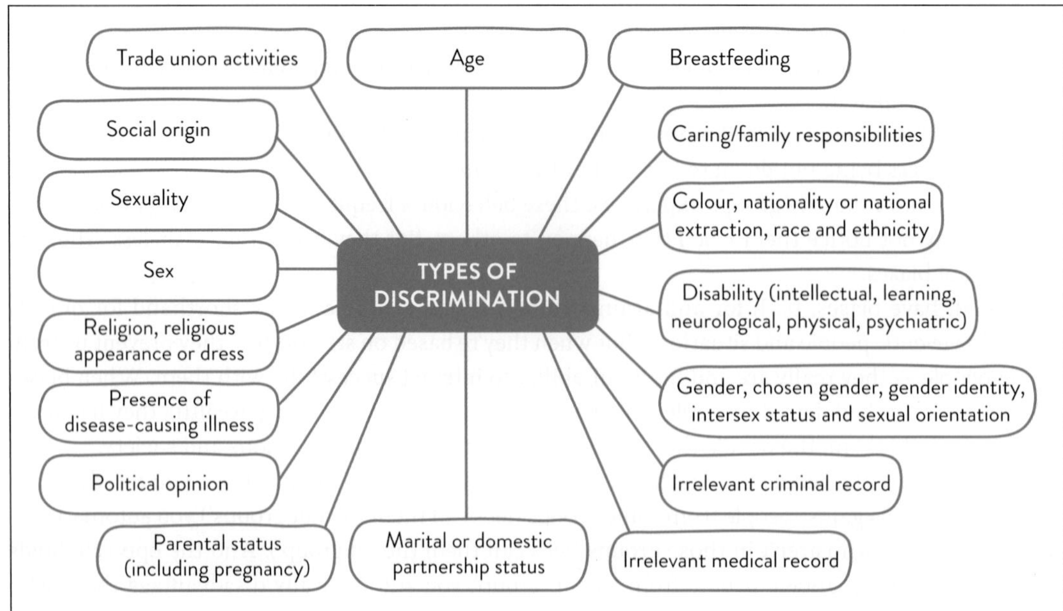

FIGURE 32.1 Don't discriminate!

Anti-discrimination legislation requires organisations to examine their policies and identify and eliminate differences in employee benefits, conditions of employment, pay, perks, promotions, superannuation, transfers and a host of other job-related conditions. It requires all leader-managers to make objective decisions relating to hiring, firing, paying, promoting, training and developing, and transferring employees. Two important principles can help:

Transferable skills

1.1 Financial literacy

1.4 Business operations

2.2 Personal effectiveness

2.3 Business strategy

3.4 Leadership

1. Make *merit* – a person's ability to do a job – the sole consideration in employment decisions and ignore irrelevant factors such as age, nationality and gender.
2. Only take into account job-related characteristics, particularly skills and abilities.

You can find out more about anti-discrimination legislation at https://www.humanrights.gov.au/employers/good-practice-good-business-factsheets/quick-guide-australian-discrimination-laws and https://www.ag.gov.au/RightsAndProtections/HumanRights/Pages/Australias-Anti-Discrimination-Law.aspx.

It's comforting to have legislation, but compliance isn't the only answer. If it were, organisations would have embraced diversity by now and learnt how to make everyone feel welcome. Similarly, most organisations have a range of policies, including policies on diversity and dignity, but we've known for some time that policies are sometimes adopted for symbolic or tokenistic reasons and, as a result, do not accomplish their stated purpose. Legislation and policies aren't enough. To truly reap the benefits of diversity and inclusion, we need people to know that we need them.

Transferable skills

2.2 Personal effectiveness

2.3 Business strategy

3.4 Leadership

The merit principle

Transferable skills

1.4 Business operations

2.3 Business strategy

3.4 Leadership

The merit principle was originally intended to fight nepotism – giving your relatives the plum jobs. It has since become diversity's catchcry. But research has shown that merit might end up biasing in favour of the 'in group' anyway.[3] For example, when recruiting, selectors look first for the clear 'hires' and clear 'rejects' and then concentrate on the 'maybe' pile, which is where stereotypes of women and people from minority groups shape the decisions.

When women and others from a disadvantaged group lack one of the 'hire' criteria (e.g. business acumen, communication skills, cultural fit or maths skills), they move straight into the 'reject' pile, even when they are strong in the other areas. White men lacking in one of the 'hire' criteria are considered 'coachable' or that they 'had an off day' and remain under consideration. To reach their final decision, recruiters move from considering performance to 'gut feel' and 'personal chemistry', which buys into the tendency to hire 'people like us'.

To make matters worse, candidates in the 'maybe' pile often need a 'champion' among the selectors and 'champions' support those most like themselves. Female selectors and other selectors from minority groups champion fewer candidates, perhaps because they feel more vulnerable, since women and others from disadvantaged groups who champion diversity are penalised with lower performance ratings.

Ways to discriminate

Which of these statements do you agree with?

- A person's status is a good indicator of their value to an organisation and society.
- It's better to try to conform to the norms of the workplace than be true to yourself.
- Men are less patient and intuitive but better with numbers and decision-making than women.
- More women than men work part-time; they, and others who work part-time, are less committed to their jobs than people who work full-time.
- People with accents shouldn't work in customer service.
- People with disabilities aren't as productive as people without disabilities.

- Shy, quiet people aren't self-motivated highfliers.
- You should speak loudly and slowly to people in wheelchairs.
- Women don't need to earn as much as men.

Most people wouldn't agree with any of these statements. So why do many people behave as though they're true?

How would you define discrimination? We don't always know it when we see it because sometimes, even when discrimination is right in front of our nose, we may not notice it. People in the 'in group' generally don't notice their own unearned advantages and they generally don't notice others' unearned disadvantages – it's 'just the way things are'. Sometimes discrimination is blatant and we notice it, yet we ignore it, tacitly accepting it.

Direct discrimination

There are two types of **direct discrimination**: overt and covert. Have you ever heard someone say, 'We don't want to employ a woman because women can't handle the pressure' or 'Don't employ an Aboriginal – he'll go walkabout on you'? That is **overt discrimination** – clear, direct discrimination on the grounds of race, sex, social origin or one of the other factors listed in Figure 32.1. **Covert discrimination** is subtler and therefore more difficult to spot. People who discriminate covertly are often unaware that they are discriminating at all.

There are two types of covert discrimination. Have you ever heard someone say, 'I try not to hire newlyweds because they're likely to start a family and might take parental leave' or 'It's risky hiring students – they're just here for the beer money'? That type of covert discrimination makes assumptions about people based on characteristics that belong to *some* members of a group – but not to *everyone* in that group.

For instance, assuming that a woman plans to have a family and intends to leave paid employment to do so can make managers reluctant to promote, train or otherwise invest time, money or effort in her. Or the skills of women returning to work after taking a career break to stay at home with young children may be perceived as outdated or rusty, making some managers reluctant to hire them. Women's child-bearing role – the 'Mummy penalty' – has placed women (whether they're mothers or not) at a disadvantage in employment and employment-related matters.

A second type of covert discrimination is based on characteristics that are incorrectly or unfairly associated with people of a particular group. These are normally assumptions based on stereotypes. Saying: 'Employing someone with a physical disability would make the rest of the staff feel uncomfortable' is an example of this type of discrimination.

Indirect discrimination

Indirect discrimination occurs when policies or practices appear on the surface to be neutral but actually adversely affect a particular group of people. It often results from assumptions that everyone is the same as the policy-makers (the 'in group') and these assumptions are embedded into the organisation's policies, practices and procedures. An example of indirect discrimination is providing information about health and safety, leave policies, or training opportunities only in English.

Other examples of indirect discrimination can be less easy to spot. 'Our business can't accept cheques without a driver's licence as proof of identity'. Fair enough? What about people who are blind and don't drive and therefore don't have a driver's licence – or even those who don't have a disability, but just don't have a driver's licence. Discrimination can creep in, unnoticed, if we're not careful.

Religious discrimination

You apply for an accountancy position with a small manufacturing company through a recruitment agency. Both the recruitment agency and the company interview you and you are offered the position. The company then withdraws its offer because you need time during the day for prayer.

You register a complaint with the Australian Human Rights Commission, explaining that you advised the recruitment agency that you are Muslim and need to arrange a room at the workplace where you can conduct your daily prayers. You say that you need about three 10-minute prayer breaks during the day and could undertake one set of prayers during your lunch break.

The company says it withdrew its offer of employment for two reasons. First, it has concerns about your honesty because in the interview you did not disclose your need for additional breaks, despite being asked whether anything would prevent you from working normal office hours. Second, despite these concerns, it attempted to find a suitable location for your prayers but, because the office is open plan, the only options available were the meeting room, which has a glass wall, or a nearby park. The company says you rejected these suggestions. Therefore, the company denies it discriminated against you on the ground of your religion.

The Commission holds a conciliation conference. The company agrees to pay you compensation and provide you with a statement of regret.

Systemic discrimination

Transferable skills

2.3 Business strategy

3.4 Leadership

Many organisations have gone about as far as they can to remove the more obvious types of discrimination and it is now up to individual leader-managers to identify and remove the nearly invisible *structural,* or **systemic discrimination**, that remains. This is longstanding direct and indirect discrimination that has been common practice for so long in an organisation or industry that it seems to be the natural order of things. It is based on established employment practices and unchallenged assumptions about people from particular groups.

Unlike indirect discrimination, which can affect only a few people or occurs in isolated instances, systemic discrimination affects many people. Because it is entrenched in 'the way we do things', structural discrimination is more difficult to recognise, and potentially of greater sensitivity and difficulty to deal with.

The recruitment and performance review methods discussed in the section 'The merit principle' earlier in this chapter, are examples of systemic discrimination. Requirements to work overtime or long hours (paid or unpaid), to travel and work at home on weekends and so on, assume that someone else can look after home duties, including household management (e.g. cooking, cleaning, shopping) and care for children and the elderly; that someone is usually assumed to be a woman. The segregation of occupations is another example of systemic discrimination, as are training only male machine operators to set up machines when a vacancy for a setter-operator occurs, recruiting Asians to assemble tiny hearing aids because smaller hands suit them to this work, or considering only female applicants for personal assistant positions.

Here are some questions to help determine whether systemic discrimination is occurring:

Transferable skills

1.4 Business operations

2.1 Critical thinking

3.4 Leadership

4.1 Data literacy

- *Are people expected to comply with conditions or requirements that put them at a disadvantage?* For example, when a building has no wheelchair access or toilet facilities for people with a disability, people who use a wheelchair would find it difficult to report to work and work normally.
- *Are people with a particular characteristic expected to comply with a requirement or condition that it is not possible for them to comply with?* For example, it is unreasonable to continually

switch meetings to 5 p.m. at short notice even though some employees need to leave at 5 p.m. to pick up children from day care.

- *Are people with a particular characteristic expected to comply with a requirement or condition that the majority of people without that characteristic can comply with more easily?* For example, employees with child or parental care responsibilities may find it more difficult to attend weekend training workshops or to travel away from home for extended periods on business, things which people from the 'in group' find easy to do.

Unearned disadvantage, unearned advantage

As shown in Figure 32.2, there are really two sides of the diversity/inclusion coin – unearned disadvantage and unearned advantage. We've been looking at unearned disadvantage, which for most people is easier to talk about than unearned advantage: 'It's an Aboriginal problem'; 'It's a religious issue'; 'It's a girl thing'.

For those in the 'in group' with unearned advantages, it can be more difficult to acknowledge your success when, rather than put it down to hard work and brains, you must accept that part of it is due to the good luck of being born into the 'right' religion, race, gender, sexual orientation or class, or being the 'right' age. When you have a characteristic that isn't 'right' (not 'wrong' but not 'right' either), when you aren't Protestant, white, male, straight, economically well-off or young, you don't glide as easily through life.[4]

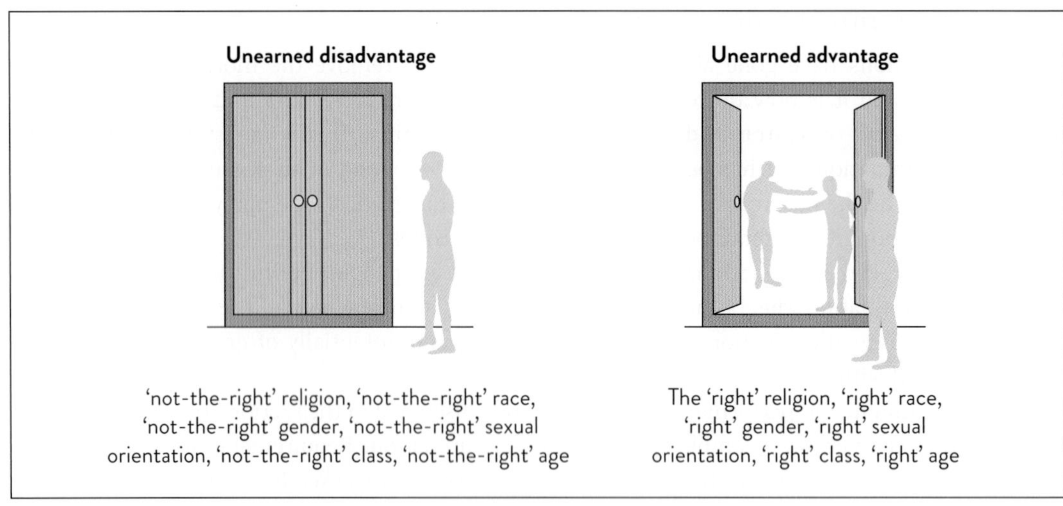

FIGURE 32.2 Unearned disadvantage, unearned advantage

The diversity dividend

Transferable skills
1.4 Business operations
2.3 Business strategy
3.1 Teamwork/relationships
3.4 Leadership

Contrary to what you might think, there are no benefits from diversity per se. None at all. The benefits come from *inclusion* – from welcoming a diverse range of people that reflect your stakeholders into all aspects of your organisation's operations. You can have a wide range of workers from all age groups and from all continents of the world, who follow various religious practices and have a range of sexual orientations and gender identities, but if they feel you don't want them to be there, if they aren't allowed to contribute fully and to be themselves, you may as well not bother.

Inclusive organisations are more 'intelligent' because people's distinctive strengths and weaknesses combine to make the whole greater than the sum of the parts. Different ways to approach challenges, make suggestions and decisions, react to problems, and think about how to solve them all increase an organisation's creativity, flexibility and ability to innovate. Given the right conditions (discussed in Section 32.3), diverse, or 'heterogeneous', teams can produce better decisions, more robust debate and more and better ideas than 'homogeneous' teams, or those made up of people with similar backgrounds.

This also makes diversity an important risk management tool because people with truly different perspectives, knowledge, skills, and work and life experiences help organisations challenge assumptions, avoid groupthink, recognise decision-making biases, spot opportunities and connect the dots to spot looming risks.

Transferable skills

1.4 Business operations

2.3 Business strategy

Workplaces filled with a range of people who reflect the customers and communities they serve and its other stakeholders can provide a greater understanding of the organisation's different customer groups than homogeneous workplaces. New ways of working and finding new and better ways to serve customers and achieve goals can result, giving culturally complex organisations a competitive advantage and more business opportunities.

A multicultural workforce can help organisations work effectively in a global marketplace, provide access to new markets and help develop internationally successful products and services.

Transferable skills

1.4 Business operations

2.3 Business strategy

A rich seedbed for innovation

PepsiCo has 'affinity groups' – associations of employees united by gender, ethnicity, race or other traits. The Hispanic employee affinity group at its Frito-Lay division worked on guacamole-flavoured potato chips, which became a US$100 million product.

A cross-cultural group at MTV Networks discovered marketing opportunities in the similarities between North American country music and Latin American music, which use many of the same instruments and have singers with similar vocal styles.[5]

Recruiting from the total labour pool, as well as using open and fair employment policies and practices, enhance an organisation's image and reputation and help it compete for quality employees. An organisation culture that respects diversity means you don't lose good people because they feel marginalised or uncomfortable and you don't spend time and money on diversity-based employee grievances. It also helps you to identify and rectify indirect discrimination through appropriately flexible measures that accommodate differences among the workforce, which builds an environment where everyone is valued, recognised and supported. This increases employee loyalty – when people know they are working for an employer who cares about them as a person, regardless of their personal characteristics, they are more likely to return this respect.

Transferable skills

1.4 Business operations

2.3 Business strategy

3.4 Leadership

Diversity can also improve retention. For example, Hewlett-Packard Australia implemented a diversity management strategy that addressed the concerns of minority employees and reduced its workforce turnover from the IT industry average of 25 per cent to about 8 per cent over a three-year period.[6]

But does diversity make money? Decades of research consistently show a strong link between an organisation's performance and harnessing the benefits of diversity and that for the public and private sectors to remain competitive and lead the world in the provision of services, they must become diverse and inclusive. For example, 30 per cent of a company's senior leaders being female leads to a 15 per cent increase in profitability for an average company.[7] A large international study found clear evidence that women in decision-making roles generate higher returns on equity, better stock performance and higher dividend payout ratios; in fact, the more women in top management, the greater the returns for shareholders.[8] The evidence is clear – organisations can avoid the doom of mediocrity by welcoming into their ranks a range of people that reflect their stakeholders.

Transferable skills

1.1 Financial literacy

1.4 Business operations

32.2 Building a diverse and inclusive workplace

> Inclusion matters because those of us who are outsiders (basically anyone who isn't white, male, Christian, under 60 and, probably, with a private school education) have different views of the world. That richness of diverse views and experiences matters.
>
> Jane Caro, 'Outsiders on the inside', *Company Director*, February 2017, p. 9.

Transferable skills

1.4 Business operations

2.3 Business strategy

3.4 Leadership

Organisations can reap benefits from including everyone and making the most of all their individual differences – but only when organisations and teams achieve *inclusion*, not just *diversity*.

It isn't enough to accept differences. The aim of diversity is not to assimilate 'outsiders' into a dominant culture, but to create a dominant heterogeneous culture that includes and values everyone, that gives everyone equal opportunity and a chance to contribute fully and add value to the organisation and its customers. This means educating people to confront their biases and prevent those biases from influencing decisions about who to recruit, train, coach, promote, reward or assign work and projects to. In short, it means basing all employment-related decisions solely on the requirements of the job and applying the merit principle (as previously discussed) – a person's actual ability to do a job – in the same way to everyone.

Should you want to exclude someone, not because of their skills and ability to contribute but because of a factor such as their age, criminal record, political opinion, religion or sex, you must be able to prove that factor is relevant to your decision to exclude them.

Build diversity into the culture

Differences can be frightening, puzzling or fascinating. When you have a variety of people on board, it isn't always easy to create a workplace that can rise above the potential friction that people's differences can kindle. For example, diversity can lead to more and different points of view, which can result in longer discussions, misunderstandings and conflict rather than creativity, insight and innovation.

To form a team of people who are basically the same is short-sighted, but to treat everyone as though they're the same is even more so. To build a diverse and successful workplace, people may need to step out of their comfort zones and accept that 'like me' doesn't have to mean people who look like them, think like them or have a similar background to them. In diverse workplaces, 'like me' means sharing common organisational and team goals, values and visions; that is, everyone agrees on the essentials – what they are there to achieve and how to achieve it.

Building a productive workplace where diversity is part of its identity means ensuring that behaviours and norms are respectful and inclusive. It means fostering a work climate that values everyone's contributions, and acknowledges and builds on the strengths of everyone in the work team. For example, unnecessarily drawing attention to someone's race, religion or any other characteristic (e.g. the Arab woman, that man in the turban, the gay guy) highlights distinctions and gives the impression that the person is different from 'us'. Stereotyping people (e.g. excitable Italian, whingeing Pom, emotional woman) implies a belief that all individuals from a particular group share that characteristic. Lumping diverse groups together (e.g. Asians, Europeans, people with disabilities) denies their individual differences.

Using language that diminishes people or casts them in a negative light (e.g. office girls, oldies) is disrespectful. Derogatory labels, offensive language and put-downs in the form of 'jokes' are also unacceptable. You don't want comments like any of these at your workplace because they can easily lead to other forms of discrimination, make people feel uncomfortable, and shatter a culture of dignity, inclusion and respect. Not standing for these types of behaviours is a good first step towards fostering an inclusive diverse culture in the workplace. Figure 32.3 outlines some other ideas that can be implemented.

Begin a mothers' support group that meets, say, every six weeks.

Build a culture of respect where every team member recognises and values the differences between, and the contributions of, the employees, customers and suppliers they work with.

Create opportunities for people from diverse backgrounds, cultures, lifestyles and so on to come together informally and to work together, for example, on projects, secondments and special assignments.

Deal quickly and firmly with anyone who does not treat fellow employees, customers or suppliers fairly and respectfully.

Ensure that men aren't assessed on their potential and people from minority groups on their performance.

Establish clear criteria before deciding, for example, who to assign to a project, who to promote, who to recruit and so on, so that people can't justify their decisions after they're made, and scrutinise your decision-making criteria to ensure they are directly related to the job.

Ensure people know and adhere to the organisation's policy and programs on dignity- and diversity-related matters.

Give everyone equal access to employment opportunities and thoughtfully apply the merit principle to all employment-related decisions and opportunities.

Initiate formal mentoring and sponsoring programs aimed at people from disadvantaged groups.

Institute flexible start and finish times and other flexible working arrangements (e.g. options to work part-time or job-share, work from home, and work to a compressed working week) for roles that can accommodate these initiatives.

Introduce cross-training and job rotation when it involves contact between different groups of employees.

Introduce networking groups for people from disadvantaged groups (e.g. women, working parents, and lesbian, bisexual, gay, transitioning/transitioned and intersex employees).

Provide clear information about where employees can seek assistance and investigate any complaints carefully, according to your organisation's policy (as discussed in Chapter 31).

Keep refresher training on discrimination and inclusion up to date and record people's attendance.

Observe the right of all employees to confidentiality.

Open a nursing mothers' room.

Open a parents' room to care for sick family members.

Provide an option to bring children to the office or work from home when necessary (e.g. during school holidays).

Provide training to help employees work effectively with a range of people and hold them accountable for doing so.

Provide ways for people on parenting leave to stay in touch with the workplace.

Recognise that each employee has individual skills and contributions to make.

Set and track quotas and publicise the organisation's performance against them.

Set up a high-level diversity task force of influential leader-managers to examine the causes of low diversity and find ways to increase diversity.

FIGURE 32.3 Becoming more welcoming

Transferable skills

2.3 Business strategy

Special measures

Sometimes, simply ceasing to discriminate isn't enough because equal treatment doesn't always result in fair treatment (see the following Reflect box). Sometimes more is needed. This can mean taking steps to help people from the 'out groups' catch up quickly so they can compete equally for jobs, training and promotion. These steps are known as *special measures*, *positive discrimination* and *affirmative action*, and the terms are used interchangeably.

REFLECT

Equal treatment and equitable treatment have very different results:

- Equal treatment: giving a person who is blind the same written standard operating procedure (SOP) that you give sighted employees.
- Equitable treatment: giving the person who is blind the SOP in braille.
  Do you recognise this in your own workplace?

Transferable skills

2.3 Business strategy

3.4 Leadership

Relatively straightforward actions, such as modifying the workplace with ramp access for wheelchairs, using different languages on signs and in safety information, or installing visual alarms for hearing-impaired people, are inexpensive and easy and can help people feel included. Mentoring and sponsoring programs and quotas (e.g. setting a goal of employing a specific number of Aboriginal and Torres Strait Islander people in management positions by a certain date) are other examples of actions to overcome the practical effects of disadvantage and discrimination. The English as a second language (ESL) courses that many TAFE colleges provide for employees whose first language isn't English is another example of a special measure.

Transferable skills

2.3 Business strategy

3.1 Teamwork/relationships

INDUSTRY INSIGHTS

Making poor use and good use of special measures

Sean spent two years in a government department as part of its Indigenous cadet program. Not having been given a phone, a computer or even an induction, he felt like his only contribution was filling a quota. He left and went to university, spending three summers working in Hewlett-Packard's business operations unit as part of HP's internship program. He was given specific goals and objectives to help develop the company's business plan around new international quality standards initiatives. Every 12 weeks his performance was reviewed, and more responsibilities were added each time. Sean was also asked to teach HP executives about Aboriginal culture.

Sean worked full-time for HP after graduation before joining KPMG, which has a number of initiatives to improve employment opportunities for Aboriginal and Torres Straight Islander peoples, including high school and tertiary scholarships, mentoring and work experience programs and cultural awareness training.[9]

The lesson: symbolic policies don't work. Support them and follow through.

The case for quotas

In an ideal world, people would be placed in roles based on merit – their ability to do the job. But a look at the numbers tells us that isn't the case. Maybe it's just human nature to hire, promote and support people who are like oneself.

The case for quotas is self-interest. When organisations 'do diversity well', they prosper. But progress towards diversity, never mind inclusion, has been glacial. Since the 1990s, progress has levelled off or gone backwards in many measures. Traditional attempts to increase organisational diversity have clearly failed. Specifically:

- recruitment testing hasn't worked – people can ignore the results
- performance ratings haven't worked – women and people from minority groups tend to receive poorer reviews whatever their performance
- robust grievance procedures haven't worked – people don't trust them and use them only when they're desperate and, as a result, complaints drop and organisations conclude they have no problem.

What does work? It is well established that increasing contact with people from disadvantaged groups works, and implementing quotas supports the opportunities for such contact.

Sponsoring

Transferable skills

2.3 Business strategy

3.4 Leadership

Mentors help people think problems through, understand unwritten rules and offer advice and support. Many organisations offer formal mentoring programs as a way to assist employees from disadvantaged groups. However, sponsoring goes a step further. Sponsors are people with influence who actively promote employees from disadvantaged groups to further their careers, providing opportunities and opening doors that wouldn't otherwise be opened. They use their networks to facilitate introductions and meetings and effect pay rises, high-level assignments and promotions.

Sponsoring is about 'getting people to the start line when previously they wouldn't even have been in the race'. A number of leading organisations have introduced sponsorship programs to help people not just enter the race but to track well in it, and informally sponsoring people is becoming more common as well.

Review and evaluate the success of your diversity and inclusion policies

Transferable skills

2.3 Business strategy

3.1 Teamwork/relationships

3.2 Verbal communication

3.3 Written communication

3.4 Leadership

Set specific, time bound, measurable and mandated SMART targets. Track what's most important to your organisation and make sure there are consequences for not achieving them so the targets aren't just a nice-to-have aspiration. Ensure your targets are:

- communicated to stakeholders
- connected to the organisation's strategy
- linked to people's measures of success to hold people accountable
- tracked and publicised regularly.

Review the effectiveness of your policies and strategies against your targets at least twice a year. Like all monitoring, this can highlight your successes and indicate areas for improvement. Publicise your progress to keep it top of mind and build momentum.

Work with your stakeholders to find where and how you can make improvements. As you make progress, build a business case to show where and how diversity builds the business. This way, resources follow. Keep moving your targets forward on various measures of diversity, such as recruitment, promotion and remuneration rates, comparing the 'in groups' with the 'out groups'. (You can find out about what and how to monitor in Chapter 20.)

32.3 Promoting inclusion in your work team

Diversity is inviting people to the party; inclusion is getting them to dance.

Brigadier Mark Abraham, Chief-of-Staff Support Command, British Army, in 'Getting the best from everyone', *Management Today*, April 2015, pp. 64–67.

Transferable skills
3.4 Leadership

Diversity is easy enough – you hire people that reflect the population of your organisation's wider community. But unless they're well led, you could end up with even worse results than you would with a homogeneous team. In fact, when led poorly, diverse teams suffer from conflict and perform less well than homogeneous teams. But when you lead them well, your results are far superior to teams where everyone is the same.[10]

So how do you lead a diverse team 'well'? You point them all in the same direction, towards a purpose and goals they all share. You make sure they appreciate each other's contributions. You make sure they have the information, equipment and other resources they need. You train and coach the team as a whole and its individual members and provide plenty of feedback. (For more detail on this, see Chapters 13, 14, 15 and 19.)

Transferable skills
1.1 Financial literacy
1.4 Business operations
2.3 Business strategy

IN PRACTICE

Diversity and innovation

Diversity can be *acquired* or *inherent*. Acquired diversity, as the name implies, is gained from experience. For example, you might work with people from different cultures and gain cultural intelligence, or acquire a physical or mental impairment. Inherent diversity refers to characteristics you're born with, such as gender, ethnicity and some physical and mental abilities.

Companies whose leader-managers possess at least three acquired and three inherent diversity traits – 2D diversity – out-innovate and outperform less diverse companies. Part of the reason is that 2D diversity increases innovation by creating an environment where people feel able to speak up and suggest novel ideas.[11]

Transferable skills
3.4 Leadership

Naturally, you also want to discuss diversity and inclusion with your team members; make sure everyone in your team knows, understands and follows your organisation's diversity policies; and train them to recognise – and avoid – all types of discrimination.

But you can do more because the goal isn't just diversity and compliance. It's inclusion. You can help team members develop their emotional intelligence and foster an environment of cultural sensitivity and global outlook to help them appreciate people's unique abilities and differences. You can encourage people to experience individuals rather than stereotypes to connect with them more easily.

Your own day-to-day actions send strong signals about how important a culture of collaboration and respect is to you, so the example you set is crucial. You can keep diversity 'on the radar' by, for example, putting it on your team meeting agenda every few meetings and putting up diversity posters.

Transferable skills
2.2 Personal effectiveness
3.1 Teamwork/relationships
3.2 Verbal communication
3.4 Leadership

Bearing in mind that training only works when it's put into practice, you and your team can participate in training and discuss how to apply what you've learnt. Training that fosters awareness of and supports diversity, and assists employees to perform in a culturally diverse environment, can include:

- the advantages of diversity and how to work effectively in diverse work groups
- cross-cultural training
- the changing work environment and marketplace

- communication skills
- equal employment opportunity and anti-discrimination awareness
- interpersonal skills.

Should a grievance concerning discrimination arise, deal with it fairly, quickly and following your organisation's **dispute settlement procedure**.

Transferable skills

1.4 Business operations

3.4 Leadership

A quick tour of diverse groups

In most work groups today, you can find men and women from five generations and from an array of cultural, ethnic and religious backgrounds. They have a range of abilities and many speak English as a second language. As well as visible attributes such as age, gender and physical ability, diversity is also about valuing invisible attributes, such as different ways of communicating, dealing with conflict, thinking and problem-solving.

Groups of people that contribute to diversity in most workplaces include people:

- with disabilities
- from different cultures and races
- of different sexes, sexual orientations and gender identities
- from different generations.

Diversity of abilities

Transferable skills

4.1 Data literacy

People with disabilities are Australia's largest minority group, made up of all genders and age groups, ethnicities, gender identities and educational and social backgrounds. It might surprise you to learn that more than one in five people in Australia have a disability and 2.1 million of these people are of working age (15–64 years).[12] You may be even more surprised to learn that in a 2010 Organisation for Economic Co-Operation and Development (OECD) report, Australia ranked a shocking 26 out of 27 countries for the percentage of disabled people living in poverty.[13]

Disability is an umbrella term for activity limitations, impairments and participation restrictions. Disabilities can be caused by accident, disease, genetics or trauma and can be permanent or temporary, partial or total, acquired or lifelong, visible or invisible.[14] There are five broad types of disability:

- head injury/stroke/brain damage: long-term effects that restrict everyday activities
- intellectual disabilities: difficulty in learning or understanding
- physical disabilities: chronic or recurrent pain, incomplete use of arms or fingers, disfigurement or deformity, and the presence of viruses such as HIV and hepatitis C
- psychological disabilities: a nervous or emotional condition
- sensory and speech: difficulties seeing, hearing or speaking.

You have probably heard the standard pretexts for not employing people with disabilities: 'It costs too much to accommodate their needs', 'They don't fit in' and so on. But these excuses ignore the following facts:

- Expensive workplace adjustments are seldom needed and, when they are, 80 per cent cost less than $500 and are paid for by the government.
- People with a disability are as productive or more productive than other employees.
- People with a disability can have lower absenteeism, higher retention rates and take less sick leave than other employees.
- People with a disability can have fewer accidents at work – workers' rehabilitation and compensation costs for people with a disability can be as low as 4 per cent of the compensation costs of other employees.

- People with a disability can build staff morale, raise management awareness of workplace practices and conditions, and increase customer and staff loyalty.
- The cost of hiring people with a disability can be as low as 13 per cent of the cost of other employees.[15]

Transferable skills

2.3 Business strategy

3.4 Leadership

When you need to make adjustments for employees with a disability, common sense serves in most situations. For instance, you may need to allow flexibility in weekly hours to allow employees to attend regular medical appointments, provide desks with adjustable heights for people using a wheelchair and provide more regular breaks for people with chronic pain or fatigue. Ask the employee to indicate the assistance you can provide and, should something seem too difficult, seek assistance from the Australian Human Rights Commission (http://www.hreoc.gov.au) or Job Access (http://www.jobaccess.gov.au). Specialist organisations across Australia work with employers and people with disabilities to match abilities to job requirements. Many also provide ongoing workplace support that helps them remain employed and achieve the outcomes expected of them.

Employing people with disabilities gives them a chance to participate, and that chance is often met with commitment, loyalty and a desire to achieve. There really are no excuses. Failing to benefit from the abilities, experience, ideas and skills of over two million working-age Australians doesn't make much sense in a country with an ageing population and skills shortages.

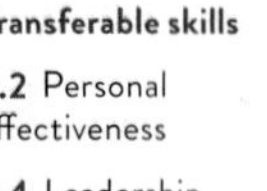

Transferable skills

2.2 Personal effectiveness

3.4 Leadership

Above all, don't think of the people you work with as deaf people, blind people, disabled people or handicapped. Although their disability is part of who they are, don't let it define them – they have families, hobbies, likes and dislikes, trials, tribulations and joys. They are just people who happen to have a disability.

FYI

Looking beyond disabilities to abilities

Having a disability doesn't mean you don't contribute. There are many prominent Australians who live with disabilities, and who are not only highly skilled and successful in their vocations but are also vocal disability activists. They include:

- Senator Jordan Steele uses a wheelchair due to cerebral palsy and has spoken in parliament on the need for the house to be wheelchair-friendly, and is an advocate for disabled prisoner's rights.
- Dylan Alcott AO is the 2022 Australian of the Year and an international wheelchair tennis and basketball champion and Olympian. He works as a motivational speaker, and is the founder of disabled rights organisation the Dylan Alcott Foundation that aims to assist Australians with disabilities to gain self-esteem and self-respect through sport and study.
- Carly Findlay is a writer and activist who lives with the debilitating skin condition ichthyosis. She was awarded the Order of Australia Medal in 2020 for 'service to people with a disability'.[16]

IN PRACTICE

Blind injustice

Josh, who is blind, has worked in a large government organisation as a desk administrative officer for many years. He performs his duties well. An opportunity for a transfer to another job arises, a job that Josh can do and would enjoy. But he is refused the transfer because, although he can carry out the duties of the position, he is not suitable for promotion to the next job up the line from the transfer position because that position requires a sighted person. That is discrimination. Failing to transfer Josh is discriminatory and unlawful because more than the required skills and abilities of the job in question have been considered.

Cultural and racial diversity

Transferable skills

3.4 Leadership

You can expect to report to and supervise people who were born overseas, many in countries where the main language is not English. Many will be from countries with cultures and economies quite different from Australia's, including different customs, behavioural expectations, and even practices regarding verbal and non-verbal communication. Some will have privileged backgrounds, while others will be from poverty-stricken countries and war-torn countries. It is important to note that although differences *within* cultures exist, there are greater differences *between* cultures. Where does your cultural intelligence lie on the scale shown in Figure 32.4? Where do you think your team members would place themselves?

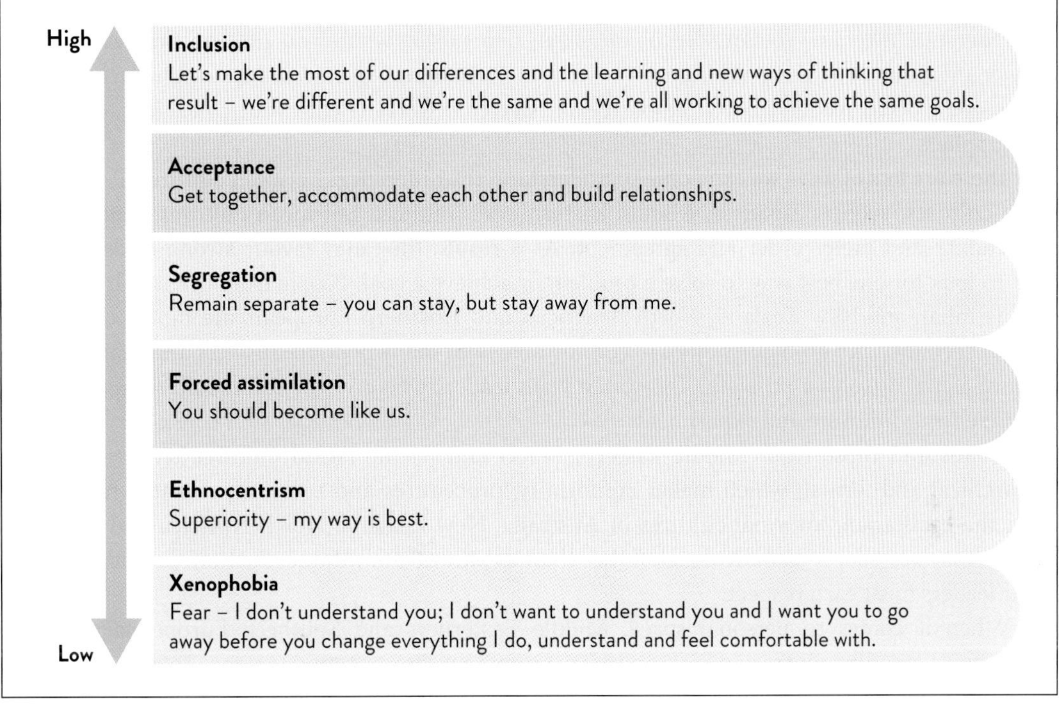

FIGURE 32.4 Degrees of cultural intelligence

Transferable skills

2.2 Personal effectiveness

3.4 Leadership

Your job is to help everyone in your team feel comfortable in their work surroundings and ensure that everyone understands and respects people's differences. To do that, you first need to understand your own cultural background. And that isn't easy – what do fish know about the water in which they swim? But when you can understand other cultures and how yours differs from others, then you can work out how to work together effectively.

Ask yourself what your own cultural expectations are. We behave as we've been brought up to behave, according to the norms of our family and community. How have you been brought up to behave? Consider the following:

Transferable skills

2.2 Personal effectiveness

- Are you comfortable speaking up in meetings or do you wait until someone asks for your opinion?
- Do interruptions indicate 'I'm engaged in the conversation' or 'I'm rude and don't care what you have to say'?
- Do you blow your nose or do you sniff when you have a head cold?
- Do you look a senior manager in the eye or do you look down?
- Do you prefer formality or informality?

- Do you shy away from conflict or explore it?
- Does silence mean 'I'm thinking' or 'I have nothing to say'?
- How close to people are you comfortable standing or sitting?
- How firm or loose is your handshake?
- Is being late for a meeting no big deal or is it a sign of disrespect?
- When you say you'll do something, is it a promise or an aim?
- When you're trying to understand someone's meaning, do you take their words at face value or do you read 'between the lines' and think about what is *not* said?
- Which do you value more: competition or cooperation, the individual or the group?

The behaviours listed above are more than personality traits. They're important differentiators between cultures that persist over generations, and they are potential sources of irritation and misunderstanding. How you answer the questions depends on where you grew up, and however you answer them (and there are no 'rights' or 'wrongs'), awareness of how others might answer them makes you a better leader, a better employee and better at working with your colleagues, customers and suppliers.

Transferable skills

2.1 Critical thinking

There are lots of ways we can come to understand the differences between cultures. People from some cultures, such as Japanese, Middle Eastern and Southern European cultures, tend to avoid uncertainty and prefer order and agreement. As a result, they may favour strong leadership and tend to look for one best way to solve a problem or achieve a goal. People from other cultures, such as Australian and New Zealand, North American and Northern European, are more comfortable with uncertainty and ambiguity and are comfortable with many possible answers and many ways to achieve a goal or solve a problem. They often want leaders who give them freedom to figure things out, take risks, innovate and experiment.

Asians and those from Middle Eastern, Māori and Pacific Island cultures tend to be more hierarchical and formal, which makes conformity, procedures and rules important, while people from the egalitarian, informal cultures of Australia, New Zealand, North America and Northern Europe may see people as individuals, rather than as part of a family, occupation, position or tribe. Their leaders must earn respect.

When it comes to personal space, Middle Easterners and Southern Europeans are often comfortable standing closer and making more eye contact than are most Asians. They gesture more and can be more facially expressive than most Asians, too. In between these two ends of the spectrum are the Northern Europeans and people from English-speaking countries.

Some cultures, known as collectivist cultures, stress the importance of being part of a group. Other cultures emphasise the importance of 'standing on your own two feet'. People from Middle Eastern, Asian, Japanese, Māori and Pacific Island cultures tend to be group oriented and cooperation, not competition, describes their general approach. This means they like to work, learn and reach decisions in small groups and they're uncomfortable being 'in the spotlight', so don't assume they'll speak up when they have something to say – they probably prefer to be asked for their thoughts. Many English-speaking and Northern European cultures are at the other end of the scale, where individuals, not relationships, take the front seat and action and results count more than consensus.

Transferable skills

2.2 Personal effectiveness

It's important to remember that these are generalisations and not all people from one culture will act or behave in an identical way as another from the same culture. We are not pre-programmed robots. But you can think of descriptions like these as scales, with some cultures lying at one end, other cultures lying at the other end and some cultures in the middle. Don't use them to stereotype people and ignore what each individual can offer but as shorthand generalisations to help you work more effectively with people from different cultures by adapting your own style to the people you're working with. Widen your comfort zone so that you can adapt gracefully and quickly to add value and achieve the outcomes you need.

Cultural intelligence and awareness helps you avoid conflict, miscommunication and misunderstanding. When you're culturally competent, you don't think of the way you do things as 'normal' or view other ways as 'different'. You don't see other cultures and ways of behaving as stereotypes and in a critical light. You don't tend to assume you know the reasons that people from other cultures do something and think you know what they mean or intend based on your own culture rather than their culture.

Transferable skills

2.2 Personal effectiveness

How to increase your cultural intelligence

To adapt to a different culture, whether it's on the other side of the world or a project team you've just joined, work out the norms and how they differ from the norms you're used to. That way, you know what behaviours you need to tone down and what you need to adopt in their place. Think through the norms in the following dimensions:

- assertiveness
- directness
- enthusiasm
- formality
- self-disclosure
- self-promotion.

Transferable skills

2.2 Personal effectiveness

3.4 Leadership

Then think about the range of behaviours in each of those dimensions. When a higher range makes you uncomfortable, you can adopt behaviours from a lower range. For instance, if you move from a culture that shows low enthusiasm to one that shows high enthusiasm, you might not want to shout 'Fantastic!' when someone asks how you are; you can adopt a lower range response instead: 'Really well, thanks!' Having worked out how to adjust your behaviours to fit into your new culture, use them over and over until they feel comfortable and second nature.[17]

 INDUSTRY INSIGHTS

The bamboo and falafel ceilings

In Australia, an applicant with a Chinese name needs to submit 68 per cent more applications than an applicant with an Anglo-Saxon name and the same qualifications and experience to get as many interviews. People with a Middle Eastern name need to submit 64 per cent more applications. Female applicants also need to apply for more jobs than their male counterparts.[18] People from these groups are not proportionately represented in Australian political life or the private sector professional workforce.

Why is it that Chinese people, people from the Middle East and women need to demonstrate, beyond a shadow of a doubt, that they are qualified and competent to win a job while white men are assumed to be qualified and competent?

Transferable skills

4.1 Data literacy

Turning cultural differences into team assets

Don't be surprised to find that many of your team members are not aware of how their teammates think about basic concepts, such as time or whether they are individually or group oriented, competitive or cooperative, and so on. Help them increase their awareness of their teammates' ways of thinking by making them transparent, using the team culture wheel shown in Figure 32.5.

Transferable skills

3.4 Leadership

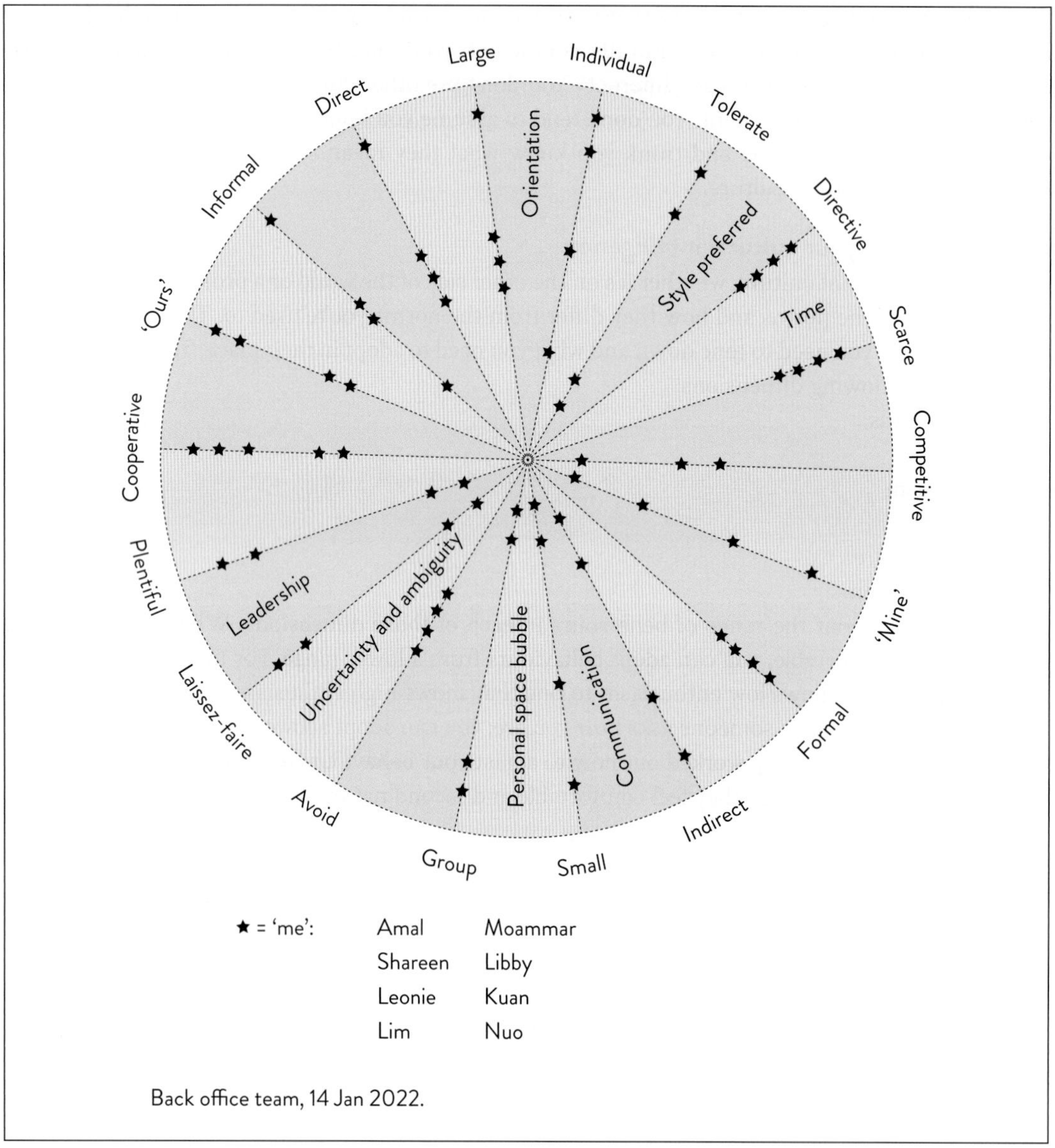

Large
Individual
Tolerate
Directive
Scarce
Competitive
'Mine'
Formal
Indirect
Small
Group
Avoid
Laissez-faire
Plentiful
Cooperative
'Ours'
Informal
Direct
Orientation
Style preferred
Time
Leadership
Uncertainty and ambiguity
Personal space bubble
Communication

★ = 'me': Amal, Moammar, Shareen, Libby, Leonie, Kuan, Lim, Nuo

Back office team, 14 Jan 2022.

FIGURE 32.5 The team culture wheel

Ask team members to think about the approaches shown on the culture wheel and then use stick-on dots to place themselves on the wheel's continuum spokes. This shows where team members' attitudes differ and highlights where discomfort and misunderstandings can occur. You can use this information to discuss which aspects of the culture wheel are central to your team's performance and agree ways to work together.

Transferable skills

3.1 Teamwork/relationships

3.2 Verbal communication

3.4 Leadership

When team members understand what they do that helps the team work effectively, what they do that disrupts teamwork, what they can do to help the team work more effectively, how others may interpret their behaviour and whether they interpret others' behaviour correctly, their cultural intelligence broadens. They have valuable information they can use to increase their ability to work well in a diverse workplace.

Leading and managing diverse employees

Transferable skills

2.1 Critical thinking

3.1 Teamwork/relationships

3.2 Verbal communication

3.4 Leadership

You can expect to lead employees from many cultures and all age groups, including 'retired' full-time workers. Some will be contract and part-time workers with several contract and part-time jobs. Many will only be with you for a few months. Yet you need to be able to encourage each one to share your vision and the organisation's vision and help them feel like important, contributing members of the organisation. Here are some ways to harness the expertise of everyone in a diverse team:

- Accommodate differences and create choices. Learn about team members and accommodate their personal needs when you can.
- Be aware of people's abilities, cultures, generations, lifestyles and personality styles, but think in terms of individuals and skills.
- Build a team culture where people appreciate different ways of thinking and communicating.
- Concentrate on output, meeting customers' needs and people working together.
- Develop a norm to ask for more information or explanation when people aren't sure what someone is saying so that they don't assume there is more shared understanding than really exists.
- Facilitate mentoring inside your team; for example, make it easy for older, more experienced employees to show younger employees 'the ropes', for younger, techno-savvy employees to help older employees improve their skills, for people from the same or similar cultures to support each other and for people from different cultures to learn from each other.
- Guard against listening more to some team members and discounting opinions, ideas and information from other team members.
- Guard against according more status and influence to high-contributing team members. Be sure to hear all voices and seek everyone's opinions.
- Help everyone learn and develop their skills.
- Shared information gets most of the 'airtime' at the expense of unique information, which can lead to groupthink; don't mistake shared information for important information.
- Stress people's similarities, not their differences.
- Tailor your leadership approach to suit different individuals with different needs, expectations and abilities.
- When managing older employees, think about what it would be like to manage your mother or father and what it would be like for your parents to be managed by someone your age.

Gender diversity

We've mentioned that women belong to a disadvantaged group in many workplaces, and in the following we will look at this further. We will also discuss other individuals disadvantaged because of their sexual orientation, sexual status, gender identity or gender expression.

The boys' club

Transferable skills

4.1 Data literacy

Mao Zedong said that 'women hold up half the sky' and that's true in that women make up 50.2 per cent of the Australian population, have similar educational levels to men and comprise 38.6 per cent of managers in Australia.[19] A record-high number of women (23) are now in charge of Global 500 businesses. This is an increase from 14 in 2020 and is the highest number of women CEOs in the Global 500 since Fortune started tracking this data in 2014. While this is encouraging, there is still a long way to go when you put this into perspective – despite women making up half of the population, these 23 female-led companies make up just 4.6 per cent of the Global 500.

The number of CEOs who are women of colour on the Global 500 list has also risen. In 2020, just one woman of colour was working as a Global 500 CEO. In just a year, that number increased to six. Steps are slowly being made in the right direction.[20]

Transferable skills
4.1 Data literacy

But there are still some double standards. It's expected that men benefit from the 'old-boy' network to 'rise through the ranks', while women who benefit from special measures are seen as rising through the ranks as a result of special treatment, not because they qualify for their positions.

What accounts for the gender wage gap mentioned in the FYI box 'Not a pretty picture' earlier in this chapter? Is the gap because women take time out to have children and can't catch up? It seems not, because that gap begins early. Straight out of university, male graduates earn over $2000 a year more, on average, than female graduates. An analysis of the gap tells us that 60 per cent of the gender wage gap is a penalty for 'being female'.[21]

The 'motherhood penalty' multiplies the 'female penalty'. For every child a woman has, her salary decreases by about 4 per cent a year, about $1200 per child for women working full-time for an average salary.[22] It literally doesn't pay to be female, even though gender diversity in the boardroom and executive ranks is a strong indicator of a well-governed, well-performing organisation.

Gender transition and gender identity

Bridging the gender gap isn't just about women. Similar laws, policies and procedures that apply to other forms of discrimination and harassment apply to people whose gender identity and gender expression are different from that on their birth certificate, as well as to people whose sexual orientation is towards the same or both sexes.

Not everyone is born male or female and many people feel uncomfortable having to tick a box that puts them into one of these categories. Some people are 'gender fluid', others 'genderless' and others 'a-gender' or 'non-gender'. Some people are transgender (as Catherine McGregor in the Snapshot that opens this chapter, former Olympian Caitlyn Jenner and Laverne Cox, who stars in the US TV series *Orange Is the New Black* along with Australian Ruby Rose who is gender fluid).

Another often marginalised group of individuals are LGBTQIA+ people, which stands for lesbian, gay, bisexual, transgender, queer (an umbrella term encompassing a variety of sexual orientations and gender identities excluding heterosexuality)/questioning (people unsure of their sexual orientation and/or gender identity), intersex, asexual. Many LGBTQIA+ employees prefer to conceal their identity or orientation from their co-workers and employers. It's a shame they feel the need to. When you feel marginalised enough to 'cover' – for example, avoiding using 'her' or 'him' when discussing your partner to avoid the 'gay penalty' (or not mentioning day care or other family responsibilities to avoid the 'motherhood penalty') – how can you possibly feel fully engaged at work and perform at your best? An important part of engagement and 'giving your all' is trusting your organisation and co-workers to value you and your capabilities as an individual, without looking through the lenses of sexual orientation or gender.

Transferable skills
3.1 Teamwork/relationships
3.2 Verbal communication
3.3 Written communication
3.4 Leadership

Getting used to someone's new name pales alongside the difficulties a transgender person faces; when an employee affirms a different gender, make sure you use the correct pronouns and use the employee's new name to reinforce that you and the organisation fully support the employee. Instruct team members to direct any concerns they have to you, not to their teammate. Make it clear to your team and the gender-affirmed or intersex employee that your policy is zero tolerance for harassment or any actions creating loss of dignity and to notify you immediately of any problems. Promptly deal with any misconduct, as explained in Chapter 31.

Educate your team so that they understand the struggle their colleague has gone through. Remember, your team are watching you for clues as to how to behave and what to say. The key is for everyone to be able to live openly as their true selves.

Should concerns be raised about a front-line employee dealing with customers, remember that 'What will the customers say?' concerns were also expressed when racial minorities, people with disabilities and even people sporting nose rings joined the workforce, and those concerns have largely been disregarded. Maybe you can go one step further and include an Mx box, as well as the standard Dr, Mr, Mrs, Ms boxes for customers and clients to tick. Small adjustments remove institutional barriers and demonstrate your respect for people's sense of self.

IN PRACTICE

Words and bathrooms

Rather than using the 'trans' prefix of the terms 'transgender' and 'transsexual', which suggest the person has changed, rather than accepted their true gender identity, the term 'gender affirmation' is currently preferred. This is seen as affirming the gender the person has always had, rather than transitioning from one gender identity to another. However, rather than make assumptions, ask the employee which term they prefer.

Language is important, and so are the bathrooms. This is often a hot issue when a team member transitions from male to female or vice versa. You can always take some interim (up to three months) steps until the team feels more comfortable. For example:

- When there is more than one bathroom, the transitioning employee could use the one closest to their workstation and others who are not comfortable can use another one.
- When there is only one bathroom, the transitioning employee might agree to use it during the first 30 minutes of every hour.
- Switch to unisex bathrooms.

Every employee is entitled to be treated with respect, to feel comfortable and safe in their workplace and to use its facilities.

Transferable skills

1.4 Business operations

3.1 Teamwork/relationships

3.4 Leadership

Generational diversity

People are living longer and retiring later and, for the first time in history, five generations make up our workforce. Older workers working alongside and reporting to employees young enough to be their children and even grandchildren becomes more common in an ageing population. You can expect people from different generations to have different values, engagement preferences and life experiences. For most organisations, this presents both challenges and opportunities. Different generations have different ways of working, different expectations, different skill sets, and different motivators and personality profiles – differences that have the potential to lead to misunderstandings and conflict.[23]

Those growing up in the cultural milieu of the dippie-hippie 1960s grew up with the Cold War, the Vietnam War, building the Berlin Wall, the first people in space and on the moon, the Chinese Cultural Revolution, mechanical typewriters, *Doctor Who* and *Star Trek*, the Beatles and the Rolling Stones. Compare that to those who grew up in the cultural milieu of the 1990s with the end of the Cold War and collapse of the Soviet Union, terrorism, the birth of the internet, mad cow disease, HIV/AIDS, *Baywatch*, Kylie Minogue, Madonna and the Spice Girls. How could these generations *not* be quite different people?

While there are obviously differences between the individuals in each generation, there are more differences between the generations themselves – people from the same generation usually have more in common with each other than they have with people from other generations. Cultural events, politics and the technology that people grow up with influence how they view and live in the world for the rest of their lives. People born in the same era tend to share similar attitudes, cultural references, motivations, outlooks on life, values and work ethics, and these are different from people born in other eras. People of the same generation feel comfortable with each other. They are on similar wavelengths, and they can think and speak in the same 'shorthand'.

Not surprisingly, marked differences between the generations have been found in their attitudes towards work, too. Surveys of employees across Australia, China, Germany, Singapore and the US found that work has a much greater focus for older employees than it does for younger people, for whom it's just one part of their life. This supports the widespread notion of a weaker work ethic in younger generations, with Baby Boomers valuing 'hard work', Generation X valuing self-discipline and self-improvement, and Generation Y valuing leisure.

Transferable skills

2.2 Personal effectiveness

3.4 Leadership

Slowly climbing the organisational ladder no longer has the pull it once had and loyalty to employers has followed loyalty to employees into the distant past. Understanding each generation's distinguishing characteristics helps you manage and work with people from different generations in ways that work for them. Your insight into the combination of factors that motivates and drives each generation helps you lead them more effectively.

However, the usual precautions apply. In the same way that seeing other cultures through your own cultural lenses is dangerous, so is seeing other generations through your own generational lenses. And just as putting everyone from the same culture in the same box is dangerous, so is putting people from the same generation in the one box.

Transferable skills

1.4 Business operations

2.2 Personal effectiveness

3.4 Leadership

Turning potential intergenerational misunderstandings and conflict into a creative, energising, positive, competitive advantage is today's challenge for leader-managers. As with any diversity, making the most of people from different age groups is not about assimilation but about adaptability and inclusion, for employees as well as for organisations. It's about valuing the abilities and talents of all generations, from the energy and enthusiasm of young people entering the workforce to the experience and thoroughness of mature-age workers.

Hiring, training and retaining people regardless of their age, and understanding the needs and goals of employees at different phases in their life cycle and career, is another way to inject diversity and dynamism into organisations and teams. Organisations that do this and can harness the diversity of a multigenerational workforce are well placed to succeed.

Transferable skills

2.2 Personal effectiveness

4.1 Data literacy

The working generations

If you aren't already, you will soon be leading, managing and working with up to five generations at the same time, including people older than yourself, and all expect different things from their jobs and different leadership and support from you. The tags for each generation, as well as the range of birth dates, vary slightly from source to source, but here's the gist:

- *Generation Z* (sometimes called *Millennials*): born between 1996 and 2009, this is the first generation to not have experienced life before the internet. The oldest of these 'digital natives' are well ensconced in the workforce.
- *Generation Y*: born between 1981 and 1995, many of this generation of tech-savvy, highly confident, mobile employees are in leader-manager roles; they need to be managed carefully to harness their innovation and creativity and to benefit from their enthusiasm and energy.
- *Generation X*: born between 1965 and 1980, some of this generation are already planning their retirement and others are leader-managers.
- *Baby Boomers*: born between 1946 and 1964, Boomers are retiring in large numbers and many are taking sabbaticals and choosing to switch to part-time and contract work before they fully retire.
- *Traditionalists*: there are still a few people in the workforce born between 1920 and 1945. Some love to work; some need to work because their superannuation hasn't worked for them as they'd hoped.

Did you notice the span of years of generations is shrinking? That's mostly because of the rapid rise and development of technology.

Transferable skills

4.1 Data literacy

Some reasons to hang onto mature-aged workers

In 1970, only 8 per cent of Australia's population was aged 65 and over. By 2016, that figure was 15.3 per cent and is projected to reach about 21 per cent by 2054. There are now almost twice as many people aged 55 and over in the workforce as there were in the 1980s.[24]

The shrinking, greying workforce means organisations face increasing competition for employees. This is one reason that retaining the participation of older workers and of women in the workforce have been identified as the two top reforms needed to ensure the supply of employees required to keep the Australian economy healthy. Boomers and women also comprise huge consumer and user markets, and as employees are able to help organisations relate to those two groups of customers better.[25]

Transferable skills

2.3 Business strategy

Living gives people, at least those who pay attention, deeper and wider life skills. The longer you live and learn, the more your emotional intelligence grows, helping you to put matters into perspective. Living and learning increases your patience and ability to think problems and decisions through. Experience and practice guide you to achieve goals in ways that work for you. In many ways, older people can hold their own against younger people and even surpass them.

One reason for this is that as people age, the two hemispheres of the brain work better together, meaning that older people have a fuller access to all their mental power. Another reason is that the brain never stops growing and reshaping itself in response to its environment and what it learns.

As time passes, people become more emotionally stable and satisfied with their lives. Their people skills and ability to avoid conflict improve. Priorities become clearer, and job-related knowledge and vocabularies grow. So does people's ability to see the big picture. Maybe that's why older employees are often called 'Wisdom Workers'. Yet many Australians over the age of 55 want to work but can't find employment, at a large personal cost to themselves as well as the economy.

STUDY TOOLS

QUICK REVIEW

KEY CONCEPT 32.1 

a Which groups of people are most likely to be discriminated against in Australia and what effect is this likely to have on their employment? Is everyone belonging to one or more of these groups disadvantaged?

b List the two types of covert discrimination and give an example of each. What other types of discrimination exist?

c Which of the following statements are discriminatory, and why?

- i 'I want to employ a woman for this job because it requires good interpersonal skills and sensitivity.'
- ii 'An Islander couldn't do this job because it requires a certain amount of previous experience.'
- iii 'We need a real Aussie to do this job because they need to deal with the public so much.'
- iv 'This job takes a lot of mental nimbleness and flexibility because the systems and technology change so often. That means we need a younger person, probably someone under 35 and preferably someone in their 20s.'
- v 'Because everyone is different, we need to tailor questions to each job applicant. For instance, while it's reasonable to ask a woman whether she has adequate child-minding arrangements, it would be silly to ask a man that question.'
- vi 'I would like to recruit someone from a minority group for this role because it's very visible and I want to show we're serious about diversity in this organisation.'
- vii 'I've noticed you never ask Duha to join you for coffee; why is that?' 'Well, she's so hard to understand, and anyway, we don't have anything in common, so she'd feel left out.'
- viii 'He did a great job for someone in a wheelchair.'

ix 'We can't hire a convicted thief or sex offender for this role because it requires going into people's homes in a position of trust.'
x 'We couldn't possibly have a transgender person in this role – what would the public say!'
xi 'Give it to Gramps – he'll know how to do it!'
xii 'We'll need to hold this training program over the weekend so as not to interfere with work time.'
xiii 'I don't want him on my project team – I can't trust him! He doesn't even look people in the eye!'

d Discuss how diversity can benefit organisations.

KEY CONCEPT 32.2 

a Explain the difference between treating people equally and treating people equitably, illustrating your explanation with three examples.
b What evidence is there that quotas are effective?
c Explain the concept of unearned disadvantage and unearned advantage and how it affects society and organisations.

KEY CONCEPT 32.3 

a Review the cultural differences you can expect to find in Australian workplaces and give some examples from your own experience to illustrate your explanation.
b Review the generational differences found in Australian workplaces and explain the tensions that can arise as a result. How can these tensions be overcome by good team leadership?

BUILD YOUR SKILLS

KEY CONCEPT 32.1 

a Have you ever been aware of bias, either for or against a person or group of people? If so, what were the effects on the 'targets' and on the people or persons responsible?
b What biases do you hold that offer either unearned advantage or unearned disadvantage? List five of them and for each, consider:
i how it may have been formed
ii whether it is logical or reasonable
iii how it serves you (perhaps it makes you feel safe or superior, or allows you to avoid certain people because they make you feel uncomfortable)
iv how you can prevent it resulting in discrimination in favour of or against people.

c The merit principle is based on US research. Do you think the findings also hold true in Australia? Why or why not? What evidence can you cite to support your opinion? What actions can organisations take to mitigate the unwanted effects of applying the merit principle?
d Provide an example of each of the three following forms of discrimination in terms of opportunity or treatment in employment: exclusion, preference and distinction. State whether the example you have given is of overt or covert discrimination and whether it is direct or indirect and explain whether the examples you have given might be systemic in nature.
e In the chapter, it is stated; 'There are no benefits from diversity per se. None at all.' Discuss.
f Including everyone improves performance. Discuss.

KEY CONCEPT 32.2 

a What is the difference between not discriminating and encouraging inclusion? How important is senior management's support of diversity? Explain your reasoning, using examples if possible.
b Explain why targets need to be mandatory, tracked and reported.
c Interview someone from a disadvantaged group. Find out whether they have ever felt discriminated against. If they have, find out how they may have been disadvantaged and how they believe their treatment might have affected the organisation in which they worked at the time.

KEY CONCEPT 32.3 

a List at least 10 actions you can take to communicate effectively with people who don't yet speak English well and 10 actions you can take to communicate effectively with people who are hearing impaired.
b Bearing in mind that not everyone fits every aspect of their generational profile, research the five generations you can find in Australian workplaces and

prepare a 300-word summary on the characteristics of each and how best to lead each. Use your generalisations as a framework, remembering that just as people are shaped by the times they live in and by their peers, they are also shaped by the values and beliefs of their cultures and personal experiences.

c Conduct an internet search to find out about three of the following cultures:
- African
- Australian/New Zealand
- Indian subcontinent
- Aboriginal and Torres Strait Islander
- Japanese
- Māori and Pacific Islander
- Middle Eastern
- North American
- Northern European
- South-East Asian
- Southern European.

Summarise your findings in terms of the work styles, including communication and decision-making styles and attitudes towards making mistakes and to time, and the best way to lead and manage people from each of these cultures. What style of leadership do people from each culture tend to prefer? Share and discuss your findings with the class. What actions can you take to prevent these generalisations from becoming stereotypes?

d How could you handle the three situations below in a way that would strengthen your team's ability to work together and value each other's differences?

i One team member freely uses the desks of other team members and when she needs a ruler or a stapler she rummages through her teammates' drawers to find one. She's naturally friendly and can't understand why her teammates give her the 'cold shoulder'. Her teammates can't stand it anymore and complain to you.

ii You value punctuality and one of your team members consistently turns up late for work and for meetings. When you point out his tardiness, he responds, 'Hey, what's a few minutes here or there? I was doing something else, and it was important!'

iii A new team member, fresh from university, often texts, checks messages and seems to consult various apps on her smartphone during meetings. Some of the other team members roll their eyes when she does this but haven't said anything either to you or to their new colleague.

e If you're from an Anglo-Celtic Australian culture, how can you adjust your communication style to be more 'in tune' with someone from an Asian culture? If you are from an Asian culture, how can you adjust your communication style to be more 'in tune' with someone from an Anglo-Celtic Australian culture?

f Research shows that in order to learn, you need to feel you 'belong'.[26] Do you believe the same holds true for being productive – you need to feel you belong in order to do your best? Discuss and provide examples from your own experience.

WORKPLACE ACTIVITIES

KEY CONCEPT 32.1 

a Watch the 17-minute talk called 'Perceiving social inequity' at https://www.youtube.com/watch?v=oVmHO_ENnOE in which the speaker discusses the difference between inequality and inequity, unearned advantage and unearned disadvantage, and how the merit system camouflages the system of privileges inside which it operates. Summarise your learnings and discuss how they apply to your workplace and how you can use what you've learnt from this video to be a better leader-manager.

b In the video referred to in the question above, the speaker related an anecdote of unearned advantage and disadvantage called the 'front row' and the 'back row'. In what ways do you sit in the 'front row'? In what ways do you sit in the 'back row'? What about the members of your work team and the other leader-managers in your organisation? What steps can you and your organisation take to mitigate 'back row' effects?

c Are you aware of any examples of bias in your workplace? What are the effects of these biases? What actions can the organisation take to mitigate their effects? What actions can you as a leader-manager take and what actions have you taken to mitigate their effects?

d How diverse is your organisation's workforce or your workplace? For example, does it employ members of all groups in the full range of jobs or are people from some groups concentrated into a few types of jobs? Are some groups of people concentrated in a few levels of the organisational structure? Are any groups or individuals disadvantaged or excluded? If so, how? Do the requirements of the jobs involved justify these disadvantages or exclusions? Here are some other measures of diversity to consider:
- educational level
- life and work experiences
- literacy and numeracy skills
- marital status
- outside-of-work commitments
- personality styles
- socio-economic background.

Based on your analysis, assess how your organisation or workplace measures up in terms of discrimination, diversity and inclusion. Outline a plan for increasing diversity and inclusion that targets specific benefits that align with your organisation's strategy, vision and values.

e List the state and federal legislation that affects your organisation's diversity and inclusion efforts. The first federal Act prohibiting discrimination was passed in 1975; since then, the four groups most at risk of discrimination have not changed. What do you think accounts for this? What measure can you suggest your organisation takes to increase its diversity and inclusiveness?

KEY CONCEPT 32.2 

a Review some of the ways organisations can encourage diversity and discuss which might be most effective in your workplace and why.

b In which of the ways listed in the chapter is your organisation diverse? Your work team?

c Do you think you're free of gender bias? You might be surprised by this 19-minute video: https://leanin.org/education/creating-a-level-playing-field. Watch it and then list the six simple and easy actions the speaker suggested you can take to limit gender bias in the workplace; summarise the studies that support each action and give an example of how each action could be, or already is, put into practice in your organisation. Would these steps help reduce or eliminate forms of discrimination other than gender discrimination?

d Describe the steps you or your organisation have taken to establish a common vision and goals and create an inclusive organisation culture. Discuss the diversity policies and programs your organisation has and, based on qualitative and quantitative measures, as discussed in Workplace activities 32.1(d), assess how effectively they have helped build a diverse organisation.

e Discuss the barriers to inclusion that still exist in your organisation and suggest how they might be overcome or diminished.

f Give three examples of what you have done to champion diversity and inclusion in your workplace.

g Explore http://www.prideindiversity.com.au and list five ways this organisation could help your organisation become more gender diverse.

KEY CONCEPT 32.3 

a What steps have you taken as a leader-manager to build a diverse work team? What steps have you taken to build an inclusive team?

EXTENSION ACTIVITIES

Referring to the Snapshot at the beginning of this chapter, answer the following questions:

1 Would the majority of others in leadership positions have been as supportive as Lieutenant-General Morrison?

2 What do you think institutions such as the Australian Defence Force can do to make such declarations and transitions easier for people to make?

3 What message would have been sent to the troops had Lieutenant-General Morrison transferred Lieutenant-Colonel McGregor to another post?

CASE STUDY 32

DAMLA'S DILEMMA

Newly arrived in Australia with limited English skills, Damla finds a casual job preparing packaged sandwiches for the retail lunch trade. Her hours are generally 3 a.m. to 8 a.m., which allows her just enough time to get home before her husband leaves for work and to care for her children, aged two, three and five years.

Damla understood that those were to be her usual hours and that she would be employed with reasonable regularity, and all goes well for eight or nine weeks. Then her boss begins asking her to stay late to help complete orders. She explains as best she can that she cannot stay because she needs to get home to her children. There are always several other workers willing to stay and Damla believes they can easily complete the work.

Then Damla's boss begins making remarks about people who aren't committed to their jobs and just there for the money. These comments soon escalate into thinly veiled remarks about people from Damla's homeland, the number of children 'they' have, 'their' lack of a 'real work ethic' and more. Before long, several of the other workers join in, commenting on the way Damla dresses, asking her pointed questions about her religion and smirking when she enters the room.

This upsets Damla but she needs her job to help pay the bills. She gets on with her duties and remains silent. Her boss continues to press her to work beyond 8 a.m. but Damla cannot. She doesn't feel able to explain her concern that her husband would be angry with her if she came home late as he has clear expectations about her role as a wife and mother.

Five weeks later, her boss fires her, saying he needs someone who is flexible enough to stay until all the work is finished. Damla is devastated. How can she face her husband now that she has lost her job? The family depends on the money she brings home to make ends meet.

Questions

1 Is it reasonable for Damla's boss to insist she stay longer than the agreed hours?
2 Assess the way Damla's boss handled the situation.
3 Does Damla have any recourse that would allow her to keep her job?

CHAPTER ENDNOTES

1 David Morrison, transcript of speech to Australian Army personnel, https://speakola.com/ideas/david-morrison-adf-investigation-2013, accessed 29 September 2021.

2 Workplace Gender Equality Agency, 'Australia's gender equality scorecard', 11 February 2022, https://www.wgea.gov.au/publications/australias-gender-equality-scorecard

3 See, for example, E. Castilla, S. Benard, 'The paradox of meritocracy in organizations', *Administrative Science Quarterly*, December 2010, Vol. 55, No. 4, pp. 543–676; Lauren Rivera, *Pedigree: How elite students get elite jobs*, Princeton University Press, New Jersey, 2016; D. Hekman, S. Johnson, M. D. Foo, W. Yang, 'Does diversity-valuing behaviour result in diminished performance ratings for nonwhite and female leaders?', *Academy of Management Journal*, 3 March 2016.

4 See 'Perceiving social inequity – Live session' at https://www.youtube.com/watch?v=3rb3Cyjm8VQ, published 19 December 2014, accessed 29 September 2021.

5 Pepsico, 'Diversity, equity and inclusion', https://www.pepsico.com/about/diversity-equity-and-inclusion, accessed 29 September 2021.

6 Robert Bean, 'Diversity dividends', *Training and Development in Australia*, February 2005.

7 'Diversity and the bottom line', *Company Director*, March 2016, p. 11.

8 Julia Dawson, Richard Kersley, Stefano Natella, *The CS Gender 3000: The reward for change,* Credit Suisse AG, Zurich, 2016.

9 'KPMG reconciliation action plan 2017–2020: KPMG's second Elevate RAP documents our 10-year reconciliation journey and our future commitment to reconciliation over the period 2017-2020', https://home.kpmg/au/en/home/about/citizenship/reconciliation-with-indigenous-australia/reconciliation-action-plan.html, accessed 29 September 2021.

10 David Rock, Heidi Grant, 'Why diverse teams are smarter', 4 November 2016, *Harvard Business* Review, https://hbr.org/2016/11/why-diverse-teams-are-smarter

11 Sylvia Ann Hewlett, Melinda Marshall, Laura Sherbin, 'How diversity can drive innovation', *Harvard Business Review*, December 2013, p. 30.

12 'Stats and facts', Australian Network on Disability, https://www.and.org.au/pages/disability-statistics.html, accessed 29 September 2021.

13 Organisation for Economic Co-operation and Development, 'Sickness and disability', https://www.oecd.org/employment/emp/sicknessdisabilityandwork.htm, accessed 29 September 2021.

14 'Stats and facts', Australian Network on Disability, op. cit.

15 Human Rights Commission, https://www.humanrightscommission.vic.gov.au, accessed 29 September 2021.

16 Aruma, 'Five of the best Australian disability activists', https://www.aruma.com.au/about-us/blog/five-of-the-best-australian-disability-activists/, accessed 29 September 2021.

17 Andy Molinsky, 'Companies don't go global, people do', *Harvard Business Review*, October 2015, pp. 82–85.

18 Tim Soutphommasane, 'Unconscious bias and the bamboo ceiling', Address to Asian Australian Lawyers Association, Melbourne, 10 June 2014, https://www.humanrights.gov.au/news/speeches/unconscious-bias-and-bamboo-ceiling, accessed 30 September 2021.

19 Australian Bureau of Statistics, 'Gender indicators, Australia', https://www.abs.gov.au/statistics/people/people-and-communities/gender-indicators-australia/latest-release#key-statistics, accessed 29 September 2021.

20 Courtney Connley, 'A record number of women are now running Global 500 businesses', *CNBC*, 2 Aug 2021 https://www.cnbc.com/2021/08/02/a-record-number-of-women-are-now-running-global-500-businesses.html, accessed 29 September 2021.

21 Workplace Gender Equality Agency, 'GradStats – Starting salaries', https://www.wgea.gov.au/sites/default/files/GradStats_factsheet_2016.pdf, accessed 29 September 2021.

22 Michelle Budig, 'Third way', 29 September 2021, https://thinkprogress.org/having-children-is-great-for-a-mans-paycheck-and-terrible-for-a-woman-s-bc320f6d4b14/, accessed 29 September 2021.

23 Keith Macky, Dianne Gardner, Stewart Forsyth, 'Generational differences at work: Introduction and overview', *Journal of Managerial Psychology*, Vol. 23, No. 8, pp. 857–861.

24 Australian Bureau of Statistics, '3101.0 – Australian demographic statistics', June 2016, https://www.abs.gov.au/statistics/people/population/national-state-and-territory-population/latest-release

25 'Engaging and retaining older workers', Discussion paper, February 2013, *AIM*, NSW and ACT Training Centre Ltd.

26 Gregory M. Walton, Geoffrey L. Cohen, 'A question of belonging: Race, social fit, and achievement', *Journal of Personality and Social Psychology*, Vol. 92, No. 1, January 2007, pp. 82–96.

GLOSSARY

360-degree feedback
A type of performance review whereby a selection of people dealing with a job-holder (peers, reports, managers, external and internal customers and suppliers) comment on the job-holder's performance. The intention is to build up a full picture of how a person does their job so that they can improve their performance and productivity; aka a multi-rater feedback.

85:15 rule
Provided people know precisely what is expected of them and are trained to do it properly, 85 per cent of the causes of poor performance and low productivity can be found in the work environment (information, job design, systems and processes, teamwork, time, and tools and equipment) and are not the direct fault of the employee. 'Acts of God' and personal problems account for the remaining 15 per cent.

absenteeism
Unplanned non-attendance of employees when they are expected to attend, which can reflect conflict between personal and work-related responsibilities, genuine illness, low motivation or a poor work culture. *See* presenteeism.

accident
An unexpected event that results in injury or damage to health or property and points to inefficient operations and lack of control over materials, people and processes. *See* incident.

acknowledgement listening
Responding to a speaker with eye contact, nods, 'uh-huhs' and other minimal encouragers.

action learning
Facilitated learning by a group (an action-learning set) that works on current problems and issues relevant to the organisation, simultaneously solving problems and providing learning opportunities that set members can transfer to other situations.

additive manufacturing
As distinct from the traditional subtractive manufacturing that removes and reshapes materials, additive manufacturing makes complex goods by adding layer upon layer of various materials, which reduces waste; aka digital manufacturing. *See* 3D manufacturing.

aggressive behaviour
Putting your own wants and needs ahead of others, often ignoring the wants and needs of others. *See* assertive behaviour and passive behaviour.

analytics
The systematic analysis of large amounts of data from sources such as digital images, mobile phone GPS signals, posts to social-networking sites, sensors, transaction records of online purchases, and videos posted online in order to find meaningful patterns and trends to analyse risks, capitalise on opportunities, inform decision-making and generate insights to increase competitiveness and predict events; aka big data.

arbitration
When agreement is not reached through conciliation, a neutral third party, having heard and considered both sides, makes a ruling by which both parties must abide; the ruling can be enforced as if it were a court order.

ask 'Why?' five times
A technique used to uncover the main cause of a problem.

assertive behaviour
A learned style of communicating and relating to others based on mutual respect that results in clear, open communication; the ability to state and work towards realising your own wants and needs while at the same time respecting the wants and needs of others. *See* aggressive behaviour and passive behaviour.

attrition
Employee turnover; aka churn. The frequency with which employees leave an organisation, usually expressed as a percentage of the total workforce; below-average turnover is generally a sign of high morale and employee engagement, while above-average turnover is generally a sign of low morale and engagement. The opposite measure is retention.

authoritarian leader
A task-centred type of leader who exercises strong control, offers followers little opportunity to participate in decision-making and provides minimal information; aka autocratic leader.

authority
The right to decide what is to be done and who is to do it; aka legitimate power.

autocratic leader
See authoritarian leader.

award
A legally enforceable order made by the Full Bench of the Fair Work Commission providing additional minimum terms and conditions supplementing the National Employment

Standards for those employees in a particular industry or group of occupations to whom it applies; unique to Australia.

B corporation
Companies that have stated their commitment to environmental and social goals, as well as profit; aka B corps.

balance sheet
One of three statements required in a financial report, it is a 'snapshot' of the financial health of a business, showing what it owns and is owed (assets and reserves) and what it owes (liabilities) on a specific date, comparing this period to the last period's position and showing the change as a percentage; aka statement of financial position; previously known as the statement of financial position. *See* cash flow statement, income statement, current, fixed, intangible and tangible assets.

balanced scorecard
Measuring customer satisfaction, internal business process efficiencies and effectiveness, and organisational learning and growth (including training and workplace culture) in addition to (and in order to 'balance') financial measures (which measure only past performance); designed to help organisations continuously improve their strategic performance and results. Also a method of reviewing performance.

bar chart
A visual display of quantities using bars, or lines, whose lengths are in proportion to those quantities.

behavioural approach to leadership
Examines what effective leaders say and do.

benchmarking
Using meaningful standard measures of performance to gauge an organisation's performance, either internally or across other similar and/or nearby organisations. *See* best practice benchmarking.

best practice
A method that has been accepted to produce optimal results compared to any other.

best practice benchmarking
Comparing measures of an organisation's performance with those of leading organisations in the same or different industries.

big data
See analytics.

biodiversity
The variety of life forms in an ecosystem (biome) or on the entire planet; a measure of the health of biological systems, measured by the Living Planet Index and the ecological footprint.

board of directors
The policy- and strategy-establishing body of a company, which represents its shareholders and guides the organisation's operations.

body language
The unspoken messages people send with their bodies – the ways they sit and stand, move and change position, and the pitches, speeds, tones and volumes of their voices.

boomerang principle
The concept that what people 'send out' to others returns to them; for example, when you are polite to someone, that person is likely to be polite in return.

brainstorming
A technique that helps produce a large number of ideas for later evaluation.

budget
A summary of objectives expressed in quantity and dollars; for example, expected income and expenses for a given period or project.

bullying
Aggressive remarks and/or behaviours that repeatedly demean, humiliate and/or undermine the recipient, carried out in person or electronically (cyberbullying) and committed by one person or several (mobbing); illegal behaviour. Ostracism, or repeated exclusion, is silent bullying.

bureaucracy
An organisation characterised by a formal chain of command, a rigid or semi-rigid hierarchy, specialisation of tasks and strict rules and procedures.

burnout
The result of unalleviated stress.

business complexity
Having numerous diverse and interdependent parts.

business continuity plan
The steps an organisation intends to take to ensure its survival in the event of a disruption to its operations.

business disruption
Revolutionary business models providing processes, products or services in a completely different way, such as additive manufacturing, Airbnb and Uber.

business model
How a business makes its offering distinctive by creating value for its customers and obtaining value from the value it creates. *See* also digital platform business model.

business process management
Using technology and systematic analytical methods to radically redesign processes and operating procedures from top to bottom to achieve breakthrough improvements in productivity; essentially, reorganising around core capabilities; aka process re-engineering, re-engineering and core process redesign.

capabilities-based competition
Creating value and competitive advantage through capabilities

in processes, such as design and marketing, delivery and invoicing, the ability to enter emerging markets successfully, to bring new products to market quickly, to respond promptly to customer complaints; aka competency-based competition.

capabilities-based organisation
One structured around its core capabilities, or business processes, executed in a way that is difficult to copy; based on cross-functional teamwork and strategic investment in support systems that span business units and functions.

capability
What an organisation excels at – information systems and workflows, logistics, marketing, people, processes, technology and so on; usually built over time and difficult to copy; a set of processes that require cross-functional teamwork and strategic investment in support systems. *See* intangible assets.

carbon footprint
A measure of the greenhouse gases released by using fossil fuels. There are several ways to calculate CF although many simply calculate the tonnes of carbon rather than demand on bioproductive area; aka CO_2 footprint. *See* ecological footprint.

carbon sink
A natural or human-made system that absorbs carbon dioxide from the atmosphere and stores it, including trees, plants and oceans; aka carbon reservoir.

cash flow statement
One of three statements required in a financial report, it reports a company's cash sources and uses, indicating its liquidity (cash and assets converting easily into cash) by showing how much working capital (money) is available; it summarises an organisation's cash flow from its operating, investing and financing activities. *See* balance sheet, income statement, intangible assets and tangible assets.

casual employee
A type of employee who has no expectation of ongoing work from the employer and who does not receive paid holiday or sick leave entitlements. They are called in on a day-to-day basis when needed by the employer and paid only for the hours worked at a higher pay rate called casual loading. *See* temporary employee.

casualisation
The increasing use of casual and temporary employees (contractors) who have less stability and security of employment but who provide employers with greater flexibility at reduced employment costs.

cause-and-effect diagram
A pictorial representation that helps to identify problems, isolate the main cause of a problem or clarify a problem by allowing you to view it in its entirety; aka Ishikawa diagrams and fishbone diagrams.

centralised organisation
One in which decision-making authority resides with management.

charismatic leadership
Leadership based on personal magnetism and other qualities.

check sheet
A method of gathering data, based on sample observations, that helps detect and isolate patterns of non-conformance and variation.

checkerboard analysis
A matrix used to analyse a problem by comparing various elements of the problem with each other.

circling
A technique to break a complex issue into its elements by circling key words to arrive at a succinct problem definition.

circular economy
One where products are designed to be reused rather than wasted.

climate change
The inadvertent effects of human-amplified modification of the natural environment resulting in long-term (decades to centuries) alteration in global weather patterns, particularly increases in average temperature and storm activity (as opposed to natural climate variability, which is years to decades fluctuations in climate; e.g. El Niño).

closed question
One that can be answered with 'yes', 'no' or a short statement of fact.

coach
A colleague or manager who helps develop another's talents, skills and understanding; or selected professionals or specialists such as accountants, computer experts or professional coaches who develop another's skills and understanding.

coaching
Passing on one's experience or skills, or using a particular process to help people develop their talents, skills and understanding.

collaborative systems technology
Software that helps people work together, such as chat systems, email and Lotus Notes ('low-end' technology), Voice-over internet Protocol and videoconferencing systems ('mid-level' technology), and software that allows people to work remotely together, in real time, on documents, spreadsheets and so on; these are underpinned by base-level technologies such as the internet, encryption (to protect data while it travels across the internet) and compression (to make the data smaller so it travels quickly, taking less time to transmit); aka groupware, application sharing and collaborative software.

common law
Principles and rules based on judicial decisions, custom and precedent; judge-made law built up over time; not written in statutes.

competency-based job description
A position description showing the knowledge and skills (i.e. competencies) required by the jobholder. *See* job description and role description.

competency-based interviewing
A method of interviewing that probes what candidates have done and been motivated by in the past and/or asking them to walk you through how they would handle a hypothetical situation and using that information to predict what they will do and be motivated by in the future; it allows interviewers to compare the candidates with the person specification to reach sound selection decisions, aka behavioural interviewing and situational interviewing.

conciliation
A neutral third party helping two disagreeing parties (e.g. an employer and a group of employees or a manager and a direct report) reach agreement.

conciliator
Takes a more direct role than mediators and may even suggest a way or ways to resolve a dispute.

confirmation bias
A tendency to interpret, search for and remember information in a manner that confirms your beliefs or values.

conscious capitalism
A business philosophy based on organisations working to benefit all stakeholders, not just shareholders, as the preferred path to long-term competitive advantage; it differentiates itself from corporate social responsibility, which it sees as a response to external pressure. *See* also corporate responsibility and B corporations.

consensus
Exploring, analysing and discussing an issue until a group reaches widespread, or near-unanimous, agreement.

constructive feedback
Guidance that helps people further improve their performance and productivity, polish their skills and build on their strengths. *See* corrective feedback, feedback, negative feedback and positive feedback.

consultation
Seeking the informed ideas and opinions of employees (and, when appropriate, other stakeholders) about the organisation's operations and important decisions; influencing a decision; not joint decision-making.

contingency planning
See risk management.

continuous improvement
Frequent small enhancements, or incremental improvements, to a process, product or service; aka continuous incremental improvements and *kaizen*.

continuous manufacturing model
Software upgrades and updates greatly extending the life of products and strengthening relationships between buyers and sellers, enabling more sustainable manufacturing and providing a continuous profit stream.

continuum of leadership styles
A model of leadership based on the amount of authority the leader retains and the corresponding amount of freedom allowed to followers, resulting in a range of leadership behaviours labelled telling, selling, consulting, sharing and delegating.

contractor
A business or an individual engaged by an organisation to perform work; for example, a company may call in a building or painting contractor to paint its offices or contract a trucking company to deliver its products rather than employ its own drivers and purchase and maintain its own fleet of delivery vehicles. Dependent contractors are sometimes called 'false self-employed' because the contractor's income is dependent on one client, making the contractor an 'in fact' employee, yet not entitled to the protections of an employment relationship; independent contractors contract to perform work for another person or organisation (the client) but are not employed by the client and are paid for results, the client having minimal control over when, where and how the work is performed.

control chart
A type of run chart showing the upper and lower acceptable limits of variation in the results of a process on either side of the average; used for quality control purposes.

corporate citizenship
An organisation's legal and moral obligations to its community and society, including support of charities and local initiatives, and care for the environment. *See* conscious capitalism.

corporate culture
The beliefs and behaviours that determine how management and employees interact with one another and also how they conduct external business dealings.

corporate governance
Managing a company and its operations according to legal requirements and regulations; the way an organisation is governed

and controlled, particularly by its board of directors. It includes the organisation's code of conduct for ethical behaviour, its policies and programs on corporate social responsibility, risk management and sustainability, and its human resource policies, programs and management systems; it is often considered to be concerned not only with compliance with the law but also with the way an organisation is run as a whole, balancing economic and social goals, and communal and individual goals.

corporate responsibility
The next iteration of corporate social responsibility, which is considered to be prescriptive, 'one-size-fits-all', while CR identifies the needs and expectations of stakeholders and seeks to meet the most important. Most major companies now have a CR, sustainability, corporate citizenship or similar department and publish a CR report. *See* also conscious capitalism and B corporations.

corporate social responsibility
Doing the right thing economically, environmentally, ethically and socially. *See* business ethics, conscious capitalism, corporate citizenship and corporate responsibility.

corporation
A business that exists independently of its owners and employees; a legal entity in its own right.

corrective feedback
Guidance given to employees who are underperforming or whose behaviour is unacceptable in some way. It describes what to do to improve performance, productivity or behaviour. *See* constructive feedback, feedback, negative feedback, positive feedback and performance counselling.

cost–benefit analysis
Weighing up the cost of introducing an initiative or making a purchase against the benefits to be gained, by quantifying and then adding all the positive factors (the benefits) and quantifying and subtracting the negatives (the costs); the difference indicates whether the course of action or purchase is advisable.

covert discrimination
Unequal treatment based on characteristics that belong to, or are connected with, some members of a group of people; often subtle and unconscious. *See* direct discrimination, discrimination, indirect discrimination, overt discrimination and systemic discrimination.

cradle-to-cradle
Taking raw materials from the earth, making them into a product and, at the end of the product's life, upcycling it to reuse the materials to make the same product again, or another product that retains the value of those raw materials (rather than downcycling them, destroying them or dumping them in landfills). *See* circular economy, cradle-to-grave, downcycling, upcycling.

cradle-to-grave
The conventional way of manufacturing that takes raw materials from the earth, makes them into a product and, at the end of the product's life, it is downcycled, dumped or destroyed, generating greenhouse gases in the process. *See* cradle-to-cradle.

critical path
The path, or series of tasks, that must start and finish on time so that a project or plan finishes on time; any delay on the critical path delays the project.

critical path analysis
A type of network diagram that shows the various activities of a plan or project as they relate to each other and when each activity should begin and finish; aka critical path method (CPM). *See* PERT diagram.

cross-functional team
See multifunctional team.

cross-skilling
Increasing the ability of employees to carry out a wider range of tasks at the same or similar levels of responsibility; aka cross-training, in the sense that employees can do each other's tasks and therefore can cover for each other. *See* job enlargement, job enrichment, multiskilling and upskilling.

cultural intelligence
The ability to operate across cultures, and not just internationally, because all groups have cultures – communities, families, generations, neighbourhoods, organisations, work teams and so on.

culture
The beliefs, customs, habits and practices of a country, a group, an organisation or a team; the collection of unwritten codes of behaviour and rules by which people operate and the shared set of values and assumptions that reflect the underling mindset.

current asset
An asset such as inventory and money in the bank.

customer–supplier chain
A systems view of an organisation that sees the internal relationships in the organisation (departments or activities) as one continuous process of supplying and receiving products, services or information and adding value at each step.

decentralised organisation
An organisation in which decision-making authority is

located as close as possible to the area affected by the decision.

delegation
Assigning work to a team member.

deliverable
A tangible or intangible, but quantifiable, end result of mental or physical effort such as a design, document, innovation or report; a building block of a job or project.

democratic leader
A people-centred type of leader who encourages participation and involves people. Sometimes called participative leaders.

demotion
Reassignment to a job of lower rank and pay.

deregulation
For the private sector: removing protection from overseas competition by reducing tariff and non-tariff barriers on trade in goods and services, floating currencies and opening financial markets by reducing barriers to direct foreign investment and other international capital flows, resulting in freer trade between countries; a major driver of globalisation. For the public sector: allowing private providers to enter markets traditionally served by the public bodies.

dictatorial leader
A negative, task-centred type of leader who rules through force and threats of punishment.

digital platform business models
Use technology to bring together the supplier/producer and the consumer; e.g. Airbnb, eBay, Uber.

digital transformation
The integration of digital technology across many or all areas of an organisation.

direct cost
A cost that is traceable to a specific cost centre or item; you can think of it as being attached to a single product or service. *See* also indirect cost.

direct discrimination
Refusal or consistent failure to treat people from disadvantaged groups equally in employment matters. *See* covert discrimination, discrimination, indirect discrimination, overt discrimination and systemic discrimination.

disability
A physical or mental impairment or restriction in activities.

disaster recovery plans
The steps an organisation plans to take to recover its IT systems and infrastructure after a disruptive event. *See* business continuity plans.

discipline
Addressing employee behaviour or work performance or productivity that is below the expected standard of conduct or output.

discrimination
Bias or prejudice resulting in denial of opportunity or unfair treatment; unequal treatment before, during or after employment; a distinction, exclusion or preference based on one or more of the above grounds. See covert discrimination, direct discrimination, indirect discrimination, overt discrimination and systemic discrimination.

dismissal
When an employer ends a contract of employment; this should be done with notice and the employee paid any leave owing. *See* constructive dismissal, instant dismissal, unfair dismissal and unlawful dismissal.

dispute settlement procedure
A clear procedure detailing the steps for dealing with conflict, disagreements and grievances between employers and employees, either in groups (e.g. concerning the application of an award or workplace agreement) or individually (e.g. concerning a performance review or unfair treatment by a line manager) that should be clearly set out in all workplace agreements and preferably confirmed in a separate policy; aka grievance-handling procedure.

diversity
A general term indicating that people with a variety of differences (e.g. ability, age, cultural, ethnicity, gender, language, race, religion, sexual orientation) are present, welcome and productive in an organisation.

downcycling
Reuse, but in a way that lessens the item's original value; for example, melting a computer casing into a speed bump. *See* cradle-to-cradle, cradle-to-grave and upcycling.

downsizing
Reducing the number of employees in an organisation in an effort to lower costs, increase profitability and be more responsive in the marketplace by streamlining internal operations.

drivers of success
The factors that work together to propel an organisation forward towards achieving its strategic goals; these are different for each organisation but may include, for example, organisation culture, growth, human capital, information capital and innovation.

duty of care
The legal obligation to avoid causing harm to others. In health, safety and welfare, the legal obligation of employers to ensure that their business, so far as is practicable, does not harm employees or the general public. In risk management, it refers to understanding the organisation's

risk profile and developing plans to manage risks for the continuity and survival of the organisation.

ecological footprint
Expressed in global hectares (gha) and widely used as a measure of environmental sustainability and the extent of human demand, or impact, on the planet's ecosystems, the EF estimates how many planet earths are needed to support humanity if everyone lived a given lifestyle. It measures the amount of biologically productive land and water area required to produce the resources an individual, a population or an activity consumes and to absorb the waste generated, given prevailing technology and resource management; therefore, small is better.

economies of scale
Efficiencies associated with the quantity produced – the more products or services an organisation produces, the cheaper each becomes.

ecosystem
A localised and interdependent dynamic community of plants, animals, insects and micro-organisms that interact and depend on each other as well as on the non-living aspects of the environment (e.g. air, climate, sunlight and water) to function as a unit (lakes and even some suburban gardens are ecosystems). (A biome is a large ecosystem. The Great Barrier Reef, deserts, oceans and rainforests are examples of biomes.)

emotional intelligence (EI or EQ)
The (largely learnt) ability to monitor your own and other people's emotions and use that information to guide your thinking and actions.

empathic leadership
A way of leading that considers followers' perspectives and uses empathy when giving advice, directions and support.

empathy
The ability to see problems and situations from another person's point of view.

employee assistance program (EAP)
A program that help employees, and often members of their immediate families as well, through difficult or traumatic events, incidents or issues; some programs concentrate on events in employees' working lives while others also deal with issues in employees' private lives to help create a generally healthier, happier, more productive workforce.

employee engagement
The psychological commitment employees feel towards their employer, based on identifying with the organisation's values and vision and ways of operating.

employer brand
An organisation's image that attracts potential employees and retains current employees, made up of factors such as its practices, products and services, reputation for quality and customer service, how it treats its employees, how it delivers its promises and corporate social responsibility.

employer value proposition
The total package of an organisation's offering to employees that attracts and helps retain the employees it needs at all levels; it includes its career- and performance-management systems, culture, values, vision and mission, employer brand, health and wellness policies, reputation for corporate social responsibility, management practices, technologies, learning and development processes, and working benefits and arrangements (e.g. for flexible working).

empowerment
See job empowerment.

engagement
See employee engagement.

equity
The difference between assets and liabilities; the investment in the organisation by its owners.

eustress
A positive form of stress having a beneficial effect on health, motivation, performance and emotional wellbeing.

executive directors
Members of the board who also work in the company. *See* non-executive directors.

exit interview
A discussion, usually held between a neutral party, such as a human resources officer, and an employee who has resigned, to discover the reason for the resignation. The information is used to improve the organisation's ability to retain valued employees.

external board
A board of directors made up entirely of directors not employed by the company in another capacity; aka a non-executive board. *See* inside board and mixed board.

external customer
A person or organisation who purchases or uses an organisation's products or services. *See* internal customer.

external locus of control
An inability to control one's emotions, actions and reactions to people and events; as a result, other people and events dictate a person's behaviour and actions; thought to result from seeing the cause of events as outside oneself, resulting from, for example, luck, chance or fate.

feedback
Guidance or information about performance, productivity or behaviour used to make or

maintain improvements. *See* constructive feedback, corrective feedback, negative feedback and positive feedback.

fight, flight or freeze response
An instinctive reaction to a dangerous or an unpleasant situation: to stay and fight, to turn and flee from it or to freeze when there is no hope, when fight or flight is impossible.

first-line leader-managers
The level of management between the non-management workforce and the rest of management. (Note: the terms first-line manager, management and team leader are used interchangeably in this text.)

Five Keys
The Five Keys that unlock performance excellence and high productivity: people need to know What To do; they need to Want To do it and know How To do it; they need a Chance To do it and be appropriately Led To do it.

fixed asset
An asset expected to last more than a year, such as a building and equipment.

fixed cost
A cost of running an organisation that doesn't change for a specific period of time, such as insurance, rent and tax. *See* also variable costs.

flexible working
Measures, such as annualised hours, banked time, compressed working weeks, flexitime and purchased leave, intended to help balance work and personal responsibilities and increase workforce flexibility and organisational effectiveness.

flow chart
A pictorial representation showing all the steps of a process or an activity.

force-field analysis
A technique that helps to ensure the smooth implementation of a plan or decision by highlighting factors working against you (resisting forces), to diminish or remove them, and factors in your favour (driving forces), to capitalise on in order to move from the current to the desired situation.

framing statement
A short sentence used to nominate and introduce a topic for discussion or to describe a problem or decision to be made.

functional leadership
Satisfying three areas of need in order to be an effective leader: the task, the team and the individual; aka action-centred leadership.

functions
Specialised activities such as customer service, distribution, finance, information technology, marketing, production and research and development grouped into departments; sometimes referred to (censoriously) as 'silos'.

Gantt chart
A planning and monitoring aid that lists planned activities vertically and time periods horizontally, showing what needs to be done and when.

gap analysis
Answering the questions: 'Where are we now?' (current situation), 'Where do we want to be?' (desired situation) and 'How will we get there?' (the plan or strategy) in order to establish how to bridge the gap, or move from the current to the desired situation.

globalisation
Treating the world as one marketplace; the integration of the world's economic, financial, trade and communications systems. Driven by national and international deregulation of trade and investment and enabled by the IT-related revolution, the central feature of which is the ability to manipulate, store and transmit large quantities of information at very low cost.

goodwill
An intangible asset that raises the price of a business or shares in a listed company above its actual market value of its tangible assets less its liabilities; based on the total of its other intangible assets.

green electricity
See renewable energy.

greenhouse gases (GHG)
Gases that contribute to the warming of the Earth's atmosphere by trapping and reflecting heat back to the earth's surface; they include carbon dioxide (CO_2), which is of the greatest concern because it generates just over 55 per cent of human-induced greenhouse gases and remains in the atmosphere for about 100 years, halocarbons (compressed gas) and chlorofluorocarbons (CFCs), methane (CH_4), nitrous oxide (N_2O), ozone (O_3), sulphur hexafluoride (SF_6) and water vapour. Greenhouse gases are released by human activities, including cutting down forests, driving cars and flying aircraft, growing crops and keeping livestock (animal waste gives off methane), industrial processes, and power plants that use fossil fuels for electricity.

grievance
A complaint or an objection that employees, either singly or collectively, have formally registered with a trade union or a management official according to the organisation's agreed dispute-settlement procedure.

group dynamics
The unique pattern of forces operating in a group that affects particularly the interactions between members and their relationships with each other; the way people work together and

their behaviour towards each other, which influences how they go about achieving their goals.

groupthink
A phenomenon of highly cohesive groups that occurs when group members would rather maintain a group's equanimity than cause friction by challenging ideas, stating an opposing point of view or putting forward contrary evidence; this inhibits constructive criticism, disagreement and a full assessment of alternatives, and filters out contraindications to a decision or chosen course of action.

groupware
See collaborative systems technology.

halo effect
Forming a positive opinion about a person based on some other unrelated trait or characteristic.

halo/horns effect
Allowing a positive or a negative characteristic of a person or situation to 'spread' and influence your perception of other characteristics, even though they are not connected, causing you to see the person or situation in an artificially positive or negative light.

harassment
Unwanted or unwelcome behaviour of a sexual nature, including verbal as well as non-verbal behaviour and innuendo; illegal behaviour.

hazard
Anything with the potential to harm life, health or property.

hierarchy of needs
Six levels of basic human needs that people are motivated to fulfil; aka Maslow's hierarchy of needs.

histogram
A bar chart that displays the distribution of measurement data in graph form, illustrating how often these events occur, to show the amount of variation in a process and help people to identify and describe a problem and monitor its solution.

holacracy
Comprehensive practice for structuring, governing and running an organisation that removes power from a management hierarchy and distributes it across clear roles, which can then be executed autonomously without a micromanaging boss.

horizontal integration
Horizontally integrated organisations seek complementary products or uses for their products and facilities. *See* vertical integration.

horns effect
Forming a negative opinion about a person based on some other unrelated trait or characteristic.

hot-stove principle
Providing advanced warning about the need to comply with important rules and regulations, followed by immediate, consistent and impartial discipline when they are not followed.

hub working
See workplace hub.

hygiene factors
Factors in the job environment which, when satisfactory, put people in 'neutral' so that they can be motivated; poor hygiene factors dishearten and 'demotivate' workers. *See* motivation factors.

'I' language
An assertive style of communication that involves taking responsibility for and communicating your own feelings, thoughts and opinions.

'I' message
A clear, succinct and blame-free statement of how someone's actions affect you and/or the team, and the behaviour you want instead.

incident
An event which, on this occasion, did not result in injury or damage to property; aka a near miss. *See* notifiable incident.

income statement
One of three statements required in a financial report, it shows a company's trading result (profit or loss) from sales and other income minus direct costs and overheads over a weekly, monthly, quarterly or yearly period, incurred to the date of preparing the statement; commonly called the profit and loss (P&L) account; previously known as the profit and loss statement and now also known as the statement of financial performance. *See* balance sheet, cash flow statement, current, fixed, intangible and tangible assets.

indirect cost
A cost that is not tied to a particular cost centre or item but is part of the ordinary running of an organisation and benefits the entire organisation; the total of all indirect costs is called overheads. *See* also direct cost.

indirect discrimination
Policies and practices that appear on the surface to be neutral but which act to disadvantage members of some disadvantaged groups. *See* covert discrimination, direct discrimination, discrimination, overt discrimination, and systemic discrimination.

influence
The informal power a person holds.

informal leader
The person with the most influence in a group or team.

inherent risk
The risk with no controls in place.

inside board
A board of directors made up entirely of executive directors; aka an executive board. *See* external board and mixed board.

intangible assets
Items such as brand and image in the marketplace, capabilities, customer and supplier relationships, goodwill, intellectual capital, organisation structure and strategies, all of which can increase competitiveness because they are difficult for competitors to replicate; considered to account for up to 75 per cent of a company's value even though they are difficult to measure in dollars; aka organisational capabilities. *See* balance sheet, cash flow statement, goodwill, income statement, current, fixed and tangible assets.

intellectual capital
How much an organisation knows and is able to use; its knowledge, made up of human capital, relationship capital and structural capital.

intellectual property
The intangible assets resulting from creativity and innovation such as brands, copyrights, designs, formulas and recipes, images, patents, pricing, processes and methodologies, proprietary and confidential information, symbols and trademarks, and tender documents.

internal customer
A person within an organisation who benefits from other employees' efforts in the organisation. *See* external customer.

internal locus of control
The ability to control one's emotions, actions and reactions to people and events.

internal suppliers
People and departments inside the organisation who provide information, materials and services. *See* external suppliers.

International Organization for Standardization (ISO)
The world's largest developer and publisher of international quality standards that are used around the world to assure product and service quality; there are currently more than 19 500 standards covering most aspects of technology and business. The ISO's Central Secretariat in Geneva in Switzerland coordinates the network of 157 national standards institutes of its member countries.

is/is not comparison
A technique that helps identify and analyse problems by comparing the what, where, when, who, extent, frequency and so on of something that is a problem with something similar that is not a problem.

ISO
See International Organization for Standardization.

job breakdown
An instruction tool that divides a job or task into its stages and key points.

job design
The way a position is structured in terms of its specific duties, responsibilities and tasks; an important source of job satisfaction and an enabler of high performance and productivity. *See* job redesign.

job empowerment
The training and workplace conditions that enable employees or work teams to increase their range of decision-making authority and responsibility.

job enlargement
Expanding a job horizontally, at the same or similar level of authority and responsibility. *See* cross-skilling.

job enrichment
Expanding a job vertically, to a higher level of authority and responsibility. *See* upskilling.

job placement
Assigning duties to suit an employee's aptitudes, interests, knowledge, skills, temperament and work-style preferences.

job purpose
A succinct, motivational statement that expresses the main reason a job exists.

Johari Window
A model for self-awareness based on two dimensions: aspects of yourself known or not known to yourself and aspects of yourself known or not known to others, resulting in four 'windows' or areas of knowledge about yourself.

kaizen
See continuous improvement.

key performance indicators (KPIs)
Measures of success in reaching goals for activities, processes or projects; a series of KPIs helps manage, monitor and assess the effectiveness of activities and employees; aka key success indicators.

key result areas (KRAs)
The main areas of accountability and responsibility of a job.

knowledge economy
An economy based not on what people make but on what people know.

knowledge worker
An employee who develops or uses information and knowledges in their work, such as academics, people in information technology, professional workers, researchers, scientists, systems analysts and technical writers.

labour market
The availability of labour both in terms of demand and supply to fill available positions.

lag indicator
A measure of results after a process is completed; an historical measure. *See* lead indicator.

laissez-faire leader
A non-directive, delegative leader who provides information and leaves employees to do their jobs, with little or no directions or other input; aka free-rein leader.

lead indicator
A measure taken during a process; a current measure of what is happening as the process occurs. *See* lag indicator.

lean
A methodology for innovating and making improvements to existing work flows, or processes.

lean Six Sigma
Combines lean production with Six Sigma; more robust than lean and less rigorous than Six Sigma.

learning culture
The value an organisation and its employees place on learning; a strong learning culture is one in which employees at all levels continually learn and share their learning, building their competencies and their organisation's capabilities at the same time.

learning cycle
A way to improve individual or team performance by reviewing what was done, which actions worked well and what could have been done better and how, and planning to apply this insight to improve subsequent performance; aka after-action review.

life cycle analysis
Investigating and assessing the environmental impacts of a product or service throughout its life in order to choose the least burdensome one; aka cradle-to-grave analysis, ecobalance and life cycle assessment. *See* upcycling.

lost-time injury
An event resulting in a fatality, permanent disability or time lost from work of one day or a shift or more.

management by exception
Asking people to report only important deviations; when nothing is reported, work is going according to plan and agreed targets are being reached.

management by objectives (MBO)
A performance management system whereby employees and managers agree specific performance objectives and targets, aligned with corporate goals and strategy, to be accomplished within a given time period.

managerial grid
A system that describes five possible leadership styles based on how much attention a leader pays to output and to people.

matrix organisation
An organisation in which relationships and activities are arranged so that individuals report to different managers for different activities.

matrix teams
Teams whose members belong to two or more teams.

meaningful work
A task or job role that enables individuals to utilise skills and knowledge aligned to their values. This work is seen as important, valuable and worthwhile, causing the person to feel happy and fulfilled.

measures of success
Also called key performance indicators, objectives and targets, they quantify and measure important aspects of a job, task or project to track how well it is being performed.

mediation
The process of assisting disputing parties to clarify the disputed issue(s) and develop and agree ways to reach agreement.

mediator
A neutral person trained to lead parties of a grievance or dispute through a mediation process to reach a mutually acceptable agreement without advising on or determining the outcome.

mental health
Psychological and emotional wellbeing. It affects how we think, feel and act. It also helps determine how we deal with personal and work-related stress, how we relate to others and how we make personal and business choices.

mentor
A person (usually older, more senior or experienced) who takes an interest in someone's career and provides advice, encouragement, help and support.

mentoring
Assisting and advising someone to build their expertise and career.

middle management
The level of management between senior management and first-line management.

milestone
A clear, specific measuring post, or interim objective, indicating progress towards achieving a goal; significant events or major stages in a project schedule or plan.

mindfulness
The ability of being aware and open to the present moment and environment, and taking a stance of non-judgemental acceptance.

mindset
The often unconscious and unquestioned beliefs a person

holds about themselves, others and the world around them that guide their behaviour; aka mental model, paradigm and world view.

minutes
A record of what has been discussed and agreed during a meeting, also indicating the attendees, date, time and place of the meeting.

mirroring
Consciously or unconsciously, subtly matching another's body position, gestures, speech patterns, tone of voice, which induces rapport.

mission
The overriding or overall strategic goal set by senior managers and directors of an organisation, answering the questions, 'What business are we in?' and 'How will we achieve our vision?'

mixed board
One in which the board of directors is made up of both executive and non-executive directors. *See* inside board and external board.

moments of truth
Any contact a person has with an organisation, personally or electronically.

monitor
Regularly checking actual performance and productivity against desired output of employees or processes.

morale
Inclination to perform tasks well and willingly, which can be high or low; aka *esprit de corps*.

motivation factors
Factors in the job itself that provide job satisfaction and encourage people to perform enthusiastically. *See* hygiene factors.

multifunctional team
A team responsible for delivering an entire product or service, including design, marketing, manufacture, after-sales service and delivery. Also, a temporary team made up of people from several operational areas of the organisation; aka a cross-functional team.

multiskilling
Training across a broad range of skills, enabling employees to carry out a wider range of tasks. *See* cross-skilling, job enlargement, job enrichment and upskilling.

narcissistic leader
A strong type of leader with personal dynamism and magnetism who can become convinced of their invincibility, distrustful of others and emotionally isolated.

near miss
An event that could have potentially caused injury, death or damage but did not on this occasion. *See* incident.

negative feedback
Unspecific criticism that makes people feel unimportant and unappreciated, lowering morale and self-esteem. When specific, it is constructive feedback or corrective feedback and can reduce or eliminate the behaviour in question or improve results. *See* feedback and positive feedback.

network diagram
A chart or schematic representation showing the sequence and relationships of the steps in an activity or a process (e.g. critical path analysis, flow charts and PERT diagrams); used for scheduling and monitoring plans and projects.

networking
Building a range of mutually supportive, informal relationships with others inside and outside the organisation in order to advise, help and support each other.

non-executive directors
Members of the board of directors who are not involved in the business in any other capacity. *See* executive directors.

norm
Unwritten rules or codes of behaviour by which people in an organisation or a team operate ('It's how we do things around here').

not-for-profit (NFP) sector
Non-government organisations whose purpose is to fulfil a mission other than make a profit.

notifiable incident
An incident involving death, serious injury or illness (one that results in treatment as an in-patient in a hospital or medical treatment within 48 hours of exposure to a substance) or a dangerous incident (one that exposes someone to a serious risk to their physical or psychological health and safety, such as an uncontrolled escape, spillage or leakage of a substance; an uncontrolled implosion, explosion or fire; an electric shock; psychological abuse). These must be reported to Comcare as soon as reasonably possible.

occupational violence
Any incident in which an employee is physically attacked or threatened with violence in the workplace, including the direct or indirect application of force to their body, equipment or clothing; illegal behaviour.

onboarding
The process of familiarising employees who are new to an organisation with the requirements and responsibilities of their position and integrating them into the organisation's culture through the building and nurturing of ongoing relationships through organisationally based programs, systems and arrangements.

open question
One that encourages a full response, not just 'yes', 'no' or a short statement of fact.

opportunity cost
Benefits you could have gained by taking a different action.

organisation design
Creating or developing the most suitable organisation structure.

organisation structure
The way an organisation links its employees and capabilities or functions together, depicted in an organisation chart.

organisational politics
Building alliances to help achieve the organisation's goals.

outsourcing
Contracting out non-essential or non-core functions and operations to independent providers; contracting work to, or purchasing parts from, outside the organisation that are not integral to the organisation's operations, usually to cut costs or benefit from efficiencies and expertise not available within, or not worth keeping within, the organisation; aka contracting out.

overt discrimination
Direct, clear discrimination on the grounds of, for example, national origin, race or sex. *See* covert discrimination, direct discrimination, discrimination, overt discrimination, and systemic discrimination.

paradigm
See mindset.

Pareto chart
A vertical bar chart that displays the relative importance of problems or events, showing attribute data in descending order of quantity.

Pareto principle
The 80:20 rule of Vilfredo Pareto that says that 20 per cent of people's efforts gain 80 per cent of their results, and vice versa.

participative leader
See democratic leader.

partnership
An enterprise in which two or more people share the ownership of a business and have unlimited liability.

passive behaviour
Putting other people's wants and needs ahead of your own. *See* aggressive behaviour and assertive behaviour.

P–D–C–A cycle
The Plan–Do–Check–Act system for making and maintaining improvements to a process; aka the PDSA (for Plan–Do–Study–Act) cycle and the Shewhart Learning and Improvement Cycle, after the person who developed it, Walter Shewhart.

performance
How well work is done; a measure of quality. *See* productivity.

performance counselling
Discussing an employee's performance with a view to improving it so that performance expectations are met. *See* corrective feedback.

performance gap
The difference between expected performance and actual performance, preferably measurable, although it can be behavioural (i.e. something you see or hear).

performance improvement plan
A document that outlines what the employee is aiming to improve and ways in which this will be achieved.

performance management
Part of an organisation's human capital management systems to align the organisation's strategic and business plans with individual employees' performance plans, and assisting and enabling employees to attain them by managing the Five Keys to peak performance and productivity.

performance plan
Agreed goals and SMART targets.

performance review
A formal, systematic assessment and discussion of an employee's past performance and productivity, agreeing goals and success measures for future output and planning for future development and training; aka performance appraisal and formal performance discussion.

person specification
A description of the abilities, knowledge and skills, or competencies, required by an ideal job-holder.

personal power
Authority derived from personal attributes.

PERT diagram
Program Evaluation and Review Technique: a type of network diagram that shows a plan's or project's various activities as they relate to each other and when each activity should begin and finish; used to schedule, organise and coordinate plans and projects. *See* critical path analysis.

pie chart
A circular graph showing percentages of the data being studied displayed like slices of a pie.

Plan–Do–Check–Act
See P–D–C–A cycle.

position description
See competency-based job description, job description and role description.

position power
Formal authority derived from a person's job.

positive feedback
When specific, it provides information about actions and outcomes that you appreciate, which makes it more likely they will continue. When general, it

helps build a positive working climate and raises self-confidence.

presenteeism
Being unproductive while at work, physically present but psychologically absent; can reflect a lack of work–life balance, low motivation, longer-term health problems such as arthritis, asthma or depression, short-term health problems such as an allergy or a cold, an unhealthy lifestyle, underemployment or a poor work culture. *See* absenteeism.

private company
The term for a proprietary company in Queensland.

private sector
Corporations, firms and partnerships whose primary goal is to make money for their owners through the provision of goods or services.

probation
A 'getting to know you' period of a few weeks to a few months; a recruit's employment can be terminated during this period if they are found to be unsuited to the job; the period should be written into the employment agreement.

procedural fairness
The right to be given a fair hearing with the opportunity to present one's case and to have a logic-based decision made by an unbiased decision-maker; called due process in the USA and fundamental justice in Canada.

process capability chart
A graph used to show whether a process, or the way work is carried out, is capable of meeting the specifications and to monitor the performance of a system.

productivity
A ratio of the output of goods and services to the cost of the various resources used to achieve that output; when an organisation produces more with the same resources or produces the same with fewer resources, its productivity has improved. *See* performance.

programmed decision
A routine decision for which one answer consistently applies; aka standing plans. *See* standard operating procedure.

project
A temporary undertaking with a defined beginning and end, aimed at creating a product, a service or some other result, such as tackling a problem, identifying and capitalising on an emerging opportunityor redesigning or improving a process.

project charter
A project's terms of reference detailing its scope and limitations; aka the project mandate.

project manager
The person who guides a project from conception to finalisation.

project sponsor
A senior manager with overall 'ownership' of a project.

project team
A temporary team brought together to undertake a specific assignment, such as developing a new product or service, procuring, installing and testing new equipment, or building, refurbishing or updating a facility.

proprietary limited company
A corporation with limited liability that has up to 50 owners; signified by the abbreviation Pty Ltd after its name.

psychological contract
The unwritten and often unstated expectations and norms about what employers and employees expect from each other; for example, 'the organisation offers stable employment and training in return for faithful and loyal service'.

public company
A corporation with limited liability that has any number of owners and is quoted on the Australian Securities Exchange (ASX); signified by the abbreviation Ltd or the word Limited after its name.

public sector
Organisations involved either directly or indirectly in the business of governing the country.

Pygmalion effect
A person's beliefs about another, causing them to live up (or down) to their expectations.

quality certification
Recognition by an auditing body that an organisation is capable of reliably producing a product or service that meets requirements, based on its quality management systems and conformance to the relevant Australian or international quality standards; such organisations are known as 'certified' or 'registered'.

quality culture
The value and importance an organisation and its employees place on quality; a strong quality culture is one in which employees at all levels, in all areas of the organisation, pay attention to the small details that add up to providing a quality product or service and continually seek to improve their offering.

quality standard
A document that provides guidelines, requirements or specifications that can be used to ensure that processes, products and services consistently meet requirements.

quality systems
The internal procedures and processes an organisation has in place to formally control its activities to manage and ensure the quality of its products and services.

racial vilification
Illegal behaviour that humiliates, insults, intimidates or offends a person or group of people because of their colour, national or ethnic origin, or race.

rapport
The feeling of being 'in sync' or in harmony with another person; a feeling of comfortable affinity.

redundancy
Termination of employment because the position has been eliminated, usually due to job redesign, outsourcing or restructuring.

re-engineering
See business process management.

reflective listening
Briefly stating your understanding of the speaker's feelings and/or meaning; aka active listening.

religious vilification
Illegal behaviour that humiliates, insults, intimidates or offends a person or group of people because of their religion.

remuneration
An employee's total reward package, including, for example, base pay (or compensation), plus fringe benefits, such as allowances, bonuses, loadings, penalty rates and provision of a motor vehicle.

renewable energy
One hundred per cent 'clean' energy, or power generation, sourced from the sun, wind, waste or water; aka green electricity and green power.

residual risk
The risk remaining after the original risk (inherent risk) has been treated.

resilience
The (largely learnt) ability to recover swiftly from problems and setbacks.

restructuring
The process of altering the organisational design.

retention
The opposite of attrition. The ability to keep employees; an important measure of organisational culture, employee engagement and morale. Strategies for retention include career management, training and development programs, flexible working, job design and monitoring staff concerns.

retrenchment
Lay-offs caused by lack of work to keep people fully occupied.

risk
In health and safety, the measure of the likelihood and severity of potential illness or injury (psychological or physical) to people or damage to the environment or property resulting from a hazard. In risk management, an adverse or favourable event resulting from an organisation's operations or its operating environment that could advantage or jeopardise the organisation's ability to achieve its goals.

risk analysis
Deciding what could go wrong with (or enhance the outcome of) a plan, project, potential event or strategy; considering the likelihood, or probability, of the event occurring; and examining the consequences of the negative (or positive) event to determine how best to deal with it.

risk appetite
Pertains to an organisation's overall preparedness to accept risk for all objectives.

risk culture
How an organisation and its employees approach risk; a strong risk culture is one in which employees at all levels, in all areas of the organisation, are aware of potential risks and opportunities and their role in controlling or optimising them.

risk management
The coordinated set of activities and systems that identify and manage the many risks that can affect an organisation's ability to achieve its objectives; systematically applying policies, practices and procedures to identify, analyse, evaluate, prioritise, treat, monitor and report on both positive and negative risks, or potential events, in order to minimise or optimise them.

risk management framework
The way an organisation designs, implements, monitors, reviews and continually improves its risk management processes.

risk management plan
The organisation's intended approach and the resources to be applied to dealing with a risk by enhancing, removing or controlling it before the event (risk management systems) and/ or dealing with it should it occur (contingency plans) and, in the case of extreme negative risk events, to ensure the continuity and survival of the organisation; ideally, critical operations and services can continue and, should they be disrupted, they are resumed as rapidly as required. The RMP can be applied to a process, product or project, and part of or all of the organisation.

risk register
A master document listing identified inherent and residual risks, showing an analysis of the risk severity and possible mitigations (i.e. preventions) for each risk; generally presented in a spreadsheet; aka risk log and risk and opportunity register. See also ongoing risk register.

risk tolerance
Pertains to the risk associated with a particular objective.

role clarity
Knowing what is expected of you in terms of clear standards of behaviour, performance and productivity.

role conflict
When the various roles a person plays require different and incompatible behaviour, beliefs or attitudes.

role description
A document outlining the value-adding behaviours expected of a job-holder and the key functions, goals, relationships and responsibilities of a position without prescribing how to achieve them; used for more open-ended positions. *See* competency-based job description and job description.

role expectations
The expectations that others hold about a role.

role model
A person whose behaviour and actions others emulate in order to develop those skills and attributes in themselves.

role perception
A person's idea of what their role demands regarding behaviour, attitudes, behaviours, dress and so on.

run chart
A simple way to graph trends in a process.

S-curve of change
The natural order of growth, prosperity, plateauing and fading that governs living systems.

safety analysis
Examining a task or job to pinpoint its hazards and safety requirements.

safety audit
An examination of the workplace to identify specific health, safety and welfare hazards present and check the effectiveness of existing controls; aka hazard identification survey and hazard inspection.

safety culture
The value and importance an organisation and its employees place on safety; a strong safety culture is one in which employees at all levels, in all areas of the organisation, are aware of physical and psychological hazards and consistently follow safe working procedures.

scatter diagram
A way of displaying what happens to one variable when you change another variable, revealing any relationships, or correlations, between those variables.

scenario planning
A technique that helps strategic planners and risk managers envision different ways the future might unfold and plan appropriate responses to each.

self-awareness
The degree to which a person understands their own attitudes, beliefs, feelings, motivations, perceptions of the world and values as the underlying causes of their actions; aka personal skills and self-understanding.

self-esteem
A person's feelings of self-respect and self-worth.

self-fulfilling prophecy
The way people's beliefs and paradigms influence the way they perceive the world and others and drive their behaviour; people tend to see what they expect, which reinforces their beliefs and, in turn, people tend to respond by living up (or down) to others' expectations.

self-managed teams
Work teams that are empowered to make their own decisions.

self-paced learning
Employees learn by themselves using purpose-designed learning modules or study guides, as and when time permits, either during or after working hours.

self-talk
The often unconscious thoughts or messages people give themselves, which direct their behaviour.

senior management
The level of management in an organisation that falls between middle management and top-level management; aka executives.

servant leader
A type of leader who is unselfish and has a genuine desire to help people achieve their potential.

service economy
An economy based on services such as accounting and finance, aged care, banking, entertainment, home services, hospitality, insurance, law, media, technology and tourism rather than, for example, agriculture, knowledge or manufacturing.

service partners
Internal customers and internal suppliers.

service–profit chain
The roll-on effect of high-quality internal service, raising employee satisfaction, which fuels employee loyalty and productivity, which boosts external service value, which increases customer satisfaction and loyalty.

sexual harassment
Illegal behaviour that includes unwanted or unwelcome sexual advances, comments or conduct of a sexual nature, including verbal and non-verbal behaviour and innuendo, or requests for sexual favours that are embarrassing, humiliating, intimidating or offensive; unrelated to mutual attraction or friendship.

shareholder
A person (natural or corporate) who owns a share (portion) of a company, having 'lent' the company money in return for a share of its profits.

sigma
A statistical measure of variation used to measure defects per million. The greater the sigma number, the fewer the defects. *See* Six Sigma.

situational approach to leadership
Modifying the style of leadership to suit the circumstances.

Six Sigma
3.4 defects per million – virtually error-free.

SMART targets
Targets that are specific (which usually means measurable and time-framed), motivating, ambitious, related to the organisation's vision and goals, and trackable.

sole trader
A person who is the single owner of a business with unlimited liability.

stakeholder
A person or group affected by, or who perceive themselves to be affected by, the operations of the organisation or the outcome of a project; in organisations they are considered to be customers/ clients, employees, owners, suppliers, the wider society and the closer community; in project management, the people and groups affected by, or who perceive themselves to be affected by, the outcome of a project.

standard operating procedure
A document listing the step-by-step method for carrying out a task or procedure, to be followed at all times.

strategic alliance
Collaborating with non-competitor organisations to combine strengths to each produce a better service or product; aka business collaboration.

stratification chart
A way to graph and analyse data by breaking it down into meaningful categories, helping to isolate a problem.

subculture
The culture of subgroups that form part of a larger group.

supply chain
The network of organisations, people, information, resources and technology that contribute to the creation of a product or service, beginning with and including external suppliers and ending with and including external customers; aka integrated value chain. *See* supply-chain management, trading partnerships and value chain analysis.

supply-chain management
Working with suppliers and customers to create a smooth and efficient supply chain, or integrated value chain, that offers value to all parties.

sustainability
Using natural resources without destroying the ecological balance, enabling their continued use; a subset of corporate social responsibility.

SWOT analysis
A systematic way to identify an organisation's internal *strengths* and *weaknesses* and external *opportunities* and *threats*.

synergy
The ability of the whole team to achieve more than its individual members could achieve singly.

systemic discrimination
The result of longstanding direct and indirect discrimination that seems to be the 'natural order of things'. *See* covert discrimination, covert discrimination, direct discrimination, discrimination, indirect and overt discrimination.

tangible assets
Physical assets such as buildings, equipment and money in the bank. *See* current, fixed and intangible assets.

task-readiness level
An employee's ability and willingness to carry out a particular task; used to determine the most appropriate leadership style.

team building
Assisting a team to clarify its overall team purpose and goals (its task) and agree ways to work better together (its process) to achieve its purpose and goals.

team life cycle
A model that describes the five predictable stages through which teams mature: forming, storming, norming, performing and adjourning.

team maintenance
See maintenance functions.

team purpose
A succinct statement that expresses why a team exists; a team mission statement.

teleworkers and remote workers
People who work from home, a satellite office near home or a mobile office such as a vehicle.

teleworking
Working from home, from a satellite office near home or from a mobile office, such as a vehicle, for all, most or some of the time, linked to the employer's office through information and communications technology; aka telecommuting.

temporary employee
A type of employee that works only a specific number of weeks on a fixed-term contract. *See* casual employee.

termination of employment
A permanent separation from the organisation.

Theory X
A type of leadership style. Theory X leaders believe that employees are lazy and work only for money and therefore need to be managed with coercion and threats of punishment. *See* Theory Y.

Theory Y
A type of leadership style. Theory Y leaders believe that employees want to do their jobs well and seek responsibility and challenge; they therefore have high expectations of them, set challenging targets and coach followers to achieve them. *See* Theory X.

top-level management
The most senior level of management in an organisation, consisting of the chief executive officer or managing director, and the members of the board of directors.

total quality management (TQM)
The culture, mindsets and methods that drive quality in an organisation in order to improve customer satisfaction, performance, productivity and profitability; finding ways to work that are cheaper, easier, faster and more reliable; aka quality management.

toxic culture
A workplace culture plagued by fighting, drama and unhappy employees to the point that productivity and the wellbeing of the people in the office is affected.

trading partnership
Organisations working with their external customers and suppliers in mutually beneficial relationships.

trait approach to leadership
Examines the personal qualities a leader possesses, such as intelligence, height and self-assurance.

transactional approach to leadership
A way of thinking about leadership that relies on rewards and punishments to elicit good performance and productivity.

transformational leadership
Leadership that takes an organisation in new directions, largely through the leader's personal dynamism and drive.

triple bottom line
A framework to measure and report financial, social and environmental results of an organisation's activities; aka 3BL and TBL.

turnover (employee)
See attrition.

unity of command
A principle that states that each employee should receive instructions from only one person about a task, job or project.

universal precautions approach
The view that harassment, vilification and violence can happen to anyone, either in or out of the workplace, and still be covered by an employer's duty of care responsibilities.

unlawful dismissal
Dismissal for reasons that are discriminatory; for temporary absence from work because of illness, injury, maternity or parental leave or for engaging in a voluntary emergency management activity; for trade union membership or non-membership; or for filing a complaint or participating in proceedings against an employer. *See* instant dismissal and unfair dismissal.

upcycling
Planning beyond the end of a product's life to use its constituent materials in a way that maintains their value, without loss of quality or performance; aka virtuous cycle and cradle-to-cradle. *See* downcycling and life cycle analysis.

upskilling
Increasing employees' skills to enable them to take on increased responsibility and/or work at a higher level. *See* cross-skilling, job enrichment and multiskilling.

value chain
See supply chain.

value chain analysis
Working with customers to identify and agree on the critical few outcomes that make a difference to them and then examining the organisation's service delivery in this light, step by step, with a view to improving it.

variable cost
A cost that increases depending on the amount or number of products or services produced. *See* also fixed cost.

vertical integration
Vertically integrated organisations attempt to secure control of critical suppliers and customers of their products and services. *See* horizontal integration.

virtual meeting
A meeting between remote participants run electronically, such as a webconference, videoconference or teleconference, or a simultaneous text-messaging meeting using the internet or an organisation's intranet.

virtual teams
Teams made up of members based in different geographical locations.

virtual working
Working at locations different from the rest of one's team and manager and using advanced communications, collaborative systems and information technologies to facilitate team working.

vision
A statement describing the beliefs, culture and operating philosophy an organisation, team or project aspires to, answering the questions, 'Who are we?' and 'How do we operate?'

wellbeing
The state of being comfortable, healthy or happy due to balanced physical and psychological health.

wirearchy
Coined in 1999 by Jon Husband; describes how power and authority flow dynamically, in a way that is based on trust, information, credibility and an emphasis on results, aided by interconnected technology and people.

workers' compensation
See workers' rehabilitation and compensation.

workers' rehabilitation and compensation
Insurance for occupational injury designed to cover lost income resulting from an industrial accident or disease, the associated medical expenses and, when necessary, retraining costs; aimed at no-fault compensation and getting people back into the workforce as quickly as possible.

work–life balance
The ability to honour both work and home commitments.

work–life blending
Integrating work and private life, made possible by technology, so that, for example, an employee might take the afternoon off to care for a child or parent or attend a child's school play, and make up the time working at home after hours. The idea is that where you work is fluid and shifting and need not be just from the office or cubicle; aka 'bleisure' (business and leisure).

work–life integration
A means by which we can prioritise – and integrate – both of these parts of our identity.

workplace agreement
An employment agreement negotiated between an employer and representatives of a group of employees, or an employer directly with a group of employees under Fair Work legislation; aka collective agreement, industrial agreement and enterprise agreement.

workplace hub
Independent or company-provided informal, shared workspaces for telecommuters, freelancers and corporate remote workers, often based around 'communities' of workers engaged in similar work, to come together; aka coworking centre, coworking space.

INDEX

F

I

J

N

Q

R

T

U

Z